SPECIAL EDITION
USING
Microsoft®
Office Word 2003

Bill Camarda

Pearson Education
800 East 96th Street
Indianapolis, Indiana 46240

SPECIAL EDITION USING MICROSOFT® OFFICE WORD 2003

International Standard Book Number: 0-7897-2958-X

Library of Congress Catalog Card Number: 2003108698

Printed in the United States of America

First Printing: December 2003

06 05 04 03   4 3 2 1

Trademarks

All terms mentioned in this book that are known to be trademarks or service marks have been appropriately capitalized. Que Publishing cannot attest to the accuracy of this information. Use of a term in this book should not be regarded as affecting the validity of any trademark or service mark.

Warning and Disclaimer

Bulk Sales

Que Publishing offers excellent discounts on this book when ordered in quantity for bulk purchases or special sales. For more information, please contact

U.S. Corporate and Government Sales
1-800-382-3419
corpsales@pearsontechgroup.com

For sales outside of the U.S., please contact

International Sales
1-317-428-3341
international@pearsontechgroup.com

Publisher
Paul Boger

Associate Publisher
Greg Wiegand

Acquisitions Editor
Stephanie J. McComb

Development Editor
Kevin Howard

Managing Editor
Charlotte Clapp

Project Editor
Tricia Liebig

Copy Editor
Cheri Clark

Indexer
Chris Barrick

Proofreader
Suzanne Thomas

Technical Editors
Bill Rodgers
J. Boyd Nolan

Team Coordinator
Sharry Lee Gregory

Multimedia Developer
Dan Scherf

Interior Designer
Anne Jones

Cover Designer
Anne Jones

Page Layout
Tim Osborn
Plan-it Publishing

Graphics
Tammy Graham
Tara Lipscomb

CONTENTS AT A GLANCE

CONTENTS

IV Industrial-Strength Document Production Techniques

VI The Corporate Word

Troubleshooting Table of Contents

ABOUT THE AUTHOR

Bill Camarda (www.billcamarda.com) is a consultant and writer who specializes in helping leading technology companies deploy and market advanced computing and Internet technologies and services. His 17 previous books include Que's best-selling *Special Edition Using Word 2002*, *Special Edition Using Word 2000*, and *Special Edition Using Word 97*, as well as *Microsoft Office Deployment and Administration* and *Microsoft Office Administrator's Desk Reference*.

ABOUT THE CONTRIBUTING AUTHORS

Patricia Cardoza didn't plan on spending her life working with computers. She graduated from the University of California, Davis with a degree in Environmental Sciences, but every job she has ever had has involved computers. Finally, in 1996, she stopped fighting the inevitable and took a job as an IT manager for a telecommunications company in Sacramento, California. For the past five years, she's been working as the co-network administrator, Exchange administrator, programmer, and resident Outlook expert for a box company in central California. In 2001, Microsoft awarded Patricia Most Valuable Professional status for Microsoft Outlook.

For the past four years, Patricia has been writing about Exchange and Outlook for various online technical journals, including *TechRepublic*, *.NET Magazine*, and Microsoft's Office Communities page. She takes on small independent consulting projects in her spare time, mostly related to programming Outlook forms and Access databases. Patricia is also a gadget geek and loves playing with the latest wireless devices. She is currently implementing an 802.11g network in her home and has a Pocket PC Phone Edition that goes everywhere with her. Patricia wrote Chapter 27 and revised Chapters 30 and 32.

J. Boyd Nolan is a senior software developer working for NetIQ Corporation. Boyd has been in the computing industry for over 15 years, with experience including system/network administration, database administration and development, and general application development. He has experience architecting and developing security and auditing applications, as well as large-scale n-tier Web applications for business and engineering uses. He holds bachelor and master's degrees in Mechanical Engineering from the University of Oklahoma (Boomer Sooner!). Boyd currently lives in Norman, Oklahoma, with the two loves of his life: his wife, Lisa, and son, Justin. Boyd wrote Chapter 25 and revised Chapter 35.

Faithe Wempen, M.A., is a Microsoft Office Specialist Master Instructor and an A+ certified PC technician. A 12-year veteran in the computer book publishing industry, she is the author of more than 70 books on computer operating systems, office applications, and hardware/A+ certification. She teaches Computer Information Technology and Technical Communications courses at Indiana University/Purdue University at Indianapolis and is in the process of developing a graduate-level course in writing effective software documentation. She also co-owns Sycamore Knoll Bed and Breakfast (www.sycamoreknoll.com) in Noblesville, Indiana. Faithe revised Chapters 24 and 34.

DEDICATION

To my wife, Barbara.

To my son, Matthew.

You put up with me.

You give my life purpose.

And you make me very happy.

I can't believe how lucky I am to have you.

I love you.

ACKNOWLEDGMENTS

I'd like to thank an excellent team at Que. (You guys are *always* great.)

We'll start with Kevin Howard, my talented development editor, for making sure this book covers what really matters, and for coordinating an awful lot of professionals doing an awful lot of hard work.

Thanks to tech editors J. Boyd Nolan and Bill Rodgers for adding insights and catching errors (any that they've missed are, of course, mine). They added enormous value—both where I expected it and where I didn't.

Thanks, also, to copy editor Cheri Clark, who not only smoothed the rough edges to make this book far more readable, but also went beyond the call to raise technical issues and make this book significantly more accurate.

Thanks to Stephanie McComb, my very capable acquisitions editor, and the excellent contributing authors she acquired—Faithe Wempen, Patricia Cardoza, and Boyd Nolan.

And behind these behind-the-scenes talents, there are the terrific Que production folks who transform marked-up manuscripts into attractive, inviting books, with amazing speed and efficiency, including (but not limited to) project editor Tricia Liebig, proofreader Suzanne Thomas, indexer Chris Barrick, and series designer Anne Jones.

Thanks to my agent, Lisa Swayne, who got me involved with this project even before she *was* an agent. A personal, heartfelt thanks to the marketing, promotion, and sales teams who've made previous editions of this book a best-seller.

This time around, I'd especially like to thank the late Bill Ray for the valuable contributions he made to earlier editions of this book. He was a good man, gone far too soon. He will be deeply missed.

Finally, thanks to *you* for choosing this book. I sincerely hope you'll find it to be a trusted companion as you work with Word for years to come.

WE WANT TO HEAR FROM YOU!

As the reader of this book, *you* are our most important critic and commentator. We value your opinion and want to know what we're doing right, what we could do better, what areas you'd like to see us publish in, and any other words of wisdom you're willing to pass our way.

As an associate publisher for Que Publishing, I welcome your comments. You can email or write me directly to let me know what you did or didn't like about this book—as well as what we can do to make our books better.

Please note that I cannot help you with technical problems related to the topic of this book. We do have a User Services group, however, where I will forward specific technical questions related to the book.

When you write, please be sure to include this book's title and author, as well as your name, e-mail address, and phone number. I will carefully review your comments and share them with the author and editors who worked on the book.

Email: feedback@quepublishing.com

Mail: Greg Wiegand
          Associate Publisher
          Que Publishing
          800 East 96th Street
          Indianapolis, IN 46240 USA

For more information about this book or another Que Publishing title, visit our Web site at www.quepublishing.com. Type the ISBN (excluding hyphens) or the title of a book in the Search field to find the page you're looking for.

INTRODUCTION

In this introduction

This book has one—and only one—goal: *to make you the most productive Word 2003 user on the block, no matter what kind of documents you create.*

From letters to manuals, reports to email merges, Web sites to XML content, you'll find a relentless focus on productivity here. I intend to show you

- The fastest, easiest way to get the job done
- Techniques for streamlining and automating those annoying tasks you've been doing by hand
- Ideas for doing more with Word than you ever thought possible

Even if you're experienced with Word, you'll be amazed at how much more it can do for you—and how easily—once you know how to utilize it.

For instance, you probably know about *some* of these features, but you're a rare and special Word user if you already know how to get Word to do *all* this:

- Prevent a document from being read after a certain date
- Design, organize, and create links for an entire business email newsletter *in 15 minutes*
- Automatically format your document and fix hundreds of common spelling mistakes without even being asked
- Compare two older drafts of a document and show you every single text and formatting change
- Remove hidden personal information from your documents so they can't be identified
- Automatically reformat your document from U.S. to European A4 page size
- Apply numbered headings throughout your document that stay up-to-date automatically
- Build a meeting agenda with Word in a matter of minutes
- Automatically insert large blocks of formatted text—even pictures—when you type a few characters of your choice
- Automatically build an index based on a list of words you provide
- Automatically add a numbered caption to every graphic or table in your document
- Print a list of every change you've made in a document using Tracked Changes
- Reveal all the formatting associated with any text in your document
- Display a document onscreen in a manner designed for easy review—without changing the document's actual formatting
- Use XML to automatically extract useful data from Word documents

There are dozens more examples, but you get the point. The time you invest in learning Word's productivity features can pay extraordinary dividends.

If you've ever suspected that there was a more efficient way to get the job done, or avoided a feature because you were worried about its complexity, now's the time to *go for it*. *Special Edition Using Microsoft Office Word 2003* will be with you every step of the way.

WHO SHOULD READ THIS BOOK?

This book has been carefully designed to benefit virtually *any* Word user:

- If you've been around the block a few (or a *thousand*) times with Word, you'll appreciate the focus on productivity. Sure you might already know how to get the job done, but do you also know the most *efficient* way to do it?

- If you're an experienced Word user, but you're new to Word 2003, you'll appreciate the detailed coverage of Word's powerful new features—especially the practical, step-by-step coverage of Word's improved document collaboration, privacy, and security features, and new XML support.

- If you're completely new to Word, first of all, welcome aboard! *Special Edition Using Microsoft Office Word 2003* will help you quickly learn skills and good habits that might otherwise take you years to learn.

- If you're using Word in a business setting, you'll welcome this book's extensive practical examples drawn from the requirements and experiences of actual companies. You'll also appreciate its detailed coverage of business features, such as managing revisions, SharePoint collaboration, integrating Excel worksheets, and creating mass mailings.

- If you're using Word as a Web editor—or if you're thinking about it—we'll show you how to turn out great pages and sites with minimal hassle.

- If you use Word to write books or other long documents, you'll appreciate this book's practical, hands-on coverage of powerful features such as outlining, tables of contents, indexing, master documents, footnotes, and cross-references.

HOW THIS BOOK IS ORGANIZED

Special Edition Using Microsoft Office Word 2003 is organized into six parts:

Part I: Word Basics: Get Productive Fast

You'll start with a quick introduction to Word 2003's improved interface, navigation tools, and formatting features. The emphasis, of course, is on productivity: new Word conveniences, plus old shortcuts you might not have noticed before. You'll also find a full chapter on printing and faxing in Word, as well as extensive coverage of Word's powerful new voice control and dictation features. If you're new to Word, odds are you need to get productive in a hurry. Part I delivers the quick-start basics you need *right now*.

Part II: Building Slicker Documents Faster

In Part II, you'll learn how to make the most of Word's bread-and-butter document development tools, including proofing tools, brand-new research tools, styles, templates, AutoText, tables, and much more. Most Word users, even experienced ones, only scratch the surface of these tools. We've made sure to provide plenty of real-world examples that show exactly how to get the best results from these powerful tools—old *and* new.

Part III: The Visual Word: Making Documents Look Great

Whether you create documents for print or electronic use, odds are your documents are growing more visual every year. Part III shows how to use Word's powerful design and graphics tools to build documents that are highly visual—and highly effective.

You'll learn how to bring images into your document from any source—online photographs, Office clip art, WordArt typography, or your own images, whether scanned, captured with a digital camera, or hand-drawn with Word's drawing tools. You'll also find a full chapter of coverage of Word's impressive tools for creating graphs, business diagrams, and organizational charts.

Part IV: Industrial-Strength Document Production Techniques

Next, you'll focus on Word's core features for streamlining complex document projects, including outlining, master documents, tables of contents, captioning, indexes, footnotes, endnotes, cross-references, and fields. You'll find comprehensive coverage of Word 2003's elegant mail-merge feature. And, of course, you'll find plenty of practical examples to show when you should use these features—and how to use them most effectively.

Part V: Word, the Internet, and XML

Part V begins with hands-on coverage of using Word to create Web pages and Web sites. If you're upgrading from an older version of Word—say, Word 97 or Word 2000—you'll be pleasantly surprised at how much Word's Web capabilities have improved.

This part of the book also contains a detailed, practical introduction to XML—so you can begin leveraging Word 2003's powerful XML support in your own business environment.

Part VI: The Corporate Word

If you use Word in a corporate setting, or if you're responsible for managing Word, Part VI is aimed at *you*. In this part of the book, you'll discover practical, easy ways to leverage Word's supercharged document collaboration features and make the most of Word's integration with the rest of Microsoft Office. You'll learn how to record macros that automate the tasks you and your colleagues perform every day.

You'll find a full chapter on Word 2003's significantly enhanced security and privacy features—as well as coverage of networking issues, cross-platform and file export issues, using Word in multilingual environments, and accessibility features. Simply put, it's everything you need to know in order to use Word anywhere—and help others in your organization to do so as well.

HOW THIS BOOK IS DESIGNED

Here's a quick look at a few structural features designed to help you get the most out of this book. To begin with, you'll find the following features.

TIP

> *Tips* are designed to point out especially quick ways to get the job done, good ideas, or techniques you might not discover on your own. These aren't wimpy, run-of-the-mill tips you learned the first week you used Word and don't need a book to tell you.

NOTE

> *Notes* offer even more insight into features or issues that may be of special interest— without distracting you from the meat-and-potatoes answers you're looking for.

CAUTION

> Cautions, as you'd expect, warn you away from those sharp edges that still remain in Word after nearly two decades of sanding and polishing.

Often, when a subject is covered in greater detail elsewhere in the book, you'll find a marker like this, which points you to the location where the topic can be found:

→ For more information about Word's automated spelling and grammar checker, **see** "Using Automatic Spelling and Grammar Checking," **p. 254**.

New icons are placed before text throughout the book. This indicates a feature that has been added to this version of Word 2003.

> *Although it's rare that you'll get yourself in deep trouble with Word, it's not so rare for a feature to work unexpectedly—in other words, for it not to do what you wanted. At times like those, you need answers fast. Wherever you're likely to get into trouble, you're equally likely to find a Troubleshooting icon that serves as a cross-reference to a proven troubleshooting solution at the end of the chapter.*

WHAT'S ON THE COMPANION WEB SITE

Special Edition Using Microsoft Office Word 2003—along with Que's other excellent Special Edition books for Office 2003—shares an excellent companion Web site at www.quehelp.com. Here, you'll find

- Bonus software resources
- Bonus chapters from other *Special Edition Using Microsoft Office 2003* books
- Updates, corrections, and much more

CONVENTIONS USED IN THIS BOOK

Que's Special Edition conventions are designed to be completely predictable—so it's easy to understand what you're reading and what you're supposed to do.

For example, you'll often read about key combinations such as Ctrl+B, Word's shortcut for boldfacing text you've selected. Ctrl+B means hold down the Control key, press B, and then release both keys.

Also, when you're instructed to select a menu item, you'll find that the menu name and item have one letter underlined in the text just as they do onscreen. For example, to display Word's Print dialog box, select File, Print. The underlined keys (F in File and P in Print) are the shortcut keys you can use to select the command with the keyboard instead of the mouse. In the case of menu items, you'll need to press Alt to activate the menu bar and then press the underlined keys to select the menu and command.

You'll occasionally run across a few other types of formatted text, as explained here:

- Internet addresses are specified in a monospace font, for example, `www.microsoft.com`. If a Web address must continue on the following line due to page-width restrictions, the address will be divided at the backslash. This indicates that the same Web address continues on the following line due to page-width restrictions, but that you should treat it as one line of text, without pressing Enter or entering spaces. You can see this in the following example:

  ```
  www.google.com/
  search?q=Microsoft+Word+%2B+watermark+%2B+PostScript&hl=en&lr=&safe=off
  ```

- Terms introduced and defined for the first time are formatted in *italic*.

- Text that you are supposed to type is formatted in monospaced type as in the following example:

  Run Setup using a command such as `setup.exe /q1 /b1`.

- Finally, text formatted in "typewriter" type represents code listings, such as Visual Basic for Applications program listings, as in the following example:

  ```
  Sub Macro7()
  '
  ' Macro7 Macro
  ' Macro recorded 07/10/01 by Bill Camarda
  '
   Selection.Font.Bold = wdToggle
  End Sub
  ```

One last point: with this version of Office, Microsoft has added the word "Office" to the name of every product in the "Office family." That means Word 2003's official name is "Microsoft Office Word 2003."

Rather than wasting dozens of pages repeating that mouthful, we'll just call the product "Word" or "Word 2003." Obviously it's Microsoft Office Word 2003 we're referring to.

That's all you need to know to get the most out of this book. Now fire up your copy of Word 2003, and let's see what this baby can do.

PART

I

WORD BASICS: GET PRODUCTIVE FAST

CHAPTER 1

WHAT'S NEW IN MICROSOFT OFFICE WORD 2003

In this chapter

1

DISCOVERING MICROSOFT'S KEY WORD 2003 ENHANCEMENTS

On September 29, 2003, Microsoft Word turned 20 years old. What could possibly be added to software this mature and comprehensive? *A lot*. In Word 2003, Microsoft has focused on extending Word in several key areas. These include

- Research tools
- Collaboration improvements
- Document security
- Productivity
- XML support

In this chapter, we'll briefly review the most significant enhancements to Word 2003 in these areas, and point you to locations in the book where these new features are covered in even greater depth.

RESEARCH TOOLS

Word's new Research task pane builds on the basic thesaurus and translation tools provided in earlier versions of Word, connecting you to a wide range of online research resources (see Figure 1.1). Some of these services cost money, but most of them are free.

Figure 1.1
Word's Research task pane, showing an online stock quote.

→ For more information about Word's Research task pane, **see** "Working with Additional Research Services," **p. 276**.

Assuming that you have an Internet connection, Word can connect you to

- The online Encarta English language dictionary (North American edition, for users throughout North America)

- Automated translation services for generating rough translations between English and more than a dozen other languages—from brief phrases through entire documents (see Figure 1.2)

- Thesauruses for English, French, and Spanish

- MSN Search, Microsoft's Web search engine

- Thomson Gale basic company profiles of public companies (with more detailed profiles available for a fee)

- MSN Money Stock Quotes (delayed at least 20 minutes)

- Subscription-only research services, including eLibrary and Factiva

Figure 1.2
Retrieving text translation across the Internet from within Word.

Word's research tools make it significantly easier to find the external information you need to include or reflect in your document.

REVIEW AND COLLABORATION IMPROVEMENTS

Nowadays, many—if not most—business documents are developed through a collaborative process, in which many individuals participate as reviewers or contributors. With each new version of Office, Microsoft improves the collaborative tools available to Word users—and to the organizations that employ them.

Word 2003's collaboration improvements fall primarily into two categories:

- Tools that give you better control over how your documents are reviewed

- Tools that simplify team-based collaboration, relying on Microsoft network or Internet-based software such as SharePoint Team Services

1

NEW DOCUMENT REVIEW TOOLS

If you've ever been responsible for producing a large document that requires contributions from many individuals, you know how frustrating the process can be. People comment on areas of the document they know little about. They introduce inconsistent formatting. Their changes are difficult to integrate and resolve. Word 2003 adds two new features to help overcome these problems:

- **Range Permissions and Editing Restrictions.** Word 2003's improved Protect Document feature allows you to restrict individuals to editing only the portions of a document you want them to edit. You can, if you want, allow them to comment on other parts of the document without actually making changes to those parts of the document.

- **Formatting Restrictions, aka Style Lockdown.** Organizations that want their documents to remain absolutely consistent in appearance can prevent users from applying direct formatting that introduces unwanted inconsistencies. Word now allows the "owner" of a document to limit formatting to a specific selection of styles.

To do so, choose Tools, Protect Document. The Protect Document task pane appears (see Figure 1.3). Then, check the Limit Formatting to a Selection of Styles check box. Next, click Yes, Start Enforcing Protection. The Start Enforcing Protection dialog box opens. To use a password to protect your formatting, enter it in both the Enter New Password and the Reenter Password to Confirm boxes, and click OK.

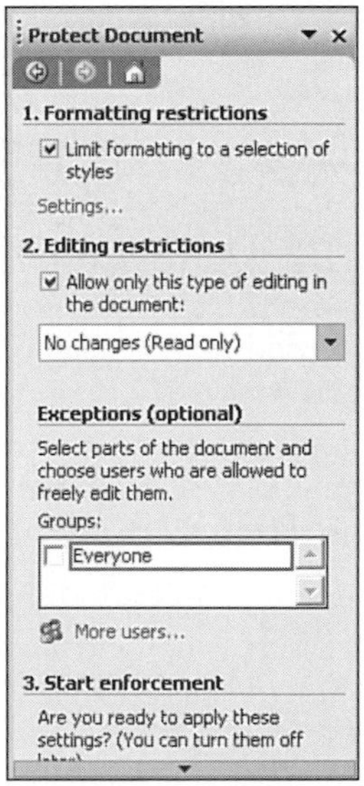

Figure 1.3
Protecting a document against unwanted formatting or editing changes.

→ For more information about protecting documents with either passwords or server-based user authentication features, **see** "Limiting the Changes Reviewers Can Make in Your Document," **p. 892**.

NEW TEAM-BASED COLLABORATION TOOLS

If you are running Microsoft Office 2003 and Windows Server 2003 with SharePoint Team Services Version 2, you can construct Shared Workspaces from within Word 2003—locations where you and your colleagues can collaborate on all aspects of a project (see Figure 1.4).

Figure 1.4
Creating a Shared Workspace from the Shared Workspace task pane.

These Shared Workspaces can bring together all the documents and information related to a project in a single *document library*. Shared Workspaces also provide extensive tools for keeping all project participants up-to-date on a project's status and on their individual responsibilities.

You can also create Document Workspaces to store central copies of an individual document. Through a Document Workspace, you can assign tasks to others who are working on your document. You can also provide links to other resources inside and outside the company—resources that your colleagues can use to work on your document or project.

NOTE

> If you're using Outlook 2003 with Exchange 2003, you can also create Meeting Workspaces, which give you and your colleagues tools for planning and managing meetings: tracking attendance and sharing agendas, documents, decisions, action items, and more.

→ For more information about using SharePoint Team Services from Microsoft Word, **see** Chapter 27, "Online Document Collaboration Using SharePoint Team Services," **p. 909**.

TIP

If you and your colleagues use Microsoft instant messaging services (Microsoft Windows Messenger, Microsoft MSN Messenger, or Microsoft Exchange Instant Messaging Service), you can send instant messages to anyone who is available to receive them.

To do so, you must first make sure Word can recognize the names of your IM contacts. Choose Tools, AutoCorrect Options, Smart Tags. In the Recognizers box, check Person Name (English) and Person Name (Outlook email recipients).

When you type a name in your document corresponding to an individual whose name is recognized, a thin red underline and Smart Tag icon appear in the document. When you click on the icon, you are given all your available options for communicating with the individual. If the individual is currently available on Microsoft Instant Messaging, sending an instant message will be one of the options you can choose. If you are using shared calendars through Outlook 2003 and Microsoft Exchange, the Smart Tag can even display your colleagues' availability based on their Outlook calendars.

DOCUMENT SECURITY WITH INFORMATION RIGHTS MANAGEMENT (IRM)

Microsoft's new Information Rights Management (IRM) technology can give organizations unprecedented control over the information they generate. Using IRM, Word and Office users can not only restrict who can read documents, but prevent documents (or even excerpts from documents) from being printed, forwarded, or copied (see Figure 1.5).

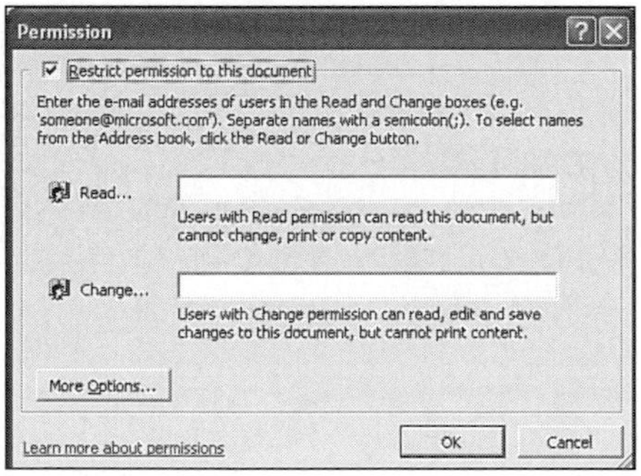

Figure 1.5
Controlling rights to a document from the Permission dialog box.

The limits remain in place no matter where the document is sent—dramatically reducing the risk of sensitive information falling into unauthorized hands. What's more, document creators can establish a document expiration date. After that date, the document becomes inaccessible to *anyone*.

→ For more information about Information Rights Management and Permissions, **see** Chapter 33, "Word Document Privacy and Security Options," **p. 1087**.

PRODUCTIVITY IMPROVEMENTS

Microsoft has added various new features intended to help users get their work done more quickly, efficiently, and conveniently. Word 2003's most important productivity improvements include the following:

- **Reading Layout** (see Chapter 2, "Navigating Word 2003"). Word 2003 provides the new Reading Layout view, which has been designed specifically to make it easy to read and review documents. By default, Reading Layout uses Microsoft's ClearType technology, which is intended to increase legibility (see Figure 1.6).

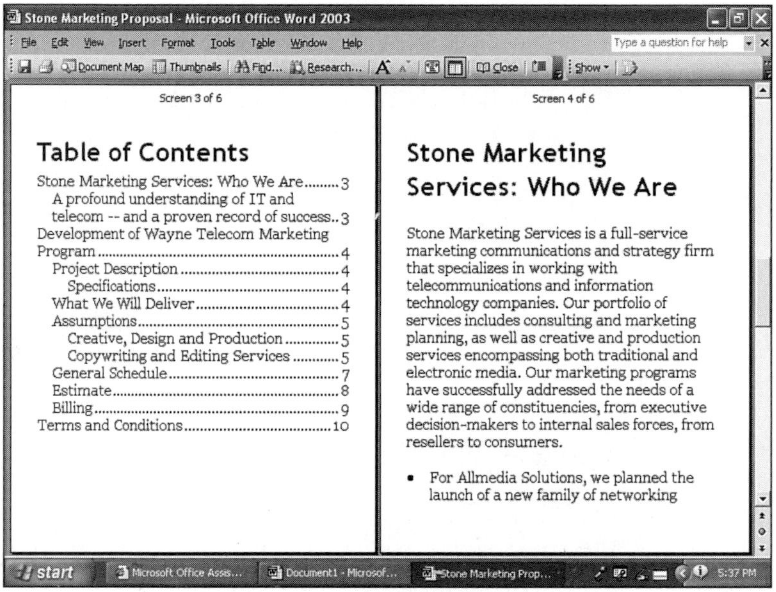

Figure 1.6
Word 2003's Reading Layout view.

- **Thumbnails** (see Chapter 2). Word 2003's new Thumbnails make it easy to browse through your document. When you display Thumbnails, the left side of your screen displays a row of small "thumbnail" images of your document's pages; to go to a page, click on its image (see Figure 1.7).

- **Internet Faxing** (see Chapter 6, "Printing and Faxing in Word"). Word and Office 2003 support Internet faxing via Venali Internet Fax Desktop Solutions. Using Venali's paid subscription service, you can send faxes to any fax number worldwide, directly from Word, without using a fax modem. Venali will also receive faxes on your behalf, and forward them to your email account—eliminating the need for a separate fax line.

- **Improved Task Panes** (see Chapter 2). In Office XP and Word 2002, Microsoft introduced *task panes*, which made it easier for users to perform common tasks by bringing all relevant options together in a single, easy-to-access pane appearing on the right side of the screen. In Word and Office 2003, Microsoft has refined these task panes, making them easier to use and navigate—and added several new ones. Figure 1.8 shows the new Getting Started task pane.

Figure 1.7
Working with thumb-nails.

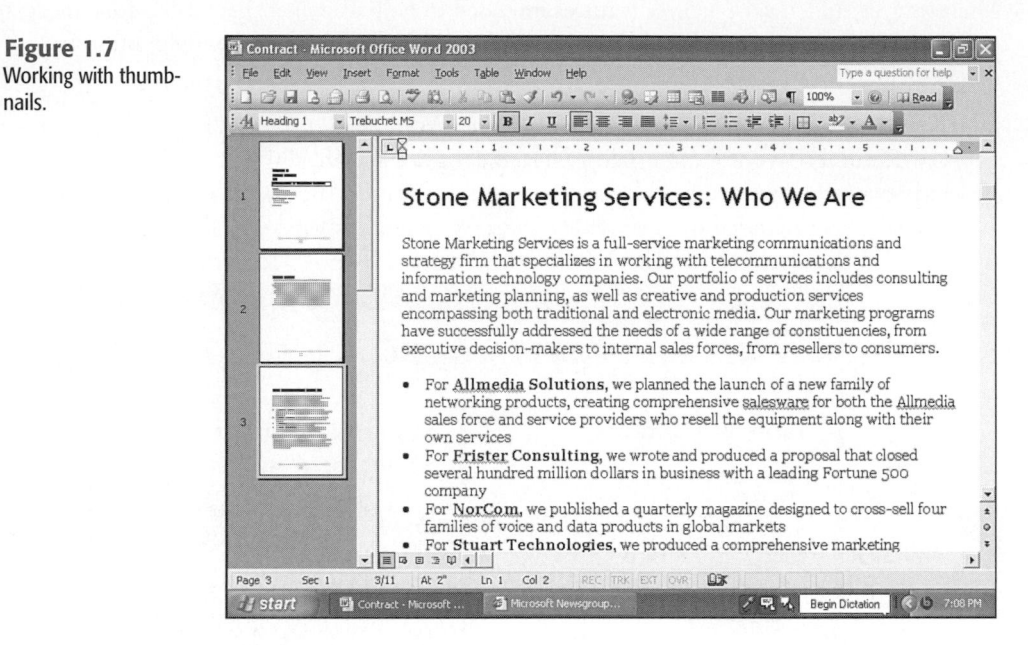

Figure 1.8
Word's new Getting Started task pane.

■ **Better Smart Tags and New Smart Documents** (see Chapter 9, "Automating Your Documents"). In Office XP and Word 2002, Microsoft introduced *smart tags*. When Word recognizes certain information in your document, such as names, it places a smart tag in your document. Clicking on the smart tag gives you options for using that information—for example, sending an email to an individual whose name has been recognized. Office 2003 adds new Smart Tags and makes it easier for professional developers to customize their own.

Word 2003 also supports Smart Documents: documents that provide built-in tools for completing them, drawing on information from throughout and beyond the organization. For example, a professional developer working for your company might create a smart document for building proposals. Such a document might include custom smart tags connecting users to product lists, pricing tools, commands for routing the document to specific reviewers, and more. Smart Documents have the potential to dramatically reduce the effort involved in building complex business documents.

- **Better Ink Support** (see Chapter 2). In Word 2002 and Office XP, Microsoft supported Tablet PCs through an add-on, the Microsoft Office XP for Tablet PC (Tablet Pack). Office 2003 more tightly integrates Tablet PC "ink" support into Word (as well as Excel and PowerPoint).

  Some of Word 2003's ink support is available to users of any PC with a writing tablet, not just a Tablet PC. For example, after a reviewer marks up a document by handwriting, you can display or hide the handwritten markup from the Reviewing toolbar.

- **Easier Interface Customization** (see Chapter 31, "Customizing Word"). Word's new Rearrange Commands dialog box (available through Tools, Customize, Commands) makes customizing Word toolbars and menus easier and more intuitive.

- **More Online Help Resources** (see Chapter 2). Word and Office 2003 go beyond conventional built-in product help files, offering extensive product assistance from across the Internet. For example, you can retrieve relevant Microsoft Knowledge Base articles from within Word, or even access product newsgroups to ask other Office users your question (see Figure 1.9).

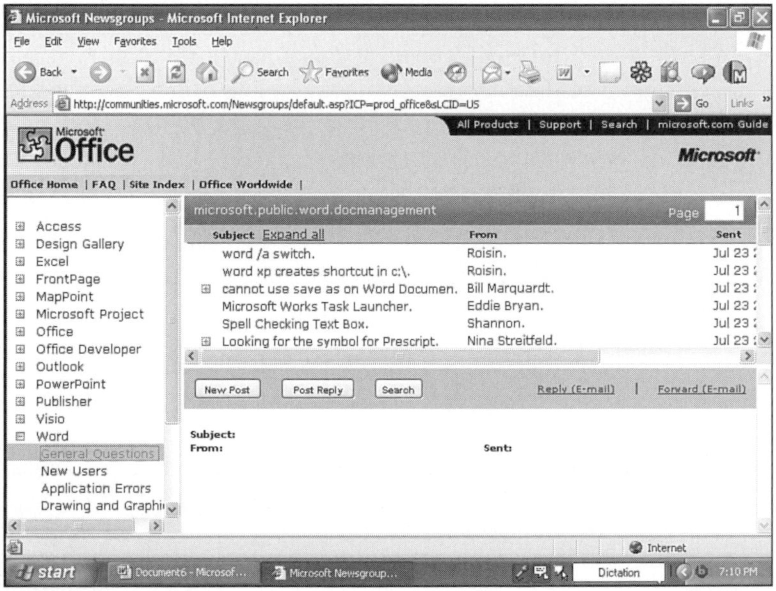

Figure 1.9
Accessing product newsgroups from within Word.

XML SUPPORT

Finally, Microsoft has added extensive support for XML throughout Microsoft Office Professional and the standalone version of Microsoft Word. Word's XML support has received extensive publicity and is covered in detail in Chapter 25, "Using Word to Develop XML Content and Use XML Applications." This section briefly summarizes what XML is, and what Word's support can (and cannot) do for you.

XML is a widely accepted standard for representing any form of structured data—from text to database entries, and far beyond. Like HTML, XML is a markup language—you attach "tags" to data, and the tags indicate how the data should be handled. Like HTML files, XML files are composed of text; they are not binary files like conventional Word documents.

XML has at least three attributes that set it apart from HTML, and make it potentially far more useful—especially in business.

First, the rules for creating XML documents are far more restrictive than those for creating HTML documents. This means you can rely on XML to accurately communicate information between computer systems that cannot interpret the ambiguities and outright errors that are commonplace in HTML documents. As a result, XML is rapidly becoming the data exchange format of choice for an enormous range of business applications. *Word's XML support means you can use Word to generate data for use by these XML-based applications, and that you can use Word to access data those applications already contain.*

Second, unlike HTML, XML separates content from presentation. You won't find an XML tag to boldface text. Instead, you'll find tags that specify what information *is*—and what it *means*. This means it's easier to use XML as the format for documents that must be repurposed later; you merely attach a different style sheet that provides new instructions for how to format and display each type of data contained in the document.

Consider the widely quoted example of a pharmaceutical company that must use consistent, accurate, and up-to-date information on everything from consumer advertising to FDA reports. XML makes it possible to draw on the same information for all these uses, without having to worry about the inconsistencies that arise when source data must be stored in dozens of separate forms and locations.

Finally, unlike HTML, XML establishes rules that can be used to create a virtually infinite number of markup languages for specialized purposes and environments. To give you a sense of XML's breadth, consider these examples—just a few of the *hundreds* of XML dialects that have already been created:

- XBRL, which standardizes the communication of financial reporting data among corporations
- MathML, which provides a standard format for mathematical equations
- WML, which provides a stripped down markup language for displaying Web applications on wireless phones

- VoiceXML, which provides a standard language for controlling voice applications such as automated voicemail or call center systems

- SVG, which defines an efficient format for 2D vector graphics

If you are using the standalone version of Word 2003, or the version of Word 2003 in Office 2003 Enterprise and Office 2003 Professional, you can work with any XML dialect supported by its own "XML Schema," using the XML Schema tab of the Templates and Add-ins dialog box (see Figure 1.10). You can even create your own internal schema, and use that.

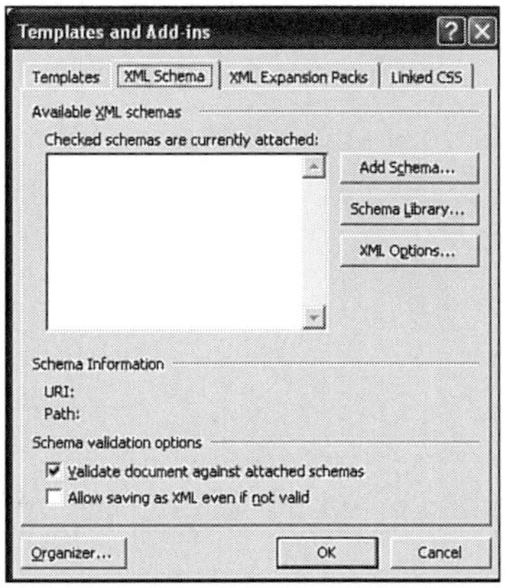

Figure 1.10
Adding a custom schema in Word 2003.

However, the version of Word provided in less expensive versions of Office can only store and read documents using Microsoft's own proprietary, undocumented WordML schema—significantly limiting its usefulness in data exchange.

It's worth mentioning that, for most organizations, taking full advantage of Word's XML support will require planning, technical sophistication, and in many cases, custom programming.

Having said that, the versions of Word and Office that contain full XML support give organizations powerful new options for streamlining business processes, interacting with business partners, and delivering up-to-the-minute data to the people who need it, in a form they find easy to use.

→ For more information about Word's XML capabilities, **see** Chapter 25, "Using Word to Develop XML Content and Use XML Applications," **p. 837**.

Navigating Word 2003

QUICK TOUR OF THE "COCKPIT"

Typically, the easiest way to start Word is to click Start, All Programs, Microsoft Office, Microsoft Office Word 2003. Word opens with a new blank document ready for editing. In Figure 2.1, you can see the basic Word interface with each of its components marked.

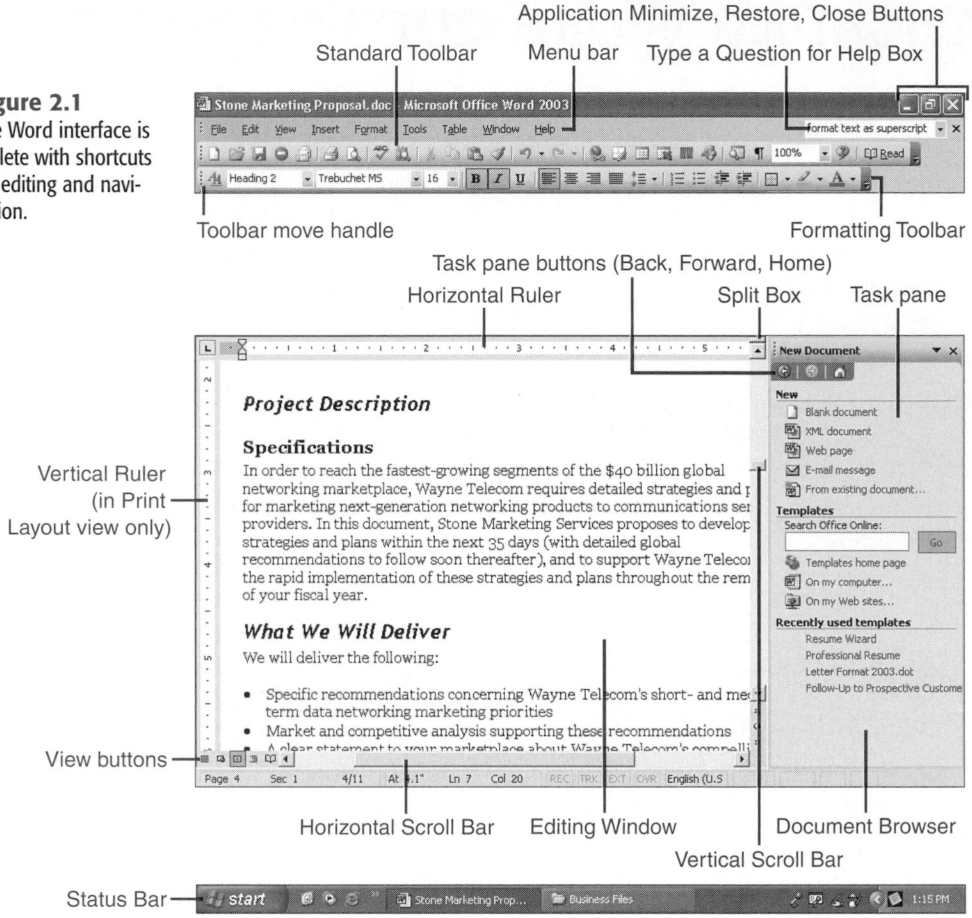

Figure 2.1
The Word interface is replete with shortcuts for editing and navigation.

The next few sections take a closer look at each important element of the Word interface.

USING WORD'S IMPROVED TASK PANES

Task panes, first introduced in Word 2003, are designed to make Word easier to use by bringing together all the options available to perform a task, and placing them conveniently on the right side of Word's editing window. For example, the New Document task pane appears when you first open Word. This task pane shows your options for opening existing documents or creating a new one (refer to Figure 2.1).

Each option in a task pane appears as a blue hyperlink; when you move your mouse over the option, it appears underlined. To choose the option, click on it.

In some cases, clicking an option executes the option; for example, clicking on the name of a document opens that document. In other cases, clicking an option opens a related dialog box, where you can make appropriate choices. For example, if you click On My Computer in the New Documents task pane, Word displays the Open dialog box, which you can use to browse to and select the document of your choice.

Word offers many task panes. These include

- The new Getting Started task pane, which provides easy connections to Microsoft Office Online and allows you to open one of the documents you were working on most recently. (To view, display any task pane and click the Home icon.)

- The Help task pane, which brings together all of Microsoft Word's online and offline help features (and is covered later in this chapter, in the "Getting Help" section).

- The Clip Art task pane, which allows you to choose an image to insert in your document (to view, choose Insert, Picture, Clip Art.)

- The Research task pane, which gives you access to all of Word's research tools, as well as translation tools that can translate single words among the languages installed on your computer file searches (to view, choose Tools, Research, or Tools, Language, Translate).

- The Clipboard task pane, which allows you to paste any of multiple items you have cut or copied into the Clipboard.

- The Basic File Search task pane, which controls file searches (to view, choose File, File Search).

- The New Document task pane, which lets you specify which type of new document you want to create.

- The Shared Workspace task pane, which lets you control the way you collaborate with others using SharePoint to work on the same documents.

- The Document Updates task pane, which allows you to check for updates to your document that may have been made by collaborators using SharePoint.

- The Protect Document task pane, which lets you control which types of edits and formatting others can make to your document.

- The Styles and Formatting task pane, which allows you to control all the styles and formatting associated with text you've selected. (To view, choose Format, Styles and Formatting, or click the Styles and Formatting button on the Formatting toolbar.)

- The Reveal Formatting task pane, which shows all the formatting associated with specific text. (To view, choose Format, Reveal Formatting.)

- The Mail Merge task pane, which walks you through the process of building a mass mailing or an emailing. (To view, choose Tools, Letters and Mailings, Mail Merge.)

■ The XML Structure task pane, which allows you to apply new XML elements to a Word document saved in XML format, using an XML schema you have already created. (For more on working with XML, see Chapter 25, "Using Word to Develop XML Content and Use XML Applications."

To view any task pane, including the Clipboard task pane (which does not have its own menu command), choose View, Task Pane. A task pane appears; click the down arrow to the right of the task pane's name. Then, choose the task pane you want from the drop-down menu.

In Word 2003, you can also move among task panes you have already viewed: Use the Back and Forward buttons at the top of the task pane. You can also move to the Home task pane at any time, by clicking the Home button.

USING WORD'S PERSONALIZED MENUS

As in any Windows application, you can choose a wide range of commands from menus. However, in Word there's a difference: If you want them, you can have Personalized Menus.

If you choose to work with Personalized Menus, when you first choose a menu Word displays an abbreviated list of commands. To see the complete list, point the mouse pointer to the double arrow at the bottom of the menu and wait a moment.

When Personalized Menus are enabled, if you choose a menu item that isn't on the "short" list, Word adds it to the short list the next time you display the menu. In this way, Word attempts to personalize itself for you, showing the commands you use while eliminating the clutter associated with those you don't use.

You can control whether Word uses Personalized Menus. Choose Tools, Customize; click the Options tab; and clear or check the Always Show Full Menus check box.

NOTE

> Throughout this book, you'll find references to commands that don't appear on abbreviated Personalized Menus. If you are using Personalized Menus, and a command is mentioned that doesn't appear in your copy of Word, position your mouse pointer over the double arrow at the bottom of the menu, and the command will appear.

MOVING AROUND FAST WITH THE SCROLLBARS

As with most Windows applications, Word provides a vertical scrollbar that enables you to move throughout a document rapidly. To move to a specific location, click the scroll box and drag it up or down. As you drag the scroll box, Word displays a ScreenTip showing the page number to which you've scrolled. To move up or down by one screen, click anywhere in the vertical scrollbar above or below the scroll box.

TIP

> If you use Word heading styles to identify your document's headings, Word provides even more useful ScreenTips, displaying the headings as you move past them (see Figure 2.2). This way, you don't even need to know the page number you're looking for—just the subject matter.

Figure 2.2
As you scroll through a document that uses heading styles, Word displays a ScreenTip showing the names of the headings you pass.

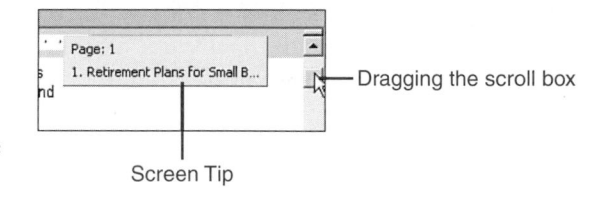

Dragging the scroll box

Screen Tip

Word also provides a horizontal scrollbar that enables you to move from left to right in a document. You'll find this most useful when you're working in documents wider than your editing window, such as documents formatted horizontally in landscape orientation.

If your document is only slightly wider than your window, you might find it more comfortable to display all your text at the same time, rather than scrolling horizontally back and forth. One way to do this is to choose Tools, Options, View, and check the Wrap to Window check box. Another option is to type a smaller number in the Zoom box on the Standard toolbar—perhaps 90% or 95% instead of 100%.

TIP

> Another option is to set the Zoom control to Page Width. Word will then automatically display your page as large as it can be displayed while still fitting entirely in your editing window. To do so, click the down arrow next to the Zoom setting in the Standard toolbar, and choose Page Width from the drop-down list.

TIP

> If you have a Microsoft IntelliMouse (or compatible mouse), you can also scroll through a document by rolling the scroll wheel between the left and right mouse buttons.

DOCUMENT BROWSER: BROWSE ANY WAY YOU WANT

At the bottom of the vertical scrollbar is a powerful tool for moving around your document: Word's Document Browser (sometimes called Select Browse Object), shown in Figure 2.3. Document Browser enables you to jump quickly between document elements. You can choose from a wide range of document elements, including pages, footnotes, tables, drawings, and several others.

Figure 2.3
With Document Browser, it's easy to move to the preceding (or next) page.

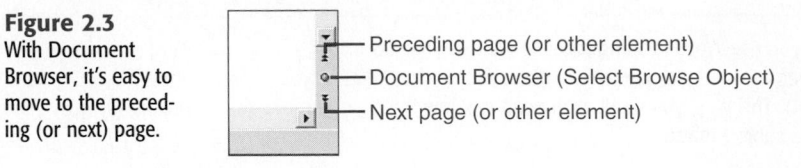

Preceding page (or other element)
Document Browser (Select Browse Object)
Next page (or other element)

By default, Document Browser is set to work with pages. If you click the double up-arrow button, you move up one page, and if you click the double down-arrow button, you move down one page. However, you can use Document Browser to move among many other document elements as well. Click the Select Browse Object ball, and Word displays icons representing several document elements (see Figure 2.4).

Figure 2.4
When you click the Select Browse Object ball, Word enables you to choose the document element you want to browse.

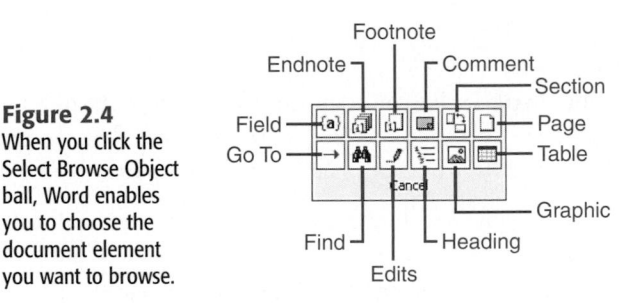

Footnote
Endnote
Comment
Section
Field
Page
Go To
Table
Graphic
Find
Heading
Edits

After you choose the one you want, the double arrows turn blue, indicating that they no longer move to the next or preceding page but rather move to a different element in your document. They remain blue for the rest of your editing session or until you click the Page icon to browse by page again.

You can always check to see which element type the Document Browser is set to search for by using ScreenTips. Just position the mouse pointer on one of the double-arrow buttons until the ScreenTip opens. When you want to revert to browsing by page, click the Select Browse Object icon and choose Page.

TIP

What if it's not enough to view the next or preceding document element—you want to move ahead or back by several elements? Or what if you want to browse for an element that Select Browse Object doesn't control? Use Word's Go To dialog box: Press F5 to display it. Go To is covered in detail later in this chapter, in the section "Go To Practically Anything You Want."

GET THE BEST VIEW OF YOUR DOCUMENT

There's more than one way to look at anything—especially your Word documents. Word lets you choose the right view for whatever purpose suits you at the moment, including editing speed, previewing, or document organization, to name a few. You can navigate and edit your document in any of these five Word views:

- Normal view
- Web Layout view
- Print Layout view
- Outline view
- Reading Layout view

The fastest way to choose your view is to click a View button at the left of the horizontal scrollbar, near the bottom of the screen (see Figure 2.5).

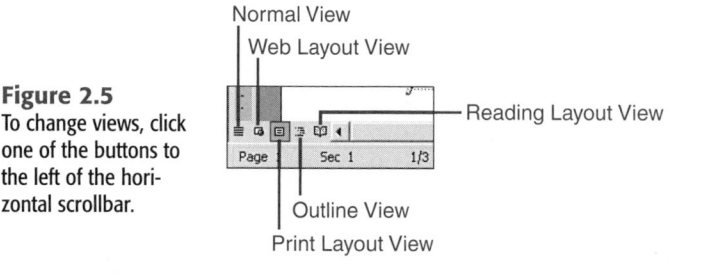

Figure 2.5
To change views, click one of the buttons to the left of the horizontal scrollbar.

NOTE

A sixth way of viewing your Document, Document Map, allows you to view (and quickly move among) the headings of your document. Document Maps are covered later in this chapter, in the "Document Map" section.

WORKING IN NORMAL VIEW

Normal view is Word's default setting (refer to Figure 2.1). It represents a trade-off between accuracy and speed. In Normal view, you see your document much as it will appear when printed, with some significant exceptions. For example:

- You can't use Word's drawing tools. (If you do, you've switched automatically into Print Layout view.)
- If your document consists of multiple columns, Normal view displays a single column instead.
- Headers and footers aren't displayed unless you choose <u>V</u>iew, <u>H</u>eader and Footer (which also switches you into Print Layout view).
- Page breaks appear as dotted lines. Page breaks you enter manually appear darker, and contain the words "Page Break." (Section breaks appear as dark double-dotted lines, with the words "Section Break.")

TIP

> Occasionally, even Normal view is too slow. For example, you may be using a relatively slow computer to edit an extremely long, complex document. One option is to display the contents of your document in Draft Font. Because this hides all text formatting, Word runs noticeably faster. To do this, first make sure that you're in Normal or Outline view. Then select Tools, Options, View and check the Draft Font check box.

WORKING IN WEB LAYOUT VIEW

Web Layout view is designed to show how text will appear when viewed through a Web browser. For example, Web Layout view wraps text to the width of your screen, as a browser does, rather than allowing it to stretch beyond the screen's borders (see Figure 2.6).

Figure 2.6
Web Layout view enhances your document's appearance for onscreen viewing.

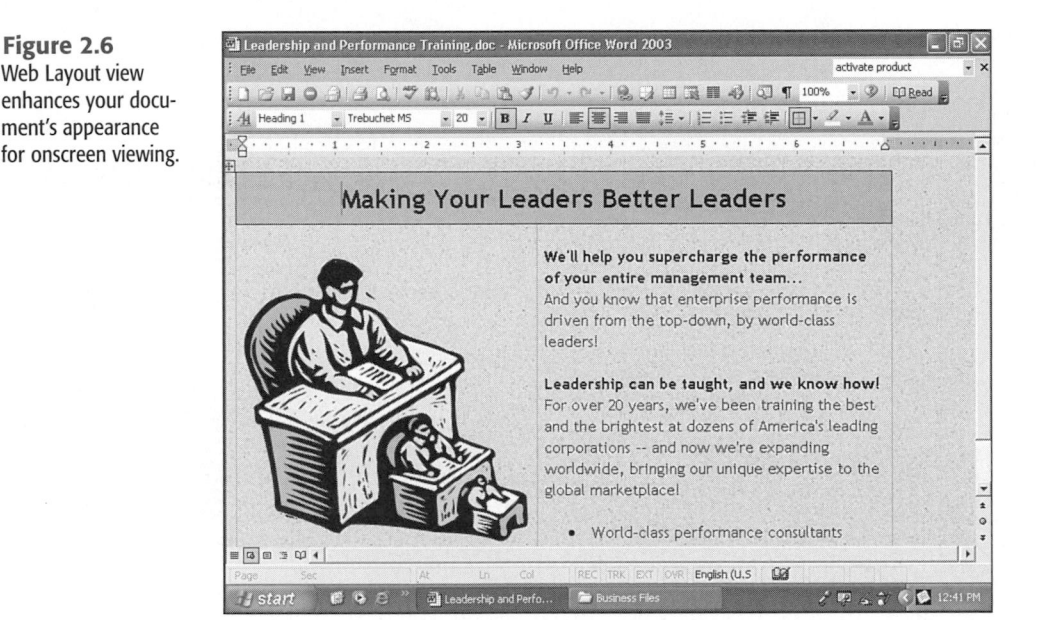

WORKING IN PRINT LAYOUT VIEW

Print Layout view (see Figure 2.7) shows your document exactly as it will appear when you print it, with all headers, footers, images, columns, and other elements in place. The trade-off is that Print Layout view is slower because Word, Windows, and your computer must all work harder to continually display these elements accurately.

TIP

> If that Print Layout view runs too slowly, yet you need to see accurate page layouts, there is a compromise: Keep the layout but hide any images contained in the document. To do this, first make sure that you are in Print Layout view. Next, select Tools, Options, View. Check the Picture Placeholders check box and clear the Drawings check box.

Figure 2.7
In this figure, the document is displayed in Print Layout view. Note that all elements

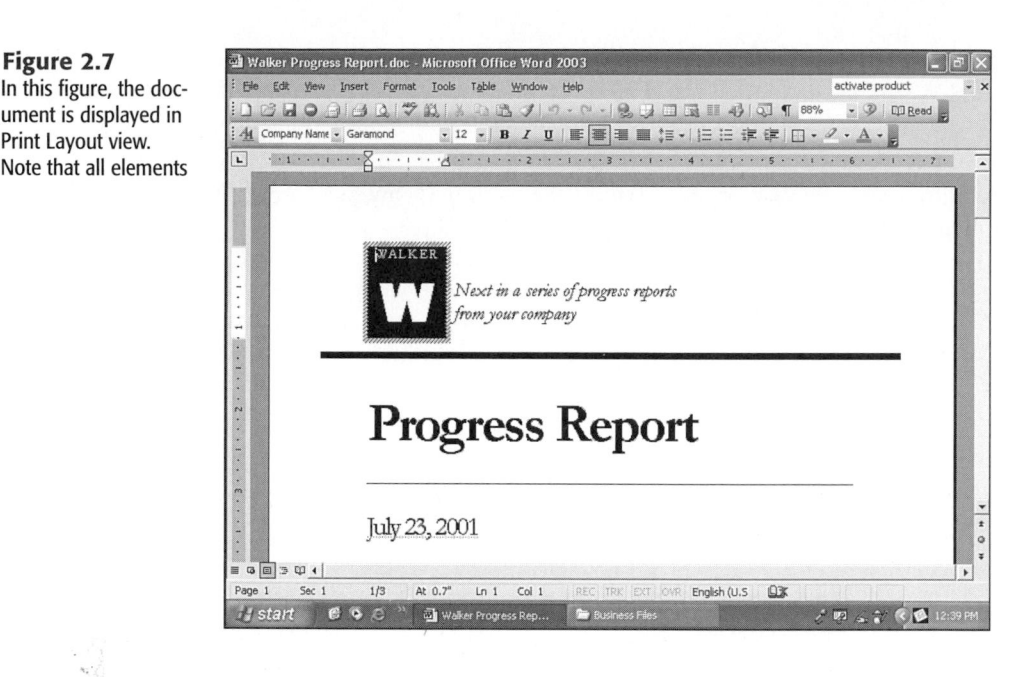

WORKING IN OUTLINE VIEW

Outline view (see Figure 2.8) displays the outline structure embedded in your document so that you can quickly see (and change) the way your document is organized.

Figure 2.8
In Outline view, you can see exactly how your document is structured and move

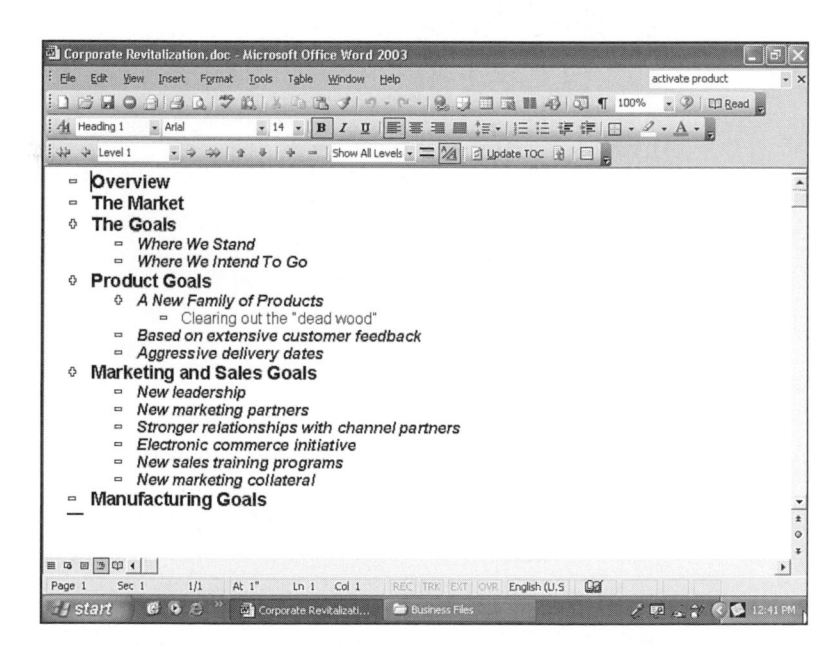

You won't see much of a difference between Outline view and other views unless you've used Word's Heading Styles or Outline Levels features to establish distinctions between levels of text. But if you do use these features, Outline view gives you exceptional control over your document that's available in no other way. (For a close look at what you can do in Outline view, see Chapter 18, "Outlining: Practical Techniques for Organizing Any Document.")

TIP

> If you haven't used Heading Styles, you can often add them quickly using Word's AutoFormat feature, as discussed in Chapter 9, "Automating Your Documents."

WORKING IN READING LAYOUT VIEW

NEW In Word 2003, Microsoft introduces Reading Layout view, a special view designed primarily for reading documents rather than editing them (see Figure 2.9).

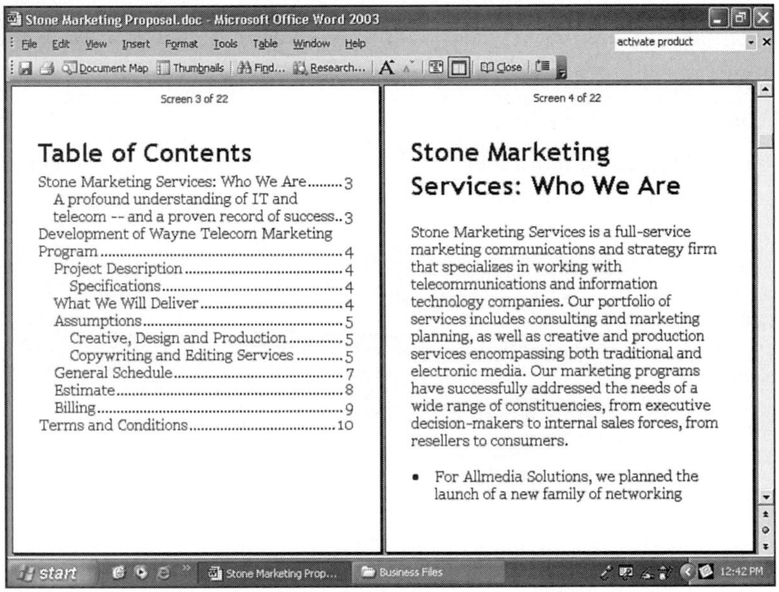

Figure 2.9
Reading Layout view is optimized for reading documents onscreen.

You can choose Reading Layout view by clicking the Reading Layout view button at the lower left of the editing window, or by clicking Read on the Standard toolbar, or choosing View, Reading Layout. When you display Reading Layout view, Word changes your page display in the following ways:

- Text is enlarged significantly. (This affects only the onscreen display, not how the text will be printed.)
- Depending on your video settings, two "screens" of text may be shown at once.

- Word uses Microsoft's ClearType technology to slightly improve legibility.
- All toolbars are hidden except the Reading Layout Toolbar, which brings together the tools Microsoft expects you to use most often while reading a document (see Figure 2.10). (You can, however, restore any toolbar by choosing View, Toolbars and selecting the toolbar you want to appear.)

Figure 2.10
The Reading Layout toolbar brings together the tools you may use most often while reading a document onscreen.

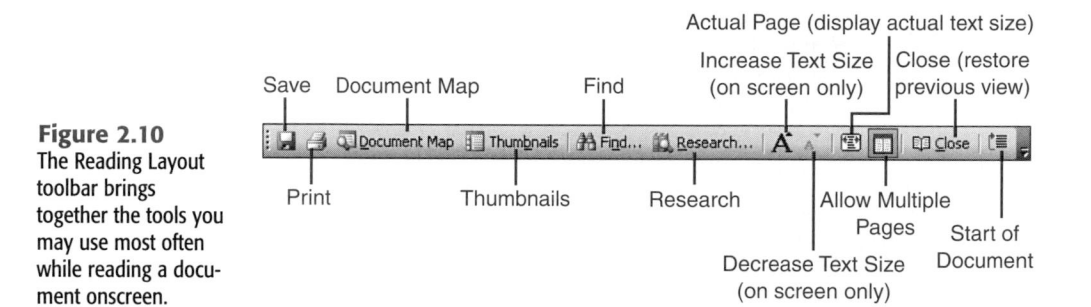

Although Reading Layout view is optimized for reading, you can also edit and format text the same way you normally do. However, if you depend on toolbar buttons, you will have to redisplay those toolbars.

When you are finished working with Reading Layout view, click Close. Word will display the view you were using previously.

DOCUMENT MAP

If your document includes headings or custom styles that Word can use as mileposts throughout your document, you'll also find the Document Map valuable. To display the Document Map, choose View, Document Map.

With Document Map (see Figure 2.11), you can see both your document's text and a map of your document at the same time. Click an element on the map, and you move to that location—just as you would if you clicked on a hyperlink on a Web page.

WORKING WITH THUMBNAILS

Word 2003 introduces thumbnails, which allow you to move among pages by clicking on a small image of the page displayed to the left of the editing window (see Figure 2.12). To display thumbnails (or hide thumbnails already displayed), choose View, Thumbnails.

TIP

> If you are working in Reading Layout view, you can also display or hide thumbnails by clicking the Thumbnails button on the Reading Layout toolbar.

Document Map

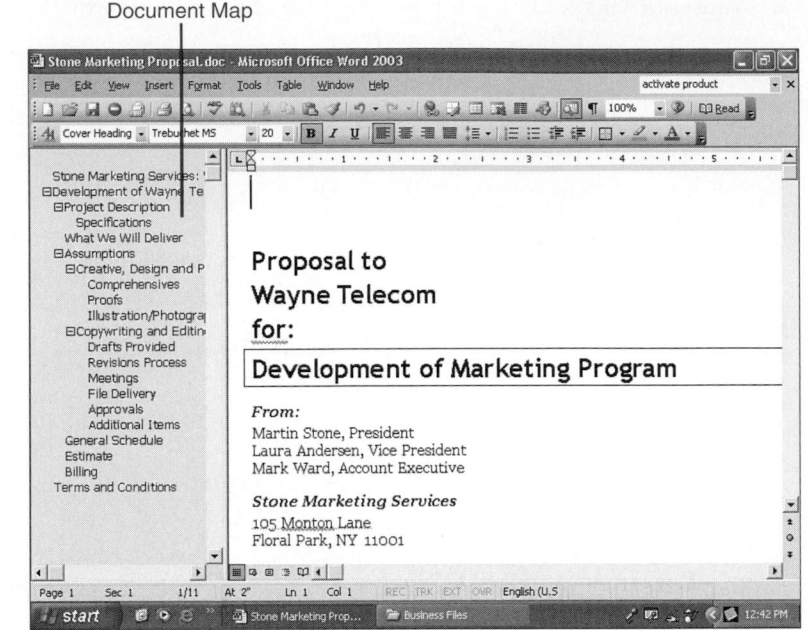

Thumbnails

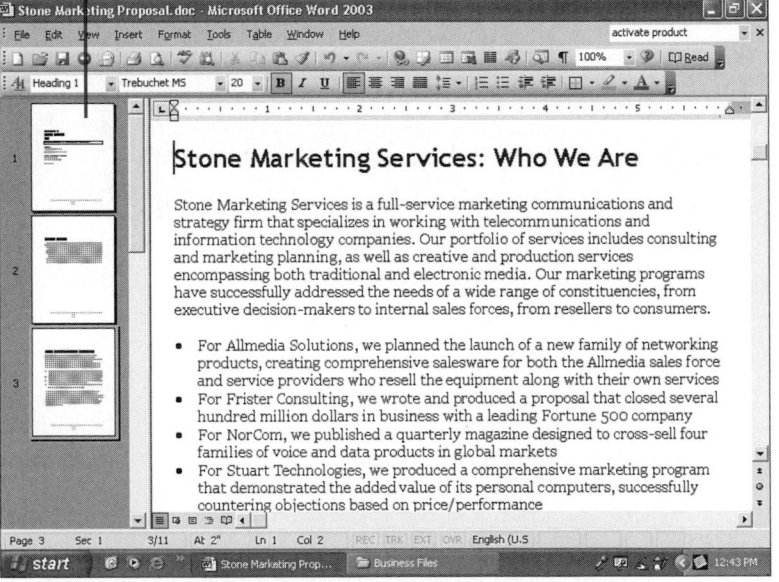

SEEING MORE OF YOUR DOCUMENT

Some people find Word's interface just too much: All those buttons seem to get in the way of their work. If you're one of those people, you'll appreciate knowing that you can hide as much of the Word interface as you want. You can even hide all of it.

HIDING SOME INTERFACE ELEMENTS

Much of Word's interface can be hidden or displayed via the View menu. For example, selecting View, Ruler toggles Word's rulers on or off. Selecting View, Toolbars displays a cascaded list of all available Word toolbars; you can then clear the check marks associated with each toolbar you want to hide.

Other interface elements can be hidden using Word's Options dialog box. Choose Tools, Options to display this dialog box; then display the View tab (see Figure 2.13).

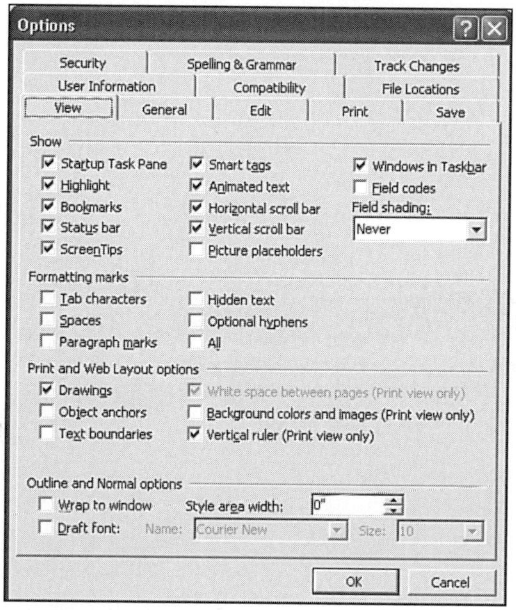

Figure 2.13
The View tab of the Options dialog box enables you to show or hide scrollbars and the status bar.

From here, clearing any or all of the Vertical Scroll Bar, Horizontal Scroll Bar, or Status Bar check boxes removes them from view in Word.

WORKING WITH A BLANK SCREEN

If you want, you can hide Word's interface almost entirely. It's easy: Choose View, Full Screen. Your document editing window expands to cover the entire screen, and the Full Screen toolbar appears, containing one button: Close Full Screen (see Figure 2.14). You still have access to Word's menus: Point your mouse at the very top edge of the screen, and they will appear.

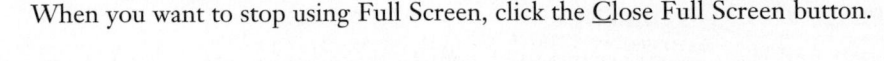

When you want to stop using Full Screen, click the Close Full Screen button.

Figure 2.14
Displaying Word's Full Screen interface.

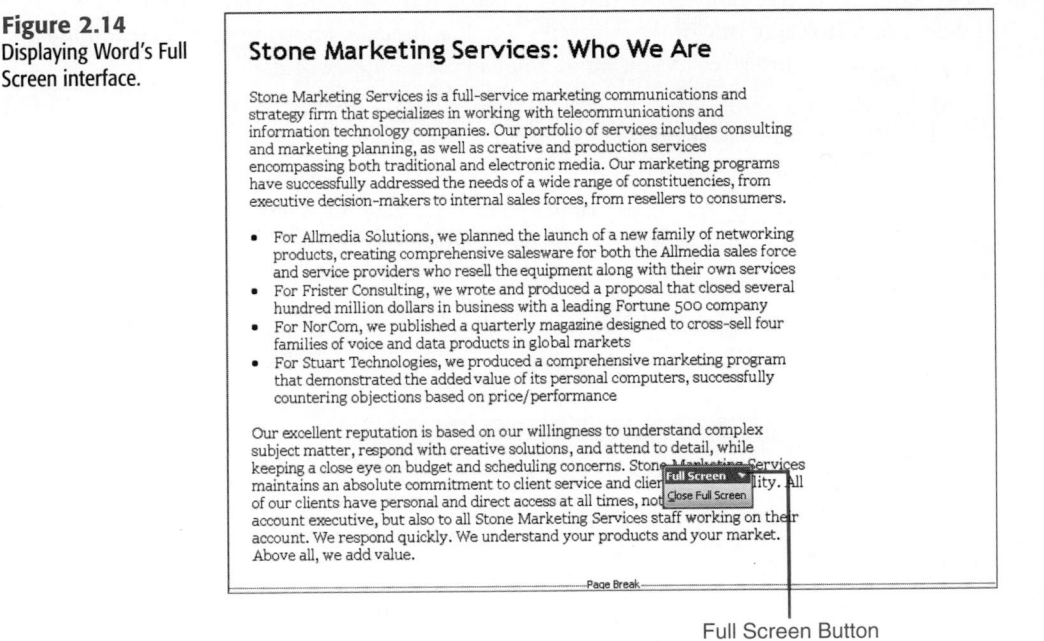

Full Screen Button

TIP

If the Full Screen toolbar disappears, or if you inadvertently close it, you can press Esc to display Word's interface again. You can also move your mouse pointer to the top of the screen, displaying Word's row of menu commands, and then choose View, Full Screen again to toggle the Full Screen view off.

ZOOMING IN ON WHAT YOU WANT TO SEE

By default, Word displays your text at full size in Normal view: 100%. However, you may occasionally want to change this. For example, to view the intricate details of a drawing, you might want to zoom in to 200% or more; or to see most or all of a page in Print Layout view, you might want to zoom out to 80% or less. Word makes this easy with the Zoom drop-down box in the Standard toolbar (see Figure 2.15).

Figure 2.15
Use the Zoom drop-down box to specify how much you want to enlarge or reduce your document

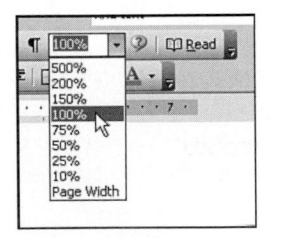

NOTE

> The Zoom drop-down list box displays different options depending on the view you've selected.

You can click the down arrow next to the Zoom drop-down box and choose from among Word's built-in ratios: 10%, 25%, 50%, 75%, 100%, 150%, 200%, and 500%, as well as Page Width, which ensures that all your text fits horizontally on your screen. (Page Width saves you the trouble of trying to figure out how much to reduce your document to see all its text.)

Sometimes you may want to specify an exact proportion not included on Word's drop-down list. For example, many people find their documents easier to edit if the type is enlarged to 110% or 120%. To specify an exact proportion, click inside the Zoom drop-down box and enter the value you want. Any whole digit between 10% and 500% works.

Changes you make in the Zoom drop-down box do not affect the way your document appears when printed or published online. They also do not affect how the document is displayed in other views; for example, if you change the 100% setting to 75% in Normal view, your document will still be displayed at 100% in Print Layout view.

Word uses the new setting you establish in any new documents you create. Word retains the Zoom settings that are associated with each view when you close a document. In other words, if you reopen a document that was displayed at 75% in Normal view during your preceding editing session, it will be displayed at 75% in Normal view now as well.

GAINING FINER CONTROL OVER ZOOM WITH THE ZOOM DIALOG BOX

You can gain even finer control over your Zoom settings. Choose View, Zoom to display the Zoom dialog box (see Figure 2.16).

Figure 2.16
Use the Zoom dialog box to gain finer control over zooming.

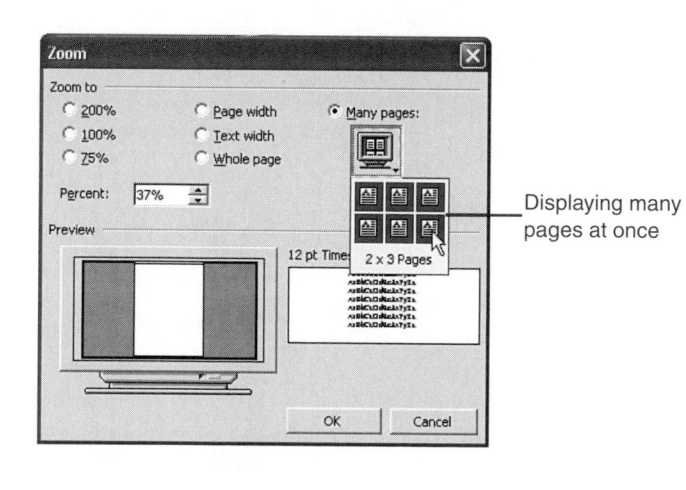

Displaying many pages at once

In addition to the standard settings accessible from the drop-down box, you can also zoom to <u>T</u>ext width (which hides most of the left and right margins, allowing for slightly larger and more readable text than zooming to page width).

You can also choose Whole Page, which displays the entire page at once. And, if you are working in Print Layout view or Print Preview, you can display several pages at once. To do so, click the Many Pages button, and drag under it to display the number of pages you specify.

> **NOTE**
> Options available in the zoom dialog differ depending on the current view you have selected.

TRACKING YOUR PROGRESS WITH THE STATUS BAR

Often, you'll want to know exactly where you are in your document, or on your page—especially if you're working in Normal view, where your location on the page isn't always apparent. You can always get this information—and more—from the Word status bar. You can find the status bar at the bottom of the Word screen (see Figure 2.17).

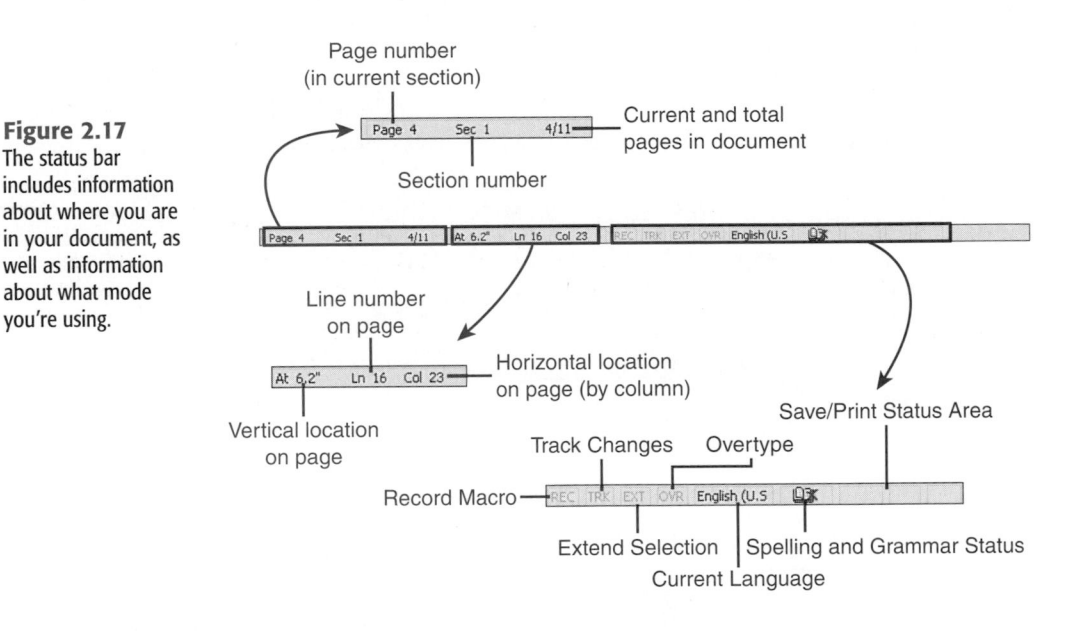

Figure 2.17
The status bar includes information about where you are in your document, as well as information about what mode you're using.

TRACKING WHERE YOU ARE

The location information section of the status bar tells you what page and section you're in and how many pages are in your entire document. If you have more than one section, and you've told Word to start numbering new sections with page 1, Word tells you both the correct page number within the section and the number of the page in the overall document. (See Chapter 5, "Controlling Page Features," to learn about document sections.)

Location information also tells you where you are on a given page. The information is provided vertically by inches and line numbers and horizontally by columns, with each character of text on the line counted as one column. (Don't confuse the columns Word uses for this column numbering with those it creates with multiple-column documents such as newsletters.)

TIP

> Double-clicking on the Page, Section, or Current and Total Pages indicator displays the Go To tab of the Find dialog box, which you can use to navigate to another location in your document.

2

TRACKING YOUR CURRENT MODE

Most of the time, you'll work in Word's standard editing mode, but some tasks require you to be in another mode. For example, when you ask Word to track changes in your document, you're in Track Changes mode. Any active modes are displayed in the status bar; grayed-out modes are inactive:

Abbreviation	Description
REC	A macro is currently being recorded.
TRK	Revisions are currently being tracked.
EXT	A text selection is currently being extended.
OVR	Word is currently overtyping (replacing text as you type over it). OVR is not available when Tracked Changes is turned on.

At the far right of the status bar, the Spelling and Grammar Status animated icon appears. When it resembles a pencil writing in a book, Word is busy displaying your current keystrokes. When you stop momentarily, the icon changes to display a large red × over the book, indicating that Word is checking your grammar and spelling.

→ For more information about Word's automated spelling and grammar checker, **see** "Using Automatic Spelling and Grammar Checking," **p. 254**.

TIP

> You can activate or deactivate any of these four modes by double-clicking on its icon in the status bar. (If the icon is grayed out, it is inactive; double-clicking on it activates it.)

VIEWING TWO PARTS OF THE DOCUMENT AT THE SAME TIME: THE SPLIT BOX

Word's split box (see Figure 2.18) enables you to view and edit two parts of your document at the same time. For example, if you change one clause of a contract, you might want to view another clause at the same time, to see how it should be edited. Or if you're creating a cross-reference (as is covered in Chapter 22, "Using Footnotes, Bookmarks, and Cross-References"), you might want to view both the referenced text and the place where you're inserting the reference.

Figure 2.18
The split box appears above the vertical scrollbar at the right edge of the screen.

Split box

The split box is a tiny beveled rectangle placed above the vertical scrollbar. To split the screen with the split box, follow these steps:

1. Place your mouse pointer on the split box.

2. Click and drag the mouse pointer down to the location in the editing window where you want your screen to split. While you are dragging, a split pointer is visible.

3. Release the mouse button. The document is now displayed in two separate windows.

You can navigate and edit in either window (see Figure 2.19). Your edits appear in both windows because you are still working on only one document. In Word, each split box window contains its own ruler, scrollbars, Document Browser, and View buttons, each of which works independently.

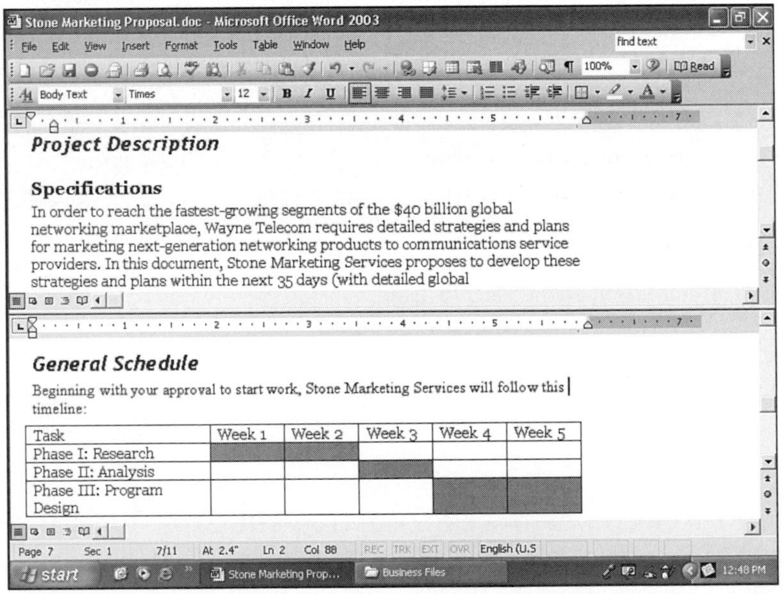

Figure 2.19
Working with a document split into two windows.

When you no longer want a split screen, click and drag the split pointer above the top or below the bottom of the editing window. Your screen returns to normal.

NOTE

> If you can't find the split box, make sure that Document Map is not displayed, and make sure that the vertical scroll box is displayed (choose Tools, Options, View; check Vertical Scroll Box; and choose OK).

TOOLBARS: USUALLY THE FASTEST WAY TO GET THE JOB DONE

In Word, there's little you can't do by clicking a single button. In fact, sometimes the hardest part is finding the right button to click. If you're not sure what some of Word's button icons mean, position your mouse pointer over the icon, and a ScreenTip appears, displaying the button's name.

TIP

> Occasionally, you might prefer to start using a keyboard shortcut in place of a toolbar button. To learn more of the keyboard shortcuts associated with Word toolbar buttons, tell Word to display the keyboard shortcut whenever it displays a ScreenTip.
>
> To do so, select View, Toolbars, Customize and choose the Options tab. Make sure that Show ScreenTips on Toolbars is checked and that Show Shortcut Keys in ScreenTips is also checked.

Word comes with more than a dozen toolbars, each containing a series of buttons you can click to perform common tasks. For example, Word's Drawing toolbar contains a series of tools for drawing, coloring, and manipulating lines, shapes, and text. You can display most of Word's toolbars anytime you want, by selecting View, Toolbars. A cascaded list appears. Check the toolbar you want. Table 2.1 lists the toolbars you can display using View, Toolbars.

TABLE 2.1   WORD TOOLBARS AVAILABLE BY CHOOSING VIEW, TOOLBARS

Toolbar Name	What It Does
Standard	File management and editing
Formatting	Font (character) and paragraph formatting
AutoText	Insertion and management of boilerplate text
Control Toolbox	Insertion and management of ActiveX controls
Database	Control of Word database tables and external queries
Drawing	Graphics, image management, text boxes, and text-based graphics (WordArt)
Email	Email editing tools
Forms	Electronic forms
Frames	Creation of frames in Web pages
Ink Comment	Tools for marking up documents with an electronic pen

continues

TABLE 2.1 CONTINUED

Toolbar Name	What It Does
Mail Merge	Organizing and performing mail or email merges
Outlining	Document outlining features
Picture	Insertion and manipulation of clip art
Reviewing	Tracking reviewers' changes
Tables and Borders	Table and cell creation, formatting, manipulation, and sorting
Task Pane	Displays Task Pane to the right of the editing window
Visual Basic	Running and working with Visual Basic macros
Web	Accessing Web resources; creating documents to be published on the Web
Web Tools	Insertion of automated elements in Web forms
Word Count	Displays word counts and allows you to quickly update them
WordArt	Creation of graphics from text

Other toolbars, such as Header and Footer, automatically appear when you're performing the tasks they're designed to assist, and they don't appear at any other time.

Another option, Customize, allows you to make changes to your toolbars' behavior and contents, and create new toolbars. Some toolbar customization tasks were covered earlier in this chapter, in the "Using Word's Personalized Menus" section. Most are covered in Chapter 31, "Customizing Word."

DISPLAYING THE FULL STANDARD AND FORMATTING TOOLBARS

Two toolbars are especially important: the Standard toolbar, which contains basic file management and editing tools, and the Formatting toolbar, which contains basic formatting tools.

If you rarely use some of these toolbar buttons, you might be willing to trade them for increased editing space. To combine the most common Standard and Formatting toolbars onto a single row, choose Tools, Customize and click Options. Then clear the Show Standard and Formatting Toolbars on Two Rows check box, and click Close.

NOTE

> Most users prefer to display full toolbars. In addition, you'll find references to Standard and Formatting buttons throughout this book that appear on only the full toolbars.

A CLOSER LOOK AT THE STANDARD AND FORMATTING TOOLBARS

As you've learned, Word clusters the most commonly used tasks on two Word toolbars: the Standard toolbar and the Formatting toolbar.

The Standard toolbar (see Figure 2.20) contains basic file management and editing tools, along with one-button shortcuts for common tasks, such as inserting tables, columns, or drawings.

Figure 2.20
The Standard toolbar organizes many of Word's most common file management and editing tools.

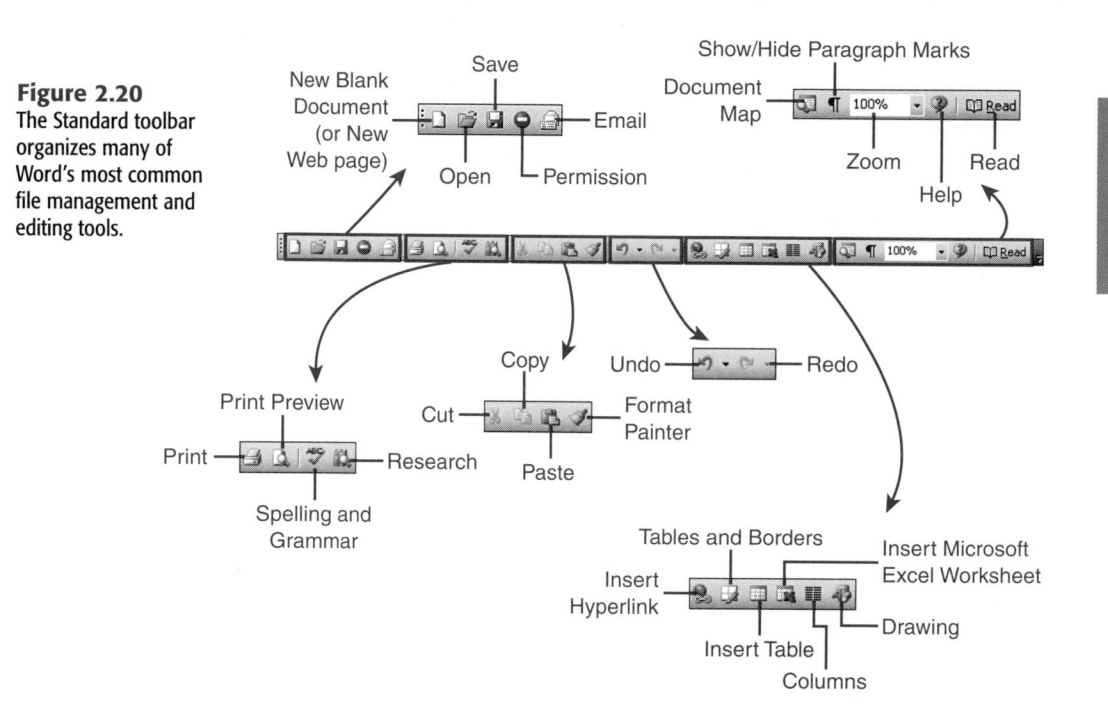

The Formatting toolbar (see Figure 2.21) contains shortcuts for formatting text, aligning paragraphs, inserting bullets and numbering, adjusting indentation, and adding borders and highlighting. Formatting is covered in detail in Chapter 4, "Quick and Effective Formatting Techniques."

TIP

> If you often edit text in foreign languages, or if you create documents that utilize phonetics, you may want to display Word's Extended Formatting toolbar, which contains a set of tools for these applications.
>
> You can't display the Extended Formatting toolbar through View, Toolbars, however. To display it, choose Tools, Customize; then click the Toolbars tab if it doesn't already appear. In the Toolbars scroll box, check the Extended Formatting check box and click Close.

ADDING RELATED BUTTONS TO A WORD TOOLBAR

If you wish that one of Word's toolbars had slightly different buttons, Word makes it easy to do something about it. Click the down arrow at the far right of any Word toolbar, click Add or Remove Buttons, and click the name of the toolbar from the cascading menu. An extensive list of buttons appears (see Figure 2.22). If you want to add a button that doesn't currently appear, click to place a check mark next to it. If you want to remove a button, click on it to clear its check mark.

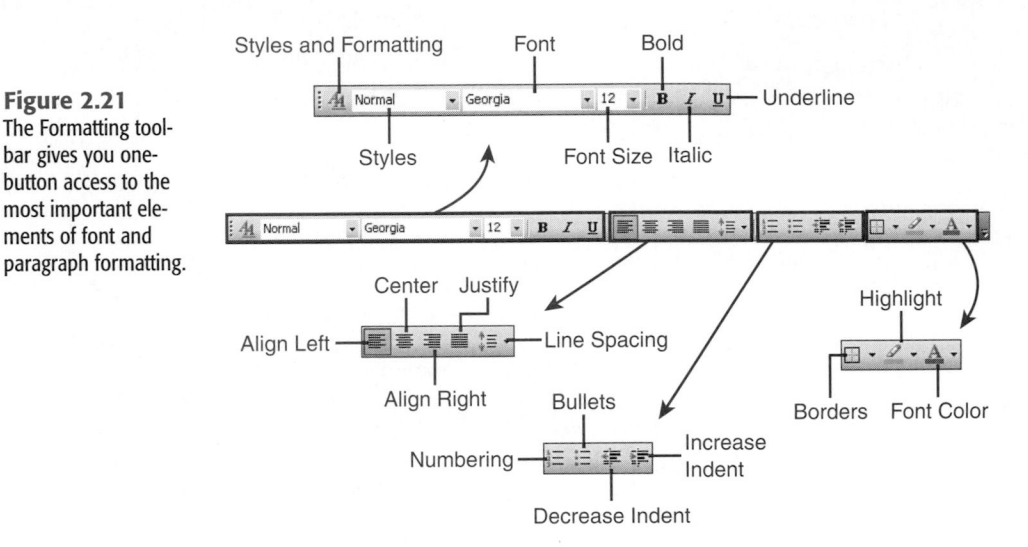

Figure 2.21
The Formatting toolbar gives you one-button access to the most important elements of font and paragraph formatting.

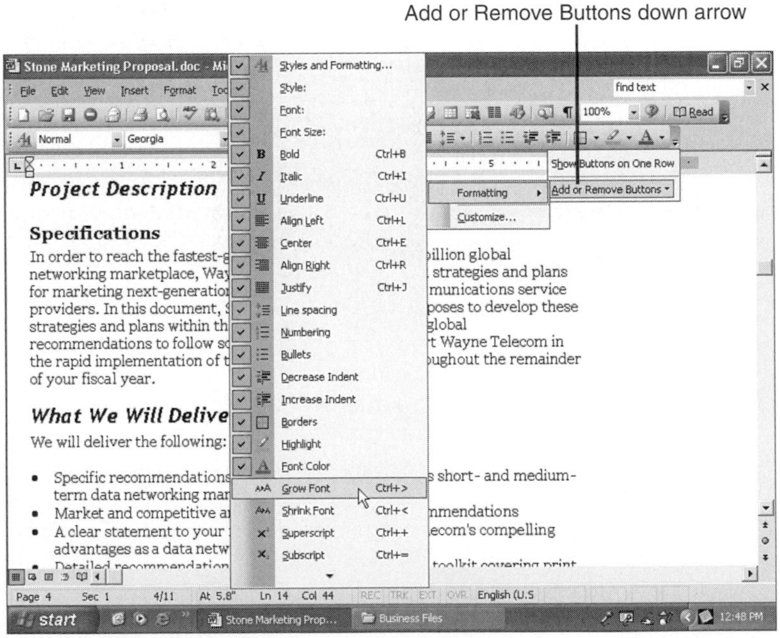

Figure 2.22
Adding related buttons to a toolbar.

➔ To learn how to create new toolbars, add other buttons to existing toolbars, and move buttons between toolbars, **see** "Customizing Toolbars and Menus," **p. 1023**.

MOVING TOOLBARS

You don't have to settle for where Word places your toolbars; you can drag them anywhere you want. You may especially want to move toolbars (and display extra toolbars) if you have a high-resolution monitor and a lot of space in your editing window.

If a toolbar is locked in place at the top of the screen, you can drag it by clicking and dragging the notch at the left edge of the toolbar, which is called a *move handle*. If the toolbar is floating in midscreen, you can drag it by its title bar.

If you drag a toolbar to the edge of the screen, it locks in place. If you drag a toolbar to the center of the screen, it floats. Examples are shown in Figure 2.23.

Figure 2.23
Locked and floating toolbars.

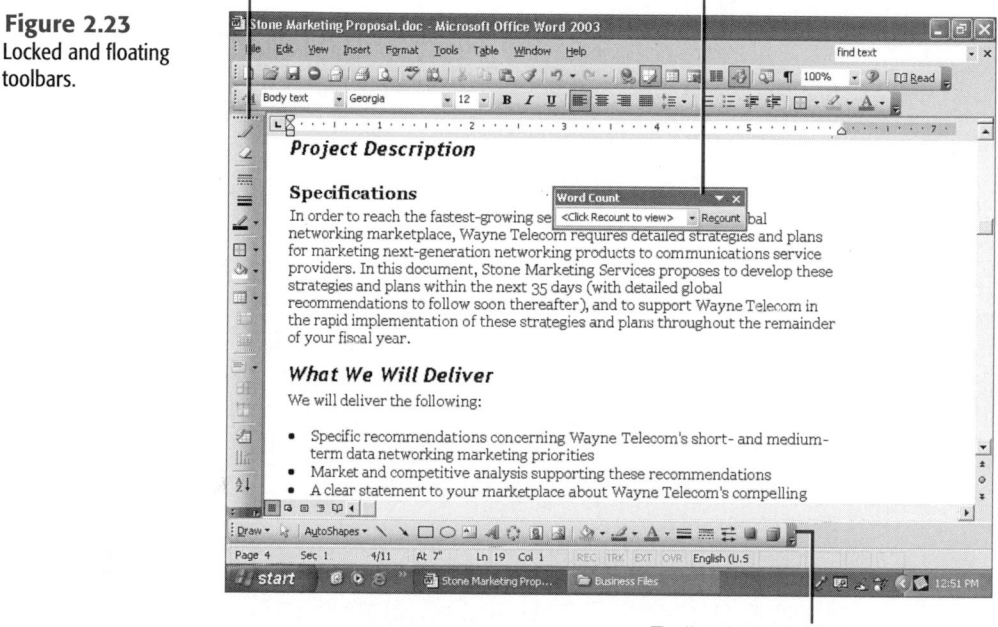

Toolbar locked at side of screen   Toolbar floating on screen

Toolbar locked at bottom of screen

USING THE RULER

Word's ruler (see Figure 2.24) displays by default, providing an easy, "hands-on" way to control margins, indents, and tabs. You'll take a closer look at using the ruler to control indents and tabs in Chapter 3, "Essential Document Creation and Management Techniques," and margins in Chapter 4, "Quick and Effective Formatting Techniques."

KEYBOARD SHORTCUTS: GETTING THE JOB DONE EVEN FASTER

So far, this chapter has focused primarily on shortcuts that involve clicking or dragging elements of the Word interface, such as toolbar buttons and scrollbars. But many people prefer

2

to work from the keyboard whenever possible—and often, even confirmed mouse users are sure to find some of Word's 250-plus keyboard shortcuts more convenient than its corresponding mouse shortcuts.

Figure 2.24
You can control margins, indents, and tabs by clicking and dragging elements of the ruler.

Word's keyboard shortcuts fall into several categories, including navigation, file management, editing, selecting text, viewing the document, inserting document elements, formatting, proofing, outlining, and several more. You may find the keyboard shortcuts for navigating your document, as listed in Table 2.2, to be especially handy.

TABLE 2.2   KEYBOARD SHORTCUTS FOR NAVIGATING YOUR DOCUMENT

Task	Keyboard Shortcut
Go to a specific location	Arrow keys
Display the Go To window	F5 or Ctrl+G
Go to previous insertion point	Shift+F5 or Alt+Ctrl+Z
Beginning of document	Ctrl+Home
End of document	Ctrl+End
Top of window	Ctrl+Page Up
Bottom of window	Ctrl+Page Down
Next screen	Page Down
Previous screen	Page Up
Next page	Alt+Ctrl+Page Down
Previous page	Alt+Ctrl+Page Up
Next paragraph	Ctrl+down arrow
Previous paragraph	Ctrl+up arrow
Next window	Ctrl+F6
Previous window	Ctrl+Shift+F6
Open Document Browser	Alt+Ctrl+Home
Beginning of column	Alt+Page Up
End of column	Alt+Page Down

Task	Keyboard Shortcut
Beginning of line	Home
End of line	End
Next line	Down arrow
Previous line	Up arrow
Left one word	Ctrl+left arrow
Right one word	Ctrl+right arrow

TIP

> If you press Shift before pressing most of the cursor movement keyboard shortcuts listed in Table 2.2, Word selects the text between your current insertion point and where the shortcut takes you. For example, if you press Shift+down arrow, Word selects all the text going down one line.

DISPLAYING COMMONLY USED FUNCTION KEYS

Word's Function Key Display enables you to see the most important function keys and click them onscreen. The Function Key Display works much like a toolbar; you can see it in Figure 2.25. You can't view it the same way as you view a toolbar, however. To view it, choose Tools, Customize and click the Toolbars tab if it doesn't already appear. In the Toolbars scroll box, check the Function Key Display check box; then click Close.

Figure 2.25
Click on any button in the Function Key Display to perform the action.

After the Function Key Display is open, you can close it by clicking the close box in the upper-right corner. If the Function Key Display is locked at a corner of the screen, drag it to the middle so that it floats; then click the Close box.

USING SHORTCUT MENUS

Word also provides shortcut menus that bring together many of the options you're most likely to need while editing your document.

Different choices appear in Word's shortcut menus depending on what you're doing. For example, if you've selected text, Word's shortcut menus include choices for cutting, copying, pasting, or formatting that text. On the other hand, if you're working within a table, you find options to insert rows, delete cells, and format table borders.

2

To view a shortcut menu, right-click on the text or graphic you are working with. You can see a typical shortcut menu in Figure 2.26.

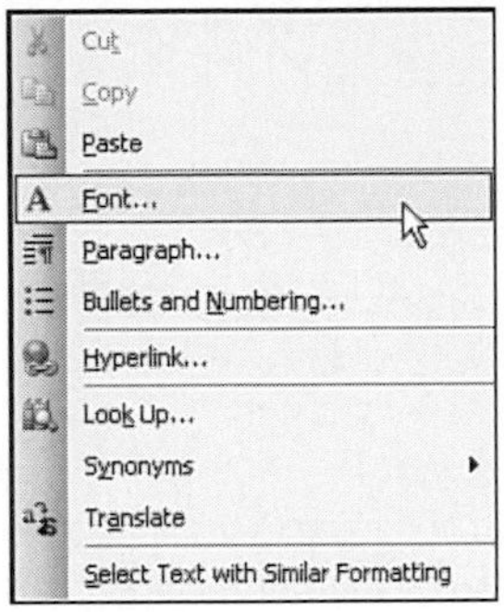

Figure 2.26
The shortcut menu that appears when you right-click ordinary text.

✂	Cu_t_
📋	_C_opy
📋	_P_aste
A	_F_ont...
≣	_P_aragraph...
≔	Bullets and _N_umbering...
🔗	_H_yperlink...
📖	Loo_k_ Up...
	S_y_nonyms ▶
🔤	T_r_anslate
	Se_l_ect Text with Similar Formatting

USING FIND, REPLACE, AND GO TO

If dialog boxes could get worn out, for many users the Find and Replace dialog boxes would be the first to go. They're real workhorses: easy to use and extremely powerful. The next few sections show you how to make the most of them.

In this section, you'll learn the fundamentals of searching for text—but you'll also discover that Find and Replace can work with nearly anything you can put into a Word document: formatting, graphics—you name it. You'll also discover how to use the related Go To command, which can find much more than most users realize.

Word brings together its Find, Replace, and Go To tools in a single dialog box, so it's easy to switch between them if you realize that you need to use a different tool. You can open this Find and Replace dialog box in several ways:

- To display the Find tab, press Ctrl+F; or choose Edit, Find; or click Select Browse Object and click the Find button (refer to Figure 2.4).
- To display the Replace tab, press Ctrl+H or choose Edit, Replace.
- To display the Go To tab, press F5 (or Ctrl+G); or choose Edit, Go To; or click Select Browse Object and click the Go To button.

> **TIP**
>
> To get one-click access to Find, add Word's optional Find button to the Standard toolbar. Click the down-arrow button at the right edge of the Standard toolbar and move the mouse over Add or Remove Buttons. Choose Find from the list of buttons that appears. (It's at the bottom of the list.)

FINDING TEXT QUICKLY

When all you want to do is find text, Word makes things simple:

1. Display the Find and Replace dialog box by pressing Ctrl+F (see Figure 2.27).

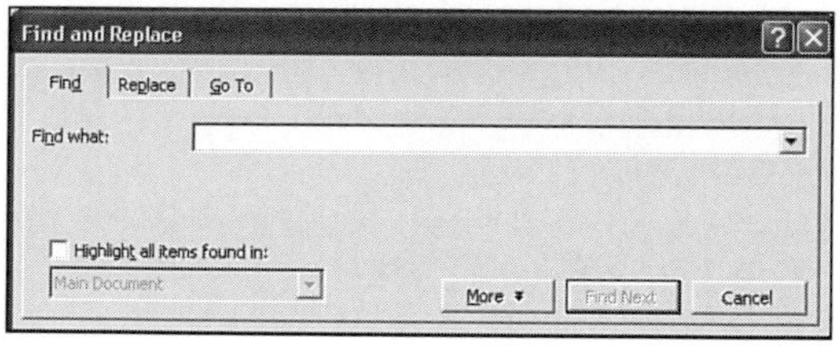

Figure 2.27
Word's Find tab, with complex options hidden.

2. Enter the text you want to locate in the Find What text box.
3. Click Find Next. If the text is found in your document, Word selects it.

After Word locates the text, the Find and Replace dialog box remains open so that you can search for something else—or edit the document after you locate the text you want to edit.

> **TIP**
>
> Sometimes, after you find text, you might decide that you want to replace it—either in one location or globally.
>
> With the Find and Replace dialog box open, click the Replace tab: The text you originally entered in the Find What text box is still there. The Replace tab is discussed in detail in the next section.

After you close the Find and Replace dialog box, you don't have to reopen it to find the next instance of the same text. Just press Shift+F4, and Word moves to the next location where the text can be found. (This will not happen if you change Browse objects. Choosing a new Browse object resets the Find Next operation to use the Browse setting, not the Find setting.)

REPLACING TEXT QUICKLY

Often, you know in advance that you want to replace text, not just find it. To replace text without first finding it, follow these steps:

1. Press Ctrl+H to display the Replace tab of the Find and Replace dialog box (see Figure 2.28).
2. In the Find What text box, enter the text you want to replace.
3. In the Replace With text box, enter the text you want to use instead.
4. You now have a few options as to what you do next:
   - To find the next occurrence of the text and then decide whether to make the replacement, click Find Next.
   - To replace the next occurrence of the text and wait for instruction about what to do after that, click Replace.

- To replace all occurrences of the text immediately, click Replace All.

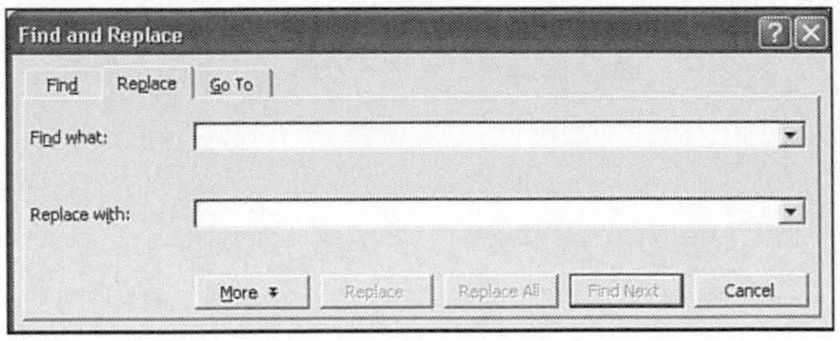

Figure 2.28
In the Replace tab, you can specify the text you want to find and the text with which you want to replace it.

2

5. When you're finished replacing text, click Close (or Cancel if the search text was not found).

HIGHLIGHTING ALL APPEARANCES OF AN ITEM IN A DOCUMENT

In Word 2003, instead of displaying found text one instance at a time, you can have Word select them all at once. After you've selected them all, you can cut or reformat them all at once.

To select all text references at once, press Ctrl+F to display the Find tab of the Find and Replace dialog box and enter what you are looking for in the Find What text box. Check the Highlight All Items Found In check box.

If necessary, you can also select the part of the document where you want to display highlighting. You may have only one option: Main Document. If your document contains headers or footers, these may appear as a second option. If you selected text before displaying the Find dialog box, Current Selection will also appear as an option.

TAKING MORE CONTROL OVER FIND AND REPLACE

Thus far, all the searches and replaces you've performed have used Word's default settings. For example, Word searches the entire document and disregards capitalization and formatting. (By default, a phrase is found whether or not it is capitalized, and whether or not it is boldfaced.)

You can, however, exercise much more control over how Find and Replace works. To begin, in either the Find or the Replace tab, click the More button. Word displays several additional options (see Figure 2.29).

CONTROLLING THE DIRECTION OF A SEARCH

Usually, you'll want to search an entire document for the text you want—but not always. For example, suppose that you realize partway through editing a document that you've been using a product name incorrectly; you may want to search backward to find incorrect references that appear earlier in your document.

Figure 2.29
The Find dialog box with "More" options displayed.

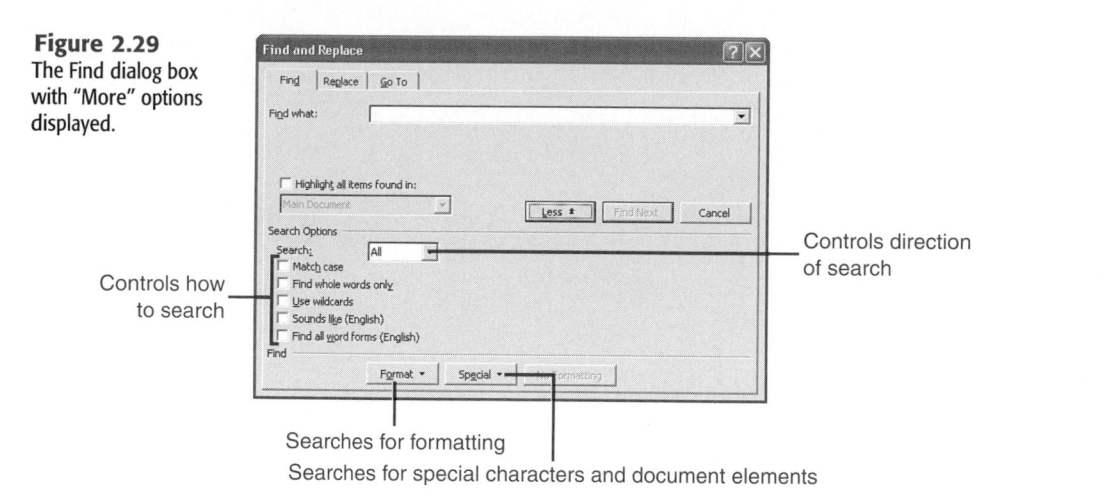

Controls how to search

Controls direction of search

Searches for formatting

Searches for special characters and document elements

The Search: drop-down list box enables you to control the direction in which Word searches for the text you specify in the Find What box. You can search the entire document by leaving the setting at All. Or you can search forward through the document by choosing Down or backward through the document by choosing Up.

NOTE

> When you choose All, Word searches in a circular fashion from the current position of the insertion point forward in your document. When Word reaches the end of your document, it automatically goes to the top of the document and starts searching from there until it reaches your current insertion point.

PERFORMING CASE-SENSITIVE SEARCHES

By default, when you ask Word to find text, Word ignores any capitalization you may have used when specifying words or phrases in the Find What and Replace With text boxes. Similarly, if you ask Word to replace text, Word inserts the new text using the same capitalization it found in the original text. For instance, when Word replaces text at the beginning of a sentence, it capitalizes the sentence properly—even if you lowercased the text when you entered it in the Find and Replace dialog box.

This is usually what you want, but not always. For example, words like "Walker" are capitalized when used as last names but may be lowercased in other contexts. To find only text capitalized a certain way, type the text using the correct case in both the Find What and the Replace With text boxes. Then check the Match Case check box.

Word now finds only selections that match the case you typed in the Find What text box and replaces that text using the case you typed in the Replace With text box.

FINDING ALL OCCURRENCES OR ONLY WHOLE WORDS

Sometimes, the word for which you are searching may also be contained within another word. Consider "establish" and "establishment" or "when" and "whenever." This can slow down searches by burdening you with text you don't care to see. Worse, it can lead Word to replace text incorrectly.

If you search with default settings, Word finds every occurrence of the characters you type in the Find What text box. However, to find "establish" without looking at words that contain it—such as "establishment"—place a check in the Find Whole Words Only check box.

IMPROVING A SEARCH WITH WILDCARDS

If you've ever played poker, you may be familiar with *wildcards*; if you pick up a wildcard, you can use it as if it were any card you wanted. In Word searches, a wildcard is a symbol that stands for any character you want. Using wildcards helps you widen your searches. Word also provides several parameters you can use to not just widen searches, but refine them.

Table 2.3 describes the wildcards recognized by Word's Find and Replace dialog box, with examples of how these wildcards can be used. In the table, asterisks (*) are used to represent strings of text, question marks (?) to represent single characters, and exclamation points (!) to represent that you want to find any single character except those specified next to it.

For example, you'll notice that including a ? within the characters in the Find What text box tells Word to find any character in the position of the question mark. Here are a few pointers for using wildcards and parameters:

- If the character you're searching for happens to be one of the ones Word uses for wildcards, such as the asterisk (*), type a backslash (\) before the character.

- Suppose that you have a name that appears several times in your document, ordered last name first. You can use the \n wildcard, combined with parentheses, to search to rearrange the name so that it appears in first name, last name order. For example, if the name appears as Smith, John, then type (Smith), (John) in the Find What text box and \2 \1 in the Replace With text box. Word finds Smith, John and replaces it with John Smith. Note that placing the comma outside the parentheses in the Find What text box eliminates it when you replace the text.

TABLE 2.3 WILDCARD CHARACTERS USED TO SEARCH A WORD DOCUMENT

Use This Wildcard	To Find	Examples
?	Any single character	w?n finds win, wan, and won.
*	Any string of characters	l*d finds learned and limped

Use This Wildcard	To Find	Examples
[ ]	One of the specified characters	s[uo]n finds sun and son.
[-]	Any single character in this range	[b-d]rown finds brown, crown, and drown. Ranges must be in ascending order.
[!]	Any single character except the characters inside the brackets	l[!a]st finds list, lost, and lust, but not last.
[!x-z]	Any single character except characters in the range inside the brackets	cl[!a-m]ck finds clock and cluck, but not clack or click.
{n,}	At least *n* occurrences of the preceding character or expression	We{1,}d finds wed and weed.
@	One or more occurrences of the preceding character or expression	fe@d finds fed and feed.
{n}	Exactly *n* occurrences of the preceding character or expression	we{2}d finds weed but not wed.
{n,m}	From *n* to *m* occurrences of the preceding character or expression	10{1,3} finds 10, 100, and 1000.
<	The beginning of a word	<(ex) finds except, exempt, and exercise, but not text.
>	The end of a word	(al)> finds exceptional and diagonal, but not albatross or alarm.

CAUTION

If you're not careful about how you specify a wildcard search, you may get more than you bargained for. Searching for l*d will find "learned" and "limped" but will also find "license to d" in "license to drive" and even much longer strings between any *l* and the next *d*. And searching for 10{1,3} will find not only 10, 100, and 1000, but also the first four digits of 10000, 100000, and similar numbers.

FINDING WORDS WITH SPELLING VARIATIONS

Do you have trouble distinguishing there, their, and they're? How about its and it's? You can review your document for words that sound alike but are spelled differently using Word's Sounds Like (English) feature.

TIP

As an alternative, let Word's Grammar Checker correct mistakes for you.

→ For more information on working with Word's grammar checker, **see** "Using Automatic Spelling and Grammar Checking," **p. 254**.

FINDING OTHER WORD FORMS

Have you ever decided, after you're already several pages into a document, that the verb you've chosen to describe an action should be replaced with one that's more precise or effective? Changing each occurrence of the verb, in its various incarnations (for example, singular, plural, or adverbial) can be tedious. Instead, use Word's Find All Word Forms feature.

When you place a check in the Find All Word Forms check box, Word finds all forms of the word you type in the Find What text box. For example, if you type forbid in the Find What box, Word finds "forbid," "forbids," "forbidden," "forbade," and "forbidding."

When Word finds an instance of the word you are replacing, it provides a drop-down list of forms of the word that could be used as replacements. So, continuing with the "forbid" example, if you search and replace "forbid" with "prohibit," when Word finds any form of the word "forbid" listed, the list of possible replacements will include "prohibit," "prohibits," "prohibiting," and "prohibited."

Word selects the form of the word that the grammar rules pick as being the correct form. However, you can pick a different form of the word from the drop-down list. It's a good idea to replace these one by one so that you can review and approve each replaced form.

If you use different parts of speech in the Find What and Replace With text boxes, pay especially close attention to the word forms Word suggests for the replacement. Word conjugates the verb for you if the Replace With word can serve as a verb, even if your target is a noun. Make sure that the result is what you wanted.

NOTE

The Find All Word Forms feature is not available if you have checked either the Use Wildcards check box or the Sounds Like check box. All three of these choices are mutually exclusive.

NOTE

If you don't see the Find All Word Forms check box, you may need to run Setup again to install this feature."

SUPERCHARGED FIND AND REPLACE TECHNIQUES

Although Find and Replace basics are powerful, you can use Find and Replace in even more powerful ways. For example, you can use it to

- Clean up imported documents, such as emails containing line breaks after every line
- Find and replace formatting; for example, to replace all boldface in a document with italics
- Find and replace styles, to improve the visual consistency of a document
- Find and replace symbols and other special characters

CLEANING UP IMPORTED DOCUMENTS

Many documents contain paragraph marks you want to keep, as well as paragraph marks you want to eliminate. Often, imported documents contain two consecutive paragraph marks wherever a new paragraph begins. To eliminate the single paragraph marks you don't need, while retaining the double paragraph marks you do need, follow these steps:

NOTE

Don't use Replace All to replace every paragraph mark with nothing. Word not only strips out the single paragraph marks that appear at the end of every line, but also strips out the double paragraph marks that indicate the end of paragraphs. You obviously need that "end of paragraph" information; the procedure that follows shows you how to retain it.

TIP

In certain documents, you can also use Word's Format, AutoFormat feature to eliminate much of the stray formatting you don't need.

1. Open the Find and Replace dialog box and select the Replace tab (press Ctrl+H).
2. Clear any text you see in either the Find What text box or the Replace With text box, and place the insertion point in the Find What text box.
3. If the Search Options portion is not displayed, click the More button. Then click the Special button. A pop-up list appears, showing you the special characters for which you can search (see Figure 2.30).
4. Choose Paragraph Mark from the list; then click More again and choose it a second time. The characters ^p^p should now appear in the Find What text box.
5. In the Replace With text box, enter placeholder text that doesn't appear elsewhere in your document, such as QQQQ.
6. Click Replace All to replace every instance of double paragraph marks (^p^p) with QQQQ.
7. Type ^p in the Find What text box and the appropriate replacement in the Replace With text box. If your document's end-of-line paragraph marks include no spaces, type a space in Replace With; if they do include spaces, type nothing.

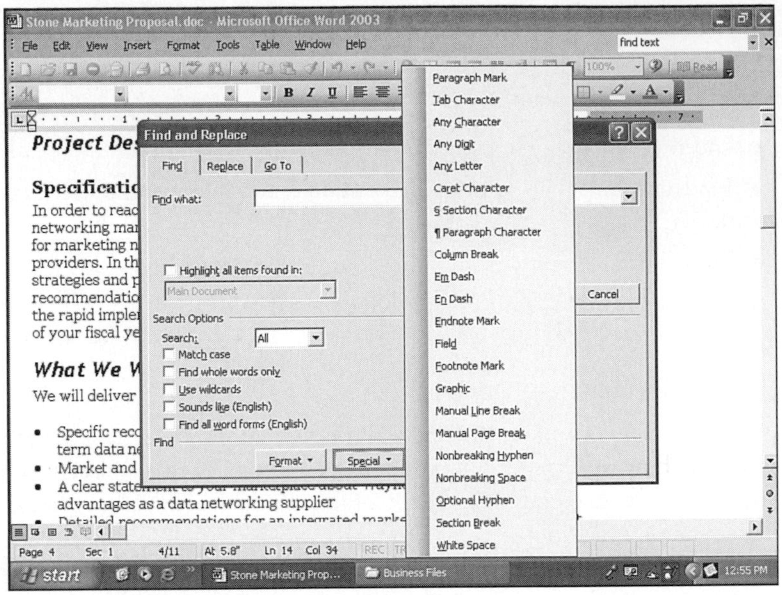

Figure 2.30
You can search for any character on this list and even replace it with any other character on the list.

8. Click Replace All to replace every unwanted paragraph mark with a space.

9. Now type QQQQ in the Find What text box and ^p in the Replace With text box.

10. Finally, click Replace All to replace every instance of QQQQ with true paragraph breaks.

TIP

Clicking the Special button displays a long list of special characters Word can search for, including

- Em dashes, en dashes, and quarter em spaces
- Column, line, and page breaks
- Graphics
- Endnote and footnote marks
- Any character, digit, or letter (wildcards)
- Column, line, and page breaks
- Graphics
- Endnote and footnote marks
- Ellipses
- Tabs

After a while, you may become familiar with the special characters Word inserts when you search for some of these document elements—for example, paragraph marks (^p). You don't have to choose them from the Special drop-down list; you can enter them directly.

Always start with the ^ caret character, and if the second character is a letter, enter the letter as lowercase. For example, to search for a footnote mark, enter ^f, never ^F.

Finding and Replacing Formatting

You can search for formatting of various types and replace it with other formatting. For example, you can search for and replace font and paragraph formatting, tab settings, frames, highlighting, language formatting, and styles. (Finding and replacing language formatting and styles are discussed in the next two sections.)

Place the insertion point in the appropriate text box (Find What or Replace With). If you are searching for text containing formatting, type the text for which you want to search.

TIP

> If you want to search for all occurrences of some formatting (for example, italic) don't type any text in the Find What text box.

Click the Format button. A pop-up list appears, showing the categories of formatting for which you can search (see Figure 2.31).

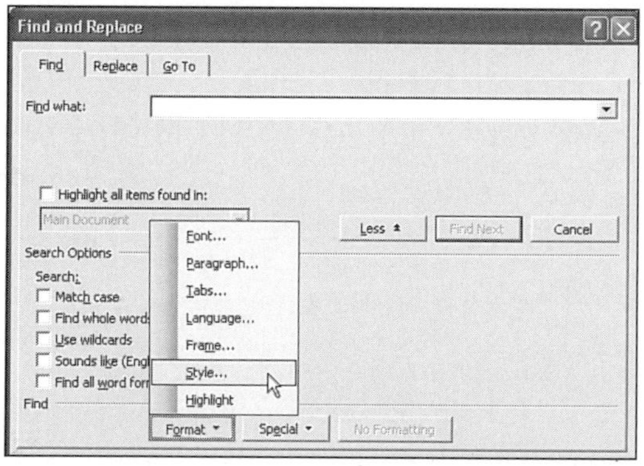

Figure 2.31
You can search for various categories of formatting by clicking the Format button.

If you choose Font, Paragraph, Tabs, or Frame, Word displays a dialog box similar to the dialog box you would use to apply this type of formatting.

→ For more information on formatting text in Word, **see** Chapter 4, "Quick and Effective Formatting Techniques," **p. 107**.

After you've opened the appropriate dialog box, select the formatting you want Word to search for, and click OK. Word then displays the Find and Replace dialog box again, listing the formatting you selected. If you choose Paragraph, the Find Paragraph dialog box appears. If you choose Highlight, you don't see a dialog box; Word simply changes the Find and Replace dialog box to include highlighting in either the search or the replacement (see Figure 2.32).

To clear formatting from the Find and Replace dialog box, place the insertion point in the Find What text box or the Replace With text box, as appropriate, and click the No Formatting button.

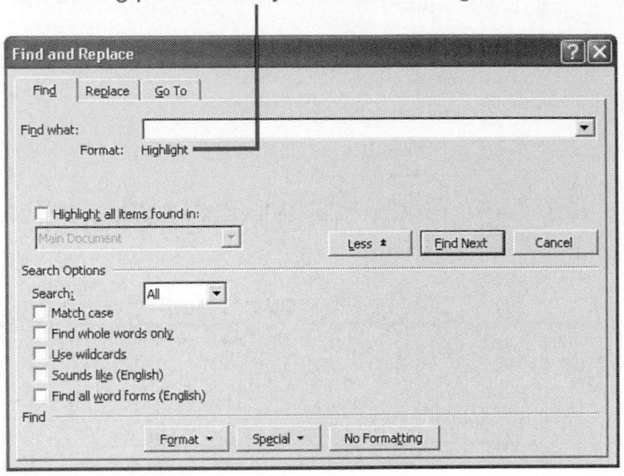

Formatting parameters you are searching for

Figure 2.32
After you select Highlight (or other parameters), Word adds the parameters in the Find and Replace dialog box.

NOTE

For character formatting (bold, italic, highlight, and so on), you can search for text that does not contain this formatting. For Highlight, select the option twice from the Format menu, and Word changes the Find and Replace dialog box so that you see Not Highlight. (Select it again to clear it entirely.)

For character formatting that you select from the Find Font dialog box, select the opposite of the formatting; that is, select Not Bold or Not Italic, or click any check box twice to remove the check.

FINDING AND REPLACING STYLES

In Chapter 10, "Streamlining Your Formatting with Styles," you'll learn how to use styles to make your document formatting easier and more consistent. When you use styles regularly, you'll find occasions when you want to switch some or all occurrences of one style in your document with another style. Using Find and Replace, you can search for styles and replace them with other styles.

Place the insertion point in the Find What text box (make sure that the box contains text only if you want to search for text formatted in a particular style), and click the Format button. A list appears, showing the formatting for which you can search. When you choose Style, the Find Style dialog box appears (see Figure 2.33). Select a style and click OK.

NOTE

You can find not only paragraph and character styles but also list styles. However, you cannot find table styles.

Repeat this process after you place the insertion point in the Replace With text box. When you choose Style, the Replace Style dialog box appears; it looks just like the Find Style dialog box shown in Figure 2.33.

Figure 2.33
From this dialog box, select the style you want to find.

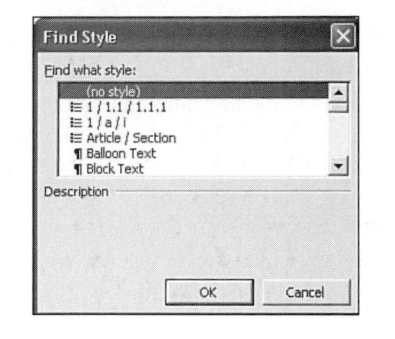

To remove styles from the Find and Replace dialog box, place the insertion point in the Find What text box or the Replace With text box, as appropriate, and click the No Formatting button.

FINDING AND REPLACING LANGUAGE

As you'll learn in Chapter 35, "Using Word's Multilingual and Accessibility Features," Word text can be tagged with specific languages so that Word knows which set of proofing tools to use with it. You can use Find and Replace to change the language associated with specific blocks of text, or to assign the No Proofing language to certain blocks of text (such as product or company names) that you don't want proofed in any language.

Place the insertion point in the Find What text box (make sure that the box contains text only if you want to search for text formatted in a particular language). Click the Format button; a pop-up list appears, showing the formatting for which you can search. Choose Language, and the Find Language dialog box appears (see Figure 2.34). Select a language and click OK. The selection appears in the Find and Replace dialog box.

Figure 2.34
Use the Find Language dialog box to find portions of the document formatted in another language or with No Proofing.

You can clear the language from the Find and Replace dialog box by placing the insertion point in the Find What text box or the Replace With text box, as appropriate, and clicking the No Formatting button.

USING FIND AND REPLACE TO INSERT THE CONTENTS OF YOUR CLIPBOARD

You've already learned how to replace text and formatting. But Word offers a little-known shortcut that lets you use Replace to insert virtually anything in your document. This feature can be invaluable. For instance, you can use it to replace a block of text with

- An icon such as the "Note" and "Caution" icons that appear throughout many books and manuals

- A field code or a block of text that includes a field code; for example, a standard line of text that contains cross-references or captions that automatically update themselves

- A heavily formatted table that might include formulas you intend to reuse in many places

To work with the feature, insert the same block of text throughout your document, wherever you want to replace it with something else. Use a block of placeholder text that isn't likely to appear anywhere else in your document; for instance, QQQQQ. Next, copy the document element you want to insert throughout the document. (You can copy it from a Word document or any other Windows application.) This places the information in the Clipboard—an area of your computer's memory set aside to store information that can be pasted elsewhere.

Choose Edit, Replace and enter the placeholder text in the Find What text box. In the Replace With text box, enter ^c; then click Replace All. Word replaces the placeholder text with whatever appears in your Clipboard.

GO TO PRACTICALLY ANYTHING YOU WANT

No matter what you're doing, there are going to be times when you'll want to go elsewhere in your document. Word's Go To command makes it convenient to go to almost anything. To display the Go To tab of the Find and Replace dialog box (see Figure 2.35), use any of the following techniques:

- Press F5.
- Open the Find and Replace dialog box and click the Go To tab.
- Press Ctrl+G.
- Click Select Browse Object and click Go To.
- Double-click on the page number in the status bar.

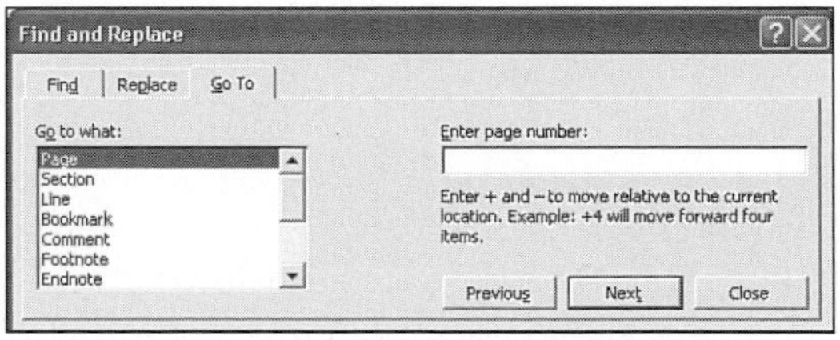

Figure 2.35
Use the Go To dialog box to move around documents quickly.

As you scroll through the G<u>o</u> to What list box, you'll see that you can go to the following objects in a Word document:

- Page
- Section
- Line
- Bookmark
- Comment
- Footnote
- Endnote

- Field
- Table
- Graphic
- Equation
- Object
- Heading

USING BOOKMARKS TO GO TO A LOCATION

If you expect to return to a location regularly, create a *bookmark* there. Then you can use the Go To dialog box to find the bookmark. You can get the job done by following these steps:

1. Place your insertion point where you want the bookmark.
2. Choose <u>I</u>nsert, Boo<u>k</u>mark.
3. In the <u>B</u>ookmark Name text box, enter a name for your bookmark.
4. Click <u>A</u>dd.

Now that you have the bookmark, you can find it like this:

1. Press F5 to display the <u>G</u>o To tab of the Find and Replace dialog box.
2. Choose Bookmark in the G<u>o</u> to What list box.
3. Choose the bookmark you want from the <u>E</u>nter Bookmark Name drop-down box.
4. Click Go <u>T</u>o.

→ For more information on working with bookmarks, **see** "Using Bookmarks," **p. 755**.

> **TIP**
>
> If you know the name of the bookmark you want to locate, just type it in Word's <u>G</u>o To tab, and Word can find it, even if you don't select Bookmark in the G<u>o</u> to What list box. So you can type the bookmark name in the text box even if it reads <u>E</u>nter Page Number, <u>E</u>nter Section Number, or one of the other options.

GOING TO YOUR MOST RECENT LOCATION

If you simply want to return to the location where you were last, press Shift+F5. This key combination recalls the last three locations in which you clicked before your current location. Keep pressing Shift+F5 until you arrive at the location you want.

2

TIP

> Many Word users get in the habit of using only a few of the navigation tools available to them. But an eclectic mix of keyboard and mouse may well get the job done fastest.
>
> For example, you may want to try a strategy such as this:
>
> - Use the arrow and Ctrl+arrow combinations to move a few letters or words.
> - Use the scrollbar (or mouse wheel) to move large distances if you don't know the exact location to which you're going.
> - Use the Go To tab of the Find and Replace dialog box if you do know where you're going.

SEARCHING FOR ITEMS

Regardless of what you choose to go to, you can go to the next or preceding occurrence of the same type of object using the navigator buttons that appear on either side of the Select Browse Object button at the bottom of the vertical scrollbar (refer to Figure 2.4).

But what if you want to go to a specific numbered item or location? Earlier in this chapter, you learned how to use a bookmark to mark your place in a document. When you use the Go To command to return to that location, you go to a named location. The same method works if you want to go to a comment (you enter the reviewer's name), a field (you enter the field's name), or an object (you provide an object type, such as an Excel worksheet).

You also can use the Go To tab of the Find and Replace dialog box to move the insertion point to a specific numbered item or location. For example, if you want to go to page 4, select Page from the Go to What list box and type 4 in the text box to the right. You can use numbers for pages, sections, lines, footnotes, endnotes, tables, graphics, equations, or headings.

Word numbers these items sequentially as they appear in your document. For example, to go to the 23rd graphic in your document, choose Graphic in the Go to What scroll box and enter 23 in the Enter Graphic Number text box.

Similarly, you can use plus and minus signs to move your cursor a specific number of items forward or backward in your document. For example, to move forward three footnotes, choose Footnote in the Go to What scroll box, and type +3 in the Enter Footnote Number text box.

TIP

> You also can specify how far into a document you want to go as a percentage of the whole document. For example, to move to a location 25% from the beginning of the document, type 25% in the Enter Page Number text box and click Go To.

GETTING HELP

Word provides extensive online help, easily accessible through the Type a Question for Help box and the Help task pane. These tools bring together Help resources that were placed on your hard disk when you installed Word, as well as Help resources at Microsoft Office Online, part of Microsoft's Web site. In the following sections, you'll learn how to make the most of both sets of resources.

HELP FROM THE TYPE A QUESTION FOR HELP BOX

The easiest way to get help is to type a question in the Type a Question for Help box on the right edge of the menu bar. After you type the question, press Enter; Word displays the Search Results task pane, listing pages that may contain the answer (see Figure 2.36). If you are connected to the Internet, Word will draw on the Help content stored on your computer, as well as additional help from Microsoft Office Online.

If the first several page names do not appear to contain the answer, you can scroll down to see more. To view one of the help pages, click on its name.

Enter your query in the Type a Question for Help Box…
When you do, the Search Results task pane appears

Figure 2.36
Working with the Type a Question for Help box (in this case, asking about Styles).

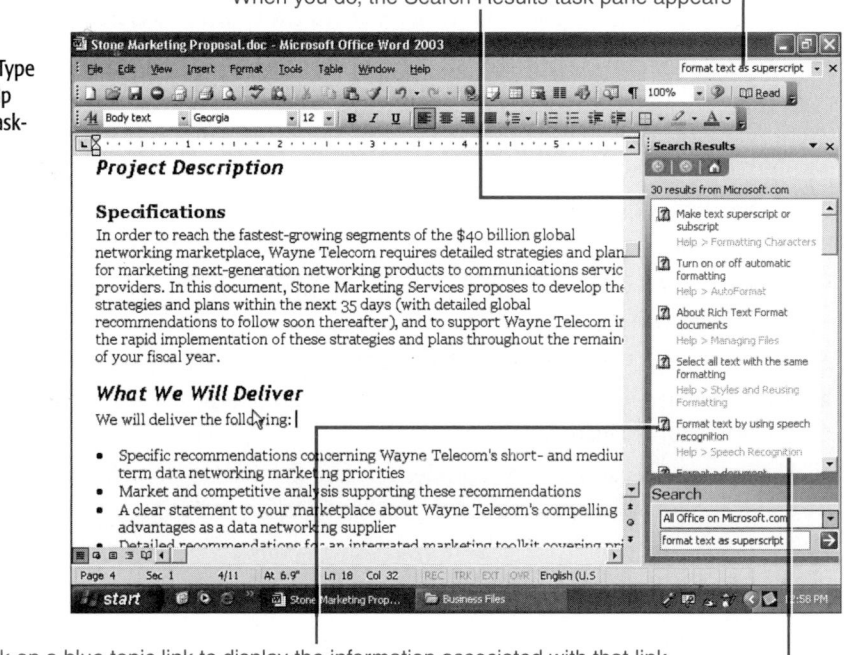

Click on a blue topic link to display the information associated with that link
Or click on a gray category link to display more information related to that category of topics

When you do, Microsoft Word Help appears, displaying a page of help. This page may itself contain blue hyperlinks that connect you to more help; for example, if you asked for help troubleshooting a feature, Word may list several problems. Clicking one provides the solution.

TIP

This isn't "Jeopardy": You don't have to phrase your query in the form of a question. If you just know a term or phrase—such as "word count" or "insert date"—you can usually get the help you're looking for.

TIP

Word remembers questions you've asked recently. If you need help on the same topic again, you can select a question you asked previously from the Type a Question for Help drop-down list box.

NOTE

In Word 2003, as in previous versions of Word, you can also get online help by asking questions of the animated Office Assistant. However, in Word 2003, the Office Assistant appears only when you summon it by choosing Help, Show the Office Assistant.

Type a question in the What Would You Like to Do box, and Word displays the Help pages it thinks are most likely to include the answers.

REFINING YOUR HELP SEARCHES

Sometimes the first set of results you get doesn't include the specific answer you're looking for. You may be able to get better results by refining your search, as described here:

- Rephrase the terminology in your question. If you know it, use Microsoft's terminology for the feature you're interested in. For example, if you wanted to know how to create styles for large text headlines, use Word's term—headings—rather than headlines.

- Add more detail to your query: "format text as superscript" will get you a more targeted answer than "formatting."

- If one answer is closer to being relevant than the others, click the gray *category link* under it, to display closely related content

- Make sure that your query doesn't contain any misspellings

BROWSING THE MICROSOFT WORD HELP BOOK

Some users prefer to browse Microsoft Word's help system as if it were a book. To do so, choose Help, Microsoft Word Help to display the Microsoft Word Help task pane. Then, click Table of Contents, and browse to the help page you want to read (see Figure 2.37).

USING AUTOTILING TO KEEP HELP VISIBLE AS YOU WORK

By default, when you display a help window, the help window is superimposed over your editing window. However, you'll often want to display the help window and the editing window next to each other so that you can more easily follow the step-by-step instructions that appear in the help window.

Figure 2.37
Browsing the Table of Contents to find a specific Help page.

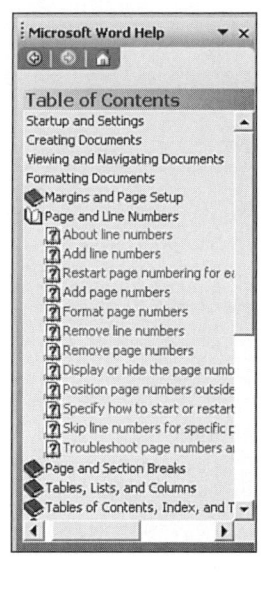

In Word 2003, it is easy to display both windows side by side. In the Microsoft Word Help window, click the AutoTile button (see Figure 2.38). When you do, Word hides the Help (Search Results) task pane to leave more room for you to work.

AutoTile

Figure 2.38
The Microsoft Word Help window, untiled.

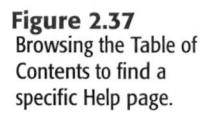

Sometimes you'll want to turn off AutoTiling and display the help window above the Word editing window again—perhaps to view lengthier instructions. To toggle AutoTiling off, click the Untile button (see Figure 2.39). When you do, Word displays the Help (Search Results) task pane again.

Untile

Figure 2.39
The Microsoft Word
Help window, tiled.

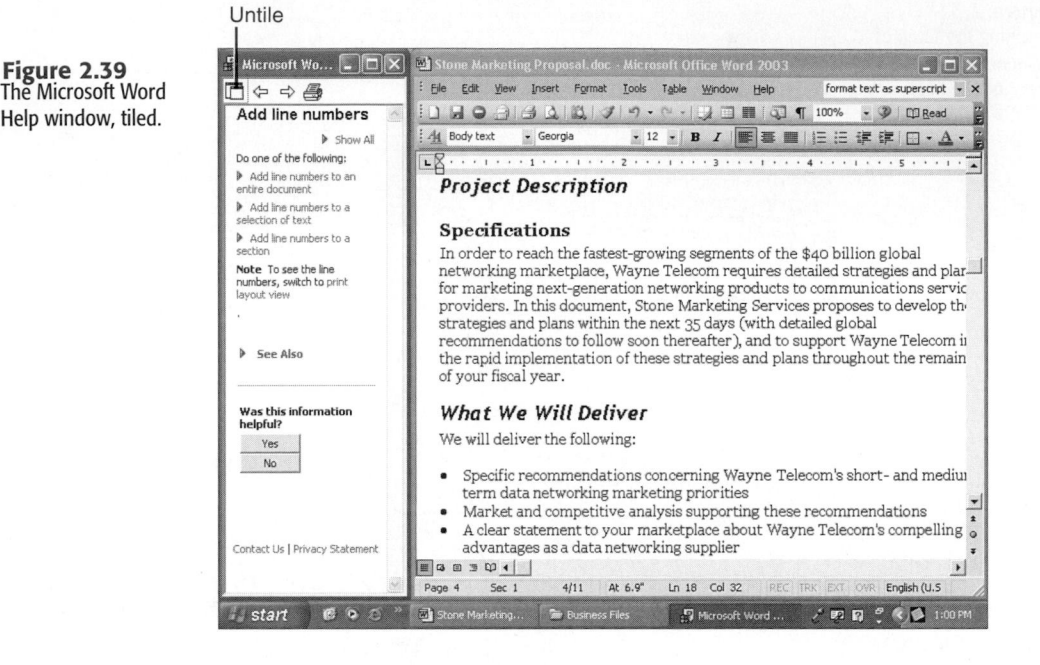

GETTING HELP FROM OTHER OFFICE USERS

Microsoft maintains heavily trafficked newsgroups in which users can ask questions about Microsoft Word (and other Office applications), and other users can volunteer answers. In some cases, official "Microsoft Most Valuable Professional" expert volunteers may answer your questions.

In Word 2003, you can get to these newsgroups straight from the Search Results task pane. To do so, scroll down the list of results Word has displayed, and click Ask Other Office Users.

Internet Explorer loads, displaying the main page of Microsoft's Newsgroup application (see Figure 2.40). Click Word to display Microsoft's list of Word newsgroups; then click on the newsgroup you want to browse or participate in.

In some cases, your question will already have been asked and answered. If not, you can ask a new question by clicking New Post. The Post a New Message window appears; enter your name, email address, subject, and message, and click Send.

USING OTHER WEB-BASED HELP FROM OFFICE ON MICROSOFT.COM

Microsoft brings together many additional online Help resources in the Microsoft Word Help task pane (see Figure 2.41). You can click

- **Connect to Office on Microsoft.com** to display the main page of Microsoft's online support site in Internet Explorer. From here, you can connect to news about Office, feature articles displaying help on selected topics, and new Office-related downloads.

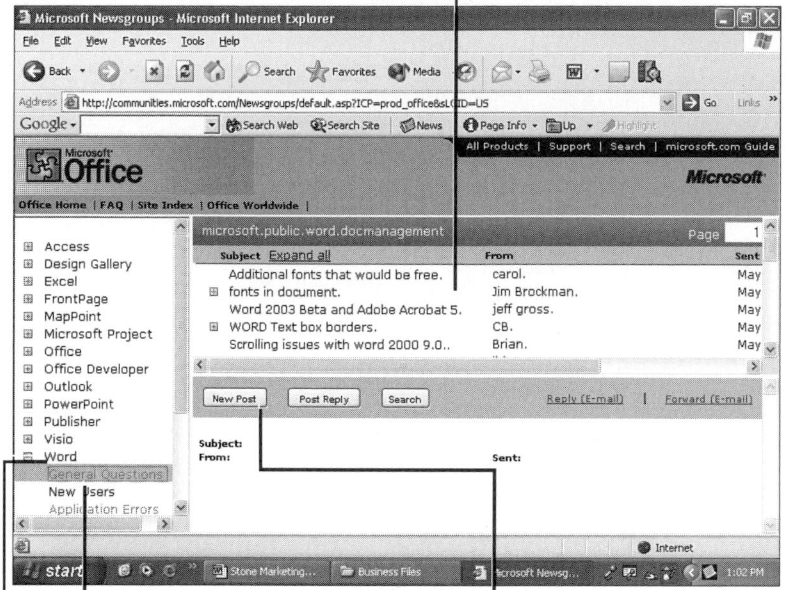

Browse this box to view posted questions and answers

Figure 2.40
Microsoft's online
newsgroup commu-
nity.

Click Word to display list of Word newsgroups

Click specific newsgroup to see postings

Click New Post to post a new question or answer

- **Get the Latest News About Microsoft Word** to display the main page of Microsoft's Word support site—step-by-step help organized around categories such as Mass Mailings and Security and Privacy.

- **Automatically Update This List from the Web** to retrieve brand-new information about Office into your Microsoft Word Help task pane.

- **Assistance** to display online suggestions and resources for using Word and Office in new and better ways.

- **Training** to link to Microsoft's new online training courses for Word and Office, designed to walk you through selected tasks visually.

- **Communities** to link to Microsoft's online newsgroups, discussed earlier in this chapter in the section "Getting Help from Other Office Users."

- **Office Update** to connect with a Microsoft Web page that can scan Word or Office to determine whether you need to install updates.

- **What's New** to display a list of new features in Word 2003.

- **Contact Us** to display a list of options for getting additional help from Microsoft.

- **Accessibility Help** to display Help about features that make Word more accessible to users with limited dexterity, low vision, or other disabilities.

- **Online Content Settings** to display the Service Options dialog box, from where you control which online Help resources are sent to your computer, and how they are displayed.

Figure 2.41
Microsoft Word Help
task pane.

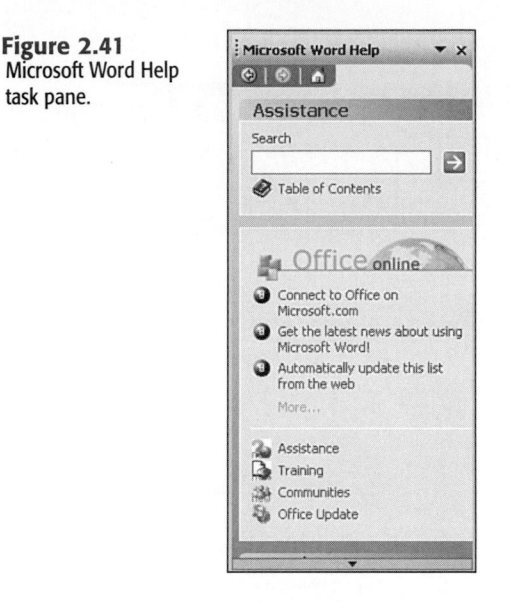

ACTIVATING WORD OR OFFICE

When you first install Microsoft Word 2003 or Office 2003, you are asked to activate the software, either by connecting briefly to Microsoft's Web site or by phone. Activation allows Microsoft to verify that your copy of Word or Office is legitimate, and that it is not running on more computers than it is licensed to run on.

If you do not activate Word or Office within 30 days, you will lose the ability to edit or create new content with it (though you will still be able to read existing files).

To activate Word, choose Help, Activate Product. The Microsoft Product Activation Wizard appears. Follow its step-by-step instructions to connect to the Internet and activate your product (or, if you are not connected to the Internet, follow its instructions for calling Microsoft).

TROUBLESHOOTING

HOW TO MOVE A TOOLBAR BACK WHERE YOU WANT IT

It's easy to inadvertently move a toolbar to a location where you don't want it. If the toolbar is docked to the top, side, or bottom of the screen, drag its *move handle* (refer to Figure 2.1). If the toolbar is floating in the middle of the screen, drag it by its title bar.

HOW TO TROUBLESHOOT FIND AND REPLACE

If Word doesn't find or replace text or graphics you believe are present in your document, check the following:

- Double-check your typing.

- Make sure that you haven't restricted your search to text formatted in a specific way. With Find What selected, click the No Formatting button. (If the button is not high-lighted, you don't need to worry about this.)

- Clear other check boxes that may be inadvertently limiting your search, including Match Case, Find Whole Words Only, and Use Wildcards. (If these check boxes do not appear, click the More button to display them.)

CHAPTER

3

ESSENTIAL DOCUMENT CREATION AND MANAGEMENT TECHNIQUES

In this chapter

CREATING NEW DOCUMENTS

Now that you've completed your tour of the Word interface, it's time to get to work. In the rest of this chapter, you'll learn the basic techniques you need to create, open, edit, and save Word documents. In Chapter 4, "Quick and Effective Formatting Techniques," you'll build on what you learn here, understanding how to format the text you've created.

Let's start with creating new documents. As you've already seen, Word opens with a blank document already displayed, ready for editing. At this point, you have several choices:

- You can start working in the blank document that's already open, entering text and other elements. When you're ready, you can save the file as either a Word document or a Web page. (See the "Saving Your Documents" section, later in this chapter.)

- You can start with one of Word's built-in templates, which may already contain some of the text and much of the formatting you need.

- You can create a blank Web page, email message, or XML page.

> **TIP**
>
> Any time you want to create a new blank document, the quickest way to do it is to click the New button on the Standard toolbar or to use the keyboard shortcut Ctrl+N.
>
> These commands create a blank document based on Word's default Normal template. If you use File, New instead, you can choose to create a document based on a different template.

USING THE NEW DOCUMENT TASK PANE

Word 2003 brings together your options for opening or creating files in the New Document task pane (see Figure 3.1). This task pane appears when you choose File, New. Depending on how your computer is configured, it may also appear automatically when you start Word. You can also display it like this: Choose View, Task Pane; click the down arrow at the upper right of the task pane; and choose New Document.

> **NOTE**
>
> To display the New Document task pane at startup, choose Tools, Options, View; then check the Startup Task Pane check box and click OK.

From the New Document task pane, you can

- Choose a document you worked on recently, or another document on any drive accessible to you
- Create a blank document, Web page, XML document, or email message
- Browse to an existing document and create a new document based on it
- Create a new document based on a template (see the following section for an overview of what templates can do)

- Find and use additional templates at Microsoft Office Online
- Find additional templates on your Web sites, including your MSN Communities Web site if you have one

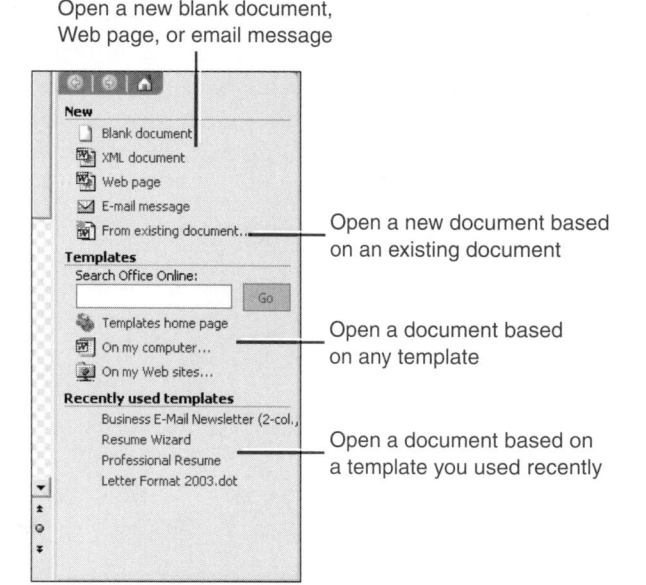

Figure 3.1
The New Document task pane.

Open a new blank document, Web page, or email message

Open a new document based on an existing document

Open a document based on any template

Open a document based on a template you used recently

CREATING A BLANK DOCUMENT

Whenever you want to create a document from scratch, Word provides several ways to display a blank document for editing and formatting. You can

- Click Blank Document on the New Document task pane
- Click the New Blank Document button on the Standard toolbar
- Press Ctrl+N

Although a blank document contains no text, it has access to all of Word's built-in styles and shortcuts, and draws on Word's default formatting settings (reflecting any changes you may have made to the defaults, of course).

CHOOSING A TEMPLATE THAT HAS ALREADY DONE THE WORK FOR YOU

Why start from scratch if you can get Word to do much of the work for you? For example, you might want to create a memo that follows a standard format, with a standard memo header and To, CC, From, Date, and Re lines already included and formatted. You don't have to enter all those lines; you can choose a built-in Word template that already contains them.

Templates are patterns Word can use to build new documents. You'll learn about them in detail in Chapter 11, "Templates, Wizards, and Add-Ins." The quickest way to access templates is from the New Document task pane.

If you've used a template recently, you can select it from the templates that appear in the Recently Used Templates section.

If you want to browse all the templates stored on your computer (as well as any workgroup templates stored on your network server), click On My Computer. The General tab of the Templates dialog box opens (see Figure 3.2). Click the tab corresponding to the type of template you are seeking, and double-click the template you want to use.

Figure 3.2
The Templates dialog box organizes all Word's built-in templates and any you create.

Word offers an extensive library of built-in templates for the following types of documents:

- Agendas
- Brochures
- Directories
- Letters & Faxes
- Legal Pleadings
- Mail Merges

- Manuals
- Memos
- Reports
- Resumes
- Theses

Some of these templates, such as Memos, appear in their own tabs in the New dialog box. Several, such as Brochures and Directories, appear in the Publications tab. Several others, such as Agendas and Resumes, appear in the Other Documents tab.

For many categories of printed documents, Word offers three consistent approaches to document formatting: Contemporary, Elegant, and Professional. By choosing one of these approaches and using it in all your documents, you can have the benefits of consistent professional design without the expense.

If you don't want your documents to potentially look exactly the same as those of another Word user, you can change fonts and other aspects of the base styles on which these documents are built (see Chapter 10, "Streamlining Your Formatting with Styles"). If you're careful, you can establish a distinctive, high-quality set of design standards for your business with remarkably little effort and expense.

→ For more information about Word's wizards for building newsletters and other documents, **see** "Using Word Wizards," **p. 380**.

If the Templates dialog box does not contain a template appropriate for your task, click Templates on Office Online. Microsoft opens your Web browser, connects to the Internet (or uses your currently active Internet connection), and displays the Microsoft Office Online Templates Home Page.

This is your gateway to a large, well-organized, easy-to-search collection of Word and Office templates. You can browse among the categories of templates listed on the bottom of the page. Or you can choose Templates from the Web page's Search drop-down box, enter the type of template you're looking for, enter the topic you're looking for, and click the green right arrow to perform your search.

For more information on using these templates, see the "Using Templates from Microsoft Office Online" section of Chapter 11.

CREATING A WEB PAGE

As mentioned earlier, Microsoft expects users to often use Word 2003 to create Web and intranet pages. To create a blank Web page, display the New Document task pane and click Web Page.

While you are editing a Web page, you can create a new Web page by clicking the New Web Page button on the Standard toolbar, or by pressing Ctrl+N.

CREATING A BLANK EMAIL MESSAGE

To create a blank email message, display the New Document task pane and click E-mail Message. A blank email message appears, containing tools for specifying recipients, adding subject lines, and inserting attachments.

→ For a detailed look at using Word to edit email, **see** Chapter 30, "Using Word As an Email Editor," **p. 999**.

CREATING AN XML DOCUMENT

To create an empty XML document, display the New Document task pane and click XML Document. Word opens an empty XML document.

To add your own XML tags to your XML document, you first need to attach an XML schema to your document, through the Tools, Templates and Add-Ins dialog box. Working with XML schema and editing XML documents is covered in detail in Chapter 25, "Using Word to Develop XML Content and Use XML Applications."

You can add your own XML tags to a document only if you are using either Microsoft Office Professional 2003 or the standalone version of Microsoft Word 2003.

BASIC EDITING

To enter text in a new or existing document, just start typing in the editing window. If the text doesn't appear, make sure that Word is the active application by clicking anywhere in the Word window.

A blinking vertical line, the *insertion point*, is displayed in your document at the location where your text will appear. As you type, your words are placed to the left of the insertion point as the insertion point moves to the right. After you've added content, you can move the insertion point by clicking elsewhere in the editing window.

SELECTING TEXT

In Word, you can manipulate text in virtually any way imaginable—but before you do any of that, you have to select it. You can select text in several ways. If you're new to Word, you might try each method to see which seems most comfortable. If you're an experienced Word user, you already select text dozens of times a day. Now might be a good time to see whether you can do it more efficiently.

MOUSE SHORTCUTS

The most basic way to select text is with the mouse, as follows:

1. Click the left mouse button when the pointer is where you want your selection to start.
2. Keep the left mouse button pressed down while you drag the mouse to where you want the selection to end.
3. Release the mouse button.

You can drag the mouse in any direction. If you drag it across, you select text on the same line. If you drag it up or down, you can select many lines.

Selecting text this way is simple, and it's especially convenient if the text you're selecting doesn't fit simple boundaries, such as adjacent parts of two paragraphs or several consecutive words. However, if you are selecting a specific word, line, sentence, or paragraph, or the entire document, other alternatives might be quicker.

To select the current word, double-click in it; to select the current paragraph, triple-click in it. To select the current line, click at the left edge of the screen, outside your margin. (You know you are in the right place when your mouse pointer faces your text.) You can then extend your selection to multiple lines by dragging the mouse pointer up and down.

KEYBOARD SHORTCUTS

Often, the easiest way to select a precise block of text is with a keyboard shortcut. Table 3.1 lists several convenient keyboard shortcuts for selecting text.

TABLE 3.1   KEYBOARD SHORTCUTS FOR SELECTING TEXT

Extend Selection	Keyboard Shortcut
Entire document	Ctrl+A
To beginning of document	Ctrl+Shift+Home
To end of document	Ctrl+Shift+End
To top of window	Ctrl+Shift+Page Up
To bottom of window	Ctrl+Shift+Page Down
Down one page	Shift+Page Down
Up one page	Shift+Page Up
Down one paragraph	Ctrl+Shift+down arrow
Up one paragraph	Ctrl+Shift+up arrow
Current sentence	F8, F8, F8
Up one line	Shift+up arrow
Down one line	Shift+down arrow
To beginning of line	Shift+Home
To end of line	Shift+End
Left one word	Ctrl+Shift+left arrow
Right one word	Ctrl+Shift+right arrow
Current word	F8, F8
Left one character	Shift+left arrow
Right one character	Shift+right arrow

In addition, the keyboard shortcut F8 begins extending a selection; you can then continue extending the selection with the mouse, or any other way you choose. You can tell Word to stop extending your selection by double-clicking EXT on the status bar, or by pressing Esc.

> **TIP**
>
> If you need to select large blocks of text in a document that contains heading styles or outline numbering, do so in Outline view. There, double-clicking a heading selects all the contents subordinate to it; you can then cut, copy, or paste all those contents at once. See Chapter 18, "Outlining: Practical Techniques for Organizing Any Document," for more tips on cutting and pasting in Outline view.

CUT, COPY, AND PASTE

The heart of word processing—what first made it superior to the typewriter 25 years ago—is the ease with which you can cut, copy, and paste text. Using Word, you can move text around at will, until you're satisfied with its content and organization.

To cut, copy, or paste text (or any other document element, such as a graphic), first select it. Then, right-click and choose Cut, Copy, or Paste from the shortcut menu. Or, if you prefer, use any of the mouse, menu, or keyboard shortcuts shown in Table 3.2.

TABLE 3.2   METHODS FOR CUTTING AND PASTING IN WORD

Action	Via Menu	Via Keyboard	Via Standard Toolbar
Cut	Edit, Cut	Ctrl+X	✂
Copy	Edit, Copy	Ctrl+C	🗐
Paste	Edit, Paste	Ctrl+V	📋

You can cut, copy, or paste within the same Word document, among open Word documents, or among multiple Windows programs. For example, you can copy worksheet data from an Excel report and paste it into an executive summary created in Word.

→ For more information on sharing information between Word and Excel, **see** "Integrating Excel and Word," **p. 962**.

WORKING WITH MULTIPLE CLIPBOARD ITEMS THROUGH THE OFFICE CLIPBOARD TASK PANE

Ever need to collect several blocks of text and deposit them all in the same place? Most people cut one block of text, go to the new location, paste it, and then go looking for the next block of text to paste. Word 2003 provides an easier solution: the Clipboard task pane.

When you first copy text (or anything else), Word 2003 works as it always has: It stores the information in the Office Clipboard waiting for you to paste it somewhere. However, if there's already text in the Office Clipboard, and you copy more text into the Clipboard, Word 2003 copies that into the Office Clipboard separately.

The Office Clipboard can contain up to 24 elements, including text, images, and elements from other Office 2003 applications, such as Excel and PowerPoint. If you attempt to copy a 25th item, Word displays a message warning you that it will delete the oldest (the one that was copied into the Clipboard first) of the 24 items currently stored in the Clipboard.

When you're ready to paste multiple items into the Office Clipboard, display the Clipboard task pane. To do so, click the Office Clipboard icon in the Windows taskbar (see Figure 3.3), or choose Edit, Office Clipboard. If another task pane is already open, click the down arrow at the top of the task pane, and choose Clipboard from the drop-down menu.

In Word 2003, you can also open the Clipboard task pane by pressing Ctrl+C twice.

You can use Word's usual Copy and Cut commands and buttons to place material in the Clipboard. Then, scroll through the items in the Office Clipboard. When you find one you want to paste, click on it. If you want to paste all the elements in your Office Clipboard at once, click the Paste All button.

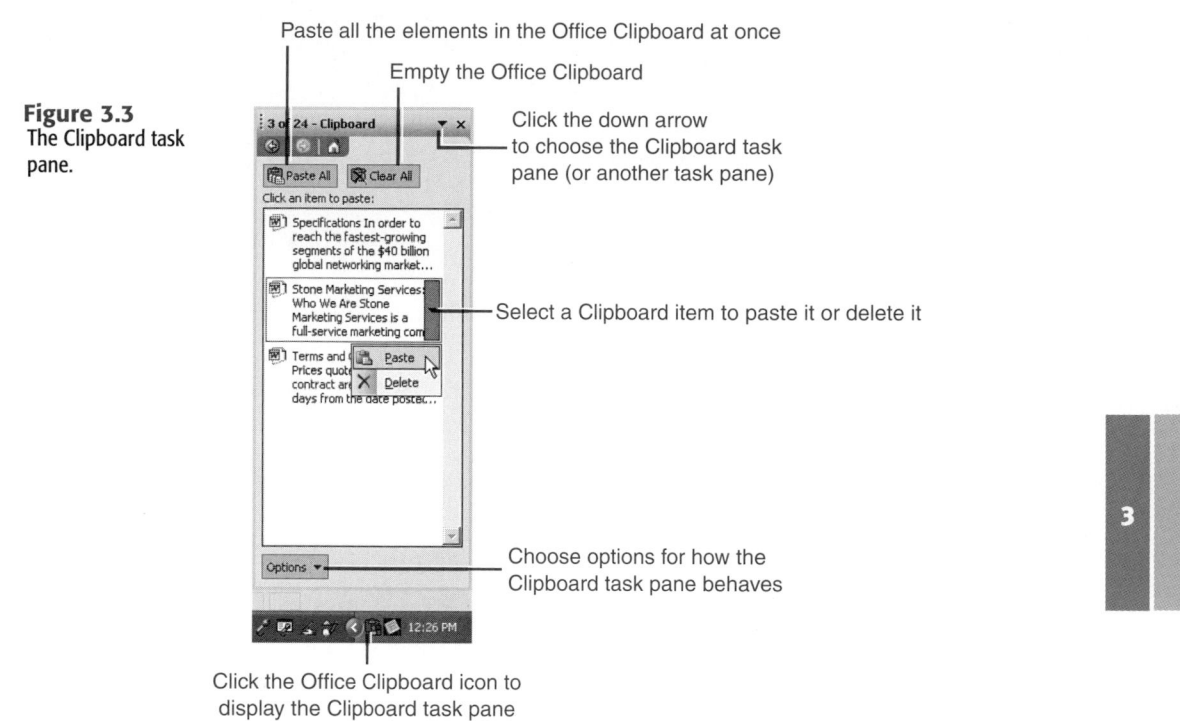

Figure 3.3
The Clipboard task pane.

You have several options for controlling the behavior of the Office Clipboard task pane and managing its contents:

- To delete a single item in the Office Clipboard, click on the down arrow next to that item and choose Delete from the menu that appears.
- To delete all the items in the Office Clipboard, click the Clear All button.
- To automatically display the Clipboard task pane whenever you copy or cut anything, click Options, and select Show Office Clipboard Automatically from the menu that appears.
- To instruct Word to store multiple items in the Office Clipboard even when the Clipboard task pane isn't displayed, click Options, and select Collect Without Showing Office Clipboard from the menu that appears.

USING THE PASTE OPTIONS BUTTON

When you paste text into a Word 2003 document, a Paste Options button appears (see Figure 3.4). Clicking this button gives you control over how the text you are pasting will be formatted. The options available vary depending on what you are pasting, and where you are pasting it. But if you are pasting one block of text into another, your options are typically these:

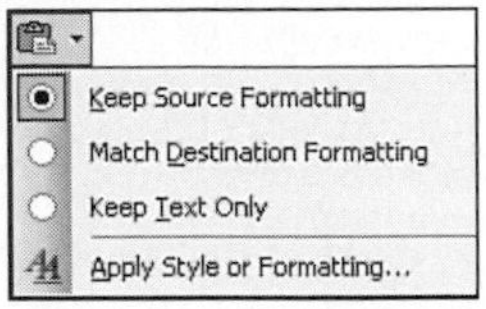

Figure 3.4
Clicking the Paste Options button gives you options for how your pasted text will be formatted.

- Underline{K}eep Source Formatting tells Word to format the text exactly as it was formatted in the document you pasted it from.

- Match Destination Formatting tells Word to format the text to match surrounding text in the location where you pasted it.

- Keep Text Only clears all manual formatting and styles from the text, displaying it in the style Word uses as its default, Normal. Unless you've made changes, this means that your text will be formatted as 12-point Times New Roman, with no italics, bold-face, or other character formatting.

- Apply Style or Formatting displays the Styles and Formatting task pane, where you can choose the formatting or style you want to use. (See Chapter 4 for more information on this feature.)

CLICK AND TYPE: EDITING ANYWHERE ON THE PAGE

Word's Click and Type feature allows you to start entering text anywhere on a page, regardless of whether any other text exists nearby. To use Click and Type, make sure that you're working in Print Layout view (choose View, Print Layout). Then, double-click where you want to enter text and start typing.

Word sets a tab at that location. If you start typing beyond the end of the text already in your document, Word adds paragraph marks between the text that was already there and the new location.

NOTE

If Click and Type isn't working in Print Layout view, choose Tools, Options; click the Edit tab; and check the Enable Click and Type check box.

TIP

If you keep typing past the right margin, Word starts the next line at the left margin. If you want all your text to be lined up under the beginning of the first line you created, select the paragraph and press Ctrl+Shift+T. This creates a hanging indent at the location where you double-clicked to start typing.

→ You can also create hanging indents with Word's ruler. To learn how, **see** "Indenting with the Ruler," **p. 129**.

DRAG-AND-DROP: WHEN TO USE IT

In the real world, if you want to move something, you don't cut it and paste it somewhere else. You pick it up and put it down where you want it. You can do the same thing with Word's drag-and-drop feature. Select the text you want to move. Then left-click inside the area you've highlighted and drag the text to the insertion point where you want it to appear.

In Word, you can also move text by highlighting it and click and dragging it with the right mouse button. When you right-click and drag the text to a new location, Word displays a shortcut menu asking whether you want to move, copy, link, or hyperlink the text (see Figure 3.5). For copying text, you might find this quicker than using the Copy toolbar button, and it's an especially handy way to create hyperlinks.

NOTE

> The Link Here option creates a link to the original text using Windows object linking and embedding (OLE). Word inserts a field at the Link Here location. If you update the text in the original location, Word automatically updates the same text in the linked location (though it may take a few moments in a large document).

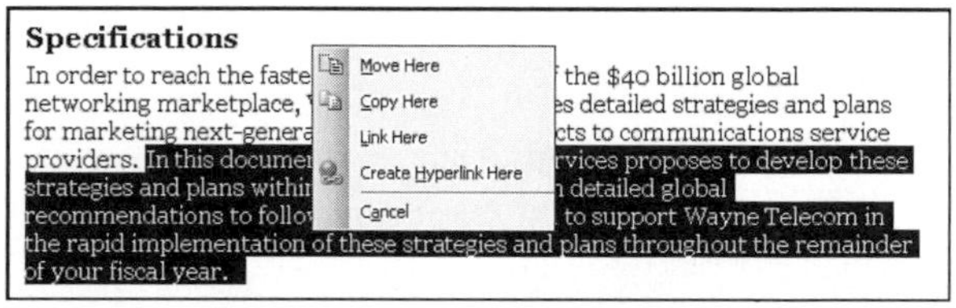

3

Figure 3.5
The shortcut menu that appears when you right-click to drag and drop text.

USING WORD'S UNDO AND REDO CAPABILITIES

With all this cutting, pasting, dragging, and dropping, it's easy to make a mistake. Word's Undo feature reverses the effects of an action and returns your document to the way it was before you performed it.

Word Undo stores not one, but 100 or more actions, so you have more time to realize you've made a mistake. There are several ways to invoke Undo. The keyboard shortcut Ctrl+Z and the menu selection Edit, Undo will each undo your last action. So does the Undo button on the Standard toolbar. However, if you want to undo several actions at the same time, you must use the toolbar button:

1. Click the down arrow next to the Undo toolbar button. A list of your most recent actions appears.

2. Scroll to and select the action you want to undo. Word will undo that action, as well as all subsequent actions. (You can't pick and choose: You have to undo all of them.)

Certain types of changes take quite a bit of memory to store. One example is finding and replacing blocks of text that occur repeatedly through a large document. In some cases, Word warns you that it cannot store Undo information if you go through with a requested change. If you're sure that you won't need to undo this or any prior actions, you can go ahead. After you've made the change, Word again starts tracking new changes that can be undone.

CAUTION

> One important thing Undo doesn't undo is a file save. When you save over a previous file, the old file is gone for good. In addition, Word undoes only those actions that change the contents of a document. It doesn't, for example, undo a switch to Print Layout view or retrieve a document that you just sent via email.

SAVING YOUR DOCUMENTS

Now that you've learned the basics of editing your document, let's discuss saving it—which you should do often.

TIP

> If you have several files open at once, you can save them all at once by pressing Shift while you choose File, Save All.
>
> The Save All option does not normally appear on the File menu, except when you press Shift. Alternatively, you can customize Word to always include it (as covered in Chapter 31, "Customizing Word.")

SAVING AN EXISTING FILE IN ITS CURRENT LOCATION

Most of the time you'll just want to save your existing document in its existing location, and Word provides several quick ways to do so. You can click the Save button on the Standard toolbar, use the Ctrl+S or Shift+F12 keyboard shortcut, or choose File, Save.

SAVING FILES USING A DIFFERENT NAME, FORMAT, OR LOCATION

Often, you want to make changes in the way you save a file. In particular, you may want to save a file to a different location on your computer or on your network. Or you may want to save it in a different file format so that people who run software other than Word can use it. In each case, you use the Save As dialog box (see Figure 3.6). To display it, choose File, Save As, or press F12.

Up one level ¬   ┌ Search the Web (Web folders)

Previous folder (returns   ┌ Delete (Delete selected file or folder
to folder you displayed last) ¬

Save in (Choose folder or computer)   ┌ Create new folder
        View (Specify how files are listed)

Figure 3.6
The Save As dialog
box enables you to
save files to different
locations or in differ-
ent formats.

Tools (Control
options related
to saving
this or all files)

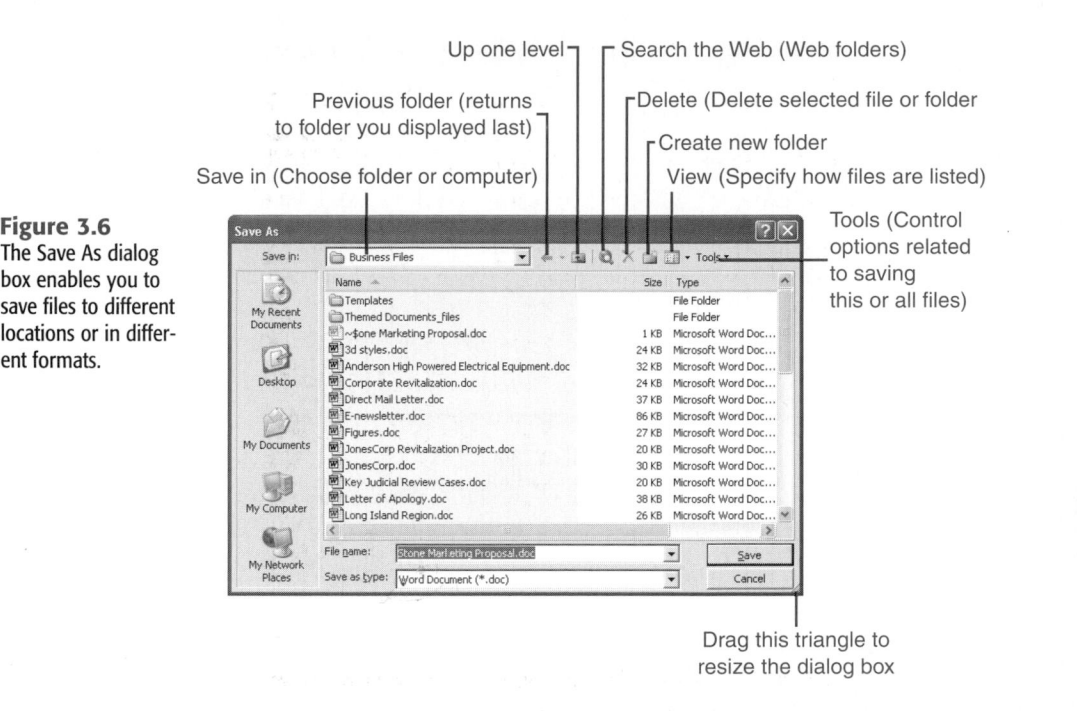

Drag this triangle to
resize the dialog box

NOTE

Because new documents require you to specify a name and location for the file, Word
also displays the Save As dialog box when you save a file for the first time. By default,
Word expects you to save your file in the My Documents folder. (In Windows 2000 and
Windows XP, these folders are stored as subfolders within the folders associated with
your user profile.)

Word also inserts the first word or phrase of your document in the File Name text box,
guessing that these words might be your document's title. If Word has made correct
assumptions, all you need to do is click Save to store the file. Otherwise, type in a new
name before saving the file.

If you want to change the standard location Word uses for saving files, display Tools,
Options; click the File Locations tab; select Documents from the File Types scroll box; and
click Modify. Browse to a new location and click OK twice.

SAVING TO A DIFFERENT LOCATION

Word's Save As dialog box gives you extensive control over where you save your files. Save a
copy of your file in a different folder or drive as instructed here:

1. Click anywhere in the Save In drop-down box. A list of available drives and resources is
   displayed (see Figure 3.7).

2. Click the drive or resource where you want to store your file. A list of existing documents and folders already stored on that drive is displayed.

Figure 3.7
You can choose a folder, drive, network, or Internet FTP resource from the Save In drop-down box.

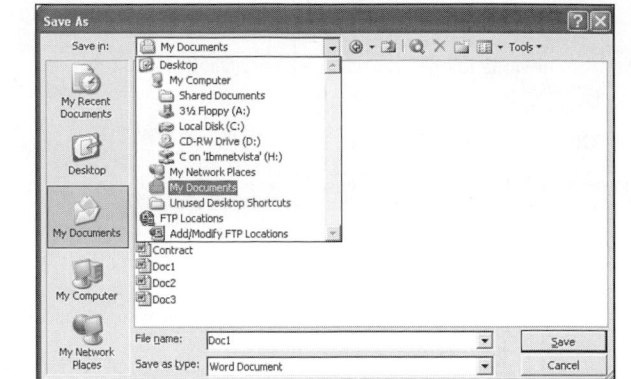

3. If you want to store your file in one of the subfolders, double-click it; repeat the process until you arrive at the folder you want.

4. Make sure that the filename and file format are correct and click Save.

NOTE

> If you are using Save As to save an existing file in a new location, Word leaves the earlier version where you originally stored it.

Sometimes the only change in file location you want to make when using the Save As dialog box is to go up one level in your folder structure. Or you may want to move around on the same drive rather than choose a different drive. In this case, click the Up One Level toolbar button (or press Alt+2) to display the next higher level folder or drive. From there, browse the file and folder lists until you find where you want to save the file.

Occasionally, you may want to save a file in a folder that doesn't exist yet. To create a new folder within your current folder, click the Create New Folder button. The New Folder dialog box opens; enter the name of your new folder and click OK. The folder now appears within your current file and folder list. To save your file in the new folder, first double-click the new folder to open it and then click Save.

SAVING ACROSS A NETWORK

Most Word users are now connected to a network. If your computer connects to a networked folder at startup and assigns that folder a drive name, this mapped network drive appears in the list of drives under My Computer in the Save In drop-down list box. Choose the mapped drive as you would any other drive, find the folder within that drive if necessary, and click Save to save the file.

If the network drive or folder where you want to save the file is not a mapped drive, but you have unrestricted access to it, you can reach it through My Network Places:

1. Click inside the Save In drop-down list box.

2. Click My Network Places. Word displays a list of computers and mapped drives accessible to you on the network.

3. Double-click the computer or mapped drive where you want to store the file.

4. After that computer's name appears in the Save In drop-down box, browse for the drive and folder where you want to store the file.

5. Make sure that the filename and format are correct and click Save.

In certain instances, you may be asked to provide a password when you attempt to access a computer or drive. For example, if you are attempting to access a drive on Windows 2000 Server for the first time during a session, you may be asked for a password. Enter your password, or if you don't have one, speak to your network administrator about getting access.

NOTE

> If you don't have access to a computer on the network, it may not even appear on the list of computers in My Network Places.

3

SAVING IN A DIFFERENT FORMAT

What if you want to save a file for use by someone who works with a different word processor or an older version of Word? Or what about saving it as text-only for transmission over an email system that can't handle formatting or HTML? In each case, you need to save your file in a different format.

To choose a format other than Word, display the Save As dialog box and click in the Save as Type drop-down box. Scroll to the file type you want to use and click it. If the filename uses a different extension (as will be the case unless you are saving to an older version of Word for Windows or DOS, or to WordPerfect), Word automatically changes it accordingly in the File Name text box. Click Save to save the file.

NOTE

> In some cases, Word may prompt you to install a filter— from either your CD-ROM or the network installation you installed Office from—before you can save to other formats.

Table 3.3 lists the file formats available in Word.

TABLE 3.3 FILE FORMATS AVAILABLE AS SAVE AS OPTIONS	
Format	**Description**
Web Page	Saves in HTML/XML format for use on Web or intranet pages (see Chapter 24, "Using Word to Develop Web Content").

continues

TABLE 3.3 CONTINUED

Format	Description
Web Page, Filtered	Saves a more stripped-down version of HTML that doesn't contain code intended to support Word-only features (see Chapter 24).
Single File Web Page	Saves a single .mht or .mhtml Web archive file that contains any graphics included on your Web page (as opposed to saving the graphics in a separate new folder). Note that Web Archive files can be read only by Microsoft Internet Explorer.
Document Template	Saves files as Word templates for creating other similar files.
Rich Text Format (RTF)	Saves in a Microsoft standard file format for exchanging word processing data in text file format. RTF preserves most, but not all, Word formatting. Some software can import RTF files but not Word 2003 files; in addition, saving to RTF can sometimes fix a damaged Word file.
Plain Text	Eliminates all formatting; converts line, section, and page breaks to paragraph marks; uses the ANSI character set. Useful if you're uncertain about your file's ultimate destination.
Word 97-2002 & 6.0/95—RTF	Saves to a version of Rich Text Format that can be read by Word 6, 95, 97, 2000, and XP.
XML Document	Saves to XML format using Microsoft Word's built-in XML schema.
WordPerfect 5.x Formats	Provides multiple options for saving to various WordPerfect 5.x formats.
Microsoft Works	Provides multiple options for saving to various Microsoft Works formats, from Works 3.0 for Windows through Works 2000.

If you need a file converter that isn't on this list, you have several options. In some cases, the converter you need is available in the Microsoft Office 2003 Resource Kit at www.microsoft.com/office/ork/, or free from Microsoft's Web site.

If you need to convert a file that doesn't have an official Microsoft converter, consider Dataviz Conversions Plus Suite.

What if you need to view or work with a file someone else has sent? First, note that Word can open files in a few formats that it cannot use to save files, notably WordPerfect 6.x for Windows and Lotus 1-2-3.

If you need to merely view the contents of a file, try Quick View, which comes with Windows 2000 and Windows XP. (It's an optional component; you might have to run your Windows setup program to install it.)

A third-party product, Stellent Quick View Plus, supports more than 200 file formats, most of which aren't included in Quick View. Unlike the free Quick View, Quick View Plus enables you to print files.

TIP

> Often, the easiest solution is to ask whoever sent you the file to resave it in a format you can read. For example, most current word processors—such as Sun's widely used StarOffice Writer—will save in one of Microsoft Word's native formats.

TIP

> What if you need the text from a file right now; you can't afford to wait for a third-party product to arrive, and you can live without the formatting? Or what if you have a file that you can't even identify? Try Word's Recover Text from Any File filter, available through the File, Open dialog box. You'll learn how to use File, Open and Word's document filters in the next section.

Finally, it's important to note that Word's built-in file conversions aren't always perfect. Many of these limitations are minor; for example, Word's decimal table cell alignments are converted to WordPerfect right-aligned paragraphs, and centering codes may have to be individually repositioned. Taken together, however, they mean you can't assume that what you see in Word is what you get in WordPerfect.

Ideally, you should double-check the results of any file conversion in the program to which you've converted. In the real world, however, you may not have access to that program, so just do your best to give your file's recipient enough time to check it and make any necessary adjustments.

→ For more information about file conversions, **see** Chapter 34, "Managing Word More Effectively," **p. 1113**.

TAKING A CLOSER LOOK AT WORD'S SAVE AS AND OPEN DIALOG BOXES

Word 2003's Save As and Open dialog boxes are full of productivity tools and shortcuts you may not have noticed. Take a few moments to look over these dialog boxes—it will pay off many times over in improved efficiency.

TIP

> Word 2003 Save As and Open dialog boxes are resizable, so you can view longer or wider lists of documents. To resize one of these dialog boxes, drag on the triangle at the bottom right of the dialog box (refer to Figure 3.6).

THE PLACES BAR: QUICK ACCESS TO KEY FOLDERS

At the left side of the Open and Save As dialog boxes, you'll see a vertical bar displaying five folders Microsoft expects you to use heavily as you work with Word. These work like shortcuts: Clicking on one displays the contents of the corresponding folder. These are the folders:

- **My Recent Documents.** The My Recent Documents folder stores Windows shortcuts for every file you've used and lists them in date order, with the most recent first. If you've worked on the same file several times, the shortcut takes you to the latest version. It's a great way to find a file that you've used in the past few days but that may no longer be on Word's most recently used file list.

- **Desktop.** This is the top-level folder on your computer. Although you probably won't store files in the Desktop folder, clicking Desktop gives you a quick high-level view of your drives and network resources. From the desktop, you can browse to just about anywhere.

- **My Documents.** This is Word's default document folder. Word places all the new files you save here unless you've specified otherwise in Tools, Options, File Locations.

- **My Computer.** Like the Desktop, the My Computer view shows you all the local and mapped network drives you have access to. It also shows you shared document folders, as well as all the My Documents folders you have access to. For example, if you are logged on as Administrator, you will be able to access the Administrator's Documents folder as well as folders belonging to other users you have the rights to access.

- **My Network Places.** This folder gives you a one-click connection to the folders on your network, Web, or FTP server—including files you may have published on your intranet or Web site.

You can customize the Places Bar with additional folders you use regularly. To add a folder to the Places Bar, select the folder in either the Open or the Save As dialog box; then click the Tools button at the top of the dialog box and choose the Add To "My Places" option. The folder now appears on the Places Bar in all major Microsoft Office 2003 applications. An arrow may also appear at the bottom of the Places Bar, if its contents are now too long to fit.

To reorganize the Places Bar, right-click on an item; then choose Remove, Move Up, Move Down, or Rename. You can also choose Small Icons to squeeze more icons onto the Places Bar (see Figure 3.8).

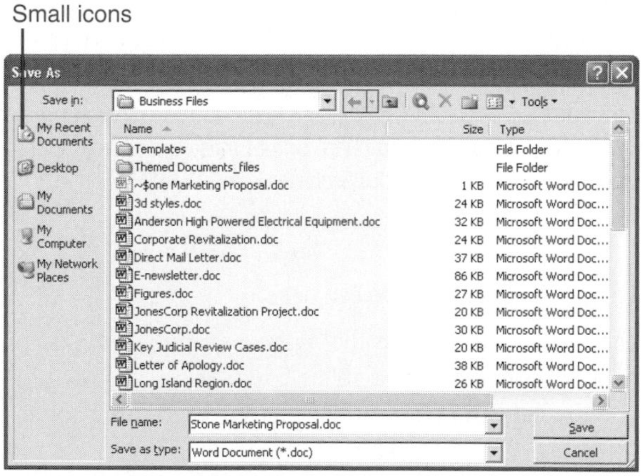

Small icons

Figure 3.8
Displaying small icons to fit more locations on the Places Bar.

CONTROLLING HOW YOU VIEW LISTS OF DOCUMENTS

Word can list your document in several ways. You can choose a different view of your document list by clicking the down arrow next to the Views button on the Save As (or Open) toolbar (see Figure 3.9). A drop-down list appears, containing these choices:

Figure 3.9
Choosing how to view a list of documents.

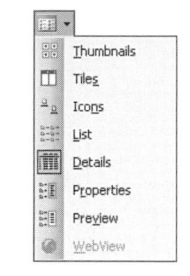

- **Thumbnails.** Displays thumbnail images of documents. Note, however, that in many cases Word cannot display a thumbnail and simply presents an icon.
- **Tiles.** Displays large icons representing each file and folder, with the name of each file or folder appearing to its right. Typically, the Tiles view can display only 10 files or folders at a time.
- **Icons.** Displays rows of icons representing each file and folder, with the name of each file or folder appearing beneath it. Typically, the Icons view can display approximately 24 files or folders at a time.
- **List.** Displays a list of the names of your documents and folders, typically in two columns.
- **Details.** Displays the size, type, and last modification date of each file and folder. You can sort files by clicking on the heading you want to sort by, such as Name, Size, Type, or Modified.
- **Properties.** Enables you to select a file and get information about it (see Figure 3.10).
- **Preview.** Displays the first page of the document.

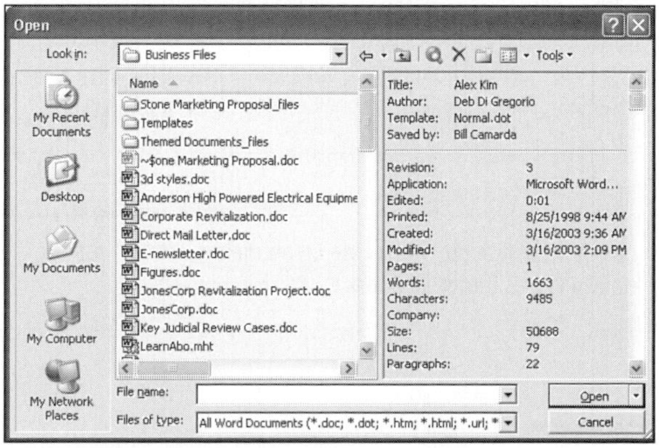

Figure 3.10
The Properties view within the Save As dialog box.

USING TOOLS IN THE SAVE AS AND OPEN DIALOG BOXES

For your convenience, Word brings together a series of file-related tools in the Tools menu of the Save As dialog box. To view these tools, click the Tools button (see Figure 3.11).

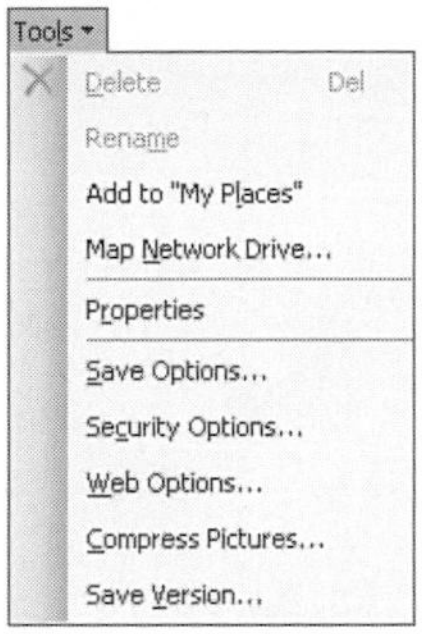

Figure 3.11
Choosing among the tools available in the Save As dialog box.

> Tools ▾
>
> ✕ Delete   Del
>   Rename
>   Add to "My Places"
>   Map Network Drive...
>   Properties
>   Save Options...
>   Security Options...
>   Web Options...
>   Compress Pictures...
>   Save Version...

3

> **NOTE**
>
> Some of these tools are also available in the Open dialog box, as is another tool—Search—which you can use to search for files. Search is covered later in this chapter.
>
> Additionally, some of the tools described previously, as well as other options, are also available from shortcut menus that display when you right-click on a filename.

You can select a file, click Tools, and then Delete it or Rename it. Or, if you prefer, click Properties to display the document's properties. (To learn more about using document properties, see Chapter 34.)

If you select a networked drive, you can choose Map Network Drive to map that drive so that it appears as another drive letter on your local drive.

> **NOTE**
>
> Several additional options are available in the Tools menu; these are covered elsewhere in the book. Save Options is covered in Chapter 31, "Customizing Word." Security Options is covered in Chapter 33, "Word Document Privacy and Security Options." Web Options is covered in Chapter 24, "Using Word to Develop Web Content." Compress Pictures, which shrinks file sizes by compressing images within the files, is covered in Chapter 13, "Getting Images into Your Documents." Finally, Save Version is covered in Chapter 26, "Managing Document Collaboration and Revisions."

> **TIP**
>
> You can select multiple files in the Open dialog box and use the Tools menu to add them to the My Places folder all at once.

USING MSN WEB COMMUNITIES TO STORE CONTENT ON THE WEB

Microsoft's MSN Web Communities offers 30 megabytes of storage space on the Web at no charge. You can use this space from within Office as

- Supplemental file storage
- An easy way to share large files with clients and business partners
- An easy way to transfer files you'll need on a trip

In the following procedure, you'll walk through claiming and using your Web-based storage space.

NOTE

> The following procedure assumes that you have a Microsoft Passport user ID, which gives you access to all of Microsoft's services on the Web, including Hotmail. If you don't have one, you can get one at www.hotmail.com and a variety of other sites on the Web. As with any other free Web resource, before you sign up for Passport, carefully read Microsoft's posted privacy policies.

1. Choose File, Open (or File, Save As).
2. In the Open (or Save As) dialog box, choose My Network Places from the Places Bar.
3. Double-click on My Web Sites on MSN. The Sign In with Microsoft .NET Passport dialog box appears (see Figure 3.12).

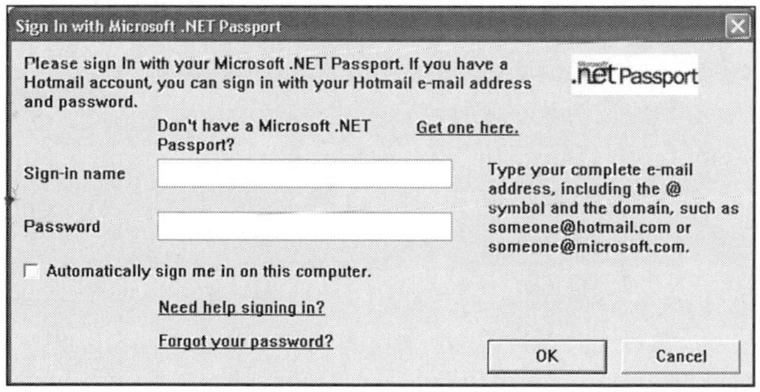

Figure 3.12
The Sign In with Microsoft .NET Passport dialog box.

4. Enter your sign-in name (typically your Hotmail email address) and your password; then click OK.

TIP

> If you're unconcerned about the security of your computer, and you don't want to be bothered with signing in to Passport every time you use your Web storage, check the Automatically Sign Me In on This Computer check box.

5. Microsoft now provides you with a folder bearing your sign-in name (you cannot rename this folder). Double-click this folder.

If you want to create a new folder within this folder, click the New Folder button in the Save As toolbar. The New Folder dialog box appears (see Figure 3.13). Enter a folder name in the Name text box and click OK. The folder now appears in your list of folders.

Figure 3.13
The New Folder dialog box.

Now that you have Web storage, you can browse to it, save files to it, and open files from it, just like any other drive you have access to. If you are accessing the drive for the first time in a session, you may be asked for your Microsoft Passport ID and password.

USING WORD'S PROGRAM AND FILE RECOVERY FEATURES

Word 2003 and Office 2003 include features designed to make them more resilient, and more capable of fixing both themselves and damaged document files.

These features cannot solve every problem you encounter with Word 2003; however, they should assist with many, if not most, of them—and, especially, help avoid much of the lost work and inefficiency that results from crashes and damaged files.

In the following sections, we introduce the Word 2003 program and file recovery features that will be most important to day-to-day users.

RECOVERING DOCUMENTS WITH THE DOCUMENT RECOVERY TASK PANE

If Word 2003 crashes, it displays a dialog box that gives you options for what to do next. By default, Word restarts and attempts to recover your work; if you don't want this to happen, clear the Recover My Work and Restart Microsoft Word check box.

If you have an Internet connection, you can also send Microsoft an error report that summarizes the technical aspects of the crash. To see what the report contains, click the Click Here link. Microsoft says it will treat the report as confidential and anonymous.

If you want to send the report, click Send Error Report. Word transfers the report, keeping you updated as to its status.

When the error report has been submitted, if Microsoft has information about how to prevent the problem, a dialog box appears containing a More Information link. If you click

More Information, a Web page appears containing information on the problem and how it might be prevented or worked around.

If you prefer not to send an error report to Microsoft, click Don't Send. Word closes. Unless you specified otherwise, Word then restarts, displaying the Document Recovery task pane (see Figure 3.14).

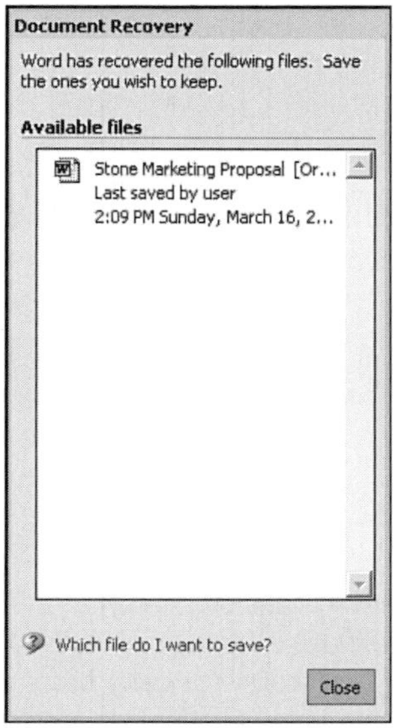

Figure 3.14
From the Document Recovery task pane, you can attempt to recover files that may have been damaged when Word crashed.

Document Recovery

Word has recovered the following files. Save the ones you wish to keep.

Available files

Stone Marketing Proposal [Or...
Last saved by user
2:09 PM Sunday, March 16, 2...

Which file do I want to save?

Close

To view a file, click on it, or click on the right arrow next to it and choose View from the drop-down menu. To save a file with a new name, click the down arrow to its right, and choose Save As from the drop-down menu. (If you choose Save As but use the original file-name, Word overwrites the existing version of the file.) It makes sense to resave your file immediately, in case there's still a problem with Word that might cause it to crash again, and risk the possibility that the crash might even prevent Word from recovering your data next time.

In some cases, the Document Recovery task pane contains more than one version of the file. If a version is marked [Recovered], it contains recent edits you never saved. If a version is marked [Original], it contains the last saved version of the file.

You can review each document and then decide which to save or, possibly, save both, by saving one under a different name.

To close a file without saving it, click Close. Word displays a dialog box asking you to confirm whether you want to abandon the file. If the file was marked [Recovered], this damaged version of the file is lost.

USING AUTORECOVER TO RECOVER INFORMATION FROM DAMAGED FILES

By default, Word stores AutoRecover information about your document every 10 minutes. Word uses this AutoRecover to attempt to restore your files in the event of a system crash or power failure.

It's important to understand that AutoRecover information isn't a substitute for saving your file regularly; in fact, Microsoft changed the name of this feature from Automatic Save to emphasize this. You should still save regularly, for two reasons. First, if you save regularly, your saved file may contain more up-to-date information than the AutoRecover file. Second, AutoRecover files aren't foolproof; they can't always be used to generate reliable, complete files.

If you're concerned about the stability of your system, you can tell Word to create AutoRecover files more often. Conversely, if you find that Word slows down to create AutoRecover files too frequently, you can tell Word to create them less often. The schedule Word uses to create AutoRecover files is set in the Save tab of the Options dialog box. To change how often AutoRecover saves a file, choose Tools, Options and click the Save tab. Then, in the Save AutoRecover Info Every scroll box, enter a new setting from 1 to 120 minutes.

NOTE

> By default, AutoRecover files are stored in the \Application Data\Microsoft\Word sub-folder of your Windows folder, a subfolder of your profile folder. You can change this through the File Locations tab of the Tools, Options dialog box. If you do change it, how-ever, use a local folder on your own computer, rather than a location on a network server, to maximize reliability.

CREATING AUTOMATIC BACKUPS

If you want, every time you save your file, Word can rename the previously saved version with the .bak extension, ensuring that you always have a fairly recent backup of your work. This, too, is controlled from the Save tab of the Options dialog box. Check the Always Create Backup Copy check box.

When you use this feature, Word disables Fast Saves, so your saves will be somewhat slower, especially if you are working with long documents.

NOTE

> Fast Saves are fast for the same reason it's faster to throw your clothes on the chair rather than hang them in the closet. With Fast Saves, Word doesn't actually put the changes where they belong; it simply makes a list of the changes that will be integrated the next time Word saves normally. (In fact, if you open a Fast Saved file in a text editor such as Notepad, you may well see text you thought you deleted.) When the list of changes gets very long, Word does a normal save to put things back in order.

CAUTION

> If you're using Fast Saves, turn it off before you save a Word file that will be exported to another program. Other software may not understand Word's Fast Saves "to-do lists."
>
> Also be aware that because Fast Save may not immediately delete information from your document that you *think* you've deleted, it can be a security risk.
>
> To turn off Fast Saves, choose Tools, Options and click the Save tab; then clear the Allow Fast Saves check box.

SAVING LOCAL BACKUPS

If you typically save to a network drive or a removable disk such as a Zip disk, you can tell Word to automatically save a duplicate copy of your file on your local hard disk. To do so, choose Tools, Options and click the Save tab; then check the Make Local Copy of Files Stored on Network or Removable Drives check box.

MICROSOFT OFFICE APPLICATION RECOVERY

If Word stops responding, Office 2003 includes a tool you can use to try to kick start Word: Microsoft Office Application Recovery. To run it, choose Start, Programs, Microsoft Office Tools, Microsoft Office Application Recovery. The Microsoft Office Application Recovery dialog box appears (see Figure 3.15).

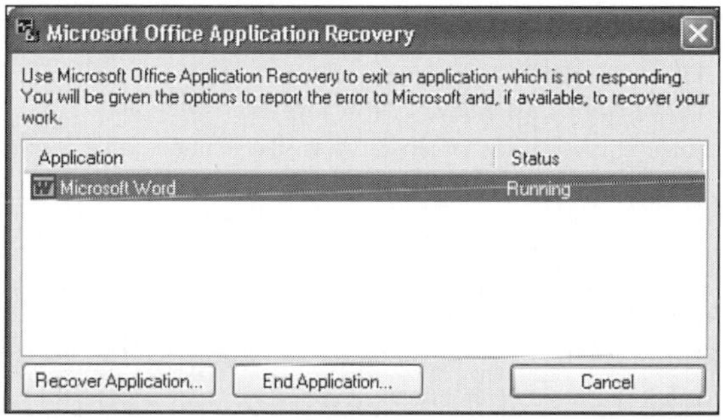

Figure 3.15
Using Microsoft Office Application Recovery, you can attempt to get an unresponsive Word to start working again, or simply exit Word.

Any Office 2003 application that Windows reports as frozen is listed in this dialog box. To attempt to start Word running again, select Word from the list and click Recover Application. To close Word, click End Application.

If Microsoft Office Application Recovery cannot recover Word, try closing it instead, using the End Application command. If you can't close it through the Application Recovery applet, press Ctrl+Alt+Delete. Select Microsoft Word from the Windows Task Manager, and choose End Task.

USING OFFICE SAFE MODE

Over the years, Word users have sometimes encountered startup problems—and these startup problems have often been caused by errant add-ins or extensions, or damaged templates. Word 2003 and Office 2003 contain their own Safe Mode that allows Word to start, while disabling a component causing a problem.

In Automated Safe Mode, when Word encounters a problem that prevents startup, it displays a message identifying the component that appears to be causing the problem and offers you an opportunity to disable that component. If you disable the component, Word typically starts. Of course, you won't have access to the capabilities of that component.

To view a list of the components Word has currently disabled, choose Help, About Microsoft Word and click the Disabled Items button.

If any components are listed in the Disabled Items dialog box, you can select one and click Enable to manually enable it. In certain cases, the component may then work properly. However, if you reenable an item that Word has trouble with loading at startup, the item may be automatically disabled again the next time you start Word.

Keep in mind that Safe Mode disables certain Word features. Most notably, your interface and AutoCorrect customizations aren't loaded, and you can't save new or changed templates. For a more detailed list of Safe Mode restrictions, search the Help system for "Safe Mode."

NOTE

If a component is disabled, visit the component provider's Web site to see whether a fix, workaround, or new version is available.

TIP

You can start any Office application in Safe Mode manually. Press the Ctrl button while you're starting Word. (Microsoft calls this User-Initiated Safe Mode.)

RETRIEVING YOUR DOCUMENTS

You can retrieve and open any saved document by clicking the Open button on the Standard toolbar, using the keyboard shortcut Ctrl+O, or choosing File, Open. Each of these steps opens the Open dialog box, shown in Figure 3.16.

After the dialog box is open, browse the drives and folders as you've already learned how to do. Select the file you want to open and click Open.

TIP

In particular, keep in mind that you can click the My Recent Documents icon to view a list of all the files you've worked on, in chronological order, starting with the most recent. The My Recent Documents folder stores shortcuts to the files. If you've worked on the same file several times, the shortcut takes you to the latest version.

Figure 3.16
You can retrieve any file from the Open dialog box.

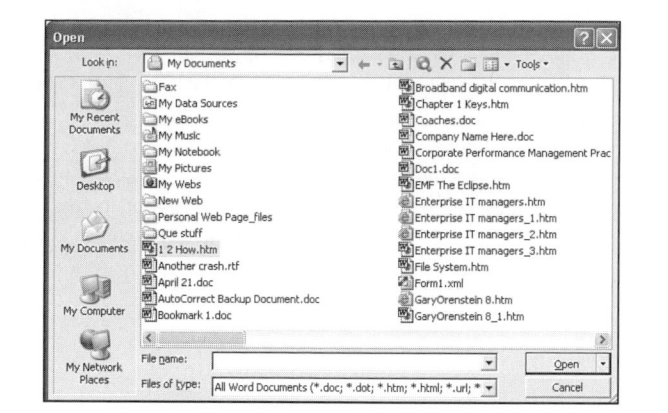

CAUTION

> The My Recent Documents folder may be a security risk; other users can explore it to see which files you've worked on. The My Recent Documents folder even records the names of encrypted files you've worked on (though a password is still required to open those files).
>
> To empty the contents of the My Recent Documents folder, click My Recent Documents in the Open dialog box to display its contents; then choose Tools, Clear Document History.

By default, Word's Open dialog box displays only files Word is designed to edit. In Word 2003, these include .doc files, .dot (document template) files, .htm and .html Web pages, .mht and .mhtml Web archive files, .xml XML files, .url files (links to Internet addresses), .rtf (Rich Text Format) files, and .txt (text only) files.

If you can't find a file where you expect it to be, it may be there but have a different extension. To find out, click in the Files of Type drop-down box and select All Files (*.*). Word now displays all files in the current folder.

If you know the extension of the file you want to open, you can choose to display only files of a specific type. If the file uses an extension Word recognizes, such as .wps for Microsoft Works files, you can select the extension from the Files of Type drop-down box. Otherwise, enter the extension in the File Name drop-down box, using the * wildcard. For example, to display all files with the extension .rpt, enter *.rpt.

You can open many files at the same time. Display the Open dialog box and browse to the folder you want. Press and hold Ctrl while you click each file you want to open. When your files are all selected, click Open.

If you want to open several files listed consecutively in the same folder, press and hold Shift; then choose the first and last files you want. Word automatically selects all the files in between as well.

TIP

> Increasingly, the files you want may be found on the World Wide Web. Using Microsoft Internet Explorer, you can look for a file on the Web from inside the Open dialog box.
>
> Click the Search the Web button; Internet Explorer opens. If you are already connected to the Internet, Internet Explorer displays a Microsoft-owned Web page where you can specify a search and the search engine you want to use. If you are not already connected, and must connect via dial-up, the Dial-Up Networking window appears; you can use it to connect. After you're connected, Internet Explorer displays Microsoft's search page.

Next, click Search, and the Web search engine you've chosen returns a list of pages containing the information you want.

USING THE MOST RECENTLY USED FILE LIST

Sometimes, you don't have to go anywhere near the Open dialog box; there are faster ways to find what you need.

If you've used the file recently, it may appear on the most recently used file list that appears at the bottom of the File menu. The same list appears at the bottom of the Getting Started task pane.

By default, Word keeps track of the last four files you use; you can reopen one of these files by selecting it from the File menu.

You might want Word to keep track of more than four files (Word can track up to nine). To change the number of files Word tracks, choose Tools, Options and click the General tab. In the Recently Used File List scroll box, select the number of files you want to track, from 0 to 9. Click OK. Word begins tracking the new number of files. (Of course, Word doesn't immediately display additional files you opened earlier; it hasn't been tracking them.)

USING THE WINDOWS RECENT DOCUMENTS LIST

Windows keeps track of the last 15 documents you've used. This includes all files you may have used: Excel worksheets, compressed Zip files, text files, or anything else. If you primarily use Word, you may find that all the Word files you've worked with for the past few days are automatically being tracked by your operating system. To open one, click Start on the taskbar; then click Documents (or My Recent Documents, in Windows XP). The list of files appears. Click the one you want to open.

OPENING A FILE AS READ-ONLY OR AS A COPY

Normally, when you find the file you want, you simply click Open to open and work in it. However, Word gives you some additional one-click options. To see these choices in the Open dialog box, right-click on the down arrow next to the Open button (see Figure 3.17).

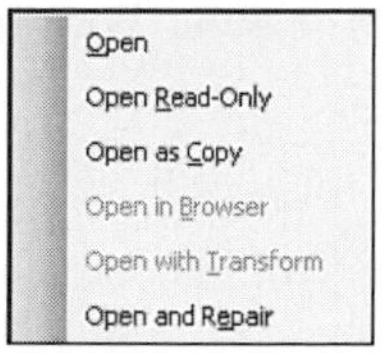

Figure 3.17
Choosing how you
want to open a file.

O̲pen
Open R̲ead-Only
Open as C̲opy
Open in B̲rowser
Open with T̲ransform
Open and R̲epair

- **Open R̲ead-Only.** Word opens the file but prevents you from making changes to it.

- **Open as C̲opy.** Word creates a new copy of the file and opens the copy. Word starts the filename with the words Copy of. (In other words, if the original file was called STONE.DOC, the copy is named Copy of STONE.DOC.) Open as Copy does not work with Web pages.

- **Open in B̲rowser.** This option works only if you've selected an HTML or HTM file. Choosing Open in B̲rowser displays the file in Internet Explorer (or whatever browser you've registered as your primary browser) instead of in Word. If you're using Internet Explorer, you can later edit the document in Word by clicking the arrow next to the Edit button on the Internet Explorer Standard Buttons toolbar and choosing Edit with Microsoft Word from the drop-down box.

- **Open with T̲ransform.** This option works only if you've selected an XML file. Choosing Open with T̲ransform opens the Choose an XML Transform dialog box; here, you can select an XSL or XSLT file that will apply appropriate formatting to your XML file.

- **Open and R̲epair.** Word attempts to open a damaged file and make repairs.

FINDING THE FILE YOU'RE SEEKING

Until now, it's been assumed that you know the name and location of the file you want to open. But that's not always the case. How often have you scratched your head and wondered, *Where did I put that file? What did I call it?* For those times, Word 2003 provides extraordinarily powerful Search features.

NOTE

> In older versions of Word, the feature that allowed you to search for files was called Find. It has been renamed Search to distinguish it from Word's Find and Replace features for locating text within an open document.

The Search features are accessible in two separate ways:

- You can work in the File Search dialog box. To get there, choose F̲ile, O̲pen; then choose S̲earch from the Tool̲s menu.

- You can use Word's Basic and Advanced File Search task panes. To access them, choose F̲ile, File Searc̲h.

Whichever approach you choose, Search works exactly the same. Both the dialog box and the task panes offer two approaches to searching:

- *Basic File Search*ing, designed to simplify searching for specific text
- *Advanced File Search*ing, which allows you to create complex searches based on a broad range of criteria

Both approaches to searching share common tools for specifying where to search and what types of documents to search for.

The following sections cover Basic File Searches, introduce the common tools available in both Basic and Advanced File Searches, and show you how to make the most of Advanced File Searches. But first, a word about Office 2003's Fast Search capabilities.

UNDERSTANDING FAST SEARCH

If you have accumulated hundreds or thousands of documents, it can take Word a good deal of time to search them. To streamline the process, Word can build an index of the words in each document and search the index instead of the documents themselves. This is called Fast Searching.

Fast Searching is generally turned on by default. To check whether it is turned on, choose File, File Search. The Basic File Search task pane appears (see Figure 3.18).

Figure 3.18
The Basic File Search task pane.

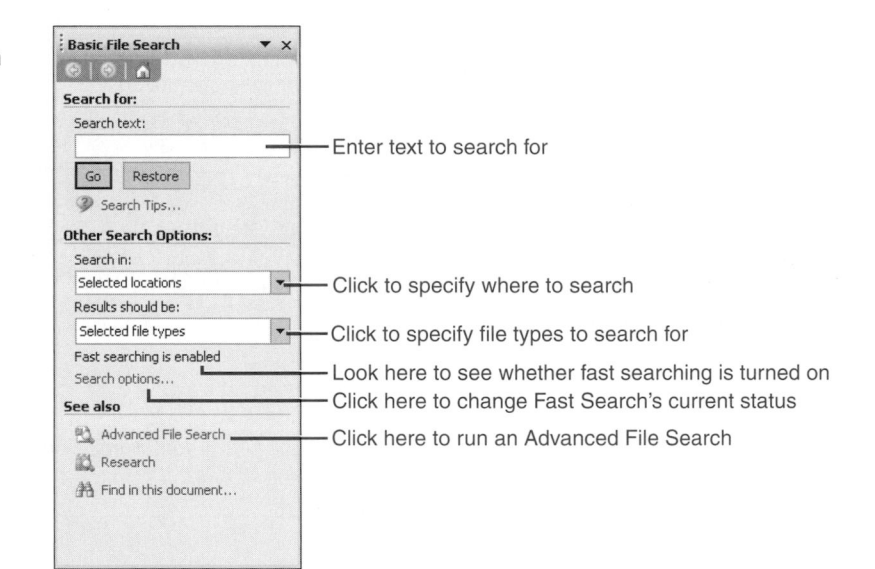

To turn Fast Search on or off, click Search Options. The Indexing Service Settings dialog box appears. To turn on the indexing service that makes Fast Search work, click Yes, Enable Indexing Service and Run When My Computer Is Idle. To turn it off, click No, Do Not Enable Indexing Service. Click OK.

PERFORMING A BASIC FILE SEARCH FOR SPECIFIC TEXT

As mentioned earlier, basic searches make it easy to search for documents containing specific text. Basic File Searches also search the full contents of each file's Properties dialog box, including information such as the file's author and subject.

To run a Basic File Search from the Basic File Search task pane, choose File, File Search. The Basic File Search task pane appears (refer to Figure 3.18).

If you prefer to work in a larger dialog box, choose File, Open; then click the Tools button and choose Search. The Basic tab of the File Search dialog box appears (see Figure 3.19).

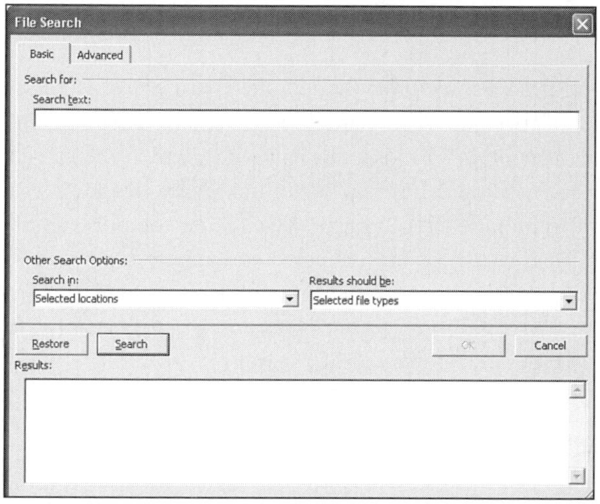

Figure 3.19
The Basic tab of the File Search dialog box.

Whether you're working in the task pane or the dialog box, the remaining steps are the same:

1. Enter the text you're looking for in the Search Text box.

> **TIP**
>
> You can make a Basic File Search more powerful by using wildcards. Word supports two wildcards:
>
> - * (the asterisk character) represents any group of one or more characters. For example, S*artz finds both Schwartz and Swartz.
> - ? (the question mark) represents a single character. For example, gr?p would find grip, but not grasp.

2. Specify where you want to search by clicking the down arrow in the Search In drop-down box. A list of file locations appears. You can expand an item to include its sub-folders by clicking the plus sign. Check the boxes corresponding to where you want to search; clear the boxes corresponding to locations you don't want to search.

TIP

By default, Word searches My Computer—in other words, all the folders on your computer. However, many people store all their Word files in the My Documents folder or a few other folders or subfolders. Don't search your entire computer if all your files are in a few locations—specify those locations, and you'll get done far more quickly.

NOTE

You can also search one or more of your Network Places. However, searching networks can be inherently slow due to bandwidth constraints, and there's no guarantee that every location on the network contains a Fast Search index.

3. Specify types of files to search for. By default, Word searches all files created in any Office 2003 application; all Web pages; and all email messages, appointments, contacts, tasks, and notes created in Outlook. To narrow or widen the search, click the down arrow in the Results Should Be drop-down box. A list of file types appears. You can expand an item to include subcategories by clicking the plus sign; for example, if you click the + sign next to Office files, check boxes appear for Word Files, Excel Files, PowerPoint Files, Access Files, Data Connection Files, and Document Imaging Files. Check the boxes corresponding to file types you want to search; clear the boxes corresponding to file types you don't want to search.

4. When you're ready to search, click Go if you are using the Basic File Search task pane (or Search if you are using the File Search dialog box).

Word builds a list of all the files it finds. Figure 3.20 shows search results in the Search Results task pane; Figure 3.21 shows search results in the File Search dialog box.

Figure 3.20
In the Search Results task pane, Word displays a list of all the files it finds.

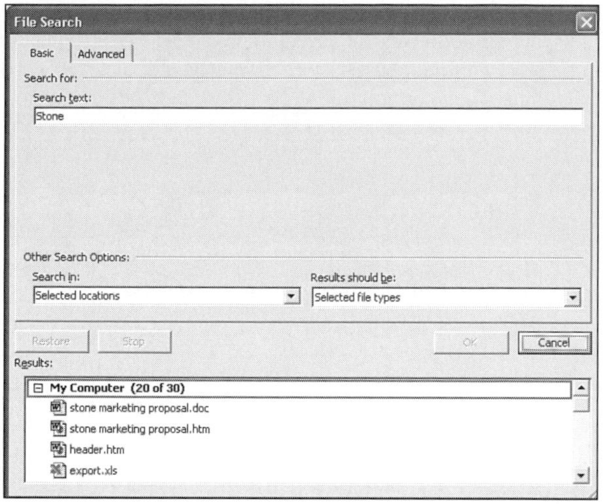

Figure 3.21
In the File Search dialog box, Word displays a list of all the files it finds.

You now have several options:

- To open a file from the Basic File Search task pane, click on the file. To open the file from the Basic tab of the File Search dialog box, double-click on it; then click Open in the Open dialog box.

> **TIP**
>
> Unfortunately, you can't open several found files at the same time (though the Search Results pane remains open as you open files one at a time).
>
> You can, however, open multiple files at once using the file search feature built into Windows itself. To use the Windows file search, choose Start, Search, For Files or Folders (in Windows XP this is called All Files and Folders). Create your search query and click Search. When Windows returns a list of found files, press Ctrl and select each file you want to open, right-click, and choose Open. All the files will open.

- To create a new file with the same contents as the existing file, click the down arrow to the right of the filename and choose New From This File from the drop-down list.
- To copy a hyperlink to the file into the Office Clipboard, from where you can paste it into any document, click the down arrow and choose Copy Link to Clipboard.
- To view the file's Properties dialog box, click the down arrow and choose Properties.
- If the file is a Web page, to view it in your default browser, choose Open in Browser.

> **NOTE**
>
> In older versions of Word, if you wanted Word to find documents containing all related forms of Word you specified, you had to check a Match All Word Forms check box. Word 2003 finds all word forms automatically—whether you want it to or not.

NOTE

> One feature unfortunately removed from Word's file search feature is the capability to save a search for future use. However, when you display the Search task pane, it shows the last query you performed.

ADVANCED FILE SEARCH: SPECIFYING PROPERTIES TO SEARCH FOR

Word enables you to refine your search, creating Advanced File Searches that use an extraordinary collection of document properties and attributes. Examples of properties you'll use often are

- Filename
- Text or property (searches for specific text in the document, as well as text in the Properties dialog box)
- Last modified (date the file was most recently edited)

However, when necessary, you can search by many other properties. For example, imagine that you're reviewing the past year's work and you want to know which projects took the longest to complete. You might use Search to find all Word files that had a "total editing time" of more than 20 hours. Or, if you're looking for reports that contain embedded audio comments, you could search for documents in which the "Number of multimedia clips" is at least 1.

To perform an Advanced File Search from the Advanced File Search task pane, choose File, File Search and click Advanced File Search (see Figure 3.22).

Figure 3.22
Creating an Advanced File Search from the Advanced File Search task pane.

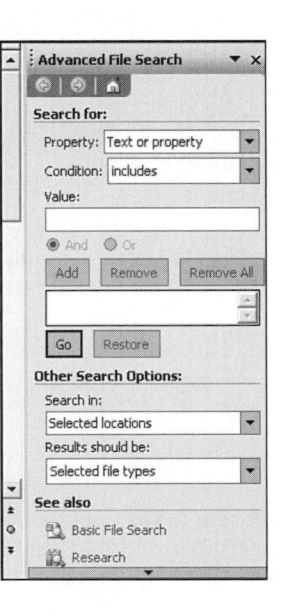

To perform an Advanced File Search from the File Search dialog box, choose File, Open; click Tools; choose Search; and click the Advanced tab (see Figure 3.23).

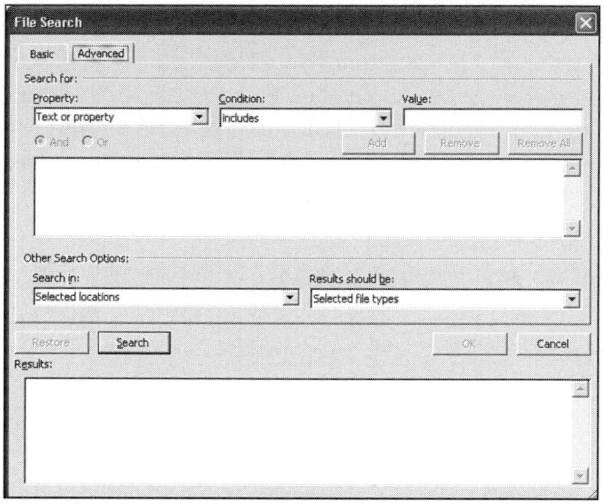

Figure 3.23
Creating an Advanced File Search from the File Search dialog box.

Whether you work from the task pane or the dialog box, Advanced File Search works the same way. Using the Property, Condition, and Value boxes, you first establish criteria for your search, one at a time. For example, you might add the criterion that the file must have been created within the past seven days, or that it must contain the word "Stevenson."

NOTE

As described in the "Performing a Basic File Search for Specific Text" section earlier in this chapter, you can also specify the following:

- Locations where Word should search, via the Search In drop-down box
- File types to search for, via the Results Should Be drop-down box

TIP

You can specify text to search for in the Basic tab (or Basic File Search task pane) and then switch to Advanced File Search. The text you specified will be included in the search.

After you set a criterion, click Add to include it in the list of criteria Word is to consider. When you've listed the appropriate criteria to narrow your file list, click Search. Word searches for the files, displaying the results.

You add criteria using the Property and Condition drop-down boxes and the Value text box. Choose a property from the drop-down list of properties and document elements for which Word can search.

Depending on the property, Word may display a list of available choices in the Condition drop-down box. For example, if you're searching for documents based on the number of pages they contain, your condition choices will include arithmetical conditions, such as equals and more than. After you've set the condition, you need to specify a value.

If you want to search for all files containing specific text, you can choose Text or Property from the Property drop-down box and enter the text in the Value text box. You can narrow searches by requiring that documents include multiple blocks of text, by specifying each block of text as a separate criterion. Because this can be confusing, an example is shown in Figure 3.24.

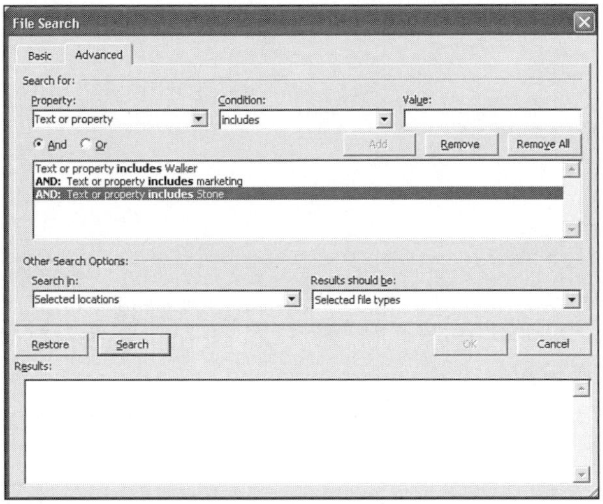

Figure 3.24
An example of searching for specific text.

TIP

To search for a phrase (multiple adjacent words), surround the phrase with quotation marks.

To search for files by the dates they were last modified, click the Property drop-down list box and select Last Modified. In the Condition drop-down list, choose one of the following options: Today, Last Week, This Week, Last Month, This Month, or Any Time.

Here are two examples of how the criteria you set in the Find Files That Match These Criteria window correspond to what Word actually searches for.

If you set the criterion Comments Include the Word Smith, Word searches the properties associated with every document, returning all files that contain the word "Smith" in the Comments property. (The Comments box may be found in the Summary tab of the Properties dialog box.)

If you set the criterion Last Saved By Is Not Walker, Word searches for the Last Saved By property, which you can find in the Statistics tab of the Properties dialog box. If the name stored there does not include "Walker," Word includes the file in its listings. (Note that Word bases Last Saved By information on the name stored in the User Information tab of the Tools, Options dialog box.)

→ For more information on using document properties to track your documents, **see** "Using Document Properties to Simplify Document Management," **p. 1122**.

Before you finalize a search criterion, you need to take one more step, which relates to the breadth of the search you want. In some cases, you are designing criterion to find many files; for example, you might want to take a look at all the work you did for a specific client last month. In such cases, you may want each criterion to add more files to the list that Word provides. In other cases, you may be looking for one specific file. Then, you'll want to design your searches as narrowly as possible, ideally to return only that one file.

To create a broader search, click the Or button. Word then returns files that meet either this criterion *or* the other criteria you include. To create a narrower search, click the And button. Then, Word displays only those files that meet this criterion as well as the others.

When you're satisfied with one search criterion, click Add, and Word places it under the other criteria. You can then add other criteria until you're satisfied. Then, click Search, and Word displays the files you've requested.

If Word's Search feature isn't locating the files you expect, see "What to Do If Advanced File Search Doesn't Locate What You Need," in the "Troubleshooting" section of this chapter.

SWITCHING AMONG FILES YOU'VE OPENED

Often, you'll have many files open at once. If you are running Word 2003 in Windows 2000, each file you open gets its own icon on the Windows taskbar. You can have multiple icons on the taskbar while only one copy of Word is open. To display any open file, click its taskbar icon.

This behavior, which contrasts with most Windows programs, has not met with universal acclaim. In Word 2003, the choice is yours. If you prefer to set aside only one taskbar icon for Word—and to switch among files using the Window menu or other traditional techniques—you can have what you want.

To switch back to the classic "multiple document interface," choose Tools, Options, View; clear the Windows in Taskbar check box; and choose OK.

Windows XP largely solves the problem. If you are running Word 2003 in Windows XP, by default each file is listed within a single group displayed on the taskbar. Click the group to display all the files listed in it, and click to choose the one you want to view.

If you clear the Windows in Taskbar check box while you are running Windows XP, only the current document icon will appear in the taskbar; you'll have to switch between files using the Window menu.

TROUBLESHOOTING

WHAT TO DO IF ADVANCED FILE SEARCH DOESN'T LOCATE WHAT YOU NEED

You can use the following tips to troubleshoot problems with Word's Advanced File Search feature.

It's easy to make a mistake in designing a search and get results that aren't quite what you wanted—or an error message. If that happens, check your search with these troubleshooting questions:

- Did you forget to add one criterion to the list by clicking <u>A</u>dd?

- Are your values correct? Word may not care whether you were brought up well, but it will care if you incorrectly spell a keyword or another search value.

- Are your *and*s and *or*s correct? Be aware that order matters. These two similar-looking searches return different results:

Search 1:

`Author includes the words Stewart.`

`Creation date today.`

OR: `Keywords includes the words Jones.`

Search 2:

`Creation date today.`

OR: `Keywords includes the words Jones.`

AND: `Author includes the words Stewart.`

In the first search, a file created last year whose keywords include Jones will be found. In the second search, Word first locates files created today and files with the keyword Jones, but then eliminates all those files except the ones authored by Stewart.

- Are any of your search criteria mutually contradictory? Have you asked for files created after June 1 and before February 24? No such files exist, of course, and Word usually flags the mistake with an error message. More subtly, have you asked for files that could exist, but are unlikely to? For example, have you asked for files saved on certain dates by someone who was on vacation at the time, or files created today that have been edited for more than 20 hours?

CHAPTER 4

QUICK AND EFFECTIVE FORMATTING TECHNIQUES

In this chapter

UNDERSTANDING THE BASICS OF DIRECT FORMATTING

The techniques you'll learn in this chapter are often called *direct* formatting because they involve applying formatting directly to text in your document. Even if you've been using Word for some time, this chapter presents many direct formatting techniques and shortcuts you might not be familiar with.

Later, in Chapter 10, "Streamlining Your Formatting with Styles," you'll learn *indirect* formatting techniques based on *styles*. In indirect formatting, you create a style that includes specific formats. Whenever you want a block of text to use those formats, you apply the style, and Word, in turn, applies the formats.

→ To learn more about indirect formatting with styles, **see** "What Styles Are and How They Work," **p. 331**.

Direct formatting is easier to learn and often quicker to apply, whereas indirect formatting is more flexible and often more powerful. When should you use each approach? In general,

- Use direct formatting when you're concerned only with formatting a specific block of text, especially short blocks of text that don't compose whole paragraphs. For example, use direct formatting when you need to italicize the name of a book or magazine. Also rely on direct formatting when you're creating a quick document that won't need to be repeated or built on later.

- Use indirect formatting when you are applying text formats that you'll need to use frequently throughout your document or in other documents—or for text that might need to be reformatted later; for instance, if your company redesigns all its documents and you must quickly apply new formatting to existing styles. You should especially rely on indirect formatting in large documents, where styles can help you organize both the formats and the content of your document.

As you become increasingly comfortable with Word, you should increasingly depend on indirect formatting: It will help you build more consistent documents, and even automate your documents. However, before you can master indirect formatting, you need to understand the basics of direct formatting covered in this chapter.

UNDERSTANDING WORD'S MULTIPLE LEVELS OF FORMATTING

If you've ever wondered why Word formatting behaves in a certain way, it helps to know how Word "thinks" about formatting. Word has three levels of formatting, all of which work together:

- *Font formatting* applies to specific characters. The Format, Font dialog box (also accessible by pressing Ctrl+D) brings together many of Word's font formatting controls.

- *Paragraph formatting* applies to entire paragraphs. The Format, Paragraph dialog box brings together many of Word's paragraph formatting controls.

- *Section formatting* applies to entire sections of a document. Word allows you to divide a document into sections corresponding to its major components, such as chapters in a manual, and establish margins, headers/footers, and other section formatting individually for each section. Section formatting controls can be found in the File, Page Setup dialog box and a few other locations.

Most day-to-day text formatting is font and paragraph formatting. This chapter covers font formatting first and then reviews several of the most common paragraph formatting techniques. *Section formatting* includes margins, headers and footers, and other elements that are often established once and then left alone.

→ For more information on formatting sections of a document, **see** "Using Word's Page Setup Features," **p. 158**.

WORKING WITH THE REVEAL FORMATTING TASK PANE

Word enables you to view and manage all your document formatting—both direct formatting, such as font, paragraph, and section formatting, and indirect formatting, such as styles—from a single location: the Reveal Formatting task pane.

To view all the formatting associated with a block of text, select the text (or click the insertion point at the location you are interested in). Then choose Format, Reveal Formatting, or press Shift+F1. The Reveal Formatting task pane appears (see Figure 4.1).

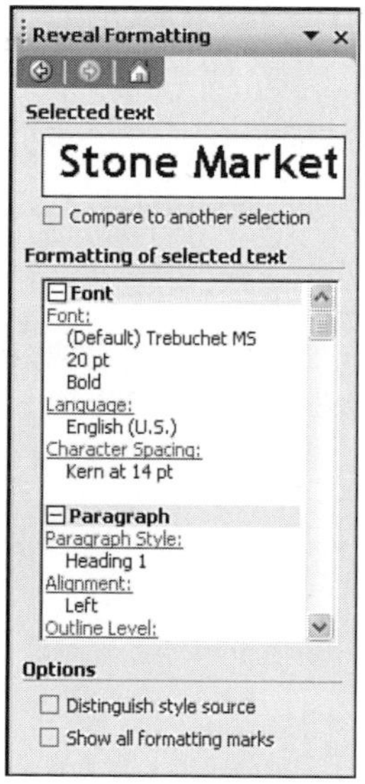

Figure 4.1
The Reveal Formatting task pane.

All formatting associated with the selected text (or insertion point location) is listed in the Formatting of Selected Text scroll box.

To change a formatting attribute, click the hyperlink associated with the category of formatting you want to change. Word displays the dialog box associated with that formatting—the same dialog box that would appear if you chose a menu command to view it. You can then make the changes there.

As discussed earlier—and covered in greater depth in Chapter 10—many attributes of Word formatting are associated with built-in styles or custom styles you create. In other words, the formatting of a specific block of text may be a combination of direct formatting you apply and indirect formatting applied by the styles. If you want the Reveal Formatting task pane to distinguish between direct formatting and formatting applied by a style, check the Distinguish Style Source check box.

To make fine adjustments to formatting, it sometimes helps to see the formatting marks Word places in a document—such as paragraph marks, manual line breaks, and tabs, which are normally invisible. To view the formatting marks in a document, check the Show All Formatting Marks check box.

NOTE

> You can also view formatting marks by clicking the Paragraph Mark button on the Standard toolbar.

→ To use Reveal Formatting to compare the formatting of two blocks of text, **see** "Comparing the Formatting of One Text Selection to Another," **p. 149**.

INTRODUCING FONT FORMATTING

Formatted text is capable of communicating far more effectively than unformatted text. Editors and publishers have long recognized the value of italics, boldface, and other character formatting in calling attention to text. Choices of font communicate subtly (or not so subtly) about the type of information contained in text, and how that information should be viewed.

In Word, you can apply an extraordinarily wide range of formats to specific characters. As already mentioned, Word calls this font formatting. It includes the following:

- Choice of font
- Font size (measured in points)
- Font style (for example, bold or italic)
- Underlining
- Font effects (for example, strikethrough, superscript, or emboss)
- Font color
- Scaling (font stretching)
- Spacing between groups of letters
- Position of text on a line
- Kerning (spacing between specific pairs of letters)
- Text animation

As already mentioned, you can control any type of font formatting through the Format, Font dialog box (see Figure 4.2).

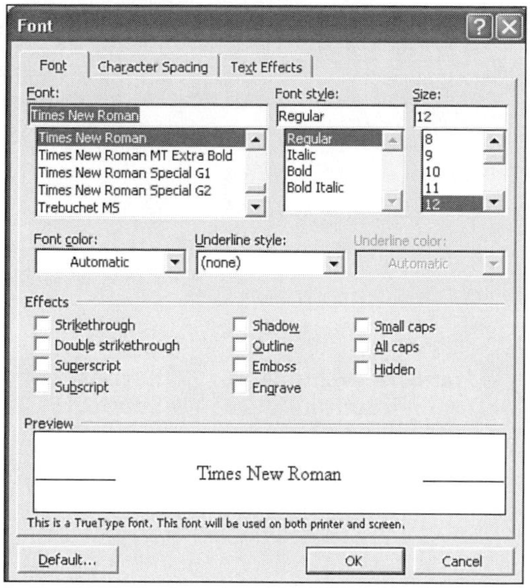

Figure 4.2
The Font tab of the Font dialog box brings together Word's most commonly used Font

Every aspect of controlling a font's formatting can be found here. However, when it comes to the formatting you do most, Word usually has quicker ways to get the job done than by using this dialog box.

QUICK AND EASY FONT FORMATTING

In many cases, the fastest way to apply a format is to use Word's Formatting toolbar (see Figure 4.3). In other cases, it can be easier to use a keyboard shortcut. For example, pressing Ctrl+B may be a faster way of boldfacing selected text than locating and clicking the Bold button on the Formatting toolbar. Either way, you first select the text you want to format and then click the button or press the keyboard shortcut to format your text.

NOTE

> Most formatting toolbar buttons and keyboard shortcuts toggle formatting both on and off. For example, if you select text that is bold, clicking the Bold button eliminates the Bold formatting.
>
> Some toolbar buttons offer multiple options, accessible by clicking the down arrow next to them. For example, clicking the down arrow next to the Line Spacing toolbar button allows you to choose from 1.0, 1.5, 2.0, and several other line spacing options.

There are plenty of keyboard shortcuts for formatting text, including many that don't have Formatting toolbar counterparts. Table 4.1 lists the Formatting toolbar buttons that apply to font (character) formatting and corresponding keyboard shortcuts where they exist.

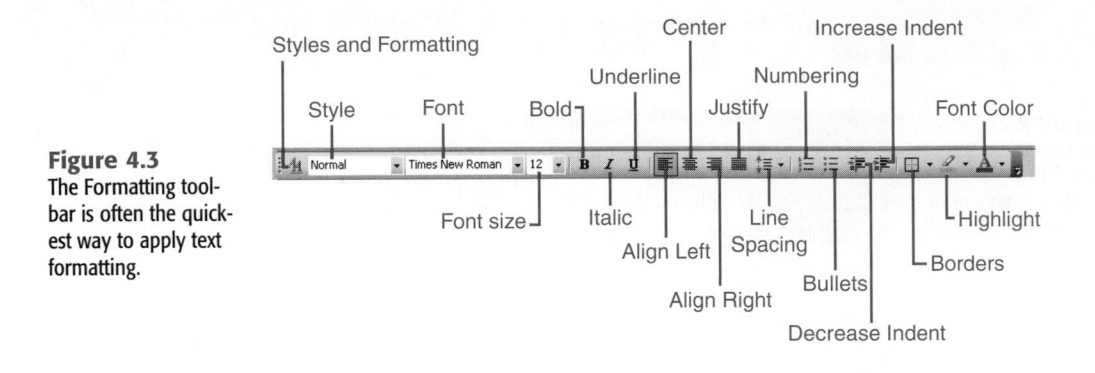

Figure 4.3
The Formatting toolbar is often the quickest way to apply text formatting.

TABLE 4.1   TOOLBAR BUTTONS AND KEYBOARD SHORTCUTS FOR FONT FORMATTING

Task	Standard or Formatting Toolbar Button	Keyboard Shortcut
Boldface	**B**	Ctrl+B
Italicize	*I*	Ctrl+I
Underline	U	Ctrl+U
Underline words only (not spaces)		Ctrl+Shift+W
Double underline		Ctrl+Shift+D
All caps		Ctrl+Shift+A
Small caps		Ctrl+Shift+K
Toggle capitalization		Shift+F3
Subscript	x_2	Ctrl+= (Equal sign)
Superscript	x^2	Ctrl++ (Plus sign)
Format as hidden text		Ctrl+Shift+H
Apply Symbol font		Ctrl+Shift+Q
Clear all font formatting		Ctrl+spacebar

NOTE

Some toolbar buttons listed in Table 4.1, such as Underline, do not appear if Word has been customized so that the Standard and Formatting toolbars share one row. To display the Formatting toolbar on its own row, choose Tools, Customize, Options and check the

Show Standard and Formatting Toolbars on Two Rows check box. (You can also drag any toolbar down to its own line, or even undock it to float free.)

Superscript, Subscript, Grow Font, Shrink Font, and Language toolbar buttons can be added manually, using the Add or Remove Buttons option at the right edge of the Formatting toolbar.

CHOOSING FONTS AND SIZES

Word can work with thousands of Windows-compatible fonts, including TrueType fonts (by default) and Adobe PostScript fonts.

NOTE

TrueType and PostScript are competing "scalable font" formats—in other words, formats for organizing the information that allows computers to scale characters in a font to any size without losing clarity. PostScript font support is provided automatically in Windows 2000 and Windows XP.

The easiest way to choose a font is via the Font drop-down box on the Formatting toolbar (see Figure 4.4). To do this, select the text you want to format, click the down arrow next to the Font drop-down box or press Ctrl+Shift+F, and scroll to and select the font you want.

NOTE

You can also change formatting without any text selected. If you do so, all text you type immediately following the insertion point will take on the new formatting.

Figure 4.4
Selecting a font through the Font drop-down box. The fonts at the top are the ones you've used most recently.

Each font name in this list is formatted to reflect the appearance of the corresponding font. This makes choosing the most appropriate font much easier.

TIP

> In choosing fonts, be sensitive to the visual tone communicated by the font. It is traditional or cutting-edge? Sophisticated or cartoony? Commonplace—such as Times New Roman and Arial—or unfamiliar? If you're choosing fonts for text (as opposed to headlines), readability is Job #1: Never select a display font such as Algerian or Wide Latin for text.
>
> You may also want to pay attention to the width of characters in a font, because this affects how much text can appear in a given number of pages. For example, Times New Roman was designed to fit far more text than Courier New without compromising readability.
>
> If you're choosing fonts for Web pages, don't count on your audience having fonts other than those installed with Windows or Office. Microsoft Web fonts such as Georgia and Verdana were designed for Web reading and are now sufficiently widely distributed to be relatively safe alternatives to Times New Roman and Arial.

If Word doesn't display a font you expect to see listed, see "What to Do If Fonts Seem to Be Missing," in "Troubleshooting" at the end of this chapter.

If Word substitutes a font you don't like for one you don't have, see "What to Do If Word Substitutes Fonts You Don't Like," in "Troubleshooting" at the end of this chapter.

Now that you've specified a font, you can specify its size, using the Font Size drop-down box on the Formatting toolbar. Select the text you want to format, click in the Font Size drop-down box (or press Ctrl+Shift+P), type or select the size you want, and press Enter.

TIP

> Sometimes you want to increase or decrease text size by only a point or two. Save time with these keyboard shortcuts:
>
> | **Task** | **Keyboard Shortcut** |
> | --- | --- |
> | Enlarge font 1 point | Ctrl+] |
> | Shrink font 1 point | Ctrl+[|
> | Enlarge size 1 increment | Ctrl+Shift+> |
> | Decrease size 1 increment | Ctrl+Shift+< |
>
> At smaller sizes, the increments Word uses with the Ctrl+Shift+> and Ctrl+Shift+< shortcuts are 1 point, no different from Ctrl+] and Ctrl+[. However, at larger sizes the increments grow. So, for example, you can use Ctrl+Shift+> to jump from 36-point to 48-point in a single keystroke.

NOTE

> Word can actually format text as large as 1,638 points—nearly 2 feet high—though not all fonts can scale that large. To format text larger than 999 points, you must work in the Format, Font dialog box.

CHOOSING FONT STYLES, UNDERLINING, COLOR, AND EFFECTS

You've probably noticed that you can apply font styles from the Formatting toolbar by clicking the Bold, Italic, or Underline button, or that you can apply font styles by using the keyboard shortcuts shown earlier in Table 4.1. These and many additional options are available to you in the Font dialog box as well (refer to Figure 4.2). A quick way to display these options is to select the text you want to format, right-click it, and choose Font from the shortcut menu (make sure the Font tab is selected).

Using the Font dialog box, you can conveniently change all elements of font formatting at the same time: font, style, size, underlining, color, and effects. Choose from the corresponding Font, Font Style, and Size scroll boxes and the Effects check boxes.

NOTE

> Any changes you make in the Font dialog box are previewed in the Preview window at the bottom of the dialog box.

SELECTING FONT UNDERLINING

You can select the Underline Style of your selected text from the drop-down box. Word provides several underlining choices, including dotted, thick, dash, dot-dash, dot-dot-dash, and wave underlining. Underlining is a separate control; you can use it with any other font style or text effect.

SETTING A FONT COLOR

In the Font Color drop-down box, you can select a text color from among 40 font colors—plus Automatic, the default setting. Automatic is black, unless one of the following situations occurs:

- You have (perhaps inadvertently) changed Windows's overall text color using the Windows Control Panel.

- You are formatting text in a table, against a background shaded with a very dark color, in which case Automatic reformats the text color to white for readability.

NOTE

> Automatic text color doesn't change when you format a page background with Format, Background—because backgrounds formatted this way do not print.

Word, however, does not limit you to a basic palette of predefined colors. To choose another color, click More Colors at the bottom of the Font Color list; the Colors tabbed dialog box opens. In the Standard tab, you can pick from a wider palette of 124 colors, as well as 15 shades of gray. If that still isn't enough, you can manufacture a custom color through the Custom tab (see Figure 4.5).

Figure 4.5
Specifying a custom color using the Custom tab of the Colors dialog box.

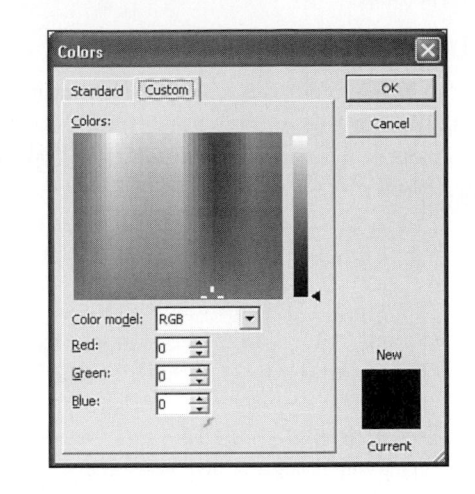

To start creating a custom color, click a color in the Colors box. The color now appears on a slider, in varying shades from very light to very dark. You can drag the slider triangle to get the shade you want. After you choose a color, through either the Standard or the Custom tab, click OK. The color now appears in your Color box and in the text you selected in your document.

→ For more information about choosing a custom color, **see** "Changing Fills and Line Colors," **p. 497**.

CAUTION

Word's text color controls might be thought of as "business color"; they are perfectly adequate for business uses (or, for that matter, most home uses) but are not really up to sophisticated design tasks.

To start with, the colors available to you depend on the colors displayed on your monitor. If you create a custom color on a system that can display 16-bit "high color" or 24-bit "true color" and then display it on a system limited to 15 or 256 colors, Word uses the nearest color available, which is probably not what you intended.

Also, be aware that Word does not offer the built-in color precision or color matching of a professional desktop publishing program such as QuarkXPress, so if you're planning to print a Word document professionally, your printed document might not maintain the precise colors you saw onscreen.

In some cases, you might be able to achieve the results you want with Microsoft Publisher 2003, which is designed to work closely with Word 2003. However, before you assume that either Word's or Publisher's color matching will achieve the results you want, consult with a representative of the printing company you plan to work with.

Similar issues apply if you are setting colors for a Web page: If precise colors are important to you, check them in various Web browsers and with various computers and monitors.

SETTING TEXT EFFECTS

Text effects provide even more ways to distinguish text, from basics like subscript and super-script (for formulas and trademarks) to far more decorative effects. You might be surprised at how many text effects Word provides:

- Strikethrough
- Superscript
- Subscript
- Hidden
- Small Caps
- All Caps

- Double Strikethrough
- Shadow
- Outline
- Emboss
- Engrave

NOTE

Additional animated text effects are available through the Text Effects tab of the Font dialog box, covered later in this chapter.

Figure 4.6 shows samples of all 10 visible effects. Not all of these effects can be applied together. Sometimes, the limitations are obvious. For example, you cannot apply strikethrough and double strikethrough to the same text. Sometimes the limitations are not so obvious. For example, you cannot apply shadow or outline to text you also intend to emboss.

Figure 4.6
Samples of Word's text effects.

~~**Strikethrough**~~	Outline
~~**Double Strikethrough**~~	Emboss
Superscript	Engrave
Subscript	SMALL CAPS
Shadow	ALL CAPS

Notice that subscript lowers text by 3 points and reduces its size at the same time; super-script raises text by 3 points and reduces its size. If you want to change the position of sub-script or superscript text, select it and use the Position controls on the Character Spacing tab of the Font dialog box.

→ For more information about character spacing, **see** "Character Spacing: Creating Typographer-Quality Documents," **p. 119**.

TIP

If you need more sophisticated text effects than those provided here, use the WordArt applet provided with Word (choose Insert, Picture, WordArt).

→ For more information about WordArt, **see** "Using WordArt," **p. 468**.

CHANGING CASE

One of the most common effects-related tasks is to change the case (capitalization) of selected text to (or from) all caps. You don't have to bother with displaying the Font dialog box to do this: Just press Ctrl+Shift+A.

Word also recognizes that there are several common ways to capitalize blocks of text you've selected. For example, you might want to format text as a sentence, in which only the first word is capitalized, or as a title, in which every word is capitalized. Or you might want to format text entirely lowercase.

You can quickly toggle selected text through five types of capitalization by pressing Shift+F3 repeatedly. Or you can choose the capitalization you want by selecting Format, Change Case, and selecting an option there.

HIDING TEXT

Hidden text is most valuable as a way to make temporary notes to yourself. (You don't have to use the Font dialog box to format text as hidden; try the Ctrl+Shift+H keyboard shortcut.) Formatting text as hidden makes it invisible by default, though you can see it by clicking the Show/Hide Paragraph Marks button. Word automatically uses hidden text to hide the contents of certain fields, notably index and table of contents entry fields.

If you print a document while hidden text is displayed, the hidden text also prints. Also, make sure that you "hide" your hidden text before you create tables of contents or indexes. Otherwise, Word might miscalculate your document's length and apply incorrect page numbers to referenced locations.

CAUTION

Because hidden text is so easy to view, don't consider it a security tool. If you really want to secure your document, use passwords, encryption, or permissions, as covered in Chapter 33, "Word Document Privacy and Security Options."

TIP

You've just carefully applied a series of formatting commands in the Font dialog box. Now you want to apply them again elsewhere, without returning to the Font dialog box and selecting everything again.

Select the new text and press either F4 or Ctrl+Y, Word's shortcuts for repeating the last editing or formatting command you've made. F4 and Ctrl+Y repeat only one command made by a toolbar button or keyboard shortcut; however, if you click either shortcut after using a dialog box, it repeats all the commands you applied through that dialog box.

CHARACTER SPACING: CREATING TYPOGRAPHER-QUALITY DOCUMENTS

Word includes character spacing controls that were once available only on typesetting systems that cost tens of thousands of dollars. You don't have to be a typographer to use them, either. Simply display the Font dialog box and click the Character Spacing tab (see Figure 4.7).

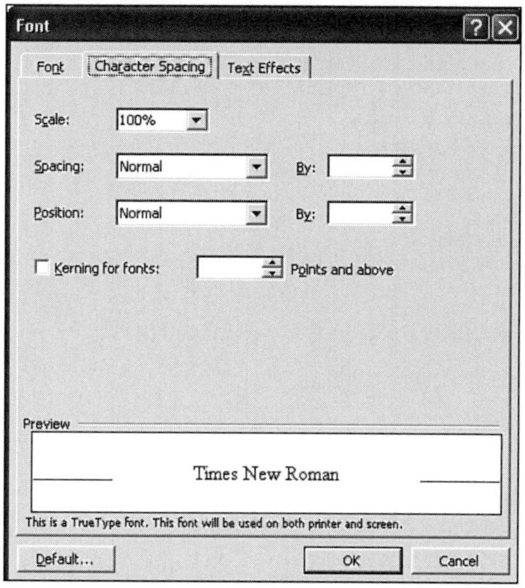

Figure 4.7
The Character Spacing tab controls spacing between characters, kerning between pairs of characters, the height and depth of characters, and their scale.

There are three reasons to use the controls on this tab:

- They can help you improve the look of your documents, typically in subtle ways. Your readers will believe that your documents look a cut above the rest—even if they don't know why.

- You can use some of these features, especially scaling, to create interesting text effects without inserting graphics into your document.

- Some character spacing features can help you control the size of your document, squeezing one or more pages out—which can save you money on production, printing, and/or mailing.

NOTE

The settings in the Character Spacing tab are primarily intended for print documents. Word does retain them when you save a file as a Web page, and they are displayed properly in Internet Explorer 4.0 and higher; but they do not display correctly in Netscape Navigator 4.0 or earlier versions of Navigator.

STRETCHING YOUR TYPE WITH WORD'S SCALING FEATURE

Scaling allows you to stretch individual characters either horizontally or vertically. Why scale text? Generally, for design reasons. For instance, you might want to create a *drop cap* that drops down more than three lines at the beginning of a newsletter article. If the character is a wide one, such as W, it's likely to stretch wider than you might want. You can narrow it by scaling. (If you scale one drop cap in a document, be sure to scale all of the other drop caps equally, to be consistent.)

You can see an example of a scaled drop cap in Figure 4.8.

Figure 4.8
Sometimes scaling a drop cap can improve its appearance and, not incidentally, make it fit better.

> W hat's the easiest way to get your product to market? Thousands of companies worldwide have discovered the advantages of working with a partner like Stuart Anderson Enterprises. |

Scaling body text slightly can also help you fit more of it on a specific page. This is an issue especially in large directories and catalogs, where narrower text translates directly into fewer pages and lower cost.

Normally, you would use a condensed font such as Arial Narrow for this purpose. However, you might not have a condensed font available that meets your needs and fits with the rest of your document's design. Scaling lets you "fake" a condensed font. The results won't thrill a professional typographer who is familiar with the subtleties of quality font design, but for day-to-day business work, scaling does the job.

Figure 4.9 shows the difference in appearance (and size) between standard Times New Roman text and text narrowed to 95% of its normal width.

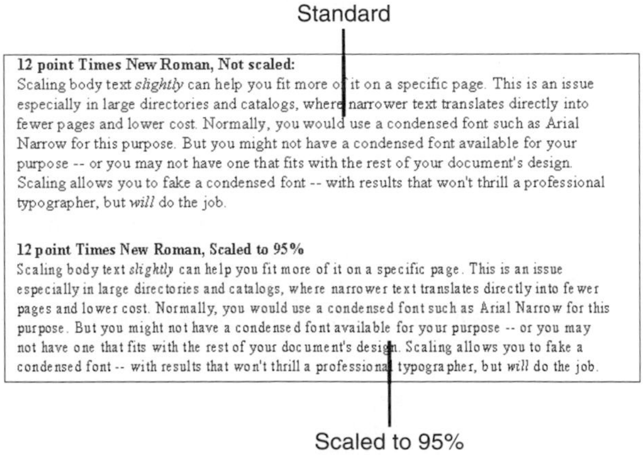

Standard

Figure 4.9
Standard Times New Roman text, compared with text narrowed to 95% of normal width.

12 point Times New Roman, Not scaled:
Scaling body text *slightly* can help you fit more of it on a specific page. This is an issue especially in large directories and catalogs, where narrower text translates directly into fewer pages and lower cost. Normally, you would use a condensed font such as Arial Narrow for this purpose. But you might not have a condensed font available for your purpose -- or you may not have one that fits with the rest of your document's design. Scaling allows you to fake a condensed font -- with results that won't thrill a professional typographer, but *will* do the job.

12 point Times New Roman, Scaled to 95%
Scaling body text *slightly* can help you fit more of it on a specific page. This is an issue especially in large directories and catalogs, where narrower text translates directly into fewer pages and lower cost. Normally, you would use a condensed font such as Arial Narrow for this purpose. But you might not have a condensed font available for your purpose -- or you may not have one that fits with the rest of your document's design. Scaling allows you to fake a condensed font -- with results that won't thrill a professional typographer, but *will* do the job.

Scaled to 95%

CAUTION

> Don't narrow body text by more than 10%. Beyond that, readability deteriorates significantly.

TIP

> Although the Scale drop-down box includes only eight choices, you can manually enter any value from 1% to 600%.

If you set scaling to one of Word's predefined settings, Word automatically shows you an immediate preview at the bottom of the Font dialog box. If you enter a custom setting, you can preview what your selected type will look like by pressing Tab to move out of the Scale drop-down box.

CONTROLLING SPACING

Spacing complements scaling. Scaling narrows or widens the characters themselves; spacing changes the space between characters. Professional designers sometimes call this *tracking*.

Word's default spacing is called Normal; you can tighten or loosen spacing as much as you want. As with scaling, use spacing judiciously. Tightening your spacing just a little can save space and might even make type read faster. That's one reason advertising copy is spaced a little tighter than normal. On the other hand, over-tightening type quickly renders it illegible.

To control spacing for selected text, select either Expanded or Condensed in the Spacing drop-down box on the Font dialog box's Character Spacing tab.

In the By scroll box, set the amount by which you want to expand or narrow your spacing. The default is 1 point, and the scroll buttons increase or reduce spacing by tenths of a point. However, you can manually enter spacing values in twentieths of a point if you want (for example, 1.05 points).

KERNING: ONE SECRET TO GREAT-LOOKING TEXT

Kerning is similar to spacing in that it adjusts the space between letters. But whereas spacing controls the space between all letters, kerning adjusts the spacing between special pairs of letters—and then only if kerning data has been included with your font by its designer. It's used most commonly with larger font sizes.

NOTE

> Depending on the quality of a font, there might be as many as 500 *kerning pairs* stored within it—pairs of letters that come with kerning instructions. This is one way expensive fonts can be superior to cheap ones.

4

You can see in Figure 4.10 why kerning matters. In the unkerned word WATCH at the top, the letters *W* and *A* are far apart; so are the letters *A* and *T*. The effect is subtly distracting; the word looks uneven, not quite natural. In the bottom example, kerning has been turned on. You can see that the *A* now slips slightly under the *W*, and the *T* is also closer to the *A*. It just looks better. You'll hardly ever see a professionally produced advertisement that hasn't been carefully kerned.

Figure 4.10
Notice the difference between the unkerned word at the top and the kerned version under it.

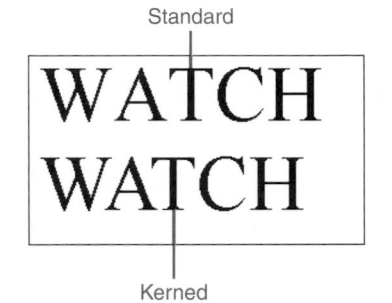

Why not turn on kerning all the time, for every font, size, and kerning pair that supports it? Technically, as long as the font supports it, you can. However, it might slow down your computer, plus kerning isn't really necessary for very small text, such as in classified advertisements. Here's how to decide when and whether to kern:

- First, test your computer. If you don't notice a speed difference with kerning turned on, make it part of your default settings for all text that is 7 points or higher. You'll learn how to change your font formatting defaults later in this chapter.

- For day-to-day newsletters, it's usually sufficient to turn on kerning for all headlines but skip the body text. You might set kerning to begin at 12- or 14-point text.

- For more sophisticated publications, or for high-end customer proposals, kern body text as well. Set kerning to start as low as 7-point text. Especially consider kerning if you are printing on a relatively high-resolution printer, such as a 600 dpi (dots per inch) laser printer.

- If kerning does slow down your computer, consider doing all your editing with kerning turned off, and then select the entire document and apply kerning to it before you take care of final "design tweaks," such as fixing line and page breaks. If you want, you can record a macro to select and kern your entire document.

To turn on kerning for selected text, place a check in the <u>K</u>erning for Fonts check box on the Character Spacing tab. Word sets kerning to 12 P<u>o</u>ints and Above. If you want, enter a new font size in the P<u>o</u>ints and Above scroll box.

TIP

> Some desktop publishing programs, such as QuarkXPress, not only enable you to auto-matically kern all text larger than a specific size, but also allow you to manually adjust the kerning of individual pairs of letters. Often, you can manually improve the look of your headlines by kerning them beyond the settings that come with your font, especially when you are using large type—48-point or higher.
>
> You can do manual kerning with Word, even though there's no formal setting for it. If you want to tighten or loosen the spacing between two letters, select the first letter and apply a small amount of Condensed or Expanded Spacing to it. Word can control spacing down to 1/20 of a point, which should be as precise as you'll ever need to get.

CONTROLLING POSITION

The Character Spacing tab has one more feature: Position. Look at a line of text and visualize an imaginary line where the text is "sitting." That's called the *baseline*. The Position setting determines how far above or below the baseline text should appear.

Most users will rarely need to use Position. For instance, it's usually easier to create superscript or subscript characters using Word's keyboard shortcuts, Ctrl++ (plus sign) for superscript, and Ctrl+= (equal sign) for subscript. These keyboard shortcuts also shrink the characters in the way true subscript and superscripts should appear. However, some users find that these keyboard shortcuts shrink the size of text too much or too little, or they want more control over exactly how far from the baseline their subscripted or superscripted text moves. Position offers this control.

To set the position for selected text, choose Raised or Lowered in the Position drop-down box. Word sets the change in position to 3 points. You can scroll to increase or decrease the baseline shift, or type in a position in 1/2-point increments (for example, 2.5 points).

ANIMATING YOUR TEXT

Now, after studying the subtleties of kerning and baseline shifts, it's time to shift to one of the most garish features ever to be found in Word: text animation.

You can apply one of six simple animations to any block of text, calling attention to it when it is viewed onscreen in Word or in Internet Explorer 3.0 or higher. Netscape Navigator or other Web browsers do not recognize text animations. They are also not recognized by Word 95, Word 6, or other older versions of Word—and, of course, they don't print. Table 4.2 describes each of these animations.

TABLE 4.2   DESCRIPTIONS OF WORD'S ANIMATED TEXT OPTIONS

Animation	What It Does
Blinking Background	Blinks reverse text on and off
Las Vegas Lights	Borders text with rapidly changing colored shapes

continues

4

TABLE 4.2	CONTINUED
Animation	**What It Does**
Marching Black Ants	Borders text with black dotted lines that constantly move to the right
Marching Red Ants	Borders text with red dotted lines that constantly move to the right
Shimmer	Repeatedly blurs and unblurs text
Sparkle Text	Superimposes moving colored sparkles on text

You might use text animation when you are sharing a document file (or displaying it on a corporate intranet running Internet Explorer) and you want to be especially sure that your reader looks at a specific block of text. To animate text, select it, press Ctrl+D, choose the Text Effects tab, and choose an animation from the Animations scroll box. (The Preview box shows what it will look like.)

TIP

> Learn from the experience of Web designers who alienated many of their visitors through heavy use of blinking text—use text animations sparingly. If you must use text animation at all, stick with the animations that are least intrusive, such as Marching Black Ants. Apply them only to small blocks of text—possibly even single characters, such as Wingding symbols.

SETTING DEFAULT FONT FORMATS

By default, Word formats your text as 12-point Times New Roman. If you find yourself changing this setting in every new document, you can save yourself some time and effort by changing Word's default settings. Follow these steps:

1. Select some text that's formatted as you want your default text to look.

2. Right-click on the text you've selected and choose Font from the shortcut menu (or press Ctrl+D).

3. Check all the settings and change any that you want to change. For example, do you want to turn on automatic kerning?

4. Click the Default button and then choose Yes to confirm the change.

The new default font formatting will apply to your current document in the future, and to every document you create with the same template you're currently using.

→ To learn more about the relationship between styles and templates, **see** "Understanding the Relationship Between Styles and Templates," **p. 366**.

WORKING WITH PARAGRAPH FORMATTING

So far, you've worked with only font formatting—formatting that affects individual characters. Next, you'll learn about formatting that Word can apply to paragraphs. In Word, paragraph formatting includes the following:

- Paragraph alignment
- Outline levels
- Indentation
- Spacing between lines
- Spacing before and after paragraphs
- Line and page breaks
- Tabs

The following sections review all these aspects of formatting, except for outline levels.

→ To learn more about working with outline levels, **see** "Applying Outline Levels to Specific Text," **p. 635**.

First, however, it's important to understand what Word interprets as a paragraph, and where Word stores the information it uses to format paragraphs.

How Word Stores Paragraph Formatting

Word considers a paragraph to be any block of text that ends with a paragraph mark (±). In fact, Word actually stores the paragraph formatting with the paragraph mark. If you understand this, you can avoid many problems that arise in paragraph formatting. The fact that Word stores paragraph formatting with the paragraph mark has several implications:

- You can copy paragraph formatting to a new location by copying the paragraph mark (or any part of the paragraph that includes the mark).
- You might inadvertently copy paragraph formatting that you don't want if you copy the paragraph mark by mistake. If you want to copy a paragraph to a new location but keep the existing formatting of the surrounding text, don't copy the paragraph mark.
- If you finish a paragraph and start a new paragraph by pressing Enter, your new paragraph shares the same paragraph formatting (and styles) as the previous one. This is because pressing Enter creates a paragraph mark that stores the same formatting as the previous paragraph.
- If you delete text that includes a paragraph mark, any remaining text from that paragraph is reformatted to match the formatting and styles in the following paragraph.

Of course, to work with paragraph marks, it helps to see them. Click the Show/Hide Paragraph Marks button on the Standard toolbar, and they all appear.

TIP

> Or, with the Reveal Formatting task pane open, display paragraph marks by checking the Show All Formatting Marks check box.

Some other things appear, too: tab markers and dots that correspond to spaces between the words in your document. Seeing all this can be helpful, but many people find it distracting.

4

If all you want to see is paragraph marks, adjust the following settings in Tools, Options, View:

- Clear the All check box.
- Check the Paragraph Marks check box.
- Clear any other check boxes in the Formatting Marks area.

TIP

Because paragraph marks are so fraught with meaning, you might occasionally want to jump text to the next line without entering the mark. You can use Shift+Enter for this purpose; Word adds a line break but not a paragraph mark. (Line breaks are sometimes called soft returns.)

Line breaks have many uses. For example, if you have an automatically numbered list, you might want to enter more text under a numbered item without having Word automatically enter the next number. If you use a line break rather than a paragraph mark, you can. Then, when you're ready to move on to the next item in your numbered sequence, press Enter to generate a paragraph mark, and Word continues automatic numbering as if nothing unusual had happened.

→ To learn more about automatic numbering, **see** "Using Bullets and Numbered Lists," later in this chapter.

PARAGRAPH ALIGNMENT

The first aspect of paragraph formatting to understand is paragraph alignment. Word offers four types of paragraph alignment: Align Left, Center, Align Right, and Justify.

Align Left, Word's default setting, starts every line at the left margin but doesn't reach all the way to the right margin (except on rare occasions when the word fits precisely without tweaking). When a word comes along that is too long to be squeezed onto the first line, Word jumps it onto the next line, leaving the previous line unfinished. Align Left is sometimes called *flush left* or *ragged right*.

Align Right, of course, works the opposite way: It squeezes all text toward the right margin. Center keeps text anchored in the middle of the page, so it usually leaves room at both margins when it jumps to the next line. Justify stretches text from the left to right margin edges.

TIP

Word justifies text by inserting extra space between words. If you choose to justify text, consider using Word's hyphenation controls (choose Tools, Language, Hyphenation) to make sure that no text is stretched too much to be read easily. One way to do so is to manually hyphenate long words that appear immediately following lines that are too spread out:

1. Select a word to manually hyphenate.
2. Choose Tools, Language, Hyphenation.

3. Click Manual.

4. Click the insertion point at the location where you want the word hyphenated. (Word may suggest natural locations at syllable breaks.)

5. Click Yes.

Table 4.3 lists the toolbar buttons and keyboard shortcuts for each alignment option and explains when each option is most widely used.

TABLE 4.3   PARAGRAPH ALIGNMENT CHOICES: HOW AND WHEN

Task	Keyboard Shortcut	Toolbar Button	Uses
Align Left	Ctrl+L		Most informal documents
Center	Ctrl+E		Some headings and short copy blocks
Align Right	Ctrl+R		Occasional artistic/design uses
Justify	Ctrl+J		Some traditional books, magazines, reports, and formal business documents

INDENTING TEXT

Word also provides total control over the way you indent your paragraphs. You can create the following four kinds of indents:

- **Left indents.** Adjust the left edge of every line in a paragraph.
- **Right indents.** Adjust the right edge of every line in a paragraph.
- **Hanging indents.** Leave the first line alone but move every line under it.
- **First line indents.** Move only the first line in a paragraph.

You can see examples of all four kinds of indents (left, right, hanging, and first line) in Figure 4.11.

Left and right indents are often used together to indent blocks of text such as quotations. Hanging indents are often used in numbered and bulleted lists; in fact, Word automatically adds them when you create lists using the Numbering or Bullets buttons on the Standard toolbar.

Word also provides four ways to create indents: via the Formatting toolbar, keyboard shortcuts, the ruler, and the Formatting toolbar. Each approach has advantages, depending on your work style and what you're trying to accomplish.

4

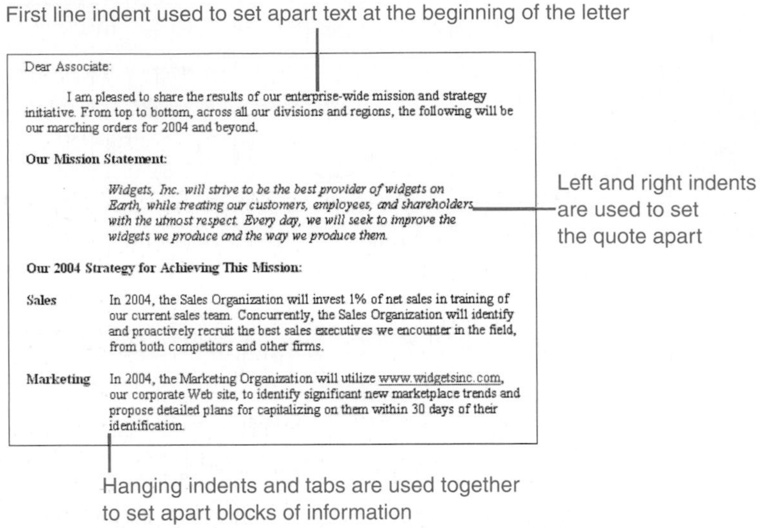

First line indent used to set apart text at the beginning of the letter

Figure 4.11
Left, right, hanging, and first line indents.

Left and right indents are used to set the quote apart

Hanging indents and tabs are used together to set apart blocks of information

INDENTING WITH KEYBOARD SHORTCUTS

Word provides quick and easy keyboard shortcuts for working with indents. These keyboard shortcuts are listed in Table 4.4.

TABLE 4.4 KEYBOARD SHORTCUTS FOR WORKING WITH INDENTS

Task	Keyboard Shortcut
Indent	Ctrl+M
Decrease Indent	Ctrl+Shift+M
Hanging Indent	Ctrl+T
Decrease Hanging Indent	Ctrl+Shift+T

NOTE

To create a traditional paragraph indent of 0.5" in which the first line is indented and the others are not indented, select one or more paragraphs and press Ctrl+M; then press Ctrl+Shift+T.

The size of the indent created by toolbar buttons or keyboard shortcuts is based on Word's default tab settings, which are 0.5" unless you change them. If you change the defaults, you also change any new indents you create afterward using the toolbar or keyboard shortcuts.

NOTE

You can change the default tab settings through the Format, Tabs dialog box. To learn more about using this dialog box, see "Setting Tabs," later in this chapter.

INDENTING WITH THE RULER

If you're visually oriented, you may want to use Word's ruler to control indents—much as you might have controlled tabs on a typewriter many years ago.

Word displays the horizontal ruler by default. If you don't see it, choose View, Ruler. In Figure 4.12, you can take a closer look at the ruler and its indent settings.

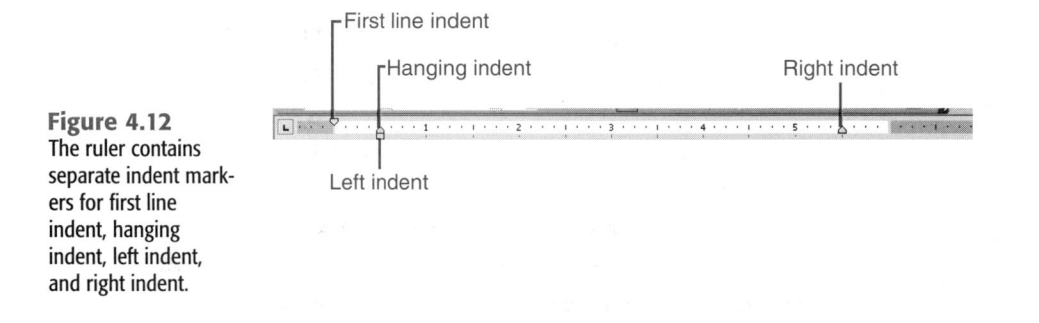

Figure 4.12
The ruler contains separate indent markers for first line indent, hanging indent, left indent, and right indent.

4

Notice that 0" on Word's horizontal ruler corresponds to wherever you have the left margin set. (By default, this means it is 1.25" from the left edge of an 8.5" sheet of paper. The right margin is 1.25" from the right edge. Accordingly, a default document has 6 inches between margins.) Indents you create with the ruler start at the margin and work inward or outward from there.

To create a new indent using the ruler, first click in the paragraph you want to change, or select multiple paragraphs. Then drag the upper indent marker to where you want it and release the mouse button.

TIP

If you want all the paragraphs in your document to start with a 0.5" indent automatically, change your Normal style to include a 0.5" first line indent.

→ For more information on creating styles, **see** "Creating and Changing Styles," **p. 339**.

CREATING PRECISE INDENTS IN THE PARAGRAPH DIALOG BOX

You can also create paragraph indents in the Paragraph dialog box. Given that there are so many other easy ways to create indents, when would you bother? You would want to use the dialog box in these instances:

■ You need a precise indent that you can't reliably set from the ruler. In the Paragraph dialog box, you can set indents to a precision of 1/100 of an inch. The ruler only works to 1/16 of an inch—and then only if your eyes are very good!

■ You want to set other paragraph formats, such as line spacing, at the same time.

To set an indent from the Paragraph dialog box, follow these steps:

1. Right-click on the paragraph you've selected and choose <u>P</u>aragraph from the shortcut menu.

2. Click the <u>I</u>ndents and Spacing tab (see Figure 4.13).

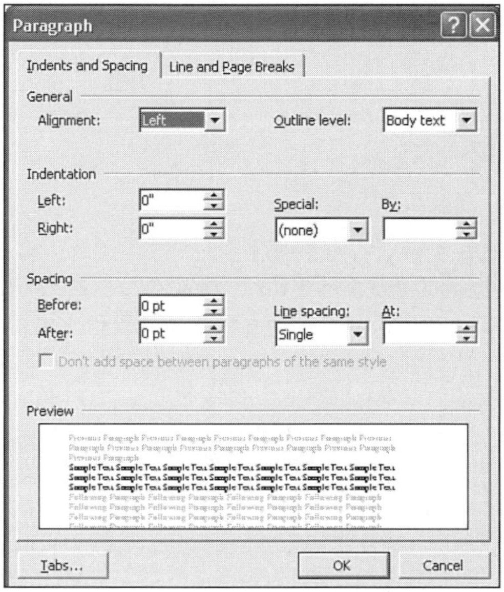

Figure 4.13
The <u>I</u>ndents and Spacing tab controls paragraph alignment, indentation, and spacing, including line spacing.

3. Set any left or right indent from the <u>L</u>eft or <u>R</u>ight scroll box.

4. If you want to set either a paragraph or a hanging indent, choose the indent you want from the <u>S</u>pecial drop-down box. Word displays the default indent, 0.5"; if you want to change the setting, enter the new one in the B<u>y</u> scroll box.

5. When you're finished, click OK.

TIP

> Indents normally extend from the margin toward the center of your page. However, you can also set indents that extend toward the edge of the page. These are called *outdents*, and they can be quite useful. For example, you can use outdents to place headings or icons in the margins of your documents.
>
> To set an outdent, enter a negative value (such as –0.5") in the <u>L</u>eft or <u>R</u>ight scroll box of the <u>I</u>ndents and Spacing tab. Or drag one of the ruler's indent markers into the dark gray area outside your current margin.

SETTING PARAGRAPH SPACING

As with indents, Word gives you extensive control over paragraph spacing. Using keyboard shortcuts, you can instantly set single-spaced (Ctrl+1), double-spaced (Ctrl+2), and 1.5-line-spaced (Ctrl+5) paragraphs.

Word also provides control over paragraph spacing through the Line Spacing button on the Formatting toolbar. To change the spacing of text, first select the paragraphs you want to adjust. Next, click the down arrow next to the Line Spacing button (see Figure 4.14) and choose the spacing you want.

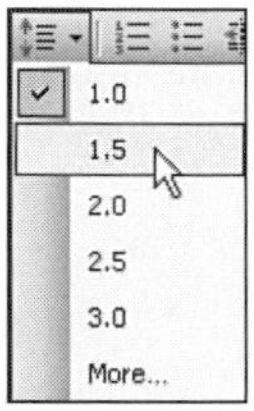

Figure 4.14
Setting paragraph spacing using the Line Spacing button on the Formatting toolbar.

If you want finer control than you can get from this list, choose More to open the Indents and Spacing tab of the Paragraph dialog box. From here you can specify line spacing to a precision of 1/10 of a point. You can even set exact spacing that Word applies before or after each paragraph.

Word line spacing can be controlled from the Line Spacing scroll box. By default, Word uses single line spacing. This means Word keeps track of the font size you're using and adjusts line spacing so that there's just enough room between lines for comfortable reading. In body text, 1/72 inch is added between the characters that reach down farthest from one line (descenders such as p and q) and those that reach up farthest from the next (ascenders such as b and k). Of course, the larger the text, the more space Word adds to keep single-spaced lines readable.

In addition to single spacing, 1.5 line spacing, and double spacing, Word provides several other line spacing options:

- **At Least.** This spacing sets a minimum space from one line to the next, but it enables Word to increase spacing if it encounters larger font sizes or graphics that wouldn't fit in the minimum space.

- **Exactly.** This spacing tells Word exactly what spacing to use no matter what text or graphics it encounters. If text or a graphic is too large, portions of it may be cut off. You might use Exactly if you're creating a form or another document that must fit on a single page no matter what.

- **Multiple.** This spacing enables you to specify any multiple of Word's single spacing (which, as mentioned previously, can vary depending on the font size you are using). For example, to triple–space, you set the multiple to 3. You can choose any multiple spacing increment from 0 to 132 lines, in increments of 1/100 of a line. You're unlikely to use settings quite this fine, but Multiple does provide welcome control over document size and appearance.

TIP

> If you need to shrink your document by just one page, try Word's Shrink to Fit feature. Click the Print Preview toolbar button; then click the Shrink to Fit toolbar button on the Print Preview toolbar.

→ To learn more about reducing document size using the Shrink to Fit button, **see** "Shrinking Your Document Automatically," **p. 220**.

If you include a large text character in a single-, double-, or multiple-spaced line of text, Word accommodates it by increasing line spacing for that line only. If you would prefer that Word cut off the top of the character (or nearly cut off) rather than using uneven line spacing, select the paragraph and use the Exactly setting.

ADDING EXTRA SPACE BEFORE AND AFTER PARAGRAPHS

You've just learned how to set spacing between lines in your document (or within selected paragraphs). You can also add extra space between paragraphs, as shown here:

1. Right-click inside the first paragraph and choose <u>P</u>aragraph from the shortcut menu.
2. Choose the <u>I</u>ndents and Spacing tab.
3. Enter a new value in the <u>B</u>efore or Aft<u>e</u>r scroll box. (You'll generally use one or the other, not both.)
4. Click OK.

This is far superior to using the old-fashioned technique of pressing Enter twice at the end of each paragraph. First, you have more precise control. If you only want to add a half-line of space between each paragraph, it's easy to do so. Second, it's easier to change the spacing between paragraphs. If your document is running slightly long, and you decide you want to cut the space after paragraphs from 8 points to 6, select the entire document, display the <u>I</u>ndents and Spacing tab, enter the new setting, and click OK—that's all there is to it.

TIP

> It's best to include the setting for spacing after paragraph in a style so that you can easily change it and include it automatically in new paragraphs you create.

→ To learn how to change paragraph formats in a style, **see** "Creating Paragraph Styles Easily with Style by Example," **p. 339**.

TIP

> To add a full line of space before one or more selected paragraphs, use the keyboard shortcut Ctrl+0 (zero).

SETTING TABS

If you ever learned how to use a typewriter, you know what tabs are—stopping points along a horizontal line of text that you can use to align text or numbers.

In the early days of word processing, tabs were the state-of-the-art way to create row-and-column tables of information. Now, in Word, tables offer a much easier, more powerful way to create these row-and-column matrices.

→ To learn more about working with tables, **see** Chapter 12, "Structuring and Organizing Information with Tables," **p. 387**.

But even now, for some tasks, nothing beats tabs. In particular, tabs are the best way to

- Add a dot leader that connects text at the left margin with text at the right margin, as you might use in a table of contents
- Align a row of numbers that contain varying decimal places
- Center text over a precise horizontal location on your page

Word provides five kinds of tabs, as described in the following list and shown in Figure 4.15. (The icons shown next to each paragraph are the ones Word inserts in your ruler to reflect each kind of tab.)

Click this marker to choose which type of tab you want to set (example shows Left tab)

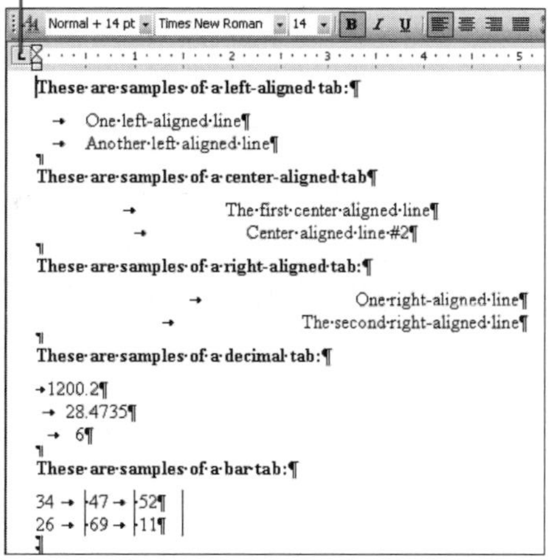

Figure 4.15
Samples of left, center, right, decimal, and bar tabs.

These are the various types of Word tabs:

- **Left tabs.** After you enter a left tab, additional text begins at the tab stop and continues to its right.
- **Center tabs.** After you enter a center tab, additional text moves to the left and right, remaining centered on the location where the tab stop appears.

- **Right tabs.** After you enter a right tab, additional text begins at the tab stop and continues to its left. The more text you enter, the closer to the left margin the text moves.

- **Decimal tabs.** After you enter a decimal tab, rows of numbers that you enter all align on the decimal point, regardless of how many integer and decimal places they contain.

- **Bar tabs.** With these auspiciously named tabs, you have a quick and easy way to draw a vertical line extending through as many horizontal lines of text as you want.

Word automatically places a default left-aligned tab stop at every 0.5", without displaying these tabs in the ruler. (You'll notice this if you keep pressing the Tab key in a blank document: Word moves the insertion point 0.5" to the right each time you do so.)

However, you may need tabs in different locations than these. If so, you can create tabs in two ways:

- Using the ruler, which is typically the quickest way to get the job done

- Using the Tabs dialog box, which offers more precision and gives you access to advanced features such as tab leaders and bar tabs

Many Word users don't realize that tab settings may vary between paragraphs.

Whether you use the ruler or the Tabs dialog box, the tab stops you create apply to only the paragraphs you have selected. If you don't select a paragraph, they apply to the current paragraph and any paragraphs you add immediately following it by pressing Enter and continuing to type.

To add a tab setting that applies to the entire document, press Ctrl+A to select the entire document, and then add the tab(s) using either the ruler or the Tabs dialog box. Other tab stops you created are still present. However, it's possible that some text affected by tabs you've placed in the document will move to reflect the new tab stops you've added.

For instance, imagine that you have a paragraph of text that contains two tabs, set at 1.25" and 4.25". You now add a new document-wide tab stop at 3.75". That 3.75" tab stop is now the second tab stop Word finds in the paragraph we're discussing—so the second tab's location in that paragraph moves from 4.25" to 3.75".

CREATING TABS WITH THE RULER

To set a tab with the ruler, click inside the ruler—either in the middle of the ruler where the numbers appear or anywhere along the gray line at the bottom of the ruler. Word inserts a left-aligned tab marker.

If you want to create a different type of tab, follow these steps:

1. Click the tab marker to the left of the ruler (refer to Figure 4.15). By default, the tab marker is set to create a left tab. If you do not want a left tab, keep clicking to display the tab you want. The icons change in the following order: first center tab, then right tab, then decimal tab, and then bar tab.

TIP

> If you keep clicking, the tab marker offers two indent options, first line indent and hanging indent, before cycling back to left tab.

2. After you choose the right kind of tab, click the ruler where you want the tab to be set.

TIP

> To see tabs in your document, click Show/Hide Paragraph Marks. The tabs appear as right arrow marks.

After you place a tab on the ruler, you can move it by dragging it to the left or right. In the paragraphs you've selected, any text affected by the tab moves to the left or right as well.

CREATING TABS AND LEADERS USING THE TABS DIALOG BOX

You can tabs from the Tabs dialog box (see Figure 4.16). To view this dialog box, choose Format, Tabs. Or, if you're already working with paragraph formatting, you can click the Tabs button at the lower left of the Paragraph dialog box. Or double-click any tab you've already set on the ruler.

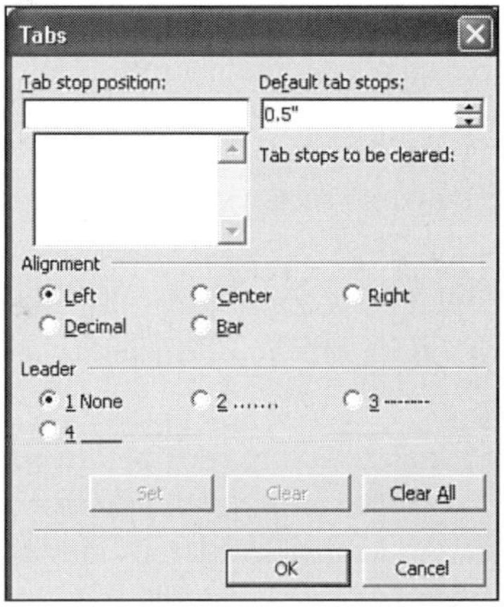

Figure 4.16
The Tabs dialog box controls tab stops, tab alignment, and leaders.

4

If you have manually set any tabs that apply to the currently selected paragraph(s), they appear in the Tab Stop Position text box. To set a new tab, follow these steps:

1. Enter the location where you want the tab to appear in the Tab Stop Position text box.

2. In the Alignment area, choose the type of tab you want: Left, Center, Right, Decimal, or Bar.

3. If you want to use a tab leader, select it from the Leader area. You can choose a dot leader, dash leader, or solid line leader.

4. Click <u>S</u>et.

5. Repeat steps 1–4 for any additional tabs you want to set.

6. Click OK.

CHANGING DEFAULT TAB STOPS

As you may recall, Word provides default tab stops every 0.5" and uses these tab stops to determine how far to indent text when you click the Increase Indent/Decrease Indent buttons on the Formatting toolbar (or use the equivalent keyboard shortcuts).

You might want to change the default tab stop locations. For example, your document's design might call for indents and tabs at 0.75" increments. To change the default tab stops, choose F<u>o</u>rmat, <u>T</u>abs; enter a new value in the De<u>f</u>ault Tab Stops scroll box; and click OK.

REMOVING TABS

You may at some point want to remove a tab you have created manually. To clear all the tab settings in a specific part of your document (or in the entire document), select the text or the entire document; choose F<u>o</u>rmat, <u>T</u>abs; choose Clear A<u>l</u>l; and click OK.

To clear a specific tab setting, select all the paragraphs that contain the tab setting you want to clear and drag the tab setting off the bottom of the ruler so that it disappears.

Unfortunately, Word doesn't provide an easy way to know where a tab setting begins and ends in your document. As a result, you may find eliminating tab settings to be a trial-and-error process. Here are some tips that help a little:

- If all the text you've selected contains the tab setting, the tab setting appears in solid black on your ruler.

- If some of the text you've selected contains the tab setting, the tab setting appears in gray on your ruler. Dragging the tab setting off the ruler deletes it for those paragraphs you've selected.

- If you've selected a large number of paragraphs that start before you applied the tab setting and end after the tab setting is no longer present, you don't see the tab setting on your ruler—even though it is still present in some of the paragraphs you've selected.

> **NOTE**
>
> If you remove a tab setting that text in your document depends on, the tabs in your text revert to Word's default tab settings. If this changes your document in ways you don't like, click Undo to restore the tab setting you had before.

 If Word's tabs start acting strangely, see "What to Do If Your Tabs Don't Work as You Expect," in "Troubleshooting" at the end of this chapter.

CONTROLLING HOW PARAGRAPHS BREAK BETWEEN PAGES

In documents, a *widow* is the last line of a paragraph that appears by itself at the top of a page. An *orphan* is the first line of a paragraph left to fend for itself at the bottom of a page. To readers, a widow or an orphan can easily be confused with a subhead. For years, typographers and graphic designers have done everything possible to eliminate widows and orphans.

You rarely see a widow or an orphan in a Word document, because Word includes a feature called Widow/Orphan control. If Word encounters a paragraph that will be split at the bottom of the page, separating one line from all the rest, Word automatically makes sure that the entire paragraph prints together. For example, it moves the potentially orphaned line to the top of the next page with the rest of its "family."

Widow/Orphan Control is one of four Pagination settings Word provides in the Line and Page Breaks tab of the Paragraph dialog box (see Figure 4.17). You can use these settings to make sure that your page breaks don't unnecessarily interrupt or inconvenience your readers.

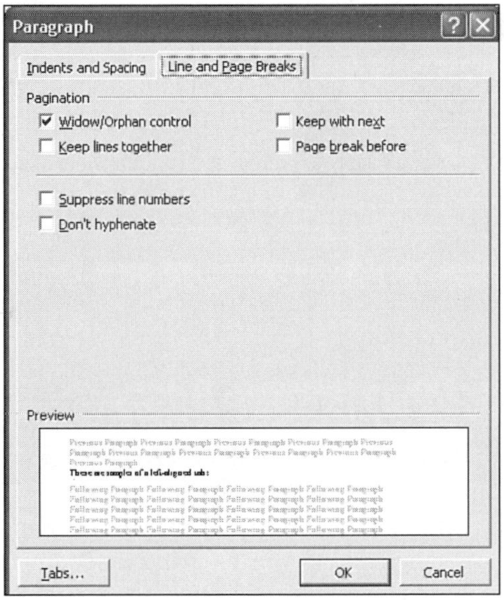

Figure 4.17
The Line and Page Breaks tab controls pagination and whether line numbers or hyphenation will be applied to selected text.

Although Widow/Orphan Control is turned on by default, the other three settings are turned off unless you check them.

As with the other paragraph formatting elements you've seen, you can apply Pagination controls to a specific paragraph or paragraphs you select, or you can select the entire document and apply them universally. You can also include Pagination controls in styles so that they can be used automatically throughout your document.

The various settings available are as listed here:

- **Keep Lines Together.** Whereas <u>W</u>idow/Orphan Control prevents page breaks that leave single lines by themselves, <u>K</u>eep Lines Together prevents all page breaks that interrupt paragraphs. When a page break is needed, Word simply jumps the entire paragraph to the next page. <u>K</u>eep Lines Together can be especially handy in tables, where it prevents a few lines of a table (or, worse, parts of a single table row) from jumping onto the next page by themselves.

- **Keep with Ne<u>x</u>t.** Sometimes you have two paragraphs that must stay together. For example, you might have a figure caption that needs to stay with an accompanying table. Or you might have space on a contract for signatures that need to be on the same page as other contract clauses.

- **Page <u>B</u>reak Before.** This option forces a manual page break before a paragraph. You might use this feature if you expect a paragraph to create pagination problems and you're not sure that Word will handle them properly.

TIP

If you have a document that must have one paragraph on each page, use Page <u>B</u>reak Before rather than manual page breaks. It's quicker, easier to keep consistent, and easier to change if necessary.

NOTE

Pagination controls don't apply to Web pages, which by definition consist of only one page apiece.

→ To learn more about line numbering, **see** "Using Line Numbering," **p. 172**.

USING BULLETS AND NUMBERED LISTS

Bullets and numbered lists provide an excellent way to segregate, list, and organize information for a reader. You can control the appearance, or *format*, of a bulleted or numbered list. The bullet or numbering format you use last becomes the default format; that is, the next time you create a bulleted or numbered list, Word uses the same format you used the last time you created a bulleted or numbered list. As you'll learn in this section, you can easily change the default bullet or numbering format by choosing one of seven default bullet formats or one of seven default numbering formats. You can modify any of these to create your own formats.

→ The bullet and numbering features covered here are designed for simple lists. If you need to build complex automated multilevel numbering schemes based on your outline headings, **see** "Using Word's Automatic Outline Numbering," **p. 636**.

NOTE

Here's a quick refresher on when to use bulleted lists and when to use numbered lists:

- Use a bulleted list when you have several related items, but the order in which the reader sees them doesn't matter much.
- Use a numbered list when you have several related items, but the order does matter—for instance, in describing a procedure containing steps that must be followed consecutively.

STARTING AND STOPPING A BULLETED LIST

Using the Formatting toolbar, you can quickly create a bulleted list. Place the insertion point in the paragraph where you want to add bullets, and click the Bullets button on the Formatting toolbar. Word inserts a bullet and automatically indents text so that, as word wrap takes over, your text aligns itself correctly.

NOTE

If you've already typed in your list without bullets, you can easily add them by highlighting the text and clicking the Bullets button. Word adds bullets to each individual paragraph.

Press Enter to start a new paragraph preceded by a bullet. By default, Word continues to add bullets after every paragraph mark you add.

To end a list—stopping Word from adding bullets (or numbering) after paragraph marks that follow—take one of these actions:

- When the insertion point appears in the first paragraph you don't want preceded by a bullet, click the Bullets button to toggle it off.
- Press Enter twice at the end of the last paragraph you want to contain a bullet.
- Press Backspace when the insertion point appears at the beginning of an empty bulleted paragraph.

TIP

By default, Word's AutoFormat feature creates Automatic Bulleted Lists. (This setting is controlled in the AutoFormat As You Type tab of the Tools, AutoCorrect Options dialog box.) With this feature turned on, you can type an asterisk at the beginning of the paragraph to which you want to add a bullet. Follow the asterisk with a space and type. When you press Enter, Word converts the asterisk to a bullet character and adds a bullet character to the next paragraph.

CAUTION

In some cases, you won't want Word to automatically create bulleted or numbered lists—you'll need to retain control over your numbering. For these situations, choose Tools, AutoCorrect Options, AutoFormat As You Type, and clear the Automatic Bulleted Lists and Automatic Numbered Lists check boxes.

4

CHANGING THE APPEARANCE OF WORD'S BULLETS

If you don't like the bullet you get when using the Formatting toolbar, you can open the Bullets and Numbering dialog box and select a different one.

With the insertion point in the paragraph you want to change, choose Format, Bullets and Numbering, or right-click and choose Bullets and Numbering from the shortcut menu. The Bullets and Numbering dialog box appears (see Figure 4.18).

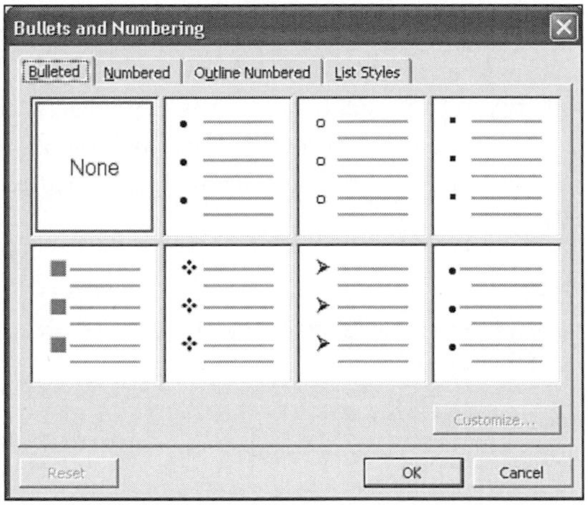

Figure 4.18
Select one of these standard bullet characters or choose your own.

With the Bulleted tab displayed, you can choose one of seven standard bullets by clicking on the one you want and clicking OK.

As you'll see, you can also customize your bullet with another character or use a picture in place of a bullet—as is commonly done on Web pages. Whatever bullet character or picture you choose becomes the default and appears if you add bullets to a paragraph using the Bullets button on the Formatting toolbar.

NOTE

> You can't actually select a bullet or number in an automatic bulleted or numbered list. To change the format of a bullet or number, you must work through the Bullets and Numbering dialog box. To delete the character, place the insertion point in the paragraph and click the appropriate Standard toolbar button: Bullets or Numbering.
>
> If you create a custom bullet and later decide you want a different one, choose Format, Bullets and Numbering again. In the Bulleted tab, click the thumbnail sketch corresponding to the Custom bullet you created. Then click Customize and make the changes you want, using the Customize Bulleted List dialog box. (As you work in that dialog box, you may have to click Font to choose new font formatting, or click Bullet to choose a new symbol.)

CUSTOMIZING YOUR BULLET'S APPEARANCE

If none of Word's seven standard bullet characters is what you want, choose one of them and click Customize. The Customize Bulleted List dialog box opens (see Figure 4.19). Here, you can control virtually every aspect of a bullet's appearance, including its font formatting, the character you use, and the bullet's indentation.

Figure 4.19
You can control any aspect of a bullet character's appearance in the Customize Bulleted List dialog box.

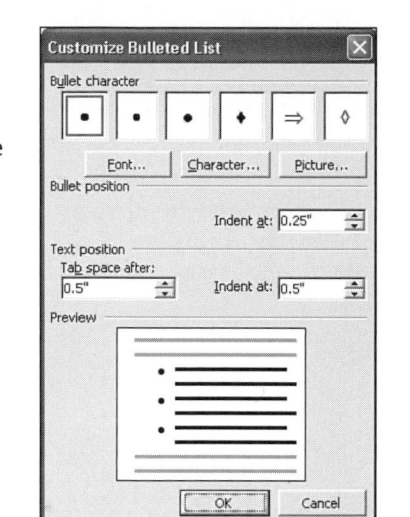

TIP

If you hit on a bullet format that you particularly like, you may want to make it available all the time. Open the template you use most often and modify the List Bullet style, using your favorite bullet format. All new documents you create based on this template will contain the updated List Bullet style, which you can apply to paragraphs you want preceded by bullets.

When you're finished customizing your bullet, click OK, and the new custom bullet appears as an option in the Bulleted tab from now on.

→ To reset your custom bullets to the ones that came with Word, **see** "Resetting Numbering or Bullet Formats to Word's 'Factory Defaults,'" **p. 148**.

CHANGING A BULLET'S FONT FORMATTING

To change the font formatting used to produce a bullet, do the following:

1. Choose Format, Bullets and Numbering.
2. From the Bulleted tab, choose one of Word's seven standard bullets. Use a standard bullet you don't expect to need in your current document because the custom bullet you're creating will replace it.

4

3. Click Customize to display the Customize Bulleted List dialog box (refer to Figure 4.19). The bullet character you selected in the Bullets and Numbering dialog box appears selected in the Bullet Character box.

4. To control the bullet's font formatting, click the Font button. Word's standard Font dialog box appears. Here, you can choose a different font, font size, character spacing, or text effect.

5. When you're satisfied, click OK.

As you select fonts (or make any other change), the Preview box shows you how the change will affect the appearance of your bullet.

CAUTION

> If you change fonts, check the Preview box to make sure that you haven't changed the character Word is using. For example, a bullet character in the Symbol font corresponds to an icon in the Wingdings font.

CHANGING A BULLET CHARACTER

To change the character used for a bullet, follow these steps:

1. Choose Format, Bullets and Numbering.

2. From the Bulleted tab, choose one of Word's seven standard bullets (or one of your custom bullets, if you've already created one).

3. Click Customize to display the Customize Bulleted List dialog box (refer to Figure 4.19).

4. Click Font and choose the font formatting you want your bullets to follow; click OK when you're finished doing so.

5. If you prefer one of the other five bullets displayed in the Bullet Character area, click on it. Otherwise, click Character to display Word's Symbol dialog box (see Figure 4.20).

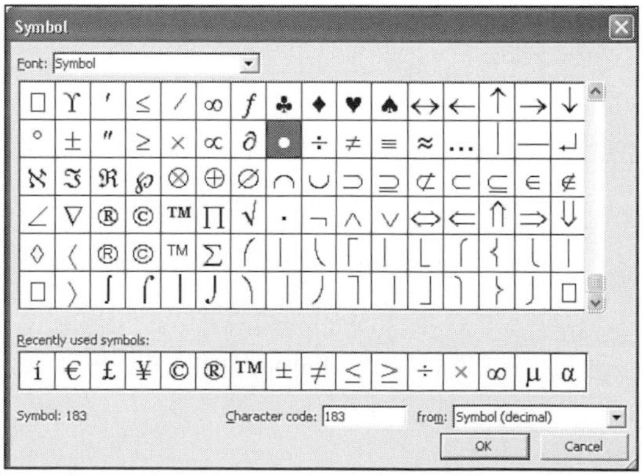

Figure 4.20
Select a character for the bullet from the Symbol dialog box.

6. Choose the bullet you want and click OK to close the Symbol dialog box.

7. Click OK again.

TIP

> Note that some fonts are especially valuable sources of bullets. In addition to the Symbol font that Word normally uses, others include Wingdings; the newer Wingdings 2 and Wingdings 3; Webdings, Microsoft's free font for Web applications; and the Adobe PostScript font Zapf Dingbats.

SPECIFYING A PICTURE BULLET

You can use a picture or series of pictures as your bullets. This is most commonly done on Web pages, but you can do it in print documents as well. To select an image for use as a bullet, follow these steps:

1. Choose Format, Bullets and Numbering.

2. From the Bulleted tab, choose one of Word's seven standard bullets (or one of your custom bullets, if you've already created one).

3. Click Customize to display the Customize Bulleted List dialog box (refer to Figure 4.19).

4. Click Picture. The Picture Bullet dialog box appears (see Figure 4.21).

Figure 4.21
Selecting a picture for use as a bullet.

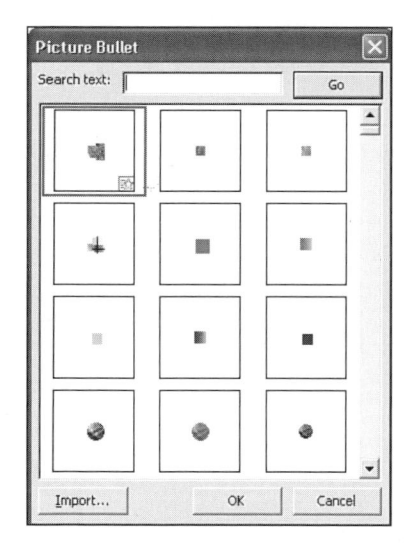

5. Select a bullet. Or, if you want to use a bullet not contained in the dialog box, click Import to open the Add Clips to Gallery dialog box.

6. From the Add Clips to Gallery dialog box, browse to and select the bullet image you want to use; then click Add.

7. From the Picture Bullet dialog box, make sure that the bullet you want is selected and click OK.

→ To learn how to specify a different picture bullet for multiple levels of your list, **see** "Adding a New List Style," **p. 646**.

CONTROLLING BULLET INDENTATION AND TEXT POSITION

By default, Word indents the bullet character 0.25" from the left margin and indents the text after the bullet 0.50" from the left margin.

You can change either of these settings using the Customize Bulleted List dialog box. Open the Bullets and Numbering dialog box (choose Format, Bullets and Numbering). With the Bulleted tab displayed, choose a bullet. Then click Customize. The Customize Bulleted List dialog box appears (refer to Figure 4.19).

To change the position of the bullet, enter a new value in the Bullet Position Indent At spin box. To change the position of text following the bullet, enter a new value in the Text Position Indent At spin box. When you finish, click OK.

Word also allows you to control the length of the tab Word inserts immediately following a bullet. By default, this is set to 0.5". The result is a hanging indent where all text lines up accurately. However, if you need to change the tab setting, you can enter a new setting in the Tab Space After scroll box.

STARTING AND STOPPING A NUMBERED LIST

Numbered lists work much like bulleted lists. To quickly create a numbered list, do the following:

1. Click in the paragraph you want to number (or select the paragraphs you want to number).
2. Click the Numbering button on the Formatting toolbar.

Word numbers each paragraph you selected. Then, as you work, each time you press Enter to start a new paragraph, Word adds the next consecutive number to that paragraph. If you move paragraphs within a numbered list, Word automatically renumbers them, keeping the numbering consecutive.

Figure 4.22 shows a sample numbered list.

TIP

> You can convert a bulleted list to a numbered list by selecting the bulleted list and clicking the Numbering button. Use the same technique to convert a numbered list to a bulleted list.

To stop Word from numbering new paragraphs, do one of the following:

■ Press Enter twice at the end of a numbered list.

- Press Enter once at the end of a numbered list and then press Backspace.
- Place the insertion point in the first paragraph you don't want to contain a number and click the Numbering button on the Standard toolbar.

Figure 4.22
An example of Word's default numbered list.

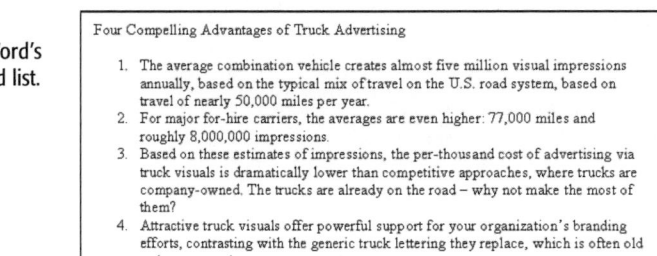

Four Compelling Advantages of Truck Advertising

1. The average combination vehicle creates almost five million visual impressions annually, based on the typical mix of travel on the U.S. road system, based on travel of nearly 50,000 miles per year.
2. For major for-hire carriers, the averages are even higher: 77,000 miles and roughly 8,000,000 impressions.
3. Based on these estimates of impressions, the per-thousand cost of advertising via truck visuals is dramatically lower than competitive approaches, where trucks are company-owned. The trucks are already on the road – why not make the most of them?
4. Attractive truck visuals offer powerful support for your organization's branding efforts, contrasting with the generic truck lettering they replace, which is often old or in poor repair.

TIP

Occasionally, you may want to skip numbering one paragraph but continue numbering in paragraphs afterward. Word adds numbers to every selected paragraph or every line ending with a paragraph mark. To avoid numbering a line, use a line break (Shift+Enter) rather than a paragraph break (Enter) to start the line you do not want to number.

However, if you do this, you lose all other benefits of the paragraph's formatting. For example, if the paragraph has 6 points of Space Before, this new line won't get it. In other words, in an attempt to discard one paragraph format, you discard all of them.

If you want to maintain other formatting and skip numbering of one or more paragraphs, place the insertion point in the first paragraph of the new list. Then right-click, choose Bullets and Numbering, and click the Continue Previous List button. Then click OK.

By default, you can also start numbering a list manually, using a number followed by a period, hyphen, or closed parentheses mark and a space. As soon as you press Enter, Word reformats the list as an automatically numbered list. Word also recognizes numbered lists that start with the letter A or a; an uppercase or lowercase Roman numeral; or a letter or number placed between parentheses, such as (1).

NOTE

If Word does not start a numbered list automatically, choose Tools, AutoCorrect Options; click the AutoFormat As You Type tab; and check the Automatic Numbered Lists check box.

NOTE

You can't edit the numbers in an automatic list directly. As you'll see in a moment, however, you can customize them through the Customize Numbered List dialog box.

4

CHANGING HOW NUMBERED LISTS WORK

If you don't like the appearance of the number you get when using the Formatting toolbar, choose Format, Bullets and Numbering to display the Bullets and Numbering dialog box. Click the Numbered tab (see Figure 4.23). Then select one of the seven standard number patterns available in Word.

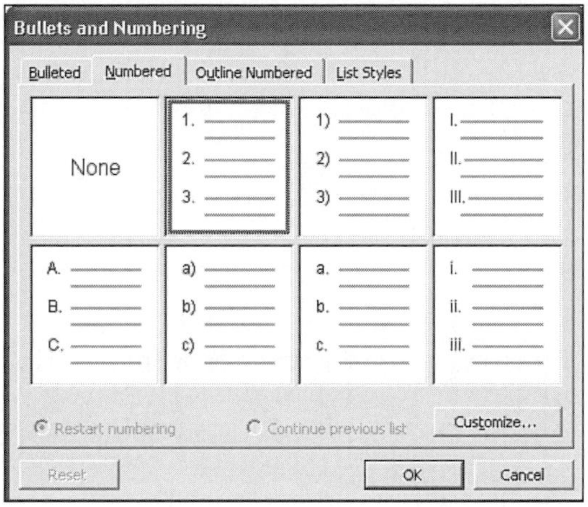

Figure 4.23
Select one of these seven standard numbering patterns.

As with bullets, you can choose one of seven standard numbering styles. And if that's not enough, you can take even more control of your numbering options.

NOTE

> Whatever number pattern you settle on becomes your default setting for the current document, and Word uses that setting whenever you click the Numbering button on the Formatting toolbar.

If none of the numbering patterns in the Bullets and Numbering dialog box is sufficient for your needs, choose one that you don't expect to use in your document and click Customize.

NOTE

> When you customize a numbering pattern, the customized version replaces the original version as a choice in the Numbered tab of the Bullets and Numbering dialog box. The original is no longer available unless you click Reset to return to Word's factory defaults.

→ For more on resetting number formats, **see** "Resetting Numbering or Bullet Formats to Word's 'Factory Defaults,'" **p. 148**.

The Customize Numbered List dialog box opens (see Figure 4.24). Here, you can customize your numbered list by changing the font used to produce the number, the style of the list, the starting number, and how the numbers and text indent and align. As you make changes, you can view their effects in the Preview box.

Figure 4.24
Customizing a numbered list.

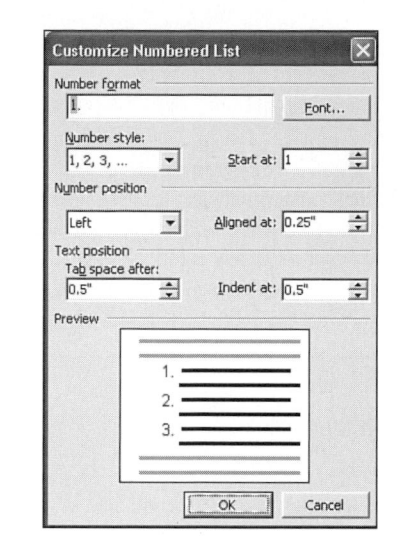

CHANGING A NUMBERED LIST'S FONT

To change the font used to produce a number, display the Customize Numbered List dialog box (refer to Figure 4.24). The number character you selected in the Numbered tab of the Bullets and Numbering dialog box appears selected in the Number Format box. Click the Font button, and the Font dialog box appears; here, you can change fonts, font sizes, character spacing, and effects.

When you're satisfied with your selection, click OK to close the Font dialog box, click OK again to close the Customize Numbered List dialog box, and click OK again to close the Bullets and Numbering dialog box.

CHANGING NUMBER STYLE

Using the Number Style boxes in the Customize Numbered List dialog box, you can choose different numbering sequences and a different starting number for your list. Word enables you to choose from the following sequences:

- 1, 2, 3...
- I, II, III...
- i, ii, iii...
- A, B, C...
- a, b, c...

- 1st, 2nd, 3rd...
- One, Two, Three...
- First, Second, Third...
- 01, 02, 03...

You can also choose no numbering at all by selecting (none) in the Number Style drop-down list box. This feature enables you to type several characters in the Number Format box and use them as if they were single bullets—so you could create a numbered list such as the following:

BONUS! Free software!

BONUS! 30-day free access!

BONUS! CD-ROM packed with sample ideas!

NOTE

> If you create a numbered list that contains only text (as described previously), be sure to use a font that is consistent or complementary with the surrounding text in your document. For instance, if the text in your document is formatted in Times New Roman, use either Times New Roman or a complementary *sans serif* face such as Arial for your list text.

Changing the Starting Number in a Numbered List

In some cases, you might want to change the number your list starts with. For instance, your list might need to correspond with a set of serial numbers that begins with 101. To set a new number format, display the Customize Numbered List dialog box and enter the new value in the Start At spin box.

TIP

> If you simply want to restart numbering at 1 partway through a numbered list, you don't need to work with the Customize Numbered List dialog box. Instead, simply right-click on the numbered list element you want to renumber as 1; then choose Restart Numbering from the shortcut menu.
>
> Later, if you want to restore consecutive numbering, right-click on the numbered list element you restarted at 1 and choose Continue Numbering from the shortcut menu.

Changing Number Position and Alignment

By default, Word indents the number in a numbered list by 0.25" from the left margin. It indents the text following the number by 0.5" from the left margin.

To change how Word aligns the number, enter a new value in the Aligned At spin box. (You can also choose to center or right-align the number in the Number Position drop-down box.)

To change how Word indents the text that follows the number, enter a new value in the Indent At spin box.

Resetting Numbering or Bullet Formats to Word's "Factory Defaults"

Suppose you've been changing bullet and numbering formats so that when you open the Bullets and Numbering dialog box, you don't see the format you want anymore—and you know it was there when you first started using Word. You can reset your numbering formats to reinstate Word's defaults.

In the Bullets and Numbering dialog box, click the Bulleted or Numbered tab, as appropriate. Then, click a format. If the Reset button is available, you have customized the selected format. Click the Reset button; then click Yes to confirm that you want to restore the original formatting.

COMPARING, SELECTING, AND COPYING FORMATTED TEXT

Word 2003 offers powerful new techniques for comparing the formatting of two blocks of copy, selecting all the text formatted in a specific manner, and copying formatting from one block of text to another. In the next sections, we'll cover these techniques.

COMPARING THE FORMATTING OF ONE TEXT SELECTION TO ANOTHER

Occasionally, you may want to compare the formatting of one text selection to another, to identify an inconsistency or a problem. You can use the Reveal Formatting task pane to do so, like this:

1. Select Format, Reveal Formatting to display the Reveal Formatting task pane.
2. Select the first text element you want to compare.
3. In the Reveal Formatting task pane, check the Compare to Another Selection check box.
4. Select the second text element you want to compare.

Word displays the differences in formatting, organized by category. For example, in Figure 4.25, Word has found that one block of text uses single line spacing, whereas the other uses 1.5 line spacing. If you click the Spacing hyperlink, Word displays the Format, Paragraph dialog box, displaying the tab that contains spacing controls.

COPYING FORMATTING USING THE STYLES AND FORMATTING TASK PANE

Imagine that you've worked really hard to format a block of text just the way you want it. Let's say that it's formatted with the New Century Schoolbook font, 24-point italic, centered, and bordered with a box. Perhaps you've even added an effect, such as embossing.

Now imagine that you've created several equally complex formats throughout your document—and you want to apply the same formats in new locations. You *could* create a style—and if you plan to reuse the format repeatedly, you probably should. But in this case, maybe you don't care about saving the formatting for posterity; maybe you just want a quick, easy way to apply the formats once or twice more.

To simplify this, Word provides the new Styles and Formatting task pane. This task pane makes it easy to reapply any combination of formatting you have already used in your document—direct formatting, as discussed in this chapter, as well as styles, discussed in Chapter 10.

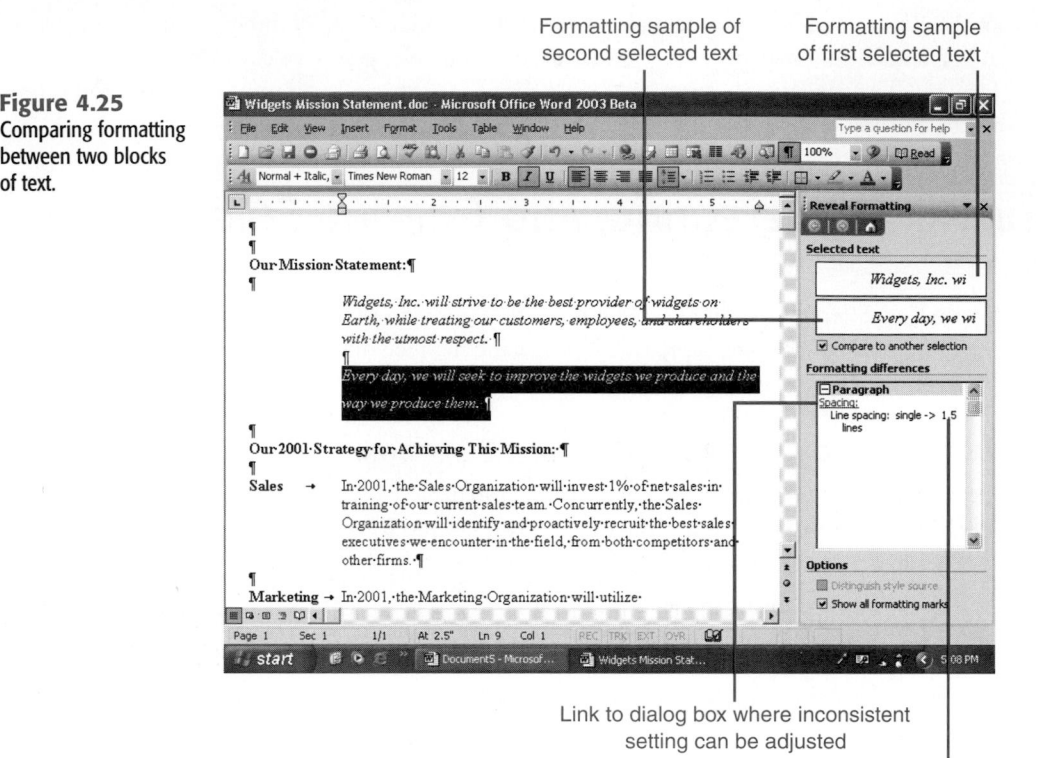

Formatting sample of
second selected text

Formatting sample
of first selected text

Figure 4.25
Comparing formatting
between two blocks
of text.

Link to dialog box where inconsistent
setting can be adjusted

Difference found in line spacing

→ For more on using the Styles and Formatting task pane with styles, **see** "Changing Styles Using the
Styles and Formatting Task Pane," **p. 345**.

To apply direct formatting with the Styles and Formatting task pane, follow these steps:

1. Select the text you want to reformat.

2. Click the Styles and Formatting button on the Formatting toolbar, or choose F<u>o</u>rmat,
   <u>S</u>tyles and Formatting. Word displays the Styles and Formatting task pane (see Figure
   4.26).

3. In the Pick Formatting to Apply scroll box, choose the formatting you want to apply.
   Word displays actual samples of each type of formatting available in the document.

TIP

> To see a detailed description of a format, hover your mouse pointer over it; a ScreenTip
> appears containing detailed formatting and/or style attributes.

If Word's list of formats is too long or confusing and you know you have already used the
format you want to apply, choose Formatting in Use from the Show drop-down box. Word
hides styles that are available but have not yet been used in the document.

Figure 4.26
The Styles and
Formatting task pane.

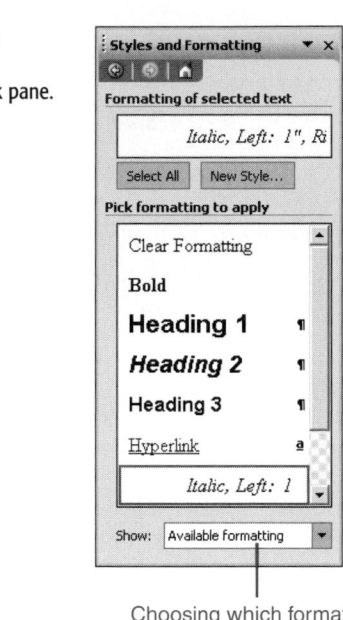

Choosing which formatting
and styles to display

If you want to choose a format that isn't already in the document, choose All Styles. If you want to control exactly which styles appear in the list, choose Custom, and place check boxes next to the styles you want to make visible (see Figure 4.27).

Figure 4.27
The Format Settings
dialog box.

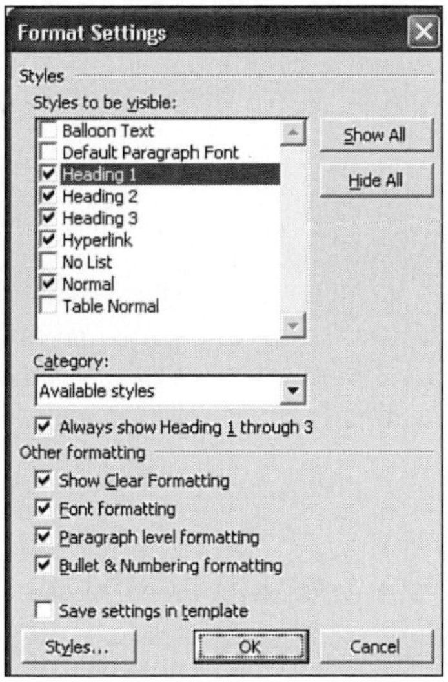

4

SELECTING ALL TEXT WITH SIMILAR FORMATTING

The Styles and Formatting task pane also makes it easy to identify all text in a document that shares the same formatting. To do so, follow these steps:

1. Select one block of text that contains formatting you want to change.

2. Open the Styles and Formatting task pane. The formatting associated with your block of text is already selected with a blue box surrounding it.

3. Click the down arrow next to the selected format and choose <u>S</u>elect All Instance(s), as shown in Figure 4.28. Word selects all locations in your document that use the same formatting.

Figure 4.28
Selecting all instances of a format, using the Styles and Formatting task pane.

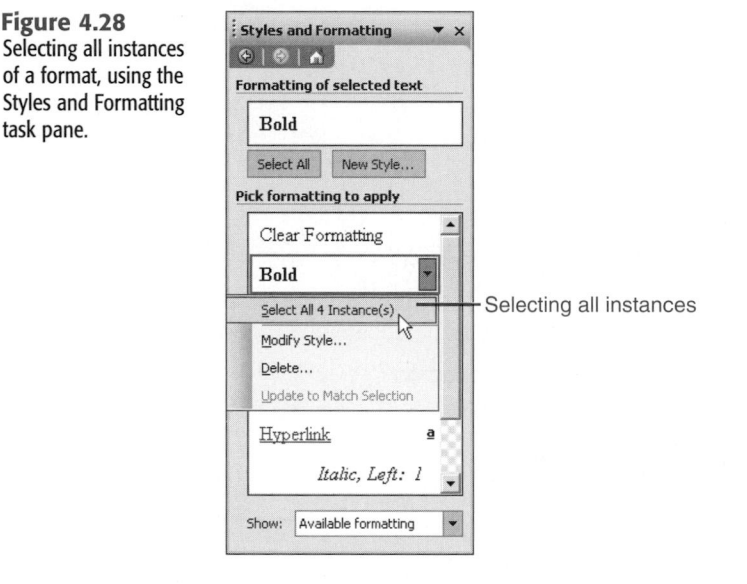

COPYING FORMATTING TO MULTIPLE LOCATIONS AT ONCE

To build a more consistent document, you'll often want to change the formatting of multiple text selections at once. The Styles and Formatting task pane makes this easy. First, follow the steps described in the preceding section to select all blocks of text containing the formatting you want to change.

After you've done so, you can choose a different format or style from the Pick Formatting to Apply list. Or, if you prefer, you can

■ Clear all formatting and styles from the text you've selected by choosing <u>D</u>elete from the shortcut menu. This reformats all selected text in the Normal Style—typically, 12-point Times New Roman.

■ Change the formatting associated with all the selected text by choosing <u>M</u>odify from the shortcut menu. The Modify Style dialog box appears (see Figure 4.29).

From here, you can control a wide range of formatting elements and style behaviors. For example, if you want to reformat all selected text as 14-point, you can choose 14-point text from the Font Size drop-down box in the Modify Style dialog box. When you're finished working with Modify Style, click OK.

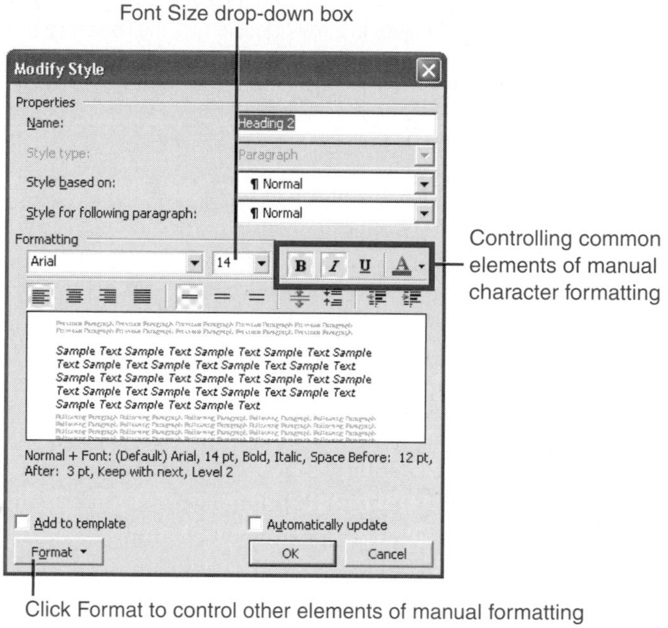

Figure 4.29
The Modify Style dialog box provides a single set of controls for adjusting a wide range of formatting elements and style behaviors.

Font Size drop-down box

Controlling common elements of manual character formatting

Click Format to control other elements of manual formatting

You can also eliminate styles and formatting from a block of text by selecting it and choosing Clear Formatting from the Pick Formatting to Apply scroll box in the Styles and Formatting task pane. Word applies the Normal style to the text and removes any manual formatting.

→ To learn more about the Modify Style dialog box, **see** "Changing Styles," **p. 345**.

USING FORMAT PAINTER TO COPY FORMATS

If you simply want to reapply direct formatting from one location to another, and you already know where to find the formatting you want in your document, you don't need to use the Styles and Formatting task pane. You can use Format Painter.

To use Format Painter, first select the text with the formats you want to copy. Then click the Format Painter button on the Standard toolbar. Select the text to which you want to apply the formats. You can select text anywhere in the same document or in other documents to apply the copied formats to.

The first time you release the mouse pointer, the formats are applied to the text you selected. That means some ways of selecting text work with the mouse pointer, and others don't. For example, you can drag your mouse pointer across text to select it for format painting. However, if you click in a new location intending to select text with a keyboard shortcut, you're too late; you've already let go of the mouse pointer, and the text you select afterward won't be reformatted.

TIP

In the preceding example, you applied a set of text formats once. What if you want to apply them several times in a row? Double-click the Format Painter button. Then select the blocks of text you want to format paint, one at a time. When you're finished, press Esc or click the Format Painter button again.

Format Painter copies all font formatting, including bold, italic, underlining, effects, character spacing, and animation. If you copy the formatting from an entire paragraph (including the paragraph mark at the end), it copies all paragraph formatting and paragraph styles as well.

USING ON-THE-FLY FORMAT CHECKING

In the past few sections, we've introduced Word's tools for eliminating formatting inconsistencies throughout your documents. But you can avoid those inconsistencies in the first place—and Word can help you systematically eliminate them in existing documents, much as it provides "on-the-fly" and "full document" spell checking.

ON-THE-FLY FORMAT CHECKING

To activate on-the-fly format checking, choose Tools, Options; click the Edit tab; check the Mark Formatting Inconsistencies check box; and choose OK. Word marks formatting inconsistencies it identifies in your document with a blue wavy underline, as shown in Figure 4.30. In this example, Word identified some text that was manually formatted to match a heading style (without actually using that heading style).

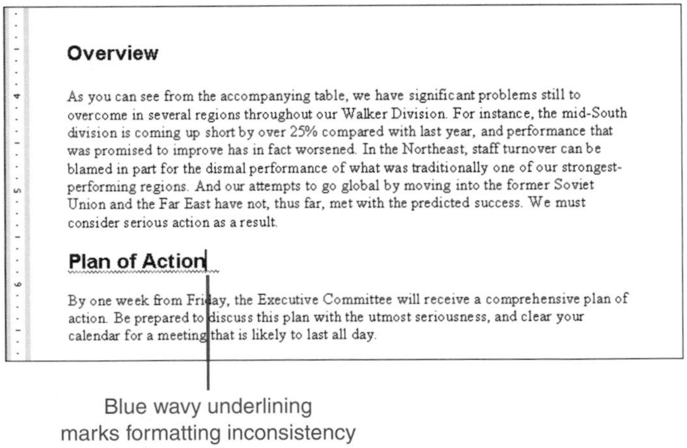

Figure 4.30
With Mark Formatting Inconsistencies selected, Word flags formatting inconsistencies as you type with blue wavy underlining.

Overview

As you can see from the accompanying table, we have significant problems still to overcome in several regions throughout our Walker Division. For instance, the mid-South division is coming up short by over 25% compared with last year, and performance that was promised to improve has in fact worsened. In the Northeast, staff turnover can be blamed in part for the dismal performance of what was traditionally one of our strongest-performing regions. And our attempts to go global by moving into the former Soviet Union and the Far East have not, thus far, met with the predicted success. We must consider serious action as a result.

Plan of Action

By one week from Friday, the Executive Committee will receive a comprehensive plan of action. Be prepared to discuss this plan with the utmost seriousness, and clear your calendar for a meeting that is likely to last all day.

Blue wavy underlining
marks formatting inconsistency

To resolve the formatting inconsistency, right-click on the text that Word has flagged. A shortcut menu appears, as shown in Figure 4.31. At the top, Word recommends a change to resolve the formatting inconsistency—in this case, Replace Direct Formatting with Style Heading 1.

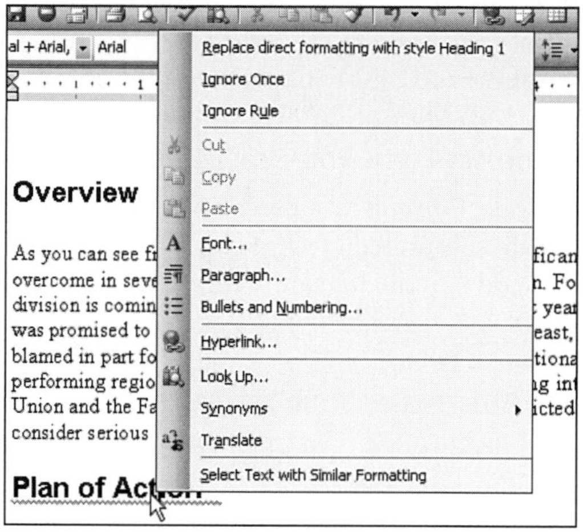

Figure 4.31
Word's options for resolving a formatting inconsistency appear at the top of the shortcut menu.

If you agree, select Word's change. To disregard this formatting inconsistency only in this case, choose Ignore Once. To always disregard similar formatting inconsistencies in this document, choose Ignore Rule.

TIP

If you suspect that the same formatting inconsistency appears throughout your document, you can fix it everywhere at once, like this:

1. Right-click to display the shortcut menu.

2. Choose Select Text with Similar Formatting.

3. Click the Styles and Formatting button on the Formatting toolbar (or choose Format, Styles and Formatting) to display the Styles and Formatting task pane.

4. In the Pick Formatting to Apply scroll box, choose the formatting you want to use instead. Word applies the correct, consistent formatting to all the text you've selected.

TROUBLESHOOTING

WHAT TO DO IF FONTS SEEM TO BE MISSING

If the font is a PostScript font, make sure that PostScript fonts are available. On the taskbar, click Start, Settings, Control Panel (or, in Windows XP, Start, Control Panel). Double-click the Fonts folder. Choose Tools, Folder Options, TrueType, and make sure that the Show Only TrueType Fonts in the Programs on My Computer check box is cleared.

WHAT TO DO IF WORD SUBSTITUTES FONTS YOU DON'T LIKE

If you open a document that calls for fonts you don't have, Word substitutes other fonts. You can control which fonts are substituted by choosing Tools, Options, Compatibility and clicking Font Substitution. Word lists the fonts it is currently substituting and lets you choose different ones.

WHAT TO DO IF THE TOPS OR BOTTOMS OF YOUR LETTERS ARE CUT OFF

Check the Format, Paragraph dialog box to see whether you've set Line Spacing with an Exactly setting that is too small for the font size you're using.

WHAT TO DO IF YOUR TABS DON'T WORK AS YOU EXPECT

Did you add or remove tab stops in ways that affected the tabs you placed in your document? Are stray tab stops still in your document that you thought you deleted? One way to find out is to display the tabs in your document by clicking the Show/Hide Paragraph Marks button on the Standard toolbar, pressing Shift+F1, and then clicking on a tab that is behaving oddly. Word's Format, Reveal Formatting task pane will display complete information about your current paragraph and tab formatting.

WHAT TO DO IF WORD ISN'T KEEPING TRACK OF FORMATTING

For Word to mark formatting inconsistencies, you must check the Mark Formatting Inconsistencies check box in the Edit tab of the Tools, Options dialog box. This check box is available only if you first check the Keep Track of Formatting check box immediately above it.

CHAPTER 5

CONTROLLING PAGE FEATURES

In this chapter

USING WORD'S PAGE SETUP FEATURES

You've created a document. But before you print it, you want to make sure that all your margins and other page settings are correct. You can control the following aspects of page formatting from the Page Setup dialog box:

- Change margins (including setting up a document for binding)
- Set the size and orientation of your paper
- Choose the tray from which your printer is to print
- Divide your document into sections
- Add line numbers
- Control the vertical alignment of text on the page

Each of these elements can be controlled for your entire document, or for individual sections you've created. To view the Page Setup dialog box, choose File, Page Setup.

NOTE

> Much of what is discussed in the remainder of this chapter applies only to documents that you print, not to Web or other online documents. Specifically, these features and the settings related to them do not have any effect or meaning in documents saved as Web pages, and you will not see the effects of changing them in Web Page view: margins, headers and footers, page numbers, page borders, paper size, paper orientation, sections and section breaks, vertical alignment of text on pages, and line numbering.
>
> Of course, the paper size, orientation, and printer paper tray settings do matter if you print your Web pages. See Chapter 24, "Using Word to Develop Web Content," for more detail on what Word features do work with Web pages and how to best use them.

Word's default page settings appear in Table 5.1. In subsequent sections of this chapter, you'll learn how to change these settings, both for new documents and for only the current document.

NOTE

> These default settings apply if you haven't already made changes or customizations to the Normal template.

TABLE 5.1 DEFAULT PAGE SETTINGS IN U.S. VERSION OF WORD

Feature	Setting
Top and bottom margins	1"
Left and right margins	1.25"
Header and footer margins	.5"

Feature	Setting
Paper size	Letter (8.5"×11")
Paper	Orientation Portrait
Paper source	Printer-dependent
Section starts	On a new page
Headers and footers	The same throughout your document
Vertical alignment	Top
Line numbers	Off

WORKING WITH SECTIONS

By default, any change made to the options shown in Table 5.1 applies to your entire document. If this isn't what you want, you can use sections to apply any setting you establish in the Page Setup dialog box to only specific portions of your document.

Sections give you a way to establish different settings for different parts of the same document. For example, suppose that your document is formatted (like most documents) in Portrait mode—the pages are taller than they are wide. What if you need to insert a page containing a table that appears sideways? You can make that page a separate section. Splitting a document into sections enables you to customize the following formats for any part of a document:

- Column formatting
- Footnote and endnote appearance and location
- Headers and footers
- Page and line numbering
- Paper size and orientation

Often, Word automatically creates sections for you when necessary. For example, if you use Word's columns feature to make your document two columns wide from "This Point Forward," Word inserts a section break at your insertion point. Later in this chapter, when you learn to change margins, you'll see another example of how Word can automatically insert section breaks when needed.

→ For more information about creating documents with more than one column, **see** "Working with Multiple Columns," **p. 182**.

→ To learn another way to control the behavior of section breaks after you insert them, **see** "Specifying Where to Start a Section," **p. 172**.

Often, however, you need to insert section breaks and assign settings to them manually.

CREATING A SECTION

You can divide a document into sections at any time by choosing Insert, Break and creating the section in the Break dialog box (see Figure 5.1).

5

Figure 5.1
Use the Break dialog box to start a new section in your document.

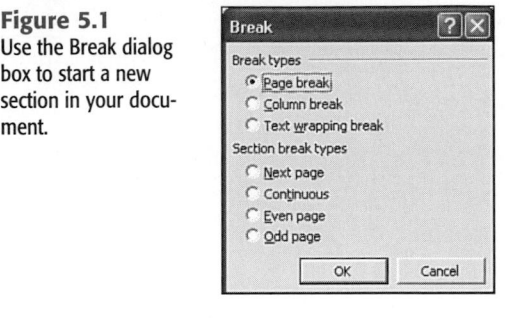

TIP

Notice that you can insert a manual page break from this dialog box. You may find it easier, however, to place the insertion point wherever you want the new page to begin and press Ctrl+Enter.

After you select the type of break you want to use, Word inserts the break immediately before the insertion point.

NOTE

The section break is inserted at your insertion point, but (as with anything you insert at the insertion point) it moves the insertion point forward. In other words, after you insert the break, text you type appears after the break unless you move the insertion point elsewhere.

SELECTING A TYPE OF SECTION BREAK

You can create several types of section breaks. In Draft mode or Normal view onscreen, they look similar, but their differences are apparent in Print Layout view or when you print the document:

- A Next Page section break starts the new section at the top of the next page in your document. Both onscreen and when you print, Word starts a new page at the section break.

- A Continuous section break starts the new section at the insertion point. Onscreen in Normal view, you see a section break, but in Print Layout and Web views and when you print, the break is transparent.

- An Even Page section break starts the new section on the next even-numbered page. If the section break falls on an even-numbered page, Word leaves the next odd-numbered page blank.

- An Odd Page section break starts the new section on the next odd-numbered page. Similar to the Even Page section break, if the section break falls on an odd-numbered page, Word leaves the next even-numbered page blank. This is commonly required in books, which often start all new chapters on a right-hand page.

You see section breaks in your document automatically in Normal view. To see them in Print Layout view, click the Show/Hide Paragraph Marks button on the Standard toolbar, or click the Show All Formatting Marks check box on the Reveal Formatting side pane. Figure 5.2 shows a Next Page section break displayed in Normal view.

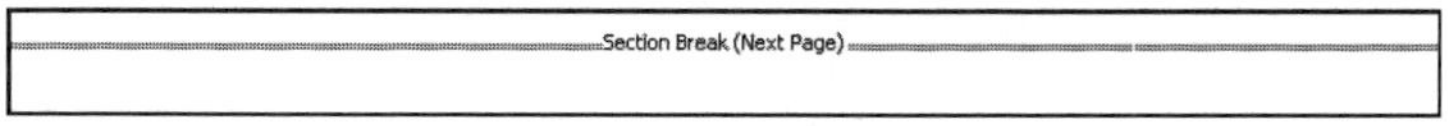

Figure 5.2
In Normal view, section breaks appear in your document as double-dotted lines.

Section Break (Next Page)

After you insert a section break, you have two sections that contain the same page formatting. To change the formatting in one section, place the insertion point anywhere within that section and make your format changes using the Page Setup dialog box. Page Setup formatting changes such as changing the paper orientation from portrait to landscape to accommodate a wide table in the section then apply just to the section unless you change the Apply To setting to Whole Document.

COPYING A SECTION'S FORMATTING

In the same way that paragraph marks store all the formatting for a paragraph, the section break mark that appears after a section stores all the section formatting for that section. After you establish formatting for a section, you may want to copy that formatting to another section, and you can do so easily by copying the section break mark. Simply select the section break and click the Copy button. Then, move the insertion point to the end of the text you want to format and click the Paste button. You get a new section break that includes all the same formatting as the one you copied.

TIP

> You can search for section breaks. Open the Find dialog box and, if necessary, click the More button to display the additional Find options. Then, click the Special button and choose Section Break.

DELETING A SECTION BREAK

You can delete a section break the same way you delete any text. For example, you can place the insertion point on the section break and press the Delete key.

Before deleting a section break, remember that a section break mark stores all the formatting for the section preceding the break mark. If you delete a section break, the text before the break mark merges with the text after the break mark and assumes the formatting characteristics of the section after the break mark.

5

NOTE

> Word provides no easy way to change a section break after you have inserted it. This is unfortunate because if you delete a section break, you lose any differences in page formatting that you have applied separately in each section.
>
> There is, however, a workaround.
>
> If you inadvertently create the wrong type of section break, insert a correct section break immediately after the incorrect one. Then, select them both. Choose File, Page Setup and click the Layout tab. In the Section Start drop-down box, choose the type of break you want—for example, New Page or Continuous. Click OK. You now have two identical section breaks in your document. Delete the first one. The result: one section break containing the formatting you need.

CHANGING MARGINS

Margins measure the amount of space that appears on a page between the edge of the page and the text. Margin space surrounds the text of your document. Margin settings initially apply to your entire document, but you can establish different margin settings for different portions of your document. You can change margins using the following two techniques:

- Using the ruler
- Using the Page Setup dialog box

CHANGING MARGINS USING THE RULER

Use the ruler to change margins if

- You like to get immediate, interactive visual feedback about your margin settings
- You have the good hand-eye coordination needed to establish precise margin settings with the ruler
- You want to change margin settings for your entire document

To change margins using the ruler, follow these steps:

1. Open the View menu and make sure that you see a check mark next to Ruler. If you don't, choose Ruler.
2. Choose View, Print Layout.
3. Slide the mouse pointer into the ruler at the edge where you want to change the margin (see Figure 5.3). If Word's triangular indent markers appear at the left edge of the ruler (where the white area meets the gray area), position the mouse pointer between the triangular indent markers.
4. When the mouse pointer changes to a two-headed arrow, click and drag the mouse. Drag a side margin to the left or right; drag a top or bottom margin up or down. When you release the mouse pointer, the new margin is applied.

Double-arrow mouse pointer indicates
you can drag to change a margin

Figure 5.3
Drag a left margin to
the right to make the
margin larger and to
the left to make the
margin smaller.

While you drag the mouse
pointer, a vertical line indicates
the current location of the margin

The ruler can show current measurements, making it a precise tool. Press Alt while you drag the mouse pointer, and the measurements appear, as shown in Figure 5.4.

Left margin
measurement

Right margin
measurement

Figure 5.4
If you press Alt while
you drag the mouse
pointer, Word dis-
plays measurements
as you move.

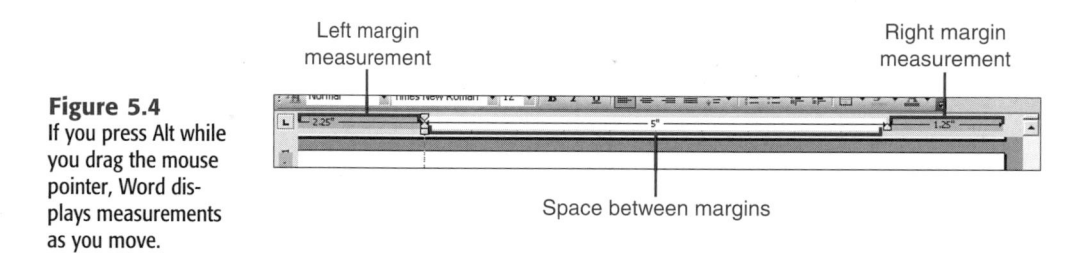

Space between margins

TIP

> If the vertical ruler doesn't appear in Print Layout view, choose Tools, Options; click the View tab; and check the Vertical Ruler (Print View Only) check box.

5

CHANGING MARGINS USING THE PAGE SETUP DIALOG BOX

You also can use the Page Setup dialog box to change the margins in your document. Use the Page Setup dialog box to change margins when you need very precise margin settings or when you want the change to affect only part of your document.

NOTE

> If you have not divided your document into sections before opening the Page Setup dia-log box, you can choose This Point Forward in the Apply To drop-down box on any tab, and Word inserts a section break at your insertion point—applying all your section for-matting changes only after the section break.

continues

continued

> If you select text before opening the dialog box, you see Whole Document and Selected Text as the choices in the Apply To list box. If your document already has at least one section break in it, you also see Selected Sections in the list. If you don't select text, you see Whole Document and This Point Forward as the choices in the list box. If you choose Selected Text while making Page Setup choices, Word automatically creates sections in your document.

Place the insertion point at the location where you want the new margins to begin. If you want to change the margins for a certain portion of your document even if you have not divided your document into sections, select the text you want affected by the new margins.

Choose File, Page Setup. The Page Setup dialog box appears (see Figure 5.5). Use the Top, Bottom, Left, and Right boxes to increase or decrease margins. If you selected text and want the settings to apply to selected text only, choose Selected Text from the Apply To drop-down list box. If you didn't select text and you want the settings to apply to the rest of your document, choose This Point Forward instead. You can also, of course, stick with the default option of applying the margins to the entire document.

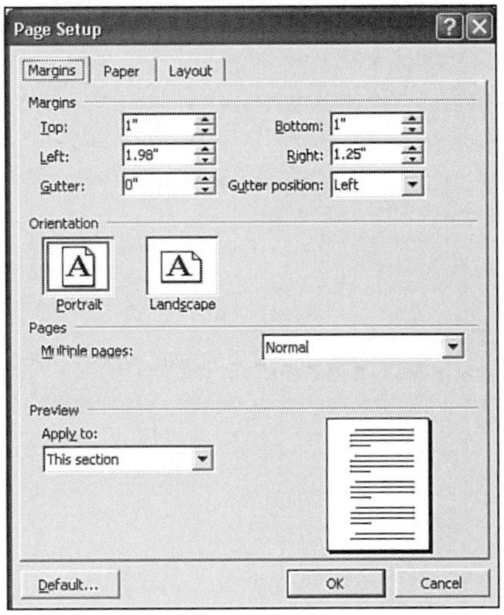

Figure 5.5
Change margins from the Margins tab of the Page Setup dialog box.

> *If you find yourself inadvertently indenting paragraphs instead of changing page margins, see "How to Avoid Accidentally Changing Paragraph Marks Instead of Margins," in the "Troubleshooting" section of this chapter.*

USING LANDSCAPE MODE TO PRINT WIDE PAGES

The Margins tab of the Page Setup dialog box includes an option that controls the orientation of documents sent to the printer. To understand the difference between *portrait* and *landscape* orientation, consider the text on an 8 1/2×11-inch page:

- When you choose <u>P</u>ortrait orientation, the text flows across the 8 1/2-inch side of the page between the left and right margins, and the page is taller than it is wide.

- When you choose Land<u>s</u>cape orientation, the text flows across the 11-inch side of the page between the left and right margins and the page is wider than it is tall.

Landscape mode is useful for financial reports with wide lists of numbers, and it also adds visual interest to proposal documents, newsletters, and many other documents. To switch a document from Portrait to Landscape mode, choose <u>F</u>ile, Page Set<u>u</u>p and click the Margins tab. Then click the Land<u>s</u>cape button and click OK.

CREATING GUTTERS FOR BOUND BOOKS AND DOCUMENTS

Suppose you're producing a report that will be bound or stapled. You probably want to leave extra space on the left margin of each page to accommodate the binding. Or, if you're producing a book or booklet that will be printed on both sides of every sheet and then bound together, you'll probably want to leave extra space on both the inside margins, near the binding.

Page Setup's Margins tab provides a separate setting, <u>G</u>utter, for these purposes. When you enter a number in the <u>G</u>utter scroll box, Word adds that value to the left side of your page, in addition to your left margin.

If you prefer, you can place the gutter on the top of the page instead of at the left. (This is common in documents oriented in Landscape mode.) To do so, choose Top from the <u>G</u>utter Position drop-down box. But occasionally you may want to create gutters for a binding that appears at the top of a sheet.

SETTING MULTIPLE PAGES OPTIONS

With Word 2002, Microsoft significantly improved Word's support for printing multiple-page documents such as books and folded brochures. The first step in preparing such documents is to specify a setting from the <u>M</u>ultiple Pages drop-down box in the Margins tab of the Page Setup dialog box.

SETTING MIRRORED MARGINS

Word 2003 brings together settings for controlling the behavior of multiple pages. You can choose any four from the <u>M</u>ultiple Pages drop-down box on the Margins tab of the Page Setup dialog box.

For example, if you plan to print on both the front and the back sides of each page, choose Mirror Margins from the <u>M</u>ultiple Pages drop-down box. When you check this box, Word automatically sets up your document so that it uses facing pages. If you fold and staple your document, when you open it, you'll see two pages: an even numbered page on the left and a consecutive odd numbered page on the right. Word displays a thumbnail sketch of both pages. Figure 5.6 shows an example of mirror margins.

5

NOTE

As shown in Figure 5.6, you may have to add gutter space to account for binding.

Gutters at center of two-page spread

Figure 5.6
You can use mirrored margins to set up your document to print with facing pages.

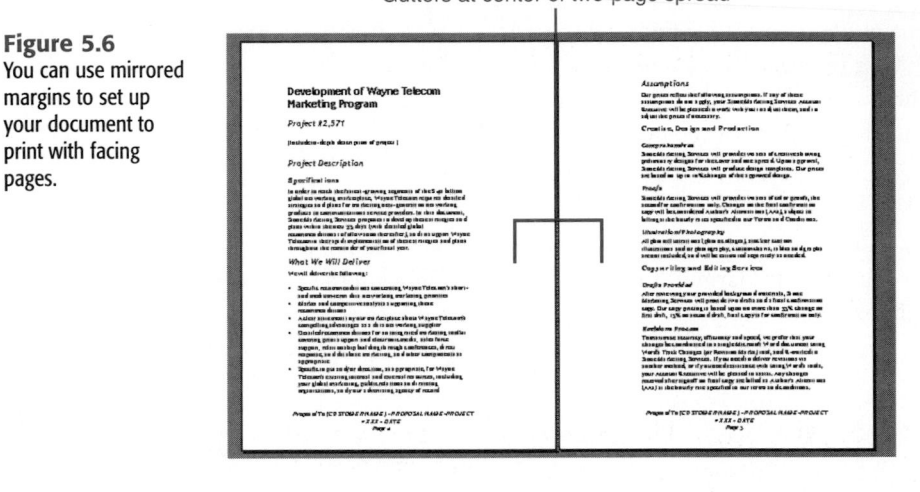

NOTE

If you plan to bind your document and print on only one side of each page, you'll still want to leave extra space at the left margin for binding. In this case, don't select Mirror Margins from the <u>M</u>ultiple Pages option, but do set a <u>G</u>utter size.

PLACING TWO PAGES ON THE SAME SHEET

Word now provides a way to print two half-sheet landscape pages on the same sheet, as shown in Figure 5.7. To print two pages on a sheet choose <u>F</u>ile, Page Set<u>u</u>p and click the Margins tab. Choose 2 Pages Per Sheet from the <u>M</u>ultiple Pages drop-down box.

When you print two pages to a sheet, Word reduces the size of each page by 50%. For example, on an 8 1/2×11-inch sheet printed in Portrait mode, each page will be 5 1/2×8 1/2 inches. Page 1 and Page 2 will print on the same sheet, Page 3 and Page 4 will print on the next sheet, and so forth.

USING BOOK FOLD TO PRINT FOLIOS, BOOKLETS, AND PAMPHLETS

The 2 Pages Per Sheet option is ideal if you're distributing informal documents. However, more complex documents, such as books, require pages to be arranged differently to be professionally printed correctly.

For example, in an eight-page booklet, page 8 and page 1 need to be on the same side of the same sheet; similarly, page 7 and page 2 need to be adjacent. When the printed document is folded and bound, the pages then appear in the correct order for reading.

Figure 5.7
Placing two horizontal pages on the same sheet.

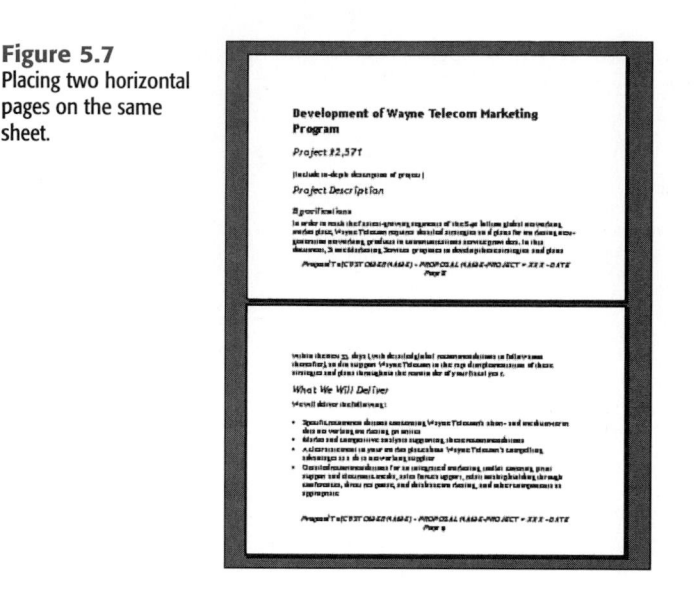

In the printing trade, the organization of pages for printing is called *imposition*, and the specific arrangement of pages is commonly called *printer spreads*, to distinguish from *reader spreads*, which represent the order in which the reader wants to see pages.

Word enables you to organize pages for printing as booklets or books. To use this capability, choose Book Fold from the Multiple Pages drop-down box.

NOTE

Because Book Fold significantly affects the formatting of your pages, if possible, try to establish this setting when you start working with your document. If you establish it after entering all your text, formatting, page, and section breaks, you will have to check your document carefully—and often make adjustments.

After you've done so, a new drop-down box appears: Sheets per Booklet. Here, you can specify how many sheets will be printed together. The printer's term for this is *signature*. For example, many books are printed in signatures of 32 pages. In other words, the books are printed in 32-page sections, and then bound together.

NOTE

Book Fold requires your pages to be oriented in Landscape mode; if they aren't, Word switches that setting as well.

Of course, the specific arrangement of pages Word applies depends on the size of the signature. A simple example: On an 8-page signature, the front of the first sheet contains pages 1 and 8, whereas on a 32-page signature, it contains pages 1 and 32. Figure 5.8 presents a simple example of the difference between reader spreads and printer spreads (Book Fold) in an eight-page document or signature.

Figure 5.8
Reader spreads (left) and printer spreads (right).

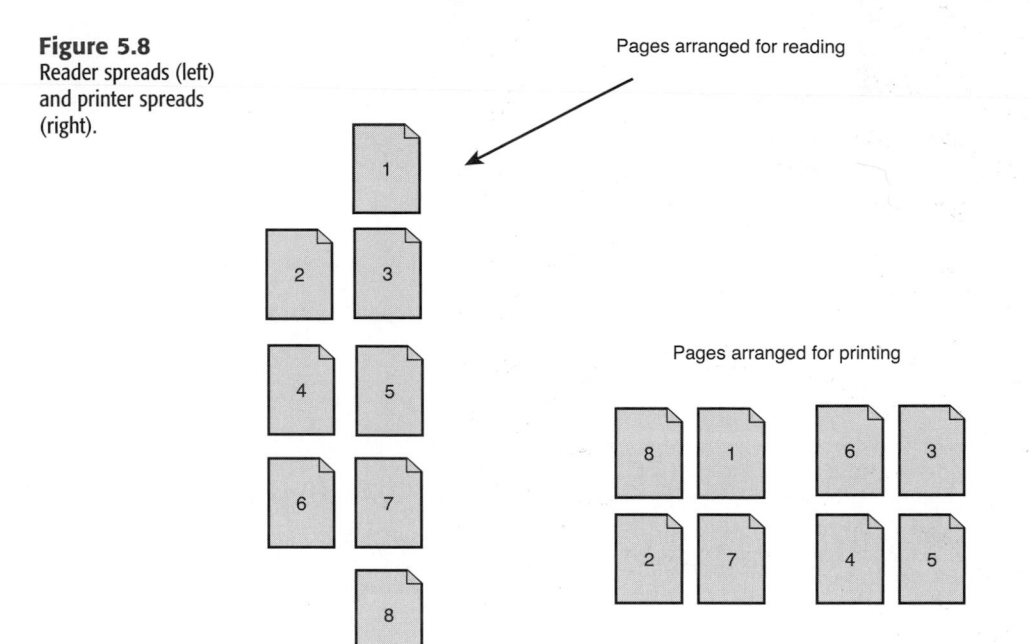

Pages arranged for reading

Pages arranged for printing

For shorter documents printed in-house, you may be able to leave the default setting, All—in which case, Word prints all the pages in your document as a single signature. For longer documents, and documents that will ultimately be printed by a professional printing shop, consult with your printer to determine the appropriate setting. It also makes sense to provide your printer with a test set of pages to ensure that they are, in fact, organized correctly.

→ In some cases, your printer wants to print from a PostScript file rather than a Word document. For information on creating a PostScript file from a Word document, **see** "Creating a Print File from Which You Can Print Later," **p. 202**.

NOTE

For Book Fold documents you are printing yourself, remember to print on both sides of the paper. If your printer can do this automatically, specify that it does so. (Choose File, Print and click Properties to display the settings associated with your printer driver.)

If your printer cannot physically print on both sides of the page at once, use Word's Manual Duplex printing feature. (Choose File, Print; check the Manual Duplex check box; and click OK to print. Word prints all the pages on one side and then prompts you to turn over the sheets of paper and feed them into your printer again for printing on the reverse sides.)

Permanently Changing Default Page Setup

Suppose, for example, that you prefer 1-inch rather than 1.25-inch left and right margins for all your documents. With every new document, you find yourself manually changing the margin settings. Why not change Word's defaults instead?

Choose File, Page Setup to open the Page Setup dialog box. Select the settings you want to apply to every document and then click the Default button in the lower-left corner of the dialog box. Word displays the dialog box shown in Figure 5.9.

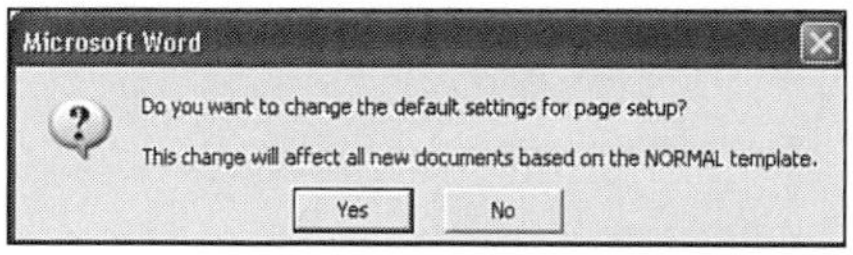

Figure 5.9
When you click the Default button in the Page Setup dialog box, Word displays a confirmation dialog box.

Choose Yes to accept your changes or No to reject them. Keep the following in mind:

- You are changing defaults for a specific template—the one on which the current document is based.

- When you change defaults, you change them for new documents you create based on the selected template, not for existing documents. If you want to change the settings of existing documents, you must edit each of them individually.

Setting Paper Size and Source

You can set the size and source of paper from the Paper tab of the Page Setup dialog box (see Figure 5.10). If the Page Setup dialog box isn't open, choose File, Page Setup and click the Paper tab.

Choosing a Paper Size

Word 2003 provides several paper sizes; these may vary depending on the printer you use. The following list shows *some* of the more common paper types Word supports:

- Letter (8 1/2"×11")
- Legal (8 1/2"×14")
- Executive (7 1/4"×10 1/2")
- A4 (210×297mm)
- A5 (148×210mm)
- A6 Index card (105×148mm)
- #10 Envelope (4 1/8"×9 1/2")
- DL Envelope (110×220mm)

- C5 Envelope (176×250mm)
- Monarch Envelope (7.5"×3.88")
- Photo Paper (4"×6", 100×150mm, and 200×300mm)

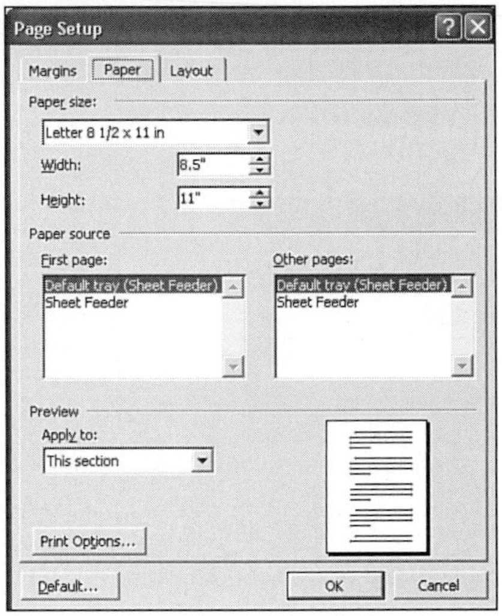

Figure 5.10
You set paper size and source from the Paper tab of the Page Setup dialog box.

You can also choose Custom Size and enter your own dimensions in the Width and Height scroll boxes below the Paper Size drop-down list.

NOTE

As you know, the United States uses 8 1/2×11-inch paper by default. Most other countries, however, use A4 as the standard paper size. If you need to print a document on 8 1/2×11-inch paper that was originally formatted for A4 paper, Word can help you convert the document and still retain most, but not all, of the document's layout. From the Paper tab of the Page Setup dialog box, click Print Options; check in the Allow A4/Letter Paper Resizing check box; and click OK.

CHOOSING YOUR PAPER SOURCE

You can also determine the paper tray from which your printer prints by using the Page Setup dialog box. Display the Paper tab in the Page Setup dialog box, if it isn't already open (refer to Figure 5.10).

NOTE

Many shared network printers have these settings locked down by the network server; users can't change such settings in Word.

If your document has only one section, the choices you make in the Paper Source area of the Paper tab apply to the entire document. If your document has multiple sections, the choices you make here apply to the section your insertion point is in, or the sections you have selected before opening the dialog box.

You can specify different paper sources for the First Page of each section and for the Other Pages. This feature is particularly useful when using letterhead for the first page of a document and second sheets for the subsequent pages. You can store the letterhead in one paper tray, and second sheets in another, and then set your Paper Source settings to match.

The paper tray choices contained in the First Page and Other Pages scroll boxes depend on the printer you have installed. Not all printers are created equal. For example, some printers have two paper trays, typically called Upper and Lower. Other printers have special trays for envelopes. Still other printers may have a multipurpose tray that fills several different roles.

TIP

> In Chapter 6, "Printing and Faxing in Word," you'll learn how to print envelopes and documents together. Because Word creates a separate section for the envelopes, you can use Paper Source settings to instruct Word to print the envelopes from a separate tray.

If your document contains one section, your Paper Source settings apply to the entire document. If you prefer, however, you can apply new settings only to portions of your document that follow the insertion point. To do so, choose This Point Forward from the Apply To drop-down box. Word then inserts a section break at your insertion point and applies your First Page and Other Page settings only to the new section that follows the insertion point.

If your document contains multiple sections, Apply To gives you three choices about where you apply your First Page and Other Page paper source settings. You can apply them to

- The section your insertion point is in (This Section or Selected Sections if you have selected text first).
- The remainder of your document, from the insertion point on (This Point Forward). Word inserts a new section break at the insertion point and applies the paper source settings to all text that follows, including any text in additional sections that follow your insertion point.
- The entire document (Whole Document).

CONTROLLING YOUR DOCUMENT'S LAYOUT

The Layout tab of the Page Setup dialog box (see Figure 5.11) brings together various features that apply to entire pages. Perhaps you need to align your page vertically so that the text is centered from top to bottom. Or you may want to number the lines of your document so that proofreaders can refer to line numbers in their comments. You control these settings here.

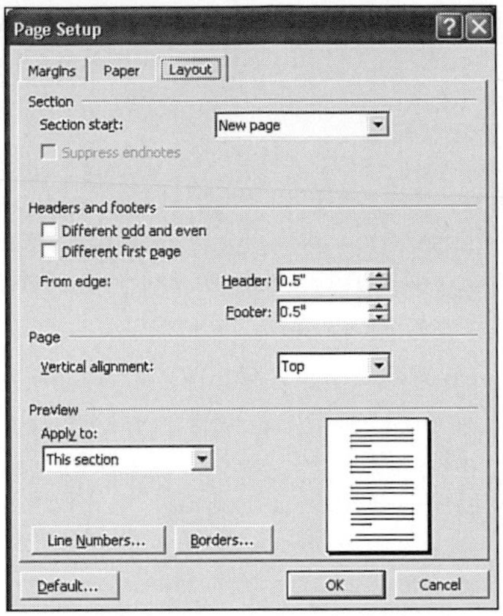

Figure 5.11
Working in the Layout tab of the Page Setup dialog box.

SPECIFYING WHERE TO START A SECTION

If your document has multiple sections, Section Start gives you a second chance to specify where Word starts each section you've selected. For example, if you originally inserted a continuous section break, you can change that setting to New Page here. (Word's default setting for section breaks is New Page: Where you insert a new section, Word starts a new page.)

SETTING VERTICAL ALIGNMENT OF TEXT ON PAGE

When you're creating a multipage document, such as a legal brief or a report, you ordinarily want the text to align vertically at the top of the page. Suppose, however, that you're creating a short letter or a cover page for a report. You may prefer to align text vertically in the center of the page.

Rather than struggling to center the title manually, let Word do it for you. Choose File, Page Setup and click the Layout tab. Then click the Vertical Alignment drop-down list box, choose Center, and then click OK.

> **TIP**
>
> You can also justify text from top to bottom on a page, which means stretching the space between lines to reach the top and bottom margins.
>
> This works only if you have sufficient text on a page; otherwise, Word gives up and places the text at the top of the page.

USING LINE NUMBERING

Line numbering is handy for various reasons. For example, it gives reviewers something to refer to when making comments on a document—and it can be essential in many legal documents.

To turn on line numbering, choose File, Page Setup and click the Layout tab. Click the Line Numbers button and place a check in the Add Line Numbering check box of the Line Numbers dialog box (see Figure 5.12).

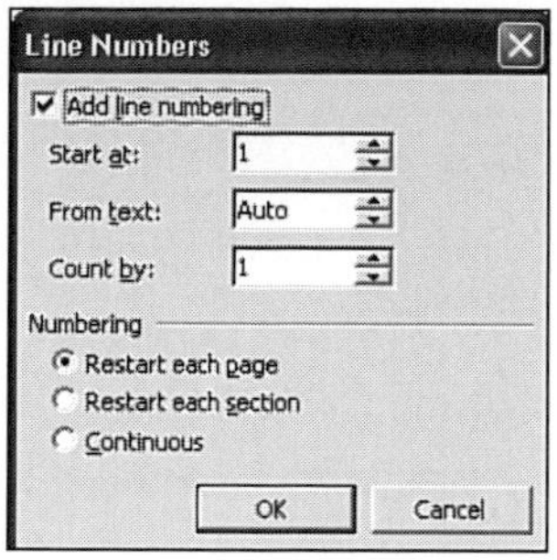
Line Numbers
Add line numbering
Start at: 1
From text: Auto
Count by: 1
Numbering
Restart each page
Restart each section
Continuous
OK
Cancel

Figure 5.12
You can number your document's lines continuously or you can restart at the beginning of each page or section.

Numbers appear in the left margin in Print Layout view, when you print, or when you preview the document (see Figure 5.13). You can control the initial number and the increments of the numbering. Use the From Text box to control the space between the numbers and the text.

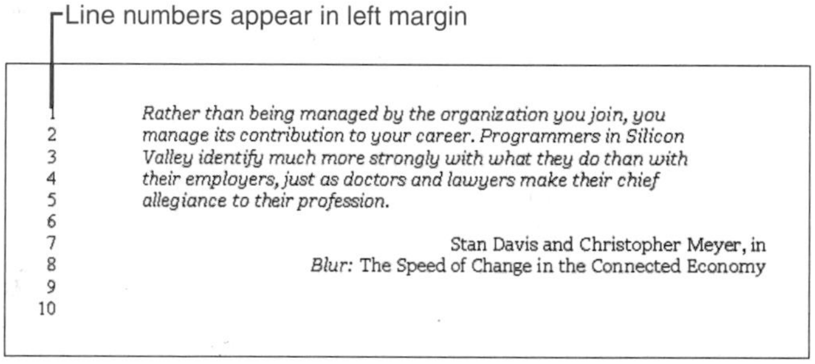
Line numbers appear in left margin
1 Rather than being managed by the organization you join, you
2 manage its contribution to your career. Programmers in Silicon
3 Valley identify much more strongly with what they do than with
4 their employers, just as doctors and lawyers make their chief
5 allegiance to their profession.
6
7 Stan Davis and Christopher Meyer, in
8 Blur: The Speed of Change in the Connected Economy
9
10

Figure 5.13
Line numbering makes reviewers' lives easier.

To remove line numbering, reopen the Line Numbers dialog box and clear the Add Line Numbering check box.

> **NOTE**
>
> From the Layout tab of the Page Setup dialog box, you can also access Word's page bordering controls. Click Borders to display the Borders and Shading dialog box.
>
> Borders and shading are covered later in this chapter in the "Using Borders and Shading" section.

Using Headers and Footers

A *header* is text that appears at the top of each page; a *footer* is text that appears at the bottom of each page. Typically, headers and footers appear at the top or bottom of every page, perhaps with modifications (such as page numbers that change with every page). Word gives you extensive control over headers and footers. For example, you can

- Enter any text (or insert other elements, such as images)
- Create different headers for odd and even pages, or for the first page
- Automatically number header or footer pages
- Automatically add dates or times to headers and footers
- Create different headers for different sections of your document; or reconnect headers in different sections so that they are all consistent

To work with headers, choose View, Header and Footer. Word switches you to Print Layout view, if you're not already there, and displays your header surrounded by nonprinting dotted lines that represent its location and size (see Figure 5.14).

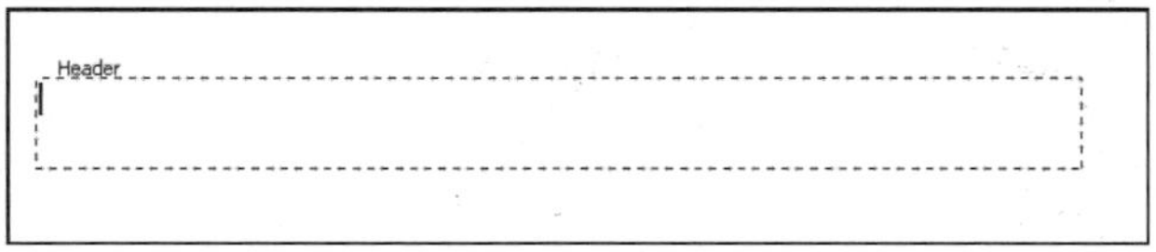

Figure 5.14
Displaying an empty
header.

If you want to work with a footer rather than a header, click the Switch Between Header and Footer button on the Header and Footer toolbar.

To enter text, simply start typing. Nearly any editing or formatting you can do in a regular Word editing window you can do in a header or footer area. You have access to the Standard toolbar, Formatting toolbar, and ruler shortcuts; all basic editing and formatting menu selections; and most keyboard shortcuts.

Word normally styles both headers and footers with left-aligned, Times New Roman 12-point type. You can change this manually, or by changing the built-in Header style in the same way you would change any document style.

By default, two tabs are set as part of the formatting in the Header and Footer styles: a center tab and a right tab. Text you type at the left margin is aligned, of course, with the left margin of the header or footer pane. If you press Tab and type, the text you type appears centered between the left and right margins. Similarly, if you press Tab again and type, text you type aligns with the right margin.

Also by default, the header and footer you create appear on every page of the current section of your document—if your document contains only one section, the header or footer appears on every page of the entire document. Every page's header contains the same information, except for information that is automatically adjusted through fields, such as page numbering. Footers work the same way: When you enter your first footer, that footer is applied to every page in your document. Later in this chapter, you'll learn how to vary the headers and footers throughout your document.

WORKING WITH THE HEADER AND FOOTER TOOLBAR

When you display a header or footer, Word also shows the Header and Footer toolbar (see Figure 5.15).

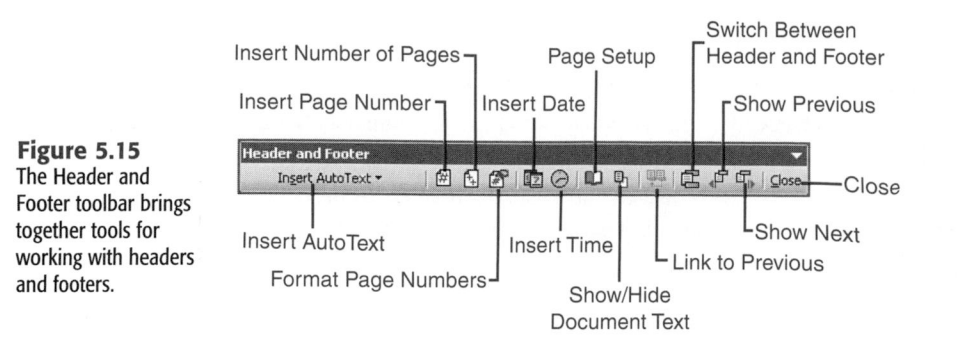

Figure 5.15
The Header and Footer toolbar brings together tools for working with headers and footers.

The buttons on the Header and Footer toolbar help you create headers and footers (see Table 5.2):

- The six tools on the left side of the Header and Footer Toolbar (Insert AutoText, Insert Page Number, Insert Number of Pages, Format Page Number, Insert Date, and Insert Time) help you insert and format commonly used header and footer text.

- The next tool, the Page Setup button, gives you access to Word's features for controlling page margins, paper size, and layout.

- To the right of these tools, the Show/Hide Document Text button toggles the surrounding document text on and off so that you can see how your header, footer, and document text look next to each other.

- The Link to Previous button helps you control whether headers and footers in separate sections are identical or not.

- Finally, the three tools immediately to the left of the Close button (Switch Between Header and Footer, Show Previous, and Show Next) help you navigate between headers and footers in your document.

For example, if you are viewing the Header pane and you click the Switch Between Header and Footer button, you'll view the Footer pane. The Link to Previous, Show Previous, and Show Next buttons become useful when you create different headers and footers for various portions of your document.

TABLE 5.2   HEADER AND FOOTER TOOLBAR

Button	Function
Insert AutoText	Enables you to choose from a series of preformatted headers and footers that specify page numbers, author's name, date, filename, or other information
Insert Page Number	Inserts a field that displays the correct page number on all pages
Insert Number of Pages	Inserts a field that displays the number of pages in the entire document
Format Page Number	Displays the Page Number Format dialog box, which enables you to control page number formatting and numbering
Insert Date	Inserts a field that displays the current date
Insert Time	Inserts a field that displays the current time
Page Setup	Displays the Layout tab of the Page Setup dialog box, where you can specify different headers and footers for odd and even pages, or for the first page
Show/Hide Document Text	Toggles between displaying document text in the background (in gray) or showing no text in the background
Link to Previous	Specifies that a header (or footer) contain the same text as the header or footer in the preceding section
Switch Between Header and Footer	Toggles between displaying the current section's header or footer
Show Previous	Displays the header associated with the preceding section, if any
Show Next	Displays the header associated with the next section, if any
Close	Closes the Header and Footer pane

TIP

> After you have created a header or footer, you can edit it by reopening the Header or Footer pane. Either use the menus or double-click any header or footer in Print Layout view that contains text.

Word's Header and Footer toolbar also includes buttons that give you one-click access to the dialog boxes you're most likely to need from within a header or footer:

- The Page Number Format dialog box, where you can specify the appearance and numbering scheme used by page numbers
- The Layout tab of the Page Setup dialog box, where you can specify different headers and footers for odd and even pages, or for the first page of your document

CREATING HEADERS AND FOOTERS THAT UPDATE THEMSELVES

The Insert AutoText button on the Header and Footer toolbar enables you to choose from a series of boilerplate AutoText entries that include much of the information people typically place in headers, such as page numbers, author's name, date, and filename, as shown in Figure 5.16.

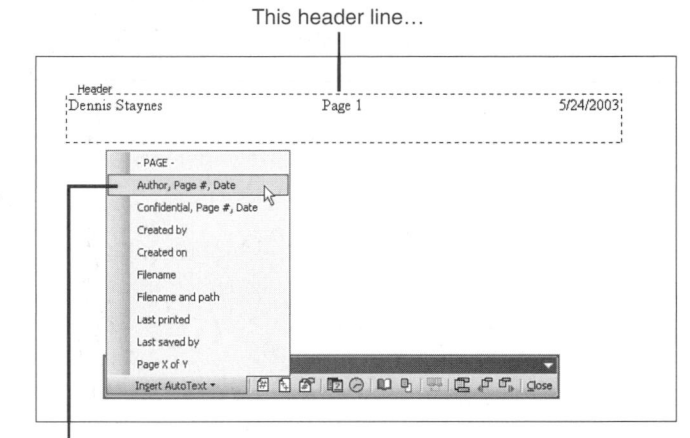

Figure 5.16
Many of the AutoText entries you can place in a header can update automatically as information in your document changes.

...comes from this AutoText entry

Much of this information is inserted in the form of fields, which Word can update automatically as you edit your document. For example, if you change the Author's name in the Summary tab of the Properties dialog box, the name changes in your header or footer the next time you update your fields.

→ For more information about working with fields, **see** Chapter 23, "Automating Your Documents with Field Codes," **p. 771**.

> **TIP**
>
> Word aligns the three-part AutoText entries that are separated by commas using the built-in tab stops associated with the Header or Footer styles.
>
> For example, if you choose Author, Page #, Date, Word displays the author's name at the left edge of the pane, the page number centered in the pane, and the date at the right edge of the pane. After you've inserted the AutoText entry, you can edit its contents and adjust its location if you want.

In addition to the AutoText entries, other buttons on the Header and Footer toolbar insert fields. For example, the Insert Date button inserts a date field. If you include this field in your header or footer and reopen your document tomorrow, Word automatically updates the date to the current date when you print the document or update all the fields in your document.

Similarly, the Time button inserts a time field that updates whenever you update fields or print your document. Or, if you include the total number of pages in your document by clicking the Insert Number of Pages button, Word updates that number as you add pages to your document.

TIP

> You can add the date or time anywhere in the body of your document. Choose Insert, Date and Time. In fact, you can add most of the fields you see on the Header and Footer toolbar to any portion of your document by using the Insert, Field command.

INSERTING PAGE NUMBERS WITHOUT VIEWING THE HEADER OR FOOTER

You can insert page numbers without working in the Header and Footer toolbar, like this:

1. With the insertion point in the document area (not the header or footer), choose Insert, Page Numbers. The Page Numbers dialog box appears (see Figure 5.17).

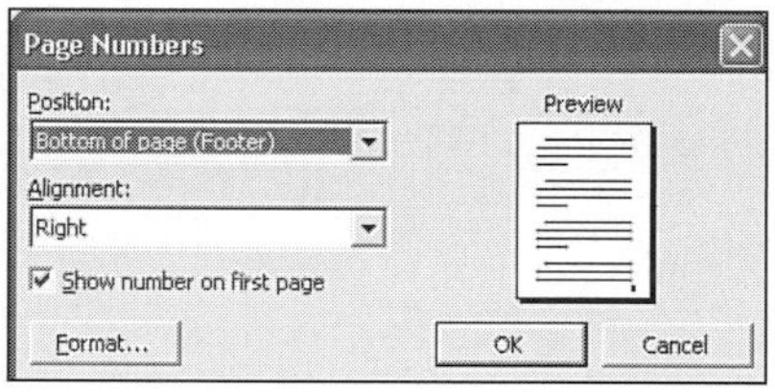

Figure 5.17
The Page Numbers dialog box.

2. In the Position drop-down box, choose whether to place the page numbers in the header or footer.

3. Choose the Alignment for the page number.

4. If you don't want a page number on the first page, clear the Show Number on First Page check box.

5. If you want more control over how your page number is formatted, click Format and establish settings in the Page Number Format dialog box (see Figure 5.18); click OK when you're finished doing so.

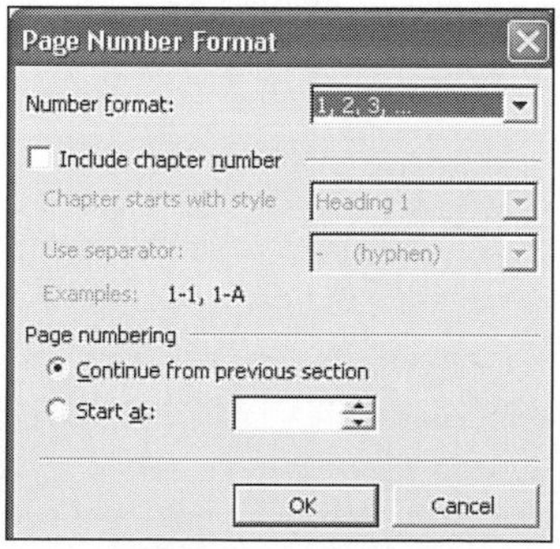

Figure 5.18
The Page Number Format dialog box.

→ To learn techniques you need to know in order to use the chapter numbering feature built into the Page Number Format dialog box, **see** "Adding Chapter Numbers to Your Captions," **p. 700**.

6. In the Page Numbers dialog box, click OK to apply the page numbering you've specified.

CREATING DIFFERENT HEADERS AND FOOTERS IN THE SAME DOCUMENT

By default, the headers and footers you create are the same on every page of your document. If you create sections in your document, however, you can create various headers and footers in your document. Specifically, for each section you can create

- A different header and footer for each section
- One header and footer for even pages and another header and footer for odd pages
- One header for the first page and another for subsequent pages

Initially, when you create a header or footer, it is linked throughout your document. That's how Word knows to use the same header and the same footer on each page of your document.

When you first divide your document into sections, the second (and any additional) section starts out with the same header as the first section. Word assumes that when you make a change in one section's header or footer, you'll want to make the same change in all your other headers or footers. Similarly, all your footers are connected to their fellow "feet."

You can tell when a header or footer is taking its cues from a previous one because the words "Same as Previous" appear at the upper right of the header or footer area (see Figure 5.19). In addition, the Link to Previous button is pressed down on the Header or Footer toolbar.

Figure 5.19
A header linked to a previous header.

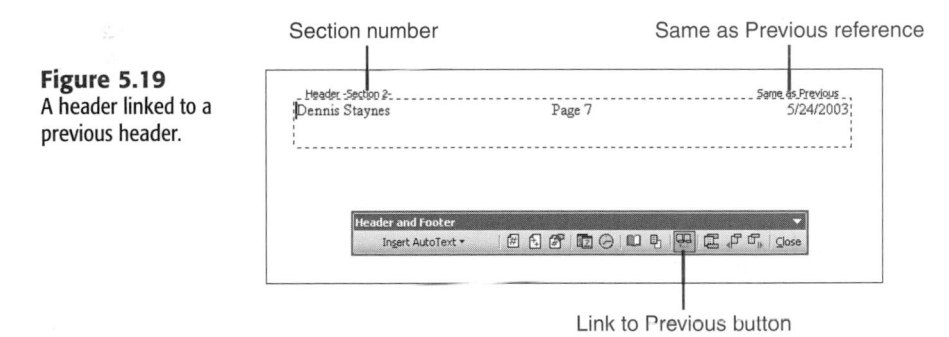

Section number

Same as Previous reference

Link to Previous button

CREATING DIFFERENT HEADERS AND FOOTERS FOR EACH SECTION

By default, when you create additional sections in a Word document, these new sections use headers and footers identical to those you created when your document contained only one section. Word enables you to create separate headers and footers for each section, by unlinking a section's header and footer from the headers and footers in the preceding section. To change a section's header or footer without changing those in other sections as well, follow these steps:

1. Choose View, Header and Footer. When the Header pane appears, you can see that it also contains a section designation.

2. Use the Show Next button to navigate to the section for which you want a different header. The Header pane for the next section appears, and the Link to Previous button on the Header and Footer toolbar becomes available.

3. Click the Link to Previous button to toggle it off (thereby disconnecting the header or footer from others in previous sections).

4. Change the header text for the section you want to change.

5. Click the Close button.

Check your document in Print Preview. The header in the section that you changed should now be different from the headers in the previous sections.

NOTE

> Changing one section's headers or footers can impact other sections you did not intend to change. To understand how, it helps to understand more clearly how Word links headers and footers through a simple example: a document containing three sections.
>
> Assume that you created your header before you divided the document into sections; as mentioned previously, the newly created sections use the same headers and footers as the original section. The third section of the document has the same heading as the first and second sections.
>
> You now decide to change the header in the second section so that it is different from the header in the first section. To do so, you first toggle off Link to Previous (as described in the preceding section) and then edit the header as needed.
>
> But the third section remains linked to the second, and Link to Previous is still enabled in the third section. Therefore, any changes made to the second section are reflected in the third section.

If you want to change the heading of one section in the middle of a sequence of sections without changing the headings in subsequent sections, do the following:

Before you change the section in the middle, go to the first section after it that you don't want changed and toggle off the Link to Previous button in the Header and Footer toolbar.

This approach has one limitation: It does not allow you to directly link the first and third sections so that changes to the first section's headers or footers are reflected in the third section as well.

You can solve this problem like this: Bookmark the text in the first heading that you also want to appear in the third heading (excluding any automatic page numbering fields). Then, in the third heading, insert a cross-reference to the bookmarked text. Whenever you edit the first heading, select the third heading and press F9 to update it; the text now matches the revised first heading.

Of course, you can disconnect a footer from previous footers by displaying the footer and then following the same steps.

NOTE

If you later decide that you want a disconnected header to once again be a reflection of the previous section's header, redisplay the Header pane and use the Show Next button to display the header for the section you changed. Click the Link to Previous button. Word displays a message asking whether you want to delete this header and connect to the header/footer in the previous section. Choose Yes.

Keep this in mind: If there are sections that follow the one you are changing that are linked to it by the Link to Previous setting in those following sections, they will change as well.

Creating Separate Headers for Odd and Even Pages

It's common for books and other long documents to utilize different headers for left and right pages. A left-hand header might, for example, include the book name or chapter, whereas a right-hand header contains a specific chapter section.

To create separate headers or footers for odd and even pages, use the Page Setup dialog box. Again, the steps listed here show you how to create different headers for odd and even pages. To create different footers, substitute *footer* for *header* throughout the next procedure. Follow these steps:

1. Choose View, Header and Footer. When the Header pane appears, you'll see that it also contains a section designation.
2. Click the Show Next button to navigate to the section for which you want different headers for odd and even pages. The header pane for the next section appears.
3. Click the Page Setup button. The Page Setup dialog box appears (refer to Figure 5.11).
4. Place a check mark in the Different Odd and Even check box.
5. Click OK. Word redisplays your document, and the Header toolbar title changes to either Even Page Header—Section X or Odd Page Header—Section X.

Type the text you want to appear in the Even Header pane and then click the Show Next or Show Previous button to find the Odd Header pane and complete it.

Creating a Different Header for the First Page

Often, regardless of the headers or footers that appear on most of your pages, you'll want a different header or footer on the first page—or no header or footer at all. Follow these steps:

1. Choose View, Header and Footer.

2. If your document has multiple sections, click Show Next to navigate to the section for which you want a different first page header. (If you want a different first page header for the entire document, you can skip this step.)

3. Click the Page Setup button. The Page Setup dialog box appears (refer to Figure 5.11).

4. Check the Different First Page check box. If you are creating a different first page header for the entire document, choose Whole Document in the Apply To drop-down list box.

5. Click OK.

Word redisplays your document, placing a blank header on the first page of the section or of the whole document, depending on what you selected in step 4. You can add text to the header, or simply leave it blank.

 If you want separate first page headers in every section, but Word only creates one in the first section, see "How to Make Word Create Separate First Page Headers in Every Section," in the "Troubleshooting" section of this chapter.

NOTE

When you no longer need a header or footer, you can simply select its contents and delete them.

WORKING WITH MULTIPLE COLUMNS

One of the hallmarks of newsletters and other desktop-published documents is the use of multiple newspaper-style columns, in which text snakes from the bottom of one column to the top of the next column.

Word gives you extensive control over columns. You can create uneven columns, specifying exact widths for each and the amount of whitespace that appears between the columns. You also can add a new column to existing columns. If columns are turned on for more than one page, Word can flow text from the bottom of the last column on one page to the top of the first column of the next page.

To help you refine your layouts, Word can also draw vertical lines between each column—although you can't control the placement or formatting of those lines.

TIP

If you need to set up a column layout for part of a page, where specific text, graphics, or other elements must remain in a rigid location and not move as you edit them, use Word tables (see Chapter 12, "Structuring and Organizing Information with Tables").

CREATING MULTIPLE COLUMNS THE EASY WAY

If you want to create multiple columns of the same width, click on the Columns toolbar button. (If you want to create multiple columns for only part of the document, select the text you want to split into columns and then choose the Columns toolbar button.)

When you choose Columns, a box appears, displaying four columns. Click on the box and drag across until the number of columns you want is highlighted (see Figure 5.20). Then release the mouse button. Word applies the columns either to your entire document or, if you have selected text, to only that text. Word also displays your document in Print Layout view so that the columns are immediately visible. You can, however, switch back to Normal (or another) view and work there, if you choose.

Figure 5.20
Selecting columns from the Standard toolbar.

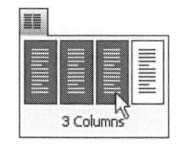

3 Columns

If you're creating multiple columns for only a selected portion of your document, Word inserts section breaks before and after the text you've selected.

NOTE

Although the Columns button displays four columns when you open it, you can use it to create up to six columns. Just click on the rightmost column (number four) and drag to the right.

TIP

The Columns button is handy for making quick headings that span multiple columns. Select the text that you want to spread across your columns, click the Columns button, and select only 1 column.

GETTING MORE CONTROL THROUGH THE COLUMNS DIALOG BOX

You may want more control than the Columns button can give you. You might want columns of different widths, for example. You might want to change the exact spacing between individual columns or add a line between columns. To do any of these things, choose Format, Columns from the menu. The Columns dialog box opens (see Figure 5.21).

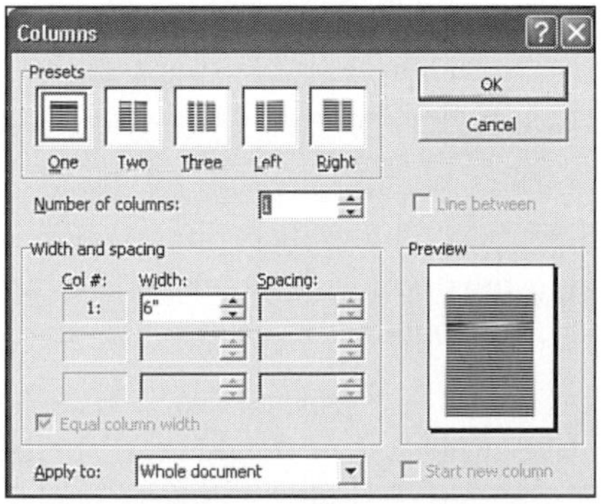

Figure 5.21
Working in the Columns dialog box.

Columns comes with five preset column formats: basic Qne column, Two-column, and Three-column formats, as well as two-column formats in which the Left or Right column is smaller.

The width of your columns depends on your left and right margins; the wider the margins, the narrower the columns will be. If you choose one of the unequal width presets, Left or Right, the "named" column is set to a little less than one-half the width of the other column. For example, on a page with 1-inch left and right margins and two columns, selecting the Left preset makes the left column 1.83" and the right column 4.17" with a 0.5" space between; selecting the Right preset switches the widths of the columns.

The gutter between your columns is controlled by the Spacing measurement. Generally, it's a good idea to keep your spacing between 0.25" and 0.5". (Word's default setting is 0.5".) You might want to use a larger measurement if you are also using the Line Between check box to place a vertical line between each column, or if you intend to use the empty space for figures.

You also can specify the number of columns directly, using the Number of Columns spin box. Word won't create columns narrower than 0.5", so if you're using Word's default formatting of 1.25" left and right margins on an 8.5" page, you can specify up to 12 columns— realistically, less, because you inevitably need at least a little space between the columns for readability.

NOTE

Left-aligned text can often remain readable with slightly narrower space between columns than justified text.

Check Line Between to tell Word to place a line between each column.

NOTE

Word does not add space between columns to compensate when you add a line between columns. If your space between columns is narrower than 0.5", check to make sure that the line you've added does not overlap the text to its right.

In the Apply To box, choose whether you want your column settings to apply to This Section, to the Whole Document, or from This Point Forward. If you choose This Point Forward, Word inserts a section break at your insertion point unless you're already at the start of a new section.

If you've selected text before opening the Columns dialog box, your choices here are Selected Text or Whole Document, if the document has only one section; the choices are Selected Text or Selected Sections if the document has more than one section.

As already mentioned, if you create columns for selected text, section breaks are added before and after the text. As you make changes, Word shows their effects in the Preview box of the Columns dialog box.

NOTE

Columns of unequal width—your first column being narrower than your others, for example—are used to add more visual variety to a large-format publication, such as a newsletter. There are no hard-and-fast rules for sizing your columns, other than to be sure that your text can still be read easily. If many of the lines in your column end in hyphenated or broken words, your column is too narrow.

CHANGING COLUMN WIDTHS WITH THE RULER

After you've created columns, you can adjust column width and the space between columns by hand, using the ruler.

If all your columns are of the same width, you can use the ruler to increase or decrease the width of all the columns (and thus the space between columns) at the same time. If you start out with columns that are all the same width, you'll end up with columns that are all the same width.

If your columns are of different widths, you can use the ruler to change the width of each column individually. In this case, as you widen or narrow a column, the space between that column and the next increases or decreases to compensate.

NOTE

Changing column widths with the ruler does not affect overall page margins.

To change column widths with the ruler, make sure that you're in Print Layout view, and that the ruler is visible (choose View, Ruler). If all the column widths are equal, click and drag the column marker on the ruler (see Figure 5.22) to make adjustments—a ScreenTip tells you whether you're working with the left or right margin of the column.

Click the left or right margin
and drag to a new column width

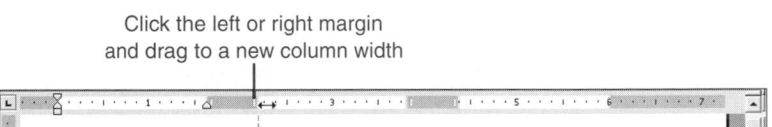

Figure 5.22
The ruler can be used to adjust column widths quickly.

If the column widths are unequal, you can drag the Left or Right Margin markers to adjust the column widths; the width of the gutter between the columns increases or decreases, as you would expect. If the column widths are unequal, though, you have one additional column marker available, called Move Column. If you click and drag on the Move Column marker, the width of the gutter stays the same, whereas the widths of the columns to the left and right of the gutter get adjusted.

5

TIP

> If you hold down the Alt key as you drag a column marker, Word shows you precise measurements for column and gutter widths in the ruler area.

TIP

> After you've moved your columns to a new place, you can use the Undo/Redo buttons to toggle between two different widths for your columns. It's a quick way to compare two choices.

NOTE

> You can't drag one column marker into the space reserved for another column. If you need to widen a column beyond the space currently available for it, you must first narrow an adjacent column to make more room for it.

GETTING MORE CONTROL OVER INDIVIDUAL COLUMN WIDTHS

You can set precise column widths in the Columns dialog box (refer to Figure 5.21). Choose Format, Columns to display the dialog box. If your current settings are for columns of equal width, clear the Equal Column Width check box. This enables you to work on any column listed in the Width and Spacing area.

For each column, set the Width and the Spacing. (You can move from one box to the next by pressing Tab.) If you have more than three columns, a scrollbar appears to the left of the Col # list. Use it to scroll to the columns you want to set.

STARTING A NEW COLUMN

Sometimes, as you edit your document, you'll realize you need to change the number of columns that appear from your insertion point onward. For example, your document might consist of only one column for the first several pages, but you now need to enter material that should be formatted in three columns. There are two ways to change the number of columns in a document from the insertion point onward:

- Select Format, Columns; apply the column settings to This Point Forward; and check the Start New Column box that appears at the bottom right of the dialog box.
- Insert a column break by choosing Insert, Break (refer to Figure 5.1). Then in the Break dialog box click the Column Break option in the Break Types section and click OK.

TIP

> If you're having trouble seeing where to insert column breaks, you can see—and edit—the whole page at the same time by clicking the arrow next to the Zoom control and selecting Whole Page.

REMOVING COLUMN BREAKS

You remove column breaks just as you would remove a manual page break. The easiest way to see the break is to switch to Normal view (see Figure 5.23) by choosing View, Normal. Then select the Column Break line and press Delete to remove it.

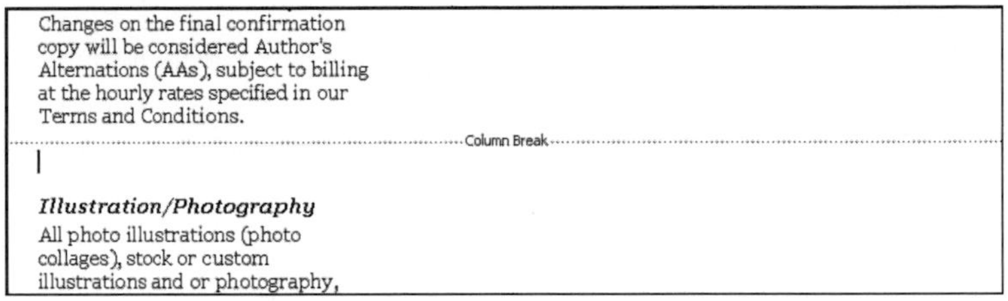

Figure 5.23
Viewing a column
break in Normal view.

Changes on the final confirmation
copy will be considered Author's
Alternations (AAs), subject to billing
at the hourly rates specified in our
Terms and Conditions.

··Column Break···

Illustration/Photography
All photo illustrations (photo
collages), stock or custom
illustrations and or photography,

MAKING YOUR COLUMNS EVEN

Sometimes you want to balance your columns so that the text is spread evenly over all your columns. This choice can be made for aesthetic or practical reasons.

It's not always easy to balance your columns and at the same time stay consistent with your paragraph pagination settings. For example, if you've specified that two paragraphs must stay together (Keep with Next), you limit Word's capability to move lines around to even things out.

Word does provide an easy solution, however: Use a continuous section break at the point where you want the column to end. Word will then end the section wherever necessary to balance the columns. Follow these steps:

1. Create your columns, if you have not already done so.
2. If necessary, switch to Print Layout view by choosing View, Print Layout.
3. At the end of the text that you want to balance, click to place the insertion point.
4. Choose Insert, Break.
5. From the Break dialog box, select a Continuous section break.
6. Click OK to close the dialog box.

USING BORDERS AND SHADING

Borders and shading add visual interest to your document. Word allows you to place a border around a page, or add a shaded background to a page. Word 2003's Borders and Shading features are covered in detail in the "Adding Table Borders and Shading" section of Chapter 12. Bordering a page is covered here.

5

NOTE

> Word's Borders and Shading features can be used with any text you select, including words, paragraphs, table cells, and tables.

CREATING PAGE BORDERS

Page borders have various uses. For example, they are effective for report title pages. Figure 5.24 shows an example.

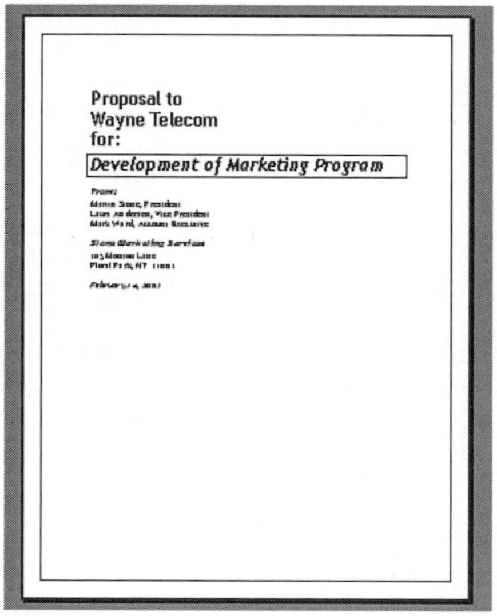

Figure 5.24
Using a page border on a report title page.

To add a border around a page, work in the Page Border tab of the Borders and Shading dialog box. To display this dialog box, choose Format, Borders and Shading, and display the Page Border tab (see Figure 5.25).

CHOOSING WHICH TYPE OF BORDER TO CREATE

In the Setting area, you can choose from among five types of borders:

- **None.** No border, the default setting. Click this setting to remove a border that already exists.

- **Box.** Places a line along each of the four sides of your page.

- **Shadow.** Borders all four sides but places a thicker border on the bottom and right sides, to create a shadow effect.

- **3-D.** Makes it appear that your page actually rises from its background.

- **Custom.** Enables you to customize your own border, one side at a time.

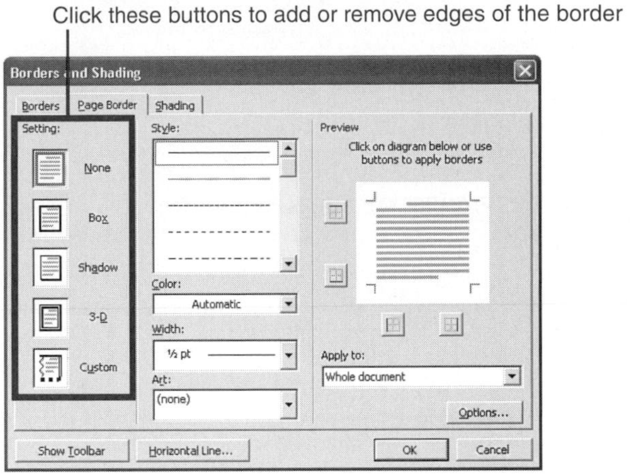

Click these buttons to add or remove edges of the border

Figure 5.25
The Page Border tab
of the Borders and
Shading dialog box.

When you choose one of these settings (except for Custom), Word reflects them in the Preview window; you can then edit each edge of the border individually, as discussed in the next section.

SETTING THE STYLE, COLOR, AND WIDTH OF YOUR PAGE BORDER

After you select a type of page border, you can control the line style, color, and width of the line you use:

- To choose a dotted, double, or triple line, select the line you want from the Style scroll box.
- To specify a color for your page border, click on the Color drop-down box and choose the color from the palette that appears. You can also click More Line Colors to choose from a wider selection of colors.
- To specify a thickness for your border lines, click on the Width drop-down box and select any of the options there, from 1/2 point to 6 point.

> **NOTE**
> As you make changes, you can view their effects in the Preview box (unless you have selected the Custom setting).

You can edit each edge individually. First, click the edge you want to reformat. Then, set the Style, Color, and/or Width settings you want; then click again on the edge you want to reformat, and the current settings are applied. If you don't click on the edge first, every change you make to the style, color, and/or width will affect all four borders.

USING A GRAPHICAL BORDER

Word provides a library of repetitive images you can use as borderlines. To use one, click the Art drop-down box and choose the image from there. Figure 5.26 shows a sample.

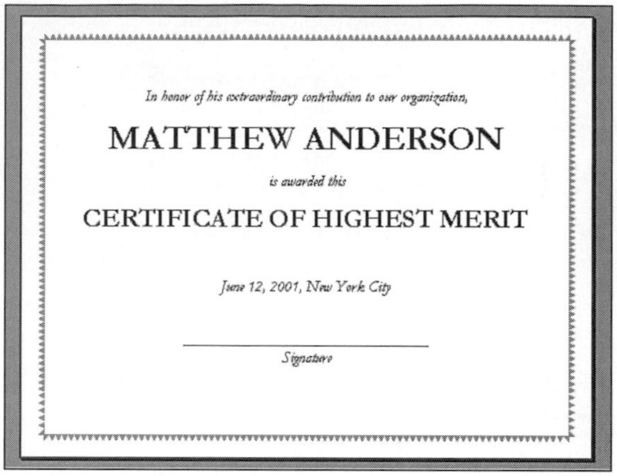

Figure 5.26
Using an image as a page border.

CAUTION

Although these images can be helpful in some documents, such as retail fliers, in many other situations they are viewed as tacky. Be careful how you use them.

SPECIFYING WHICH PAGES ARE BORDERED

As mentioned earlier, one use for page borders is to set apart the cover of your document. Word gives you complete control over which pages you border. Click the Apply To button and choose one of these options:

- **Whole Document.** Borders the entire document.
- **This Section.** Borders all pages in your insertion point's current section; if your document has one section, borders every page.
- **This Section—First Page Only.** Borders only the first page of the current section. Note that you can use this feature to border the first page of every section if you want.
- **This Section—All Except First Page.** Borders every page except the first page in the current section. Again, you can establish this setting individually for each section.

CONTROLLING THE LOCATION OF PAGE BORDERS

By default, Word places borders 24 points (1/3 inch) away from each edge of your page. You can change these settings. To do so, follow these steps:

1. Choose Format, Borders and Shading.
2. Click the Page Border tab.
3. Click the Options button. The Border and Shading Options dialog box appears (see Figure 5.27).

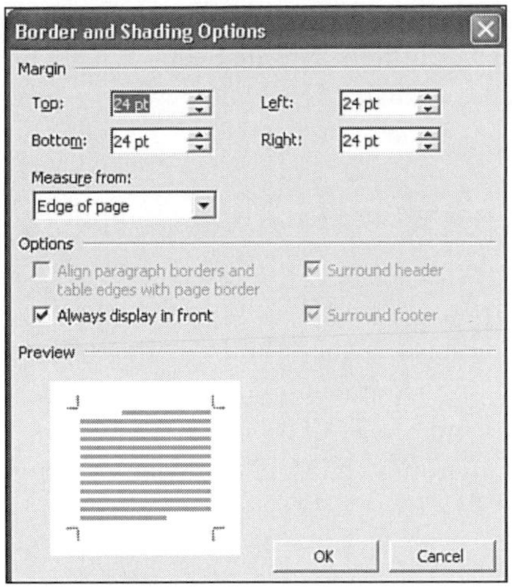

Figure 5.27
Controlling where
page borders appear
on the page.

4. Set your custom margins in the T<u>o</u>p, Bott<u>o</u>m, L<u>e</u>ft, and Right spin boxes.

5. When you're finished, click OK.

> **TIP**
>
> By default, Word measures page borders from the edge of the page. If you want to make sure that the borders always stay a specific distance from text, choose Text in the Measu<u>r</u>e From box. You can then choose whether you want the border to surround the page header or footer, or whether you want to tightly align the border to paragraph borders and table edges.

TROUBLESHOOTING

HOW TO AVOID ACCIDENTALLY CHANGING PARAGRAPH MARKS INSTEAD OF MARGINS

You may have dragged the mouse pointer when it did not resemble a two-headed arrow. You can control both page margins and paragraph indents from the ruler, and what you change depends on the mouse pointer shape at the time you drag. Hover your mouse pointer over the ruler icon you want to drag, and a ScreenTip tells you which icon you've chosen.

WHAT TO DO IF YOUR SECTION BREAKS INCORRECTLY ADD BLANK PAGES

If you select text before changing margins in the Page Setup dialog box and then choose Selected Text in the Appl<u>y</u> To drop-down box, Word creates a new section for the text you selected and starts the new section on the following page. If you already had a Next Page section break immediately preceding this, you now have two consecutive section breaks, each starting a new page. You also have one blank page. To eliminate the blank page, you can replace the first Next Page section break with a Continuous section break.

In the future, when you encounter this situation, while you are still in the Page Setup dialog box, click the Layout tab and select Continuous in the Section Start drop-down list. When you click OK to dismiss the Page Setup dialog box, the new section is created with a continuous page break, so there is no blank page.

HOW TO MAKE WORD CREATE SEPARATE FIRST PAGE HEADERS IN EVERY SECTION

To create a separate first page header in every section, you must specify the first page headers individually. There are two ways to do so. You can place the insertion point in a section, open the Page Setup dialog box, and place a check in the Different First Page check box; then move to the next section and do the same. Or you can display the Header and Footer toolbar and use the Show Previous and Show Next buttons to navigate through the document, correcting them one at a time from within the Page Setup dialog box.

CHAPTER 6

PRINTING AND FAXING IN WORD

In this chapter

PRINTING THE ENTIRE DOCUMENT

Basic Word printing is as simple as it gets. Click the Print button in the Standard toolbar. Word sends one copy of your entire document to your current printer.

> **NOTE**
>
> To print from Word or any Windows application, you must have at least one printer connected to your PC with the appropriate configuration files (called "device drivers") installed that allow it to work with Windows.

Much of the time, this is all you need to know about printing. At other times, however, you'll want to take advantage of Word's more sophisticated printing options, which require more than clicking the Print button. This chapter covers those other times.

> **TIP**
>
> You can print a Word document without opening Word. In Windows Explorer (or in a folder window you've opened on the Windows Desktop, such as My Computer or My Documents), locate and right-click on the file you want to print, and choose Print from the shortcut menu. Word opens, displaying the document you asked to print and then prints one copy of the document on your default printer. When finished sending data to the printer, Word closes.
>
> To print only selected headings from a document outline, use the buttons on the Outlining toolbar to display the document at the level of detail with which you want to print, and then click the Print button on the Standard toolbar.
>
> Creating a document outline is discussed in Chapter 18, "Outlining: Practical Techniques for Organizing Any Document."

 For various printing troubleshooting techniques, see "Troubleshooting" at the end of this chapter.

SPECIFYING WHAT TO PRINT

Suppose that you don't simply want to print one copy of your entire document. Perhaps you want to use a different printer, print several copies of the document, or print only part of a document. You can control these and other aspects of printing from the Print dialog box (see Figure 6.1). To open this box, choose File, Print.

The following sections cover options found in the Print dialog box.

CHOOSING WHICH PAGES TO PRINT

Rather than having Word print every page of your document (as it does by default), you can use the Print dialog box to control which pages or parts of your document are printed. You can

■ Print the page your insertion point (text cursor) is in by choosing Current Page from the Page Range area of the dialog box

■ Highlight specific portions of text and print that text by clicking the Selection button

■ Select specific pages to print by entering the page numbers in the text box next to the Pages button

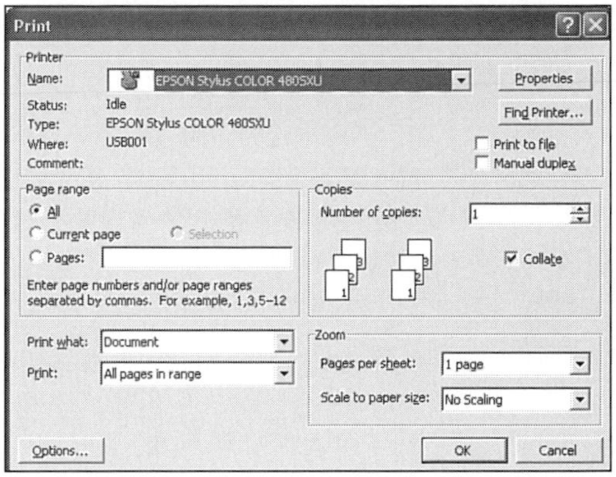

Figure 6.1
From the Print dialog box, you can specify special printing options.

If you specify individual pages, Word understands hyphens and commas, as in the following examples:

1–3	Prints pages 1 through 3
1,2,6	Prints pages 1, 2, and 6
1–3,5,8	Prints pages 1 through 3 and pages 5 and 8
p1s2–p2s4	Starts printing with page 1 of section 2 and prints all pages through page 2 of section 4

→ For more information about sections, **see** Chapter 5, "Controlling Page Features," **p. 157**.

PRINTING ODD OR EVEN PAGES

If you want to print only odd or even pages, you can make this choice from the Print drop-down list box in the Print dialog box. Choose Odd Pages or Even Pages rather than the default setting, All Pages in Range.

Some people have traditionally used this feature to print on both sides of paper even if their printers do not provide this capability. However, as is covered in the "Printing on Both Sides of Your Paper" section of this chapter, Word offers a Manual Duplex printing feature that can accomplish the same task more elegantly.

CONTROLLING NUMBER OF COPIES AND COLLATION

You can use the Number of Copies spin box to specify the number of copies you want to print. Either click the spin-box arrows or type the number of copies you want to print.

6

The Number of Copies spin box is set to 1 by default, so you can simply type a new number and click OK (or press Enter) to immediately print several copies.

By default, Word automatically *collates* multiple copies of your document by sending the document to the printer, waiting a moment, and then sending it again. This way, you get output arranged in page order. Because you usually want your document to print in page order, what could be wrong with that?

Only one thing—it may take longer. Printers typically process each page in your document separately. When the second copy of a collated document starts printing, none of the processing from the earlier pages remains in memory. The processing must be done over again. This repetitive processing can create significant bottlenecks in your print queue if your documents contain extensive graphics or formatting.

Laser printers can, however, print several consecutive copies of the same page without reprocessing them. So if you're willing to manually collate your document—or if you're lucky enough to have someone around to help—you *might* get your print job done sooner by disabling Word's collating function. To do so, clear the Collate check box.

PRINTING ON BOTH SIDES OF YOUR PAPER

A few printers are designed to print on both sides of the paper at once, allowing you to print documents such as books with all pages in consecutive order. Most printers, however, can only print on one side at a time. You can still perform duplex printing on these printers, using Word's Manual Duplex printing feature.

To use Manual Duplex printing, check the Manual Duplex printing check box. Then, wait until your printer prints all the odd-numbered pages in your document. Word displays a dialog box asking you to remove the printout and place it back in your printer's input bin. Click OK. Word prints the remaining pages.

When you place the printout back in your printer's input bin, be careful to follow your printer's directions to make sure that your pages will not print upside down, or on the wrong side (in which case you'd be printing on the same side twice).

Printing on both sides of the paper by running the paper through twice can cause some printers to jam. Check your printer's manual to make sure that this isn't a problem for your printer.

This feature does not always work well with printers that use their own spooler software for background printing–for instance, many inkjet printers. Word hands off all the "fronts" to the inkjet printer's spooler, and, assuming that the pages have actually been printed, prompts the user to turn all the sheets over—often, long before the sheets are actually ready to be turned over. Worse, when this prompt appears, you can do nothing in Word until you click OK to indicate that you actually *have* turned over the sheets.

If you encounter this problem, revert to printing even pages and then printing odd pages separately, as you might have done in earlier versions of Word.

N O T E   You may occasionally need to reverse the order in which your printer prints duplex pages (for example, print from back to front). From the Print dialog box, click Options; then check the Front of the Sheet check box, the Back of the Sheet check box, or both.

PRINTING SEVERAL PAGES ON A SHEET

You can print more than one page on a single sheet of paper. There are many applications for this. For example, this makes it easier to print a booklet with staples in the center. It also makes it easier to provide compact handouts of outlines and other document elements, much as presenters have long done with PowerPoint presentation handouts.

→ For more information about creating booklets and other documents that are printed several pages to a sheet, **see** Chapter 5, "Controlling Page Features," **p. 157**.

To print several pages on a sheet, choose an option from the Pages Per Sheet drop-down box of the Print dialog box: 1 page, 2 pages, 4 pages, 6 pages, 8 pages, or 16 pages. Click OK when you're ready to print.

Depending on the number of pages you choose, the size of your original document, and your other printer settings, Word arranges the pages on the sheet to fit as many as possible. For instance, if you choose four pages, Word prints the pages right side up, one in each of the sheet's four corners. However, if you print eight pages, Word prints the pages sideways on the sheet, in two rows of four pages apiece.

C A U T I O N   You can't combine paper saving techniques. For example, you can print drafts on both sides of the paper, or print several pages on one side of a sheet, but you can't do both.

C A U T I O N   Be careful that you don't create drafts with text that is illegibly small. Although two pages on a sheet may be barely readable, printing several pages on a sheet tends to be useful primarily for providing a quick sense of layout.

SCALING A DOCUMENT TO A DIFFERENT PAPER SIZE

Those who work in international environments know that different regions use different standards for paper sizes. Word makes it easier to deal with these differences by simplifying the process of switching between the many paper sizes.

6

To scale a document so that it prints well at another paper size, display the Print dialog box. Then choose the paper size you want from the Scale to Paper Size drop-down box. In addition to U.S. letter size (8 1/2"×11"), Word provides many other options. The following options are likely to be most useful to typical users:

- Legal
- Executive
- A4 and A5 (European/ISO standard)
- #10 Envelope
- DL, C6, or 132×220mm Envelope (European/ISO standard)
- Monarch Envelope
- Index Card (A6, 5×8" or 8×10" sizes)

NOTE

> Word can scale printing to many sizes that were once unsupported. These include three standard Photo Paper sizes, as well as A3, B3, SuperA3, US B 11×17", and Half Letter (5.5×8.5") sizes.

PRINTING ACCOMPANYING INFORMATION ABOUT YOUR DOCUMENT

You can print information about your document other than its text. Using the Print What list box, you can print any of the following information about your document:

- The document's properties (see Chapter 34, "Managing Word More Effectively")
- Document Showing Markup, the document with all comments and revision marks displayed (see Chapter 26, "Managing Document Collaboration and Revisions")
- List of Markup, a list that includes all comments and revision marks but not the entire document
- Styles you used within the document and the formatting you defined for them (see Chapter 10, "Streamlining Your Formatting with Styles")
- AutoText entries (for example, boilerplate text or graphics; see Chapter 9, "Automating Your Documents")
- Custom keyboard shortcuts you defined within this document or for the template attached to the document (see Chapter 31, "Customizing Word")

Because the controls for printing specific document elements are scattered throughout Word, Table 6.1 lists all the document-related elements you can print and specifies the command or commands used to print them. In some cases, you must display information in your document before you can print it; these cases are listed in the fourth column of the table.

TABLE 6.1   PRINTING ELEMENTS OF WORD FILES

Element	Included with Document	Prints Separately	Must Be Displayed Before Printing	Notes
Document Markup	X	X		Can be printed with document or separately
AutoText Entries		X		
Envelopes				Covered later in this chapter
Field Codes	X		X	
Hidden Text	X		X	
Shortcut Key Assignments		X		
Styles		X		
Properties		X		
Outlines				Display in Outline view before printing

OTHER USEFUL PRINT SETTINGS

In addition to the print settings you've already seen, Word enables you to control several additional settings through the Print tab of the Print Options dialog box. You can display this dialog box by choosing File, Print, and clicking Options, or by choosing Tools, Options, Print (see Figure 6.2).

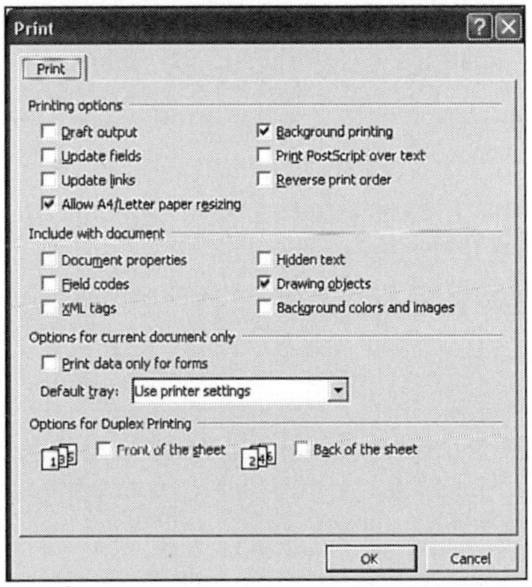

Figure 6.2
Use this dialog box to set special printing options.

6

CONTROLLING PRINT OPTIONS

Among the options Word allows you to control from the Print tab of the Print (or Options) dialog box are the following:

- **Draft Output.** Occasionally, you may want to print a document with extensive graphics and formatting, but you don't need to see the graphics or formatting right now—only the text. If so, you can often print more quickly by checking this box; Word prints your document with minimal formatting and no graphics.

- **Update Fields, and Update Links**. If your document contains fields, checking Update Fields tells Word to update those fields before you print the document. This way, the document is entirely up to date whenever you print it. Similarly, checking Update Links tells Word to update any links to other documents before printing.

CAUTION

> Although you'll often want to update fields and links before you print, sometimes you shouldn't. For instance, to accurately track a project (or for legal reasons), you may need to print a memo precisely as it appeared several months ago, with old dates and old numbers. Before you print such a document, clear the Update Fields and Update Links check boxes.

- **Allow A4/Letter Paper Resizing.** Word permits you to switch automatically between the standard 8 1/2"×11" paper size used in the United States and the slightly longer, narrower "A4" size used in most countries. To enable this automatic switching feature, check the Allow A4/Letter Paper Resizing check box. With this box checked, Word adjusts page layout and margins automatically to compensate for changes in paper size when the document is about to be printed. These changes are not stored permanently and do not affect the document as it appears onscreen. In the future, if you instruct Word to print the document at 8 1/2"×11" again, Word will do so.

TIP

> If you only want to adjust to A4 paper size for the document you're currently printing, display the Print dialog box and choose A4 210×297 mm (or Letter 8 1/2×11) from the Scale to Paper Size drop-down box.

- **Background Printing.** By default, Word prints "in the background." This means that you can go back to work in your document more quickly, but you may find that your print job runs more slowly. If you find that Word prints too slowly, try clearing this check box.

CAUTION

> The downside of disabling background printing is that Word doesn't allow you to start working in the file again until it has sent all pages to your printer (or more precisely, to Windows's print spooling file).

- **Print PostScript over Text.** Sometimes you need to accommodate watermarks or other surprinted text created in Word for the Macintosh. The Print PostScript over Text option enables PostScript code that may have been placed in a Macintosh Word document to be printed above text, not beneath it.

- **Reverse Print Order.** Occasionally, you may need to reverse the order in which your printer outputs your pages. For instance, you might have a printer that stacks pages in reverse order (the completed pages are ordered with the last page first and first page last). Many inkjet printers generate face-up output in reverse order. Many laser printers also have a face-up reverse output tray that is used to print on heavier paper stock or envelopes. To get output on those printers in the correct order, check this box.

CAUTION

Note that some of these printers, most notably Hewlett-Packard inkjet printers, allow you to change print order outside of Word, using the printer driver built into Windows. If you choose reverse printing in both Word and through the Windows printer driver, the two settings cancel each other out.

CONTROLLING WHAT TO INCLUDE WITH YOUR DOCUMENT WHEN PRINTING

Word provides six options for controlling what elements of your document print. Check the corresponding check box to include each element in your printed document.

- **Document Properties**. Prints a page of information about your document, such as file size, filename, and author information.

- **Field Codes**. Prints the field codes in your document, instead of the results generated by those field codes.

- **XML Tags**. Prints all XML markup within an XML document. This feature is new in Word 2003, the first version of Word with extensive XML support.

- **Hidden Text**. Prints all text marked as hidden.

- **Drawing Objects**. Checked by default, this instructs Word to print all drawings in your document.

- **Background Colors and Images**. Prints background colors, patterns, or images that would otherwise be ignored by Word. This feature is new in Word 2003.

Another option, Print Data Only for Forms, allows you to print a quick record of the responses to a filled-out form, without printing the form itself.

→ For more information about creating and filling in forms, **see** Chapter 28, "Creating Forms," **p. 933**.

CHANGING PAPER SOURCES

In Chapter 5, "Controlling Page Features," you learned that you can choose the size of paper to use in your printer by opening the Page Setup dialog box (choose File, Page Setup) and choosing the Paper Size tab. You also learned that if your printer is equipped with more than one paper tray, you can change the paper tray from the Paper Source tab of the Page Setup dialog box.

If you want Word (and only Word) to use a print tray different from the default setting, you can select a different one from the Print dialog box. In the Print dialog box, open the Default Tray list box and select the tray containing the paper to which you want Word to print.

CAUTION

When you choose a paper tray from the Print dialog box, you are setting a new default paper tray that remains in effect for *all* Word documents (not just the current document). When you change the paper tray from the Page Setup dialog box, you affect only the current document.

NOTE

The paper source settings in the Page Setup dialog box (select File, Page Setup) supersede any paper tray settings in the Print dialog box. In other words, if the paper tray settings are different in the Page Setup dialog box than in the Print Options dialog box, Word uses the settings in the Page Setup dialog box.

CREATING A PRINT FILE FROM WHICH YOU CAN PRINT LATER

Occasionally, you may want to prepare a file to print but not actually print it. Perhaps you want to take it to the fancy laser printer at the office, which can print at much higher resolution than your home printer does, or has color capabilities that your home laser printer doesn't. Or perhaps you're planning to print a newsletter using your local printing shop. In this case, you may need a file that the shop's computers can use directly to generate film that can be used to print your newsletter.

Whatever your reasons, Word enables you to *print to file*—that is, create a disk file that contains all the commands and information a printer needs in order to print the document. To print a document to a file, first make sure that you've installed a printer driver for the printer you ultimately intend to use—otherwise, Word won't know what commands and information to include in the file it creates.

TIP

If you're not sure about the printer's make or model, but you know it is a PostScript printer, Windows's Generic PostScript Printer driver is usually a safe substitute. It's best, however, to check with the people who will be printing your document, and use the driver they specify.

After you make sure that the correct driver is installed, follow these steps:

1. Choose File, Print.
2. In the Name drop-down box, choose the printer on which you will ultimately print the file.
3. Check the Print to File check box (toward the upper right of the Print dialog box).
4. Click OK. Word displays the Print to File dialog box, shown in Figure 6.3.

Figure 6.3
Typing a new file-name in the Print to File dialog box

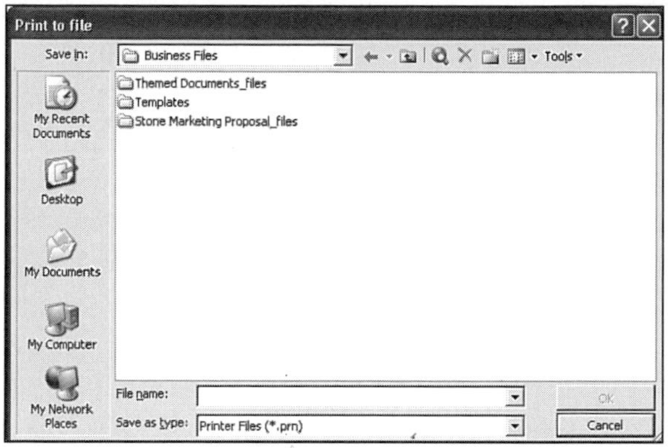

5. Type a name for the file in the File Name box.
6. Browse to the folder where you want to store the printer file.
7. Click OK.

You now have a file that can be printed. If you're having someone else print your document, send the file electronically or hand him a disk containing it—and you're done. But what if you need to print the document yourself—perhaps on your office printer?

This presents an issue. You can't open the file you've created in Word and print it. All you'd get is text interspersed with printer commands. You can't even drag the file to a printer icon because Windows wants to know what program it should open to interpret the data. If you suggest a program, you're back where you started—text interspersed with printer commands.

The solution is a throwback to the oldest days of the MS-DOS operating system that preceded Windows: Copy the file to your printer port from an MS-DOS command session. Here's how:

1. Click Start, Programs, Accessories, Command Prompt. An MS-DOS window opens, as shown in Figure 6.4.
2. At the command prompt, type the following command (where your filename replaces *FILENAME*, and your path information replaces C:*FOLDER*):
   ```
   COPY C:\FOLDER\FILENAME.PRN LPT1 /B
   ```

6

Figure 6.4
Using a DOS window to send a PRN file to your printer.

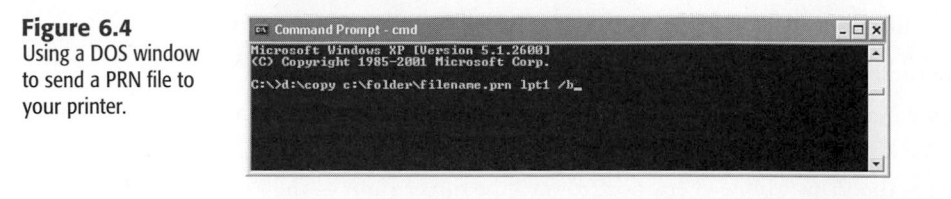

NOTE

> The /B switch used at the end of this Copy command specifies that the data is being sent to the printer in binary format. This solves various problems, including incorrect ASCII coding of higher-level characters and timeouts that can occur when a printer must take too long to process a stream of data.

Be sure to include the .PRN extension. Also be sure to include the path to your file's location.

PRINTING ENVELOPES IN WORD

Word automates envelope and label printing—a process that was once tedious and difficult, especially if you were working with large or nonstandard envelopes.

In the simplest example, assume that you've written a standard business letter, in which the recipient's name and address appear at the top, under the date. To print an accompanying envelope, choose Tools, Letters and Mailings, Envelopes and Labels. The Envelopes and Labels dialog box shown in Figure 6.5 appears (make sure that the Envelopes tab is selected).

When it opens this dialog box, Word searches your letter for the places where you're most likely to have included an address. If it finds something that looks like an address, it places this information in the Delivery Address box on the Envelopes tab. If Word cannot find an address, it leaves the space blank.

CAUTION

> Occasionally, Word may find three other lines that seem to fit the general form of an address but in fact are incorrect. Whether Word's guess is right or wrong, you can edit it in the Delivery Address scroll box.

If you've entered your own name and address in the User Information tab located in Tools, Options, Word also pulls that information into the Return Address scroll box. You can edit your address, if necessary, or if you don't want a return address—perhaps you're using preprinted envelopes that already contain one—click the Omit check box.

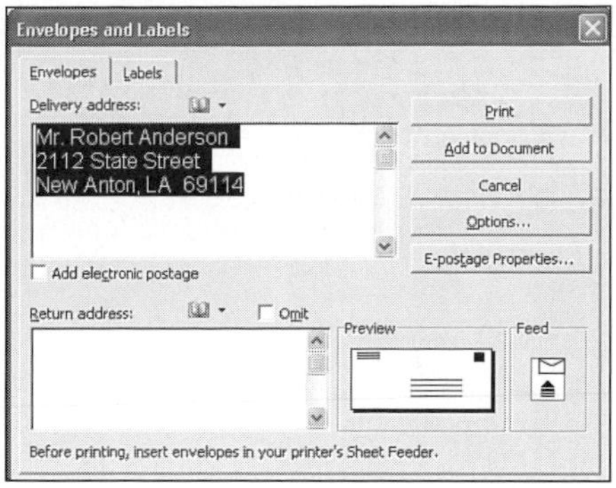

Figure 6.5
The Envelopes and
Labels dialog box,
showing the name
and address Word

TIP

If you don't want Word to find names and addresses for you automatically, you can tell it to flag specific text as the Delivery Address or Return Address text, using two bookmarks designed for this purpose: EnvelopeAddress and EnvelopeReturn.

First, select the text in an open document that you want to use as your outgoing or return address and choose Insert, Bookmark. When the Bookmark dialog box appears, select the Bookmark name box, and type EnvelopeAddress for an outgoing address, or EnvelopeReturn for a return address. (Type these as one word, with no spaces.) Finally, click Add.

→ For more information about bookmarks, **see** Chapter 22, "Using Footnotes, Bookmarks, and Cross-References," **p. 743**.

If you are using Microsoft Outlook, you can retrieve a delivery or return address from the names stored in its Contact List. In the Envelopes and Labels dialog box, click the Address Book icon (it resembles an open address book) located above the Delivery or Return address forms. The Select Name dialog box appears (see Figure 6.6). Choose a name and click OK.

NOTE

For more information on these features, see the Microsoft Knowledge Base articles Q134901, Q141874, and Q167770.

ADDING A NEW NAME TO YOUR ENVELOPE AND CONTACTS LIST

If you're adding a new name that isn't in the contacts list, click Advanced, and click New from the drop-down list. The New Entry dialog box opens; choose New Contact, and click OK.

6

Figure 6.6
Choosing a name from your Outlook contacts list, using the Select Name dialog box.

A new Outlook 2003 Contact item appears; here you can use the different tabs aligned across the top of the box to enter the recipient's address and any other information you have available (see Figure 6.7).

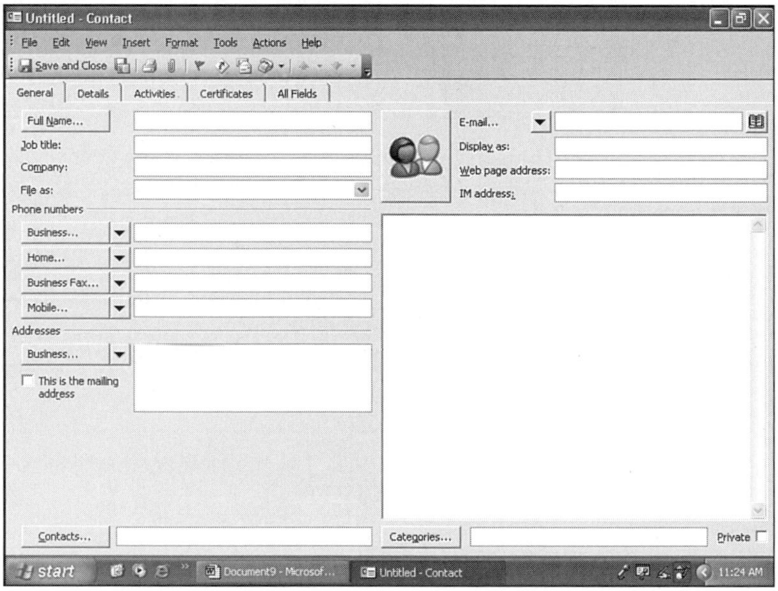

Figure 6.7
Adding a new name to your Outlook contacts list.

Click Save and Close when you're finished; Word returns you to the Envelopes and Labels dialog box and displays the recipient's name and business address in the Delivery Address scroll box. At the same time, the name is added to your Outlook contacts list.

PRINTING AN ENVELOPE—NOW OR LATER

Assuming that you use a standard (#10) business envelope and that your addresses are correct, you can simply print the envelope by clicking the Print button in the Envelopes and

Labels dialog box (refer to Figure 6.5). If necessary, Word prompts you to insert an envelope into your printer's manual feed mechanism, showing how the envelope should be inserted.

If you're not ready to print yet, you can tell Word to add the envelope to the beginning of your document as Page 0 in a separate section. Then, when you print the document, Word prompts you to insert the envelope first. To add an envelope at the beginning of your document, click Add to Document in the Envelopes and Labels dialog box. This closes the Envelopes and Labels dialog box and then, as you can see in Figure 6.8, shows how the envelope appears in your document (in Print Layout view).

Figure 6.8
The envelope, appearing as Page 0 in Print Layout view.

Mr. Robert Anderson
2112 State Street
New Anton, LA 69114

If Word prompts you to feed envelopes manually, even though you've placed a stack of envelopes in a printer tray, see "What to Do If Word Incorrectly Prompts You to Feed Envelopes Manually," in "Troubleshooting" at the end of this chapter.

ADDING GRAPHICS TO AN ENVELOPE

Most business envelope stationery includes some form of logo or graphic accompanying the return address. With Word, you can include a graphic next to the return address, without paying for printed stationery. Follow these steps to add a clip art image to your envelope:

1. Choose Tools, Letters and Mailings, Envelopes and Labels.

2. In the Envelopes tab, click Add to Document. This inserts the envelope as a new section at the beginning of your document. (As mentioned earlier, the envelope becomes Page 0, so it doesn't affect the page numbering of your document.)

3. Click the area of the envelope where you want to place the graphic.

4. Insert the picture using any of Word's tools for doing so. For example, choose Insert, Picture, From File; then browse to the picture and choose Insert.

→ For more information about inserting graphics in documents, **see** Chapter 13, "Getting Images into Your Documents," **p. 437**.

5. Resize the graphic, if necessary, by dragging one of the square sizing handles surrounding the image.

NOTE

> You can also import a graphic from Word's Media Gallery or use a scanned logo. Or you can use Microsoft WordArt to design special type effects. (WordArt and Word's other graphics tools are covered in Chapter 13 and Chapter 14, "Using Word's Quick and Easy Drawing Tools.")

After you create a design for your return address (or for some other purpose), you may want to include it on all your envelopes from now on. To do so, first select all the text and graphics you want to use; these are typically found on page 0 along with the rest of your envelope. Next, choose Insert, AutoText, New. In the Create AutoText dialog box, type EnvelopeExtra1 and click OK.

NOTE

> You actually can create *two* special AutoText entries to use on envelopes: EnvelopeExtra1 and EnvelopeExtra2. If you create these AutoText entries in the Normal template, they will be available to all templates, and, therefore, they will appear on all envelopes. If you want to use them in specialized situations only, create them in a template other than the Normal template. If you later decide you don't want to include these entries on envelopes at all, delete the AutoText entries.

UNDERSTANDING ENVELOPE PRINTING OPTIONS

You've learned the basics of envelope printing. But that's just the beginning: Word enables you to control all the following elements:

- What size of envelopes you use
- Whether the envelopes use postal bar codes
- How the delivery and return addresses look and where they appear on the envelope
- How the envelopes feed into your printer

To work with these settings, click Options in the Envelopes tab of the Envelopes and Labels dialog box. The Envelope Options dialog box appears, as shown in Figure 6.9.

CHANGING ENVELOPE SIZES

By default, Word expects you to use a standard business envelope—normally referred to as a #10 envelope. Word previews how your printed envelope should look in the Preview box of the Envelope Options dialog box (refer to Figure 6.9). If you're using a different kind of envelope, click on the Envelope Size drop-down box to choose one of Word's built-in envelope sizes.

You can also create a custom-size envelope, which you might need if you're designing a special mailing piece—though custom-size envelopes can be expensive.

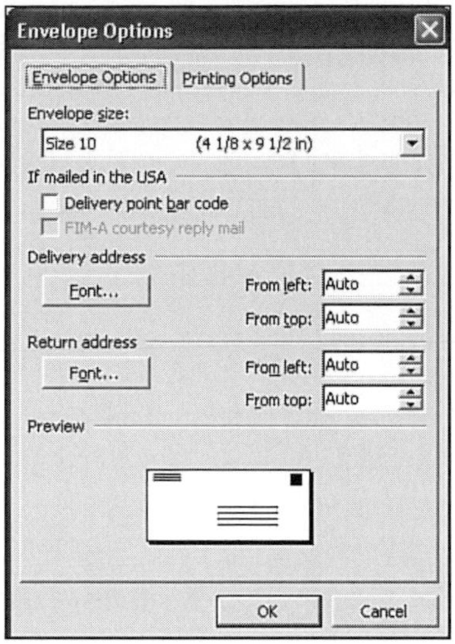

Figure 6.9
The Envelope Options dialog box is your control center for printing envelopes.

To create a custom-size envelope, choose Custom Size from the Envelope Size drop-down box. The Envelope Size dialog box appears (see Figure 6.10). Set the sizes you want (in inches) and click OK.

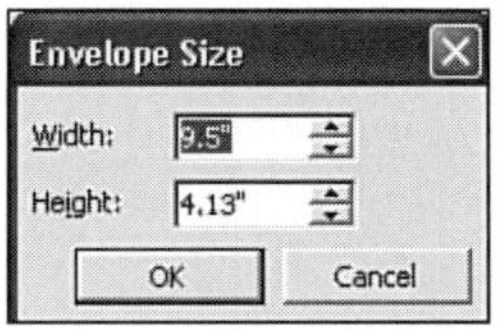

Figure 6.10
Setting a custom envelope size.

ADDING BAR CODES TO YOUR ENVELOPES

By now you've doubtless noticed that much of the mail you receive contains postal bar codes. Two kinds of postal bar codes are generally used:

- **Delivery Point Barcode (POSTNET).** These codes are ZIP codes translated into bar-code language that the U.S. Postal Service computers can read.

- **Facing Identification Marks (FIMs).** These codes flag different kinds of Courtesy Reply Mail. Most of us know this as Business Reply Mail, which uses the FIM-A mark.

Adding bar codes to your mail has two benefits. First, if you're doing mass mailings that qualify, you can get a lower postal rate. Second, bar-coded mail is sometimes delivered more quickly. Fortunately, Word can handle the bar coding for you.

To add a delivery point bar code, check the Delivery Point Bar Code check box. If you're creating Business Reply Mail, check the FIM-A Courtesy Reply Mail check box. (This box is available only if Delivery Point Bar Code is also checked, because you can't have a FIM-A bar code without a POSTNET code.)

6

CAUTION

> Word's bar-code options work only if the Windows locale is set to US. In Windows 2000, this setting appears in the General tab of the Regional Options dialog box, found in the Control Panel. In Windows XP, this setting appears in the Regional Options tab of the Regional and Language Options dialog box, also found in the Control Panel.
>
> Don't use FIM codes if you're also using Internet postage: Internet postage systems print their own FIM codes.

CHANGING ENVELOPE FORMATTING

To change the formatting of the addresses on your envelope, click the Options button in the Envelopes and Labels dialog box. The Envelope Options dialog box appears (refer to Figure 6.9). The Envelope Options tab of this dialog box provides near-total control over how your delivery and return addresses look and where they print on the envelope.

To change the appearance of the typeface used in either the delivery address or the return address, click Font in the appropriate section of the Envelope Options dialog box.

If you click the Font button in the Delivery Address section of the Envelope Options dialog box, the Envelope Address dialog box opens (see Figure 6.11). This looks much like the Font dialog box discussed in Chapter 4, "Quick and Effective Formatting Techniques."

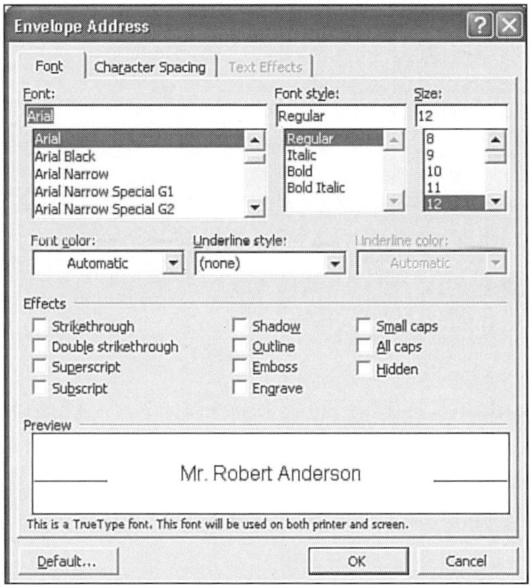

Figure 6.11
The Envelope Address dialog box contains most of the character formatting options available in the Font dialog box.

From here, you can choose a font, a font style, a size, and font effects. (Animations aren't available because they don't print.) You can also click the Character Spacing tab to control *character spacing* and *kerning*. When you have the envelope address formatting the way you want it, click OK.

→ For more information on how Word uses templates as the basis for creating both envelopes and other documents, **see** Chapter 11, "Templates, Wizards, and Add-Ins," **p. 355**.

CONTROLLING WHERE DELIVERY AND RETURN ADDRESSES ARE PRINTED

You can also control how far from the left edge or top of the envelope the delivery and return addresses appear. With the Envelope Options dialog box open (refer to Figure 6.9), change the From Left and From Top settings in either the Delivery Address or the Return Address box, or both.

NOTE

By default, Word's settings make sure that you do not enter addresses beyond the range of your printer, beyond the edges of the envelope you've specified, or beyond the areas acceptable to the U.S. Postal Service. For instance, using Word's default settings, you can't set the delivery address to be less than 1 " from the left edge or less than 1 1/2 " from the top edge of the envelope.

CONTROLLING HOW ENVELOPES FEED INTO YOUR PRINTER

Word allows you to control several aspects of how you feed envelopes to your printer while printing envelopes. To change these settings, display the Envelopes tab of the Envelopes and Labels dialog box, click Options, and choose the Printing Options tab (see Figure 6.12).

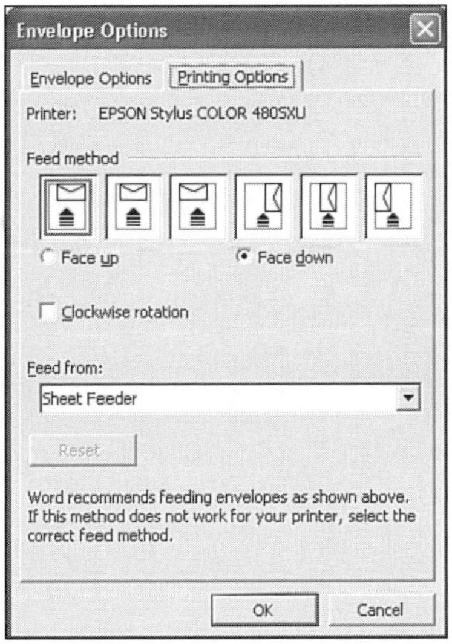

Figure 6.12
The Printing Options tab of the Envelope Options dialog box lets you control how your envelopes feed into your printer.

Word sets a default feed method based on information it finds in the printer driver you selected. You should rarely have to change this; if you do, you can click on one of the envelope images shown in the Feed Method area of the dialog box.

Similarly, based on your printer driver, Word specifies whether your envelope should be placed Face Up or Face Down. If necessary, you can change this setting as well.

Depending on the options provided by your printer, you can also control the source where your envelopes will feed from. For example, you can specify whether envelopes will be fed manually, will be placed in the default tray you ordinarily use for regular paper, or will be fed from a different tray.

In general, the default settings in this dialog box will be the appropriate ones. If you make changes, and find that the changes do not work properly (or you simply want to revert to the default settings), click the Reset button. This button is available only if you have made changes to your envelope printing options.

USING E-POSTAGE WITH WORD

Word allows you to print United States Postal Service approved electronic postage directly onto your envelopes if you subscribe to Stamps.com's electronic postage service and use Stamps.com's add-on software.

NOTE

> If you have used an earlier version of Stamps.com's service, you will need to upgrade to Stamps.com 3.1 or higher.

To sign up with Stamps.com, click E-Postage Properties on the Envelopes tab of the Envelopes and Labels dialog box; click Yes; and follow the Web links and instructions that are displayed in Internet Explorer. After you have successfully signed up for Stamps.com and installed its software, you can add postage to an envelope like this:

1. With the Envelopes tab of the Envelopes and Labels dialog box open, make sure that the correct delivery address appears in the Delivery Address text box; if it does not, either enter it manually or click the Address Book icon to select it from one of your address books.

2. Check the Add Electronic Postage check box.

3. If you want to add special services such as Certified Mail, Registered Mail, insurance, envelope graphics or logos, or postage or mail date corrections, click E-Postage Properties. Then specify the appropriate settings in the Stamps.com dialog box, and click OK.

4. Stamps.com's online postage service will check your delivery address against the USPS Address Matching System to ensure that your ZIP Code is correct. Click Accept to confirm any adjustments the USPS Address Matching System has made. (If you are sure that a change is incorrect, click Edit to make appropriate changes.)

5. The Stamps.com dialog box appears. Specify your postage options here, including weight and mailing date.

> **NOTE**
>
> If you don't have enough postage in your account, you will be prompted to purchase more. Click Buy Postage to do so, using the credit card you have on file with Stamps.com.

6. Click Print to print the envelope.

> **NOTE**
>
> For more information about printing postage with Stamps.com, see www.stamps.com/support/howto/office2003.

PRINTING LABELS

You also can print a label—or a sheet of labels—using either your delivery address or your return address. To do so, choose Tools, Letters and Mailings, Envelopes and Labels, and click the Labels tab, as shown in Figure 6.13.

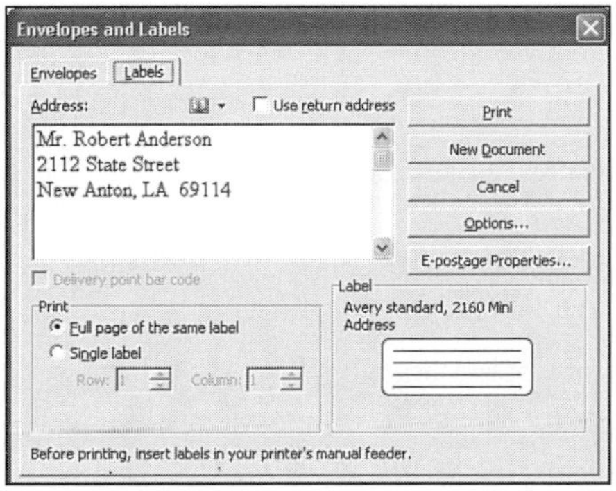

Figure 6.13
The Labels tab, showing an address borrowed from a letter.

Word follows the same rules for finding an address to include on your labels as it did for finding the address for envelopes. If you entered a specific name and address in the Envelopes tab, Word places it in the Labels tab as well. Again, you can edit it if you want. And, as with envelopes, you can click the Address Book button to insert names from your Microsoft Outlook or other address book.

> **NOTE**
>
> By default, Word assumes that you want to use the delivery address in your letter. If you prefer to use your return address, check the Use Return Address check box. You cannot print both the delivery and the return addresses on the same label.

6

TIP

> You're not limited to entering an address in the Address box. If you need a full page of identical shipping labels that say "FRAGILE," you can create these as well.
>
> You can also use Word's mail merge features, covered in Chapter 17, "Using Mail Merge Effectively," to create sets of labels for different recipients, or sets of labels based on databases—for example, a set of folder labels based on a list of clients.

By default, Word expects to print a full page of identical copies of the text in the label. Therefore, the Full Page of the Same Label button is selected. You can, however, click Single Label to print only one label. You might use this option to create a shipping label for a large envelope or package, to create a large return address label, or to allow you to reuse most of a sheet of labels in the event you need to print only one.

CAUTION

> Many label sheets cannot be run through a laser printer twice.

If you've dealt with partially used label sheets before, you know that printing a single label means choosing a specific location of the sheet to print to. So, when you choose to create just one label, Word wants to know which of the label locations on your sheet it should print on. For example, you might want to print on the second label in the third column of labels. Use the Row or Column scroll boxes to specify the row and/or column number on which you want to print.

SPECIFYING LABEL PRINTING OPTIONS

Word assumes that you feed your labels manually. To tell it otherwise, click the Options button. The Label Options dialog box opens (see Figure 6.14). Select another paper source from the Tray drop-down list in the Printer Information area of the dialog box.

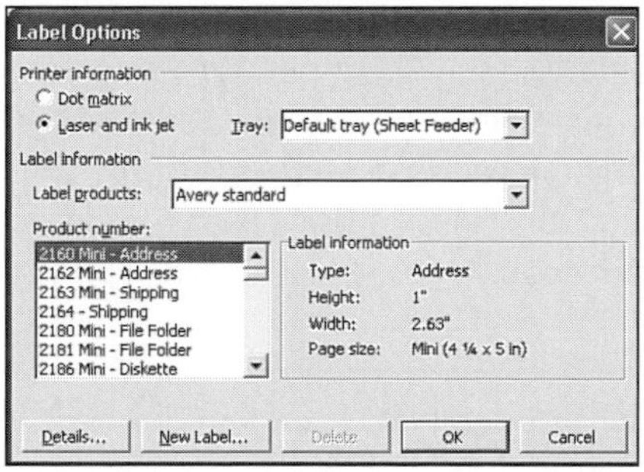

Figure 6.14
Selecting your label and its print destination.

NOTE

> If the Label Options dialog box specifies manual feed, but the Print tab of the Options dialog box specifies automatic feed, the setting in the Print tab overrides the setting here.

NOTE

It's always a good idea to spot-check your labels by printing at least some of them on regular paper and placing that on top of the label sheet to ensure that the labels are printing within the correct areas. Labels aren't cheap, and if your printer fails to print within the correct label margins, your sheet is wasted.

Word supports an extraordinary variety of labels, including labels sold both in the U.S. and in global markets. The Label Products drop-down box in the Label Options dialog box (refer to Figure 6.14) contains 14 groups of laser and inkjet labels from around the world:

- Avery standard (the default U.S. setting)
- AOne
- APLI
- Avery A4 and A5 sizes
- Devauzet
- ERO
- Formtec

- Herma
- Hisago
- Kokuyo
- MACO/Wilson Jones Standard
- Pimaco
- Rank Xerox
- Zweckform

Additional categories are available for dot-matrix printers, notably the CoStar LabelWriter. To see which label to use, see the packaging your labels came in.

The labels Word supports (or can be customized to support) include far more than just address labels: You can create disk, videotape, and CD-ROM labels; file folder labels; name badge labels; postage labels; tent cards; portfolio labels; and much more. To choose a label, select the manufacturer and product category from the Label Products drop-down box; then select the specific type of label from the Product Number scroll box. There, Word provides not only product numbers, but brief descriptions of each label as well.

CREATING A CUSTOM LABEL

If none of Word's hundreds of built-in label definitions matches yours—hard as that is to imagine—you can build your own label. In the Label Options dialog box, click New Label or click in the Label Information area. The New Custom Laser dialog box opens, as shown in Figure 6.15. (If you have specified dot matrix as your printer type, this dialog box is titled New Custom Dot Matrix, and the picture of the label is somewhat different.)

To create a custom label size, follow these steps:

1. Type a name for the label in the Label Name drop-down box.
2. Select the Page Size from the drop-down list at the bottom of the dialog box.
3. Set the Number Across. This tells Word how many labels are positioned between the left and right margins of the sheet.

6

Figure 6.15
Creating a custom label for a laser or inkjet printer.

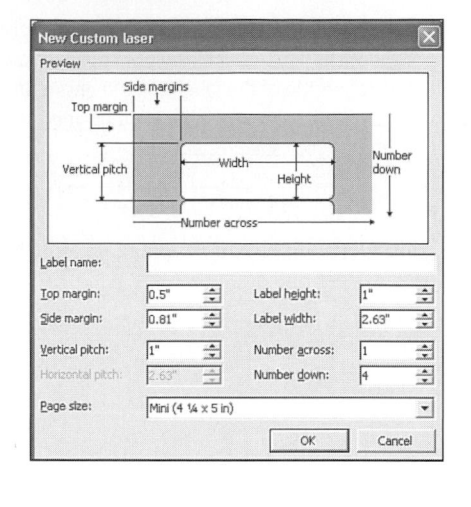

4. Set the Number Down. This tells Word how many labels are positioned between the top and bottom margins of the sheet.

5. Set the Label Height. Notice that Word automatically changes the Vertical Pitch setting. (Vertical pitch is the distance from the top of one label to the top of the next label.)

6. Set the Label Width. Notice that Word automatically changes the Horizontal Pitch setting. (Horizontal pitch is the distance from the left edge of one label to the left edge of the label in the next column.)

7. Adjust the Top Margin and Side Margin settings, if necessary.

8. Click OK to return to the Label Options dialog box. Your custom label is selected in the Product Number scroll box.

9. Click OK to return to the Envelopes and Labels dialog box.

10. Click Print or New Document, depending on whether you want to send the labels to the printer immediately.

Although you can create labels of virtually any size, you must print them on one of Word's standard paper sizes, such as 8 1/2"×11".

CREATING A FILE OF LABELS FOR LATER PRINTING

You may not want to print your labels immediately. For example, the computer you are using right now may not be attached to a printer that can print your labels; or the labels you need may be in the supply cabinet at the office while you're at home. You can create a file consisting of labels for later printing.

To do so, include the text you want to appear in your label (for example, add a name and address, as discussed in earlier sections). Establish the label settings you want (for example, choose whether you want to print a full page of the same label, or just one label). Then, click New Document. Word creates and displays a new document consisting of the labels you have created (see Figure 6.16). Be sure to save the file Word creates.

Figure 6.16
A file containing new labels for later printing.

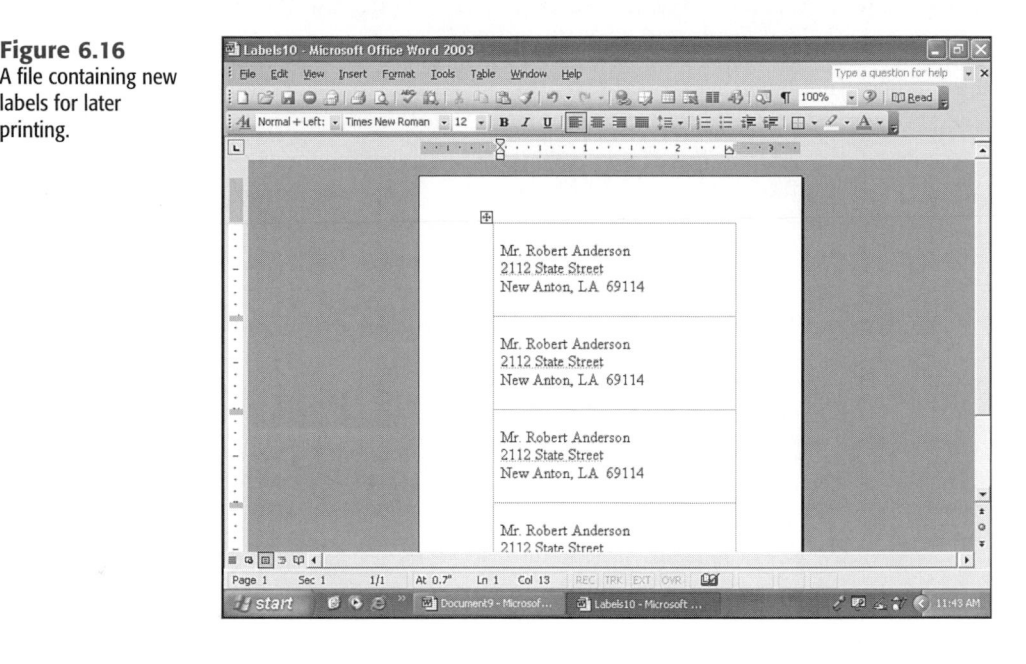

NOTE

You can edit this file manually, just as you can edit any other file. For example, you can manually replace duplicate copies of the same label with different names and addresses, or copy the entire page of labels to create a document consisting of several pages.

PRINTING MANY FILES AT THE SAME TIME

Just as you can open more than one file at a time, you can print more than one file at the same time—as long as the files are stored in the same folder. Moreover, you don't need to open the files to print them. Click the Open button on the Standard toolbar to display the Open dialog box.

Navigate to the folder containing the documents you want to print, and select each document. Right-click on the files you've selected and choose Print from the shortcut menu. Word prints one copy of each document, using the currently selected printer.

To select contiguous files, click the first file and then Shift+click the last file. To select non-contiguous files, Ctrl+click each file.

CAUTION

You don't get a chance to adjust printer settings when you use this procedure: Word sends the documents straight to the printer.

USING PRINT PREVIEW

When you want to preview a document as it will be printed, use Word's flexible Print Preview feature. To display it, click the Print Preview button on the Standard toolbar.

You can perform many tasks in Print Preview, including viewing, editing, and printing. But first, here are the basics. Figure 6.17 shows the Print Preview screen. You can see a miniature version of your current document, as well as a toolbar containing several useful options. Whenever you're ready to leave Print Preview, click Close, and Word returns you to the view of the document you were using before you selected Print Preview.

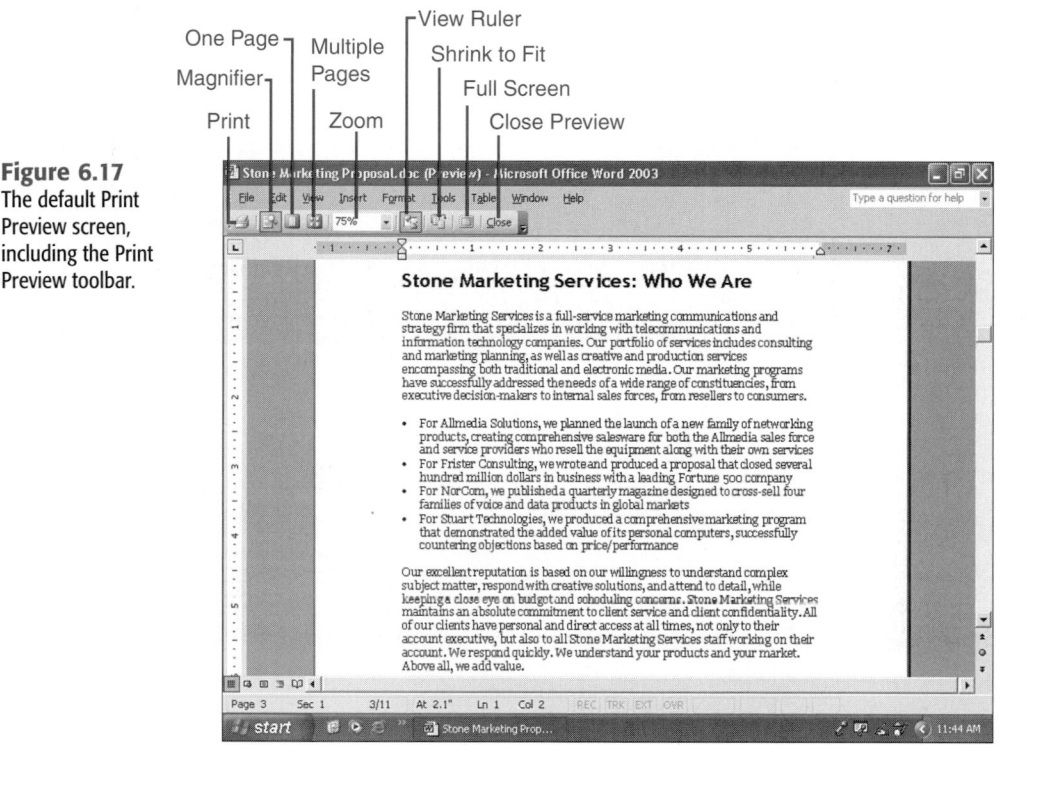

Figure 6.17
The default Print Preview screen, including the Print Preview toolbar.

VIEWING RULERS AND MARGINS IN PRINT PREVIEW

Horizontal and vertical rulers are displayed by default in Print Preview. On the rulers, the document's active text areas are displayed in white; nonprinting areas are displayed in gray.

If you want to toggle the rulers on or off, click the View Ruler toolbar button.

PRINTING FROM WITHIN PRINT PREVIEW

To print one copy of a document from within Print Preview, click the Print button. If you want more control over how your document prints, choose File, Print to display the same Print dialog box discussed earlier in this chapter.

ZOOMING IN AND MOVING AROUND

While you are viewing the document in Print Preview, the mouse pointer becomes a magnifying glass with a plus symbol. To zoom the document to full size, move the pointer to the region of the page you want to look at more closely, and click. The text enlarges to full size, as shown in Figure 6.18. You can adjust the exact proportion of the text by entering a new percentage in the Zoom box.

Figure 6.18
A document shown at 100% size in Print Preview.

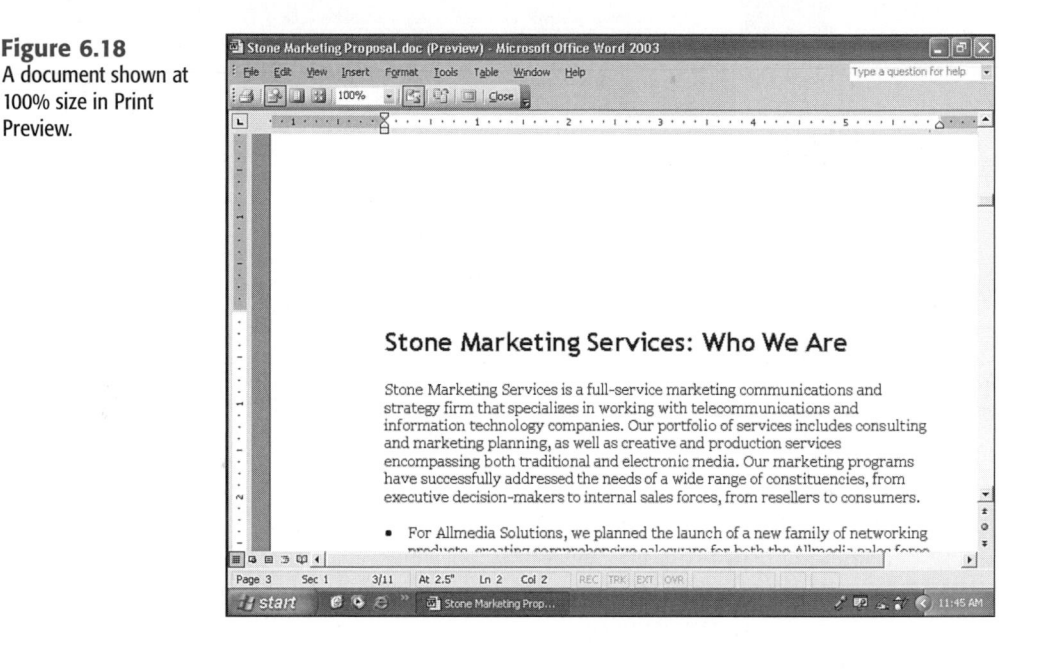

If you want to view enlarged text elsewhere on your page and the text extends beyond the current boundaries of your screen, scroll to it with the vertical or horizontal scrollbars. Keep in mind that the scrollbars take you through the entire document, not just to the top and bottom of the visible page.

NOTE

> To move forward one page in Print Preview, click the double down arrow button at the bottom of the vertical scrollbar. To move back one page, click the double up arrow.

6

You can make your text area appear a little bigger by hiding screen elements you may not need. For example, to hide everything except the Print Preview toolbar (see Figure 6.19), click the Full Screen button on the Print Preview toolbar. When you need a menu, you can make it appear by moving your mouse pointer up to the top of the screen.

When you want to switch from Full Screen view back to the standard Print Preview screen, click the Full Screen button again or click the Close Full Screen button on the Full Screen toolbar.

Figure 6.19
Previewing a document in Full Screen view.

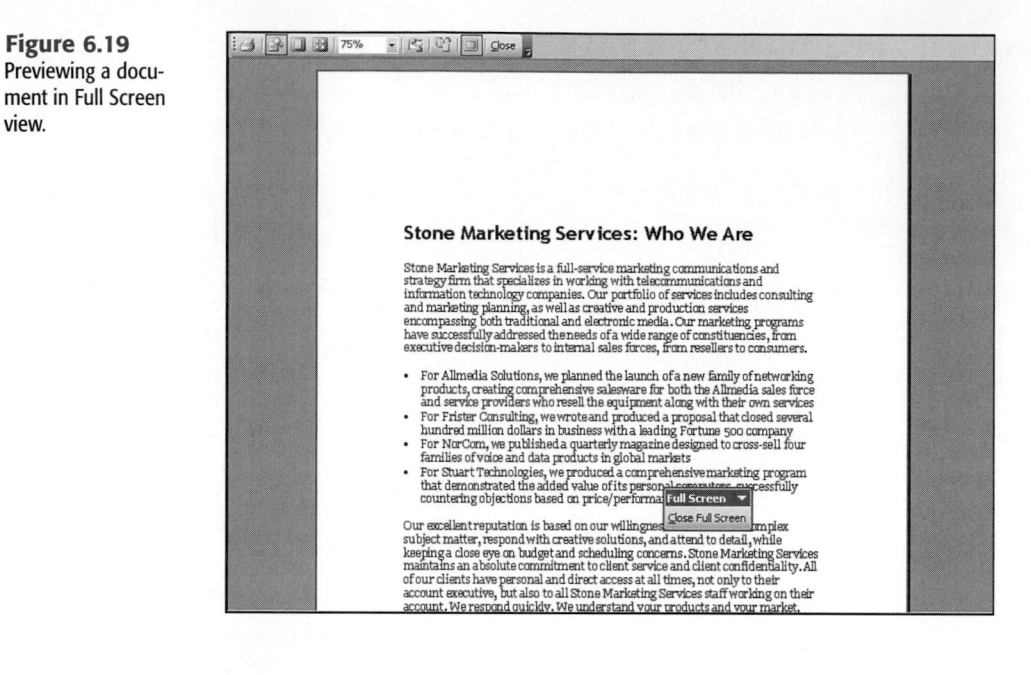

VIEWING MULTIPLE PAGES AT ONCE

You can view up to 24 thumbnail (miniature) pages at once in Print Preview. To do so, click the Multiple Pages button in the Print Preview toolbar. A box opens, as shown in Figure 6.20. Select the number of pages you want to appear by dragging the mouse across the selection grid. You can display up to three rows of pages in as many as six columns. Figure 6.21 shows six pages displayed at once.

Figure 6.20
Dragging the selection grid to display several pages at once.

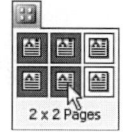

To switch back to a single-page Print Preview, click the One Page button.

> **NOTE**
>
> Realistically, you won't see much detail if you display 24 pages, especially if they're text pages. However, showing many pages at once can give you a good feel for the high-level organization and appearance of a section of a large document.

SHRINKING YOUR DOCUMENT AUTOMATICALLY

At one time or another, you've probably created a document that was just slightly too long. You hoped that report would fit on three pages, but a few lines jumped onto the fourth page. Or someone told you to make your argument in a single page, but you couldn't quite make it fit. In the past, you might have cheated by manually shrinking the type size and space between lines. Now Word does the cheating for you.

Figure 6.21
Six pages displayed at once.

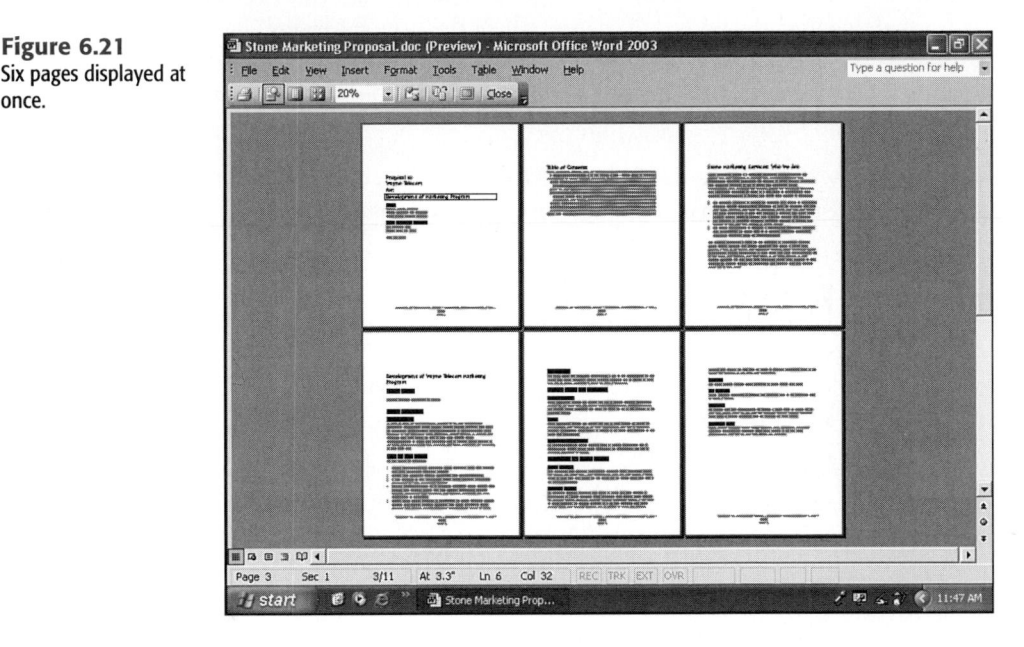

Rather than shrink your document by trial and error, you can have Word calculate and make the changes necessary to reduce your document's length by one page. Click on the Shrink to Fit button in the Print Preview toolbar.

Be warned, though, that using Shrink to Fit can be a little like setting the water temperature too hot on your washing machine. Use Shrink to Fit only when you need to save a few lines, because if you try to do more it can shrink things way too much. It can shrink text to 4-point without batting an eyelash. (On occasion, Shrink to Fit gives up and tells you it can't remove a page. But that's rare. It's pretty zealous about trying.)

N O T E

> You can undo the effects of shrinking if you click the Undo tool; however, after you save the document, you cannot undo Shrink to Fit.

EDITING IN PRINT PREVIEW

You can edit your document in Print Preview. Place the magnifying glass on the part of the page you want to edit, and click to zoom to 100% (or whatever other measurement you find most readable). Then click on the Magnifier button in the toolbar. This turns off the magnifier, leaving the current zoom in place. Now you can select text, edit it, move it around, and reformat it as if you were still in Normal or Print Layout view.

Most of the usual Word menu items are available while you're editing in the Print Preview screen, including Find and Replace, and nearly everything on the Format menu.

6

CHANGING MARGINS AND INDENTS IN PRINT PREVIEW

You can use Word's rulers to change margins and indents in Print Preview, just as you can in the normal document window. To change any of the page's margins, click the Ruler button in the Print Preview toolbar to display the ruler; then drag the margin boundary with the mouse. (Your mouse pointer changes to a double-headed arrow when it touches the margin boundary on the ruler.)

Dragging works for both horizontal and vertical margins, but on the horizontal margins you need to be careful not to inadvertently move an indent instead.

SENDING A FAX FROM WORD

NEW Microsoft Word 2003 gives you two options for faxing documents. You can fax using your own fax modem, with either the fax software built into Windows or your own third-party software, such as WinFax Pro.

Alternatively, if you don't have a fax modem (or prefer not to use it), you can use an Internet-based fax service. With an Internet-based fax service, you email your file to a service provider via Microsoft Outlook. The Internet fax service handles the faxing on your behalf and charges you based on either a monthly subscription or per-page rate.

The following sections cover both.

FAXING A DOCUMENT WITH YOUR FAX MODEM

To fax a document with your fax modem, first complete and save your document. Then, follow these steps:

1. Choose <u>F</u>ile, Sen<u>d</u> To, Recipient Using a <u>F</u>ax Modem. The Word Fax Wizard opens.

2. Click Ne<u>x</u>t. Word's Document to Fax window opens (see Figure 6.22).

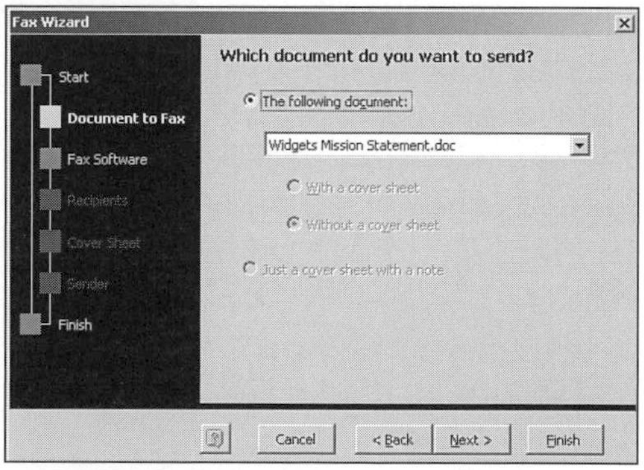

Figure 6.22
Choosing which document to fax.

3. Choose the document you want to fax; you can select any open document.

4. Click <u>N</u>ext. The Fax Software window opens (see Figure 6.23).

Figure 6.23
Choosing which software you want to use to send your fax.

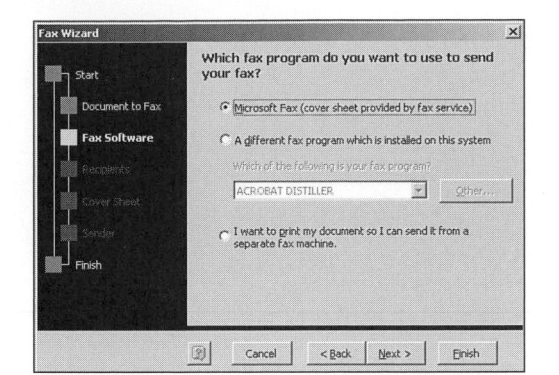

5. Specify which fax software you want to use. Most users will choose the built-in Microsoft Fax service available through Windows 2000 and Windows XP. If you choose Microsoft Fax, the Recipients, Cover Sheet, and Sender boxes of Word's Fax Wizard disappear.

> **N O T E**
>
> Microsoft Fax Service is installed by default in Windows 2000 and in Windows XP Professional. It is not installed by default in Windows XP Home, but it can be installed separately from the Windows XP Home CD-ROM.

> **N O T E**
>
> If you choose third-party software instead, such as Symantec's WinFax Pro, click Next and proceed to specify recipients, cover sheet, and sender information within Word's Fax Wizard.

6. Click Next. The Finish screen appears.

7. Click Finish. Windows's Send Fax Wizard opens.

8. Click Next. The Recipient and Dialing Information dialog box opens (see Figure 6.24).

9. Enter names and fax numbers in the To and Fax Number boxes, or retrieve them from Microsoft Outlook by clicking the Address Book button and choosing them from the Address Book dialog box. If you enter the fax numbers manually, always include the full phone number, including the area code and the country code prefix ("1" for U.S. numbers) wherever necessary.

10. Click Next. The Adding a Cover Page window appears (see Figure 6.25).

11. Choose the style of cover sheet you want to use. If you don't want a cover page, clear the Include a Cover Page check box.

12. Enter a Subject Line and any Note you want to appear on your cover page.

13. Click Next. The Scheduling Transmission window appears.

14. Specify when you want the fax sent; if you want to send it now, leave the Now button selected. If you want to associate a billing code with your fax, enter it in the Billing Code text box.

6

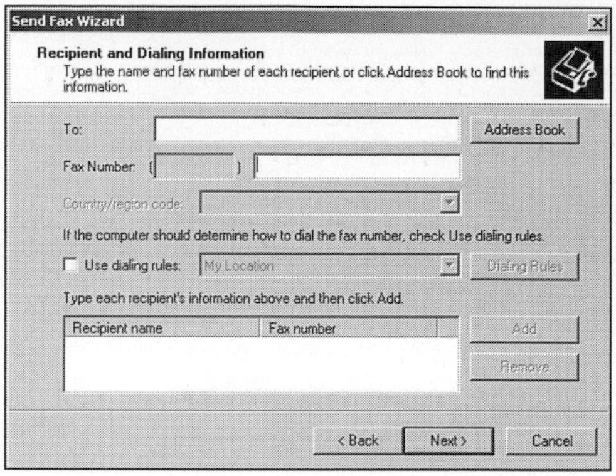

Figure 6.24
Setting recipient and dialing information through the Fax Wizard.

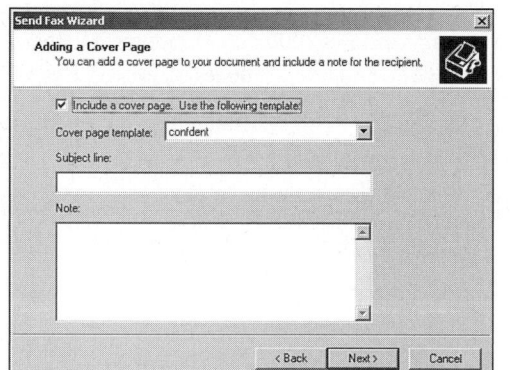

Figure 6.25
Choosing one of Word's standard fax cover sheets.

15. Click Next.
16. Click Finish.

USING THE VENALI INTERNET FAX SERVICE

Currently, one fax service is integrated with Microsoft Word 2003: Venali Internet Fax Service. This is a subscription service with base prices that range from $4.95 a month for low-volume outbound service to $19.95 per month for higher-volume inbound/outbound service.

To sign up for Venali Internet Fax Service, visit `www.venali.com/signup/msoffice/signup/select_package.aspx` and follow the instructions there. After you've signed up, follow these instructions to send a fax:

1. Save the Word document you want to fax.
2. Choose File, Send To, Recipient Using Internet Fax Service. Word converts your document to a TIFF file for delivery as a fax. Outlook's Sent with Microsoft Office 2003 Fax Service window opens (see Figure 6.26).
3. In the Fax Recipient line, enter your recipient's name.

Figure 6.26
Outlook's Sent with
Microsoft Office 2003
Fax Service
dialog box.

4. In the Fax Number box, select the country/region prefix associated with your fax destination. If you are using Word within the U.S., and faxing within the U.S., you can
   leave the default setting of United States (+1).

5. In the City/Area box, enter your recipient's area code.

6. In the Local box, enter your recipient's local fax number.

7. If you want to add another recipient, click Add More. A new recipient's line appears;
   repeat steps 3–6.

8. Edit the Subject line as you like.

9. If you want to change your cover sheet, choose a different cover sheet from the Fax
   Service task pane. (If your fax cover sheet isn't listed, click Custom, and select any
   Word template.) You can also send your fax with no cover sheet, by clearing the Use
   Cover Sheet check box.

10. If you want to preview your fax, click Preview; Microsoft Office Document Imaging
    will appear (see Figure 6.27), displaying the preview. Close it when you're finished pre-
    viewing the fax.

11. If you want to know how much your fax service provider will charge for your fax, click
    Calculate Cost. Microsoft Internet Explorer will appear, displaying a summary of the
    charges you will incur for sending this fax (see Figure 6.28).

12. Click Send. If you are asked whether to convert the file from Word document format
    to an image format, click Yes.

6

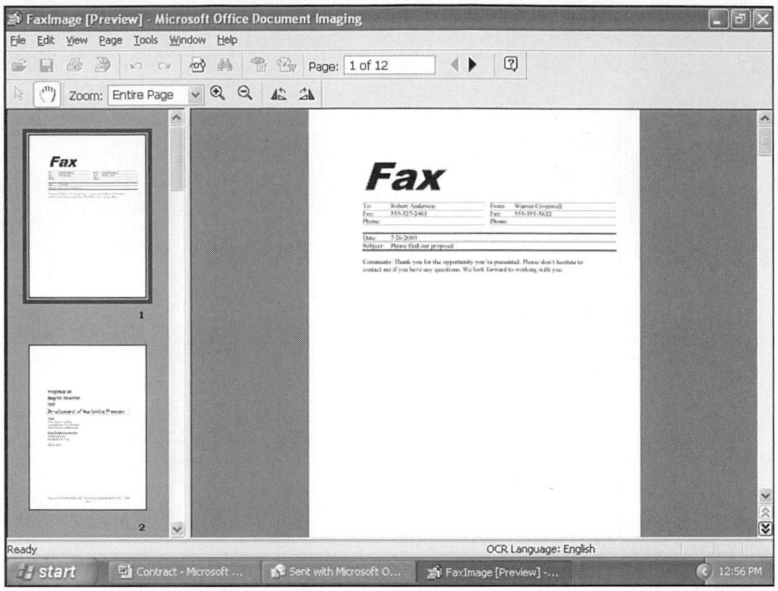

Figure 6.27
Previewing your fax with Microsoft Office Document Imaging.

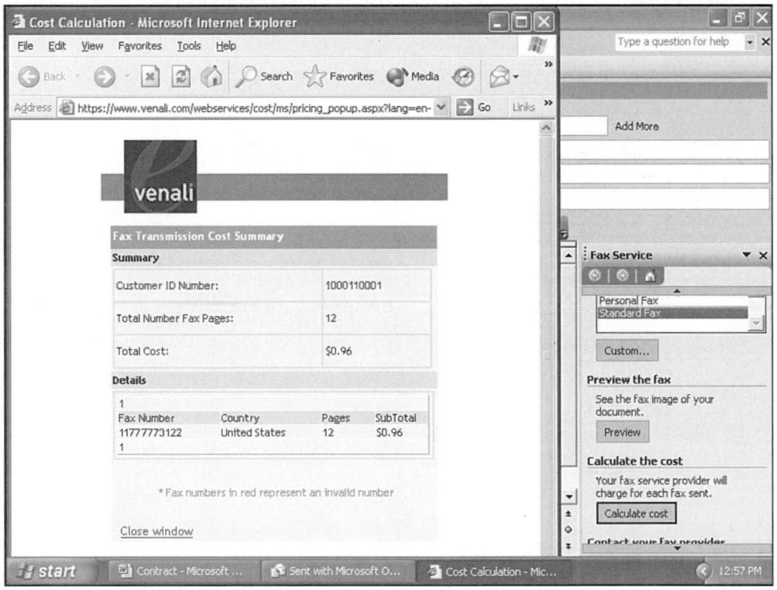

Figure 6.28
Calculating the cost of sending your fax.

TROUBLESHOOTING

WHAT TO DO IF WORD INCORRECTLY PROMPTS YOU TO FEED PAPER MANUALLY

Check to see whether the wrong paper tray is selected. Choose File, Page Setup and choose the Paper Source tab. Choose the Default Tray (Automatic/Normal) option for both the First Page and Other Pages.

What to Do If Word Fails to Print Your Document

First, make sure that no problem exists with your printer setup in Windows by using the Windows Print Troubleshooter. Click the Start button and choose Help. Click the Index tab and then search for Print Troubleshooter. Click Display and then follow the instructions in the Windows Print Troubleshooter.

If your Windows printer setup seems correct, check your Word printer settings. Choose File, Print and check the Name text box to make sure that the selected printer matches the printer attached to your computer. Then make sure that the page range you've selected in the Print dialog box corresponds to the pages you want to print.

If you are attempting to print to a network printer (a printer you are connected to via a server, a print server, or another computer on your network), be sure to do the following:

- Check whether the printer is turned on, working properly (for example, not jammed), and connected appropriately—to another computer, server, or print server. Can others print from the printer? If so, chances are that the problem is not with the printer or its network connection.

- Make sure that you're connected to the network, and logged on. Can you find and use other computers and network resources? If so, the problem is probably not with your network connection.

- Make sure that you can access the printer you're trying to use. Does it appear on your list of printers? (In Windows 2000, choose Start, Settings, Printers; in Windows XP, choose Start, Control Panel, Printers and Faxes.)

- Make sure that you have rights to use the printer you're trying to use. For example, in some organizations, the network may be configured to deny you access to specific printers at specific hours. You may need to check with your network administrator to learn your rights.

- If these solutions do not work, see the following Microsoft support pages:

  For Windows 2000:

  `http://support.microsoft.com:80/support/kb/articles/q260/1/42.asp`

  For Windows XP:

  `www.microsoft.com/insider/printhelp/oscontent_winxp_network.asp#gen`

What to Do If Text Looks Different from What You Saw Onscreen

First, make sure that you've been viewing the document in Print Layout view. If you're using a different view, the printed document will not entirely match the view onscreen. If this doesn't solve the problem, consider the following:

- Word might be displaying text using draft fonts or printing a draft of your document. Choose Tools, Options and then click the View tab. Remove the check from the Draft Font check box. This option is available only if you switch to Normal view before displaying the Options dialog box.

- The font in your document might not be available on the printer you're using, or the font may be available on your printer, but no matching screen font exists. Change the font in your document to one that is available on your printer or change the font to a TrueType font. Available fonts appear in the Font dialog box (choose Format, Font).

- Animated text effects don't print. If text in your document is animated, it prints with only the underlying text formatting.

WHAT TO DO IF YOU CAN'T ACCESS THE PRINT DIALOG BOX

If Print is grayed out on the File menu, try selecting a different printer to see whether the command becomes available. If not, your printer driver may not have been installed properly or may have become damaged. Try reinstalling the print driver. It's also possible that you've never installed a print driver at all; if so, install one corresponding to your printer.

WHAT TO DO IF A BLANK PAGE APPEARS AT THE END OF YOUR DOCUMENT

You may have created an extra blank page by adding extra paragraph marks (pressing Enter) at the end of your document. Click the Show/Hide Paragraph Marks button to view non-printing characters, and delete any spare paragraph marks that appear at the end of your document. Then check your document in Print Preview.

If you're printing to a network printer, check the printer for a form feed option. If one exists, turn it off.

WHAT TO DO IF THE "TOO MANY FONTS" ERROR MESSAGE APPEARS WHEN YOU PRINT

If you're using TrueType fonts, you may be able to avoid this message by instructing your printer to print TrueType fonts as graphics rather than fonts. Choose File, Print and then choose Properties. On the Fonts tab, choose Print TrueType as Graphics. If this option doesn't appear, the printer you're using doesn't have this feature, and the message from Word is true: You are using more fonts than your printer can handle. Eliminate some fonts from your document and try again.

WHAT TO DO IF WORD INCORRECTLY PROMPTS YOU TO FEED ENVELOPES MANUALLY

Switch to another printing tray for envelopes. Choose Tools, Letters and Mailings, Envelopes and Labels, and click the Envelopes tab. Choose Options and choose the Printing Options tab. In the Feed From box, select the name of the tray you want.

WHAT TO DO IF WORD FAILS TO DIAL PROPERLY WHEN YOU SEND A FAX

Make sure that your telephone numbers are properly formatted to include both area code and "1," if needed, in the United States (or a country code, if you are sending a fax internationally).

CHAPTER 7

USING WORD'S SPEECH CONTROL, DICTATION, AND HANDWRITING FEATURES

In this chapter

UNDERSTANDING WORD'S SPEECH FEATURES

Word contains extensive support for speech recognition—and if you are running a fast computer in a quiet environment, you may be pleasantly surprised by its performance. Word's speech-recognition features take two forms:

- Voice Command, which allows you to choose Word commands, specify formatting, and perform other tasks by speaking directions to the computer aloud
- Dictation, which allows you to speak and have Word transfer your spoken language into text onscreen

How much Word's speech-recognition features improve your productivity depends heavily on how you use your computer and on how good a typist you are. Speech recognition is, of course, especially valuable for those with repetitive stress injuries or other physical challenges that prevent them from using mice and keyboards comfortably or for long periods. Many users want to use speech recognition to supplement the way they normally work with Word, rather than to replace it.

PREPARING FOR SPEECH RECOGNITION

Before you can begin working with speech recognition in Word or Office 2003, you must check to make sure that you meet Microsoft's hardware requirements and that your microphone is working properly.

According to Microsoft, the recommended minimum hardware requirements for a computer to run speech recognition well include a Pentium II (or equivalent AMD processor) with 128MB RAM and at least a 400MHz processor. In other words, the requirements for speech are significantly higher than the system requirements for using Word or Office without speech recognition.

In fact, by default, when you install Office, speech features are not installed on systems that do not meet these hardware requirements.

TIP

> You can, however, manually install speech recognition on lower-end systems if you specify it as a feature to be installed when you run the Windows Installer setup program.

In addition, you need a microphone—not any old microphone, but a high-quality close-talk (headset) microphone with gain adjustment support and noise cancellation or filtering.

When purchasing a new headset, it is important to select one with an adjustable microphone that can be positioned about an inch to the side of your mouth. If possible, Microsoft also recommends that you select a USB microphone with a gain adjustment feature that can amplify your input so that your computer can "hear" it more clearly.

7

CAUTION

An equally important "hardware requirement" is a quiet room in which to work.

If you work in an area with a great deal of ambient noise—from colleagues, children, radios, or anything else—Word's speech-recognition accuracy degrades dramatically.

TRAINING WORD TO UNDERSTAND SPEECH

Before you can begin using Word's speech-recognition feature, you must first perform two steps:

- Adjust your microphone so that it captures your voice as clearly as possible, and test to make sure that it is working properly.
- Train Office to understand your unique voice, by reading a passage that Word can calibrate against its own speech database.

To begin the process, make sure that your microphone is connected properly to your computer. You might want to run Windows Sound Recorder (Start, Programs, Accessories, Entertainment, Sound Recorder) and attempt to record your voice; if you see jagged audio lines instead of a straight flat line as you speak, your computer is successfully recording your voice from your computer.

TIP

If you are using a microphone that connects via a sound card, most recent computers display red color-coding and a microphone icon to identify the correct sound input on the back of the card.

Next, choose Tools, Speech. The Welcome to Office Speech Recognition dialog box appears.

RUNNING THE MICROPHONE WIZARD

As already mentioned, the first step in getting Word ready to take your dictation and voice commands is to prepare your microphone. Click Next in the Microphone Wizard - Welcome dialog box to run the Microphone Wizard. Then click Next again. The Microphone Wizard - Adjust Volume dialog box appears (see Figure 7.1).

The wizard requests that you read a sentence repeatedly; as you do so, it automatically adjusts your microphone volume. When volume levels consistently remain within the green area as you read the sentence, you're ready to continue. Click Next. The Test Positioning dialog box appears (see Figure 7.2).

7

Figure 7.1
Adjusting the volume of your microphone through the Microphone Wizard.

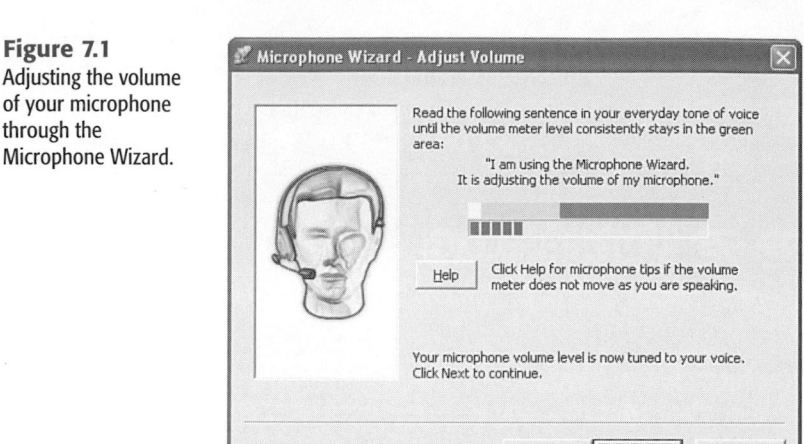

Figure 7.2
Adjusting the positioning of your microphone.

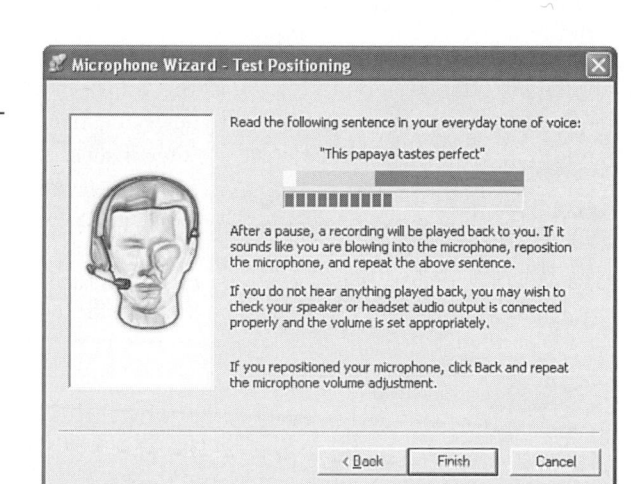

If you're not using a headset microphone, click Finish. If you are, position the microphone as shown in the picture and speak the sentence Microsoft provides: "This papaya tastes perfect."

After a few moments, Word recites the sentence back to you. If you hear it clearly, and do not hear your breathing, you're ready to continue. Click Finish; you're ready to move on.

NOTE

If you need to run the Microphone Wizard again later—perhaps to install a new microphone or readjust your existing one—here's how:

1. Display the Language Bar.

   If the Language indicator is visible on the tray at the right of the taskbar, click on it and choose Show the Language Bar. (If you are using U.S. English, the Language indicator is a blue square with the white letters EN inside it.)

7

> If the Language indicator is *not* visible, choose Start, Control Panel, Regional and Language Options. Choose the Languages tab, click Details, and click Language Bar. Finally, in the Language Bar Settings dialog box, check Show the Language Bar on the Desktop, and click OK three times.
>
> 2. From the Language Bar, choose Tools, Options.
> 3. Click Configure Microphone.

USING THE MICROSOFT SPEECH RECOGNITION TRAINING WIZARD

Word now displays the first dialog box of the Microsoft Speech Recognition Training Wizard. Here, you train Word to recognize your voice as distinct from anyone else's. To begin, click Next. You're asked to tell Word whether you're a child or an adult, male or female.

When you're finished, click Next. Word is almost ready to have you start reading aloud. Before you do, click Sample to hear the tone of voice Word wants you to use: calm, clear, and measured (but not stilted). Then, click Next to begin training. The Wizard displays several paragraphs of text (see Figure 7.3).

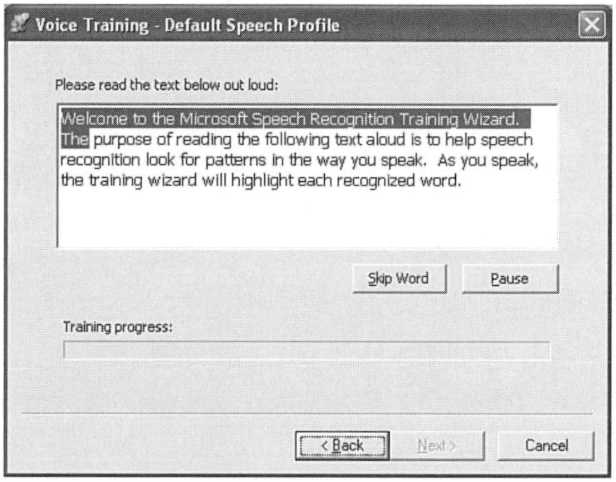

Figure 7.3
Reading a sample passage.

As you read the sample passages, Word follows along, one word or clause at a time, highlighting the words you've read. If you need to pause, click Pause. If, no matter what you say, Word can't recognize a word or phrase you're saying, click Skip Word. If you find yourself skipping quite a few words, the result is likely to be less accurate speech recognition, at least at the outset. (As you'll see later, Word gives you additional opportunities to improve speech-recognition performance as you work with the feature.)

When you've finished with the text Word asks you to read, Word processes your speech data. You can then click Finish to begin using Word's speech-recognition feature.

7

NOTE

If you're connected to the Internet, completing the wizard causes Windows to display Internet Explorer and show you a brief Flash-based movie with more information on speech recognition.

NOTE

Microsoft only promises 85%–90% accuracy when you begin working with speech recognition. This may sound reasonably good, but you'll find yourself making many corrections. To improve the efficiency of working with recognition, try the following:

- Do all your dictation first and then make your revisions all at once, afterward, to save time.
- Perform more training. You can ask Word to provide more text for you to read, or, as you'll see later, you can train Word based on a document you've written yourself.

At this point, you've now trained Word sufficiently to begin using its speech-recognition capabilities. In the following sections, you'll learn how to take advantage of these features.

TIP

You can return to this wizard to perform more training at any time. From the Language Bar, choose Tools, Training.

ISSUING VOICE COMMANDS TO WORD

You control both voice commands and dictation from Word's Language Bar (see Figure 7.4). If the Language Bar does not appear, right-click the Restore button in the Windows taskbar. To turn on Voice Command, click Voice Command.

Click Voice Command to switch
to Voice Command mode

Figure 7.4
Word's Language Bar.

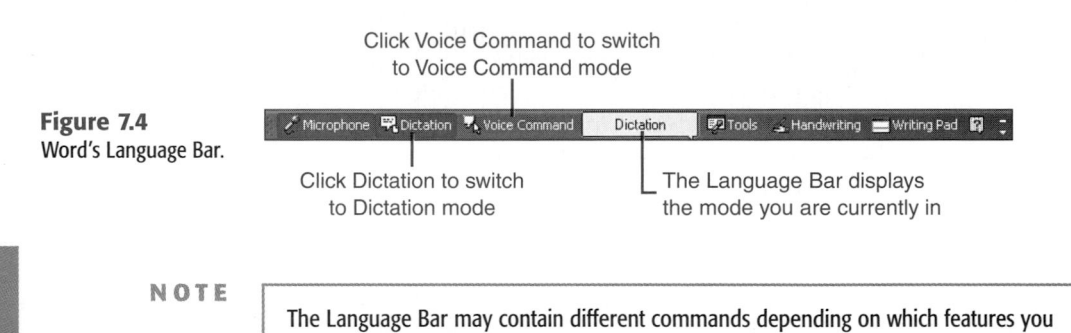

Click Dictation to switch
to Dictation mode

The Language Bar displays
the mode you are currently in

NOTE

The Language Bar may contain different commands depending on which features you are using, or have used.

Word recognizes the following commands:

- Any menu command. First say the name of the menu and then say the name of the command.
- Any command, setting, or button in a dialog box (but not numeric values in dialog boxes). To check a box, say Check, followed by the command name. To clear a box, say Uncheck, followed by the command name.
- Tabs in dialog boxes with multiple tabs.
- Any toolbar button; say the name of the button.
- The word "select," which tells Word you want to select text or other document elements next.
- The phrase "task pane," which displays the task pane.
- Various navigation settings, as listed in Table 7.1.

TABLE 7.1   NAVIGATION AND RELATED COMMANDS WORD RECOGNIZES

To Do This...	Say This...
Backspace	Backspace *or* Delete
Go back one word	Back one word *or* Last word
Go Down One Screen	Page down
Go Down	Down *or* Go down
Go forward one word	Forward one word *or* Next word
Go left	Left *or* Go left
Go right	Right *or* Go right
Go to beginning	Home *or* Go Home
Go to End	End *or* Go End
Go to next page	Next page
Go to previous page	Previous page
Go up one screen	Previous screen
Go up	Up *or* Go up
Press Escape	Escape *or* Cancel
Press the Enter key	Enter *or* Return
Press the spacebar	Space *or* Spacebar
Redo	Redo
Right-click to show a shortcut menu	Right-click *or* Context menu *or* Right-click menu
Tab	Tab
Undo	Undo

7

TIP

> It's unlikely you've memorized the names of all the toolbar buttons you'll ever want to use. For example, did you remember that the right-align button is called Align Right, not Right Align?
>
> You can always display a button's name by hovering the mouse pointer over the toolbar button. Of course, if you can hover over the button, you can also click it—but at least you'll know the name for next time.

You may find yourself using Word to format text. You can instruct Word to select text by speaking the word "select," followed by whatever you want Word to select; for example: "select word," "select paragraph," "select table," or "select all" (which selects the entire document).

When text is selected, you can speak the name of the formatting you want to apply: "bold," "italic," "underline," "bullet," "numbering," "increase indent," and so forth. You can say "font" to display the list of fonts and then speak the name of a font you want to apply, such as Arial. You can also say "font size," and then speak the font size you want to apply.

TIP

> If Word is having trouble understanding your commands, you may want to adjust the margin of error it permits in recognizing commands. To do so, follow these steps:
>
> 1. From the Language Bar, choose Tools, Options.
> 2. Click the Settings button. The Recognition Profile Settings dialog box appears (refer to Figure 7.8, later in this chapter).
> 3. In the Pronunciation Sensitivity area, drag the slider to the left, toward Low; then click OK twice.

DICTATING TO WORD

In addition to giving Word commands by voice, you can dictate to Word; Word processes the text you speak and inserts it in your document.

To begin dictation, display the Language Bar by right-clicking on the Restore icon in the Windows taskbar. If Voice Command is selected, click the Dictation button to switch into Dictation mode. Then begin speaking.

Try to speak naturally: Don't speak in the stilted "one-word-at-a-time" tone that early speech-recognition software demanded. Word actually does somewhat better with "natural" language, in which phrases run together.

As you speak, Word inserts a series of colored dots at your insertion point. As Word processes the text you've spoken, it replaces the dots with the text it believes you spoke. Depending on the speed of your computer, Word may be several seconds behind you at any time, or even further behind—don't let that distract you.

7

When you're ready to stop dictating, either click Voice Command to switch to voice commands, or click the Microphone button again to shut off the microphone.

When you start working with Word's speech-recognition feature, it's unlikely that you'll find it sufficiently reliable, even though you've already run through Word's Speech Recognition Training Wizard. There are, however, several ways you can make Word's speech recognition more accurate over time, as discussed in the following sections.

MAKING SPEECH-RECOGNITION CORRECTIONS ON-THE-FLY

If you've just spoken a sentence or phrase and Word has misheard it, you can tell Word what you meant immediately, and Word generally improves its performance the next time you speak that text. To correct a word or phrase, select and right-click on it. A shortcut menu appears, listing the first several alternatives Word considered in addition to the one it chose.

If one of these is correct, select it, and the correct text is inserted in your document. To view still more options, click More (or click Correction on the Language Bar). Word replays the word as you originally spoke it and at the same time displays a list of all the options it considered (see Figure 7.5).

Figure 7.5
Choosing from among all the possibilities Word considered when it recognized what you spoke.

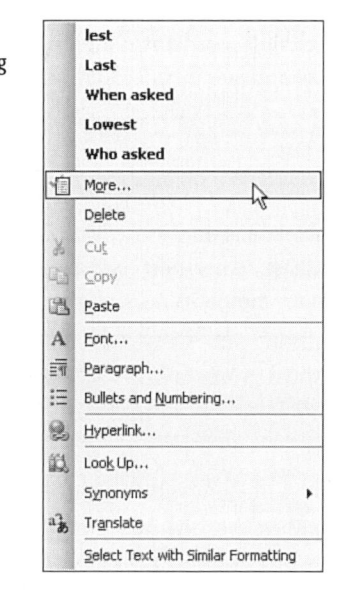

In many cases, you'll still find that none of these is what you actually said—even when Word displays as many as 20 options. What then? Add the word to Word's speech-recognition dictionary manually.

7

Adding Words to the Speech-Recognition Dictionary Manually

To add a word to the speech-recognition dictionary manually, select the word in your document that Word interpreted incorrectly, and choose Tools, Add/Delete Word(s) on the Language Bar. The Add/Delete Word(s) dialog box opens (see Figure 7.6).

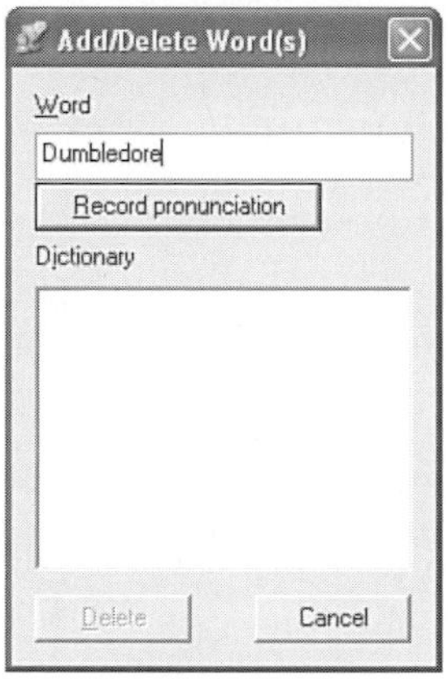

Figure 7.6
Adding or deleting a word in the speech-recognition dictionary.

With the word selected in the Word text box, click Record Pronunciation and speak the word aloud. The word or phrase you spoke now appears in the Dictionary window. To hear it read back to you, double-click on it.

NOTE

In some cases, you can tell that the problem is a phrase, not a single word. For example, Word may misinterpret the last syllable of one word as the first syllable of the next.

If the problem is with a phrase instead of a single word, don't select the phrase; just open the dialog box and type the phrase there.

If you want to add another word or phrase, you can. If you want to delete a word or phrase from the dictionary, select it and click Delete.

TIP

Usually you'll want to delete a word when, even after you recorded it, Word still gets it wrong. You can try recording it again to see whether you can speak more clearly and get better results.

Training Word from an Existing Document

As emphasized, when you begin working with Word's speech-recognition feature, your results are likely to be no better than fair—and quite likely, poor. One reason may be that Word's generic training doesn't reflect the types of content you actually create or the kinds of words you actually use.

To help solve this problem, you can "feed" Word one of your existing documents. It identifies words that aren't in its dictionary and adds them. The result: Word may now recognize these words.

Open an existing document that is representative of the work you normally do. Next, from the Language Bar, choose Tools, Learn from Document. Word builds a list of all the words in the document that do not also appear in the dictionary (see Figure 7.7).

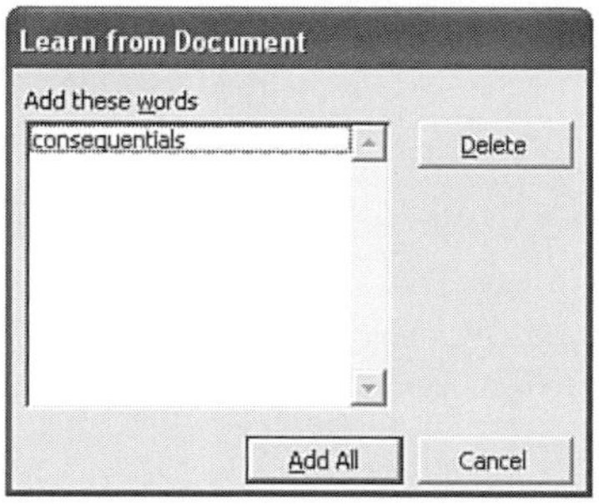

Figure 7.7
The Learn from
Document dialog box.

Select the words you want to train Word on and click Add All. Word reads each word aloud in its "text to speech" voice and adds them to the dictionary.

TRAINING WORD BY READING ADDITIONAL PASSAGES

Word provides one more tool for improving the accuracy of speech recognition: You can read additional passages that are different in content from the one you read when you first ran the Speech Recognition Wizard. These excerpts range from Aesop to Bill Gates, *The Wizard of Oz* to Edith Wharton. Click Next to begin training; as in the original wizard, Word displays a series of screens for you to read aloud.

NOTE

> These excerpts are longer than the excerpt you read to begin training Word. Set aside at least 10 minutes for each excerpt you want to read.

ADJUSTING THE TRADE-OFF BETWEEN SPEED AND ACCURACY

Speech recognition is one of the most computing-intensive tasks your computer is likely to perform, and there's a direct trade-off between speed and accuracy. Because correcting errors takes a lot of time, if you're running a fast computer you may want to adjust that trade-off, improving accuracy at the expense of speed. To do so, follow these steps:

1. From the Language Bar, choose Tools, Options.
2. Click the Settings button. The Recognition Profile Settings dialog box appears (see Figure 7.8).

7

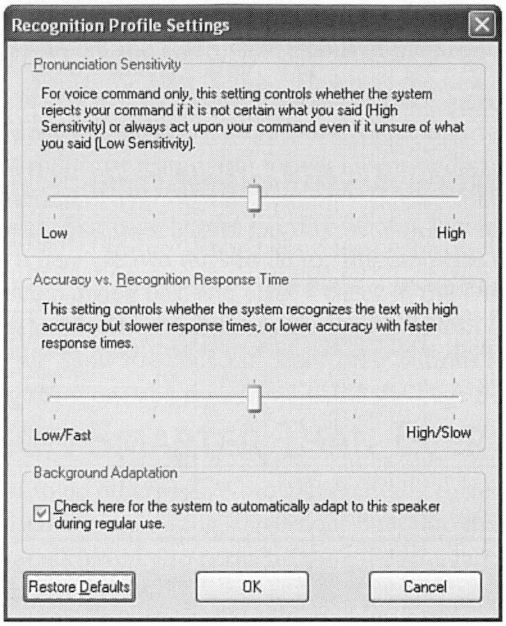

Figure 7.8
Adjusting the trade-off between accuracy and recognition.

3. In the Accuracy vs. Recognition Response Time area, drag the slider to the right, toward High/Slow; then click OK twice.

TURNING OFF THE MICROPHONE

You may find that Word hears voice commands and dictation when you're speaking to someone else, or not speaking at all. To temporarily turn off speech recognition, click the Microphone button. If you're in Voice Command mode, you can also speak the words "Microphone Off."

CREATING MULTIPLE SPEECH PROFILES

You've gone through all this effort to train your computer to recognize your voice—but what if someone else shares your computer? That person can create her own speech profile, reflecting her own training. To create a new profile, display the Language Bar; then choose Tools, Options to display the Speech Recognition tab of the Speech Properties dialog box (see Figure 7.9).

Click New to create a new profile. The Profile Wizard appears (see Figure 7.10).

7

Figure 7.9
From this dialog box, you can create new speech profiles, access more training, reconfigure your microphone, or adjust your audio inputs.

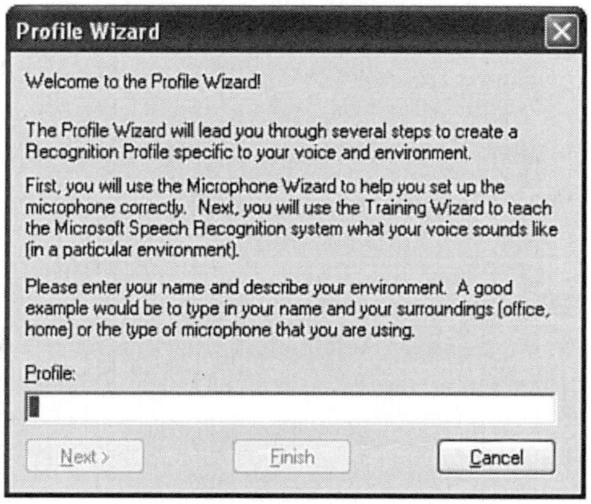

Figure 7.10
Use the Profile Wizard to create a new profile.

Enter a name for the profile and click Next. This launches the Microphone Wizard you learned about in the "Running the Microphone Wizard" section, earlier in this chapter. When the Microphone Wizard finishes running, the Microsoft Speech Recognition Training Wizard runs, as discussed earlier in the "Using the Microsoft Speech Recognition Training Wizard" section of this chapter.

When you have more than one profile, select the one you want to use from the Language Bar. Choose Tools, Current User, and select the profile you want from the list in the cascading menu.

7

CAUTION

Don't use someone else's profile, and don't let anyone use yours. Words added to the wrong profile can actually interfere with Word's recognition accuracy.

USING WORD'S HANDWRITING FEATURES

Occasionally, you may want to take handwritten notes, or you may simply prefer handwriting to typing. If you have a graphics tablet compatible with Windows, Word can read and recognize the handwritten text you create using your tablet and translate it into onscreen text you can format and edit.

NOTE

This section covers the handwriting features available when you run Word on a standard desktop or notebook PC. Later in this chapter, we cover additional ink features for the Tablet PC, in the section "Using Additional Ink Features on the Tablet PC."

NOTE

You can also use Word's handwriting support with a mouse. However, most users find it quite clumsy to write accurately with a mouse, and the resulting handwriting may be more difficult for Word to recognize.

Handwriting recognition is also available for Word in the following languages: English, Simplified Chinese, Traditional Chinese, Japanese, and Korean. It works in all major Office 2003 applications.

TIP

If you have a Windows-powered Handheld PC or PocketPC, you can convert handwritten notes you take on this device into text in Word. The steps for doing so may vary from one device to another; follow the instruction manual provided with your device.

To use Word's handwriting-recognition feature, display the Language Bar (right-click on the Language Bar icon in the tray on the Windows taskbar and choose Show the Language Bar). Next, click the Handwriting button. The Handwriting menu appears (see Figure 7.11).

Figure 7.11
The Handwriting
menu.

From here, you can choose how you want Word to work with your handwriting. You can do the following:

- If you want to write within a Writing Pad—a special window Word superimposes on your editing window—check the Writing Pad check box.
- If you want to write anywhere onscreen, check the Write Anywhere check box.
- If you want to draw an image that will be inserted as a graphic, check the Drawing Pad.
- If you want to enter characters one at a time, using an onscreen keyboard, choose On-Screen Standard Keyboard.
- If you want to enter symbols one at a time, using an onscreen keyboard, choose On-Screen Symbol Keyboard.

The Writing Pad and Write Anywhere functions are discussed in the following sections.

Using Word's Handwriting Text Recognition

If you've chosen the Writing Pad, it now appears, and you can begin writing inside its borders (see Figure 7.12). If you've chosen Write Anywhere, you can start handwriting anywhere onscreen.

Writing Pad
This course of treatment
is
Space
Tab

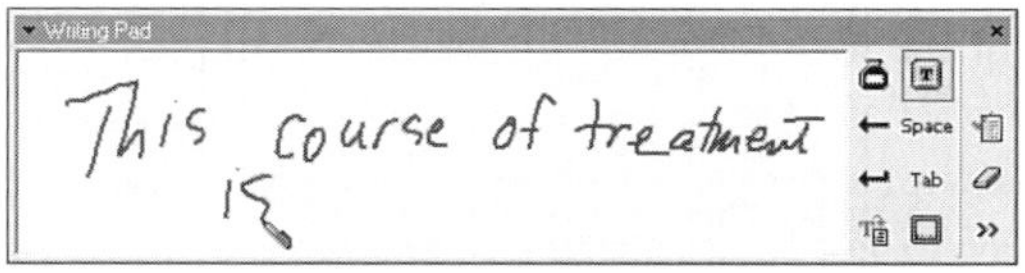

Figure 7.12
Writing inside the Writing Pad.

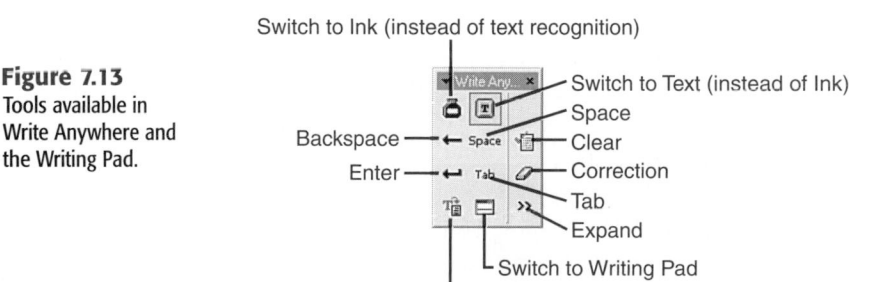

Every time you complete a word and pause momentarily, Word attempts to recognize the text you've written and then inserts the text in your document, at the insertion point.

You'll find you get the best results from printing one letter at a time, yet you may find that Word does a remarkably good job with script.

Whether you use the Writing Pad or Write Anywhere, Word provides several tools that can help you use handwriting more effectively. These appear at the right of the Writing Pad, or as a separate floating toolbar if you are using Write Anywhere (see Figure 7.13).

Switch to Ink (instead of text recognition)
Write Any...
Switch to Text (instead of Ink)
Space
Backspace
Clear
Enter
Correction
Tab
Expand
Switch to Writing Pad
Recognize Now (instead of waiting for a pause)

Figure 7.13
Tools available in Write Anywhere and the Writing Pad.

7

The toolbar provides buttons that simplify navigation and allow for the insertion of special characters, such as spaces, tabs, and paragraph marks. For even more navigation tools, click Expand. Word now adds buttons for navigating up, down, left, and right, as well as tools for displaying Word's Drawing Pad and On-Screen Keyboard (see Figure 7.14).

Figure 7.14
If you click Expand, additional tools become available.

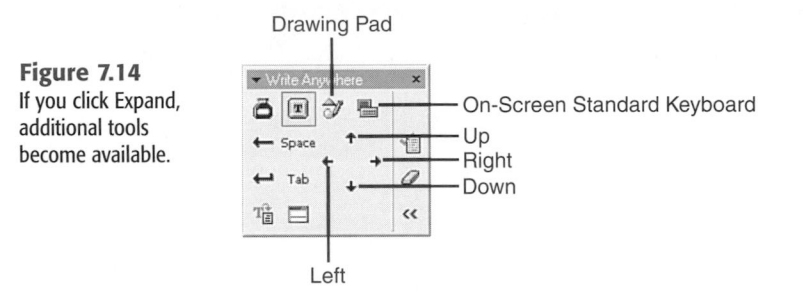

Drawing Pad

On-Screen Standard Keyboard
Up
Right
Down

Left

CORRECTING AN ERROR IN HANDWRITING RECOGNITION

When Word inserts text in your document, you may sometimes find that it has made a mistake (or, conceivably, you've made an error yourself). You can easily fix the error. Click the Correction button; then, in the document window, select the text you want to correct. When the text is selected, write your new text by hand. Word replaces the incorrect text with your replacement text.

INSERTING INK OBJECTS INTO YOUR DOCUMENT

Occasionally, you may not want to convert handwriting to text. For example, you might want to handwrite a signature and insert it in your document as a signature. For situations like these, Word provides *ink objects*.

An ink object is a picture of the handwritten text you drew, which behaves the same way as other text in your document. When an ink object appears in your document, you can select it; format it as boldface, italic, or underline; or resize it using a different font size.

In fact, you'll often want to resize ink objects because Word inserts them at the same size as surrounding text, which is often too small to be easily readable.

NOTE

> Unlike with other pictures, you cannot use most of Word's picture formatting tools with ink objects. Moreover, you can't edit the contents of an ink object after you've inserted it.
>
> You can, however, instruct Word to convert it to editable non-handwritten text, if you decide later to do so. Right-click on the ink object, and choose Ink Object, Recognize.

To insert an ink object, click Ink in the Writing Pad or Write Anywhere toolbar; then write your text, pausing a moment when you're finished. Word inserts the ink object in your document (see Figure 7.15).

7

Figure 7.15
An ink object,
enlarged to 36-point
so that it is big enough
to serve as a signature.

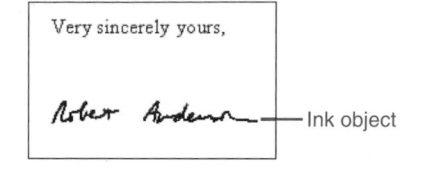

Very sincerely yours,

Robert Anderson ——— Ink object

When you want Word to begin recognizing your handwriting and inserting text again, click the Text button in the Writing Pad or Write Anywhere toolbar.

USING THE DRAWING PAD TO INSERT A HANDWRITTEN DRAWING

Word provides strong drawing tools, including powerful organization charting and business diagramming tools. However, on occasion all you need (or have time for) is a rough "back of the napkin" type of drawing—you know, the type that was supposed to launch billion-dollar companies back in the 1990s! You can now create that freehand drawing more easily than ever, from within Word.

To create a drawing and insert it in your document, follow these steps:

1. From the Language Bar, click Handwriting and select Drawing Pad from the drop-down menu. The Drawing Pad appears (see Figure 7.16).

Switch to Writing Pad

Figure 7.16
The Drawing Pad.

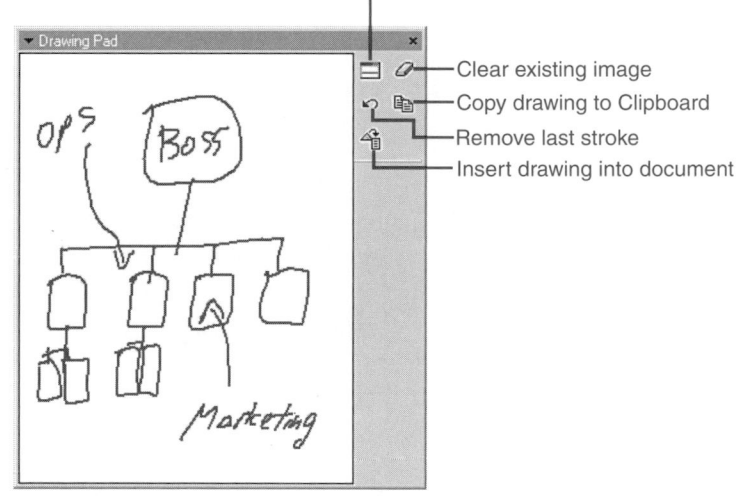

Clear existing image
Copy drawing to Clipboard
Remove last stroke
Insert drawing into document

2. Using your drawing tablet or mouse, create your drawing within the drawing area on the Drawing Pad.

3. When your drawing is complete, click Insert Drawing to insert the drawing in your document, at the current insertion point.

7

Your drawing now behaves like any other drawing. For example, it contains sizing handles you can use to resize it, and if you right-click on the drawing and choose F<u>o</u>rmat Object from the shortcut menu, you can control fill color, layout, cropping, and other attributes of the drawing.

→ For more information about formatting Word drawings, **see** "Inserting a Photo or Another Image You've Created," **p. 439**.

WORKING WITH ONSCREEN KEYBOARDS

Word provides two onscreen keyboards that allow you to enter one character at a time by selecting them onscreen instead of using a "real" keyboard. One onscreen keyboard—the On-Screen Standard Keyboard—displays the same keys as a regular keyboard. A second onscreen keyboard, the On-Screen Symbol Keyboard, displays the most commonly used symbols in languages other than English, such as è, ç, and ¥.

Onscreen keyboards are helpful for those who have trouble handling a real keyboard due to disabilities but can also be handy for anyone who wants an easy way to enter symbols.

To display the On-Screen Standard Keyboard, display the Language Bar, click Handwriting, and select On-Screen Standard Keyboard from the drop-down menu. The On-Screen Standard Keyboard appears (see Figure 7.17).

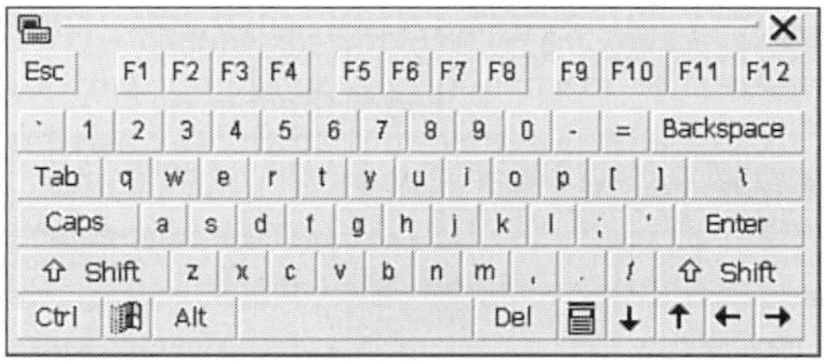

Figure 7.17
The On-Screen
Standard Keyboard.

You can now select keys by clicking on them with your mouse, or pointing to them with your graphics tablet pen. Your regular keyboard is not disabled while you use the onscreen keyboard.

When you're finished working with the onscreen keyboard, click the × at the upper right of the keyboard.

The On-Screen Symbol Keyboard works the same way as the On-Screen Standard Keyboard does. To display it from the Language Bar, click Handwriting and select On-Screen Symbol Keyboard from the drop-down menu (see Figure 7.18).

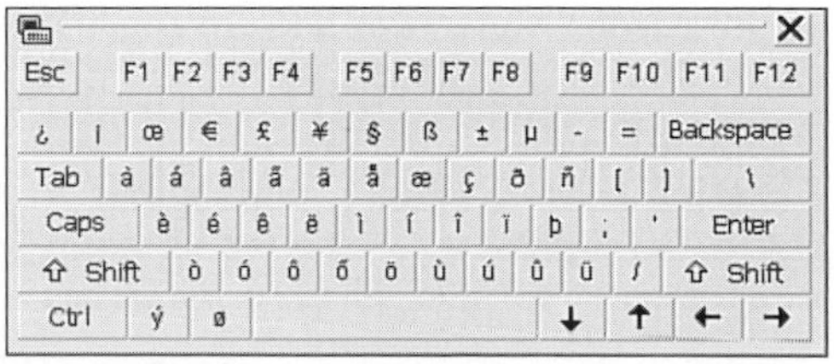

Figure 7.18
The On-Screen
Symbol Keyboard.

USING ADDITIONAL INK FEATURES ON THE TABLET PC

NEW If you are running Word on a Tablet PC, you will find additional "ink" features that permit you to integrate handwriting more thoroughly into your day-to-day work.

NOTE

> A Tablet PC is a computer running Microsoft Windows XP Tablet PC Edition. On a Tablet PC, "ink" refers to the writing or drawing strokes you make with a tablet pen (or, if you prefer, a mouse).

For example, you can

- Write or draw anywhere in a document—not just in text boxes—and then work with your text or drawing as you would work with any other graphic.
- Use a separate Ink Annotations layer to mark up an existing document by hand without changing the underlying document itself.

You can also use your tablet pen to make handwritten comments using Word's Ink Comment feature, and review them in the Reviewing Pane alongside other comments and revisions. This feature is also available to users who connect an add-on graphics tablet to an ordinary Windows XP or Windows 2000 computer.

→ For more information about formatting Word drawings, **see** "Inserting Ink Comments," **p. 882**.

WRITING IN YOUR DOCUMENT USING A TABLET PC

NEW If you are running Word on a Tablet PC, you can start writing ink in your document by following these steps:

1. Using your tablet pen, tap where you want to write.
2. Click the Ink button on the Standard toolbar, and choose Ink Drawing and Writing. The Ink Drawing and Writing toolbar appears, displaying tools for changing line color or thickness, erasing ink, selecting an object, and stopping inking in order to return to keyboard entry. A transparent Writing Canvas also appears.
3. Begin writing inside the Writing Canvas. When you're finished, tap Stop Inking on the Ink Drawing and Writing Toolbar.

TIP

> If the Writing Canvas is too large for your needs, you can shrink it like this:
> 1. Tap inside the Writing Canvas.
> 2. Tap Stop Inking.
> 3. Tap the Fit button on the Ink Drawing and Writing toolbar.
> 4. Tap outside the Ink canvas.

7

USING WORD'S INK ANNOTATIONS LAYER ON A TABLET PC

Often, you will want to mark up a document just as you would if it were printed on paper. After you've done so, you or a colleague can respond to this markup later, by making appropriate editing changes to the corresponding content. For this purpose, Word (running on a Tablet PC) provides a separate Ink Annotations layer that can be superimposed on your text.

To work with the Ink Annotations layer, first switch to Print Layout view; otherwise, your Ink Annotations may not appear exactly where you expect them to. (You can also use Reading Layout view, but you must choose the Actual Page option.)

After you've changed to an appropriate view, follow these steps:

1. Using your tablet pen, tap where you want to write.
2. Click the Ink button on the Standard toolbar, and choose Ink Annotations. The Ink Annotations toolbar appears, displaying tools for changing line color or thickness, erasing ink, displaying or hiding ink markup, and stopping inking in order to return to keyboard entry.
3. Begin writing anywhere in the editing window. When you're finished, tap Stop Inking on the Ink Annotations Toolbar.

To show or hide the Ink Annotation layer and all the annotations on it, click Markup on the Ink Annotation toolbar. Hiding Ink Annotations does not hide other inking you may have entered into your document.

CAUTION

Ink Annotations remain in the same location on your page regardless of how you edit text in your document. Accordingly, if you move text, the Ink Annotations will no longer line up correctly with that text.

TROUBLESHOOTING

SPEECH RECOGNITION ISN'T WORKING ON MY COMPUTER

In addition to the base system requirements discussed earlier (128MB RAM, 400MHz processor), Word has specific requirements for the versions of Windows that must be present in order for speech recognition to work.

In particular, if you use Windows 2000 and Microsoft Outlook/Outlook Express HTML Mail (for example, email formatted as Web pages instead of as text only), you must install Internet Explorer 5.5 with Service Pack 1 or higher.

If you are running the correct versions of Windows and Internet Explorer, check to make sure that speech features have actually been installed. Choose Start, Settings, Control Panel, Add/Remove Programs; choose Microsoft Word 2003 or Microsoft Office 2003; and click Change. Microsoft Office Setup runs; select Add or Remove Features and click Next.

Then, in the section Office Shared Features/Alternative User Input, click on Speech, and choose Run from My Computer. Finally, click Update, and Windows installs the feature.

NOTE

> You will need access to either your original Word or Office CD-ROM, or the network location from which you originally installed Word or Office.

WORD IS RECOGNIZING TEXT WHEN I DON'T WANT IT TO

It can be disconcerting to find that Word is trying to translate random noise—or your conversations with a colleague—into text onscreen. To turn speech recognition off until you need it again, click the highlighted Microphone button on the Language Bar. This should turn off the highlighting and hide the Voice Command and Dictation buttons.

MY LANGUAGE BAR DISAPPEARED

First, check to make sure you haven't moved the Language Bar somewhere it might be difficult to see, such as over another row of buttons. Second, check whether you have minimized the Language Bar to the Taskbar. If so, you can redisplay it by clicking the Restore button in the tray at the right corner of the Taskbar (see Figure 7.19).

Figure 7.19
Click the Restore button to display the Language Bar.

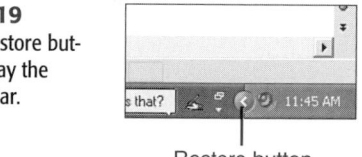

Restore button

If you have closed the Language Bar entirely, you can reopen it by choosing Tools, Speech.

WHEN I USE SPEECH OR HANDWRITING RECOGNITION, MY DOCUMENT FILES BECOME HUGE

By default, Word also stores a spoken-voice recording of the text in your document (or, if you wrote your document by hand, Word stores the handwritten text). This allows you to improve recognition: You can tell Word "what you meant to say," and Word can compare that to what it "heard."

Of course, these recordings can take up a great deal of disk space. To tell Word not to keep recordings of your voice or handwriting, choose Tools, Options, Save; then clear the Embed Linguistic Data check box, and click OK.

NOTE

> Linguistic data stored with a document is automatically deleted whenever the document is saved by versions of Word preceding Word 2002, or saved to older formats of Word, such as Word 6/95.

BUILDING SLICKER DOCUMENTS FASTER

MAKING THE MOST OF WORD'S PROOFING AND RESEARCH TOOLS

In this chapter

8

USING AUTOMATIC SPELLING AND GRAMMAR CHECKING

By default, when you open a file in Word, Word's automatic language feature checks the text to determine which language you are writing in. It then runs a spell and grammar check on all sections written in languages for which it has proofing tools. Because you probably write most documents in your default language, Word typically proofs your entire document.

Word flags all possible errors with wavy underline marks, as shown in Figure 8.1. Potential spelling errors are marked with a red wavy underline—including words not in Word's dictionary, repeated words, apparent errors in capitalization, and combinations of words with the spaces missing. Word flags potential grammar errors with a wavy green line.

NOTE

> Word can also track inconsistent formatting, if Format Tracking is turned on. To track formatting inconsistencies, choose Tools, Options, Edit, and check both the Keep Track of Formatting and the Mark Formatting Inconsistencies check boxes. Inconsistent formatting is marked with a wavy blue line. For more information on working with Format Tracking, see the "Using On-the-Fly Format Checking" section of Chapter 4, "Quick and Effective Formatting Techniques."

When Word is checking spelling or grammar, an animated icon appears in the status bar, showing a pencil writing and pages turning. When Word has completed checking spelling or grammar, the icon shown in Figure 8.1 appears.

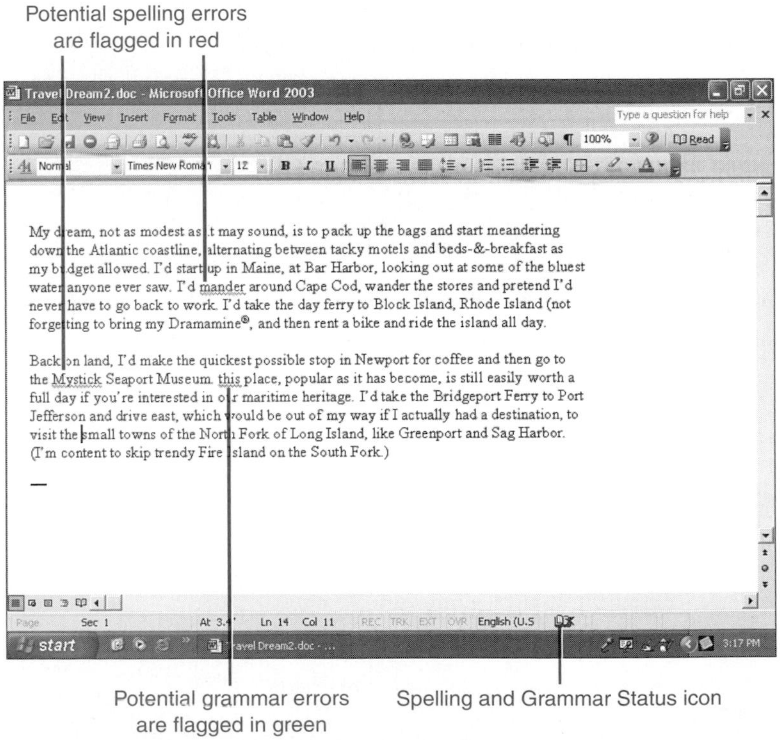

Potential spelling errors
are flagged in red

Figure 8.1
Potential spelling and grammar errors are flagged automatically by Word.

Potential grammar errors   Spelling and Grammar Status icon
are flagged in green

➔ For more information about automatic language detection, **see** "Turning on Automatic Language Detection in Word," **p. 1138**.

TIP

> Some users do not like the red and green colors Word provides for underlining potential spelling and grammar errors. In addition, some color-blind users find that Word's red and green colors look alike to them. Microsoft has provided a macro you can use to change these colors.
>
> The macro is part of Word's SUPPORT.DOT template. To use it to change the colors of Word's proofing underlining, follow the steps listed next.
>
> Unless you want to trust all macros from Microsoft, before you follow these steps, make sure that your security level is not set to High. To do so, choose Tools, Macro, Security; click the Security Level tab; choose Medium; and click OK.
>
> 1. Choose Tools, Templates and Add-Ins.
> 2. Click Add.
> 3. Browse to the SUPPORT.DOT template, which is typically found in the \Program Files\Microsoft Office\Office11\Macros folder.
> 4. Select SUPPORT.DOT, and click OK.
> 5. If a Security Warning dialog box appears, you have two options:
>   - You can check Always Trust Macros from this Publisher, and click Enable Macros. From now on, Word will automatically assume that it can run macros authenticated as coming from Microsoft.
>   - You can cancel the wizard, and reduce your security setting to Medium, as described immediately before this procedure.
> 6. Choose Tools, Macro, Macros.
> 7. From the Macros In drop-down box, choose SUPPORT.DOT (global template).
> 8. In the Macro Name scroll box, choose RegOptions, and click Run. The Word Options tab of the Set Registry Options dialog box appears.
> 9. From the Option scroll box, choose SpellingWavyUnderlineColor.
> 10. Click Choose Color.
> 11. Select the color you want Word to use when it flags a potential spelling error, and click OK.
> 12. To change the color Word uses for grammar errors, choose GrammarWavyUnderlineColor in the Option scroll box, and repeat steps 9–10.
> 13. When you're finished, click Close.

In general, Word flags as potential spelling errors any word it cannot find in its built-in dictionaries, or in any added dictionary entries you have created.

NOTE

> Word disregards certain text that would ordinarily lead to extensive "false positives," such as Internet and file addresses. Later, in the section "Controlling Spelling Settings," you'll learn how to control which text Word ignores.

The easiest way to resolve an individual potential spelling error is to right-click on the flagged word. A shortcut menu appears (see Figure 8.2), listing any suggestions Word may have about the correct spelling, as well as a set of other choices. These choices, which depend on the error Word has found, include the following:

- **Ignore All.** Tells Word to disregard all occurrences of the spelling within the current document (and to stop displaying them with red underline).

- **Add to Dictionary.** Tells Word to add the spelling to your custom dictionary; after you add it, Word won't flag the spelling as an error anymore, in any document that uses the same custom dictionary.

- **AutoCorrect.** Enables you to select a way to correct your spelling and add it to your AutoCorrect file so that Word can make the same correction automatically every time you make this (exact) mistake from now on.

- **Language.** Enables you to mark the word as being in another language. If you have proofing tools installed for that language, Word uses those proofing tools automatically to check the word. If you do not have the appropriate proofing tools, Word skips the word and any future occurrences for that document.

- **Spelling.** Opens Word's spell checker dialog box, which may provide more alternative spellings than the shortcut menu, and can allow you to save a new word in a different custom dictionary, if you have one. Custom dictionaries are covered in greater detail later in this chapter, in the "Creating Custom Dictionaries for Custom Needs" section.

- **Look Up.** Opens Word's Research task pane, and searches Encarta Dictionary and other Web reference books to see whether the word can be found—and if so, provides definitions and pronunciation information.

→ For more information about using Word's reference tools, **see** "Working with Additional Research Services," **p. 276**.

Figure 8.2
You can access Word's most commonly used proofing features from the Spelling and Grammar shortcut menu.

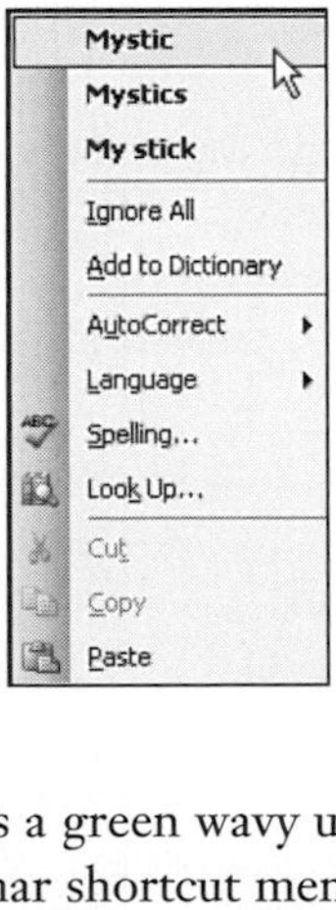

| Mystic |
| Mystics |
| My stick |
| Ignore All |
| Add to Dictionary |
| AutoCorrect ▶ |
| Language ▶ |
| Spelling... |
| Look Up... |
| Cut |
| Copy |
| Paste |

If Word shows a green wavy underline indicating a possible grammar error, right-click to see the grammar shortcut menu. Word may propose choices, as in Figure 8.3, or make general suggestions. You can also

- Instruct Word to ignore the sentence this time only (Ignore Once).

- Open the <u>G</u>rammar checker to see more options. (For more information about grammar checking, see "Checking Your Document's Grammar," later in this chapter.)

- Choose A<u>b</u>out This Sentence to see more information about the potential error Word has flagged.

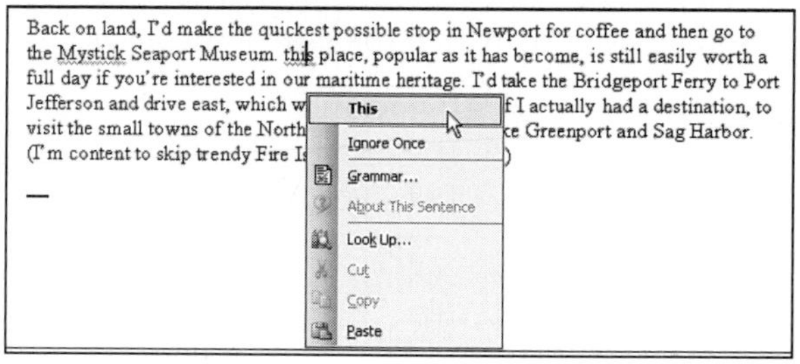

Figure 8.3
In some cases, Word presents a specific suggestion for solving the grammar problem.

You can also resolve errors without using the shortcut menu by simply editing the text. Word checks the word or sentence again as you move your insertion point away from it, and if the word is now spelled correctly or the sentence now uses correct grammar, the corresponding wavy underline disappears.

> **TIP**
>
> To quickly find the next spelling or grammar problem, double-click the Spelling and Grammar Status icon on the status bar (at the bottom of the screen), or press Alt+F7.

DISABLING OR HIDING AUTOMATIC SPELLING AND GRAMMAR CHECKING

Automatic spelling and grammar checking isn't everyone's cup of tea. Many people appreciate the way it catches typos and other inadvertent errors as they make them—without going through the trouble of a formal spelling or grammar check. Others find it distracting and want to turn it off immediately—especially the grammar checker, which has improved but is still far from perfect. Automatic spelling and grammar checking also slows down Word slightly.

If you prefer not to use automatic spell checking or automatic grammar checking, you can easily turn off one or both of them. Choose <u>T</u>ools, <u>O</u>ptions, and click the Spelling & Grammar tab in the dialog box that appears. Then, to disable automatic spell checking, clear the Check S<u>p</u>elling as You Type check box. To disable automatic grammar checking, clear the Check <u>G</u>rammar as You Type check box. When you're finished, click OK and your document is now free of red and green wavy lines.

> **TIP**
>
> You can also display Spelling & Grammar options by right-clicking the Spelling & Grammar Status icon on the status bar and choosing <u>O</u>ptions from the shortcut menu. For more information about spelling options, see "Controlling Spelling Settings," later in this chapter.

8

Another option is to enable Word to keep checking the document but prevent it from displaying the potential problems with red or green wavy underlines.

You can also do this from the Spelling & Grammar tab of the Options dialog box. Check the boxes Hide Spelling Errors in This Document and Hide Grammatical Errors in This Document. The result will be a less cluttered-looking document—but because Word is still checking your document in the background, you won't gain much performance.

Later, when you check the document's spelling or grammar using the Spelling and Grammar dialog box, the process goes faster because Word has already found the potential errors. Or, when you're ready, you can clear these check boxes and fix all your potential errors at once from within the document.

CHECKING SPELLING THROUGH THE SPELLING AND GRAMMAR DIALOG BOX

In addition to the streamlined spelling and grammar tools Word makes available through the shortcut menu, Word provides a powerful spelling- and grammar-checking dialog box that gives you even more options for fixing your current document—and improving the way you check future documents. To access it, click the Spelling and Grammar button on the Standard toolbar, or press F7.

The Spelling and Grammar dialog box opens, displaying the first potential error it finds, starting from the current text cursor position (see Figure 8.4).

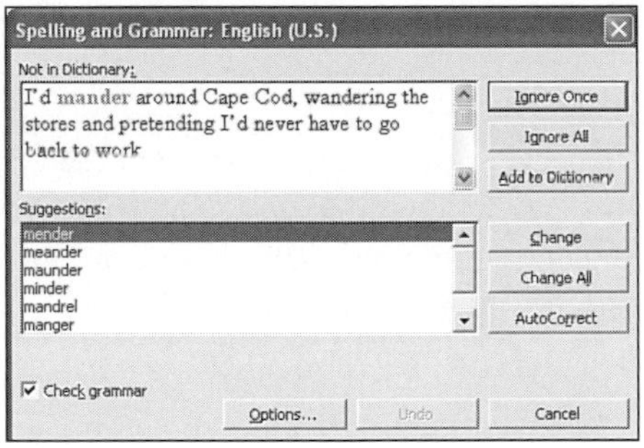

Figure 8.4
The Spelling and Grammar dialog box, showing a spelling error and offering suggestions.

NOTE

Word displays both spelling and grammar errors in the Spelling and Grammar dialog box. If you want to check only spelling, clear the Check Grammar check box.

The sentence containing the potential problem appears in the Not in Dictionary scroll box; the incorrect word appears in red. You now have several options:

- If you want to disregard the spelling error without ignoring it elsewhere in the document, choose Ignore Once.

- If you want Word to disregard the spelling error throughout the current document, choose Ignore All.

- If the word is spelled correctly and you want Word to add it to the custom dictionary (so that the word will never be flagged as wrong again), click Add to Dictionary.

- If one of the words shown in the Suggestions list is correct, click on the correct word. Then, click Change; Word changes the spelling to match that suggestion.

- If you want to change the spelling wherever it appears in the document, click on the correct word. Then, click Change All.

- If you want to add the correction to its AutoCorrect database so that Word can fix the error as soon as you make it from now on, click on the correct word. Then, click AutoCorrect.

- If Word hasn't made any acceptable suggestions, but you know how to fix the error manually, edit the word in the Not in Dictionary scroll box and click Change (or Change All or AutoCorrect).

→ For more information about AutoCorrect, **see** Chapter 9, "Automating Your Documents," **p. 287**.

No matter which option you choose, Word follows your instructions and automatically moves to the next potential error it finds. If you've chosen to proof only part of your document (by selecting that part of the document before running the spell check), Word offers to proof the rest after it finishes checking your selection. Otherwise, it reports that the spelling and grammar check is complete.

The next section has more information about proofing portions of a document.

TIP

> If a change you make to fix a word or syntax error affects surrounding text, you can edit any part of the sentence that appears in the Not in Dictionary scroll box—not just the incorrect portion.
>
> Or, if you prefer, you can click inside the document and make your edits there. The Spelling and Grammar dialog box remains open. When you finish, click inside the dialog box and click Resume.

PROOFING ONLY PART OF A DOCUMENT

Word enables you to check your entire document or any part of it, including individual words. If you don't want to check your entire document, select only the text you want to check—even if it's just a single word.

You can also tell Word to never proof a portion of your document. To do so, select the text you don't want proofed. Next, choose Tools, Language, Set Language. The Language dialog box opens. Check the Do Not Check Spelling or Grammar check box and click OK. This turns off both spelling and grammar for the portion of the document you selected.

8

UNDOING SPELLING OR GRAMMAR CHANGES YOU JUST MADE

You can always undo your most recent spelling or grammar changes (except for adding words to a custom dictionary). From within the Spelling and Grammar dialog box, click Undo.

If you've already finished spell checking, you can still click the Undo button on the Standard toolbar to undo one change at a time, starting with the last change you made. You might find this most useful if you've been spot-checking specific changes in your document, rather than spell checking the document as a whole.

REVISING A PREVIOUSLY CHECKED DOCUMENT

If you proof a document a second time, Word doesn't recheck the spelling of words (or the syntax of sentences) you already proofed and chose to ignore. If you want Word to catch previously caught errors, reopen the Spelling & Grammar Options dialog box (either choose Tools, Options and click the Spelling & Grammar tab or click the Options button inside the Spelling & Grammar dialog box) and click the Recheck Document button. Word asks you to confirm that you want to recheck text you've already proofed; choose Yes.

CONTROLLING SPELLING SETTINGS

The Spelling & Grammar tab of the Options dialog box (see Figure 8.5) gives you extensive control over how you interact with Word's spell checker. You can display this dialog box by clicking the Options button in the Spelling and Grammar dialog box, or by choosing Tools, Options, and clicking the Spelling & Grammar tab.

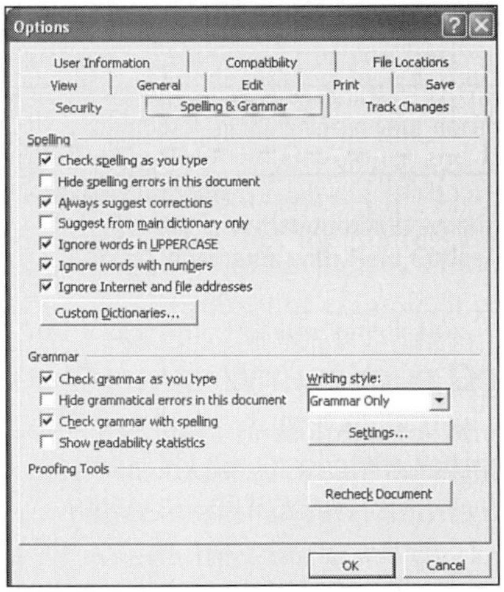

Figure 8.5
You can control the behavior of spelling and grammar from the Spelling & Grammar tab of the Options dialog box.

You've already learned about the first two options in this dialog box: Check Spelling as You Type and Hide Spelling Errors in This Document. Word also offers you several additional controls:

- **Always Suggest Corrections.** Word's spelling suggestions are often inaccurate in highly technical documents or documents that contain a lot of arcane jargon. For such documents, to save time, you might want to disable Word's suggested-spellings feature.

- **Suggest from Main Dictionary Only.** By default, Word looks in all open dictionaries to make suggestions about spelling changes. This can take time. It also means that Word may recognize as correct certain words that are actually incorrect when read in context. If you're sure your current document won't benefit from words you added to your custom dictionaries, check this box.

- **Ignore Words in UPPERCASE.** No spell checker understands all acronyms. Because most acronyms are all caps, you can tell Word not to flag words that are all caps. (This feature is turned on by default.)

- **Ignore Words with Numbers.** Some product names combine words and numbers. Suppose that you sell a 324MX computer, a D1007 CD player, and a KFE259 fire extinguisher. Word might flag each of these as incorrect—a real problem if you're proofing a long price list. Therefore, by default, Word ignores word/number combinations.

- **Ignore Internet and File Addresses.** Until recently, most spell checkers have incorrectly flagged Internet file addresses such as the Web address www.microsoft.com or the filename c:\windows\system.dat. If you leave this check box checked, Word doesn't spell check addresses such as these.

The Spelling & Grammar tab can control one additional aspect of Word spell checking: custom dictionaries. These are covered in the next section.

CREATING CUSTOM DICTIONARIES FOR CUSTOM NEEDS

When you use Word's spell checker to add words to your dictionary, Word stores these in a custom dictionary file called custom.dic. It then consults custom.dic whenever you run a spell check—thereby making sure that it doesn't flag words as incorrect that you indicated are accurate. If you want, you can also create other custom dictionaries—up to 10—for special purposes. For example, if you do legal editing on only Tuesdays and Thursdays, you can maintain a legal custom dictionary and use it on only those days.

The following sections show you how to work with Word's custom dictionaries.

CREATING A NEW CUSTOM DICTIONARY

To create a new custom dictionary, choose Tools, Options, Spelling & Grammar, and click Custom Dictionaries. The Custom Dictionaries dialog box appears (see Figure 8.6), listing custom dictionaries that already exist. Dictionaries that are currently enabled—in other words, dictionaries Word is currently using in spell checking—appear checked.

To create a new dictionary, click New. The Create Custom Dictionary dialog box opens. Enter a name for your dictionary and click Save. The dictionary now appears checked in the Custom Dictionaries dialog box. Note that words you add to custom dictionaries during a spell check are placed in the Default custom dictionary—whichever one is currently listed first.

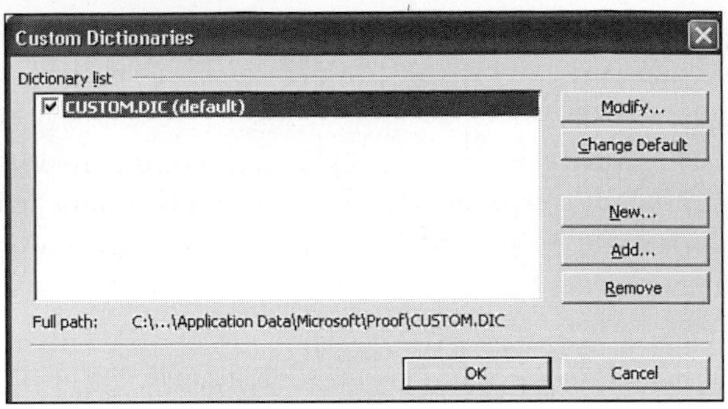

Figure 8.6
The Custom Dictionaries dialog box shows the custom dictionaries being used during a spelling and grammar check.

DISABLING A CUSTOM DICTIONARY

From the Custom Dictionaries dialog box, you can also make a custom dictionary unavailable by clearing its check box. While the dictionary is unavailable, keeping it in the list allows you to make it available again without first browsing your system to locate it.

To make the dictionary disappear entirely from the list of dictionaries, select it and click Remove. Note that this doesn't erase the dictionary file; you can use the Add button to locate it, place it back on your list, and make it available again.

CHOOSING A CUSTOM DICTIONARY WHILE SPELL CHECKING

Suppose, during a spell check, that you find a word you want to add to a custom dictionary other than the default custom.dic file that Word normally uses. To select a different custom dictionary, perform these steps:

1. Make sure that the word you want to add appears highlighted in the Spelling and Grammar dialog box.
2. Click Options.
3. Click Custom Dictionaries.
4. Make sure that a check mark appears next to the custom dictionary where you want to store words.
5. If the dictionary you want to use is not the default dictionary, select it, and click Change Default. After you change the *default* custom dictionary, Word places all words you add in *that* custom dictionary until you change it again.
6. Click OK twice to return to the Spelling and Grammar dialog box.
7. Click Add to add the word to the dictionary you've selected. Any additional words you add to the custom dictionary will be placed in the dictionary you've selected, until you choose a different one.
8. Continue checking spelling and grammar as usual. If you want to add words to a different custom dictionary, change the custom dictionary by following steps 1–5 again.

EDITING A CUSTOM DICTIONARY

While you're spell checking, it's easy to mistakenly add words to the custom dictionary that shouldn't be there. If you do enter words in a custom dictionary by mistake, however, it's easy to delete them. You can also manually add lists of words to a custom dictionary—you don't have to wait for them to show up in your documents. For example, you might want to add the last names of all the employees in your company or the company names of all your clients.

There are two ways to edit a custom dictionary. If you simply want to add or delete one word, or a few words, Word provides a dialog box that makes this easy. If you want to add many words at once, you can edit the .dic file manually. Each approach is covered next.

ADDING AND DELETING INDIVIDUAL WORDS FROM A CUSTOM DICTIONARY

To add or delete a single word from a custom dictionary, display the Spelling & Grammar tab of the Tools, Options dialog box; then follow these steps:

1. Click Custom Dictionaries.
2. Select the dictionary you want to edit.
3. Click Modify. Word displays a dialog box listing all the words in the custom dictionary you selected (see Figure 8.7).

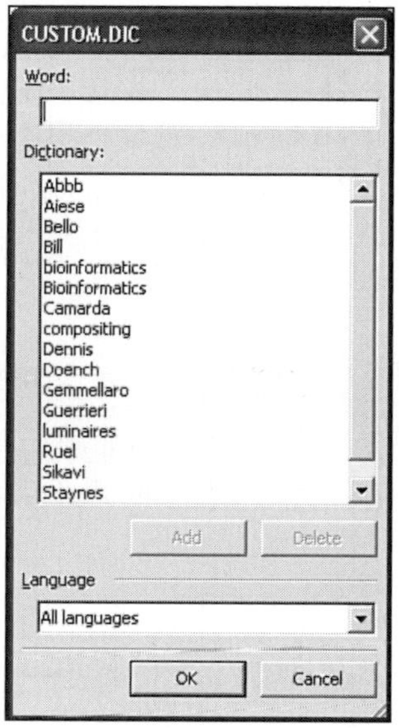

Figure 8.7
Word displays a dialog box that simplifies the editing of custom dictionaries.

4. To add a new word, type it in the Word text box and click Add.
5. To delete an existing word, choose it from the Dictionary scroll box and click Delete.
6. When you've finished making changes to your custom dictionary, click OK.

8

COPYING LARGE NUMBERS OF WORDS INTO A CUSTOM DICTIONARY

The dialog box covered in the preceding section is designed to work one word at a time. If you want to add many words to a custom dictionary, you can do so. Because word dictionary files are ASCII (text only) lists of words with a .dic extension, you can use Word to open them and look at them.

When you open a custom dictionary, you can add as many words as you want—either manually, or by cutting and pasting them from another file. The only limitation is that you must save the file as a Text Only (.txt) document and place only one word on each line.

NOTE

Word stores words in custom dictionaries in alphabetical order, with all capitalized words appearing before all lowercased words. However, you do not need to store your words in this order—you can insert them any way you want. Word reorganizes your list automatically the next time you add a word to this dictionary during a spell check.

To edit a custom dictionary manually (without using the Custom Dictionaries dialog box), perform the following steps:

1. Choose File, Open.

2. Browse to and open the custom dictionary. Typical Windows 2000 and Windows XP systems store custom dictionaries in the \Documents and Settings*profile*\application data\microsoft\proof folder, where *profile* is the user profile associated with this installation of Office.

3. Copy or type the new words into the file. One word should appear on each line, separated from other words by a paragraph mark (press Enter, *not* Shift+Enter). Figure 8.8 shows a sample dictionary file being edited.

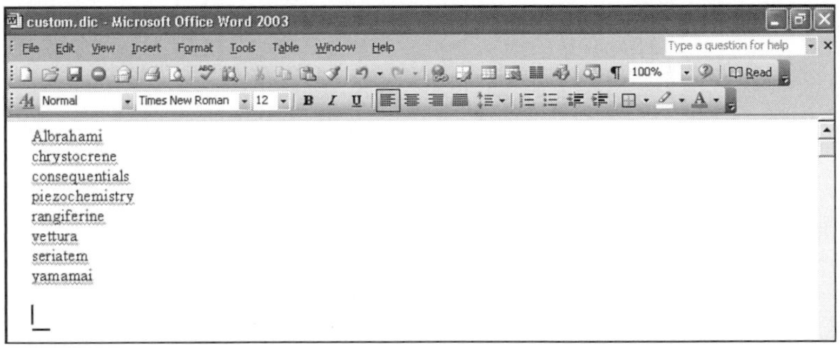

Figure 8.8
Editing a custom dictionary manually.

4. Save the file as a Plain Text (.txt) file. Be sure to change Word's default file extension from .txt to .dic.

FLAGGING "CORRECT" WORDS AS POTENTIAL ERRORS

Occasionally, you might want to have the spell checker flag a word as a possible misspelling even though the word is in the dictionary. Suppose that you often mistype "liar" as "lira," both of which are spelled correctly. Because you write crime novels, not reports on European currency exchange, wouldn't it be nifty if the spell checker would always question "lira" as a misspelling, rather than assume that you know what you're doing?

You can't remove a word from Word's basic dictionary. You can, however, create a supplemental file called an *exclude dictionary*, which includes words you want to flag as problems even if they're spelled correctly.

CAUTION

When you create an exclude dictionary, all your Office applications will use it.

Like custom dictionaries, exclude dictionaries are ASCII files with one word on each line. Exclude dictionaries use the same filename as the main dictionaries with which they're connected, except that they have an .exc extension. They are stored in the same folder as the main dictionary.

For example, if you are using the default dictionary for American English, mssp3en.lex, then the name of the exclude dictionary you will create must be mssp3en.exc.

The default location for the exclude dictionary is the following path: Windows\application data\microsoft\proof.

To create an exclude dictionary, edit it manually and save it as Text Only with the correct name and extension in the correct folder. (Make sure that Word doesn't append a .txt extension to the filename, or it won't work.)

SPELL CHECKING TEXT IN FOREIGN LANGUAGES

By default, Word is installed with spelling and grammar dictionaries for three languages: English, Spanish, and French. You can spell check text in any of these three languages, or in any other language whose proofing files you install.

To proof in a foreign language, first mark the text you want to proofread to specify the language it is written in—or ask Word to attempt to identify the language automatically. (Doing so is covered in the following section.) After the text has been properly identified, use the spell checker and grammar checker as you normally do.

NOTE

By default, Word attempts to identify the language associated with each paragraph automatically; however, in our experience, it often fails.

To tell Word not to attempt to identify languages, clear the Detect Language Automatically check box in the Language dialog box.

8

→ For more information about working with foreign languages in Word, **see** Chapter 35, "Using Word's Multilingual and Accessibility Features," **p. 1131**.

IDENTIFYING TEXT IN A FOREIGN LANGUAGE

To mark text in the language it has been written in, first select the text. Then, choose Tools, Language, Set Language. The Language dialog box opens (see Figure 8.9).

Figure 8.9
Marking selected text with the language it has been written in.

In the Mark Selected Text As scroll box, scroll to and select the language you want Word to use for proofing. Then click OK.

A CLOSER LOOK AT THE GRAMMAR CHECKER

Word's grammar checker, like all contemporary grammar checkers, follows rules that identify potential writing problems. Word's grammar checker has gradually been refined; however, it still cannot "understand" your documents the way a friend, co-worker, or English teacher would, so it's best to have modest expectations.

On a good day, the grammar checker might pleasantly surprise you—catching things you would never have noticed. On another day, it may flag many "errors" that are, in fact, not errors at all. Later, you'll learn to personalize the grammar checker to catch only the types of errors you actually make, with fewer false alarms.

CHECKING YOUR DOCUMENT'S GRAMMAR

As you learned earlier in this chapter, Word flags potential grammar problems as you work, displaying them with a green wavy underline. To get Word's suggestions, right-click anywhere in the underlined text. Word displays either potential solutions or a general description of what it thinks is wrong. For example, in Figure 8.10, Word recommends that you consider revising a double negative.

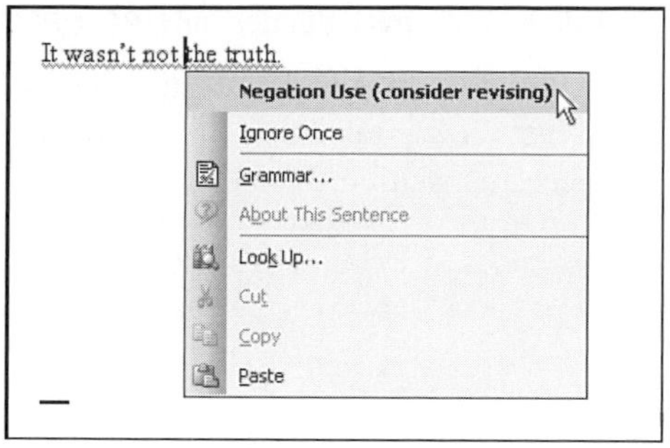

8

Figure 8.10
Viewing Word's suggested solutions for a potential grammar problem.

It wasn't not the truth.

Negation Use (consider revising)

Ignore Once

Grammar...

About This Sentence

Look Up...

Cut

Copy

Paste

If the grammar checker makes a specific recommendation, you can click that recommendation to accept it. Or you can tell Word to Ignore the flagged words altogether. If you want to take a closer look at a highlighted word or passage, choose Grammar. The Grammar dialog box opens, with the questionable phrase displayed in green (see Figure 8.11).

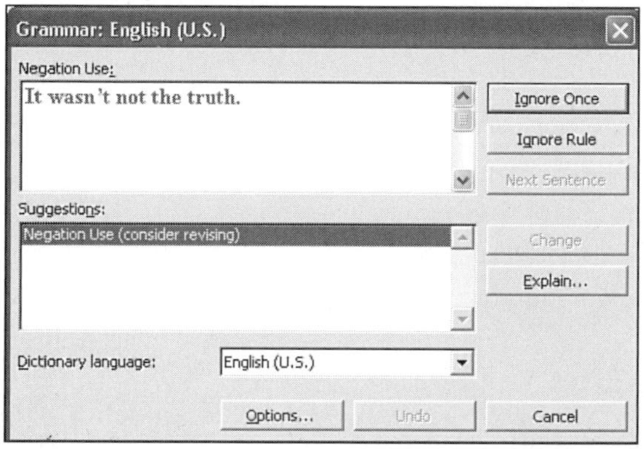

Figure 8.11
The Grammar dialog box, displaying a potential grammar error.

Grammar: English (U.S.)

Negation Use:

It wasn't not the truth.

Ignore Once

Ignore Rule

Next Sentence

Suggestions:

Negation Use (consider revising)

Change

Explain...

Dictionary language: English (U.S.)

Options... Undo Cancel

Word displays possible improvements in the Suggestions scroll box. The category of problem it has identified appears above the flagged text. Often, none of Word's suggestions is ideal; you can then edit the text manually until the green wavy underlines disappear.

It's also quite possible that you won't agree there's a problem at all. To tell Word to ignore the sentence, click Ignore Once. To tell Word never to flag problems for the same reason it flagged this one, click Ignore Rule. To leave the sentence alone without making any decisions, click Next Sentence.

Word follows your instructions and moves to the next potential error it finds—either a spelling or a grammar error. If you've chosen to proof only part of your document, after Word finishes, it offers to proof the rest. Otherwise, it reports that it has finished proofing.

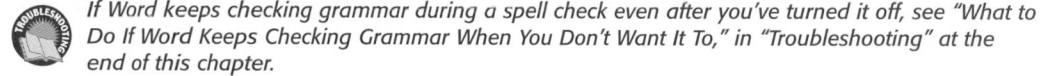 *If Word keeps checking grammar during a spell check even after you've turned it off, see "What to Do If Word Keeps Checking Grammar When You Don't Want It To," in "Troubleshooting" at the end of this chapter.*

8

Strategies for Making Grammar Checking Work More Effectively

Word's grammar checker contains 34 fundamental rules it can check in your document, ranging from determining proper sentence capitalization to recognizing clichés. Word provides two built-in approaches for checking writing. It can check the following:

Grammar Only settings:

- Capitalization
- Misused words
- Noun phrases
- Punctuation
- Relative clauses
- Verb phrases

- Fragments and run-ons
- Negation
- Possessives and plurals
- Questions
- Subject-verb agreement

Grammar and Style settings:

- All the rules in Grammar Only, plus those listed here
- Clichés, colloquialisms, and jargon
- Contractions
- Sentence fragments
- Gender-specific words
- Hyphenated and compound words
- Misused words
- Numbers
- Passive sentences
- Possessives and plurals
- Punctuation

- Relative clauses
- Sentence length
- Sentence structure
- Sentences beginning with *And*, *But*, and *Hopefully*
- Successive nouns
- Successive prepositional phrases
- Unclear phrasing
- Use of first person
- Verb phrases
- Wordiness
- Words in split infinitives

Note that several of the same rules are covered in both Grammar and Grammar and Style. If you select the rule in Grammar and Style, Word not only flags the issue, but also makes stylistic suggestions for revision.

You can change the settings for either Grammar Only or Grammar and Style to apply a "mix and match" of grammatical rules to the grammar check of your document.

One strategy for deciding how to deal with the grammar checker is to run a full grammar check on a few of your documents, noticing which types of errors you make most often, and then customize the grammar checker to flag only those errors. The grammar checker is especially good at catching passive sentences, subject-verb disagreements, incorrect punctuation, and clichés.

TIP

Writing-style preferences are stored with templates, so you can set different preferences for different templates. After you've done so, the appropriate settings are automatically used when you create a document based on the template.

→ For more information about creating templates, **see** Chapter 11, "Templates, Wizards, and Add-Ins," **p. 355**.

CHOOSING WHICH WRITING STYLE TO APPLY

To switch between Grammar Only and Grammar and Style—or back again—choose Tools, Options; then click the Spelling & Grammar tab. In the Writing Style drop-down list box, choose Grammar & Style or Grammar Only. Then click OK.

CHOOSING WHICH RULES OF GRAMMAR TO APPLY

You can edit either of Word's writing styles, Grammar Only or Grammar and Style. To do so, display the Spelling & Grammar tab of the Options dialog box and click Settings. The Grammar Settings dialog box opens, as shown in Figure 8.12.

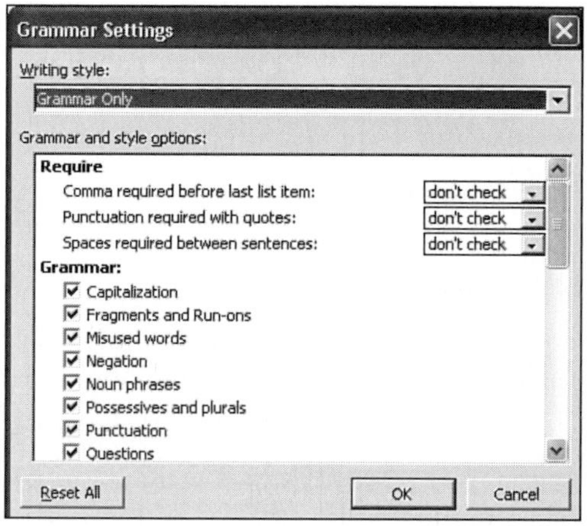

Figure 8.12
The Grammar Settings dialog box gives you control over how Word checks your grammar.

In this dialog box, follow these steps:

1. In the Writing Style drop-down box, choose the writing style you want to edit, Grammar Only or Grammar and Style.

2. Check the boxes corresponding to rules you want the grammar checker to enforce; clear the boxes corresponding to rules you want to ignore.

3. When you're finished, click OK.

If you later decide that you want to use Word's default grammar settings, reopen the Grammar Settings dialog box, choose the writing style you want to reset, and choose Reset All.

8

Looking at Figure 8.12, you'll notice that Word's grammar settings include three settings you may be interested in even if you never use grammar checking for anything else. They are listed at the top of the Grammar and Style Options scroll box, in the Require area:

- **Comma Required Before Last List Item.** Some individuals swear by serial commas; others swear against them. If you're a professional writer, you may find that even your clients disagree about them, making it easy to make mistakes! You can instruct Word to make sure that you always use a serial comma before the last item of a list, make sure that you never use one, or ignore the issue completely (don't check).

- **Punctuation Required with Quotes.** You can specify whether you prefer to place punctuation inside or outside your quote marks, or whether Word should ignore how you punctuate quotes.

- **Spaces Required Between Sentences.** If you are of a certain age, your typing teacher taught you always to place two spaces between sentences. Now, in this era of typeset and desktop published documents using attractive fonts, the standard has changed: You should generally use one space between sentences. You can use this setting to specify one or two spaces between sentences, or to instruct Word to ignore the issue altogether.

You might decide that one or more of these three settings are all the grammar you ever want to check. In that case, choose Grammar Only as your writing style; clear all the Grammar check boxes; establish the settings of your choice for commas, punctuation, and spaces between sentences; and click OK. From now on, when you check the grammar of documents associated with the current template, Word will check only the commas, punctuation, and spaces between the sentences.

USING THE WORD THESAURUS

As you write, you may sometimes find yourself getting into a rut—using the same word or phrase repeatedly when another word might make your point more clearly. That's what a thesaurus is for—and Word comes with a fairly powerful one.

To use the thesaurus, right-click on the word for which you want to see synonyms (similar meanings) and choose Synonyms on the shortcut menu (see Figure 8.13). Or select the word and press Shift+F7. Select an option to use in place of the existing word.

If you don't like any of the options Word presents and you want to explore further, choose Thesaurus from the shortcut menu. Word's Research Task Pane opens, displaying a list of synonyms—sometimes a longer list than the one you already saw, or a list that presents more meanings to choose from, each with its own synonyms (see Figure 8.14).

TIP

> If the word you want to look up isn't in the document yet, click on a blank area in the editing window and press Shift+F7. Word displays the Research task pane with the English (U.S.) thesaurus selected and all its text boxes empty. You can now enter the word in the Search For box.

The word you select appears in the Search For text box. Below, in the scroll box, Word lists several synonyms (and, in some cases, an antonym). The example in Figure 8.13 asks for synonyms for the word "place," and Word lists a series of options beginning with "put" as the most likely synonyms.

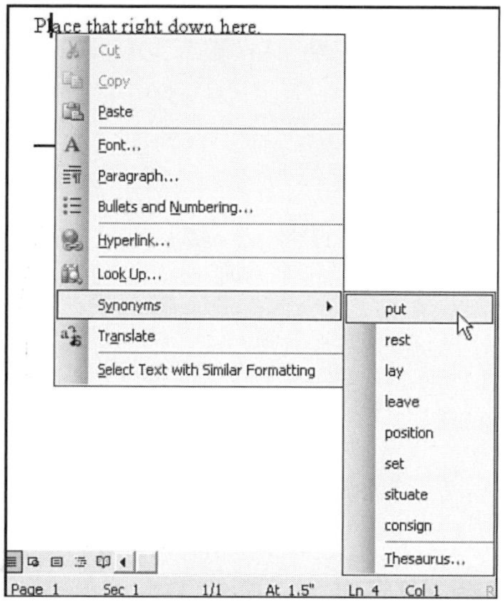

Figure 8.13
Choosing a synonym from the shortcut menu.

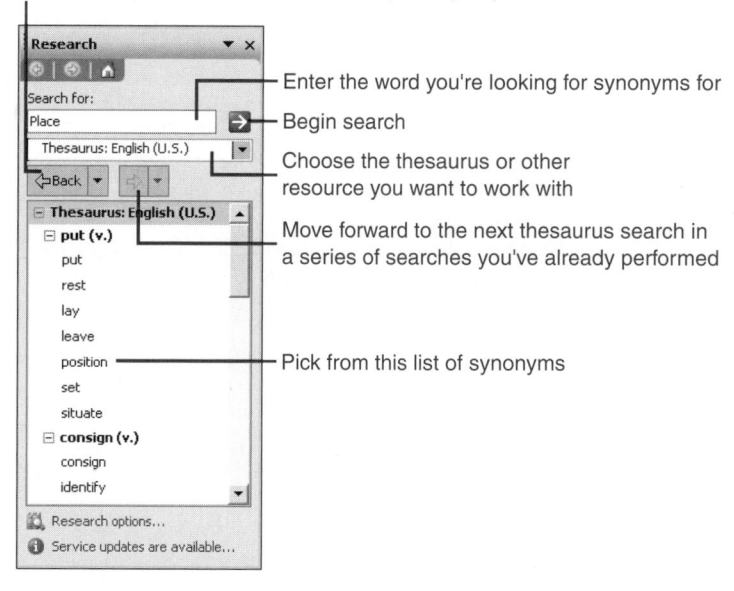

Figure 8.14
Looking up a synonym for a word.

Return to a previous thesaurus search you've just performed

Enter the word you're looking for synonyms for

Begin search

Choose the thesaurus or other resource you want to work with

Move forward to the next thesaurus search in a series of searches you've already performed

Pick from this list of synonyms

To work with one of the words listed in the scroll box, right-click on it. A drop-down box appears (see Figure 8.15).

8

Figure 8.15
Working with a synonym.

You now have three options:

- To insert the word in your document (replacing the word you selected before choosing Thesaurus), click Insert.
- To copy the word into your Clipboard so that you can place it wherever you want, click Copy.
- To look up synonyms for the word you've just selected, click Look Up.

You may often follow a trail of several suggested replacements before arriving at the word you want. If you want to return to a previous thesaurus request, you can. Click the Back button immediately above the list of words (refer to Figure 8.14).

> **NOTE**
>
> The Research task pane contains two Back buttons. Use the larger one immediately above the list of words, *not* the Back button at the top of the pane.

When a word has several meanings, the thesaurus organizes its synonyms by meaning. For example, as shown previously in Figure 8.14, the word *place* can be used in several senses. If you want to use it as a verb, similar to *put* ("Place the book on the table"), you can review meanings under "put (v.)." If you scroll down, you can find several other meanings: for example, *place* as a noun, meaning *status* ("Your place in society").

FINDING ANTONYMS

In many cases, the Word thesaurus can show you antonyms (opposite meanings) of a word or phrase. Antonyms are followed by the word "Antonym" in parentheses. As with synonyms, you can select an antonym and click Replace to place it in your document.

USING WORD'S BUILT-IN LANGUAGE TRANSLATION TOOLS

NEW Word can translate words among any languages for which it has access to a bilingual dictionary. Word 2003 can also draw on Web-based machine translation services for language pairs that are not already installed on your computer, if you are connected to the Internet. These translation services are provided by WorldLingo, a leading provider of both machine-based and human translation services.

By default, Word begins with the bilingual dictionaries it finds on your computer; then if no results are returned, it attempts to retrieve results from WorldLingo's Web-based services. If you select more than one word for translation—for example, an entire sentence or document—Word will rely on WorldLingo.

Office 2003 can translate words between the following language pairs:

- English (U.S.) and French (France)
- English (U.S.) and German (Germany)
- English (U.S.) and Italian (Italy)
- English (U.S.) and Spanish (Spain-Modern Sort)
- English (U.S.) and Japanese
- English (U.S.) and Korean
- English (U.S.) and Chinese (both People's Republic of China and Taiwan variants)

When machine translation is turned on, several additional languages are available through WorldLingo, including Russian, Dutch, Portuguese, and Greek. With machine translation, you can also translate among non-English languages; for example, directly from French to Greek.

To translate text, select it; right-click to display the shortcut menu, and choose Translate. The Research task pane opens, with the word's translation from English to French (see Figure 8.16).

TIP

> To translate a single word, you can also press the Alt key and then click on the word.

NOTE

> For the first time, translation services are available throughout Microsoft Office, not just in Word. In Office 2003, the same translation capabilities are accessible through Excel, OneNote, Outlook, PowerPoint, Publisher, Visio, and Internet Explorer.

8

NOTE

If Translation features are not available, Word may present an error message asking whether you want to install them. Click Yes to do so. You will need access either to your Word or Office CD-ROM, or to the network location you installed Word or Office from.

Specify which language
you want to translate to

Figure 8.16
Word's Research task pane displaying a translation to French.

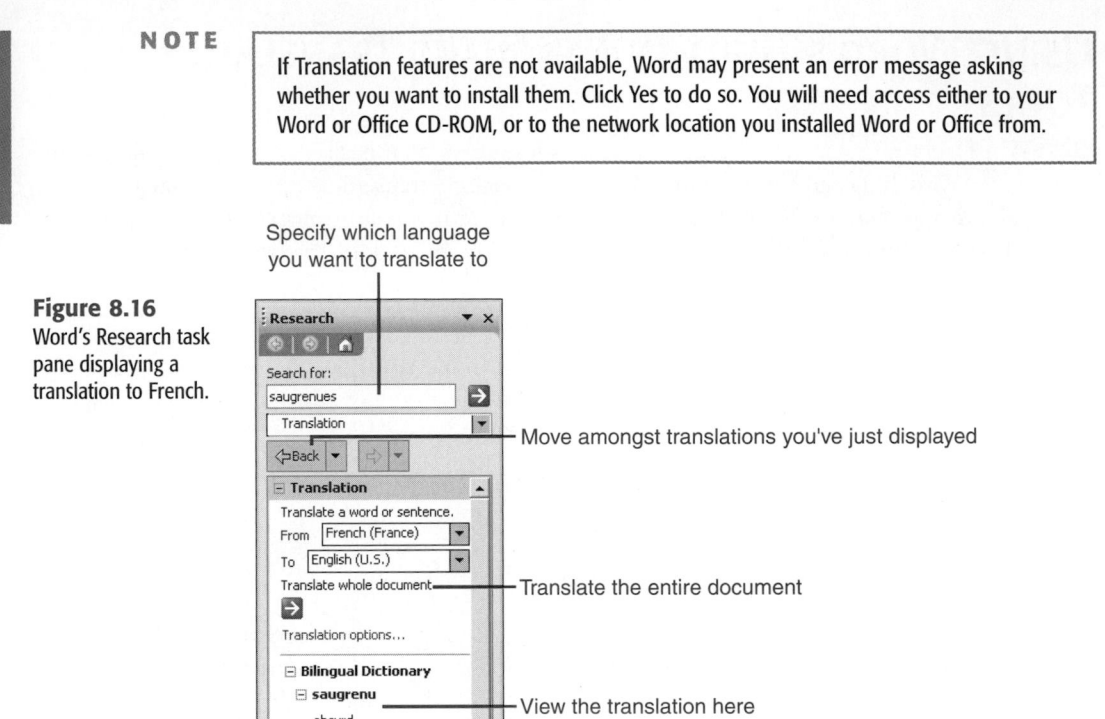

Move amongst translations you've just displayed

Translate the entire document

View the translation here

To translate into a different language, choose the language from the To drop-down box.

To copy the translated text into your document, select it within the task pane, using Word's selection tools. For example, to select a word, double-click on it; to select a paragraph, triple-click on it. Next, right-click, and choose Copy from the shortcut menu.

As with the Thesaurus feature discussed earlier in this chapter, you can use the Back and Forward buttons to move among translations you've just displayed (refer to Figure 8.14).

CONTROLLING TRANSLATION OPTIONS

To control how the Translation feature works and whether it uses Web-based resources, click Translation Options on the Research task pane. The Translation Options dialog box opens (see Figure 8.17).

By default, Word uses all the resources available to it: its own built-in bilingual dictionaries, WebLingo's online dictionaries when no dictionary is installed, and WebLingo's machine translation services.

Figure 8.17
Controlling translation options.

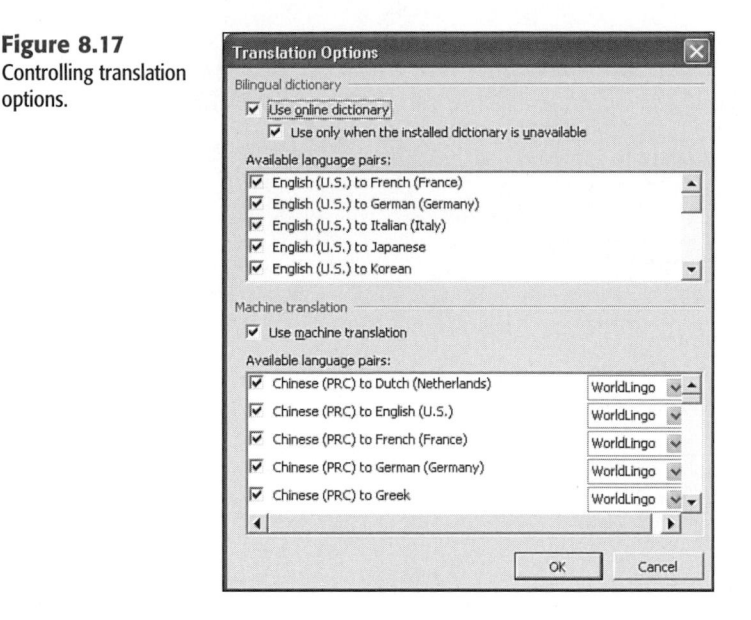

You can specify which resources Word utilizes. For example, if you prefer not to access the Internet for translation services of any kind, you can clear the Use Online Dictionary and Use Machine Translation check boxes.

Conversely, if you'd like to see what WorldLingo can come up with even if Word is capable of translating from its own built-in French or Spanish dictionaries, clear the Use Only When the Installed Dictionary is Unavailable check box.

TRANSLATING ENTIRE DOCUMENTS

You can translate an entire document using Word's Web-based machine translation services. The resulting translation appears in an Internet Explorer window.

To translate an entire document, display the Translation task pane (for example, right-click in the document and click Translate, or choose Tools, Language, Translate). Then, click the large green arrow under Translate Whole Document.

It may take a little while for your translation to appear, depending on its length and the speed of your Internet connection. When it is displayed, WorldLingo and MSN provide a quote and link that allow you to purchase a more refined translation by a human translator (see Figure 8.18).

8

Figure 8.18
Translating an entire document using WorldLingo's translation services.

Click here to hire a human translator to refine the translation

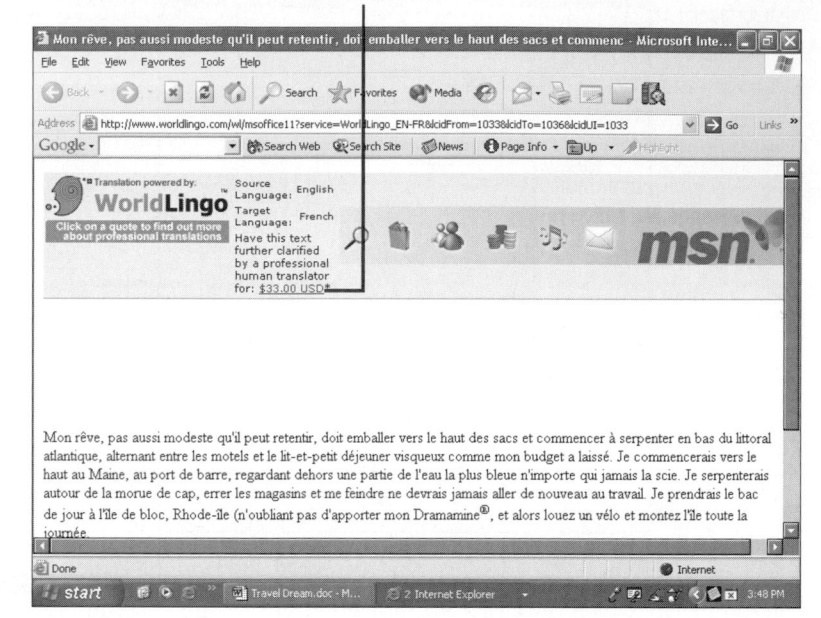

WORKING WITH ADDITIONAL RESEARCH SERVICES

In addition to the Thesaurus and Translation services discussed earlier in this chapter, Word 2003 comes with several other powerful research tools, all brought together in the Research task pane. These tools are organized into three categories:

- *Reference books*, including the Encarta dictionary along with the thesaurus and translation tools already discussed

- *Research sites*, including Encarta Encyclopedia, the MSN Search Web search engine, and two paid news and research sites

- *Business and financial sites*, including delayed MSN Money stock quotes and company profiles from Thomson Gale

Many of the information resources Word can connect you with are free; for example, the Microsoft Encarta dictionary, selected articles from the Microsoft Encarta encyclopedia, and most results returned by the MSN search engine.

On the other hand, some information sources charge for access. For example, although you can read free basic Thomson Gale company profiles, deeper information—such as executive contacts at the company you're reading about—requires payment. Similarly, although you can read free article summaries from the eLibrary online research site, full text articles must be paid for, often by subscription.

To use Word's research tools, choose Tools, Research. The Research task pane appears (see Figure 8.19). In the Search For text box, enter the word or phrase you want to research. Then, from the Research Services drop-down box choose which category of sites you want to search, and click the green arrow to the right of the Search For text box.

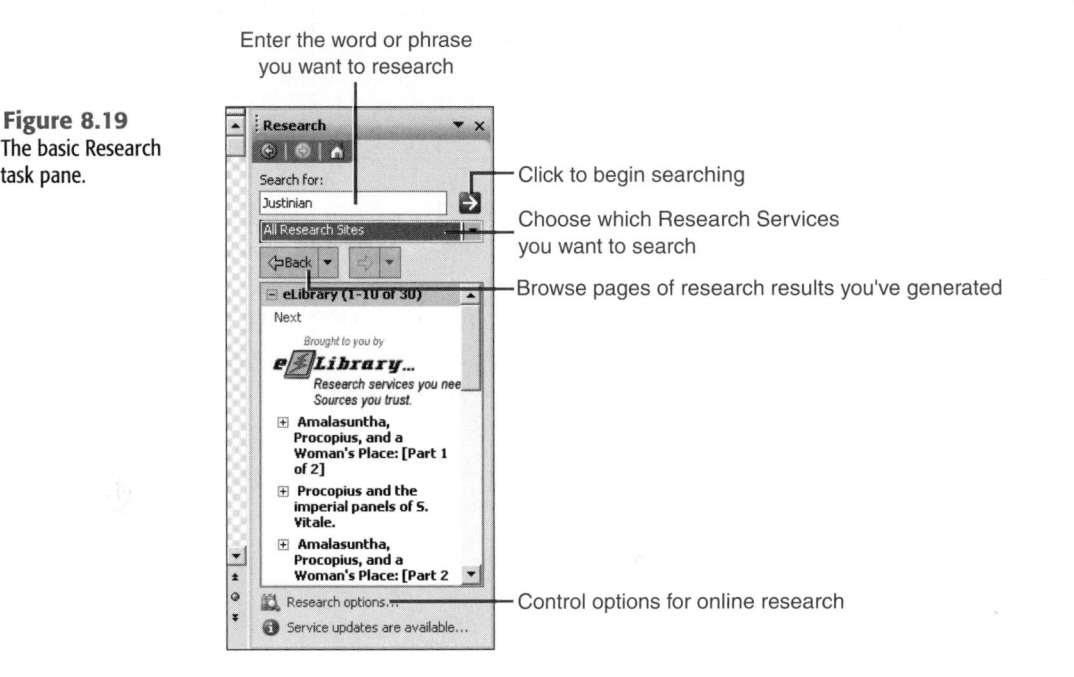

Enter the word or phrase
you want to research

Figure 8.19
The basic Research
task pane.

Click to begin searching

Choose which Research Services
you want to search

Browse pages of research results you've generated

Control options for online research

When Word returns a short piece of information, you can select it in the Research task pane, right-click, and choose Copy to copy the information into your document. In most cases, Word will return links to longer content. If you click a link, the content will be displayed in Internet Explorer. From there, you can typically select and copy text, and then paste it into your document.

CAUTION

Be aware of the copyrights that may apply to content you want to use.

CONTROLLING RESEARCH OPTIONS

As with Translation services, you can control which resources Word relies on and how it works with them. To control how Research works, click Research Options on the Research task pane. The Research Options dialog box opens (see Figure 8.20).

Check the boxes of the research sources you want Word to utilize; clear the boxes of research sources you do not want to utilize. For example:

8

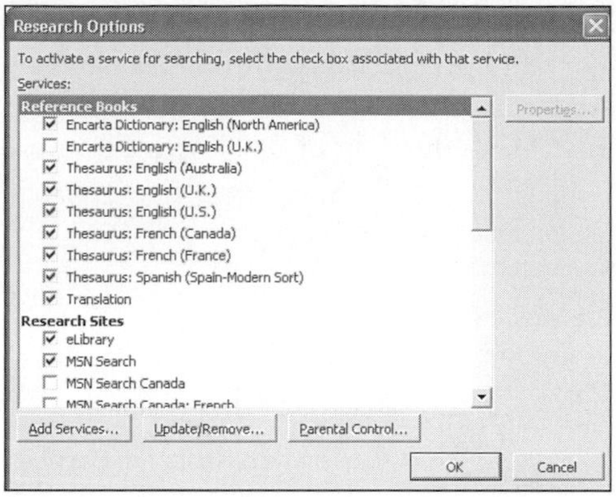

Figure 8.20
Controlling research
options.

- If you know you never want to utilize paid research services, clear the eLibrary and Factiva check boxes.

- If you want deeper information related to a specific nation or region of the world, check the boxes associated with one or more of MSN's regional search engines, such as MSN Search Singapore.

To learn more about any reference source, select it and click Properties.

ADDING RESEARCH SERVICES

Microsoft expects that others will create Research services that will be accessible from Microsoft Office 2003's Research pane. These may include third-party information sites as well as internal corporate information made available through SharePoint or even corporate databases. If one of these services is available to you, add it this way:

1. From the Research task pane, click Research Options.

2. From the Research Options dialog box, click Add Services. The Add Services dialog box appears (see Figure 8.21).

3. If the service is listed in the Advertised Services box, select it. If not, enter its Web address (URL) in the Address box.

4. Click Add.

TIP

> Microsoft SharePoint collaborative sites can be added to the Research task pane without custom programming. Use the site's address, which typically follows this format:
>
> `http://your root directory/_vti_bin/search.asmx`

NOTE

> For detailed technical information on building research services that are compatible with Microsoft Office 2003, see `msdn.microsoft.com/library/default.asp?url=/ library/en-us/dno2k3ta/html/odc_customizingtheresearchpane.asp`.

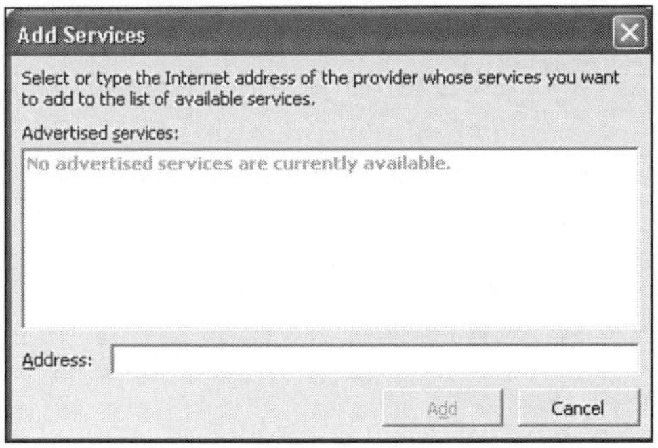

Figure 8.21
Adding a research service.

Add Services

Select or type the Internet address of the provider whose services you want to add to the list of available services.

Advertised services:

No advertised services are currently available.

Address: [   ]

Add   Cancel

USING PARENTAL CONTROLS TO LIMIT A RESEARCH SERVICE

Certain research services and Web sites contain filters that eliminate content which might be inappropriate for children. Many, of course, do not—and other sites have no need for them.

If you would like to use the parental filters that are available, or prevent your children from searching sites that do not use content filters, follow these steps:

1. From the Research task pane, click Research Options.

2. From the Research Options dialog box, click Parental Control. The Parental Control dialog box appears (see Figure 8.22).

3. Check the Turn on Content Filtering to Make Services Block Offensive Results check box.

4. If you want to prevent Word from searching sites that do not have content filters, check the Allow Users to Search Only the Services That Can Block Offensive Results check box.

5. In the Specify a Password box, enter a password that will be required in order to make changes to your Parental Control settings. Click OK.

6. In the Confirm Password dialog box, enter the same password and click OK again.

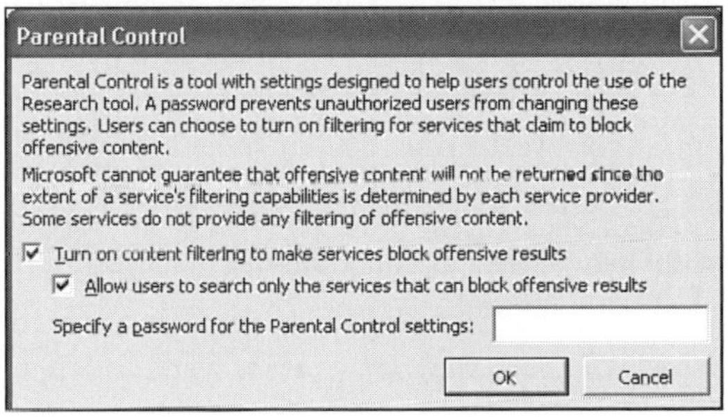

Figure 8.22
Setting parental controls for research services.

Parental Control

Parental Control is a tool with settings designed to help users control the use of the Research tool. A password prevents unauthorized users from changing these settings. Users can choose to turn on filtering for services that claim to block offensive content.

Microsoft cannot guarantee that offensive content will not be returned since the extent of a service's filtering capabilities is determined by each service provider. Some services do not provide any filtering of offensive content.

☑ Turn on content filtering to make services block offensive results

☑ Allow users to search only the services that can block offensive results

Specify a password for the Parental Control settings: [   ]

OK   Cancel

8

UPDATING OR REMOVING A RESEARCH SERVICE

NEW In some cases, you may want to update the list of Research Services available to you, or remove services from the list entirely. For example, if you choose not to renew a subscription to a third-party information provider, you might no longer want to see the results it returns. To make such changes, follow these steps:

1. From the Research task pane, click Research Options.
2. From the Research Options dialog box, click Update/Remove. The Update or Remove Services dialog box appears (see Figure 8.23).
3. Select the category of services you want to update or remove.
4. Click Update to update a service; click Remove to remove it.
5. Click Close.

Figure 8.23
Updating or removing groups of research services.

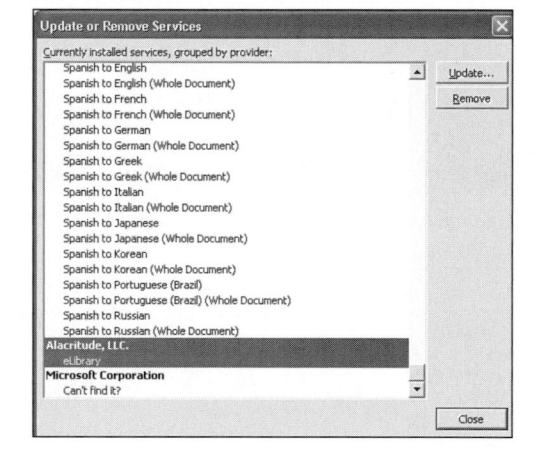

COUNTING A DOCUMENT'S WORDS, PAGES, LINES, AND CHARACTERS

Often, you need to count the words, characters, lines, paragraphs, or pages in your document. For example, in creating your document, you might have been given a word limit you aren't permitted to exceed. To get an accurate estimate of your document's current size, choose Tools, Word Count. Word reads your document and displays the Word Count dialog box (see Figure 8.24).

By default, Word does not include footnotes and endnotes in its count. If you want them included, check the Include Footnotes and Endnotes check box; Word recounts immediately.

If you frequently need word counts, you can use the Word Count toolbar to recount the words in a document in a single click. To display the word count toolbar, choose Tools, Word Count, and click the Show Toolbar button. The Word Count toolbar appears, displaying the word count (see Figure 8.25).

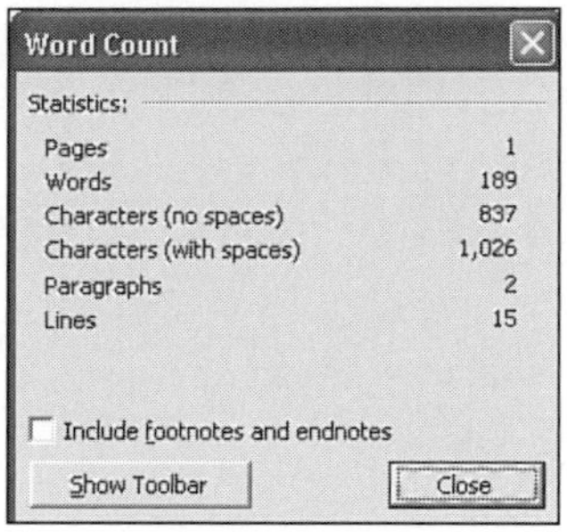

Figure 8.24
The Word Count dialog box.

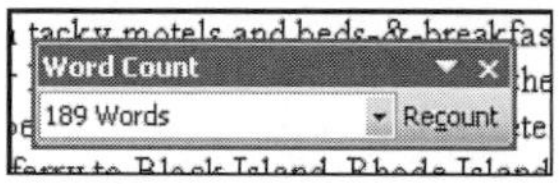

Figure 8.25
The Word Count toolbar.

When you add or delete words from your document, the word count disappears; to display a new word count, click Recount.

Counts of pages, paragraphs, lines, words, and characters are also available. Click File, Properties to display the Properties dialog box for your active document; then select the Statistics tab. Word automatically updates all of your document's statistics when you select this tab.

TIP

> You can't print the results from the Word Count dialog box, but you can use the NumChars, NumPages, and NumWords fields to insert that information in your document.

DISPLAYING READABILITY STATISTICS

Sometimes word counts aren't enough: You want to know how readable your document is and whether it is suitable for the audience that is to read it.

To display readability statistics, choose Tools, Options, and click the Spelling & Grammar tab. Check the Show Readability Statistics check box and click OK. Then check spelling and grammar in your document by pressing F7 or choosing Tools, Spelling and Grammar. Allow Word to check your document completely; at the end, it displays a dialog box similar to the one in Figure 8.26.

INTERPRETING READABILITY STATISTICS

The statistics listed in the Readability Statistics dialog box are based on an estimate of the number of words in an average sentence and the average number of syllables in each word. The Flesch Reading Ease score in the Readability field of the dialog box rates text on a scale of 1 to 100; the higher the score, the more understandable the document. You should generally shoot for at least 60 points.

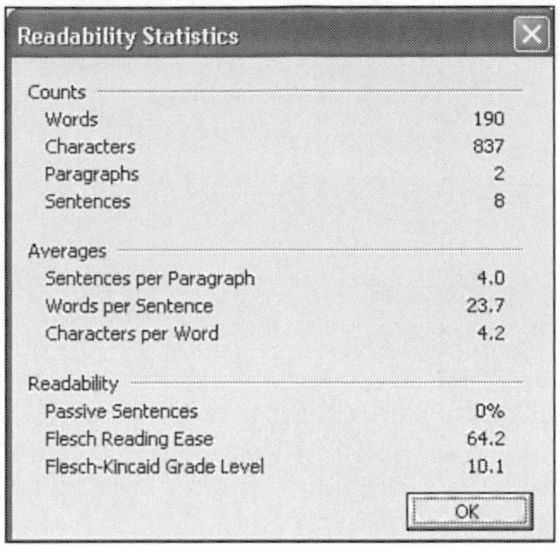

8

Figure 8.26
A sample Readability Statistics dialog box as it appears after checking spelling and grammar in a document.

Readability Statistics

Counts	
Words	190
Characters	837
Paragraphs	2
Sentences	8

Averages	
Sentences per Paragraph	4.0
Words per Sentence	23.7
Characters per Word	4.2

Readability	
Passive Sentences	0%
Flesch Reading Ease	64.2
Flesch-Kincaid Grade Level	10.1

OK

The Flesch-Kincaid Grade Level score rates text based on the average United States grade level of education needed to understand it. For example, a score of 7.0 means an average seventh-grader should understand the document. If you write a nontechnical document for a general audience, and it receives a score much higher than 8 or 9, consider editing to make the document simpler.

CONTROLLING HYPHENATION

Carefully controlling hyphenation can help you create documents that look and read better. If you justify text between margins, hyphenating can help you reduce the amount of whitespace between words. If you justify text at the left margin, hyphenating helps reduce the raggedness of the right margin. It can be particularly helpful in maintaining even line lengths in narrow columns, helping readers read smoothly, without distraction.

You can let Word hyphenate your document automatically, or you can use manual hyphenation to control where hyphens appear in words. In addition, you can use nonbreaking hyphens or optional hyphens to control where hyphenated words or phrases break.

TIP

> Wait until you've finished writing and editing to hyphenate your document because adding and deleting text affects the way the lines break.

AUTOMATICALLY HYPHENATING WORDS IN YOUR DOCUMENT

You can let Word automatically hyphenate your document. Follow these steps:

1. Choose Tools, Language, Hyphenation. The Hyphenation dialog box appears (see Figure 8.27).
2. Check the Automatically Hyphenate Document check box.
3. If you want to automatically hyphenate words that appear entirely in capital letters, check in the Hyphenate Words in CAPS check box.

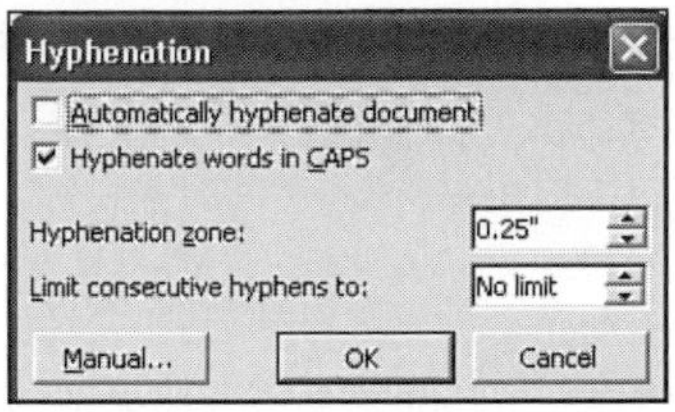

Figure 8.27
Use this dialog box to set and control hyphenation.

4. Set the Hyphenation Zone. The larger the zone, the fewer hyphens Word will insert, but the more ragged your right margin will appear.

5. Use the Limit Consecutive Hyphens To spin box to set the number of consecutive lines that Word can hyphenate.

6. Click OK.

Word will place hyphens throughout your document. If you change your mind and want to remove the hyphenation, repeat these steps and remove the check from the Automatically Hyphenate Document check box.

To remove hyphenation from part of your document, select that text, right-click, and choose Paragraph. Choose the Line and Page Breaks tab and place a check in the Don't Hyphenate check box.

MANUAL HYPHENATION: TAKING LINE-BY-LINE CONTROL

You can control Word's placement of hyphens by manually hyphenating your document. Reopen the Hyphenation dialog box (choose Tools, Language, Hyphenation) and clear the Automatically Hyphenate Document check box. Then, click the Manual button. Word switches to Print Layout view (if necessary) and displays the dialog box shown in Figure 8.28.

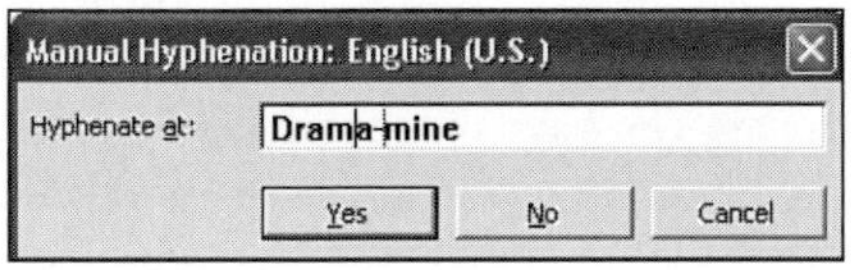

Figure 8.28
Use this dialog box to hyphenate an individual word.

If you like the location within the word that Word has chosen, click Yes. If you want to move the hyphen, use the left- and right-arrow keys to move the blinking insertion point. When the blinking insertion point appears where you want to hyphenate, click Yes. If you don't want to hyphenate the word at all, click No.

If you manually hyphenate a word, Word will display a hidden symbol in your document to indicate that the word has been manually hyphenated (see Figure 8.29). To view this symbol, click the Show/Hide Paragraph Marks button on the Standard toolbar.

Of course, if the word does not appear at the end of a line, Word will not hyphenate it.

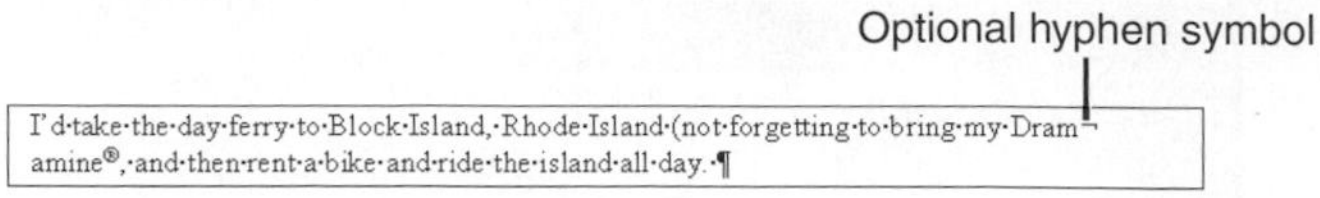

Optional hyphen symbol

Figure 8.29
Word inserts an
optional hyphen sym-
bol to flag manual
hyphenation.

> I'd·take·the·day·ferry·to·Block·Island,·Rhode·Island·(not·forgetting·to·bring·my·Dram¬
> amine®,·and·then·rent·a·bike·and·ride·the·island·all·day.·¶

TIP

> You can insert an optional hyphen at any time. Place the insertion at the location in the
> word where you want the optional hyphen to appear, and press Ctrl+Hyphen.

In addition to manual hyphenation, you can also use nonbreaking hyphens to prevent a
hyphenated word or phrase from breaking at the end of a line.

For example, suppose you want all occurrences of "add-in" to appear together on a line, and
you don't want Word to split the words so that "add" appears at the end of a line and "in"
appears at the beginning of the next line. Use a nonbreaking hyphen between the words.
Simply press Ctrl+Shift+Hyphen to insert the hyphen. Word will always keep the phrase
together on a line, forcing a new line if the phrase appears at the end of a line and won't fit.

TROUBLESHOOTING

WHAT TO DO IF YOU CAN'T EDIT YOUR CUSTOM DICTIONARY

Two causes are possible. First, your custom dictionary might be empty—you can't edit it
until it contains at least one word. Second, if you're running Word across the network, your
network administrator may have set custom.dic or its folder as Read Only. Ask permission to
create your own local copy of custom.dic, and store it where you can access it.

Custom dictionaries have size limits you need to be aware of. No word can be longer than
64 characters, and no custom dictionary can have more than 5,000 entries or exceed 64KB
in size. If you are running up against these limits, create a separate dictionary for the additional words.

WHAT TO DO IF WORD KEEPS CHECKING GRAMMAR WHEN YOU DON'T WANT IT TO

You may have hidden grammar mistakes rather than disabled grammar checking. Or you
may have disabled Check Grammar as You Type. To completely disable Grammar
Checking, choose Tools, Options, and click the Spelling & Grammar tab. Then, remove the
checks from the Check Grammar as You Type and the Check Grammar with Spelling check
boxes.

How to Spell Check Text in a Protected Form

When you protect the framework of a form from being edited, Word also prevents users from spell checking the text they enter in that form. If your form contains extensive user text, this can be a significant problem.

To solve the problem, you need a fairly complex macro. Fortunately, the Microsoft Office experts at www.mvps.org have provided one. You can find it (along with detailed directions for using it) at www.mvps.org/word/FAQs/MacrosVBA/SpellcheckProtectDoc.htm.

What to Do If Word Doesn't Find Obvious Spelling Errors

Sometimes Word doesn't find spelling errors you know it should catch. Assuming that Word's spell checker is turned on, follow these steps:

- To ensure that Word spell checks the entire document, make sure you haven't selected specific text when you run spell check. If text is selected when you run spell check, Word will only check the selected text.

- Make sure that no text is specifically marked as off-limits to the proofing tools. Select the entire document (Ctrl+A); then choose Tools, Language, Set Language. In the Language dialog box, clear the Do Not Check Spelling or Grammar check box. (Note that Word sometimes enables Do Not Check Spelling or Grammar in documents created by a mail merge, even when you haven't asked for this.)

- Run the spell checker again, like this: choose Tools, Options, Spelling and Grammar; click the Recheck Document button; and click Yes. This tells Word to recheck the entire document, not just portions of it that haven't previously been checked.

CHAPTER 9

AUTOMATING YOUR DOCUMENTS

Word provides features designed to automate and streamline many aspects of document production.

For example, Word's AutoCorrect feature can fix spelling errors on its own, and Word's AutoText feature allows you to add large blocks of content to a document with just a few clicks. Word's AutoFormat feature can format an entire document automatically, using Word's built-in styles.

Word's AutoSummarize feature can generate reasonably useful executive summaries in just moments. And, in Word 2003, Smart Tags make it incredibly simple to use the content in your document in powerful new ways. This chapter focuses on helping you make the most of all these remarkable automation tools—and avoiding their occasional pitfalls.

AUTOCORRECT: SMARTER THAN EVER

Unless you tell it to do otherwise, Word automatically corrects thousands of the most common spelling mistakes—even using suggestions built into the spell checker that it didn't use before. That's not all. Word also performs the following tasks:

- Makes sure that you start all your sentences with a capital letter
- Corrects words you inadvertently start with two capital letters
- Capitalizes days of the week, such as Tuesday
- Fixes things when you inadvertently press the Caps Lock key
- Replaces character strings such as (c) with symbols such as ©
- Replaces Internet "smileys" such as :) with Wingding symbols such as ☺

NOTE

Word's AutoCorrect features work closely with its multilingual spelling capabilities, so Word will not incorrectly AutoCorrect words that have been formatted in a foreign language.

If you're using Word's default settings, this is all happening right now in the background; you haven't had to do a thing. You can take control of the settings and make AutoCorrect back off on certain things, or stop correcting you altogether. Conversely, you can make it even smarter by adding your own entries. To control AutoCorrect, choose Tools, AutoCorrect Options to display the AutoCorrect tab of the AutoCorrect dialog box (see Figure 9.1).

TIP

AutoCorrect is invaluable if you extensively use long words or complex phrases—for instance, if you use technical, scientific, or legal terms in your work. You can set up shortcuts for words, phrases, or even paragraphs you use often and have AutoCorrect insert the lengthy text blocks automatically whenever you type the shortcut.

Simply type a few letters in the Replace text box of the AutoCorrect dialog box and copy the lengthy word or phrase into the With text box. When choosing the few letters that will serve as your shortcut, make sure that they are memorable, are easy to type, and will not appear in your document except when you intend for AutoCorrect to replace them.

Don't use a shortcut consisting of a word you type often; if you do, whenever you press the Enter key after typing that word, Word will replace it with your AutoText entry.

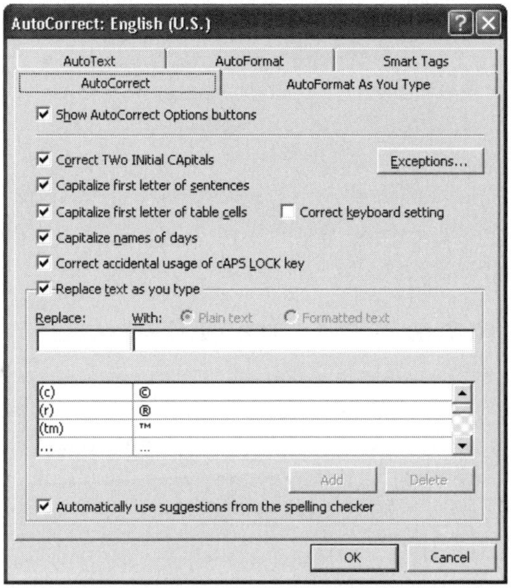

Figure 9.1
From the AutoCorrect tab, you control AutoCorrect's overall behavior and specify which text elements it automatically corrects.

NOTE

Four of Word's automation features—AutoCorrect, AutoFormat, AutoText, and Smart Tags—can be controlled from the AutoCorrect dialog box. Rather than accessing this dialog box only when you want to make a single change, consider investing a few minutes in systematically adding entries to AutoCorrect and AutoText, and setting the AutoFormatting controls that make the most sense for you.

By default, all of Word's AutoCorrect capabilities are selected. A couple of AutoCorrect options are so innocuous that few people want to turn them off. Capitalize Names of Days automatically adds a capital letter at the beginning of the seven days of the week: Sunday, Monday, Tuesday, and so on. You'll rarely, if ever, want these words lowercased.

NOTE

The Capitalize Names of Days feature doesn't change day-of-the-week abbreviations such as Tues. or Thu.; it affects only days of the week that are fully spelled out.

Another option, Correct Accidental Usage of cAPS LOCK Key, is designed for those times when your left pinkie finger inadvertently presses Caps Lock rather than A or Q at the left edge of your keyboard. If this happens partway into a word, Word recognizes that you probably didn't mean it. Rather than letting you continue typing until you notice the problem, it turns off Caps Lock and changes the capitalization on all the letters it thinks you reversed. For instance, if you typed

```
sPORTSMANSHIP
```

Word would turn off Caps Lock and edit your text to read

```
Sportsmanship
```

NOTE

This feature never changes text you capitalized by pressing and holding the Shift key.

In the following sections, you'll learn about several more of AutoCorrect's capabilities. You'll also learn how to control AutoCorrect so that it behaves as you want it to—and leaves your text alone the rest of the time.

AUTOMATICALLY CAPITALIZING THE FIRST LETTER IN TABLE CELLS

Often, table cells contain text that does not consist of complete sentences, but should nevertheless begin with a capital letter for style or consistency. You can instruct Word to capitalize the first word placed in any table cell regardless of whether the table's contents consist of a full sentence. To do so, display the AutoCorrect tab of the AutoCorrect dialog box, and check the Capitalize First Letter of Table Cells check box.

Selecting this option does not change cells whose contents begin with numbers.

AUTOMATICALLY CHANGING KEYBOARD SETTINGS TO MATCH THE LANGUAGE YOU'RE TYPING

If you commonly switch among languages as you type, you may have found it frustrating to manually switch keyboard settings in order to make sure that the correct foreign language characters are always available to you. Word can do this task for you.

If you check the Correct Keyboard Setting check box in the AutoCorrect tab of the AutoCorrect dialog box, Word will automatically change your keyboard settings to match the language you are typing. This feature works *if* Word recognizes the language you're typing (based on the dictionaries installed with Microsoft Office) and *if* the appropriate language support is installed on your computer.

AUTOCORRECTING ERRORS FLAGGED BY THE SPELL CHECKER

AutoCorrect finds errors in two ways. First, it watches for errors flagged by Word's interactive spell checker. When an error is made, and Word is sure of the correct spelling, AutoCorrect fixes the error automatically. If Word is not sure of the correct spelling—for example, if several alternative words seem reasonable—AutoCorrect leaves the word unchanged.

NOTE

> If you find AutoCorrect making spelling changes you disagree with, you can turn off this feature by choosing Tools, AutoCorrect Options and clearing the Automatically Use Suggestions from the Spelling Checker check box in the AutoCorrect tab.

AUTOCORRECTING 1,000 COMMON ERRORS

In addition to AutoCorrecting errors caught by Word's spell checker, AutoCorrect draws on a database containing more than 1,000 mistakes that writers tend to make most often. These errors fall into the following categories:

- **Spelling errors.** For example, Word replaces *acheive* with *achieve*.
- **Common typos and transpositions.** For example, Word replaces *teh* with *the*.
- **Spaces left out between words.** For example, Word replaces *saidthat* with *said that*.
- **Spaces misplaced between words.** Word fixes many pairs of words in which the space between words has been typed in the wrong place.
- **Errors in usage.** Word replaces *should of been* with *should have been* and *their are* with *there are*.
- **Missing or incorrect apostrophes.** Word replaces *wouldnt* with *wouldn't* and *you;re* with *you're*.
- **Forgotten accent characters.** Word replaces *seance* with *séance*.

In addition, Word inserts a wide variety of symbols in place of the "fake" symbols that many writers use. For example, if you type (c), Word replaces it with ©. Word also replaces various Internet/email smileys. For example, Word replaces :) with the corresponding symbol from the Wingding font: ☺. Table 9.1 shows the complete list of symbols AutoCorrect replaces.

TABLE 9.1 SYMBOLS AND SMILEYS WORD AUTOMATICALLY REPLACES

Text You Type	Symbol Word Inserts
(c)	©
(r)	®
(tm)	™
...	…
:(	L
:-(	L

continues

TABLE 9.1   CONTINUED

Text You Type	Symbol Word Inserts
:)	☺
:-)	☺
:-|	K
:|	K
<—	←
<==	←
<=>	↓
==>	→
—>	→

If you're simply not comfortable with Word changing your text, you can clear the Replace Text As You Type box, and Word will leave all your potential errors alone.

REMOVING OR CHANGING AN AUTOCORRECT ENTRY

You might be comfortable with Word's AutoCorrect feature but object to one or more of the replacements Word makes by default. For example, if you copy text formatted with the Wingdings font into an email message, that text may not appear correctly when your recipient gets it. If you are a fiction writer using dialect, you don't want Word to clean up usage like "should of had." Or perhaps you work for the CNA insurance company and want Word to stop changing your company name to "CAN."

To remove an AutoCorrect entry, choose Tools, AutoCorrect Options. In the Replace text box, type the entry you want to remove (or scroll to it in the list beneath the Replace text box); then click Delete.

The entry is removed from your AutoCorrect list. However, it remains in the Replace and With text boxes, so if you immediately change your mind, you can click Add to put it back in your list.

N O T E

If you save a Word file to text-only format, Word reverts the smileys to their original characters. For example, [sf] becomes :) again.

On occasion, rather than delete an entry, you might want to change the replacement text Word uses. From within the AutoCorrect tab, scroll to the entry you want to change and select it. The entry appears in the Replace and With text boxes. Enter the replacement text you prefer in the With text box and click Replace.

ADDING A NEW AUTOCORRECT ENTRY

Just as you can remove AutoCorrect entries you don't want, you can also add new, custom AutoCorrect entries that reflect the errors you make most often. To add a new entry, display the AutoCorrect tab by choosing Tools, AutoCorrect Options; then type the incorrect text you want Word to replace. In the With text box, type the text you want Word to insert. Click Add. The new entry now appears in the AutoCorrect list.

You can also add AutoCorrect entries while you're spell checking. In fact, that's a great time to do it, because that's when you systematically review documents and discover the errors you're most likely to make.

Click the Spelling and Grammar button on the Standard toolbar to run Word's spell checker. Word displays your first error in the Spelling and Grammar dialog box. Select the replacement text you want to use; if you want Word to correct this error from now on, click AutoCorrect.

You can also right-click an error within the document; select AutoCorrect from the shortcut menu, and select one of the choices Word provides (see Figure 9.2). Word then automatically corrects the mistake in the future.

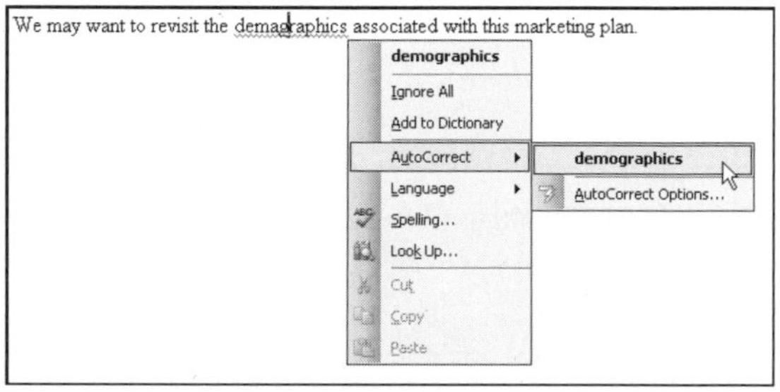

Figure 9.2
You can add an AutoCorrect entry from the shortcut menu in any document.

→ To learn more about working with Word's spell check feature, **see** Chapter 8, "Making the Most of Word's Proofing and Research Tools," **p. 253**.

TIP

A word doesn't have to be misspelled for you to ask Word to correct it. For example, if you constantly type manger rather than manager, you can tell Word to make the change automatically, even though manger is a perfectly legitimate word.

This is an example of why it's not enough to run a spell check on an important document: You have to actually *read* the document to make sure that everything's okay!

USING AUTOCORRECT TO INSERT BOILERPLATE TEXT

Later in this chapter, you'll learn about AutoText, a powerful feature that enables you to manage boilerplate text and insert it into a document with just a few keystrokes. You can also use AutoCorrect this way—not to correct errors, but to insert large blocks of formatted or unformatted text automatically.

For example, ever since securities reform legislation passed Congress, it's common to see an extremely lengthy disclaimer appear in press releases and other documents. Usually these disclaimers say something to the effect that "forward-looking statements" involve risks and uncertainties, and the company is not making an ironclad commitment that these predictions will come true. These statements can involve 100 words or more; you wouldn't want to constantly retype them, and your lawyers wouldn't want you to inadvertently leave something out.

Follow these steps to have AutoCorrect insert such a block of text automatically:

1. Select the text you want Word to add automatically. (You don't have to copy it.)

2. Choose <u>T</u>ools, <u>A</u>utoCorrect Options. The text you selected appears as <u>F</u>ormatted Text in the <u>W</u>ith text box. If necessary, the text box expands to two lines to accommodate at least some of the additional text. The text appears with the same boldface, italic, or underline character formatting you applied in the document; this formatting appears whenever Word inserts the AutoCorrect entry.

3. In the <u>R</u>eplace text box, enter a distinctive sequence of letters that you wouldn't inadvertently use for any other purpose, such as `dsclmr`.

4. Click <u>A</u>dd.

After you've added your AutoCorrect entry, every time you type `dsclmr` followed by a space, Word automatically replaces that word with the entire block of boilerplate text.

TIP

> With the AutoCorrect dialog box open, you can enter as many new entries as you want. After you click <u>A</u>dd to add an entry, type the next AutoCorrection you want in the <u>R</u>eplace and <u>W</u>ith text boxes; then click <u>A</u>dd again.

You can also use AutoCorrect to insert graphics or heavily formatted text. Follow the previous steps, selecting the graphics or formatted text before choosing <u>T</u>ools, <u>A</u>utoCorrect Options. A portion of your selected text or image appears in the <u>W</u>ith box, as shown in Figure 9.3.

CAUTION

> Word doesn't limit the length of <u>F</u>ormatted Text you can place in an AutoCorrect entry, but it does limit <u>P</u>lain Text (ASCII) entries to 255 characters and cuts off any text that extends beyond that.

TIP

> Just as you can insert formatted text or images, you also can insert fields using AutoCorrect. For instance, you might want to use AutoCorrect to replace text with { INCLUDETEXT } fields that retrieve text from an external "source" file. When you change the text in that source file, you can update the document containing the fields, and the text in that document will be updated wherever it appears.

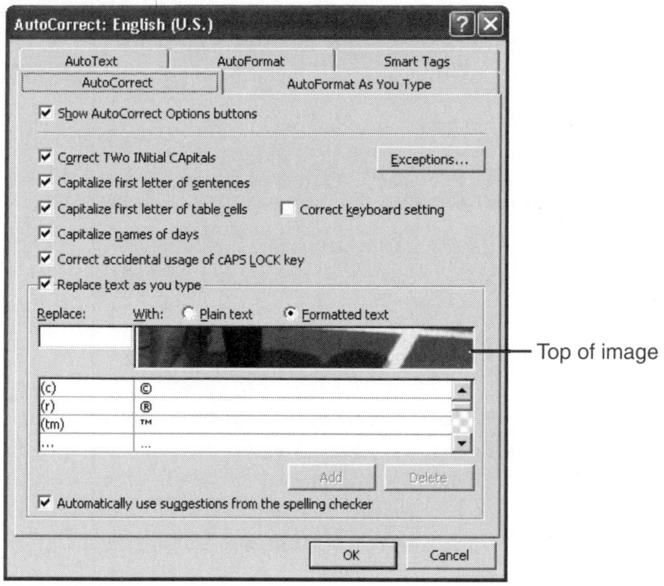

Figure 9.3
When you select an image and open AutoCorrect, part of the image appears in the <u>W</u>ith box.

Top of image

→ For more information about working with fields, **see** Chapter 23, "Automating Your Documents with Field Codes," **p. 771**.

Using AutoCorrect to Add Dummy Text

Ever need to quickly add some generic or dummy text just to get a feel for the formatting of a page? Word has a built-in AutoCorrect entry that'll do it for you. It enters paragraphs full of this classic sentence (carefully designed to use one of each letter in the alphabet): The quick brown fox jumps over the lazy dog.

To tell Word to insert a paragraph containing this sentence five times over, type =rand() and press Enter.

You can actually control how many times the sentence appears and how many paragraphs you get. Type =rand(p,s), where p equals the number of paragraphs, and s equals the number of sentences. This works only when the Replace <u>T</u>ext As You Type feature is turned on in the AutoCorrect tab.

AutoCorrecting Initial Caps and Sentence Capitalization

You might have noticed two more options in the AutoCorrect dialog box:

- **C<u>o</u>rrect Two Initial Capitals.** If you place two capital letters at the beginning of a word, AutoCorrect makes the second letter lowercase.

- **Capitalize First Letter of <u>S</u>entences.** If you start a sentence with a lowercase letter, AutoCorrect capitalizes it for you.

Most of the time, these features work as intended, fixing inadvertent mistakes. However, there are times you won't want Word to make these AutoCorrections. For example, say that you include an abbreviation within a sentence, and the abbreviation ends in a period, as follows:

```
Please contact Smith Corp. regarding their overdue invoices.
```

When AutoCorrect was first introduced, it would see the period after "Corp.," see the space after it, and assume wrongly that the word "regarding" started a new sentence. Word has since fixed this problem by enabling you to specify exceptions—words that AutoCorrect won't fix. AutoCorrect now contains a list of 128 common abbreviations. When Word sees one of these abbreviations, it doesn't assume that it has arrived at the end of a sentence, notwithstanding the period in the abbreviation.

If you use specialized abbreviations, such as those common in scientific or technical fields, you might want to add them to your Exceptions list. To do so, follow these steps:

1. Choose Tools, AutoCorrect Options.

2. Click Exceptions. The AutoCorrect Exceptions dialog box opens, as shown in Figure 9.4.

3. Click the First Letter tab.

4. Enter your new exception in the Don't Capitalize After text box.

5. Click Add.

6. Click OK.

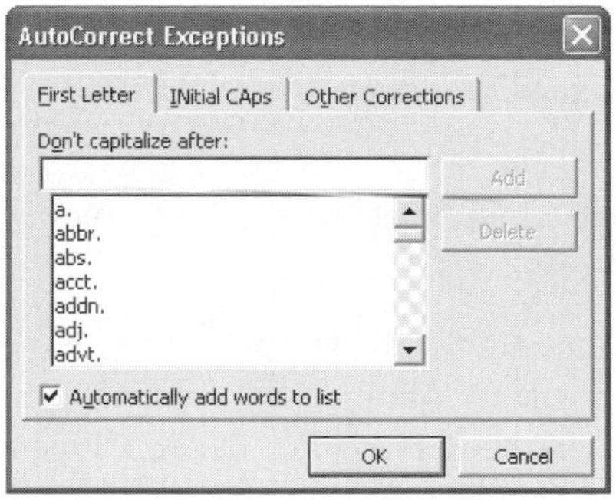

Figure 9.4
Specifying abbreviations and other words that should not be followed by capital letters.

CREATING CAPITALIZATION EXCEPTIONS FOR PRODUCT NAMES, BRAND NAMES, AND ACRONYMS

As mentioned earlier, Word also automatically "fixes" words that start with two capital letters. No standard English words begin with two capital letters, so most of the time you'll want this fix to occur. However, you may occasionally come across a product, a brand name, or an acronym that is capitalized oddly to attract attention. For example, the CompuServe online information service renamed itself "CSi." Word automatically corrects this to "Csi." You can create an exception for oddly capitalized words as shown here:

1. Choose Tools, AutoCorrect Options.
2. Click Exceptions. The AutoCorrect Exceptions dialog box opens.
3. Click INitial CAps. The INitial CAps tab appears, as shown in Figure 9.5.
4. Enter your new exception in the Don't Correct text box.
5. Click Add.
6. Click OK.

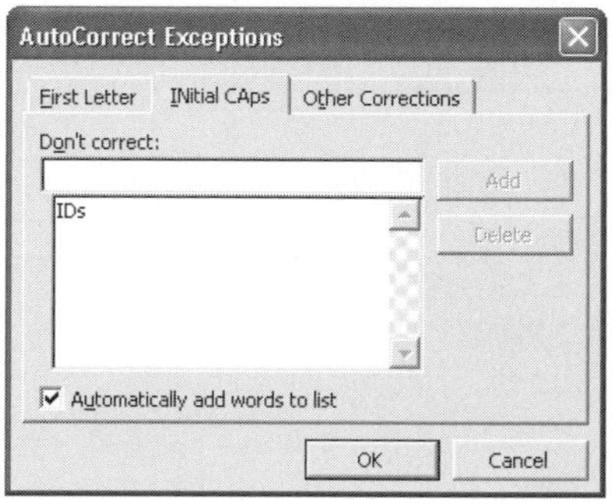

Figure 9.5
Specifying oddly capitalized words that should not be corrected.

CREATING OTHER AUTOCORRECT EXCEPTIONS

Although many of the AutoCorrect exceptions you want to create are likely to fall into the First Letter and Initial Caps categories, what happens when you encounter an exception that doesn't?

For example, what happens if you sell a product with a lowercase name similar to a "real" word? Word may automatically assume that you meant to type the word in its dictionary. (This won't happen with capitalized words, which Word recognizes as names.) Or, what happens if you occasionally use a word in a foreign language, such as the French "sollicitation," which Word AutoCorrects to "solicitation"?

Word's solution is the Other Corrections tab. Follow these steps to create an exception that doesn't fall into the First Letter or Initial Caps categories:

1. Choose Tools, AutoCorrect Options.
2. Click Exceptions. The AutoCorrect Exceptions dialog box opens.
3. Click Other Corrections. The Other Corrections tab appears, as shown in Figure 9.6.
4. Enter your new exception in the Don't Correct text box.
5. Click Add.
6. Click OK.

TELLING WORD TO CREATE EXCEPTIONS AUTOMATICALLY

Wouldn't it be nice if Word were smart enough not to make the same mistake twice? What if Word saw the fixes you made manually and added them to its Exceptions list so that you wouldn't be bothered again? It can, and it does.

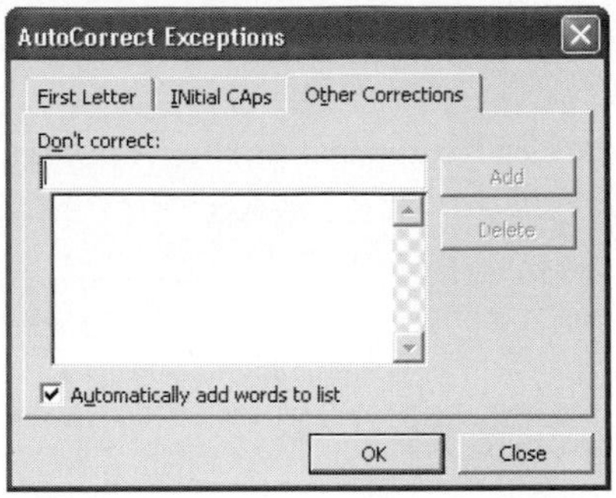

Figure 9.6
Specifying
AutoCorrect excep-
tions that don't fall
into the First Letter or
Initial Caps categories.

If you check the Automatically Add Words to List check box in any of the three AutoCorrect Exceptions tabs, Word watches as you work. If Word corrects an initial cap, a first letter, or another word, and you immediately use the left-arrow key or the Backspace key to go back and type over the correction, Word adds your correction to the exception list.

NOTE

Word won't add a correction to the exception list unless you use the Backspace or left-arrow key to make the correction. Pressing shortcut keys or using Undo does not work.

TIP

Each tab of the AutoCorrect Exceptions dialog box has separate automatic exception controls. So, for example, you can tell Word to automatically add abbreviations to the list for First Letters, but not to the list of Initial Caps or Other Corrections.

BACKING UP AND RESTORING AUTOCORRECT ENTRIES

The longer you work with Word, the more entries you're likely to add in the AutoCorrect dialog box. If you get a new computer, can you move those entries with you? Or can you share these entries with other users? Or can you restore an AutoCorrect file that has somehow been damaged, preventing AutoCorrect (or Word itself) from functioning properly? The answer in all cases is yes. Microsoft provides a special AutoCorrect utility to perform these tasks.

The AutoCorrect utility is stored in the Support.dot template. This template is installed on your hard disk when you install Office 2003 with a Complete (not Typical or Upgrade) setup; however, it is not automatically loaded and made available to you.

NOTE

If you don't want to run a Complete install, you can install the SUPPORT.DOT template by running Setup in Maintenance Mode and installing More Templates and Macros (found within the Wizards and Templates section, in the Word section).

In the following procedure, you'll first load the template, then run the macro and follow the procedure within it.

To load the template and make the macro accessible, follow the steps listed next. Unless you want to trust all macros from Microsoft, before you follow this procedure, make sure that your security level is not set to High. To do so, choose Tools, Macro, Security; click the Security Level tab; choose Medium, and click OK.

1. Choose Tools, Templates and Add-Ins.
2. Click Add.
3. Browse to and select support.dot. This template is typically found in the \Program Files\Microsoft Office\Office 11\Macros folder.
4. Click OK twice. If a Security Warning dialog box appears, you have two options:
   - You can check Always Trust Macros from This Publisher, and click Enable Macros. From now on, Word will automatically assume that it can run macros authenticated as coming from Microsoft.
   - You can cancel the wizard, and reduce your security setting to Medium, as described immediately before this procedure.

Next, to run the macro, follow these steps:

1. Choose Tools, Macro, Macros.
2. From the Macros In drop-down box, choose support.dot.
3. In the Macro Name scroll box, choose AutoCorrect Backup.
4. Click Run. The AutoCorrect Utility dialog box appears (see Figure 9.7).

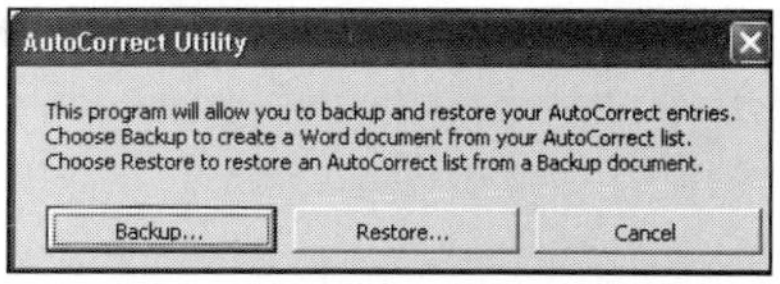

Figure 9.7
From here, you can create a Word file containing your list of AutoCorrect entries, or transform such a list into a working AutoCorrect file.

To create a backup copy of your AutoCorrect file, click Backup. Word adds each AutoCorrect entry, showing its progress on the status bar. It then reformats the information into a three-column table, making the information easier to read and edit. This process may take a minute or two.

When Word finishes, it displays the Save As dialog box, suggesting AutoCorrect Backup Document as a filename. Click Save to save the file in your My Documents folder.

Word AutoCorrect files are stored in special binary files with an ACL extension. To back up an ACL file, the AutoCorrect Utility translates it from ACL format into Word document format. To restore an ACL file, the AutoCorrect utility translates it back into the ACL format.

EDITING AN AUTOCORRECT BACKUP DOCUMENT

You can use Word to edit an AutoCorrect Backup Document to add or delete entries before restoring them to another computer. As shown in Figure 9.8, AutoCorrect Backup Document consists of three-column tables.

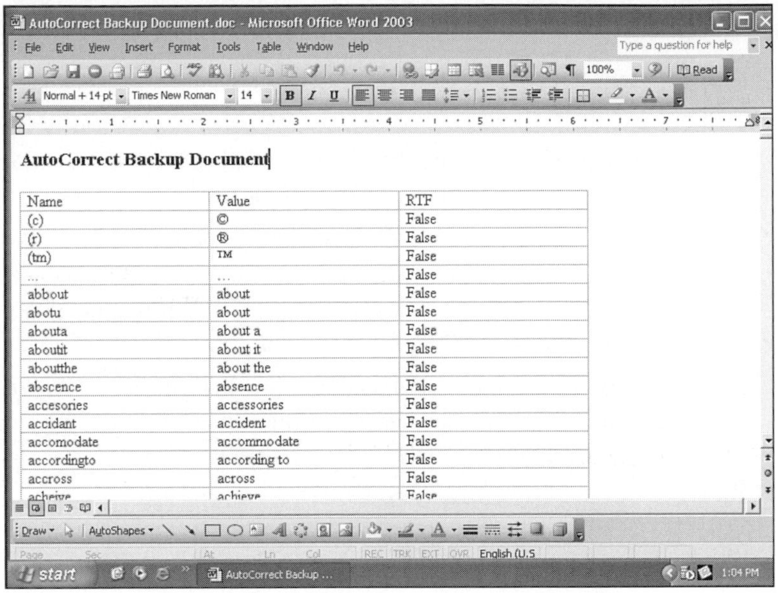

Figure 9.8
An AutoCorrect Backup Document contains a three-column table that you can edit to add, change, or delete entries.

The first column, Name, includes the word or phrase you want to change. The second column, Value, indicates the word or phrase you want to use in its place. The third column, RTF, indicates whether the replacement text should be inserted as ASCII text or as formatted text. The default setting here is False. However, if you added text with formatting (as discussed earlier in the "Using AutoCorrect to Insert Boilerplate Text" section), the RTF entry is True.

COPYING AUTOCORRECT ENTRIES TO AN AUTOCORRECT FILE

To copy an AutoCorrect Backup Document's entries into Word's AutoCorrect file, follow these steps:

1. Run the AutoCorrect utility (as described earlier in "Backing Up and Restoring AutoCorrect Entries").

2. Click Restore.

3. Click Yes to confirm that you want to replace any current AutoCorrect entries with equivalent entries in the backup document. The Open dialog box opens.

4. Browse to and select the AutoCorrect Backup Document you want to use.

5. Click Open. Word begins adding AutoCorrect entries to the computer's ACL file. This may take a few minutes.

6. When Word finishes, it presents a message that it has completed. Click OK.

AUTOTEXT: THE COMPLETE BOILERPLATE RESOURCE

You've already seen how you can use AutoCorrect to enter large blocks of boilerplate text quickly—text that you use repeatedly in many documents. However, this isn't AutoCorrect's primary function. Another Word feature, *AutoText*, is designed specifically to help you manage and quickly insert boilerplate text.

If you build a library of AutoText entries, you can dramatically reduce the amount of retyping you have to do. At the same time, you can help your colleagues build documents more quickly and more consistently. In other words, whether you're working on your own or in a corporate setting, AutoText offers enormous opportunities to improve your productivity.

AUTOTEXT ENTRIES BUILT INTO WORD

Word comes with dozens of built-in AutoText entries to help you streamline letters and other documents. The categories of entries and the text associated with each entry are listed in Table 9.2.

TABLE 9.2   WORD'S BUILT-IN AUTOTEXT ENTRY TEXT

Category (Submenu)	Entry Text Options
Attention Line	Attention:; ATTN:
Closing	Best regards; Best wishes; Cordially; Love; Regards; Respectfully Yours; Respectfully; Sincerely yours; Sincerely; Take care; Thank you; Thanks; Yours truly
Header/Footer	Page–; Author, Page # Date; Created by; Created on; Confidential, Page # Date; Last printed; Last saved by; Filename; Filename and Path; Page X of Y
Mailing Instructions	CERTIFIED MAIL; CONFIDENTIAL; PERSONAL; REGISTERED MAIL; SPECIAL DELIVERY; VIA AIRMAIL; VIA FACSIMILE; VIA OVERNIGHT MAIL; SPECIAL HANDLING
Reference Initials	Your own initials
Reference Line	In regards to; In reply to; RE:; Reference
Salutation	Dear Madam or Sir; Dear Madam; Dear Mom and Dad; Dear Mother and Father; Dear Sir or Madam; Dear Sir; Ladies and Gentlemen; To Whom It May Concern
Signature	Your signature
Subject Line	Subject:

To use one of these entries—or any other entry you create—choose Insert, AutoText and display the cascading menu containing the entry you want to use (see Figure 9.9). Click the entry, and Word inserts the corresponding entry text in your document.

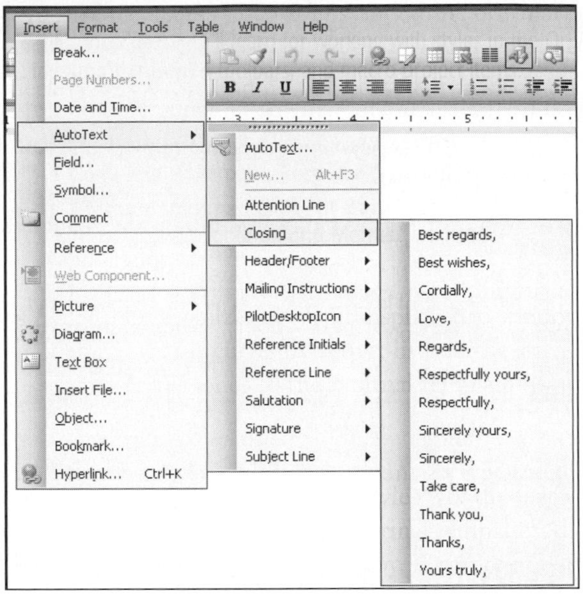

Figure 9.9
Select an existing
AutoText entry.

NOTE

Some of Word's built-in AutoText entries insert not only text but also fields that update themselves. For example, if you insert the Author, Page #, Date entry in your header or footer, Word enters three fields: the { AUTHOR } field, which reports the name of the author as it appears in your Properties dialog box; the { PAGE } field, which displays the current page number, and the { DATE } field that displays the current date.

When you create your own entries, you'll typically use short, easy-to-remember names for your AutoText entries. If you remember the name of an AutoText entry (custom or built-in), you can use it in your document without working with menus. Just type the AutoText entry name and press F3. Word replaces the AutoText entry name you typed and inserts the longer text associated with the entry.

CAUTION

The AutoText entry must be separate from the text that precedes and follows it for Word to recognize it as an AutoText entry when you press F3. However, it can be within parentheses, or immediately before punctuation such as a period, colon, or semicolon.

WORKING WITH THE AUTOTEXT TOOLBAR

If you're planning to work with quite a few AutoText entries at the same time, you may want to display the AutoText toolbar (see Figure 9.10). This toolbar contains three buttons:

- The AutoText button, which displays the AutoText dialog box, where you can control all aspects of your collection of AutoText entries.

- A button that displays all your current AutoText entries, or those associated with the style you're currently using.
- A <u>N</u>ew button that appears when you've selected text. Click it to display the Create AutoText entry you've already seen.

Figure 9.10
If you're working on many AutoText entries at the same time, display the AutoText toolbar.

9

ENTERING AUTOTEXT ENTRIES EVEN FASTER WITH AUTOCOMPLETE

Imagine that you have an AutoText entry, such as "dsclmr," that places your company's standard disclaimer clause in your document. As you've seen, if you want to use this entry, you can type `dsclmr` and press F3, and Word inserts the formatted text. But there's an even quicker way. As soon as you type the fourth letter in this (or any) AutoText entry, a ScreenTip appears showing all the text associated with the AutoText entry (or as much as will fit within the ScreenTip). You can see an example in Figure 9.11. If you are planning to use this AutoText entry, just press Enter, and Word *AutoCompletes* the entry at the current insertion point.

If you aren't planning to use the AutoText entry—for example, if you're typing another word that just happens to start the same way as an AutoText entry—just ignore the ScreenTip and keep typing.

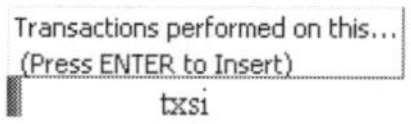

Figure 9.11
When you type the fourth letter of an AutoText entry, Word displays the beginning of the corresponding AutoText entry as a ScreenTip, along with instructions for inserting the text.

> Transactions performed on this...
> (Press ENTER to Insert)
> txsi

NOTE

> If you have two AutoText entries that start with the same four letters, Word doesn't display a ScreenTip until you've entered enough text for it to recognize which one you're most likely to want.

TIP

> AutoComplete doesn't just work with AutoText entries; it also offers to complete months of the year, days of the week, and today's date.

CREATING YOUR OWN AUTOTEXT ENTRY

Word's built-in AutoText entries are handy, but you don't get the full benefits of AutoText until you start creating your own entries. There are several ways to create your entry. The quickest way is to select the text you want to transform into an AutoText entry and press Alt+F3 to display the Create AutoText dialog box. You can also display the same dialog box by choosing Insert, AutoText, New. Figure 9.12 shows the Create AutoText dialog box.

Figure 9.12
One quick way to create an AutoText entry is to select text and then press Alt+F3 to display the Create AutoText dialog box.

Word automatically displays the first word or words in the text you've selected. Edit this text into a brief entry name you'll easily remember and click OK. Now, the entry name appears in the AutoText cascaded dialog box with any other entries you may have added.

CONTROLLING WHICH FORMATTING IS INCLUDED IN AN AUTOTEXT ENTRY

If you want your AutoText entry text to include paragraph formatting, include in your selection the paragraph mark (+) at the end of the paragraph containing that formatting.

AutoText entry text is stored with whatever character formatting you've applied to it. That saves you the trouble of duplicating complex character formats later. However, paragraph styles aren't saved unless you select a paragraph mark. When you do not select the paragraph mark, your AutoText entry text takes on the paragraph style of the surrounding text wherever you insert it.

UNDERSTANDING WHERE AUTOTEXT ENTRIES ARE STORED AND DISPLAYED

All of Word's built-in AutoText entries are stored in the Normal (Normal.dot) template. New AutoText entries are stored in the template associated with the document in which you're working. In other words, if you are working on a document based on the Normal template, any AutoText entry you create manually is also stored in the Normal template.

Then, whenever you are working on a document based on the Normal template, you have access to all the AutoText entries you've stored in the Normal template, with one major exception. If your insertion point is currently within a block of text formatted in a custom style and if that custom style has AutoText entries associated with it, Word displays only the entries associated with the custom style.

→ For more information about how Word displays AutoText entries based on specific styles, **see** "Adding New Categories of AutoText Entries," **p. 306**.

You can see this most easily when the AutoText toolbar is displayed. If you are currently working in text formatted in a custom style that has AutoText entries associated with it, that style's name appears in place of All Entries. When you click the button, you see only the entries associated with that style.

TIP

> If you need access to an AutoText entry that isn't displayed, press Shift before you display the list of AutoText entries via either the AutoText toolbar or the Insert, AutoText cascaded menu. Or click your insertion point in text formatted with any of Word's standard styles, such as Normal, Body Text, or any built-in heading style.

9

SAVING AN AUTOTEXT ENTRY IN A DIFFERENT TEMPLATE

At times you might want to store AutoText entries in a template other than Normal. For example, your AutoText entries might be relevant only when you're creating a specialized kind of document, and you always use the same custom template to create that kind of document. Why clutter up the Normal template with AutoText entries you'll never use in the documents you create with Normal?

To create AutoText entries in another template, first create or open a document based on that template; then create the AutoText entry as you normally do.

CONTROLLING THE TEMPLATES IN WHICH AUTOTEXT ENTRIES ARE AVAILABLE

By default, Word makes available AutoText entries in all templates that are currently open. For example, if you are working in a file created by a template named Smith.dot, you have access to all AutoText entries stored in Smith.dot, as well as those in Normal.dot—a global template that is always open. However, you might not want to see the more general AutoText entries you may have associated with Normal.dot if you're using a customized template.

You can choose any open template and tell Word to display only the AutoText entries associated with that template. To do so, choose Insert, AutoText, AutoText. The AutoText tab of the AutoCorrect dialog box opens (see Figure 9.13). In the Look In drop-down list box, choose the template containing the entries you want to see and click OK.

When you return to your editing window, you see that AutoText entries associated with other templates are no longer available from the AutoText menu. If you type them in your document and press F3 or use AutoComplete, nothing happens.

MOVING AUTOTEXT ENTRIES BETWEEN TEMPLATES

You can move AutoText entries between templates, using Word's Organizer feature. The Organizer is covered in detail in Chapter 11, "Templates, Wizards, and Add-Ins." Briefly, though, you follow these steps:

1. Choose Tools, Templates and Add-Ins.
2. Click the Organizer button.
3. Click the AutoText tab.

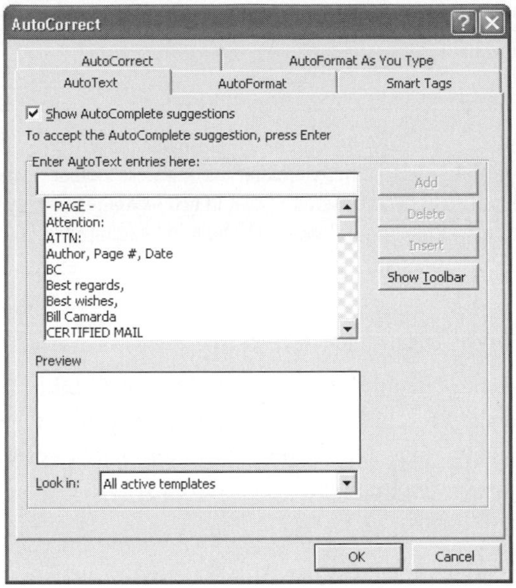

Figure 9.13
With the AutoText tab of the AutoCorrect dialog box, you can control which template's AutoText entries are active.

4. In one scroll box, display the document or template containing the AutoText entry or entries you want to move.

5. In the other scroll box, display the document or template you are moving the AutoText entry or entries to.

6. Select the entries you want to move.

7. Click Copy.

8. Click Close.

ADDING NEW CATEGORIES OF AUTOTEXT ENTRIES

You might want to add new categories of AutoText entries. That way, when you click Insert, AutoText, your new categories appear along with Word's built-in submenus. For example, imagine that you work for the sales department of Acme Corporation; you might want to add a submenu called Acme Proposals that contains AutoText entries you can include in your sales proposals.

Word organizes AutoText entries in submenus, based on the styles with which they are associated. When you want to create a new submenu, you can use this to your advantage.

First, create a new style with the name you want to appear in your custom submenu. To do so, select a paragraph, click the drop-down style box, type the new name, and press Enter. Don't worry much about how your style is formatted. When you select an AutoText entry, it uses the surrounding formatting in your document, not the formatting associated with the style you've just created.

Next, enter the first block of text for which you want to create an AutoText entry and format the text using the style you just created.

Finally, create the AutoText entry using whatever method you prefer. Repeat the process for any other text you want to appear in the same submenu; make sure to format the text with your custom style before you create the AutoText entry.

After you do this, your new AutoText entries appear in their own submenu whenever you're working in the same template where you created them.

TIP

You can use AutoText to store virtually anything you can place in a document, not just text. Here are some types of entries you might want to store as AutoText:

- Your handwritten signature and the signature of anyone else for whom you prepare documents
- Your corporate logo
- Photos and drawings
- Complex table formats
- Complex field codes, such as customized cross-references

If you are creating a Web page, you can also store AutoText entries that place custom design elements or pieces of HTML code into your document, such as customized bullets and borders.

PRINTING LISTS OF AUTOTEXT ENTRIES

The more you work with AutoText entries, the more you'll need to keep track of them. You've already seen how you can review your entire list of AutoText entries in the AutoText dialog box. You might also want to print a list of entries associated with a specific template. To print the list of entries, first create or open a new document based on the template containing the entries you want to print. Choose File, Print. In the Print What drop-down box, choose AutoText Entries and click OK.

CHANGING AN EXISTING AUTOTEXT ENTRY

You may occasionally want to change an AutoText entry. To change an entry, follow these steps:

1. Insert the AutoText entry in your document.
2. Edit the AutoText entry to reflect your changes.
3. Select the entire AutoText entry.
4. Choose Insert, AutoText, AutoText to display the AutoText dialog box.
5. Select the name of the AutoText entry you want to change.
6. Click Add. Word displays a dialog box asking whether you want to redefine your AutoText entry.
7. Click Yes.

Changing AutoText entries doesn't change any text you've previously inserted in a document using those entries—unless, that is, you use the procedure discussed in the following section.

INSERTING AUTOTEXT ENTRIES THAT UPDATE THEMSELVES

After you enter text in your document using an AutoText entry, that text looks and behaves no differently than if you had typed it manually. But what if you could enter an AutoText entry that updates itself whenever the AutoText entry is updated? Imagine that your corporate lawyers change the boilerplate disclaimer language you've been using. Wouldn't it be great if your entire workgroup could have access to the new language immediately? And wouldn't it be even better if you could automatically update your existing documents to reflect the change?

You can. Rather than inserting your AutoText entry using the methods discussed earlier, use an { AUTOTEXT } field. Follow these steps:

1. Choose Insert, Field. The Field dialog box opens.
2. Choose { AutoText } from the Field Names list. In the AutoText Name scroll box, Word displays a list of all the AutoText entries currently available to you.
3. Select the entry you want to insert.
4. Click OK.

If you display field results, your document looks exactly as if you had inserted the AutoText entry the normal way. If, however, you change the text (or other document elements) associated with this AutoText entry, Word can update the field the same way it updates any other field.

> **TIP**
>
> You can update all the fields in your document by pressing Ctrl+A and then F9.

→ For more information about working with fields, **see** Chapter 23, "Automating Your Documents with Field Codes," **p. 771**.

INSERTING AUTOTEXT OPTIONS WITHIN YOUR DOCUMENT

If you're setting up a document or template for others to work on, you can streamline their work by making it easy for them to choose the right AutoText entries wherever they're appropriate. You do this by inserting an { AUTOTEXTLIST } field at those places in your document where a choice needs to be made.

You can see { AUTOTEXTLIST } fields at work in Word's letter templates, which embed multiple options for Salutations and Closings directly in the documents they create. In Figure 9.14, if you right-click the word Sincerely, Word displays a list containing all Word's built-in choices for letter closings. If you merely pause over the word, a ScreenTip appears, telling you what to do.

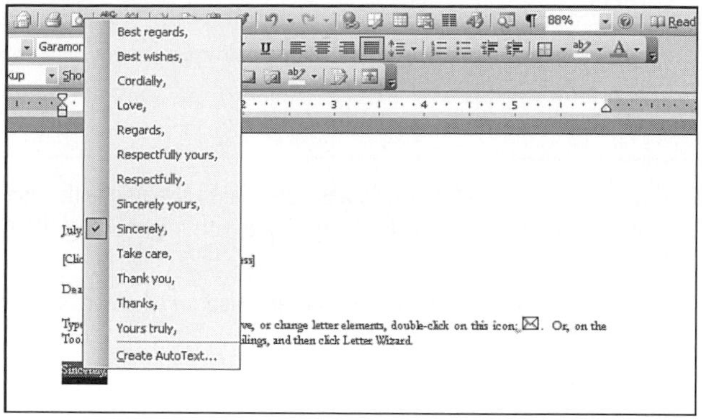

Figure 9.14
If you right-click the letter closing in a built-in Word letter template, you can choose from all of Word's AutoText entries for letter closings.

To create an AutoText field, follow these steps:

1. Choose <u>I</u>nsert, <u>F</u>ield.

2. Choose { AutoTextList } from the <u>F</u>ield Names scroll box. Word displays the options associated with the { AutoTextList } field (see Figure 9.15).

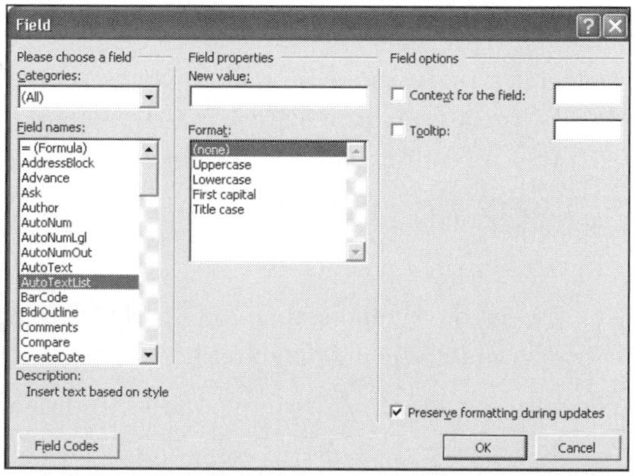

Figure 9.15
Setting properties and options for the { *AutoTextList* } field in the Field dialog box.

3. In the New Value: text box, enter the text you want to appear by default before users right-click the { AutoTextList } field. Use the text that's most likely to be the right choice. That way, your users can often ignore the field.

4. Next, enable users to choose among AutoText entries associated with a specific style. To do so, type the name of the style in the check box to the right of the Conte<u>x</u>t for the Field check box.

TIP

You don't have to specify the same style in which the field result is formatted. You can choose any style currently available to the document.

5. If you want to provide users with help, enter your Help text in the text box to the right of the Tooltip check box. This information is shown whenever a user hovers his or her mouse pointer over the field.

TIP

> The { AUTOTEXTLIST } field has potential to streamline the construction of a wide range of business documents. For example, you might use { AUTOTEXTLIST } to do the following:
>
> - Choose different text in a proposal based on whether the project schedule is normal or rushed
> - Select one of several preformatted tables
> - Insert a signature from any one of several people
> - Select the contents of a letter from a set of preestablished AutoText entries

➜ For more information about working with fields, **see** Chapter 23, "Automating Your Documents with Field Codes," **p. 771**.

AUTOFORMATTING: THE FASTEST WAY TO FORMAT

If you haven't bothered to format your document at all, or if you received it in ASCII (text-only) format via email, Word's AutoFormatting feature may be able to handle the formatting for you. Among the many tasks AutoFormat can perform are

- Creating headings and lists, including bulleted lists
- Applying styles to many document elements
- Replacing ASCII text with custom symbols, including curly "smart quotes," fractions, ordinal numbers such as 1st and 2nd, em and en dashes
- Replacing Internet and network addresses with hyperlinks to the same addresses

To use AutoFormatting, choose AutoFormat from the Format menu. The AutoFormat dialog box opens (see Figure 9.16).

Figure 9.16
You can tell AutoFormat to reformat anything it pleases, or you can review the results of AutoFormat's handiwork one change at a time.

If your document is a letter or an email, telling that to Word helps it do a better job of AutoFormatting. In the P̲lease Select a Document Type drop-down box in the AutoFormat dialog box, choose Letter or Email rather than General Document.

> **TIP**
>
> If you choose Email, Word removes extra paragraph marks that often appear at the end of every line in email messages, as well as performing other email–specific actions.

Next, click OK. Word reformats the entire document for you.

> **TIP**
>
> Sometimes it takes a couple of tries to get the best results from AutoFormat. Try running AutoFormat simply to get an idea of what AutoFormat does to your document. You may notice problems the first time around. Click Undo. Then, as is discussed in the next section, adjust AutoFormat options so that Word doesn't make changes you don't like. Finally, run AutoFormat again.

If you want, you can AutoFormat only part of a document. To do so, select the text you want formatted before you choose F̲ormat, A̲utoFormat. Don't forget that tables have a separate set of AutoFormatting controls (choose T̲able, Table AutoF̲ormat). The AutoFormat command discussed in this chapter doesn't touch the way your tables are formatted.

→ For more information about AutoFormatting tables, **see** "Using Table Styles to AutoFormat a Table," **p. 411**.

CONTROLLING THE CHANGES AUTOFORMAT MAKES

You have a good deal of control over the changes AutoFormat makes. With the AutoFormat dialog box open, click O̲ptions. The AutoFormat tab of the AutoCorrect dialog box appears (see Figure 9.17). You can now clear any check boxes corresponding to document elements you want AutoFormat to leave alone.

 *If Word makes undesirable formatting changes, see "What to Do If Word Makes Formatting Changes You Don't Want," in "Troubleshooting" at the end of this chapter.*

Here's a closer look at the document elements AutoFormat can change, along with some tips for making the most of AutoFormat:

- **Built-In Hea̲ding Styles.** One of the best reasons to use AutoFormatting is to save time in transforming a text-only file into one that can benefit from Word's outlining features and heading styles. Before you try to add heading styles manually, consider clearing every box except Built-In Hea̲ding Styles and running AutoFormat to see how many headings it can format properly.

- **L̲ist Styles.** With L̲ist Styles checked, Word automatically starts applying Word's built-in list styles (List, List 2, List 3, and so on) to any list of consecutive lines separated by paragraph marks.

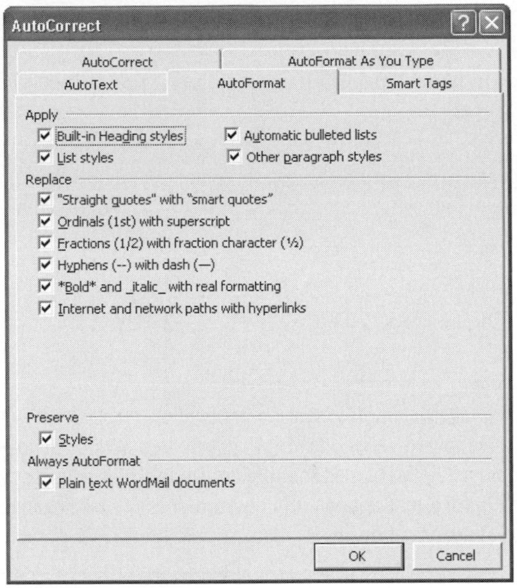

Figure 9.17
In the AutoFormat tab, you can control the formatting changes that Word makes when you run AutoFormat.

- **Automatic Bulleted Lists**. With this check box checked, Word automatically inserts bullets in place of the characters commonly used to substitute for bullets, such as dashes and asterisks.

- **Other Paragraph Styles.** By default, AutoFormat transforms all text formatted as Normal into other formats such as Body Text. In some cases, Word can recognize from the contents of text what the text is likely to be. For instance, it recognizes address lines and reformats them with the Inside Address style. However, for convenience and simplicity, you might prefer to keep all text other than headings formatted as Normal. Clear this check box if you don't want Word to change the styles associated with text paragraphs.

- **"Straight Quotes" with "Smart Quotes".** With this box checked, Word replaces straight up-and-down quotation marks and apostrophes with curly ones that look better. If you're exporting your document for use by another program, especially if you're crossing platforms (say, to the Macintosh or a Linux workstation), make sure that the other program can display SmartQuotes properly before using them.

TIP

If you're a writer, you might have one client who requires SmartQuotes and another who prohibits them. Sometimes you'll realize partway through a document that Word has been adding undesired SmartQuotes. You can turn off SmartQuotes through the AutoFormat As You Type tab of the AutoCorrect dialog box. But what about the incorrect quotation marks that are already in your document? Use Find and Replace to get rid of them.

First, choose Edit, Replace. Then, place a straight quote mark (') in the Find box and another straight quote mark (') in the Replace box. Choose Replace All. Word searches for both curly and straight quotation marks and replaces them all with straight quotation marks.

- **Ordinals (1st) with Superscript.** Word recognizes typed ordinals (1st, 2nd, 3rd, and so on) and can automatically replace them with the more attractive 1st, 2nd, 3rd, and so on. This works with any number but does not work with spelled out numbers such as "twenty-eighth."

- **Fractions (1/2) with Fraction Character ($\frac{1}{2}$).** By default, Word replaces 1/2, 1/4, and 3/4 with the better-looking symbol characters. Most fonts don't have symbol characters for other fractions, such as 1/8 or 3/16. If your document uses fractions that can't be reformatted, you may want to clear this check box to keep everything consistent.

- **Hyphens (—) with Dash (—).** When Word recognizes that you've typed characters typically used in place of dash symbols, such as two consecutive hyphens in place of an em dash (—), it can substitute the proper character automatically. As with SmartQuotes, if you're planning to export your Word document, make sure that the program you're exporting it to can handle the symbols correctly.

- ***Bold* and _Italic_ with Real Formatting.** When this check box is checked, if you type an asterisk followed by text and another asterisk, Word eliminates the asterisks and formats the text as boldface. If you type an underscore character (_) followed by text and another underscore character, Word eliminates the underscores and formats the text as italic. You might find the underline feature confusing, because text is being formatted in italic, not underline. "Pre-computer" style manuals instructed users to simulate italic on a typewriter by using underlining, but this can be confusing if you learned how to create documents using PCs, not typewriters. This option is not checked by default; it needs to be activated in the AutoFormat As You Type tab of the AutoCorrect dialog box.

- **Internet and Network Paths with Hyperlinks.** This is a welcome feature if you are creating a document that will be published on the Web, or will primarily be used in electronic format: It saves you the trouble of manually adding hyperlinks. It is not so welcome if you are creating a printed document, or if you are providing a disk file for use in another program, such as a desktop publishing program. Word replaces standard text with hyperlink fields that look different (they're blue and underlined) and act differently (they're *field codes*, which can't be understood by many programs to which you may be exporting your Word file). If this sounds like trouble, clear this check box.

- **Preserve Styles.** By default, if AutoFormat finds that you've formatted a paragraph with any style other than Normal, it leaves that paragraph alone. If you clear this check box, Word uses its judgment and reformats any paragraph it thinks necessary.

- **Plain Text WordMail Documents.** If you are on a network, if you receive email, *and* if you have selected Word as your email editor in Outlook, checking this box tells Word to AutoFormat email documents that arrive as plain ASCII text. Checking this box doesn't affect any other text-only documents, including those you retrieve as ASCII files from other email systems and display in Word via the File, Open dialog box.

AUTOFORMATTING INTERACTIVELY

You've already learned that you can run AutoFormat, undo the results if you don't like them, and then control the types of AutoFormatting that Word applies through the AutoFormat tab of the AutoCorrect dialog box. You can also run AutoFormatting interactively and make decisions one at a time.

This gives you finer control over the AutoFormatting changes Word makes. However, because Word stops everywhere that it makes even the most minor changes, this can be a slow process. (There's no way to accept all the formatting changes of a certain type.)

One approach is to first run AutoFormat automatically, selecting only the changes you're sure you would accept. Then, you can run AutoFormat again, this time interactively, using different settings that correspond to changes you want to accept or reject individually.

To AutoFormat interactively, choose Format, AutoFormat. Then choose AutoFormat and Review Each Change and click OK.

Word AutoFormats the document and displays the AutoFormat dialog box (see Figure 9.18), from where you can review each change Word has made to accept or reject that change.

Figure 9.18
From here, you can accept or reject all changes, review them one at a time, or display the Style Gallery.

The AutoFormat dialog box stays open as you move through the document. So before you start reviewing changes in detail, you might want to use the scrollbar and other Word navigation tools to get a rough idea about how close Word has come. If the document looks right on target, click Accept All. If Word's AutoFormatting is far from what you had in mind, click Reject All.

If Word landed somewhere in between, click Review Changes. The Review AutoFormat Changes dialog box opens (see Figure 9.19), describing the first change Word has made to your document. While this dialog box is open, Word also displays the text changes it made throughout your document, with revision marks. If you prefer to see the document as it would look if all the changes were accepted, click Hide Marks. If you then want to take a closer look at a specific change, click Show Marks.

To move toward the beginning of the document; click ← Find. To move toward the end, click → Find. Word selects the first AutoFormatting change it made. When you select a change, Word tells you what it changed—for example, it might say "Adjusted alignment with a tab."

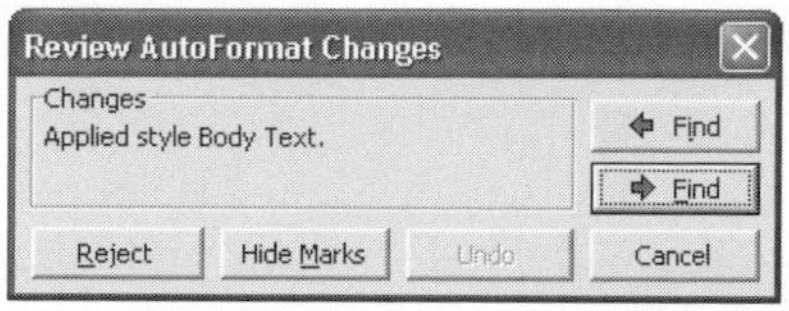

Figure 9.19
You can use this dialog box to move through your document to approve or reject individual changes.

USING STYLE GALLERY TO REFORMAT AUTOFORMATTED TEXT

The AutoFormat dialog box (refer to Figure 9.18) that appears after AutoFormat runs also gives you access to the Style Gallery. Using the Style Gallery, you can quickly reformat your styles to match the styles in a different template. Click Style Gallery to view it. Then, in the Template scroll box, choose a template containing formats you want to view. If you prefer the formats associated with the template, click OK.

As is always the case when you use Style Gallery (see Figure 9.20), Word doesn't actually change the template associated with the document with which you're working. Rather, it changes the formatting associated with the styles in your current document to make the formatting look like the formatting in the template you chose.

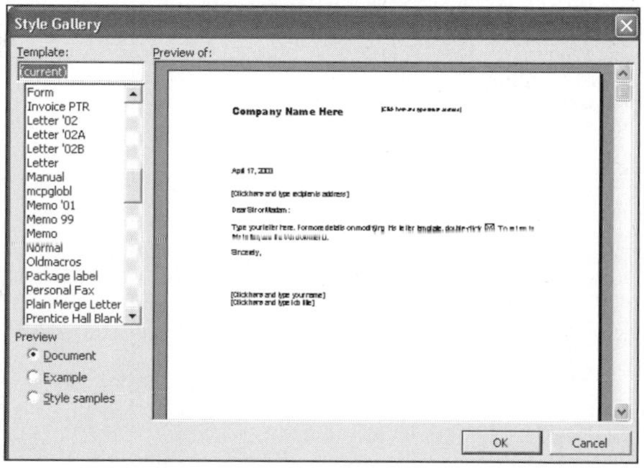

Figure 9.20
You can quickly change the look of your AutoFormatted document through Style Gallery.

→ For more information on working with the Style Gallery, **see** "Previewing New Templates with Style Gallery," **p. 372**.

Because all Word's built-in templates are based on Times New Roman and Arial, most of Word's built-in templates don't radically change the appearance of your document. However, if you've created custom templates that use Word's built-in style names, Style Gallery enables you to apply those styles quickly to an AutoFormatted document.

USING AUTOFORMAT AS YOU TYPE

Word can also AutoFormat as you type, helping make sure that your document is formatted properly as you work. In many cases, the document elements Word reformats on-the-fly are similar to those Word can AutoFormat when you choose Format, AutoFormat. In other cases, they are different.

For example, by default, Word doesn't convert text that it identifies as headings into heading styles while you work, because many people find it distracting, and because for some documents the text Word recognizes as headings may not be the same text you intend to format as headings.

On the other hand, if you're writing a document in which most of the headings consist of short blocks of text that end without a period, and are set apart from surrounding text with paragraph marks, you may find that it's a real convenience to have Word reformat those headings as you type them.

To control Word's on-the-fly AutoFormatting, choose Tools, AutoCorrect Options; then click the AutoFormat As You Type tab (see Figure 9.21). Make any changes you want to these options, and click OK. (For explanations of the options here, see the earlier discussion in "Controlling the Changes AutoFormat Makes.")

Figure 9.21
The AutoFormat As You Type tab enables you to control formatting changes Word makes while you work.

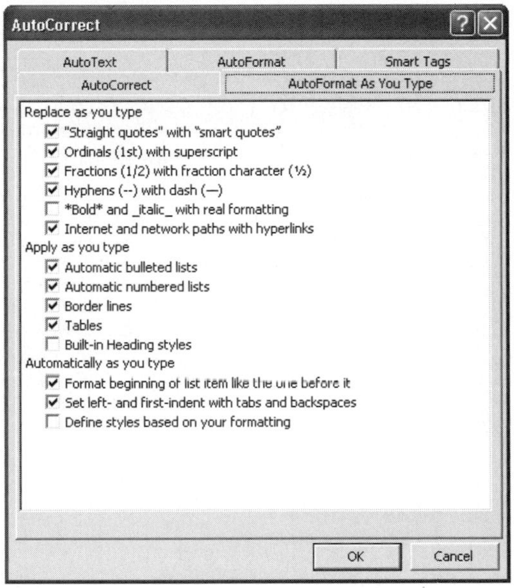

The following differences are worth pointing out:

- **Border lines.** Unlike regular AutoFormat, AutoFormat As You Type can transform rows of hyphens or underlines into true bordering. (Check the Border Lines check box.)

- **Tables.** AutoFormat As You Type transforms a row of hyphens and plus signs into a table row, with one column for each plus sign. (Check the Tables check box.)

■ **Indents.** AutoFormat As You Type replaces tabs and backspaces with indents if they appear at the beginning or end of paragraphs. (Check the Set Left- and First-Indent with Tabs and Backspaces check box.)

AUTOMATING FORMATTING FOR THE BEGINNING OF LIST ITEMS

When you are creating a list, you may occasionally format the first word or phrase in the list differently than you format the remaining text in each list paragraph. You can see an example of this in Figure 9.22. Word can recognize this specialized formatting and apply it to the new list items it creates each time you press Enter at the end of a list paragraph.

To activate this feature, check the Format Beginning of List Item Like the One Before It check box in the AutoFormat As You Type tab.

CAUTION

If you're creating a numbered or bulleted list, this feature doesn't deliver the results you want unless you also check the Automatic Bulleted Lists and/or Automatic Numbered Lists check box.

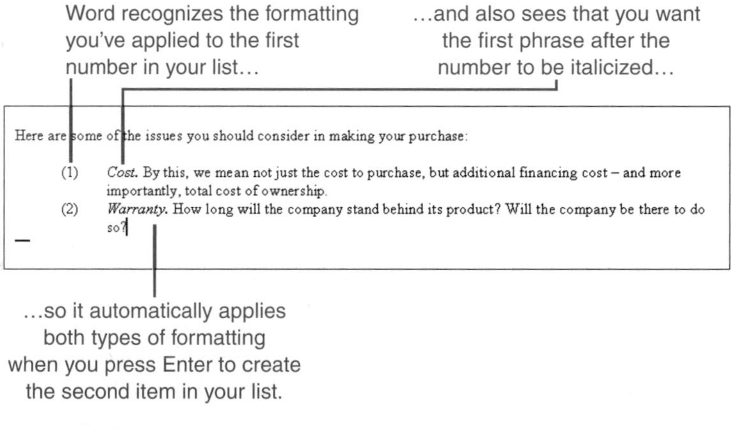

Word recognizes the formatting you've applied to the first number in your list…

…and also sees that you want the first phrase after the number to be italicized…

Figure 9.22
After you create specialized formatting to begin a list, Word can use that formatting in list items that immediately follow.

Here are some of the issues you should consider in making your purchase:

(1) *Cost.* By this, we mean not just the cost to purchase, but additional financing cost – and more importantly, total cost of ownership.

(2) *Warranty.* How long will the company stand behind its product? Will the company be there to do so?

…so it automatically applies both types of formatting when you press Enter to create the second item in your list.

USING AUTOFORMAT AS YOU TYPE TO GENERATE STYLES AUTOMATICALLY

If you can't be bothered with creating styles through the Style box, you can ask Word to watch you work and create the styles based on the manual formatting you apply. To turn on this feature, display the AutoFormat As You Type tab, check the Define Styles Based on Your Formatting check box, and click OK. Make sure that the document elements you want to AutoFormat, such as Headings, are also selected. Then click Close.

CAUTION

Many users find that this feature generates too many unwanted styles. If you turn it on, check its behavior before deciding to leave it on.

WORKING WITH AUTOSUMMARIZE

Word can summarize your documents for you—or, more precisely, *attempt* to do so. AutoSummarize reviews the entire document and then scores each sentence based on a variety of factors, such as whether a sentence contains keywords—the words used the most often throughout the document. The sentences that get the highest score are included in your summary.

Because Word can't understand the subtleties of your document, the results of running AutoSummarize are mixed—from good to terrible. In general, the more tightly structured your document is, the better chance you have of getting useful results. You also generally have better luck with documents that cover a few key topics in-depth, as opposed to documents that include just a paragraph or two on many disparate topics.

In general, AutoSummarize does a fair-to-good job on the following types of document:

- Reports
- Articles
- Scientific papers
- Theses

AutoSummarize generally does a poor job on these:

- Fiction
- Most typical correspondence
- How-to instructions (such as this book)

Of course, some documents, such as contracts, are just too important to rely on AutoSummarize; there's no alternative to reading every word.

On the other hand, there's no law that restricts you to summarizing only those documents you create. Use AutoSummarize as a tool to deal with all kinds of information overload. It's like hiring your computer to skim for you. Run AutoSummarize on any long, well-structured document that can be opened and edited in Word—such as Web pages formatted in HTML—and you can quickly see whether the document is worth reading in its entirety.

If you're creating an executive summary or abstract for a longer document, AutoSummarize rarely delivers perfection, but it often gives you a significant head start. Using the content AutoSummarize creates, you can fill in holes, polish and tighten the text, and make sure that your summary reads smoothly—all in significantly less time than it would have taken you to create it from scratch.

To AutoSummarize your document, choose Tools, AutoSummarize. Word immediately builds a summary of your document and stores it in memory pending your instructions. The AutoSummarize dialog box then opens (see Figure 9.23).

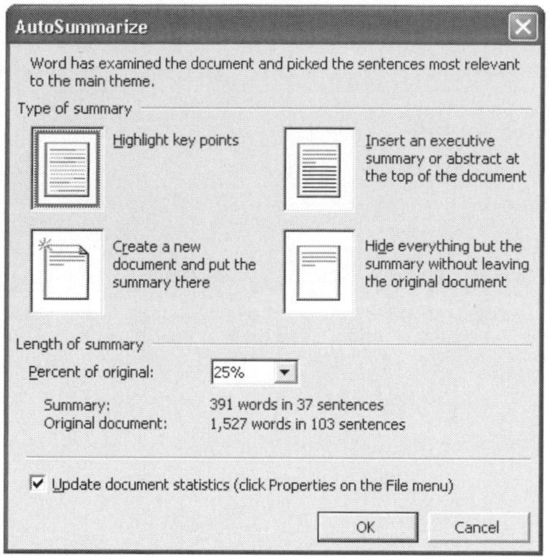

Figure 9.23
In the AutoSummarize dialog box, you specify where to place your summary and how detailed you want it to be.

You now have the following four choices:

- **Highlight Key Points.** Without changing the contents of your document or creating a new document, Word applies yellow highlighting to the sentences it deems most important, as shown in Figure 9.24. The AutoSummarize toolbar appears in your document. Other, unhighlighted paragraphs appear in gray. You can drag the Percent of Original scrollbar to highlight more or less of the document; as you drag it, more or fewer sentences are highlighted.

TIP

> Word highlights AutoSummarized text in yellow, so if you used yellow highlighting elsewhere in the document, you won't be able to tell the difference. Consider using a different highlight color in documents you plan to AutoSummarize using the Highlight Key Points feature.

- **Create a New Document and Put the Summary There.** Word creates a new document and places the summary there. This document has no link to the original document, so after the text has been inserted, there's no way to adjust it except by running AutoSummarize again. This option makes sense if you need to provide an executive summary or abstract but don't want to change the page numbering or contents of your original document.

- **Insert an Executive Summary or Abstract at the Top of the Document.** This copies the AutoSummarized text to the beginning of your document, where it can be edited and saved along with any other document contents. After you copy the text, you can't adjust the size or contents of the summary except through conventional editing techniques.

Figure 9.24
Using AutoSummarize
to highlight the most
important sentences
in your document.

Highlighted text included in summary

Close AutoSummarize

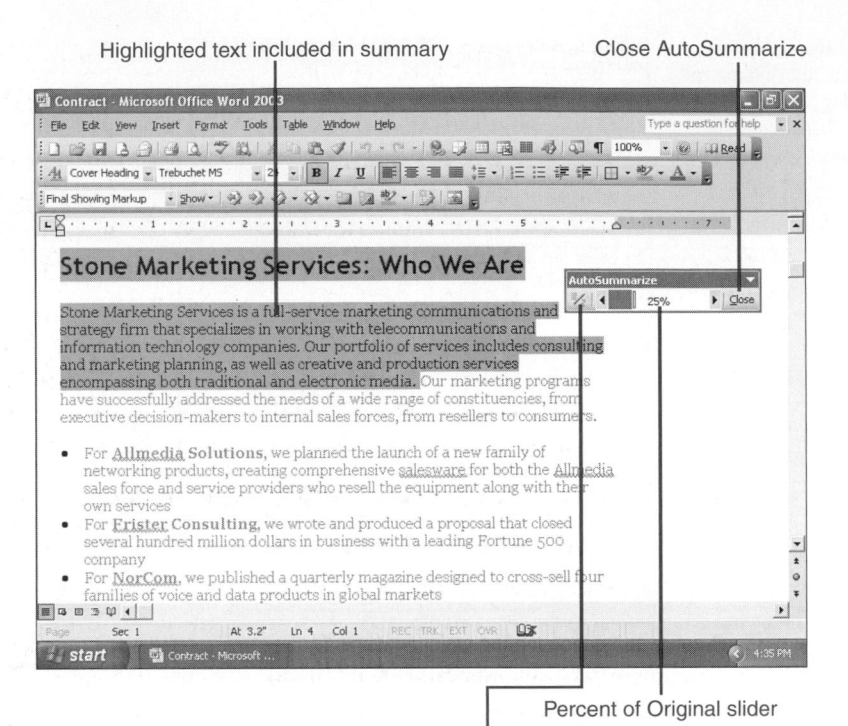

Percent of Original slider

Highlight/Show Only Summary

TIP

> If you choose either of the preceding two options, consider increasing the percentage of sentences Word inserts in your summary because it is easier to delete sentences from your summary later than to add more. You can change this value with the Percent of Original slider in the AutoSummarize dialog box.

■ **Hide Everything but the Summary Without Leaving the Original Document.**
This option makes no changes to the text in your current document. Rather, it temporarily hides all the paragraphs that weren't selected to be part of the summary. In other words, your document looks as if it contains only the summary. If you print your document with only the summary showing, only the summary prints. However, when you click Close on the AutoSummarize toolbar, all the hidden text reappears.

You can also control what percentage of your document appears in the summary by entering a value in the Percent of Original drop-down list box. You can enter any percentage. Or, using the options in the drop-down list box, you can choose a specific number of sentences or words. If you leave Word's default setting alone, Word creates a summary containing 25% of the original document. If you're creating an executive summary of a long document, you may want to shrink it to 10%–15%, or place a word limit, such as 500 words, to keep things manageable.

If you choose either Highlight Key Points or Hide Everything but the Summary Without Leaving the Original Document, you can toggle between these options using the Highlight/Show Only Summary button on the AutoSummarize toolbar. In other words, if you've chosen to hide the parts of your document not included in the summary, you can view them at any time by clicking the Highlight/Show Only Summary button.

If you chose Highlight Key Points or Hide Everything but the Summary, you can adjust the percentage of the summary by dragging the Percentage of Original slider within the AutoSummarize toolbar.

When you're done working with AutoSummarize, and you no longer want to see high-lighted text, click the Close AutoSummarize button on the AutoSummarize toolbar.

If Word is not summarizing your document as you expect, see "What to Do If Word Doesn't Summarize Your Document," in "Troubleshooting" at the end of this chapter.

If text in an AutoSummarized document seems to disappear, see "What to Do If Text Disappears from an AutoSummarized Document," in the "Troubleshooting" section of this chapter.

USING AUTOSUMMARIZE TO UPDATE FILE PROPERTIES

As you will learn in Chapter 34, "Managing Word More Effectively," you can use the Properties dialog box to track information about your document, making it easier to track and search for documents later. As you've seen, within the information that AutoSummarize generates about your document is a list of keywords. Of course, it also includes the summary itself. Because this information is already available, AutoSummarize offers to place it in your Properties dialog box.

→ To learn more about working with document properties, **see** "Using Document Properties to Simplify Document Management," **p. 1122**.

When the Update Document Statistics check box is checked, as it is by default, Word inserts the top five keywords it finds in the Keywords text box in the Summary tab of the Properties dialog box. It also inserts the first few paragraphs of the summary itself in the Comments text box, also in the same tab.

CAUTION

When would you want to clear Update Document Statistics? If you are already using Keywords or Document Contents information for another purpose, you don't want Word overwriting the information stored there. For example, you might have already specified keywords and used the { KEYWORDS } field to display those keywords in a cover sheet to your document. Unless you clear this check box, when Word displays your summary it will also replace your keywords with the ones it thinks are most important.

→ To learn more about working with keywords and other document properties, **see** "Using Document Properties to Simplify Document Management," **p. 1122**.

WORKING WITH SMART TAGS

What if a word processor could automatically tag certain phrases as belonging to specific categories, and give you tools for using that text in new ways? For example, what if your document recognized when you typed a date, and offered to schedule a meeting for you? What if it recognized a name and provided commands for adding that name to your Outlook contact list, or for sending an email to that individual? With Word 2003's *Smart Tags* feature, you can do this, and far more.

USING SMART TAGS

When Word recognizes a Smart Tag in your document, it displays a thin purple underline beneath the text, as shown in Figure 9.25. (This underline is finer than the red wavy line Word uses to mark possible spelling errors.)

Figure 9.25
Word marks Smart Tags with a faint dotted underline.

123 Main Street

After text is marked with a Smart Tag, you can choose a Smart Tag Action to perform. To do so, click on (or hover your mouse pointer above) the tagged text. A small Information icon appears; click on it, and a menu of Actions appears (see Figure 9.26). Choose the one you want to use.

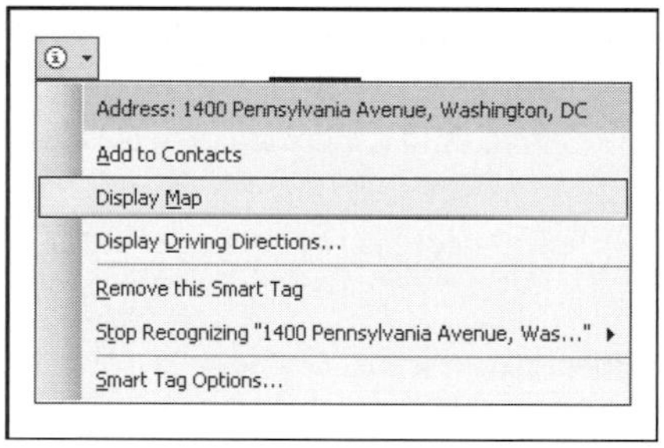

Figure 9.26
Selecting a Smart Tag Action.

Address: 1400 Pennsylvania Avenue, Washington, DC
Add to Contacts
Display Map
Display Driving Directions...
Remove this Smart Tag
Stop Recognizing "1400 Pennsylvania Avenue, Was..." ▶
Smart Tag Options...

For instance, if you click on the Smart Tag Actions associated with a date, and choose Show My Calendar, Word will open your Outlook calendar to that date. If you click on a Financial Symbol associated with a company and choose Stock Quote on MSN MoneyCentral, Word will open Internet Explorer and display that company's stock quote and related information.

CONTROLLING HOW WORD WORKS WITH SMART TAGS

Word 2003 can recognize several categories of Smart Tags:

- **Any names.** Name-related Word Smart Tag Actions allow you to send mail or instant messages, schedule meetings, open or add to Outlook contact information, and insert addresses. By default, Word recognizes only names stored in Outlook as email recipients, but in the English language version of Word, you can instruct Word to recognize other names as well. (Doing so is covered in the next section.)

- **Addresses.** Address-related Word Smart Tag Actions allow you to add an address to your Outlook contacts, or to display a map and/or driving directions to a specific location. Addresses are recognized by default.

- **Financial symbols.** Word Smart Tag Actions associated with financial symbols allow you to retrieve current MSN MoneyCentral stock quotes, company reports, or recent news about a company that corresponds to a U.S., UK, or Canadian stock symbol. (Note that the stock and funds smart tag is not installed during a "typical" installation, and that financial symbols are not recognized by default.)

- **Dates and times.** Date- and time-related Word Smart Tag Actions allow you to schedule a meeting or show your Outlook calendar for a specific date or time. Dates and times are recognized by default. (Word recognizes only dates after 1970.)

- **Selected place names.** Place-related Word Smart Tag Actions allow you to add an address to your Outlook contacts, or to display a map and/or driving directions to a specific location. Addresses are recognized by default.

- **Telephone numbers.** Phone-number–related Word Smart Tag Actions allow you to add a phone number to your Outlook Contact list. Phone numbers are not recognized by default.

To control which items Word flags as Smart Tags, and how those Smart Tags behave, choose Tools, AutoCorrect Options, and select the Smart Tags tab, as shown in Figure 9.27. (You can also display the Smart Tags tab by clicking on a Smart Tag and choosing Smart Tag Options from the shortcut menu.)

CHOOSING WHICH SMART TAGS TO RECOGNIZE

The categories of text Word can recognize as Smart Tags are listed in the Recognizers list box in the Smart Tags tab of the AutoCorrect dialog box (refer to Figure 9.27).

To instruct Word to recognize a category of text as Smart Tags, check the corresponding box; to instruct Word to stop recognizing a category, clear its box.

RECHECKING SMART TAGS IN A DOCUMENT

After you've changed Smart Tag settings for a document, you may want to recheck the document to make sure that the appropriate tags are flagged. To do so, click Recheck Document in the Smart Tags tab of the AutoCorrect dialog box.

FINDING ADDITIONAL SMART TAGS ONLINE

Microsoft and its business partners have made available several additional Smart Tags that you can download and install, assuming that you are connected to the Internet.

Figure 9.27
Smart Tag options available from the AutoCorrect box.

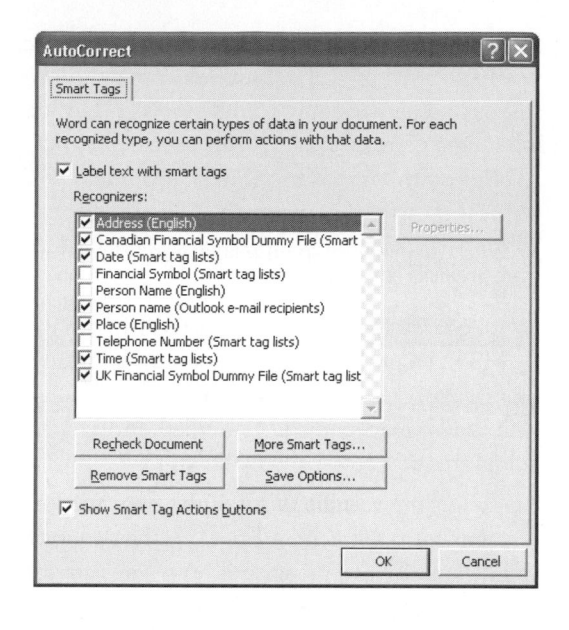

For example, you can import current news and weather information into your documents using MSNBC Smart Tags. Federal Express provides Smart Tags that link to the company's online tools for packaging tracking or creating shipping labels. (There's even an ESPN Smart Tag that recognizes the names of baseball players and teams, and can insert current statistics about them.)

Although many Smart Tags are free to download and use, some are available by monthly subscription, and others are available in connection with other software you need to buy.

To discover which Smart Tags are available, display the Smart Tags tab of the AutoCorrect dialog box, and click More Smart Tags. Internet Explorer opens, taking you to the Microsoft Office eServices Smart Tags page. From here, select the tag you're interested in, and follow the online instructions for downloading and installing it.

NOTE

> One powerful advantage of Smart Tags is that technically sophisticated organizations can create new ones. Business IT organizations might, for example, create Smart Tags for looking up and inserting information from a company database. Similarly, a company might create a Smart Tag that integrates with its accounting system, allowing a user to insert complete details of an order using a Smart Tag that recognizes order numbers.
>
> Creating original Smart Tags is beyond the scope of this book. Microsoft provides a series of free tools and resources that facilitate Smart Tag development. These are available at `http://msdn.microsoft.com/library/default.asp?url=/downloads/list/officedev.asp`. Using Microsoft's tools requires significant programming experience.
>
> Two third-party tools are available for creating Smart Tags somewhat more easily: ActiveDocs, from Keylogix (`www.keylogix.com`), and DataPortal, from Nereosoft (`www.nereosoft.com`).

TURNING OFF SMART TAGS

In certain cases, you may not want Word to recognize any Smart Tags. For example, Smart Tags can significantly increase document size, and may cause problems for third-party programs that need to import Microsoft Word documents. If you do not want Word to recognize Smart Tags in a document, display the Smart Tags tab, and clear the Label Text with Smart Tags check box.

TELLING WORD NOT TO RECOGNIZE A SMART TAG DATA TYPE OR ITEM

Word 2003 allows you to stop recognizing either individual blocks of text or entire categories of data ("data types"). To do so, click on the Smart Tag Actions icon associated with text marked as a Smart Tag. Then, choose Stop Recognizing.

A cascading menu appears. If you choose As Smart Tag, Word will stop recognizing the specific text you're working with. If you choose As Financial Symbol (or whatever data type Word has recognized), Word will stop recognizing *all* text associated with that data type.

REMOVING ALL SMART TAGS FROM A DOCUMENT

If your document already contains Smart Tags that you want to remove, display the Smart Tags tab, and click Remove Smart Tags. Click Yes to confirm that you want to do so.

CAUTION

> Removing Smart Tags removes not only the Smart Tags currently available on your computer, but also Smart Tags inserted in the same document by others, whether on your computer or theirs. The Smart Tags will also no longer be present when other users open your document on their computers (though they can recheck the document and add them back again).

REMOVING A SINGLE SMART TAG FROM A DOCUMENT

To remove a single Smart Tag from a document, click on its Smart Tag icon and choose Remove This Smart Tag from the shortcut menu.

HIDING SMART TAG BUTTONS IN A DOCUMENT

Occasionally you may want to allow Word to recognize Smart Tags in your document but turn off the icons that give users access to Smart Tag Actions. To do so, display the Smart Tags tab, and clear the Show Smart Tag Actions Buttons check box.

INSTRUCTING WORD NOT TO STORE SMART TAG DATA WITH SAVED DOCUMENTS

By default, Word stores Smart Tag data when you save a document. As already mentioned, this can enlarge your documents, and may conceivably cause problems when users of third-party software try to import your Word documents. To instruct Word not to save Smart Tag information with your document, display the Smart Tags tab of the AutoCorrect dialog box, and click Save Options. (You may also click Tools, Options, Save.) With the Save Options tab displayed, clear the Embed Smart Tags check box.

NOTE
Smart Tags can be saved in documents using only Microsoft Word .doc or Web page format. They cannot be saved in RTF, Text Only, or other formats.

SAVING SMART TAGS AS XML FOR USE BY WEB BROWSERS

If you are creating a Web page that will be viewed by Internet Explorer 5 or 6, or another Web browser that supports XML, you can store Smart Tags in an XML format that makes them visible and usable from within those browsers.

XML is increasingly being used to provide a common format for storing structured and semistructured data so that it can be used by other business applications. Saving Smart Tag data in XML formats can be one small step toward facilitating this.

To instruct Word to save Smart Tag data in XML format for use in Web browsers and by XML applications, display the Save Options tab, and check the Save Smart Tags as XML Properties in Web Pages check box.

SMART TAG LIMITATIONS

Smart tags are a great addition to Word, but they have some limitations. Word sometimes tags information incorrectly; you may find yourself deleting some incorrect smart tags. Moreover, Smart Tags created in Office 2003 are not viewable in older versions of Office, and Smart tags saved as XML aren't useful or viewable in older Web browsers.

TROUBLESHOOTING

WHAT TO DO IF WORD MAKES FORMATTING CHANGES YOU DON'T WANT

There are two places to control AutoFormatting, and it's easy to get them confused.

The settings in the AutoFormat tab are applied only when you run AutoFormat from the AutoFormat dialog box. The settings in the AutoFormat As You Type tab apply when you are editing a document—except they do not apply when you run AutoFormat from the AutoFormat dialog box.

The settings in each tab are similar but not identical. Changes you make to the settings in one tab are not automatically reflected in the other. As a result, it's all too easy to clear a check box in the AutoFormat settings tab and wonder why Word is still making AutoFormat changes automatically as you type—or vice versa. Make sure that you've made your changes in AutoFormat As You Type. Also,

- If you tell Word not to replace symbol characters with symbols, and Word keeps inserting symbols, delete the symbol entries in the AutoCorrect tab (accessible through Tools, AutoCorrect Options).
- If Word is updating a style globally whenever you change it manually in one location, first select text formatted with the style you want to prevent from updating. Then,

choose F<u>o</u>rmat, <u>S</u>tyles and Formatting; right-click on the down-arrow next to the style, choose <u>M</u>odify style from the drop-down box, and clear the A<u>u</u>tomatically Update check box in the Modify Style dialog box.

- If you told Word you don't want it to automatically format headings as you type and it keeps doing so, clear the Define Styles Based on Your Formatting check box in the AutoFormat As You Type tab of the AutoCorrect dialog box.

WHAT TO DO IF WORD DOESN'T SUMMARIZE YOUR DOCUMENT

AutoSummarize ignores the following: text formatted in a language other than English (assuming that your user interface is set to English); text formatted as "no proofing"; and text that appears inside text boxes, frames, and tables. In short documents, AutoSummarize may not display any sentences at all, unless you increase the <u>P</u>ercent of Original setting in the AutoSummarize dialog box.

Word can prepare summaries of documents written in Chinese, French, German, Italian, Japanese, Korean, Brazilian Portuguese, Spanish, or Swedish, assuming that the appropriate language files are installed. If a document contains text prepared in more than one language, AutoSummarize uses the language used most often in the document.

WHAT TO DO IF TEXT DISAPPEARS FROM AN AUTOSUMMARIZED DOCUMENT

If you run AutoSummarize using the Hi<u>d</u>e Everything but the Summary option and then save the file while only the summary is visible, Word applies hidden text formatting to all the text not included in the summary. Then, if you reopen the document, you won't see most of your text because it's now formatted as hidden text. Click Close in the AutoSummarize toolbar, and the text will reappear.

WHAT TO DO IF SMART TAGS APPEAR EVEN IF YOU'VE TURNED THEM OFF

Smart Tags can be carried into your files when they're copied from documents created by other users. To eliminate them, click on one to display the shortcut menu; choose <u>S</u>mart Tag Options, and click S<u>t</u>op Recognizing, As <u>S</u>mart Tag.

WHAT TO DO IF YOU WANT SMART TAGS BUT DON'T WANT PURPLE UNDERLINES

If you want to use Smart Tags but can't stand to see purple underlining throughout your document, choose <u>T</u>ools, <u>O</u>ptions, <u>V</u>iew; then clear the Smart Tags check box. The Smart Tags still work, but the underlining is no longer present.

CHAPTER 10

STREAMLINING YOUR FORMATTING WITH STYLES

In this chapter

WHY STYLES ARE SO VALUABLE

Styles are one of Word's most powerful time-savers, for five important reasons.

First, styles can dramatically reduce the time it takes to format a document—often by 90% or more. Second, styles can help you make sure that all your documents look consistent, with very little effort on your part. Third, if you export your Word document to a desktop publishing program, you can generally use Word styles to help automate the work done in that program. Fourth, if you need to change the way your styled document looks, you need to change only a few styles, not hundreds of manual formats.

Fifth and finally, it's much easier to take advantage of Word's powerful automation and organization features if you use styles. For example, Word can automatically build and update a table of contents based on the styles in your document. Without styles, you would have to manually apply a field to every single item you wanted to include in your table of contents. In addition to tables of contents, Word styles make it easier to use all these features:

- **Web Publishing.** See Chapter 24, "Using Word to Develop Web Content," to learn how Word uses styles in pages saved in HTML as Web pages.

- **Outlining.** See Chapter 18, "Outlining: Practical Techniques for Organizing Any Document," to learn how styles enable you to easily outline and reorganize your document.

- **AutoFormat.** See Chapter 9, "Automating Your Documents," to learn how styles enable you to format your document automatically, all at once.

- **AutoSummarize**. See Chapter 9 to learn how styles can help Word build an automatic summary of any document.

- **Outline Numbering**. See Chapter 18 to learn how styles enable you to apply automatic outline numbers to your documents and have Word track them automatically.

- **Tables of Figures**. See Chapter 20, "Tables of Contents, Figures, Authorities, and Captions," to learn how styles enable you to build and update figure tables automatically.

- **Master Documents**. See Chapter 19, "Master Documents: Control and Share Even the Largest Documents," to learn how styles enable you to automatically divide a large document into several subdocuments for easy, team-based editing.

For all these reasons, styles are a great foundation for automating your document. Best of all, Word makes styles easy to use. (In fact, as you'll see later, Word's automatic style definition feature might enable you to get the styles you need with almost no effort on your part.)

NOTE

> Word's Themes feature can help you establish a consistent format for your document quickly. Primarily intended for Web pages, themes contain formatting that visually communicates a wide variety of moods and messages, from the informal Loose Gesture to the buttoned-down Corporate.

When you choose a theme, Word changes the styles in your document to reflect the formatting in the theme and (if you want) also adds backgrounds, horizontal lines, and special graphical bullets. The backgrounds and horizontal lines can be viewed only in Web Layout. Documents with themes open in Web Layout view by default.

Themes are covered in detail in the "Using Themes to Change the Styles in Your Template" section of Chapter 11, "Templates, Wizards, and Add-Ins."

Many Word users never bother with styles; they are comfortable with Word's easy manual formatting capabilities. Others use a few styles now and then but don't take full advantage of them. If you fall into either category, this chapter can help you dramatically improve your productivity.

TIP

If you can't or won't format your document with styles, Word 2003 gives you two alternative ways to get *some* of their automation advantages.

You can specify outline levels for individual blocks of text, as covered in Chapter 18, and Word can use those outline levels rather than styles. Keep in mind, though, that it's usually more work to create outline levels than styles. Outline levels don't work with as many Word features as styles do, and you probably need the styles anyway for formatting reasons.

The alternative, as covered in Chapter 4, "Quick and Effective Formatting Techniques," lies in the capability of Word 2003 to track the manual formatting you apply to your document. This allows you to reapply existing manual formatting to other text selections through the Styles and Formatting task pane, much as you would apply styles.

However, this feature is still more cumbersome than styles. For example, you can't name a format, as you can with styles—making it difficult to connect formatting to the role of text in your document. And, as with outline levels, formats applied through the Styles and Formatting side pane don't integrate with other Word automation features that use styles.

WHAT STYLES ARE AND HOW THEY WORK

In Word, a style is a series of formats that can be applied all at once to one or more paragraphs, or one or more characters. Rather than applying formats one at a time by clicking toolbar buttons or using keyboard shortcuts or dialog boxes, you choose a style and Word automatically applies all the formatting for you. If you want or need to change the appearance of your entire document, all you have to do is change the styles. Styles can be named, making it easy to choose the right formatting for headings and other document elements and keep that formatting consistent.

➔ For more information about keeping styles consistent using Word's Format Checker and related features, **see** Chapter 4, "Quick and Effective Formatting Techniques," **p. 107**.

HOW STYLES AND TEMPLATES WORK TOGETHER

Styles are intimately linked to another Word feature, *templates*. Templates are patterns for your documents, which can include many features, including styles, boilerplate text, manually formatted text, graphics, and custom automation tools such as macros and special toolbars.

When you store your styles in a template, the styles are immediately available whenever you create a document based on that template. By default, your styles are stored in the Normal template—which makes them available to every document you create. As you'll see in Chapter 11, you can use templates to manage, organize, and distribute collections of styles—and this makes it easy to refine and standardize the look of all your documents.

→ For more information about working with templates, **see** Chapter 11, "Templates, Wizards, and Add-Ins," **p. 355**.

Word offers two kinds of styles: paragraph styles and character styles; both can be stored in your templates. Each type of style is covered next.

UNDERSTANDING PARAGRAPH STYLES

Paragraph styles control the formatting of entire paragraphs. Any manual formatting you can add to a font or paragraph can be included in a paragraph style. If you can find it in one of the following dialog boxes, you can add it to a paragraph style by choosing

- Format, Font (Font, Character Spacing, and Text Effects tabs)
- Format, Paragraph (Indents and Spacing, Line and Page Breaks tabs)
- Format, Tabs (tab stops, alignment, and leaders)
- Format, Borders and Shading (Borders and Shading tabs, but not Page Borders)
- Tools, Language, Set Language (the language in which text should be proofed)
- Format, Bullets and Numbering (Bulleted, Numbered, and Outline Numbered tabs)

UNDERSTANDING CHARACTER STYLES

Unlike paragraph styles, *character styles* can be built only from the text formatting options available in the Format, Font dialog box; the Format, Borders and Shading dialog box; and the Tools, Language, Set Language dialog box.

Chances are, you'll use paragraph styles much more often than character styles. Paragraph styles are easier to create, and they can do more. For certain purposes, however, character styles are indispensable.

For example, you might have a short block of text that must always be formatted in a specific way, such as a company name. With character styles, it's easier to make sure that this text is always formatted correctly to begin with and remains formatted correctly as a document evolves.

NOTE

Two additional types of styles are covered elsewhere in this book. Table styles, which streamline the consistent formatting of tables, are covered in Chapter 12, "Structuring and Organizing Information with Tables." List styles, which make it easy to consistently format numbered and bulleted lists, are covered in Chapter 5, "Controlling Page Features."

HOW PARAGRAPH AND CHARACTER STYLES INTERACT

Character styles are superimposed on paragraph styles. When character and paragraph styles conflict, the font specified in a character style takes precedence. However, if a character style does not specify a formatting attribute and the paragraph style does, the paragraph style is applied.

For example, imagine you have a paragraph style named Summary that specifies

> 12-point Times New Roman italic

Now, imagine you superimpose a character style named Smith, which specifies

> 14-point Impact

You get 14-point Impact just as your character style requests, but you'll also get italic because your character style hasn't expressed a preference and your paragraph style has. On the other hand, if your paragraph and character styles both specify italic, Word assumes that you want to preserve some contrast between the two styles and formats the text as not italic. Therefore, you can't count on a character style being absolute.

As is covered in the next section, manual formatting of text overrides both paragraph and character styles.

HOW MANUAL FORMATTING AND STYLES INTERACT

Manual formatting is superimposed on both paragraph and character styles. As in the preceding example, however, Word seeks to maintain contrast. So if you add italic formatting to a paragraph that's styled to use italic, Word displays non-italic text.

To see which formatting elements in a block of text have been created by styles and which have been created by manual formatting, select the text and choose Format, Reveal Formatting. The Reveal Formatting task pane appears. Character styles, if any, are listed under Font formatting. Paragraph styles are listed under Paragraph formatting (see Figure 10.1).

To clear all manual formatting and character styles, leaving only paragraph styles, select text and press Ctrl+spacebar, or display the Styles and Formatting task pane and choose Clear Formatting from the Pick Formatting to Apply scroll box.

10

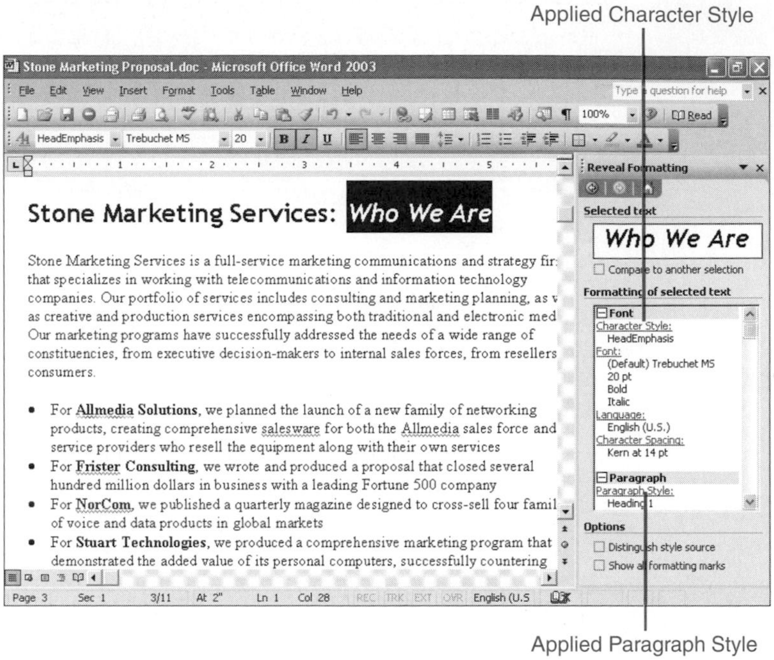

Applied Character Style

Figure 10.1
Displaying all the paragraph and font formatting associated with a block of text.

Applied Paragraph Style

DISPLAYING STYLES WITH YOUR TEXT

Sometimes you might like to view the styles in your document as you work. For example, you may have a set of corporate styles you need to follow. Or you might have styles that look similar to each other; viewing the style names helps you tell them apart.

You already know that you can view style and formatting information about selected text by displaying the Reveal Formatting task pane (choose Format, Reveal Formatting). However, Word offers a little-known way to display *all* style names alongside the text that uses them: the Style Area (see Figure 10.2).

The Style Area works only in Normal and Outline views. To display a Style Area, choose Tools, Options, View. Then specify a Style Area Width greater than 0 inches. (The default setting, 0", means that Word displays no Style Area. That's why you may never have seen one.)

TIP

> Try a measurement of 0.8 inches, sufficient to display most style names without reducing the editing area too much.

After you have a Style Area, you can resize it with the mouse. To do this, place the mouse pointer over the border of the Style Area. When the pointer changes to appear as vertical bars, click and drag the border to the width you want.

Figure 10.2
Word's Style Area, along the left side of this figure, enables you to view your styles and document at the same time.

Style area ———

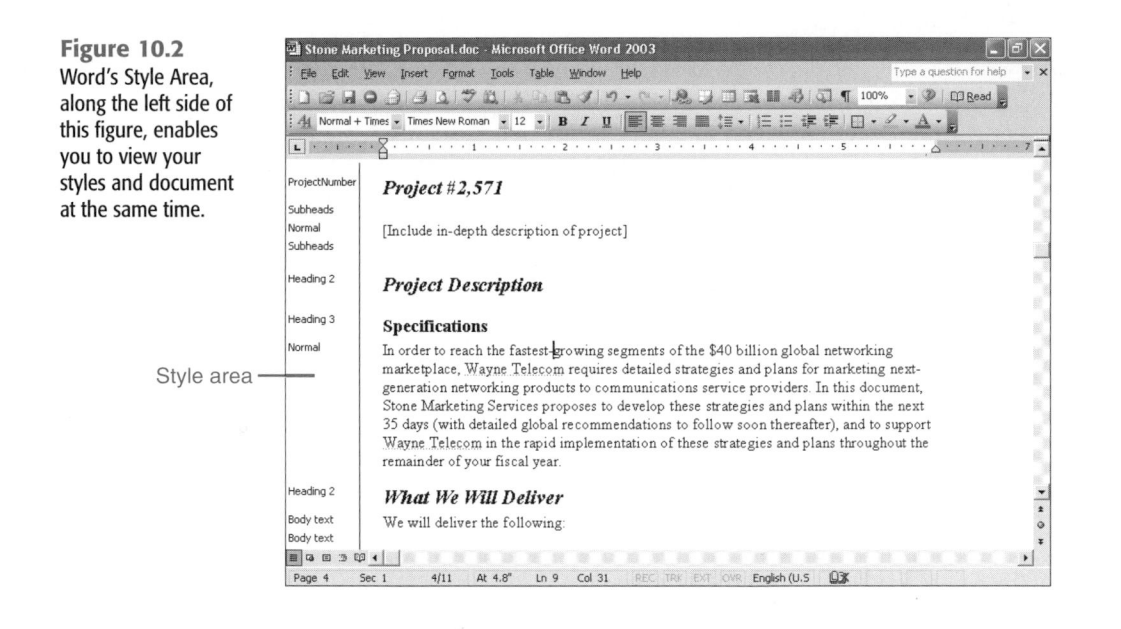

UNDERSTANDING AND USING WORD'S DEFAULT STYLES

You're using styles whether you know it or not.

Word actually contains more than 100 built-in styles. When you display a new document and begin entering text, Word enters the text using the Normal style, Word's standard style for body copy. (By default, Normal style is 12-point Times New Roman, left-aligned, single-spaced, with an outline level equivalent to body text.) Similarly, whenever you use automated features such as AutoFormat, Tables of Contents, or Indexes, Word applies built-in styles in many places to ensure overall consistency.

All of Word's built-in styles are designed to work together, creating documents that are consistently formatted, if somewhat ordinary-looking. These styles are stored together in Word's Normal template, which means that they are available to every document you create. And, as you'll see later, changing these built-in styles is the fastest way to change the overall look of *all* the documents you create.

Because Word contains so many built-in styles, the fastest way to add styles to your document is to use the ones that already exist. To apply an existing style, select the text you want to style. Then click the arrow in the Style box on the Formatting toolbar, or press Ctrl+Shift+S (see Figure 10.3) and choose the style you want from the list that appears.

In Word 2003, the Style box doesn't just list the available styles; it shows them formatted so that you can see what they look like before you apply them.

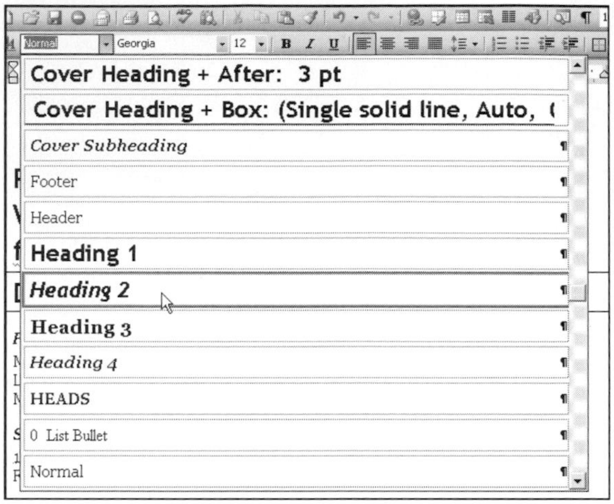

Figure 10.3
Choosing a style from the Style box on the Formatting toolbar.

10

NOTE

> Although all of Word's built-in styles are available to all your documents, this may not be true of custom styles you create.
>
> If you have stored custom styles in more than one template, the custom styles available for your use may vary depending on which templates are currently accessible to your documents. To learn more about controlling which templates are available to your documents, see "Attaching a New Template to an Existing Document," in Chapter 11.

In the next few sections, you'll learn how to make the most of Word's built-in styles—and you'll also learn techniques you can use with the custom styles you create.

APPLYING AN EXISTING STYLE FROM THE STYLES AND FORMATTING TASK PANE

Word 2003 provides yet another way to apply an existing style: the Styles and Formatting task pane. To display it, choose Format, Styles and Formatting, or click the Styles and Formatting button on the left edge of the Formatting toolbar. Next, select a style from the Pick Formatting to Display scroll box.

If the built-in style you're looking for doesn't appear, choose All Styles from the Show drop-down box.

SHORTCUTS FOR THE MOST COMMON STYLES

Five of Word's most widely used styles also have quick keyboard shortcuts:

Style	Keyboard Shortcut	Common Use
Normal	Ctrl+Shift+N	Body text
Heading 1	Alt+Ctrl+1	First-level headings
Heading 2	Alt+Ctrl+2	Second-level headings

Style	Keyboard Shortcut	Common Use
Heading 3	Alt+Ctrl+3	Third-level headings
List Bullet	Ctrl+Shift+L	Bulleted lists

Sometimes you want to apply a different paragraph style to a block of text. You can always do so by selecting any part of the paragraph and choosing a new style from the Style box.

Because many styles are heading styles, you often find yourself changing styles to change heading levels. One effective way to make these changes is to switch into Outline view and use the Promote and Demote buttons on the Outlining toolbar (covered in detail in Chapter 18). If, however, you're just changing one or two headings, simply click the Style box and use the up- or down-arrow keys to move to the style you want.

NOTE

Two additional keys allow you to change heading styles: Alt+Shift+right arrow *demotes* the paragraph you've selected. For example, if you select a paragraph formatted as Heading 1, pressing Alt+Shift+right arrow converts the paragraph to Heading 2 style.

Conversely, Alt+Shift+left arrow promotes the paragraph, for example, from Heading 3 to Heading 2.

NOTE

Later in this chapter, in the "Creating Keyboard Shortcuts for Your Styles" section, you'll learn how to provide custom keyboard shortcuts for the styles *you* create.

TIP

If you're sure of the style name you want to use, you can simply type it in the Style box. However, if you mistype, Word creates a new style formatted as your text already appears.

To minimize clutter, Word typically displays only seven built-in styles in the Style box of a new document: Normal, Heading 1, Heading 2, Heading 3, and three Table of Contents (TOC) styles. All the other styles built into Word are still available, however. If you want to apply a style that doesn't appear in the Style box, apply it from the Styles and Formatting task pane, as described earlier, in the "Applying an Existing Style from the Styles and Formatting Task Pane" section.

APPLYING MULTIPLE STYLES AT THE SAME TIME

Maybe you'd rather not have your train of thought interrupted by stopping to apply styles as you write. If so, you can write your document the way you normally do and then have Word's AutoFormat feature apply the styles for you, using the built-in styles it recognizes.

10

NOTE

You can also use AutoFormat As You Type to make similar changes as you type.

AutoFormat and AutoFormat As You Type are covered in detail in Chapter 9, but briefly, Word can recognize the following elements and assign styles to them:

- **Built-in heading styles.** If you enter one line of text without a period, ending with a paragraph mark, Word recognizes it as a heading and applies a heading style. If your headings are not already manually numbered or styled, Word typically uses Heading 1.

  If you have already formatted some headings, Word applies the next subordinate heading style beneath your headings. That's useful to know if, for example, only the name of your chapter uses Heading 1 style. Format that one line of copy manually, and Word automatically formats all the other headings it finds as Heading 2. This leaves you with fewer to correct manually.

- **List styles.** AutoFormat can recognize some lines of text as belonging to a bulleted or numbered list and reformat those with built-in list styles. For example, if either AutoFormat or AutoFormat As You Type encounters paragraphs that begin with an asterisk and a space, it reformats them as items in a bulleted list.

- **Automatic bulleted lists.** When you start a paragraph with an asterisk, one or two hyphens, the > symbol, or a "fake" arrow created by combining hyphens or equals signs with the > symbol (for example, —>), AutoFormat assumes that you want to create a bulleted list and applies a list style containing a bullet.

- **Other paragraph styles.** AutoFormat can search for other document elements it recognizes, such as addresses, and format them with its corresponding built-in styles. For paragraphs AutoFormat does not recognize as requiring special formatting, AutoFormat can apply Word's built-in Body Text style. Body Text style is identical to Normal style except that 6 points have been added after each paragraph to compensate for the extra paragraph mark AutoFormat automatically removes.

To use AutoFormat to apply several styles at once, choose Format, AutoFormat and click the Options button. Then, on the AutoFormat tab (see Figure 10.4), specify the types of styles you want Word to apply—Built-In Heading Styles, List Styles, Automatic Bulleted Lists, or Other Paragraph Styles. These options all appear in the Apply area of this tab. If you don't want Word to change any other document elements aside from these, clear the remaining check boxes elsewhere in the dialog box. Click OK twice, and Word AutoFormats the document.

Word isn't perfect. Double-check the styles Word applies. You may have to do some tweaking. However, if your document's structure isn't too unusual, using AutoFormat can often save you a good deal of time.

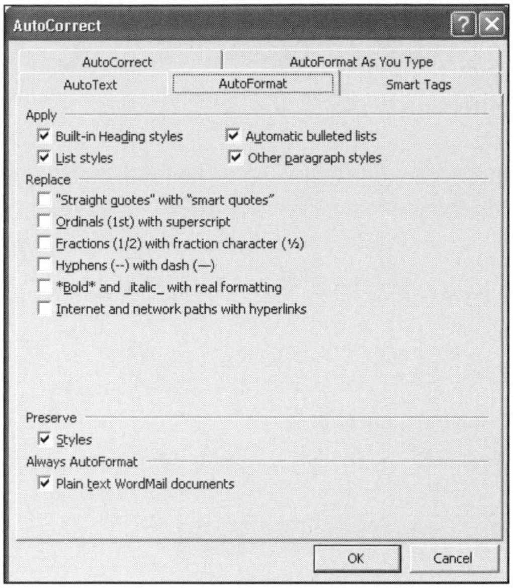

Figure 10.4
If you want Word to apply styles automatically but make no other changes to your document, check the boxes in the Apply area of the AutoFormat tab and clear the boxes in the Replace area, as shown.

CREATING STYLES

Until now, you've learned how to use the existing styles Word provides. If you do nothing more than use Word's styles, your documents will look consistent, you will spend less time formatting them, and you'll have access to all the power of Word's automation features.

However, considering that Word is—by far—the world's most popular word processor, your documents will have a tendency to look a lot like everyone else's. Moreover, you might encounter situations in which Word has no applicable built-in style. For example, Word doesn't have a built-in style for chapter summaries, or for tips, or for many other elements you find in this book.

For these reasons, you should know how to create new styles or change existing ones. Fortunately, Word makes this easy to do.

CREATING PARAGRAPH STYLES EASILY WITH STYLE BY EXAMPLE

The quickest way to create an entirely new style is to use Word's Style by Example feature, as explained here:

1. Select and format a block of text the way you want it.

2. Click inside the Style drop-down box on the Formatting toolbar (or press Ctrl+Shift+S).

3. Type the new style name in the Style box and press Enter.

DEFINING PARAGRAPH AND CHARACTER STYLES FROM THE NEW STYLE DIALOG BOX

Character styles can't be defined on the Formatting toolbar (although they can be selected from there after they've been defined); to create a character style, you must use Word's New Style dialog box.

You may also want to use the New Style dialog box when you need total control over the contents of a style. Using the New Style dialog box gives you a systematic way of making sure that all the formatting you want to incorporate in a style is, in fact, included.

To define a style using the New Style dialog box, carry out these steps:

1. Select a block of text. If you want, you can manually apply formatting to include in your style.

2. Select Format, Styles and Formatting.

3. Click New Style. The New Style dialog box opens (see Figure 10.5).

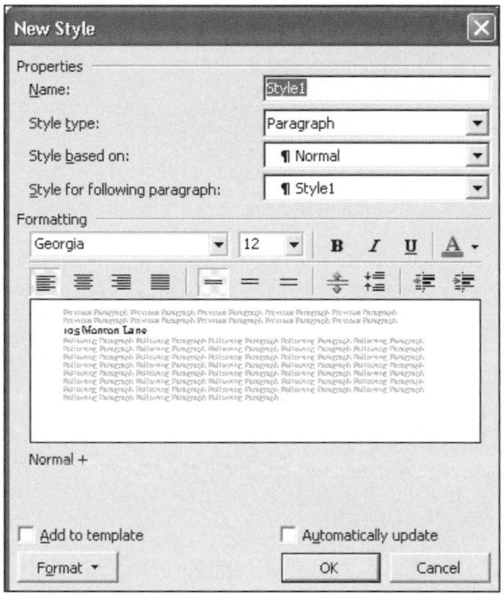

Figure 10.5
Creating a style in the New Style dialog box.

4. Enter a style name in the Name box.

5. In the Style Type drop-down box, choose the type of style you are creating: Paragraph, Character, Table, or List.

6. If you want to include additional formatting in your style (beyond any formatting you may have applied to selected text in step 1 of this procedure), apply it now.

   - Apply the most common text formatting by using the two rows of formatting buttons at the center of the New Style dialog box.

   - To add formatting unavailable through these buttons, click the Format button and choose the category of formatting you want to apply (see Figure 10.6). When you do, a dialog box appears, containing all the formatting options available in that category.

In most cases, this dialog box is identical to the one you would use elsewhere to create manual formatting. For example, clicking Font displays the Font dialog box with three tabs: Font, Character Spacing, and Text Effects. Apply your formatting in this dialog box and click OK to return to the New Style dialog box. Repeat the process for other categories of formatting you want to include.

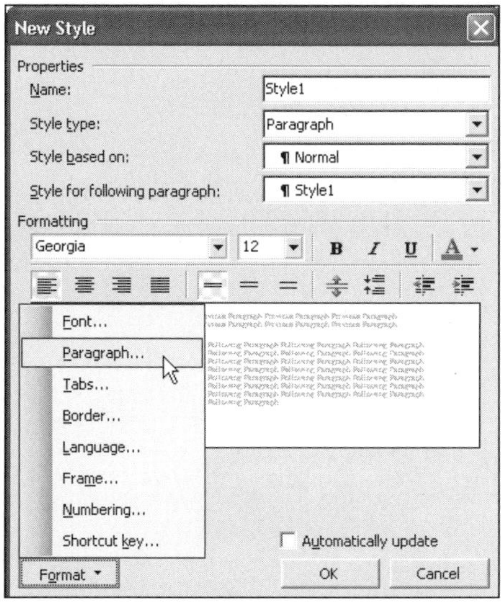

Figure 10.6
Click Format to display additional options for including formatting in your style.

7. When you've finished incorporating formatting in your style, click OK.

Working with Based On Styles

The New Style dialog box contains additional settings you can use to enhance your productivity while using styles. The first of these is Style Based On styles, which allow you to specify an existing style that your new style will be based on.

By default, most built-in Word styles are based on the Normal style, and unless you make a change, your new style is based on it also. Of course, Word uses the formats you specify, but where you do not specify a setting, Word makes assumptions based on the Normal style, which includes the following:

■ Font: Times New Roman

■ Size: 12-point

■ Proofing Language: Depends upon your location; for example, in the United States, this will be English (United States)

■ Character scale: 100%

■ Alignment: Flush left

- Line spacing: Single
- Pagination: Widow/Orphan Control
- Outline level: Body Text

At times, you might have a different style you want to use as the basis for your new style—one with formatting that closely resembles the style you are creating. For example, you might want to base all your headings on your Heading 1 style. That way, if you change the font in Heading 1, all the other headings change automatically.

With the New Style dialog box open, click the Style Based On box and choose the style you want to use as the basis for your new style. If you are working with a paragraph style, you can choose from all the styles available to your current document.

If you are working with a character style, your choices are more limited. They include several styles associated with Web pages, including Emphasis and Strong. These are styles that Web browsers have long used to control the display of text on Web sites.

TIP

If the Style Based On style you want to use appears in the Style drop-down box in the Formatting toolbar, here's a quicker way to get the same result:

1. Format a block of text using the Style Based On style.
2. Reformat the text to reflect any changes you want to make.
3. Click in the Style box.
4. Type the new style name and press Enter.

USING STYLE BASED ON TO TRANSFORM THE LOOK OF YOUR DOCUMENTS

Using Word's Style Based On feature enables you to create a unique look for all your documents with little effort. All you have to do is change the Normal style, which underlies all of Word's styles.

For example, if you're bored with Times New Roman, you can change the Normal style to a somewhat more interesting font, such as Garamond. That change cascades through all the styles based on the Normal style—except for those that already specify a different font, such as Arial.

When you make a change such as this, you probably need to make a few other changes as well. Some of Word's styles, although they are based on Normal, also specify their own fonts. For example, Heading 1 uses the Arial font. Consider changing these styles to specify a font that complements the one you've now chosen for text.

If you choose a serif font for text, generally choose a sans serif font for some or all of your headings. Serif fonts have tiny tails at the ends of each letter to improve readability; sans serif fonts don't.

Serif and sans serif fonts complement each other well and often are used in combination to make book and newspaper designs more attractive.

You should note one more thing about choosing fonts for your styles. Different fonts have different widths. Times New Roman is unusually narrow, which simply means that more words fit on a line when you're using it. If you choose a wider font, such as Bookman, you may find you've lengthened a long document by several pages.

CHOOSING A FOLLOWING PARAGRAPH STYLE

Think about your documents for a moment. In most cases, after you type a heading, you usually type body text. After you type the first element in a list, you usually type another list element. Word paragraph styles take advantage of this fact. When you specify a new paragraph style, you can also specify the style that should be used in the paragraph that follows it.

By default, the Following Paragraph style is Normal. These steps show you how to specify a different one:

1. Open the New Style dialog box (refer to Figure 10.5).
2. Click in the Style for Following Paragraph drop-down box.
3. Choose the style you want to use.
4. When you're finished with the settings in the New Style dialog box, click OK.

After you've set a Following Paragraph style, Word applies it automatically as you work. When you press Enter at the end of one paragraph, Word applies the Following Paragraph style to the next paragraph.

USING AUTOMATIC STYLE CHANGES

The same AutoFormat technology that enables you to create all your styles at the same time can also help you change existing styles automatically. For example, because Word can recognize a line of type as a heading, it can also recognize when you are formatting a line of type manually to look like a heading. It also can automatically transform your manual formatting into a heading style.

Automatic style definition is part of Word's AutoFormat As You Type feature. To use it, follow these steps:

1. Choose Format, AutoFormat.
2. Click Options.
3. Click the AutoFormat As You Type tab.
4. In the Apply As You Type area, specify the elements for which you want Word to automatically create styles: Automatic Bulleted Lists, Automatic Numbered Lists, Border Lines, Tables, and/or Built-In Heading Styles.

5. Check the Define Styles Based on Your Formatting check box in the Automatically As You Type area of the dialog box.

6. Click OK twice.

After you turn on automatic style definition, pay close attention to it for a few days to make sure that it isn't creating styles you don't want. If the formatting in your documents starts changing in ways you don't like, turn off the feature.

➜ For more information about enabling or disabling automatic style updates for specific styles, **see** "Enabling or Preventing Automatic Style Updates," **p. 344**.

TEMPLATE OR DOCUMENT? WHERE TO STORE YOUR STYLES

By default, Word adds your new style to your current document only. If you change a built-in style, that change also applies in only your existing document. However, you will sometimes want to make the style available for several documents. You can do this by adding the style to the template associated with the document in which you are working.

It's easy to add a style to a template. With the New Style dialog box open, check the Add to Template check box and click OK.

It's not quite as easy to decide whether you *should* add a style to your template. Here's what you need to know. Unless you have chosen another template, you are probably working in the Normal template. If you add a new style to the Normal template, you make it available to every document you create.

If you change a built-in style, you likewise change it globally, meaning that it is changed for all documents using this particular style. Be careful not to introduce inconsistencies with existing documents that use Word's default styles.

➜ To learn more about how templates and styles work together, **see** "How Styles and Templates Work Together," **p. 332**.

CAUTION

Because the styles in your document aren't included in your template unless you check the Add to Template check box, it's possible for different documents using the same template to have varying styles with the same style names.

ENABLING OR PREVENTING AUTOMATIC STYLE UPDATES

As you've learned, Word can create new styles automatically by transforming your manual formatting into styles as you type. If you want, Word can also change your styles automatically for you whenever you manually reformat them.

In some circumstances, this is a great shortcut, because you can manually reformat one line and your entire document is updated to match. However, it's not always appropriate. Imagine that one of your headings refers to the title of a book, which should be formatted in italic. If Word is automatically updating your styles, all the headings using this style change, even those that shouldn't be italicized.

Word enables you to specify which styles qualify for automatic updating. To set a new style for automatic updating, first create the style by clicking New Style in the Styles and Formatting task pane. From the New Style dialog box, establish the style settings you want. Then, check the Automatically Update check box and click OK.

TIP

> If you want to automatically update a style that already exists, display the Styles and Formatting task pane (Format, Styles and Formatting); right-click on a style in the Pick Formatting to Apply scroll box; and choose Modify Style from the shortcut menu. The Modify Style dialog box opens; check the Automatically Update check box and click OK.
>
> The Modify Style dialog box is covered in more detail in the "Changing Styles Using the Modify Style Dialog Box" section later in the chapter.

CHANGING STYLES

In the past few pages, you've learned how to create new styles. However, you can also make changes in existing styles. If you want to make systematic changes in a style, you can use the Modify Style dialog box. If you want to make simple changes to a style, it's easier to use the Styles and Formatting task pane.

CHANGING STYLES USING THE STYLES AND FORMATTING TASK PANE

To change a style quickly, reformat the text in your document to reflect the formatting you want the style to use. Then, in the Styles and Formatting task pane, choose the original style name associated with the style (not the modified style name that Word automatically creates when you superimpose manual formatting on the style).

Right-click on the style name and choose Update to Match Selection from the shortcut menu (see Figure 10.7).

CHANGING STYLES USING THE MODIFY STYLE DIALOG BOX

As mentioned earlier, when you want to make more systematic changes to a style, it usually makes sense to work in the Modify Style dialog box.

To display the Modify Style dialog box, first display the Styles and Formatting task pane (choose Format, Styles and Formatting). Next, right-click on a style in the Pick Formatting to Apply scroll box and choose Modify Style from the shortcut menu. The Modify Style dialog box opens (see Figure 10.8).

As you can see, the Modify Style dialog box looks much like the New Style dialog box. However, the existing style you've already chosen is listed in the Name box. The style's current settings are also listed in the Description area of the dialog box, and their appearance in your document is previewed in the Preview area.

As soon as you change a style, Word applies the change throughout your document anywhere you used the style—or anywhere you used a style based on it. If you add the changed style to a template, the change takes effect in all new documents based on that template.

10

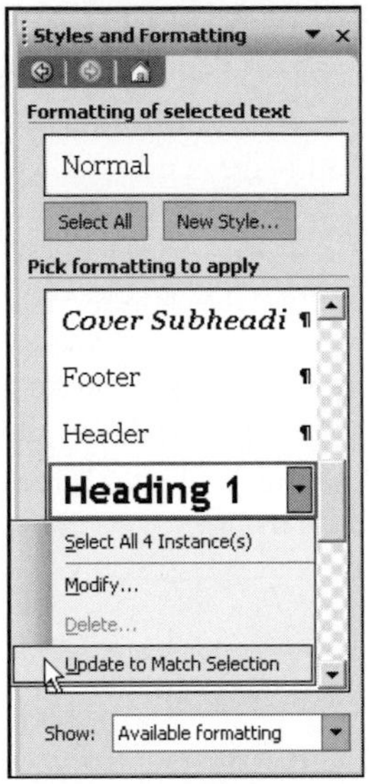

Figure 10.7
Updating a style to match the text you've selected.

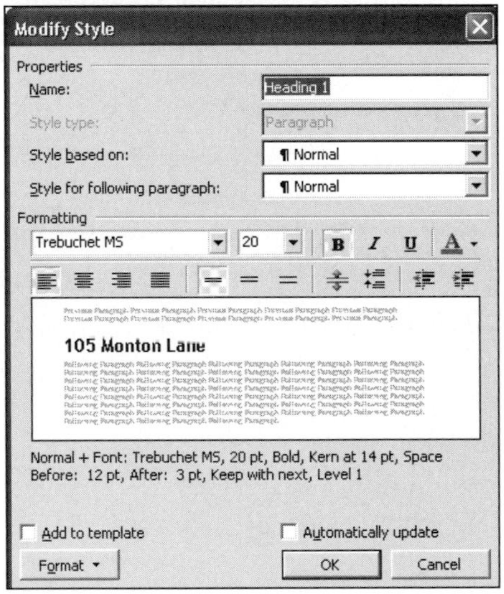

Figure 10.8
The Modify Style dialog box looks and works just like the New Style dialog box you've already seen.

However, the changes are not made automatically in existing documents. First, you have to save the changes by saving the template. Then, when you open an existing document based on that template, you have to tell Word that you want to update the styles.

To update styles based on the template, first open a document based on the template you've changed. Next, choose Tools, Templates and Add-Ins, and check the Automatically Update Document Styles check box. Click OK, and Word reformats the document to reflect any style changes you saved in the template.

If Word changes styles on its own, in ways you don't like, see "What to Do If Styles Suddenly Change When You Don't Expect Them To," in "Troubleshooting" at the end of this chapter.

If styles you create appear different from the way you expect, see "What to Do If Styles Look Different Than You Expect," in "Troubleshooting" at the end of this chapter.

CREATING KEYBOARD SHORTCUTS FOR YOUR STYLES

Earlier, you learned that Word comes with built-in keyboard shortcuts for the three highest-level heading styles, for the Normal style, and for the List style. You may discover other styles, built-in or custom, that you find yourself using quite often. To assign a keyboard shortcut to any style, follow these steps:

1. Display the Styles and Formatting task pane, by clicking the Styles and Formatting button on the Formatting toolbar or choosing Format, Styles and Formatting.

2. Right-click on the style you want to create a keyboard shortcut for and choose Modify Style from the shortcut menu.

3. In the Modify Style dialog box, click Format, Shortcut Key. The Customize Keyboard dialog box opens (see Figure 10.9).

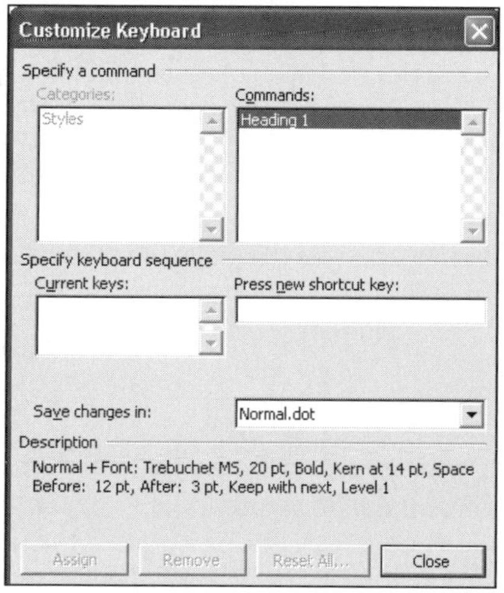

Figure 10.9
You can create a convenient keyboard shortcut for any style you expect to use often.

4. Press the keyboard shortcut combination you want to use. The combination appears in the Press New Shortcut Key box. If that combination is already in use, the current use is listed beneath the box where the keyboard combination is displayed.

5. If the combination you've chosen is acceptable to you, click Assign. If not, click inside the Press New Shortcut Key box, backspace to eliminate the shortcut that appears there, and type another keyboard combination. When you're satisfied with the combination you've typed, click Assign. (If you're not satisfied with any combination, click Close to exit the dialog box without adding a keyboard combination.)

REMOVING A KEYBOARD SHORTCUT ASSOCIATED WITH A STYLE

You might occasionally want to remove a keyboard shortcut associated with a style, possibly to use the shortcut for another purpose. To remove a keyboard shortcut associated with a style, follow these steps:

1. Display the Styles and Formatting task pane, by clicking the Styles and Formatting button on the Formatting toolbar or choosing Format, Styles and Formatting.

2. Right-click on the style you want to create a keyboard shortcut for, and choose Modify Style from the shortcut menu.

3. In the Modify Style dialog box, click Format, Shortcut Key. The Customize Keyboard dialog box opens (refer to Figure 10.9).

4. In the Current Keys scroll box, choose the keyboard shortcut you want to remove.

5. Click Remove.

6. Click Close.

→ For more information on creating custom keyboard shortcuts, **see** "Creating Keyboard Shortcuts for Your Styles," **p. 347**.

DELETING A STYLE

Sometimes you may no longer need a style. Perhaps you have created a style with a similar name and different formatting that you want to use instead.

To delete a style, right-click on it in the Styles and Formatting task pane and choose Delete from the shortcut menu. Click Yes to confirm that you want to delete all instances of the style. All text that had been formatted in the style you deleted is reformatted in the Normal style.

MANAGING STYLES

Before you start accumulating new and changed styles, give a little thought to how you'll manage them. Managing styles involves the following:

- Deciding which styles should be placed in templates, and organizing those styles in the templates associated with specific kinds of work
- Naming styles so that you and your colleagues understand their purpose
- Occasionally moving styles or deleting styles you no longer use

You can perform some management tasks in the Style dialog boxes you've already studied. For other tasks, such as moving styles between templates, you use the Organizer, described later in this chapter.

HOW TO CHOOSE STYLE NAMES

Spend a few moments thinking about how to name your styles. Keep the following tips in mind:

- Name your styles based on their function, not their appearance. Don't name a style Arial 48 Bold; what if you decide to change its appearance someday? Rather, name it based on how you expect to use it—for example, Front Page Headline. (This is one of the key disadvantages of simply using Word 2003's list of formats instead of styles—and one reason most sophisticated users will continue to work with styles instead.)

- Keep your style names as consistent as possible. Imagine that you use a set of styles for only projects involving Omega Corp. Consider starting each style name with O. That way, they'll all be listed together—and you'll be less likely to inadvertently use them in projects that don't involve Omega.

The catch with using descriptive style names is that they could also become quite wordy. This can become problematic if you also like to type your style names in the Style box to select them. It takes too long to type a long name, and if you make a mistake, Word creates a new style, which isn't what you want to happen.

You can have it both ways. Use *aliases*. An alias is an abbreviated style name that Word recognizes in place of the full style name. For example, if you have a style named Major Headline, you might want to use the alias MH.

You can create an alias from either the New Style or the Modify Style dialog box. Type the style's full name, add a comma, and then type your alias. For example, to create the style Document Summary and assign the alias DS at the same time, enter

```
Document Summary,DS
```

Both the full name and the alias appear in the Style box, but you can select the style by typing only the alias.

KEEPING TRACK OF STYLES WITH THE ORGANIZER

The Organizer (see Figure 10.10) is Word's control center for copying, deleting, and renaming styles. To display the Organizer, choose Tools, Templates and Add-Ins, and click Organizer. The Organizer opens. If the Styles tab is not displayed, click Styles to display it.

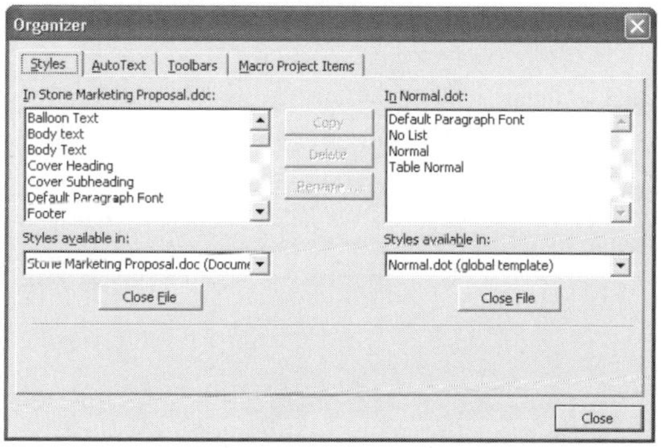

Figure 10.10
You can use the Organizer to move styles between documents or templates.

TIP

> The procedures you'll learn for working with styles in the Organizer also work for moving AutoText entries, toolbars, and macro project items.

→ For more information about working with AutoText entries, **see** "AutoText: The Complete Boilerplate Resource," **p. 301**.

→ For more information about creating and managing custom toolbars, **see** "Customizing Toolbars and Menus," **p. 1023**.

When the <u>S</u>tyles tab of the Organizer opens, it displays two windows. The left window, named after the document that is currently active, lists all the styles contained in that document. The right window corresponds to the Normal template (Normal.dot).

COPYING STYLES

When you open the Organizer and choose the <u>S</u>tyles tab, the Organizer is already set to copy styles from the current document to the Normal template. All you need to do is select the style or styles you want to copy, and click <u>C</u>opy. If you're not sure whether you want to copy a style, you can review the style's contents, which are displayed beneath its window.

You can also copy styles in the opposite direction, from the Normal template to the current document. Click one or more styles in the right window. The arrow inside the <u>C</u>opy button switches direction, now facing the Document window.

NOTE

> You'll often want to copy styles to different templates, not just different documents. To learn how, see "Working with Different Documents and Templates," later in this chapter.

If you copy styles to a destination that already has styles of the same name, Word displays a warning dialog box asking whether you're sure that you want to do so. Click <u>Y</u>es to confirm; click Yes to <u>A</u>ll if you're sure that you want to overwrite any other styles as well.

TIP

> If you want to copy a style from one document to another, and the style name isn't already used by the destination document, try this shortcut. Select some text that's already formatted using the style, and copy it. Then simply paste it into the other document.
>
> The style comes along with it and is now listed on the Style box along with all other styles in this document. It'll still be there even after you delete the text associated with the style.

RENAMING STYLES

Sometimes you might want to rename a style. For example, you might be setting up several styles associated with a specific project and template, and you want them all to begin with the same letter or word. To rename a style, select it in the Organizer and click <u>R</u>ename. Then, enter the new name in the Rename dialog box (see Figure 10.11) and click OK.

Figure 10.11
The Rename dialog box displays the current name, which you can edit or replace.

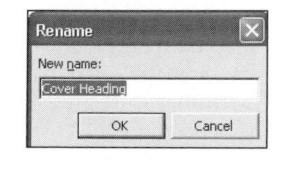

TIP

> You can also rename a style from the Modify Style dialog box. Display the Styles and Formatting task pane by clicking the Styles and Formatting button on the Formatting toolbar, or by choosing Format, Styles and Formatting. Right-click on the style you want to rename, and choose Modify Style from the shortcut menu. Then, enter a new name in the Name text box and click OK.

WORKING WITH DIFFERENT DOCUMENTS AND TEMPLATES

Until now, you've used the Organizer only to move styles between the current document and the Normal (Normal.dot) template. However, the Organizer can be used to move styles between any documents or templates. You simply need to place the appropriate documents or templates in the left and right windows. To do so, follow these steps:

1. Under either the left or the right window, click the Close File button. The window becomes empty, and the button changes to Open File.

2. Click the Open File button. Word displays the Open dialog box, showing your current list of document templates stored in the Templates folder. If you want a template, navigate to it, select the template, and click Open. If you want a document instead, choose Word Documents in the Files of Type box. Then navigate to the document you want to use and click Open.

3. Repeat the same process in the other window to display the appropriate document or template there.

You can now copy, delete, or rename styles just as you've already learned in this chapter.

TIP

> Because the Organizer's Open File button displays the same Open dialog box you normally use to open files, you have full access to the extensive file search capabilities covered in Chapter 3, "Essential Document Creation and Management Techniques."

TIP

> If you're organizing a template with several specific styles, you can create all the styles in a new, blank document, delete the styled text, and save the remaining blank document as a template. Then, use that template whenever you want to access those styles.

WORD STYLES AND DESKTOP PUBLISHING PROGRAMS

If you export files for use in separate desktop publishing programs, most of these programs can recognize Word styles. The designer working with that software is likely to want to change the specific formatting associated with each style, but the styles themselves already exist, eliminating time-consuming "tagging."

Microsoft Publisher 2003 and other recent versions of Microsoft Publisher can import Word 2003 files directly. The two leading desktop publishing programs, Adobe's InDesign 2.0 and QuarkXPress 5.0, now ship with Word filters designed to open Word 97, 2000, 2002, and 2003 files.

CAUTION

> QuarkXPress users have occasionally encountered trouble with documents created by new versions of Word, even though Word's official format has not changed. This is apparently due to very slight changes Microsoft introduces within the standard Word 97/2000/2002/2003 format in order to support new features. Moreover, relatively few QuarkXPress users have upgraded to the latest versions, so they may be using Word filters that are even more problematic.
>
> If QuarkXPress users encounter difficulty with your documents, try saving them to Word 6/95 format.

Adobe PageMaker 6.x can import Word 2003 files using the optional Word 97 filter, which you can find by searching at www.adobe.com/support/downloads/main.html. Users of QuarkXPress 4.0 and older versions can find current Word filters by searching at www.quark.com/service/desktop/downloads/.

No filter is perfect. Even the best of them don't support all of Word's myriad features. For example, PageMaker 6.5's Word filter doesn't support character styles. Instead, it reformats that text as if you had manually formatted it. However, it does a nice job with paragraph styles.

For all these caveats, though, using Word styles in desktop publishing can still save significant time and money.

TROUBLESHOOTING

WHAT TO DO IF STYLES SUDDENLY CHANGE WHEN YOU DON'T EXPECT THEM TO

Right-click on the style name in the Styles and Formatting task pane, click Modify Style, and see whether Automatically Update is turned on in the Modify Style dialog box. If it is, Word may have misinterpreted a manual formatting change as an instruction to change the style. Clear the check box.

If this doesn't solve the problem, did you change a style on which other styles are based? If so, those styles change as well, sometimes unexpectedly.

If your styles are still changing improperly, is a template that your document depends on missing? Assume that your document uses a template stored on a network drive. If you open a Word document while the server is temporarily unavailable, Word may use styles with the same name from the Normal template stored on your hard disk.

WHAT TO DO IF STYLES LOOK DIFFERENT THAN YOU EXPECT

Perhaps you added manual formatting inadvertently, or imported text that already had manual formatting. Press Shift+F1 and click the text to see whether it has any unexpected manual formatting. If so, select the text and press Ctrl+spacebar to eliminate it (or choose Clear Formatting from the Pick Formatting to Apply scroll box of the Styles and Formatting task pane).

Another possibility is that you have attached a different template to a document, or opened it as part of a master document that contains the same style names but formats those styles differently.

CHAPTER **11**

TEMPLATES, WIZARDS, AND ADD-INS

In this chapter

WHAT TEMPLATES ARE AND HOW THEY WORK

Templates are patterns for your documents. When you choose a template for your new document, you're telling Word what information—text, formatting, and graphics—you want to appear in that document automatically.

Of course, the more information you can automatically add to your new documents, the less you have to add manually. You can use templates to dramatically reduce the number of documents you create from scratch. Depending on your work, you might virtually eliminate them. Travel often? Create an expense report template. Provide a status report every month? Build a status report template with subheads for every topic you must cover and links to Excel worksheets containing the raw data you're analyzing.

But slashing the time it takes you to create new documents is only half of what templates can do for you. That's because templates don't merely place information in new documents. They enable you to create custom editing environments for specific clients, projects, or companies. They store all the tools you and your colleagues need in order to edit specific documents as efficiently as possible, including styles, automated macro procedures, AutoText boilerplate text, and more.

To make the benefits of templates seem less abstract, consider the possible applications. You might, for example, build a template designed to streamline document creation for a specific client, project, or company. Your template could include the following:

- **All relevant styles.** As discussed in Chapter 10, "Streamlining Your Formatting with Styles," you can create a system of styles that makes it easy to make specific documents look consistent. You can store this system of styles in a template, making it easy to use when you need it.

- **All relevant boilerplate text (AutoText entries).** For example, your template can include contract clauses, marketing language, and product names and descriptions that you often use in connection with a client, project, or company. You learn more about AutoText in Chapter 9, "Automating Your Documents."

- **New toolbars, menus, or menu items.** These items provide shortcuts for tasks associated with specific documents. For example, if your template helps a user run an electronic mail merge, it might include a toolbar that walks the user through each step of the process. In some cases, the toolbar might borrow buttons from Word's built-in Mail Merge toolbar, such as the Mail Merge Helper button. In other cases, the buttons might be attached to custom macros. You'll learn more about customizing Word this way in Chapter 31, "Customizing Word."

Templates such as these are extremely valuable to you, but they can be even more valuable to your colleagues and others who may be working on similar documents.

USING WORD'S BUILT-IN TEMPLATE LIBRARY

When you create a new document, you're actually choosing a template on which your document will be based. The default Blank Document template that most people use is based on Word's Normal template, an especially important Word template that you'll learn more about shortly.

Word comes with more than 40 templates for the documents you're most likely to create. These templates can be used to create letters and mail merges, faxes, memos, reports, résumés, Web pages, brochures, manuals, and many other documents.

Most of Word's templates actually contain their own directions on how to use them most effectively. For example, the Report templates explain how to insert your own company name, create consistent bulleted lists, and use AutoFormat to create a table consistent with the one already in the document.

> **NOTE**
>
> Later in this chapter, in the "Using Word Wizards" section, you'll learn more about the wizards that also appear in the Templates dialog box.

To select a template, choose File, New. The New Document task pane appears (see Figure 11.1).

Then, click the tab containing the template you want to use

Figure 11.1
The choices in the Templates dialog box are templates that contain predefined text, formatting, and graphics.

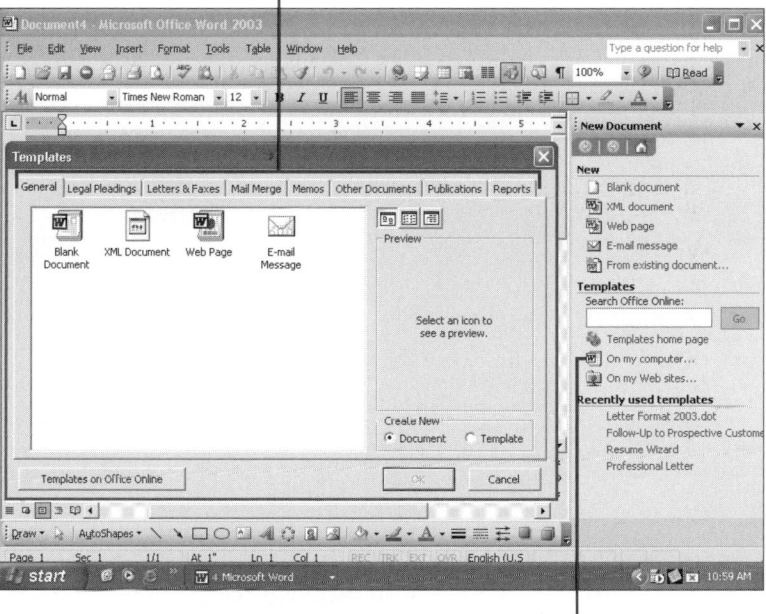

First, click On My Computer to display the Templates dialog box shown at left

Next, specify where to look for the template. For example, if you want to use a template that came with Word, or one you've created yourself on your own computer, click On My Computer. Then, click the tab containing the template you want, and double-click the template.

When you use some templates in Word 2003 for the first time, Word may need to install them before running them. If Word displays a dialog box asking permission to do so, click Yes.

NOTE

If you installed Word across the network, Word looks for templates in the network location you originally installed from. If you installed Word locally, Word prompts you to insert the Office 2003 or Word 2003 CD-ROM.

TIP

If you installed Microsoft Office 2003, you can open Word and a document based on a template of your choice, both at the same time. On the taskbar, click Start, New Office Document. Office displays a list of all the templates associated with Word (as well as other Office programs you may have installed). Double-click any Word template. (They're recognizable by their Word icons.)

11

USING TEMPLATES FROM MICROSOFT OFFICE ONLINE

Microsoft has made available a wide range of additional templates on its Web site, providing prewritten documents in the following categories:

- Calendars and Planners
- Holidays and Occasions
- Finance and Accounting
- Orders and Inventory
- Education
- Health Care and Wellness
- Home and Community
- Legal
- Marketing
- Stationery and Labels
- Meetings and Projects
- Employee Management
- Your Career
- Travel and Maps
- Charts and Diagrams

To create a file based on one of these templates, choose File, New; then click Templates Home Page.

TIP

> Or, click File, New; click On My Computer, and click the Templates on Office Online button. (By doing so, you can review the templates already available to you on your computer and private network. Then, if you don't have one that will solve your problem, you can go online to find one.)

Microsoft opens your Web browser, connects to the Internet (or uses your currently active Internet connection), and displays the Microsoft Office Online Templates Home page, a collection of Word templates organized into the categories listed previously.

Browse to the category and subcategory you want; then click on the template you want to install. Internet Explorer will display an image of a sample document built with the template (see Figure 11.2). To open a new file based on this template, click Download Now. Word displays a new document based on the template.

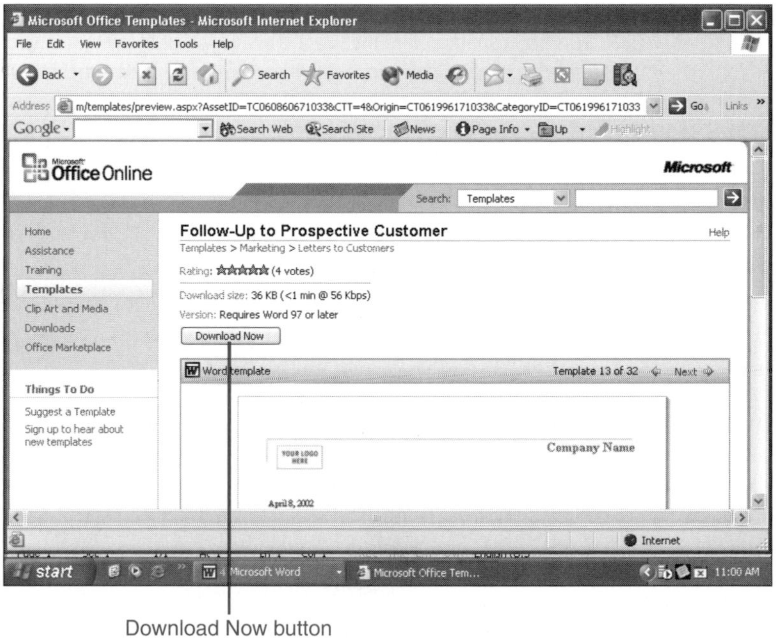

Figure 11.2
Click Download Now to open a file based on the online template you've chosen.

Download Now button

NOTE

> Microsoft does not provide a way to download the template itself. However, you can save the open file as a template on your own computer. Choose File, Save As; enter a filename in the File Name text box; choose Document Template (*.dot) from the Save As Type drop-down box; and click Save.

If Word does not display a file based on the template you are trying to download, see "What to Do If Word Does Not Properly Download a Template," in "Troubleshooting" at the end of this chapter.

THE NORMAL TEMPLATE: CRUCIAL TO ALL DOCUMENTS

No matter which template you choose for a specific document, one template is always open: the Normal template, stored as Normal.dot in Word 2003's template folder. Although the Normal template doesn't include any text, it does include the following:

- Word's built-in AutoText entries for letters and other business documents as covered in Chapter 9.
- The 90-plus built-in Word styles covered in Chapter 10.

As you work, your new styles, AutoText entries, macros, and many other customizations are stored in the Normal template, unless you deliberately choose to save them elsewhere. Therefore, the longer you work with Word, the more valuable your Normal.dot file is likely to become.

CAUTION

This file is so important that it's the first target of many macro virus authors—who, by infecting Normal.dot, can thereby infect *all* of your documents. Even if you don't back up your entire Word installation as regularly as you should, at least store a current copy of Normal.dot somewhere safe every couple of weeks.

Word looks for Normal.dot whenever it starts up. If Normal.dot is damaged or renamed, or if Word simply can't find it in the template (or Workgroup template) folder you've specified in Tools, Options, File Locations, it simply creates a new one using Word's default settings. However, the new Normal.dot won't contain any of the styles, AutoText entries, or other customizations you have added since installing Word.

You can generally use the Organizer to copy custom styles, toolbars, macros, and AutoText entries from the renamed Normal.dot to the new Normal.dot. (If your original Normal.dot was virus-infected, don't copy macros into the new one.) The Organizer is covered in Chapter 10 and is reviewed again later in this chapter, in the "Moving Elements Among Templates" section.

→ To learn more about protecting your documents from virus infection, **see** "Preventing and Controlling Word Viruses," **p. 1106**.

UNDERSTANDING WHERE WORD STORES TEMPLATES

Although Word normally manages template files well on its own, if you want to copy templates between computers manually—or if you run into problems with a template—it helps to know where and how Office 2003 stores templates. Word recognizes templates stored in several ways:

- **User-customized templates.** These are templates you create yourself. In Windows 2000 and Windows XP, they are typically stored in `C:\Documents and Settings\`*`userprofile`*`\Application Data\Microsoft\Templates\`.

- **Custom workgroup templates.** These are templates stored in a special workgroup template folder (commonly established as a read-only shared folder on a network server). When Word finds templates stored here, these templates are displayed in the General tab of the Templates dialog box.

- **Templates stored on your Web sites.** These are templates stored in folders you have designated on Web servers you control. Creating a folder on a Web Server where you can store templates is covered later in this chapter, in the section titled "Storing Templates on a Web Server."

- **"Advertised" and Installed templates.** These are templates that come with Microsoft Office 2003. They are listed in the Templates dialog box the first time you open Word, whether or not they have been copied to your hard drive. If they have not been copied to your hard drive, you will be prompted to install them the first time you use them. These are stored in the following folder: `C:\Program Files\Microsoft Office\Templates\`*`language id number`*, where *language id number* is different depending on your default language. The U.S. version of Microsoft Office uses 1033 as its ID number. You can have several separate folders, each containing Word's templates for a specific installed language.

- **"Non-file-based" templates.** These are special templates used internally by Word to create some new kinds of documents; they do not correspond to separate physical files but rather features directly built into Word.

You can change the location where Word looks for user templates and custom workgroup templates through the File Locations tab of the Tools, Options dialog box. When you make a change here, it affects all your Office applications.

CREATING A NEW TEMPLATE

Now that you've learned what templates are and how to use the ones Word provides, it's time to start creating your own. Word gives you two ways to do so: from scratch, or by saving an existing document file as a template. Answer the following questions to decide which approach makes more sense:

- Do you already have a document that can easily be transformed into a template? For example, if you're creating a template for business proposals, have you made a proposal lately with which you're especially pleased? Would it be easy to edit the contents specific to one client or project, leaving "holes" for you to fill in custom information later? If the answers to these questions are yes, it makes sense to open that file, make your changes, and save it as a template.

- Are you creating a template for a document for which there is no usable model? Then you may want to create it from scratch.

11

CREATING A TEMPLATE BASED ON AN EXISTING DOCUMENT

To create a template based on an existing document, follow these steps:

1. Open the existing document.

2. Edit the document to eliminate the specific references that you don't want to appear every time you create a new document using this template.

> **TIP**
>
> Before you delete these references, consider whether they're worth saving as AutoText entries. If you're building your template from a proposal you made to Alpha Corporation, you don't want all your Alpha-related experience to show up in proposals you might make to their fiercest competitor, Omega Corporation.
>
> But you do want to have that boilerplate conveniently available as an AutoText entry the next time you make a proposal to Alpha.

→ For more information about using AutoText entries, **see** "AutoText: The Complete Boilerplate Resource," **p. 301**.

3. Make sure that all styles, AutoText entries, macros, toolbars, or keyboard shortcuts you want are properly set up (either by default from the existing document, added manually, or copied from some other existing document or template, using the Organizer).

→ For more information about working with the Organizer, **see** "Moving Elements Among Templates," **p. 374**.

4. Choose File, Save As.

5. Choose Template in the Save as Type drop-down box. When you do, Word changes the current folder to the one where it saves user templates (see Figure 11.3).

Figure 11.3
When you tell Word you want to save a template, it switches you to the folder where you currently save all user templates.

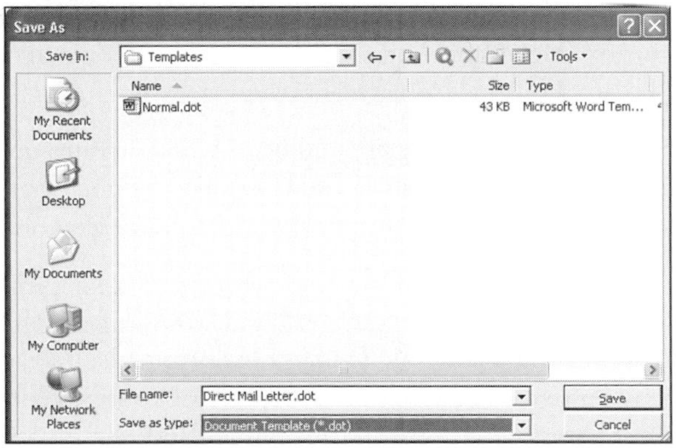

6. Enter a name for the template in the File Name text box.

7. If you want to save your template in that folder so that it appears in the General tab of the Templates dialog box, click Save. If you want it to appear in a different tab in the

Templates dialog box, double-click that folder and click Save. (You can also browse to folders on Web servers that you or your company have designated as central locations for storing templates.)

You are not limited to using the folders Word automatically provides. For example, you might want to create a new folder that contains all the custom templates you provide for your company and name that folder Company Templates. Word makes this easy to do.

After you display the Save As dialog box and choose Document Template to save your template, click the Create New Folder button. The New Folder dialog box appears. Enter the name you want to use and click OK. Word creates the new folder and opens it.

Enter an appropriate filename for your template and click Save. The next time you open the Templates dialog box, your new folder will appear with its own tab. If you click on that tab, you'll find an icon for the template you just saved.

NOTE

Word's Templates dialog box displays only subfolders containing at least one template. If you create the folder but then do not save your template, the folder will not appear in the Templates dialog box.

TIP

If you want to use your revised template with one of Word's built-in wizards (discussed later in this chapter), the filename must include the word Fax, Letter, Memo, or Résumé, and you must save the template in the corresponding subfolder. For example, if you want to make a new memo accessible to the Memo Wizard, store it in the `\Templates\Memos` folder.

CREATING A TEMPLATE BASED ON AN EXISTING TEMPLATE

Sometimes you may not have a document that's an adequate model for a template, but Word just might. You can browse the tabs in the Templates dialog box to find out.

To display the Templates dialog box, choose File, New and click General Templates on the New Document task pane. In the Templates dialog box, click on a template; Word displays a thumbnail preview of a sample document based on it.

If you find a template you want to use, click the Template button to indicate that you want to create a new template rather than a document (see Figure 11.4). Then click OK. A new template opens, containing all the contents of Word's built-in template. Adjust it any way you want and save it under a new name or in a different folder. If you change the document's formatting, consider changing its styles to match.

→ For more information about changing styles, **see** "Changing Styles," **p. 345**.

Preview a template's appearance here

Figure 11.4
Selecting a template
to open as a template.

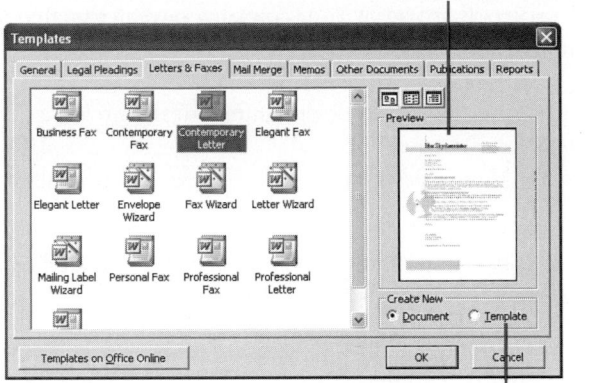

Click the Template button to open a
new template based on the existing one

CREATING A TEMPLATE FROM SCRATCH

You can also create a new template from scratch, much as you create a new document. To do so, click the New Blank Document button on the Standard toolbar or press Ctrl+N. Add the text and formatting you want to include in the document. Then click the Save button and choose Document Template (*.dot) from the Save as Type drop-down box. As mentioned earlier, Word switches folders to display your default location for user templates. From here, browse to or create the location where you want to save the template, name the document in the File Name text box, and then click Save.

UNDERSTANDING GLOBAL TEMPLATES

Global templates are templates whose styles and other settings are available to all open documents. As already mentioned, Normal is a global template. However, you can add more global templates, either for your current session or permanently. You might load a global template in the following situations:

- When you want to make sure that a set of macros, styles, or AutoText entries is available for use in all documents you plan to create during one session—but not necessarily for all sessions. For instance, if you are editing several sales proposals today, you may want to load a sales proposal template as a global template today so that you can have access to its special toolbars, shortcuts, AutoText entries, and macros. However, because you edit sales proposals only one day a week, you can avoid cluttering your editing environment with irrelevant tools and shortcuts, by not loading this global template on other days.

- When you want to make sure that third-party macros are available to all your documents, without copying them into your Normal.dot template. (In fact, many third-party templates do not permit you to copy individual macros out of them.)

Global templates are also helpful when you want to distribute a set of customizations to others. You can build them into a template and instruct your colleagues how to load the template as a global template when they need these customizations.

LOADING A GLOBAL TEMPLATE FOR THE CURRENT SESSION

You can add a global template anytime during the course of a session. Global templates are controlled in the Templates and Add-Ins dialog box, which is found by clicking Tools, Templates and Add-Ins (see Figure 11.5).

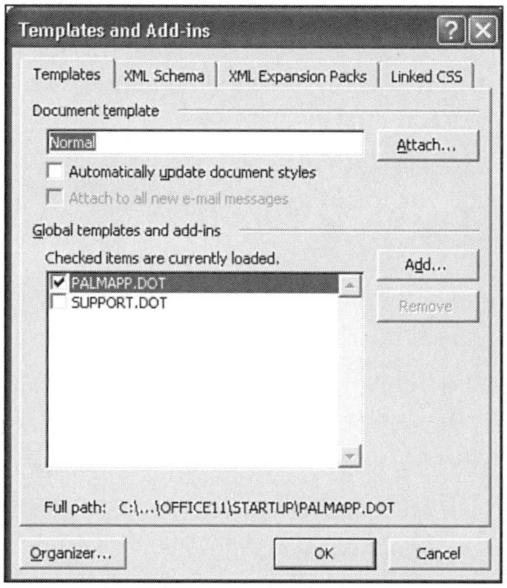

Figure 11.5
The Templates and Add-Ins dialog box enables you to add one or more global templates for use in all documents.

To add a global template, click Add from this dialog box. Then, in the Add Template dialog box (see Figure 11.6), Word displays a list of the templates currently available in the Templates folder. Browse the list to select the template you want, and click OK.

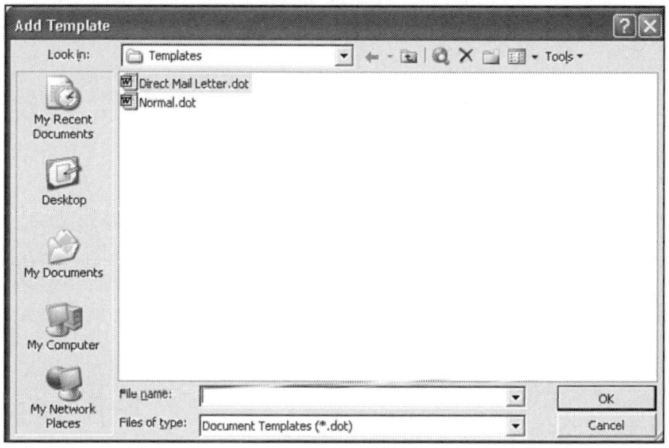

Figure 11.6
The Add Template dialog box works much as the Open dialog box does; browse for the template you want and click OK.

TIP

> Templates can be stored anywhere on your hard disk or on a networked hard drive. However, only templates stored in the Office 2003 Templates folder, one of its subfolders, or a networked folder designated as the Workgroup Templates folder appear in the Templates dialog box. (Workgroup templates are covered later in this chapter.)

When you return to the Templates and Add-Ins dialog box, the additional template appears in the Global Templates and Add-Ins scroll box with a check mark next to it. It remains loaded until you uncheck the box or exit Word. The next time you start Word, the template will be listed in the Global Templates and Add-Ins scroll box, but its check box won't be checked. You'll need to recheck it to reenable it as a global template.

If you suddenly lose access to a template that was available before, see "What to Do If You Lose Access to a Template," in "Troubleshooting" at the end of this chapter.

LOADING A GLOBAL TEMPLATE PERMANENTLY

You may want to load the same global template automatically whenever you run Word without having to fiddle around with check boxes each time. The easiest way is to copy the template into Word's Startup folder. In a typical Windows 2000 or Windows XP installation of Microsoft Office 2003, this folder is \Windows*user profile*\Application Data\Microsoft\Word\Startup.

After you copy the template, it loads automatically when you run Word, and stays loaded unless you uncheck its check box in Templates and Add-Ins.

NOTE

> Why wouldn't you load a global template permanently? Conceivably, it might contain confidential information that you wouldn't want others to access routinely. More likely, you're simply trying to save memory and make sure that Word starts as quickly as possible by not loading any more templates than necessary—or you need the template only on rare occasions.

UNDERSTANDING THE RELATIONSHIP BETWEEN STYLES AND TEMPLATES

In Chapter 10, you learned how to create a set of consistent styles and store them in a template. The styles available to your current document depend on the templates open at the time. These templates are as listed here:

- The Normal template.
- Whatever template you based the document on, if you based it on a template other than Normal.

■ Any other global templates that are currently loaded. By default, no global templates other than Normal are loaded.

What if several templates are open, and each defines the same style differently? This happens often, even if you stay with Word's built-in styles. For example, Heading 1 is 14-point Arial Bold in the Normal template, but 10-point Arial Bold in the Contemporary Letter template. If you open a document based on the Contemporary Letter template, Word uses its styles, not those in any other template, global or otherwise.

If you change the styles in your document without storing those changes in a template, the document's revised styles override all the templates available to that document.

NOTE

> Not surprisingly, templates can also store combinations of formatting that appear in the Styles and Formatting task pane. In general, however, if you are building complex documents that you want to keep consistent, it makes more sense to rely on styles than on these formatting combinations.

ATTACHING TEMPLATES TO DOCUMENTS AND EMAIL MESSAGES

In Word 2003, templates have a role to play in virtually any kind of document, from conventional business documents such as reports, to email messages, to Web pages. In the following sections, you'll learn how to attach templates to existing documents, and to email messages.

ATTACHING A NEW TEMPLATE TO AN EXISTING DOCUMENT

Every document has one template attached to it (except for documents created by wizards, which have a wizard attached to them, as you'll see later). Typically, the attached template is the one you used to create the document—whether you used the Normal template, another built-in Word template, or one of your own. However, in some instances, you may want to change the template associated with a document.

For instance, imagine that your company, Acme Chocolate, has just been purchased by Intergalactic Candies. Intergalactic has different corporate design standards than Acme. Both companies use Word, and both companies have Word templates codifying basic document formats such as headings and body text. If so, you may be able to redesign your documents to the Intergalactic standard simply by attaching the Intergalactic template to them.

NOTE

> Of course, things aren't usually quite this simple. The style names you used at Acme may not be the same as those used by Intergalactic, or Intergalactic might not have a template containing all its styles. However, you can still create a new template that combines

continues

continued

> Intergalactic's formatting rules with the style names you've already been using and achieve the same result.

To attach a different template to your document, choose Tools, Templates and Add-Ins, and click Attach. The Attach Template dialog box opens. Browse to the template you want to attach and click Open. If you want to update your existing document's styles to reflect those in the new template, check the Automatically Update Document Styles check box.

TIP

> To automate the process of migrating from one document design to another, record a macro that changes the attached template to the new template and automatically updates the document's styles. Name the macro AutoOpen and store it in the Normal template. It will run every time you open a new document, changing the formatting of the document to reflect your corporate redesign.

NOTE

> Sometimes you want to attach a new template but not update the styles. For example, you might be perfectly happy with your document's formatting, but you want access to a set of AutoText entries associated with a different template. In this case, attach the template, but do not check the Automatically Update Document Styles check box.

ATTACHING A TEMPLATE TO ALL EMAIL MESSAGES

Many Word users prefer to edit their email in Microsoft Word, rather than in Outlook or Outlook Express. Moreover, email users are increasingly using HTML-based formatting to make their email communications more powerful and effective. Word 2003 enables you to specify a document template that will be used in all new email messages you create within Word. To specify a default template for emails, follow these steps:

1. Click File, New, and choose Blank Email Message from the New Document task pane. The Word window changes to an email message window.

2. Click in the text area of the message (not the To, Cc, or Subject lines).

3. Choose Tools, Templates and Add-Ins.

4. Click Attach. The Attach Templates dialog box opens.

5. Browse to the template you want to attach to your email messages, select it, and click Open.

6. If you want this template to be applied to any future emails, check the Attach to All New Email Messages check box.

7. Choose OK.

For more information about working with Word as an email editor, see Chapter 30, "Using Word as an Email Editor."

LINKING CSS STYLE SHEETS TO WEB PAGES

If you are using Word to create Web pages that will be used in recent-vintage browsers, you can use Cascading Style Sheets (CSS) to achieve much of the same formatting control that styles and templates provide for print documents in Word.

Word's Templates and Add-Ins dialog box enables you to link a Web page to one or more Cascading Style Sheets, change links to style sheets that already exist, or change the priorities in which multiple style sheets are applied to a single document. To make these changes, follow these steps:

1. Choose Tools, Templates and Add-Ins.
2. Click the Linked CSS tab (see Figure 11.7).

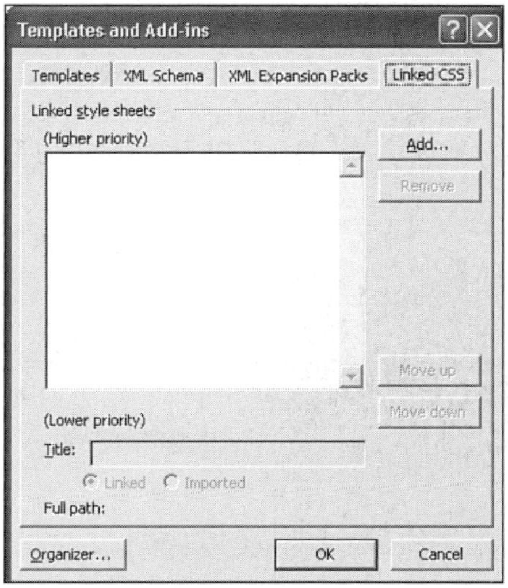

Figure 11.7
The Linked CSS tab allows you to control which style sheets are linked to a Web page, and the priority in which they are applied.

3. To add a Cascading Style Sheet, click Add. In the Add CSS Link dialog box, browse to the cascading style sheet you want to attach and click Open.
4. To remove a Cascading Style Sheet, select it from the Linked Style Sheets scroll box and click Remove.
5. To change the priority of a Cascading Style Sheet, select it from the Linked Style Sheets scroll box and click Move Up or Move Down.
6. If you want, enter a title for the style sheet in the Title text box.
7. By default, your HTML page is Linked to the style sheet: if the style sheet is updated, all linked pages will automatically reflect the changes when they are displayed in a

browser. If, however, the style sheet is not available when the Web page is eventually published, you may want to import the style sheet into the Web page itself. To do so, click the Imported button.

8. When you are finished establishing settings for CSS links, click OK.

9. Word displays a dialog box informing you that you must save and reload the document to see the formatting changes your new Cascading Style Sheets have applied. To do so, click Yes.

USING THEMES TO CHANGE THE STYLES IN YOUR TEMPLATE

In addition to templates, Word 2003 provides several dozen *themes*: sets of styles that you can copy into your current document, immediately giving it a different appearance. Themes are helpful for communicating the tone of your document. Although they're designed primarily for Web and intranet pages (or for Word documents viewed electronically), they can also be used for printed documents if you want.

CAUTION

Backgrounds in themed documents don't print. Some themes use white text against a darker background; when these print, the white text will be invisible with the background absent.

Word themes are purely concerned with the visual appearance of your document. In contrast to templates, themes do not include editing customizations, AutoText entries, macros, or other elements that may be included in templates. They do include

- Background colors and/or graphics (intended purely for online viewing; these backgrounds do not print)
- Formatting for heading styles and body text
- Formatting for Web hyperlinks and table borders
- Custom bullets and horizontal lines

Although you can switch among Word's themes, you can't change the contents of a theme. There is a workaround, however: You can create a document with a theme, change the styles in that document, and save the revised document as a template.

TIP

If you've installed FrontPage 2003, which comes with certain versions of Office 2003, you can also use the themes provided by FrontPage.

To apply a theme to your document, choose Format, Theme. The Theme dialog box opens (see Figure 11.8).

Figure 11.8
You can choose among several dozen predefined themes in the Theme dialog box.

NOTE

If Theme is grayed out on the Format menu, you need to install the feature by running Microsoft Office 2003 Setup again, in Maintenance Mode, using the Office 2003 or Word 2003 CD-ROM (or the network location where your installation files can be found). The Theme components are found in Office Shared Features, not in the Word section. You also need to choose which sets of themes to install: Typical Themes, Additional Themes, or both.

Click on each set of themes you want to select, and choose Run All from My Computer. After you've selected all the themes you want to install, click Update.

To select a theme, choose it from the Choose a Theme scroll box. You see a preview in the Sample scroll box, showing you how first- and second-level headings, text, hyperlinks, bullets, and horizontal lines will appear in your document if you choose this theme. You can also control three elements of your theme, through check boxes at the lower-left corner of the dialog box:

- Vivid Colors tells Word to use brighter colors for text than it would normally.
- Active Graphics, which is turned on by default, tells Word to use animated bullets rather than regular graphical bullets. You won't see the difference until you load your page in a Web browser, however: Word does not display animated graphics.
- Background Image, also turned on by default, tells Word to include a background. If you do not want to include the background, you can clear this check box.

Figure 11.9 shows a document created with Word's Blocks theme.

11

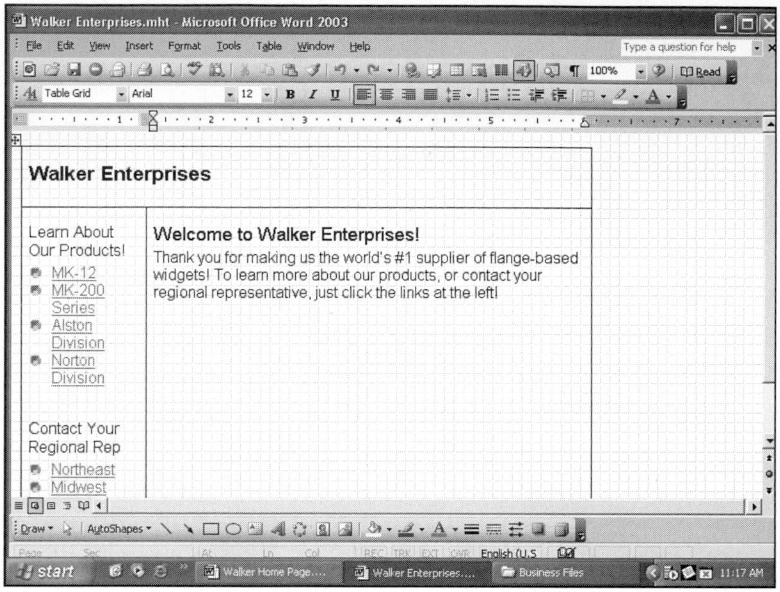

Figure 11.9
A Web page created with the Blocks theme.

11

CAUTION

Note that some themes use Microsoft fonts such as Trebuchet that, though widely available, aren't available on all platforms. For example, many Linux users will not have access to these fonts. If you need strict cross-platform font compatibility, stay with basic fonts such as Arial and Times New Roman.

If you need headlines to appear in fonts that aren't available on all platforms, consider creating your headlines as GIF graphics. Word is not the ideal tool for doing this. However, one possible solution is to use WordArt, and save the document containing your WordArt text as a Web Page. Word will create a separate GIF from the WordArt text.

→ For more information on using WordArt, **see** "Using WordArt," **p. 468**.

Previewing New Templates with Style Gallery

You may be interested in how your document would look if you used the styles from a different template. For example, in the Acme-to-Intergalactic example used earlier, you might want to preview the impact of applying Intergalactic's template to your current documents, to determine which adjustments you'd need to make to your templates to accommodate Acme's documents.

To use Word's Style Gallery to preview what your document would look like (see Figure 11.10), choose Format, Theme, and click Style Gallery.

Figure 11.10
The Style Gallery enables you to preview how a document will appear with different style formatting.

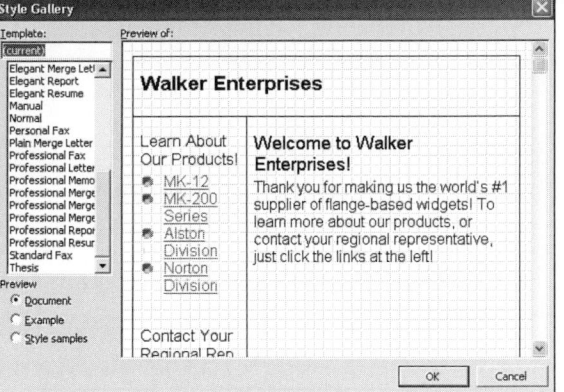

Next, select a template you want to preview from the Template scroll box. Word then shows what your document would look like if it were using the styles in that template. If some styles appear only later in the document, you can use the scrollbar to move to any location you want. If you want to apply the styles in the new template you've chosen, click OK.

It's important to understand what Style Gallery *doesn't* do. The Style Gallery does not attach a different template to your document. Rather, it copies styles from that template into your document, where they override any formatting settings from the template that is attached.

By default, Style Gallery previews how your document would look if you changed its styles to resemble those in a different template. Sometimes, however, this doesn't give you enough information to decide whether you want to apply another template's formats. Possibly, you've just started editing your document and haven't yet used the styles you're interested in previewing.

TIP

If the Preview does not change when you choose a different template, click Example, and then click Document again.

If you want to preview all the styles in a built-in Word template, you can ask Style Gallery to show you a sample document that uses all the styles in that template. With the Style Gallery dialog box displayed, choose Example. Figure 11.11 shows how Style Gallery displays an example of a Professional Letter.

11

Figure 11.11
Previewing an example document based on the Elegant Report template.

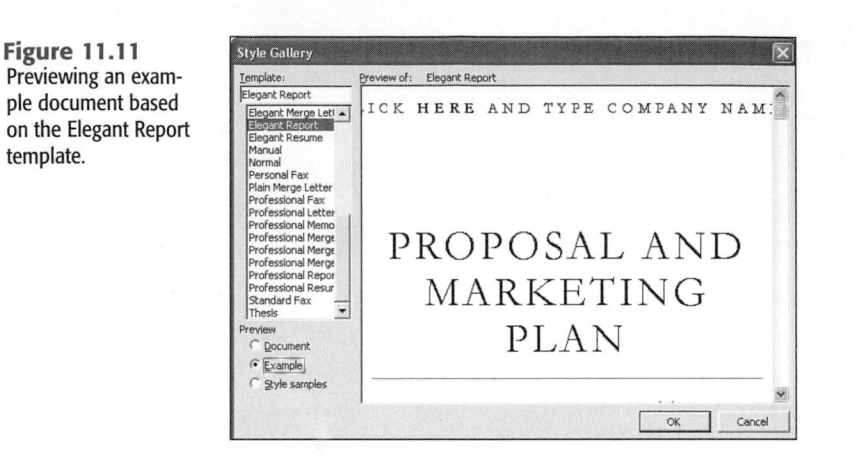

MOVING ELEMENTS AMONG TEMPLATES

The "Keeping Track of Styles with the Organizer" section of Chapter 10 explains how Word's Organizer lets you move styles among templates and documents. The Organizer doesn't just work with styles: it's Word's tool for moving a wide variety of elements between templates, including

- **AutoText entries** (boilerplate text and graphics; see Chapter 9)
- **Toolbars** (see Chapter 31)
- **Macro Project Items** (see Chapter 32)

To use the Organizer, choose <u>T</u>ools, Templates and Add-<u>I</u>ns; then click <u>O</u>rganizer. The Organizer appears, with the <u>S</u>tyles tab displayed (see Figure 11.12).

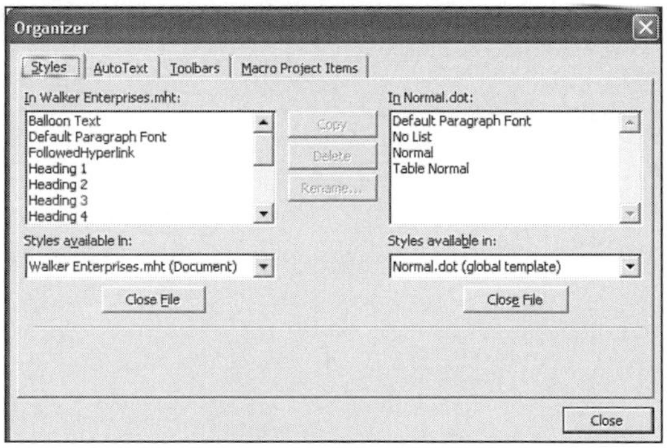

Figure 11.12
The Organizer can move styles, AutoText entries, toolbars, and Macro Project Items between templates.

➔ For more information on moving styles between templates, **see** "Keeping Track of Styles with the Organizer," **p. 349**.

➔ For more information on moving macros among templates and documents, **see** "Moving Project Items Among Templates and Documents," **p. 1083**.

If you have trouble copying elements between templates with the Organizer, see "What to Do If You Can't Copy Styles, AutoText Entries, Macros, or Toolbars," in "Troubleshooting" at the end of this chapter.

MANAGING TEMPLATES TO MINIMIZE YOUR WORK

Now that you understand the basics of using and creating templates, you're ready to plan a strategy for using templates to minimize your work and improve the efficiency of all your colleagues.

NOTE

Although our examples assume that you're in a corporation or small business, you can follow the same steps to streamline document production even if you work solo.

ORGANIZING YOUR CUSTOM TEMPLATES

The tabs of the Templates dialog box correspond to folders on your hard disk. The location of the customized *user templates* you create depends on your configuration and the version of Windows you are running. To find out what folder your user templates are stored in, choose Tools, Options, File Locations, and look for the User Templates listing in the File Types window.

Templates stored in this folder appear within the General tab of the Templates dialog box—the tab that appears when you first open the Templates dialog box. Any subfolders created under this folder appear as tabs within the Templates dialog box.

This means that you can reorganize your templates—even adding new subfolders if you need to. The easiest way to add a new folder is to choose Tools, Options, File Locations; select User Templates; click Modify; and click the Create New Folder button.

You see the results immediately in the Templates dialog box, as shown in Figure 11.13. Note that Word doesn't display empty template subfolders; you must store a template in the folder before that folder will appear in the dialog box.

It also means that you should move or copy all the templates you use most into the top-level User Templates folder, for quicker access. If you manage Word in a workgroup or department, you can hide or delete the templates or folders you don't want used.

For example, if you standardized on the Elegant family of templates for letters, faxes, and memos, you can copy those into the folder that corresponds to the General tab (in other words, the folder Word is using for your user templates). You can then consider moving unused templates and template subfolders elsewhere on your hard drive so that they do not appear in the Templates dialog box at all.

Think for a moment about how to name your most commonly used templates. Consider including your company's name (or an abbreviated version) in each of them, to make it obvious that these templates are customized to your company's needs.

11

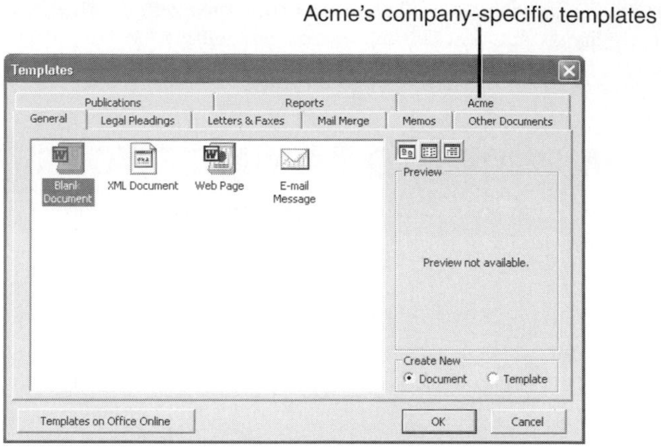

Acme's company-specific templates

Figure 11.13
A customized Templates dialog box displaying templates specific to the Acme Company.

FURTHER AUTOMATING DOCUMENTS WITH TEMPLATES

Your templates are now model documents that contain all the text and formatting common to all the documents based on them. You've already saved yourself and your colleagues many hours. Your next step is to use the other capabilities of Word templates to build custom editing environments that make you (and your colleagues) even more efficient. To do this, you can draw on various Word features covered in detail elsewhere in the book:

- **AutoText entries** (Chapter 9). Identify blocks of copy that seem to recur often in your documents. For example, many of your company's status reports might include a table that lists steps to be taken next. You can store a skeleton table as an AutoText entry. Then you can use the Organizer to copy this AutoText entry into your Report template.

- **Styles** (Chapter 10). Consider which styles should be used in the documents for which this template is being created. Create those styles, or copy them from documents that already contain them.

- **Custom toolbars and menu items** (Chapter 31). You can include custom menus and/or toolbars in a template. Then, whenever you or anyone else creates a document based on that template, these custom menus and toolbars are there to help. For example, you might create a button on your Report toolbar that inserts an Executive Summary on the first page, using Word 2003's AutoSummarize feature.

- **Macros** (Chapter 32). You can record macros to perform a wide variety of tasks, and if you're comfortable with Word's Visual Basic for Applications (VBA) programming language, you can coax Word to perform an even wider range of tasks.

As you think about your documents, you might find elements that ought to be in them but haven't been added. Now's a good time to create those elements. If you want, you can scour Word's built-in templates and wizards for ideas. An especially good source for business ideas is Word's Agenda Wizard.

If you're using a version of Office 2003 containing PowerPoint, you'll find that PowerPoint is replete with good ideas you can adapt. To find them, either run PowerPoint's AutoContent Wizard or review the templates PowerPoint provides.

> **TIP**
>
> As discussed later in this chapter, if your computers are networked, you can store your global template in a central Workgroup Templates folder that everyone can access. Then, when you make changes to this global template, you can store the new one in Workgroup Templates rather than copy it to everyone's computer.
>
> As is also discussed later in this chapter, you can utilize a folder on a Web server as a central repository for templates for people throughout your organization.

After you're familiar with the Word features involved, you can create a preliminary version of all these templates in just a few hours, excluding VBA macro programming. Try it out. If you're working as part of a team, share it with a few of your colleagues. Modify it as necessary. If you've chosen the right documents to automate, your time investment will pay for itself in just a few weeks—or possibly even a few days.

USING WORKGROUP TEMPLATES

One of the best ways to keep your entire workgroup or organization in sync is to use *workgroup templates*, which are stored centrally on a network server. All your users can share access to these templates at the same time. Better yet, you can centrally update and manage workgroup templates—eliminating the need to provide individual copies of your critical templates to every user.

Here are some of the ways you can use workgroup templates:

- Centrally store AutoText boilerplates you want everyone to use
- Provide a library of standardized documents built around the needs of your department or company
- Update everyone's user interface at the same time

You create a workgroup template the same way you create any other template. You then store it in a folder that each user's computer recognizes as the location for workgroup templates. It usually makes sense to mark workgroup templates as read-only, to prevent inadvertent or unauthorized customizations that affect everyone who uses them. To ensure that unauthorized individuals don't have access to them, consider storing them on a server with limited permissions. If you have the authority to do so yourself, browse to your workgroup template using Windows Explorer; right-click and choose Properties from the shortcut menu; check the Read-Only check box; and choose OK.

Follow these steps to specify a workgroup template location on a specific computer:

1. Choose Tools, Options.

2. Choose the File Locations tab (see Figure 11.14).

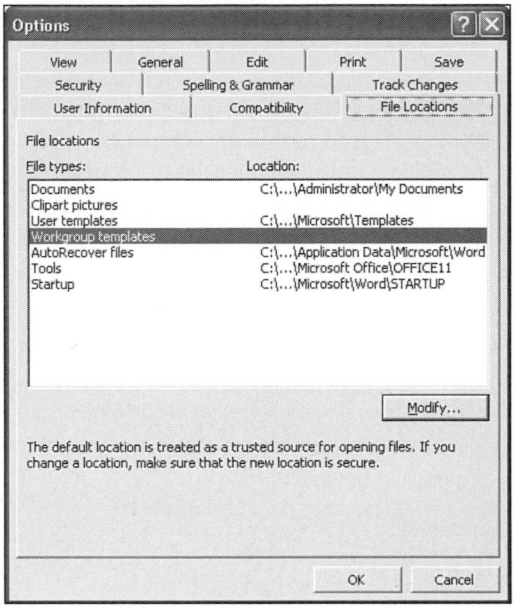

Figure 11.14
You can establish or change the Workgroup Templates folder in the File Locations tab of the Options dialog box.

3. In the File Types scroll box, click Workgroup Templates. (By default, no location is associated with workgroup templates.)

4. Click Modify to open the Modify Location dialog box.

5. Browse and select the folder you want to use.

6. Click OK twice.

TIP

> The procedure just described sets a workgroup template location for a single workstation. You can, however, specify a workgroup template location when you deploy Office throughout your organization, using tools provided in the Office 2003 Resource Kit. Alternatively, you can give your users a file containing an AutoOpen macro that changes the workgroup template location; instruct the users to open the file to change the location.

After you establish a Workgroup Templates folder, any templates you save there automatically appear in the General tab of the Templates dialog box when users open a new file, just as if they were stored locally.

CAUTION

If the Workgroup Templates folder is temporarily inaccessible, the templates stored there will be absent when a user creates a new file. Users are dependent on your network to create documents based on those templates.

STORING TEMPLATES ON A WEB SERVER

Word 2003 also enables you to centrally store templates for your entire organization on a Web or intranet server. As with workgroup templates, all users can share access to these templates concurrently, and the templates can be centrally managed and updated.

CREATING A TEMPLATE FOLDER ON A WEB SERVER

To specify or create a folder on a live Web server where you can store and retrieve templates:

1. Click File, New. The New Document task pane opens.
2. Click On My Web Sites. The New from Templates on My Web Sites dialog box opens.
3. Click the Create New Folder button (fifth button from the left along the row of buttons at the top of the dialog box). The Add Network Place Wizard opens.
4. Follow the instructions in the Add Network Place Wizard to create a shortcut to the folder you want to use. You may have to log on to your Web server using a valid password.

SAVING TEMPLATES TO A FOLDER ON A WEB SERVER

After you've created a Web folder to store your templates, you can save a template to the Web folder the same way you would save any other template.

Choose File, Save As. In the Save As Type drop-down box of the Save As dialog box, choose Document Template (*.dot). Now, browse to the folder you created (it may appear at the bottom of the list of templates displayed in the dialog box). If you are asked to log on with a password, do so. Click Save to save the template.

CREATING FILES FROM TEMPLATES STORED ON WEB SERVERS

You can create new documents based on templates stored on your Web server by browsing to the appropriate location:

1. Choose File, New.
2. In the New Document Task Pane, click On My Web Sites.
3. Browse to the Web-based location containing the template you want to use. Depending on the location and performance of your Web server and Internet connections, Word may take longer to access this folder than it does to access templates on your own computer.

11

4. Click Create New to create a new document based on the template you've stored on the Web.

USING WORD WIZARDS

In addition to templates, Word provides a set of interactive *wizards* that enable you to walk through the construction of a document step by step, making choices about how it will be built. When you finish making the choices, Word creates the document for you. Then you only need to "fill in the holes" with your specific text and graphics. The document's structure and formatting are already in place, reflecting your choices.

WIZARDS INCLUDED WITH WORD 2003

Word 2003 includes wizards for creating

- Agendas
- Calendars
- Envelopes
- Fax cover sheets
- Flyers
- Legal pleadings
- Letters

- Mailing labels
- Memos
- Newsletters
- Postcards
- Résumés
- Simple form letters
- Web pages

NOTE

Depending on how you originally installed Word, the first time you double-click on a wizard to run it, you may be prompted to install it first—from either your CD-ROM or the original network location you installed Word from.

OPENING AND WALKING THROUGH A TYPICAL WIZARD

The best way to get the flavor for how wizards work is to walk through using one. To run Word's Résumé Wizard, choose File, New; click On My Computer on the New Document task pane; click the Other Documents tab; and double-click Résumé Wizard.

The opening window of the Résumé Wizard appears. Along the left side, a subway-style map shows the entire process. A green square indicates where you are right now; you can click any other square to "hop" there. Four buttons along the bottom of the window also help you navigate through the wizard. Finally, if you click the Help button, the Office Assistant offers help about this wizard.

> You don't always have to walk through every step of a wizard. After you've included all the information you want to include, click Finish. Word generates the document based on whatever information you've given it.

Click Next to get started. The wizard asks you to choose from Word's three built-in styles for résumés: Professional, Contemporary, or Elegant. These are the same three style options available in most of Word's templates and wizards, making it easy to build a consistent set of documents. Make a choice and click Next.

The wizard next asks what type of résumé you want to create. You can choose an Entry-Level Résumé designed for individuals with little job experience; a Chronological Résumé that lists your work experience by date; a Functional Résumé that lists types of achievement; or a Professional Résumé, which is commonly used in several professions. Make your choice and click Next.

In the Address window, you're asked for the personal information that Word doesn't already know. If you entered your name when you installed Word, that name already appears in the Name text box. After you enter the personal information once, it appears automatically on this screen whenever you run the Résumé Wizard. When you're finished entering personal information, click Next.

In the Standard Headings window, Word displays a list of headings commonly included in résumés. The ones already checked are most commonly included in the type of résumé you want to create. You can check or clear any of these check boxes. Click Next.

You may have experiences or qualifications that don't fit into typical categories used by résumés. For example, if you're new in the work force, you might want to mention Extracurricular Activities or Community Activities. If you are a professional engineer, you might have Patents and Publications to your credit. You can specify these in the Optional Headings window. When you're finished, click Next.

Now, in the Add/Sort Heading window Word gives you a chance to organize the headings you've chosen or add new ones that weren't included in previous windows. If you want to add a new heading, enter it in the Are There Any Additional Headings text box and click Add.

After you add any new headings, you can make sure that your headings are organized the way you want. Select a heading in the These Are Your Résumé Headings text box and click Move Up or Move Down to move it toward the top or bottom of your résumé. If you decide upon reflection that you don't want a heading—perhaps you don't have enough to include in it, or it's inappropriate for the specific job you're seeking—select it and click Remove. When you're finished, click Next.

You're now in the final window of the Résumé Wizard. Here's your chance to review your work. You can click any box at the left edge of the window to view its current settings, or click Back repeatedly to move back through the wizard one screen at a time.

11

After you're satisfied, click Finish, and Word creates your document. You can see the results in Figure 11.15.

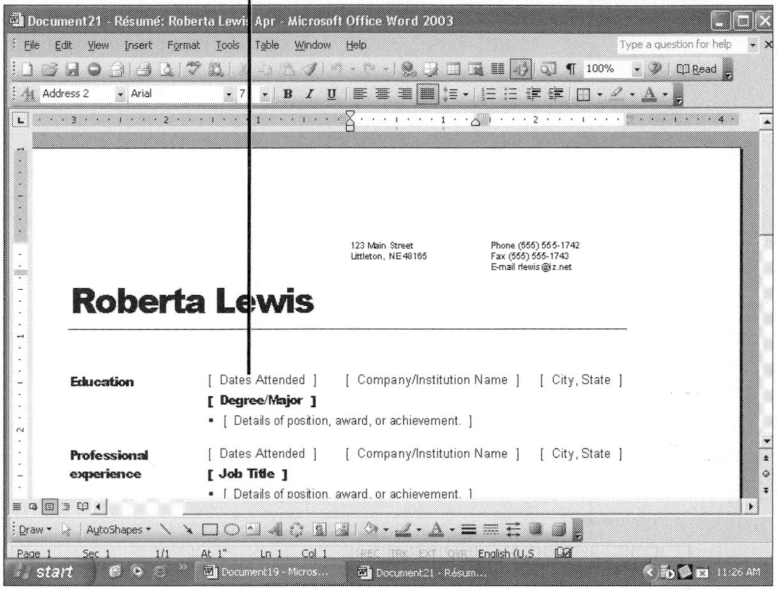

Replace text by clicking within brackets

Figure 11.15
A sample résumé created by the Résumé Wizard.

All the text in the résumé that appears within brackets is text you need to replace. Simply click inside any set of brackets; Word selects the entire block of text contained there. Start typing, and Word enters your replacement information. When you've added all the information you want to include about yourself, save the file as you normally would.

NOTE

These clickable areas are actually MacroButton fields. You can use them whenever you're creating a document in which you want others to add information in specific locations. You'll learn more about MacroButton fields in Chapter 23, "Automating Your Documents with Field Codes."

CAUTION

If you forget to replace one of these bracketed fields, the boilerplate text will print—making your omission painfully obvious to anyone who reads your résumé.

Because the Résumé Wizard stores the settings you enter in it, it's suddenly much easier to create a customized version of your résumé whenever you apply for a new job. You no longer have to create "one size fits all" résumés for mass résumé mailings; you can target your résumés to the needs of specific employers.

TIP

> If you especially like a document that results from working with a wizard, consider saving it as a template. That way, you always have access to a document that's well along the way to completion, without even having to run the wizard.

TIP

> The next time you're searching for a job, consider using another Word feature along with the Résumé Wizard. AutoText entries are perfect for saving boilerplate content you can reuse in future personalized résumés and cover letters. For example, if you have language specifically written to highlight your qualifications as an administrative assistant, store that language as an AutoText entry and reuse it the next time you apply for that position.
>
> You can use the same approach with other Word wizards as well. For example, to create a boilerplate letter that can easily be combined with standard paragraphs of contract information, create a custom letter template with AutoText entries and save it in the same subfolder as the other Letter templates.
>
> You can then use that letter template with the Letter Wizard, building the skeleton of a new letter document. After you've created the new document, you can use the AutoText entries built into it to add the contract language quickly.

→ For more information on saving blocks of text for easy reuse, **see** "AutoText: The Complete Boilerplate Resource," **p. 301**.

11

UNDERSTANDING WORD ADD-INS

Templates and wizards are powerful, but if you want to customize your Word environment even more, you should know about add-ins. These extend Word's capabilities, adding new features and custom commands. They have access to the full capabilities of the Windows operating system, and typically run faster than macros.

Many third-party Word add-ins are available. For example, Woody's Office Power Pack (WOPR) from Pinecliffe International (www.wopr.com) adds sophisticated envelope creation, file management, and many other features to Word.

Other add-ins offer specialized capabilities to Word. For example, the EndNote add-in from Thomson ISI ResearchSoft (www.endnote.com) enhances Word with extensive bibliographic reference capabilities.

When you have an add-in, either follow the instructions that come with it or install it the same way you install a global template. Choose <u>T</u>ools, Templates and Add-<u>I</u>ns; click A<u>d</u>d. Then, in the Add Templates dialog box, select the add-in you want to load and click OK.

Like global templates, add-ins normally don't load at startup unless you copy them to Word's Startup folder or run a macro that loads them.

TROUBLESHOOTING

WHAT TO DO IF WORD DOES NOT PROPERLY DOWNLOAD A TEMPLATE

Word's Template downloading feature is incompatible with Internet Explorer add-ons such as Pop-Up Stopper that immediately close pop-up windows to prevent unwanted advertising from displaying. Temporarily disable your add-on while downloading your template. For example, if you are using Pop-Up Stopper, press the Ctrl key when you click Download Now, and hold Ctrl down until the download is complete.

WHAT TO DO IF YOU LOSE ACCESS TO A TEMPLATE

If you suddenly lose access to a template that was always available before, check to see whether the corresponding template file (.dot) has been moved. If the template is part of a workgroup on a network, you should also check to see whether you have lost access to the server where it is stored. If you have exited and restarted Word, also check to see whether the template is a global template that must be reloaded.

WHAT TO DO IF YOU CAN'T COPY STYLES, AUTOTEXT ENTRIES, MACROS, OR TOOLBARS

If the Organizer won't let you copy elements between templates or documents, there are a few possible causes. First, the destination template may be set as read-only. Second, it may be password protected. Third, the template may be protected for tracked changes, comments, or forms. This means you can copy elements to the template only if you first unprotect it with the correct password. To determine the cause, open the template file for editing. (Don't open a new file based on the template—open the template itself.)

WHAT TO DO IF WORD WARNS YOU ABOUT VIRUSES WHEN YOU OPEN A TEMPLATE

If you have set macro security to High or Medium, Word might warn you that templates can contain viruses whenever you open a template (or a document based on one). This warning does not mean the template is infected, only that you should be careful about the templates you open.

If the template is one of Word's built-in templates, choose Tools, Options, Security; click the Macro Security button; click the Trusted Publishers tab, and make sure that the Trust All Installed Add-Ins and Templates check box is checked.

If Microsoft Corporation does not appear in the list of Trusted Sources, the next time a Microsoft template triggers a security warning, click Details to check whether Microsoft's digital signature is OK (not tampered with). If the template is OK, check the Always Trust Macros from This Source check box in the Security Warning dialog box, and click Enable Macros. From now on, Microsoft's own templates won't trigger security warnings.

WHAT TO DO IF CUSTOM TEMPLATES APPEAR ON THE WRONG TAB IN THE NEW DIALOG BOX

By default, all custom templates are saved to the Templates folder (typically: C:\Windows*userprofile*\Application Data\Microsoft\Templates, or in Windows 2000, C:\Documents and Settings*userprofile*\Application Data\Microsoft\Templates. This folder contains subfolders corresponding to the tabs that appear in the File, New dialog box. In Windows Explorer, browse to this folder, select the template you want to move, click the Cut button, browse to the subfolder you want the template to appear in, and click the Paste button.

CHAPTER 12

STRUCTURING AND ORGANIZING INFORMATION WITH TABLES

In this chapter

UNDERSTANDING WHAT WORD TABLES CAN DO

In Word, *tables* are collections of horizontal rows and vertical columns organized into individual cells, in which you can place text, numbers, graphics, *fields*, or other elements. Traditionally, tables were used primarily to display numbers, but you can use Word tables for any task that requires information to be displayed in a structured fashion. Use tables to

- Help build newsletters, brochures, and other "desktop published" pieces in which elements must be placed in specific locations on a page and kept there (see Chapter 16, "Word Desktop Publishing")

- Structure and organize Web pages (see Chapter 24, "Using Word to Develop Web Content")

- Write certain scripts that require audio/video directions to appear in one column with spoken narration in a second column (though this format is less common than it once was)

- Build forms that can be filled out electronically or on paper (see Chapter 28, "Creating Forms")

- Create the source data you will use in charts and graphs (see Chapter 15, "Visualizing Your Message with Graphs, Diagrams, and Org Charts")

- Build databases that can be used for mail merging (see Chapter 17, "Using Mail Merge Effectively")

NOTE

> Nearly every task that you might once have used tabs for can be performed more easily and efficiently with tables. Only a few rare tasks, such as adding dot leaders between left- and right-aligned text, still call for tabs.

When you want a complex table to perform a complex task, Word provides exceptional power and flexibility. And when all you want is an old-fashioned row-and-column table for text or numbers, Word gets the job done quickly and simply.

WORD'S MULTIPLE APPROACHES TO CREATING A TABLE

Depending on the kind of table you want, and how you prefer to work, Word offers several approaches to drawing a table:

- If you need to create a simple table and you know how many rows and columns you need, but you don't need to control anything else, you can use the Insert Table button on the Standard toolbar.

- If you want to control the number of rows and columns, but you also want to control column width at the same time, choose Table, Insert, Table to work from the Insert Table dialog box.

- If you prefer to draw your tables freehand, or if you need tables with varying row and column sizes, click the Tables and Borders button on the Standard toolbar (or choose T<u>a</u>ble, Dra<u>w</u> Table) and use the tools on the Tables and Borders toolbar.

- If you already have information in tabular form, or you've imported information in a standard format such as comma-delimited, use Word's Con<u>v</u>ert Text to Table feature, covered in the "Converting Text to Tables" section of this chapter.

- If you learned to create "fake tables" on a typewriter, using hyphens (rows) and plus signs (columns), do the same thing in Word; when you press Enter at the end of the first line, Word transforms your typing into a real table.

The following sections cover each of these methods in more detail.

TIP

> Know how your table will be used before you format it. If your document will be published in a journal, a magazine, or even a company brochure, find out what the publisher's needs are. Find out whether the table will be a graphic element placed in the text before printing or whether it will be laid out as a table within the text. Many scientific journals ask that you include your tables on separate pages at the end of your manuscript, one table per page.
>
> Unfortunately, in certain cases, your publisher may not accept Word tables at all. In this case, use Word's T<u>a</u>ble, Con<u>v</u>ert, Ta<u>b</u>le to Text feature to replace table cells with tabs or other document elements that the publisher can use. For more information, see the "Converting Tables to Text" section, later in this chapter.

CREATING NEAT ROWS AND COLUMNS WITH THE INSERT TABLE BUTTON

In many tables, each column is the same width, and each row is the same height. Word makes it easy to create tables such as these. If you need to make modifications later—perhaps adjusting the width of just one column—it's easy to do.

→ For more information about changing the width of a table, **see** "Controlling the Width of Columns," **p. 421**.

To create a table in which each column is the same width and each row is the same height, follow these steps:

1. Click the Insert Table button in the Standard toolbar. A set of rows and columns appears under the button, similar to a shortcut menu.

2. Drag the mouse pointer down as many rows as you need. Word automatically adds rows as you drag. You see the number of rows highlighted as you go.

3. Still pressing the mouse button, drag the pointer across, covering as many columns as you need. Again, you see the number of columns highlighted (see Figure 12.1).

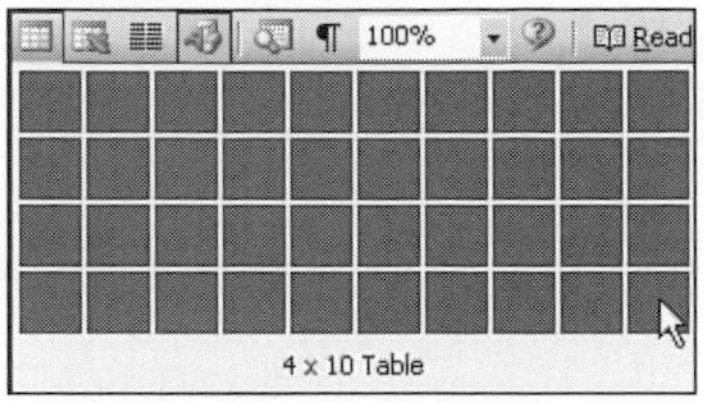

Figure 12.1
Clicking the Insert Table button displays a white grid of cells. Drag down and across to specify the number of rows and columns you want.

TIP

It helps to have a rough idea of how many rows and columns you'll ultimately need, but don't worry about it too much. After the table is created, it's easy to add and delete rows and columns.

4. When you are satisfied, let go of the mouse. Word creates a table, as shown in Figure 12.2.

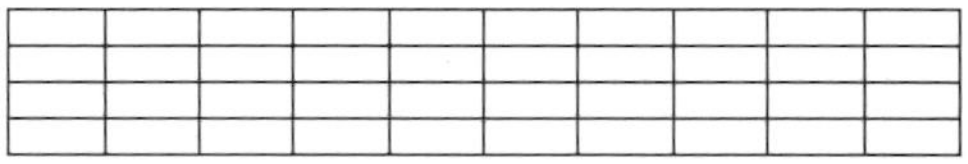

Figure 12.2
When you release the mouse pointer, the table appears in your document.

Word sets the height of each row in your table to match the height of surrounding paragraphs. By default, this is 12-point (in other words, six lines to an inch). However, if your surrounding paragraphs use different line-spacing settings, your tables match those instead.

Word sets the width of each column by calculating the width between the margins you've set and dividing that width equally among the number of columns you specify.

CONTROLLING COLUMN WIDTHS WHEN YOU CREATE A TABLE

Although you can change the width of a column anytime you want, sometimes you may want to set widths precisely as you insert the table—or tell Word how to automatically set them for you. To do so, use the Insert Table dialog box, as described here:

1. Click in your document where you want the table to appear.

2. Choose Table, Insert, Table, and the Insert Table dialog box appears (see Figure 12.3).

3. Specify the Number of Columns and Number of Rows you want in the table.

4. Next, specify column width, choosing one of three options:

   • You can set a precise width to be used by all the columns in your table by clicking in the Fixed Column Width scroll box and entering (or scrolling to) the value there, which is set in inches by default.

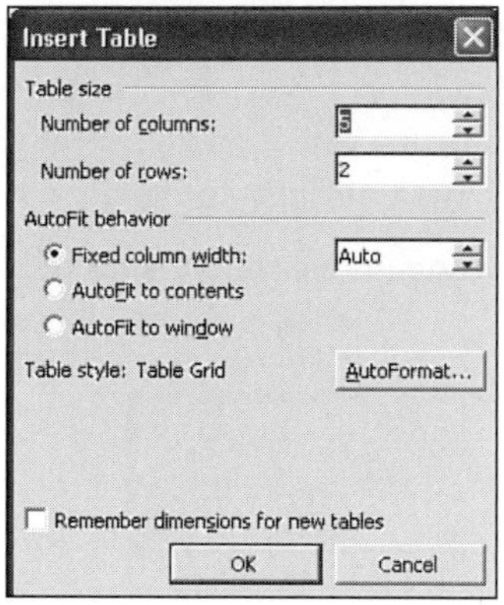

Figure 12.3
Inserting a table using the Insert Table dialog box.

- You can choose AutoFit to Contents, which enables Word to widen or narrow columns based on the contents you insert in them. Word adjusts the columns as you type within the cells. This feature works in regular Word documents as well as documents saved as Web pages.

- You can choose AutoFit to Window, which adjusts the width of every cell based on the width of the screen of the individual viewing it. For example, if you change your monitor from displaying at 640×480 to 800×600, your cells widen. This feature works only with documents saved as Web pages and viewed from within Word or a Web browser.

5. If you want to use one of Word's built-in AutoFormats to format your table now, click AutoFormat and work in the AutoFormat dialog box. (This feature is covered later in the chapter, in the section "Using Table Styles to AutoFormat a Table.")

6. If the settings you've established reflect the way you'll usually want your tables to look, check the Remember Dimensions for New Tables check box.

7. When you're finished, click OK. Word inserts your table into your document.

NOTE

After you create a table, it's easy to change its AutoFit setting. Select the table; choose Table, AutoFit; and choose whichever setting you prefer: AutoFit to Contents, AutoFit to Window, or Fixed Column Width.

TIP

A quick way to AutoFit a column containing a single word or number is to double-click the column boundary at its right. When cells contain multiple words or numbers, each double-click expands the column incrementally until all the data fits on a single line.

12

DRAWING TABLES FREEHAND WITH WORD'S DRAW TABLE FEATURE

Word provides an even more intuitive way to insert tables: You can simply draw them with your mouse, much as you might draw them with a pencil on a piece of paper. Don't worry if you can't draw a straight line; Word straightens your lines for you.

Draw Table is ideal for creating tables that contain uneven columns or rows—similar to the table you see in Figure 12.4.

Figure 12.4
Using the Draw Table feature, you can easily create a table similar to this one.

Region and State		1998			
		Q1	Q2	Q3	Q4
E	New York	320	310	302	343
a	Massachusetts	222	236	239	256
s	Maine	243	240	225	232
t	New Hampshire	261	275	230	260
	Region Total	1046	1061	996	1091
W	California	334	380	392	418
e	Oregon	267	290	299	311
s	Nevada	276	276	289	302
t	Region Total	877	946	980	1031
Company Total		1923	2007	1986	2122

To draw a table, follow these steps:

1. Click the Tables and Borders button on the Standard toolbar. If you're not there already, Word switches to Print Layout view and displays the Tables and Borders toolbar. (Most of this toolbar's buttons remain gray until you create a table.) See Table 12.1, later in the chapter, for a description of each button on the Tables and Borders toolbar.

2. Click in the document where you want to begin drawing the table. The mouse pointer icon changes to a pencil.

3. Drag the mouse pointer down and to the right margin until the outline that you see while dragging appears to be the approximate size you want for the outside boundaries of the table.

4. When you release the mouse button, the insertion point appears inside the table, which looks like a box; the Tables and Borders toolbar also appears, as shown in Figure 12.5.

You now have a table consisting of one large *cell* (the intersection of a row and a column). To create multiple cells that appear in rows and columns, you can draw additional columns and rows inside the original cell, roughly where you want them to appear. As long as you start or finish the lines near a cell border, Word automatically extends and straightens lines that you've drawn only part way. Word provides a visual cue to tell you whether you've connected to a border: When you have, the border is temporarily shaded blue.

NOTE

> If your lines come nowhere near an existing cell border, Word may insert a nested table instead—a second table within a table. If this isn't what you want, click Undo to back up a step.

Insertion point inside one-cell table

Figure 12.5
Drawing a table.

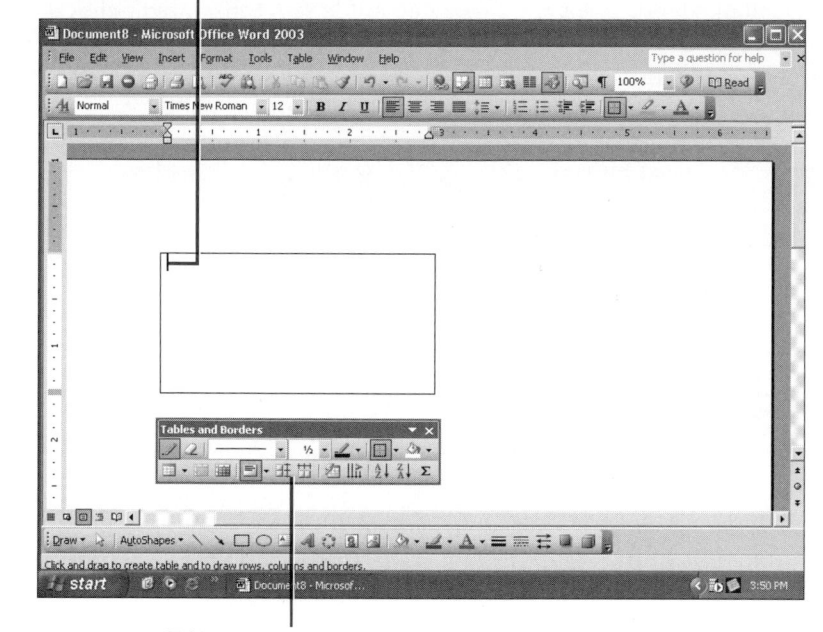

Tables and Borders toolbar

If you draw a line where you don't want one, click the Eraser button on the Tables and Borders toolbar and drag across the line until it disappears.

You can also use Draw Table to draw diagonal lines that extend across an individual cell. To do so, click the Draw Table toolbar button; then click in one corner of a cell and drag to the other corner.

You can use diagonal lines to call attention to the fact that a cell contains no data, as shown in Figure 12.6. Notice that drawing diagonal lines does not actually divide a rectangular cell into smaller triangular cells: If you type in the cell, your text will overlap the diagonal line.

Diagonal line in a table cell

Figure 12.6
Creating diagonal
lines in a table cell.

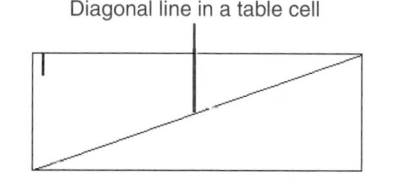

When you finish drawing the table's rows and columns, click the Draw Table toolbar button again, and your mouse pointer reverts to its normal state. You can now edit or format the table as you want (or work elsewhere in the document).

Now that you have a table, you can polish it any way you want. For example, if you want several of your columns to be the same width, select them, right-click on them, and choose Distribute Columns Evenly from the shortcut menu. Or, after you enter text in a cell, you can turn that text sideways by clicking Change Text Direction on the Tables and Borders toolbar. Table 12.1 shows the options available on this toolbar.

TABLE 12.1   THE TABLES AND BORDERS TOOLBAR

Button	Function
	Draws a table.
	Erases borders in a table.
	Specifies the style of line used when drawing.
	Specifies the thickness of the line used when drawing.
	Specifies the color of the line used when drawing.
	Specifies where borders should appear around a cell, group of cells, or table.
	Specifies a cell shading color.
	Displays the Table shortcut menu, offering choices for inserting columns, rows, and cells, and controlling column width.
	Merges selected cells.
	Splits a selected cell into multiple cells.
	Enables you to choose the alignment of text in a cell or cells you select.
	Formats the rows you select with equal heights.
	Formats the columns you select with equal widths.
	Displays the AutoFormat dialog box, where you can choose how you want to automatically format the table.
	Changes the direction of text in a cell.
	Sorts selected entries in ascending order (A–Z).
	Sorts selected entries in descending order (Z–A).
	Adds the values above or to the left of the cell containing the insertion point and inserts the sum in the cell in which you've clicked.

In addition to the Tables and Borders toolbar, you can find tools for working with tables in the Table menu and in the Table shortcut menu that appears whenever you right-click inside a table (see Figure 12.7).

Figure 12.7
The Table shortcut menu appears whenever you right-click inside a table.

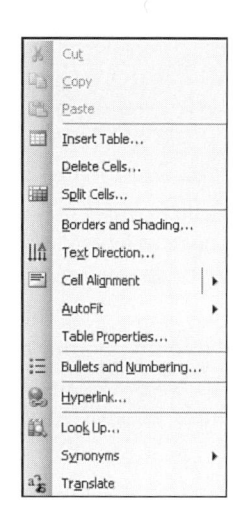

CREATING A TABLE FROM THE KEYBOARD

If you're more comfortable working with the keyboard, you can also type a pattern that represents the kind of table you want, with plus signs corresponding to cell borders and minus signs corresponding to units of width within a cell. Here is an example:

```
+-----+-----+-----+
```

After you type the line, press Enter. Word inserts a one-row table. Each cell is the same width as the number of hyphens you typed between plus signs.

NOTE

If this feature does not work, make sure it is turned on in the AutoFormat As You Type tab of the AutoCorrect dialog box. Choose Tools, AutoCorrect Options; click the AutoFormat As You Type tab; check the Tables check box; and click OK.

CREATING SIDE-BY-SIDE TABLES

Word can create tables that appear side by side on your page, as shown in Figure 12.8.

To create two tables on the same line, follow these steps:

1. Insert the first table using Draw Table on the Tables and Borders toolbar, or the Insert Table dialog box (choose Table, Insert, Table).

Figure 12.8
An example of side-by-side tables.

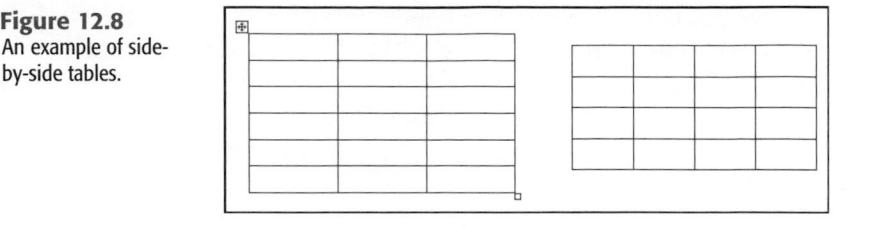

CAUTION

Don't use the Insert Table button on the Standard toolbar–it uses up all the space between your left and right margins, leaving no room for another table.

2. To the right of the existing table, use Draw Table to draw another table. Word inserts the table with a .5" border and adds unbordered table cells between the two tables (creating the illusion of a second table but actually simply extending the first table).

CREATING NESTED TABLES

Word enables you to create tables within tables, called *nested tables*. This technique is primarily used in building Web pages. It can give you more control over the appearance of your table, by allowing you to more precisely control where information in your table appears. Sample nested tables are shown in Figure 12.9.

Figure 12.9
An example of nested tables.

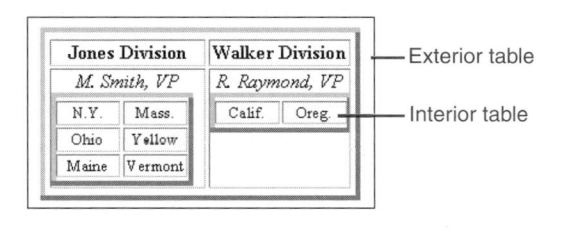

— Exterior table

— Interior table

12

To create a nested table within an existing table, first click inside the table where you want the nested table to appear. Then create a new table, using any of Word's table creation tools: the Insert Table button on the Standard toolbar, the Draw Table button on the Tables and Borders toolbar, or the Insert Table dialog box.

CAUTION

If you're concerned about how quickly your Web pages will display on browsers, use nested tables sparingly; they tend to display more slowly than ordinary tables. In particular, avoid creating complex nested tables. Especially avoid nesting tables within other nested tables.

TIP

> You can copy existing nested tables into Word from a Web browser and edit them to meet your needs. Nested tables copy into Word with surprising fidelity.

EDITING IN A TABLE

After you create a new empty table, the next step is to put something in it—and that can be anything you want: text, graphics, you name it.

When Word creates a new table, it positions the insertion point in the table's first cell. Typing in a table is similar to typing anywhere else in a document, with a few significant exceptions. Unless you selected AutoFit to Contents when you created the table, when you reach the right edge of a cell, Word wraps text back to the left edge, as if you were at the end of a line. Also, some keystrokes behave differently within a table. In particular, pressing Tab within a table cell moves you to the next cell; if you need a conventional tab, press Ctrl+Tab instead.

Within a cell, you can enter paragraph marks or line breaks the same way you normally do: Press Enter to add a paragraph mark, or Shift+Enter to add a line break. These breaks add lines to the row the cell is in and to all other cells in the same row, as shown in Figure 12.10. (To view paragraph marks and line breaks within cells, click the Paragraph button on the Standard toolbar.)

Figure 12.10
Adding line breaks within a cell.

Paragraph mark

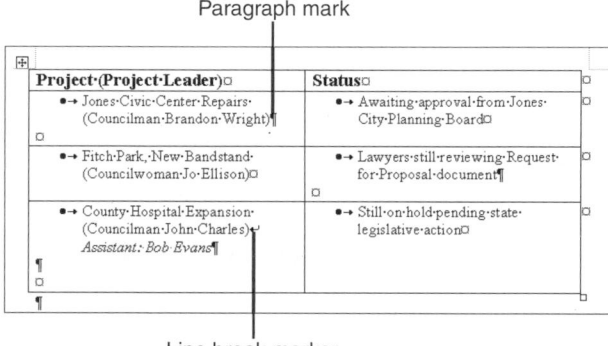

Line break marker

To move within a table, click the cell to which you want to go. Word also offers many keyboard shortcuts. For example, Tab moves you to the next cell; Shift+Tab moves you back. A complete list of keyboard navigation shortcuts appears in Table 12.2.

TABLE 12.2   KEYBOARD SHORTCUTS FOR NAVIGATING WITHIN TABLES

This Key	Moves the Insertion Point
Up arrow	Up one line within a cell. If at the top of a cell, moves up one cell. If already at the top of the table, moves one line above the table.

continues

TABLE 12.2	CONTINUED
This Key	**Moves the Insertion Point**
Tab	To the next cell.
Shift+Tab	To the preceding cell.
Down arrow	Down one line within a cell. If at the bottom of a cell, moves down one cell. If already at the bottom of the table, moves one line below the table.
Left arrow	Left one character within a cell. If at the beginning of a cell, moves to the end of the preceding cell.
Right arrow	Right one character within a cell. If at the end of a cell, moves to the start of the next cell.
Home	To the beginning of the current line in the current cell.
End	To the end of the current line in the current cell.
Alt+Home	To the beginning of the first cell in the current row.
Alt+End	To the end of the last cell in the current row.
Alt+Page Up	To the beginning of the first cell in the current column.
Alt+Page Down	To the beginning of the last cell in the current column.

TIP

If you are building a list of names in table format, Word capitalizes them automatically for you, by default. If you do not want this to happen, toggle this AutoCorrect setting off. Choose Tools, AutoCorrect Options; display the AutoCorrect tab; and clear the Capitalize First Letter of Table Cells check box.

12

CHANGING A TABLE'S STRUCTURE OR FORMATTING

As you begin to edit the contents of your table, you may find that you want to adjust its structure or formatting. This may include

- Changing the column widths and row heights, perhaps to accommodate more or less information than you originally anticipated, or to adjust Word's automatic settings.
- Adding or deleting rows or columns, again to accommodate more information (or less).
- Merging two or more cells into one, perhaps to create complex table designs that are often used in forms.
- Splitting one cell into two or more.
- Changing the appearance of individual cells or the entire table.

When you create a table, it takes on the character and paragraph formatting of the paragraph preceding it. In other words, if the preceding paragraph uses Times New Roman 14-point type, double-spaced, so will your table unless you change it. You can change any of this formatting by using any of the character and paragraph formatting techniques discussed in Chapter 4, "Quick and Effective Formatting Techniques."

SELECTING PART OR ALL OF A TABLE

As with other formatting tasks in Word, your first step is often to select the elements of the table you want to change. You need to know a few special techniques to select part or all of a table.

You can use the following techniques to select elements of a table:

- To select a column, move the mouse pointer over the top of the column. When the mouse pointer changes to a black arrow pointing downward, click the mouse. Or click anywhere in the column you want to select, and choose Table, Select, Column.

- To select a row, move the mouse pointer to the immediate left edge of the row. Click when the pointer changes to a black arrow pointing up and to the right. Or click anywhere in the row you want to select, and choose Table, Select, Row.

- To select a cell, move the mouse pointer to the left boundary of the cell. When the pointer changes to a black arrow pointing up and to the right, click. Or click inside the cell and choose Table, Select, Cell.

- To select a block of cells, click in the upper-left cell you want to select and drag the mouse pointer across all the other cells you want to select, highlighting them. Or select the first cell, row, or column you want to select, and press Shift as you select the last cell, row, or column you want to select. Make sure that you don't click and drag until the cursor changes; otherwise, you may inadvertently resize your row or column.

- To select the entire table, hover the mouse pointer over the table or click anywhere inside it; a table selection icon appears at the upper-left corner of the table (see Figure 12.11). Click the table selection icon.

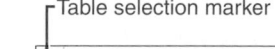
Table selection marker

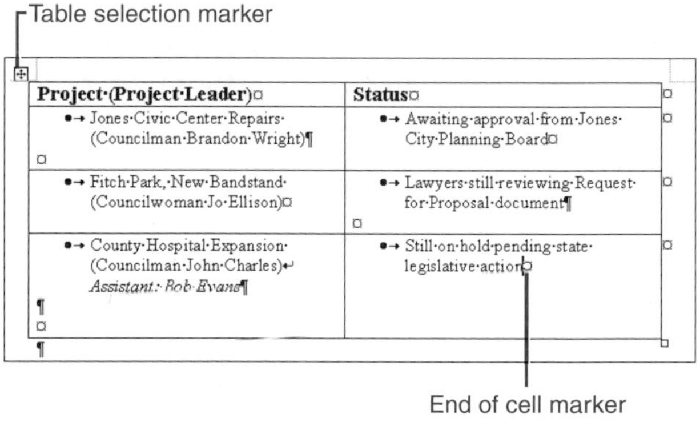

Figure 12.11
When you hover your mouse pointer over a table, a table selection icon appears at the upper left of the table.

Project (Project Leader)	Status
• → Jones Civic Center Repairs (Councilman Brandon Wright)¶	• → Awaiting approval from Jones City Planning Board
• → Fitch Park, New Bandstand (Councilwoman Jo Ellison)	• → Lawyers still reviewing Request for Proposal document¶
• → County Hospital Expansion (Councilman John Charles)↵ Assistant: Rob Evans¶	• → Still on hold pending state legislative action

End of cell marker

 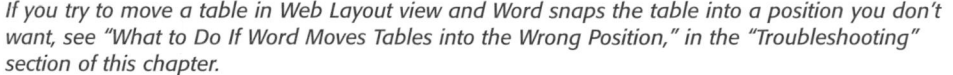

If you try to move a table in Web Layout view and Word snaps the table into a position you don't want, see "What to Do If Word Moves Tables into the Wrong Position," in the "Troubleshooting" section of this chapter.

12

SELECTING PART OR ALL OF A CELL

Thus far, you've learned to select entire cells, rows, columns, and tables. However, at times you want to select only the text within a specific cell, not the entire cell. For example, if you copy an entire cell to another location in your document, you create a new one-cell table. Often, however, that's not what you intend: You want to copy the contents of the table cell, not the cell itself.

As shown previously in Figure 12.11, every cell in a Word table contains an end-of-cell marker. To avoid copying the cell itself, you must avoid copying this marker.

To see end-of-cell markers in your table, click the Show/Hide Paragraph Marks button on the Standard toolbar. As you type in a cell, the end-of-cell marker moves to stay just ahead of your typing.

Pay attention to end-of-cell markers when you format your tables. When an end-of-cell marker is selected, your formatting affects the entire table cell surrounding it. When an end-of-cell marker is not selected, your formatting affects only the text or graphics within that cell.

INSERTING ADDITIONAL ROWS, COLUMNS, AND CELLS

You may sometimes want to add a new row, column, or block of cells to your table. For example, in a year-to-date financial report, you might need to add a column containing the latest month's results, or a row reflecting the addition of a new department or sales channel. Word makes this easy.

INSERTING NEW ROWS

To add a new row to the bottom of your table, position your insertion point in the last cell and press Tab. A new row appears in the same format as the preceding row.

To add a new row anywhere else in your table, select the row where you want a new row to be placed. The standard Table toolbar button changes to an Insert Row button. Clicking the Insert Row button inserts a row above the row you selected. Alternatively, you can right-click on a table row and choose Insert Rows from the shortcut menu. (This option is available only when a table row is selected.)

Whichever method you choose, a new row appears, using the height, widths, and formatting of the row in which your insertion point is currently located. Other rows are pushed down to make room.

If you want to insert a row below the one you've selected, choose Table, Insert, Rows Below.

TIP

> You can insert several rows at the same time by selecting the same number of rows in the table, before you choose the menu command to insert rows. In other words, if you select six rows before choosing Table, Insert, Rows Above, Word places six empty rows above the rows you selected.

INSERTING NEW COLUMNS

To add a new column within your table, select a column to the right of the location where you want your new column. The Insert Table button in the Standard toolbar changes to an Insert Column button. Click it, and the new column is inserted; the other column widths are adjusted to compensate, so the entire table is no wider than it was before.

If you do not want to change the widths of existing columns when you insert a new one, there is a different procedure to follow. If you want the new column to appear to the left of the column you selected, choose Table, Insert, Columns to the Left. If you want the column to appear to the right, choose Table, Insert, Columns to the Right.

A new column appears where you specified, and columns to the right of it are pushed further to the right to make room. To add a new column at the right edge of your table, select the column at the far right of the existing table and choose Table, Insert, Columns to the Right.

When you insert a new column, it takes the same formatting as the column you selected before inserting it.

TIP

As with rows, you can insert several columns at the same time by selecting the same number of columns in the table, before you choose the menu command to insert columns.

TIP

Often, you'll want to insert a column containing a list of consecutive numbers, such as serial numbers. Use Table, Insert, Columns to the Left to insert a blank column. Then, with the blank column selected, click the Numbering icon on the Formatting toolbar.

12

INSERTING NEW CELLS

You also can insert cells anywhere within a table. Select a cell adjacent to where you want your new cell to appear. The Insert Table button on the Standard toolbar changes to the Insert Cells button. Click it, and the Insert Cells dialog box appears, as shown in Figure 12.12.

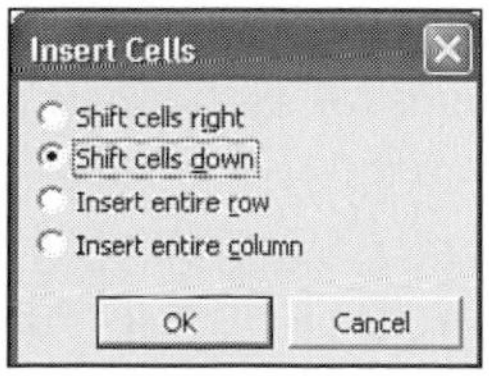

Figure 12.12
Telling Word how you want it to insert cells.

Insert Cells

- ○ Shift cells right
- ● Shift cells down
- ○ Insert entire row
- ○ Insert entire column

[OK] [Cancel]

NOTE

You can also display the Insert Cells dialog box from the Tables and Borders toolbar. If the Tables and Borders toolbar is displayed, click the down arrow next to the Insert Table button, and choose Insert Cells from the shortcut menu.

Tell Word where you want to move the cells you are displacing: Shift Cells Right or Shift Cells Down. If this is what you want, click OK in the dialog box to confirm. Some of the time, you may want to make further adjustments. For instance, you might really want to add an entire row or column, so Word also offers those options.

If you choose to Shift Cells Right or Shift Cells Down, Word shifts only these cells— leaving you with a table that has additional cells in some rows or columns, as shown in Figure 12.13.

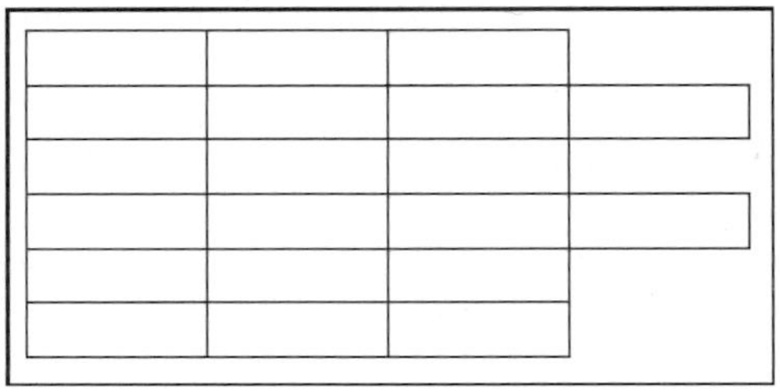

Figure 12.13
A table with extra cells in some rows.

CAUTION

If you intend to perform calculations that use cell references in your table, be careful about adding or removing cells from rows; this can make it difficult to accurately identify cells in your formulas.

Deleting Rows, Columns, or Cells

Word makes it easy to delete portions of a table—or the entire table. Simply click one of the cells you want to delete, or (if you are deleting more than one row or column) select all the rows and columns you want to delete. Then,

- To delete the column in which your insertion point is (or all the columns you've selected), choose Table, Delete, Columns; or select the column, right-click, and choose Delete Column from the shortcut menu.
- To delete the row in which your insertion point is (or all the rows you've selected), choose Table, Delete, Rows; or select the row, right-click, and choose Delete Row from the shortcut menu.
- To delete the entire table, choose Table, Delete, Table; or select the table by clicking on the icon at its upper left, and press Backspace or Delete.

To delete individual cells, select them, right-click, and choose Delete Cells from the short-cut menu. A dialog box appears, asking you how to adjust the table after deleting the cells (see Figure 12.14). Be aware that you can inadvertently create a lopsided table by deleting single cells, thereby leaving fewer cells in one row or column than are contained in the other rows or columns in the table.

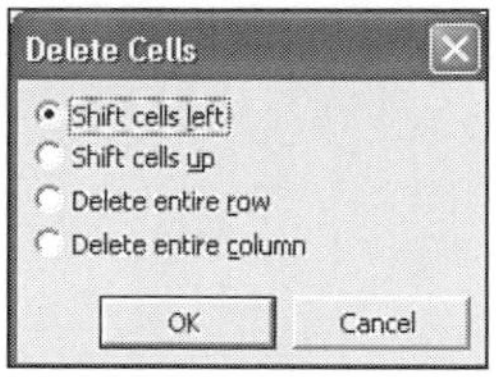

Figure 12.14
Choose the adjust-ment you want to make to the table's structure after you delete a single cell.

MERGING AND SPLITTING CELLS

Occasionally, you create a table with information in separate cells that you later decide should be merged into a single cell. Perhaps you realize that there isn't enough width to create all the columns you wanted, but you do have room to extend the information verti-cally, in deeper rows.

Merging cells solves this problem. Select the cells you want to merge and choose Table, Merge Cells; or from the Tables and Borders toolbar, click the Merge Cells button; or right-click and choose Merge Cells from the shortcut menu.

Word combines all the selected cells in each row into a single cell. The information that originally was in separate cells is separated with a paragraph marker within each new cell. The new cell is the same width as all the previous cells combined and can be adjusted with any of Word's column width tools. The overall width of the row is not changed; nor are the widths of other cells in the same column that you did not select.

Figure 12.15 and Figure 12.16 show a typical before-and-after example of using Merge Cells.

NOTE

> You can also merge cells from two rows, or merge cells in both rows and columns at the same time. It always works the same way: Select the cells you want to merge, and then choose Merge Cells from the menu, shortcut menu, or Tables and Borders toolbar.

Conversely, you may sometimes find that you need to split one table cell into two, perhaps to customize a form or some other complex layout. To do so, follow these steps:

1. Right-click inside the table cell you want to split.
2. Choose Split Cells from the shortcut menu. Word displays the dialog box you see in Figure 12.17.

12

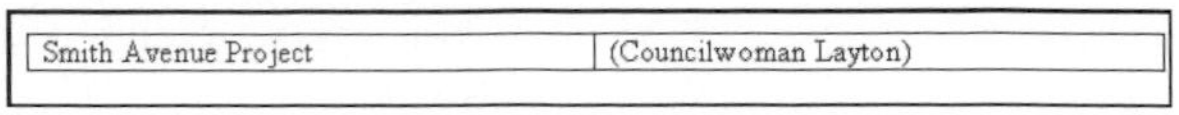

Figure 12.15
Cells before merging…

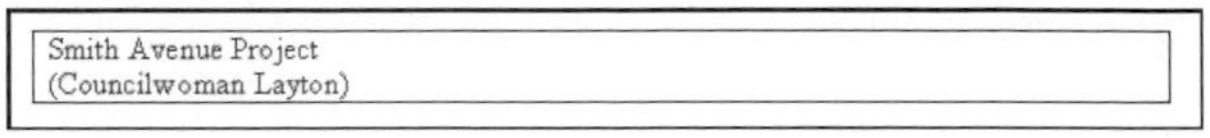

Smith Avenue Project	(Councilwoman Layton)

Figure 12.16
…and after merging.

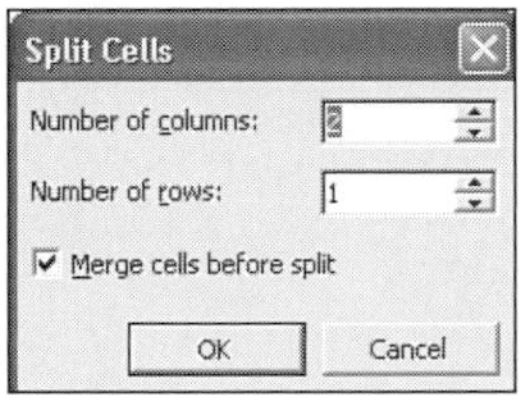

Smith Avenue Project
(Councilwoman Layton)

Figure 12.17
Use this dialog box to split cells in a table.

Split Cells

Number of columns: 2

Number of rows: 1

☑ Merge cells before split

OK   Cancel

3. In the Number of Columns scroll box, specify into how many columns you want to split the cell.

4. In the Number of Rows scroll box, specify into how many rows you want to split the cell.

5. Click OK. Word divides the cell you've chosen into the number of rows and columns specified.

All the text that appeared in the original cell now appears in the first cell, unless one or more paragraph marks appeared in the original cell. In that case, Word will follow your paragraph marks, placing text after the first paragraph mark into the second cell, text after the next paragraph mark into the next cell, and so forth.

TIP

You can use this technique to quickly create an entire table with rows and columns of equal size. Use the Draw Table toolbar button to draw a large one-cell table, and use Split Cells to create the correct number of rows and columns, while retaining the overall dimensions of the table.

CUTTING OR COPYING TABLE INFORMATION

To move or copy information from one cell to another, select the text and use standard drag-and-drop methods (drag to move, Ctrl+drag to copy), or use the Cut, Copy, and Paste commands. To replace the contents of the destination cell, select the entire source cell, including its end-of-cell marker. To retain the contents of the destination cell, select text but not the end-of-cell marker in the source cell.

If the text you move or copy contains character formatting, both the text and its formatting appear in the destination cell; however, you cannot move or copy any cell formatting, even if you include end-of-cell markers. Cell formatting includes borders, shading, text alignment, and text direction.

You can also use standard drag-and-drop or Cut, Copy, and Paste commands to move entire rows or columns by selecting entire rows or columns before you move. When you move or copy a row or column, Word automatically overwrites the destination cells with the source information because the source selection contains end-of-cell markers.

COPYING AND MOVING ENTIRE TABLES

After you have a table looking the way you want, you might want to copy or move it elsewhere in your document. To do so, choose Table, Select, Table to select the table. Then cut or copy it, and paste the table using whatever methods you prefer.

Word also enables you to move or copy entire tables by dragging and dropping them:

- To move a table, click and hold the selection handle at its upper-left corner, drag the table to its new location, and release the selection handle.
- To copy a table, click and hold the selection handle at its upper-left corner, press and hold the Ctrl key, drag the table to its new location, and release the selection handle.

TIP

You can select a formatted table and store it as an AutoText entry, making it easy to insert anytime you want. Choose Table, Select, Table; then choose Insert, AutoText, New. Enter a one-word name for the AutoText entry in the Create AutoText dialog box and click OK.

ADDING TABLE BORDERS AND SHADING

12

You can format tables with borders and shading any way you want, calling attention to specific cells or headings.

NOTE

Don't overdo borders and shading. For instance, if you have a table in which all the cells contain approximately the same amount of text, try simply placing one horizontal line under the headings and another at the end of the table. The whitespaces formed by the cell padding can create the illusion of vertical lines separating the columns.

This works best on tables when the cell contents within each column are relatively close to the same widths.

CONTROLLING THE BORDERS OF TABLES AND INDIVIDUAL CELLS

By default, Word inserts tables with a .5-point border around each cell. You can adjust or remove these borders, or specify which cells are bordered and which ones are not.

To work with the borders of a table, select the table by clicking the Select Table icon at the upper-left corner of the table, or by clicking inside the table and typing Alt+NumPad5 on your keyboard. You can also select specific cells for which you want to change bordering. Then choose Format, Borders and Shading, and choose the Borders tab (see Figure 12.18).

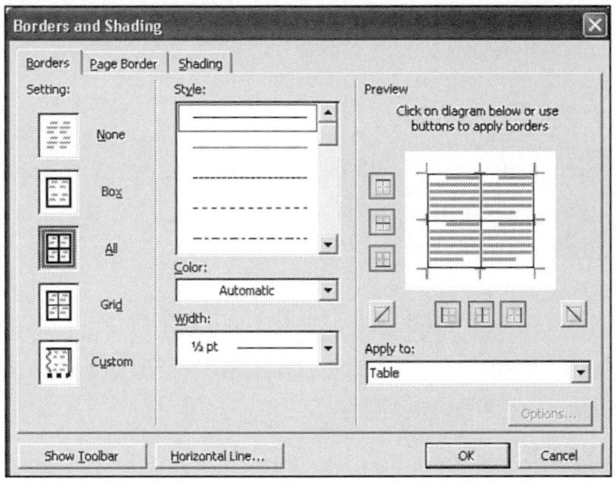

Figure 12.18
Working in the
Borders and Shading
dialog box.

TIP

> The Borders and Shading dialog box is also accessible by right-clicking on a table and choosing Borders and Shading from the shortcut menu.
>
> Yet another way to reach this dialog box is to choose Table, Table Properties; click the Table tab; and click Borders and Shading.

At the left, Word presents the border approaches it expects you to use most often: None, Box, All, Grid, and Custom.

- None clears all borders from the cells you've selected.
- Box places a border around the edges of the block of cells you've selected. If you select the entire table, a border appears around the outside edges of the table but not around each individual cell.
- All is the default setting. Word places a border at the top, bottom, left, and right of every cell you've selected.
- Like All, Grid places a .5-point border around the edge of the table. However, it allows you to specify a different border line around the edges of the table than is used around interior cells. For example, you might specify a 1.5-point border around the edges of the table, and a .5-point border around every cell.

The Grid and All boxes appear only if you choose multiple cells within a table and nothing else. If you choose one cell, or if you choose text inside and outside a table, the Shadow and 3-D boxes appear instead. Samples of Box, All, and Grid borders are shown in Figure 12.19.

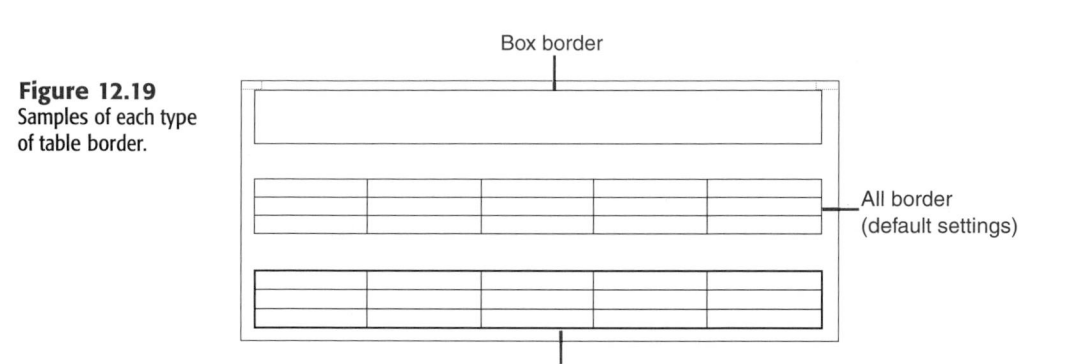

Box border

All border
(default settings)

Grid border (thicker outside border)

Figure 12.19
Samples of each type of table border.

You can also individually control the left, right, top, and bottom borders of your table or any cells within it. To set or clear the border of one side of a table, click the edge you want to change in the Preview box. If you've chosen to set the border, after you select it, you can control its appearance through the other tools in this tab: Style, Color, and Width.

You also can choose a color for your border. Click on the Color drop-down box and select from the options listed there (see Figure 12.20), or click More Line Colors to create a custom palette.

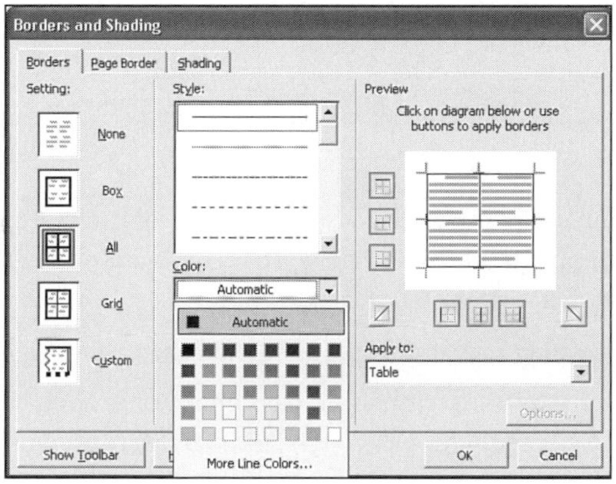

Figure 12.20
Choosing a line color.

Although Word has default settings for its boxes and grids, you can change them. To change the Box border, first select it and then choose a different border from the Style area.

To change the Grid area, first select it. To change the outside borders, choose a different border from the Style area. To change the inside borders of each individual cell, click in the middle of the thumbnail sketch and then choose a new border from the Style area.

12

NOTE

> If you use tables without borders, you may find it difficult to recognize where one cell ends and another begins. Choose Table, Show Gridlines to display light gray lines that show the edges of each cell onscreen but do not print.

CONTROLLING THE SHADING OF TABLES AND INDIVIDUAL CELLS

Often, you'll want to call attention to the contents of a specific cell or portion of a table. One of the most powerful ways to do so is with shading.

To use shading, select the cell or cells you want; then choose Format, Borders and Shading, and choose the Shading tab, as shown in Figure 12.21.

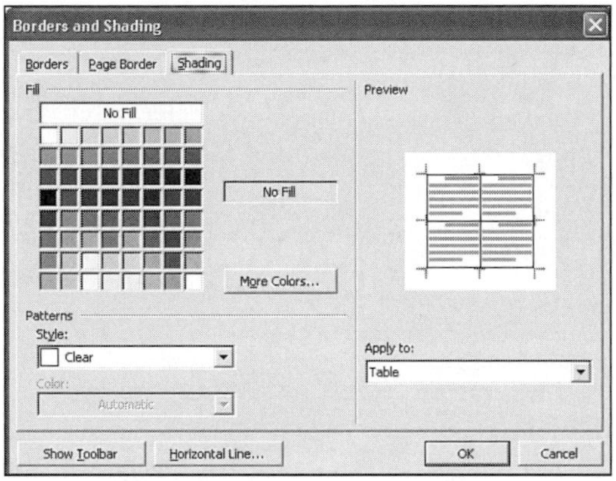

Figure 12.21
Creating shading for a table or specific cells.

To choose a color, click the color in the Fill area; the name of the color appears to the right, and a sample of the color appears in the Preview area. If you cannot find a satisfactory color, click More Colors to choose a custom color.

→ For more information about creating custom colors, **see** "Controlling Colors," **p. 497**.

You can also superimpose a pattern over a color. To choose one, click the Style drop-down box. The patterns showing percentages (5%, 10%, and so on) can be used to lighten the color you've selected. Additional patterns (such as Dk Horizontal and Lt Trellis) can be used as design elements.

NOTE

> Be careful with shading. Text that is printed over shading is much less readable—especially text printed over patterns such as Dk Horizontal.
>
> For most printers, unless the cell is intentionally left blank (as, for example, some cells on tax forms are), don't use more than 20% shading for text that is to be printed on a laser or inkjet printer. However, the higher the resolution of your printer, the more shading you can use without compromising readability.

If you are working on a Web page and you plan to add shading to individual cells, test the results on the browsers your site's visitors are likely to use. Some old browsers cannot recognize colors applied to only portions of a table.

CONTROLLING TABLE BREAKS AND TABLE HEADERS

Even after you create, edit, and format your table, you may need to take more control over it, and Word offers various techniques for taking that control. For example, you can

- Split one table into two
- Control where page breaks appear within tables
- Set a header that appears on every page of your table, even though you entered it in your document only once
- Resize all the rows and columns in a table instantly

In the next few sections, you learn these techniques, which give you more control over your tables than you've ever had before.

USING SPLIT TABLE TO ADD SPACE ABOVE OR BETWEEN TABLES

What if you need to split a table in order to place a paragraph of text between the top and bottom of the table? Use Word's Split Table feature. Click in the row you want to become the first row of the second table. Then choose Table, Split Table. Word divides the table into two tables and places the insertion point in a paragraph that appears between the two new tables.

> **TIP**
>
> Occasionally, you'll set up your entire table at the top of the page and then realize that you need to add text before the table. You can't move your insertion point in front of the table. Even moving to the beginning of the document (Ctrl+Home) doesn't do it. Word's Split Table feature solves the problem. Click in the upper-left cell of the table and choose Table, Split Table. Word adds a paragraph mark above the table and places the insertion point in that paragraph.
>
> Another way to add space before a table at the beginning of a document is to click the insertion point in the first cell and press Ctrl+Shift+Enter.

12

SPECIFYING RECURRING HEADERS

What happens when you have a table that continues for several pages, and you want each page to share the same headings? Use Word's Heading Rows Repeat feature.

This feature allows you to specify a heading row (or rows) that will appear on every page the table appears on. In other words, if a table jumps to a second page, the header rows will appear at the top of the second page; if the table continues on third pages, or beyond, the same header row(s) will appear at the top of those pages as well.

The heading row (or rows) you use must include the first row of the table. To create a repeating heading row, select the row you want to include in the repeating headers and choose Table, Heading Rows Repeat. Alternatively, you can work from the Table Properties dialog box. Choose Table, Table Properties (or right-click on the table and choose Table Properties from the shortcut menu). Click the Row tab; then check the Repeat as Header Row at the Top of Each Page check box.

PREVENTING ROWS FROM BREAKING ACROSS PAGES

Table rows can easily break across pages, leaving hard-to-understand text (or blank space) on the following page. Such "widow" and "orphan" lines can be difficult for readers to understand, especially if you haven't bordered the cells in your table. Fortunately, you can select specific rows (or an entire table) and tell Word to keep them on the same page. When you do so, Word will either squeeze all the rows you selected onto the previous page or move all of them together, to the top of the following page.

Right-click on the row you want to remain intact on one page. (Or, if you prefer, select several rows or the entire table and then right-click.) Next, choose Table Properties from the shortcut menu and click the Row tab. Clear the Allow Row to Break Across Pages check box and click OK.

Now, if one of the rows you selected does not fit entirely on the first page, Word jumps all the contents of that row onto the next page.

TIP

The procedure previously described allows you to keep the contents of a single row together on the same page. But what if you want to make sure *several* rows stay together on the same page? Use Word's Paragraph controls:

1. Select the contents of the rows you want to keep together.
2. Choose Format, Paragraph.
3. Choose the Line and Page Breaks tab.
4. Check Keep with Next.
5. Click OK.

TIP

If you don't mind breaking a table into two tables, you can separate the tables by inserting a manual page break (Ctrl+Enter) at the end of the row after which you want the break to be inserted.

The disadvantage: You can no longer use table selection, formatting, Header Rows Repeat, or sorting tools that assume you're working within a single table.

RESIZING YOUR TABLE AUTOMATICALLY

Often, you want to resize a table to fit a predefined space on a page. In some earlier versions of Word, this required manual resizing of individual rows and columns. In Word, you can resize every row and column in a single motion.

Hover your mouse pointer over the table you want to resize. At the lower-right corner of the table, a resizing handle appears. Drag the resizing icon until your table is the correct size. As you drag the icon, all column widths and row heights automatically adjust proportionally to the new size of the overall table (see Figure 12.22). Text within the table automatically rewraps to reflect the new column widths and row heights. The text, however, does not resize itself.

Figure 12.22
Dragging the table resize handle to resize a table.

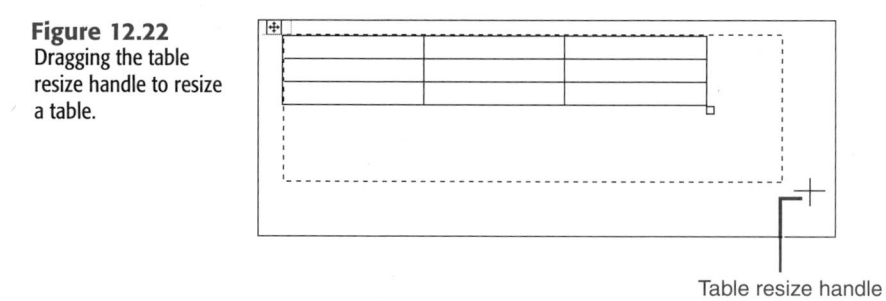

Table resize handle

If Word is resizing your table when you don't want it to, see "What to Do If Word Resizes Cells Inappropriately," in the "Troubleshooting" section of this chapter.

USING TABLE STYLES

Word's table styles feature makes it easier to reuse complex table formats after you've created them. Conceptually, table styles are similar to other Word styles: They allow you to store a set of formats and reapply them all at once. Table styles can incorporate

- Borders and shading
- Font, font size, font attributes, and font color
- Alignment of text or images within each cell
- Paragraph formatting, such as indents
- Table properties, such as alignment of the entire table, text wrapping, and whether rows can break between pages
- Whether stripes will appear in row or column bands
- Tab settings within table cells

Word provides dozens of sets of built-in table styles through the Table AutoFormat dialog box. These are covered in the following section. You can also create your own table styles. This is covered later, in the section "Creating a New Table Style."

USING TABLE STYLES TO AUTOFORMAT A TABLE

Formatting a table attractively can be a time-consuming task. Fortunately, Word can do it for you. You can automatically format your table by choosing from one of 45 prefabricated table styles available in Word.

12

To automatically format an existing table, place your insertion point anywhere inside the table and choose Table, Table AutoFormat. The Table AutoFormat dialog box appears, as shown in Figure 12.23.

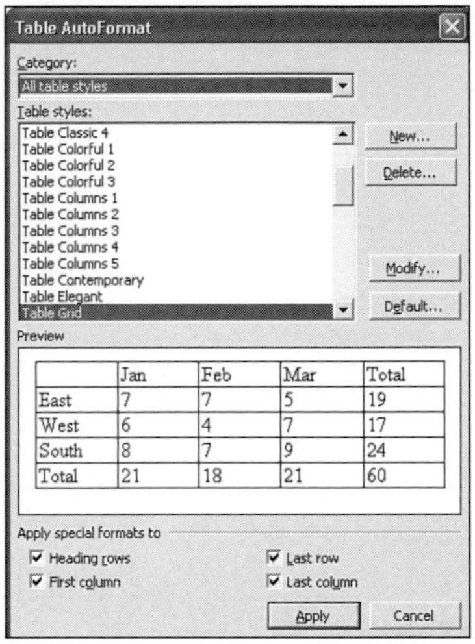

Figure 12.23
Choosing a table style from the Table AutoFormat dialog box.

Choose the table style you want to use, and click Apply. Figure 12.24 shows a table AutoFormatted with the Table Web 1 table style.

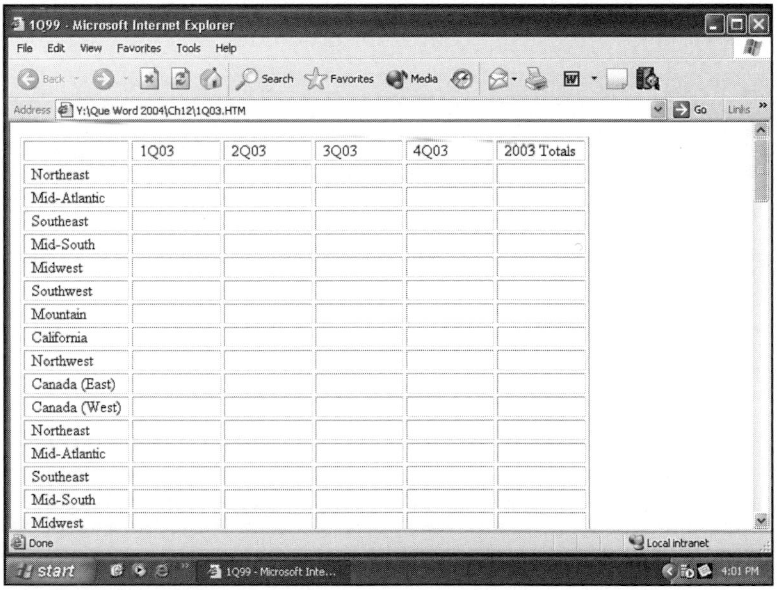

Figure 12.24
A table AutoFormatted in Word's Table Web 1 style and displayed in Internet Explorer 6.

TIP

If you want to apply a table style instantly, there's a shortcut that uses Word's default settings (and doesn't give you control over which rows and columns of your table are reformatted). Select the table, click the Styles and Formatting button on the Standard toolbar, and choose the table style from the Pick Formatting to Apply scroll box.

To AutoFormat a new table, choose Table, Insert, Table; set the number of rows and columns (and optionally the column width); then click AutoFormat. Then, to choose a table style, select it from the Table Styles list box. The style's built-in settings are shown in the Preview box.

By default, Table AutoFormat applies borders, shading, and font color from the built-in table style. It does not override other settings you may have applied manually, such as your choice of font, or how you've chosen to align text within cells.

Word's built-in table styles often include special formatting for Heading Rows and for the First Column. These are turned on by default. Word assumes that you are actually putting something special in the top row and first column—such as headings. If you are not, clear these check boxes. Word will then format the corresponding cells as it formats other cells containing ordinary data.

Alternatively, you might want the last row or column to contain special formatting; perhaps you're showing a total there. Check Last Row or Last Column to place special formatting there. Again, the Preview box shows you what to expect. When you have your AutoFormat the way you want it, click OK. (If you don't like the results, click Undo.)

CREATING A NEW TABLE STYLE

If none of Word's built-in table styles meets your needs, you can create your own or modify a table style Word provides. To do so, click inside a table and follow these steps:

1. Choose Table, Table AutoFormat.

2. If you want to create a new table style, click New. The New Style dialog box opens (see Figure 12.25). If you instead want to modify the settings associated with an existing table style, select it from the Table Styles list and choose Modify. Both the New Style and the Modify Style dialog boxes offer the same options, and they are both similar to the Style dialog boxes you learned about in Chapter 10, "Streamlining Your Formatting with Styles."

3. In the Name text box, enter the name of your new table style.

4. If you want to base your table style on one that already exists, choose the style from the Style Based On drop-down box. The Preview box changes to reflect the style you've chosen to work from.

5. Set the formats you want to include in your style, using the Apply Formatting To drop-down box and the associated formatting options. Again, the Preview box reflects the changes.

12

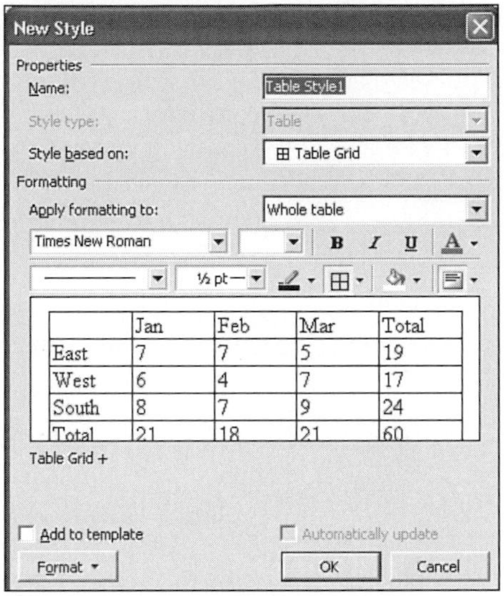

Figure 12.25
Creating a new table style from the New Style dialog box.

6. If you want greater control over the formatting of your table style, click the Format button. Then choose the category of formatting you want to adjust: Table Properties, Borders and Shading, Stripes, Font, Paragraph, or Tabs. Clicking any of these options opens its corresponding dialog box; make changes there and click OK to return to the New Style or Modify Style dialog boxes.

7. If you want to include the new table style in the template associated with your current document, check the Add to Template check box.

8. When you're finished establishing settings for your new table style, click OK. The new style now appears selected in the Table AutoFormat dialog box. If you want to use it on the table you've already selected, click Apply. Otherwise, click Close.

WORKING WITH TABLE PROPERTIES

Microsoft provides extensive control over tables through the Table Properties dialog box. From here, you can control all these options and more:

- Table height and width
- The height of individual rows
- The width of individual columns
- The alignment of your table on a printed or Web page
- Whether text should wrap around your table, and if so, how it should wrap
- The vertical alignment of text within individual cells
- Whether a header row should repeat across multiple pages
- Cell margins and whether any individual cells should have unique margins

The following sections walk you through the use of Table Properties—and in some cases, show you faster or easier ways to achieve the same goals.

SETTING THE PROPERTIES FOR AN ENTIRE TABLE

Word provides settings you can use to control the appearance or behavior of an entire table. To work with these settings, right-click on the table and choose Table Properties from the shortcut menu. Then click the Table tab, shown in Figure 12.26.

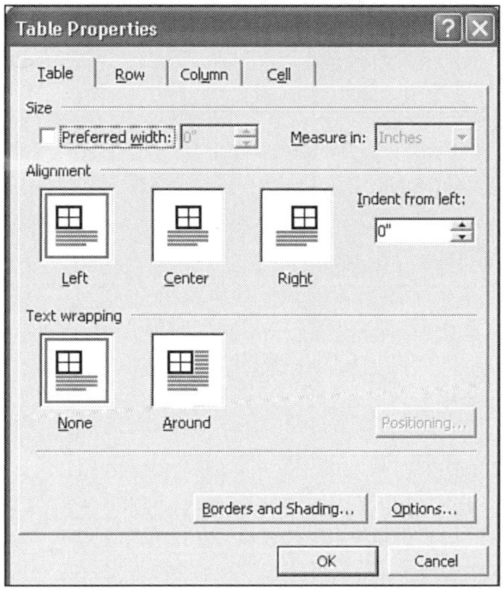

Figure 12.26
Controlling table settings that affect the entire table.

CONTROLLING THE PREFERRED WIDTH OF A TABLE

The first option in the Table tab allows you to specify a preferred width for your table—an overall table width that is to be used unless you choose other settings or display the table on a browser or monitor that makes your preferred width impossible to use. To set a preferred width for the entire table, check the Preferred Width check box and enter the width in the scroll box that appears next to it.

As with many of Word's measurement-related features, you can set your measurement either in inches or in percent—a percentage of the width of the screen. If you're creating a Web page, using percentages enables a viewer's browser to adjust how it displays your table so that the entire table is visible no matter what monitor (or monitor settings) your viewer is using. The browser formats the table as a percentage of the width available.

CAUTION

As always when creating Web pages, test your pages to see how they will actually display on the browsers and monitors you expect your site's visitors to use.

12

CONTROLLING THE ALIGNMENT OF A TABLE

By default, Word tables start at the left margin, but you can choose to start them anywhere on your page. If you're inserting a new table, you can use the Draw Table button on the Tables and Borders toolbar and start drawing the table anywhere on the page. No matter how you insert the table, however, you can adjust its alignment any way you want, using the Alignment settings on the Table tab of the Table Properties dialog box.

To specify whether your table is left-aligned, center-aligned, or right-aligned on the page, click the sample table above the Left, Center, or Right windows. Or, to set a precise indentation from the left margin, enter the value in the Indent from Left scroll box.

Using an Indent from Left setting is often the best way to get precise control over alignment because your table doesn't move unless you change the left margin. With centering, in contrast, your table adjusts every time the total width of all its columns changes. This tends to happen often.

NOTE

> These table alignment settings don't affect the alignment of text within each cell of a table. You can control horizontal text alignment using the same tools you use outside a table, including the Left Align, Center Align, and Right Align buttons on the Formatting toolbar.
>
> And, as you'll see later in this chapter, you can control vertical alignment of text within a cell by using the Cell tab of the Table Properties dialog box.

CONTROLLING TEXT WRAPPING AROUND A TABLE

Word permits you to run text around a table, just as you could if it were a graphic.

To do so, locate the Text Wrapping portion of the Table tab in the Table Properties dialog box, and click the Around table sample. After you click Around, the Positioning button becomes available.

To adjust how text wraps around your table, click Positioning; the Table Positioning dialog box appears, as shown in Figure 12.27.

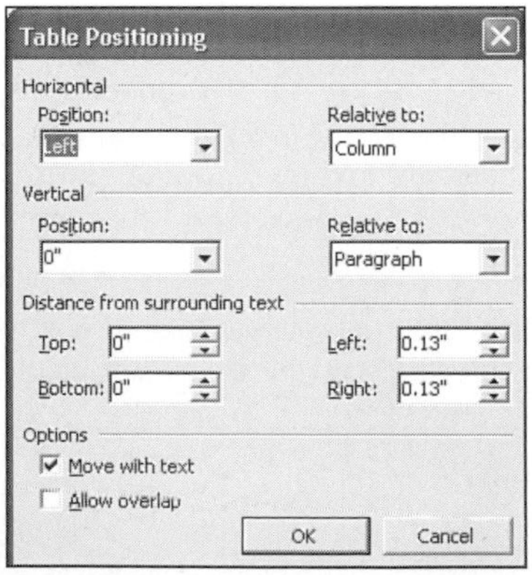

Figure 12.27
Controlling how text wraps around a table.

The Horizontal and Vertical controls specify where the table appears in relation to the surrounding text, and the Distance from Surrounding Text section of this dialog box controls how far text appears from the table when wrapping around it.

CONTROLLING THE HORIZONTAL RELATIONSHIP OF A TABLE TO SURROUNDING ELEMENTS By default, the Horizontal controls set the table so that it appears to the left of surrounding text. You can, however, choose Center or Right instead; these move the table to the center of the page or the right margin, respectively.

You can also set the Horizontal position to choose Inside and Outside; these settings move the table to the inside or outside the page and then adjust the location of the table automatically if an odd-numbered page becomes an even-numbered page, or vice versa.

For example, in most books, page 1 is a right-hand page; choosing Outside would display the table toward the right edge of that page. However, if you edit the book so that the table now appears on page 2, Word moves it automatically to the left edge of the page—and moves the surrounding copy to the right edge.

As covered in Chapter 5, "Controlling Page Features," Word enables you to create multiple-column documents, in which text snakes from the bottom of one column to the top of the next. This is a technique you might use in newsletters and magazines.

In one-column documents, of course, it makes no difference whether you measure a table from the margin of your current column or your page margin. In multiple-column documents, however, there is a difference—and Word allows you to control the position of your table in reference to either the column margin or the page margin.

Use the Relative To drop-down box to specify what you want Word to measure your table's position against: Margin, Page, or Column.

CONTROLLING THE VERTICAL RELATIONSHIP OF A TABLE TO SURROUNDING ELEMENTS The settings described in the preceding section cover the table's horizontal relationship to its surroundings; you can also control its vertical relationship. By default, the table and its surrounding text both start at the same point on a page, as shown in Figure 12.28. However, if you choose, you can specify that the table begin higher or lower by setting a different value in the Vertical Position combo box. For example, specifying .75" tells Word to insert .75" of the surrounding text before starting the table, as shown in Figure 12.29.

By default, this measurement is set off against the surrounding paragraphs of text, but you can tell Word to set the vertical position against the top or bottom page margin, or against the edge of the page itself. To do so, choose Margin, Page, or Paragraph in the Vertical Relative To scroll box.

CONTROLLING THE DISTANCE BETWEEN A TABLE AND SURROUNDING TEXT When you wrap text around a table, Word places no extra space above or below a table; it places .13" to the left or right of the table. Using the Table Positioning dialog box, you can change each of these settings by entering new values in the Top, Bottom, Left, and Right scroll boxes.

12

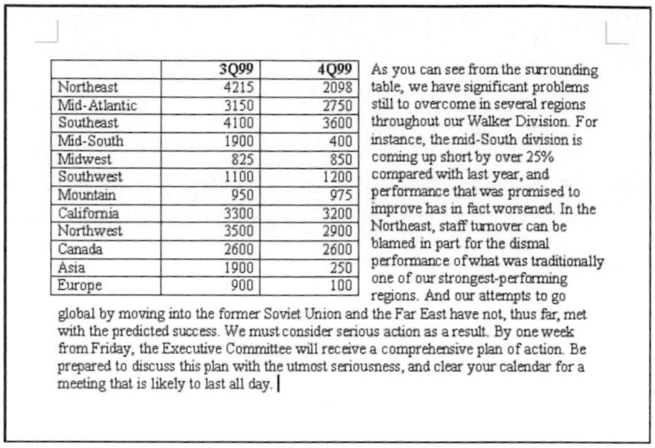

Figure 12.28
Word's default setting:
Table and text begin
together.

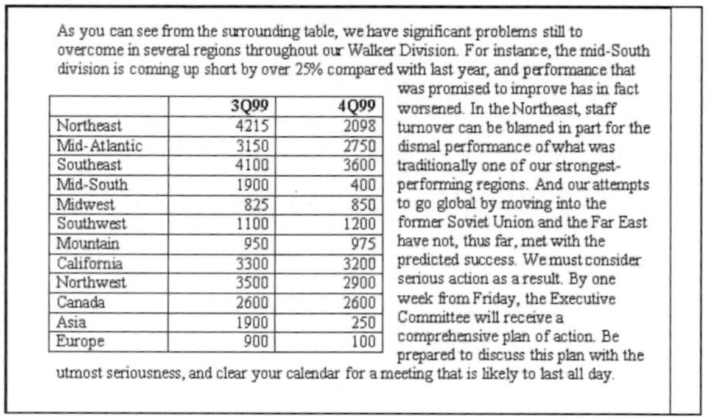

	3Q99	4Q99
Northeast	4215	2098
Mid-Atlantic	3150	2750
Southeast	4100	3600
Mid-South	1900	400
Midwest	825	850
Southwest	1100	1200
Mountain	950	975
California	3300	3200
Northwest	3500	2900
Canada	2600	2600
Asia	1900	250
Europe	900	100

As you can see from the surrounding table, we have significant problems still to overcome in several regions throughout our Walker Division. For instance, the mid-South division is coming up short by over 25% compared with last year, and performance that was promised to improve has in fact worsened. In the Northeast, staff turnover can be blamed in part for the dismal performance of what was traditionally one of our strongest-performing regions. And our attempts to go global by moving into the former Soviet Union and the Far East have not, thus far, met with the predicted success. We must consider serious action as a result. By one week from Friday, the Executive Committee will receive a comprehensive plan of action. Be prepared to discuss this plan with the utmost seriousness, and clear your calendar for a meeting that is likely to last all day.

Figure 12.29
Using Vertical Position
to start a table .75 "
lower on the page
than the surrounding

As you can see from the surrounding table, we have significant problems still to overcome in several regions throughout our Walker Division. For instance, the mid-South division is coming up short by over 25% compared with last year, and performance that was promised to improve has in fact worsened. In the Northeast, staff turnover can be blamed in part for the dismal performance of what was traditionally one of our strongest-performing regions. And our attempts to go global by moving into the former Soviet Union and the Far East have not, thus far, met with the predicted success. We must consider serious action as a result. By one week from Friday, the Executive Committee will receive a comprehensive plan of action. Be prepared to discuss this plan with the utmost seriousness, and clear your calendar for a meeting that is likely to last all day.

	3Q99	4Q99
Northeast	4215	2098
Mid-Atlantic	3150	2750
Southeast	4100	3600
Mid-South	1900	400
Midwest	825	850
Southwest	1100	1200
Mountain	950	975
California	3300	3200
Northwest	3500	2900
Canada	2600	2600
Asia	1900	250
Europe	900	100

Word moves your table *with* the surrounding text as you make edits to your document. If you want the table to remain anchored in a specific location even as surrounding paragraphs move, clear the Move with Text check box.

By default, Word prevents tables from overlapping text or pictures in documents saved as Web pages. If you want to permit overlap—perhaps for reasons of graphic design—check the Allow Overlap check box.

SETTING DEFAULT MARGINS FOR ALL THE CELLS IN A TABLE

Each cell in a Word table has its own left, right, top, and bottom margins: the space between the edge of text and the border of the cell. (In an HTML document, this is known as *cellpadding*.) By default, the top and bottom margins of cells are zero; the left and right margins are .08". Similarly, Word does not typically provide for any spacing between cells.

It's unlikely that you'll need to change these margins in printed documents, but many Web designers need more control over cell margins and spacing—and Word provides that control. To control these settings, return to the Table tab of the Table Properties dialog box and click the Options button. The Table Options dialog box appears (see Figure 12.30).

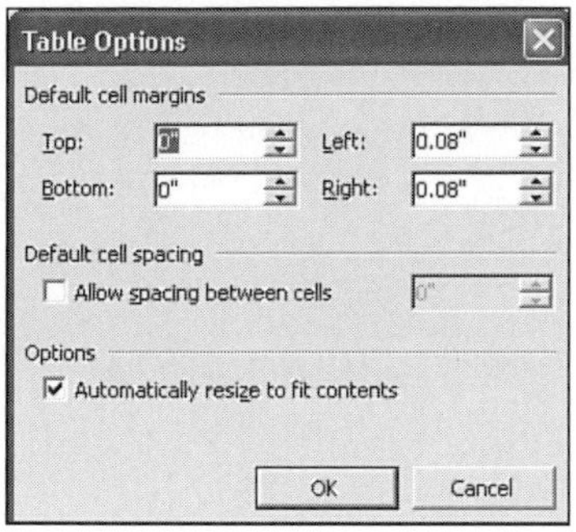

Figure 12.30
Make changes to your table in this dialog box.

To change the default cell margins in your current table, enter new values in the Top, Bottom, Left, or Right scroll boxes. To change Word's default setting of no spacing between cells, check the Allow Spacing Between Cells check box and enter a value in the scroll box next to it.

By default, Word automatically resizes columns in a table to accommodate the content you place in them—for example, extending a column as you type text too long to fit in it. If you don't like this feature—and many Word users find it annoying—clear the related check box.

Controlling the Height of Rows

By default, when you create a table, Word uses a row height of "one line." "One line" starts out equal to one line in the preceding paragraph. As you work within the table, "one line" can grow or shrink depending on the type size you use on each row. When Word shrinks or enlarges a row's height, it generally does so for all the cells in the row.

Word provides several ways to change row height. The first involves simply dragging the row's borders where you want them. This is visual and easy, but it works on only one row at a time—and unless your eye-hand precision is outstanding, it's also approximate. The second method takes you into the Table Properties dialog box, so it involves a few more steps; but it is highly precise and can control many rows (or an entire table) at once.

You might want to take a hybrid approach. First, manually adjust one row as described previously. Examine its properties to see the measurements you created. Then, display the Table Properties dialog box and change all rows to match the same measurement.

Changing a Row's Height by Dragging Its Borders

In Print Layout or Web Layout views, you can change the height of one row within a table by dragging its borders, as described here:

1. In the table, point the mouse pointer to the bottom of the row you want to change. The mouse pointer changes to display vertical arrows.
2. Click and drag the row's border up or down to shrink or enlarge the row's height.
3. Release the mouse pointer when you're finished.

TIP

You can also use the vertical ruler to move a row's border: Drag the dark gray band immediately to the left of the row you're adjusting.

TIP

If you want to see the exact measurements of rows or columns as you drag their borders, press the Alt key as you drag; the changing measurements will appear in the vertical or horizontal ruler.

CHANGING ROW HEIGHT THROUGH THE TABLE PROPERTIES DIALOG BOX

To change the height of table rows using the Table Properties dialog box, follow these steps:

1. Select the row or rows you want to adjust.
2. Choose Table, Table Properties.
3. Click the Row tab.
4. Check the Specify Height check box.
5. Enter the row height you want in the Specify Height scroll box.
6. In the Row Height Is drop-down box, choose whether Word must follow your row height Exactly, or whether Word can use your row height as a minimum (At Least).
7. If you want to control rows above the ones you selected, click Previous Row. If you want to control rows below the ones you selected, click Next Row.
8. When you're finished, click OK.

If Word is displaying only part of the text in a table cell, see "What to Do If Word Cuts Off the Tops of Letters in a Table Cell," in "Troubleshooting" at the end of this chapter.

MAKING SURE SEVERAL ROWS HAVE THE SAME HEIGHT

Sometimes, you're not that concerned with the precise height of rows in a table, but you do want them all to have the same height so that the table looks as professional as possible.

To accomplish this, first select the rows you want to adjust. Then choose Table, AutoFit, Distribute Rows Evenly. (Or, if the Tables and Borders toolbar is displayed, click the Distribute Rows Evenly button.)

Word reformats the rows you selected so that they are all the same height. If the rows are empty, or have text that is all the same size, Word distributes the rows so that they take up the same amount of height they did before; in short, if all the rows together were 3" high before, they will still be 3" high. However, if the rows contain text of differing sizes, Word distributes the rows to reflect the largest text so that no letters are cut off in any row—even if this means that some rows are much larger than necessary.

CONTROLLING THE WIDTH OF COLUMNS

Often, the column widths you set when you create your table need to be adjusted later, as you modify the content that goes into the table. For example, you may have created a descriptive first column followed by many shorter columns of numbers. Or, in a glossary, your first column might include just a word or a phrase, but your second column might include a detailed explanation.

Earlier in this chapter, you learned how to use AutoFit to enable Word to control your column widths. However, you sometimes need to control your column widths manually, and Word provides several ways to do so. As with rows, you can adjust column widths directly by dragging their borders, or via the ruler, or through the Table Properties dialog box.

CHANGING COLUMN WIDTH BY DRAGGING ITS EDGE

The easiest way to adjust a column's width is usually to drag the edge of the column with the mouse pointer. To do so, position the mouse pointer anywhere on the column's right gridline or border. Next, drag the gridline or border left or right to the location you want, and release the mouse pointer.

Unless you're adjusting the last column in your table, the width of the following column changes to compensate for the widening or narrowing you've just done, so your overall table retains the same width.

CHANGING COLUMN WIDTH USING THE HORIZONTAL RULER

You also can change column width in the horizontal ruler. As you can see in Figure 12.31, when you are within a table, the table's column borders are shown on the horizontal ruler. You can change these column borders by positioning the mouse pointer on the border shown in the ruler (avoiding the indent markers) and dragging to the new border that you want. The columns that follow shrink or enlarge to compensate, unless you are changing the last column.

CHANGING COLUMN WIDTH THROUGH THE TABLE PROPERTIES DIALOG BOX

If you need more precise control over your column width, or if you want to change a column's width without changing the width of the others, display the Column tab of the Table Properties dialog box, and perform these steps:

1. Check the Specify Width check box.
2. Enter the Column Width you want in the Specify Width scroll box.
3. In the Column Width Is drop-down box, choose whether Word should measure your column width in inches or as a percentage of the overall width of your table (Percent of Table).

12

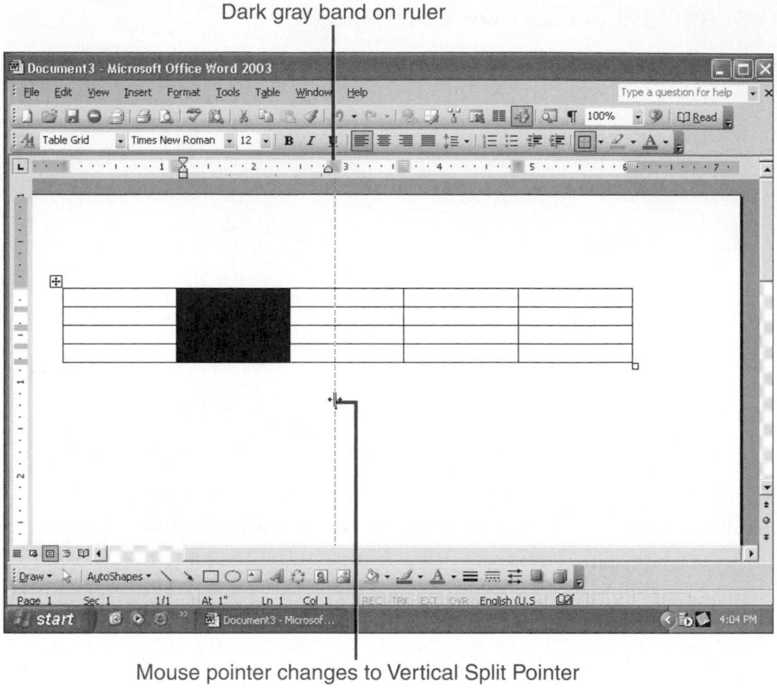

Dark gray band on ruler

Figure 12.31
Changing a column's width with the horizontal ruler.

Mouse pointer changes to Vertical Split Pointer

NOTE

> The Percent of Table setting is used primarily on Web pages and enables your columns to adjust themselves automatically based on your other settings and the monitor and browser being used to show your page.

4. If you want to control columns to the left of the ones you selected, click Previous Column. If you want to control columns to the right of the ones you selected, click Next Column.

5. When you're finished, click OK.

MAKING SURE SEVERAL COLUMNS HAVE THE SAME WIDTH

Sometimes, you're not that concerned with the precise width of columns in a table, but you do want them all to be the same width. To accomplish this, first select the columns you want to adjust. Right-click anywhere on the columns you selected, and choose Distribute Columns Evenly from the shortcut menu.

CONTROLLING THE PROPERTIES OF INDIVIDUAL CELLS

Just as Word gives you extensive control over the properties of tables, rows, and columns, you can also control the properties of individual cells. These include

- The width of the specific cell

- The vertical alignment of text or other elements within the cell

- Whether the cell shares the same margins and wrapping options as the rest of the cells in the table

CHANGING A CELL'S WIDTH BY DRAGGING ITS EDGE

The easiest way to adjust a cell's width is to drag the edge of the cell with the mouse pointer. To do so, select the cell; then place the mouse pointer anywhere on the cell's right gridline or border. Next, drag the gridline or border left or right to the location you want, and release the mouse pointer.

Unless you're adjusting a cell in a column that's on the right edge of your table, the width of the adjacent cell changes to compensate for the widening or narrowing you've just done, so your overall table retains the same width.

If you're widening the last column, your cell "bulges outward" to the right. Conversely, if you're narrowing the last column, your cell may be indented inward. Make sure that this is what you really intend. Often, it isn't.

CHANGING THE WIDTH OF CELLS THROUGH THE TABLE PROPERTIES DIALOG BOX

Sometimes you need more precise control over the width of an individual cell (or cells). Or you may want to adjust a block of cells at once, without changing entire rows or columns. Or you may want to adjust one cell without also changing the adjacent cell.

In these cases, you need to work from the Table Properties dialog box. To change the width of cells using the Table Properties dialog box, do the following:

1. Select the cell or cells you want to adjust.

2. Choose Table, Table Properties.

3. Click the Cell tab.

4. Check the Preferred Width check box.

5. Enter the cell width you want in the Preferred Width scroll box.

6. In the Measure In drop-down box, choose whether Word should measure your column width in inches or as a percentage of the overall width of your table (Percent of Table).

7. Click OK.

CONTROLLING THE VERTICAL ALIGNMENT OF A CELL'S CONTENTS

By default, Word starts the contents of individual cells at the upper-left corner of the cell, but this may not always be what you want. For example, if some of the cells in a row are very deep, the result can be an unbalanced, unattractive design.

Word enables you to control both vertical and horizontal alignment at the same time. Select the cell or cells you want to adjust, right-click to display the shortcut menu, and click the right arrow next to the Cell Alignment command. Then choose one of the nine options that appear (see Figure 12.32).

Figure 12.32
Choosing a cell alignment from the shortcut menu.

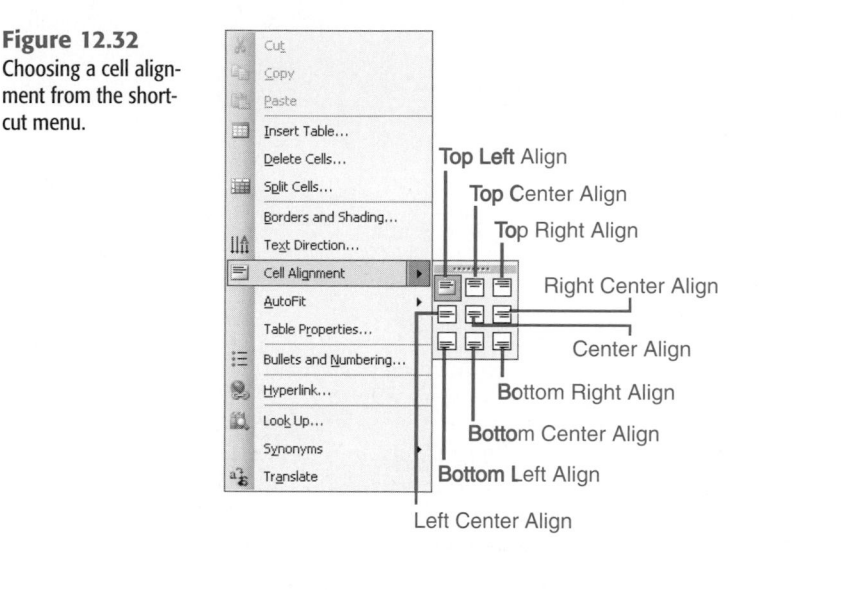

TIP

If you've displayed the Tables and Borders toolbar, you can get the same choices by clicking the Cell Alignment (Align Top Left) button.

CONVERTING TEXT TO TABLES

Sometimes you might need to convert text into a table format, or the other way around. For example:

- You might have an old table created using tabs; you now want to revise it, and it is easier to make the revisions by using tables.

- You might have a print merge or database file that was created or exported in tab-delimited or comma-delimited (comma-separated) format.

- You might have text that you decide would simply look better in table format.

To create a table using existing text, first make sure that the text contains a separator character Word can use to identify where it should start new table cells and rows. It's common for documents to use tabs or commas in locations where you'll want new cells and to use paragraph marks in locations where you'll want new rows. However, as long as the document is consistent, Word lets you work with any separator characters that may be present.

After you've checked the document, select the text you want to convert; then choose Table, Convert, Text to Table. The Convert Text to Table dialog box appears, as shown in Figure 12.33.

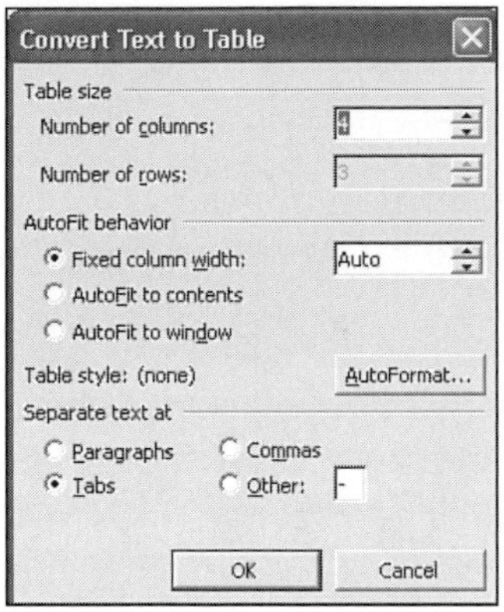

Figure 12.33
The Convert Text to Table dialog box gives you extensive control over how Word transforms text into a table.

When the dialog box opens, Word shows you its best guess as to the Number of Columns required and how you want the text to be separated. If, for example, you have selected tabbed material, Word is likely to assume that you want to Separate Text at Tabs. The result: Word starts a new cell every time it encounters a tab mark.

If the only breaks Word can find are paragraph marks, Separate Text at Paragraphs is likely to be marked. If you leave this marked, Word starts a new cell every time it encounters a paragraph mark. You can also change the setting to Tabs, Commas, or Other. This last option allows you to enter whatever separator character you want in the text box next to the button.

SOME TIPS FOR BETTER TEXT-TO-TABLE CONVERSIONS

It is generally easier to convert text in which tabs or commas split cells than those in which all you have are paragraph marks. First, much of the text you will want to reformat as tables was probably originally created with tabs. (Commas are often used to separate fields in exported database files.) A more important reason, however, is the difference in how Word handles the text-to-table conversion.

When you are converting from tabbed or comma-delimited material, Word recognizes a paragraph mark (or line break) as its cue to start a new row. Word also is smart enough to create a table that accommodates the line with the most commas or tabs. All this means is that you can easily convert long lists of text into tables.

However, if you choose paragraph marks, Word can no longer tell when to end a row. It places each paragraph (or each chunk of text ending with a line break) in its own row. The result is a one-column table.

If you have a table of moderate length, you can use Edit, Replace to swap all the paragraph marks (^p) in the selected text for tabs (^t). Then manually restore the paragraph marks where you want each row to end. Finally, use Table, Convert Text to Table.

12

If you are converting from tabbed text, whenever Word sees a tab, it places the text that follows the tab in a new cell to its right. Sometimes people use extra tabs (in the place of blank data) to make sure that all the text lines up properly.

Extra tabs can create havoc when you convert from text to table because Word creates unwanted empty cells. Of course, this does not happen if custom tabs are set, replacing the 0.5" default tabs.

If you are converting from comma-delimited text, make sure that your document contains commas only where you want cell breaks. Sometimes a comma is really just a comma. It is easy to be thrown off by city/state addresses ("Fort Myers, FL" would be split into two columns) and by numbers ("1,000,000" would be split into three columns).

CONTROLLING WIDTHS AND AUTOFITTING WHEN CONVERTING TEXT TO A TABLE

Working from the Convert Text to Table dialog box, you can specify the column width manually by setting a Fixed Column Width. Or, if you prefer, you can specify one of Word's AutoFit options to enable Word to control your column widths. AutoFit to Window adapts your column widths depending on the display device and browser software with which your page is being displayed. AutoFit to Contents adapts the column's width based on the width of text in the column. You can also click AutoFormat to select an automatic table format from Word's AutoFormatting dialog box.

When you finish establishing settings, click OK, and Word converts your text to a table.

TIP

> If you don't like the results of your text-to-table conversion, use Undo Text Table immediately. If you change your mind later, you can still revert to text by using Convert Table to Text, as described next. But you have to accurately specify whether Word should use paragraph marks, tabs, or commas to divide the contents of the table.
>
> If you use tabs, you might also need to adjust the tab settings Word creates, which match the cell borders of the table you just eliminated.

CONVERTING TABLES TO TEXT

As you might expect, just as you can create a table from text, you can also convert a table back to straight paragraph text. To do so, follow these steps:

1. Select the entire table you want to convert.

2. Choose Tables, Convert Table to Text. The Convert Table to Text dialog box appears (see Figure 12.34).

3. As with creating a table from text, you need to choose how Word separates the text. In the Separate Text With area, choose one of the following options: Paragraph Marks, Tabs, Commas, or Other. If you choose Other, type the character you want Word to insert when it comes to the end of each row.

Figure 12.34
Deciding what settings to use in converting a table to text.

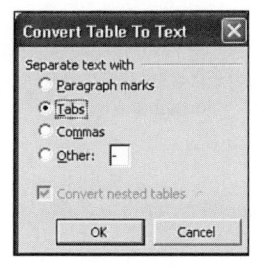

4. Click OK. Word converts the selected table into regular text, breaking at the separator you chose.

TIP

> Word also converts nested tables, but only if you specify Separate Text with Paragraph Marks.

CALCULATING WITH TABLES

Basic tables look tantalizingly like spreadsheets. In fact, a Word table can actually be made to perform a wide variety of calculations. In this section, you'll learn how to use tables as if they were spreadsheets.

NOTE

> If you find that Word's table calculation capabilities are not sufficient for your needs, or if your source data is already stored in an Excel worksheet, see Chapter 29, "Leveraging Microsoft Office 2003's Power from Word," to learn how to embed Excel worksheet data and calculations in your Word documents.

ADDING A LIST OF NUMBERS USING AUTOSUM

Perhaps the most common calculation you'll want to perform in a table is to add a list of numbers. Word's AutoSum feature makes this easy.

Place your insertion point in an empty cell under (or to the right of) the list. Then, from the Tables and Borders toolbar, click the AutoSum button. Word enters a field in the cell containing a { SUM } function that calculates all the cells above it, or to its left.

Because the calculation is entered as a field, it can be updated automatically after you change the numbers in the table. To update the calculation, select the field (or, if you want to update all its fields, press Ctrl+A to select the entire document) and press F9.

CAUTION

In most cases, formulas will not update themselves automatically when the values they depend on change. Therefore, don't assume that a value is correct unless you know you have updated the field to reflect the latest information.

 If AutoSum doesn't add all the numbers it should, see "What to Do If AutoSum Doesn't Add All the Numbers in a Row or Column," in the "Troubleshooting" section of this chapter.

CREATING MORE COMPLEX FORMULAS THROUGH THE FORMULA DIALOG BOX

Sometimes your calculation requires more than a simple sum, or you may want to control the way Word inserts a value into your table. For these purposes, choose Table, Formula.

The Formula dialog box appears, as shown in Figure 12.35. If you've opened the Formula dialog box while your insertion point is at the bottom or to the right of a list of numbers, the formula text box will already contain a formula such as =SUM(ABOVE) or =SUM(LEFT). If all you want to do is add the list of numbers, you can click OK and Word inserts the calculation field just as if you clicked the AutoSum button.

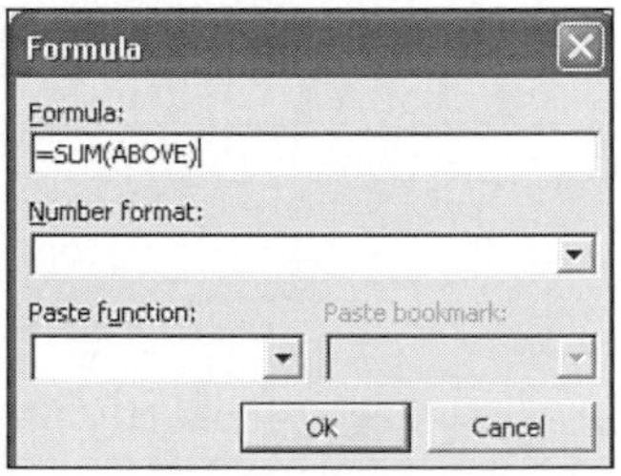

Figure 12.35
Creating a formula in the Formula dialog box.

Formula	
Formula:	
=SUM(ABOVE)	
Number format:	
	▼
Paste function:	Paste bookmark:
▼	▼
OK	Cancel

However, that's just the beginning of what you can do here. You can create fairly complex calculations, based on either values in the table or data that can be found elsewhere. You can also control the formatting of the values that result from your calculations.

From within the Formula dialog box, you can write your own formula. Formulas that you create within this dialog box are placed in your document as fields and can be updated the way other fields are updated: by selecting them and pressing F9.

To make your formulas calculate the contents of other cells, you can use cell references, much like those in Excel. The upper-left cell in a table is called A1. Rows are numbered; columns are lettered. Accordingly, to subtract cell A1 from cell A2, use the following formula:

=A2-A1

To multiply cell A1 by cell A2, use the following formula:

=A1*A2

To divide cell A1 by cell A2, use the following formula:

=A1/A2

Word also offers various functions that can be used in table formulas. These are available in the Paste Function box. See Table 12.3 for a brief description of what each function does.

TABLE 12.3   FUNCTIONS AVAILABLE IN TABLES

Function	Purpose
ABS	Displays the absolute value of a number or formula, regardless of its actual positive or negative value.
AND(x,y)	Used in logical expressions, AND returns the value 1 if both x and y are true, or the value 0 (zero) if either expression is false.
AVERAGE()	Calculates the average of a list of numbers that appear, separated by commas, in the parentheses.
COUNT()	Displays the number of items in a list. The list appears in the parentheses, with list items separated by commas.
DEFINED	Displays 1 if the expression x is valid, or 0 if x cannot be computed.
FALSE	Displays 0 (zero).
IF(x,y,z)	Evaluates x and displays y if x is true, or z if x is false. Note that x is a conditional expression, and y and z (usually 1 and 0) can be either any numeric value or the words True and False.
INT	Displays the numbers to the left of the decimal place in the value or formula.
MIN()	Displays the smallest number in a list. The list appears in parentheses with its items separated by commas.
MAX()	Displays the largest number in a list. The list appears in the parentheses, with its items separated by commas.
MOD(x,y)	Displays the remainder that results from dividing x by y a whole number of times.
NOT (x)	Returns the value 0 (zero), meaning false, if the x is true, or the value 1, meaning true, if x is false. X is a logical expression.
OR(x,y)	Returns the value 1, meaning true, if either or both x and y are true, or the value 0 (zero), meaning false, if both x and y are false.
PRODUCT()	Displays the result of multiplying a list of values. The list of values appears in the parentheses, with the values separated by commas.
ROUND(x,y)	Displays the value of x rounded to y number of decimal places; x can be either a number or the result of a formula.
SIGN (x)	Displays the value 1 if x is a positive number, or the value –1 if x is a negative number.
SUM()	Returns the sum of a list of numbers or formulas that appear, separated by commas, in the parentheses.
TRUE	Displays 1.

12

Your formulas aren't limited to calculating numbers stored in the table in which you're working. You can include numbers from other tables in your document, or from anywhere else in your document. To use a number in a formula when it isn't in the table you're working in, first mark the number as a bookmark:

1. Select the number.
2. Choose Insert, Bookmark.
3. Type a one-word name in the Bookmark Name text box.
4. Click Add.
5. Click where you want to create the formula.
6. Choose Table, Formula.
7. Edit your formula.
8. When you get to the place in your formula where you want Word to reference the bookmark, choose the bookmark from the Paste Bookmark drop-down box. Word inserts the bookmark name in your formula.
9. Finish editing your formula if necessary.
10. Click OK.

TIP

If the "number" you select to bookmark is itself a formula, updating the entire document's fields will update both formulas. You can update all the fields in a document by pressing Ctrl+A and then F9.

→ For more information about bookmarks, **see** Chapter 22, "Using Footnotes, Bookmarks, and Cross-References," **p. 743**.

FORMATTING FORMULA RESULTS

Often, you'll create a formula that inserts an accurate value, but you'll want to format it differently from the default format Word may use. For instance, you may want to round the number at three decimal points, or present it as a percentage.

To control the format Word uses to insert a value it calculates, you can select a generic number format from the Number Format drop-down box. Table 12.4 lists the number formats and shows samples of the numbers they return.

TABLE 12.4 NUMBER FORMATS AND HOW THEY LOOK

Number Format	Sample
#,##0	12,580 or –12,580
#,##0.00	12,580.00 or –12,580.00
$#,##0.00;($#,##0.00)	$12,580.00 or ($12,580.00)

Number Format	Sample
0	12580 or –12580
0%	12580% or –12580%
0.00	12580.00 or –12580.00
0.00%	12580.00% or –12580.00%

→ For more information about using Numeric Picture techniques, **see** "Customizing Numeric Formats to Your Specific Needs," **p. 792**.

SORTING THE CONTENTS OF TABLES

Often, you'll want to sort items in a table—perhaps to alphabetize them, place them in numeric order, or organize them by date. Word provides two sorting tools that make this easy:

- If you simply want to alphabetize a list, click in the column you want to sort by, and click the Sort Ascending or Sort Descending button on the Tables and Borders toolbar.

- If you want more control over how Word sorts your information, choose Table, Sort, and work from the Sort dialog box.

> **TIP**
>
> Although you're most likely to use sorting within tables, it works with any text in your document.

> **TIP**
>
> Some Word users like to organize documents in Outline view using Word's sorting feature. Start with a document that hasn't had outline numbering applied; then click Show Heading 1 to view only the highest-level headings and manually assign numbers to them, based on the order you want them to appear in. Finally, select all the high-level headings (again, with nothing else showing) and click Sort Ascending on the Tables and Borders toolbar to arrange them in the order you want.

Now imagine that you have a slightly more complex list, such as the list of customers in Figure 12.36.

Select the table and choose Table, Sort. The Sort dialog box appears, as shown in Figure 12.37. You can specify up to three levels of sorting. Imagine that you have a table in which column 1 includes last name, column 2 includes first name, and column 3 includes phone numbers. You might tell Word to sort first based on company names; after those are in order, to sort based on cities; and finally to sort on the sales representatives' names.

Word gives you a neatly ordered list of companies, in which each company's listings are sorted by city and each company's city listings are sorted alphabetically by name.

12

Figure 12.36
Sorting a list of customers.

Last Name	First Name	Phone
Smith	Robert	555-222-1800
Louisa	Mark	555-264-3720
Anderson	Kenneth	555-217-3420
Demby	Mark	555-264-3278
Alliana	Stuart	555-273-4120
Smith	Adrianna	555-296-1840
Talbot	Cari	555-802-4917
Schmidt	Fraser	555-497-1906

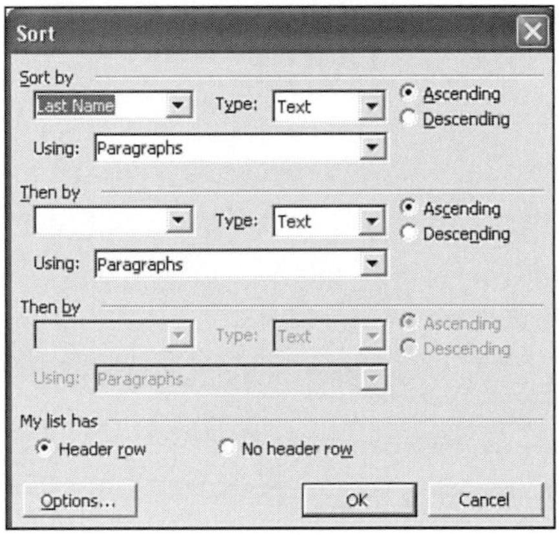

Figure 12.37
Using the Sort dialog box to sort rows of a table.

You also can tell Word to sort a table alphabetically based on text, sort a field based on date order, or sort a field in numeric order. (These sorts can have different results.) You also can specify whether each sort should appear in ascending or descending order.

Often, you'll have a table with a header row that contains information you don't want to sort. To avoid sorting the top row, click Header Row.

Although the sorting options you've already learned will usually be all you need, occasionally you may need to refine your sorts even further. To do so, click Options in the Sort dialog box. The Sort Options dialog box appears (see Figure 12.38).

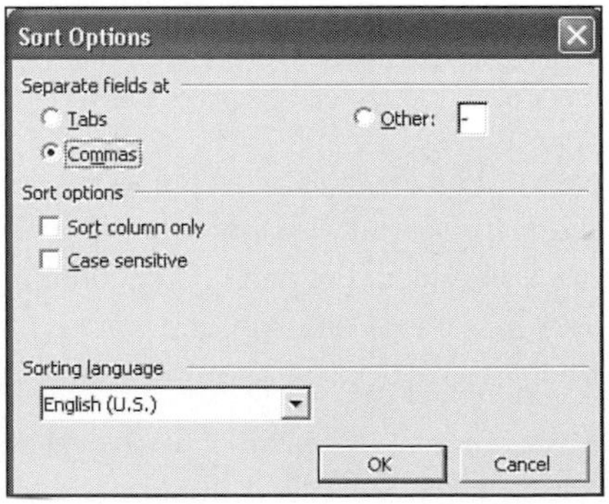

Figure 12.38
The Sort Options dialog box.

If you want to sort only the contents of a single column without also moving text in other columns, choose Sort Column Only. This option is available only if you've selected multiple columns for sorting.

NOTE

> Word can sort across multiple columns. For example, if first names and last names are stored in separate columns, you can select both columns and sort them together.

Normally, Word sorts are not case sensitive; march and March are listed next to each other. If you want Word to separate them, listing all capitalized words before lowercase words, choose Case Sensitive in the Sort Options box.

Finally, if you are sorting text that is not in a table or separated by paragraph marks, specify the separator you want Word to use in sorting the text. Other than paragraph marks, the most common separators are Tabs or Commas. However, if you want to use another character, you can enter that character in the Other text box.

TROUBLESHOOTING

WHAT TO DO IF WORD RESIZES CELLS INAPPROPRIATELY

Word automatically resizes cells as you type more information into them. This can be disconcerting and can also result in table layouts you don't like. To turn off this feature, select the table and choose Table, AutoFit, Fixed Column Width.

WHAT TO DO IF WORD MOVES TABLES INTO THE WRONG POSITION

If you're working in Web Layout view, when you move a table, Word may automatically snap it to the left or right of where you intend it to go. If this occurs, you need to clear Text Wrapping for the table. Right-click on the table, choose Table Properties from the shortcut menu, and click the Table tab. Click None in the Text Wrapping area and click OK.

WHAT TO DO IF AUTOSUM DOESN'T ADD ALL THE NUMBERS IN A ROW OR COLUMN

If you use AutoSum to add the contents of an entire column or row, you might find that AutoSum misses some of the numbers you want included. This occurs when blank cells appear in the row or column AutoSum is asked to add—AutoSum stops adding when it encounters a blank cell. Replace the blank cell with 0 and update the cell containing your AutoSum formula. This can also occur when you have inserted rows or columns without updating the formula. If you insert rows or columns and your sums aren't working properly, remove the formula and reinsert it.

WHAT TO DO IF WORD CUTS OFF THE TOPS OF LETTERS IN A TABLE CELL

If you use the Exactly setting to set a row height shorter than the text in the row, Word cannot display all the text in the row and cuts off some of the top. Instead, use the At Least setting, unless you have specific typographical or design reasons for setting exact measurements. If you must use Exactly, increase the size of the row.

A similar problem can occur—within or outside a table—when you set the line spacing of paragraphs to Exactly in the Format, Paragraph dialog box. (This sometimes can occur without your knowledge when you import a document from another word processing format.) Again, the solution is to use the At Least line spacing setting if at all possible, and if you must use the Exactly setting, to increase the value.

PART III

The Visual Word: Making Documents Look Great

CHAPTER 13

GETTING IMAGES INTO YOUR DOCUMENTS

In this chapter

OPPORTUNITIES TO USE GRAPHICS EFFECTIVELY

Every year, your documents must compete for attention in an increasingly sophisticated visual environment. Using Times New Roman and Arial fonts isn't enough anymore; today's best documents are visually rich, incorporating high-quality graphics and various other visual techniques. This chapter focuses on Word's powerful capabilities and resources for importing and using graphics—along with some "dos and don'ts" for using graphics effectively.

Word permits you to add virtually any image to a document:

- Images you capture with a digital camera or scanner
- Images provided by your organization, such as company logos
- Bitmapped images you create or edit using software such as Adobe Photoshop or JASC Paint Shop Pro, or that you adjust and import from Microsoft Office Picture Manager, a new application included with Microsoft Office 2003
- Vector images you create or edit using software such as Adobe Illustrator
- Vector images you import from Microsoft Word and Microsoft Office's built-in Clip Art library, or clip art Microsoft provides on its Web site

Before going further, you may find it valuable to perform a brief inventory of your graphics resources and the opportunities you may have to improve your documents through the use of graphics:

- Can you more effectively promote your corporate identity by adding your corporate logo or signature to more of your forms and documents?
- Do you create documents that would benefit from directly relevant photographs? For example, if you appraise real estate, would it improve your reports to include scanned photos, or photos taken on a digital camera of homes and properties?
- Would it save you time to send documents by fax directly from your computer, rather than printing them on stationery? If so, consider creating stationery templates that incorporate your logo and scanned digital signatures that can easily be imported into your documents.
- Are your newsletters and other customer communications too "gray"—all text and headlines, with no visuals to keep your reader's attention? Consider using a mix of original photography and digital clip art resources available through Microsoft Office Online, other Web sites, and low-cost CD-ROMs.

All these scenarios and options are covered in this chapter.

13

INSERTING A PHOTO OR ANOTHER IMAGE YOU'VE CREATED

The simplest way to insert an image in your document is to insert it directly, from a file stored on your hard drive, your network, your intranet, or the Internet. To do so, follow these steps:

1. Choose Insert, Picture, From File. The Insert Picture dialog box appears, typically displaying the My Pictures folder (see Figure 13.1). This is the folder Word provides as a default for storing all the photos you personally use.

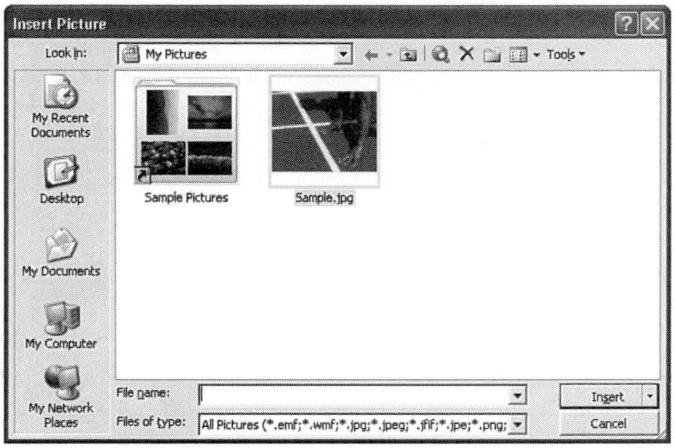

Figure 13.1
From the Insert Picture dialog box, you can browse to any picture.

NOTE

> My Pictures is a subfolder within your My Documents folder. By default, each user of your computer has her own My Documents and My Pictures folders, so images stored inside yours won't be displayed by default when others use your PC.
>
> Windows XP also provides a Shared Pictures folder within the Shared Documents folder inside My Documents. If you store images in the Shared Pictures folder, they will be more easily accessible to all users who share your computer.

2. Browse to and select the image file you want to use. You can browse to any location on your network, as well as Web or FTP sites you've set up as Network Places.

→ To learn more about browsing to and setting up Network Places, **see** "Saving Across a Network," **p. 82**.

3. If you want to see a larger preview of your image, choose Preview from the View button in the Insert Picture dialog box. The Preview window at the right side of the screen shows a large preview of the image (see Figure 13.2).

4. When you're satisfied with the image you've chosen, click Insert.

13

Figure 13.2
When you use Insert Picture to select an image, it's previewed in the Preview window.

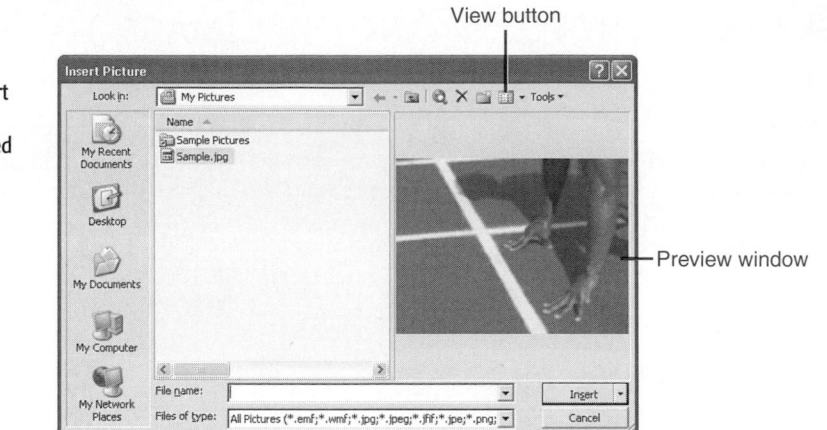

LINKING TO A PHOTO STORED ON YOUR HARD DRIVE OR NETWORK

Inserting images into your documents can significantly increase the document's file size. You can avoid this problem if you insert only a link to the original image instead.

CAUTION

If you plan to distribute a document containing links to images, you need to distribute the images as well, and they must be in the same relative paths as in your document. Otherwise, Word will fail to find them and will display blank spaces in place of your images.

One option is to place all your images in the same folder before you create links to them. Another is simply to forget about linking, and place entire images in your document.

Follow the steps in the preceding procedure, but instead of clicking Insert to insert the image itself, click the down arrow next to the Insert button (see Figure 13.3). Then, choose Link to File.

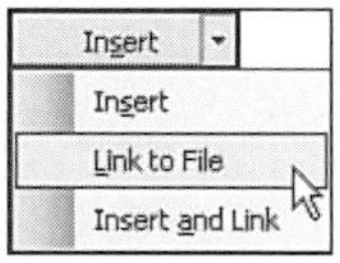

Figure 13.3
Linking to a file instead of inserting the image itself.

The image still appears in your document, but your document will be smaller because it doesn't contain the actual image. The image is automatically updated whenever you open your Word document or edit the graphic while the Word document is open. However, if the image is moved, renamed or deleted, it will no longer appear.

If Word doesn't recognize the file type you're importing, see "What to Do When Word Doesn't Recognize the File Type You've Tried to Import," in the "Troubleshooting" section of this chapter.

INSERTING AN IMAGE AS AN EDITABLE OBJECT

In some cases, you will want to insert an image that you created in a graphics program. However, you may also want to edit that image after you've inserted it into Word. To insert an image in a form that can easily be edited by the original graphics program, insert it as an object. By doing so, you maintain a connection to the graphics program you used to create the image, and can open the graphics program by double-clicking on the image within Word. Follow these steps:

1. Choose Insert, Object.
2. Select the Create from File tab and click Browse.
3. In the Browse dialog box, browse to and select the image file you want to insert.

> **TIP**
> To preview the image, click the down arrow next to the Views button and choose Preview.

4. Click Insert.

> **NOTE**
> Word also gives you the option of displaying an icon in place of the object; the default icon corresponds to the program your computer uses to edit the object.
>
> To display an icon in place of an image, click the Display as Icon check box in the Create from File tab of the Object dialog box. When you do, the Change Icon button appears; you can click this button to select a different icon for your image.

INSERTING AN IMAGE YOU CAPTURE WITH A SCANNER OR DIGITAL CAMERA

Word 2003 enables you to insert images directly from a scanner or digital camera, without using an additional application. To do so, Word uses the scanner or digital camera drivers you've already installed. To place a picture from a scanner or digital camera, follow these steps:

1. Place your insertion point in the document where you want the image to appear.
2. Make sure that your scanner or digital camera is properly connected. If you're using a scanner, place the printed image on the scanner.
3. Choose Insert, Picture, From Scanner or Camera. The Insert Picture from Scanner or Camera dialog box appears (see Figure 13.4).
4. If you have more than one scanner and/or digital camera available, choose the source from the Device drop-down box (if you have only one device, it should be displayed by default).

13

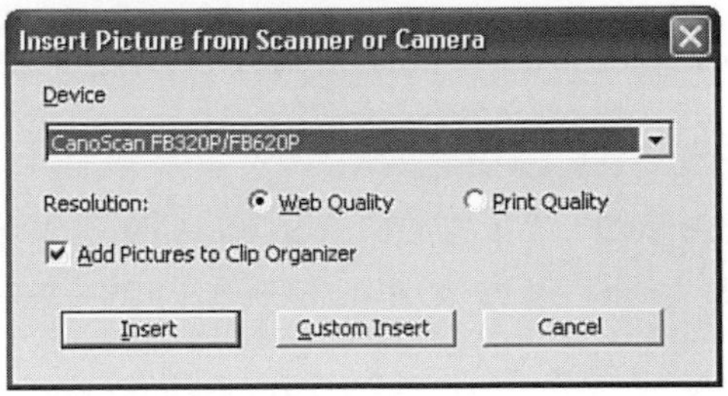

Figure 13.4
The Insert Picture from Scanner or Camera dialog box.

5. If you intend to use your scanned image on a Web or intranet site, choose Web Quality. Word scans your image at a lower resolution that is usually sufficient for onscreen display. If you plan to use the image in a printed document, use Print Quality. Word scans the image at higher resolution (better picture quality), creating a significantly larger file.

6. By default, Microsoft Clip Organizer automatically catalogs imported images alongside the other images it has cataloged. If you don't want it to do this, clear the Add Pictures to Clip Organizer check box.

7. Click Insert. Word captures the image using its built-in scanner/camera settings and places the image in your document. If Word doesn't scan after you click Insert, your scanner may not support automatic scanning. Click Custom Insert instead, and follow the instructions in the dialog box that appears next.

If Word still can't scan after you click Custom Insert, see "What to Do When Word Doesn't Work with Your Scanner," in the "Troubleshooting" section of this chapter.

CAUTION

Word works only with scanners and digital cameras that support the industry-standard TWAIN interface. In addition, you must install the device's driver, connect the device, and turn it on before using Word's Insert Picture from Scanner or Camera feature. For driver installation issues you should refer to the manual that should have come with your scanner or digital camera.

TIP

If you plan to edit the document later, using an image editor such as Paint Shop Pro or Adobe Photoshop, choose Print Quality. This gives you a higher quality image to start with, and you can use the image editor to prepare a lower-resolution Web file later, after you've refined the image.

FINDING AND INSERTING IMAGES THROUGH THE CLIP ART TASK PANE

Microsoft Word and Office come with their own library of clip art, as well as two related tools for accessing it: the Clip Art task pane and the Microsoft Clip Organizer applet.

NOTE

> The Clip Art task pane and Clip Organizer are primarily intended for working with clip art. Microsoft Office now contains a third tool, Microsoft Office Picture Manager, which provides basic tools for managing, editing, and sharing photos you create.
>
> Microsoft Office Picture Manager is a standalone application that can work with any Office application—or any other Windows application. It is introduced later in this chapter, in the section "Working with Microsoft Office Picture Manager."

In general, it's easiest and quickest to use the Clip Art task pane to find and insert an image. Although you can also find and insert images through Clip Organizer, it's generally easier to use the Clip Organizer primarily for organizing your clip art.

To find and insert a clip art image from the Clip Art task pane, follow these steps:

1. Choose <u>I</u>nsert, <u>P</u>icture, <u>C</u>lip Art. The Clip Art task pane opens (see Figure 13.5).

Enter your search
word or phrase here

Figure 13.5
The Clip Art task pane, displaying search results.

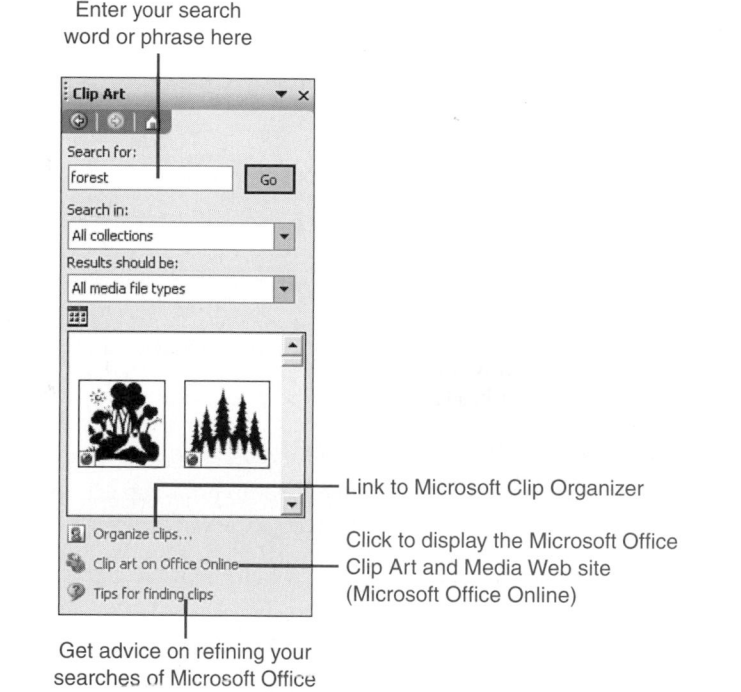

Link to Microsoft Clip Organizer

Click to display the Microsoft Office
Clip Art and Media Web site
(Microsoft Office Online)

Get advice on refining your
searches of Microsoft Office

2. Enter one or more keywords corresponding to the contents of the image you're looking for. For example, you can enter a broad keyword, such as business; two keywords that narrow your search, such as business + money; or a very narrow keyword search, such as Yen.

3. Click Go. Word searches all its clip art resources. If you are connected to the Internet, it also searches clips available through the Microsoft Office Clip Art and Media Web

site. You may see images that are stored on your hard drive or network in a matter of seconds, but Clip Art may continue to search for minutes, adding images it finds on the Web.

4. The Clip Art task pane displays thumbnails of the images it has found. If you want to see more images in each row, click Expand Results (see Figure 13.6). To insert an image in your document, click on its thumbnail image, or drag the thumbnail to the location where you want the image to appear in your document.

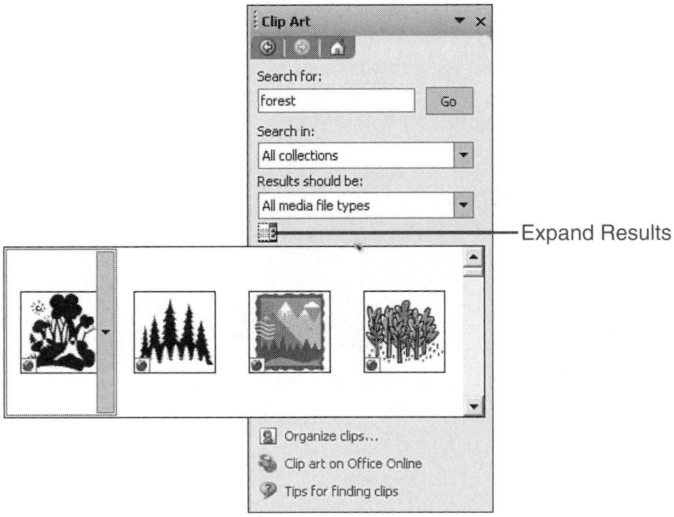

Figure 13.6
Seeing more results on each row.

Expand Results

If you haven't found the image you're looking for, enter new text in the Search For text box, and search again.

CONTROLLING WHERE TO SEARCH FOR CLIP ART

To speed up your search, you can control where to search for clip art. Microsoft organizes clip art into three "collections":

■ **My Collections**—Images you already own, which can be organized and displayed through the Clip Art task pane and Microsoft Clip Organizer.

→ To learn how to add clips, **see** "Cataloging Images on Your Computer," **p. 448**.

■ **Office Collections**—Images that were installed with Microsoft Office.

■ **Web Collections**—Additional images found on Microsoft Office Online.

By default, the Clip Art task pane searches all three sources (All Collections). To limit the search, click the Search In down arrow; then clear the check boxes corresponding to collections and folders you do not want to search (see Figure 13.7). When you're finished, click Go to search the collections and folders you've specified.

Figure 13.7
Choosing collections
and folders you do
not want to search.

For example, if you want an image of a Yen symbol, you can clear all collections and then check the Business folders within Office Collections and Microsoft Office Online. Then, Word won't search folders you know are unlikely to include a Yen symbol.

CONTROLLING WHAT TYPES OF CLIPS TO SEARCH FOR

Graphics include photographs, drawings, and anything else designed primarily to communicate visually. All graphics files stored on a computer are stored in some type of graphics file format. Most of them differ by the degree of image quality they offer and how big the files are they store them in. Word recognizes and has support for most of the major graphic file formats. By default, the Clip Art task pane searches for every type of media clip, including

- Editable clip art provided in WMF and other vector formats
- Photographs in JPG and other bitmap formats
- Movies provided in AVI, MPEG, and other video formats
- Sounds provided in WAV, MP3, and other audio formats

NOTE

> This chapter focuses primarily on "still image" graphics such as photographs and drawings, rather than movies and audio files, which still have far more limited application in most business environments.

Of course, in many cases, you already know what kind of clip you need. For example, if you're creating a printed flier, it's unlikely you'll need a movie or audio clip. To tell Word not to bother searching for some types of clips, follow these steps:

1. In the Clip Art task pane, click the Results Should Be down arrow. The list in this drop-down box is formatted similarly to the one shown earlier, in Figure 13.7.

2. Clear the check boxes corresponding to media file types you don't need.

TIP

> If you know exactly what format of clip you are looking for, it's much easier to clear an entire group of formats and enable one or two, than it is to clear all the ones you don't need. The simplest way to do this is to clear the check box associated with the high-level category of clip (for example, Clip Art or Movies); this clears the check boxes for all the types it contains. Then click the + symbol to expand the list and enable only the check box for the category (or categories) you do want (for example, Windows Metafile *.wmf or Animated GIF *.gif).

3. When you're finished, click Go to search the media types you've specified.

WORKING WITH A CLIP YOU'VE SELECTED

You've already learned that you can insert a clip by clicking on its thumbnail image in the Clip Art task pane. But sometimes you might not be ready to insert the image immediately. For example, you might want to learn more about the image before you insert it. Or you might want to add the image to a specific collection of images so that it is easier to find the next time you're looking for it.

If you simply want a brief description of an image, hover your mouse pointer over it; Word displays a ScreenTip describing the image's format, keyword descriptions, and size in pixels and kilobytes. This can be especially helpful if you're creating a Web page and are concerned about download speed (large files slow download speeds considerably).

For more options, click the gray down arrow on the right side of the image. Word displays a shortcut menu (see Figure 13.8).

- Insert places the image in your document.
- Copy copies the image into the Clipboard; from there, you can insert it into any document, in Word or another program.
- Delete from Clip Organizer removes the clip from Clip Organizer altogether.
- Open Clip In, if available, allows you to choose a different program stored on your computer to edit the image with.
- Make Available Offline copies a clip file from Microsoft Office Online so that it will be available to you even if you aren't connected to the Internet.
- Move to Collection allows you to move an image from one collection of images on your computer to another.
- Edit Keywords allows you to change the keywords associated with a clip. Editing keywords and other properties associated with an image is covered later in this chapter, in the section "Editing an Image's Keywords and Properties." Adding keywords, of course,

makes the clip easier to find later. (You cannot, unfortunately, change, add, or delete the keywords associated with clips provided by Microsoft—only your own and third-party clips.)

Figure 13.8
The Clip Art shortcut menu offers several options for working with an image.

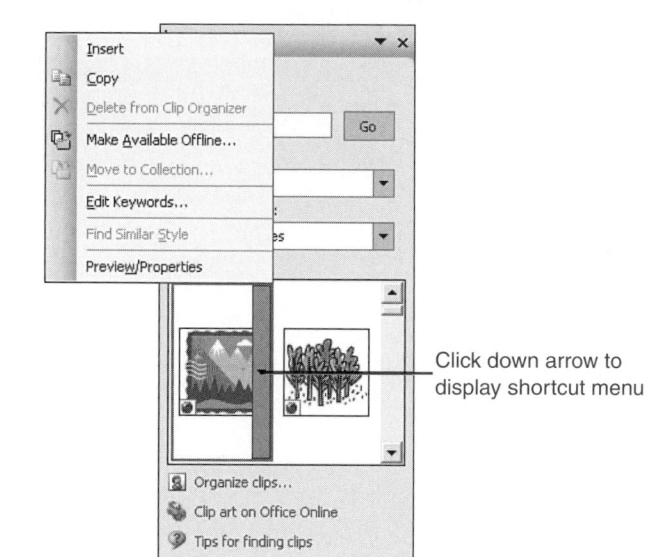

Click down arrow to display shortcut menu

- Find Similar Style instructs Word to search for other images from Office's built-in library of clips that are complementary in look and feel.

- Preview/Properties displays a larger version of the image and lists its properties and keywords.

WORKING WITH MICROSOFT CLIP ORGANIZER

To organize your images and other media clips, work with Microsoft Clip Organizer, an applet shared by all Office applications.

To display Microsoft Clip Organizer, choose Insert, Picture, Clip Art; then click the Organize Clips hyperlink at the bottom of the Clip Art task pane.

When you open Microsoft Clip Organizer, it displays a detailed Collection List—a list of all the collections and subfolders you already have. The My Collections list corresponds to folders on your computer that contain media clips; Office Collections lists the 39 categories of images provided with Office; Web Collections lists the 46 similar categories of images provided by Microsoft Office Online.

To view all the images in one subfolder, click on the subfolder; Clip Organizer displays a list of images (see Figure 13.9).

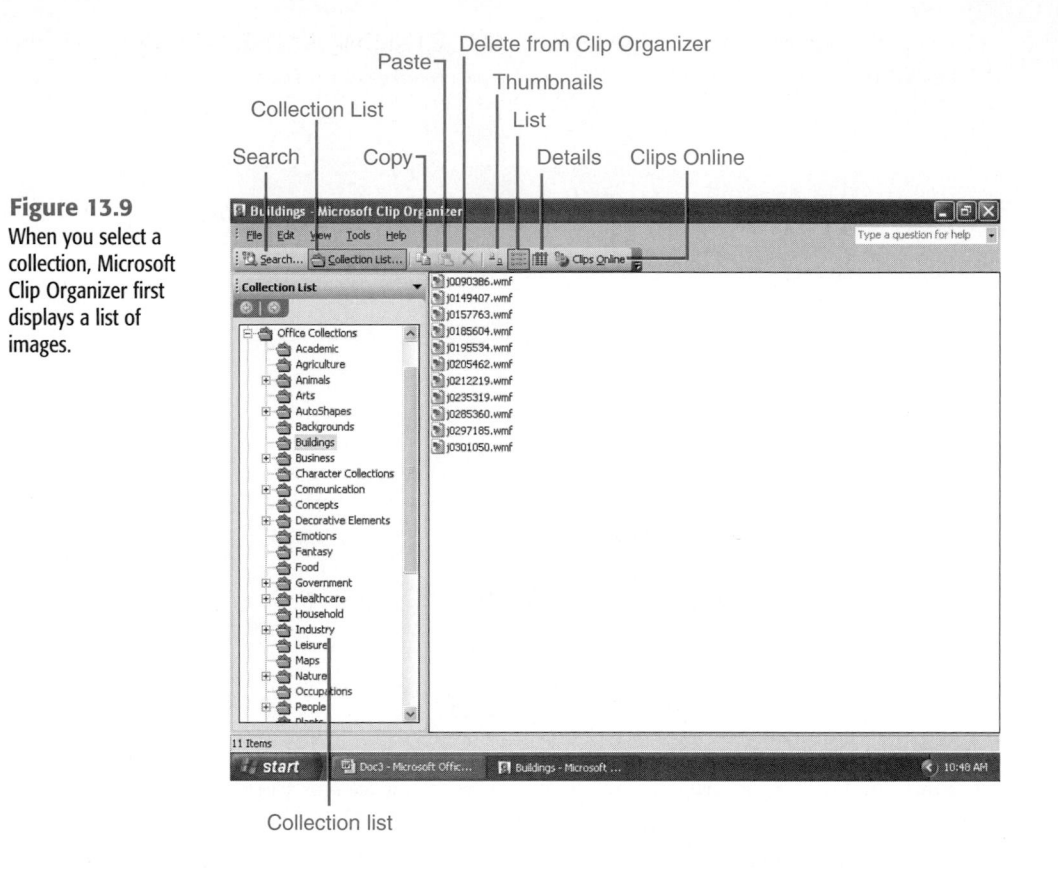

Figure 13.9
When you select a collection, Microsoft Clip Organizer first displays a list of images.

Collection list

To display thumbnails of your images, click the Thumbnails button. After you've displayed thumbnails (see Figure 13.10), you can click on an image to insert it in your document, or click the gray down arrow next to the image to view options for working with it.

If you prefer to view a list of images instead of thumbnails, click the List button; if you prefer to view detailed information about each image, click the Details button.

To search for an image from within Microsoft Clip Organizer, click the Search button. A Search pane appears that is identical to the Clip Art task pane covered earlier in this chapter.

CATALOGING IMAGES ON YOUR COMPUTER

You can have Microsoft Clip Organizer create thumbnails and keywords for all the images and clip media on your computer so that you can search for them just as you search for clips provided by Microsoft.

The first time you open Microsoft Clip Organizer, the Add Clips to Gallery dialog box appears (see Figure 13.11). If you want to catalog all the files on your computer, click Now.

Figure 13.10
Viewing thumbnails of
the images in a collec-
tion.

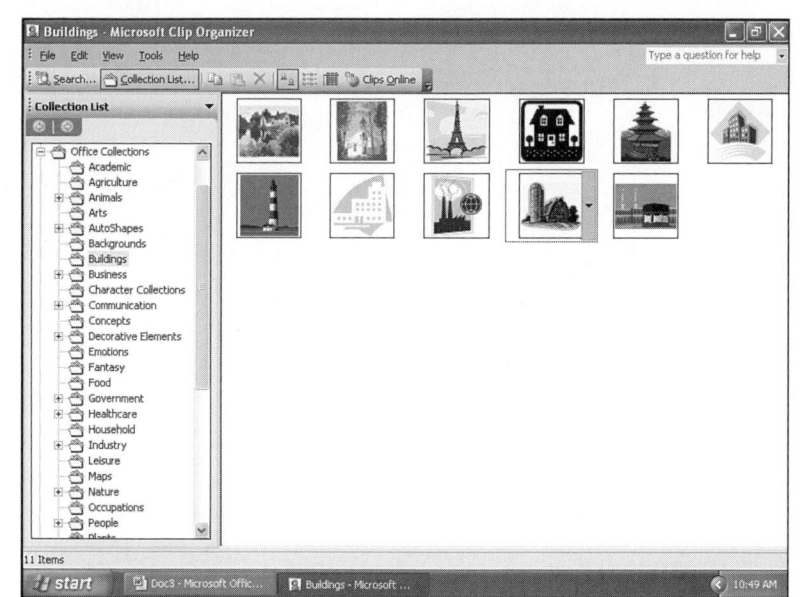

Figure 13.11
Choosing whether to
catalog clips now or
later.

Cataloging images may take several minutes or more, depending on how many you have, and how fast your computer is. If you prefer to defer cataloging to another time, click Later. You can always ask to catalog your images by choosing File, Add Clips to Gallery, Automatically.

If you want to control which images are cataloged, click Options; the Auto Import Settings dialog box appears. Clip Organizer searches your computer to determine which folders contain images; you can then clear the check boxes next to folders you do *not* want to catalog (see Figure 13.12). After you've made the selections you want, click Catalog to create the catalog.

Occasionally, you might copy several images to your computer, or perhaps an entire folder full of images. Rather than recataloging the entire computer, you can catalog only the images in that folder. To do so, choose File, Add Clips to Gallery, On My Own. The Add Clips to Gallery dialog box opens.

Figure 13.12
Clear check boxes next to folders that contain images you do *not* want to catalog.

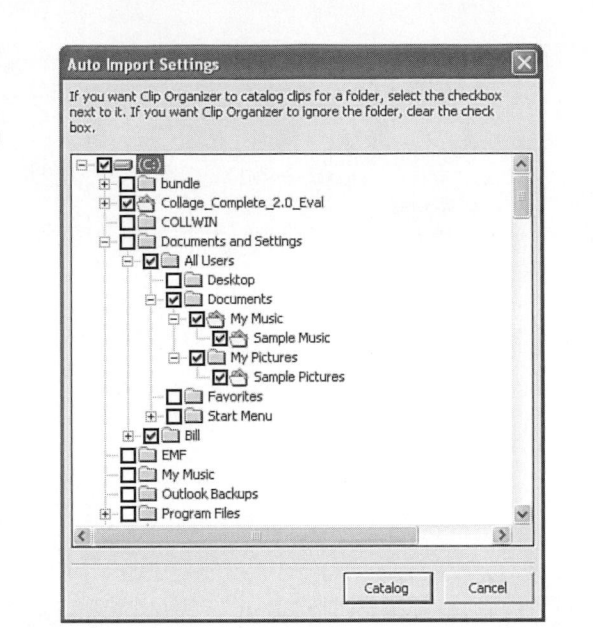

From this dialog box, you can browse to and select the images you want to add. To choose the gallery or folder where you want the images to be added, click Add To, which opens the Import to Collection dialog box.

Here, you can select the collection you want to add your images to, or, if you want to create an entirely new collection, click New to open the New Collection dialog box (see Figure 13.13). Enter the name of the new collection and click the folder you want to place it in.

Figure 13.13
Creating a new collection and choosing which folder to store it in.

Click OK in the New Collection dialog box to set the name of the new collection; then click OK to confirm that you want to import new images to the collection (be it a new collection you've just created, or an existing one). In the Add Clips to Gallery dialog box, make sure that the images you want to add are selected, and click the Add button. Thumbnails of the images you created are added to the collection you chose.

EDITING AN IMAGE'S KEYWORDS AND PROPERTIES

Like Word document files, each image in the Clip Organizer database has a set of properties that contain information about the image. For example, each image that Microsoft provides with Office, or via the Microsoft Office Online Web site, contains a list of keywords that make the image easy to search for. Images can also contain a caption that describes them.

When Clip Organizer catalogs your own images, it adds keywords based on the folder and file type of the images it finds and a caption corresponding to the filename. However, in many cases, these keywords and captions will not be very descriptive. If you want your images to be as easy to search for as Microsoft's, you'll often want to add your own keywords and captions.

To review the keywords, captions, and other properties associated with an image, select the image in Microsoft Clip Organizer (or in the Clip Art task pane); then right-click on the image (or click on the gray down arrow) and choose Preview/Properties. The Preview/Properties dialog box opens (see Figure 13.14).

Figure 13.14
From the Preview/Properties dialog box, you can review the properties associated with any cataloged image.

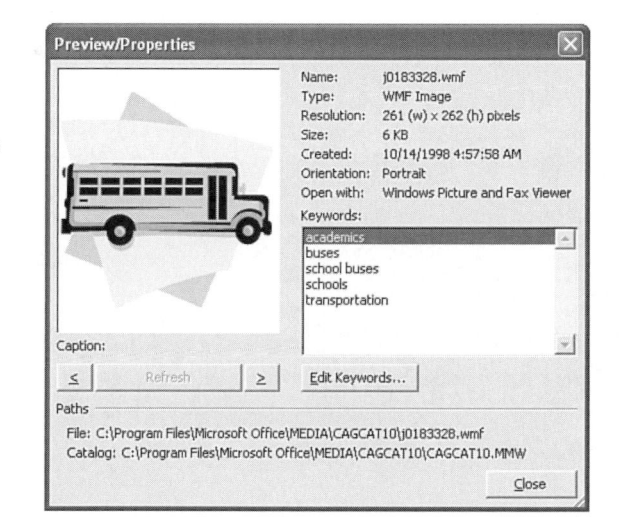

If the image has a caption, it appears immediately under the image preview. Information about the image appears on the right, including a scrolling list of keywords.

> **TIP**
>
> Clicking the left-arrow and right-arrow buttons under the image preview allows you to browse among images in a folder.

To edit an image's keywords and captions, click Edit Keywords to open the Keywords dialog box. (This dialog box is similar in appearance to Figure 13.15, which is shown in the next section.)

CAUTION

> You can't edit keywords or captions associated with an image provided by Microsoft, either with Office or via Microsoft Office Online.

To change the caption associated with an image, enter a new caption in the Caption text box. To add a keyword, enter it in the Keyword text box and click Add. To remove an existing keyword, select it from the Keywords for Current Clip list and click Delete. To change an existing keyword, select it, edit it in the Keyword text box, and click Modify. When you're finished making changes to the keywords and captions associated with an image, click Apply.

NOTE

> Although you can delete the caption and all keywords associated with an image you've added to the Clip Organizer, doing makes it nearly impossible to find your clip. (You can still find it by searching all clips in a folder.)

If you want to change the keywords and captions associated with another image in the same folder, click Previous or Next to display that image. When you've finished making changes to keywords or captions, click OK.

ADDING KEYWORDS TO MULTIPLE IMAGES AT ONCE

In some cases, several related pictures will use some or all of the same keywords. You can add the same keywords to multiple images at once. To do so, display the Collection List in Microsoft Clip Organizer; display the folder containing the images; click List or Details to display all the images in the folder; and select multiple images (using either the Ctrl or Shift key and clicking them).

Then, right-click on the images, choose Edit Keywords from the shortcut menu, and click the All Clips at Once tab (see Figure 13.15).

Now, edit the keywords and captions as you want and click OK. Your changes will be applied to all the images you selected.

RESTORING OR COMPACTING A CLIP ORGANIZER DATABASE

Clip Organizer's keywords, categories, descriptions, and image thumbnails are stored in a database. As time passes, it is possible for this database to become corrupted. Failing that, Clip Organizer may start to run slowly as you add many more images. To alleviate this problem, Clip Organizer provides the Compact tool, which squeezes unused space out of the Clip Organizer database so that it will run faster. It also attempts to repair your database if it is damaged.

Figure 13.15
Adding keywords or captions to multiple images at once, through the All Clips at Once tab of the Keywords dialog box.

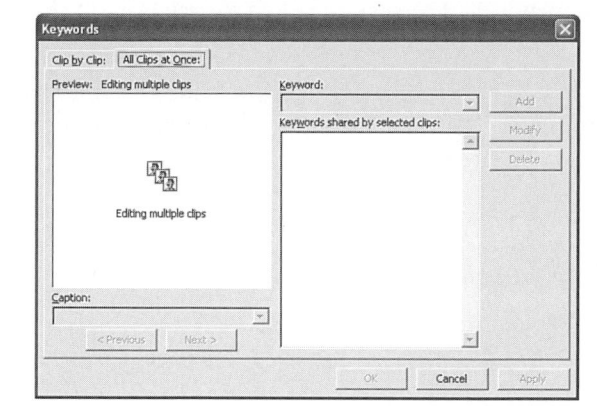

To run Compact, choose Tools, Compact. Note that Compact has no settings; as soon as you select it, it runs.

FINDING OTHER SOURCES OF IMAGES

You may find that the clip art you need cannot be found on the Office CD-ROM, or even at Microsoft Office Online. Fortunately, many other sources of clip art are available. In the following sections, we review two of them: clip art libraries available on CD-ROM, and non-Microsoft Web resources.

CLIP ART AND PHOTOGRAPHS ON CD-ROM

Inexpensive CD-ROMs have revolutionized the clip art industry, transforming clip art from a scarce commodity to an item that should rarely cost you more than a fraction of a penny per image. If the images you need can't be found on your Office CD-ROM or Microsoft's Web site, consider these clip art products:

- Hemera's The Big Box of Art 100,000 for Windows (www.hemera.com)
- Nova Development Art Explosion 150,000 Images (www.novadevelopment.com)
- IMSI ClipArt&More 2,000,000 (www.imsisoft.com)

These products change rapidly, so check the Web sites for the latest information.

NOTE

> Images from third-party CD-ROMs or Web sites don't import into Clip Organizer automatically, but you can import them by following the steps in the "Cataloging Images on Your Computer" section, earlier in this chapter. Or you can use them directly, using Insert, Picture, From File. This technique is discussed in "Inserting a Photo or Another Image You've Created," at the beginning of this chapter.

13

WEB-BASED IMAGE RESOURCES

If you can't find the image you need on the CD-ROM or at Microsoft's site, don't despair. There are literally thousands of Web sites dedicated to graphics and clip art. There are two approaches to finding images on the Web:

- Searching Web sites that exist primarily to provide images, either for a fee or at no charge. Many "free" image sites support themselves with extensive, occasionally intrusive, advertising. Others are simply nonprofit sites provided as a service to the Web community.

- Searching the entire Web, using a Web image search engine.

In the following sections, we cover both techniques.

FINDING IMAGE SITES ON THE WEB

The Web contains hundreds of sites that either are in the business of providing images or provide them free (as a service or as part of an advertising-supported business).

In most cases, you get what you pay for: The sites with the most professional, highest-quality images generally charge for those images, though the prices vary widely, and in some cases promotional prices are available. Sites that charge for images typically do so in one of two ways:

- **Rights Managed/Rights Protected:** You pay for the right to use an image in one or more specific ways. For example, you pay for the right to use an image on your Web site; if you later decide to use it in your corporate brochure, you must pay an additional fee. Image companies often employ staff or third-party services to scour the Web and the print media to ensure that their images are not being "hijacked" for unpaid use.

- **Royalty-Free:** You pay for the image once and can then use it whenever and wherever you like.

High-quality paying sites for professional photography and imagery include

- **Corbis** (www.corbis.com)
- **Comstock** (www.comstock.com)
- **Superstock** (www.superstock.com)
- **Getty Images Imagebank** (http://creative.gettyimages.com/imagebank/)
- **Digital Vision** (www.digitalvisiononline.com)

The Web is also replete with sites that provide images at lower cost, or at no cost. There are simply too many to list here, but the following Web-based directories can help you find the source you're looking for:

- **DropBears Image Libraries** (www.dropbears.com/l/links/images.htm)
- **Desktop Publishing.com Image Paradise** (www.desktoppublishing.com/commclip.html)

- **CSU Libraries Art Resources** (`http://lib.colostate.edu/research/hum/art.html`)
- **Berkeley Digital Library SunSite Image Finder** (`http://sunsite.berkeley.edu/ImageFinder`)

USING WEB IMAGE SEARCH ENGINES

Looking for the right image on the Web might seem like trying to find a needle in a stack of other needles, but luckily there are some excellent "needle finders" available: specialized areas of Web search engines that focus on identifying images.

Most search engines work in a fashion similar to the Clip Organizer keyword search: Type a word or phrase into the search text box and press the Search button (or Go! or Find It! or such). In a few moments, your search results are returned as a list of Web-linked addresses. If you see something promising, click the link and check it out.

Searching with only the keyword has a major drawback, though, when you're looking for clip art: You'll usually be forced to sift through thousands of unrelated links. To avoid this kind of scenario, a number of the search engines have special tools to help you to limit your search to only graphics. The following list outlines how some of the search engines work:

- Google Image Search (`http://images.google.com`) allows you to search for any image by entering it in the Google search box and clicking Google Search. To refine your search, click Advanced Image Search. On the Advanced Image Search page, Google allows you to control your search more finely based on search text, file size, image formats, domain searched, and even whether you want to see only full color, black-and-white, or grayscale images. Google Image Search also includes filtering capabilities that can help avoid inappropriate images. Figure 13.16 shows the results of a search for images related to Denver, Colorado. After a search is displayed, you can click on an image to see a larger version. Google also provides a link to the original page where the image was found.
- AltaVista Image Search (`www.altavista.com/image/default`) enables you to search for photos, graphics, and/or buttons/banners. You can choose to search color or black-and-white images; images from all sources or selected sources, such as Corbis.com and RollingStone.com; or images of any size. (For example, AltaVista can return images of desktop wallpaper size.)
- Yahoo Picture Gallery (`http://gallery.yahoo.com/`) is Yahoo!'s dedicated graphics search engine. You can do a keyword search of the entire gallery, Corbis.com pictures, or NBA basketball-related pictures. Alternatively, you can browse Yahoo's categories (Arts, Entertainment, People, and so on) and subcategories to locate the pictures you want.

CAUTION

> Be sure that you read the copyright information associated with each collection. Many, but not all, images are free to use privately. Most ask to be contacted by you if you're using their artwork for a profit-making venture.

13

Figure 13.16
Using Google Image Search to return images related to Denver, Colorado.

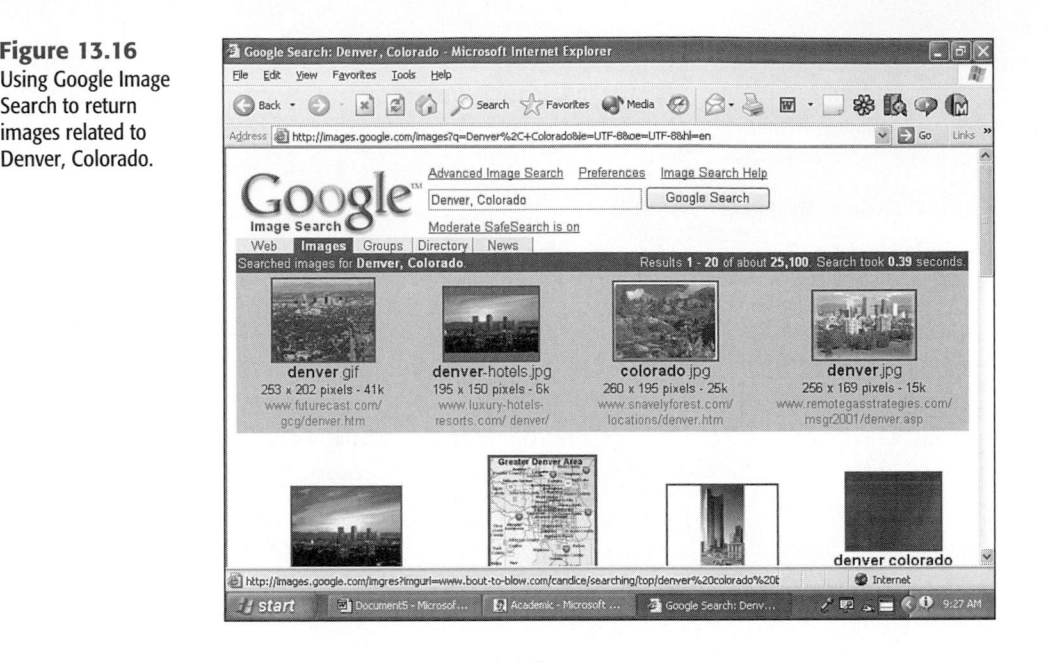

To download a graphic you find using an image search engine, right-click on the image in Internet Explorer. Choose Save Picture As from the shortcut menu; the Save As dialog box opens. Browse to the location where you want to resave the file; rename the file if you want to do so. Click Save. The image is copied onto your hard drive.

CAUTION

Be *especially* careful to make sure you have the rights to use images you capture in this fashion. Most images on commercial sites are copyrighted, and even sites that permit reuse often ask you to contact them if you intend to use their artwork for a profit-making venture.

EDITING IMAGES TO SERVE YOUR NEEDS

Regardless of how you've inserted images into your documents, you may need to modify them to serve your needs more effectively.

At the least, you'll probably need to reposition and perhaps resize your images to integrate them into your document. However, you can do much more. Graphics can be cropped, brightened, recolored, and even redrawn. You can also adjust how graphics work with other page elements.

POSITIONING AND SIZING IMAGES

Before you insert an image, you position your insertion point where you want the image to appear. Still, it's likely that you'll have to make adjustments to the image's size or position after it is placed in your document. The next few sections show you how.

RESIZING IMAGES USING SIZING HANDLES

The easiest way to resize an image is by dragging its edges to match the size and shape you want. To do so, click the image once to select it. A box appears around the image with eight sizing handles (see Figure 13.17).

Figure 13.17
Selecting and dragging an image.

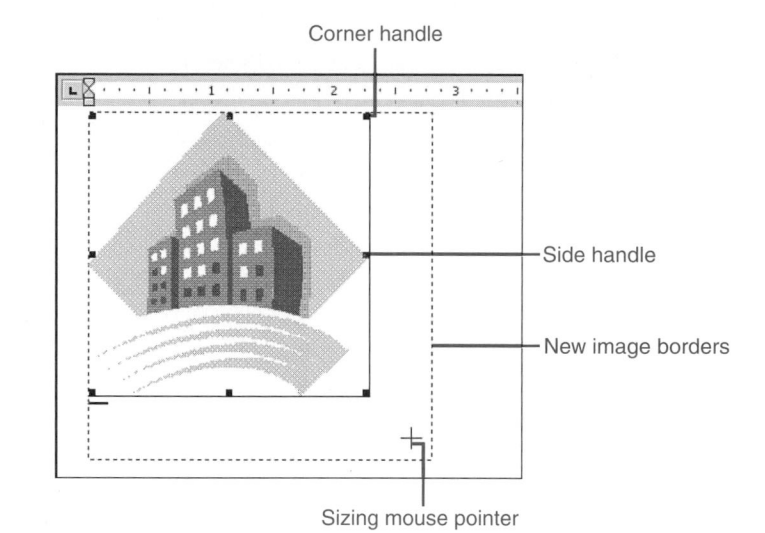

Corner handle

Side handle

New image borders

Sizing mouse pointer

The different handles have different effects:

- Dragging the corner handles resizes your image diagonally, making it wider and taller (or narrower and shorter) at the same time. By default, the aspect ratio of the image remains the same—so the image doesn't appear oddly stretched in any direction.

- Dragging the middle handles resizes the object only vertically (using just the top and bottom handles) or only horizontally (using the handles on the side). Of course, this does change the aspect ratio—stretching the image out of its original proportion.

TIP

The results you get from resizing a graphic can depend on the type of graphic you are resizing.

Generally, vector graphics—graphics built from lines, such as WMF files—adjust well to being enlarged or stretched. Bitmap graphics—graphics composed of pixels, such as JPEG photographs—do not survive with the same quality. Stretching can introduce unattractive roughness into these images.

NOTE

The size of the image Word inserts is equal to the size of the original image. If the image is quite large, you will likely want to reduce the size of the image after you've inserted it, to accommodate text and graphics in a layout that gives appropriate importance to each.

13

RESIZING IMAGES PRECISELY, BY USING FORMAT, PICTURE

Word also has a way for you to resize an image more precisely than you can by dragging its edges by hand. If you want to resize an image while retaining all its contents, right-click the image and choose Format Picture from the shortcut menu. Select the Size tab of the Format Picture dialog box that appears (see Figure 13.18).

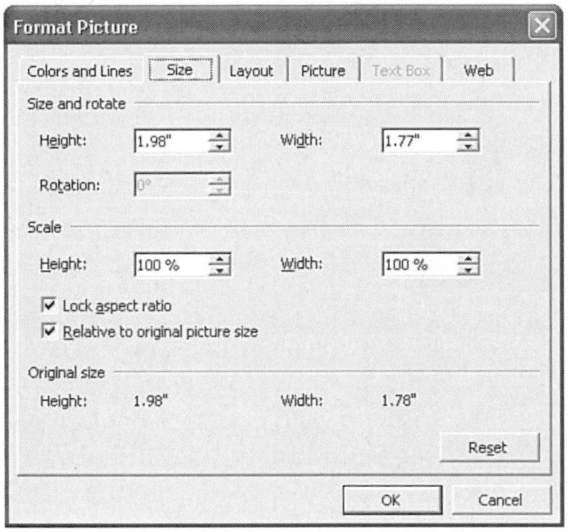

Figure 13.18
Resizing images through the Size tab of the Format Picture dialog box.

NOTE

Notice that the Rotation scroll box is grayed out. Rotation is available for only those images you create in Word using Word's AutoShape and WordArt drawing tools. These tools are covered in Chapter 14, "Using Word's Quick and Easy Drawing Tools."

In the Height scroll box (in the Size and Rotate area), enter the exact height you want the picture to be. When you do so, the value in the Width scroll box changes as well to maintain the picture's proper proportions (aspect ratio).

Alternatively, you can resize an image by scaling it up or down. To do so, enter a new value in the Height scroll box in the Scale area. Again, the value in the accompanying Width box changes proportionally.

If you want to stretch an image out of proportion, clear the Lock Aspect Ratio check box before you make changes in the height or width scroll boxes.

TIP

Even if the Lock Aspect Ratio check box is cleared, you can still use sizing handles to stretch an image proportionally if you need to do so. Select the image, press and hold the Shift key, and drag the corner sizing handles. Word resizes the image proportionally as you drag its borders. Release the mouse pointer; then release the Shift key.

NOTE

> If you want to resize an image by cutting out (cropping) parts of it, see the section "Cropping an Image," later in this chapter.

WRAPPING TEXT AROUND YOUR IMAGES

After you've placed an image in your document and sized it appropriately, the next thing to control is how text flows around that image. In Word, this is called *text wrapping*.

In Word 2003, pictures are placed "in line with text" by default. That means that a picture, no matter how large, acts just like any other character of text you might insert. Figure 13.19 shows how this works, and how to control text wrapping from the Text Wrapping button on the Picture toolbar.

Figure 13.19
Graphics placed "inline," such as this one, are placed just as if they were characters in text.

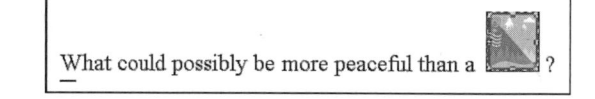

The options that appear in the Text Wrapping toolbar work as explained here:

- **In Line with Text**—As already mentioned, this option allows the picture to move as surrounding text moves around it. In other words, the picture behaves just like a character in the document's flow of text, always staying immediately ahead of the character behind it.

- **Square**—This option wraps text to the left and right of the bounding box that contains the picture. If the picture is inserted at the left margin, Square wraps to the right only (see Figure 13.20).

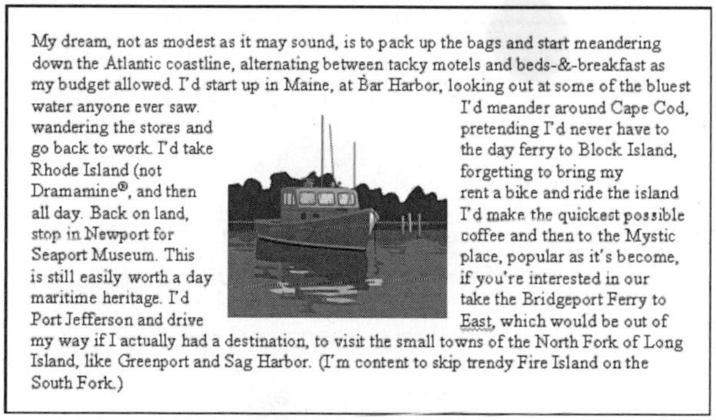

Figure 13.20
Graphics placed using Square wrapping.

> My dream, not as modest as it may sound, is to pack up the bags and start meandering down the Atlantic coastline, alternating between tacky motels and beds-&-breakfast as my budget allowed. I'd start up in Maine, at Bar Harbor, looking out at some of the bluest water anyone ever saw. wandering the stores and go back to work. I'd take Rhode Island (not Dramamine®, and then all day. Back on land, stop in Newport for Seaport Museum. This is still easily worth a day maritime heritage. I'd Port Jefferson and drive I'd meander around Cape Cod, pretending I'd never have to the day ferry to Block Island, forgetting to bring my rent a bike and ride the island I'd make the quickest possible coffee and then to the Mystic place, popular as it's become, if you're interested in our take the Bridgeport Ferry to East, which would be out of my way if I actually had a destination, to visit the small towns of the North Fork of Long Island, like Greenport and Sag Harbor. (I'm content to skip trendy Fire Island on the South Fork.)

13

- **Tight**—This option wraps text so that it follows the left and right edges of the actual image, not just the bounding box (see Figure 13.21).

Figure 13.21
Graphics placed using
Tight wrapping.

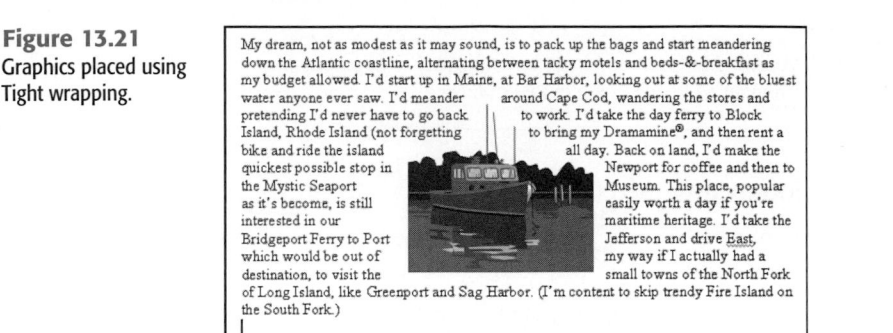

- **Behind Text**—Choosing this option enables text to be superimposed on the picture. This is the setting normally used with watermarks (see Figure 13.22).

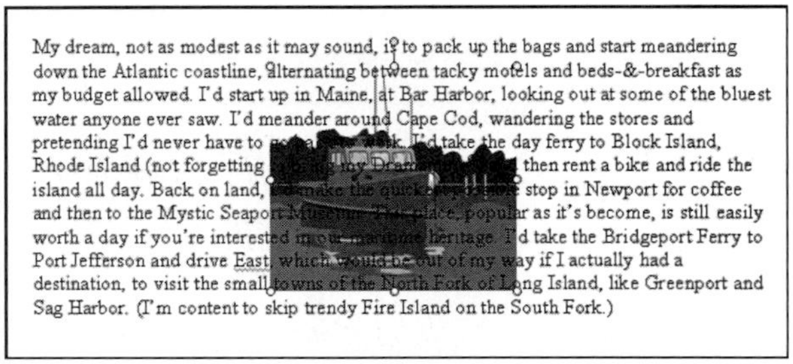

Figure 13.22
Graphics placed
behind text.

My dream, not as modest as it may sound, is to pack up the bags and start meandering down the Atlantic coastline, alternating between tacky motels and beds-&-breakfast as my budget allowed. I'd start up in Maine, at Bar Harbor, looking out at some of the bluest water anyone ever saw. I'd meander around Cape Cod, wandering the stores and pretending I'd never have to go back to work. I'd take the day ferry to Block Island, Rhode Island (not forgetting my Dramamine®) and then rent a bike and ride the island all day. Back on land, I'd make the quickest possible stop in Newport for coffee and then to the Mystic Seaport Museum. This place, popular as it's become, is still easily worth a day if you're interested in our maritime heritage. I'd take the Bridgeport Ferry to Port Jefferson and drive East which would be out of my way if I actually had a destination, to visit the small towns of the North Fork of Long Island, like Greenport and Sag Harbor. (I'm content to skip trendy Fire Island on the South Fork.)

- **In Front of Text**—With this option selected, the picture is superimposed on top of the text. With many graphics, this makes the text unreadable. In other cases, such as GIFs with transparent backgrounds or text created with WordArt, the text can still show through. Use this option sparingly, however, because even when the text is visible, it is often difficult to read (see Figure 13.23).

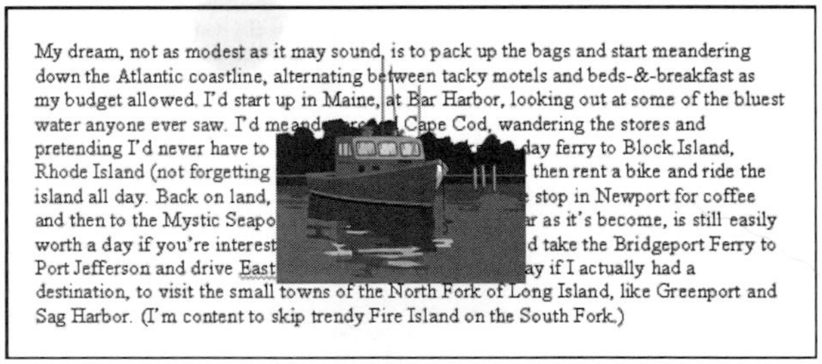

Figure 13.23
Graphics placed in
front of text.

My dream, not as modest as it may sound, is to pack up the bags and start meandering down the Atlantic coastline, alternating between tacky motels and beds-&-breakfast as my budget allowed. I'd start up in Maine, at Bar Harbor, looking out at some of the bluest water anyone ever saw. I'd meander around Cape Cod, wandering the stores and pretending I'd never have to day ferry to Block Island, Rhode Island (not forgetting then rent a bike and ride the island all day. Back on land, stop in Newport for coffee and then to the Mystic Seapo ar as it's become, is still easily worth a day if you're interest d take the Bridgeport Ferry to Port Jefferson and drive East ay if I actually had a destination, to visit the small towns of the North Fork of Long Island, like Greenport and Sag Harbor. (I'm content to skip trendy Fire Island on the South Fork.)

- **Top and Bottom**—Choosing this option prevents text from wrapping around the image; the text instead jumps from above the image to below it (see Figure 13.24).

Figure 13.24
Graphics placed using top and bottom wrapping.

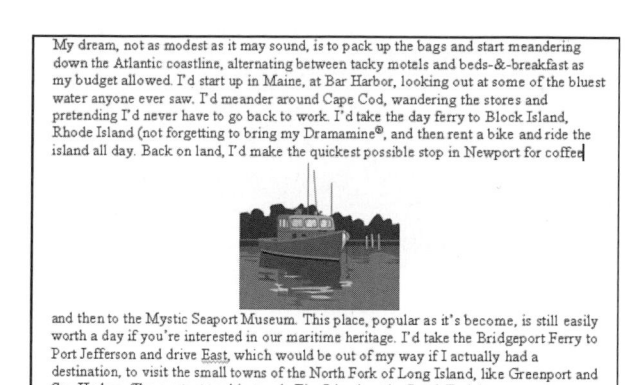

■ **Through**—Same as Tight, but without a fixed outer wrapping boundary. This option lets text fill gaps in the image (if there are any). Use Edit Wrap Points to allow more or less text in each gap (see Figure 13.25).

Figure 13.25
Graphics placed using Through wrapping.

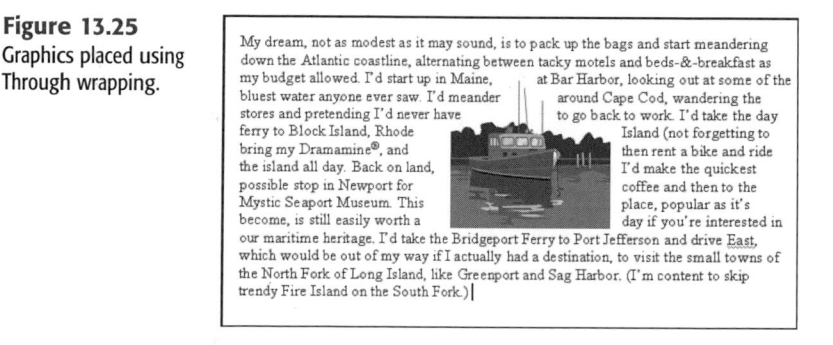

■ **Edit Wrap Points**—This enables you to wrap text around any corner or edge of an image, as discussed in the next section.

SETTING PRECISE TEXT WRAPPING WITH EDIT WRAP POINTS   The final text wrapping option available through the Text Wrapping button is called Edit Wrap Points. This option enables you to control precisely where text wraps to refine your page layout—for example, to accommodate a long word that would otherwise wrap oddly. If you click Edit Wrap Points, all the edges of the image are highlighted. Figure 13.26 shows the wrap points in a vector image. (In a bitmap image, the only wrap points are the edges of the bounding box.)

When wrap points are displayed, you can click and drag any small square to adjust the edge of the image Word recognizes for text wrapping. When you're finished editing wrap points, click outside the image to deselect it.

NOTE

Changes you make to Edit Wrap Points don't change the actual content of the image.

13

Dragging a wrap point

Figure 13.26
Dragging wrap points
to customize the way
text wraps around
and through an
image.

Wrap point

SETTING TEXT WRAPPING FROM THE FORMAT PICTURE DIALOG BOX   Word's "one click" toolbar options are all you need in most cases. But you can get even more control through the
Layout tab of the Format Picture dialog box (see Figure 13.27). Select your image, right-
click and choose Format Picture from the shortcut menu, and click the Layout tab.

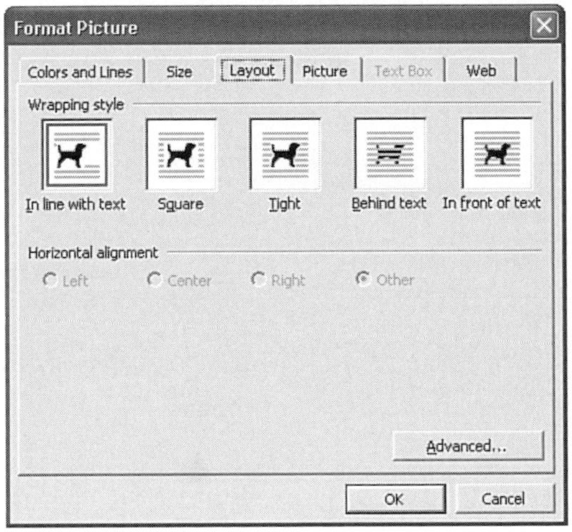

Figure 13.27
Adjusting wrapping
styles and horizontal
alignment.

After you've displayed the Layout tab, follow these steps to control the layout of your
image:

1. Choose the wrapping style you want: In Line with Text (the default setting), Square,
   Tight, Behind Text, or In Front of Text (the pictures associated with each option depict
   their effect).

2. If you choose a setting other than In Line with Text, you can also choose where you
   want the text to wrap: to the Left, Center, Right, or Other.

3. For even more control, click <u>A</u>dvanced to display the Advanced Layout dialog box. There, in the Text Wrapping tab, you can control whether text wraps on both sides of your image and exactly how far from the image the text appears.

4. If you want to control any of the following, work from the Picture Position tab:
   - The alignment of your image
   - How images fit into a book layout (for example, whether they always appear nearest the spine or the edge of the page)
   - The absolute position of an image on a page
   - Whether images should move when text moves

CROPPING AN IMAGE

Cropping means cutting away a portion of an image. Images are typically cropped to eliminate extraneous elements, to focus the reader's attention on a particular area, or simply to make the graphic fit on a page. When you use Word's cropping tools, you merely hide part of the image you're cropping—you can restore it later, if necessary.

Word provides two ways to crop an image: with the Crop tool, and through the Format Picture dialog box. To use the Crop tool, first display the Picture toolbar. To do so, select the image. If the Picture toolbar doesn't appear, choose <u>V</u>iew, <u>T</u>oolbars, Picture (see Figure 13.28).

Figure 13.28
Display the Picture toolbar to show Word's Picture tools.

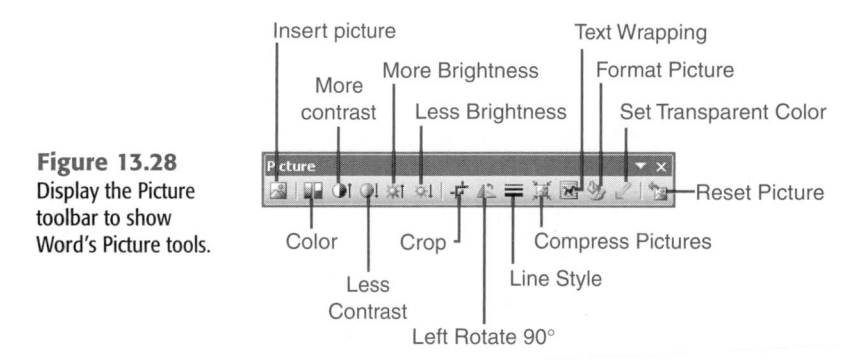

After the Picture toolbar is displayed, click on the image to select it. Next, click the Crop button on the Picture toolbar. Then, click and drag any sizing handle on the edges of the image. The handles enlarge or shrink the borders of the image just as they do with resizing.

To reveal a cropped section of a picture, you must reverse the process. Follow these steps:

1. Select the graphic.

2. Click the Crop tool from the Picture toolbar.

3. Click a sizing handle and drag away from the picture to "uncrop" the image, displaying the parts of the image that were hidden when it was originally cropped.

13

TIP

> Just as you can precisely resize an image using the Format Picture dialog box, you can crop an image "by the numbers." Select your image and then choose Format, Picture to open the dialog box. Click the Picture tab. In the Crop From section, change the values in the Left, Right, Top, and/or Bottom boxes.

RECOLORING WHOLE IMAGES

Most images today are produced in color. Word enables you to convert any image from full color to *grayscale*, consisting of levels of gray, or to straight black and white. You can also adjust the brightness and the contrast of an image to deemphasize it or make it stand out even more. Finally, Word includes a default watermark setting that converts your picture to one that works well behind text. Change your image in any of these ways:

1. Click the image to select it.
2. Display the Picture toolbar if it isn't already displayed.
3. Click the Color button.
4. Make a choice from the drop-down list that appears. Word eliminates or softens the colors in your picture, displaying it as you've requested:
   - **Automatic** uses the same colors as your original image. Use it to reset the colors, if necessary.
   - **Grayscale** converts colors to their gray equivalent, preserving relative contrast and brightness.
   - **Black & White** changes multicolored images to two colors. It is useful for creating high-contrast line art.
   - **Washout**, formerly called Watermark, sets Brightness to 85% and the Contrast to 15%. This usually results in an image that is visible, but which can appear underneath text without reducing legibility much.

NOTE

> The same settings are available through the Color drop-down box in the Picture tab of the Format Picture dialog box.

13

INSERTING A PRINTED WATERMARK

Word's Printed Watermark feature makes it easy to insert watermarks: very light images or text that appear "behind" the other contents of your document. In the following two sections, you learn how to create watermarks first from pictures, and then from text.

INSERTING A PICTURE WATERMARK

To create a watermark using a picture, follow these steps:

1. Choose Format, Background, Printed Watermark. The Printed Watermark dialog box opens (see Figure 13.29).

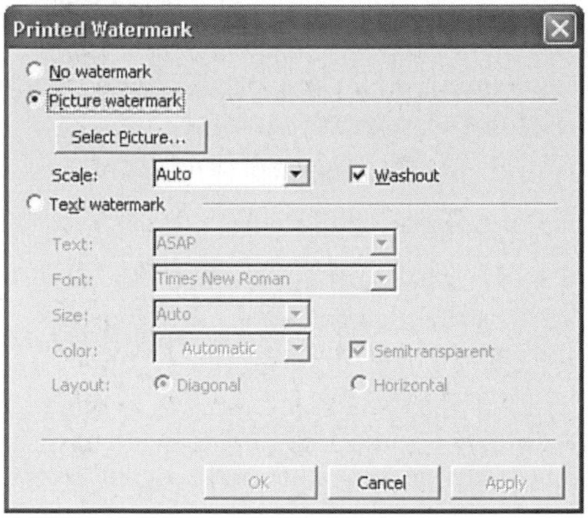

Figure 13.29
Inserting a printed watermark.

Figure 13.29
Inserting a printed watermark.

NOTE

The Printed Watermark option is not available in Web Layout or Reading Layout view.

2. Choose Picture Watermark.

3. Click Select Picture; the Insert Picture dialog box opens.

4. Browse to, and select the picture; then click OK.

5. In the Scale drop-down box, specify whether you want to enlarge or shrink the picture, or use Word's Auto setting (which enlarges or shrinks the picture to fit the left and right margins of the page).

6. By default, your picture watermark appears in light, "washed out" colors that make it easier to read the type that may be superimposed on it. If you want the picture to appear with its original brightness and contrast, clear the Washout check box.

7. Click OK.

INSERTING A TEXT WATERMARK

To create a watermark using text, follow these steps:

1. Choose Format, Background, Printed Watermark. The Printed Watermark dialog box opens.

NOTE

The Printed Watermark option is not available in Web Layout or Reading Layout view.

2. Choose Te**x**t Watermark.

3. In the **T**ext drop-down box, enter the text you want to appear (or select one of Word's built-in watermark text blocks, such as ASAP or CONFIDENTIAL.

4. In the **F**ont drop-down box, choose a font.

5. In the **S**ize drop-down box, specify a font size, or use Word's Auto setting (which enlarges the text to fit the left and right margins of the page).

6. In the **C**olor drop-down box, choose a color.

7. Choose either a **D**iagonal or a **H**orizontal layout.

8. If you want your text to appear partially transparent, check **S**emitransparent.

9. Click OK.

CONTROLLING IMAGE BRIGHTNESS AND CONTRAST

You may sometimes want to brighten or darken an image, or adjust its contrast. You can do so from the Picture toolbar; or if you need more precise control, you can use the Format Picture dialog box. First, select the image you want to adjust.

To brighten the image, click the More Brightness button, or to darken the image, click the Less Brightness button. Each time you click the button, Word adjusts the image's brightness by 3%.

To sharpen the image's contrast, click the More Contrast button, or to reduce the contrast, click the Less Contrast button. Each time you click the button, Word adjusts the image's contrast by 3%.

If you need more precise control, select the image and click Format Picture. In the Picture tab, enter precise values in the Bri**gh**tness or Co**n**trast scroll boxes. Click OK to see the results.

MINIMIZING GRAPHICS FILE SIZE BY COMPRESSING PICTURES

13

Now that Word is increasingly used as a Web editor, controlling the file size of images is becoming even more important. Word provides a Compress Pictures feature that gives you greater control over image size, in both Web pages and conventional documents.

To display the Compress Pictures options that Word provides, display the Picture toolbar and click the Compress Pictures button. The Compress Pictures dialog box appears (see Figure 13.30).

If you have selected a picture, Compress Pictures will compress only the selected picture, unless you choose the **A**ll Pictures in Document radio button.

You can then change the resolution of one (or all) images in the document. If you choose **W**eb/Screen, Word cuts the image's resolution to 96 dpi—adequate for screen or Web, but not for print or other applications. If you choose Print, Word cuts the image's resolution to 200 dpi—adequate for desktop printing or Web, but not for high-resolution professional offset printing.

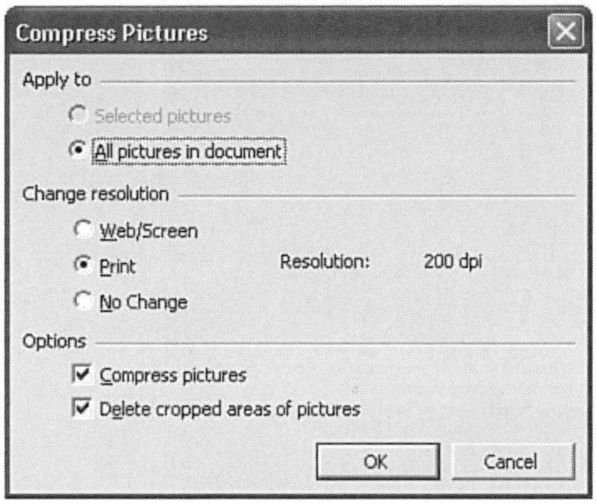

Figure 13.30
The Compress
Pictures dialog box.

CAUTION

After you use Compress Pictures, Word discards excess file information stored in your document. You cannot reverse this except by removing an image and reinserting it using the source image file.

If you Compress a linked picture, Word does not compress the source image.

If you check the Compress Pictures check box, Word applies JPEG compression to the images you have selected. Because JPEG is a "lossy" image compression technique, this reduces image quality—though, in many cases, the reduction is not serious.

If you check Delete Cropped Areas of Pictures, Word deletes the image information associated with areas you've cropped. The images are smaller, but you can no longer uncrop them.

ADDING ALTERNATIVE TEXT TO YOUR IMAGE

If you're creating Web pages, always include alternative text that can appear in place of images. Alternative text appears in the following circumstances:

- When a Web page is displayed in a browser with images turned off (to increase speed)
- When a Web page is displayed in a browser customized for an individual with a visual disability (the alternative text can be read aloud by the computer, whereas an image cannot)
- When an image cannot be accessed from the Web server
- In Internet Explorer, as a ScreenTip that can be used to explain an image

13

To create alternative text, right-click on an image, choose Format Picture from the shortcut menu, and click the Web tab. The Web tab of the Format Picture dialog box appears (see Figure 13.31).

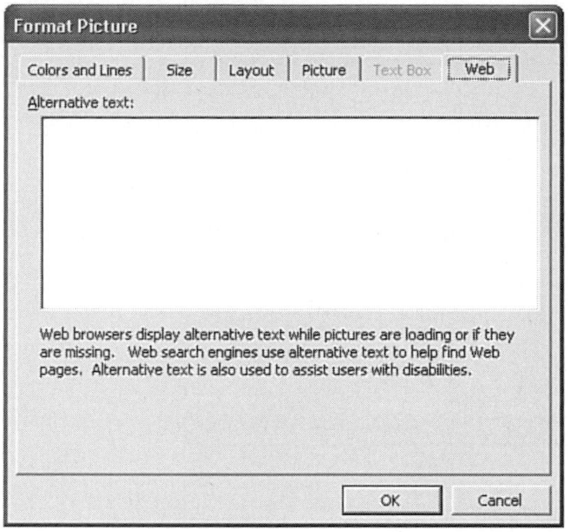

Figure 13.31
Entering alternative text for an image included on a Web page.

In the Web tab's Alternative Text box, enter the descriptive text. Though the dialog box is large, it's usually best to keep the text as concise as possible. If the alternative text is associated with a navigation button or another graphical element, make sure that readers know what clicking the button will do. When you're finished, click OK.

USING WORDART

You can often create powerful visual impact using nothing more than text. Word and Office provide a special tool for creating text effects: WordArt.

Using WordArt, you can give your text added dimension, color, and style. Moreover, your WordArt creation is completely customizable after you've created it—you can even change the text you included.

WordArt tends to be most useful when you need to attract attention—for example, in retail advertising or brochures, on report cover pages, or for the banner at the top of a newsletter. WordArt tends to be less useful when you need highly refined imagery for a highly sophisticated and discriminating audience. Use WordArt for no more than a few words at a time so that you can achieve maximum impact without compromising readability.

NOTE

> WordArt objects work much like other objects, such as drawing objects. You can resize them by selecting them and dragging their resizing handles; you can also drag them to new locations.
>
> Unfortunately, they also have the drawbacks of other Word objects: They cannot be checked for spelling, nor can their text be located through Find and Replace.

INSERTING A WORDART OBJECT

To create a WordArt object, follow these steps:

1. Choose Insert, Picture, WordArt. The WordArt Gallery appears (see Figure 13.32).

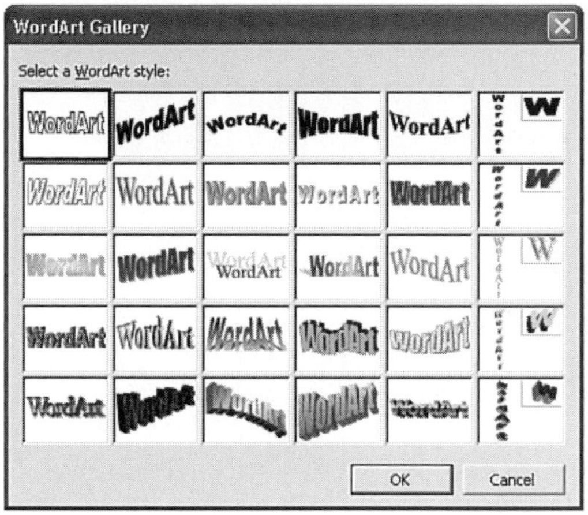

Figure 13.32
The WordArt Gallery offers 30 customizable preset designs.

2. Double-click any of the 30 preset designs, which opens the Edit WordArt Text dialog box.

3. Type in your text to replace the "Your Text Here" phrase.

4. Make any font changes you want and click OK. WordArt creates your object with sizing handles around it and opens the WordArt toolbar.

When you're finished, you can click outside the WordArt object to return to the regular document. Later, you can change the text in your WordArt object by double-clicking it to reopen the Edit WordArt Text dialog box.

TIP

> If you select a word or phrase prior to starting the WordArt process, your text automatically appears in the Edit WordArt Text dialog box.

MODIFYING YOUR WORDART OBJECT

It's easy to modify a WordArt object after you've created it. You can either try different preset effects through the WordArt Gallery or combine a preset with one of 40 shapes. Your new shape can then be stretched, resized, and rotated. Experimentation with the various shapes is the best way to understand what generates the best look for your particular WordArt object. Often, trying to achieve one effect leads you to a completely unexpected, but attractive, result.

To modify your WordArt object, first select it. This typically displays the WordArt toolbar (see Figure 13.33); if the toolbar doesn't appear, choose <u>V</u>iew, <u>T</u>oolbars, WordArt.

Figure 13.33
A sample WordArt object and the WordArt toolbar.

CHANGING WORDART CONTENT AND STYLING

If you're not satisfied with the content or the appearance of the WordArt image you already have, you can use the WordArt toolbar to change it entirely. Click the Edit Te<u>x</u>t button to return to the Edit WordArt Text dialog box and change your text, or click the WordArt Gallery button to choose a different prestyled effect.

ADJUSTING THE SHAPE OF A WORDART OBJECT

If you are reasonably satisfied with your WordArt image, you can use the WordArt toolbar to make adjustments to get exactly the effect you're looking for.

For instance, to change the shape into which your WordArt object is warped, select your WordArt object; then click the WordArt Shape button (see Figure 13.34) and select one of the 40 available shapes.

Figure 13.34
Click the WordArt Shape button to choose from 40 shapes for your text.

USING VERTICAL TEXT IN A WORDART OBJECT

WordArt offers several options for adjusting text. For example, you can stack letters on top of each other by clicking the WordArt Vertical Text button (see Figure 13.35).

Figure 13.35
Stacking the text in a WordArt image.

TIP

You can create columns of text in a WordArt object. When you enter the text for your WordArt object, place a paragraph mark at the end of each word or phrase you want in a separate row. Then, after you display the WordArt object, click the Vertical Text button.

USING WORDART'S SAME LETTER HEIGHTS OPTION

You can also click WordArt's Same Letter Heights button to make your lowercase letters as large as your capital letters.

TIP

The Same Letter Heights tool, like all the WordArt toolbar formatting options, affects the entire WordArt object and can't be selectively applied to one word or a part of a phrase. To achieve that result, you need to create two (or more) WordArt objects, applying the Same Letter Heights formatting to only the object or objects you want. If you then want to group the objects so that you can treat them as a single object, click all the objects by using Select Objects from the Drawing toolbar. Finally, click the Draw button and then the Group button.

13

ALIGNING OR STRETCHING YOUR WORDART TEXT

You can align or stretch your text using the options that display when you click the WordArt Alignment button (see Figure 13.36). Table 13.1 takes a closer look at the available options.

Figure 13.36
Aligning the text in a
WordArt image.

TABLE 13.1 WORDART ALIGNMENT OPTIONS

Button	Name	Description
	Left Align	Paragraphs are aligned to the left edge of the bounding box.
	Center	Paragraphs are centered in the bounding box.
	Right Align	Paragraphs are aligned to the right edge of the bounding box.
	Word Justify	Word justifies paragraphs to the edges of the bounding box by stretching the spaces between words. If there is only one word on a line, the letters are spaced out equally.
	Letter Justify	Word justifies paragraphs to the edges of the bounding box by spacing the letters and the spaces between words equally. Single-word lines are treated the same as with Word Justify.
	Stretch Justify	Word justifies paragraphs to the edges of the bounding box by stretching the letters and the spaces between words equally.

ADJUSTING LETTER SPACING IN WORDART TEXT

As with regular Word text, you can tighten or loosen the letter spacing of text in WordArt objects. Normal spacing is 100%; condensed or tighter spacing is less, and expanded or looser spacing is more.

With regular text, letter spacing moves the letters closer together or farther apart. WordArt works differently. Here, letter spacing narrows or widens the characters themselves.

To alter a WordArt object's spacing, click the WordArt Character Spacing button. WordArt provides five preset values (Very Tight, Tight, Normal, Loose, and Very Loose), as well as a Custom box. You can also fit characters such as "A" and "V" more tightly together by enabling the Kern Character Pairs. Figure 13.37 contrasts the two preset extremes, Very Tight and Very Loose.

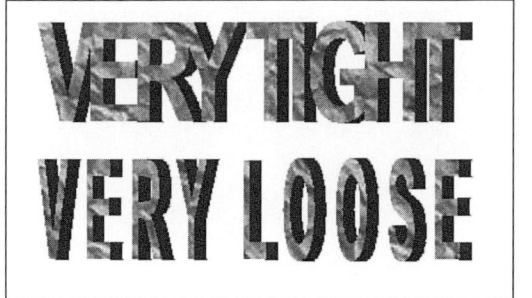

Figure 13.37
Controlling the letter spacing of text in a WordArt image.

ADJUSTING A WORDART OBJECT WITH THE ADJUSTMENT HANDLE

By default, WordArt objects are inserted inline. This means they are placed at your insertion point, on a line of text—and they move as your text moves. You can tell that a WordArt object has been inserted inline by the square sizing handles that surround it.

Sometimes you may want more control over the appearance of your WordArt object. For example, you may want to stretch or rotate it. You can't do this with inline WordArt objects, but you can do it with WordArt objects that utilize a different "wrapping style"—for example, objects that will be displayed in a square area that will not move on the page, or objects that will appear behind or in front of text.

To change a WordArt object's wrapping style so that you can stretch or rotate it, follow these steps:

1. Right-click on the WordArt object to display the shortcut menu.
2. Choose Format WordArt.
3. Display the Layout tab, and choose any Wrapping Style except In Line with Text.
4. Click OK.

Your WordArt object now has three sets of handles (see Figure 13.38):

- Circular sizing handles: Drag one of them outward to enlarge the object, or inward to shrink it.
- A green rotate handle: Drag it to rotate the object.
- A yellow, diamond-shaped adjustment handle for changing the angle of text: Drag it inward to increase the angle of the text.

Depending on the form of the shape, dragging an adjustment handle may have different effects. For example, in a shape with a curved bottom, the adjustment handle alters the degree of the curve. In a shape that fades out at the right, the adjustment handle moves the vanishing point.

13

Figure 13.38
Additional handles
that appear in non-
inline WordArt
objects.

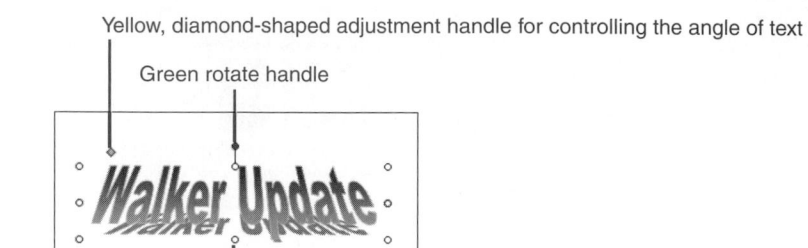

Yellow, diamond-shaped adjustment handle for controlling the angle of text

Green rotate handle

Circular sizing handles

USING THE FORMAT WORDART DIALOG BOX

Much like other Word objects, WordArt objects have a Formatting dialog box that brings together many of their formatting options (see Figure 13.39). To view this dialog box, select the object and click Format WordArt on the WordArt toolbar (or right-click on the object and choose Format WordArt from the shortcut menu).

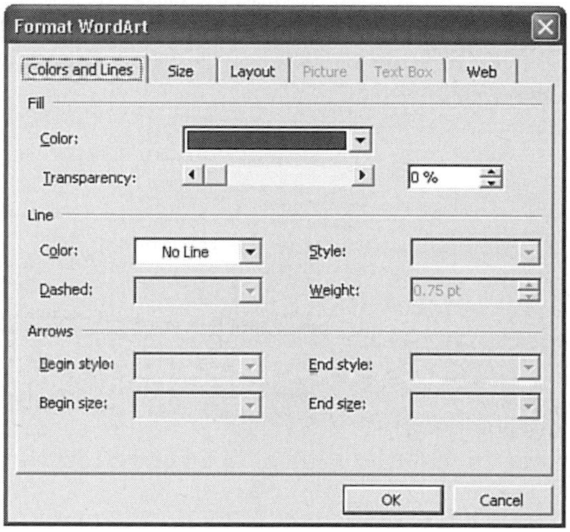

Figure 13.39
Using the Format
WordArt dialog box.

Many of the elements in this dialog box, such as Size and Layout, are similar to those you learned about in the discussion of the Format Picture dialog box, earlier in this chapter. Two options are worth pointing out, however:

- In the Colors and Lines tab, you can change the fill color, line color, and line weight of your WordArt object.

- In the Web tab, Word automatically inserts a copy of the same text that appears in your WordArt object so that viewers can see the text even if they cannot see the formatting.

WORKING WITH MICROSOFT OFFICE PICTURE MANAGER

NEW Word 2003 and Office 2003 include a new tool for managing, editing, and sharing pictures: Microsoft Office Picture Manager. As a standalone Windows application, Microsoft Office Picture Manager can work with any Office application—or virtually any other Windows application as well.

CAUTION

> Microsoft Office Picture Manager replaces Microsoft Photo Editor. However, Microsoft Photo Editor had several features that are not present in Microsoft Office Picture Manager—for example, effects such as posterization and embossing. (Note also that Microsoft Office Picture Manager and Microsoft Photo Editor in Office XP/Word 2002 have lost support for the older .PCX graphics format.)
>
> If you own an older version of Word or Office, you may want to keep both Microsoft Office Picture Manager and Microsoft Photo Editor on your computer.

To work with Microsoft Office Picture Manager, choose Start, Programs (or in Windows XP, All Programs), Microsoft Office, Microsoft Office Picture Manager. Microsoft Office Picture Manager appears, showing thumbnails of any images that appear in your My Pictures folder (see Figure 13.40).

Figure 13.40
Microsoft Office Picture Manager shows thumbnails of images in your My Pictures folder.

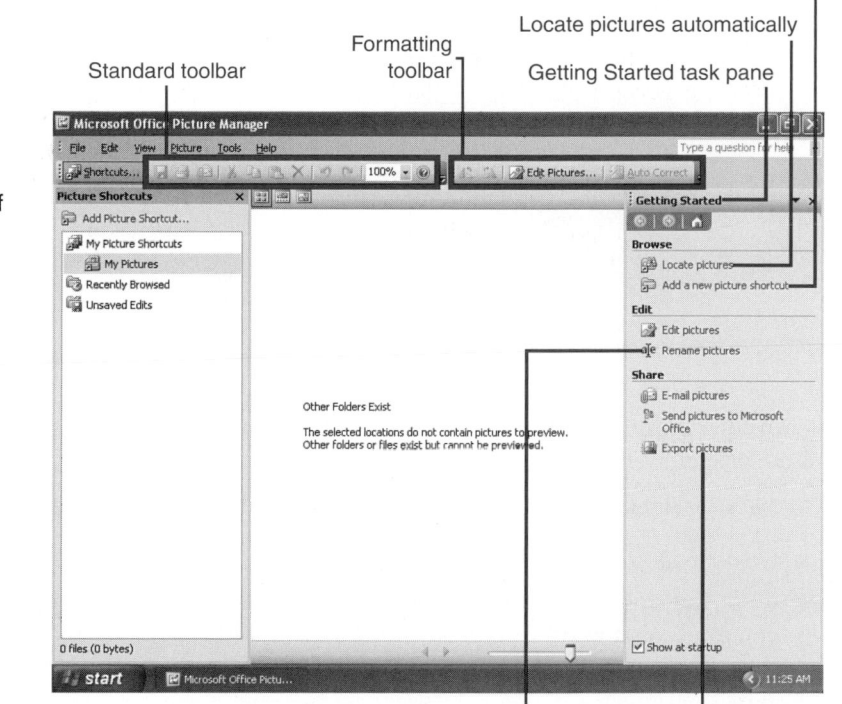

Add picture shortcuts individually

Locate pictures automatically

Getting Started task pane

Standard toolbar

Formatting toolbar

Tools for editing pictures   Tools for sharing pictures

LOCATING YOUR PICTURES

Microsoft Office Picture Manager makes it easy to work with your pictures by displaying a visual thumbnail "picture shortcut" to every picture it knows about. When you run it for the first time, however, Microsoft Office Picture Manager has no picture shortcuts, and displays only the sample pictures in your My Pictures folder—or, in some cases, no pictures at all.

To locate other pictures available on your computer, click Locate Pictures on the Getting Started task pane. The Locate Picture Shortcuts task pane appears (see Figure 13.41). Click the Look In drop-down box, and choose the drive you want to search. Click OK to begin the search.

Microsoft Office Picture Manager can search any drive on your computer or any mapped drive on your network. Depending on network performance, searching mapped drives may take some time.

Figure 13.41
Specifying which drives to search for pictures.

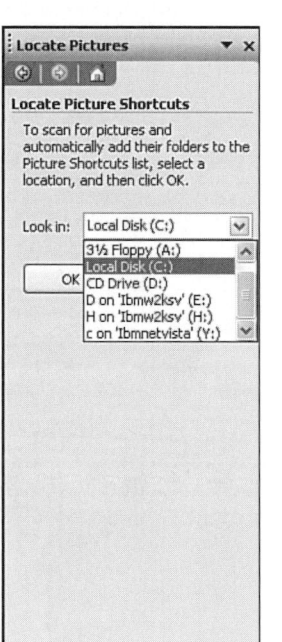

When Microsoft Office Picture Manager finishes searching, it displays picture shortcuts for all the images it finds (see Figure 13.42).

You can now right-click on the image to work with it from the shortcut menu:

- Click Send To, Mail Recipient to send the picture by email using Outlook.
- Click Cut or Copy to place a copy of the image in the Windows Clipboard; from there, you can copy it into Word or any other application.
- Click Delete to delete a picture and its picture shortcut.
- Click Rename to rename a picture from the Rename task pane.

Figure 13.42
Microsoft Office Picture Manager displays picture shortcuts for all the images it finds.

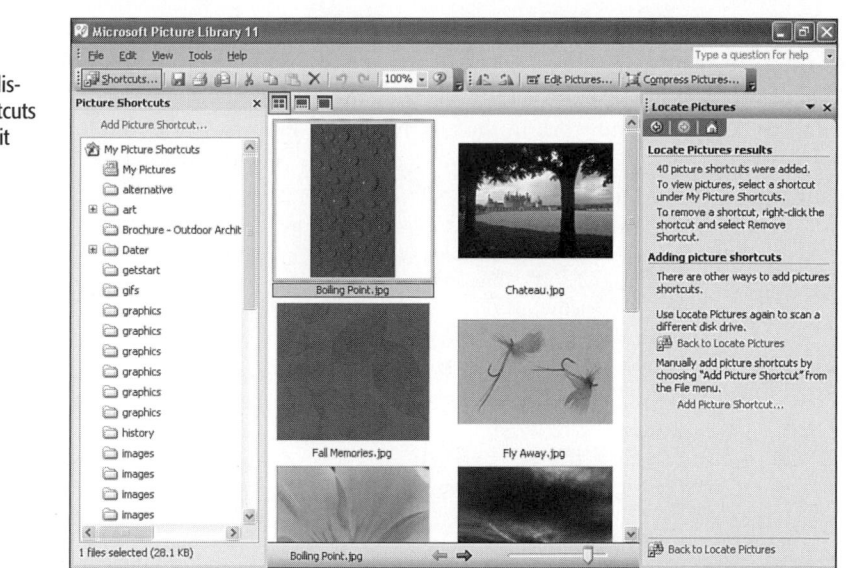

EDITING PICTURES WITH MICROSOFT OFFICE PICTURE MANAGER

To edit a picture using Microsoft Office Picture Manager, right-click on the picture, and choose Edit Pictures from the shortcut menu; or click the Edit Pictures button on the Formatting toolbar. The Edit Pictures task pane (see Figure 13.43) appears.

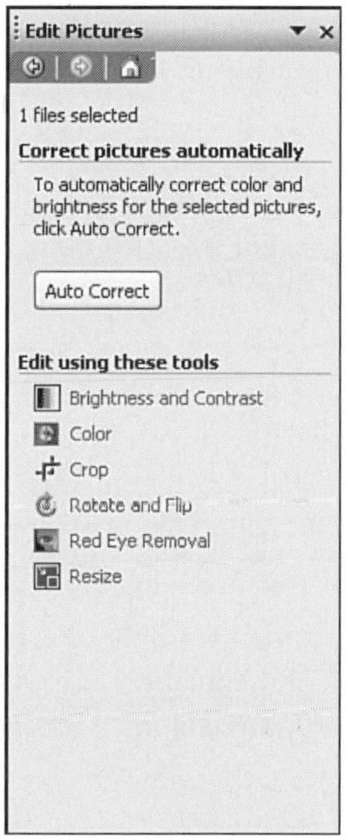

Figure 13.43
When you choose Edit Pictures, the Edit Pictures task pane presents tools for editing the picture you've selected.

13

From here, you can control brightness and contrast, color, and cropping. You also can rotate or flip your picture, remove unwanted red eye from photographic portraits, or resize your picture. To perform any of these tasks, click the corresponding hyperlink on the Edit Pictures task pane, and work in the task pane that appears. For example, to correct brightness and contrast, click Brightness and Contrast to view the Brightness and Contrast task pane (see Figure 13.44).

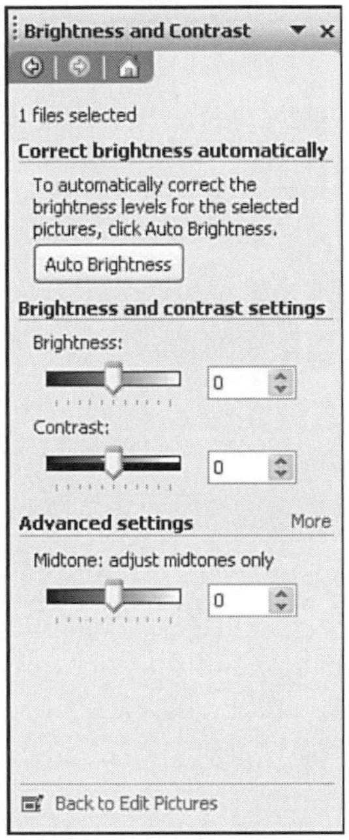

Figure 13.44
Controlling brightness and contrast from the Brightness and Contrast task pane.

You can then either work from the Brightness, Contrast, and Midtone slider bars, or click Auto Brightness to let Microsoft Office Picture Manager attempt to automatically correct your image. If you aren't satisfied with the results, you can click Undo.

VIEWING DETAILED INFORMATION ABOUT AN IMAGE

You may occasionally want to learn more about an image. For example, before using an image on a Web page, you may want to know how large it is so that you can determine whether it will take too long to load. To view detailed information about an image, right-click on it and choose Properties from the shortcut menu. The Properties task pane opens (see Figure 13.45).

The Properties task pane displays detailed information about file size, format, dimensions, file location, and most recent edit date, as well as (if the image was captured with certain digital cameras) additional technical information captured along with the image.

Figure 13.45
Displaying detailed information about an image in the Properties task pane.

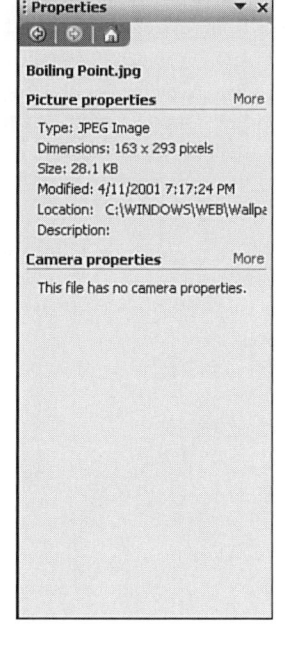

COMPRESSING IMAGES WITH MICROSOFT OFFICE PICTURE MANAGER

To reduce file sizes, you can also compress images from Microsoft Office Picture Manager. To do so, select the image (or images) you want to compress. Next, choose Picture, Compress Pictures. The Compress Pictures task pane appears (see Figure 13.46).

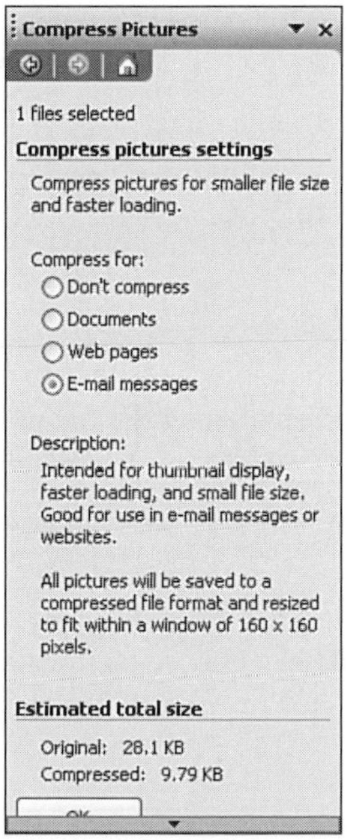

Figure 13.46
Choosing how to compress images from the Compress Pictures task pane.

13

NOTE

Many images, such as JPGs, are already compressed. Compressing them again will have little or no impact on file size; in some cases, the images may even get bigger.

Compression will, however, dramatically reduce the size of BMP and TIF or TIFF images, among other formats. And Compress Pictures can still significantly reduce an image's file size by shrinking the image (as in the case of the E-mail Messages setting).

You can now choose which purpose you intend to use the compressed image for:

- **Documents**: The image is compressed using JPG compression. If it is very large, it is also shrunk to fit within a 1,024×768 window.

- **Web Pages**: The image is compressed using JPG compression, and (if necessary) shrunk to fit within a 448×336 window.

- **E-mail Messages**: The image is compressed using JPG compression, and (if necessary) shrunk to fit within a 160×160 window for especially quick delivery.

At the bottom of the Compress Pictures task pane, Word tells you how small the image will become, based on the option you've selected. When you've made your selection, click OK.

CAUTION

Don't compress images that you intend to use for photo-quality printing. Remember, after an image is compressed, data is removed from it permanently and cannot be restored unless you have a duplicate copy of the original.

TROUBLESHOOTING

WHAT TO DO WHEN WORD DOESN'T RECOGNIZE THE FILE TYPE YOU'VE TRIED TO IMPORT

Make sure that you have installed the necessary graphics filter. The easiest way to do this is to choose Insert, Picture, From File to open the Insert Picture dialog box. Next check the list of filters in the Files of Type box. If the filter you need is not listed, run Setup again and install the filters you need.

If the file you need is not supplied by Microsoft, but you can still open it with another graphics program, you have two choices. First, after opening the file in a drawing program, select the graphic, copy it, and paste it into your Word document. The graphic becomes a Windows metafile (.wmf). If you later resave the Word document as a Web page, the graphic is resaved as a .jpg.

Alternatively, open your image file in the program that created it, copy it to the Clipboard, switch to Word, and choose Edit, Paste Special. Then choose the format in which you want the file to be pasted; for example, choose the original format so that the original drawing program can continue to edit the image.

Yet another option is to open the file in another graphics program and then resave it in a format that can be imported into Word.

WHAT TO DO WHEN A FILE THAT SHOULD CONTAIN GRAPHICS DISPLAYS ONLY TEXT

First, check the View tab of the Options dialog box—the Picture Placeholders options might be enabled. When enabled, Picture Placeholders shows all graphics as an empty box; this is intended to speed up the display for graphic-intensive documents. Choose Tools, Options and click the View tab. If the Picture Placeholders box is checked, click to clear it. While you're on the Options dialog box View tab, double-check the Drawings check box. If this is not selected, you won't see any of the drawing objects—including text boxes. To see all your graphics, check the Drawings box and clear the Picture Placeholders box.

If this doesn't work, check whether the images were incorporated in your document as links. If so, it's possible that the document or linked images have been moved, breaking the links. Choose Edit, Links; then click the Change Source button. Browse to the new location of the linked files, select them, and click Open.

WHAT TO DO IF YOUR CLIP ORGANIZER DATABASE IS DAMAGED BEYOND REPAIR

If compacting a database doesn't fix damage that prevents you from using it, you will need to create a new main catalog. To do so, find and rename the file Mstore10.mgc; Clip Organizer will create a new database with none of the customizations or additions you have made since installing Word or Office.

CAUTION

> If you are on a computer with several users, be sure to delete only the Mstore10.mgc associated with your own user profile.

WHAT TO DO IF WORD DISPLAYS MESSAGES ABOUT MISSING OR INCOMPATIBLE GRAPHICS FILTERS

If you insert a graphics file and Word displays a message indicating that a required graphics filter is missing or incompatible, follow these steps:

1. If you believe you have the correct filters installed, try to open another file with the same format (and the same file extension). If that file opens, the first image file itself may have been damaged.

2. If the filter is still reported as missing, run Setup again (through Start, Settings, Control Panel, Add/Remove Programs) and install the missing filters. In addition to the filters Office installs by default, Office ships with the following filters that *do not* install by default: CGM, CDR, FPX, MIX, PCD, PCT, PCX, and WPG.

3. If your file is in a format other than these, open the file in the program used to create it, and export it to a format Office can read.

WHAT TO DO WHEN WORD DOESN'T WORK WITH YOUR SCANNER

If your scanner does not work with Microsoft Word or Office, check to make sure that all your scanner software has been installed, including appropriate drivers. Test your scanner by scanning with the software your scanner manufacturer provided, or with other software packages.

You may want to visit your scanner's Web site to see whether newer drivers exist, especially if you have upgraded your computer to Windows 2000 or Windows XP since the last time you used your scanner.

A few older scanners are not compatible with the TWAIN standard and therefore will not work with Office.

CHAPTER 14

USING WORD'S QUICK AND EASY DRAWING TOOLS

In this chapter

UNDERSTANDING HOW WORD DRAWINGS WORK

Before you start working with Word's drawing tools, it's helpful to understand the types of images they create. Word's drawing tools create vector graphics. This is to say that they create digital images through commands and mathematical statements that instruct your computer where to place points, lines, and shapes. This is in contrast to bitmapped graphics, such as digital photos, which simply assign color data to each pixel in an image. Vector graphics have two important advantages over bitmapped graphics. First, they can be enlarged or stretched without blurring. Second, they are generally far smaller, leading to smaller files.

Word calls its vector graphics *drawing objects*. These drawing objects can be edited separately or grouped so that they can be edited together. They can also be layered so that some components of your drawing appear "on top of" others. You'll learn how to use the grouping and layering tools later in the chapter.

Because Word drawing objects are made of lines and shapes, you can often edit drawings to remove elements you don't need and add elements you do want.

WHEN TO USE WORD'S DRAWING TOOLS—AND WHEN NOT TO

Chapter 13, "Getting Images into Your Documents," discusses how to import existing graphics into Word. But what if the graphic you want doesn't exist? Often, you can create it yourself, using Word's drawing tools.

It's helpful to understand what Word's drawing tools can do well—and what they can't do well. Word's drawing tools can be invaluable when you need

- Simple flowcharts and other diagrams that can't be created automatically with Word's Diagram Gallery or Organization Chart applets
- Annotations for text or other elements in your document (using arrows, lines, or callouts)
- Starbursts and other shapes for advertisements or fliers
- Simple room or office designs using prefabricated shapes
- Edits to a vector image you already have—such as a .WMF clip art file—especially to delete an element you don't want to include
- Images that can be built from simple, regular shapes such as rectangles and circles

In short, Word's drawing tools are well suited for solving a wide variety of specific business problems. But they're poorly suited for projects in which superb aesthetics are required, such as complex freehand illustrations, images that must be printed with precise coloring, or "painted" bitmapped graphics. In such cases, use another tool for the job. For example:

- To edit photographs or scanned images, use professional-quality tools such as Adobe Photoshop or JASC PaintShop Pro, or consumer tools such as Adobe Photoshop Elements or Microsoft Picture It! For simple tasks such as adjusting brightness or

14

contrast, use Microsoft Office Picture Manager, which is included in Microsoft Office 2003 and is covered in Chapter 13.

- To create complex freehand vector illustrations, use Adobe Illustrator or Microsoft Freehand.

- To create professional-quality sketches and paintings that mimic the output of traditional media, use Corel Painter.

USING WORD 2003'S DRAWING TOOLBAR

To draw in Word, first display the Drawing toolbar. To do so, either click the Drawing button on the Standard toolbar or choose View, Toolbars, Drawing. The Drawing toolbar appears at the bottom of the Word application window (see Figure 14.1).

Figure 14.1
The Drawing toolbar centralizes all of Word's tools for drawing objects.

The Drawing toolbar brings together all of Word's tools for drawing. Some of these tools—such as callouts—are valuable even if you never create an image from scratch. Table 14.1 presents an overview of each button and what it does.

TABLE 14.1 DRAWING TOOLBAR FEATURES

Button	Name	Description
 Draw ▾	Draw	Contains editing controls for manipulating drawing objects
	Select Objects	Enables the selection of one or more drawing objects
 AutoShapes ▾	AutoShapes	Contains the library of automatic shapes, including lines, basic shapes, block arrows, flowchart elements, stars and banners, and callouts
	Line	Enables you to click and drag a line
	Arrow	Enables you to click and drag an arrow
	Rectangle	Enables you to click and drag a rectangle
	Oval	Enables you to click and drag an oval
	Text Box	Enables you to click and drag out a text box
	WordArt	Starts the creation of a fancy text object

continues

TABLE 14.1 CONTINUED

Button	Name	Description
	Insert Diagram or Organization Chart	Displays the Diagram Gallery for inserting diagrams or organization charts
	Insert Clip Art	Displays the Clip Gallery for inserting clip art
	Insert Picture	Displays the Insert Picture dialog box for inserting image files of any kind
	Fill Color	Controls the color, pattern, or effect inside a drawing object
	Line Color	Controls the color, pattern, or effect of a drawing object's border
	Font Color	Controls the color of selected text
	Line Style	Enables quick formatting for a line's thickness and style
	Dash Style	Enables quick formatting for a line's appearance
	Arrow Style	Enables quick selection from a variety of arrowhead styles
	Shadow Style	Controls shadow appearance for any drawing object
	3D Style	Controls the 3D appearance for any drawing object

→ For information on WordArt, **see** Chapter 13, "Getting Images into Your Documents," **p. 437**; on text boxes, **see** Chapter 16, "Word Desktop Publishing," **p. 557**; and on diagrams and organization charts, **see** Chapter 15, "Visualizing Your Message with Graphs, Diagrams, and Org Charts," **p. 511**.

UNDERSTANDING THE DRAWING CANVAS

Long-time Word users have sometimes encountered difficulties in controlling the position and elements of their images—especially the way images interact with surrounding text and page breaks. To help address this problem, Microsoft introduced the *Drawing Canvas*.

The Drawing Canvas is, in essence, a separate layer of a Word document for drawings. All drawing objects placed within a Drawing Canvas have an absolute position and remain together as you placed them, regardless of where the Drawing Canvas itself may move as you edit surrounding text.

When you insert a new line, shape, or other drawing element in Word 2003, Word switches to Print Layout view and displays the Drawing Canvas, as shown in Figure 14.2. If you want, you can then create your image within the borders of the Drawing Canvas. By default, the Drawing Canvas extends from your left to right margins and is 4.5" high.

Figure 14.2
Word 2003's Drawing Canvas.

Create your drawing here.

NOTE

If you are superimposing a drawing object on an existing graphic, the Drawing Canvas does not appear. You simply draw the new object on top of the graphic.

Word's Drawing Canvas toolbar (see Figure 14.3) provides four tools that make it easier to use the Drawing Canvas. To display the toolbar, right-click within the Drawing Canvas and choose Show Drawing Canvas Toolbar.

Eliminates blank Drawing Canvas space beyond the edges of your drawing objects

Provides choices for controlling how text wraps around the Drawing Canvas

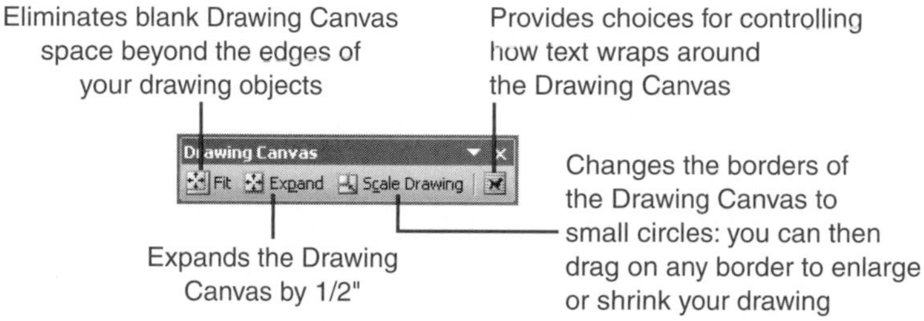

Figure 14.3
The Drawing Canvas toolbar.

Drawing Canvas
Fit   Expand   Scale Drawing

Changes the borders of the Drawing Canvas to small circles: you can then drag on any border to enlarge or shrink your drawing

Expands the Drawing Canvas by 1/2"

You can format other elements of a Drawing Canvas by right-clicking on it and choosing Format Drawing Canvas from the shortcut menu. The Format Drawing Canvas dialog box appears (see Figure 14.4).

From here, you can control the following:

- **Colors and Lines**—Fill colors, transparency, and the appearance of borders around the Drawing Canvas
- **Size**—The size and scale of the Drawing Canvas
- **Layout**—Text wrapping options for the Drawing Canvas, including horizontal alignment options not available from the Drawing Canvas toolbar
- **Web**—Alternative text that can appear in place of (or before) graphics appear, if your document is saved as a Web page or viewed on a browser

14

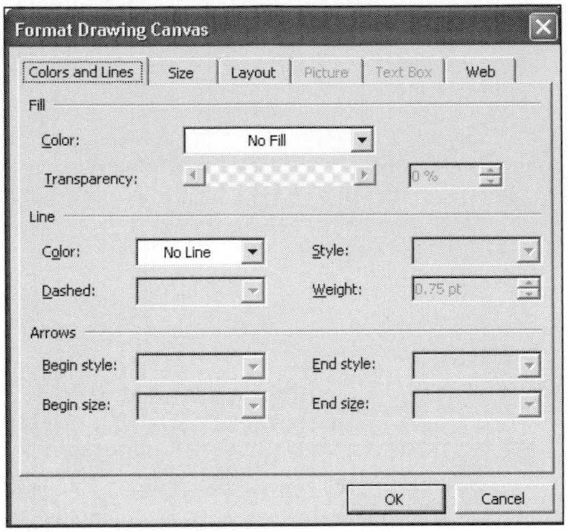

Figure 14.4
The Format Drawing
Canvas dialog box.

The settings provided in the Format Drawing Canvas dialog box are similar to those in the Format Picture dialog box covered in Chapter 13.

DRAWING WITHOUT USING THE DRAWING CANVAS

You may not always want to use the Drawing Canvas. For example, if your drawing is simple, and you don't expect to encounter problems aligning your drawing with other document elements, you may not need the Drawing Canvas. If your drawing is far smaller than the default Drawing Canvas, you may not want to take the trouble to resize the canvas. In certain cases, the Drawing Canvas can introduce new problems; for example, it can make creating accurate callouts more difficult.

To avoid using the Drawing Canvas, press Esc after Word inserts it. The Drawing Canvas will disappear.

If you really can't stand the Drawing Canvas, you can instruct Word not to display it automatically. Choose Tools, Options, General; then clear the Automatically Create Drawing Canvas When Inserting AutoShapes check box.

DRAWING LINES AND OTHER BASIC SHAPES

The simplest objects of a Word drawing are lines and basic shapes. You'll often find simple elements such as these at the heart of even complex drawings. In the next few sections, you'll learn how to create these graphical elements using Word's drawing tools.

DRAWING A STRAIGHT LINE

To draw a straight line in Word, click on the Line button on the Drawing toolbar; the mouse pointer changes to crosshairs. Next, click in the editing window where you want to begin the line, and drag the mouse pointer to where you want the line to end (see Figure 14.5). Release the mouse pointer, and a line appears selected in your document.

Figure 14.5
Dragging the mouse
pointer to draw a line.

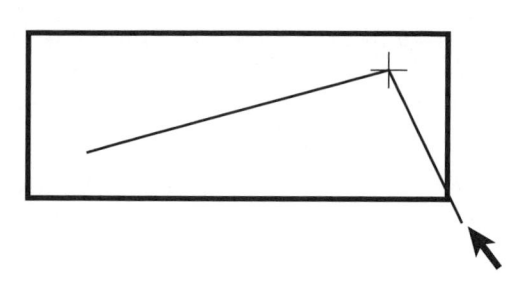

After you've created a line, you may want to adjust it. For example, you may want it to be thicker or narrower than Word's default 3/4-point line. Or you may want a dotted line instead of Word's default solid line. To change a solid line to a dotted or dashed line, select it by clicking on it. Then click the Dash Style button on the Drawing toolbar (see Figure 14.6) and select a style for the line.

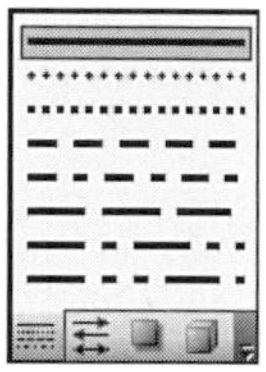

Figure 14.6
Choosing a dotted or
dashed line using the
Dash Style button.

To change a line's thickness, select it, click the Line Style button, and select a thickness for the line.

If none of Word's built-in line styles suffices, click <u>M</u>ore Lines to display the Colors and Lines tab of the Format AutoShape dialog box (see Figure 14.7).

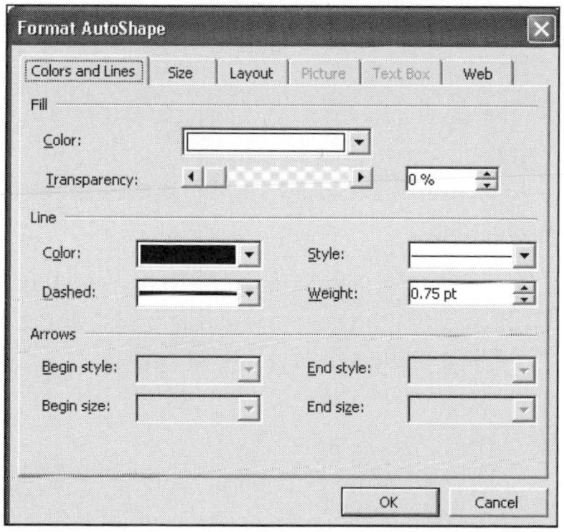

Figure 14.7
The Colors and Lines
tab of the Format
AutoShape
dialog box.

14

Each type of Word shape has its own Format AutoShape dialog box, where you can control elements such as color, thickness, size, and text wrapping. Format AutoShape dialog boxes are much like the Format Picture dialog boxes you learned about in Chapter 13. A few points about the Colors and Lines tab are especially worth mentioning:

■ From the <u>C</u>olor drop-down box, you can choose one of 40 built-in colors; click <u>M</u>ore Colors to choose a custom color, or choose <u>P</u>atterned Lines to select a pattern for your line or arrow.

■ From the <u>W</u>eight text box, you can set your line to be as thick or as narrow as you want. If you use the built-in spin controls, you can set the weight in increments of 0.25 points. If you enter the value directly, you can use increments of 0.01 points.

■ The <u>S</u>tyle drop-down box contains the same options as the Line Style button on the Drawing toolbar. The <u>D</u>ashed drop-down box contains the same options as the Dash Style button on the Drawing toolbar.

■ You can use the Size tab of the Format AutoShape dialog box to set an exact height, width, and angle of rotation for your line or shape.

■ In the Web tab, you can type alternative text that appears on Web pages when your shape cannot be displayed.

→ For more information about the Format Picture dialog box, **see** "Resizing Images Precisely, by Using Format, Picture," **p. 458**; "Setting Text Wrapping from the Format Picture Dialog Box," **p. 462**; and "Adding Alternative Text to Your Image," **p. 467**.

DRAWING ARROWS

To insert Word's default arrow, click the Arrow button on the Drawing toolbar; the mouse pointer changes to crosshairs. Click where you want the arrow's "tail" to begin; then drag it to where you want its "arrowhead" to appear and release the mouse pointer.

Sometimes, you may want to format your arrow differently. For example, Word's default arrow may not be readable if it points into a dark background. Or you may want an arrow that points in both directions.

To use one of Word's built-in arrows, first insert either an arrow or a line. (You can turn a line into an arrow by following the same steps for changing an arrow.) Next, with the arrow selected, click the Arrow Style button (see Figure 14.8) and click on a style. The line or arrow is reformatted as you specified.

If none of Word's standard arrow styles meets your needs, choose <u>M</u>ore Arrows. The Format AutoShape dialog box appears (you saw this dialog box in Figure 14.7). Here, you can choose from a wide variety of thicknesses, styles, and sizes.

DRAWING RECTANGLES AND OVALS

Drawing basic squares, rectangles, and ovals works much the same way as drawing lines. Click the Rectangle or Oval button. Then click in the document and drag the mouse pointer to set the shape's borders. Release the pointer, and the shape appears in your document.

14

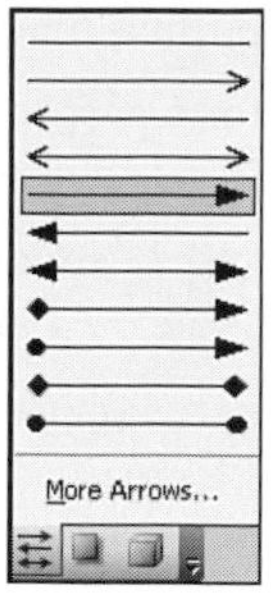

Figure 14.8
Displaying Word's basic arrow styles by clicking the Arrow Style button.

TIP

> If you want an exact square or circle, click the Rectangle or Oval button and press Shift while you drag the mouse.
>
> You can also use the Shift key to make straight lines or arrows that are precisely horizontal, vertical, or diagonal. If you press Shift while you drag the Line tool, you're limited to increments of 15°.

TIP

> To enter text in a shape such as a rectangle or an oval, right-click on it and choose Add Text from the shortcut menu. This transforms the shape into a text box and displays a cursor inside it. You can then type or format the text.

TIP

> If you simply want to place a box around a block of text, don't bother with Word's drawing tools. Just select the text and click the Outside Border button on the Formatting toolbar.

AutoShapes: Word's Library of Predrawn Shapes

You may find that you need more complicated shapes than are easily drawn manually. Fortunately, Word may have done much of the work for you, with AutoShapes. Word's AutoShapes collection gives you arrows, banners, callouts, and many other predrawn shapes, all of them easy to insert into your document and customize to your precise needs. Word provides these categories of predrawn AutoShapes:

- **Lines**—Word's tools for creating free-form shapes and "scribbles."
- **Connectors**—Straight lines, angled lines, curly lines, and arrows that can help you neatly connect any shapes you've drawn.
- **Basic Shapes**—Both 2D and 3D shapes, lightning bolts, suns, moons, hearts, smiley faces, and other commonly used shapes.
- **Block Arrows**—Both 2D and 3D arrows that are fancier than the arrows covered earlier and can be filled with colors, patterns, or gradients.

14

- **Flowchart**—Twenty-eight symbols most commonly used in building flowcharts.
- **Stars and Banners**—Starbursts and other objects ideal for newspaper advertising and fliers.
- **Callouts**—Text boxes connected to arrows; these allow you to annotate anything on a page in a single step.
- **More AutoShapes**—Displays the Clip Art task pane, where you can choose from more than 100 additional AutoShapes—including, for example, drawings of computer equipment and furniture for use in network and office layouts.

All AutoShapes can be resized, rotated, flipped, colored, and combined with other shapes (or your basic ovals and rectangles) to make even more intricate shapes.

To use an AutoShape, click AutoShapes on the Drawing toolbar, choose a category, and choose an AutoShape (see Figure 14.9). Then, click in your document and drag the AutoShape to the proportions you want.

NOTE

You can also choose More AutoShapes to display the Clip Art task pane, with many more AutoShapes that can be dragged directly into your document.

→ For more information on working with More AutoShapes, **see** "Using More AutoShapes to Create Room Designs and Other Drawings," **p. 495**.

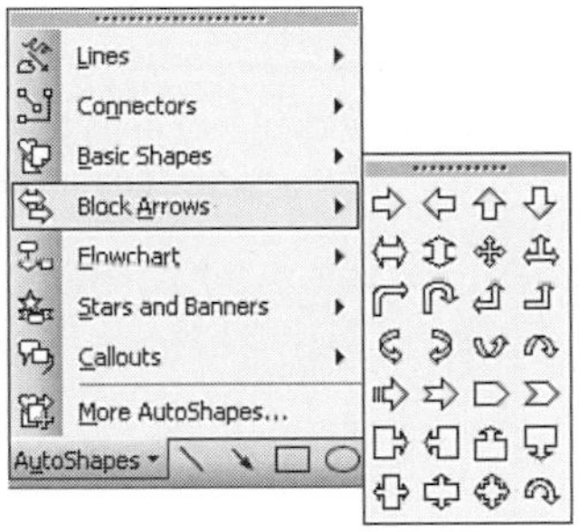

Figure 14.9
Word provides an extensive library of predefined graphic AutoShapes.

SETTING AUTOSHAPE DEFAULTS

Often, it can take some effort to get an AutoShape formatted just the way you want it. After you've done so, you may want all the AutoShapes you create in the same document to use the same formatting. If so, right-click on the shape you've formatted and choose Set AutoShape Defaults from the shortcut menu. Among the attributes you can adjust with Set AutoShape Defaults are line width, color, and style; fill color; fill effects such as textures; types of arrows; and transparency.

14

CAUTION

> Setting AutoShape defaults changes the formatting of all the AutoShapes you create in the same document from now on—not just AutoShapes identical to the one you formatted. In other words, if you choose Set AutoShape Defaults with a rectangle selected, your new defaults will affect circles, callouts, flowchart shapes, and any other AutoShape you create.

TIP

> Unfortunately, Set AutoShape Defaults works only for a single document; if you open a new document, you will have to set them all over again. One workaround is to format a shape exactly as you want it—including colors, borders, types of lines, and (if it's a text box) text size, color, and margins. Having done so, select the shape and save it as an AutoText entry: Choose Insert, AutoText, New; type the shortcut name you want to use for the AutoText entry; and click OK. Then, you can insert a properly formatted shape simply by typing the AutoText shortcut and pressing F3.

USING WORD'S STARS AND BANNERS AUTOSHAPES

Stars and Banners AutoShapes are ideal for retail advertising and fliers but might also have uses in newsletters and company publications. Be careful how you use them, though: They can be a bit garish.

Figure 14.10 shows part of a sales flier created using AutoShape starbursts. This was created by right-clicking on the AutoShape, choosing Format AutoShape from the shortcut menu, clicking the Colors and Lines tab, clicking Color in the Fill section, choosing Fill Effects from the drop-down list, and choosing a one-color horizontal gradient. You'll learn more about these formatting options later in the chapter.

Figure 14.10
An AutoShape starburst used as part of a sales flier.

MAKING FLOWCHARTS WITH WORD'S FLOWCHART AUTOSHAPES

Word's library of 28 flowchart AutoShapes is sufficient for a wide variety of flowcharting tasks. In fact, you may find that you'll be able to do all you need with a small fraction of them. Table 14.2 lists several of the most commonly used flowchart icons.

TABLE 14.2   COMMONLY USED FLOWCHART ICONS

Icon	What It Represents
☐	A process.
⬭	An alternative process.
◇	A point where a decision must be made.
⬡	A point where preparation is required.
▽	A manual operation that must be performed.
⬓	A document is generated.
⬓	Many documents are generated.

Among the tasks you may be able to perform with Word's flowchart AutoShapes are

- Simple process descriptions and business process reengineering
- Charting for ISO quality management
- Planning a small to moderate-sized project or Web site

NOTE

> If you find that Word's flowchart tools are insufficient to meet your needs, two popular (but expensive) alternatives from Microsoft are the Visio drawing program and Microsoft Project. Less costly alternatives include FlowCharts&More from IMSI (www.imsisoft.com).

Using Callouts

What do you do if you need to annotate a visual element of your document, such as a logo or photograph? Use callouts. A *callout* combines an arrow with a text box in which you can type. To use one of the 20 types of callouts provided, follow these steps:

1. From the Drawing toolbar, click the AutoShapes button.

2. Choose Callouts and then select the particular callout you want to insert. The pointer changes to a small crosshair.

3. To use a line callout, click the subject of your callout first and then hold down the mouse pointer while you drag away from it to the point where you want the callout box to appear. Release the mouse pointer. Word inserts both a line (called a *leader*) and a text box where you can enter the text of your callout. An insertion point flashes within the text box.

   To use a rectangular (non-line) callout, first click where you want to place the callout. If you want to enlarge the callout, select it; then hold down the mouse pointer and drag it outward.

Note that when you choose Callouts, Word inserts a drawing canvas, but you need not use it. You can point your callout anywhere in your document, inside or outside the drawing canvas, and if you point it outside, the drawing canvas will disappear. Many users find the drawing canvas an annoyance. If you want to get rid of it permanently, choose Tools, Options, General; clear the Automatically Create Drawing Canvas When Inserting AutoShapes check box, and click OK.

4. Type your text and apply any formatting.

5. If necessary, resize the callout box by clicking and dragging any of the sizing handles.

6. You can adjust the placement of the leader by clicking the yellow diamond adjustment handle at the end of the line, as seen in Figure 14.11. Some callouts have multiple adjustment handles, enabling you to manipulate the angles of the line that stretches between the callout and the element to which you are calling attention.

Figure 14.11
Callouts can be used to label parts of an image.

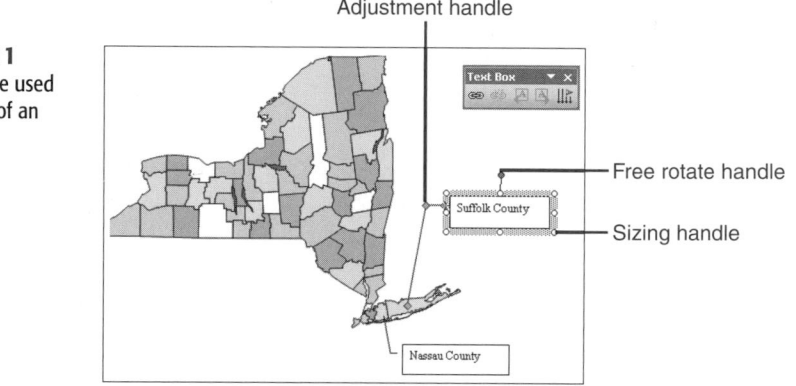

7. Click anywhere outside the callout box to return to the regular document.

USING MORE AUTOSHAPES TO CREATE ROOM DESIGNS AND OTHER DRAWINGS

In addition to the six categories of AutoShapes you've already learned about, Word provides a separate library called More AutoShapes. This library's contents include outlined images of furniture, electronic appliances, and widely used symbols such as padlocks and puzzle pieces.

To display More AutoShapes, click AutoShapes on the Drawing toolbar and choose More AutoShapes. The Clip Art task pane appears, displaying more AutoShapes (see Figure 14.12).

After you've displayed the Clip Art task pane by choosing More AutoShapes, you can browse to the image you want, and click on it. The image is inserted.

→ For more information about inserting clip art, **see** "Working with Microsoft Clip Organizer," **p. 447**.

14

Figure 14.12
The Clip Art task pane contains many additional widely used symbols.

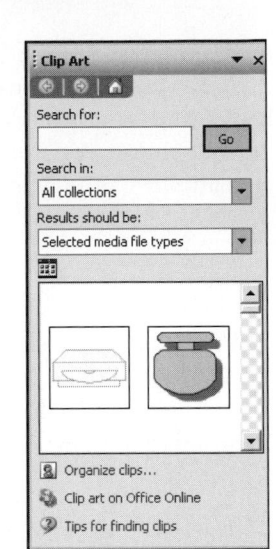

FREEHAND DRAWING

Although Word offers many preset shapes to choose from, sooner or later you are likely to need a graphic that isn't provided. The Drawing toolbar gives you access to three freehand drawing tools. You can choose from a tool that creates curves, one that uses a combination of straight lines and freehand drawing, and one that relies entirely on freehand drawing.

The freehand drawing tools are all located under the Lines submenu of the AutoShapes button (see Figure 14.13). (Lines also contains a basic Line tool, a regular Arrow tool, and a Double Arrow tool along the top row of the submenu. You create any of these shapes by clicking and dragging.)

Figure 14.13
Options on the AutoShape Lines submenu.

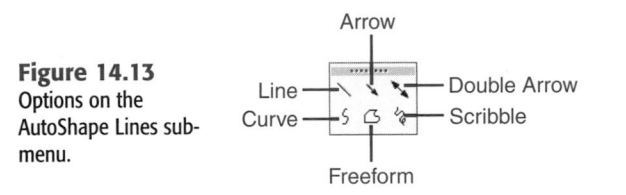

Line and Arrow tools work just like the Line and Arrow tools covered earlier in this chapter, in the "Drawing Lines and Other Basic Shapes" section. Double Arrow works just like the Arrow tool, except that it creates an arrow with arrowheads at both ends. The other three tools—Curve, Freeform, and Scribble—are covered in the next three sections.

DRAWING CURVES WITH THE CURVE TOOL

Use the Curve tool to create a smooth-turning line or shape. After selecting the Curve tool, click where you want your shape to start, and move the mouse—a line follows your movement. Click again where you want the line to begin to curve. Continue clicking and moving the mouse to build your shape. Press Esc or double-click where you want the shape to stop. To close a shape, click your starting point instead.

NOTE

> You can't convert a closed freehand shape to a text box, so you can't add text inside it, except by superimposing a separate text box on it.

DRAWING FREEHAND WITH THE FREEFORM TOOL

The Freeform tool enables you to draw freehand, using a mixture of straight lines and "hand-drawn" shapes that do not follow straight lines. After selecting Freeform from the Lines submenu, you can draw freehand, without straight lines, by clicking, holding down the mouse button, and dragging the mouse. A freehand line follows as you drag. If part of your drawing needs to be a straight line, release the mouse button; then drag to extend your drawing with a straight line. If you need to extend your drawing further with a hand-drawn (non-straight) line, click and hold down the mouse button again as you draw.

You can keep drawing until you're finished. When you're finished, press Esc or double-click to end the line. Or, if you want to close the shape, click on its starting point.

DRAWING FREEHAND WITH THE SCRIBBLE TOOL

To draw freehand, with no straight lines at all, use the Scribble tool. Click the Scribble icon, click in the document, and start dragging. Word inserts lines as you drag, until you release the mouse pointer. Because your mouse isn't a precise input tool, drawings you make with the Scribble tool are likely to look, well, scribbled.

CONTROLLING COLORS

Without color, your drawing objects are merely outlines. Word enables you to choose from a full range of colors—including shades of gray—to fill your objects, change your borders, and modify your text. In addition, you can fill your shapes with multicolor gradient blends, preset textures, and even user-selectable pictures.

CAUTION

> Not all printers and monitors accurately reproduce the colors you choose. If accurate color is important, print a test copy, or display a test file using the monitor/printer combination where you expect your document to be viewed.

CHANGING FILLS AND LINE COLORS

Shapes you create with Word's drawing tools (except for lines and arrows) have two parts that can be colored. Although the *interior* fill color is the most obvious, you can also control the *border* color separately.

14

The easiest way to change a fill or line color is by clicking the correct button on the Drawing toolbar. The Fill Color and Line Color buttons both have option arrows that open similar Color menus with 40 color swatches and extended options. Click any of the onscreen colors to change either the fill or the line color of your selected drawing object. Clicking the No Fill or No Line options makes those respective choices transparent.

If you choose More Fill Colors from the Fill Color button, or More Line Colors from the Line Color button, the Colors dialog box appears (see Figure 14.14). The Standard tab displays a default color palette in a hexagon shape, as well as a 16-step grayscale blend between black and white.

Figure 14.14
Choosing a color from the Standard color palette.

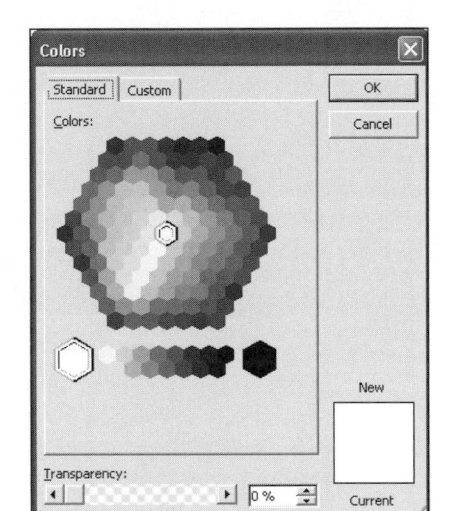

If your color palette is set to 16- or 32-bit color (also called High Color or True Color), you can use the Custom tab shown in Figure 14.15. This tab allows you to select a color that isn't in Word's standard palette.

Word 2003 supports two color models—formal descriptions of how human beings perceive color. The first, RGB, specifies color by how much red, green, and blue are present. The second color model, HSL, measures color by hue, saturation, and luminance. HSL and RGB are actually quite similar, and both are designed primarily for documents that will be displayed onscreen. HSL is generally viewed as more intuitive; RGB is more widely adopted. When you choose a color model, the appropriate settings for that model appear.

Word does not provide built-in support for the CMYK and PANTONE color models that are typically used for professional print production.

If you want to work with HSL, choose HSL from the Color Model drop-down box of the Colors dialog box. Click anywhere in the large rectangular Colors area to choose a basic color. (This sets Hue and Saturation.) Then, select its intensity (Luminance) by dragging the arrow on the long vertical strip on the right.

14

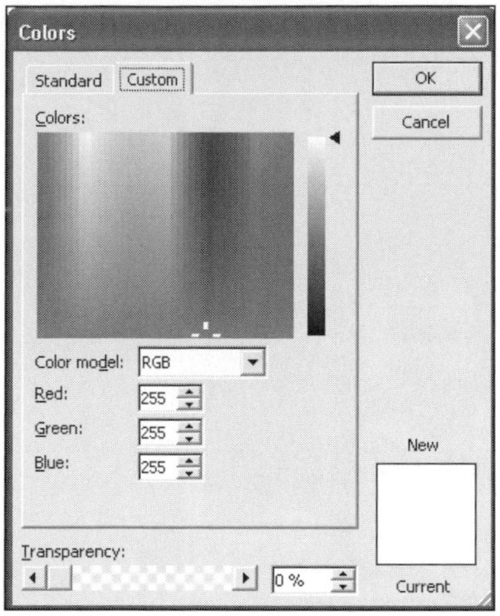

Figure 14.15
Using the Custom tab of the Colors dialog box, you can choose any color in the RGB or HSL color space.

Or, if you know the precise HSL or RGB settings you want, you can enter them in the H<u>ue</u>, <u>S</u>aturation, and <u>L</u>uminance or <u>R</u>ed, <u>G</u>reen, and <u>B</u>lue spin boxes directly.

TIP

> If you've worked hard to get a color just the way you want it, and you want to use the same color in another drawing object, here's a shortcut.
>
> Select the shape whose color you want to match. Click Format Painter on the Standard toolbar. Click the second shape. The lines and colors on the first shape now appear on the second.

ADDING FILL EFFECTS TO YOUR SHAPES

You can add fancy backgrounds to shapes you create in Word. These include gradients, textures, patterns, and even pictures. Word refers to these backgrounds as *fill effects*. To add a fill effect to a shape, first select the shape. Then, click the down arrow next to the Fill Color button on the Drawing toolbar and click <u>F</u>ill Effects. The Fill Effects dialog box appears; from here, you can work with all of Word's fill effects.

USING GRADIENTS

A *gradient* is an area of color that moves from dark to light, or from one color to another. To work with gradients, choose the Gradient tab of the Fill Effects dialog box (see Figure 14.16) to select—or custom-blend—a special gradient.

You can choose whether your gradients should contain one color or two; if you choose two colors, you can specify which colors you want. You can specify how the gradients change: from top to bottom (Horizontal), from left to right (Vertical), diagonally, from the corner, or from the center. Try experimenting—each option offers a different, interesting effect.

14

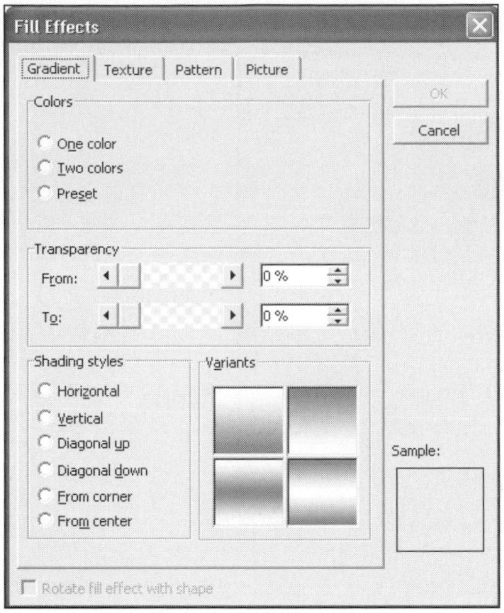

Figure 14.16
Choosing a gradient from the Gradient tab of the Fill Effects dialog box.

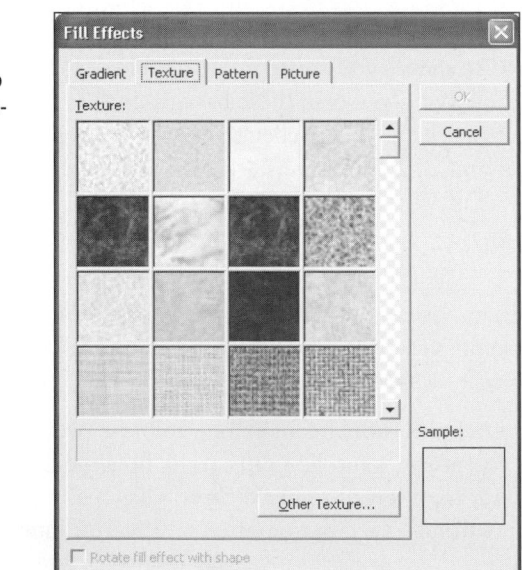

You can also choose from among a series of preset gradients, designed to communicate a certain mood. These include Early Sunset, Horizon, Desert, Rainbow, Calm Water, Gold, Brass, Chrome, and several others.

USING TEXTURES

Word also provides 24 textures you can place in a shape you've created. To browse them, click the Texture tab of the Fill Effects dialog box (see Figure 14.17). Click a texture and click OK.

Figure 14.17
Choosing a texture from the Texture tab of the Fill Effects dialog box.

TIP

You can use any bitmapped image as a texture. To do so, display the Texture tab of the Fill Effects dialog box, and click Other Texture. The Select Texture dialog box appears. Browse to the image you want to use, and click Insert. The image now appears as a choice in the Texture list. Select it, and click OK.

USING PATTERNS

Word also provides 48 patterns you can use in any shape you create. As with other fill effects, be careful—lest you create a garish effect. Used with care, though, patterns can add visual interest and help you call attention to specific elements of your drawing.

To browse Word's patterns, display the Fill Effects dialog box and click the Pattern tab.

By default, patterns are displayed in the fill color of the object you've selected. However, you can choose from Word's entire color palette for both the background and the foreground colors. Click the down arrow under Foreground or Background to change the color; an updated sample appears at the right.

Figure 14.18 shows one of Word's built-in clip art images, made more striking through the use of a white-on-black pattern.

Figure 14.18
Using a pattern to add drama.

INSERTING PICTURES INTO YOUR SHAPES

Thus far, you've learned how to make your shapes more attractive using gradients, textures, and patterns. When even these options aren't sufficient, Word also allows you to insert pictures in shapes. To insert a picture into a shape, carry out these instructions:

1. Select the shape.
2. Click the down arrow on the Fill Color button and choose Fill Effects.
3. Click on the Picture tab of the Fill Effects dialog box.
4. Click Select Picture. The Select Picture dialog box opens.
5. Browse to and select the picture you want.
6. Click Insert to close the Select Picture dialog box.

14

7. If you want to make sure that your picture is not distorted even if you stretch the shape it appears in, check the Lock Picture Aspect Ratio check box.

8. Click OK to apply the picture.

The picture appears in your document.

ADDING DEPTH TO YOUR GRAPHICS

Word 2003 includes two effective tools to make your graphics appear to leap off the page. First, any drawing object—including lines, free-form drawings, and clip art—can cast a shadow, in almost any direction and in any color. Shadows help separate a graphic from its background on the page. Second, you can apply 3D effects to drawing objects. Both tools are available through the Drawing toolbar.

CAUTION

> You can't apply shadowing and 3D to the same object. If you apply a shadow effect to an object formatted as 3D, the shadow replaces the 3D effect.

USING SHADOWING

You can instantly add a 50% gray drop-shadow to the border of a line or shape. The shadow appears on any side of an object, appears on top of the object, or surrounds the object like a picture frame.

To add a drop-shadow, first select the object you want to shadow. Next, click the Shadow button on the Drawing toolbar and choose from among the 20 preset shadows displayed in Figure 14.19. To adjust the shadow's position and color, select Shadow Settings. The Shadow Settings toolbar appears; there, you can select the settings you want.

Figure 14.19
Choosing a shadow from the list of shadows available.

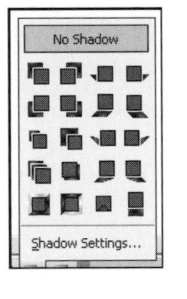

If you don't like the way the shadow looks, choose a different shadow. If you decide that you don't want a shadow after all, select the shape and choose No Shadow from the Shadow palette.

You can change the shadow's style settings by choosing the Shadow Settings command on the Shadow palette. The Shadow Settings toolbar appears, as shown in Figure 14.20.

From this toolbar, you can choose several options to change the look of a shadow. To add or remove a shadow, click the Shadow On/Off button. You can even move the shadow a little

14

bit at a time in a particular direction. Choose Nudge Shadow Up, Nudge Shadow Down, Nudge Shadow Left, or Nudge Shadow Right.

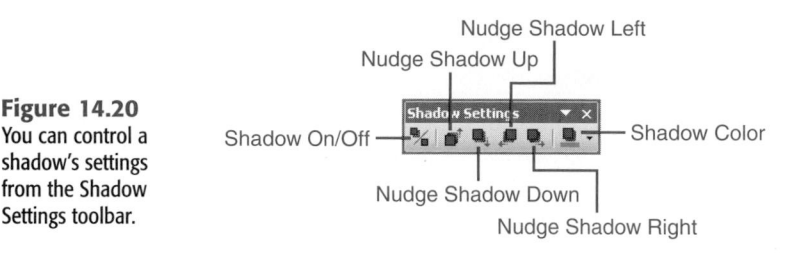

Figure 14.20
You can control a shadow's settings from the Shadow Settings toolbar.

To change the color of the shadow, click the Shadow Color drop-down arrow and select the color of your choice. Clicking More Shadow Colors displays the Colors dialog box. From there, you can choose from a wider set of colors or create a custom color.

The Shadow Color settings include a special Semitransparent Shadow option that enables text to be seen through the shadow. When combining text and an object's shadow, however, it's usually a better idea to move the object behind the text via the Order command (covered later in this chapter).

USING 3D EFFECTS

Word 2003's 3D tool goes beyond shadowing, giving 2D drawing objects apparent depth by extending their edges and rotating them to any angle.

Expanding an object's edges is called *extruding*. You can control both the depth of the extrusion and the direction. What makes the extrusion look three-dimensional is the use of a computer-generated light source that creates an illusion of light and shadow. Word even gives you control over the direction and intensity of the light. Finally, you can choose from four different surface types: Wire Frame, Matte, Plastic, or Metal.

The 3D tool works much like the Shadow tool. Select a drawing object and click the 3D button on the Drawing toolbar. Choose any of the 20 preset 3D effects. Figure 14.21 shows what four standard 3D styles look like when applied to the same object.

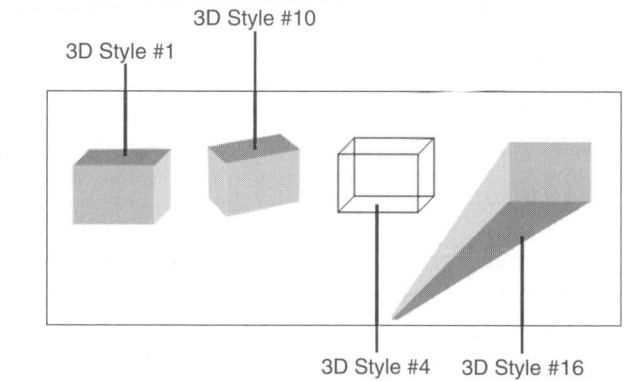

Figure 14.21
Any drawing object can be extended into the third dimension with the 3D tool.

14

After you have applied a basic 3D style, you can adjust the settings by selecting the 3-D Settings option from the 3D menu. Table 14.3 outlines the options available.

TABLE 14.3	3D SETTINGS	
Button	**Name**	**Description**
	3D On/Off	Enables or disables the 3D effect.
	Tilt Down	Each mouse click tilts the object down 5°. Shift+click tilts the object in 45° increments. Ctrl+click tilts the object in 1° increments.
	Tilt Up	Each mouse click tilts the object up 5°. Shift+click tilts the object in 45° increments. Ctrl+click tilts the object in 1° increments.
	Tilt Left	Each mouse click tilts the object 5° to the left. Shift+click tilts the object in 45° increments. Ctrl+click tilts the object in 1° increments.
	Tilt Right	Each mouse click tilts the object 5° to the right. Shift+click tilts the object in 45° increments. Ctrl+click tilts the object in 1° increments.
	Depth	Controls the size of the extrusion. There are six preset values, including Infinity for 3D extrusions that have perspective (direction), as well as a Custom option.
	Direction	Controls the direction of the extrusion. There are nine preset values and Parallel or Perspective options.
	Lighting	Controls the direction and intensity of the light. There are nine preset directions and three preset intensities.
	Surface	Controls the reflectiveness of the extruded surface. Surface types include Wire Frame, Matte, Plastic, and Metal.
	3D Color	Controls the color of the extrusion. Displays the color palette; choosing More 3D Colors displays the Colors dialog box.

The depth of your 3D object is expressed in point size—the preset values include 0 pt. (no extrusion), 36 pt., 72 pt., and so on. Think of the depth as how thick your object appears; a depth of 72 pt. makes your object an inch thick. (There are 72 points in an inch.)

In addition to the Custom option, which enables you to enter your own depth value, there is an Infinity alternative for objects that have perspective. Selecting Infinity causes your object to extrude to its *vanishing point*—a term used in perspective drawing to indicate the place where all lines meet.

Perspective also comes into play when selecting the direction of your 3D object. You can choose between Parallel and Perspective style for any direction. Perspective uses the vanishing point when drawing the extrusion, whereas P̲arallel continues all edges in their original direction. In general, P̲erspective gives a more three-dimensional appearance.

NOTE

> You can use 3D effects only on AutoShapes and WordArt. With text boxes, you have access to all 3D options, but only the frame around the text is affected, not the text itself.

EDITING OBJECTS IN A WORD DRAWING

To work with a line, a rectangle, a circle, an AutoShape, or another object, you must first select it. Lines and shapes are selected when you first place them in your document. After that, you can select a line or shape at any time by clicking on it. When the object is selected, small circles called *sizing handles* appear at the ends or corners of the shape.

After you select a shape, you can

- Move the shape by dragging it
- Shrink or enlarge the shape by clicking on a sizing handle and dragging it
- Delete the shape by pressing the Backspace or Delete key

SELECTING MULTIPLE DRAWING OBJECTS AT ONCE

Most of your original drawings—and virtually any piece of editable Office clip art—contain more than one shape. You'll often want to select many shapes in a drawing at the same time.

You can select more than one object at a time. To do so, select the first object, press Shift, and select each additional object you want. Release the Shift key; the objects remain selected, and you can format them together.

Or, click the Select Objects button on the Drawing toolbar and drag the pointer across all the drawing objects you want to select. The Select Objects pointer selects only objects entirely within the area you select—if a corner peeks off to the side, that object won't be selected. Figure 14.22 shows a simple drawing with all its different objects selected.

Figure 14.22
A drawing with all its objects selected.

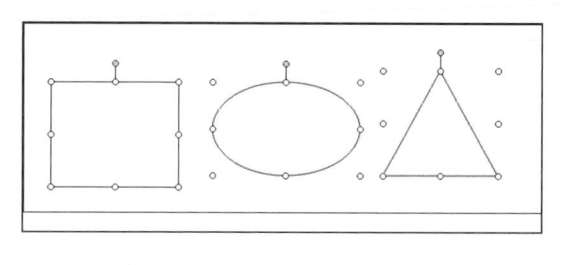

14

NOTE

> If you are selecting objects in clip art that you've inserted, first right-click the clip art and choose Edit Picture from the shortcut menu so that you can edit it.

GROUPING AND UNGROUPING

At some point, you might have several shapes and lines you want to move, format, or delete together. For example, if you're building an organization chart, you might need to move half the boxes an inch to the left to make room for a new division.

You've already learned that you can select many objects at once by dragging the Select Object pointer around them, or by selecting the objects one at a time while you keep the Shift key pressed down. However, if you do this, it's easy for the individual images to get separated.

If you group the objects you're using, they stay together no matter what. To do so, select the objects you want to group, release the Shift key, right-click on one of the selected objects, and choose Grouping, Group from the shortcut menu. Notice that selection handles now surround the group of objects, not each individual object, as shown in Figure 14.23. You can now work with all the objects as if they were one object.

Figure 14.23
When grouped objects in a drawing are selected, one set of handles surrounds them all.

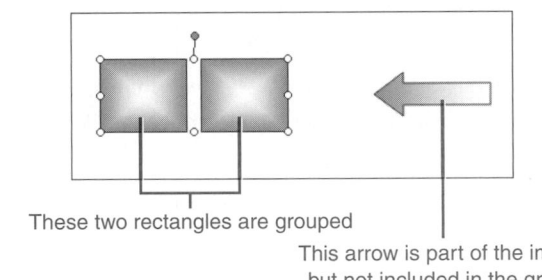

These two rectangles are grouped

This arrow is part of the image but not included in the group

If you later need to reformat or edit text in one of the grouped objects, you can do so without separating ("ungrouping") it from the rest of the group. To do so, click anywhere in the group to select it. Then, click on the object you want to edit. Round object handles appear (see Figure 14.24). Next, right-click to display the shortcut menu, and choose the task you want to perform.

Round handles indicate that the grouped object can be edited or reformatted

Figure 14.24
Editing a single object within a set of grouped objects.

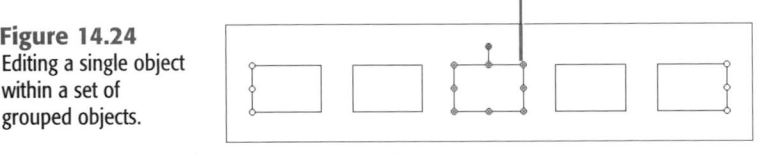

Certain tasks, such as resizing an object, cannot be performed while the object is still part of a group. For these tasks, you must first ungroup the objects, then perform the task, and then (if you want) regroup the objects. To ungroup a grouped collection of objects, right-click on them, and choose Grouping, Ungroup from the shortcut menu.

If objects have ever been grouped, Word remembers how they were grouped even after you ungroup them. To regroup a set of objects as they were before being ungrouped, right-click on one object and choose Grouping, Regroup from the shortcut menu.

Layering Your Drawing

Each drawing object you create is placed in an individual layer. By default, your text layer is on the bottom. Every time you add another object, it is drawn in the layer on top of the previous object. The stacking order becomes noticeable when objects overlap each other—the object last drawn is on top and obscures a portion of any objects that were drawn earlier.

You can move objects to a different position in a stack, much as you might reshuffle a deck of cards. This is referred to as changing the stacking or *Z-order*. (In describing coordinates on paper, X refers to the horizontal; Y, the vertical; and Z, the depth.) For example, you can move objects up or down within a stack one layer at a time, or you can move them to the top or bottom of a stack in one move. Naturally, this means that you don't have to draw the bottom object first—you can always move it later. Because text is on its own layer, Word has two special commands for moving an object behind or in front of text.

To change the Z-order of any object, click the Draw button on the Drawing toolbar and choose Order. The Order submenu appears, giving you several choices. For example, you can move an object to the front or back, forward or back one layer, or in front or behind text.

Rotating Illustrations

Word can rotate shapes and illustrations. To rotate an image 90° on its z-axis, first select it. A green rotation handle appears on the object you selected. Click and drag the handles to rotate the object around its z-axis until it arrives at the position you want.

Flipping Illustrations

Word also allows you to flip objects horizontally or vertically. A good analogy might be turning over transparent cards in a deck of cards—or, possibly, flipping transparent pancakes.

To flip an image, first select it. Then, click the Draw button on the Drawing toolbar, and choose Rotate or Flip. Finally, choose either Flip Horizontal or Flip Vertical.

Flip Horizontal swaps the left and right sides of an image. For example, a baseball player playing first base would suddenly appear to be playing third base. Flip Vertical flips the top and bottom parts of an image. For example, a landscape flipped vertically would show the sky at the bottom.

Using the Grid to Line Up Objects

Word automatically divides pages into an invisible grid, with each square in the grid set to 0.13" by 0.13". By default, objects you draw are lined up against the nearest gridlines, making it much easier to align multiple objects consistently. This automatic feature is called Snap to Grid.

You can adjust the increments used by Word's grid, up to a fineness of 0.01". You can turn off the grid, make the gridlines visible, or even specify where on the page you want the grid to begin.

To access the Grid controls, click the Draw button on the Drawing toolbar. Choose Grid to open the Drawing Grid dialog box (see Figure 14.25). You can input new values for both the Horizontal Spacing and Vertical Spacing by either typing in the values directly or using the spinner arrows.

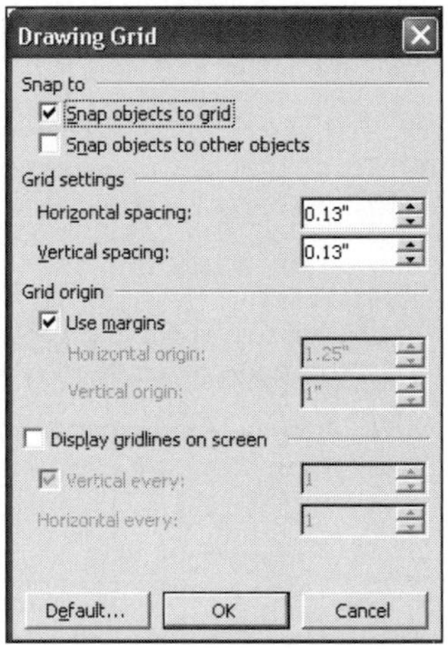

Figure 14.25
Controlling how the grid behaves and appears.

The Horizontal Spacing controls the amount of horizontal space between vertical gridlines, and the Vertical Spacing controls the amount of vertical space between horizontal gridlines.

The two Snap options can be used either independently or together. If you check Snap Objects to Grid, objects will always settle their upper-left sizing handles at the intersection of two gridlines. If you check Snap Objects to Other Objects, objects will always settle their upper-left sizing handles with each other. If both are checked, Snap Objects to Other Objects overrides Snap Objects to Grid.

You can also display gridlines onscreen to help you design pages more precisely. To do so, choose View, Gridlines. If you want more control over how your gridlines appear onscreen, click Draw, Grid; then check the Display Gridlines on Screen box. Then set values in the Horizontal Every and Vertical Every scroll boxes. The lower the values you set, the finer the gridlines.

> **TIP**
>
> You can turn off the Snap to Grid option temporarily by pressing Alt while moving your drawing object.

NUDGING AN OBJECT

If you've ever tried to use your mouse to precisely position an object, you'll appreciate Word's nudging feature. You can move your object in increments as small as one pixel at a time using the Nudge option found under the Draw button of the Drawing toolbar. You can nudge an object in any direction—Left, Right, Up, or Down.

The distance the object moves depends on your Grid options; if you have Snap Objects to Grid selected, a nudge moves your object one grid measurement. If this Snap option is not enabled, your object moves one pixel in the chosen direction.

TIP

> You can also nudge any selected object by selecting the object and pressing any arrow key. Using this technique, your object always moves one pixel at a time in the direction you've chosen. (If you have Snap Objects to Grid enabled, pressing the arrow key nudges the object one unit of grid space, instead of one pixel.)

ALIGNING AND DISTRIBUTING DRAWING OBJECTS

In addition to precise positioning of an object on the page, Word offers *relative positioning*. A drawing object can be aligned relative to another object or to the page itself. This means that multiple objects can be lined up along any of their edges or centers. They can also be centered on the page or aligned along the edge of the page. Furthermore, you can have Word evenly space your objects across (or down) the page. A tremendous amount of power is packed into the Align or Distribute commands, accessed by clicking the Draw button on the Drawing toolbar.

To align or distribute objects, first select the objects you want to align. Next, click Draw, Align or Distribute from the Drawing toolbar. Then, from the Align or Distribute submenu, select one of the following:

- **Align Left**—Aligns selected objects along the left edge of the object farthest to the left.
- **Align Center**—Aligns selected objects along the vertical center of the selected objects.
- **Align Right**—Aligns selected objects along the right edge of the object farthest to the right.
- **Align Top**—Aligns selected objects along the top edge of the highest object.
- **Align Middle**—Aligns selected objects along the horizontal center of the selected objects.
- **Align Bottom**—Aligns selected objects along the bottom edge of the lowest object.
- **Distribute Horizontally**—Distributes selected objects evenly along the same horizontal line, leaving the same amount of space between each one.
- **Distribute Vertically**—Distributes selected objects evenly along the same vertical line, leaving the same amount of space between each one.

14

- **Relative to Canvas**—Aligns selected objects relative to the Drawing Canvas. When this option is selected, all align or distribute commands use the Drawing Canvas as a super object that controls their positioning. For example, if you check Relative to Canvas and then choose Align Center, your selected object(s) is centered horizontally inside the Drawing Canvas. (This option becomes Relative to Page if you choose not to use the Drawing Canvas.)

When objects are distributed, they are arranged evenly with an equal amount of space between them, either horizontally or vertically.

You may often use the Align and Distribute commands consecutively. First, create your objects, roughing out their placement. Next, choose Align Top to line them up. Finally, select Distribute Horizontally to arrange the objects across the page or Drawing Canvas.

TROUBLESHOOTING

WHAT TO DO IF WORDS DISAPPEAR FROM A DRAWING OBJECT

Text within drawing objects is not automatically resized to fit; you must either reduce the size of the text or enlarge the drawing object by clicking and dragging the sizing handles. To adjust text placement, you have to use all the formatting options at your disposal to get the effect you want—the alignment buttons, paragraph marks, tabs, nonbreaking spaces (Ctrl+Shift+spacebar), and so on—and move the text where you want it.

WHAT TO DO IF DRAWINGS DON'T APPEAR IN PRINTED DOCUMENTS

Make sure you've specified that drawing objects should be printed. Choose Tools, Options; click the Print tab; and then check the Drawing Objects check box, if it is not already checked.

Some printers have graphics settings that override Word's options. Check your printer settings by choosing File, Print, and then clicking the Properties button on the Print dialog box.

CHAPTER 15

VISUALIZING YOUR MESSAGE WITH GRAPHS, DIAGRAMS, AND ORG CHARTS

In this chapter

15

UNDERSTANDING GRAPHS AND CHARTS

If a picture is worth a thousand words, it's easily worth a thousand numbers. Tables or columns of numbers often appear dry, uninteresting, and difficult to understand—but a chart that shows a graphical representation of the same information can impart instant understanding. It can enable you to see both individual data points and patterns so that you can spot developing trends you'd never notice just by looking at numbers. It can consolidate facts that communicate the big picture more clearly. Not least, well-designed charts make documents look better.

NOTE

If you want to know more about communicating effectively and honestly with charts, graphs, and statistics, consider these two classic books:

The Visual Display of Quantitative Information, Edward R. Tufte, Graphics Press.

How to Lie with Statistics, Darrell Huff, Irving Geis, W.W. Norton & Co.

To help you include dynamic graphs in your documents, Word 2003 calls on Microsoft Graph whenever you ask to create or insert a chart.

You can create many types of charts with Graph. All of them, however, have one thing in common: a *data source*. Your source data can be on the same page, elsewhere in the same document, in another Word file, or in a file created in Excel or some other program.

→ For more information about building charts in Word that use Excel data, **see** "Establishing a Link with Microsoft Excel," **p. 541**.

Although it still requires thought to produce high-quality, usable, and effective graphs, Word does make the mechanics of creating a graph very straightforward. Following is a high-level overview of the process of creating a chart in Word, using Graph:

1. Select the values in your Word document that you want to graph. (As you'll see, this step is optional; you can enter your source data directly in a Microsoft Graph datasheet. However, in most cases you'll already have created the data you want to graph; you may as well use that data rather than starting from scratch.)

2. Choose Insert, Picture, Chart to run Microsoft Graph. Graph inserts a basic chart in your document, immediately under the source data.

3. Right-click on the chart and choose Chart Type from the shortcut menu.

4. Set the Chart Type. In other words, tell Word what kind of chart you want. Your choices include bar charts, line chart, pie charts, and many others.

5. Right-click on the chart and choose Chart Options.

6. In the Chart Options dialog box, specify the elements you want the chart to include, such as titles, gridlines, legends, and data labels.

7. Format the chart and its elements, selecting fonts, colors, backgrounds, and other attributes.

8. Take another look at the chart and make any changes you want, using Graph's editing, formatting, and drawing tools.

9. Click outside the chart area to return to Word.

The following sections take a closer look at each step of the process.

NOTE

> Microsoft uses the terms "graph" and "chart" interchangeably throughout Microsoft Graph. This chapter does as well.

CREATING DATA TO BE GRAPHED

If you create business documents with Word, you're likely to encounter many places where charts can help you communicate more effectively: summaries of results and projections, coverage of trends, changes in the value of assets and investments, and so on. In this chapter, you'll learn several ways to provide the source data for a chart. In many cases, the easiest is to first enter your data in a Word table, as shown in Figure 15.1.

Figure 15.1
Creating data for charting.

	1Q03	2Q03	3Q03	4Q03
New York	750	772	784	779
California	886	911	937	958
Texas	456	512	528	556
Florida	398	433	465	499

→ For more information on working with charts, **see** Chapter 12, "Structuring and Organizing Information with Tables," **p. 387**.

To create a chart from a table, first select the information in your table that you want to chart. To get a chart that says what you want to say, you must select the correct information from your data source. Here are some tips to keep in mind:

- Include at least one header row or column in your selection.

- If your table includes a cell, row, or column that contains totals, you might not want to select those totals, unless they measure an average rather than a quantity. Otherwise, including totals can skew the scale of your graph, making all the other data points look small in relation to the data point or points that contain the total. If you're creating a pie chart, exactly half the pie will contain your total. This is probably not the result you had in mind.

- Select only the data and headings you need. In particular, avoid selecting the table's overall title. If your first selected row or column does not have heading information, Graph might not read your selection properly, and the result will be a generic chart with dummy data.

After you've selected the data you want charted, choose Insert, Picture, Chart. Word then enters Microsoft Graph mode and inserts a 3D column chart based on your data, below your table, in a floating frame—as shown in Figure 15.2.

15

Figure 15.2
Graph can quickly convert your table data into a movable, resizable chart.

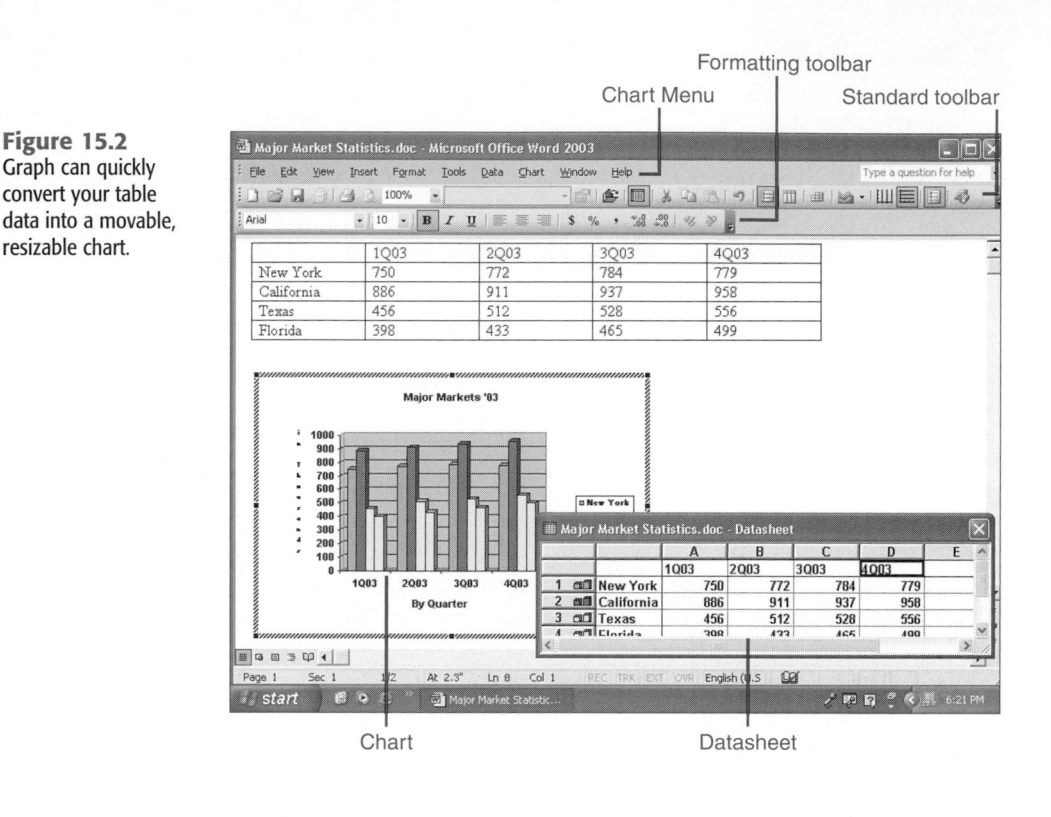

As you can see, in addition to the framed chart, Graph toolbars and menus temporarily replace Word 2003 toolbars and menus, and a datasheet window opens with an Excel-like view of the chart's data.

NOTE

From now on, the values this chart is based on will be the values displayed in the datasheet. To change the chart's contents, change the values in the datasheet.

Changing the values in the source Word table will not change the values in the chart.

→ For more information on interacting with datasheets, **see** "Creating a Chart from Scratch," **p. 531**.

When Word inserts a chart based on your information, it selects the chart. As long as the chart or any part of it is selected, you are working in Microsoft Graph. (Clicking outside the chart returns you to Word's normal menus, toolbars, and commands. You then must double-click on the chart to return to Microsoft Graph.)

To get more comfortable with chart editing, take a quick look at the menus on Microsoft Graph's menu bar and the buttons on your Standard and Formatting toolbars. These now reflect Microsoft Graph's commands rather than Word's (refer to Figure 15.2). Using these toolbars and menu commands, you can

- Format the chart or elements of it
- Change the data that the chart graphs
- Add or change elements of the chart, such as data points, legends, or data labels
- Add a background pattern, shading, or a picture to the chart—or to individual chart elements or to the chart's background

NOTE

The first time you run Graph, it displays a one-line toolbar combining the most commonly used toolbar buttons from its Standard and Formatting toolbars. Most users want to display both complete toolbars to get access to all the menu commands. This chapter refers to buttons on the full toolbars whenever they provide the fastest way to get the job done.

To view the full toolbars, click on the toolbar handle at the left of the Formatting toolbar and drag it under the Standard toolbar.

Many of these toolbar buttons should be familiar to you because they are the same as buttons on the Standard and Formatting toolbars in Word. A few of the toolbar buttons shown in Figure 15.2 will be especially handy later, when you start formatting and editing elements of your chart. For example, the Chart Objects drop-down list box enables you to select a specific chart element so that you can format or edit that element. You'll find it especially helpful when you need to select a chart element that's difficult to click on, such as a thin gridline.

The Import File button enables you to open a Microsoft Excel or other file and add information from that file to the chart you already have open. The Chart Type button gives you a quick way to switch among the most popular types of charts.

And, on the Formatting toolbar, the Currency Style, Percent Style, Increase Decimal, and Decrease Decimal buttons give you a quick way to make sure that your axes and other chart elements display numbers formatted as you like.

→ For more about formatting data in datasheets, **see** "Formatting Data in the Datasheet," **p. 534**.

CAUTION

If you use Undo, be aware that Graph's Undo button enables you to undo only your last action—not any of the last 100 or more actions, as in Word.

CHOOSING AMONG WORD'S EXTENSIVE SELECTION OF CHARTS

By default, Graph displays your information in its default chart format: a 3D column chart using standard colors against a gray background with gridlines and a legend. Graph's default chart makes sense in many situations, but you'll often want something else.

15

Graph gives you plenty of choices. For openers, you can choose from 14 different chart types, most with five to eight variations or subtypes. From there, you can modify every feature of the chart—titles, legends, grids, data series, size, placement, and wrapping—and you can use Word's powerful fill and color capabilities to include gradients, textures, and patterns.

Your first decision, however, must be to determine what kind of chart you want. Microsoft Graph chart types include

- **Column charts**—Each data point corresponds to a vertical line; each series of data uses vertical lines of the same color.

- **Bar charts**—This is probably the most popular type of chart. It shows data as a series of horizontal bars. Bar charts can be used effectively with three or four series of data over a period of time (such as monthly sales figures from four different regions).

- **Line charts**—Line charts are almost always used to display changes in data over time. You can display the changes over time in one data series, or many. Several styles of line charts are available, including stacked and unstacked options. Stacked charts show the lines above one another; unstacked charts do not.

NOTE

A *data point* is a single piece of data, such as the sales associated with one product in one month. A *data series* is a set of related data, such as the sales associated with one product in each month of the current year.

- **Pie charts**—This type of chart is particularly useful for showing the relationship or degree of relationship between numeric values in separate groups of data.

- **Scatter charts**—These help you identify patterns or trends and determine whether variables depend on or affect one another.

- **Area charts**—This chart shows data as areas filled with different colors or patterns. Area charts are best suited for charts that don't have large numbers of data points and that use several data series. They look particularly dramatic in 3D form.

- **Doughnut charts**—This is basically a pie chart but with more flexibility—and a hole in the middle. Each ring of the doughnut chart represents a data series. Use this chart to compare the parts to the whole in one or more data categories.

- **Radar charts**—This chart resembles a cobweb and shows changes in data or data frequency relative to a center point. Lines connect all the values in the same data series.

- **3D surface charts**—This chart resembles a rubber sheet stretched over a 3D column chart. A 3D surface chart can help show relationships among large amounts of data. Colors or patterns delineate areas that share the same value. Use this chart for finding the best combinations between two sets of data.

- **Bubble charts**—These are similar to an XY (scatter) chart. The bubble size is a third value type that is relative to the x-axis and y-axis data. Use this for depicting the relationship between two kinds of related data.

15

Word also provides three variants: cylinder charts, pyramid charts, and cone charts. You can use these just as you use bar or column charts, except that the data points are displayed as cylinders, pyramids, or cones.

NOTE

> Not every set of data can be used with every chart type. Worse, in some cases, you can chart the data, but the results are misleading or incomprehensible. After you create a chart, read it carefully to make sure that it communicates what you have in mind.
>
> If you have data that is continuous, such as time, or concentrated data, consider using a scatter or XY plot. If your data is categorical, such as the number of red cars versus the number of blue cars, you can use a larger variety of charts such as the bar chart and the column chart.
>
> The main difference between the types of data is that if you have measurements on a continuous scale, the intervals between your measurements do not have to be equal and may even be impossible to make equal. The scatter or XY plot takes the variable intervals into account. The bar chart and column charts will plot the data using equal intervals.

CHANGING CHART TYPE WITH A SINGLE CLICK

To select a different chart type from the one that Graph has used to build your chart, first make sure that Graph is open. The easiest way to tell which mode you're in (Word or Graph) is to check which toolbars you have active. If Word's menus and toolbars are active instead of Graph's, simply double-click anywhere in your chart to activate Graph.

When in Graph, click on the down arrow to the right of the Chart Type button on the Standard toolbar. Next, choose one of the chart types that appear (see Figure 15.3). Word replaces your chart with its default version of the chart type you selected.

Figure 15.3
Choosing a new chart type from the Standard toolbar.

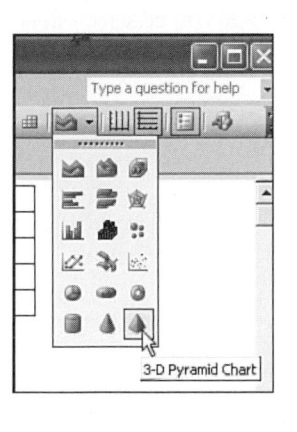

PREVIEWING AND SELECTING CHART TYPES

Choosing a chart with the Chart Type toolbar button is quick—but what if you aren't satisfied with the chart it places in your document? Change it, with Word's extensive tools for

15

selecting and adjusting chart types. To preview and choose a different chart, follow these steps:

1. Either choose Chart Type from the Chart menu, or (with Microsoft Graph open) right-click in a blank part of the chart area and choose Chart Type from the shortcut menu that appears. The Chart Type dialog box appears (see Figure 15.4).

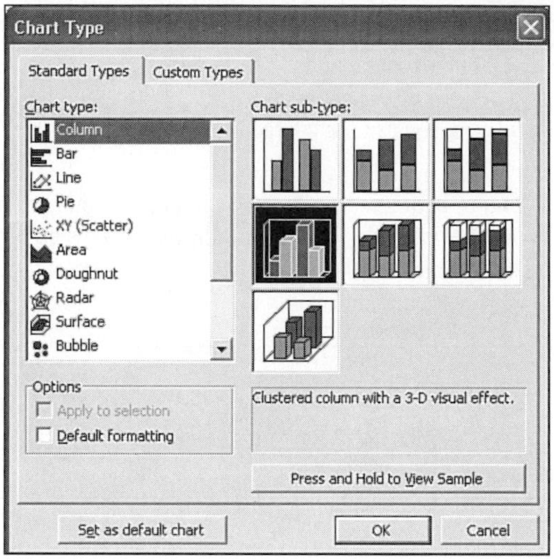

Figure 15.4
Changing the type of standard chart you use.

2. From the Standard Types tab of the Chart Type dialog box, click any of the Chart Types in the left column to see the corresponding Chart Sub-Types on the right. Use the scroll button to see additional selections. Select the desired subtype.

3. To see how your data looks using the chart type you've selected, click the Press and Hold to View Sample button.

4. When you're finished, click OK.

CHANGING YOUR DEFAULT CHART TYPE

As you've learned, Word's default chart type is a 3D bar chart. However, you might prefer to use a different standard or custom chart type as your default for all charts from now on.

CAUTION

> Some users find that Microsoft Graph's 3D effect can distort their data, or that its charts do not reproduce well on low-end printers. In addition, most technical users avoid 3D charts if they're based on fewer than three sets of data.

To choose a different default chart, right-click on your chart and choose Chart Type from the shortcut menu. In the Standard Types tab of the Chart Type dialog box, select the chart type and subtype you want as your new default. Click the Set as Default Chart button near the bottom of the dialog box, and click OK.

Now every time you create a chart, Graph uses your new default.

CHOOSING FROM WORD'S LIBRARY OF CUSTOM CHARTS

In addition to Word's standard charts, you can choose from 20 built-in custom charts. With these custom charts, Word provides not only a chart type (such as an area or pie chart), but also a set of consistent formatting. If you find one you like, using a built-in custom chart saves you the time and effort of formatting your charts one element at a time.

The Chart Types dialog box contains two tabs: the Standard Types tab you've already used, and a tab labeled Custom Types. To choose a custom chart from within Microsoft Graph, bring up the Chart Types dialog box by right-clicking on a chart and choosing Chart Type from the shortcut menu. Click the Custom Types tab, shown in Figure 15.5. Select the chart type you want. In the Sample box, Word displays a preview of how your data will appear if you choose this chart. Finally, click OK.

Figure 15.5
Word provides a broad range of custom chart types to complete the standard types discussed earlier.

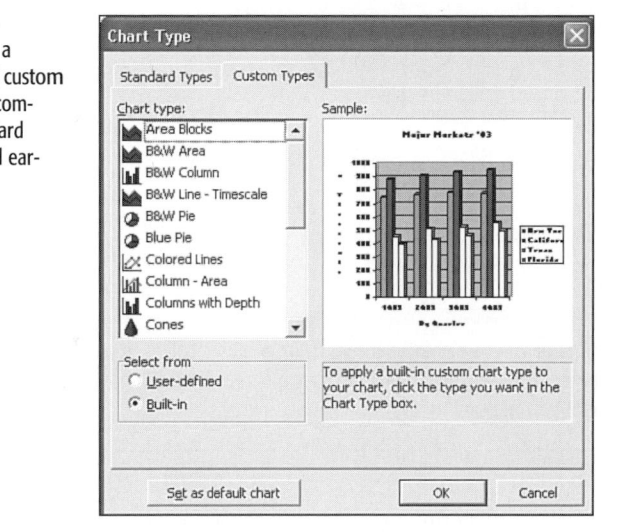

→ To create your own user-defined chart, **see** "Creating and Using Custom Chart Types," **p. 535**.

WORKING WITH CHART OPTIONS

After you've decided what type of chart to create, you can set a wide variety of options for your chart. For example, you may want to annotate the chart with a title, a legend, and titles for each individual chart axis, depending on the number of axes the chart has. All these elements become part of the chart, and if you resize or move the chart, they are resized or moved as well.

15

Before you start working with chart options or with chart formatting, however, it's helpful to take a look at the elements that can appear in charts and the nomenclature Graph uses to describe these elements—which may not always be familiar.

INSPECTING A CHART

Figure 15.6 shows a typical 3D column chart. This chart's elements include the plot area (the main part of the chart), which is bounded by the axes: the x-axis, y-axis, and (in some three-dimensional charts) z-axis.

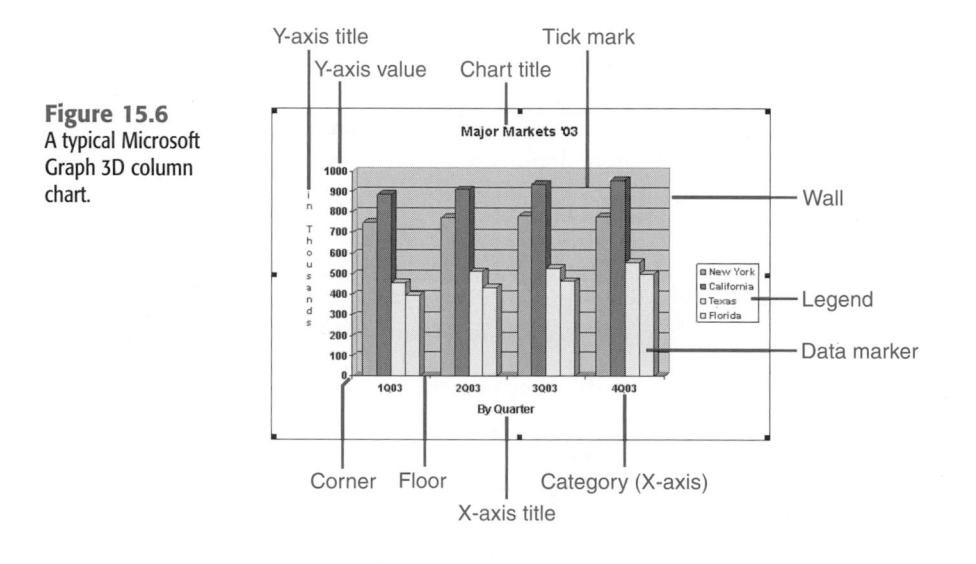

Figure 15.6
A typical Microsoft Graph 3D column chart.

> **TIP**
>
> If you're not sure where a chart element is, or what it's called, move the mouse pointer over an element on the chart. Word displays a ScreenTip that shows you the name of the chart element you're pointing to.

Within the plot area, the chart depicts one or more data series, each representing a row or column of data from your Word table or other source. The individual bars, columns, or other elements representing each data point within the data series are called *data markers*.

The plot area can also contain several optional text elements, such as *axis titles* that describe what each axis is measuring, and *data labels* that show the exact values (or names) for each data marker. *Gridlines* help the eye keep track of multiple lines.

A *chart title* appears at the top of the chart. In this example, the y-axis is the scale Microsoft Graph uses to generate the chart. This is true with most charts, with the notable exception of pie charts. If all your data points are between 0 and 500, for example, Graph places 0 at the bottom of the scale and 500 at the top.

Each increment on the y-axis is called a *tick mark*. Graph also features a y-axis title you can use to tell your audience what you're measuring. Some examples might be

Profit, in millions of dollars

Commissions, by percentage

Hard disk speed, in milliseconds

Land, in square miles

The y-axis normally tells which data series is being measured. Often, the x-axis displays the passage of time. For example, it might show four quarters in a year, or monthly results. Or it might also show results from various locations or divisions.

By default, Graph displays each data series in a different color, with like information displayed in the same color. Graph generally maintains contrast between adjacent bars, pie slices, and so on. This contrast enables you to understand the data clearly, even when it's printed in black and white. As you'll see later, however, you can change color, add patterns, or change the background Graph normally uses.

In 3D charts, such as the one shown in Figure 15.6, Graph also includes a wall, corner, and floor. These make up the 3D background to the "room" where the chart appears. Walls and floors can each be formatted separately.

Finally, most charts (except those that use only one data series) also contain a *legend*—an explanation of what each color or pattern represents. Graph inserts a legend by default.

SETTING CHART OPTIONS

To control the options available for your specific chart, select the chart and choose Chart Options from the Chart menu. Or right-click on an empty area within the chart and choose Chart Options from the shortcut menu. The Chart Options dialog box appears, as shown in Figure 15.7. From here, depending on the type of chart you've created, you can control elements such as these:

- **Titles**—You can specify names for the chart and each of its axes.
- **Axes**—You can specify which axis will be set as primary, among other attributes.
- **Gridlines**—You can specify whether gridlines will appear, and if so, where.
- **Legend**—You can specify whether a legend will appear, and if so, where.
- **Data Labels**—You can specify whether data labels will appear, and if so, what they will contain.
- **Data Table**—You can specify whether your chart will be accompanied by a data table presenting all the values used to construct the chart.

Again, the options available to you depend on the chart you've chosen. For example, a column chart has two axes that can be titled, whereas a radar chart has none. Most charts have gridlines; pie charts and doughnut charts do not.

Figure 15.7
You can control the elements included in your chart through the Chart Options dialog box.

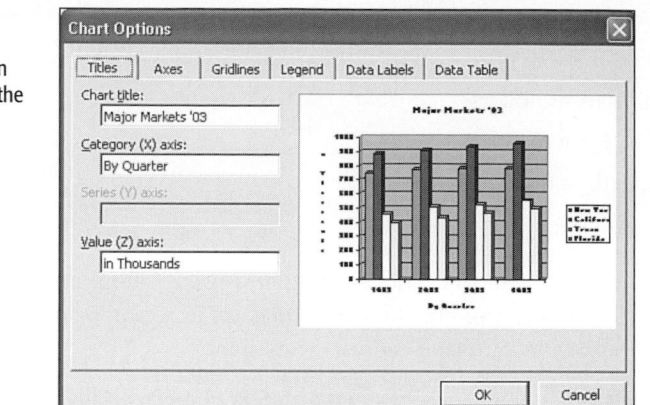

Some controls are available no matter what kind of chart you have, however. For example, you can always specify a title for your chart in the Titles tab, or a legend in the Legend tab.

As you work in the tabs of the Chart Options dialog box, you can see the effects of your changes in a preview that appears on the right side of the dialog box.

The next few sections discuss each set of chart options available through the Chart Options dialog box.

INSERTING TITLES FOR YOUR CHART AND AXES

To add a title to your chart, display the Chart Options dialog box and select the Titles tab. Graph displays title options, as shown earlier in Figure 15.7. Here, you can specify which titles you want to add: a Chart Title and, in most cases, titles for at least one axis. Type the titles in the text boxes and click OK. Graph now displays the titles in the chart, inserted as text boxes.

You can now edit or format the titles manually by clicking inside the title you want to edit. As you edit and format the title, you have access to Standard toolbar buttons, such as Cut, Copy, and Paste, and Formatting toolbar buttons, such as Font, Font Size, Bold, Italic, and Underline. These work just as they do in Word. To move any title, click it once to highlight its text box and then click and drag the borders of the box.

→ For more information about formatting chart elements, **see** "Formatting Chart Elements," **p. 527**.

CAUTION

Any text in a chart automatically resizes when the overall chart is resized. This can lead to text being far too small to read or, in some cases, to text that is disproportionately large. To turn off automatic resizing, right-click inside the title and choose Format Chart Title from the shortcut menu. Then, in the Font tab of the Format Chart Title dialog box, clear the Auto Scale check box.

Controlling Axes

By default, Graph displays tick-mark labels about each axis of data it is graphing. You can use the Axes tab of the Chart Options dialog box to hide tick-mark labels for some of the axes in your chart, or to change the labels displayed on your chart's primary axis (see Figure 15.8).

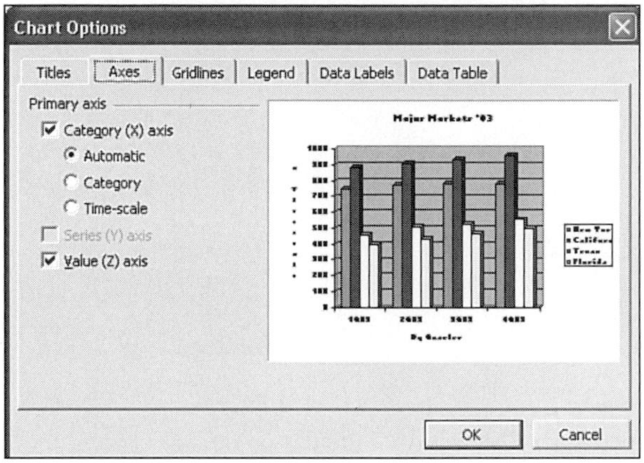

Figure 15.8
Controlling how axes display through the Chart Options dialog box.

To hide the tick-mark labels associated with any axis, clear the check box next to that axis. Click OK.

To change the contents of your primary axis tick-mark labels, first make sure that the primary axis is checked; then click the Automatic, Category, or Time-Scale button and click OK.

If you choose Automatic, Word presents a timescale x-axis if the data appears to be time-based (for example, if it is based on months or minutes); otherwise, it displays a default "category" x-axis.

A timescale axis places all *times or dates* based on how far apart they are on the clock or calendar. For example, if your chart contained sets of data points for January, March, and April, Word would place a blank space where February should have appeared.

A category axis, in contrast, simply places all sets of data points equidistant from each other. If you choose Category, Word will follow this approach even if your data points are based on times or dates.

Controlling Gridlines

Gridlines can make your chart more readable—or, if you overdo them, they can make your chart more obscure. Graph gives you complete control over the gridlines along each axis. You can easily turn them on or off, or format them any way you want.

15

To enable or disable a gridline, click its corresponding button in the Standard toolbar. The Value Axis Gridline button controls horizontal lines; the Category Axis Gridline button controls vertical lines.

If you want more control over your gridlines, return to the Chart Options dialog box and choose the Gridlines tab (see Figure 15.9).

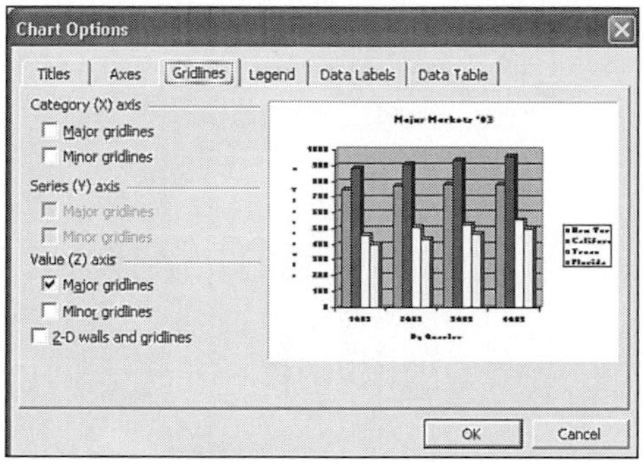

Figure 15.9
Controlling gridlines through the Chart Options dialog box.

By default, Graph places gridlines perpendicular to the data being charted, at the same points where values are shown along the axis. For example, if you create a bar graph in which the columns appear horizontally, the value axis is the x-axis, and the gridlines are displayed vertically from that axis. However, you can add gridlines for another axis, as shown in Figure 15.10.

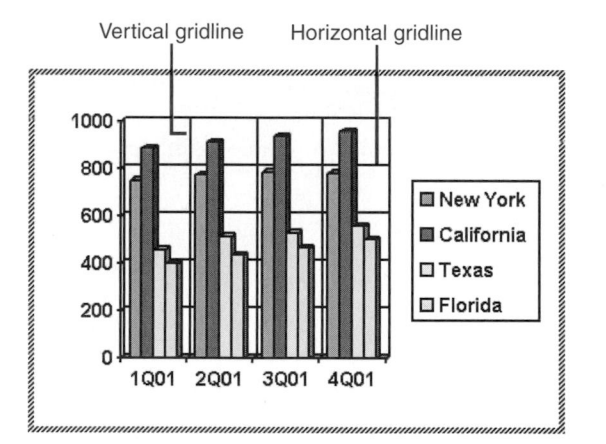

Figure 15.10
Gridlines running both horizontally and vertically.

Gridlines placed at the same points as values are called *major gridlines*. If you want additional gridlines to appear between major gridlines, add *minor gridlines*. By default, Word does not display gridlines parallel to the data being charted (in other words, on another axis). But you can add these as well—both major and minor gridlines.

By default, Word displays gridlines in 3D so that it appears that they are at the "front wall" of the background behind your data points. If you prefer a 2D background—perhaps to deemphasize the background in contrast to the foreground data points—check the 2-D Walls and Gridlines check box.

INSERTING A LEGEND

Legends are used to explain the color or pattern conventions used in a chart. Word enables them by default, but you can toggle a chart's legend on or off by clicking the Legend button on the Graph toolbar. Or, if you want to specify where the legend appears in your chart, display the Legend tab of the Chart Options dialog box (see Figure 15.11).

Figure 15.11
You can place a legend to the left, right, top, or bottom of the chart.

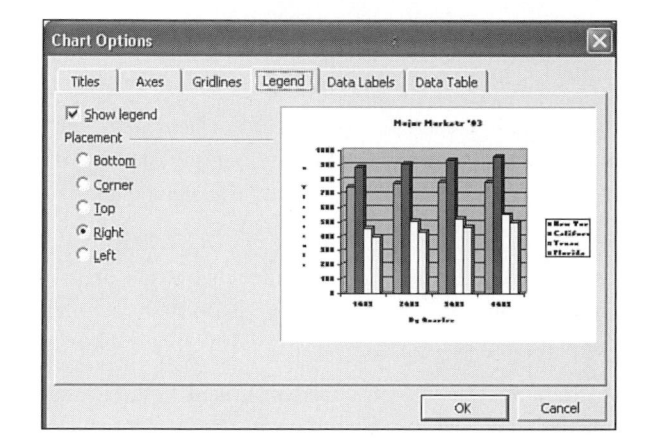

If Legends are disabled, check the Show Legend check box to place a legend in your chart; then choose Bottom, Corner, Top, Right, or Left to specify where the legend appears. (If you choose Corner, the legend appears at the upper right of the chart object.) Whichever choice you make, Word makes sure that the legend does not overlap other chart elements—unless you drag the legend to an overlapping location manually.

ADDING OR CHANGING DATA LABELS

By default, Graph inserts a chart without including the specific values or names associated with each data point. However, if your readers need to know specific values or names, you can add them. From the Chart Options dialog box, click the Data Labels tab (see Figure 15.12).

NOTE

The Data Labels tab can also be found in the Format Data Series dialog box. You can open this dialog box by right-clicking a data marker and selecting Format Data Series from the shortcut menu.

Figure 15.12
Inserting data labels through the Chart Options dialog box.

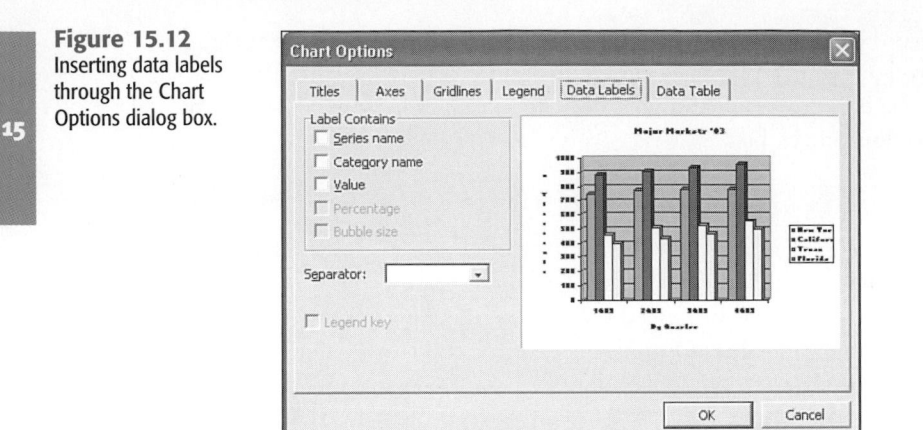

You can display the Series Name each data point is associated with; the name of the x-axis column each data point is associated with (Category Name); or the Value associated with each data point. If you choose Value, Graph displays the same data that would appear in your legend.

In Figure 15.12 you can see that some of the Data labels buttons are completely disabled. Which options are available in this dialog box depends on the type of chart you're using. If your chart already has data labels and you want to remove them, clear each check box.

The data labels that Graph inserts in your chart are linked to the headings of the columns and rows displayed in the datasheet that Graph creates from your source data. Therefore, if you change the headings in your datasheet, Graph updates the label on your chart—whether or not you change the headings in your source document.

If data labels disappear when you resize your chart, see "What to Do If Your Chart Loses Data Labels After Resizing," in the "Troubleshooting" section of this chapter.

ADDING DATA TABLES

You can use *data tables* to make sure that readers not only get the visual gist of the chart but also see the actual data on which it is based.

Data tables can be especially helpful if your data comes from a source other than the Word document where you are placing the chart. You can see an example of a data table in Figure 15.13.

To insert a data table in your chart, click the Data Table button on the Standard toolbar. You can also insert a data table through the Chart Options dialog box, via the Data Table tab (see Figure 15.14).

This tab displays two check boxes. As its name implies, you can enable (or disable) data tables by clicking the Show Data Table check box.

Figure 15.13
A data table displays
figures right on the
chart.

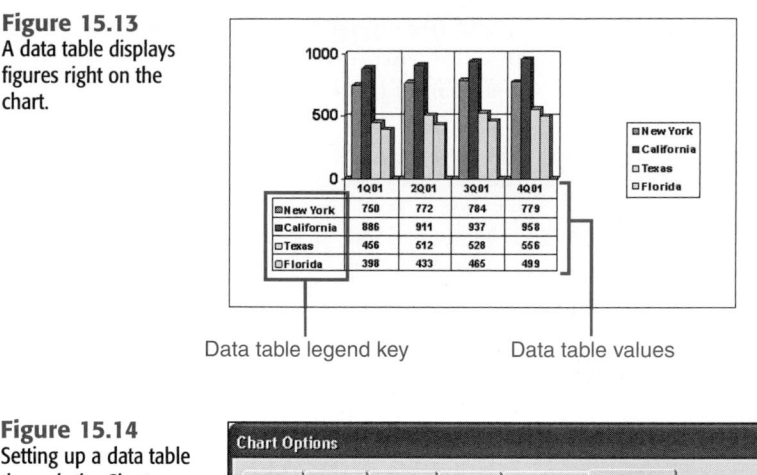

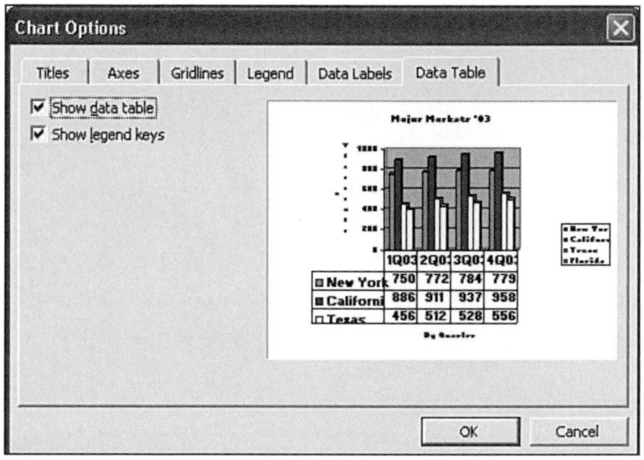

Data table legend key   Data table values

Figure 15.14
Setting up a data table
through the Chart
Options dialog box.

The default data table includes *legend keys* next to its headings (refer to Figure 15.13).
Legend keys give you the same color and pattern information you would normally place in a
legend—so you don't need to use both. However, if you don't want to include the color and
pattern information, you can clear the Show Legend Keys check box in the Data Table tab
of the Chart Options dialog box.

FORMATTING CHART ELEMENTS

Any element of a chart that you can insert, you can also format.

In some cases, as mentioned earlier, you can format a chart element directly. For example,
you can select text in a title and apply font formatting to it. You can also move elements,
such as your chart's legend or plot area, by dragging them with the mouse.

However, in most cases you'll work with dialog boxes to access the formatting controls you
need. To format a chart element, double-click on it; or right-click on it and choose the format command that appears at the top of the shortcut menu.

15

For example, if you right-click on your chart's title, the Format Chart Title command appears, and if you select it, the Format Chart Title dialog box appears—which contains tabs for formatting the Patterns, Font, and Alignment of text in the title (see Figure 15.15).

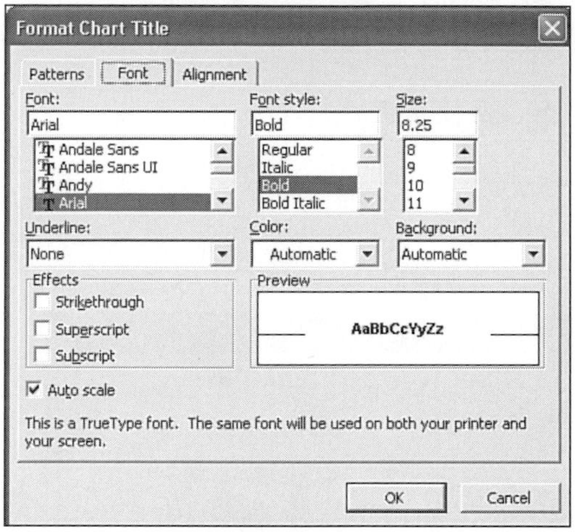

Figure 15.15
The Format Chart Title dialog box is an example of the dialog boxes available for formatting individual chart elements.

If you're having trouble precisely positioning the mouse pointer on the chart element you want to click, you can select it from the Chart Objects drop-down box on the Standard toolbar (see Figure 15.16).

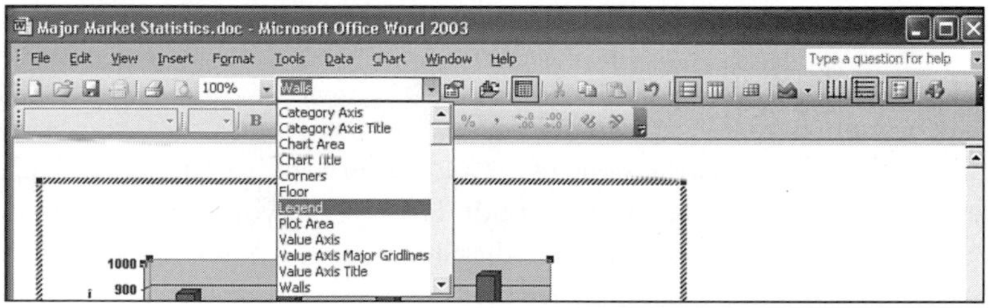

Figure 15.16
Selecting a chart element from the Chart Objects drop-down box.

Table 15.1 lists the chart elements that can be formatted and the formatting categories available to you through that chart element's Format dialog box.

TABLE 15.1   CHART ELEMENTS AND AVAILABLE FORMATTING

Chart Element	Available Formatting
Axis	Patterns, Scale, Font, Number, Alignment
Chart Area	Patterns, Font
Chart Title	Patterns, Font, Alignment
Data Labels	Patterns, Font, Number, Alignment

Chart Element	Available Formatting
Data Points	Patterns, Data Labels, Options
Data Series	Patterns, Axis, Y Error Bars, Data Labels, Options (varies with chart type)
Data Table	Patterns, Font
Error Bars	Patterns, Y Error Bars
Floors	Patterns
Gridlines	Patterns, Scale
Legend	Patterns, Font, Placement
Legend Entry	Font
Plot Area	Patterns
Trendline	Patterns, Type, Options
Walls	Patterns

WORKING WITH PATTERNS

Chapter 14, "Using Word's Quick and Easy Drawing Tools," shows you how to use Word's backgrounds and fill effects in your document. Many of these features are available in Graph as well. For example, as listed in Table 15.1, nearly all the elements in a Microsoft Graph chart contain patterns. You can adjust these patterns using the same color and fill effects available to drawing objects in Word.

→ For more information on working with fill effects, **see** "Adding Fill Effects to Your Shapes," **p. 499**, and "Controlling Colors," **p. 497**.

In addition to colors, you can give your charts textures, patterns, and gradient fills; you can even fill an element with a picture of your own choosing. To give a chart element a different fill color or effect, follow these steps:

1. Right-click on the chart object you want to format, and choose the F_ormat option on the shortcut menu. The appropriate Format dialog box opens.

2. If necessary, click the Patterns tab.

3. To choose a standard color, click one of the color swatches in the Color section. For additional color options, click the _More Colors button.

4. To choose one of the enhanced effects (gradients, textures, patterns, or picture), click Fill Effects. Choose the appropriate tab and fill effect.

5. Click OK.

Figure 15.17 shows a chart with a Chart Area formatted with a gradient that is dark at the bottom and light at the top.

Often, when you start adding textures such as these to the background, you have to adjust text fonts and other elements as well. In this example, the chart title is formatted in dark

15

type to be visible against the lightest part of the gradient, whereas the legend and axes are formatted with a white background to make them easier to read against the darker areas of the gradient.

Figure 15.17
Adding textures and fill effects to a chart is an easy way to make it look more interesting.

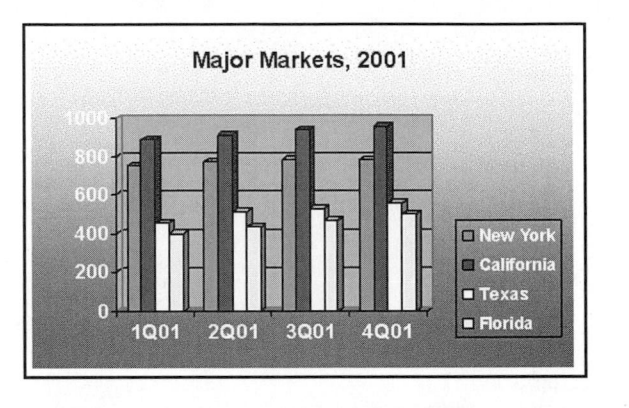

CAUTION

Be aware that many of the color schemes Microsoft Graph proposes may not reproduce with sufficient contrast on a black-and-white printer. Even some black-and-white gradients can be difficult to read, depending on the quality and resolution of your printer.

TIP

You can select an individual element of a data series and reformat it for emphasis, without changing the other elements. To do so, double-click on the data point. The Format Data Point dialog box opens, containing formatting controls that affect no other data point except the one you selected.

ADDING CALLOUTS WITH GRAPH'S DRAWING TOOLS

As discussed in Chapter 14, callouts can be used to call attention to specific text or graphics in your document. You can also use callouts to comment on charts you produce in Graph, as shown in Figure 15.18. The tools and the techniques are the same. As in Word, Graph's callout feature can be found on a special Drawing toolbar (use the steps in the following text to view this toolbar).

To place a callout in your Graph chart, follow these instructions:

1. Click the Drawing button on the Standard toolbar (or choose View, Toolbars, Drawing).

2. Click the AutoShapes button on the Drawing toolbar.

3. Select Callouts and then choose a callout to insert. The pointer changes into a small crosshair.

Figure 15.18
Callouts enable you to emphasize and comment on your Graph chart.

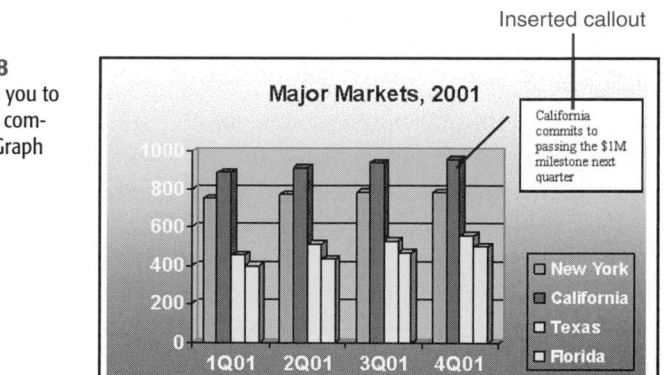

4. Click the object you want called out first, and then, holding down the mouse button, drag to the location you want your callout's text to appear. Release the mouse button. An insertion pointer appears in the callout box.

5. Input your text and apply any formatting desired.

6. If necessary, resize the callout box by clicking and dragging any of the sizing handles.

7. If you want, you can adjust the placement of the leader—the line that connects the text box to the location in the chart you're pointing to. To do so, click the yellow diamond adjustment handle on one end of the leader, and then drag the line until it appears as you want it to.

8. Click anywhere outside the callout box to return to the chart.

→ For more information about working with callouts, **see** "Using Callouts," **p. 494**.

TIP

> You can also use Graph's other drawing tools to add text boxes, arrows, and any other shape that might clarify your chart's contents.

CREATING A CHART FROM SCRATCH

You don't have to have an existing table in your document to build a chart. You don't even need a preexisting data source. You can open Graph by using a set of dummy (fake) data that Word generates and then replace that data with your real data.

To do so, place your insertion point where you want the chart to appear. Then choose Insert, Picture, Chart. Word's default chart uses dummy values to create a two-series 3D column chart.

15

WORKING IN THE DATASHEET WINDOW

Alongside the chart is a datasheet window containing the dummy data, as shown in Figure 15.19. The datasheet looks much like a basic spreadsheet, except that you can enter only numbers and letters in it—it cannot handle formulas. The only purpose of the datasheet is to control the data that creates a chart in Microsoft Graph.

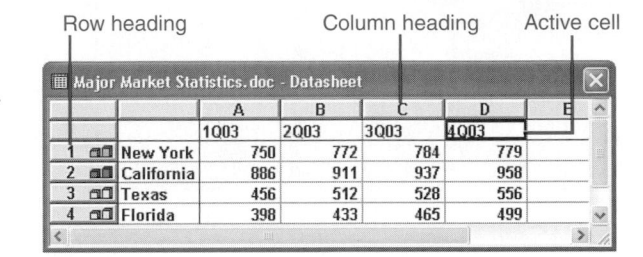

Row heading   Column heading   Active cell

Figure 15.19
A datasheet accompanying a Microsoft Graph chart.

Major Market Statistics.doc - Datasheet		A	B	C	D	E
		1Q03	2Q03	3Q03	4Q03	
1	New York	750	772	784	779	
2	California	886	911	937	958	
3	Texas	456	512	528	556	
4	Florida	398	433	465	499	

When you first insert a chart, the datasheet appears in a separate window near the chart. You can toggle the datasheet on or off by clicking the Datasheet button on Microsoft Graph's Standard toolbar.

If you create your chart from data in a Word document, that data appears in your datasheet when you open it. In this example, where we're creating the chart from scratch, the datasheet shows the dummy placeholder data. To change a value, click in its cell and enter the new value. When you change a value in the datasheet, the chart reflects the change immediately.

CAUTION

Remember that changes you make in the datasheet are not automatically reflected in the table or other data source from which you may have built the chart. To link the values in your document to the contents of your chart automatically, see "Establishing an OLE Link Between Word and Graph," later in this chapter.

Notice that each row of the datasheet also contains a *data series graphic*. This chart icon shows the color and pattern of the corresponding data series as it now appears in the chart.

If you've ever worked in a spreadsheet program such as Excel, you'll be comfortable working in the datasheet. Here are some brief pointers on datasheet editing:

- To clear any section of the datasheet, select an area by clicking and dragging over it, and then press Delete.
- You can quickly select the entire sheet by clicking the unmarked button at the upper-left corner of the columns and rows.

- To overwrite any existing data, just click the cell and input your new value or label.

- To edit existing data without removing and retyping it, double-click in the cell, or select the cell and press F2.

- After entering any new values or labels, you must confirm them by pressing Enter, Tab, or any arrow key, or by clicking another cell, thereby moving out of the present cell.

- Graph reserves the first column and row for data series labels (except in XY [scatter] and bubble charts, in which the first row or column contains values). No matter how far you scroll to the right, the first column remains visible; no matter how far you scroll down, the first row remains visible. This way, you can always see your headings.

- If your label or data is too wide to fit in the width of the column, you can adjust the column by clicking and dragging the line on the right between the column headings. When your pointer is positioned correctly, it changes into a double-headed arrow. When a column is too narrow to properly display a value, Graph shows a series of symbols (for example, "#####") until the column is widened. (Datasheets do not support multiple-line labels.)

- You can exclude a data series from the chart without erasing it by double-clicking the corresponding row or column heading. The row or column turns a light gray to indicate that it is inactive. To activate it again, double-click it.

If you need a hard copy of your datasheet, see "How to Print a Copy of Your Datasheet," in the "Troubleshooting" section of this chapter.

MOVING DATA IN THE DATASHEET

Datasheet contents can be cut and pasted like most other elements in Word. To highlight a cell on the datasheet, click it once. From there, Cut, Copy, and Paste work as in Word.

You can also drag and drop your cells to replace one value with another. To drag and drop a cell, position your pointer on the black border around a selected cell and then click and drag your cell to a new location. Release the mouse button. If the new location already contains a value, Graph asks you to confirm that you want to replace it.

CAUTION

If you find that the drag-and-drop feature is not working, it may have been disabled. With Graph open, choose Tools, Options, and click the Datasheet Options tab. Make sure that the Cell Drag-and-Drop check box is checked.

15

FORMATTING DATA IN THE DATASHEET

Graph enables you to apply formats in your datasheet. Most of these formats—including font format, cell alignments, and column width—are available simply to help make your datasheet more readable. They are not reflected in either your chart or your Word document. You can access these by choosing Format, Font or Format, Column Width, or by clicking buttons on Graph's Formatting toolbar.

However, there is one set of formatting options that is also reflected in your chart when set in your datasheet: number formats. You have two ways to specify how numbers are formatted in your charts. The quickest way is to use the five number-related toolbar buttons on Graph's Formatting toolbar:

- **Currency Style**—This button adds a leading currency symbol. In the U.S., this means that the figure 1234 is shown as $1,234.00.

- **Percent Style**—This button displays the value times 100, followed by a percent sign. To depict 50%, the value would need to be 0.5.

- **Comma Style**—This button adds a thousands separator, a decimal separator, and decimals to two places. If applied to the value 1234, the number displays as 1,234.00.

- **Increase Decimals**—This button is used with the previous styles. Each time you click this button, one additional decimal place is shown in your chart.

- **Decrease Decimals**—This button is used with the previous styles. Each time you click this button, one fewer decimal place is shown in your chart.

For more complex number formatting, right-click on a number in an individual cell and choose Number from the shortcut menu. This opens the Format Number dialog box (see Figure 15.20).

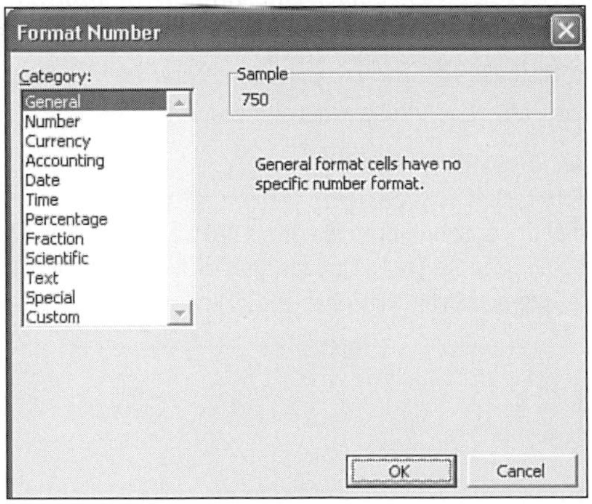

Figure 15.20
Using the Format Number dialog box to control the formatting of numbers in a datasheet.

Here, you can choose from a dozen format categories, including Currency, Accounting, Date, Time, Percentage, and Scientific. In each category are numerous subcategories

15

detailing different options involving negative numbers and other choices. You can also use a Custom category to construct your own formatting option. Click Custom in the Category scroll box; then enter your choice in the Type text box.

CREATING AND USING CUSTOM CHART TYPES

Word allows you to create custom chart types of your own—in essence, reusable chart Templates that are at your fingertips whenever you need them. Custom Chart Types allow you to create sophisticated chart designs and use them consistently in all your business diagrams. In the following sections, you'll learn how to create them, how to use them, and how they can fit into your corporate graphic design strategies.

CREATING A CUSTOM CHART TYPE

Earlier, you learned that you can use the Chart Type dialog box to choose from two sets of built-in charts: standard types and custom types. Custom chart types are similar to templates in Word: They bring together a collection of styles and settings that you can use over and over.

Each custom chart type Word provides is based on a standard chart type. The difference is that they may contain additional formatting and options, such as a legend, gridlines, data labels, a secondary axis, colors, patterns, fills, and placement choices for various chart items not found in the standard chart types.

Now that you've learned how to customize a chart's elements and formatting, you may want to create your own custom chart. To do so, you can start from one of the custom charts Microsoft provides or build your own from scratch.

HOW TO CREATE A CUSTOM CHART

You create a custom chart by first creating an example. Format a chart as you want it, complete with specific fills, typefaces, chart options, and colors. After you've built your "model," follow these steps to build its settings into a reusable custom chart:

1. Right-click on the chart and choose Chart Type from the shortcut menu.
2. When the Chart Type dialog box opens, click the Custom Types tab.
3. Click the User-Defined radio button in the Select From section.
4. Click the Add button. The Add Custom Chart Type dialog box opens (see Figure 15.21).
5. Type the name for this new chart type in the Name text box. If you want, you can also type a brief description in the Description text box. This section could include when the chart was previously used, what it is ideally used for, who created it, and so on.
6. Click OK on the Add dialog box and then the Chart Type dialog box.

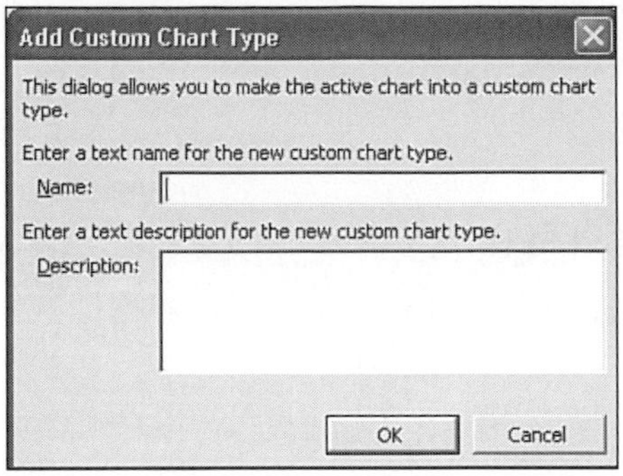

15

Figure 15.21
In this dialog box, you can specify a name and description for your Custom Chart Type.

HOW TO USE A CUSTOM CHART YOU'VE CREATED

After you've created a custom chart, here's how to use it:

1. Insert a chart in your document.

2. With Microsoft Graph open, choose Chart, Chart Type.

3. Click the Custom Types tab.

4. Click the User-Defined button.

5. In the Chart Type scroll box, select the name of the chart you created. A thumbnail of your chart appears in the preview section. Note that it may not be perfectly representative of how your data will ultimately look.

6. Click OK. Word reformats your chart based on your custom chart type.

HOW CUSTOM CHART TYPES CAN SUPPORT YOUR CORPORATE DESIGN STANDARDS

If you're working in a large office, you may want to standardize on a set of custom chart types that reflect your company's design standards. Word and Graph provide several ways to share custom chart types.

The first method is to have each user open a document that contains the chart you want, select the chart, and store the format as a custom format—using the procedure previously described in "How to Create a Custom Chart."

The alternative is to embed your custom charts in a template you can distribute or place in the workgroup templates folder.

→ For more information about working with templates, **see** Chapter 11, "Templates, Wizards, and Add-Ins," **p. 355**.

In most cases, however, the best alternative is to copy the file GRUSRGAL.GRA, which stores custom charts, to each computer that you want to have access to them. In Word 2003 running on Windows 2000 or Windows XP, this file is typically stored in the C:\Documents and Settings*Username*\Application Data\Microsoft\Graph folder, where *Username* corresponds to whichever profile is associated with your user logon.

Copying this file to another computer makes its custom charts available to that user.

CAUTION

> If you copy your GRUSRGAL.GRA file over a user's existing GRUSRGAL.GRA file, you will delete any custom charts that user has created. Ideally, create and store your custom charts before you install Microsoft Word or Microsoft Graph on your colleagues' computers—in other words, before your colleagues have had time to create their own custom charts.

USING TRENDLINES

Spotting trends is a major use of charts and data. Trendlines extend your actual data forward to predict where future data points may fall. You can also test your data and analysis by extending the data backward and comparing it against actual, older figures.

Trendlines can be used in various chart types: unstacked area, bar, column, line, stock, XY (scatter), and bubble charts. However, you cannot add trendlines to a 3D, stacked, radar, pie, or doughnut chart. If you have trendlines in place and you convert your chart to one that does not support trendlines, the trendlines disappear.

It's easy to add a trendline to your chart. Choose Chart, Add Trendlines. (If Add Trendlines is not active, your chart type doesn't support this option.) The Add Trendline dialog box opens, as shown in Figure 15.22.

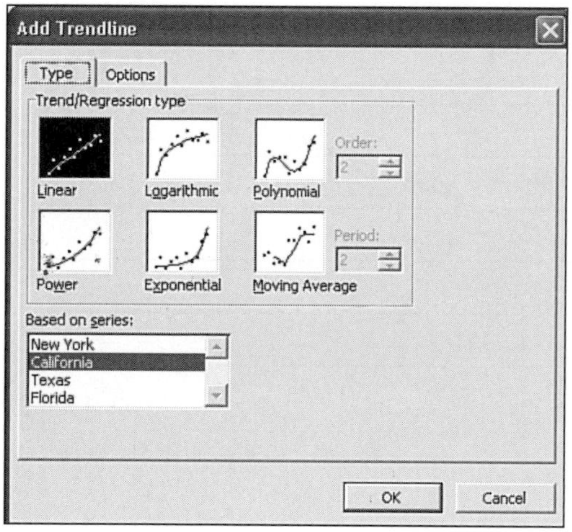

Figure 15.22
Choose a trend analysis from six different formulas.

On the Type tab, you can choose from six Trend/Regression formulas: Linear, Logarithmic, Polynomial, Power, Exponential, and Moving Average. After you've chosen a formula type for your trendline, click the Options tab of the Add Trendline dialog box. Here, you can give your trendline a custom name and set the number of periods your trendline is to forecast both forward and backward.

Table 15.2 lists the trendline options and their key uses.

TABLE 15.2 TRENDLINE OPTIONS AND THEIR USES	
Chart Element	**Use When the Pattern in Your Data Points Indicates...**
Linear	Growth or decline at an approximately steady rate.
Logarithmic	Rapid growth or decline followed by a leveling out.
Polynomial	Ongoing fluctuations in data (hills and valleys).
Power	Increase or decrease at a roughly constant rate (for example, acceleration or deceleration). Cannot be used if any of your data points is zero or negative.
Exponential	Increase or decrease at accelerating or decelerating rates. Cannot be used if any of your data points is zero or negative.
Moving Average	Smoothes out temporary fluctuations which might otherwise obscure a pattern of data.

After you set these options, your chart will contain a trendline similar to the one in Figure 15.23. You can change the color, style, and weight of the trendline (and reset any of the previously chosen options, as well) by selecting the line and clicking the Format button on Graph's Standard toolbar.

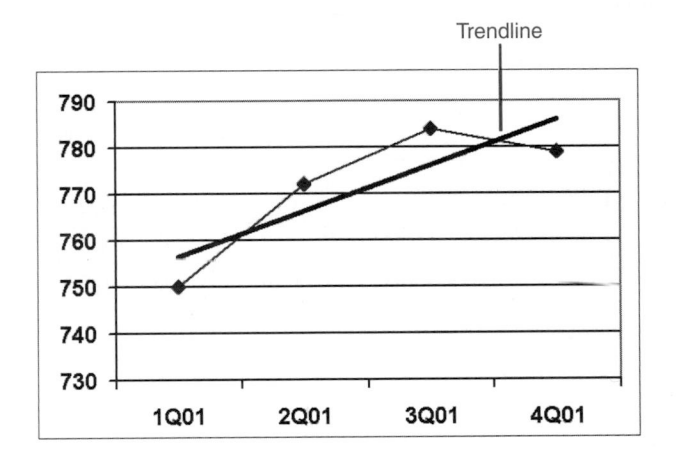

Figure 15.23
Trendlines predict future developments based on current data.

USING ERROR BARS

Error bars show degrees of uncertainty relative to each data marker in a series. They're often used in engineering applications and also are common in polling and market research, where they're used to visually represent the potential error in a survey. (If you hear that a poll is accurate to within plus or minus 3%, you can represent that statistical statement with error bars.)

Error bars display as small T-shaped lines, upright to show error in the positive range and inverted to show error in the negative range. Error bars can be added to data series in area, bar, column, line, XY (scatter), and bubble charts. To add error bars to your chart, follow these steps:

15

1. Click on a data marker to select the data series to which you want to add error bars.

2. Choose Format, Data Series.

3. In the Format Data Series dialog box, click the Y Error Bars tab shown in Figure 15.24. (If you are working with XY [scatter] and bubble charts, your dialog box will also have an X Error Bar tab.)

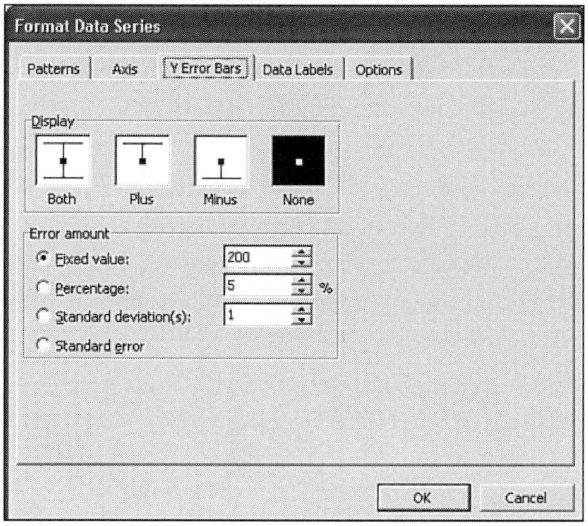

Figure 15.24
Setting error bars in the Format Data Series dialog box.

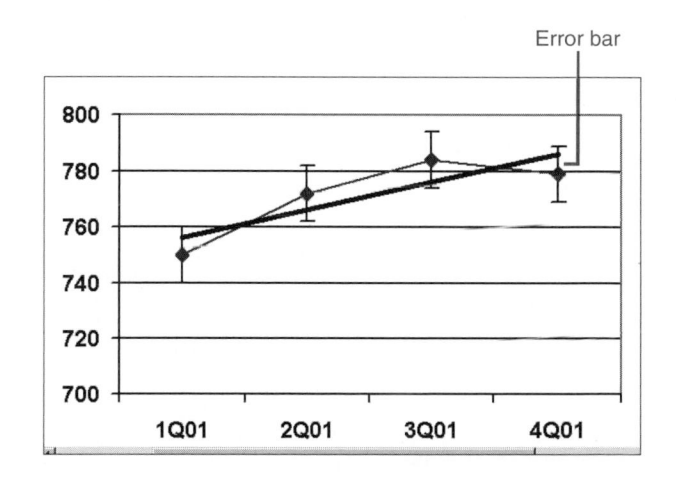

4. In the Display section, select a positive/negative range for the margin of error. You can choose from these options: Both, Plus, Minus, or None.

5. In the Error Amount section, choose from Fixed Value, Percentage, Standard Deviation(s), or Standard Error. You can enter values for all but Standard Error.

6. Click OK when you've completed your choices. The error bars appear in your chart, as shown in Figure 15.25.

Figure 15.25
Error bars depict the potential error amounts relative to each data marker.

15

REVISING CHARTS AUTOMATICALLY

Earlier, you learned that charts created from Word tables are no longer connected to those tables, so changes you make in the datasheet aren't reflected in the source data. Of course, this may not be ideal. You may well want to maintain one consistent set of data that appears in both your data source and your charts. Moreover, you don't want to keep rebuilding and reformatting the same chart as you update it; you simply want the data to change—automatically.

The next two sections show you how to build enduring links between your charts and your data source—first using Word data and then using data from an Excel worksheet.

ESTABLISHING AN OLE LINK BETWEEN WORD AND GRAPH

If you want tight and permanent links between your chart and your Word document, so that the chart changes whenever data changes in your document, you can establish an OLE (object linking and embedding) link between the Word document's original chart data and the contents of the chart itself. Here's how to create an OLE link:

1. Select and copy the Word data you want to graph. (You could also copy data from another document, an Excel worksheet, or another OLE-compliant source.)

2. Choose Insert, Picture, Chart to open Microsoft Graph. Graph opens with dummy (fake) data in its datasheet.

3. If the datasheet does not appear, click the Datasheet button on Microsoft Graph's Standard toolbar to display it.

4. Click your insertion point in the upper-left cell of the datasheet.

5. Choose Edit, Paste Link.

6. Word asks you to confirm that you want to replace the dummy data currently in your datasheet. Click OK.

7. Graph displays the chart, as well as the datasheet window containing the data you pasted.

When you establish the link in this way, the accompanying graph and datasheet are automatically updated whenever you make changes to the Word table.

Not only can you change the data figures of your chart, but you can also change the column or row headings. The chart is updated as soon as you confirm your entry by pressing Tab or otherwise moving from the cell.

You can even add a data series through a linked table, by adding another row or column in the table. Graph creates a new entry in the chart's legend and fills in the information as it is entered.

TIP

> If you no longer want the link, you can break it. Double-click on your chart to open Microsoft Graph and choose Edit, Links. In the Links dialog box, click the Break Link button and click OK.

ESTABLISHING A LINK WITH MICROSOFT EXCEL

The process for linking a chart with Excel (or any other OLE-compatible program) is basically the same as the one described previously for linking a table and chart in the same document. You select and copy the information in Excel, switch to Word, and insert a chart, if one is not already in the document. After selecting the datasheet in Graph, you choose Edit, Paste Link.

However, because you are working with two separate files now, the updating is not instantaneous unless Excel is open, Word is open, and you've double-clicked on your chart to open Microsoft Graph.

After you have changed, saved, and closed your Excel file, you can update your chart by opening your Word document and double-clicking the chart to invoke Graph. The same holds true if your source data is in another Word document or a file created by another program.

CAUTION

> If you use Paste Link, and then make manual changes in the datasheet, your changes disappear the next time you open the file, because Word automatically updates the chart based on the data stored in the source spreadsheet.

TIP

> If you don't want to link your data to an external file, you have another option: Simply import it. Open Graph by double-clicking your chart. Choose Edit, Import File and select the file from the dialog box. You can then choose to import either the entire sheet or a selected data range.

CAUTION

> If you create a live link to an Excel worksheet (or another data source), be careful not to move the source file, or Graph may not be able to update it properly.

ABOUT WORD'S ORGANIZATION CHART FEATURE

One of the most dreaded assignments any white-collar worker can get is to draw up a new organization chart—a diagram that shows the relationships between people working in an organization. Trying to keep all the boxes and lines straight with Word's regular drawing

15

tools can be challenging at best. Fortunately, Word 2003 contains a powerful, easy-to-use tool specifically designed for building organization charts.

TIP

> Beyond organization charts, you can use Word's organization chart tool to create any diagram that requires a hierarchical structure. For example, you might use it to present the high-level organization of a Web site.

NOTE

> Word 2003 also provides several other types of business diagrams, including cycle, radial, pyramid, Venn, and target diagrams. These are covered later in this chapter.

You can access Word's organization chart tool by choosing Insert, Picture, Organization Chart. You can also click the Diagram Gallery button on the Drawing toolbar (use View, Toolbars, Drawing to enable this toolbar), and then double-click the Organization Chart icon.

Whichever method you choose, Word displays a default organization chart with one top-level employee and three subordinates (see Figure 15.26). Word also displays the Organization Chart toolbar, which contains all of Word's tools for organizing and editing organization charts. This toolbar's buttons are described in Table 15.3.

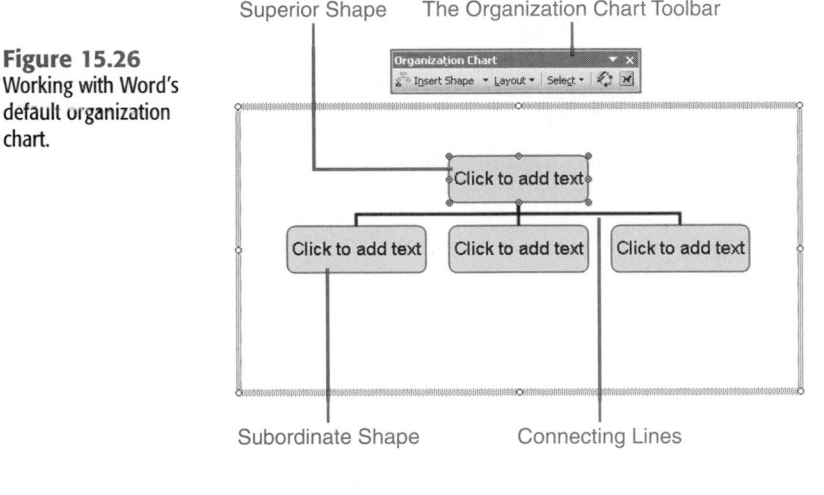

Figure 15.26
Working with Word's default organization chart.

TABLE 15.3 THE ORGANIZATION CHART TOOLBAR

Button	Function
Insert Shape ▾	Inserts boxes for subordinates, assistants, and co-workers

Button	Function
Layout ▾	Selects layouts and controls the size of your organization chart and drawing canvas
Select ▾	Selects portions of an organization chart, including levels, branches, assistants, and connecting lines
🔳	Displays options for reformatting organization charts
🔳	Displays options for wrapping text around or through organization charts

After you've inserted an organization chart, here are some of the tasks you can perform:

■ Enter and format text in text boxes representing each individual

■ Insert new shapes representing subordinates, co-workers, and assistants

■ Format individual shapes using tools similar to those available for formatting text boxes

■ Adjust the layout of your overall organization chart; you can, for example, utilize hanging layouts that represent lists of employees vertically

■ Select elements of your organization chart, such as levels or branches, and perform limited formatting on them

■ Reformat the entire organization chart using one of 15 built-in diagram styles

■ Specify certain formatting that applies to the organization chart as a whole; for example, a background or text wrapping settings

CAUTION

When you are working with organization charts and other diagrams from the Diagram Gallery, Word's Undo feature is somewhat limited. Although you can undo text entries, you cannot undo adding or deleting a box for an employee.

NOTE

You can delete a box by right-clicking on it and choosing Delete from the shortcut menu.

ENTERING AND FORMATTING TEXT IN AN ORGANIZATION CHART BOX

After you've inserted an organization chart, you'll want to begin entering text corresponding to the names of each individual. To enter text inside a shape in your organization chart, click on it and begin typing.

TIP

You can move among boxes in an organization chart by using the arrow keys—up, down, left, and right.

Each shape contains a text box, and these text boxes work much as they do elsewhere in Word. For example, you can select text and format it using the controls on the Standard toolbar (such as the alignment and font formatting buttons).

You can also change the size, color, borders, or inside margins of a text box by right-clicking on it and choosing Format AutoShape from the shortcut menu.

→ For more information about text boxes and Format AutoShape controls, **see** Chapter 14, "Using Word's Quick and Easy Drawing Tools," **p. 483**.

 If Word won't let you adjust the colors or lines of a text box in an organization chart, see "What to Do If Word Won't Let You Control AutoShape Formatting in Organization Charts or Diagrams," in the "Troubleshooting" section of this chapter.

INSERTING NEW SHAPES IN AN ORGANIZATION CHART

It's unlikely that your organization consists of exactly one superior and three subordinates. To add a box for another employee, follow these steps:

1. Click on the box representing the individual your new employee will report to, or work with.

2. On the Organization Chart toolbar, click the down arrow next to Insert Shape.

3. Choose the relationship your new employee has to the employee you selected: Subordinate, Coworker, or Assistant.

If you choose Subordinate, Word inserts a new box below the employee you have selected, with a vertical connecting line between them.

If you choose Coworker, Word inserts the new employee to the right of the employee you selected, on the same level of the organization chart.

If you choose Assistant, Word inserts the new employee below, and to the left or right, of the existing employee. The new assistant is connected to the existing employee with a right-angle "elbow" connecting line.

If necessary, when Word inserts a new employee, it adjusts the rest of your organization chart layout to make room.

MOVING A SHAPE IN AN ORGANIZATION CHART

As companies reorganize, responsibilities and reporting arrangements change constantly. You'll often be called on to move boxes in an organization chart. To do so, select the box you want to move, and drag it over the box containing the individual's new supervisor. Word places the box under the new supervisor and adds a reporting line between them.

If you want to move an individual *and* all the individuals who report to him or her, click Select, Branch on the Organization Chart toolbar; then drag the individual over the box containing his or her new supervisor. All of the individual's subordinates will follow as well.

→ For more on selecting parts of an organization chart or diagram, **see** "Selecting Elements of an Organization Chart," **p. 546**.

DELETING A SHAPE FROM AN ORGANIZATION CHART

Occasionally, you'll need to remove an employee from an organization chart. To do so, right-click on the employee's box and choose <u>D</u>elete from the shortcut menu. If you delete an individual with subordinates, all the subordinates are deleted as well.

CHANGING ORGANIZATION CHART LAYOUTS

By default, Word formats its organization charts using a Standard format in which all employees at the same level of the organization appear on the same horizontal level of the chart. This layout works well in many, but not all, circumstances. For example, it can be problematic when you have many employees at the same level: Either your organization chart will become too wide for practical use, or each box will become illegibly narrow.

In these cases, you may want to stack some or all of your organization chart vertically, facing to the left, to the right, or both. Word provides both options. To change the layout of an organization chart, follow these steps:

1. Click on the box at the top of the branch containing all the boxes you want to change. If you want to change the entire organization chart, click on the box at the top of the organization chart; for example, your company's top executive.

2. Click the Layout button on the Organization Chart toolbar and choose the setting you want.

Figure 15.27 shows a portion of an organization chart that has been reformatted with a <u>L</u>eft Hanging layout.

Figure 15.27
A portion of an organization chart formatted with a Left Hanging layout.

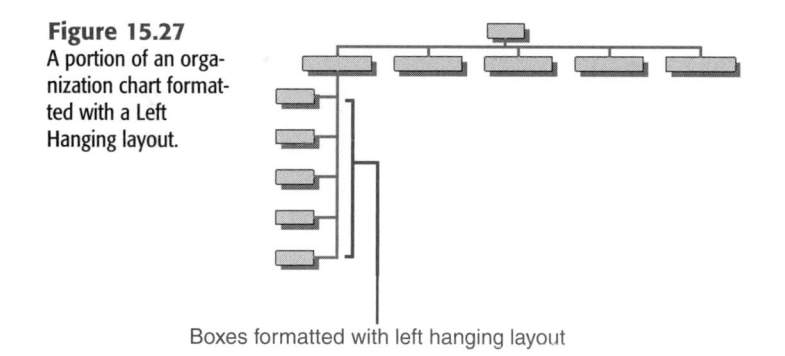

Boxes formatted with left hanging layout

Word provides three other layout options. Unlike the hanging layouts used in the figure, these do not affect the structure of the chart.

- <u>F</u>it Organization Chart to Contents shrinks the drawing canvas to fit snugly around whatever boxes you have placed in your cell.

- <u>E</u>xpand Organization Chart slightly increases the size of your organization chart.

15

- **S**cale Organization Chart places circular sizing handles around the edges of your organization chart's drawing canvas. You can then drag any of these handles to enlarge or shrink the organization chart.

You can also control the way text wraps around an organization chart, just as you can control how text wraps around any other drawing canvas. To do so, click the Text Wrapping button on the Organization Chart toolbar and select the text wrapping option you prefer.

→ For more details on text wrapping options **see** Chapter 14, "Using Word's Quick and Easy Drawing Tools," **p. 483**.

MANUALLY CONTROLLING THE LAYOUT OF DIAGRAM ELEMENTS

By default, when you create a diagram or an organization chart, Word controls most of the layout features for you. You may at times, however, want more control over the layout than Word is providing. For example, you might want to move, resize, or reshape a circle in a Venn diagram, or add spaces between the triangles in a pyramid diagram.

To gain access to this control, click **L**ayout on either the Diagram or the Organization Chart toolbar, and clear the **A**utoLayout check box.

CAUTION

> While clearing AutoLayout gives you more control over the appearance of individual shapes, it prevents you from performing several other key tasks, including inserting additional shapes, or changing the type of diagram (for example, from a pyramid to a cycle diagram).
>
> If you try to perform one of these tasks, Word prompts you to turn AutoLayout back on. Doing so eliminates all the customizations you have made with AutoLayout turned off.
>
> The best way to handle this is to make sure you have included all the shapes you need, and have chosen the correct diagram, before turning AutoLayout off to make any final layout tweaks you may need.

SELECTING ELEMENTS OF AN ORGANIZATION CHART

At times, you may want to select elements of an organization chart to make global formatting changes to them. You've already learned that you can select an individual box by clicking on it. You can also select

- An entire *branch* of an organization chart: everyone who reports to a specific individual
- An entire *level* of an organization chart: everyone at the same level in the organizational hierarchy
- All *assistants*, regardless of their level or location in the organization

NOTE

> Word defines assistants as individuals whose primary job responsibility is to support *one* individual, rather than to operate as a manager in the corporate hierarchy—for example, executive and administrative assistants.

- All *connecting lines*. Having done so, you can then right-click, choose Format AutoShape, and adjust line colors and line weight.

To select one of these elements, click the Select button on the Organization Chart toolbar and choose what you want to select from the drop-down list. After you've selected an element of your organization chart (or other diagram), round gray selection handles appear around all the boxes you've selected, as shown in Figure 15.28.

Figure 15.28
Gray selection handles appear around organization chart elements you've selected.

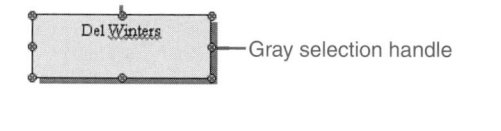

Gray selection handle

These selection handles are different from the sizing handles Word's drawing tools provide, and they cannot be used to resize elements of an organization chart or a diagram.

→ To learn how to resize elements of an organization chart or a diagram, **see** "Manually Controlling the Layout of Diagram Elements," **p. 546**.

TIP

> Using Format AutoShape, you can also change solid lines into dotted lines, indicating that one individual has certain reporting responsibilities to another but is not a direct report. Of course, it's more likely that you'll want to do this with only one or a few connecting lines, rather than the entire organization.

CHANGING THE OVERALL FORMAT OF AN ORGANIZATION CHART

Word's default style for organization charts displays every box in turquoise with a 3/4-point solid black border. Although you can change the formatting of individual boxes by choosing Format AutoShape from the Organization Chart shortcut menu, Word also provides 15 predefined AutoFormats that can give your organization chart an entirely new look with just a few clicks. To choose one, follow these steps:

1. Click the AutoFormat icon on the Organization Chart toolbar. The Organization Chart Style Gallery opens (see Figure 15.29).

2. In the Select a Diagram Style box, choose a style. If you're unsure which style fits your needs or if you want to experiment, use the preview window on the right side of the dialog box to see a sample representation of the selected style.

3. After you've selected the style you want, click Apply.

Figure 15.30 shows an organization chart created with Word's Vibrant format.

Figure 15.29
Choose a new
AutoFormat from the
Organization Chart
Style Gallery.

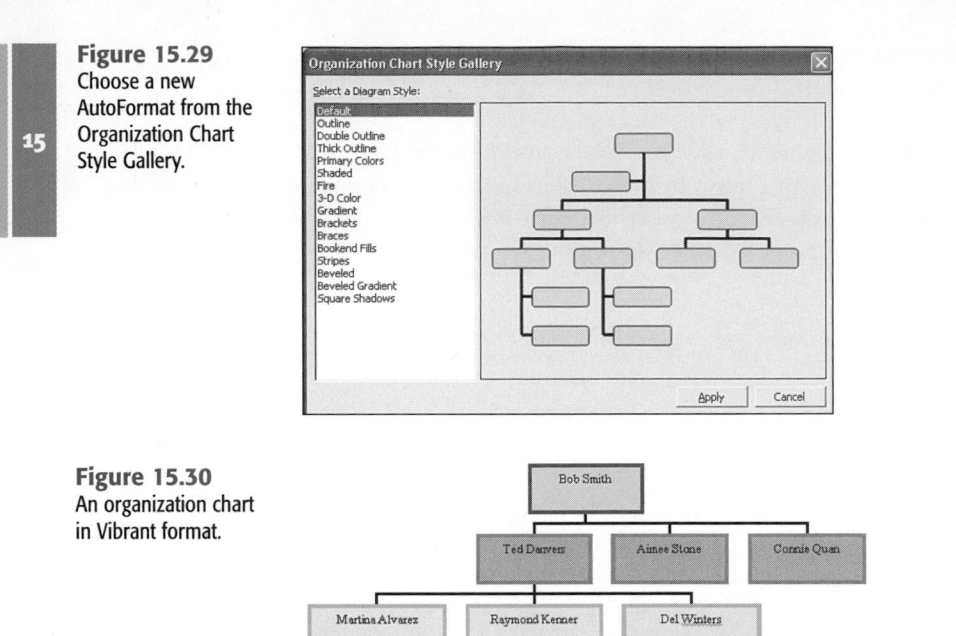

Figure 15.30
An organization chart
in Vibrant format.

ABOUT WORD'S BUSINESS DIAGRAMS CAPABILITIES

In addition to organization charts, Word can instantly build five more key types of business charts:

- *Cycle diagrams* are commonly used to explain continuous processes. Figure 15.31 shows a cycle diagram for a software development project. This project starts with planning, but after software has eventually been delivered, it cycles back into planning for new enhancements.

Figure 15.31
A cycle diagram for a
software development
project.

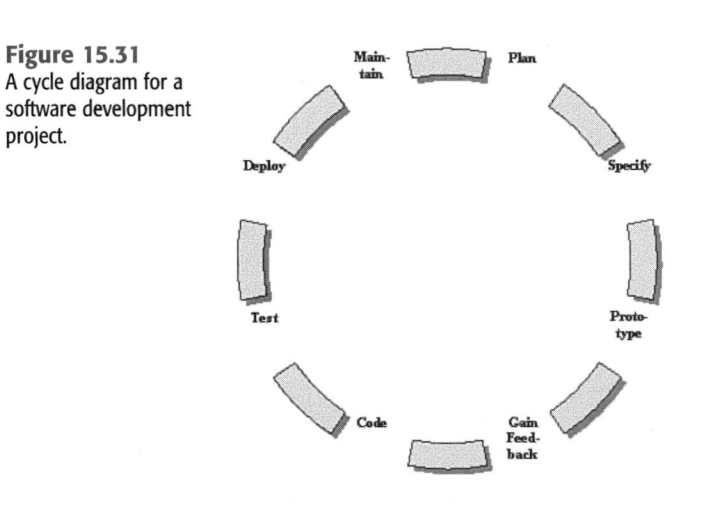

- *Radial diagrams* (as in Figure 15.32) are commonly used to describe processes that all center on, or radiate from, a single core element.

Figure 15.32
A simple radial diagram.

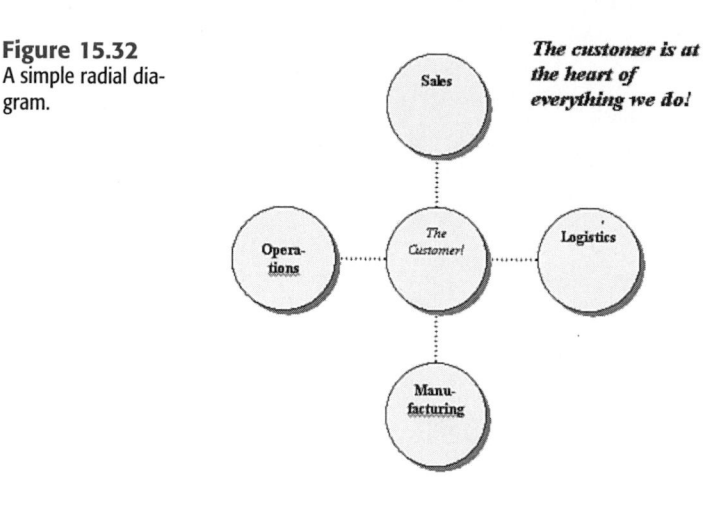

- *Pyramid diagrams* are commonly used to explain how elements of a project or process build on each other. Figure 15.33 shows a pyramid diagram showing how computers are organized conceptually.

Figure 15.33
A simple pyramid diagram.

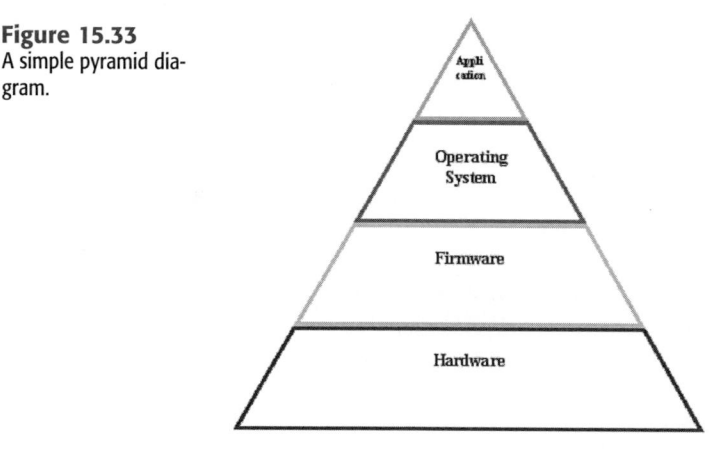

- *Venn diagrams* are commonly used to explain aspects or characteristics of a system that are different and point out aspects or characteristics that overlap. Figure 15.34 shows a simple Venn diagram.

TIP

> For more Venn diagram applications than you ever imagined possible, visit www.venndiagram.com, where Thomas Leonard has already compiled nearly 800 real-world Venn diagrams.

Figure 15.34
A simple Venn diagram.

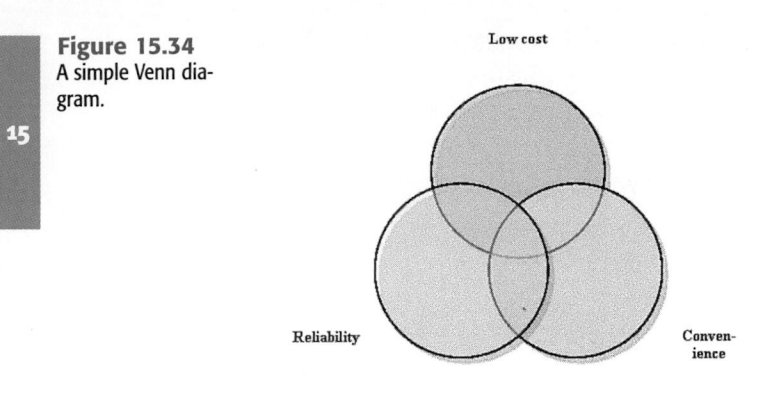

- *Target diagrams* are commonly used to present steps toward a goal, as shown in Figure 15.35.

Figure 15.35
A simple target diagram.

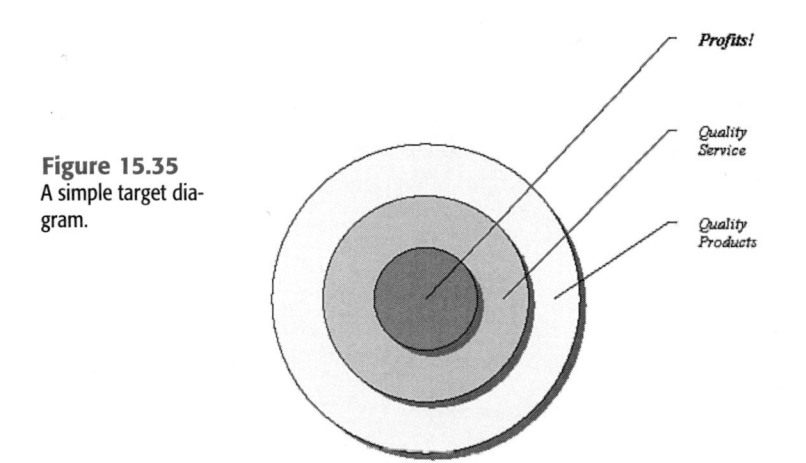

To create any of these charts, choose Insert, Diagram, or display the Drawing toolbar (by choosing View, Toolbars, Drawing); then click the Insert Diagram or Organization Chart button. The Diagram Gallery dialog box opens (see Figure 15.36).

Figure 15.36
The Diagram Gallery dialog box.

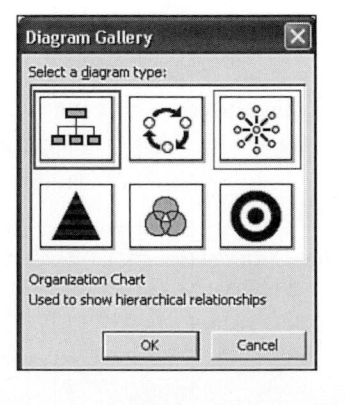

Choose the type of diagram you want to create and click OK; Word inserts a generic diagram within a drawing canvas. Word also displays the Diagram toolbar, which contains Word's features for formatting and managing diagrams. Table 15.4 presents the tools available on the Diagram toolbar.

TABLE 15.4   THE DIAGRAM TOOLBAR

Button	Function
Insert Shape ▾	Inserts additional shapes into your diagram, such as a new 3D circle that surrounds the 3D circles already present in a target diagram.
⟳	Moves all the diagram's shapes (and their text contents) one element backward. For example, in a cycle chart, moves every element counterclockwise.
⟲	Moves all the diagram's shapes (and their text contents) one element forward. For example, in a cycle chart, moves every element clockwise.
⇆	Reverses the locations of all text elements in the diagram.
Layout ▾	Controls the size and scale of the diagram and drawing canvas.
⟳	Displays Autoformat options for reformatting diagrams.
Change to ▾	Changes one type of diagram to another.
⊠	Displays options for wrapping text around or through organization charts.

Many of the tools Word provides for working with diagrams are similar to those you learned about in the discussion of organization charts, earlier in this chapter.

For example, each type of diagram has its own Diagram Gallery with AutoFormat designs you can use to change the look and feel of your diagrams, and the designs Microsoft has provided for each type of diagram are consistent with those it has provided for organization charts. By consistently using the design with the same name, you can have consistent, attractively formatted diagrams and organization charts throughout your documents.

Similarly, you can use the tools on the Layout button to shrink your drawing canvas around the edges of your diagram (Fit Diagram to Contents); to slightly enlarge the diagram (Expand Diagram); or to display sizing handles for the entire drawing canvas (Scale Diagram).

A few tools, however, are unique to the Diagram toolbar. For example, if you decide partway through working on a diagram that your message would be communicated more effectively with a different type of diagram, you can click the Change To button and choose from any of the other four types of diagrams.

15

You can also move information between elements of your diagrams with a single click. For example, imagine that after you create a pyramid diagram, you realize that the text in the second and third shapes on the pyramid should be switched. Select the third shape and click the Move Shape Backwards button. Word switches the third item with the one above it.

NOTE

The Move Shape Backwards and Move Shape Forwards buttons on the Diagram toolbar look different depending on the type of diagram you are working with, but they are always located in the same position and perform the same tasks.

Occasionally, you may want to "turn a diagram upside down": reverse the location of *all* the contents in your diagram. For example, in a pyramid diagram, you might want to move the text that appears in the wide foundation layer all the way to the point at the top, while reversing the order of all the other layers as well. To do so, click the Reverse Diagram button.

A NOTE ON FORMATTING DIAGRAMS

Word offers only limited control over formatting of business diagrams. As you've seen, you can click AutoFormat to choose a new format for the entire diagram. You can also format the text in each text box. For example, you can center the text in an individual text box instead of left-aligning it, you can change its font, and you can use borders and shading.

However, you cannot move or resize a text box or shape within a diagram. For example, if you want to enlarge the circle at the center of a radial diagram, Word's diagram feature provides no way to do it.

If you want to reformat a text box, you can right-click to select it and choose Format AutoShape—but after you do, you'll find that most controls are unavailable. You can only set internal margins and define alternative text that appears in place of the diagram when viewed by Web browsers without graphics.

Occasionally, you may find these limitations extremely frustrating. There are two possible workarounds, neither of them ideal.

You can create and polish your diagram using Word's tools and then superimpose additional shapes or elements over the diagram using Word's drawing tools (see Figure 15.37). For example, as in the previous example, if you want to place a larger circle in the middle of a radial diagram, you can create that circle using the Oval tool on the Drawing toolbar (press Ctrl to get a perfect circle). You can then drag the circle to the appropriate location; right-click on it and choose Add Text to enter text in it. You can then format it as you want. The disadvantage: Diagrams become more complicated to manage, especially if others must update them. Also, some of Word's diagram shapes are difficult to replicate with Word's drawing tools.

Figure 15.37
Using a callout from the Drawing toolbar to display text in the intersection of a Venn diagram.

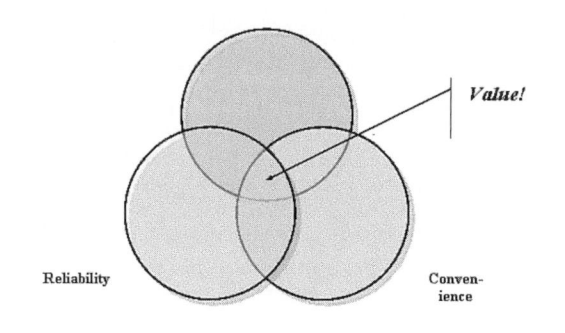

TIP

> Don't hesitate to use Word's drawing tools along with a diagram when it makes sense. For example, Word's diagram tools provide no way to enter text in the intersecting area of a Venn diagram, but as Figure 15.37 shows, you can do it easily with a callout.

If you still have access to a computer running Word 97 or Word 2000, you can open the file containing the diagram in one of these versions of Word, right-click inside the diagram, and choose Ungroup from the shortcut menu. You can then edit each individual element of your drawing, as if you had created them with Word's drawing tools. The disadvantage: When you reopen the document in Word 2003, Word no longer recognizes it as a diagram—if you have more changes to make, you must continue to make them manually, using Word's drawing tools. Also, of course, many individuals and businesses no longer have access to copies of Word 97 or 2000.

TROUBLESHOOTING

WHAT TO DO IF YOUR CHART LOSES DATA LABELS AFTER RESIZING

If you find that when your chart is reduced the text disappears, the font size is probably too small to display properly when the labels are aligned horizontally. You can either enlarge the chart by clicking and dragging the sizing handles or by double-clicking the axis. Then from the Alignment tab of the Format Axis dialog box, switch to a vertical or angled text.

HOW TO PRINT A COPY OF YOUR DATASHEET

You can't print the datasheet directly in Graph. You can, however, include a data table in your chart. Click the Data Table button on the Graph toolbar to do this. (For more information, see "Adding Data Tables," earlier in this chapter.)

Another option is to copy the information where it can be printed. Click the Select All button in the datasheet (the gray cell at the upper left of the datasheet). Click Copy. Click outside the chart and click New in Word to open a new document. Click Paste to place the datasheet's information there. You can convert the information into table format by choosing Table, Convert, Text to Table. In the Convert Text to Table dialog box, make sure that Tabs are selected in the Separate Text At section. Click OK.

THE WRONG MENUS AND COMMANDS ARE DISPLAYED

To adjust a chart, you must display Microsoft Graph's menus instead of Microsoft Word's. Merely clicking on a chart isn't enough; you must double-click on the chart.

When you're working in Graph, you may occasionally find it difficult to display the formatting options you want. Remember that you must select the chart element you want to format before the formatting options for that element become available. For example, if you click on the Legend in a chart, you can then choose Format Legend from the right-click shortcut menu, or Selected Legend from the Format menu.

Because some chart elements—such as Walls, Gridlines, and Vertical Axes—overlap or are close to each other, it can be difficult to select the element you want. Use the Zoom drop-down box on the Standard menu to enlarge your chart, making it easier to distinguish between elements.

DATA LABELS ON MY CHART DON'T CHANGE WHEN I CHANGE THEM ON THE DATASHEET

Many charts contain data labels that specify the values associated with each data point. These data labels can be edited directly on the chart itself.

> **TIP**
>
> To edit text in a data label, double-click on it. A box appears; you can now enter new text in the box.

However, after you edit text in a data label directly, any changes you make to the values in the datasheet are no longer updated in the data label.

To fix the problem, first select all the data labels, right-click, and choose Clear to eliminate all the data labels.

Next, reapply the labels by selecting the data series on the chart; choosing Format, Selected Data Series; clicking the Data Labels tab; checking boxes to specify the information your data labels should contain; and clicking OK.

WHAT TO DO IF WORD WON'T LET YOU CONTROL AUTOSHAPE FORMATTING IN ORGANIZATION CHARTS OR DIAGRAMS

As you've seen, Word provides only limited flexibility in formatting the shapes within organization charts and diagrams. But in some cases, you may find that you have no options at all.

First, make sure that you have actually selected the element you want to reformat. If you want to reformat the shape itself, you should see gray, circular selection handles.

If you want to reformat a text box or its contents, you should see gray cross-hatching around the text box.

If you want to format the entire diagram (perhaps to add background color or a border), no individual components should be selected. Right-click on an empty part of the diagram and choose Format Diagram from the shortcut menu.

WHAT TO DO IF WORD SHRINKS YOUR DIAGRAM WHEN YOU SHRINK YOUR CANVAS

You may sometimes want to reduce the size of the Drawing Canvas Word places around your diagram or organization chart, in order to place surrounding text nearer to your diagram or organization chart. However, when you do so, Word may shrink the diagram as well—not what you had in mind.

To fit the canvas tightly around your diagram so that the diagram does not shrink except when necessary to fit the corners of your resized drawing canvas itself, click Layout on the Diagram toolbar; then choose Fit Diagram to Contents.

WHAT TO DO IF TEXT WON'T FIT IN THE DIAGRAM TEXT BOXES WORD PROVIDES

In some cases, you may need to enter more text in a diagram text box than Word provides. If this occurs, you have two choices:

- Complete the rest of your diagram, and then click Layout on the Diagram toolbar and clear the AutoLayout check box. You can then resize the text box—but remember, if you reenable AutoLayout, your adjustments are deleted.
- Alternatively, place no text at all in the text box Word provides, but superimpose a new text box of the correct size, using the Text Box button on the Drawing toolbar. You may have to adjust the formatting of this text box to match the surrounding diagram. For example, you may have to eliminate its border. To make changes like these, right-click on the text box, and choose Format Text Box from the shortcut menu.

CHAPTER 16

WORD DESKTOP PUBLISHING

In this chapter

WORD 2003: *Almost* A FULL-FLEDGED DESKTOP PUBLISHING PROGRAM

What program comes with the capability to create multicolumn layouts, smoothly import any kind of graphics, use slick design techniques such as drop caps, and even embed fonts for delivery to a professional printer? It's the same program that provides built-in brochure designs, custom fonts, clip art images, and drawing and font effects software. Yes, Word 2003 does all that.

Word isn't a full-fledged desktop publishing program. But if you know your way around Word, you can create a pretty fair newsletter or brochure. Chapter 13, "Getting Images into Your Documents," and Chapter 14, "Using Word's Quick and Easy Drawing Tools," cover many of the features you can use to build visual documents, including

- Importing graphics (Chapter 13)
- Creating text-based graphics with WordArt (Chapter 13)
- Scanning graphics or acquiring them with a digital camera (Chapter 13)
- Controlling text wrapping and other aspects of picture formatting (Chapter 13)
- Drawing with Word's drawing tools (Chapter 14)
- Editing elements into and out of existing images (Chapter 14)
- Using prefabricated AutoShape images (Chapter 14)
- Working with colors, patterns, and fill effects (Chapter 14)
- Using shadowing and 3D (Chapter 14)
- Controlling layers and grouping in drawings (Chapter 14)
- Working with the drawing grid (Chapter 14)

Other chapters containing valuable techniques for use in this chapter appear earlier in this book:

- Formatting characters and paragraphs (Chapter 4, "Quick and Effective Formatting Techniques")
- Using styles to build consistent visual documents (Chapter 10, "Streamlining Your Formatting with Styles")
- Using templates to automate the production of visual—and other—documents (Chapter 11, "Templates, Wizards, and Add-Ins")
- Using tables as a layout tool (Chapter 12, "Structuring and Organizing Information with Tables")

> **NOTE**
>
> Chapter 15, "Visualizing Your Message with Graphs, Diagrams, and Org Charts," also covers additional Word tools for bringing visuals into your documents, including Microsoft Graph, Diagram Gallery, and Organization Chart.

In this chapter, you'll learn about several more features that you can use in any document, but that also lend themselves especially well to newsletters, brochures, and other traditionally desktop published documents.

TIP

> To use most of the techniques in this chapter, you should switch to Print Layout view (if you aren't there already).

When to Use Word—And When *Not* To

Should you use Word as a desktop publishing program, or should you use a different piece of software designed specifically for publishing? For example, it's one thing to create a monthly newsletter (or e-newsletter) for your sales force—a task for which Word is well suited. It's another to create a full-color brochure that depends on high-quality photography—which Word simply isn't designed to handle.

In general, consider using Word if

- You're creating a fairly simple publication, especially one that can be built from one of Word's built-in templates or wizards.
- You expect to customize your documents and need access to Word features such as mail merge to do so.
- Your desktop-published document links to other documents stored on your computer, such as Excel worksheets.
- You want to do it yourself and you already know how to use Word.
- You don't have access to desktop publishing software.

Consider using a dedicated desktop publishing program if

- Your publication will require the use of full-color photography and will be printed professionally—in other words, not on a desktop printer (Word does not support four-color separations, a requirement for high-fidelity color reproduction).
- Your layouts will be especially complex or precise.
- You will be delegating your project to a professional designer, or you already have and know how to use a desktop publishing package well.

TIP

> Even if you export your Word documents to a desktop publishing program, include styles as you work; these can easily be imported into most leading desktop publishing programs.

16

NOTE

> If you need a professional desktop publishing program, but you're worried about the complexity or are reluctant to invest a sizable amount of money, consider Microsoft Publisher.
>
> This is an easy-to-learn program with all the bells and whistles necessary to produce a wide range of publications. Publisher comes with various templates and wizards that make it easy to produce everything from a newsletter to a business form, change color schemes quickly, and even repurpose printed materials for the Web. Publisher also supports four-color separations for professional color printing.
>
> Just as Word uses text boxes, Publisher makes extensive use of text frames (and, for graphics, picture frames). As a result, much of what you learn in this chapter is applicable in Publisher.
>
> Not only does Publisher import Word files, but it also enables you to set Word as your primary editor—so that you can do all your extensive editing in the familiar Word environment, while you benefit from Publisher's more sophisticated layout capabilities.

PLANNING YOUR DOCUMENT

Before you start using Word's desktop publishing tools, consider quickly sketching out a preliminary layout by hand, especially if there are specific ways you want to lay out information or if you're using any kind of graphic such as logos, clip art, or photographs. Getting your ideas on paper, even roughly, can give you a better idea of what size your images should be, how large you can make your headings, and how much room you'll have for your basic text.

NOTE

> When you plan a document, start by asking yourself what is the key message you're trying to communicate. Make sure that the headlines, graphics, and choice of typography work together to support that message. For example, don't use the Comic Sans typeface to promote investment services.

When you are putting together a larger publication, such as a newsletter or quarterly report, it's best to gather all your materials before you begin designing the document. One of the biggest problems you'll have as a layout artist is getting the text to fit within a specific number of pages. Whether you have too much text or too little, it is much easier to make it fit when you have all the pieces. If you must lay out a document without all the elements in hand, use rectangles and text boxes approximately the right size to serve as placeholders. This gives you a truer picture of how your text is going to fit.

TIP

> If you want to see how text will flow around a picture or an AutoShape but don't have the text yet, you can use Word's built-in text generator. Place your insertion point where you want the text to start, type =Rand(), and press Enter. Word inserts three

> paragraphs. Each paragraph contains the same sentence repeated three times: "The quick brown fox jumps over the lazy dog."
>
> If you need more or fewer than three paragraphs, you can specify the exact number of paragraphs and the number of sentences in each paragraph, using the =Rand() function. The syntax is
>
> ```
> =rand(p,s)
> ```
>
> where p equals the number of paragraphs, and s equals the number of sentences in each paragraph.

Keep all the files for a project together. Create a single folder to hold the document itself; any subsidiary Word files; and all the pictures, graphs, and anything else you may need in order to assemble and maintain the document.

One final word about planning your document: moderation. When you're choosing fonts, font sizes, and styles for your publication, select the smallest number of options that can do the job. Two fonts and three font sizes are adequate for most publications. An advertisement or other document with too many changes in fonts and/or font sizes is difficult to read and detracts from your message. Just because you can change fonts every letter doesn't mean you should.

QUICK AND EASY BROCHURES WITH THE BROCHURE TEMPLATE

Word includes a handy template for creating trifold brochures, the kind printed on the front and back of plain sheets of paper (8 1/2"×11", or A4) and then folded twice.

TIP

> You aren't limited to using the built-in template, of course; if your printer can handle 8 1/2"×14" paper, consider printing a four-column brochure, assembled by folding three times.

The built-in Brochure template includes most of the standard brochure features: columns, graphics, headlines, and advanced paragraph formatting. Besides providing a tool that can make your brochures shine even if you have no layout talent, the Brochure template also offers a tutorial on useful techniques.

To create a brochure, choose File, New; click On My Computer in the New Document task pane; and click the Publications tab. Double-click on the Brochure icon. You'll get a complete brochure, with pictures in appropriate places, various text samples, and hints for making changes (see Figure 16.1).

NOTE

Depending on how you installed Word or Office, the first time you use the Brochure template, you may need to install it from your CD-ROM or the network location you originally installed the program from.

Figure 16.1
Creating a new brochure from the built-in template.

16

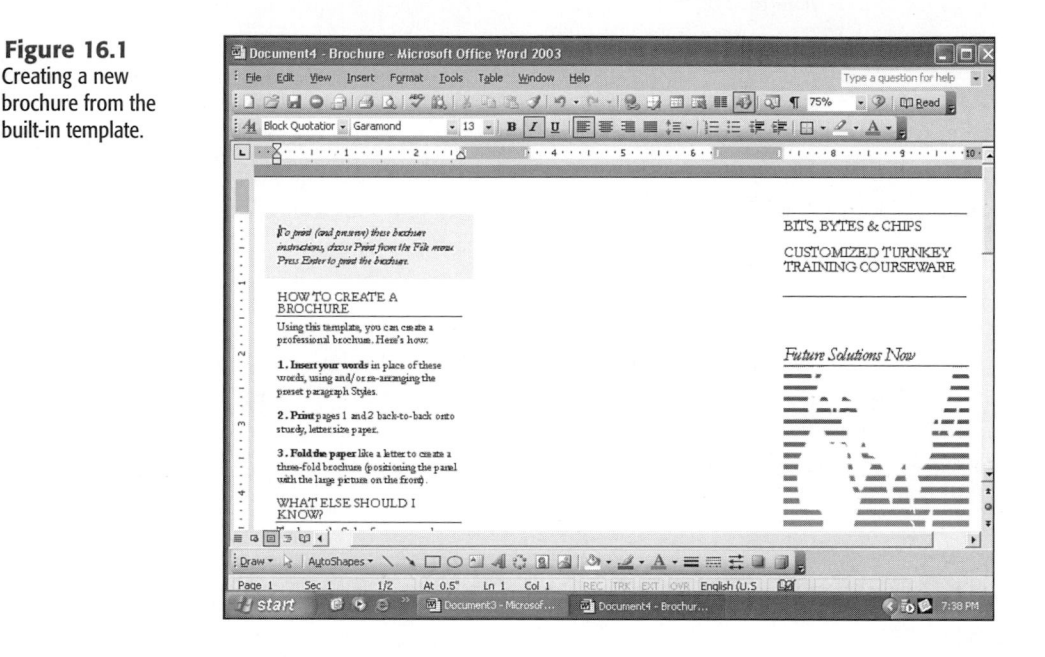

TIP

The tips in the brochure template are used as sample text that gets replaced with your own as you create your brochure. Because many of these tips and instructions are very useful, print the brochure template before you start changing it.

Start by modifying the brochure in ways that will apply to all the brochures you might want to make: Change the business name, address, tag line, logo, and so on.

Because you started with Microsoft's brochure template, you gain the formatting benefits built into that template. Most important, each newsletter element—including main headings, body text, cover title, subtitle, numbered lists, and return address—is formatted to complement the others. Moreover, each style is based on the document's Normal style, so you can quickly modify the overall look of the newsletter by changing the font used in the Normal style from Garamond to another font.

→ For more information about working with styles, **see** Chapter 10, "Streamlining Your Formatting with Styles," **p. 329**.

To customize the brochure, follow the tips in the template to replace the placeholder text; change the formatting of styles, individual paragraphs, or blocks of text; and replace the pictures in the template with your own.

NOTE

> Don't try to squeeze in too much. Readers turn off too dense layouts; strategically placed whitespace makes any document more inviting and gives the eye a place to rest. Word's nicely designed three-panel "Slim-Jim" brochure template contains space for only about 650 words.

16

To replace a picture, first select the picture by clicking it. Then, use one of the commands on Word's Insert, Picture cascaded menu to choose a new picture to replace it.

For example, if you want to use a picture stored on your hard drive, choose Insert, Picture, From File; browse to the picture; click to select it; and click Insert. Word replaces your picture with the new one. You may need to resize the picture to better fit the needs of your brochure.

→ For more information about inserting images into your document and resizing them after you insert them, **see** Chapter 13, "Getting Images into Your Documents," **p. 437**.

After you've replaced Word's generic content (text and images) with your own "boilerplate" materials—and modified design and content elements to reflect your own needs, save a copy of the brochure as a template. That way, in the future, you won't have to start all over again with Word's "generic" template: You can start with your revamped template.

USING PUBLICATION LAYOUTS FROM MICROSOFT OFFICE ONLINE

Microsoft provides a growing collection of publication templates through the Microsoft Office Online Web site. To choose "desktop publishing" templates for Word, do this:

1. Choose File, New.
2. In the New Document Task Pane, click Templates Home Page. Internet Explorer displays the Microsoft Office Online home page.
3. Click Marketing Materials (in the Marketing section).
4. Browse among the brochures, booklets, ads, flyers, posters, print and email newsletters, and other materials provided there. Templates with the Microsoft Word icon are designed for Word; other templates are designed for Publisher and other Office programs.
5. Click the Hyperlink of the template you want.
6. On the next screen, click Download Now.
7. Click Accept to accept Microsoft's License Agreement.
8. Click Continue. Word reopens, showing a new document based on the template you downloaded.

USING DROP CAPS

Word can easily create large initial capitals, more commonly known as *drop caps*, that give your documents a distinct, magazine-style appearance. Drop caps work well in newsletters, particularly those formatted with columns.

Figure 16.2 shows an example of a drop cap: One letter has been "dropped into" a paragraph, and the first lines of text in the paragraph have been pushed to the right.

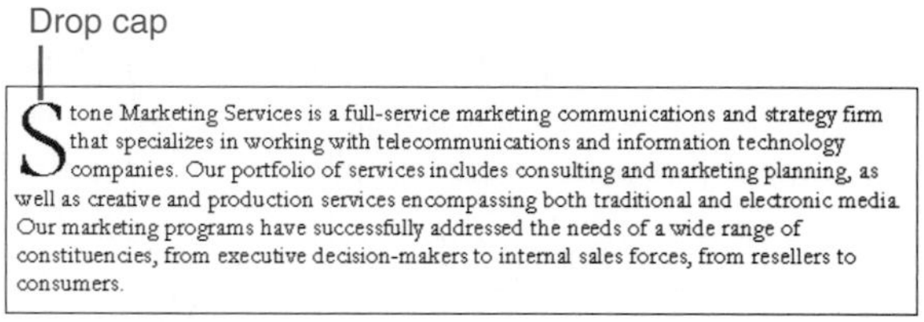
Drop cap
Stone Marketing Services is a full-service marketing communications and strategy firm that specializes in working with telecommunications and information technology companies. Our portfolio of services includes consulting and marketing planning, as well as creative and production services encompassing both traditional and electronic media. Our marketing programs have successfully addressed the needs of a wide range of constituencies, from executive decision-makers to internal sales forces, from resellers to consumers.

Figure 16.2
A drop cap adds visual spice to a page.

Follow these steps to add a drop cap to any paragraph:

1. Highlight the letter(s) or word(s) you want to convert to a drop cap.
2. Choose Format, Drop Cap. The Drop Cap dialog box appears (see Figure 16.3).

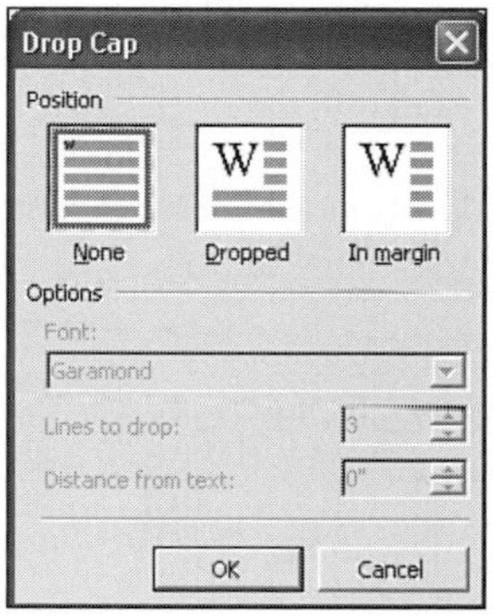
Drop Cap
Position
None
Dropped
In margin
Options
Font:
Garamond
Lines to drop:
3
Distance from text:
0"
OK
Cancel

Figure 16.3
Working in the Drop Cap dialog box.

3. Use the visuals this dialog box provides to select the position in which you want your drop cap to appear. Click either Dropped or In Margin.
4. If you want, select a different font for the drop cap by clicking the arrow next to the Font text box.
5. To change the size of the drop cap, enter a new value in the Lines to Drop text box.
6. To alter the amount of space between the drop cap and the surrounding text, enter a new value in the Distance from Text box.
7. Click OK to see the result.

Word makes your drop cap by putting your selected text into a frame. To alter your options and get a different look, click the frame with the drop cap and select F*o*rmat, *D*rop Cap again. To remove a drop cap, click the frame, select F*o*rmat, *D*rop Cap, and choose *N*one.

Drop caps are one of the few remaining Word features that use old-fashioned Word frames rather than text boxes. To format a frame, select it and choose F*o*rmat, F*r*ame. The Frame dialog box appears (see Figure 16.4).

Figure 16.4
Formatting the frame surrounding a drop cap.

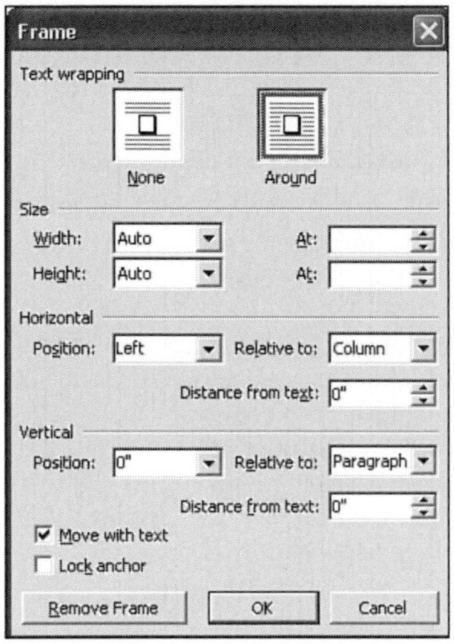

16

Here you can specify the following settings for the drop caps frame:

- Whether text wraps around the frame
- Horizontal and vertical positioning
- Width and height of the frame (not the letter itself)
- Whether the frame moves with text or locks (anchors) in place

You can also add borders or shading to a frame by right-clicking on it and choosing *B*orders and Shading from the shortcut menu. Borders and shading are covered in detail in Chapter 4.

TIP

> A classic designer's trick is to pick a font for the drop cap that's from a different typeface than the one used for the body of the paragraph. For example, if your paragraph is in a serif font such as Times New Roman, use a sans-serif font such as Arial for your drop cap.

INSERTING SYMBOLS AND SPECIAL CHARACTERS

Often, you'll want to use characters other than those shown on a standard keyboard. In some cases, you'll need foreign language characters such as é or n~. In other cases, you may need special characters, such as the section character §, which is often used in legal documents. In still other cases, you may want to use special-purpose symbols, such as the No Smoking icon available on Microsoft's free Webdings font. Finally, you may want to use symbols as decoration to spruce up newsletters and other documents. In the next few sections, you'll learn how to access symbols like these and use them most effectively.

WORKING WITH SYMBOLS

Chapter 13 discusses how you can use WordArt to transform ordinary text into attractive artwork. But often you can achieve surprisingly attractive results simply by using characters in the fonts already installed on your computer.

Sometimes it's the small touches that make the difference—like settling on a "slug" that you'll use at the end of every article. Slugs, as shown in Figure 16.5, tell the reader that the article ends here—and if you pick the right one, they also add a touch of attractiveness and professionalism.

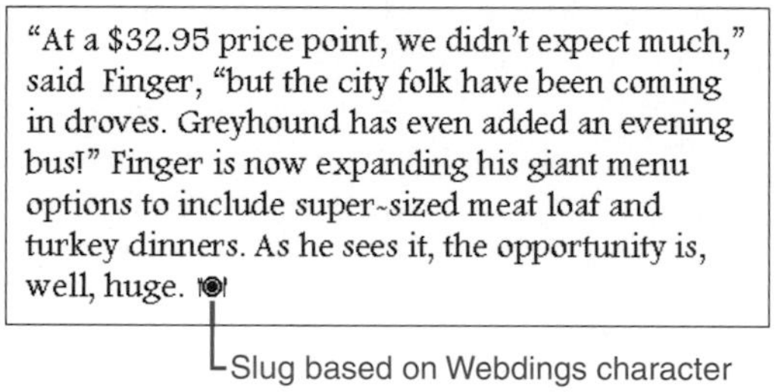
"At a $32.95 price point, we didn't expect much," said Finger, "but the city folk have been coming in droves. Greyhound has even added an evening bus!" Finger is now expanding his giant menu options to include super-sized meat loaf and turkey dinners. As he sees it, the opportunity is, well, huge.
Slug based on Webdings character

Figure 16.5
Using a symbol as a slug.

Word's tool for accessing symbols and other special characters is the Symbol dialog box. In addition to selecting symbols and other characters one at a time, the Symbol dialog box also enables you to set up various shortcuts for characters you use often. Follow these steps to insert a symbol:

1. Place your insertion point where you want the special character to appear.
2. Choose Insert, Symbol. The Symbol dialog box opens (see Figure 16.6).

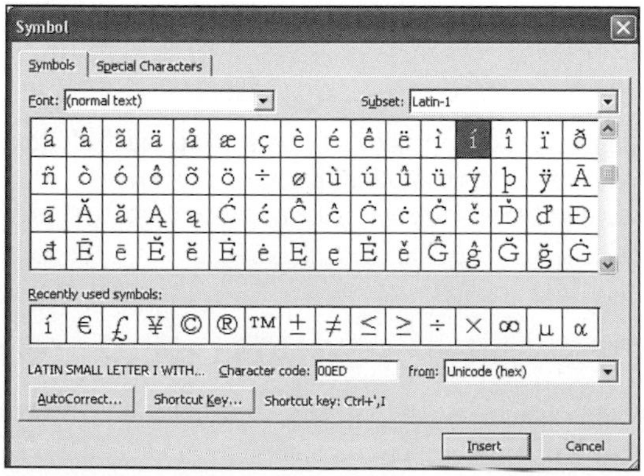
Symbol
Symbols
Special Characters
Font: (normal text)
Subset: Latin-1
Recently used symbols:
LATIN SMALL LETTER I WITH...
Character code: 00ED
from: Unicode (hex)
AutoCorrect...
Shortcut Key...
Shortcut key: Ctrl+',I
Insert
Cancel

Figure 16.6
The Symbol dialog box shows you characters from the font you've selected.

3. If you want to display only a portion of the characters available to you—to locate the character you need more quickly—click the Subset drop-down box, and choose the subset of characters you want to view.

4. To select a character or special symbol from a different font, click the arrow next to the Font text box and choose a font from the drop-down list.

5. When you're ready to insert a character, select it and click Insert. The Symbol dialog box remains open in case you want to enter more characters (however, the Cancel button changes to read Close).

6. When you finish working in the Symbol dialog box, click the Close button (or Cancel button if you did not insert any characters).

16

TIP

> If you know a symbol's character code, you can select that symbol by entering the code in the Character Code text box in the Symbol dialog box.
>
> By default, Word expects character codes to be numbered using the international Unicode standard. However, many longtime Windows users have become familiar with the character code numbering displayed in the ASCII decimal format. (The ASCII character set has 255 characters, numbered from 0 to 255.)
>
> To enter a character code in the ASCII decimal format, choose ASCII (decimal) from the From drop-down box at the lower right of the Symbol dialog box; then enter the code in the Character Code text box.

→ To learn how to create a keyboard shortcut for symbols you reuse often, **see** "Creating a Keyboard Shortcut for a Symbol or Special Character," **p. 568**.

In Word 2003, the Symbol dialog box contains a row of Recently Used Symbols that makes it easier for you to select symbols you've used before. When you use Word for the first time, the Recently Used Symbols row displays commonly used symbols, such as the Euro and other currency symbols, copyright, trademark, and math symbols.

TIP

> When you know you'll need to insert characters in a document, just select and insert all of them at the very beginning. Even if you have to move them later, it's easier to cut and paste characters from a specific part of your document than to reopen and relocate characters in the Symbol dialog box every time you need one.

WORKING WITH SPECIAL CHARACTERS

Traditionally, typographers have improved the look of documents by turning to some characters that do not appear on typewriter keyboards, such as copyright and registered trademark symbols, em dashes (—), and en dashes (–). By default, Word's AutoFormat As You Type feature adds many of these characters automatically.

→ For more information about AutoFormat As You Type, **see** Chapter 9, "Automating Your Documents," **p. 287**.

Sometimes, however, you may need to add characters such as these directly. To do so, choose Insert, Symbol and click the Special Characters tab (see Figure 16.7).

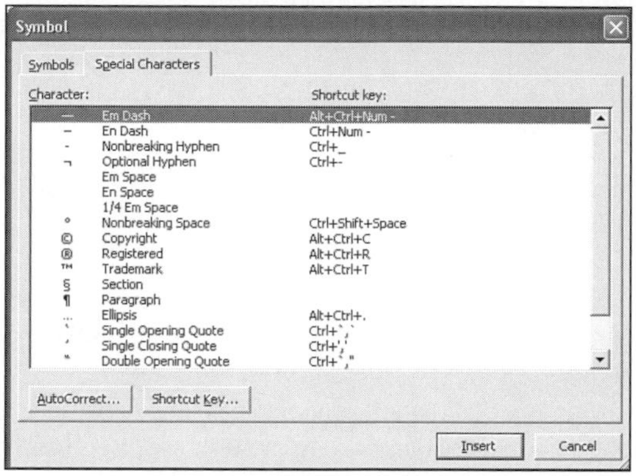

Figure 16.7
Entering a special character through the Special Characters tab of the Symbol dialog box.

This dialog box contains a long list of special characters, along with their names and any shortcut keys they've been set up with. If you see the symbol you want in this list, simply select it and click Insert (you can also just double-click it).

CREATING AN AUTOCORRECT SHORTCUT FOR A SYMBOL OR SPECIAL CHARACTER

As discussed in Chapter 9, Word allows you to create AutoCorrect entries that allow you to automatically substitute one block of text for another. For example, you can create an AutoCorrect entry that automatically inserts a lengthy paragraph of contract language whenever you type a few characters to invoke it.

You can also use AutoCorrect to insert symbols in place of ordinary text—thereby avoiding the need to open the Symbol dialog box. Word 2003 makes it easy to create new shortcuts of this nature. From within the Symbol dialog box, select the symbol character you want to create a shortcut for; then click AutoCorrect.

The AutoCorrect dialog box opens, with the symbol already appearing in the With text box. In the Replace text box, enter the text you want Word to replace with your symbol. For example, if you want Word to enter the Greek symbol omega (Ω), you might use the text "omega." Better yet, use a slight variation, such as "omegas," so Word doesn't enter the Ω symbol when you intend to type the word omega instead.

CREATING A KEYBOARD SHORTCUT FOR A SYMBOL OR SPECIAL CHARACTER

Several special characters have keyboard shortcuts assigned to them. It pays to become familiar with these keyboard shortcuts—they can save you a lot of time.

However, many special characters don't have keyboard shortcuts—and neither do symbols you entered in the Symbols tab. If you expect to make extensive use of one of these characters, it might be a good idea to create a custom keyboard shortcut for it. To do so, follow these steps:

1. Choose Insert, Symbol.
2. Locate and select the character in either the Symbols or Special Characters tab.
3. Click Shortcut Key. The Customize Keyboard dialog box opens (see Figure 16.8).

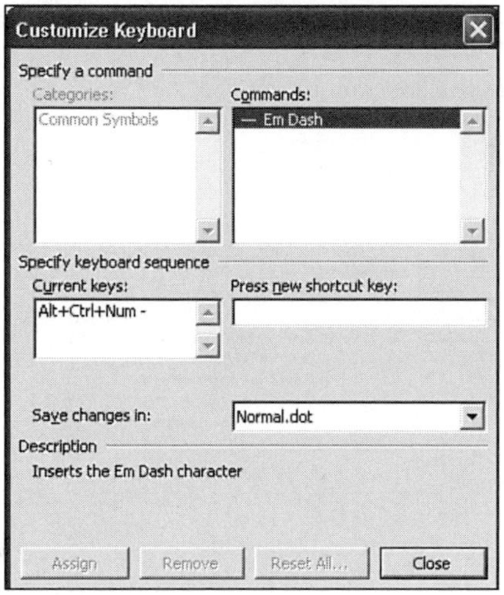

Figure 16.8
Assigning a shortcut key to a symbol or special character.

4. Press the shortcut key combination you want to use. If that combination is already assigned, Word tells you so. If this happens, the best solution is to try another combination.
5. When you've chosen a combination you want to use, click Assign.
6. Click Close twice (once for the Customize Keyboard dialog box and once for the Symbol dialog box).

After you've created the shortcut key, you can insert the corresponding symbol at any time, by clicking where you want it to appear and then pressing the shortcut key.

> **TIP**
>
> If you've created several keyboard shortcuts for commonly used symbols, you might want to print a list of them. To do so, choose File, Print; then choose Key Assignments from the Print What drop-down box, and click OK.

USING TEXT BOXES

Normally, when you work in Word, your text adjusts up, down, or sideways when you make other editing changes. But sometimes you want something—text, a graphic, a table, or some other document element—to stay put, no matter what.

Perhaps you want to include sidebar or pullquote text in your document and make sure that the other text flows around it (see Figure 16.9). Or perhaps you want to create copy that flows between one location and the next—as you would if you were producing a newsletter with a story that "jumped" from one page to another. You might want an address block on the back cover or a form that recipients could return. These are some of the many valuable uses for Word's text box feature.

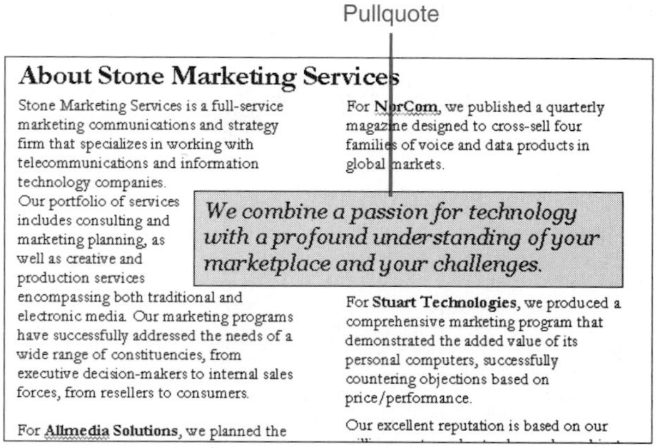

Figure 16.9
Text box used for a pullquote.

Pullquote

About Stone Marketing Services

Stone Marketing Services is a full-service marketing communications and strategy firm that specializes in working with telecommunications and information technology companies.

Our portfolio of services includes consulting and marketing planning, as well as creative and production services encompassing both traditional and electronic media. Our marketing programs have successfully addressed the needs of a wide range of constituencies, from executive decision-makers to internal sales forces, from resellers to consumers.

For **Allmedia Solutions**, we planned the

For **NorCom**, we published a quarterly magazine designed to cross-sell four families of voice and data products in global markets.

We combine a passion for technology with a profound understanding of your marketplace and your challenges.

For **Stuart Technologies**, we produced a comprehensive marketing program that demonstrated the added value of its personal computers, successfully countering objections based on price/performance.

Our excellent reputation is based on our

Text boxes are free-floating objects, independent of your regular document. You can specify precise locations and sizes for text boxes, as well as borders, fills, and other formatting.

TIP

Because it's also possible to wrap text around tables, you can sometimes use tables rather than text boxes for sidebars and similar applications.

This is a valuable alternative whenever you have a multiple-column document and you need to call attention to information that is tightly structured, such as a row-and-column set of names, products, or financial results. More information on tables can be found in Chapter 12.

INSERTING A TEXT BOX

To insert a text box, follow these steps:

1. Choose Insert, Text Box. Your pointer becomes a small crosshair, and Word switches to Print Layout view (if you aren't already in that view). Unless you have turned off the Drawing Canvas, Word also inserts a Drawing Canvas containing the text "Create your drawing here."

2. Click where you want the upper-left corner of your text box to appear.

   If you want your text box to appear within the Drawing Canvas, click inside the Drawing Canvas. If you want your text box to appear outside the Drawing Canvas, click outside it; the canvas will disappear.

→ For more information about working with Drawing Canvases, **see** Chapter 14, "Using Word's Quick and Easy Drawing Tools," **p. 483**.

3. Drag out a rectangle to the size and shape you want your text box to have.

4. Release the mouse button. Word displays a text box with shaded borders, as shown in Figure 16.10.

Figure 16.10
A typical text box, selected.

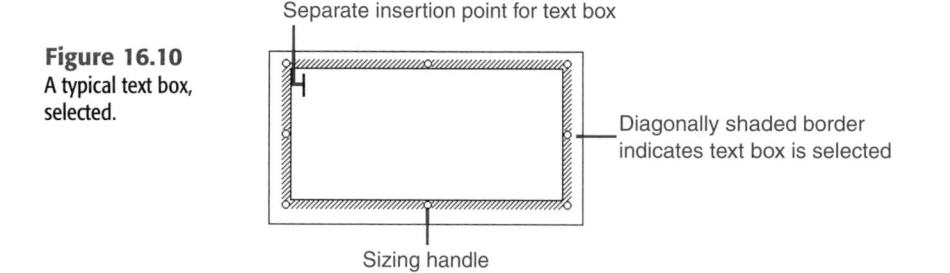

Separate insertion point for text box

Diagonally shaded border indicates text box is selected

Sizing handle

Your text box has its own insertion point, which you can use to enter text. You can also insert graphics, tables, fields, or virtually anything else Word can place in a document, with the following exceptions:

- Page and column breaks
- Comment marks
- Footnotes and endnotes
- Indexes and tables of contents (note that although entries for your index and table of contents can be placed in text boxes, Word won't find them when it compiles your index and table of contents)
- Columns
- Drop caps

NOTE

> You can use frames for these tasks, as is covered in the following section.

When a text box is selected (refer to Figure 16.11), it has a special diagonal-line border with eight sizing handles around it. The text box also has its own ruler settings, which enable you to set tabs independently from the rest of the document. Setting a tab works the same inside a text box as it does outside.

→ For more information about setting tabs, **see** Chapter 4, "Quick and Effective Formatting Techniques," **p. 107**.

Whenever you're finished working with a text box, you can deselect the text box by clicking outside it.

16

> If you're not sure how large you want your text box to be, you can use Word's default size. Choose Insert, Text Box; when the pointer becomes a small crosshair, just click once. A default text box appears. You can later size it as needed by using the sizing handles.

When you create a text box, Word displays the Text Box toolbar (see Figure 16.11). The Change Text Direction button can turn text in a text box sideways. As you click, the direction toggles, first to the right (read top to bottom), then to the left (read bottom to top), then back to normal (read left to right). You can't turn text upside down, nor can you turn only some of the text in a text box—it's all or nothing.

Figure 16.11
The Text Box toolbar.

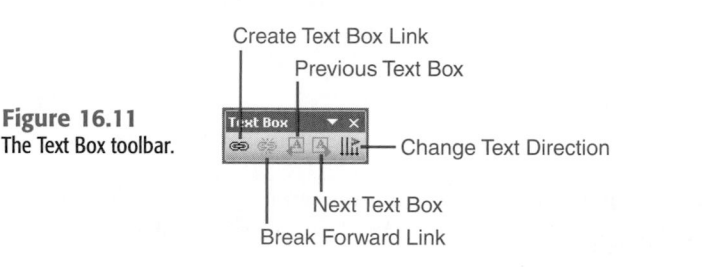

NOTE

> Using text boxes can add a bit of extra work because you have to worry about how they're positioned and formatted. For example, default text boxes have .75-point borders that you may not want. If you get a text box formatted perfectly and want to use it as a pattern for others you create, right-click to select it and choose Set AutoShape Defaults.

CONVERTING TEXT BOXES TO FRAMES

Many of the tasks now performed by text boxes were performed by frames. Word largely abandoned frames several years ago. Although they still exist in Word 2003, they are rarely used. (These frames should not be confused with Web frames, which you can use to structure Web pages. Although the names are identical, the concepts are completely different.) Use a frame if

- You want to insert text or graphics that contain comments or refer to footnotes or endnotes.
- You want to insert certain fields, including AUTONUM, AUTONUMLGL, and AUTONUMOUT (used for numbering lists and paragraphs in legal documents).

Word also ignores certain fields if they are placed in a text box; these fields *are* recognized if they are placed in a frame instead. They are

- TC (Table of Contents Entry)
- TOC (Table of Contents)

- RD (Referenced Document)
- XE (Index Entry)
- TA (Table of Authorities Entry)
- TOA (Table of Authority)

If you want to create an index or table of contents entry in a text box, use a frame instead.

Because frames are rarely used, there is no built-in menu command for creating them. To create a frame, follow these steps:

1. Insert a text box, as described in the preceding section.
2. Choose Format, Text Box.
3. Click the Text Box tab.
4. Click Convert to Frame.
5. Click OK to confirm.

OTHER TYPES OF TEXT BOXES

Word text boxes aren't limited to rectangles. As you learned in Chapter 14, Word provides more than 100 AutoShapes that enable you to include practically any shape in your document, from flowchart symbols to starbursts to cartoon-style callouts. You can easily transform any of these to a text box (except for lines and arrows, which lack an inside area where text could be entered). Follow these steps:

1. Click the Drawing button on the Standard toolbar (or choose View, Toolbars, Drawing) to display the Drawing toolbar.
2. Click AutoShapes on the Drawing toolbar and select the AutoShape you would like to insert.
3. Your mouse pointer changes to a crosshair; drag the shape to the size and proportions you want.
4. Right-click the shape to display its shortcut menu.
5. Select Add Text. Word displays an insertion point inside it (see Figure 16.12), and you can type your text.

From here, you can use your shape like any other text box. However, even though the AutoShape itself can be irregular, the area in which you can edit text is still rectangular, fitting entirely inside the AutoShape. This means that your editing area can be much smaller than you might expect.

FORMATTING YOUR TEXT BOX

By default, text boxes are surrounded by thin (.75-point) black lines; the interior is white (but not transparent). Text boxes are also set to appear in front of text, which means that they will obscure text behind them.

16

Editable area

Figure 16.12
An AutoShape, for-matted and converted into a text box, dis-playing text.

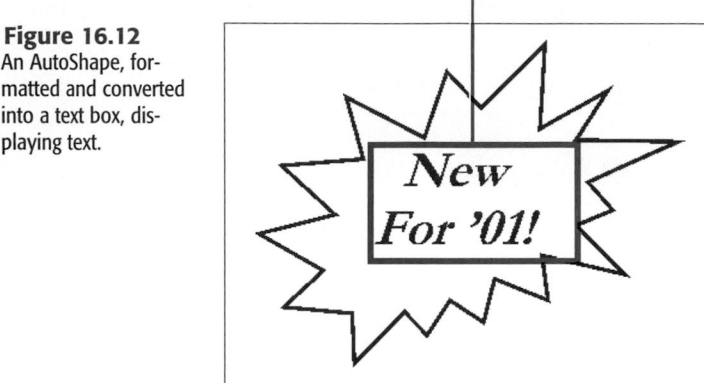

New For '01!

All these settings can be changed, using essentially the same techniques that are covered in Chapter 14 for formatting pictures with the Format, Picture dialog box. To display text box formatting controls, select a text box and choose Format, Text Box. (If you converted an AutoShape to a text box, choose Format, AutoShape.) Or select the text box, right-click, and choose Format Text Box or choose Format, AutoShape from the shortcut menu.

Whatever procedure you follow, the Format Text Box dialog box, along with its various tabs, opens (see Figure 16.13).

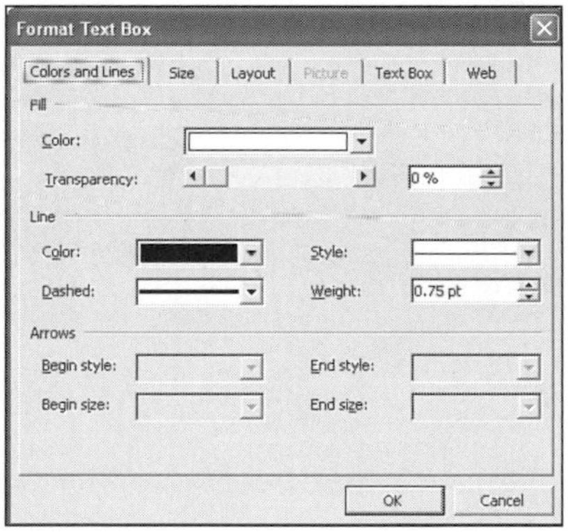

Figure 16.13
The Format Text Box dialog box.

Each tab gives you control over a different aspect of your text box's appearance. These tabs are covered in detail in Chapter 14. Briefly, here's what you can do with each of them:

- In the Colors and Lines tab, you can control the Fill Color that appears within a text box, and the Line Color, Style, and Weight that appear at the edge of the text box.

- In the Size tab, you can control the size, rotation, and scale of the text box.

- In the Layout tab, you can control text wrapping, the precise position of a text box on a page, and how (or whether) the text box moves if surrounding page elements move.

- In the Text Box tab, you control the internal <u>L</u>eft, <u>R</u>ight, T<u>o</u>p, and <u>B</u>ottom margins of the text box; the default settings are 0.1" at the left and right, and 0.05" at the top and bottom.

- Finally, in the Web tab, you can specify <u>A</u>lternative Text that appears in Web browsers when the text box itself does not appear. If your text box contains text, Word automatically uses that text as the alternative text.

TIP

> You can also format text inside a text box using any of Word's Font and Paragraph formatting tools, or use tools on the Drawing toolbar, such as Fill Color, Line Color, Shadow, and 3D (see Chapter 14).

16

LINKING TEXT BOXES

If you've ever tried to create a newsletter, you know that it can be difficult to manage the "jumps" from one page to another within an article—especially if you're still editing that article. You may have found yourself moving small chunks of copy manually from one page to the next—and then having to do it again after you made more edits.

With Word's linked text box feature, that's not necessary. As you edit an article to become longer or shorter, the contents of each linked text box can automatically adjust accordingly.

You can create links between as many as 31 text boxes; if you need to link more, you can link a separate set of 31 text boxes together. In Word, a set of linked text boxes is called a *story*.

After you've linked text boxes, if you start entering text in the first text box and run out of room, the text flows into the next linked text box in the story, and continues flowing from one linked text box to the next. If there's not enough text to fill them all, the text boxes at the end of the chain remain empty. If you have too much text to fit in all the text boxes, the excess text will run below the borders of the last text box. You may notice part of a line of text, depending on how the last text box has been sized.

Linked text boxes were traditionally found only in dedicated desktop publishing applications such as Adobe PageMaker and Microsoft Publisher. Using text boxes, you may be able to publish many documents in Word that you once could create only with desktop publishing software.

Follow these steps to link one text box to another:

1. Create at least two text boxes.
2. Select the first text box.
3. Click the Create Text Box Link button from the Text Box toolbar. The pointer changes to an upright pitcher (see Figure 16.14).

Figure 16.14
After you click the Create Text Box Link button, the mouse pointer changes to an upright pitcher shape.

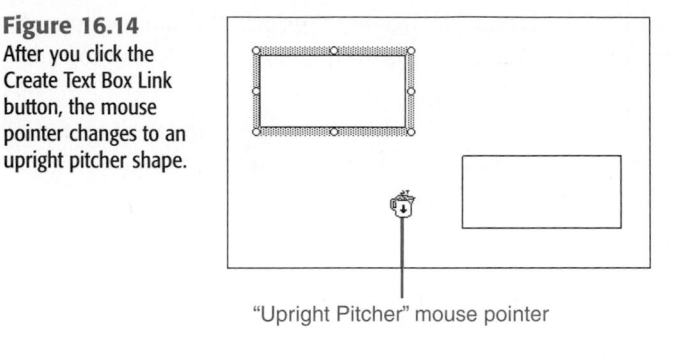

"Upright Pitcher" mouse pointer

4. Move through the document until you find the second text box. Note that when you are over a text box available for linking, the upright pitcher changes into a pouring pitcher (see Figure 16.15).

"Pouring Pitcher" mouse pointer

Figure 16.15
When you're over a linkable text box, the pitcher mouse pointer changes to a pouring pitcher shape.

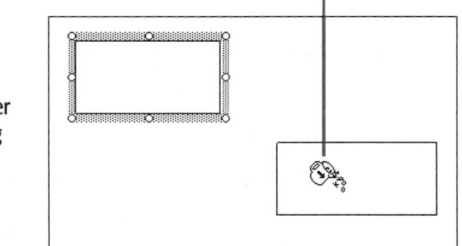

5. Click the second text box.

You can now create another text box and link it to the second box by again following steps 2 through 5. You can either create and link all your text boxes ahead of time—when you are designing your newsletter—or add your boxes and link them as needed.

CAUTION

Word doesn't display any markers to indicate whether overflow text exists.

TIP

If you place an end-of-article slug first and then insert all your linked text before it, you can quickly tell whether the entire article has fit into the text boxes you've created. If you see the slug, you know that everything fit into the available text boxes. If you don't see the slug, you know there is overflow copy.

You can format the contents of all linked text boxes at the same time. Press Ctrl+A within one text box to select all the text in all text boxes linked to it. (Conversely, if you press Ctrl+A to select all text outside a text box, no text inside any text box is selected.)

After you've linked text boxes, you can easily move from one text box to the next by clicking the Previous Text Box or Next Text Box buttons on the Text Box toolbar. You can also break links between text boxes whenever you want, as covered in the next section of this chapter.

NOTE

> You can have multiple articles running through separate sets of links. From a practical point of view, you don't want to do this with every item in your newsletter; it makes the articles too difficult to follow.

16

Breaking Links Between Text Boxes

Occasionally you need to break a link between text boxes—maybe you need to reflow some text and start over, or perhaps the wrong text boxes were linked. Whatever the reason, it's simple to break a link between two text boxes. Select the text box where you want the text to end and then click the Break Forward Link button on the Text Box toolbar.

CAUTION

> If you break a link between two text boxes (say, "Text Box A" and "Text Box B"), all the links connecting after the second text box are also lost (such as Text Box C and Text Box D, in this example).

When you break a link, all the text that previously appeared in the linked (second) text box is now moved into the first text box. Of course, if the first text box is too small, not all the text you have moved into it will be visible. To make the text visible, either reformat its text in a smaller font size or expand the remaining text box. You can expand a text box manually, by dragging its sizing handles. You can also do so automatically, like this:

1. Right-click on the text box, and choose Format Text Box from the shortcut menu.
2. Click the Text Box tab.
3. Check the Resize AutoShape to Fit Text check box.
4. Click OK.

Following a Link

After your text boxes are linked, you can follow the links, forward or backward. When you have finished editing a story or an article, it's good practice to follow your text through all the linked boxes to make sure that it looks the way you want it to.

It's common for the last line of text in a series of linked text boxes to appear by itself at the top of a text box, much as "orphan" text sometimes appears at the top of a page. This can be unsightly: You can fix the problem by enlarging the preceding text box slightly, adjusting the font size, or, in some cases, condensing the text slightly from the Character Spacing tab of the Format, Font dialog box.

To follow a series of linked text boxes, select the first text box and then

- To move to the next linked text box, click the Next Text Box button.
- To move to the previous linked text box, click the Previous Text Box button.

CAUTION

> Linked text boxes must stay within one document; you can't link a text box to another in a separate file. Nor can you link text boxes between subdocuments when you're using a Master Document structure.

TROUBLESHOOTING

I CAN'T CREATE LINKED TEXT BOXES

You've clicked on a text box and now want to link it to another check box, but the "pitcher" cursor icon does not appear, and you can't do so.

Make sure that the text box you're linking to is

- Empty
- In the same document (or in the same subdocument within a master document)
- Not part of another set of linked text boxes

You cannot link more than 31 text boxes in the same story.

I DON'T WANT TO DISPLAY DRAWING CANVASES WHEN I CREATE A TEXT BOX

Whenever you click the Text Box button on the Drawing toolbar to create a text box, Word first inserts a drawing canvas. If you don't like this behavior, choose Tools, Options, General; then clear the Automatically Create Drawing Canvas When Inserting AutoShapes check box, and click OK.

WORD INSERTS SYMBOLS I DON'T WANT

When you insert text such as (c), Word may substitute symbols such as ©. These symbols may not always be recognized accurately by other software or non-Windows computers. To prevent these substitutions from occurring, choose Tools, AutoCorrect Options; select the first substitutions you don't want Word to make; and click Delete. Repeat the process for each additional substitution you don't want. (The first 20 items in the AutoCorrect list substitute symbols for conventional text, but you may only use a few of these, such as © and ®.)

After you've done this, click the AutoFormat As You Type tab, and consider clearing the following check boxes:

- "Straight Quotes" with "Smart Quotes"
- Fractions (1/2) with Fraction Character
- Hyphens with Dash

MY EDITED BROCHURE HAS STRANGE FORMATTING AND COLUMN BREAKS

You may have inadvertently deleted a section break or column break in the document created by Word's Brochure template. If the problem has recently occurred, try clicking Undo (and repeat the process until the document is restored to its normal layout. To prevent the problem from occurring again, work in Print Layout View, and show all formatting marks (choose Tools, Options, View; check All, and click OK).

PART IV

INDUSTRIAL-STRENGTH DOCUMENT PRODUCTION TECHNIQUES

CHAPTER 17

USING MAIL MERGE EFFECTIVELY

In this chapter

AN OVERVIEW OF WORD'S MAIL MERGE

Mail merge is the process of creating custom mailings (or other documents) that combine unique information with standard text to create a set of unique documents—typically, one for every recipient. Word's mail-merge feature gives you the power to customize your message for just a few people—or for thousands at the same time.

To successfully run a mail merge, you need to understand two fundamental concepts. The first concept is this: You need a main document and a data source.

The *main document* contains the text that you want to remain constant. The main document also contains instructions about which changeable text Word should import and at which point it should import it. These instructions are called *merge fields*.

Your second file, the *data source*, contains the text that is to change from one form letter (or envelope or label or directory page) to the next. Your data-source file can consist of a table in a Word document, or it can be an Access database, Outlook contact list, or Excel worksheet. It can also come from various other sources, such as dBASE-compatible (DBF) database files.

The second concept is this: Merging is a step-by-step process, far more than many other tasks you perform in Word. Microsoft thoroughly revamped Word's mail-merge feature in Word 2002 to make this step-by-step process easier to follow, introducing a new Mail Merge Wizard task pane to replace the Mail Merge Wizard dialog box that was used for nearly a decade. If you've shied away from Word mail merges in the past, due to their complexity, you'll find that the revamping of the process has made the job far easier. Having radically changed mail merge in Word 2002, Microsoft has left it virtually unchanged in Word 2003.

Word's Mail Merge Wizard task pane enables you to create mail merges for five types of documents:

- **Letters**. When you create a form letter, Word creates a new letter for each set of merge data (that is, each individual recipient).
- **E-mail messages**. When you create an email merge, Word creates a new email for each recipient.
- **Envelopes**. When you create envelopes, Word creates a new envelope for each recipient.
- **Labels**. When you create labels, Word creates new labels for each recipient.
- **Directories** (called "catalogs" prior to Word 2002). When you create a directory, Word creates only one new document that contains all the merged data. Word repeats any standard text you add to the directory main document for each set of data.

TIP

> Directory mail merges have many uses. For example, they're ideal for creating parts lists. They're also a handy solution for generating a list of people you've already sent mail to so that you can follow up by telephone or other means.

STARTING A MAIL MERGE WITH THE MAIL MERGE WIZARD TASK PANE

To help organize and structure the mail merge process, Word provides the Mail Merge Wizard task pane, shown in Figure 17.1. The Mail Merge Wizard task pane guides you step-by-step through a mail merge. To open it, choose Tools, Letters and Mailings, Mail Merge Wizard.

Arrows allow you to revisit mail-merge
steps you've already performed

Figure 17.1
The Mail Merge
Wizard task pane, as
it appears when you
begin a mail merge.

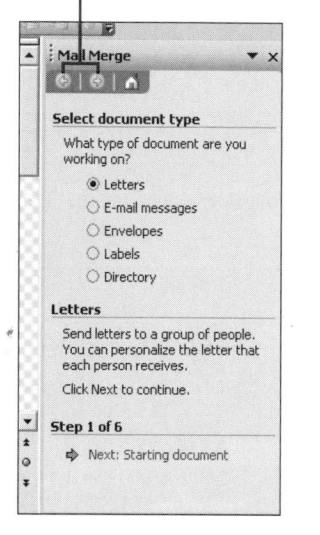

In the first window of the Mail Merge Wizard task pane, you choose the type of mail merge you want to create: Letters, E-mail Messages, Envelopes, Labels, or a Directory. When you've done so, click Next: Starting Document.

NOTE

To combine any type of standard text with unique information that is listed in a *separate* document, follow the steps for letters. You can use this basic process to create legal documents, contracts, and many other types of customizable documents. To print a list of information from a database in a *single* document, such as a parts list or a membership directory, follow the steps for directories.

NOTE

If you are working on a mailing that requires both a form letter and a set of envelopes or labels, create the form letter first and use the same merge settings later to create your envelopes or mailing labels. This way, you can make sure that you print corresponding labels or envelopes for each letter and that the labels or envelopes print in the same order.

Most of the process of merging is identical regardless of which type of merge document you are creating. The next several sections walk through the merge process in the context of merging letters. Wherever the process varies for a different type of document, we will present the key differences and nuances.

Working with the Mail Merge Toolbar

As you become comfortable working with Word 2003 mail merges, you can take advantage of the Mail Merge toolbar as a shortcut to many of the capabilities mail merge provides. You can use the toolbar either as an alternative to the task pane or as a supplement to it.

To display the Mail Merge toolbar if it is not already displayed, choose Tools, Letters and Mailings, Show Mail Merge Toolbar. The Mail Merge toolbar appears in Figure 17.2; its contents are described in Table 17.1.

NOTE

Mail Merge toolbar buttons become available only as you reach the stage of the mail-merge process where they can be used.

Figure 17.2
The Mail Merge toolbar.

Table 17.1 Mail Merge Buttons

Button	Name	Function
	Main Document Setup	Lets you choose what type of mail-merge document to create
	Open Data Source	Displays the Open Data Source dialog box, where you can choose a data source
	Mail Merge Recipients	Displays the Mail Merge Recipients dialog box, where you can specify who will receive your message
	Insert Address Block	Displays the Insert Address Block dialog box, where you can specify the contents and format of your Address Block
	Insert Greeting Line	Displays the Insert Greeting Line dialog box, where you can specify the contents and format of your Greeting Line
	Insert Merge Fields	Adds fields to a form letter or other mail merge documents

Button	Name	Function
Insert Word Field ▾	Insert Word Field	Places a Word field in the main document to customize the document
	View Merged Data	Shows what the main document would look like if it contained information from the data source in place of merge fields
	Highlight Merge Fields	Displays all merge fields in your document with gray highlighting
	Match Fields	Displays the Match Fields dialog box, where you can make sure that Word has associated the correct database fields with each element in your address block and salutation
	Propagate Labels	Makes all your labels contain the same content as the one you've already specified
	First Record	Shows what the main document would look like if it contained information from the first record of the data source in place of merge fields
	Previous Record	Shows what the main document would look like if it contained information from the previous record of the data source in place of merge fields
1	Go to Record	Enables you to specify a record from the data source and see how your main document would look if it contained that record's data, in place of merge fields
	Next Record	Shows what the main document would look like if it contained information from the next record of the data source in place of merge fields
	Last Record	Shows what the main document would look like if it contained information from the last record of the data source in place of merge fields
	Find Entry	Enables you to search for a particular record in the data source document
	Check for Errors	Checks the merge for errors

continues

17

TABLE 17.1   CONTINUED

Button	Name	Function
	Merge to New Document	Performs the merge and places the results in a new document (or documents, depending on the type of merge you are performing)
	Merge to Printer	Performs the merge and prints the resulting merged pages
	Merge to E-mail	Performs the merge and emails the resulting merged pages
	Merge to Fax	Performs the merge and faxes the resulting merged pages
	Toolbar Options	Adds or removes buttons from the Mail Merge toolbar

SELECTING A STARTING DOCUMENT

Your next step in merging a document is to choose or create the document you will use as your *main document*. This, again, is the document that contains any boilerplate text that should appear in all your merged documents and instructions about which kinds of information should be merged into them (known as *mail-merge fields*). Typically, Word gives you three choices (see Figure 17.3):

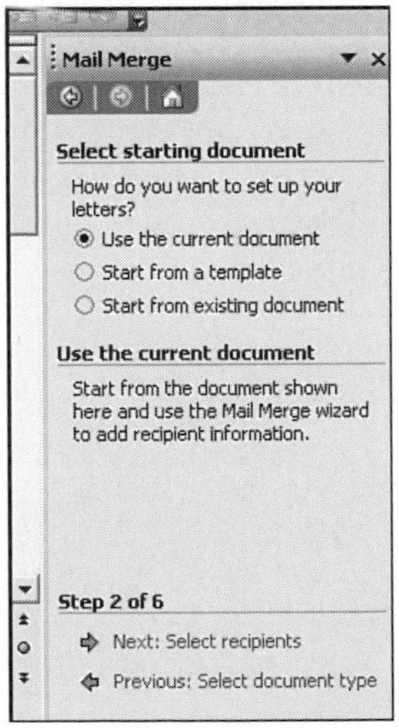

Figure 17.3
Choosing which document to use for your merge.

- If you choose Use the Current Document, you can go on immediately to select your document's recipients. In fact, you *must*—Word 2003 doesn't allow you to edit your current document until you've done so.

- If you choose Start from Existing Document, Word displays a list of any mail-merge documents you've worked with recently. If the document you want is not on that list, click Open; then browse to and select the document you want. Word 2003 can use mail-merge main documents built with Word 2002, 2000, Word 98 for the Macintosh, Word 97, Word 95, Word 6 for Windows and the Macintosh, and Word 2. It can also use documents from even older versions of Word, which may use DATA fields to identify their data sources.

- If you choose Start from a Template, you can then click select Template to choose from the mail-merge templates Word makes available for letters, faxes, and address lists (see Figure 17.4). Several of these templates are similar to Word's Letter & Faxes templates, with the addition of built-in mail-merge fields that simplify the process of building a mail merge.

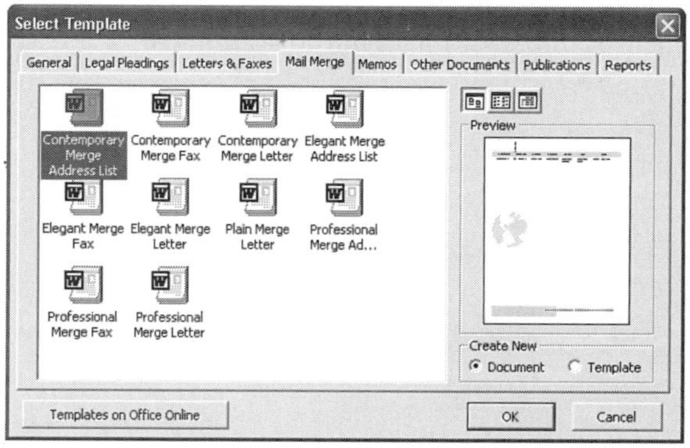

Figure 17.4
Choosing one of Word 2003's mail-merge templates.

TIP

> If you plan to create several mailings to the same set of individuals, consider saving your finished mail-merge document as a template. The finished document not only contains your text, but also reflects the settings you've created by walking through the Mail Merge Wizard's steps—such as your database connections and the specific individuals who receive your message.

TIP

> If you turn an existing document into a mail-merge main document and later want to turn it back into a regular document, click Main Document Setup on the Mail Merge toolbar, choose Normal Word Document, and click OK.

SETTING OPTIONS FOR ENVELOPES OR LABELS

If you are merging labels or envelopes, and your current document is not in a label or envelope format, the Use the Current Document option is grayed out and unavailable. Start from Current Document is replaced with Change the Current Document. If you choose this option, Word replaces the contents of your current document with a generic label or envelope format that you can adjust immediately.

The Mail Merge Wizard task pane presents a new blue hyperlink: for envelopes, Envelope Options, and for labels, Label Options. When you click this option, Word displays the Envelope Options or Label Options dialog box, as appropriate. Here, you can establish detailed settings for your labels or envelopes.

→ These dialog boxes are covered in detail in Chapter 6, "Printing and Faxing in Word." To learn more about label options, **see** the section "Printing Labels," **p. 213**. To learn more about envelope options, **see** the section "Changing Envelope Formatting," **p. 210**.

After you've selected a main document of any kind or created a new one from a template, click Next: Select Recipients.

SELECTING RECIPIENTS

In the following window of the Mail Merge Wizard task pane, you choose a data source. This is the file that already contains contact information for the people who will receive your message or, if you are creating a directory, the file that contains the data you want to incorporate into it (see Figure 17.5).

Figure 17.5
Selecting recipients for your mailing or the content source for your directory.

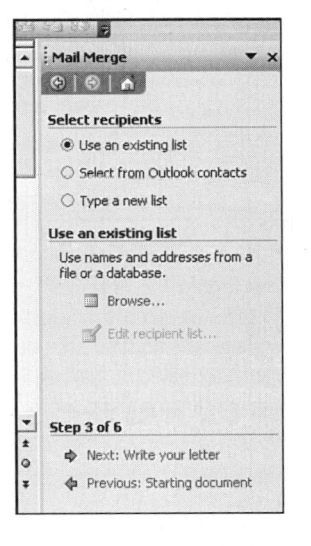

You need to create or select a data-source document to accompany your main document. Your data source must contain the information that will change in each of your merged documents. Ideally, it should also contain headings or fields that identify each specific category of data, such as first names or ZIP Codes.

NOTE

Your data source need not contain names and contact information. For example, if you're building a directory, you could specify a data source containing lists of products, together with their features and prices.

Once again, Word gives you several choices; these are covered next.

SELECTING AN EXISTING FILE CONTAINING THE NAMES YOU WANT TO USE

Select Recipients actually consists of two tasks: first, selecting or creating the data source that contains information about potential recipients; and then, choosing exactly who will receive your message from among the names in the list you've just selected. You choose your database file first.

If you already have a list of names you want to draw on—stored in a database, a spreadsheet, a Word table, or some other document—choose Use an Existing List. A Browse button appears; click it to display the Select Data Source dialog box.

Next, browse to and select the file containing the data you want to use.

If you are connecting to an enterprise database such as SQL Server 2000 or Oracle 8i, Word 2003 contains a Data Connection Wizard that streamlines the process.

To run this wizard, click the New Source button on the Select Data Source dialog box next to the Open button. This opens the Data Connection Wizard. Choose the type of database you want to connect with, click Next, and follow the steps provided in the wizard to establish the connection you need.

In some cases, you won't have a choice about where your data comes from. In other cases, you may be in charge of organizing and managing the data as well as the mail-merge process. In the latter situation, you need to decide which program makes the most sense to use for entering and managing the data you will merge with Word. Fortunately, there are some rules of thumb you can use to make that decision.

Word tables lend themselves best to small mail merges, typically 100–200 data records or fewer. Of course, if your data is already stored in Outlook, Access, Excel, or a third-party database, it usually makes more sense to use your existing data source than to create a new one. If you're building a data source from scratch, however, consider these factors:

- With which program are you most comfortable? If, instead of investing many hours in learning a new program, you can achieve identical results with a program you already know, consider using the program you already know.

- How big is your database? As your database grows—to many hundreds or thousands—it makes sense to use a dedicated database program such as Microsoft Access. If your database is very large—say, containing 100,000 records or more—consider migrating to an enterprise-scale database such as Oracle, Sybase, Informix, IBM DB2, or Microsoft SQL Server 2000.

17

- **How else do you intend to use your data?** If you're sending a sales mailing to all your business contacts, and you plan to follow up with telephone calls, use a contact manager such as Microsoft Outlook or Symantec's ACT!.

- **Where does your data come from?** If you input all your own data, Microsoft Word or Outlook may be all you need. If others help input your data, consider a database program such as Microsoft Access, which enables you to create forms that streamline and simplify the process. If your data is imported from another source, consider Excel or Access for their excellent data import and cleanup (parsing) capabilities.

SELECTING AN OUTLOOK CONTACT LIST CONTAINING THE NAMES YOU WANT TO USE

If you want to use names stored in an Outlook contact list, choose Select from Outlook Contacts; then click Choose Contacts Folder. If you are asked which profile contains the names you want to use (see Figure 17.6), choose the correct profile.

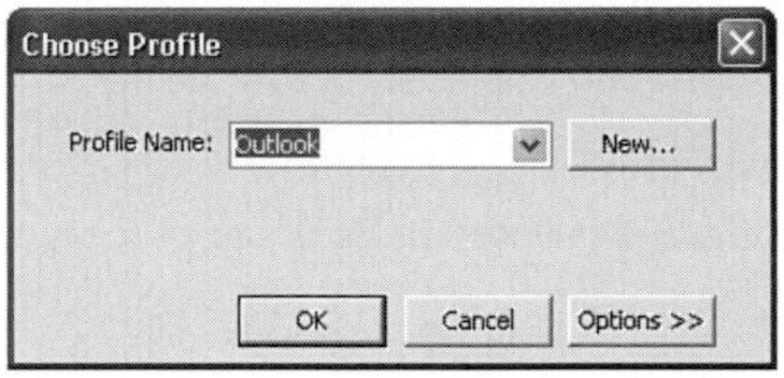

Figure 17.6
Choosing the profile associated with your Outlook contact list.

Next, choose the contact list folder you want to use—typically, Contacts. Word will display the Mail Merge Recipients dialog box, containing all the names that appear in your Outlook Contacts list. (If Outlook contains large numbers of contacts, it may take a few moments for the names to appear within the dialog box.)

After you've done so, you're ready to move forward to the next step.

CREATING A NEW LIST OF NAMES

Occasionally, you may want to create your list of names at the same time you create your mail merge. Although large lists are best created in Access, Excel, or Outlook, shorter lists can be created in Word, directly from the Select Recipients pane of the Mail Merge Wizard.

Choose Type a New List; then click Create. Word displays the New Address List dialog box (see Figure 17.7).

In this dialog box, you can customize a Word table that serves as your database and then enter detailed information (new database records) for each individual who receives your mailing. You can also find, filter, and sort names in your database table.

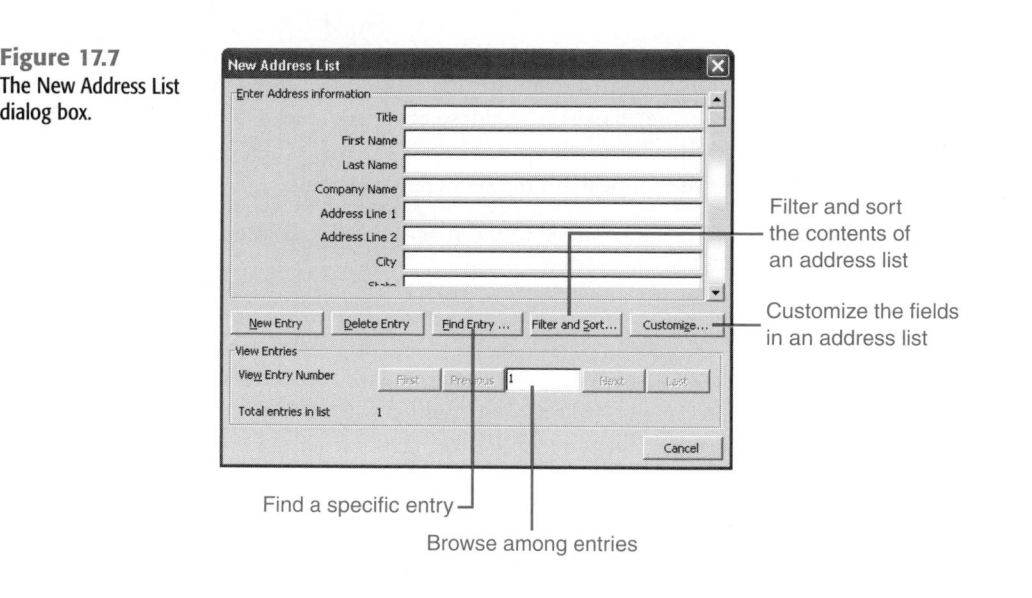

Figure 17.7
The New Address List dialog box.

Filter and sort the contents of an address list

Customize the fields in an address list

Find a specific entry

Browse among entries

CUSTOMIZING THE ADDRESS INFORMATION TABLE WORD PROVIDES

Word's Default New Address List table contains fields corresponding to the most commonly used categories needed for mass mailings: first name, last name, company name, address lines, email addresses, and so forth.

However, you may occasionally need a new category (and if you're creating a directory of parts, services, or other information unrelated to contacts, you may need many new categories). You might also need to tweak the names of a category to correspond with a mail-merge document you've already created or reorganize the fields in Word's Address List for faster data entry.

To make changes like these, click Customize. The Customize Address List dialog box opens (see Figure 17.8).

Figure 17.8
The Customize Address List dialog box.

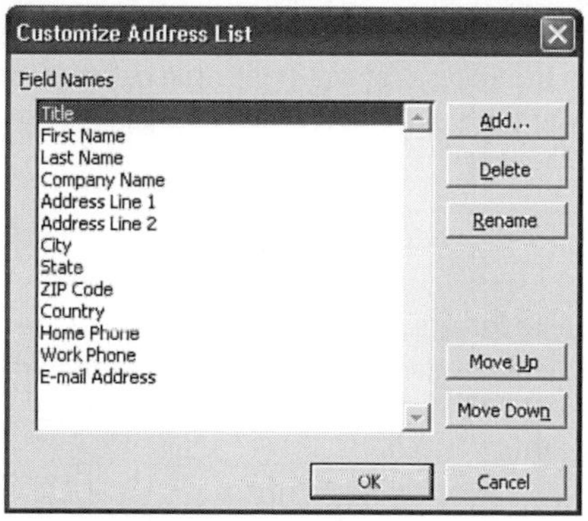

If you want to add a new field to your Word database, click Add; then type the new field's name and click OK. If you want to delete an existing field, select it in the Field Names scroll box and click Delete. To rename an existing field, select it and click Rename; then type the new field's name and click OK. To rearrange fields, select a field; then click Move Up or Move Down repeatedly, until it appears in the sequence you want.

When you're finished making adjustments to the structure of your address list, click OK to return to the New Address List dialog box.

WORKING WITH THE NEW ADDRESS LIST

In the New Address List dialog box, you can enter new data—such as the names and addresses of each mailing recipient—just as you would if you were using database software. In fact, the database you create is stored in .mdb format—the same format Microsoft's Access database software uses.

When you open the New Address List dialog box for the first time (refer to Figure 17.7), you see the first empty record. To fill in the record, click on the field you want to enter (or press Tab to move to it). Then start typing. To move from one field to the next, press Enter or Tab.

> **TIP**
>
> You can copy information from one field to another (even on different records) by using the standard Windows keyboard shortcuts for Copy (Ctrl+C) and Paste (Ctrl+V).

If you want to create another record after you finish entering the data in the current record, click New Entry. A new blank record appears. If at some point you no longer need a record, click Delete Entry to eliminate it.

> **TIP**
>
> As you edit your address list, keep in mind these pointers:
>
> Don't duplicate information included as boilerplate text in the main document. For example, don't add a comma after the city, because then you have to add a comma after every city name. Plan to include a comma in the main document immediately after the City merge field. (If you chose one of Word's mail-merge templates as your main document, this was done for you.)

> **CAUTION**
>
> You can't enter character formatting such as italic and boldface in an address list. Word disregards any character formatting that may appear in records in an underlying Word table.

> **CAUTION**
>
> Word's Undo feature isn't available from within the New Address List dialog box.

FINDING INFORMATION IN RECORDS

To move quickly among records in the New Address List dialog box, you can use the View Entry Number box, which allows you to move to the First, Last, Next, or Previous record, or to select a record number (refer to Figure 17.7).

You can also search for specific information within the address list. To do so, click Find Entry. The Find Entry dialog box opens.

Type the information you want to find in the Find text box. If you want Word to search the entire database, choose All Fields; if you want Word to search only a specific field within all records, choose the field from the This Field drop-down box. Then click Find Next. Word finds the first reference. To find the next instance of the same text, click Find Next again.

SAVING YOUR ADDRESS LIST DATABASE

When you're finished creating new database entries and managing existing entries, click Close; the Save Address List dialog box opens. Enter a name for your address list in the File Name box; then browse to and select a location for your database.

> **TIP**
>
> By default, Word stores your database in a new My Data Sources folder created when you installed Word 2003 or Office 2003 and looks in this folder first whenever you search for a data source or database.

FILTERING AND SORTING RECIPIENTS

In the previous sections, you learned how to choose your data source: the file that contains the information you want to add to your main documents. After you've chosen or created that file, you need to specify exactly who will get your message. Your primary tool for doing so is the Mail Merge Recipients dialog box, which opens automatically after you select a data source (see Figure 17.9).

> **TIP**
>
> If you're working with a large database, you may want to enlarge the Mail Merge Recipients dialog box to show more records at once. To do so, drag the triangle at the lower-right corner of the dialog box.

The Mail Merge Recipients dialog box gives Word users more direct control over who gets their messages than ever before.

To begin with, if you want to remove one individual from your mailing, you can simply clear the check box next to his or her name.

To restore all the names whose check boxes you've cleared, click Select All.

17

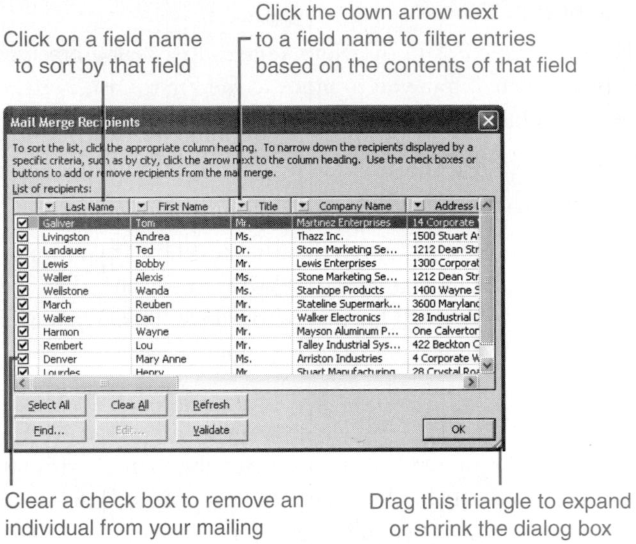

Click on a field name
to sort by that field

Click the down arrow next
to a field name to filter entries
based on the contents of that field

Figure 17.9
The Mail Merge
Recipients dialog box.

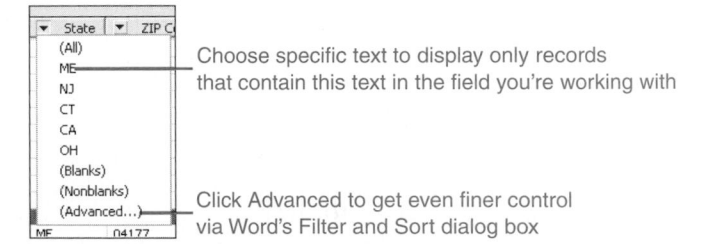

Clear a check box to remove an
individual from your mailing

Drag this triangle to expand
or shrink the dialog box

To clear all the check boxes at once, click Clear All. You might want to do this if you're building a mailing that will go to only a few of the names on your list; you can then check those recipients' check boxes individually.

To sort all the names in your mailing list, click on the field name you want to sort by.

TIP

> You can often lower the cost of a mass mailing by bundling letters going to the same ZIP Code, which is practical only if you print your letters in ZIP Code order.

→ To achieve even greater control over sorting and filtering, **see** "Advanced Filtering and Sorting," **p. 597**.

To filter names, click the down arrow next to a field (see Figure 17.10). Word lists all your options for filtering that field:

Figure 17.10
The Mail Merge
Recipients dialog box
provides powerful fil-
tering capabilities.

Choose specific text to display only records
that contain this text in the field you're working with

Click Advanced to get even finer control
via Word's Filter and Sort dialog box

■ Choose (All) to display all records. (Choosing All turns off filtering based on a specific field.)

- Choose (Blanks) to display only records containing no information in that field.

- Choose (Nonblanks) to display only records that do contain information in that field. You may often want to use Nonblanks, to avoid creating messages that don't contain key information they need in order to be delivered. For example, there's little point in creating an email message for someone whose email address you don't have.

- Choose a name from the list that appears, to filter out all items that do not contain that name. For example, use this feature to create a mailing that is sent only to individuals at a specific company. (Names may not appear if you are using an Excel database or Word table as your data source, or if there are too many different names for Word to list easily.)

Using this feature, you can filter based on multiple elements. For example, if you're planning a sales trip to a specific location of a major company, you might filter records based on that company's name, displaying all records of people who work for that company. You might then filter this subset of records, displaying only individuals in the city you'll be visiting.

ADVANCED FILTERING AND SORTING

In many cases, the Mail Merge Recipients dialog box provides all the filtering and sorting power you'll need. But in some cases, you'll want even more control. To get it, click the down arrow next to any field name and choose Advanced from the drop-down box that appears. The Filter and Sort dialog box appears (see Figure 17.11).

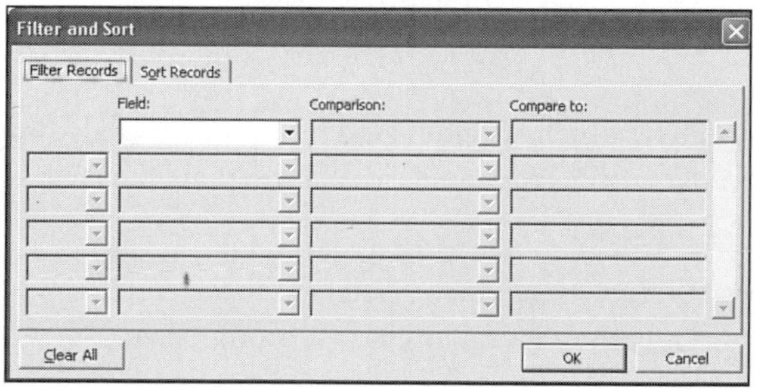

Figure 17.11
Use the Filter Records tab to specify criteria for Word to use when selecting records to merge.

NOTE

If you've used mail merge in previous versions, you may recognize this dialog box: It was previously called Query Options and is one of the few parts of mail merge that haven't changed significantly.

The Filter Records tab enables you to choose which records to print based on detailed criteria you specify. First, you tell Word the field on which you want to base your selection. Then you tell Word which comparison to make to decide whether to include a record. You can make several kinds of comparisons:

- Equal To
- Not Equal To
- Less Than
- Greater Than

- Less Than or Equal To
- Greater Than or Equal To
- Is Blank
- Is Not Blank

In most cases, you must provide a type of comparison *and* tell Word what it should compare the text or number with. ("Equal to what?") Here are a few examples of how filtering records works, first in English and then in Word's query language.

To create messages for all records in which the company name is AT&T, enter the following:

```
Field: Comparison: Compare To:
Company Equal to AT&T
```

To create messages for all records in which the order size is less than $1,000, enter the following:

```
Field: Comparison: Compare To:
Order Size Less than $1,000
```

To create a message for every record except those that don't have a name, enter this:

```
Field: Comparison:
Name Is not blank
```

NOTE

The last example does not require you to enter anything in the Compare To box.

Using the list box at the left, which specifies And by default (but also can specify Or), you can make up to six comparisons at the same time in the same query. Here's an example that uses the And operator.

To create messages for all records in which Postal Code is greater than 11700 but less than 11999 (thereby creating only messages addressed to Long Island, New York) enter this:

```
Field: Comparison: Compare To:
Postal Code Greater than or Equal 11700
And Postal Code Less than or Equal 11999
```

Here's another example, this time using the Or operator. To create messages for all records in which the addressee's company is AT&T, IBM, or General Electric, enter the following:

```
Field: Comparison: Compare To:
Company Equal to AT&T
Or Company Equal to IBM
Or Company Equal to General Electric
```

If you tell Word to print only records that meet one condition and another condition, you almost always get fewer records than if you select records that meet one condition or the other (and you never get more records).

The order in which you use the Ands and Ors makes a difference in the records Word prints. Word performs each operation in order, and the result from one operation is used when it performs the next operation.

For instance, suppose Word sees this query:

```
Field: Comparison: Compare To:
 Job Title Equal to Vice President
Or City Equal to Cincinnati
And Title Equal to Mr.
```

Word finds all the vice presidents in your database and adds to it everyone from Cincinnati. Having done this, Word next subtracts all the women. But swap things around a bit, and it's a different story:

```
Field: Comparison: Compare To:
 Job Title Equal to Vice President
And Title Equal to Mr.
Or City Equal to Cincinnati
```

Word first finds all the vice presidents in the list, next excludes the women vice presidents, and then adds anyone from Cincinnati, without regard to gender.

TIP

> If you create a set of filtering rules that don't seem to work properly, you can start over again by choosing Clear All.

SORTING MERGED RECORDS

You've already learned that you can perform simple sorts on any field by clicking that field name in the Mail Merge Recipients dialog box. However, you'll often need greater control. For example, you might want to sort by one field and then sort the results by another field.

To control the order in which your records print, click the down arrow next to any field name and choose Advanced from the drop-down box that appears. The Filter and Sort dialog box appears. Click the Sort Records tab (see Figure 17.12).

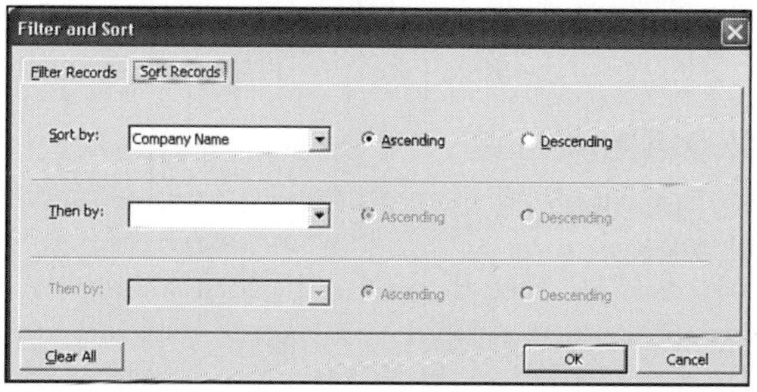

Figure 17.12
Controlling the order in which your records print.

In the Sort By drop-down box, you choose a field on which to base your sort. You also can choose whether to sort in ascending or descending order. *Ascending* sorts from 0 to 9 and then from A to Z (in other words, any entries starting with a number appear before entries starting with a letter). *Descending* sorts from Z to A and then from 9 to 0; in other words, letters appear before numbers.

You can sort up to three levels. Word first sorts by the field you choose in the Sort By box. Next, Word sorts by the field in your first Then By box. If you've specified another Then By field, Word then sorts by that field's contents.

In essence, Word uses the second and third fields as "tie-breakers": If it finds two or more records that meet the same criterion, it looks for the next criterion and then the third to determine which order to use. So, for example, you might sort your letters first by ZIP Code and then alphabetically by last name; all letters to the same ZIP Code would be printed together, but within each ZIP Code, the letters would be alphabetized.

When you're finished using Word's advanced filtering and sorting tools, click OK to return to the Mail Merge Recipients dialog box.

EDITING DATA FROM ANY DATA SOURCE

As you work with Word's filtering and sorting tools, you may find that you need to make adjustments to your database. For example, you may need to add new records, or resolve slight inconsistencies in company names and addresses, to build a mailing that reaches exactly the people who should get it.

Earlier, in the section "Creating a New List of Names," you learned that you can create a new database and then add names to it using the New Address List dialog box. Regardless of where you got your data, you can use a similar dialog box to make adjustments to it. From the Mail Merge Recipients dialog box, click Edit.

> **TIP**
>
> After you've selected your recipient list, you can edit it at any time. With the Mail Merge Wizard task pane open, click the left or right arrow until the Select Recipients window appears; then click Edit Recipient List.

→ For more information on working with the New Address List dialog box, **see** "Creating a New List of Names," **p. 592**.

REFRESHING YOUR DATA SOURCE

If you are working with live data from an enterprise database, that data may change between the time you start building your mail merge and when you're ready to run it. To update the data your mail merge is based on, click Refresh in the Mail Merge Recipients dialog box. Word reloads your data source, displaying the most up-to-date information available.

UNDERSTANDING ADDRESS VALIDATION

If you're looking to get maximum postal discounts on your mailings, you must first validate the accuracy of your address and ZIP Code information.

Neither Word 2003 nor Office 2003 contains address validation software. However, if you click Validate in the Mail Merge Recipients dialog box, Word connects you to a page on its Web site containing information about online address validation services from ThinkDirectMarketing that integrate with Microsoft Word.

By now, you've done the following:

- Identified the document you want to use as your main document
- Chosen a file as your data source
- Identified the specific individuals who should receive your letter

In the following sections, you'll walk through the process of getting your document ready for mailing.

PREPARING THE CONTENT OF YOUR MAIN DOCUMENT

To prepare the content of your letter or email message, from the Select Recipients window of the Mail Merge Wizard task pane, click Next: Write Your Letter. The Write Your Letter page appears (see Figure 17.13). From here, you can add text to your letter, as well as the mail-merge fields and other elements that customize your letter to your precise needs.

If you are creating a directory, instead of Next: Write Your Letter, the following option will be Next: Arrange Your Directory. If you are creating labels or envelopes, the option available will be Next: Arrange Your Envelope or Next: Arrange Your Label. The options described in the following sections are identical, with one addition: If you are creating labels, you can define the contents and appearance of one label, and click the Update All Labels button to apply the same settings to all the others.

Figure 17.13
The Write Your Letter page of the Mail Merge Wizard task pane.

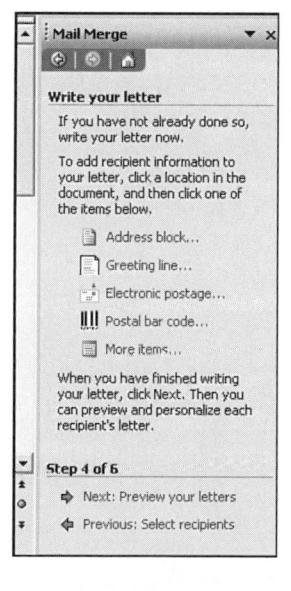

You can now write the content of your letter in the editing window—or copy existing content from another document. Beyond this, Word provides tools for organizing your letter's address block, greeting line, and other elements that will vary from one printed letter to the next. These are covered in the following sections.

SETTING YOUR ADDRESS BLOCK

Word uses the term "address block" to refer to the portion of a main document containing its recipient's name and address, and potentially company and title information. In previous versions of Word, you needed to individually add mail-merge fields for each of these elements: First Name, Last Name, Company, Address Line 1, and so forth. This was time-consuming and error prone.

Word 2003 simplifies matters by allowing you to choose the address block format you want and automatically specifying the fields that deliver this format. Of course, Word's results may not always be perfect, and you may need your address block customized in a way Word hasn't considered. If so, you can easily make manual adjustments.

To specify your address block, first click in your letter or envelope to place your insertion point where you want the address to appear.

CAUTION

> If you are creating an envelope, Word places a text box in the middle of the envelope. This is an ideal location for your outgoing mailing address. However, if you don't deliberately click inside this text box, Word instead inserts your outgoing address at the upper-left corner of the envelope, where your return address should go instead.

Then, click Address Block in the Mail Merge Wizard task pane. The Insert Address Block dialog box appears (see Figure 17.14).

From the Insert Recipient's Name in This Format scroll box, choose the format you want from the list of samples provided. (If you don't want to include the user's name at all, clear the Insert Recipient's Name in This Format check box.)

If you want to include the recipient's company name in your address block, leave the Insert Company Name check box checked.

If you want to include the recipient's postal address in your address block, leave the Insert Postal Address check box checked; then specify whether you want to include a country or region in the address.

If your messages are primarily sent within the U.S., leave the Insert Company Name check box checked. You may want a country to be listed in your address block only if the message is going abroad. If so, click Only Include the Country/Region If Different Than, and select United States in the drop-down list below.

Figure 17.14
Use the Insert Address Block dialog box to control which information will appear in your address block.

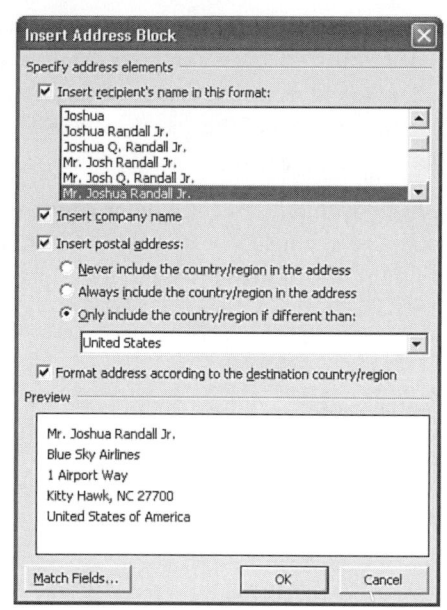

MATCHING THE FIELDS IN YOUR ADDRESS BLOCK

In many cases, Word can automatically match the field names in your data source with the field names it uses in its address block. For example, if you've used an Outlook contact list as your data source, Word can generally map fields from there without difficulty.

However, in most cases you'll want to check Word's field matching before you run your mail merge—and if changes are necessary, you need a way to make them. To check Word's field mapping, click Match Fields in the Insert Address Block dialog box. The Match Fields dialog box appears (see Figure 17.15).

Figure 17.15
In the Match Fields dialog box, you can specify which database fields from your data source correspond to each element of your address block.

Match Fields
Mail Merge has special features for easily working with addresses. Please specify address field components to simplify address insertion.

Required information

Last Name	Last Name
First Name	First Name
Courtesy Title	Title
Company	Company Name
Address 1	Address Line 1
City	City
State	State
Postal Code	ZIP Code
Spouse First Name	(not available)

Optional information

Middle Name	(not available)
Suffix	(not available)

Use the drop-down lists to choose the field from your database that corresponds to the address information Mail Merge expects (listed on the left.)

OK   Cancel

The fields Word expects to place in an address block appear in the scroll box, under Required Information. The fields Word has discovered in your database are correlated at the right. For example, Word expects a field named Courtesy Title (which might contain data such as "Dr." or "Ms."). The database used as the data source in Figure 17.15 contains a corresponding field named Title.

To change the database field associated with an element in your address block, click the box to the right of the field name and choose the field you want to use from the drop-down box, which lists all the fields Word found in your database (see Figure 17.16).

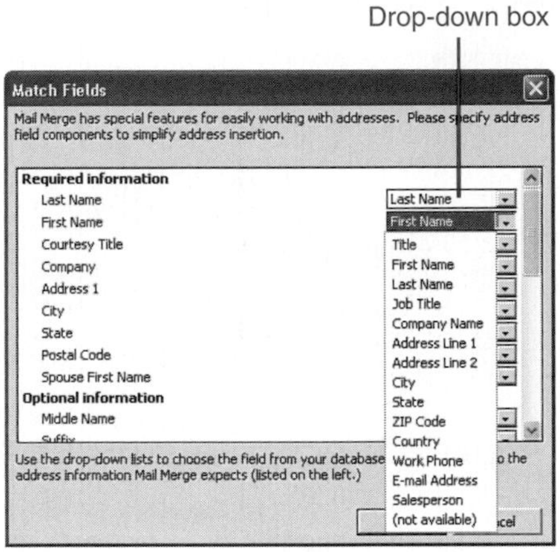

Figure 17.16
To map a different field to one of Word's address-block elements, choose it from the corresponding drop-down box.

When you've finished mapping fields, click OK to return to the Insert Address Block dialog box. When you've finished reviewing your address block, click OK.

NOTE

> If Word can't find a field that it needs for your address block or greeting line, it displays the Match Fields dialog box without being asked—expecting you to resolve the problem by locating the data within your database.

SPECIFYING A GREETING LINE

Most letters contain a greeting line, such as "Dear Mr. Jones" or "Dear Bob." Word 2003 allows you to specify this greeting line and even include a generic greeting when your database doesn't have appropriate information. To control your greeting line, click Greeting Line in the Write Your Letter window of the Mail Merge Wizard task pane. The Greeting Line dialog box opens (see Figure 17.17).

You can first choose a salutation. Two options are built-in: Dear and To. If you want a different salutation, you can type it yourself. If you want no salutation at all, choose None from the salutation drop-down box.

Choose or enter a salutation

Choose a name format

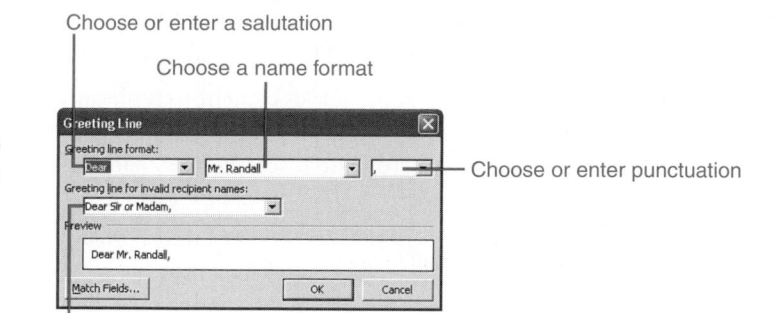

Figure 17.17
In the Greeting Line dialog box, you can specify how your message's greeting will read.

Choose or enter punctuation

Specify an alternative greeting in case database
information is unavailable for personalization

Next, choose a name format. By default, Word expects your mailing to be formal: "Dear Mr. Randall." If your mailings are more informal, you might choose a first name instead. You can choose various options, if your database contains the information to support them. For example, if you're mailing to couples, you can use a format like "Dear Joshua and Cynthia."

Then choose (or type) the punctuation you want to follow the recipient's name. By default, Word uses a comma; many letter writers prefer a colon.

Occasionally, your database won't contain the information needed to follow the format you specify. Rather than leaving your greeting blank or partially blank, Word allows you to choose or type a default Greeting Line for Invalid Recipient Names, such as Dear Sir or Madam. Many direct mail letter-writers will want to enter a generic greeting line that is more contemporary, such as Dear Colleague; or more specific, such as Dear Fellow Stamp Collector.

NOTE

> Like the Insert Address Block dialog box covered earlier (refer to Figure 17.14), the Greeting Line dialog box contains a <u>M</u>atch Fields button, which displays a dialog box that allows you to double-check whether Word has identified fields that contain the correct information to include in a greeting.

When you've finished editing your Greeting Line, click OK to return to the Write Your Letter window of the Mail Merge Wizard task pane.

CUSTOMIZING THE BODY OF YOUR MAIN DOCUMENT

You might occasionally want to add fields to the *body* of your letter or email message—not just to the address block or salutation. For example, you might want to include a paragraph that says something like this:

> *Like many of your neighbors in Longwood, you may suspect you're paying too much for auto insurance. Why not do what many of them have already done, and check out Bob's Discount Auto Insurance?*

By inserting the City field from your database into your message, you can instruct Word to customize each message with its recipient's hometown.

To make customizations like these, click in your document to position your cursor where you want the mail-merge field to be placed. Then click More Items in the Write Your Letter window of the Mail Merge Wizard. The Insert Merge Field dialog box opens (see Figure 17.18).

Figure 17.18
The Insert Merge Field dialog box.

You can choose from two sets of merge fields, by clicking the corresponding Insert button at the top of the dialog box:

- Database Fields, which must correspond to specific database field names in your database

- Address Fields, which still must be mapped to fields in your database, but need not have names identical to those in your database

Choose a field in the Fields scroll box, click Insert, and click Close. The field appears in your document, surrounded by double brackets.

CAUTION

> Be sure to place appropriate spacing before and after the field you insert to avoid unsightly gaps—or words that run together—in your final message.
>
> You may find this easier to do if you first display hidden characters such as spaces and paragraph marks by clicking the Show/Hide Paragraph Marks button on the Standard toolbar.

ADDING A POSTAL BAR CODE TO YOUR ENVELOPES

If you are creating envelopes, Word allows you to print postal bar codes that allow the U.S. Postal Service to process mail more efficiently and may qualify you for a mailing discount.

NOTE

> Word supports only U.S. postal codes.

To add postal bar codes, click Postal Bar Code on the Arrange Your Envelope window of the Mail Merge Wizard. The Insert Postal Bar Code dialog box appears (see Figure 17.19).

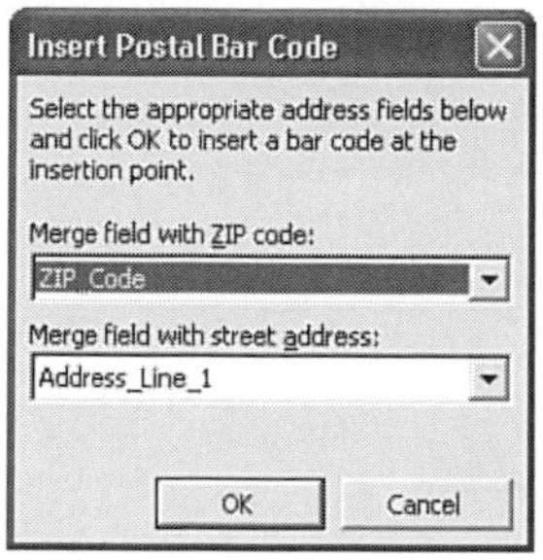

Figure 17.19
The Insert Postal Bar Code dialog box.

In the Merge Field with ZIP Code drop-down box, Word shows you the database field it intends to use to generate your five-digit ZIP Code. In the Merge Field with Street Address drop-down box, Word shows you the street address database field it intends to use to create the remaining four digits of your ZIP Code.

If either of these fields does *not* correlate with the database fields that actually contain ZIP Code or street information, make appropriate changes; then click OK. Word inserts a bar code on the envelope, in a location that meets postal regulations.

To move on with your mail merge, click Next: Preview Your Letters (or Preview Your Envelopes, or Preview Your Labels).

PREVIEWING LETTERS OR OTHER DOCUMENTS

In the Preview window of the Mail Merge Wizard (see Figure 17.20), you can review how each of your finished letters looks before you actually print it.

The first letter in your mail merge appears in the editing window. You can scroll through your database by clicking the double-arrow keys in the Preview Your Letters window, or click Find a Recipient to check the letter to a specific individual.

You may occasionally see a letter to an individual who shouldn't receive one—perhaps it's someone to whom you've already made a special private offer that is inconsistent with the direct mail offer everyone else is receiving. To remove a recipient from your mail merge, click Exclude This Recipient. To check and adjust your entire recipient list, click Edit Recipient List. The Mail Merge Recipients dialog box appears (refer to Figure 17.9); make your changes there and click OK.

Figure 17.20
Previewing a letter in the editing window.

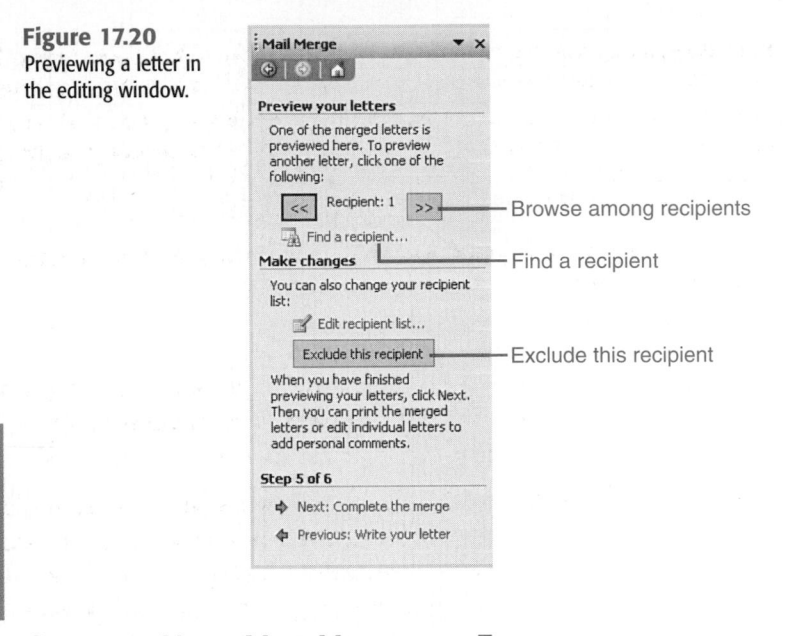

— Browse among recipients

— Find a recipient

— Exclude this recipient

CHECKING YOUR MAIL MERGE FOR ERRORS

Before you're ready to finalize your merge, you can also preview individual form letters (or other merged documents) by clicking View Merged Data while your main document is displayed. Keep in mind that in a large mailing, it may be impractical to check every document individually. It's simply too easy to miss potentially disastrous problems, such as discrepancies between merge fields in the main document and field names in the data source, or incorrect sort order.

That's where Word's Check Errors feature comes in. To run error checking, click Check Errors on the Mail Merge toolbar. The Checking and Reporting Errors dialog box appears (see Figure 17.21).

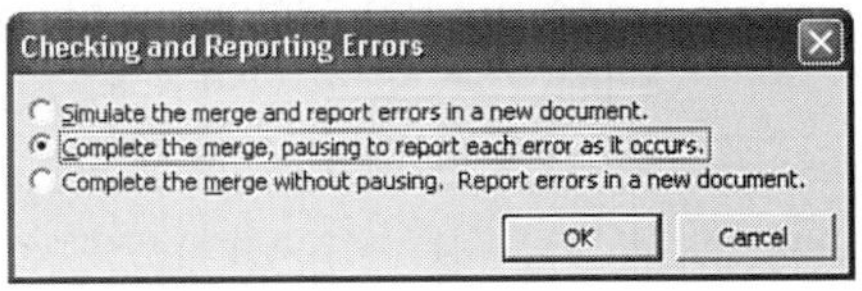

Figure 17.21
Choosing how you want Word to check and report on potential errors in your mail merge.

You have three choices. The first and third choices list your errors in a new document, named Mail Merge Errors1. The middle choice runs the merge, displaying a dialog box onscreen if an error occurs.

One common error Word may find is an invalid merge field. This often occurs when you enter merge fields and later change your data source. If the new data source includes different field names from those you used originally, Word can't find the information it needs to include in your merged documents.

When the Invalid Merge Field dialog box appears, you can click Remove Field to remove the field from your main document. Word continues checking for errors immediately without asking you to confirm the change.

To move on with your mail merge, click Next: Complete the Merge.

EDITING INDIVIDUAL LETTERS, ENVELOPES, OR LABELS BEFORE PRINTING

In the Complete the Merge window of the Mail Merge Wizard task pane (see Figure 17.22), you're given two choices about how you want to complete your mail merge.

Figure 17.22
From the Complete the Merge window, you can either print your merged documents or create an editable file containing them.

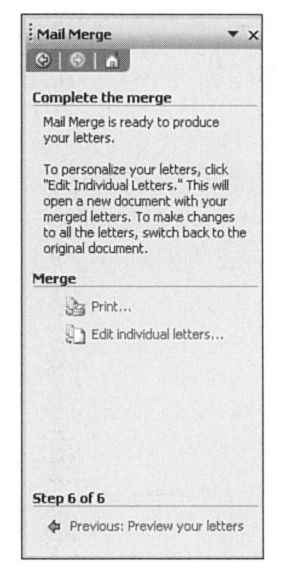

Of course, you can go straight to print—but if you're not sure that your letters, labels, or envelopes are perfect yet, or if you want to make further customizations to them, you can instead merge your letters to a single Word document. After you've done so, you can edit that document just like any other Word document.

To merge to a Word document, click Edit Individual Letters (or Edit Individual Labels or Edit Individual Envelopes). The Merge to New Document dialog box opens (see Figure 17.23). Here, you get another opportunity to specify which database records to merge. For example, imagine that your entire mailing will consist of 10,000 letters; you might simply want to spot-check 50 of them.

To merge only the current record, choose Current Record. To merge a specific set of records, click From and enter the range of records you want to merge, in the From and To text boxes. Then click OK. Word creates a new file, with each letter in a separate section. You can edit the letters and print them as you would the contents of any other Word document.

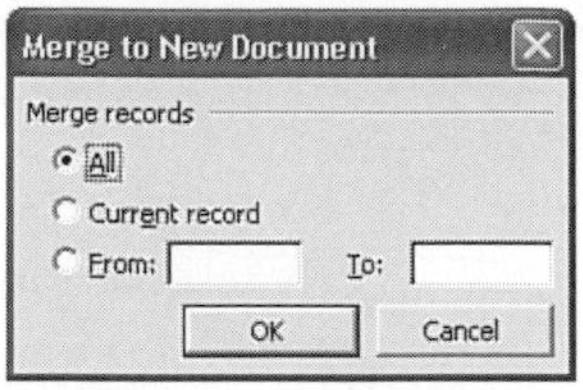

Figure 17.23
The Merge to New
Document dialog box.

PRINTING OR DELIVERING YOUR MERGED DOCUMENTS

You're finally ready to print your merged documents (or deliver them electronically). Word provides different tools for controlling how your merged documents will be printed or delivered, depending on the type of merged documents you're creating. These are covered in the following sections.

PRINTING MERGED LETTERS, ENVELOPES, OR LABELS

If you don't need to edit individual merged letters, envelopes, or labels, you can print them directly from the Complete the Merge window of the Mail Merge Wizard. Click Print; the Merge to Printer dialog box opens.

This dialog box contains the same options as were available in Merge to New Document: You can print all letters, just the currently selected letter, or a specific range of letters. Make your selections and click OK. The Print dialog box opens; choose a printer and print settings, and click OK.

After all the copies of your letter print, the Save As dialog box appears. You can now save the merge letter you created, including all merge fields, database links, and selected recipients.

MERGING TO EMAIL

If you are merging to email, the final step in the process is to click the Electronic Mail button in the Complete the Merge window of the Mail Merge Wizard. The Merge to E-mail dialog box opens (see Figure 17.24).

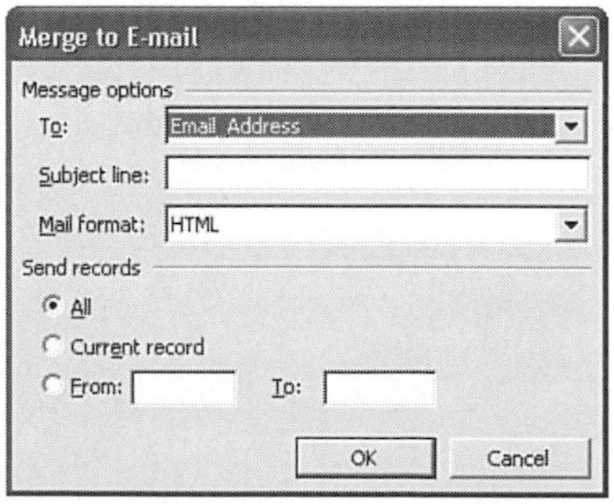

Figure 17.24
The Merge to E-mail
dialog box.

Here, in addition to specifying *which* messages to send, you can

- Make sure that Word is using the database field that contains the email addresses you want to use; if not, choose a different database field from the To drop-down box.
- Enter a Subject Line that appears at the top of all your messages.
- Specify whether your message should be sent in Plain Text format, in HTML format, or as an attachment.

When you're finished, click OK, and Word sends the messages, using Outlook (or whatever MAPI-compatible program you've chosen as your default email software).

MERGING TO A DIRECTORY

If you are merging a directory, Word provides only one option for completing the merge: creating a new document containing the contents of the directory. To perform this step, click To New Document in the Complete the Merge window of the Mail Merge Wizard. The Merge to New Document dialog box opens (refer to Figure 17.23).

As you've already seen, you can choose a specific record or a range of records for inclusion in your directory, or choose All records. After you've done so, click OK, and Word creates the new document.

CUSTOMIZING MERGED DOCUMENTS WITH WORD FIELDS

In many mailings, every form letter is alike, except for a personalized name, address, and salutation (Dear Mr. Jones). However, in other mailings you may want to customize your form letters further, varying your message depending on the individual recipient. In still other cases, you may want to skip certain recipients altogether, while still retaining them in your data source. Word provides a set of special fields that can be used to customize your letters in ways like these.

→ For more information about Word fields in general, **see** Chapter 23, "Automating Your Documents with Field Codes," **p. 771**.

These mail-merge fields provide many ways in which you can customize a merge. To insert any Word field, place the insertion point in the main document where you want the field to appear, click the Insert Word Field button, and choose a Word field.

Table 17.2 lists the Word fields available from the Insert Word Field toolbar button and briefly describes what they do. Many of these fields are discussed in more detail in the following sections.

TABLE 17.2   WORD FIELDS ESPECIALLY WELL-SUITED FOR MAIL MERGE

Field	What It Does
Ask	Asks the user for input and assigns that input to a *bookmark*. With the Set and/or { REF } fields, you can use that bookmark throughout your document.
Fill-in	Asks the user for input at each new mail-merge document and places that input in the document.
If...Then...Else...	Specifies text to print if a certain condition is met, and different text or an alternative merge field otherwise.
Merge Record #	Inserts the number of your data record in your main document.
Merge Sequence #	Inserts the number of data records successfully merged into a main document. (Often used with Merge Record # to include text such as "Letter 12 of 148.")
Next Record	Tells Word to print the next record without starting a new page. Often used with labels.
Next Record If	Starts the next record on the same page only if certain conditions are met. This command is a left over from very old versions of Word; using Filter and Sort, as discussed later in this chapter, accomplishes the same task with more flexibility.
Set Bookmark	Marks text as a bookmark that you can insert repeatedly throughout a document.
Skip Record If	Skips printing the current record if a specified condition is met. This command is a left over from very old versions of Word; using Filter and Sort, as discussed later in this chapter, accomplishes the same task with more flexibility.

TIP

These fields can be used in any type of mail-merge main document. Some, such as Ask and Fill-in, are available in any Word document.

You can also use other Word fields to customize your form letters. For example, using { DATE } can enable Word to insert the current date into your letters.

You can also use Word formula fields to perform calculations. For example, perhaps you're sending a letter confirming a customer order. You can use merge fields to place dollar amounts for each item in your letters and use the AutoSum button on the Tables and Borders toolbar to insert a formula field that tallies the value of all those items.

USING THE FILL-IN FIELD

Perhaps the most straightforward Word field is Fill-In. When you insert a Fill-In field, Word stops before printing each document and asks the user for input to place in the location specified by the Fill-In field.

To insert a Fill-In field, click on Insert Word Field and choose Fill-in. The Insert Word Field: Fill-In dialog box opens (see Figure 17.25).

Figure 17.25
Use the Insert Word Field: Fill-In dialog box to create the Fill-In field.

In the Prompt box, insert the question you want to ask whoever is running the mail merge—for example, "How big a discount for this customer?"

If you want the same text in every letter, check the Ask Once check box. Then, after the user inserts the information once, Word repeats that information in all letters that the mail merge generates.

To specify default text that prints unless you choose different text for a specific letter, type the default text in the Default Fill-In Text box.

When you (or a colleague) start the merge process, Word displays a Fill-In dialog box that displays the question or information you supplied when you created the Fill-In field and prompts you to type information (see Figure 17.26).

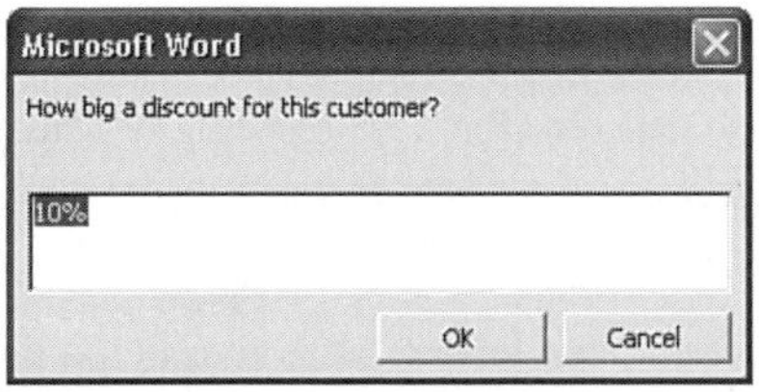

Figure 17.26
A sample Fill-In prompt dialog box.

USING THE ASK FIELD

The Ask field takes this concept of requesting user input one step further. Rather than placing your response directly in text, the Ask field transforms your response into the contents of a bookmark. Wherever you place that bookmark in your text, these contents appear. Therefore, Ask is ideal for inserting the same text repeatedly throughout a letter.

After you click Insert Word Field and choose Ask, type the name of the bookmark you want Word to create (see Figure 17.27). The bookmark's name can be up to 40 characters long but cannot include spaces. In the Prompt text box, type the text you want Word to display when it prompts you for the bookmark. In the Default Bookmark Text box, type the information you want Word to include in the main document when you type nothing in the Ask dialog box that appears when you start the merge process.

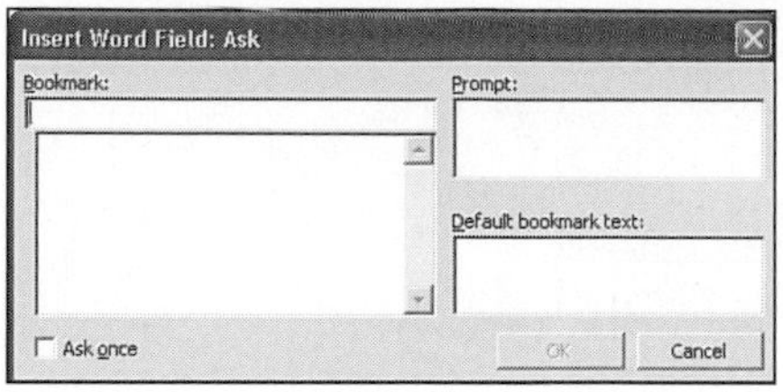

Figure 17.27
Inserting an Ask field.

All Ask does is create a bookmark; it doesn't place anything in your letter by itself. You have to place a bookmark field wherever you want the text. You can insert this field manually before you use the Ask field. First, press Ctrl+F9 where you want the bookmark to appear. Field brackets appear. Then type the bookmark name between the field brackets; for example, { offer }.

The Ask field also displays a prompt during the merge so that you can add personal notes to clients or add other information that is not suitable to store in a data source. As with the Fill-In field, the prompt appears each time Word merges a new data-source document record with the main document unless you instruct Word otherwise.

> **TIP**
>
> The information you supply when you include an Ask field can be used in other fields; for example, if you supply a number as the response to an Ask field, you can later use that number as a basis of comparison in an If...Then...Else... field.

USING THE IF...THEN...ELSE... FIELD

The If...Then...Else... field uses the following syntax: If such-and-such happens, Then do this; Else do something different. You can use this field (especially in conjunction with other merge fields and Word fields) to customize the text of each letter, based on any attribute of the recipient you choose.

Suppose, for example, that some of your form letters go to recipients in Tampa, whereas others go to recipients in Orlando. If you're asking your recipient to make an appointment, you may need to provide different phone numbers for Tampa and Orlando residents to call. In this case, you could use an If...Then...Else... statement to tell Word which phone number to include if the city is Tampa and which phone number to include if the city is Orlando.

To create an If...Then...Else... field, follow these steps:

1. Click your insertion point at the place in the document where you want the customized text to appear.

2. Click Insert Word Field, and choose If...Then...Else.... The Insert Word Field: IF dialog box opens (see Figure 17.28).

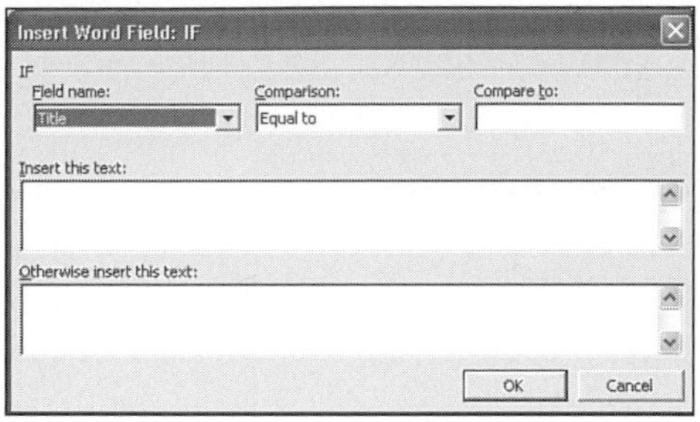

Figure 17.28
You can use this dialog box to build an If...Then...Else... field.

3. In the <u>F</u>ield Name list box, choose the field you want Word to use when making the comparison.

4. In the <u>C</u>omparison list box, choose the comparison operator; for example, whether you want text inserted only if a value is Greater Than the value found in the field. You can choose from the following comparisons: Equal To, Not Equal To, Less Than, Greater Than, Less Than or Equal, Greater Than or Equal, Is Blank, or Is Not Blank.

5. Unless you've chosen Is Blank or Is Not Blank, you also need to fill in the Compare <u>T</u>o box. Enter the number or text you want Word to search for in the selected field.

6. In the <u>I</u>nsert This Text box, type the text you want Word to insert if the comparison is true.

7. In the <u>O</u>therwise Insert This Text box, type the text you want Word to insert if the comparison is false.

> **TIP**
>
> If you edit the field directly (by right-clicking it in the document, choosing Toggle Field Codes, and then entering text and field codes within the field brackets that appear), you can gain even more control of your If...Then...Else... field.
>
> For example, you can insert an { INCLUDETEXT } field as either the Then or the Else value, and the { INCLUDETEXT } field can retrieve a large block of text from the source document you choose. In fact, the source document that { INCLUDETEXT } brings into your merge document can even have its own merge fields, as long as they access the same data source.

This technique makes it convenient to create mail merges that send two entirely different letters to two categories of recipients—for example, those who are on time with their payments and those who are late.

USING THE SET BOOKMARK FIELD

The Set Bookmark field (which actually inserts a field simply called Set) sets the contents of a bookmark, much as you've already seen Ask do. But there's one big difference: The user isn't prompted for the contents of these bookmarks during the mail merge. Rather, you set the contents of the bookmark ahead of time. You can then include the bookmark in another field, such as an If...Then...Else... field.

To create a { SET } field in your main document, click the Insert Word Field button and choose Set Bookmark. The Insert Word Field: Set dialog box opens (see Figure 17.29).

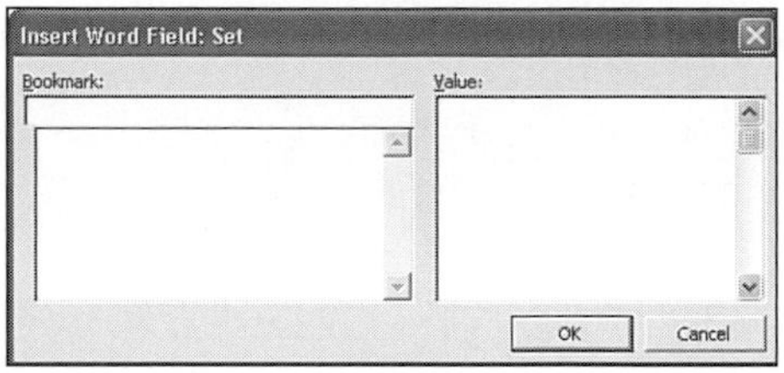

Figure 17.29
You can define a bookmark in advance using the Insert Word Field: Set dialog box.

In the Bookmark text box, type the name you want to give to the bookmark. In the Value text box, type the text you want the bookmark to represent. To print the information, you must insert a Ref or Bookmark field in the document or include the bookmark in an Ask or If…Then…Else… field.

USING THE MERGE RECORD # AND MERGE SEQUENCE # FIELDS

Sometimes, in a direct mail campaign, you want to include a unique serial number on each letter you send; it's a quick way for recipients to identify themselves. Word provides two ways to include such a serial number: the Merge Record # and Merge Sequence # fields. The distinction between these fields is subtle: Both generate a unique number in each merged document; however, the number they generate may be different.

Merge Record # returns a record number based on the number of the first record in your data source that you actually used in your merge. So if you created a merge that ignored the first five records in your data source, your first letter would display the number 6.

Merge Sequence # always inserts the number 1 in the first merged letter (or other document) you create, the number 2 in the second letter, and so forth—incrementing each additional letter by 1.

TIP

You can use { MERGEREC } inside a formula field to generate numbers from any starting point you want. For example, if you want your first letter to be numbered 101 instead of 1, insert the following field:

{ 100 + { MERGEREC } }

USING THE NEXT RECORD AND NEXT RECORD IF FIELDS

When you choose Next Record from the Insert Word Field list, you instruct Word to merge the next data record into the current document, rather than starting a new merged document. Word automatically does this when you are setting up a mailing label, an envelope, or a directory, but it's rarely needed in form letters.

TROUBLESHOOTING

WHAT TO DO WHEN WORD DISREGARDS CHARACTER FORMATTING IN YOUR DATA SOURCE

Mail-merged information takes on the formatting of the merge field in the main document; any formatting you apply in the data-source document is ignored. Format your merge fields in the main document to make merged data appear the way you want. You may also be able to use formatting switches available to Word fields to achieve the formatting you're looking for.

→ For more information about using field switches to control the appearance of text, dates, and values, **see** "A Closer Look at Field Formatting," **p. 789**.

WHAT TO DO WHEN MERGE FIELDS PRINT INSTEAD OF INFORMATION FROM THE CORRESPONDING RECORDS

Adjust your Print options—they're probably set to print field codes rather than field results. Choose Tools, Options, and click the Print tab. Then, remove the check from the Field Codes check box in the Include with Document section.

WHAT TO DO WHEN YOUR MERGED DOCUMENTS CONTAIN BLANK LINES YOU DON'T WANT

Sometimes you can solve this problem by clicking the Merge button to display the Merge dialog box, and clicking the Don't Print Blank Lines When Data Fields Are Empty option button. If blank lines are appearing where you've used an If, Ask, or Set field, try to insert the field within an existing paragraph, not in its own paragraph. If your document format won't allow this, format the paragraph mark as hidden text.

Then, before you print, make sure that hidden text doesn't print. Choose Tools, Options; click the Print tab; clear the Hidden Text check box; and click OK.

Another way to print text inserted by an If field as a separate paragraph is to insert the paragraph mark directly into the field code that generates the text, surrounded by quotation marks.

→ For more information about creating and editing field codes manually, **see** "Placing Fields Directly into a Document," **p. 780**.

CHAPTER 18

OUTLINING: PRACTICAL TECHNIQUES FOR ORGANIZING ANY DOCUMENT

In this chapter

THE BENEFITS OF OUTLINING

Word's outlining feature gives you a quick and convenient way to organize (and reorganize) any document or Web page. The larger your documents, the more valuable you will find the organizing capabilities that outlining provides. As you'll see, with outlining it's easy to view your document at a very high level, then drill down to any specific element that needs attention, and move large blocks of text easily. In other words, you can see the forest and the trees—and work with both.

You can use outlining to plan your document before you start to write. First, brainstorm—and enter the content you want to include in rough form. Then use Word's outlining tools to reorganize the text and decide what should be emphasized and which areas are minor details subordinate to more important points.

THE ROLE OF HEADING STYLES AND OUTLINE LEVELS IN OUTLINING

To understand outlining, you must understand three concepts: heading styles, outline levels, and body text.

- **Heading styles** are built-in styles that Word provides for each level of heading in your document, from Heading 1 to Heading 9. These styles don't just carry formatting information; they also carry information about where the text fits in the hierarchy of your document. In other words, Word recognizes that Heading 1 is a first-level heading, Heading 2 is a second-level heading, and so forth.

- **Outline levels** provide a way for you to give the same hierarchical information for paragraphs in your outline that are not headings. For example, you may have a quotation that you want to treat as a second-level element in your outline for the purposes of your table of contents.

- **Body text** is text that is formatted with the Body Text outline level—in other words, text that does *not* have an Outline Level from 1 to 9 assigned to it. Typically, the paragraphs of text between headings in a document are body text. By default, text formatted in Word's built-in Normal or Body Text style carries the Body Text Outline Level. In an outline, if body text follows a heading, or if it follows other text formatted with an outline level from 1 to 9, Word treats the body text as subordinate.

Word's outlining feature works seamlessly with the heading styles or outline levels you may already have inserted in your documents. If you haven't applied heading styles, Word can add them for you automatically, while you work on your outline.

→ For more information about styles, **see** Chapter 10, "Streamlining Your Formatting with Styles," **p. 329**.

→ For more information about assigning outline levels to styles, **see** "Applying Outline Levels to Specific Text," **p. 635**.

You can't change the outline level associated with a built-in heading style. However, as you'll see later in this chapter, you can assign any outline level from 1 to 9 to other styles, and use *those* styles as the basis for your outline.

TIP

> After your heading styles are in place, you can use them to automate many Word features. Later in this chapter, in the section "Using Word's Automatic Outline Numbering," you'll discover one of the most powerful of these features: Word's simple, quick Outline Numbering feature. You'll learn how Word can instantly number all your headings and subheads—and keep them numbered properly, come what may.

CREATING A NEW OUTLINE

An outline is embedded in every document you create, but unless you deliberately look for it, you might never realize it because Word treats an outline as just another way to view a document. This means that you don't have to actively create an outline to get one. It also means that when you do want a polished outline, you can simply refine the one that's already built into your document.

Outlines can be created in two ways. The first is to work from scratch. Open a new blank document and click the Outline View button on the lower-left corner of your screen to display it in Outline view (see Figure 18.1). You can also switch to this view by selecting Outline from Word's View menu.

Outlining toolbar

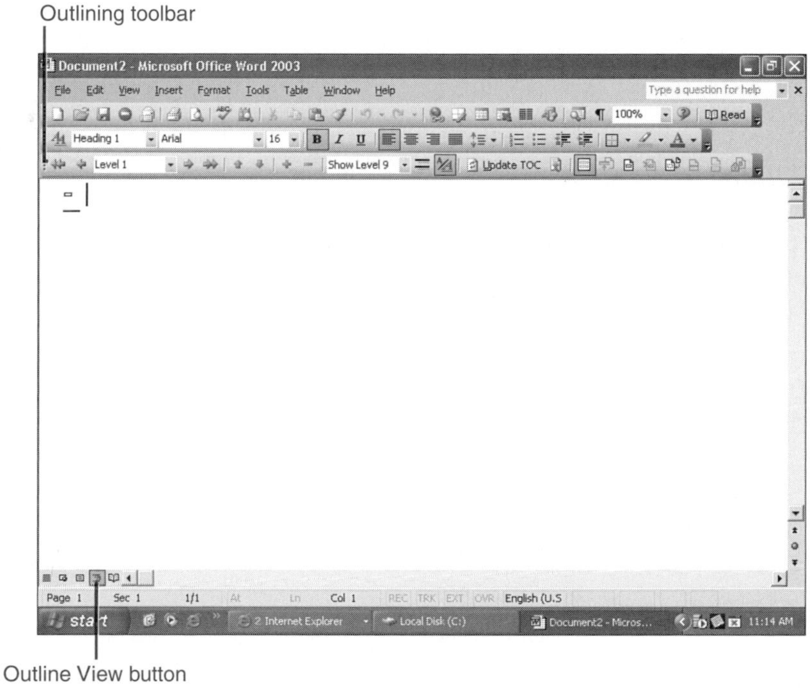

Figure 18.1
When you display a blank document in Outline view, an "outlined" minus sign appears.

Outline View button

You can create an outline from scratch if you're starting a major new project, such as a book or manual, and you don't yet have any text. Working from scratch is convenient because you don't have to worry about moving existing blocks of text or reorganizing material that should have been handled differently from the outset. You can organize the document the best way right from the beginning. If you're leading a team of writers, you can divide your outline into sections and delegate each part.

TIP

> With Word's closely related Master Document feature, you can divide the document into subdocuments, assign each subdocument to a different writer, and then edit and manage all the subdocuments together, as if they were still part of one longer document.

→ For more information about master documents, **see** Chapter 19, "Master Documents: Control and Share Even the Largest Documents," **p. 635**.

TIP

> Use Outline view in connection with Word's document collaboration and revision tools to streamline the process of getting your outline approved.

→ For more information about tracking changes, **see** "Introducing Word's Reviewing Interface," **p. 876**.

The second way to create an outline is to do nothing at all. Work as you normally do, but be sure to apply heading styles as you format your document. Then, whenever you're ready, switch to Outline view. Word displays your existing document as an outline.

Figure 18.2 shows a typical document displayed as an outline: Each first-level heading appears farthest to the left, with second-level headings and body text subordinate to it. As you can see, this works only if you use heading styles; without them, this document would appear as a one-level outline, with no apparent structure or organization.

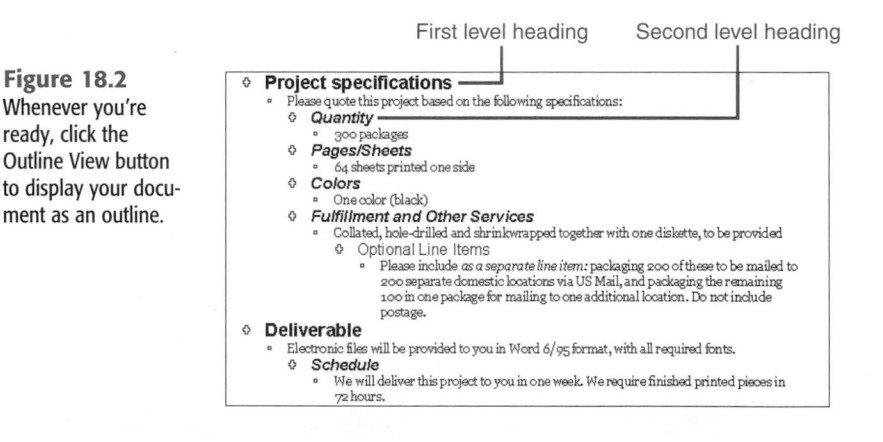

Figure 18.2
Whenever you're ready, click the Outline View button to display your document as an outline.

The problem many people have with using the heading styles to create an outline is that they don't like the text formatting these styles use. If you want the organizational benefits of outlining but don't like the appearance of Word's heading styles, you can change the formatting associated with the heading styles.

To do so, enter some text with the heading style of your choice; then manually reformat so that it looks as you want. Click in the Style box on the Standard toolbar and press Enter. The Modify Style dialog box appears; specify that you want to Update the Style to Reflect Recent Changes and click OK.

Another alternative is to use the styles you prefer but assign outline levels to those styles, as discussed later in this chapter in the "Applying Outline Levels to Specific Text" section.

Your style changes will be reflected in all views within this document, including Outline view. Repeat the process for each heading you intend to use.

 To learn more about formatting text with an existing style, **see** "Applying an Existing Style from the Styles and Formatting Task Pane," **p. 336**.

If you want to copy only the headings from one document to another, see "How to Copy Only a Document's Headings Without Copying All the Subordinate Text," in the "Troubleshooting" section of this chapter.

UNDERSTANDING OUTLINE VIEW

Soon, you'll learn techniques for polishing your outline to make sure that your document is actually structured the way you want. First, however, notice three things about Outline view:

- **Each paragraph has a symbol to its left.** These symbols tell you what you need to know about the paragraph's relationship to surrounding text:
  - A plus sign (+) tells you the paragraph has subordinate text. This text may consist of lower-level headings, paragraphs formatted in styles that Word does not recognize as a heading or outline level, or both.
  - A minus sign (–) tells you the paragraph has no subordinate text. In other words, the paragraph has a heading style or an outline level but no subheads or body text are under it.
  - A small square tells you the paragraph is body text.
- **Paragraph formatting, such as indents and line spacing, disappears.** In fact, Word grays out the Format, Paragraph menu command so that you can't use it to add new paragraph formatting. In its place, Word displays its own outline indenting to make it obvious which paragraphs are most important (for example, which appear at the highest level of your outline) and which are subordinate.
- **The Outlining toolbar appears.** This toolbar contains all the tools you need in order to edit and manage your outline.

18

You can use keyboard shortcuts or the Increase Indent and Decrease Indent buttons on the Formatting toolbar to set standard indents without changing the outline level of your heading. You can also right-click to access a shortcut menu that includes some formatting controls (see Figure 18.3).

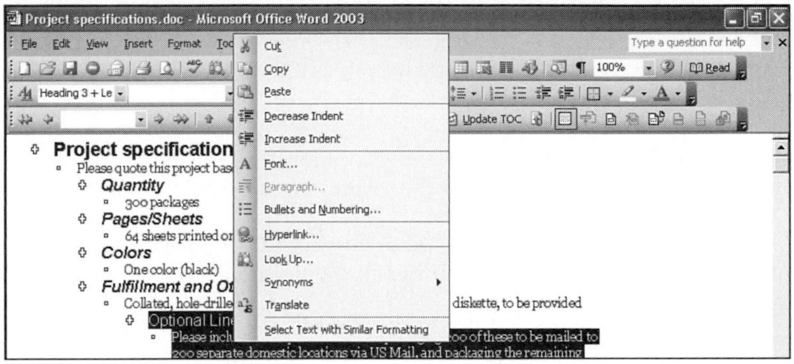

Figure 18.3
Right-click anywhere in Outline view to see its shortcut menu.

TIP

> You can switch back and forth between views at any time. You might use Outline view when you're organizing your document, Normal view when you're editing content, and Print Layout view when you're primarily concerned about graphics and the appearance of your pages.
>
> If you're working in Normal view and you decide to change a heading level, you might want to switch into Outline view so that you can quickly change all the subordinate headings at the same time.

USING THE OUTLINING TOOLBAR

Take a closer look at the Outlining toolbar (see Figure 18.4), which includes Word's tools for organizing and managing your outline. These buttons fall into the following four categories:

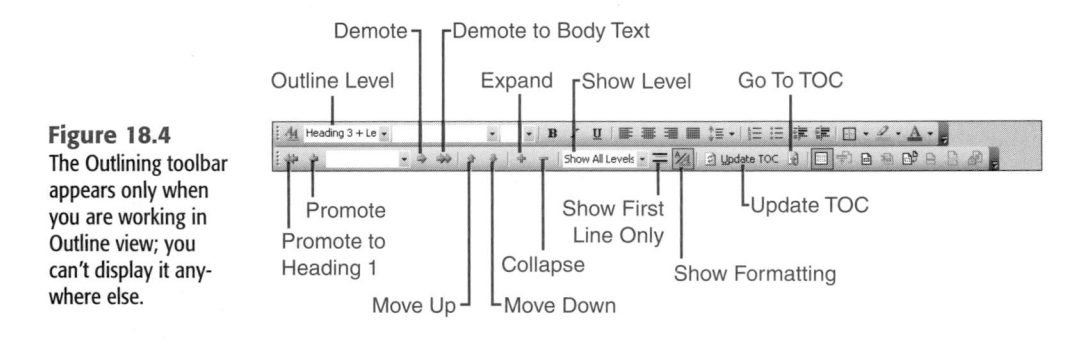

Figure 18.4
The Outlining toolbar appears only when you are working in Outline view; you can't display it anywhere else.

- Tools for increasing or decreasing the relative importance of paragraphs (Promote to Level 1, Promote, Outline Level, Demote, and Demote to Body Text).

- Tools for moving paragraphs up or down in the document (Move Up, Move Down).

- Tools for controlling which paragraphs display and how they look (Expand, Collapse, Show Level, Show First Line Only, and Show Formatting).

- Tools for working with Tables of Contents in Outline view (Update TOC and Go to TOC). These buttons are covered in Chapter 20, "Tables of Contents, Figures, Authorities, and Captions."

→ For more information about working with master document tools, **see** "Creating Master Documents and Subdocuments," **p. 655**.

Most of these buttons also have a keyboard shortcut equivalent, as listed in Table 18.1.

TABLE 18.1   KEYBOARD AND TOOLBAR SHORTCUTS FOR WORKING IN OUTLINE VIEW

Button Shortcut	Toolbar Task	Keyboard
⬅	Promote paragraph	Alt+Shift+left arrow
➡	Demote paragraph	Alt+Shift+right arrow
⏩	Demote to body text	Ctrl+Shift+N
⬆	Move selected paragraph(s) up	Alt+Shift+up arrow
⬇	Move selected paragraph(s) down	Alt+Shift+down arrow
➕	Expand text under heading	Alt+Shift++ (plus sign)
➖	Collapse text under heading	Alt+Shift+– (minus sign)
	Expand/collapse all text or headings	Alt+Shift+A
	Toggle character formatting	/ (on numeric keypad)
≡	Toggle to displayonly first line of body text	Alt+Shift+L
	Show only Level 1 headings/text	Alt+Shift+1
	Show all levels through [a number]	Alt+Shift+[number from 1 to 7]

18

T I P

> The Promote to Level 1, Promote, Demote, Demote to Body Text, Move Up, and Move Down keyboard shortcuts work in every view, not just Outline view. These shortcuts provide a quick way to change heading styles or move paragraphs.

It's helpful to understand what the Outlining toolbar buttons and symbols *don't* do so that you don't make the common mistakes that trip up many first-time outliners:

- The right-arrow button does *not* insert a tab, even though it looks as if it might. It does indent text much as a tab does, but this happens only because that text is being demoted to the next lower level.

- The numbered buttons do *not* specify heading or outline levels. They simply control how many levels you can see at the same time.

- The plus and minus buttons do *not* increase or decrease the importance of selected text. Rather, they hide or display all the subordinate text and headings under the paragraph you've chosen.

Similarly, the plus and minus symbols next to each paragraph say *nothing* about the heading level associated with the paragraph. All they tell you is whether the paragraph has text subordinate to it. It's common to have two headings next to each other, both formatted in the same style, but one adorned with a plus sign and the other with a minus sign.

ADDING NEW SUBHEADINGS

Now that you've taken a tour of Word's outlining tools, it's time to start using them. If you open a blank document and switch to Outline view, Word typically displays a minus sign. This indicates that, for the moment at least, no text is subordinate to the line in which you are working.

If you start typing the first line of an outline, Word formats your text as a first-level heading, using the Heading 1 style. If you finish your paragraph and press Enter to start a new one, Word creates a new paragraph, also with the Heading 1 style. You can see this in Figure 18.5, which shows an outline with style names displayed in the Style Area.

> **NOTE**
>
> To set a Style Area, choose Tools, Options; click View, enter a value in the Style Area Width spin box, and click OK.

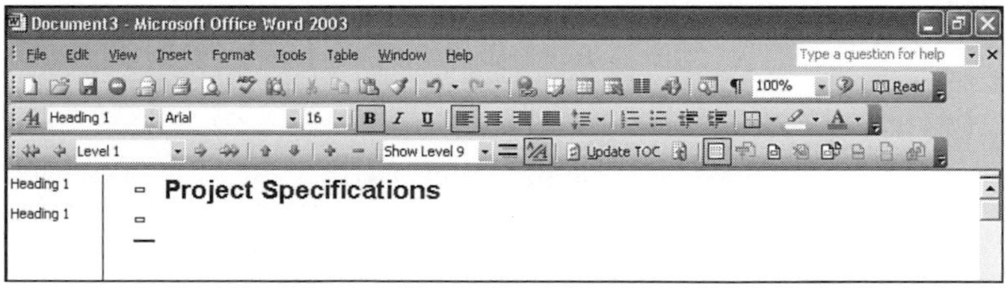

Figure 18.5
If you press Enter after creating a first-level heading in Outline view, Word starts another first-level heading.

NOTE

In this respect, Word behaves differently in Outline view than in other views. Elsewhere in Word, if you press Enter to create a new paragraph after a heading, Word assumes that you want to create Normal text–text formatted with the Normal style. (That's what Word's built-in Heading style settings tell it to do.) However, people rarely create large blocks of Normal or body text in Outline view, so Word assumes that you are creating an outline and want another heading like the one you've just finished.

PROMOTING AND DEMOTING HEADINGS

Often, you don't want another heading at the same level as the one you've just completed. Instead, you want a subordinate heading or body text. To demote any heading by one level, position your insertion point anywhere in the paragraph and click Demote, or use the keyboard shortcut Alt+Shift+right arrow.

When you demote a heading, Word indents it and also changes the heading style. For example, if you demote a first-level heading, Word changes the style associated with it to Heading 2. If the heading contains text, the character formatting also changes to reflect the new style.

Of course, you can promote subordinate headings as well. Click the Promote button or press Alt+Shift+left arrow. Again, Word changes the style and formatting as well as the indentation.

You can also drag a heading to a new level. Click the outline symbol next to the heading; your mouse pointer changes to a crosshair, and Word selects the heading and its subordinate contents. Then drag the mouse to the right. The mouse pointer changes to a horizontal double arrow, and you'll see a gray vertical line that moves as you jump from one heading level to the next (see Figure 18.6). When you've arrived at the heading level you want, release the mouse pointer.

TIP

If you want to move a heading by several levels, it's often quicker to change the style instead. For example, to move a heading from second to sixth level, choose Heading 6 in the Style drop-down list box.

DEMOTING HEADINGS TO BODY TEXT

To demote any heading to body text, click Demote to Body Text or press Ctrl+Shift+N. Word reformats that text in the Normal style and displays the small square Body Text symbol next to it. When you finish a paragraph of body text, you can start a new one by pressing Enter; another Body Text symbol appears to the left of the new paragraph.

TIP

In most cases, it's inconvenient to edit your whole document in Outline view, but you might have some ideas you'd like to jot down while you're organizing a new document in Outline view. Click Demote to Body Text in a new paragraph and start typing.

18

Figure 18.6
You can drag a paragraph left or right to a new heading level.

Vertical line
indicates level
to which selected
text is being moved

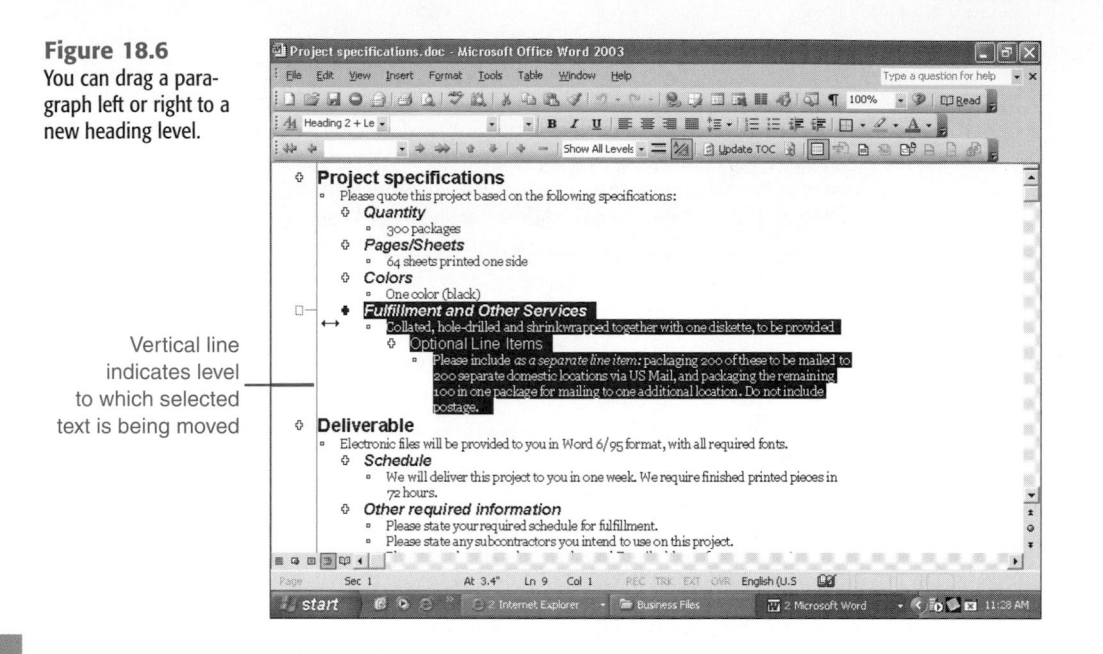

It's important to keep in mind that Word uses the term "body text" to refer to two different things: a style and an outline level. As you'll see, this can cause confusion for the unwary.

Some people format all body text using Word's Body Text style rather than the Normal style. In fact, Word often makes this change automatically when you run AutoFormat. However, Normal and Body Text are two different styles. In particular, Body Text adds 6 points of space after each paragraph, and Normal does not.

Surprisingly, when you use Demote to Body Text, you reformat text with the Normal style, not the Body Text style (though this *does* apply the Body Text outline level). As a result, if your document utilizes the Body Text style but you also click Demote to Body Text in Outline view, you may inadvertently introduce small formatting inconsistencies.

If you want to standardize on the Body Text style rather than the Normal style, spend a few minutes recording a quick macro that replaces the Normal style with the Body Text style throughout your document.

NOTE

Just as you can demote a heading to body text, you can also promote body text to a heading by selecting it and clicking Promote. Doing so transforms body text into a first-level heading formatted with the Heading 1 style; if necessary, you can then click Demote once or more to transform the text into a lower-level heading.

You can promote several consecutive paragraphs of body text at once, as long as your selection doesn't contain any headings. Select all the paragraphs and click Promote.

PROMOTING OR DEMOTING SEVERAL HEADINGS AT THE SAME TIME

If you select one heading and promote or demote it, nothing changes elsewhere in your document. That might be just fine with you. Often, however, when you promote or demote a heading, you want all your subordinate headings to be carried along with it.

Word makes this easy to do. Rather than selecting the paragraph, click the outline symbol next to it. This selects both the current paragraph and all the paragraphs subordinate to it. In Figure 18.7 you can see a first-level heading that has been selected along with the second-level heading and subordinate body text under it.

Figure 18.7
Clicking the outline symbol next to a paragraph selects the paragraph and all the subordinate headings and body text under it.

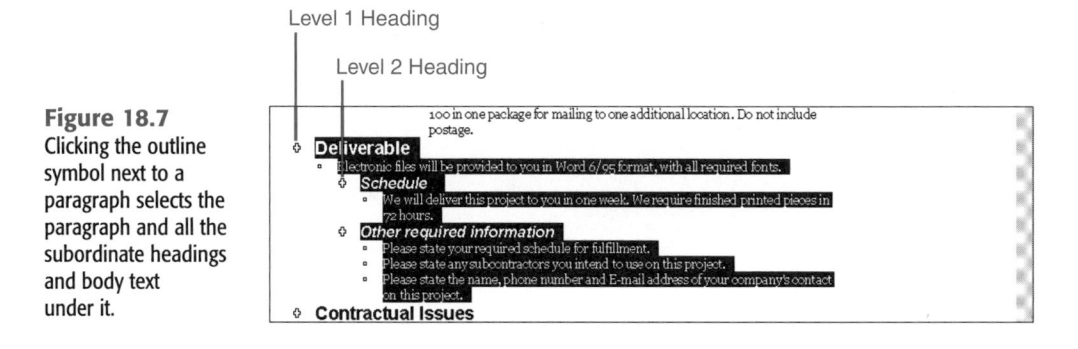

Figure 18.8 shows what happens after you click Demote. The second-level head is now a third-level head; the third-level head is now a fourth-level head, and so on. Text formatted in a style other than a Heading style does not change, however, regardless of which headings it is subordinate to. To transform body text into a heading, you must select and promote it.

Figure 18.8
After you click Demote, all the selected heading levels are demoted, but text formatted with other styles does not change.

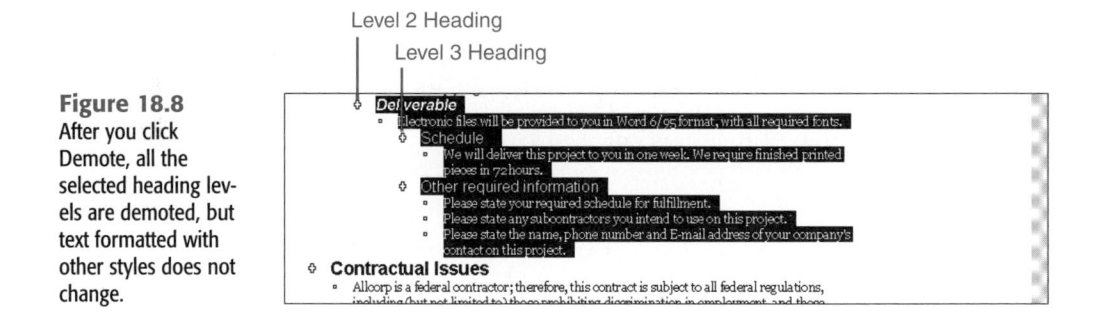

MOVING PARAGRAPHS WITHIN AN OUTLINE

As you organize your outline, you might find a heading or a block of text that you want to move toward the front or rear of the document. Word's Cut and Paste tools work within Outline view. However, if you are simply moving a heading or text by one paragraph (or a few paragraphs), there's a quicker alternative.

Place your insertion point in the paragraph you want to move, and click the Move Up or Move Down button on the Outlining toolbar. The entire paragraph moves. If you want to move more than one paragraph, select them all before clicking Move Up or Move Down.

If you're moving text farther than a paragraph or two, there's still a quicker solution than using Cut and Paste: Drag and drop it. Click the Outline symbol next to a paragraph. Your mouse pointer changes to a crosshair. Drag the mouse up or down. The pointer changes to a vertical double-arrow, and a gray horizontal line appears, moving as you jump from one paragraph to the next (see Figure 18.9). When you arrive at the location you want, release the mouse pointer.

Figure 18.9
Dragging text up or down in Outline view.

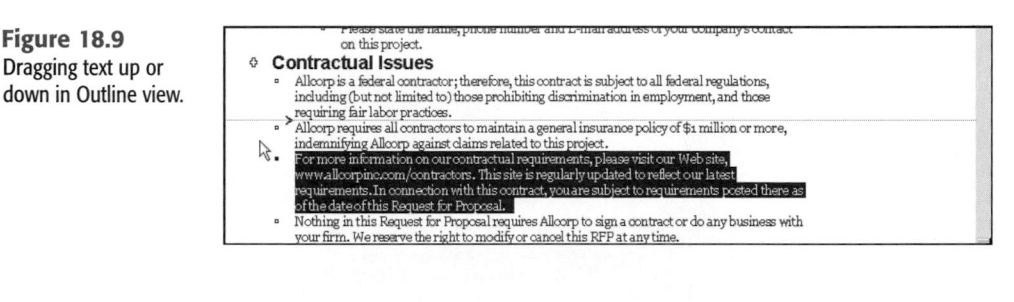

TIP

> The technique you've just learned works if you're moving just one paragraph (and its subordinate contents). However, what if you want to move several consecutive paragraphs that all share the same heading level?
>
> First, select all the paragraphs. Next, press the Alt key and click the Outline symbol next to the first paragraph of the text you've selected. Finally, drag the paragraphs to their new location.

If you have a long, complex document that needs to be thoroughly reorganized, here's a shortcut for organizing it without manually moving every heading:

1. Click Show Heading 1 to display only first-level headings (this is covered in the next section).

2. Manually enter heading numbers to reflect the order in which you want the first-level headings to appear. (Don't use any of Word's automatic numbering features.)

3. Press Ctrl+A (or choose Edit, Select All) to select all the first-level headings.

4. Choose Table, Sort.

5. Click OK. Word sorts the headings in number order—thereby reorganizing the entire document at the same time.

If you want, after your document is organized, you can use Word's Outline Numbering feature to replace your manual heading numbers with heading numbers that can automatically update themselves as you edit. (Word will automatically delete your heading numbers when adding its own.)

TIP

> If, rather than moving outline headings around within a document, you want to move them to a new document entirely, the process can get tricky. Word doesn't provide an easy way of copying outline headings only into a new document. One workaround does the job as long as you're careful. First, save a copy of your file. Then, find all text formatted using the Normal style and replace it with nothing at all. Repeat the process with each style in your document that uses the Body Text outline level. (The fewer styles that appear in your document, the less time this will take.)
>
> To replace text formatted in a specific style with no text at all, follow these steps:
>
> 1. Press Ctrl+H or choose Edit, Replace to display the Find and Replace dialog box.
>
> 2. Enter ^? in the Find What text box.
>
> 3. Click More to make sure that all the Find and Replace options are available.
>
> 4. Click Format, Style.
>
> 5. In the Find Style dialog box, choose whichever style you want to eliminate (such as Normal or Body Text) and click OK.
>
> 6. Make sure that the Replace With text box is empty, and click Replace All.
>
> The result is a document containing only text formatted as headings and text formatted with styles that use outline levels other than those you deleted.

NAVIGATING AN OUTLINE DOCUMENT WITH DOCUMENT MAP AND BROWSE OBJECT

18

Word's Document Map (see Figure 18.10) makes it easier to navigate through complex outlined documents. Document Map compiles all your headings (and text to which you've assigned outline levels) in a separate window.

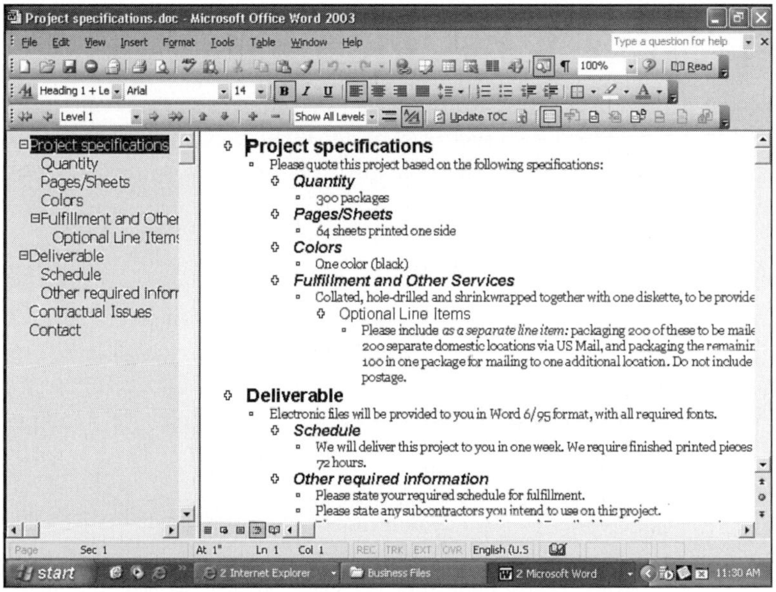

Figure 18.10
Document Map compiles all your headings and outline levels in a separate window to the left of your document.

To see the Document Map, click the Document Map button on the Standard toolbar, or choose View, Document Map. After Document Map opens, you can click any entry and move to the corresponding location in your document.

NOTE

> Document Map works in all Word document views, but if you switch to Outline view while it's open, Document Map closes. Word assumes that you're already looking at an outline, so you don't need it. When you switch out of Outline view to any view in which you opened the Document Map, the map is again displayed. Unfortunately, if you want the Document Map to remain open when switching to Outline view, you have to reopen it by clicking the Document Map button again.

You can also use Word's Browse Object feature to move quickly from one heading to the next.

To set up Word to browse headings, first click the Select Browse Object button under the vertical scrollbar. With the Browse options displayed, choose Browse by Heading. The Previous Heading/Next Heading double-arrow buttons turn blue. Then click Previous Heading to find the preceding heading, or click Next Heading to find the next one, as shown in Figure 18.11.

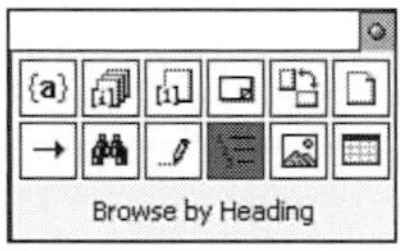

Figure 18.11
Browsing headings through Select Browse Object.

Browse by Heading

CONTROLLING YOUR OUTLINE VIEW

You've already heard that Word's outlines enable you to "view the forest and the trees." In fact, you can control the exact level of detail you view at any time. It's as if you could not only view the forest or the trees but also specific leaves, branches, trunks, individual trees, or groups of trees as well.

DISPLAYING ONLY SELECTED HEADING LEVELS

Imagine that you're reviewing a complex document with several levels of headings. You might want to start by looking at the document at a very high level—viewing only first-level headings. Choose Show Level 1 from the Show Level button on the Outlining toolbar, and Word hides all paragraphs except those formatted as first-level headings (see Figure 18.12). The gray underlining under these headings tells you they have subordinate text you aren't seeing.

After you're satisfied with the high-level organization of the document, you can drill deeper. Choose Show Level 2 from the Show Level drop-down box to view both first-level and second-level headings; choose Show Level 3 to view the first three levels of headings; and so on.

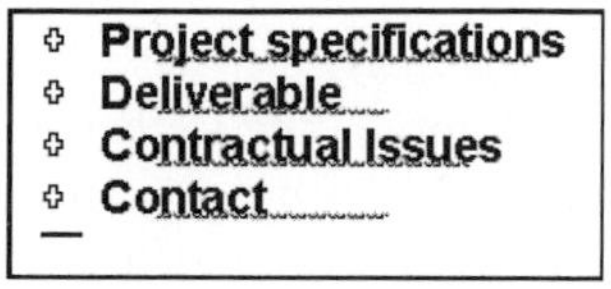

Figure 18.12
A document showing only first-level headings.

⬦ **Project specifications**
⬦ **Deliverable**
⬦ **Contractual Issues**
⬦ **Contact**

TIP

Displaying only one or two levels of headings can make it much easier to find a distant location in a large document. After you find it, you can click its heading and start editing there—in Outline view, or any other view you choose.

CONTROLLING HOW WORD DISPLAYS BODY TEXT

Sometimes headings aren't enough to tell you the gist of a paragraph. You may want to view the entire document, including body text. Choose Show All Headings from the Show Level drop-down box on the Outlining toolbar. The entire document appears, appropriately indented and marked with outlining symbols.

If your document has a lot of body text, though, viewing entire paragraphs takes up so much space that you can lose track of the document's structure and context. Word also allows you to view the first line of text in every paragraph of body text.

To do so, first choose Show All Headings from the Show Level drop-down box to display all heading and body text. Next, click the Show First Line Only button. Word displays the first line of text in every paragraph in the document (see Figure 18.13), including both headings and body text. Ellipses (…) indicate where body text has been cut off.

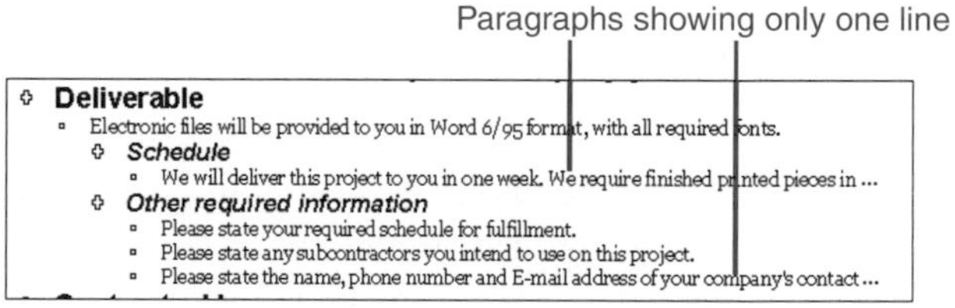

Paragraphs showing only one line

Figure 18.13
Show First Line Only shows the first line of every paragraph, giving you a better idea of the paragraph's contents.

⬦ **Deliverable**
  ▫ Electronic files will be provided to you in Word 6/95 format, with all required fonts.
    ⬦ *Schedule*
      ▫ We will deliver this project to you in one week. We require finished printed pieces in …
    ⬦ *Other required information*
      ▫ Please state your required schedule for fulfillment.
      ▫ Please state any subcontractors you intend to use on this project.
      ▫ Please state the name, phone number and E-mail address of your company's contact …

NOTE

Show First Line Only displays the first lines of paragraphs only if they would otherwise have been displayed in full. For example, if you have chosen Show Level 3 from the Show Level drop-down box to show only the first three levels of headings, Show First Line Only won't display any body text.

HIDING CHARACTER FORMATTING

You've already learned that Word hides paragraph formatting while you're working in Outline view. However, it displays font (character) formatting. If your headings are especially large, or if they are formatted in display typefaces, you might find that character formatting makes working with your outline difficult.

To display text without displaying its formatting, click the Show/Hide Formatting button on the Outlining toolbar. You can see the results in Figure 18.14.

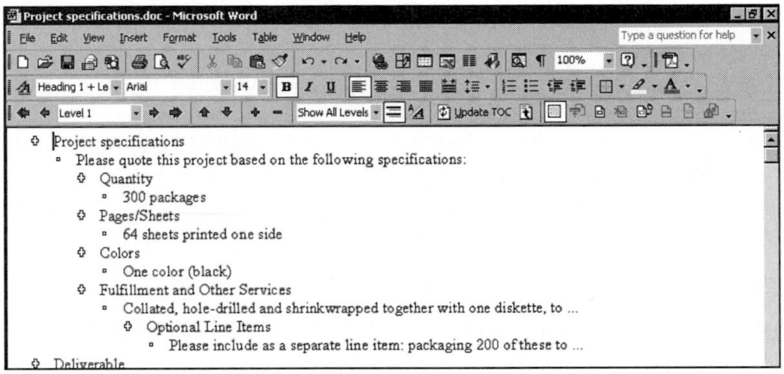

Figure 18.14
Word can display all outline headings and body text as unformatted text.

> **TIP**
>
> If Word displays unformatted text that is too small to read, use the Zoom control on the Standard toolbar to enlarge it.

EXPANDING/COLLAPSING HEADINGS

Sometimes you want to focus on a specific section of your document and review it in much greater detail than the rest. You can double-click the Outline symbol next to any paragraph to alter how it displays body text subordinate to it. Double-clicking on a heading with a + symbol causes Word to display all the headings and body text subordinate to it. Word calls this *expanding* the heading. Notice that the symbol changes to a – sign. Double-click it again and Word hides the subordinate contents. Word calls this *collapsing* the heading. Headings marked with a box cannot be expanded or collapsed.

You can use the Expand and Collapse toolbar buttons on the Outlining toolbar to precisely control the detail at which you view a section of a document so that you can better understand how that section is organized and make appropriate changes to either structure or text.

For instance, imagine that all headings and body text are currently displayed, but you want to view one paragraph at a higher level—with only its first- and second-level headings visible, not lower-level headings or body text.

Click the paragraph you want to adjust to select it. Next, click Collapse to hide all body text. Only headings remain visible. Click Collapse again to hide the lowest heading level subordinate to the paragraph with which you are working. Keep clicking Collapse to hide heading levels until you've reached the level you want.

TIP

If you have a Microsoft IntelliMouse or a compatible mouse with a wheel, you can expand or collapse selected paragraphs using the wheel between the two mouse buttons as detailed here:

1. Click the Outline symbol you want to expand or collapse (or hover the mouse pointer over the symbol until the four-headed arrow pointer appears).
2. Press and hold Shift. Roll the wheel forward to expand the selected text one level at a time; roll it back to collapse it one level at a time.
3. When you're at the level you want, leave the wheel in the current position and release the Shift key.

APPLYING OUTLINE LEVELS TO SPECIFIC TEXT

Throughout this chapter, you've seen that when you change the level of a heading in Outline view, Word also reformats the heading using the appropriate heading style. Fourth-level paragraphs are automatically formatted in Heading 4 style, and so on. Any heading levels you apply anywhere in Word automatically correspond to outline levels in Outline view.

At one time, using heading styles was the only way to define outline levels. Heading 1 was a first-level heading by definition, Heading 2 was a second-level heading, and so on. But there were some problems with this approach.

For example, what if you want to organize the levels of your document using different style names than the heading names Word provides? By default, Outline view displays any style name other than Heading 1–9 at the level of body text. What if you have titles, subtitles, or other elements that should appear at a higher level in your outline?

Or what if you have blocks of body text that you want to be included in the first level of your outline? This text is important, but it's still body text; you don't want to format it using the Heading 1 style.

Word's outline levels solve the problem. You can use them to format any paragraph for any of nine levels of importance (or format it as Body Text, which is the least important of all). Then, when you work in Outline view, those paragraphs are displayed based on their outline level, regardless of their style.

Word offers two ways to format text with an outline level. From the Outlining toolbar, you can choose a level from the Outline Level drop-down box.

18

NOTE

> The Outlining toolbar can be displayed in *any* document view, by choosing View, Toolbars, Outlining; it appears by default in Outline view.

Alternatively, you can set outline levels as you establish other paragraph formatting in the Paragraph dialog box. To do so, first select the paragraphs you want to assign outline levels for. Choose Format, Paragraph. In the Outline Level drop-down list box, choose the outline level you want: Level 1 through 9 or Body Text. Click OK.

NOTE

> You cannot change the outline levels associated with Word's built-in heading styles.

TIP

> You might find you always want text formatted in one of your custom styles to be treated as a first-level outline element. In that case, modify the style to include Outline Level 1 as one of its attributes.

→ For more information about changing the paragraph formatting in a style, **see** "Changing Styles Using the Modify Style Dialog Box," **p. 345**.

PRINTING YOUR OUTLINE

Occasionally, you might want a printed copy of your outline. For example, you might need approval for an outline before proceeding to draft your entire document.

To print an outline, first display your document in Outline view. Next, display the elements of your outline that you want to print. For example, specify how many levels of headings you want and whether you want to collapse or expand any parts of your document. Finally, click the Print button on the Standard toolbar.

 If Word prints pages with uneven page breaks, see "What to Do If Manual Page Breaks Print from Outline View," in the "Troubleshooting" section of this chapter.

USING WORD'S AUTOMATIC OUTLINE NUMBERING

Have you ever had to number multilevel headings in a document—and then change the numbering every time you add or move one of them? In this section, you'll learn how to let Word insert and manage all your multilevel outline numbering for you.

Word includes seven built-in multilevel outline numbering schemes that can handle many of the documents or Web pages you're likely to create. To use one of them, first select the paragraphs you want to number. If you want to add numbering throughout the document, press Ctrl+A to select the entire document. Right-click in the editing window and choose

Bullets and Numbering from the shortcut menu; then click the Outline Numbered tab (see Figure 18.15).

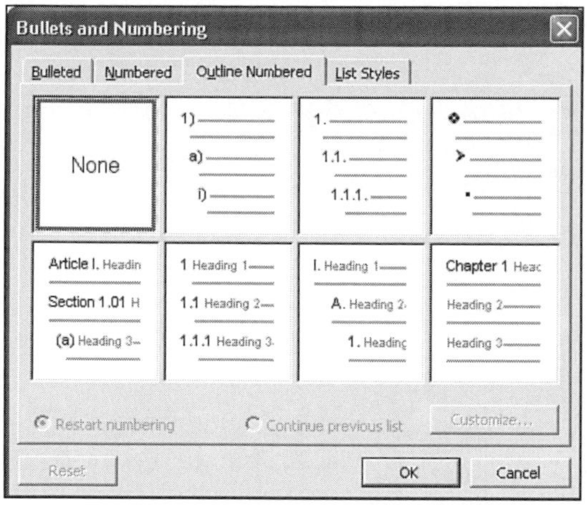

Figure 18.15
The Outline Numbered tab gives you seven choices from which to select; or select one and click Customize to adapt it to your needs.

Bullets and Numbering

| Bulleted | Numbered | Outline Numbered | List Styles |

> NOTE
>
> In addition to the Outline Numbering procedures discussed in this section, Word offers an alternative approach to creating both numbered and unnumbered lists, called List Styles.
>
> If you need to create complex list formats and then reuse them in new documents, you might find List Styles more convenient than Outline Numbering. To learn more about List Styles, see "Using List Styles," later in this chapter.

> CAUTION
>
> If you want to number only headings, not paragraphs of body text, be sure to use one of the numbering schemes in the bottom row of the Outline Numbered tab. The schemes in the top row number both headings and body text.

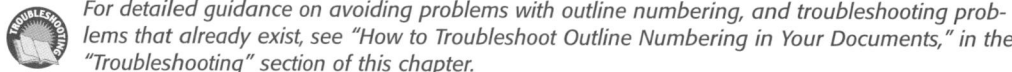

For detailed guidance on avoiding problems with outline numbering, and troubleshooting problems that already exist, see "How to Troubleshoot Outline Numbering in Your Documents," in the "Troubleshooting" section of this chapter.

Choose the scheme you want; then click OK. Figure 18.16 shows outline numbering applied to a sample document.

CREATING CUSTOMIZED OUTLINE NUMBERING

If you're in a position to decide how you want your outline numbering to appear, try to use one of Word's defaults; it saves you some trouble. However, your document may require a numbering scheme that isn't one of Word's default settings. That's where Word's extensive Outline Numbering customization capabilities come in handy.

Figure 18.16
Outline numbering based on the second numbering scheme in the bottom row of the Outline Numbered tab.

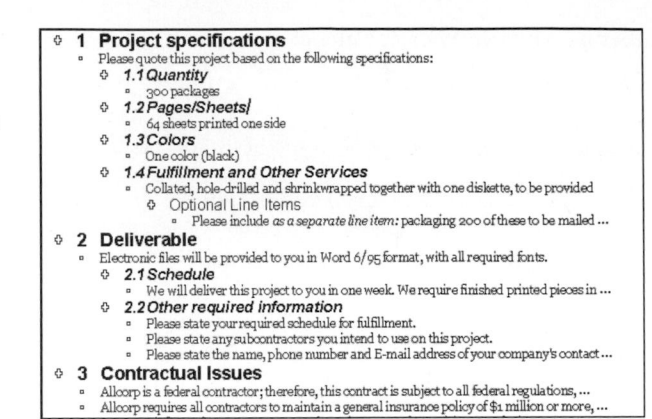

To customize outline numbering, right-click in the editing window and choose Bullets and Numbering from the shortcut menu; then click the Outline Numbered tab.

Select the numbering scheme closest to the one you want and click Customize. The Customize Outline Numbered List dialog box opens (see Figure 18.17). In the Preview box, you can see how the entire outline numbering scheme behaves; any changes you make are shown there immediately.

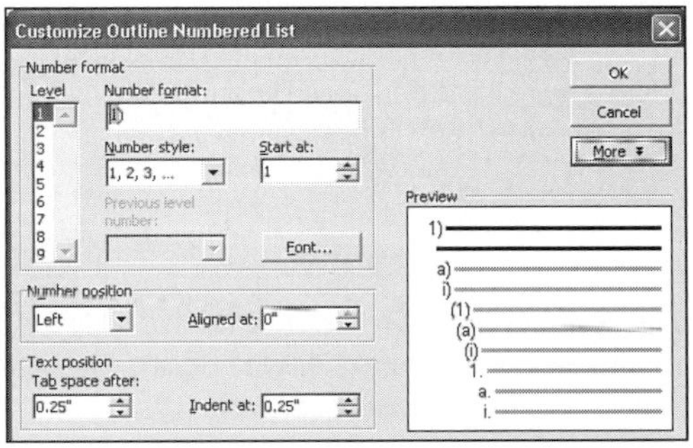

Figure 18.17
In the Customize Outline Numbered List dialog box, you can change and preview virtually any aspect of a numbered list.

CHOOSING THE OUTLINE LEVEL YOU WANT TO CUSTOMIZE

You can customize each of Word's nine levels of outline numbering separately. Choose the level you want from the Level drop-down list box at the upper left. Word displays the current settings for the level you've selected. These settings vary not just based on outline level, but also based on the scheme from which you chose to start.

TIP

It's easy to forget in which level you're working. While you're customizing your outline numbering, glance at the Level drop-down list box every now and then to make sure that you're customizing what you think you're customizing. Or if you prefer, check in the Preview box; the currently selected level is displayed in black while others are displayed in light gray.

Choosing Text to Accompany Your Lettering or Numbering

In the Number Format text box, you can specify the text or symbols you want to appear before or after the number or letter Word inserts next to your heading or paragraph. You do this by editing the text surrounding the grayed-out number or letter.

For instance, in the example shown in Figure 18.17, Word adds a closed parenthesis mark. You might, for example, want to place an open parenthesis mark before the number as well so that Word inserts numbers as (1) rather than 1).

Choosing a Pattern for Your Numbering or Lettering

You can't use the Number Format text box to control the automatic lettering or numbering that Word adds to your document. Rather, you select the lettering or numbering pattern you want Word to choose from the Number Style scroll box. Word's lettering and numbering schemes include these and other options:

- 1, 2, 3,...
- I, II, III,...
- i, ii, iii,...
- A, B, C,...
- a, b, c,...

- 1st, 2nd, 3rd,...
- One, Two, Three,...
- First, Second, Third,...
- 01, 02, 03,...

Word also includes several bullet or symbol styles from which you can choose. If you prefer to choose your own bullet, you can choose New Bullet to select a different bullet character from the Symbol dialog box. Word also offers the option New Picture, which allows you to select a picture of your choice.

CAUTION

Although Word will insert any picture you like, pictures with complex detail (such as photographs of people) will not work well as small bullets.

TIP

You can also choose no lettering and numbering at all. If you choose (none) in the Number Style drop-down list, Word inserts only the text you enter in the Number Format text box. Imagine that you're writing the feature description of a product and you want to add the word "NEW!" before every second-level heading in your document. You could use this feature to do so.

Choosing a Number or Letter from Which to Start

By default, Word assumes that you want your numbering to start at 1 and your lettering to start at A. But that won't always be the case. For example, if you're contributing the fourth chapter of a book, you might want your first-level heading to start with the number 4. In the Start At scroll box located to the right of Number Style, choose the number you want to appear next to the first heading of the current level.

INCLUDING A PREVIOUS OUTLINE LEVEL WITH YOUR NUMBERING

It's common to see documents that include multilevel numbering like that shown in the following examples:

> 1.A.
>
> 4.4.2.
>
> II.C.

You can instruct Word to insert numbering such as this. To do so, in the Previous Level Number drop-down list box (located under Number Style), choose the level of outline numbering that you want to appear next to your lower-level headings or paragraphs. For example, if your first-level headings are numbered (1), (2), (3), and you want your second-level headings to be numbered (1A), (1B), (1C), and so on, select Level 1 in the Previous Level Number box.

Notice that Word doesn't add the surrounding text you included in the Number Format text box for the preceding heading level—just the letter or number itself. Otherwise, you could easily wind up with ((1)A) or something equally unattractive.

NOTE Because there is no level prior to Level 1, the Previous Level Number drop-down list box is grayed out when you're customizing Level 1 headings.

CUSTOMIZING FONT FORMATTING

You can spice up your outline numbers with almost any character formatting you want. From the Customize Outline Numbered List dialog box, click Font. The Font dialog box opens. You can choose any character formatting, spacing, or animation.

NOTE Every font formatting option you normally have is available for numbered headings with two exceptions: You cannot use the Outline or Small Caps text effects.

CUSTOMIZING THE POSITION AND ALIGNMENT OF OUTLINE NUMBERS

Some of Word's built-in schemes left-align all outline numbers, regardless of levels. Other schemes indent outline numbers; the deeper the outline level, the greater the indent. You might want to change these built-in settings. For example, you might like everything about a scheme except the way it indents paragraphs.

Outline numbering alignment is controlled from the Number Position drop-down list box in the Customize Outline Numbered List dialog box. You can choose to left-align, center, or right-align outline numbers. You can also specify against what the outline numbering is aligned. The Aligned At scroll box specifies how far from the left margin the alignment point is. For example, if you choose Centered as the number position and 1" as the Aligned At location, your outline number is centered over a point 1 inch from the left margin.

NOTE

> The Aligned At setting doesn't control whether the entire line is left-aligned, centered, or right-aligned. It only controls how the outline numbering within the line is aligned.
>
> Remember, you have to change the number position separately for each outline level you expect to use.

To see the effect of these changes in your document, switch to Normal or Print Layout view; changes are not accurately reflected in Outline view.

CUSTOMIZING THE POSITION AND ALIGNMENT OF TEXT NEAR OUTLINE NUMBERS

You can also control the distance between the end of Word's automatic outline number and the start of the paragraph's text. To do so, enter a setting in the Indent At scroll box, in the Text Position area of the Customize Outline Numbered List dialog box.

The Indent At setting is measured from the left margin. If the Indent At setting is very small, it may have no effect on the first line of a paragraph because the outline number itself already extends beyond the indent. (Word doesn't overlap an outline number on top of paragraph text.)

Indent At behaves as a hanging indent. In Figure 18.18, you can see first-level headings that are left-aligned at 0.25" with text indented at 1.5".

Figure 18.18
The first-level headings in this sample are left-aligned at 0.25" with text indented at 1.5".

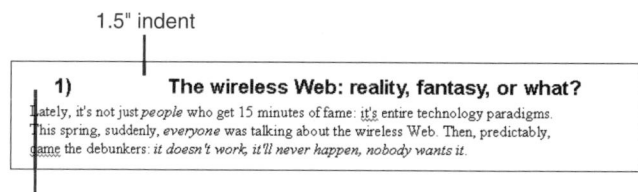

ADVANCED OUTLINE NUMBERING OPTIONS

Some outline numbering customizations are rarely used, but when they're needed, they're needed badly. You can control these by clicking More in the Customize Outline Numbered List dialog box. More options appear (see Figure 18.19).

LINKING AN OUTLINE LEVEL TO A STYLE

The Link Level to Style drop-down list box in the Customize Outline Numbered List dialog box enables you to attach any style to an outline numbering level. That way, whenever

18

you enter or format a paragraph using that style, Word automatically includes numbering, just as it includes all the other formatting associated with the style.

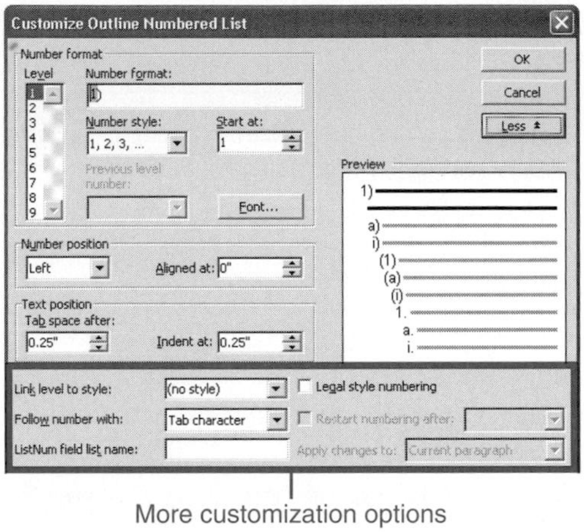

Figure 18.19
You can control more advanced aspects of outline numbering from the "expanded" version of the Customize Outline Numbered List dialog box.

More customization options

CHOOSING A SPACER CHARACTER

The Follow Number With drop-down list box in the Customize Outline Numbered List dialog box enables you to choose the non-editable character that Word places between your outline number and your paragraph text. By default, Word uses a tab, but you can change this to a space, or instruct Word not to insert a character at all.

PLACING TWO OUTLINE NUMBERS ON THE SAME LINE

In some documents, notably contracts, you may be required to include two outline numbers on the same line, as in the following example:

Article I.

    Section 1.01 (i)

        (ii)

Word lets you do this. But to do so, you must work with a little-known field, { LISTNUM }. First, set up your headings as you normally would. Then place your insertion point where you want the first extra heading to appear, and do the following:

1. Choose Insert, Field.
2. Select ListNum from the Field Names box (see Figure 18.20).
3. In the List Name scroll box, choose the name of the list you want to use. Word provides three built-in lists: LegalDefault, NumberDefault, and OutlineDefault. The numbering schemes associated with each of these are shown in Table 18.2.

Figure 18.20
Setting up a
{ *LISTNUM* }
field in the Field
dialog box.

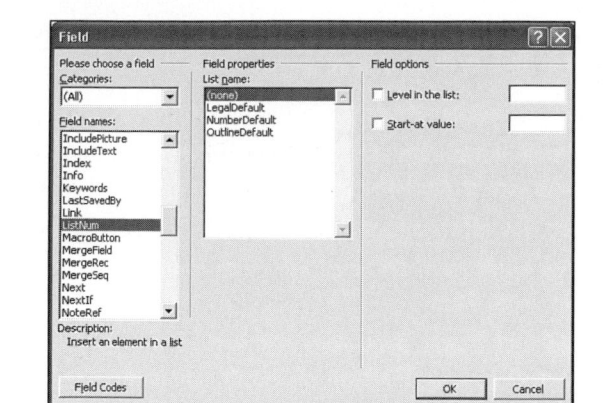

TABLE 18.2   NUMBERING SCHEMES ASSOCIATED WITH WORD'S LISTNUM LISTS

Level	NumberDefault	OutlineDefault	LegalDefault
1	1)	I.	1.
2	a)	A.	1.1.
3	i)	1.	1.1.1.
4	(1)	a)	1.1.1.1.
5	(a)	(1)	1.1.1.1.1.
6	(i)	(a)	1.1.1.1.1.1.
7	1.	(i)	1.1.1.1.1.1.1.
8	a.	(a)	1.1.1.1.1.1.1.1.
9	i.	(i)	1.1.1.1.1.1.1.1.1.

If you don't choose a list name, Word uses NumberDefault, unless you have specified other lists elsewhere in your document, in which case Word uses the last list you specified.

4. Choose which, if any, field options you want to include with your { LISTNUM } field. The first allows you to specify the Level in the List, overriding Word's default settings. The second allows you to set a Start-At Value—a number that Word will use for the first heading that reflects the { LISTNUM } field. If you don't choose a Start-At Value, Word uses 1.

5. Select the entire field and copy it to every other location where you want a heading just like it.

If you view the field results, you can see that you've now added a basic heading, such as

a)

Follow these steps to attach all the headings in the same sequence to a level in your outline numbering scheme so that they look exactly as you want them to:

1. Choose Format, Bullets and Numbering, Outline Numbered.

2. Extra headings are most commonly used with the Section and Article scheme (the scheme on the bottom row at the left). Select this scheme and click Customize.

3. Click More to display the advanced options.

4. Make sure that you're working at the level you want and that the Number Format settings are the way you want them.

5. In the ListNum Field List Name drop-down list box, enter the same word you used in your ListNum field, such as LegalDefault or NumberDefault.

6. Click OK.

You now have normal outline numbering as well as an extra outline number that uses the number format of the level immediately under the first outline number. In other words, if the outline number you applied through Format, Bullets and Numbering is formatted as Level 1, the outline number you applied through Insert, Field is Level 2.

→ To learn more about working with fields, **see** Chapter 23, "Automating Your Documents with Field Codes," **p. 771**.

APPLYING LEGAL STYLE NUMBERING

Some legal documents must use Arabic numbering (1, 2, 3…) throughout. For example, even though Word's numbering scheme for legal documents may specify that Articles use Roman numerals in some levels (for example, Article I, II, and so on), this may not be appropriate for your document. You could change every level's number style to Roman numerals individually. However, Word provides a shortcut; you can simply check Legal Style Numbering in the Customize Outline Numbered List dialog box, and Word does it for you.

INCREMENTING LIST NUMBERS IN A SPECIFIC LEVEL

By default, Word restarts numbering whenever an item in a list follows an item one level above it. You can see this behavior in Figure 18.21.

However, if you clear the Restart Numbering After check box near the bottom of the expanded Customize Outline Numbered List dialog box, Word continues to increment the numbers from where they left off (see Figure 18.22).

In Word, you can also choose which level of heading you want to trigger the restarting of numbering. This choice can be different for each outline level. To change the outline level that triggers renumbering, follow these steps:

1. Make sure that you're working in the outline level you want to change. (This feature is unavailable if you're working in Outline Level 1.)

2. Make sure that the <u>R</u>estart Numbering After check box is checked.

3. Choose the level you want from the <u>R</u>estart Numbering After drop-down box.

4. Click OK.

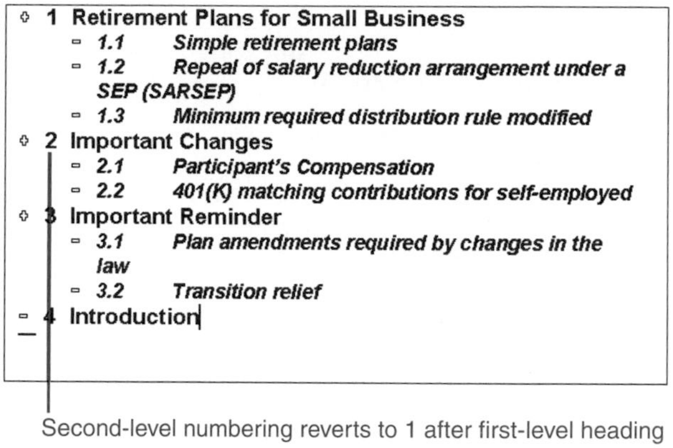

Figure 18.21
By default, Word restarts numbering whenever a lower list level follows a higher list level.

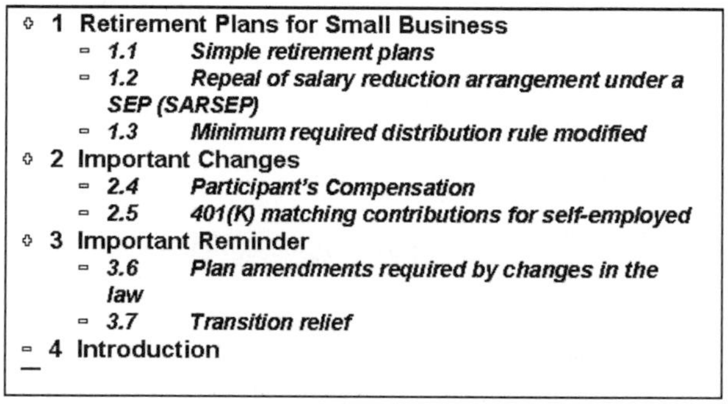

```
◇ 1  Retirement Plans for Small Business
     ▫ 1.1      Simple retirement plans
     ▫ 1.2      Repeal of salary reduction arrangement under a
                SEP (SARSEP)
     ▫ 1.3      Minimum required distribution rule modified
◇ 2  Important Changes
     ▫ 2.1      Participant's Compensation
     ▫ 2.2      401(K) matching contributions for self-employed
◇ 3  Important Reminder
     ▫ 3.1      Plan amendments required by changes in the
                law
     ▫ 3.2      Transition relief
▫ 4  Introduction
```

Second-level numbering reverts to 1 after first-level heading

Figure 18.22
Clearing the <u>R</u>estart Numbering After check box instructs Word to keep incrementing lower-level headings rather than restarting them at 1.

```
◇ 1  Retirement Plans for Small Business
     ▫ 1.1      Simple retirement plans
     ▫ 1.2      Repeal of salary reduction arrangement under a
                SEP (SARSEP)
     ▫ 1.3      Minimum required distribution rule modified
◇ 2  Important Changes
     ▫ 2.4      Participant's Compensation
     ▫ 2.5      401(K) matching contributions for self-employed
◇ 3  Important Reminder
     ▫ 3.6      Plan amendments required by changes in the
                law
     ▫ 3.7      Transition relief
▫ 4  Introduction
```

SPECIFYING WHERE YOUR CHANGES SHOULD APPLY

By default, if you make changes anywhere in the Customize Outline Numbered List dialog box, they apply globally to the entire document as soon as you click OK to exit. However, you might have a portion of a document that you want to treat differently. You have more options available through the Apply <u>C</u>hanges To drop-down list box:

- Choosing Current Paragraph tells Word to apply changes only to the paragraph where your insertion point is currently located.

- Choosing This Point Forward tells Word to apply your changes to the rest of your document, starting at the insertion point.

- Choosing Whole List tells Word to apply your changes to the entire outline.

USING LIST STYLES

Word allows you to create custom lists using the List Styles feature. You can easily create and reuse lists of any kind, both *ordered* lists (such as the alphabetical and numerical lists available in Outline Numbering) and *unordered* lists (such as lists that use different symbols or icons).

Word provides three predefined list styles:

- 1 / 1.1 / 1.1.1 (for purely numeric sequences)
- 1 / a / i (for sequences mixing numbers and letters)
- Article / Section (for sequences such as are commonly used in legal documents)

Each of these list styles corresponds to options you've already seen in the Outline Numbered tab of the Bullets and Numbering dialog box. To use one of these sequences, do the following:

1. Select the paragraphs you want to apply a list style to.
2. Choose Format, Bullets and Numbering.
3. Click the List Styles tab (see Figure 18.23).
4. Select a list style from the List Styles scroll box. Word previews the list style you've chosen in the List Preview box.
5. Click OK. Word applies the list style you've chosen.

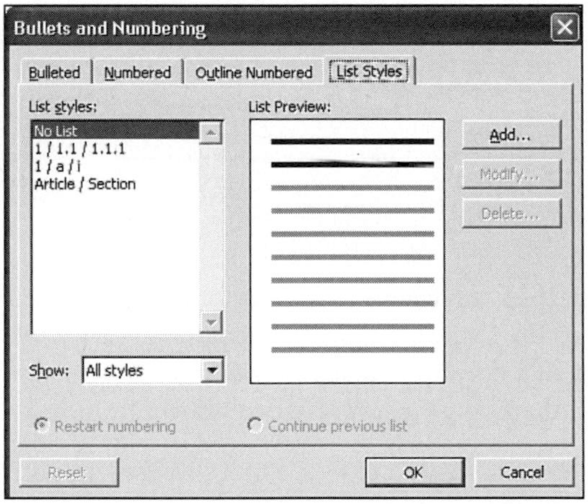

Figure 18.23
You can choose one of three built-in list styles or create your own.

ADDING A NEW LIST STYLE

Sometimes you might want to create a list style of your own. For example, you might want to use a set of bullets or symbols drawn from the Wingdings or Webdings font, or precisely control numbering in ways that cannot easily be done through the Customize Outline Numbered List dialog box. To create a new list style, follow these steps:

1. Select the paragraphs you want to apply a list style to.

2. Choose Format, Bullets and Numbering.

3. Click the List Styles tab.

4. Click Add. The New Style dialog box appears (see Figure 18.24).

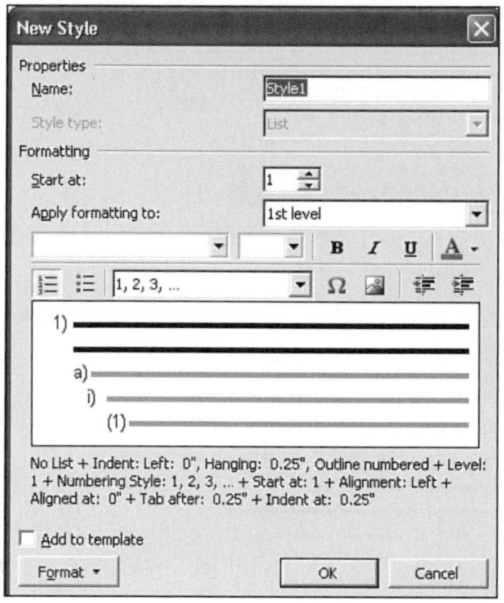

Figure 18.24
You can create a new list style in the New Style dialog box.

5. In the Name text box, enter a descriptive name for your list style that will help you identify it in the future.

6. In the Start At spin box, specify where in the sequence you want Word to begin numbering; by default, Word begins with the first number, element, symbol, or picture you define.

7. In the Apply Formatting To drop-down box, specify which outline level you want to create formatting for.

8. Use the formatting tools on the following two rows to specify formatting for the outline level you just chose. For example, if you want to specify a different font, choose it from the Font drop-down box. If you want to use a specific symbol, click the Insert Symbol button and choose it from the Symbol dialog box.

   You can control the font, font size, whether text is boldface and/or italic, whether your list style uses Latin or Asian character sets, or whether numbering or bullets are included. You can also start from a built-in sequence (such as 1, 2, 3... or First, Second, Third...), or use pictures or symbols in place of numbers and letters.

9. If you want to store your new list style in the template associated with the current document, check the Add to Template check box. If you plan to reuse the list style in other documents that use the same template, it makes sense to check this box.

18

10. If you want to control formatting for a different outline level, choose the next outline level from the Apply Formatting To drop-down box. Then repeat step 8.

11. When you have finished setting formatting for all outline levels, click OK.

MODIFYING AN EXISTING LIST STYLE

Word allows you to modify both its existing list styles and any you may have created. To do so, choose Format, Bullets and Numbering, and click the List Styles tab. Select the style you want to change; then click Modify. The Modify Style dialog box appears (see Figure 18.25).

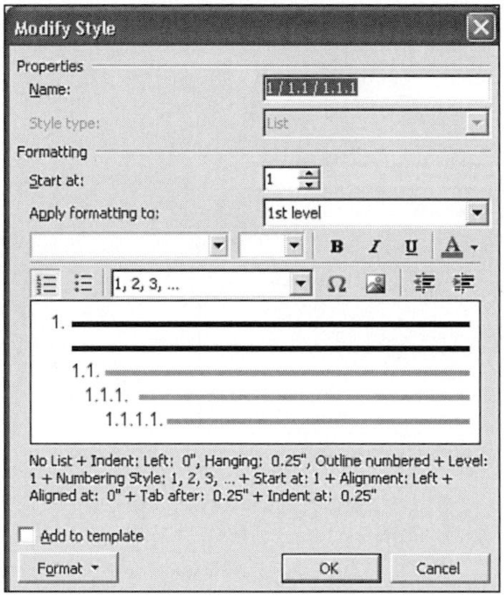

Figure 18.25
You can modify a list style through the Modify Style dialog box.

This dialog box offers identical choices to the New Style dialog box discussed in the preceding section. The current name of the list style is displayed in the Name text box; if you want to create a second list style instead of simply modifying the one that already exists, enter a new name there.

As with the New Style dialog box, you can use the Modify Style dialog box to change formatting for each outline level individually. You can control the font, font size, whether text is boldface and/or italic, whether your list style uses Latin or Asian character sets, or whether numbering or bullets are included. You can also start from one of Word's built-in sequences, or use pictures or symbols in place of numbers and letters. Finally, if you have not done so already, you can add your list style to the template associated with the current document.

When you have finished making the changes you want to make, choose OK.

NOTE

> If you want to delete a custom list style you created, display the List Styles tab of the Bullets and Numbering dialog box, choose the list style in the List Styles scroll box, and click Delete. Click Yes to confirm that you want to delete the style.
>
> You cannot delete list styles that are built into Word.

TROUBLESHOOTING

WHAT TO DO IF YOUR OUTLINING TOOLBAR DISAPPEARS

First make sure that you're in Outline view by clicking the Outline View button on the status bar. If the Outlining toolbar is still not visible, choose View, Toolbars, Outlining to display it.

HOW TO COPY ONLY A DOCUMENT'S HEADINGS WITHOUT COPYING ALL THE SUBORDINATE TEXT

You can't, but here's a workaround that accomplishes the same goal. Insert a table of contents in your document that does not contain page numbers. Select it and press Ctrl+Shift+F9 to convert it into text. You can now cut and paste it to any location or document you want.

WHAT TO DO IF MANUAL PAGE BREAKS PRINT FROM OUTLINE VIEW

One problem with printing outlines is that Word leaves manual page breaks in—and these can create pages that have only a few headings on them. The only way to avoid this is to temporarily remove the page breaks. You can do so by using Edit, Replace to replace page breaks with no text at all. (Entering ^m in the Find What box tells Word to search for a page break.)

Print the document; then click Undo to restore the page breaks.

Alternatively, save a copy of the document, delete the page breaks, and print from the copy.

HOW TO NUMBER HEADINGS, BUT NOT BODY TEXT

Outline Numbering has been redesigned to number body text paragraphs as well as headings by default. However, if (in the Outline Numbered tab of the Bullets and Numbering dialog box) you choose a numbering scheme that includes the word "Heading," Word numbers only headings.

HOW TO TROUBLESHOOT OUTLINE NUMBERING IN YOUR DOCUMENTS

Multilevel outline numbering in Word documents can be confusing, and can sometimes deliver unexpected results that are difficult to troubleshoot. In this section, we offer some high-level guidance, as well as Web links to even more detailed discussions of Word numbering problems.

Word sometimes changes its outline numbering scheme inexplicably when you change computers, or after you make additional numbering customizations elsewhere in your document. If this occurs, you've fallen victim to a feature that was architected in a very confusing manner, and is presented to you with an equally confusing interface.

When you display the Outline Numbered tab of the Bullets and Numbering dialog box, Word displays a *List Gallery* containing the first seven outline numbering schemes available to it. When you apply outline numbering by selecting one of these, Word does *not* internally store all the details of the outline numbering scheme. Rather, it stores the position of the item you chose; for example, top row, third from the left. Unfortunately, the schemes in the List Gallery can shift position as you customize them, and they may differ on others' computers—so a document opened on a different computer may display a different outline numbering scheme.

If you're having trouble with this, choose Format, Bullets and Numbering, Outline Numbered. Select the numbering scheme that is causing problems, and click Reset. Word then restores the numbering scheme that was originally located in that position on the List Gallery. If you've been unsuccessfully messing with outline numbering for some time, you may want to individually Reset every position in the Outline Numbered tab.

Here are some additional tips for making outline numbering work properly:

- Link outline numbering directly to heading styles, instead of starting out from the Bullets and Numbering dialog box. Choose Format, Styles and Formatting to display the Styles and Formatting task pane. Right-click on a style, and choose Modify. Click Format, Numbering in the Modify Style dialog box. The Bullets and Numbering dialog box now opens. Click Outline Numbered. Then, choose or customize an outline numbering scheme that will be associated with your heading style throughout the document.

- Don't mix outline numbering created by modifying styles (as described in the preceding bullet) with outline numbering applied directly through the Format, Bullets and Numbering dialog box.

- Create your outline numbering scheme first, in its entirety, *before* you begin editing your document.

- Never delete a style you've incorporated in your outline numbering scheme.

- Don't copy outline numbered paragraphs between documents. If you must copy numbered text between paragraphs, when you paste it into the new document, choose Keep Text Only from the Paste Options button, and reapply the outline numbering manually.

- If you apply outline numbering to several paragraphs, remove it, and then reapply it, Word may reapply numbering to only one paragraph: the paragraph with the insertion point. This can occur when outline numbering formats have been customized to link to specific document styles. You need to first reset paragraph formatting before you reapply outline numbering. To do so, select *all* the paragraphs you removed outline numbering from, and press Ctrl+Q to clear paragraph formatting. With the paragraphs selected, choose Format, Bullets and Numbering; click the Outline Numbered tab; choose an Outline Numbered format; and click OK.

- Consider using { SEQ } fields instead of outline numbering.
- After you get outline numbering exactly the way you want it, consider saving a copy of your document as a template that you can use whenever you need the same outline numbering in another document. (Delete all text before you save as a template.)

If you find that you're still having trouble with numbering, review the following Web resources:

```
www.mvps.org/word/FAQs/Numbering/WordsNumberingExplained.htm

www.shaunakelly.com/word/numbering/OutlineNumbering.html

www.addbalance.com/usersguide/numbering.htm

www.microsystems.com/fra_sevenlawsofoutlinenumbering.htm
```

If you're still having problems, you might want to consider a third-party Word add-in for outline numbering, such as Outliner from DocTools (www.doc-tools.com).

CHAPTER 19

MASTER DOCUMENTS: CONTROL AND SHARE EVEN THE LARGEST DOCUMENTS

In this chapter

THE ADVANTAGES OF MASTER DOCUMENTS

A master document is a document that provides a gathering place for multiple smaller documents—called *subdocuments*. Each of these subdocuments can be developed and edited separately, by separate users on separate computers. All of these subdocuments can be controlled centrally, through the master document. Subdocuments can be divided and combined as needed by the project's participants.

Master documents make it possible for many people to work on parts of a document while one person still controls the entire document.

After you've created a master document, you can reopen it any time you want, displaying all the subdocuments together. This gives you a quick, efficient way to see how all the components of your document relate to each other, even if individual subdocuments have been heavily edited by your colleagues since you viewed them last. You can use Word's navigation tools as if you were working with a conventional document rather than a collection of documents. You can also handle all the tasks that generally should be performed on the entire document at the same time, such as the following:

- Ensuring consistent formatting throughout
- Spell checking and ensuring consistent spelling of specialized terms
- Building an index and a table of contents
- Reorganizing the document, moving large blocks of text among chapters
- Printing

→ To learn more about creating a table of contents in a master document, **see** "Creating a Table of Contents, an Index, or Cross-References for a Master Document," **p. 673**.

The master document doesn't merely gather the subdocuments in one place: It integrates them, enabling you to set unified styles and document templates that can apply to every subdocument. Using master documents thereby helps you maintain visual consistency throughout large documents, even if many authors are contributing to them.

No matter what formatting is attached to styles in your subdocuments, when those subdocuments are displayed as part of a master document, they all use the formatting associated with styles in the master document's template. So if you stay with a basic set of headings and other styles, you're virtually assured of consistent formatting.

In addition, when you display subdocuments as part of a master document, all cross-references, footnotes, outline numbers, and page numbers are automatically updated to reflect the new location of the subdocument within the larger document. In fact, master documents behave very much like regular Word documents. You can format them, save them, and print them just as you would any other document.

Master documents are extremely helpful in organizing complex projects. As you'll learn later, you can organize a project using a Word outline, divide the project into subdocuments, and delegate those subdocuments to your colleagues as needed.

Because Word usually works faster when editing smaller documents, working in subdocuments rather than a much larger main document can significantly improve Word's performance during mundane editing tasks. This, of course, tends to be most important if you are using a slower computer.

CAUTION

> Before going further, it's worth pointing out that master documents have traditionally been buggier than most other Word features. We've found them fairly reliable thus far in Word 2003; however, if you choose to use them, it makes sense to save backups often.
>
> Corruption in master documents typically occurs because Word can encounter problems resolving inconsistencies among the master and subdocuments. You can improve their reliability by doing the following:
>
> - Limiting the amount of text in the master document itself: for example, only a table of contents and/or an index.
> - Opening subdocuments using File, Open instead of through the master document except when necessary
> - Using the same template for both your master document and your subdocuments
>
> For more information about issues that have arisen with master documents, see `www.addbalance.com/word/masterdocuments.htm` and `www.raycomm.com/techwhirl/masterdocs.doc`.
>
> If you find yourself encountering difficulties with master documents, you may want to consider a third-party alternative: the free Tech-Tav macro suite, available at `www.tech-tav.com/guides.html` is worth a look.

CREATING MASTER DOCUMENTS AND SUBDOCUMENTS

19

If you've learned how to use outlines, you're halfway to understanding master documents too. Master documents closely resemble outlines, and you control them in Outline view, using the buttons on Word's Outlining toolbar. The primary difference: You're outlining material that comes from several documents rather than one.

→ To learn more about outlining, **see** Chapter 18, "Outlining: Practical Techniques for Organizing Any Document," **p. 619**.

You can create master documents in two ways:

- You can do it from scratch, by outlining your document and then dividing it into subdocuments (see Figure 19.1).
- You can make separate existing documents part of your master document (see Figure 19.2).

Whenever possible, you're better off creating your master documents from scratch. It's quick, it's easy, and you have total control over all the subdocuments you create. If you start from scratch, it's also much easier to maintain consistency throughout the editing process. Here's why:

Figure 19.1
Creating a master document from scratch.

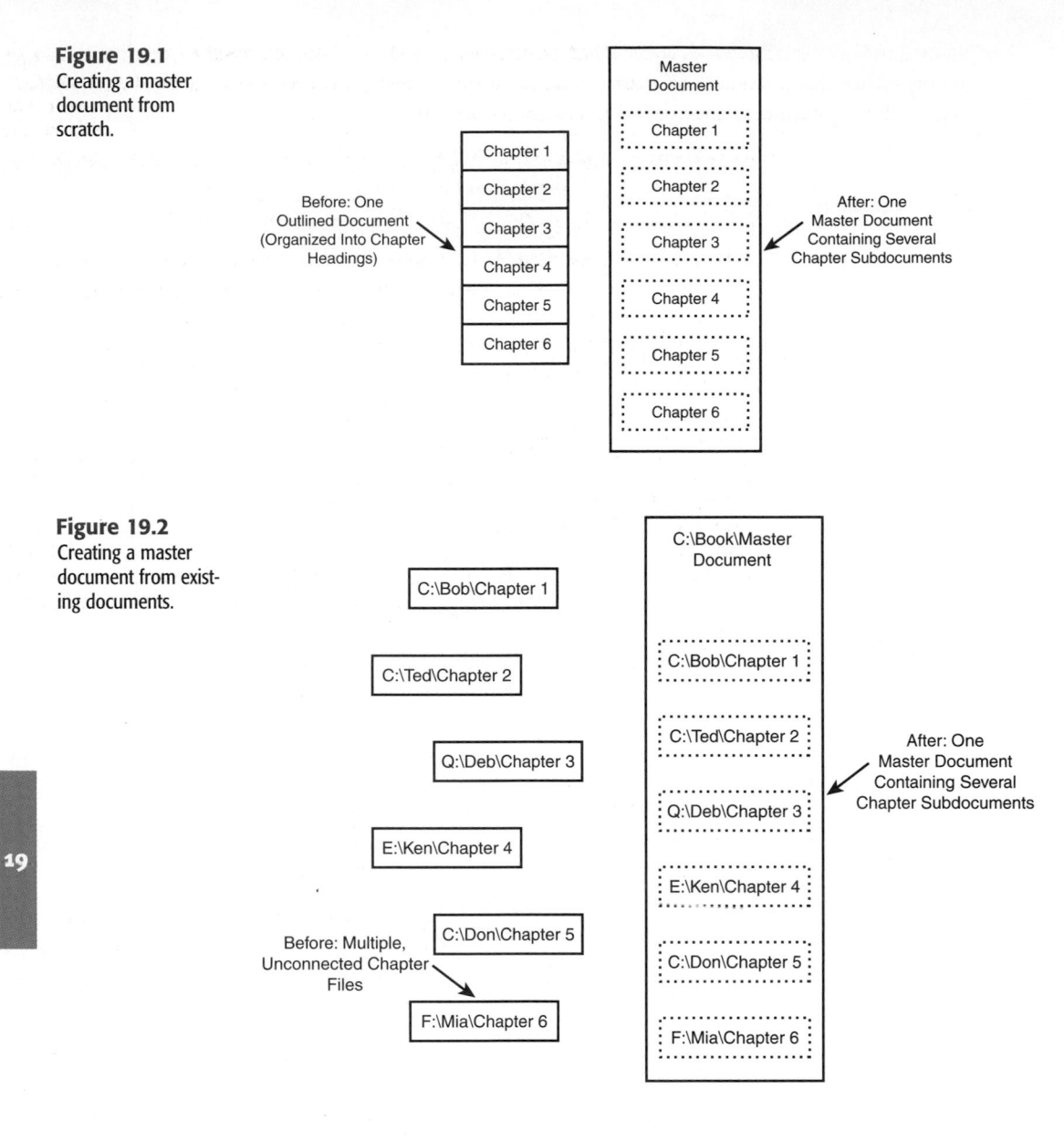

Figure 19.2
Creating a master document from existing documents.

- You usually don't have to worry about users working from different templates. Because all your subdocuments automatically share the same template, they also share the same styles, AutoText entries, and macros. In addition to promoting consistency, this can make your master documents more reliable.

- You don't have to worry about tracking the locations of your subdocuments. You can just place them all in the same folder on your local hard disk or shared network drive, and tell people to leave them there.

■ You usually don't have to worry about people inadvertently editing the wrong version of the file. There is only one: the subdocument you created.

However, you may not always have the luxury of starting from scratch. You may be asked to build on existing text—updating it, including new topics, broadening coverage with new chapters. So Word makes it easy to incorporate existing documents into your master document.

You may also find yourself taking a hybrid approach: outlining the entire master document from scratch, inserting existing documents that contain some of the content you need, and reorganizing the master document to reflect the contents you've added from existing documents.

Finally, remember that a master document can contain anything a regular document can, while containing subdocuments at the same time. So you might choose to create and edit some of your text in your master document, and use subdocuments for only the chapters others are creating.

CREATING A NEW MASTER DOCUMENT FROM SCRATCH

Because a master document is simply a document that contains subdocuments, adding subdocuments to any normal document transforms it into a master document.

So, to create a master document from scratch, start by opening a blank document and clicking the Outline View button on the status bar (or choosing View, Outline). Word switches into Outline view and displays the Outlining toolbar, which includes both outlining tools and master document tools.

NOTE

Prior to Word 2000, you were required to select Master Document view to work with master documents. In Word 2003, master document tools are built into Outline view so there is no Master Document option on the View menu.

There is still, however, a Master Document view. You can access it by clicking the Master Document View button on the Outlining toolbar. Using Master Document view makes the borders between your subdocuments easier to see and work with.

Figure 19.3 shows the master document tools at the right side of the Outlining toolbar. You'll find tools for inserting, removing, and managing the subdocuments that are the components of a master document. Each tool is explained in Table 19.1.

NOTE

The Master Document toolbar buttons appear grayed out if all your subdocuments are collapsed, or if they are expanded but locked to prevent them from being edited.

Figure 19.3
The Master Document toolbar includes Word's tools for managing subdocuments and master documents.

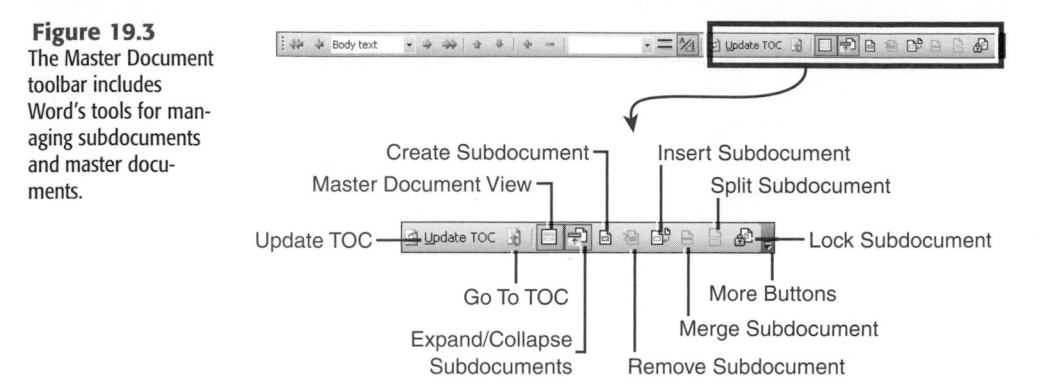

TABLE 19.1	MASTER DOCUMENT BUTTONS ON THE OUTLINING TOOLBAR
Name	**What It Does**
Update TOC	Updates a table of contents in your document
Go to TOC	Moves the cursor to the table of contents in your document
Master Document View	Toggles between Master Document view and displaying subdocuments as sections within the same document
Expand/Collapse Subdocuments	Toggles between showing all the contents of a master document and showing hyperlinks to the subdocuments in place of the subdocuments themselves
Create Subdocument	Creates a new subdocument from selected text, or creates multiple subdocuments from text selections that incorporate several headings of the same level
Remove Subdocument	Eliminates a subdocument and places its text in the master document
Insert Subdocument	Inserts an existing document as a subdocument in the current master document
Merge Subdocument	Combines two or more subdocuments into one
Split Subdocument	Divides one subdocument into two, at the insertion point
Lock Document	Toggles between locking and unlocking a subdocument

Now that you've opened a new document and displayed it in Outline view, you can create and organize the outline of your document, using Word's outlining tools, just as you would if you weren't intending to create a master document. (See Chapter 18 for details on outlining.)

TIP

> If your outline needs to be approved, get the approvals you need before you divide it into subdocuments—and especially before you delegate those subdocuments to individual contributors.

CREATING SUBDOCUMENTS

After you have the outline the way you want it, you can divide it into subdocuments. If you set up your document properly, Word can organize your entire document into subdocuments with one click. Of course, you can also set up individual subdocuments manually, if you prefer.

The quickest and most intuitive way to set up subdocuments is to create an outline in which every first-level heading—in other words, every paragraph formatted with the Heading 1 style—corresponds to a new subdocument.

For example, if you're writing a manual or book, you might format chapter titles with the Heading 1 style so that each subdocument you create corresponds to a separate chapter. Of course, these subdocuments contain all the headings and body text subordinate to the Heading 1 paragraph with which they start.

CAUTION

> When Word creates subdocuments, it places continuous section breaks between them. Therefore, after you've established subdocuments, you need to be aware of how each section handles headers, footers, and page numbering. It's usually best to establish these settings globally for your whole document before you divide the document into subdocuments.
>
> Because the section breaks Word inserts are continuous section breaks, you may want to add manual page breaks at the end of each section to start the next section on a new page.

19

To create a subdocument for every Heading 1 style in your document, select all the sections that include the Heading 1 main headings you want to break into subdocuments. (Be sure to select all the subordinate text under the Heading 1 subheadings you are dividing.) Then, click the Create Subdocument button on the Master Document toolbar.

CAUTION

> Don't use Heading 1 style for any block of text you don't want set apart in its own subdocument.

Word divides the entire document into subdocuments automatically, starting each new subdocument at the point where it finds another paragraph formatted as Heading 1.

The first time you save the document after dividing it, each subdocument will be saved with a different name. After you divide the documents, the text is stored in each subdocument rather than the master document.

→ To learn more about how subdocuments are saved, **see** "Saving a Master Document," **p. 663**.

> **TIP**
>
> You can collapse or expand subdocuments by pressing Ctrl+\. This is the only master document tool with a corresponding keyboard shortcut.

CREATING MULTIPLE SUBDOCUMENTS FROM LOWER-LEVEL HEADINGS

Although you're most likely to use Heading 1 styles as the dividing lines between your subdocuments, you can divide subdocuments by lower-level headings as well to share smaller chunks of your document for editing by colleagues. You can select any group of headings, as long as

- Your selection includes more than one heading of the same level.
- The first heading in your selection is styled with the heading level you want to use as your dividing line between subdocuments.

For example, you could select all the Heading 2 paragraphs (and subordinate text) beneath a single Heading 1. If you created subdocuments based on such a selection, Word would provide a separate subdocument for each Heading 2.

When might you divide a document based on lower-level headings? Perhaps you're making a sales proposal that covers a wide range of products, each to be covered in only a page. You can create subdocuments for second- or third-level headings corresponding to each product.

> **TIP**
>
> After you create these small, modular subdocuments, you can insert them in future documents as well. As your products are updated, have your product managers revise and resave their subdocuments. You can then include these subdocuments in future proposals and be assured that you're including the most current information about each product.
>
> You might even record macros that automatically insert each subdocument, and attach these macros to a special toolbar so that your salespeople can insert current information about any specific product with a single click.

CREATING A SINGLE SUBDOCUMENT

You don't have to create multiple subdocuments at the same time. You can create a single subdocument from any block of text that includes one top-level heading. For example, if you select a Heading 1 paragraph and all the subordinate headings and text under it, Word creates a single subdocument based on all the headings and text you selected. To do so, select the text you want to incorporate in a subdocument. After the text is selected, click Create Subdocument.

CAUTION

As mentioned earlier, however, if you inadvertently include two Heading 1 paragraphs within your selection, Word creates two corresponding subdocuments. Similarly, if you neglect to include a Heading 1, but include several Heading 2 paragraphs, Word creates separate subdocuments for each Heading 2.

TIP

Usually, the quickest way to select text for inclusion in a subdocument is to click the outline symbol next to the highest-level heading you want to use. Word then selects all text subordinate to that heading.

If you want to build a subdocument that doesn't have neat Heading level boundaries, such as including a block of text with multiple Heading 1's, you need to first create the subdocument using just the initial heading level. You can then move elements of your outline around, across subdocument boundaries. Techniques for refining the organization of your subdocuments are covered later in this chapter, in the "Reorganizing a Master Document" section.

TAKING A CLOSER LOOK AT SUBDOCUMENTS

Within the master document, Word marks the subdocuments you create in two ways (see Figure 19.4). First, text in a subdocument is surrounded by a thin, gray border. Second, a subdocument icon appears at the upper left of the first heading in the subdocument.

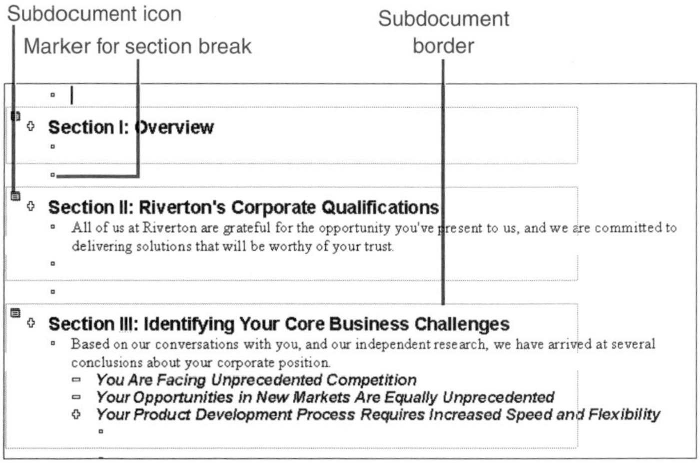

Figure 19.4
Text that has been selected as a subdocument is bordered with a gray rectangle; a subdocument icon also appears at its upper left.

Subdocument icon
Marker for section break
Subdocument border

Section I: Overview

Section II: Riverton's Corporate Qualifications
  All of us at Riverton are grateful for the opportunity you've present to us, and we are committed to delivering solutions that will be worthy of your trust.

Section III: Identifying Your Core Business Challenges
  Based on our conversations with you, and our independent research, we have arrived at several conclusions about your corporate position.
    You Are Facing Unprecedented Competition
    Your Opportunities in New Markets Are Equally Unprecedented
    Your Product Development Process Requires Increased Speed and Flexibility

In Master Document view, you can select the entire subdocument by clicking this subdocument icon. You can open the subdocument in its own editing window by double-clicking the subdocument icon. Later in this chapter, you'll learn more about organizing, formatting, and editing subdocuments.

When Word creates subdocuments, it separates them by adding continuous section breaks, which are section breaks that start the next section on the same page. As with any section breaks, these allow you to create separate formatting for each section—for example, different margins, paper size, borders, headers and footers, and column arrangements. You can delete the section breaks without damaging your subdocuments, but if you plan to adjust these types of formatting in each section, you should leave them alone.

If you switch to Normal view (see Figure 19.5), you can see the section break markers.

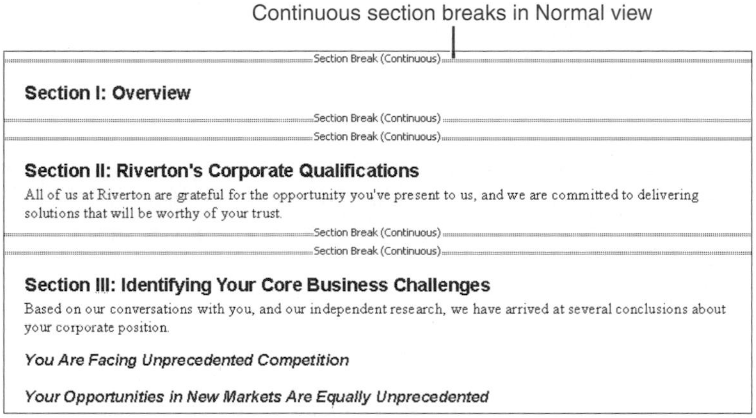

Figure 19.5
In Normal view, Word separates subdocuments with section break markers.

Continuous section breaks in Normal view

Section Break (Continuous)

Section I: Overview
Section Break (Continuous)
Section Break (Continuous)

Section II: Riverton's Corporate Qualifications
All of us at Riverton are grateful for the opportunity you've present to us, and we are committed to delivering solutions that will be worthy of your trust.
Section Break (Continuous)
Section Break (Continuous)

Section III: Identifying Your Core Business Challenges
Based on our conversations with you, and our independent research, we have arrived at several conclusions about your corporate position.

You Are Facing Unprecedented Competition

Your Opportunities in New Markets Are Equally Unprecedented

→ For more information about sections and section formatting, **see** Chapter 5, "Controlling Page Features," **p. 157**.

TRANSFORMING AN EXISTING DOCUMENT INTO A MASTER DOCUMENT

Until now, this chapter has discussed creating a new master document from scratch. However, what if you already have a document you want to turn into a master document? Follow these steps:

1. Open the document and choose View, Outline to display it in Outline view.

2. Use Word's outline tools to organize the document, if necessary. Ideally, arrange the document so that each first-level heading corresponds to one of the subdocuments you want to create. If the document hasn't used heading styles, consider using Find and Replace, or possibly AutoFormat, to insert them.

3. Create your subdocuments using one of the methods described in the previous sections. You can create them one at a time by selecting text and clicking the Create Subdocument button on the Master Document toolbar. Or if you've been able to

organize your document by first-level headings, select the entire document and click Create Subdocument to create all your subdocuments at the same time.

WORKING WITH MASTER DOCUMENT AND SUBDOCUMENT FILES

After you've created your master document and subdocuments, the next step is to begin working with them. In the following sections, we'll show you the fundamentals of opening, saving, and editing master documents and subdocuments. Then, later in the chapter, you'll learn essential techniques for reorganizing them.

SAVING A MASTER DOCUMENT

You can save a master document the same way you save any other Word file: by clicking the Save button, pressing Ctrl+S, or choosing File, Save.

When you save a master document that contains new subdocuments, Word creates new files for each subdocument and stores them in the same folder as the master document. Word automatically names your subdocuments, using the first letters or phrase at the beginning of each subdocument. If the names of more than one subdocument would be identical, or if another identical filename already exists in the same folder, Word adds a number to distinguish the files. For example, if the subdocuments all start with the word "Chapter," they would be named

```
Chapter.doc
Chapter1.doc
Chapter2.doc
```

Word is capable of creating subdocument names that are exceptionally long: up to 229 characters. However, Word will stop a subdocument name whenever it encounters punctuation—even an apostrophe. The result? You can have one subdocument name that is a full sentence long, and another one named Don, from a heading that starts with the word "Don't."

CAUTION

Double-check the filenames Word chooses to make sure that they're appropriate. If you save a subdocument named Section 1 to a folder that already has a file named Section1, Word renames your file Section2. Then it names your Section 2 subdocument Section3. The result could be confusing.

If you create your master document from a clean outline, by default, the master document itself will be named after the first Heading 1 entry. If that Heading 1 entry is "Chapter 1," the first subdocument may be called Chapter 2 even if it contains the first chapter on your document. If you want, you can choose a different name when you save the master document.

continues

continued

If Word ever chooses a subdocument name that you don't like, open the subdocument from within the master document, choose File, Save As, and rename it. The master document will then contain the renamed file.

If you insert an existing document into a master document—making it a subdocument—Word retains the existing document's name instead of assigning it a new one when you save the master document and all subdocuments.

The existing document also stays in its previous location on your hard disk or network. To simplify management of the document, you should copy the existing document into the master document folder *before* you insert it into your master document. By doing so, you can ensure that all subdocuments in your master document remain in the same folder. This makes it easier to track your master document, makes it less likely that you will misplace or lose the subdocument, and makes it easier to ensure that all appropriate users have access to the subdocuments they need to work with.

To avoid this problem, consider setting up a new folder that will contain both your master document and your subdocuments.

➔ To learn more about working with subdocuments from within a master document, **see** "Editing a Subdocument from Within the Master Document," **p. 665**.

SAVING A SUBDOCUMENT

When you save a master document, Word also saves all subdocuments. You can also save any individual subdocument you have opened from within the master document, using any of Word's tools for saving files (the Save button on the Standard toolbar, the Ctrl+S keyboard shortcut, or the File, Save menu command).

After you create and save a subdocument, Word stores its contents in the subdocument—not in the master document. This has two important implications.

First, as you'll see shortly, it means that you (or a colleague) can edit a subdocument without opening the master document. You simply open the subdocument as you would any other Word document. Assuming that nobody else is using the file, nothing tells you you're working on a subdocument rather than a normal document.

Second, it means that if you delete a subdocument, move it, or rename it—without doing so from within the master document—the subdocument will disappear from the master document. The link will still appear in the master document, but when you try to expand the subdocument to view its contents, Word will display a message that the file is missing.

CAUTION

Users who don't realize they are working on subdocuments can cause problems for others who are responsible for managing a master document containing those subdocuments. For example, a user may rename a file or save it somewhere else, and, suddenly,

> a gap appears in the master document. Or worse, the user–working outside the master document–resaves the file under another name. Then, the old version of the file stays in the master document (because a link to that file still exists)–and nobody ever realizes that there's a newer, revised version.

OPENING A MASTER DOCUMENT

After you create, save, and close a master document, you can open it the same way you open any other document. When you first open a master document, however, rather than headings that correspond to the top-level headings of each subdocument, you see hyperlinks that show the name and location of each subdocument in your master document (see Figure 19.6).

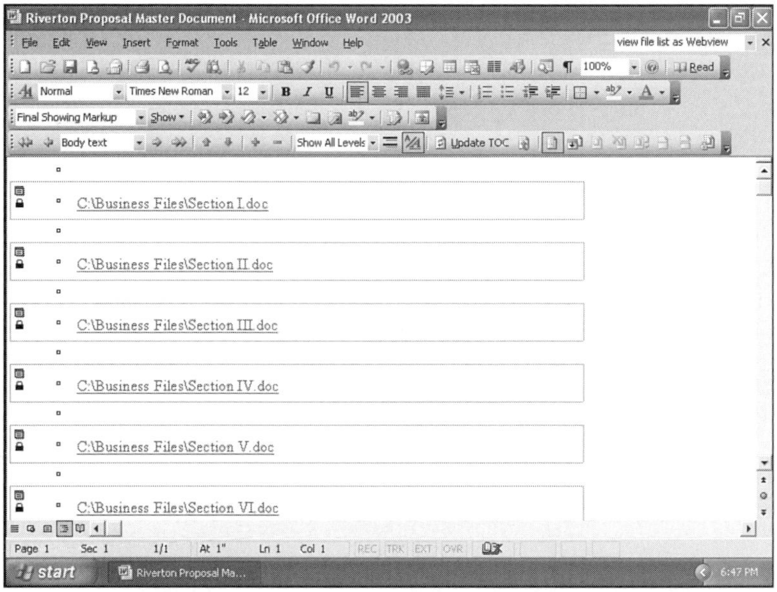

Figure 19.6
When you reopen a master document, you see hyperlinks to each subdocument

If you prefer to see formatted headings and text rather than hyperlinks, click the Expand Subdocuments button. You can then use Outlining toolbar buttons such as Show Heading 1 and Show Heading 2 to control how much detail you see in your subdocuments.

EDITING A SUBDOCUMENT FROM WITHIN THE MASTER DOCUMENT

After you've opened the master document, you can either edit individual subdocuments from within the master document or display only the subdocument for editing.

CAUTION

> For reliability reasons, some Word experts recommend opening subdocuments through File, Open whenever possible, not from the master document. However, as discussed throughout this section, at times you will have little practical alternative but to work through the master document.

To display an individual subdocument file for editing, Ctrl+click on the hyperlink. The subdocument now appears in its own window. Section breaks appear at the end of the document, as discussed earlier. The original master document remains open even while you're editing a subdocument this way. If you are using Word 2003's default "single document interface," in which each open document gets its own taskbar icon, you can view the original master document at any time by clicking its taskbar icon (see Figure 19.7).

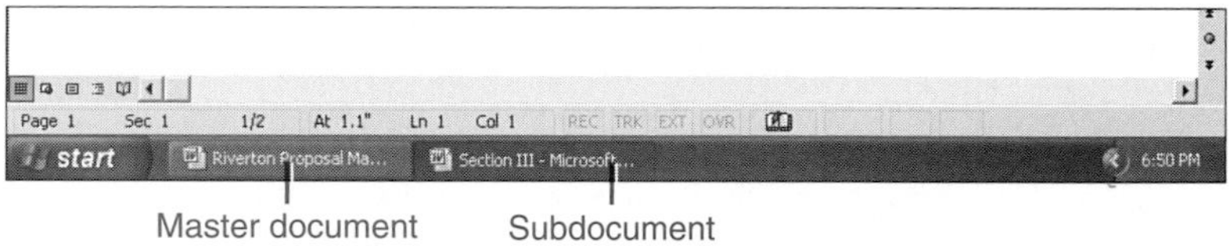

Figure 19.7
You can switch from a subdocument to a master document by clicking on the master document's icon in the taskbar.

Master document   Subdocument

NOTE

> Hyperlinks in a master document change color from blue to magenta after you Ctrl+click them once to open them. However, when you close the master document, they revert to blue and will appear blue the next time you open it. Moreover, if you edit and save a subdocument, its hyperlink also reverts to blue.

Sometimes, you may prefer to edit a subdocument with the rest of the master document's contents visible. For example, you may want to move text from one subdocument to another, or to create references to text in another subdocument. To view the contents of the entire master document, click Expand Subdocuments and then use Word's Outlining toolbar buttons to focus on the specific areas of text you want to edit.

No matter how you open a subdocument, you're not limited to viewing and editing it in Outline view. Select whatever view makes the most sense for the editing you need to do.

NOTE

> If you have both a subdocument and its master document open, you cannot edit the subdocument's text in the master document—you will find it locked. You must click the subdocument icon on the taskbar and edit the subdocument directly.

EDITING SUBDOCUMENTS OUTSIDE THE MASTER DOCUMENT

As you've learned, you don't have to open a master document to edit one of its subdocuments. You can open the subdocument directly, by using the Open dialog box or by double-clicking on its icon in Windows Explorer. If you're using master documents to manage a document with several authors, this is how your colleagues typically open the subdocuments you delegate to them.

Here's a rule of thumb: Open subdocuments separately when you intend to make changes that affect only the subdocument. For example, it's fine to open the subdocument separately if you plan to do any of the following:

- Edit text within the subdocument
- Create footnotes to appear at the bottom of the page or at the end of the subdocument
- Create temporary headers or footers that you only want to print from within the subdocument
- Check spelling within the subdocument
- Print only the subdocument

TIP

> You might add a subdocument footer that includes the words PRELIMINARY DRAFT. This footer prints whenever you open the subdocument on its own. However, the "official" master document footer you establish for your final document appears instead whenever the subdocument is printed from the master document.

→ For more information about creating headers and footers, **see** Chapter 5, "Controlling Page Features," **p. 157**.

19

On the other hand, if you plan to make organizational, formatting, or editing changes that affect the entire document, open the subdocument from within the master document as described previously.

After you've completed work on the subdocument, you can save and close it the same way you would save any normal Word document.

CAUTION

> Never rename or move a subdocument that you've opened outside the master document. Word has no way of tracking the change. The next time you open the master document, the renamed or moved subdocument will be missing.
>
> To rename or move a subdocument, open it from within the master document; choose File, Save As; enter the new name or location in the Save As dialog box; and click Save.
>
> Don't forget, this leaves the obsolete file on your hard drive in its original location. If you're responsible for managing a master document, you may want to manually delete or move the obsolete file so that others will not inadvertently edit it, assuming that it is still current.

STYLE BEHAVIOR IN MASTER DOCUMENTS AND SUBDOCUMENTS

If you open a subdocument from within a master document, the subdocument uses all the styles stored in the master document's template. If you open it separately and make style changes or apply a different template, your subdocument reflects those style changes as long as you're editing it outside the master document. However, if you save it, open the master document, and reopen the subdocument, you'll find that the master document's styles now take precedence wherever the styles conflict. If you insert an existing document into a master document, and the existing document is based on a different template, once again the master document's template takes precedence.

→ For more information about inserting an existing document into a master document, **see** "Adding an Existing Document to a Master Document," **p. 672**.

If you create a new style within a subdocument and later open that subdocument from within the master document, your new style is listed in the master document as well. However, if the style is based on a style that looks different in the master and subdocuments, text formatted with the new style may also look different depending on whether you're working on it in the master document or in a separate subdocument editing window.

Because this is complicated, here's an example:

Imagine that you're working in a subdocument that appears in its own editing window. You create a style named BookText and base it on the Normal style (which, by default, is 12-point Times New Roman). You add the extra formatting you want BookText to include: a first-line 1/2" indent and 8 points after each paragraph.

You now close the subdocument and open the master document that contains the subdocument. When you do so, the BookText style appears in your list of styles. Text formatted in the BookText style still has a 1/2" indent and 8 points after each paragraph. However, what if your master document used a different version of the Normal style, calling for text to be displayed in 11-point Georgia (instead of Times New Roman). Because your BookText is based on the Normal style, it would display your style in 11-point Georgia.

In other words, the elements you add to a style remain intact regardless of whether you display the text from within a master document or as a separate subdocument. However, where elements are based on another style, Word looks for that style in different places depending on how you are displaying the text. If you are displaying it as part of the master document, Word uses the underlying styles from the master document. If you are displaying it as a subdocument, in its own editing window, Word uses the underlying styles from the subdocument.

→ To learn more about based-on styles, **see** "Working with Based On Styles," **p. 341**.

REORGANIZING A MASTER DOCUMENT

The outlining skills you learned in Chapter 18, "Outlining: Practical Techniques for Organizing Any Document," are especially handy when you need to reorganize a master document. Display your document in Outline view and click Expand Subdocuments to view all the contents of your subdocuments. Now you can use Word's Outlining toolbar and keyboard shortcuts to rearrange any elements of your master document.

MOVING AN ENTIRE SUBDOCUMENT

You might decide that you want to move an entire subdocument to a different location in your master document. First, use Word's Outlining and Master Documents toolbar buttons to display the portions of the master document you need to see to know exactly where you want to move the subdocument. Next, click the subdocument symbol to select the entire subdocument (see Figure 19.8).

Figure 19.8
You can select an entire subdocument by clicking its subdocument icon.

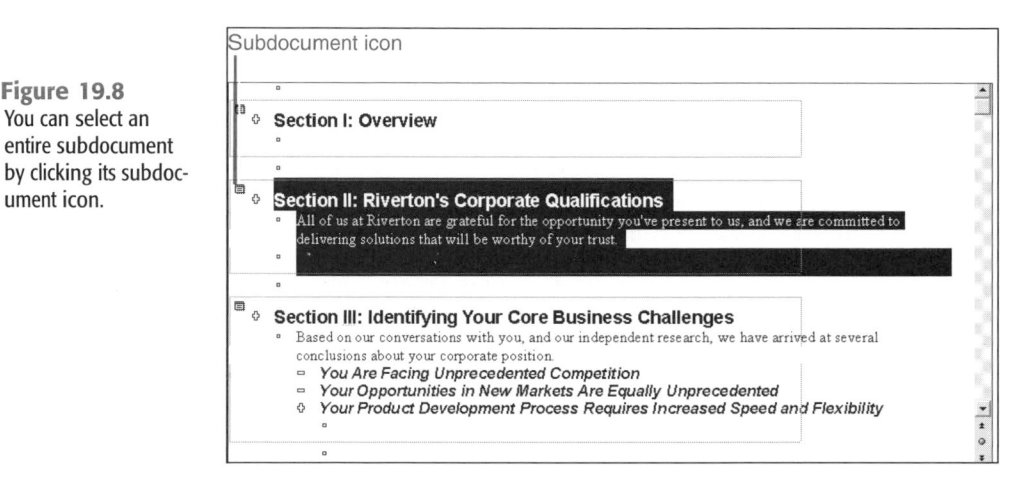

Now you can perform any of the following actions:

- **Move the subdocument intact to another location in your document**. Drag the subdocument into the empty space between two other subdocuments. (By default, when you create subdocuments, Word leaves one paragraph of body text between them, just for this purpose.)

- **Move an entire subdocument into another subdocument, by using the Move Up or Move Down buttons**. You get the same result as you would by merging subdocuments: The text in both subdocuments is now part of the same subdocument. (The subdocument you removed, however, remains on the hard disk—consider manually moving or deleting it to avoid confusion.)

NOTE

> If you use Move Up/Move Down to move a subdocument into another subdocument and then move it back out, the text is placed in the master document. It is no longer a separate subdocument. You have to click Create Subdocument to make it a subdocument again—or click the Undo button until you revert to your starting point.

- **Use drag and drop to move an entire subdocument into another subdocument.** This behaves differently than Move Up or Move Down. Now the subdocument where you've dropped the file contains its own subdocument. You're likely to use this feature only in exceptionally complex documents, where you may delegate a large section to someone who will in turn delegate smaller portions to others.

As you move subdocuments or the elements within them, a gray line appears, showing where your selected text will land if you release the mouse button.

TIP

> If you move a subdocument to the wrong place, click Undo to move it back, and try again.

MOVING PARTS OF SUBDOCUMENTS

When it comes to moving or reorganizing individual headings and subordinate text, there's no difference between master documents and conventional documents. First, display your master document in Outline view and click the Master Document View button on the Outlining toolbar to access all your outlining and master document tools.

Next you can click on the plus sign next to the heading (in Outline view) to select all the text subordinate to it—or select just one paragraph. You can then use cut and paste, drag and drop, or the Move Up/Move Down buttons and keyboard shortcuts to move your selected text anywhere in the master document. It all works—whether your destination is the same subdocument, a different subdocument, or the master document itself.

SPLITTING A SUBDOCUMENT INTO TWO

Sometimes as you develop a large document, the contents of one subdocument may grow larger than you expected. Or, perhaps, your company might reorganize, and two people may have to divide responsibility for a chapter that was previously assigned to one individual. You might also discover that part of a chapter requires someone else's specialized knowledge.

In short, there are many reasons you might decide that one subdocument needs to be split into two. To split a subdocument, first display the subdocument's contents from within the master document. Next, click your insertion point where you want to split the subdocument. (You can split subdocuments before or after headings or paragraphs, but not in the middle of a paragraph.) Finally, click Split Subdocument.

You now have two subdocuments. The second subdocument contains all the text that originally followed the insertion point in your first subdocument.

COMBINING MULTIPLE SUBDOCUMENTS

Alternatively, you might find that two subdocuments are more closely related than you expected, and that a single individual should handle them both as part of the same document. In that case, you can combine two or more subdocuments into one.

> You can only combine adjacent subdocuments; if the subdocuments you want to combine are not adjacent, you can drag the subdocument symbol on one subdocument until it is immediately before or after the other subdocument.

To combine two or more subdocuments, follow these steps:

1. Open the document and display it in Master Document view.
2. Click Expand Subdocuments.
3. Make sure that the subdocuments are adjacent; use Word's outlining tools to move them if necessary.
4. Click the subdocument icon next to the first subdocument you want to combine.
5. Press Shift and click the subdocument icon next to the last subdocument you want to combine. You have now selected the first and last subdocuments, and any subdocuments in between.
6. Click Merge Subdocument. The first of the subdocuments you selected now contains all the text that previously appeared in all the individual subdocuments you selected.

NOTE

> You can't combine subdocuments if they're marked with a padlock icon. Locking and unlocking subdocuments is discussed later in this chapter.

CAUTION

> The other subdocuments you merged into the first subdocument no longer appear as separate subdocuments within your master document. However, they still exist as separate files on your hard disk. Either delete or move these "stranded" files so that nobody edits them, mistakenly believing they are working on the current version of the document.

19

REMOVING A SUBDOCUMENT

Sometimes you want to keep the information contained in one or more subdocuments, but you no longer want to store that information in separate subdocuments. Possibly your colleagues have finished with their reviews, and you want to merge their subdocuments back into the master document, converting it back into a single document.

Follow these steps to eliminate the subdocument while moving its contents to the master document. First, expand the subdocuments, and click the subdocument icon to select the entire subdocument you want to convert. Next, click the Remove Subdocument button. The subdocument no longer appears in the master document, and all its text is copied into the master document, from where it can be edited. The outline of the overall master document is unchanged; all of its contents still appear in the same order as they did before.

CAUTION

The original subdocument file remains on disk after you remove a subdocument. If you no longer need it, you may want to move or delete it.

ADDING AN EXISTING DOCUMENT TO A MASTER DOCUMENT

What if you have a document you want to add to an existing master document? (Or what if you want to add your document to a conventional document, thereby turning it into a master document?)

First, open the master document and click Expand Subdocuments. Next, click in the master document where you want to insert your subdocument and click Insert Subdocument. The Insert Subdocument dialog box opens (see Figure 19.9). Browse to select the document you want and click <u>O</u>pen.

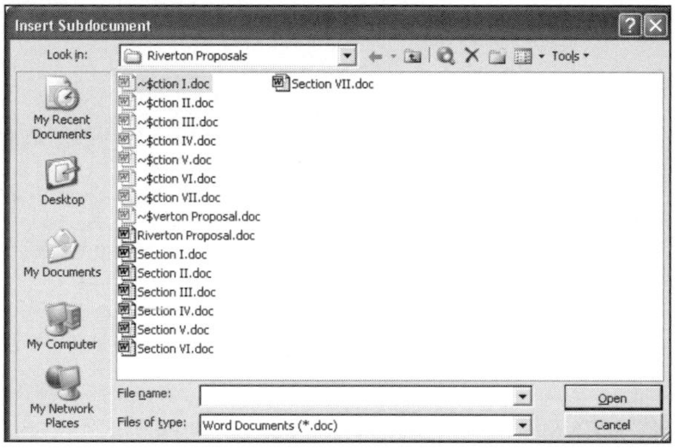

Figure 19.9
The Insert Subdocument dialog box enables you to make any document part of your master document.

NOTE

After you expand subdocuments, the toolbar button changes to the Collapse Subdocuments button. Click this button when you need to collapse the subdocuments again.

CAUTION

Before you insert an existing document into a master document, consider applying the same template that is used in the master document. This can reduce the need for Word to resolve style conflicts, one of the causes of corruption in master documents.

Word inserts the subdocument into your outline at your current insertion point. If any text is formatted with styles that have the same names as those in your master document, those styles are displayed to match the rest of your master document.

CREATING A TABLE OF CONTENTS, AN INDEX, OR CROSS-REFERENCES FOR A MASTER DOCUMENT

From within your master document, you can create tables of contents and indexes that reflect the contents of all your subdocuments. Follow these steps:

1. Open the master document, display it in Outline view, and click the Master Document View toolbar button.

2. Click Expand Subdocuments to make the contents of all subdocuments visible.

3. Position your insertion point where you want to create your table of contents, index, or cross-reference.

4. Follow Word's procedures for inserting an index, a table of contents, or cross-references. You can work from the Insert, Reference, Index and Tables dialog box or the Insert, Reference, Cross-Reference dialog box; or insert index fields directly by pressing Alt+Shift+X and working from the Mark Index Entry dialog box; or enter fields directly by pressing Ctrl+F9 and editing the text between the field brackets.

→ For more information on creating tables of contents, **see** "Quick and Easy Tables of Contents," **p. 682**.

→ For more information on creating indexes, **see** "Creating a New Index Entry," **p. 716**, and "Compiling Your Index," **p. 724**.

→ For more information on building and using cross-references, **see** "Working with Cross-References," **p. 758**.

You can enter your fields in the master document, in a subdocument displayed in the master document, or in a subdocument displayed in its own editing window.

CAUTION

> If you open a subdocument using File, Open rather than opening it from within the master document, any table of contents, index, or cross-reference you create won't reflect the contents of the master document.

19

After you have created a table of contents in a master document, you can work with it using the Go To TOC and Update TOC buttons on Word's Master Document toolbar.

If you click the Go to TOC button, Word selects your document's table of contents. If you click the Update TOC button, Word updates your table of contents, allowing you to choose whether you want to update only page numbers or the entire table of contents including the text of each listing.

PRINTING MASTER DOCUMENTS AND SUBDOCUMENTS

You print master documents and subdocuments the same way you print any other documents. You can click the Print button on the Standard toolbar to get one complete copy of whatever master document or subdocument you're working in. Or you can choose File, Print to display the Print dialog box and select printing options manually.

In general, what you see is what you print:

- If you click Expand Subdocuments and then print a master document in Normal view, Word prints the entire master document, including all subdocuments. All styles, headers/footers, and page numbering are defined by the master document, not by individual subdocuments.

- If you print a master document with hyperlinks showing, the hyperlinks print rather than the document text. It's a handy way to get a list of your subdocuments, complete with their drive and folder locations.

- If you print a master document from Outline view, Word prints whatever headings and body text are currently displayed; for example, if you collapse part of the master document or display only the first line of body text paragraphs, only the elements that appear onscreen print.

- If you double-click a subdocument icon in a master document and display a subdocument in its own window, clicking Print prints only the subdocument—using the master document's styles and template.

- If you open a subdocument without first opening the master document, the subdocument prints as if it were an independent document—using its own styles and template.

WORKING WITH OTHERS ON THE SAME MASTER DOCUMENT

19

You've learned that master documents can simplify collaboration. You can delegate parts of your document for others to edit while working on other elements yourself; then when you're ready, you can review and edit the document as a whole.

By default, Word gives you complete access to any subdocument of which you are the author (assuming that the subdocument is stored in a folder you have rights to access). Word gives you more limited access to subdocuments you did not author.

NOTE

Word determines who the author is by looking in the Author field of the File, Properties dialog box. How does the name of the author get there in the first place? It comes from the information you gave Word when you installed it (or changes you've made since in the User Information tab of the Tools, Options dialog box).

To make sure that your colleagues have priority in accessing the documents for which they're responsible, you can enter their names in the Properties dialog box of each subdocument. Remember that if you give other users priority over yourself, you won't be able to edit their submissions until they finish working and close the files.

If you did not author a subdocument, you may find that it is locked when you try to open it. You can tell that a subdocument is locked when a small padlock icon appears beneath the subdocument icon (see Figure 19.10).

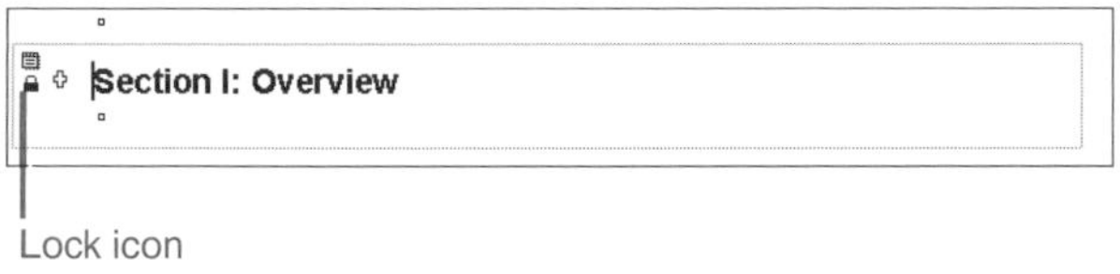

Figure 19.10
The padlock icon appears whenever a subdocument is locked.

Lock icon

When you first open a master document, displaying subdocuments as hyperlinks, all sub-documents are locked, no matter who authored them. If you click Expand Subdocuments, the Lock icons disappear, except in the following cases:

- If someone else is already working on a subdocument and you attempt to open it, Word displays a message offering you several options. You can create a copy to work on; if you do so, the words "Read Only" appear in the title bar of the document you create. When you then save the copy, you're prompted to save it in another location, and Word adds the phrase "'original name'—for merge" to the name in the title bar. Later, you can merge changes from your local copy into the original.

  Alternatively, you can wait until the first user has finished; Word will notify you when the original copy becomes available.

- When the subdocument's author saves it as Read-Only Recommended, using the check box in the Security Options dialog box. (This dialog box is accessible by choosing File, Save As; then clicking the Tools button and choosing Security Options.) When you try to open a Read-Only Recommended file, Word displays a dialog box asking, in effect, whether you want to respect this preference. You can click No and edit the document.

- When the subdocument's author has established a Password to Modify, also using options in the Security Options dialog box. You can read this subdocument, but you can't edit it without knowing the password.

- When the subdocument is stored in a shared folder to which you have only Read-Only rights. Again, you can read the file, but you can't edit it unless you convince your network administrator to upgrade your rights. The words "Read Only" appear in the title bar of a read-only document.

If a subdocument is locked, you can attempt to unlock it like this:

1. Open the master document, display it in Outline view, and click the Master Document View button.

2. Click Expand Subdocuments. (Until you expand your subdocuments, they're all locked.)

3. If the subdocument you want to edit is still locked, click anywhere in it.

4. Click the Lock Document button on the Master Document toolbar. (If the file is in use, Word displays a message that the file cannot be opened with write privileges.)

19

If the document remains locked, you may need to contact the individual using it and ask him to close the document. A last resort is to copy the contents into another document, add that document as a subdocument, and remove the subdocument that caused the problem.

Locking Others Out of a Master Document or Subdocument

If you own a master document or subdocument, you can lock others out of it. To lock a master document, click anywhere in the master document (not in a subdocument); then click the Lock Document button on the Outlining toolbar. To lock a subdocument, click in the subdocument; then click the Lock Document button. To unlock a master document or subdocument you own, click the Lock Document button again to toggle locking off.

Locking a master document does the following:

- Makes the master document read-only (though subdocuments can still be edited by those who have the right to do so).
- Disables the following buttons on the Outlining toolbar: Create Subdocument, Remove Subdocument, Insert Subdocument, Merge Subdocument, Split Subdocument.

Note that when you lock a master document and then save it, the lock is removed, and the file can be opened "writable." The same applies to manually locked subdocuments. In short, locking a file is not a significant security protection. If your goal is security, use passwords or Word 2003's Information Rights Management (both covered in Chapter 33).

Inserting Files Rather Than Using Master Documents

If you need to include some or all of the contents of multiple Word files in a single document, and you don't need the flexibility that master documents give you, Word offers another option: the Insert File feature. With Insert File, you simply browse to another Word file and insert its contents into the Word file you have open. You can do one of the following:

- Insert the contents without establishing a link—essentially copying an entire document into your file, without going through the trouble of opening the file and selecting all its text.
- Insert the contents as a link so that changes to the original file can automatically be reflected in the file you're working in.

Inserting an Entire File

The most common use for Insert File is to insert the entire contents of a file. Follow these steps to do so:

1. Click where you want to insert a file.

2. Choose Insert, File. The Insert File dialog box appears (see Figure 19.11).

Figure 19.11
Inserting a file from the Insert File dialog box.

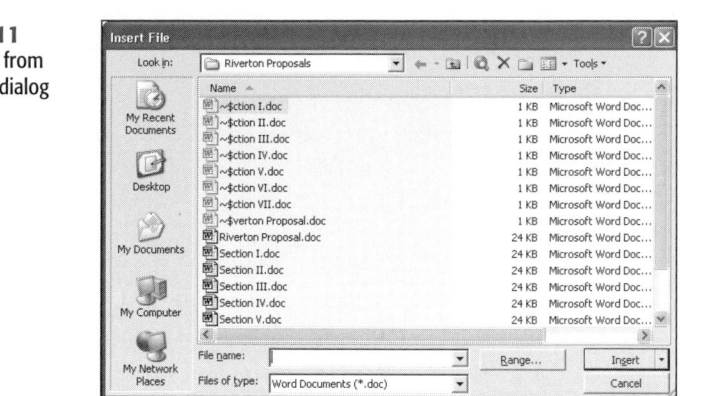

3. Browse to the file you want to insert and select it.

4. If you simply want to insert the file's text without creating a link, click the Insert button. If you prefer to create a link, click the down arrow to the right of the Insert button, and choose Insert as Link.

> **NOTE**
>
> If you're inserting a file that doesn't use Word's current file format (for example, a file from an older version of Word, such as Word 95 or Word 6, or from a competitive word processor such as WordPerfect), Word attempts to convert it first. If the file can be converted, Word inserts it. If not, Word displays an error message.
>
> For more information on Word's capability to convert documents from WordPerfect files, go to www.microsystems.com/PDFS/whitepaper.pdf.

If you insert the file using a link, Insert File actually inserts an { INCLUDETEXT } field in your document that includes a reference to the document you inserted. As with master documents, you can reflect the latest information in the source document, though the process is slightly less automatic. You have to select the field and press F9 to update it, just as you would with any other Word field.

→ For more information on how fields work and how you update them, **see** "Understanding Fields," **p. 772**, and "Updating Your Fields," **p. 783**.

Insert File also lets you build tables of contents, indexes, and cross-references that take into account the text from another document. One major difference, however, limits the usefulness of Insert File: You can't click the field to open and edit the file you've inserted.

You can, however, edit the text you've inserted. After you do, you can press Ctrl+Shift+F7 to update the source document so that it reflects your edits.

19

USING INSERT FILE TO INSERT PART OF A DOCUMENT

You can also use Insert File to insert part of any document into your current document. For example, you might want to quote a portion of a current price list. Inserting part of a document is a two-step process.

First, open the source document that contains the text you want to insert, and do the following:

1. Select the text you want to insert.
2. Choose Insert, Bookmark.
3. In the Bookmark Name text box, enter the name of a bookmark that you want to associate with this text, and click Add. (Keep the bookmark name short so that you'll remember it.)
4. Save and close the document.

Next, open the destination document where you want to insert the text, and do the following:

1. Place your insertion point where you want to insert the text.
2. Choose Insert, File.
3. Select the document containing the source text.
4. Click Range. The Set Range dialog box appears.
5. In the Range text box, enter the name of the bookmark you've just inserted in the source document.
6. Click OK to close the Set Range dialog box.
7. Click Insert to insert the text in the document. If you want to maintain a link to the source document, click the right arrow next to Insert, and choose Insert as Link.

The source document's bookmarked text appears in the destination document. Afterward, if you inserted the text as a link, you can update the destination document to reflect any changes in the source document by selecting the field and pressing F9.

NOTE

> Other valuable field shortcuts include
> - Temporarily preventing changes to the field by pressing Ctrl+F11
> - Allowing changes again by pressing Ctrl+Shift+F11
> - Transforming the field into text by pressing Ctrl+Shift+F9—thereby permanently preventing automatic updates.

CAUTION

> You can't update the text if the source document is moved, or if it is edited to eliminate the bookmark.

→ To learn more about working with bookmarks, see "Using Bookmarks," **p. 755**.

TROUBLESHOOTING

WHAT TO DO IF WORD WON'T SAVE A MASTER DOCUMENT

Word's capacity for managing subdocuments varies with the number of files and programs you have open, how much memory your computer has, and other factors specific to your system. It is possible to run out of resources while you're trying to save a master document. If Word won't save a master document, try this:

- First, cancel the save; close any other open programs and files, and try again.
- If this doesn't work, convert some subdocuments into text in the master document by selecting them and clicking Remove Subdocuments. Then try saving again.

If you find that your system can't support the master document you're trying to create, you have some alternatives. You can, of course, simply copy text from your source documents. Or you can use Word's Insert File feature, covered earlier in the "Inserting Files Rather Than Using Master Documents" section of this chapter.

WHAT TO DO IF YOUR SUBDOCUMENTS DISAPPEAR

Did you select a level from the Show Level drop-down list on the Outlining toolbar, while only hyperlinks were displayed in your master document? Word thinks you want to see only headings and body text, and it can't find any—all it can see are hyperlinks. First click Expand Subdocuments and then click Show All Headings.

WHAT TO DO IF A MASTER DOCUMENT BECOMES DAMAGED

Recovering a damaged master document can be a very complex process—one that takes several pages to explain. You can find a comprehensive explanation of the process at www.mvps.org/word/FAQs/General/RecoverMasterDocs.htm.

WHAT TO DO IF YOU CAN'T ACCESS SUBDOCUMENT CONTROLS ON THE OUTLINING TOOLBAR

If the subdocument controls on the Outlining toolbar are unavailable, first click Expand Subdocuments. If they are still unavailable, your master document or subdocuments may be locked. Click the Lock Documents button to toggle locking off. If you cannot unlock the subdocument or master document, contact the document's owner to be given permission to do so.

If none of the master document controls is available, click the Master Document View button on the Outlining toolbar.

WHAT TO DO IF YOU SAVE A MASTER DOCUMENT TO A NEW LOCATION AND SUBDOCUMENTS DON'T FOLLOW

Unfortunately, if you save a master document to a new folder, Word does not automatically save all subdocuments to the new folder; it keeps them in their original location. You must open each subdocument from within the master document, and resave it to the same location where you saved the master document.

CHAPTER 20

TABLES OF CONTENTS, FIGURES, AUTHORITIES, AND CAPTIONS

In this chapter

TABLES OF CONTENTS

If you've ever had to prepare a table of contents manually, you'll appreciate how thoroughly Word automates the process. Word can do in moments what used to take hours.

In the next few sections, you'll learn the quickest ways to compile tables in your documents. You'll learn a few tricks for getting your tables of contents to look exactly the way you want them to, when Word doesn't do the job as automatically as you might like. You'll even learn how to instantly create a table of contents that appears in a frame on a Web page—a task that previously required painstaking HTML coding.

NOTE

> If you're planning a document that will have a table of contents, be sure to use Word's heading styles (Heading 1, Heading 2, Heading 3, and so forth). It's far easier to auto-mate the construction of your table of contents if you've done so.

QUICK AND EASY TABLES OF CONTENTS

Sometimes you need a table of contents but you don't especially care what it looks like. If you used heading styles in your document, you can have your table of contents in less than 60 seconds.

To create a default table of contents, click where you want it to appear. Choose Insert, Reference, Index and Tables; click the Table of Contents tab (see Figure 20.1), and click OK.

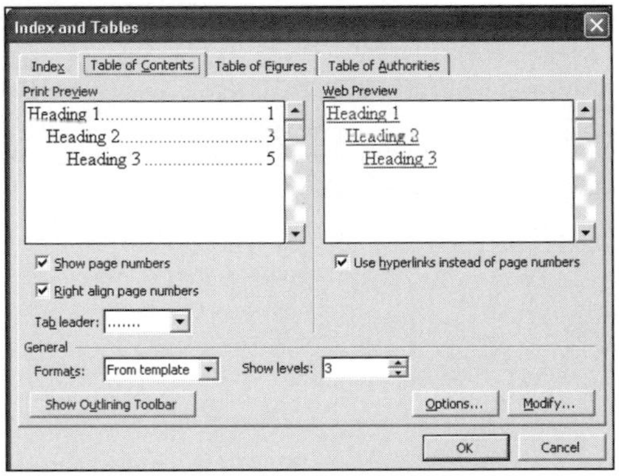

Figure 20.1
From here, you can control all aspects of your table of contents' appearance—or simply click OK to get a default table of contents using heading styles.

Word inserts a table of contents based on the first three heading levels in your document, using the built-in table of contents styles in your current template, with a dotted-line tab leader and right-aligned page numbers. If you already inserted specially formatted page numbers in your document, such as page numbers that include chapter numbers, those appear in your table of contents.

In short, you now have Word's default table of contents (see Figure 20.2). If that isn't enough for you, the rest of this section shows how to change Word's default settings to get the exact table of contents you have in mind.

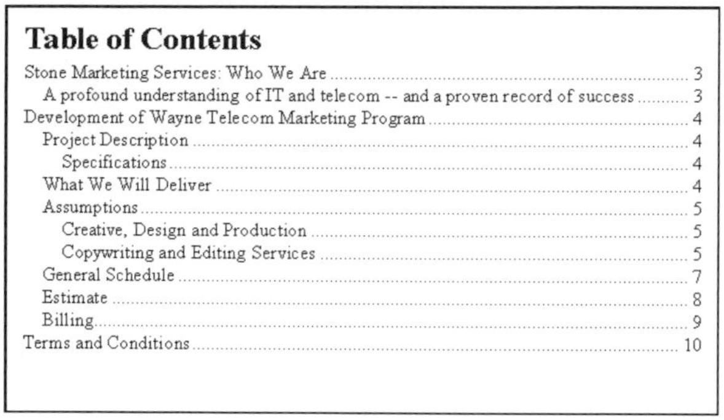

Figure 20.2
A sample table of contents built with Word's default styles and settings, and displayed in Normal view.

Table of Contents

Stone Marketing Services: Who We Are 3
   A profound understanding of IT and telecom -- and a proven record of success 3
Development of Wayne Telecom Marketing Program 4
   Project Description 4
     Specifications 4
   What We Will Deliver 4
   Assumptions 5
     Creative, Design and Production 5
     Copywriting and Editing Services 5
   General Schedule 7
   Estimate 8
   Billing 9
Terms and Conditions 10

TIP

When you work in Normal, Print Layout, or Reading Layout view, table of contents entries act as hyperlinks, even though they appear as regular text. Except in Reading Layout, you can Ctrl+click on any table of contents entry to move to the corresponding location in your document.

If you display your page in Web Layout view, by default the table of contents entries look like Word hyperlinks—in other words, they appear as blue underlined text. By default, the page numbers disappear (because page numbers are largely irrelevant on Web sites). If you would rather display page numbers instead of hyperlinks, clear the Use Hyperlinks Instead of Page Numbers check box in the Table of Contents tab of the Index and Tables dialog box.

When Word inserts a table of contents in your document, it's actually inserting a TOC field with the specific instructions you gave Word about how to build the table of contents. Later in this chapter, you'll learn a little more about this field so that you can manually control some aspects of your tables of contents that can't easily be controlled through the Table of Contents tab of the Index and Tables dialog box.

→ For more information about controlling tables of contents with TOC fields, **see** "Creating a Table of Contents for Part of a Document," **p. 695**.

TIP

Before you compile a table of contents for a printed document, take these steps to make sure you get an accurate one:

1. Make sure you've used heading styles for all the headings you want Word to include in your table of contents. As you'll see later (in the section "Setting the Styles and Outline Levels Word Compiles in Your Table of Contents"), you can include other styles and text in a table of contents if you're willing to invest a little extra time. But it's usually simplest to stay with headings.

continues

continued

> 2. Make sure you properly set margins and other section formatting that can affect page count.
>
> 3. Make sure hidden text is actually hidden. (When displayed, hidden text appears with a thin dotted underline. To hide it, click on the Show/Hide Paragraph Marks button on the Standard toolbar.)
>
> 4. Make sure your document is displaying field results rather than the fields themselves. If you see field codes within curly brackets, press Alt+F9 to display field results throughout the document.
>
> 5. Unless you have fields you do not want to update, update all your field results this way: Press Ctrl+A to select the entire document and then press F9.

CREATING TABLES OF CONTENTS IN WEB FRAMES

In Chapter 24, "Using Word to Develop Web Content," you will learn how Word makes it easy to create frames that divide Web pages into sections that can be browsed independently. One common Web design technique involves using one frame as a table of contents, which remains displayed as the user navigates the site. Each item in the table of contents is displayed as a hyperlink that the user can click to display the corresponding location in another frame.

Traditionally, creating tables of contents in frames has been a labor-intensive, complex process. In Word 2003, it's simple—again, assuming that you build your table of contents from heading styles. When you're ready to create your table of contents, choose Format, Frames, Table of Contents in Frame. Word creates a new frame at the left side of the screen and inserts table of contents hyperlinks corresponding to any heading in your document based on a heading style from Heading 1 through Heading 9. Figure 20.3 shows an example.

Figure 20.3
Word inserts table of contents hyperlinks in a new frame at the left side of the screen.

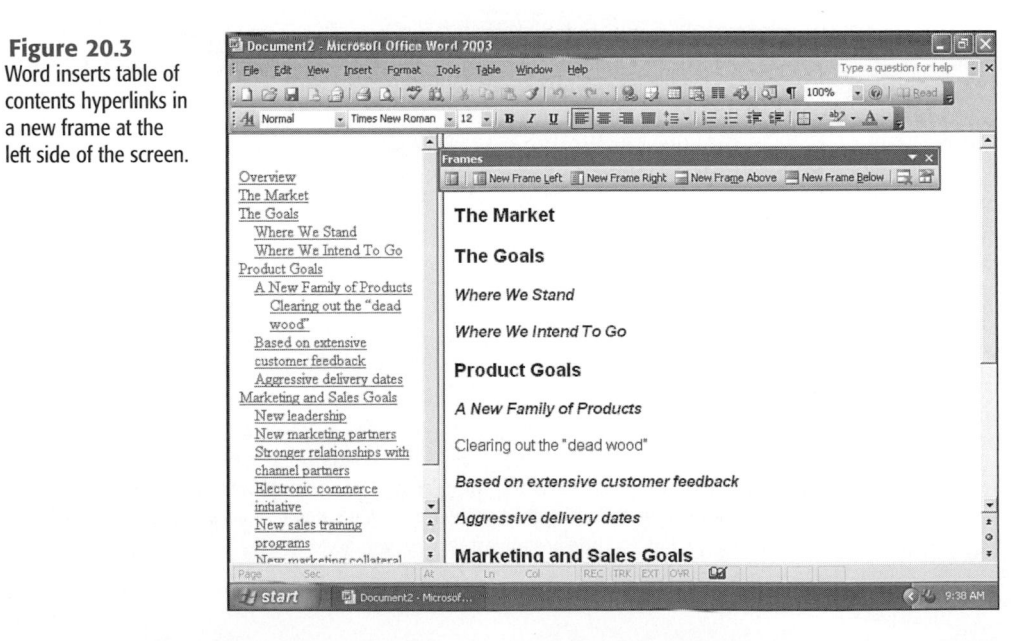

After you create a frame containing a table of contents, you can format it as needed. For example, you might want to consider

- Adding a company logo and a heading at the top of the Table of Contents frame

- Increasing the size of the hyperlinks (12-point Times New Roman by default), though the text's actual size may depend on the browser displaying it

- Deleting low-level headings (such as headings built from third- or fourth-level heading styles, or lower) if they make the table of contents too cumbersome, or too lengthy to fit on a single screen

- Editing some of your hyperlinks for brevity and clarity. Headings that work well in print, or at the top of a page, may be too long or formal to attract clicks on an intranet or a Web site. Figure 20.4 shows how the table of contents created in Figure 20.3 has been adapted for more effective Web use.

Figure 20.4
Editing and formatting a table of contents for more effective Web use.

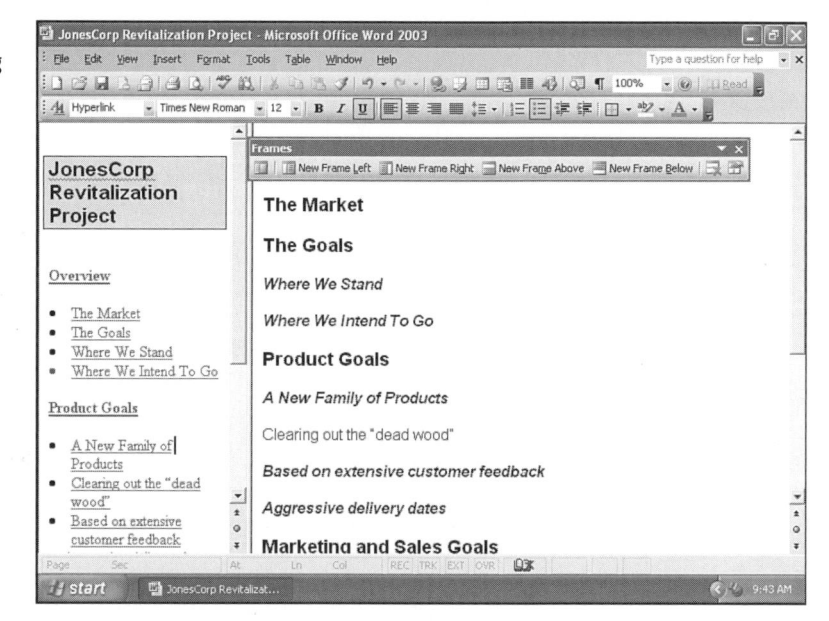

CAUTION

Be careful not to overuse frames, or to create frames that take up too much screen "real estate"—leaving too little space for the content you want to communicate.

You can find a more detailed discussion of the advantages and disadvantages of frames in Chapter 24.

NOTE

When you use Format, Frames, Table of Contents in Frame, Word inserts a separate { HYPERLINK } field for each line of the table of contents, placing these hyperlinks in a new left frame.

continues

continued

> However, if you have a Word document that contains a table of contents, and you save
> that table of contents as a Web page, the table of contents will remain a single TOC field.
> The table of contents remains in the same location where you originally placed it. If you
> created the TOC using default settings, the page numbers and leader lines will disappear
> when displayed as a Web page. However, if you display the Web page in Print Layout
> view, or resave it as a printed document, the page numbers and leaders reappear.

FORMATTING YOUR TABLE OF CONTENTS

Sometimes the default table of contents format Word applies isn't appropriate for your document. If so, you have two choices:

- Try out one of the six additional table of contents formats Word provides.
- Adapt Word's built-in table of contents styles to your specific needs.

CHOOSING ONE OF WORD'S BUILT-IN FORMATS

Word offers six built-in table of contents formats for use in printed documents: Classic, Distinctive, Fancy, Modern, Formal, and Simple. One of these might do the job if you don't have sophisticated requirements or a set of graphics standards with which to comply. (In truth, none of Word's built-in formats is especially classic, distinctive, fancy, modern, or formal, though Simple *is* reasonably simple.)

To try out a built-in format, first choose Insert, Reference, Index and Tables, Table of Contents. Next, choose the format in the Formats drop-down box. In the Print Preview box, Word shows a generic table of contents for a printed document that uses this format. In the Web Preview box, you can see how the same format would look if you saved the page as HTML and displayed it on a Web browser.

If you like what you see, click OK, and Word builds a table of contents that follows the format you've chosen.

BUILDING YOUR OWN TABLE OF CONTENTS FORMAT

The appearance of your table of contents is defined in part by the formatting of nine built-in styles, TOC 1 through TOC 9. If you are building a document that uses custom fonts and formatting throughout, it's likely that you'll want to adapt Word's built-in TOC styles as well. Word's Index and Tables dialog box includes a Modify option, which connects you to Word's Style dialog boxes where you can change these styles.

→ **See** "Changing Styles," **p. 345**.

Working through Word's nested Style dialog boxes can be time-consuming, however. There's a quicker way to change your TOC styles:

1. Choose Insert, Reference, Index and Tables.
2. Choose the Table of Contents tab.

3. Click OK to insert a table of contents in your document. Don't worry about how it looks just yet.

4. After the table of contents is inserted, select any first-level TOC entry formatted with the TOC 1 style. Be careful not to select the entire table of contents.

> **TIP**
>
> Sometimes, Word doesn't let you select the first line of a field result without selecting the entire field (for example, the entire table of contents). There are two workarounds.
>
> If your table of contents includes several lines formatted as TOC 1, select one from the middle (instead of the beginning) of your table of contents.
>
> If your table of contents has only one line formatted as TOC 1, do the following. First, right-click after the first character in the first line, press Esc to hide the shortcut menu, and press Enter. Now, you can select the new second line, reformat it, and then edit it to place the first character back where it belongs.

5. Reformat the TOC 1 entry the way you want it to look.

6. Repeat steps 2–3 for each additional TOC style in your table of contents.

> **TIP**
>
> It's often easiest to navigate and select text from within a table of contents by using keyboard shortcuts. Use Ctrl+Shift+left arrow to select words to the left, or Ctrl+Shift+right arrow to select words to the right.
>
> If you left-click in a table of contents, Word jumps to the location corresponding to the table of contents listing you clicked on. Alternatively, you can right-click in the table of contents and press Esc to hide the shortcut menu that appears, while leaving your insertion point in the table of contents.

If you used Word's default settings, which capture only heading levels 1 through 3 in a table of contents, you have to reformat only two more styles: TOC 2 and TOC 3. As you change each style, Word immediately updates all the TOC entries that use the same style to reflect the new formatting.

20

> **CAUTION**
>
> After you have the TOC styles you want, don't choose another format in the Table of Contents tabbed dialog box. By default, Word doesn't just reformat your table of contents; it reformats your custom styles with the built-in formats you just chose.
>
> (This automatic style updating won't occur if you clear the Automatically Update check box in each style's Modify Style dialog box—the dialog box that appears if you click Modify from within the Table of Contents tab of the Index and Tables dialog box.)

TIP

> If you want to make adjustments to individual heading styles and outline levels directly in the document, click Show Outlining Toolbar. Word displays the Outlining toolbar, containing tools you can use to do so. To learn more about the Outlining toolbar, see Chapter 18, "Outlining: Practical Techniques for Organizing Any Document."

CONTROLLING PAGE NUMBERS AND LEADERS IN TABLES OF CONTENTS

Occasionally, you might want to compile printed tables of contents that do not include page numbers. For instance, many people insert tables of contents without page numbers as a way to generate a quick hard-copy document outline for use in a meeting.

To tell Word not to include page numbers in a printed table of contents, display the Table of Contents tab, clear the Show Page Numbers box, and click OK.

In many cases you will want Word to include page numbers, but you'll want more control over where they appear. In most cases, the page numbers that Word includes in its built-in table of contents formats are right-aligned, as shown earlier in Figure 20.2. However, you can tell Word to place the page numbers next to the table of contents entries rather than right-align them.

To tell Word not to right-align page numbers in a table of contents, display the Table of Contents tab, clear the Right Align Page Numbers check box, and click OK.

Finally, in printed documents, if you create a table of contents based on the TOC styles in the Normal template (for example, if you use the From Template format in the Table of Contents tabbed dialog box), Word inserts a tab leader on each line (refer to Figure 20.2). By default, this tab leader is a series of dots that runs from the end of the table of contents text entry to the page number.

NOTE

> Tab leaders disappear in Web Layout view unless you clear the Use Hyperlinks Instead of Page Numbers check box.

20

You can change the tab leader, or eliminate it altogether. Display the Table of Contents tab and choose the leader you want in the Tab Leader drop-down list box. Word offers dots, dashes, and solid underlines—or you can choose (none) to show no leader.

CHOOSING THE NUMBER OF LEVELS IN YOUR TABLE OF CONTENTS

By default, Word builds tables of contents from the first three heading levels. In other words, it collects all text formatted with the Heading 1, Heading 2, and Heading 3 styles and incorporates that text in the table of contents.

NOTE

> If you want, you can also include text you have manually formatted with specific outline levels—even if that text is not formatted with a heading style. To learn how, see the following section, "Setting the Styles and Outline Levels Word Compiles in Your Table of Contents."
>
> To change the outline level associated with a block of text (other than a heading), choose Format, Paragraph; click on the Outline Level drop-down box; and choose the level you want.

Of course, this means your table of contents won't include Heading 4 through Heading 9 text. This may be a problem, especially if you used Heading 1 as only a chapter heading. In that case, your table of contents has only two levels to cover everything important that's going on within your chapters.

TIP

> One way to avoid this problem is to format chapter headings using Word's Title style instead of the Heading 1 style.

You can tell Word to place from one to nine levels in a Word table of contents. To do so, first display the Table of Contents tab of the Index and Tables dialog box. Choose a number from 1 to 9 in the Show Levels scroll box and click OK.

Word builds the table of contents using all the outline levels you've selected. For example, if you set Show Levels to 5, your table of contents would be built from headings formatted as Heading 1, Heading 2, Heading 3, Heading 4, and Heading 5, plus any other text formatted using Outline Levels 1 through 5.

You've just learned how to control the number of levels included in your table of contents. But, in the example described earlier, for instance, you may not want Heading 1 included at all—because you've used it as a chapter title, not a subheading. Word allows you to specify exactly which styles Word looks for when it builds your table of contents—and in the next section, you'll learn how.

20

SETTING THE STYLES AND OUTLINE LEVELS WORD COMPILES IN YOUR TABLE OF CONTENTS

Sometimes you may want to compile tables of contents based on styles other than Heading 1 through Heading 9. Word enables you to pick any styles you want and choose the order in which they'll be placed in your table of contents. Display the Table of Contents tab and click Options. The Table of Contents Options dialog box opens (see Figure 20.5).

Check marks appear next to all styles already in your table of contents. If you want to remove a style, delete the number in its corresponding TOC Level box. To add any style that's already in your document, click its TOC Level text box and enter a number from 1 to 9 there. More than one style can share the same level.

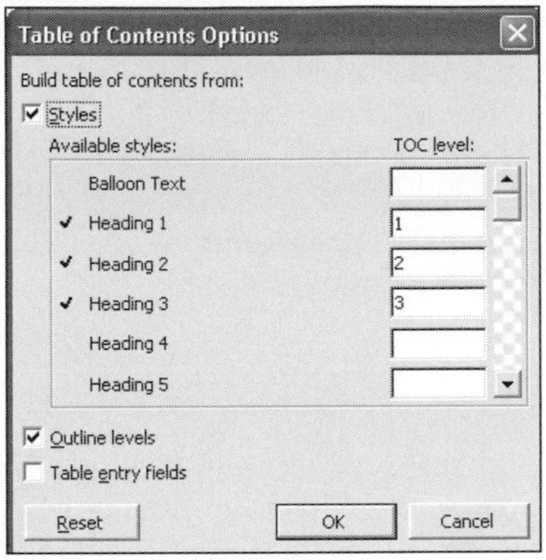

Figure 20.5
The Table of Contents Options dialog box lets you specify what styles and table entry fields Word compiles into your table of contents.

By default, Word does not include text formatted with specific outline levels in your table of contents, unless that text is also formatted with corresponding Heading styles. You might occasionally want to change this behavior. For example, you might have formatted a block of body text as Outline Level 1, 2, or 3, using the Format, Paragraph dialog box. You might now want to include that block of text in your table of contents. To do so, check the Outline Levels check box.

NOTE

Because you can choose only from styles that already exist in your document, make sure you've added all the styles you want before building your table of contents.

When you're finished setting the styles and outline levels you want to include in your table of contents, click OK to return to the Index and Tables dialog box. If your other settings are the way you want them, click OK again to compile your table of contents.

NOTE

If you decide to revert to Word's default styles (Headings 1 through 3), click the Reset button in the Table of Contents Options dialog box.

WHEN YOU CAN'T USE STYLES OR OUTLINE LEVELS: TABLE OF CONTENTS ENTRY FIELDS

On occasion, you might want your table of contents to include entries that aren't associated with either styles or outline levels. For example, you might want the first sentence of certain sections of your document to appear in your table of contents, but you might prefer *not* to create a style for the paragraphs where these sentences appear. In some instances, you could reformat these paragraphs with a certain outline level, but this often causes problems with your outlines or numbering schemes.

In some other situations you might prefer to create at least some of your table of contents entries without using styles, as well:

- You want to include an entry that paraphrases text in your document rather than repeating it precisely.

- You want to include only one entry formatted with a given style, not all of them.

- You want to suppress page numbering for selected table of contents entries, but not for all of them.

You can use Table Entry fields to instruct Word to include any text in a table of contents. It's a two-step process. First insert the fields in your document, and then instruct Word to use them in building the table of contents by checking the Table Entry Fields check box in the Table of Contents Options dialog box. The following two sections walk you through the process.

→ **See** "Inserting a Field Using the Field Dialog Box," **p. 775**.

INSERTING TC FIELDS USING THE MARK TABLE OF CONTENTS ENTRY DIALOG BOX *TC fields* are markers that Word can use in compiling a table of contents. You can place a TC field in any location in your document for which you want a table of contents entry. When Word builds the table of contents, it creates the entry by including

- Entry text you've specified within the TC field

- A page number corresponding to the location of the TC field in your document

If you intend to insert only a few TC fields, or if you're uncomfortable working with field codes, use the Mark Table of Contents Entry dialog box. If you intend to create many TC fields, you may find it faster to enter them directly into your document by pressing Ctrl+F9 to display field brackets and entering the syntax between the brackets. Both approaches are covered next.

To enter a TC entry field using the Mark Table of Contents Entry dialog box, follow these steps:

1. Click where you want your TC entry (*not* the table of contents itself) to appear.
2. Press Alt+Shift+O to display the Mark Table of Contents Entry dialog box (see Figure 20.6).

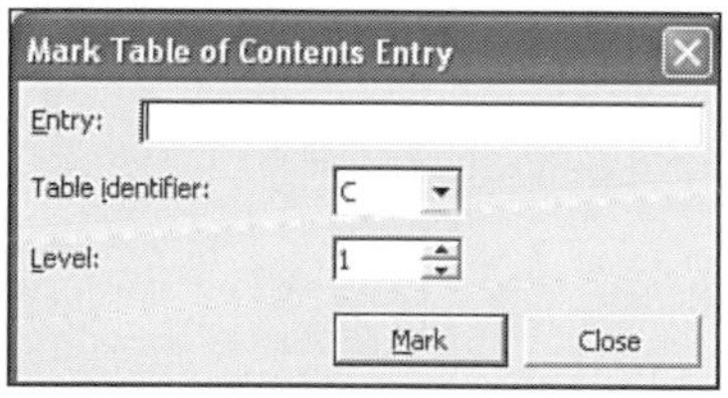

Figure 20.6
The Mark Table of Contents entry dialog box.

3. Type or edit the text of your entry in the Entry text box.
4. In the Level scroll box, enter the outline level you want to assign to your TC field. You can enter any level from 1 to 9. If you don't enter a number, Word assigns the entry to Outline Level 1.

5. If you want to place this entry in a separate table of contents from the main table of contents, enter a table identifier letter.

→ For more about creating multiple tables of contents in the same document, **see** "Adding a Second Table of Contents to Your Document," on **p. 694**.

6. Click Mark. Word inserts a TC entry at the current location in the document.

7. Click Close.

Inserting TC Fields Using the Mark Table of Contents Entry Dialog Box   If you plan to insert many TC fields at once, or if you need to use specialized options not available through the Mark Table of Contents Entry dialog box, you might prefer to enter TC fields directly in your document—that is, without using the Mark Table of Contents Entry dialog box.

As soon as you enter a TC field, Word immediately formats it as hidden text that isn't visible for editing. Before you enter TC fields, therefore, toggle the Show/Hide Paragraph Marks button on the Standard toolbar to display hidden text.

Next, press Ctrl+F9 to display field brackets and enter the appropriate syntax for the TC field. TC fields use the following syntax:

```
{ TC "Words you want to appear in table of contents" [Switches] }
```

In other words, immediately after the field name TC, enter the text you want Word to place in your table of contents, within quotation marks.

When you enter TC entries directly in your document by inserting field codes, you have all the options described previously, as well as some additional options—for example, the option to suppress page numbers in your table of contents. These options are available by adding switches to your field code, as presented in Table 20.1.

TABLE 20.1   Switches Available for Adjusting TC Fields

Switch	What It Does
\l *Level*	Specifies which level of your table of contents to use. If no switch is included, Word assumes Level 1. Example: { TC "Continental League" \l 3 } tells Word to insert a third-level entry consisting of the words *Continental League* and formatted using the TOC 3 style. (Corresponds to Outline Level in the Field dialog box.)
\n	Tells Word not to include a page number for this entry. Example: { TC "Bonus Coverage" \n } tells Word to include the words *Bonus Coverage* in the table of contents, but not to include the page number on which the field appears. (Corresponds to Suppresses Page Number in the Field dialog box.)
\f *Type*	Specifies in which list of figures to include this entry. *Type* corresponds to any character of the alphabet; all TC fields that use the same character are compiled together in the same table of contents. Example: { TC "Mona Lisa" \f m } tells Word to include a table of figures entry named Mona

Switch	What It Does
	Lisa whenever a table of contents is compiled from all the TC fields that use the \f m switch. The field { TC "Warhol" \f x } would not be included in the same table of figures, because a different letter—x, instead of m—has been used. This switch is used only for tables of figures, not for tables of contents. (You can add an \f switch by checking TC Entry in Doc with Multiple Tables in the Field dialog box; however, the Field dialog box provides no way to add the letter you need to place after the switch.)

→ To learn more about working with switches in field codes, **see** "Viewing and Editing the Field Code Directly," on **p. 780**.

→ To learn more about tables of figures, **see** "Building Tables of Figures," on **p. 706**.

Here are two more examples: Table 20.2 presents examples of TC fields and what they do.

TABLE 20.2   EXAMPLES OF TC FIELDS

Sample Field	What It Does
{TC "Marketing Reorg" \l 2 }	Inserts a second-level table of contents entry Marketing Reorg (including page numbers)
{ TC "Smith" \l 1 \n }	Inserts a first-level entry Smith, with no page number

TIP

> After you have the TC syntax correct, you can copy TC fields wherever you need them, changing only the elements that need to change, such as the text that Word places in the table of contents.
>
> There is a workaround you can use to keep TC fields (and other hidden fields) visible while you're working on them.

TIP

> After you enter field brackets, type an unusual character, such as ^, before you enter the letters TC. Word won't recognize that you're creating a hidden field.
>
> Create all your fields this way, and with your field codes displayed, use Word's Replace feature to replace all the ^ characters with no text. Word now recognizes the fields as hidden and hides them all (unless you've set Word to display hidden text).

20

TELLING WORD TO USE YOUR TC FIELDS   After you enter TC fields wherever you need them, choose Insert, Reference, Index and Tables to reopen the Table of Contents tab. Click Options to view the Table of Contents Options dialog box. Next, make sure the Table Entry Fields check box is checked. (In Word 2003, this check box is cleared by default.)

If you want your table of contents to be built from TC fields only, clear the Styles and Outline Levels check boxes. Click OK to return to the Table of Contents tab; click OK again to compile the table of contents.

UPDATING A TABLE OF CONTENTS

Your table of contents entries are likely to change after you first create your table of contents. Perhaps edits or margin changes will affect your page numbering. Possibly new headings will be added to your document, or you may be called on to reorganize existing headings. Or maybe you've used Word's outlining tools to change heading levels. Whatever the reason, you may need to update your table of contents to reflect changes in your document. Follow these steps:

1. Right-click on the table of contents and choose Update Field from the shortcut menu.

2. Choose whether you want to update only page numbers or the entire table (see Figure 20.7). If you update the entire table, you lose any manual formatting or editing you've done within it. However, you may have no choice if you've added or reorganized headings; these changes aren't reflected if you update only page numbers.

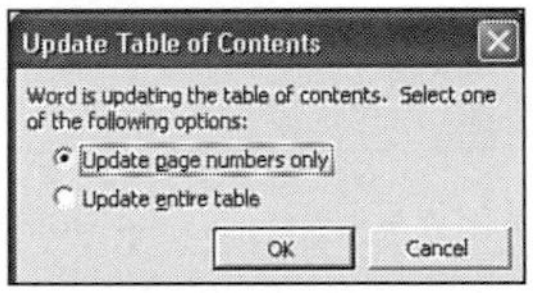

Figure 20.7
Choosing whether to update only page numbers or the entire table.

TIP

> What if you've done extensive formatting and editing in your table of contents? It seems a shame to lose all that work for just one or two new headings. You don't have to. You can patch your table of contents to reflect the new headings. Click where the new heading should appear in your table of contents and type it in manually.
>
> Even better, use Word's Cross-Reference feature twice—first to insert the heading text and then again to insert the page reference. You may also have to manually apply the heading style that corresponds to the heading level you want and polish up the formatting to make sure it matches its surroundings.
>
> As a result, you have a cross-referenced field that updates just as the rest of the table of contents does. Everything works fine—unless you forget to tell Word to update the entire table rather than just page numbers. (That's what Undo is for!)

→ To learn more about cross-references, **see** "Working with Cross-References," **p. 758**.

ADDING A SECOND TABLE OF CONTENTS TO YOUR DOCUMENT

You might want to add a second table of contents to your document. What kinds of documents have two tables of contents? It's increasingly common for how-to manuals and books (such as this book) to have a high-level, "at a glance" table of contents, as well as a more detailed, conventional table of contents that goes several levels into the document.

You might also want to insert separate tables of contents for each major section of a book, as well as an overall table of contents in the front. Whatever your reason, adding a second table of contents is easy to do.

After you insert your first table of contents, click where you want the second one to appear, establish its settings in the Table of Contents tab, and click OK. Word asks whether you want to replace your existing table of contents. Click No, and the second table of contents appears.

TIP

If you need more than two tables of contents, you can add them by following the same procedure described here. When you have two tables of contents, each one can be updated separately. (In fact, updating one doesn't automatically update the other.)

CREATING A TABLE OF CONTENTS FOR PART OF A DOCUMENT

The procedures you've just learned for creating and updating tables of contents work fine most of the time. For example, they're perfect for including a second high-level table of contents that includes only one or two heading levels. But what if you want to insert a table of contents for only part of a document? Use a TOC field.

As you learned earlier, when Word inserts a table of contents, it's actually inserting a TOC field with switches that correspond to the choices you made in the Table of Contents dialog box. However, you can do a few things with the TOC field directly that you can't do through a dialog box, and compiling a table of contents for only part of a document is one of them.

First, select the part of the document for which you want to create a table of contents. Next, *bookmark* it. To do so, choose Insert, Bookmark; enter the name of the bookmark; and click Add.

Now that you have a bookmark, insert a TOC field where you want your table of contents to appear. Include the \b switch and the bookmark name. Here's a bare-bones example which assumes that you've already created a bookmark named Jones:

```
{ TOC \b Jones }
```

TIP

The TOC field has many switches. Follow these steps to get the exact partial table of contents you want without learning them all:

1. Create your bookmark, as described previously.
2. Create and insert your table of contents the conventional way by making choices in the Table of Contents tab of the Index and Tables dialog box.
3. Select the entire table of contents, right-click, and choose Toggle Field Codes from the shortcut menu.
4. Click inside the field code, next to the right bracket.
5. Type \b followed by the name of the bookmark you created.
6. Right-click on the field and choose Update Field from the shortcut menu. The Update Table of Contents dialog box appears.

20

continues

continued

> 7. Click Update Entire Table, and choose OK.
>
> If you're sure that nothing will change in your table of contents except page numbers, there's an easier way to get a partial table of contents. Insert a table of contents the way you normally would, and just edit out the entries you don't need.
>
> Alternatively, you can copy the entries you want and paste them beneath the table of contents; then delete the original table of contents. The entries paste into the document as hyperlinks, formatted with blue underlining. You can reformat them as needed; they will still update correctly when your page numbers change.
>
> After you do this, remember to update only page numbers, not the entire table.

BUILDING TABLES OF CONTENTS FROM MULTIPLE DOCUMENTS

It's common for large documents to be composed of multiple smaller documents that need to be brought together into a single table of contents. The easiest way to do this is to work with Word's master document feature, discussed in Chapter 19, "Master Documents: Control and Share Even the Largest Documents."

First, display your document in Outline view and set up your subdocuments (or insert subdocuments using documents that already exist). Place your insertion point where you want the table of contents to appear. Next, choose Insert, Reference, Index and Tables. If you are asked whether to open all subdocuments before continuing, choose Yes. (If you choose No, Word doesn't include the missing subdocuments in your table of contents.)

The Index and Tables dialog box opens. Establish the settings you want for your table of contents and click OK. Word inserts your table of contents at the insertion point.

NOTE

> In Outline view, your table of contents appears as 10-point body text. To view your table of contents as it will print, choose Print Layout view. To view your table of contents as it would appear on the Web, choose Web Layout view.

20 INCLUDING TABLE OF CONTENTS ENTRIES FROM ANOTHER DOCUMENT

Although master documents are often the best way to build tables of contents incorporating several documents, you may occasionally want to make reference to a table of contents in another document without using master documents.

For instance, you might be sending a memo summarizing the contents of a document now being developed; or you may prefer not to use master documents because they have a reputation for being somewhat susceptible to corruption.

Word provides a special field, the Referenced Document (RD) field, for tasks such as these. Using the RD field to build a table of contents is a two-step process: First you create the RD field, specifying which file you want to reference. Next, you insert your table of contents.

NOTE

> When you build a table of contents with the RD feature, Word incorporates entries from both the referenced document and your current document. The entries associated with your referenced document are located as if the entire referenced document were located at the spot where you inserted the RD field.

As discussed earlier in this chapter, there are two ways to enter a field such as RD: from the Field dialog box, or by pressing Ctrl+F9 to display field brackets and entering the syntax between the brackets.

To enter the RD field from the Field dialog box, choose Insert, Field, and choose RD from the Field Names scroll box. In the Filename or URL: text box, enter the name of the document you want to reference, along with its path.

If you are using a path relative to the current document (in which the referenced document will always be in the same folder as the current document, or in a subfolder with the same hierarchical relationship to the current document), check the Path is Relative to Current Document check box. Click OK.

If you prefer to enter field codes directly, before you do so, be sure to click the Show/Hide Paragraph Marks button on the Standard toolbar to display hidden text. RD fields are invisible, and if you don't display hidden text, Word hides them as soon as you enter the letters RD within the field—even before you finish editing the field.

RD fields use the following syntax (notice the double backslashes in the pathname, which are required to specify a path in a Word field):

```
{ RD "c:\\folder\\filename.doc" }
```

If the file you want to reference happens to be in the same folder as your current document, you can simply specify the filename, as shown here:

```
{ RD "filename.doc" }
```

CAUTION

> Whether you use a full pathname or reference a file in the current folder, if you move the referenced file, the link is lost. This is true whether you create the field using the Field dialog box or create it directly in the document using field brackets.
>
> There is one exception: If you reference a file in the current folder and move both the file you're working on and the file you're referencing, the link remains intact as long as both files are in the same folder.

20

Now that you've entered the RD field, you can insert your table of contents the way you normally would: Click in the document where you want it to appear; choose Insert, Reference, Index and Tables; choose the Table of Contents tab; establish the settings you want; and click OK.

TIP

> When you use the RD field for applications like the ones discussed earlier, you may want to make some changes to Word's default settings in the Table of Contents tab.
>
> For example, if you are summarizing another document's table of contents and you want only high-level headings to appear, adjust the Show Levels spin box to 1 or 2. In many cases, your readers don't need to know the page numbers of the referenced document, and you can also clear the Show Page Numbers check box.

Figure 20.8 shows an RD field and TOC field in a memo; Figure 20.9 shows the corresponding field results. Note that the table of contents has been manually reformatted to fit with its surroundings.

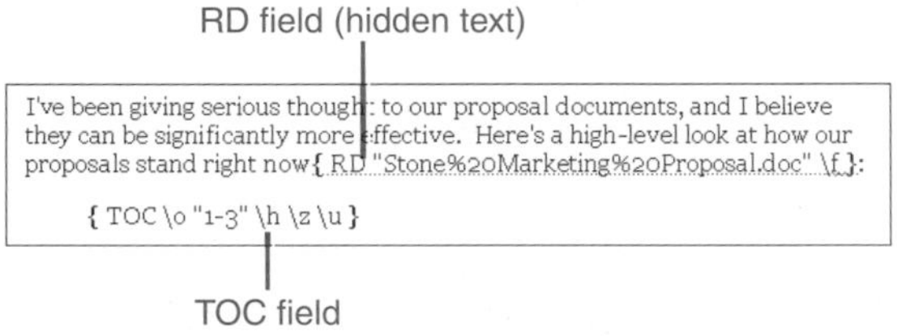

RD field (hidden text)

Figure 20.8
Inserting an RD field and Table of Contents (TOC field) in a memo…

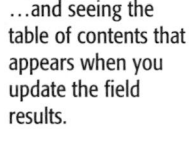

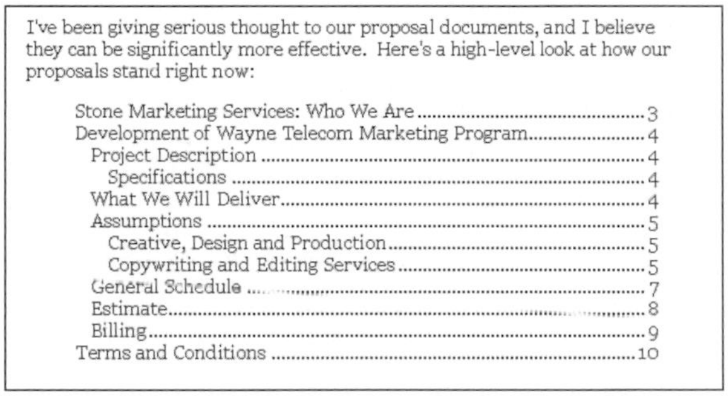

I've been giving serious thought to our proposal documents, and I believe they can be significantly more effective. Here's a high-level look at how our proposals stand right now{ RD "Stone%20Marketing%20Proposal.doc" \f }:

{ TOC \o "1-3" \h \z \u }

TOC field

Figure 20.9
…and seeing the table of contents that appears when you update the field results.

I've been giving serious thought to our proposal documents, and I believe they can be significantly more effective. Here's a high-level look at how our proposals stand right now:

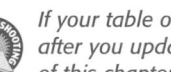

If your table of contents contains the words `Error! Cannot open file referenced on page` *after you update it, see "How to Fix Update Problems in Tables," in "Troubleshooting" at the end of this chapter.*

If your table of contents displays incorrect page numbers, see "How to Fix Incorrect Page Numbers in Tables," in "Troubleshooting" at the end of this chapter.

INTRODUCING TABLES OF FIGURES AND CAPTIONS

Often, you want other tables in your document besides a table of contents. For example, you may want a table that compiles all the figures in your document, or all the equations, or, for that matter, all the Word tables. You can build tables such as these in much the same way you've just learned how to build tables of contents.

However, Word contains a few extra tricks that might make your life even easier. For example, it can automatically insert captions for you—and then build your table of figures from the captions it has inserted. The next sections review Word's powerful captioning features. After you understand captioning, you'll learn how to compile your captions into tables of figures—or any tables you want.

USING WORD'S CAPTION FEATURE

You can't have a table of figures if you don't have any figure captions to compile into your table. So your first step is to get some figure captions into your document and let Word know that they're figures. There are three ways to do that.

You can insert your figure captions manually, using a style that you won't use for anything except captions. Word has a built-in style, Caption, that's perfectly suited for this purpose. You also can use Word's Caption feature. Or, best of all, you can tell Word to automatically insert a caption whenever it sees you inserting something that ought to be captioned.

To use Word's Caption feature to streamline captioning, first click where you want a caption to appear. Then, choose Insert, Reference, Caption to display the Caption dialog box, as shown in Figure 20.10. Word displays its default caption, Figure 1, in the Caption text box. If you want to add a description of the figure, you can type it after the figure number and click OK, and Word inserts the entire caption at your insertion point.

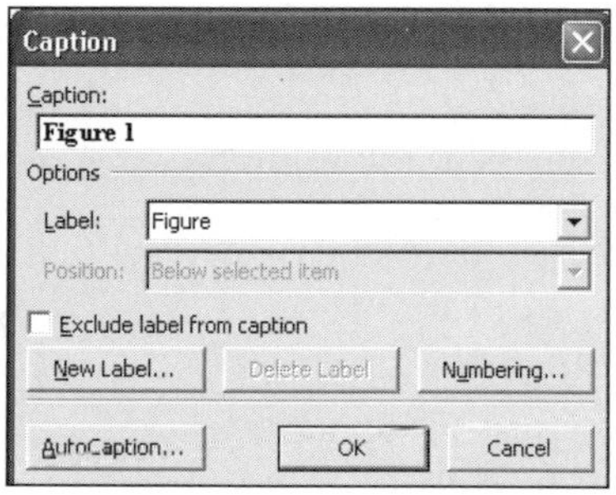

Figure 20.10
The Caption dialog box enables you to enter specific caption information while Word handles boiler-plate text and automatic caption numbering.

Click OK to return to the Captions dialog box; then click Numbering, clear the Include Chapter Number check box from the Caption Numbering dialog box, and click OK twice.

20

> **TIP**
>
> If you insert new captions or move existing ones, Word automatically renumbers all the captions for you whenever you display the document in Print Preview, print the document, or update your fields. To see the new numbering right away, choose Edit, Select All (or press Ctrl+A) to select the entire document.
>
> If you already have a table of contents, you'll be asked whether you want to update the entire table or only page numbers. Remember to choose Update Page Numbers Only if you've added custom formatting to your table of contents that you don't want to lose.

CREATING CAPTIONS FOR OTHER DOCUMENT ELEMENTS

What if you aren't creating captions for figures? If you're creating captions for equations or tables instead, choose Equation or Table in the Label drop-down list box of the Caption dialog box. If you're creating another element, such as a photo or map, you can create a special label by clicking New Label. The New Label dialog box opens (see Figure 20.11). Type your label and click OK.

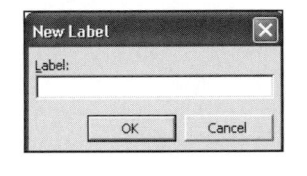

Figure 20.11
If you're creating captions for something other than a figure, table, or equation, enter your custom label in the New Label dialog box.

The new label now appears in the Caption text box, and it is added to the list of available labels for future use within the current document. If you decide you no longer need it at some point, choose Insert, Caption; then display the label in the Label drop-down box, and click Delete Label.

CHANGING THE SEQUENCE WORD USES TO NUMBER CAPTIONS

By default, Word numbers captions with Arabic numbers (1, 2, 3,…). However, you can change this. In the Caption dialog box, click Numbering; the Caption Numbering dialog box opens (see Figure 20.12). In the Format drop-down list box, choose a new sequence, such as capital letters or lowercase Roman numerals. Click OK.

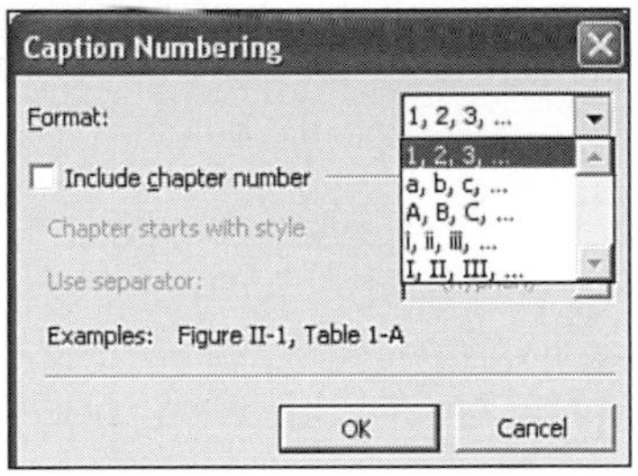

Figure 20.12
The Caption Numbering dialog box enables you to change the sequence Word uses to number captions, or to add a chapter number to your caption numbers.

ADDING CHAPTER NUMBERS TO YOUR CAPTIONS

Often, you want your captions to include chapter numbers as well as sequence numbers, as is the case with the captions in this book. Word's "official" approach to inserting chapter numbers is surprisingly complex, and it makes sense only if you have multiple chapters in your document. If you are editing a document that contains only one or a few chapters (even if it's part of a larger book), skip to the "Easier Ways to Add Chapter Numbers" section for some quicker ways to accomplish this.

Word connects chapter numbering in captions with the Outline Numbering feature. That means you have to insert outline numbers in your document before you can get chapter numbers in your captions. If you request chapter numbers by checking the Include <u>C</u>hapter Number check box in the Caption Numbering dialog box, you're likely to encounter the bewildering message box shown in Figure 20.13.

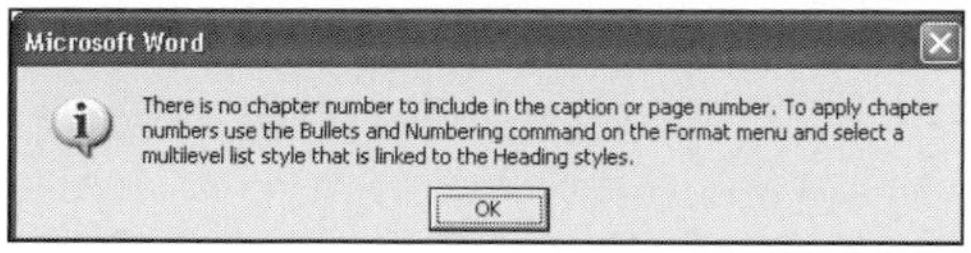

Figure 20.13
Word doesn't want to insert chapter numbers in your captions because you haven't inserted outline numbers throughout your document.

> **→   See** "Using Word's Automatic Outline Numbering," **p. 636**.

By connecting captions to chapter numbers, Word can use { STYLEREF } fields that look for the most recent example of a style and borrow the text they need from there. This way, Word knows when a caption should read Figure 1.1 and when it should read Figure 2.1.

This is a hassle, especially if you weren't intending to use outline numbering, but go along with it—for now.

SET UP YOUR DOCUMENT FOR OUTLINE NUMBERING   Start by using Word's outlining tools to make sure you used heading styles throughout your document. This procedure won't work if you simply use outline levels. You must use the heading styles Heading 1, Heading 2, Heading 3, and so on. Set aside one heading level—typically Heading 1—specifically for your chapter names. Figure 20.14 shows how your first-level headings should look in Outline view.

Figure 20.14
Make sure you use Heading 1 only for chapter names and you include nothing but chapter names in your Heading 1s.

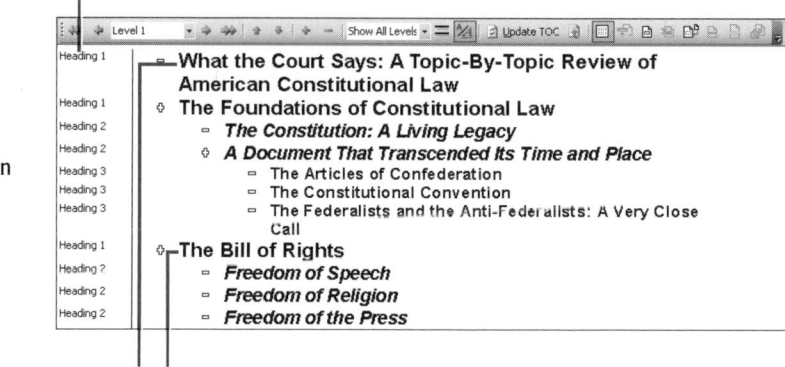

Style area displaying style names

First-level headings

TIP

> To display the styles used in a document (as shown in Figure 20.14), choose Tools, Options, View; and set the Style Area Width to a width wide enough for all your styles to be visible, such as 0.8".

INSERT YOUR OUTLINE NUMBERING   Next, insert your outline numbering, as shown here:

1. Select the entire document (or at least all sections where you want to add captions).

2. Choose Format, Bullets and Numbering.

3. Choose the Outline Numbered tab.

4. Select a heading numbering scheme from the bottom row of four options. (If you choose from the top row, Word numbers all your paragraphs, not just headings, so your figure numbers won't match your chapter numbers.)

5. Click Customize to make any changes to your outline numbering scheme, or just click OK to insert the outline numbers.

INSERT YOUR CAPTIONS   Now that you have outline numbers in your document, follow these steps to insert your captions:

1. Place the insertion point where you want your first caption.

2. Choose Insert, Reference, Caption.

3. In the Caption dialog box, add any information you want to your caption. If necessary, add a new label.

4. Click Numbering. The Caption Numbering dialog box opens.

5. Check the Include Chapter Number check box, if it is not already checked.

6. Choose Heading 1 in the Chapter Starts with Style drop-down list box. (This example assumes that chapter numbers are formatted with Heading 1 style—and, as already discussed, they are the only text formatted with that style.)

7. In the Use Separator drop-down list box, choose the separator character you want from the following selection: hyphen, period, colon, em dash, en dash. Separator characters appear between the chapter number and figure number, as in the following examples: 1.1, 1-1, 1:1.

8. Click OK twice.

The caption appears in your document, containing the number of the current chapter. Underneath the hood, here's what's happened. Word has inserted a { STYLEREF } field that searches toward the beginning of the document for the first Heading 1 style. When a Heading 1 style is found, the text formatted in that style is displayed as the field result.

TIP

> If you've gone through all this, and then decide you don't want outline numbers after all, there is a possible solution. When the document is absolutely finished, select it all (Ctrl+A). Then follow these steps:
>
> 1. Press Ctrl+Shift+F9 to *unlink* all the fields in your document so that none of them will update ever again. (This affects all fields, including the fields that track caption numbering within the chapter—so be careful!)
> 2. With the entire document selected, choose Format, Bullets and Numbering, Outline Numbered.
> 3. In the Outline Numbered tab choose None and click OK. The outline numbers disappear, but the captions stay the way they were.

EASIER WAYS TO ADD CHAPTER NUMBERS

Boy, that was hard work. Isn't there an easier way? You'd better believe it. You really don't have to include outline numbering to get chapter numbers in your captions.

ADDING CHAPTER NUMBERS TO CAPTIONS IN ONE-CHAPTER DOCUMENTS   Consider the easiest case: a document containing only one chapter. Maybe you've been asked to write Chapter 12 of a book. You're not working from within someone else's master document (or, if you are, they aren't requiring you to use Word's outline numbering approach to captions).

Follow these steps to insert chapter numbers:

1. Use Word's Insert, Reference, Caption feature to insert captions without chapter numbers.
2. Choose Edit, Replace and then use Word's Find and Replace feature to search for all references to the word "figure" that are styled using the Caption style. Replace them with "figure" followed by your chapter number and whatever separator character you want to use. You can search for a style by clicking the Format button in the Replace tab, clicking Style, and choosing the style for which you want to search.

➜ **See** "Creating Styles," **p. 339**.

CREATING CUSTOM CAPTION NUMBERING FOR ALL YOUR DOCUMENTS   You can go a step further and create a chapter numbering solution you can reuse in all your documents, no matter how many chapters they contain—without ever using outline numbering unless you want to. Follow these steps:

1. Select the chapter number anywhere in your document and format it with a new character style through the New Style dialog box (see Figure 20.15), accessible through Format, Styles and Numbering, New Style. For this example, name the character style chapnum.

➜ **See** "Understanding Character Styles," **p. 332**.

2. Use Insert, Reference, Caption (refer to Figure 20.10) to insert a caption that doesn't contain a chapter number. (If the chapter number appears in the Caption text box, click Numbering and clear the Include Chapter Number check box from the Caption Numbering dialog box.)

20

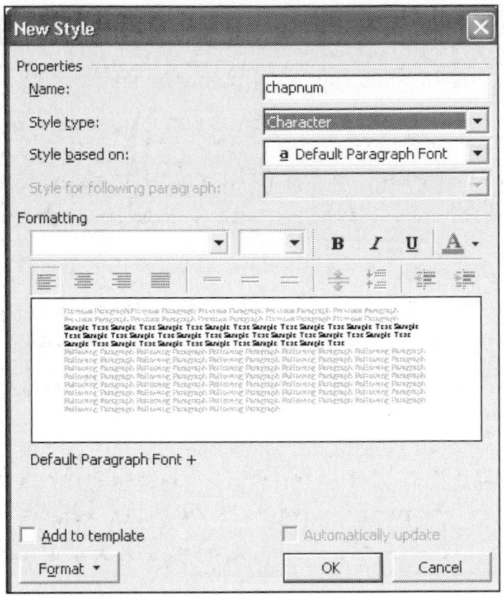

Figure 20.15
Creating a character style named chapnum in the New Style dialog box.

3. If you want, reformat the caption to your tastes and update the caption style to reflect your changes. After you reformat the caption, click in the Style drop-down box on the Formatting toolbar, press Enter, and click OK in the Modify Style dialog box that appears.

4. Click where you want the chapter number to appear within your caption.

5. Press Ctrl+F9 to insert field brackets.

6. Type the following within the field brackets (see Figure 20.16): `styleref chapnum`. This inserts a STYLEREF field that looks for text you formatted in the chapnum character style.

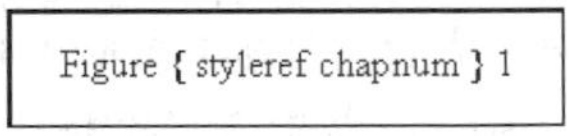

Figure 20.16
How the field looks when placed in your document (and toggled to display field codes rather than results).

Figure { styleref chapnum } 1

7. Press F9 to update the field. It should now display the chapter number to which you applied the character style (see Figure 20.17). After you update the STYLEREF field, it should display the chapter number.

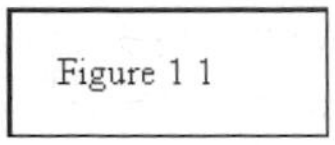

Figure 20.17
How the same field looks when updated to show results.

Figure 1 1

8. Manually enter any separator characters you need (see Figure 20.18). In this example, a period is added to separate the chapter number and figure number.

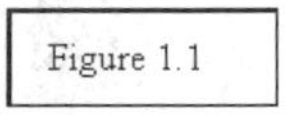

Figure 20.18
The same field, manually adjusted to include separator characters.

Figure 1.1

9. Create an *AutoText entry* based on your caption. To do so, select the caption, choose Insert, <u>A</u>utoText, New; type an entry name such as figr (see Figure 20.19); and click OK. Finally, make the entire caption an AutoText entry so that it's easy to reuse.

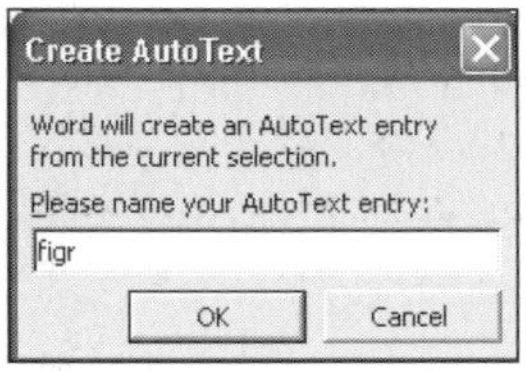

Figure 20.19
Creating an AutoText entry that makes this customized caption easy to reuse.

Create AutoText ☒

Word will create an AutoText entry from the current selection.

<u>P</u>lease name your AutoText entry:

figr

OK   Cancel

Now, whenever you start a new document that you want to contain automatically numbered captions, do this: First, type the chapter number and mark it as a bookmark named chapnum. Then, wherever you want to insert a caption, type the AutoText entry and press F3 to turn it into a complete caption.

AUTOMATING CAPTIONS

You can take Word's captioning feature one giant step further. Word can automatically add captions any time you add specific graphics or other elements to your document. To use Word's AutoCaption feature, choose <u>I</u>nsert, Refere<u>n</u>ce, <u>C</u>aption to display the Caption dialog box. Then, click <u>A</u>utoCaption. The AutoCaption dialog box opens (see Figure 20.20).

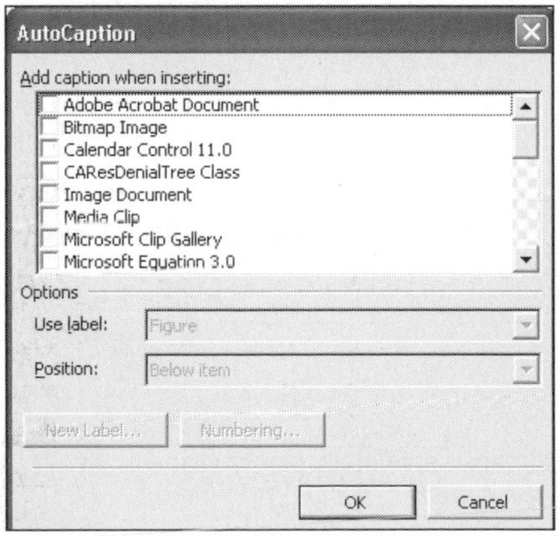

Figure 20.20
From the AutoCaption dialog box, you can tell Word which document elements to caption automatically, which label to use, and where those captions should appear.

AutoCaption ☒

Add caption when inserting:

☐ Adobe Acrobat Document
☐ Bitmap Image
☐ Calendar Control 11.0
☐ CAResDenialTree Class
☐ Image Document
☐ Media Clip
☐ Microsoft Clip Gallery
☐ Microsoft Equation 3.0

Options

Use <u>l</u>abel: Figure

<u>P</u>osition: Below item

New Label...   Numbering...

OK   Cancel

20

In the Add Caption When Inserting scroll box, you see a list of document elements. This list varies depending on the software installed on your computer. It can include elements created by other Microsoft Office programs; for example, PowerPoint slides or Excel worksheets. It can also include a wide range of elements that can be created by Microsoft Office's common tools, including charts, graphics, and drawings, as well as equations built with Microsoft Equation 3.0. It can also include files generated with a wide range of third-party programs, such as Adobe Acrobat, Adobe Photoshop, and Macromedia Fireworks.

Check the box next to every item you want Word to caption. Then, specify the label you want to use (or create a new label, if you want). In the Position drop-down list box, choose whether you want your caption to automatically appear below or above the item you insert. If you want to change automatic caption numbering, click Numbering and make your changes in the Caption Numbering dialog box you learned about earlier.

If you choose, whenever you check a box to automatically caption another type of document element, you can also click New Label to customize the text of the caption that will accompany that specific element. These customized labels are attached to the document's current template, which means that you can associate different caption text with the same file types if you work with a document attached to a different template.

When you finish, click OK in the AutoCaption dialog box. Word begins adding captions automatically whenever you insert a document element you told it to caption. Existing elements already in the document are not automatically captioned, however.

BUILDING TABLES OF FIGURES

Now that you understand captions, it's time to discuss ways you can compile those captions into tables of figures. First, choose Insert, Reference, Index and Tables, and click the Table of Figures tab (see Figure 20.21).

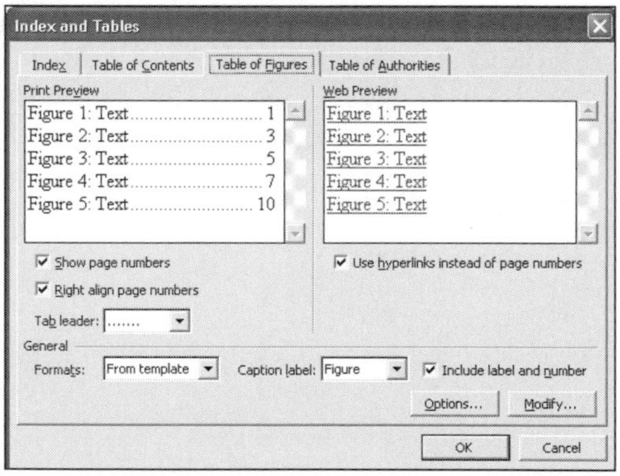

Figure 20.21
The Table of Figures tab offers many of the same options as the Table of Contents tab.

N O T E

Tables of "figures" can list a range of document elements: images, equations, row-and-column tables, and many others.

The Table of Figures tab looks similar to the Table of Contents tab you learned about earlier in this chapter. For example, you can choose whether page numbers should appear in your table, and if so, whether they should be right-aligned or appear next to the caption text. If you right-align your figure listings, you can choose a tab leader. You can also choose from five formats: Classic, Distinctive, Centered, Formal, and Simple.

You can see the effects of any change you make in two separate preview boxes: Print Preview shows how your table of figures will appear in a printed document, and Web Preview shows how it will appear if saved as a Web page and displayed through a Web browser.

NOTE

> These formats are designed to complement the table of contents formats, and they use the same names as Word's table of contents formats. However, they are not identical to the table of contents formats. As with tables of contents, you can see what a format will look like in the Preview box.
>
> When you choose a Table of Figures format and click OK, Word inserts the table in your document. Word applies its built-in Table of Figures style, after changing the style to reflect the format you chose.

Each table of figures Word compiles is based on one set of captions in your document. In other words, if you created some captions using the Table label, and others using the Figure label, each set has to be compiled separately into its own table of figures—but then, that's probably what you want.

In the Caption Label drop-down list box, choose the type of captions you want to compile. If you want to include the labels and numbers as well as the caption text, check the Include Label and Number check box; otherwise, clear it. If you're now satisfied with your table, click OK, and Word inserts it in your document. Figure 20.22 shows a default table of figures using the built-in styles in the Normal template.

Figure 1. Typical network hub. 3
Figure 2. Network routers. 7
Figure 3. The architecture of the Internet. 9
Figure 4. Configuring an IP client workstation. 10
Figure 5. How IPv6 changes typical IP networks. 15

Figure 20.22
The default table of figures.

20

BUILDING TABLES OF FIGURES FROM A DIFFERENT STYLE

Until now, you've learned how to build tables of figures by telling Word to collect the contents of every figure formatted with the Caption style. Because Word automatically uses the Caption style for all the captions it creates, you're in good shape as long as you use Word's automatic captioning feature. But what if you want to compile a table from text formatted in a different style?

Choose Insert, Reference, Index and Tables; then choose the Table of Figures tab; and click Options. The Table of Figures Options dialog box opens (see Figure 20.23).

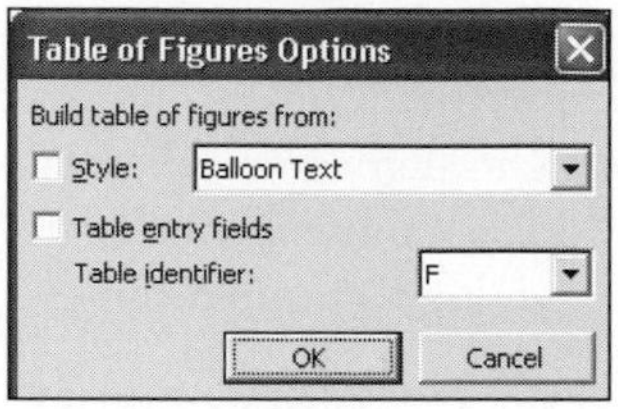

Figure 20.23
In the Table of Figures Options dialog box, you can choose another style from which to build your table—or, as you'll see later, you can choose a set of table entry fields.

To choose another style, check the Style check box and select the style from the drop-down box next to it. Click OK to return to the Table of Figures tab, and click OK again to insert the table in your document.

BUILDING TABLES FROM FIGURES WITH DIFFERENT STYLES

Occasionally, you might want to create a table of figures based on document elements that don't share a common style. For example, you might want a table of figures that contains all the quotations in your document. Because those quotations appear within paragraphs of various types scattered throughout your document, you can't compile them into a single figure table based on one style.

Earlier in this chapter, you learned about TC fields, which Word can use to build tables of contents without using styles. TC fields come to your rescue again now. Follow this procedure:

1. Select the text you want to incorporate into your table of contents.
2. Choose Insert, Field.
3. Choose TC from the Field Names scroll box.
4. Click Field Codes.
5. Click Options.
6. In the Description text box, enter the text you want to appear for this reference when the table of figures is compiled. Be sure to place the text within quotation marks.
7. After the close quotation mark, enter \f followed by a letter of the alphabet that will identify all entries for this table of figures.
8. Click OK.

Continuing with the quotation example, imagine that your document has a quotation by Alvin Toffler. You might enter the TC field:

```
{ TC "Toffler" \f q }
```

Then, later, you come across a quotation by Tom Peters you want to flag:

```
{ TC "Peters" \f q }
```

Because they both use the \f q switch, you can compile them by following these steps:

1. Choose Insert, Reference, Index and Tables, Table of Figures to display the Table of Figures tab.

2. Click Options to display the Table of Figures Options dialog box.

3. Check the Table Entry Fields check box.

4. Choose Q (or whatever letter you've inserted after \f in your TC fields) in the Table Identifier drop-down list box.

5. Click OK twice.

Word builds a table of figures that contains the names of all the people you've quoted and the page numbers where the quotes may be found.

INTRODUCING CITATIONS

If you're responsible for preparing legal documents, you know that special techniques are required to insert and track *citations*, which are references to cases, statutes, or other legal documents. Word streamlines both the process of marking citations and the process of collecting them into *tables of authorities*.

> **TIP**
>
> If you prepare legal documents, you may be interested in the Legal Pleading Wizard, which streamlines the process of creating reusable document templates that follow the requirements of the courts you work with.
>
> To work with the Legal Pleading Wizard, choose File, New; click On My Computer on the New Document Task Pane; click the Legal Pleadings tab; and double-click the Pleading Wizard icon.

MARKING CITATIONS

There's nothing unusual about entering the text of your citations: You simply type them as you normally would, wherever they are needed in your document. Commonly, in the first reference to a citation, you'll enter the long (full) version, which typically includes case numbers, dates, and other essential information. In later references, you'll usually enter a short version, which typically includes only the name of the case.

The next step is to mark the citations you've entered so that Word can compile them into a table of authorities. Select the first long citation in your document and press Alt+Shift+I to open the Mark Citation dialog box (see Figure 20.24).

> **TIP**
>
> If you use Mark Citation extensively, you can add it to your Insert menu through the Tools, Customize dialog box, as covered in the "Customizing Toolbars and Menus" section of Chapter 31, "Customizing Word."

20

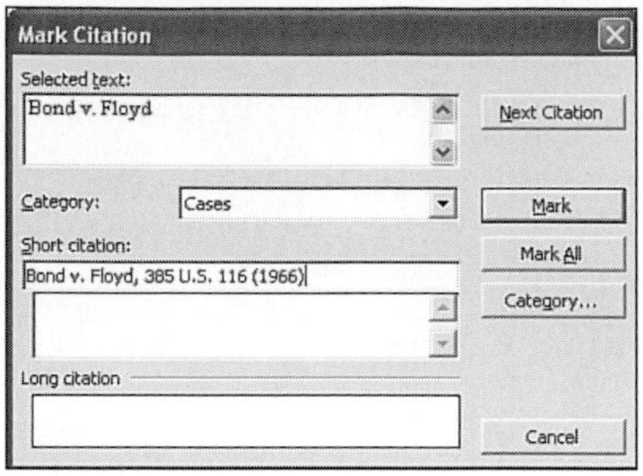

Figure 20.24
You can insert and manage citations in a legal document through the Mark Citation dialog box.

Your citation appears in the Selected Text box. Edit and format it so that it looks the way you want it to appear in your table of authorities. Your citation also appears in the Short Citation text box. Edit the short citation so that it matches the short citations you've placed in your document. Typically, this means deleting everything except the case name.

Because some tables of authorities are organized by category (for example, cases in one table, statutes in another), choose a Category from the drop-down list box. Word includes seven built-in categories: Cases, Statutes, Other Authorities, Rules, Treatises, Regulations, and Constitutional Provisions. If you need to create a table of authorities for a different category, you can create the category yourself. Word provides nine generic categories, numbered 8 through 16, which you can rename any way you want. Follow these steps to create a custom category:

1. In the Mark Citation dialog box, select one of the numbered categories.

2. Click Category. The Edit Category dialog box opens (see Figure 20.25).

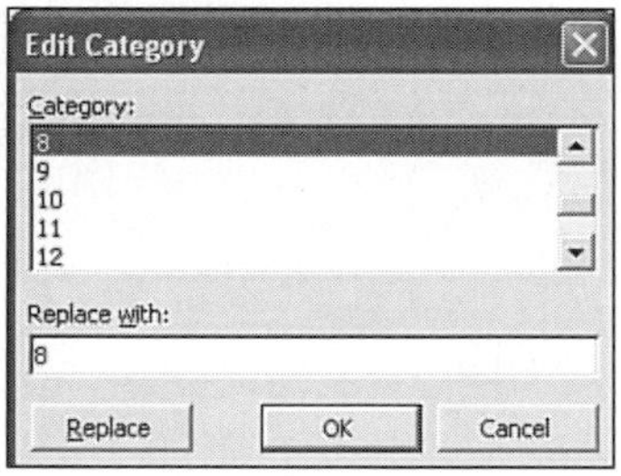

Figure 20.25
You can add up to nine custom categories of citations using the Edit Category dialog box.

3. Enter the new name in the Replace With text box.

4. Click Replace.

5. Click OK. You return to the Mark Citation dialog box with your new category already selected.

You've now prepared your citation for marking. If you want to mark only the long citation you've already selected, click Mark. If you want Word to search your entire document and mark all references to the same citation, long and short, click Mark All.

Now that you've marked all references to the first citation, you can move on to the next. Click Next Citation. Word searches your document for the next block of text it thinks might be part of a citation. For example, Word flags the abbreviation "v." and the phrase "In re," both commonly used in case names. Word also flags the symbol § that often appears in statute citations.

If Word has flagged a citation you want to mark, click the document and select the entire citation. Open the Mark Citation dialog box; the citation you selected appears in both the Selected Text and the Short Citation text boxes. You can then edit and mark it following the steps you've already learned.

NOTE

> When you mark a citation, Word inserts a TA (Table of Authorities) field in your document. This field stores the information that will be compiled when you create your table of authorities. For long citations, the TA field looks like this:
>
> ```
> { TA \l "Marbury v. Madison, 5 U.S. (3)" \s "Marbury v.
> Madison" \c 1 }
> ```
>
> As you can see, the TA field for a long citation includes both the detailed text of the long citation and the abbreviated version Word uses to search for short citations. The Mark Citation dialog box doesn't let you edit a long citation after you've marked it, but if you need to, you can edit the field directly.
>
> For short citations, the TA field looks like this:
>
> ```
> { TA \s "Marbury v. Madison" }
> ```
>
> Word inserts TA field codes formatted as hidden text. If you press Alt+F9 to toggle field codes and you still don't see your TA field codes, click the Show/Hide Paragraph Marks button on the Standard toolbar to display them.

ADDING MORE CITATIONS LATER

Imagine you've already marked the citations in your document, and you return to add new citations—either long citations or additional references to short citations you've already marked elsewhere. To mark them, press Alt+Shift+I to open the Mark Citation dialog box and click Next Citation; Word searches for the first citation it hasn't already marked. If Word doesn't find one of your new citations, select it yourself and then press Alt+Shift+I; the citation is displayed in the Mark Citation dialog box when it opens.

COMPILING TABLES OF AUTHORITIES FROM CITATIONS

After you've created your citations, you can compile them into tables of authorities. Choose Insert, Reference, Index and Tables, and click the Table of Authorities tab (see Figure 20.26).

If you've used tables of contents or figures, this dialog box certainly looks familiar. By default, Word builds your table of authorities from styles in your current template. Or you can choose from one of four formats: Classic, Distinctive, Formal, and Simple. You can also

20

specify the tab leader to use—or no tab leader at all. A default table of authorities is shown in Figure 20.27.

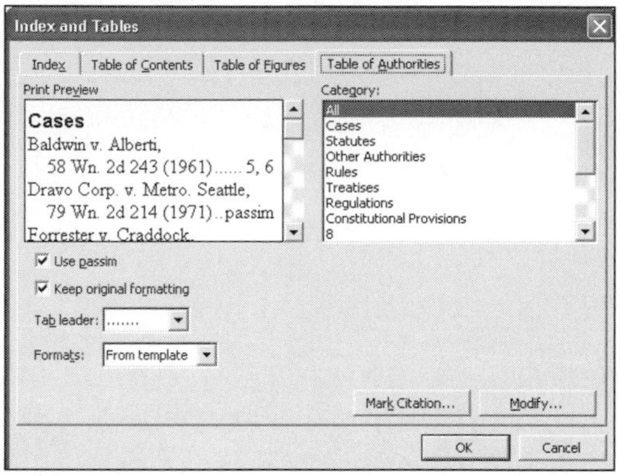

Figure 20.26
The Table of Authorities tab of the Index and Tables dialog box gives you extensive control over how your tables of authorities compile.

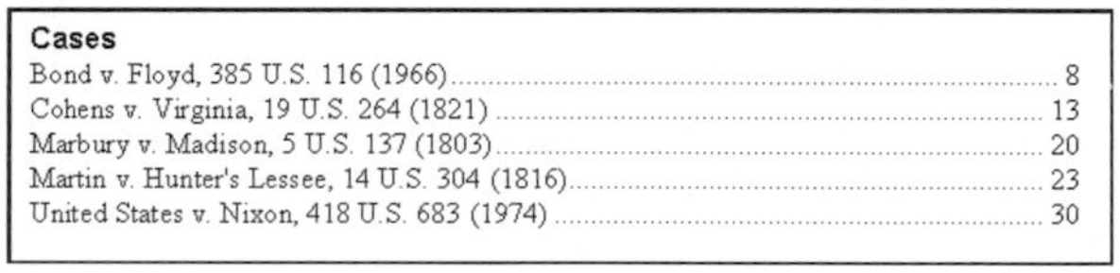

Cases

Bond v. Floyd, 385 U.S. 116 (1966)	8
Cohens v. Virginia, 19 U.S. 264 (1821)	13
Marbury v. Madison, 5 U.S. 137 (1803)	20
Martin v. Hunter's Lessee, 14 U.S. 304 (1816)	23
United States v. Nixon, 418 U.S. 683 (1974)	30

Figure 20.27
A default table of authorities using the built-in styles in Word's Normal template.

CAUTION

Word's built-in Tables of Citations formats meet the requirements of most courts and jurisdictions, but you should still compare your table of authorities with similar documents the court has accepted, and double-check with the court clerk if you're not sure.

TIP

You can also click Modify on the Table of Authorities tab to change the TOA Heading style Word uses to build tables of authorities–but as discussed in the table of contents section of this chapter, it's faster to reformat and update the styles in your document.

20

By default, Word includes every citation in your table of authorities. If you want a separate table for one category of citation, choose it from the Category drop-down box located on the Tables of Authorities tab.

It's common practice, when listing citations that appear repeatedly in a legal document, to substitute the word *passim* for the multiple page references. By default, Word substitutes *passim* whenever you have at least five references to the same citation. To display the actual page numbers instead, clear the Use Passim check box on the Tables of Authorities tab.

Many citations contain complex character formatting, especially boldface, italic, and underlining. By default, Word carries that formatting into your table of authorities. However, you can tell Word not to do so by clearing the Keep Original Formatting check box on the Tables of Authorities tab.

TROUBLESHOOTING

HOW TO FIX UPDATE PROBLEMS IN TABLES

It's common for the words Error! Bookmark not defined to appear in a table in place of page numbers. If this occurs, it's possible that you deleted one or more headings or TC entry fields from your document and then updated the table of contents using the Update Page Numbers Only option. You have three options:

- Restore the heading in your document.
- Delete the offending line from your table of contents manually.
- Update the table of contents, and when Word displays the dialog box asking whether you want to update the entire table, choose the Update Entire Table option (thereby also removing any manual formatting or editing you may have added).

Another possibility is that you may have separated the table of contents from the material it was built from. For example, you may have copied the table of contents into another document, or you may have built a table of contents in a master document and broken the links to the subdocuments.

To create a separate document that contains only a table of contents, while preserving the accurate page numbering, do this:

1. Choose File, Save As to make a separate copy of your document.
2. Working in the duplicate file you just created, select your table of contents.
3. Press F9 to update your table of contents.
4. With the table of contents still selected, press Ctrl+Shift+F9. This eliminates the underlying TOC field but retains all the text it displayed, including page numbers.
5. Delete everything else in the duplicate document except the table of contents.

→ For more information about managing links between master documents and subdocuments, **see** Chapter 19, "Master Documents: Control and Share Even the Largest Documents," **p. 653**.

HOW TO FIX INCORRECT PAGE NUMBERS IN TABLES

Occasionally, tables may contain incorrect page numbers. This may be caused by

- Hidden text that was visible when you last updated your table of contents
- Changes in margins or other document elements that affect page numbering

Make sure your document looks exactly as it should when you print it; then select the table of contents and press F9 to update it. Unless you've removed or added headings or TC entries, choose Update Page Numbers Only when asked how you want the table to be updated.

HOW TO ELIMINATE BODY TEXT IN TABLES OF CONTENTS

Occasionally, tables of contents may incorrectly include paragraphs of text from your document. If this occurs, search for the paragraph and make sure it is not formatted with a heading style or formatted with an outline level other than Body Text.

Often, this problem occurs when you place a line break (Shift+Enter) between a heading and the following paragraph, instead of a paragraph break (Enter).

→ For more information about outline levels, **see** "Applying Outline Levels to Specific Text," **p. 635**.

If you must format paragraphs in an outline level other than Body Text, but you still do not want them in your table of contents, one workaround is to delete them manually from your table of contents after you build it. Remember that when you update your table of contents, you must choose Update Page Numbers Only instead of Update Entire Table; otherwise, the paragraphs will reappear.

CHAPTER 21

BUILDING MORE EFFECTIVE INDEXES

In this chapter

HOW WORD INDEXES WORK

A quality index is an invaluable tool for helping your readers quickly access the specific information they're looking for—not just in books, but in any document that's long enough to make browsing for specific information inefficient. Word's indexing features are intended to automate those aspects of indexing that a computer is smart enough to do on its own and streamline those for which there's no substitute for your human judgment.

Building an index with Word is a three-step process:

1. Mark your index entries—either one by one or a batch at a time.
2. Tell Word how to format the index.
3. Compile the index. (That's the easy part.)

In general, compiling your index should be one of the last things you do with your document. Indexing last reduces the number of times you have to rebuild your index. It also tends to increase the quality of your index because you have access to the entire, final document while you're making decisions about how individual entries should be handled.

> **TIP**
>
> If you are indexing multiple documents–such as chapters in a book–you may want to build a mini-index to view all your index entries for one chapter, before you start to work on the next. By doing so, you can improve the consistency of the index entries you create and minimize the amount of index editing you'll have to do later.
>
> To create an index for a single chapter, open the file containing that chapter and insert the index using the procedure described later in this chapter, in the "Compiling Your Index" section. Select the index; press Ctrl+Shift+F9 to unlink the index field and convert it into ordinary text. Then cut it from the document and paste it into a blank document that you can print or view for reference while working on other chapters.

CREATING A NEW INDEX ENTRY

The quickest way to mark an index entry is to select the text you want to appear in your index and press Alt+Shift+X. Alternatively, you can choose Insert, Reference, Index and Tables; click the Index tab; and click Mark Entry. Either way, the Mark Index Entry dialog box opens (see Figure 21.1). The text you've selected appears in the Main Entry text box. In some cases, that text serves perfectly well as your index entry.

> **TIP**
>
> If you plan to create an index entry that doesn't use any of the words in the surrounding text, don't select any text before pressing Alt+Shift+X. The Mark Index Entry dialog box appears with no text already present in the Main Entry or Subentry text boxes.
>
> Although it's convenient to display the Mark Index Entry dialog box with text already present, many professional indexers find it quicker to type the entry they want than it is to edit the text Word inserts automatically.

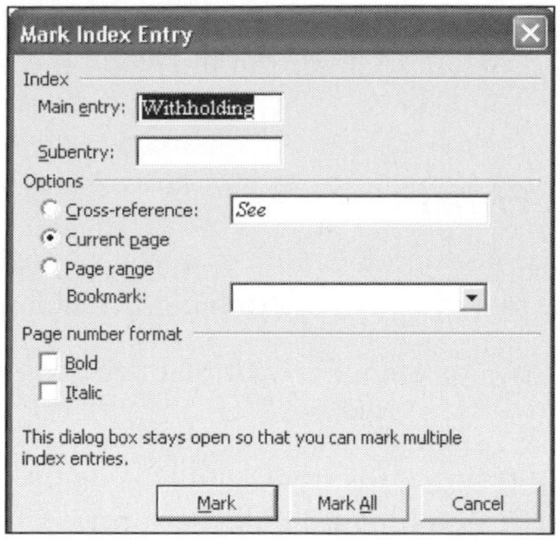

Figure 21.1

You can control all elements of your index entries through the Mark Index Entry dialog box.

If you're satisfied with your entry, click <u>M</u>ark. Word inserts an { XE } *field code* in your document that contains the text of your entry. Because the field code is hidden text, you don't see it unless you display hidden text by clicking the Show/Hide Paragraph Marks button on the Standard toolbar.

In many cases, you'll want to modify the main entry. For example, you'll often find that the text in your document is not quite the same as the text you're using for index entries about the same subject elsewhere in the document. To make sure that readers find all references to the same subject, you need to make the index entries consistent. Even when this is not an issue, you'll often need to edit your index entries to make them more concise and precise.

You can make these edits directly, in the Main <u>E</u>ntry text box. Because the entry appears highlighted when the text box opens, you can replace it by simply starting to type your new entry. Or if you only want to edit the entry slightly, click in the box and start editing text.

TIP

> If you select text within your document that includes symbols, such as copyright marks, these will be included in your index entry unless you manually edit them out.
>
> You can also select a picture and create an index entry for it, but you will have to specify text for the entry—Word will not insert a picture in an index.

After you mark the index entry, the dialog box remains open. If you want, you can create a second entry in the same location. This is called *double-posting,* and it reflects the fact that different readers will look in different places in your index for the same information. In professional indexing, double-posting is widespread, and even *triple-posting*—three different entries for the same location in the document—can be common.

Whether you double-post or triple-post, the Mark Index Entry dialog box stays open, assuming you'll want to create another entry. To create another entry elsewhere in the document, click the document, select the text you want to index, and then click again in the Mark Index Entry dialog box. The text you've selected now appears in the Main <u>E</u>ntry text box.

21

You can move throughout the document this way, using Word's navigation tools, creating entries as you go. When you're finished, click Close, and the Mark Index Entry dialog box closes.

IDEAS FOR IMPROVING YOUR INDEX ENTRIES

Often, simply copying text from your document doesn't give you an index entry that's as useful as it could be. Here are some ideas you can use to build better index entries:

- Switch last and first names so that, for example, your main entry reads "Gerstner, Lou" rather than "Lou Gerstner."

- Spell out and explain abbreviations using the most familiar version first so that, for example, references to "PCI boards" appear as "PCI (Peripheral Component Interconnect) boards."

  Consider having your index "double-post" acronyms like these so that a second entry in the index would say "Peripheral Component Interconnect, see PCI." To learn how to create index entries that use syntax like this, see "Creating Cross-Referenced 'See' Index Entries," later in this chapter.

- Change word forms for consistency or simplicity so that your entry reads "law" rather than "legalities." Avoid multiple entries that might confuse the reader, such as separate entries for "installing," "installations," and "install procedures."

- Make sure your index entries are clear and concise. Avoid vagueness, and avoid words like "understanding" or "using" that are implied with every entry.

- Avoid adjectives, especially at the beginning of index entries. Readers are much less likely to look up an entry such as "multiple tables" than they are to look up "tables" and find "multiple" as a subentry beneath it.

- Make sure your index reflects the level of your audience, with simpler entries for audiences new to the subject matter, and more complex entries for readers who already have a substantial base of knowledge to draw on.

NOTE

> You can edit field codes after you insert them. To do so, display hidden text by choosing Tools, Options, View, and checking the Hidden Text check box. Next, insert your cursor directly in an { XE } field code; then, using any of Word's text entry or editing features, including cut, copy, and paste.

CREATING INDEX CODES MANUALLY

When you use the Mark Index Entry dialog box, you are inserting an { XE } field in your document. If you are planning to do quite a bit of indexing, you might want to dispense with the dialog box altogether and create a macro that inserts an { XE } field in your document and positions your insertion point at the appropriate location within it.

To create such a macro, follow these steps:

1. Make sure that the Show/Hide Paragraph Marks icon on the Standard toolbar (next to the Zoom drop-down box) is toggled on; if it isn't, click it. ({ XE } field codes are invisible unless you show them, and this is usually the easiest way to do so.)

2. Choose Tools, Macro, Record New Macro.

3. In the Record Macro dialog box (see Figure 21.2), assign the macro a name, such as IndexEntry.

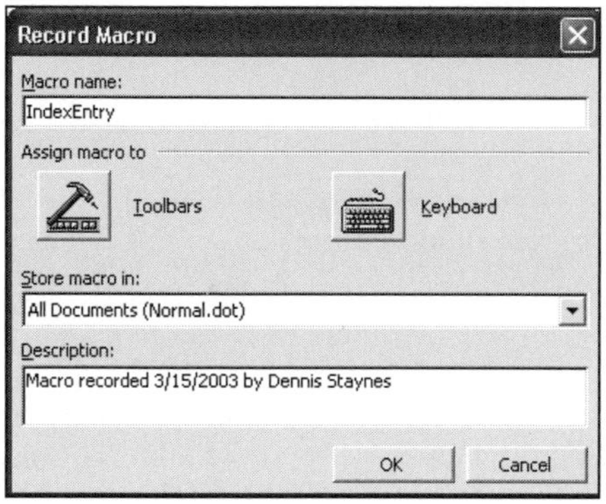

Figure 21.2
Preparing to record a macro named IndexEntry.

Record Macro

Macro name:
IndexEntry

Assign macro to

Toolbars   Keyboard

Store macro in:
All Documents (Normal.dot)

Description:
Macro recorded 3/15/2003 by Dennis Staynes

OK   Cancel

4. Click Keyboard, choose a keyboard shortcut for the macro, such as Alt+X, and click Assign.

5. Click Close. The Macro Recorder begins working.

6. Press Ctrl+F9 to insert field brackets.

7. Type the following between the field brackets:
   XE " "

8. Press the left-arrow key once to position the insertion point between the field brackets.

9. Click the Stop Recording button on the Stop Recording toolbar.

Now, every time you need to enter an index entry, you can simply press Alt+X and type the entry between the quotation marks.

→ For more about entering index entries directly in field codes, **see** "Creating Subentries," **p. 721**.

→ For more information on recording macros, **see** Chapter 32, "Recording and Running Visual Basic Macros," **p. 1069**.

If you plan to create many index entries and you prefer to use the Mark Index Entry dialog box rather than entering the entries directly into field codes, it may be worth your time to create a toolbar button that displays the Mark Index Entry dialog box. Drag Mark Index Entry (under Insert) from the Commands tab of the Customize dialog box to your favorite toolbar.

21

TIP

> Adding a toolbar button for Mark Index Entry actually causes a new toolbar button to appear, containing the words *Mark Index Entry*. If the toolbar button is too wide for you, right-click it while the Customize dialog box is displayed, click the Name command, and edit the name. (You might shorten it to XE, the name of the field code it inserts.) When you're finished, close the Customize dialog box.

→ For more information on customizing toolbars, **see** "Customizing Toolbars and Menus," **p. 1023**.

FORMATTING INDEX ENTRIES

You can apply boldface, italic, or underlining to any index text you enter in the Mark Index Entry dialog box. Simply select and format all or part of the text. This enables you to create index entries for book titles that require italics. It also helps you call attention to special aspects of an entry, as in the following example:

```
Harris, Katherine, quoted, 307
```

Within the Mark Index Entry dialog box, you can select text and press Ctrl+B to boldface it, Ctrl+I to italicize it, or Ctrl+U to underline it. This saves you the trouble of editing or formatting field codes in your document.

Although these formats are probably the most common in indexes, others—such as superscript and subscript—can be applied if needed just as easily with their usual keyboard shortcuts—for example, Ctrl+PlusSign for subscript, and Ctrl+Shift+PlusSign for superscript.

→ For a list of keyboard shortcuts for formatting text, **see** Table 4.1, "Toolbar Buttons and Keyboard Shortcuts for Font Formatting," **p. 112**.

You might also set aside boldface to call special attention to exceptionally detailed discussions of a topic.

In addition to being able to format a specific index entry as boldface or italic, many indexers prefer to call attention to some entries by boldfacing or italicizing the page numbers associated with the entry. For example, it's common to italicize page numbers associated with entries that refer to photos rather than body text.

Formatting the text of an index entry doesn't affect the formatting of the page number. If you want to add formatting to a page number, check the Bold or Italic check box in the Mark Index Entry dialog box.

MARKING MULTIPLE ENTRIES AT ONCE

If you want, you can tell Word to mark all references to specific text. Follow these steps:

1. Select the text you want to index. (You can mark multiple entries only if you select text before you open the Mark Index Entry dialog box.)
2. Press Alt+Shift+X; the Mark Index Entry dialog box opens.

3. Because you want this index entry to be applicable to every relevant reference throughout your document, edit the Main Entry box to reflect the wording that will best apply to all of these references.

4. Click Mark All. Word then marks all locations in your document where it finds the exact text you originally selected (not the edited version in the Mark Entry box).

Although this procedure marks every instance of a specific word or phrase, the "Automating Indexing with Index AutoMark Files" section of this chapter shows how to mark every instance of many different words or phrases at the same time.

CAUTION

So that you can see the index entries you're placing in your document, Word displays hidden text after you enter your first index entry—not just field codes but also other document text you may really want to stay hidden! When you're finished marking index entries, you need to rehide this hidden text manually, by clicking the Show/Hide Paragraph Marks button on the Standard toolbar. This text must be hidden before you compile either an index or a table of contents because, if you don't, your page numbering is likely to be incorrect.

The Show/Hide Paragraph Marks button also displays other types of hidden text. If you find this annoying, an alternative is to choose Tools, Options; display the View tab; clear the All check box; and check the Hidden Text check box. Now, hidden text is displayed, but other elements—such as paragraph marks and dots corresponding to spaces between words—remain hidden.

CREATING SUBENTRIES

Often, it's not enough to create an index entry. You might also want a subentry that gives your readers a better sense of what they'll find. Subentries are typically used when you expect to make several references to an item in your index, and each reference covers significantly different points, as in the following index excerpts:

```
Brinkley, J.R.
    goat gland prostate surgery, 24
    medical license suspended, 32
    XER radio station, 27
Bryan, William Jennings
    Cross of Gold speech, 106
    Scopes trial prosecuting attorney, 148
    Spokesman for Florida real estate, 127
```

To create an index entry that contains a subentry, either select text to be indexed or click where you want the index entry to be placed; then click Alt+Shift+X to display the Mark Index Entry dialog box again. Enter or edit your main entry. Be careful to be consistent about the text you specify for entries you will use more than once. Then, enter text in the Subentry text box as well and click Mark.

21

CAUTION

> Consistency is crucial in indexing. If you aren't careful about this, your final index will contain references to the same topic scattered under many separate headings—making it virtually impossible for readers to find all the references they're looking for, and misleading readers into thinking that they've already found all references when they've found only some of them.

TIP

> It's sometimes quicker to enter a subentry in the Main Entry box. To do this, type the main entry followed by a colon. Type the subentry in the same text box. Don't add a space between the colon and the subentry unless you want Word to use the space when it alphabetizes your subentries (placing subentries that begin with a space before those that don't).
>
> Including the entry and subentry on the same line is especially convenient when you are using the same index entry for several different blocks of text because you can copy the entry into the Clipboard and paste it into the Main Entry text box for each entry you want to create.
>
> If you prefer to work with { XE } fields directly, you can also copy an entire { XE } field and paste it anywhere you need the same index entry.

NOTE

> If the text of your index entry contains a colon or quotation marks, Word inserts a \ before the character in the field to avoid confusion with subentries, which also use colons.

CREATING MULTILEVEL SUBENTRIES

In some respects, building an index isn't much different from creating an outline: You might want more than two levels of index entries. Occasionally, you'll find that an index entry fits most naturally as a subentry to another subentry. Here's an example:

```
Procter & Gamble
        Peanut Butter, 47
        Soap, 113-121
                Camay brand, 116
                Ivory brand, 113-117
                        Repackaging, 114
                Oil of Olay brand, 118
                Safeguard brand, 120
                Zest brand, 121
```

To create a multilevel subentry, press Alt+Shift+X to display the Mark Index Entry dialog box. In the Main Entry text box, enter each level of entry and the subentry, all separated by colons. Don't leave space between levels. For example:

```
Procter & Gamble:Soap:Ivory brand:Repackaging
```

Word supports up to seven levels of index entries, though it's unlikely you'll ever need more than three or four.

CREATING CROSS-REFERENCED "SEE" INDEX ENTRIES

By default, Word includes a page number along with each index entry: the page number where it finds the { XE } field when it compiles the index. This is how Word behaves when the Current Page option button is selected in the Mark Index Entry dialog box. Sometimes, however, you don't want a page reference. Instead, you want to refer people to a different index entry, as in the following examples:

AMEX, *See* American Stock Exchange

Family and Medical Leave Act, *See also* Parental leave

To create a cross-reference in your index, set up the rest of the entry as you normally would; then click the Cross-Reference option button and enter the cross-reference text you want to include, next to the word "See."

TIP

> Because page numbers aren't displayed for cross-references, it doesn't matter where you add them. You can create cross-references hundreds of pages from the text you are indexing or referencing. This is helpful if you think of something you want to cross-reference that isn't related to the part of the text you are currently working on—or that appears in a separate chapter file you may not have access to yet.

You don't have to use the word "See," which Word provides as a suggestion. You can edit or replace it if you prefer a different way of referring to other index entries.

These cross-references are unrelated to the automated cross-references you can place throughout your document via the Insert, Cross-Reference dialog box covered in Chapter 22, "Using Footnotes, Bookmarks, and Cross-References."

NOTE

> Two types of references are used within most professional indexes, and they are easy to confuse.
>
> "See" references should be used to lead the reader to a reference when the topic is indexed under another main entry. For example, if you have chosen to index all the vocalists mentioned in a document under "Singers" and not under "Vocalists," you might include "Vocalists, See *Singers*" to redirect readers if they look up "Vocalists." A "see" reference is most commonly used for acronyms and synonyms.
>
> The other type of reference, a "See also" reference, is used to direct readers to related subject matter. So along with the subentries for singers under "Singers," you might also include a subentry "See also *choruses*."

21

SETTING PAGE NUMBERS FOR MULTIPLE-PAGE INDEX ENTRIES

Sometimes you want to create an index entry for a discussion that stretches across two or more pages. Word makes this easy: first you create a *bookmark* corresponding to the block of text you want to index; then you specify the bookmark as part of the index entry.

To create the bookmark, select the text for which you want to create the entry and choose Insert, Bookmark. Then enter a name for the bookmark and click Add.

Now, build the index entry using the bookmark:

1. Click Alt+Shift+X to display the Mark Index Entry dialog box.
2. Enter the main entry and/or subentry text you want.
3. Select the Page Range option.
4. Choose the appropriate bookmark from the Bookmark drop-down list.
5. Click Mark.

→ For more information about using bookmarks, **see** Chapter 22, "Using Footnotes, Bookmarks, and Cross-References," **p. 743**.

COMPILING YOUR INDEX

Now that you've learned how to create index entries, you can move on to compiling them. To prepare your index for compilation, place your insertion point where you want the index (typically at the end of the document). Then, choose Insert, Reference, Index and Tables, and click the Index tab (see Figure 21.3).

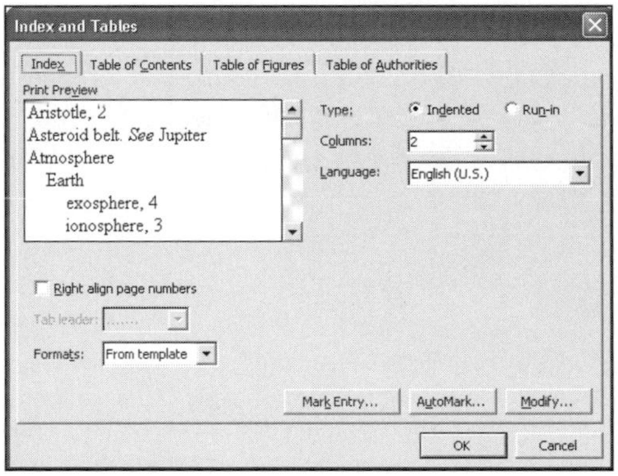

Figure 21.3
You can control nearly all aspects of compiling an index through the Index tab of the Index and Tables dialog box.

If you've read the coverage of tables of contents in Chapter 20, "Tables of Contents, Figures, Authorities, and Captions," you will see some familiar elements in this dialog box. For instance, as with tables of contents, Word's default format for indexes is From Template, which means that it uses the Index styles built into whichever template you're using.

Word also provides several more formats: Classic, Fancy, Modern, Bulleted, Formal, and Simple. If you've chosen one of these formats for your table of contents, you should probably choose the same format for your index for a consistent look. When you change a format (or make most other changes), Word shows what you can expect in the Print Preview box.

After you've finished making changes throughout the Index tab of the Index and Tables dialog box, click OK. Word inserts an index in your document. Notice that the index appears in a section of its own. Word places the index in its own section because most indexes use a different number of columns than the surrounding text. Figure 21.4 shows an excerpt from an index built with Word's default settings.

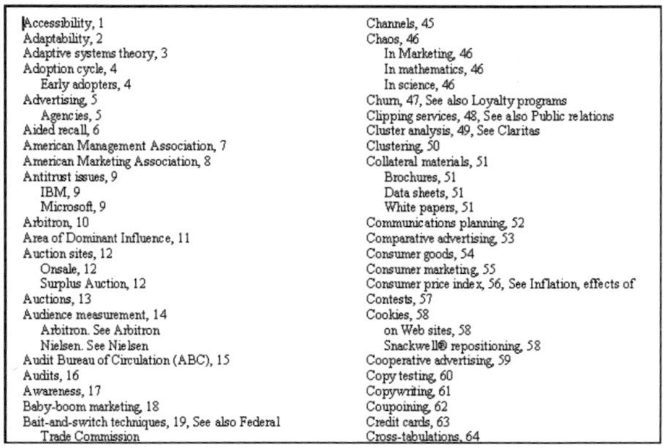

Figure 21.4
An excerpt from an index built using Word's default settings.

Accessibility, 1	Channels, 45
Adaptability, 2	Chaos, 46
Adaptive systems theory, 3	In Marketing, 46
Adoption cycle, 4	In mathematics, 46
Early adopters, 4	In science, 46
Advertising, 5	Churn, 47, See also Loyalty programs
Agencies, 5	Clipping services, 48, See also Public relations
Aided recall, 6	Cluster analysis, 49, See Claritas
American Management Association, 7	Clustering, 50
American Marketing Association, 8	Collateral materials, 51
Antitrust issues, 9	Brochures, 51
IBM, 9	Data sheets, 51
Microsoft, 9	White papers, 51
Arbitron, 10	Communications planning, 52
Area of Dominant Influence, 11	Comparative advertising, 53
Auction sites, 12	Consumer goods, 54
Onsale, 12	Consumer marketing, 55
Surplus Auction, 12	Consumer price index, 56, See Inflation, effects of
Auctions, 13	Contests, 57
Audience measurement, 14	Cookies, 58
Arbitron. See Arbitron	on Web sites, 58
Nielsen. See Nielsen	Snackwell® repositioning, 58
Audit Bureau of Circulation (ABC), 15	Cooperative advertising, 59
Audits, 16	Copy testing, 60
Awareness, 17	Copywriting, 61
Baby-boom marketing, 18	Coupoining, 62
Bait-and-switch techniques, 19, See also Federal	Credit cards, 63
Trade Commission	Cross-tabulations, 64

TIP

Because the index is contained in its own section, you can create a separate header or footer for it, or customize its page numbering.

Unlike the From Template format, all of Word's alternative index formats, with the exception of the Simple format, also add headings for each letter of the alphabet. Figure 21.5 shows a sample index formatted with the Fancy format. If you want headings like these, use any of the alternative formats except Simple.

CHANGING INDEX FORMATTING

The *Normal template* contains nine index levels, all formatted as 12-point Times New Roman, with each level indented 0.17 inches more than the level before it. If you want to change these formats manually, follow these steps:

1. Insert an index in your document.

2. Select an entry that uses the index heading style you want to change. (Be sure to include the paragraph mark at the end of the entry.) Reformat the entry. Word immediately reformats all entries that use the same index heading style.

3. Repeat step 2 for any other index heading styles you want to modify.

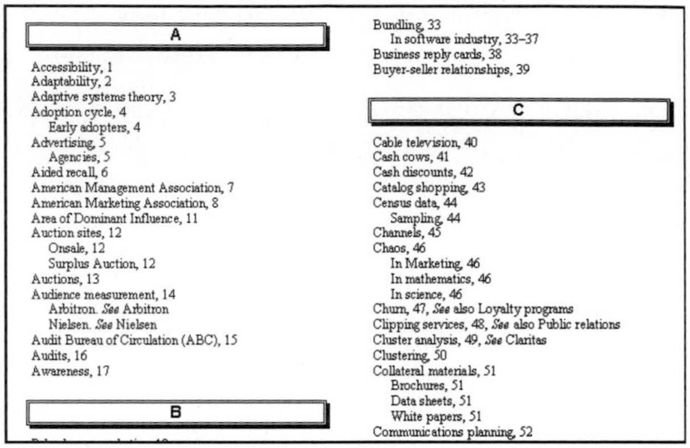

Figure 21.5
In this index, built with Word's Fancy format, each letter that contains an index entry has its own heading. Word skips letters without index entries.

If you reformat an index entry, but Word doesn't reformat the others consistently, see "What to Do If Word Doesn't Reformat All Index Entries Consistently," in the "Troubleshooting" section of this chapter.

APPLYING INDEX FORMATTING CHANGES TO A TEMPLATE

If you want, you can make formatting changes used in an existing index apply to all future indexes created through the template used to create the original index.

To copy formatting changes into a template—such as the Normal template, which defines styles for most Word documents—use the Organizer:

1. Choose Tools, Templates and Add-Ins.
2. Click the Organizer button (see Figure 21.6).

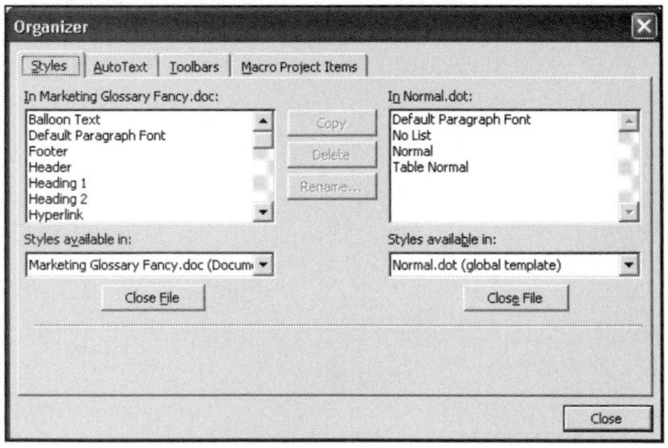

Figure 21.6
Displaying the Organizer in order to apply index formatting changes to your template.

3. In the left window (the window with your filename), select the styles you want to copy.

4. Look at the right window to make sure that it displays the styles in the template you want to use. If it does, click <u>C</u>opy. You may be asked to confirm that you want Word to overwrite existing styles in the target template; choose <u>Y</u>es.

NOTE

If you want to store your index styles in a different template than the one Word displays, click Clos<u>e</u> File in the right window; then click Op<u>e</u>n File, browse to the template you want, and choose <u>O</u>pen.

CONTROLLING SPACE WITH RUN-IN INDEXES AND COLUMNS

If you're short on space, you may want to create a run-in index, such as the one shown in Figure 21.7. A run-in index places subentries on the same line as the main entry. Often, using the Ru<u>n</u>-In option can shorten your index by as much as 30% to 40%. The more subentries you use, the more space you save. To create a run-in index, use the radio buttons in the Type section of the Index and Tables dialog box to change from In<u>d</u>ented to Ru<u>n</u>-In.

Figure 21.7
Using the Ru<u>n</u>-In option can substantially reduce the number of pages required for your index.

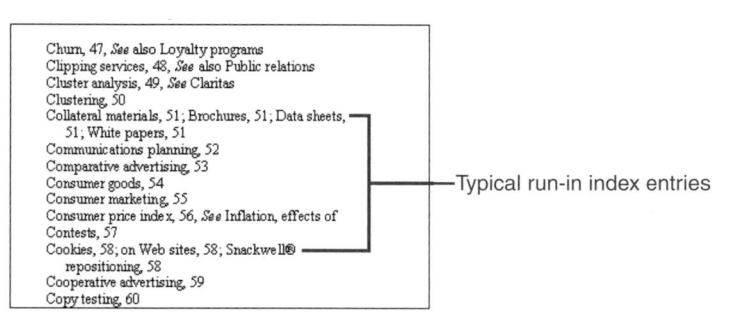

Typical run-in index entries

Another way to conserve the amount of space an index takes up is to alter the number of columns used on each page. By default, Word creates two-column indexes. Most books use two-column indexes, and in most cases, so should you. However, you may occasionally want to change this setting, especially if

- You're using a relatively wide page size
- You're using relatively small type for your index entries

Word builds indexes of up to four columns. Enter the number of columns you want in the C<u>o</u>lumns list box of the Inde<u>x</u> tab.

CREATING INDEXES IN DIFFERENT LANGUAGES

You may need to index a document written entirely, or in part, in a language that uses letters not in the English alphabet, such as Å (Swedish), Ö (German), or CH and LL in Spanish. These letters generally require custom alphabetization according to the rules of the language; if you simply work in English, they will be alphabetized incorrectly.

21

To do so, choose Insert, Reference, Index and Tables and choose the Index tab. Then select a language from the Language drop-down box, make any other setting changes you need, and click OK to compile your index. Word alphabetizes the index based on the alphabetization conventions of the language you selected.

Figure 21.8
This index is styled in the Classic format and uses right-aligned page numbers with a dot leader.

RIGHT-ALIGNING PAGE NUMBERS IN AN INDEX

Except for Word's Formal index style, all Word's built-in index styles place the page number next to the end of the index entry text. If you prefer to right-align the page numbers (see Figure 21.8), check the Right Align Page Numbers check box in the Index tab.

If you choose to right-align page numbers, Word also lets you select the Tab Leader that Word is to use between the entry text and the page numbers: a dotted, dashed, or solid line.

ADDING CHAPTER NUMBERING TO YOUR INDEX

If your document has multiple chapters, each renumbered from the first page of the chapter, you probably want an index that includes chapter numbers prior to the page number of each listing, as in the following example:

```
Van Diemen's Land (Tasmania), 4-2, 12-29, 14-10
```

Word automatically includes chapter numbering in your document if you have used Word's page numbering feature (Insert, Page Numbers) to insert chapter numbers in your header or footer. In the preceding example, the separator character that separates the chapter number from the page number is a hyphen. However, when you establish your page numbers, you can choose a period, a colon, an em dash, or an en dash instead, and the separator character you choose will apply in your index as well.

CAUTION

To use Word's page numbering feature to insert chapter numbers, you have to first use Outline Numbering. This feature is discussed at length in Chapter 18, "Outlining: Practical Techniques for Organizing Any Document."

BUILDING INDEXES FROM MULTIPLE DOCUMENTS

You may be called on to create an index that includes entries from multiple documents—for example, chapters in a book, or components of a report created by different individuals. As with tables of contents (covered in Chapter 20), you have two alternatives:

- You can incorporate each document in a master document, expand all the subdocuments to make them visible in the master document, and then insert your index at the end of the master document. Word searches each subdocument for index entries and incorporates them in an overall index. This approach takes a bit more time to organize up front, but gives you more control over how your documents work together. You can learn more about master documents in Chapter 19, "Master Documents: Control and Share Even the Largest Documents."

NOTE

> If you create an index for a master document, it usually makes the most sense to place the index in the master document itself, typically at the end of the document.
>
> If you choose to place the index in a subdocument, you may encounter trouble later in the editing process. In the event you open the subdocument outside the master document (for example, opening it from Windows Explorer instead of by clicking on its hyperlink within the master document), the index may not update properly. If you update an index in a subdocument opened in this fashion, only entries within the subdocument will be updated—Word will not be able to find entries in other subdocuments or the master document itself.

- You can use { RD } (Referenced Document) fields to incorporate other documents into your indexes without using master documents. An { RD } field simply instructs Word to search another file and reflect its contents in any index or table of contents you create in your current document. Using { RD } fields can make for smaller, more manageable files, but it doesn't do anything to help you standardize styles, headers, footers, or page numbers throughout a large document.

NOTE

> If you include more than one { RD } field, be sure to insert them in the order in which you want Word to include them in your index or table of contents.

BUILDING AN INDEX IN A MASTER DOCUMENT

To build an index in a master document, follow these steps:

1. Open or create your master document and display it in Outline view.
2. Click Expand Subdocuments on the Master Document toolbar to display all the contents of your master document and subdocuments. (If you don't, Word builds your index without the index entries contained in those subdocuments.)

21

3. Insert your index entries as appropriate, if you haven't already done so.

4. Click your insertion point where you want the index to appear.

5. Choose Insert, References, Index and Tables.

NOTE

If you didn't expand the subdocuments as directed in step 2, Word prompts you, asking whether you want to expand the subdocuments. Click Yes to include the index entries for the subdocuments. If you click No, Word creates an index but does not include entries from the subdocuments.

6. Click the Index tab and establish the index settings you need there.

7. Click OK. Word inserts your index at the insertion point. If you already have an index, Word offers to replace it.

CAUTION

If you need to move or change the name of a subdocument file, make sure the master document knows about the change. If it doesn't, updating the index could cause entries to disappear or (if the master document is looking at an old version of a subdocument) result in one with inaccurate or outdated entries. You can, however, safely change the name or location of a subdocument without harming your index as long as you move it from within the master document:

1. Open the master document and display it in Outline view.

2. Ctrl+click the hyperlink associated with the document you want to move. The document opens in its own window.

3. Choose File, Save As. The Save As dialog box opens, allowing you to save the document under a new name, in a new location, or both. The next time you open the master document, Word will look in the file's new location. Remember, though, that this does not delete the original file. If this file is no longer needed, it's usually best to delete it.

USING { RD } FIELDS TO INCLUDE INDEX ENTRIES FROM OTHER DOCUMENTS

When you incorporate index entries using an { RD } field, the page numbers Word places in the index are those in the referenced document. Make sure that the numbers are sequenced as you want them and that they do not overlap page numbers in other documents included in your index. One solution is to use chapter numbers in your index, as discussed in the "Adding Chapter Numbering to Your Index" section, earlier in this chapter.

After you've made sure that the page numbering in your referenced document is appropriate, follow these steps to incorporate the { RD } field:

1. Choose Insert, Field.

2. Choose RD from the list of Field Names.

21

3. Enter the Filename (and, if necessary, the path) of the file you want to include.

4. If the path to the file is relative to the current document, check the Path Is Relative to the Current Document check box.

5. Click OK.

CAUTION

{ RD } fields make no provision for moved or renamed documents. If you change the name or location of a linked file, you must remember to edit the fields manually to reflect the change.

REVIEWING AND UPDATING THE CONTENTS OF YOUR INDEX

What if you make content changes in your document after you create your index? You can update your index by clicking anywhere in it and pressing F9, or by right-clicking on the index and choosing Update Field from the shortcut menu.

TIP

Often it's easier to select the entire document (Ctrl+A) and press F9. That way, you update all your other fields at the same time—making sure that the page numbering in your index is accurate and up-to-date.

You should update your index, of course, any time you make significant changes in your document. However, you should also walk through your index systematically after you create it for the first time, to fix corresponding entries that aren't quite right. As you do so, update the { XE } index entry fields to fix the problems you find. For example, look for

- Redundant entries that use slightly different variations on a word, or duplicate entries for a word in capitalized and lowercase form
- Better ways of organizing high-level concepts
- Misspellings

CAUTION

Make sure that you fix errors in your index by fixing the individual { XE } index entry fields, not by editing the compiled index itself. If you edit the compiled index, the next time you update it, your edits will be removed. Moreover, by editing your index manually, you may inadvertently introduce page numbering errors.

CAUTION

Word's spell checker does not check spellings in a compiled index. This isn't a problem if you use only index entries that are identical to text in the document, which can be proofread. However, if you heavily edit your index entries, you may want to proofread them separately.

21

continues

continued

> There are two workarounds, neither of them ideal. First, you can wait until your index is absolutely final, select the index, and press Ctrl+Shift+F9 to unlink the index field. This changes the index field into text, which can be proofread. However, you can no longer update the index—a potential disaster if page numbers start changing again. You'll have to delete the entire index, insert a new one, and start over again with editing and spell checking it. (Before you unlink your index, make a backup copy of your document.)
>
> Second, you can click the Show/Hide Paragraph Marks button on the Standard toolbar to display all the index entry { XE } fields within your document and then run a spell check on the entire document. That spell check includes these index entry fields when it checks your document.

The best way to review an index is to open a second window on your file and set up Word so that you can view the index in one window while you view the document in another. To do so, follow these steps:

1. Open the document containing the index. (It should be the only document you have open.)

2. If your { XE } index entry fields are not visible, click the Show/Hide Paragraph Marks button on the Standard toolbar to make them visible.

3. Switch to Normal view if you aren't already there.

4. Choose <u>T</u>ools, <u>O</u>ptions, View, and check the <u>W</u>rap to Window check box if it isn't already checked. This ensures that you can see all your text no matter how narrow your windows are. Click OK.

5. Create a new window by choosing <u>W</u>indow, New Window.

6. Choose <u>W</u>indow, Compare Side <u>b</u>y Side to display one window on the left, and the other on the right.

7. Resize the windows so that you have a narrower window for the index column and a wider window for the document, as shown in Figure 21.9.

Now you can move through the index one item at a time. Whenever you find an item that needs changing, click in the window that displays the document, navigate to the { XE } field code that caused the problem, and edit it. When you're finished, click in the index (or select the entire document) and press F9 to update the index. Pressing F9 updates both windows (which are, as mentioned earlier, viewing the same document).

21

Index entry   Corresponding text

Figure 21.9
Setup to review an index alongside the document being indexed.

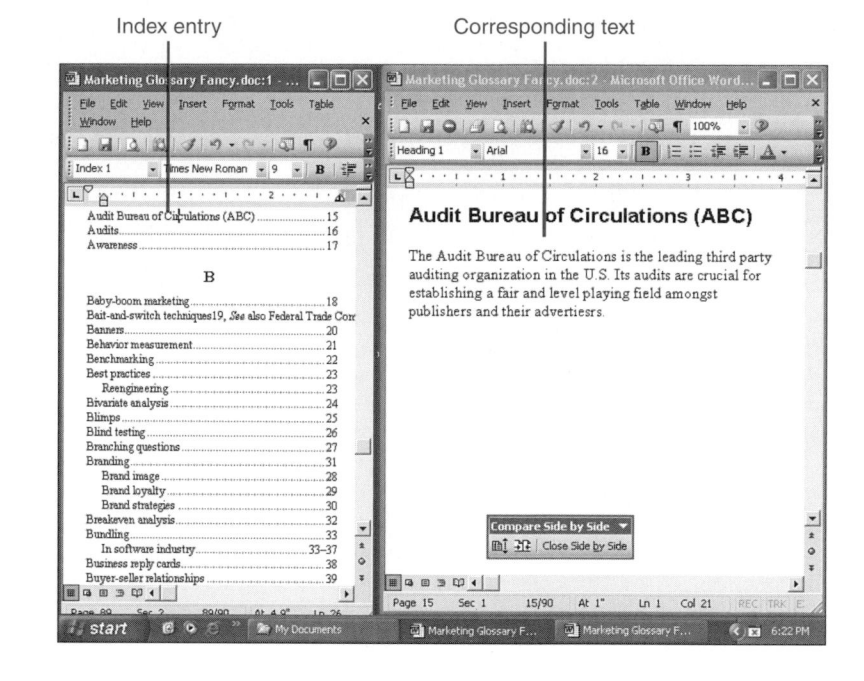

AUTOMATING INDEXING WITH INDEX AUTOMARK FILES

Earlier, you learned how to mark all the references to specific text in a document at the same time, by selecting the text, pressing Alt+Shift+X to display the Mark Index Entry dialog box, and clicking Mark All. You can go much further than this, telling Word to automatically mark (AutoMark) all references to many different words and phrases at the same time.

To do so, you first create a special file called an *Index AutoMark file*. Then you tell Word to use that Index AutoMark file to identify text for AutoMarking and to specify what each automated index entry will say. In a moment, you'll walk through AutoMarking a document. But first, you need to decide whether AutoMarking is worth your time.

NOTE

Index files built with AutoMarking are sometimes confused with *concordances*. Traditionally, a concordance is an alphabetical listing of every word in a text, showing the context in which every occurrence of the word appears. An AutoMarked index is usually built only from words selected for their relevance.

IS AUTOMARKING WORTH YOUR TIME?

To decide whether it will really save time to build and use an Index AutoMark file, scroll through your document looking for elements that lend themselves to automatic indexing. Names of any kind are excellent candidates, including people's names, product names, and brand names. Also, look for words and phrases that are

21

- Typically used in a context that you want to index.
- Used consistently throughout your document.
- Important enough to index. Look for words that are relevant and specific, and that Word can find. Avoid words that are so common as to appear in your index on every page.

Don't be surprised if you find that an Index AutoMark file handles only a quarter or a third of the index entries you need to create. If it can do even that much, however, it can still save you quite a bit of time in indexing a large document. Of course, you can still manually mark additional items by using the techniques discussed previously. But you can use AutoMarking to handle the mind-numbing, repetitive aspects of indexing, leaving you with the more interesting entries—the ones that require judgment.

CREATING AN INDEX AUTOMARK FILE

To create an Index AutoMark file, click New Blank Document on the Standard toolbar to display a new blank document (or choose File, New, and click Blank Document on the New Document task pane).

Then, insert a two-column table. You can do so in several ways; the easiest is to click the Insert Table button, drag across the matrix to create a two-column table, and release the mouse button.

Now start adding entries. In the left column, type words or phrases for which you want to search. Tab to the right column, and type the entry the way you want it to appear in your index, including colons and subentries where needed, as discussed earlier in the "Creating Subentries" section of this chapter. You can also boldface or italicize an entry in the right column, and Word will format it to match when you compile your index. To add a row for a new entry, press Tab in the right-hand column of the last row of the table.

If you don't enter anything in the right column of any row, Word creates an entry using the text in the left column of that row.

Because indexing is case sensitive, make sure that your left column includes all variations of words that might appear both uppercase and lowercase. However, make sure that you standardize on either lowercase or uppercase for the right column so that Word doesn't generate duplicate entries you don't want. Also make sure that you capture all forms of a word, such as "explode," "exploding," and "explosion."

Some people find it easier to set up the editing window so that the Index AutoMark file appears at the left and the document to be indexed appears at the right. You learned how to display the same document in two windows earlier in this chapter, in the section "Reviewing and Updating the Contents of Your Index." If both documents are visible, it's easy (and more accurate) to copy entries from one window to the other.

When you finish adding entries, save and close the file.

USING THE INDEX AUTOMARK FILE FOR AUTOMARKING

To build index entries from the Index AutoMark file you just created, follow these steps:

1. Open the document you want to index, if it isn't already open.
2. Choose Insert, Reference, Index and Tables, and display the Index tab.
3. Click AutoMark. Word displays the Open Index AutoMark File dialog box.
4. Browse to, and select the Index AutoMark file you just created.
5. Click Open. Word inserts index entries wherever you told it to.

> **TIP**
>
> If you create an AutoMark file that will have value in many documents, consider recording a macro for running that file and giving the macro a keyboard shortcut or toolbar button. If you want, you can include index entries that appear in only some of your documents but should be marked wherever they do appear. Doing so enables users to build detailed preliminary indexes even if they have no indexing expertise.

→ For more information on recording macros, **see** "Recording and Running Visual Basic Macros," **p. 1069**.

PLACING MORE THAN ONE INDEX IN A DOCUMENT

Occasionally, you might want to include more than one index in your document. For example, you might want a separate index for all quotes in your document. Using the method that follows, Word enables you to create as many different indexes in the same document as you need.

First, mark your index entries. Then, create a bookmark that covers all the text you want to incorporate in one of your indexes. To do this, select the area of your document for which you want to create a separate index and choose Insert, Bookmark. Then enter a name for the bookmark. (In this example, we use Index2, although you can use any name you want.) Click Add.

Now, position your insertion point where you want to create your index, and follow these steps:

1. Choose Insert, Field.
2. Select Index from the Field Names scroll box.
3. Click Field Codes.
4. Click Options.
5. Select \b from the Switches scroll box, and click Add to Field.
6. In the field description, after INDEX \b, add the following text: Index2. The line of text should appear as follows:
   ```
   INDEX \b Index2
   ```

21

This field tells Word to create an index covering only the block of text corresponding to the bookmark named Index2.

7. Click OK twice.

8. Press Ctrl+A (or choose Edit, Select All) to select the entire document.

9. Press F9 to update all the fields, including the { INDEX } field you just entered.

NOTE

In this example and some examples that follow, other switches you might need have been excluded for simplicity. The best way to edit the { INDEX } field code is to first use the Index tab of the Index and Tables dialog box to create as many settings as possible and then display the field code to add the settings you can't make elsewhere.

INDEXING ONLY SELECTED ENTRIES

As mentioned earlier, you might want to create multiple indexes, one containing only certain entries, such as quotes, that are not contained in the other indexes within the same document. Doing so is a two-step process.

You first manually insert { XE } fields for the entries you want to include in a specific index. Each of these { XE } fields must include the \f switch, as well as an initial (other than "i") that corresponds to the index you will create later.

NOTE

Including the initial "i" tells Word to include the field in its default index.

For example, you might decide to use the initial "q" for each index entry that will be compiled into an index of quotes, and then create fields that read like this:

```
{ XE "To be or not to be" \f "q" }
```

After you've set up all the index entries you want to include in this custom index, you can insert the index itself, using a manual { INDEX } field that contains the same switch. For example:

```
{ INDEX \f "q" }
```

NOTE

Your { INDEX } field may also contain other switches specifying formatting, language, and other elements.

The easiest way to create this field is to work through the Insert, Reference, Index and Tables dialog box as you normally would. After you've inserted your index, right-click on it, choose Toggle Field Codes, and add the \f switch and letter manually.

INDEXING ONLY SELECTED LETTERS OF THE ALPHABET

If your index is especially large, you may want to split it into two or more indexes to improve Word's performance. You might, for example, create one index that covers letters A through M and another for N through Z.

> **TIP**
>
> Even if Word is performing perfectly well, you might occasionally want to compile an index based on only part of the alphabet for review purposes. Large indexes require careful review; you might ask one reviewer to handle letters A through M and another reviewer to handle N through Z.

To create an index covering only some letters of the alphabet, follow these steps:

1. Create all your index entries as you normally do.
2. Insert the index into your document the way you normally do.
3. Right-click anywhere in the index and choose <u>T</u>oggle Field Codes to display the field code rather than the field result.
4. Add the following to your { INDEX } field code:

    `\p n--z`

Notice the double hyphens. In this example, you've told Word to compile the index from N to Z.

COMPILING AN INDEX WITH ONLY THE ENTRIES YOU SELECT

Word indexes typically contain all the index entries you selected. However, you can create custom indexes that contain only the items you specify. For example, you might be forwarding a large document to a reviewer with expertise about one specific topic. If you create a custom index, you can call attention to the pages that contain information you want reviewed. That saves the reviewer time. It might also discourage the reviewer from slowing you down with gratuitous comments about other areas of the document!

Assuming that you've already indexed the document, click Show/Hide Paragraph Marks to display hidden text, including the contents of your { XE } index entry fields. Now, in each entry you want to appear in your specialized index, add the \f switch, a space, and any letter of the alphabet except *I*. (You can also use numerals and any symbol characters that appear in the ANSI character set. However, in most situations, the 25 characters and the numbers 0 through 9 should provide you more than enough custom indexes without your resorting to ANSI codes.) You cannot use *I* because Word interprets it as a direction to include an entry in the default index. Use the same letter for every entry you want to compile as a group. So, for example, you might have an index entry that reads

`{ XE "MP3 and Copyright Law" \f r }`

21

TIP

> Does marking entries for a special index sound like a lot of work? Here's how to stream-line it. With all the field codes visible, use Word's Edit, Replace dialog box to add the \f r switch to all identical fields at once.
>
> In the preceding example, you might include
>
> ```
>     XE "MP3 and Copyright Law"
> ```
>
> in the Find What box and add the following in the Replace With box:
>
> ```
>     XE "MP3 and Copyright Law" \f r
> ```
>
> Then click Replace All, and Word fixes all instances at the same time. You can use this technique any time you need to make a global change in many fields at the same time.

After you finish customizing your index entries, create and insert your index the way you normally do. Click anywhere inside the index and press Shift+F9 to view the { INDEX } field code. Click inside the field code and add the same switch at the end. For example:

```
{ INDEX \f r }
```

Then update the index by any means you choose (such as right-clicking the field and choosing Update Field). This inserts the updated custom index and returns to the view of the index rather than the { INDEX } field code.

TIP

> If you need an index entry to appear in both the default index and a custom index, create two separate XE index entries: one that includes the custom index instruction (for example, { XE \f "r" }), and one adjacent to it that does not.

USING { INDEX } FIELD CODES TO CONTROL OTHER INDEX FORMATTING

You've already seen how manually editing an { INDEX } field code can enable you to create partial indexes based on letters of the alphabet or specific index entries. Occasionally, you may have to use other { INDEX } field switches to generate index formatting you can't get any other way.

CREATING SEPARATOR CHARACTERS

The \d switch sets the separator character that Word places between chapter numbers and page numbers in index entries. By default, Word uses a hyphen, as in the following example:

```
Hedge funds, 3-8, 5-6
```

However, it's not uncommon to use colons or other characters:

```
Derivatives, 4:6, 9:12
```

You can separate chapter numbers from page numbers with any character. You can even use several characters (up to five). Within your { INDEX } field, add the \d switch and a space.

21

Then add quotation marks containing the characters you want to use, as in the following example, which replaces the hyphen with a colon:

```
{ INDEX \d ":" }
```

→ Creating chapter numbers in Word is not straightforward; **see** "Adding Chapter Numbers to Your Captions," **p. 700**.

CREATING SEPARATOR CHARACTERS FOR PAGE RANGES

Just as you can create separator characters that go between chapter numbers and page numbers, you can also create *separator characters* that go between the numbers in ranges of pages. By default, Word uses an en dash, as in the following example:

```
Wireless Internet services, 62-68, 104-113
```

Use the \g switch to change the separator. The syntax is exactly the same as for the \d switch. For example, to use a colon as a separator, enter the following:

```
{ INDEX \g ":" }
```

CONTROLLING THE APPEARANCE OF ALPHABETICAL HEADINGS

Earlier, you saw that Word can insert headings before the index listings associated with each letter of the alphabet using special index formats in the Index tab of the Index and Tables dialog box. You can use the \h switch in the { INDEX } field to control the appearance of these headings. You're most likely to use this switch in two ways: to insert a blank line rather than a heading between letters, or to lowercase the letters in your headings for design reasons.

To insert a blank line, edit your existing { INDEX } field code to include the following:

```
\h " "
```

Be sure to include the space between the quotation marks. Even though Word's Help file says this isn't needed, Word will not insert a blank line without the space.

To lowercase your headings, edit the \h switch in your existing { INDEX } field code to include the following:

```
\*lower
```

For example, if your current field code reads

```
{ INDEX \h "A" \c "2" }
```

you would then edit it to read

```
{ INDEX \h "A" \*lower \c "2" }
```

You can also use the \h switch to custom design your own heading styles with special symbols or characters before or after the letter in the heading. To do this, enter the characters you want along with the letter *A* between quotes after the \h switch, like this:

```
{ INDEX \h "***A***" \c "2" }
```

21

This inserts three asterisks before and after each heading letter. In place of asterisks, you can use any symbol character in a normal text font except for letters of the alphabet. This feature will not properly generate characters from fonts such as Symbol or Wingdings, however.

TROUBLESHOOTING

WHAT TO DO IF CHAPTER NUMBERING IS INCORRECT IN INDEXES BUILT WITH MASTER DOCUMENTS

Sometimes, indexes in master documents don't show chapter numbers when they're supposed to, or they refer to Chapter 0 rather than the correct numbers. You may have included chapter numbering in your subdocuments but not in your master document, or vice versa. It must be turned on in both locations. To do so, carry out these steps:

1. Insert Outline Numbering in each subdocument if it is not already present. (Choose Format, Bullets and Numbering, click the Outline Numbered tab, choose one of the available sequences, and click OK.)

2. Add chapter numbering to each subdocument, by choosing Insert, Page Numbers, and clicking Format to display the Page Number Format dialog box. (To do this, you must tell Word which style is used for chapter numbers throughout your document—a fairly complex procedure that is explained in the "Adding Chapter Numbers to Your Captions" section of Chapter 20, "Tables of Contents, Figures, Authorities, and Captions.")

3. Open the master document and click Expand Subdocuments to display all your subdocuments.

4. Choose Format, Bullets and Numbering, click the Outline Numbered tab, choose a heading numbering sequence for the master document, and click OK.

5. Rebuild the index.

WHAT TO DO IF PAGE NUMBERING IN YOUR INDEX IS INCORRECT

Be sure to hide the hidden text in your document before building the index. Also, select the index and rebuild it (by pressing F9) after you create tables of contents and other document elements that affect page numbering.

→ For more information about using Outline Numbering throughout your documents, **see** "Using Word's Automatic Outline Numbering," **p. 636**.

WHAT TO DO IF WORD DOESN'T REFORMAT ALL INDEX ENTRIES CONSISTENTLY

If you change the formatting for an index entry, Word should update the formatting for all other entries that use the same style. If this doesn't happen, make sure that automatic style updating is turned on for this style. Follow these steps:

1. Choose Format, Styles and Formatting.

2. In the Styles and Formatting task pane, choose the style with which you're having problems. (If it does not appear, choose All Styles from the Show drop-down box.)

3. Right-click on the style name and choose Modify Style from the shortcut menu. The Modify Style dialog box opens.

4. Check the Automatically Update check box.

5. Click OK.

What to Do If You See { INDEX } in Your Document Instead of Your Index

If you see the { INDEX } field Word inserted in your document instead of the results generated by that field, right-click on the { INDEX } field, and choose Toggle Field Codes from the shortcut menu.

What to Do If a Marked Index Entry Doesn't Appear in Your Index

First, check to see that the index entry has been marked properly. Then, check the following:

- Is the spelling of the entry and subentry correct? (If not, the entry may appear incorrectly in the wrong location within your index.)

- If you specified subentries, are they each separated by colons?

- If you entered the field manually, is your field syntax correct? In particular, if the text in your index entry includes colons, did you add backslashes where needed, as discussed in the "Creating Subentries" section of this chapter?

- If you marked an entry corresponding to a bookmark, has that bookmarked text since been removed from your document?

- If you used an \f switch (such as \f "q") to specify that your { XE } index entry should appear only in a certain index, did you use the same \f switch in your { INDEX } field?

- Does your index entry appear in a subdocument that isn't currently available to the master document where you've placed your index?

CHAPTER **22**

USING FOOTNOTES, BOOKMARKS, AND CROSS-REFERENCES

In this chapter

USING FOOTNOTES AND ENDNOTES

Footnotes and endnotes are notes that provide more information about specific text in your document. In Word, *footnotes* appear at the bottom of your current page. Notes compiled at the end of a document—or at the end of a section—are called *endnotes*. Both footnotes and endnotes are equally easy to insert—and easy to work with after you add them. You can use them both in the same document.

Word can automate the most annoying aspects of managing footnotes and endnotes: sequencing and placing them properly. When you use Word's footnote and endnote features, you get extensive control over your footnotes and endnotes. Of course, you can control the text that appears in your footnotes and endnotes—and how that text is formatted. But you can also control

- Where your footnotes appear on your page and exactly where your endnotes are placed at the end of your document
- How your footnotes and endnotes are sequenced
- What kind of footnote or endnote marks (called *note reference marks*) you use
- How footnotes are separated from other text on your pages

By using Word's controls, you can customize your footnotes or endnotes for any type of document, including specialized documents such as legal documents, which may have strict footnote or endnote requirements.

INSERTING FOOTNOTES AND ENDNOTES

To insert a standard footnote, place your insertion point where you want the footnote mark to appear, and press Alt+Ctrl+F. Word inserts a *note reference mark* containing a number. If this is the first footnote in your document, the number is 1; if you have already inserted footnotes, Word uses the next number after your last footnote, using the sequence 1, 2, 3, and so on.

To insert a standard endnote, place your insertion point where you want the endnote mark to appear, and press Alt+Ctrl+D. Word inserts a note reference mark containing a lowercase letter. If this is the first endnote in your document, the letter is "i"; if you have already inserted endnotes, Word uses the next letter after your last endnote, following the sequence i, ii, iii, and so on.

→ To change the appearance of your footnotes or endnotes, **see** "Customizing Your Footnotes and Endnotes," **p. 748**.

TIP

> If you use footnotes and endnotes often, you can add them to the shortcut menu that appears when you right-click on text in your document. To do so, follow these steps:
>
> 1. Choose Tools, Customize, and click the Toolbars tab.
> 2. Check the Shortcut Menus check box in the Toolbars scroll box. The Shortcut Menus toolbar appears.

22

> 3. Click the Commands tab and choose Insert from the Categories scroll box.
>
> 4. In the Commands scroll box, click on the command you want to add—in this case, either Footnote or Insert Endnote Now.
>
> 5. Drag the command to the Text button on the shortcut toolbar; drag down to choose the shortcut menu you want to use (Text); then drag across the cascaded menu and release the mouse pointer where you want the command to appear.
>
> 6. Click Close in the Customize dialog box.

In *Normal view*, when you insert a footnote or an endnote, Word also typically displays the *note pane*. Figure 22.1 shows how this note pane looks immediately after you insert your first footnote. If you were to insert an endnote instead, it would look much the same except that it would use "i" for notation and the note pane would be set for endnotes.

NOTE

If the note pane does not appear, choose View, Footnotes to display it, or double-click on any footnote or endnote reference mark.

In Print Layout view, there is no separate note pane (see Figure 22.2). You simply edit footnotes wherever they are located on the page—typically under a footnote separator line that stretches about one-third of the way across the page.

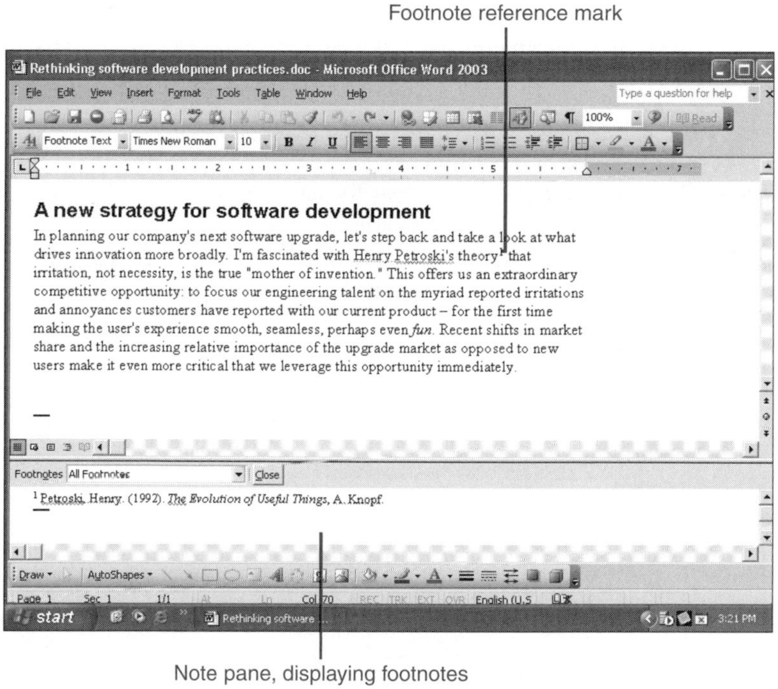

Footnote reference mark

Figure 22.1
When you press Alt+Ctrl+F to enter a footnote, Word places a footnote reference mark at your insertion point and opens the Footnote pane for editing.

Note pane, displaying footnotes

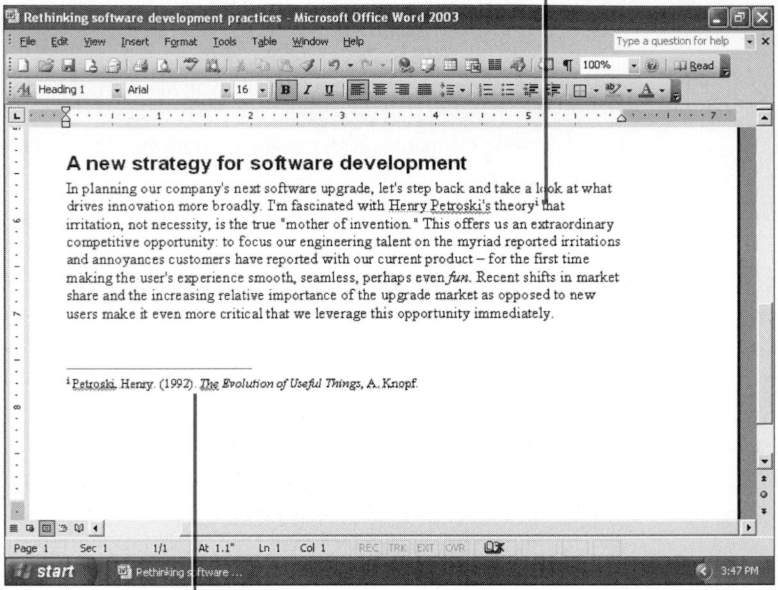

Endnote reference mark

Figure 22.2
In Print Layout view, the footnote appears in its location on the page; you can edit it there in the same way that you edit other text in your document.

Endnote pane

If you're creating endnotes, it is usually best to work in Normal view. If you create an endnote in Print Layout view, Word moves you to the list of endnotes at the end of the document or section. You can edit the endnote there, but often you can't see the document text to which it relates.

EDITING FOOTNOTES AND ENDNOTES

Within the note pane, you can edit or format text in most of the ways you're familiar with. You can even add images or tables. A few of Word's features are off-limits, but not many. For example, you can't use Word 2003's drawing tools, insert comments, or insert captions. You can't create multiple columns, either, but multicolumn tables are a possible workaround.

> **TIP**
>
> Even though you can't use drawing tools, it is possible to place a drawing inside a footnote or an endnote. Create the drawing in Word's editing window, copy it to the Clipboard, and then paste it into the note pane.

If you are working in your document and you want to edit the text associated with a footnote or an endnote, double-click its note reference mark. The note pane opens, displaying the corresponding note. In Normal view, you can also view the note pane by choosing View,

22

Footnotes. If the note pane is open for viewing footnotes, but you would prefer to view end-notes, you can choose All Endnotes from the drop-down box within the note pane.

If you don't need to *edit* the text of a note but want to *see* it, hover your mouse pointer over the accompanying note reference mark in your document. The mouse pointer changes shape to resemble a piece of note paper; then a ScreenTip appears displaying the contents of the note (see Figure 22.3).

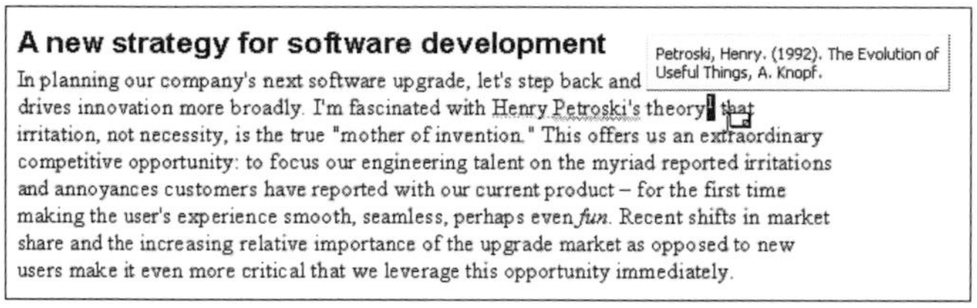

Figure 22.3
Hover your mouse pointer over a note reference mark, and Word displays the note's contents in a ScreenTip.

If you're working in a document with many footnotes or endnotes, you might want to view more than those that appear in the size of the default note pane. To adjust the size of the note pane, place the mouse pointer over the border until it changes to double vertical arrows (see Figure 22.4). Drag the border up or down to resize the pane.

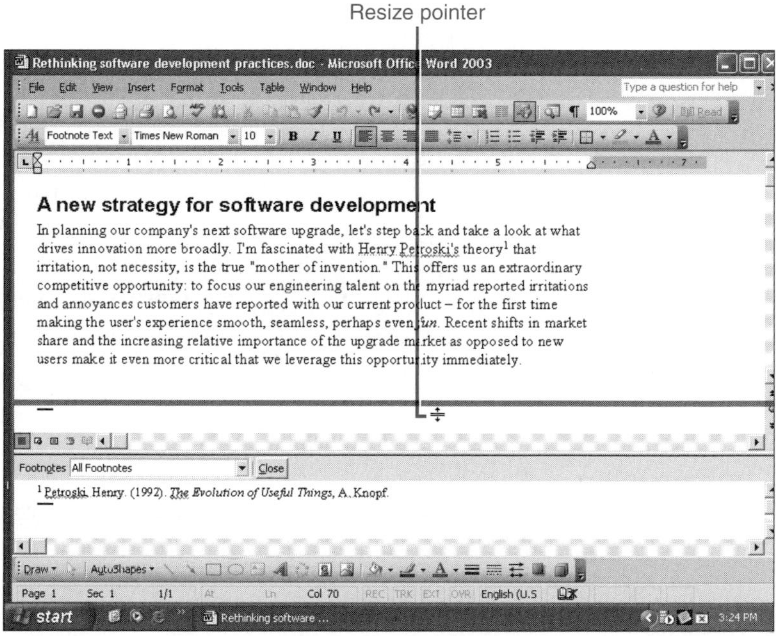

Figure 22.4
Resizing a note pane by dragging its top border.

22

CUSTOMIZING YOUR FOOTNOTES AND ENDNOTES

Word gives you total control over the appearance, sequence, and location of footnotes and endnotes. This control is available through the Footnotes and Endnotes dialog box. To display it, click Insert, Reference, Footnote (see Figure 22.5). If Footnote does not appear in the Insert menu, first click the double-down arrow to make Word display its full menu.

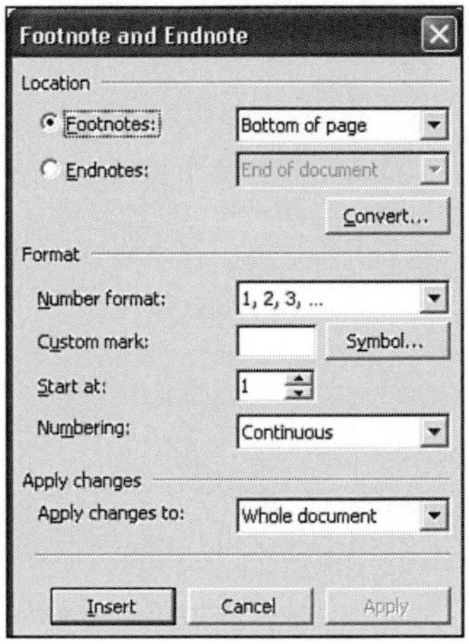

Figure 22.5
You can control the formatting and numbering of footnotes and endnotes in the Footnote and Endnote dialog box.

NOTE

Many publishers, especially in specialized fields, require customized formatting for footnotes. In some cases, their footnote styles are adapted from *The Chicago Manual of Style*. Before creating references in footnotes or endnotes, make sure that you are formatting them appropriately.

In the next few pages, you'll learn how to change each of Word's default settings, beginning with the change you're likely to make most often: customizing the character Word uses as its note reference mark.

INSERTING A CUSTOM MARK

In documents in which you have only a few footnotes or endnotes, you may want to use a *custom mark*—a special character that appears in place of the number or letter Word normally uses as a note reference mark. To create a custom mark, place your insertion point where you want the footnote or endnote, and open the Footnote and Endnote dialog box. From there,

1. Choose Footnotes or Endnotes to specify what kind of note you're creating.
2. Click in the Custom Mark text box and enter the character(s) you want to use in your note reference mark. (You can insert up to 10 characters in a note reference mark.)
3. Click Insert.

NOTE

If you want to change an existing note reference mark into a custom mark, select the mark in your document before you follow these steps.

TIP

You can use custom marks in documents that also use conventional note reference marks. When Word numbers the conventional note reference marks, it skips any custom marks in your document.

You can't edit a note reference mark directly; you must create a custom mark (or change Word's automatic footnote/endnote numbering sequence, as you'll learn how to do shortly).

You might want to use a symbol as your custom mark, such as † or ‡. If so, rather than entering text in the Custom mark field, click the Symbol button next to it. The Symbol dialog box appears (see Figure 22.6). Choose the symbol you want to use and click OK. The symbol you chose now appears in the Custom Mark box. Click Insert to finish creating the footnote or endnote.

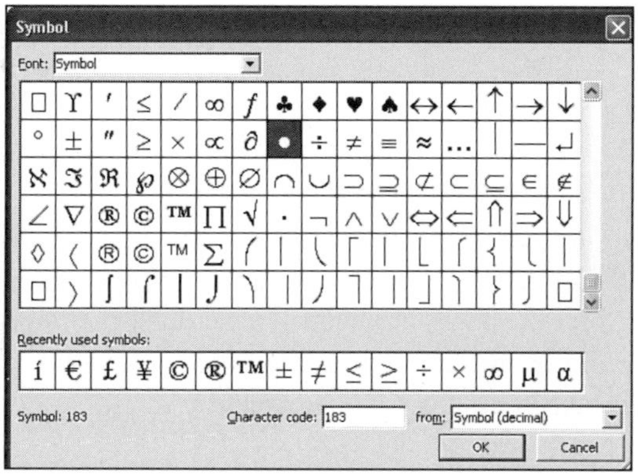

Figure 22.6
Choose a symbol from the Symbol dialog box. To choose from a different character set, select another symbol font (such as Wingdings) from the Font drop-down box.

CONTROLLING FOOTNOTE LOCATION

Word assumes that you want your footnotes to appear at the bottom of each page, but in many cases that may not be what you need.

NOTE

If you want to change footnote or endnote settings for only a portion of your document, first select the text containing the reference marks you want to control.

You can change these default settings in the Footnote and Endnote dialog box (refer to Figure 22.5). The controls for changing where footnotes or endnotes appear are located in the drop-down boxes to the right of the corresponding note type (you can work with only one type at a time).

NOTE

> Any changes you make in the Footnote and Endnote dialog box affect both the notes you *will* insert and those you've *already* inserted.

If you're working with footnotes, your choices are Bottom of Page (the default setting) or Beneath Text. If you choose Beneath Text, your footnotes are placed directly under the last line of text on each page. This means that the location of footnotes can vary, depending on how far down the page your document text extends.

If you're working with endnotes, your choices are End of Document (the default setting) and End of Section. If you choose End of Section, all the endnotes in each section are compiled after the last line of that section.

→ For more information on how section breaks affect your documents, **see** "Working with Sections," **p. 159**.

CONTROLLING FOOTNOTE NUMBERING

As you've seen, Word automatically numbers footnotes using the sequence 1, 2, 3.... Word also assumes that you want your footnotes to number consecutively throughout your document, beginning with the number 1.

→ If you need to create multiple footnotes that share the same footnote number and refer to the same text, **see** "Cross-Referencing a Footnote or an Endnote," **p. 762**.

If you allow Word to automatically sequence your footnotes or endnotes (rather than manually creating custom marks yourself), Word gives you control over the numbering and lettering sequences it uses. You can specify the sequence through the Number Format drop-down box in the Footnote and Endnote dialog box. Your choices are the same whether you're working with footnotes or endnotes. They include

> 1, 2, 3...
> a, b, c...
> A, B, C...
> i, ii, iii...
> I, II, III...
> *, †, ‡, §...

The *, †, ‡, §... option inserts a series of the most commonly used footnote symbols. After you go past four footnotes or endnotes, Word "doubles up" the characters. The reference mark associated with footnote #5 is **; footnote #6 is ††; and so on. Then, after you go past eight footnotes or endnotes, Word "triples up" the characters, and so on.

NOTE

> You can't set Word to automatically use a single custom character repeatedly in all your footnotes or endnotes, but you can manually insert the same custom mark every time you add a footnote or an endnote.

CONTROLLING THE STARTING NUMBER OF FOOTNOTES OR ENDNOTES Word assumes that you want your footnotes to begin numbering with 1 and your endnotes to begin numbering (or, perhaps, lettering) with i. You might, however, be creating a chapter of a book that already contains footnotes or endnotes. You know that several notes appear before yours. To start with a different number (or letter), select it in the Start At spin box of the Footnote and Endnote dialog box.

NOTE

> The letters or numbers in the Start At spin box change, based on the Number Format you've chosen. If you enter a different number, letter, or symbol in the Start At spin box and later change the Number Format, your starting number automatically changes to the corresponding number or letter in the new sequence.

RESTARTING NUMBERING FOR EACH SECTION OR PAGE By default, Word numbers footnotes or endnotes sequentially through the entire document. However, you might want your notes to begin numbering again with 1 (or whatever starting number you've chosen) at the beginning of each new document section. If so, choose Restart Each Section from the Numbering drop-down list box in the Footnote and Endnote dialog box.

If you're working with footnotes, you have an additional option: to restart footnote numbering with each new page. To choose this option, choose Restart Each Page from the Numbering drop-down list box.

CONVERTING FROM FOOTNOTES TO ENDNOTES (AND VICE VERSA)

Occasionally, you might start out creating footnotes and later decide that you want endnotes instead. Or perhaps you start out with endnotes and discover that your client, publisher, or organization prefers footnotes. You can convert between footnotes and endnotes whenever you want; you can even swap endnotes and footnotes at the same time.

To convert all your footnotes or endnotes at once, choose Insert, Reference, Footnote, and click the Convert button. The Convert Notes dialog box opens (see Figure 22.7). Select one of the available options and click OK.

When you convert footnotes to endnotes, or vice versa, Word correctly renumbers them, taking into account any notes that already exist. For instance, if you convert two footnotes to endnotes and you already have one endnote, Word will correctly sequence all three endnotes, from i to iii.

Figure 22.7
You can convert all footnotes to endnotes, all endnotes to footnotes, or swap footnotes and endnotes at the same time.

22

To convert only one footnote to an endnote (or vice versa), display the note in the Footnote or Endnote pane, right-click on it to display the footnote shortcut menu and choose Convert to Endnote (or Convert to Footnote).

WORKING WITH FOOTNOTES AND ENDNOTES: A CLOSER LOOK

You've already learned that you can edit any footnote or endnote in the note pane. The note reference mark in your document and the text of your footnote or endnote are connected. Whenever the note reference mark moves in your document, the footnote/endnote text moves with it. This means that you can

- Duplicate a footnote by selecting, copying, and pasting the note reference mark.
- Move a footnote by cutting and pasting (or dragging and dropping) the note reference mark.
- Delete a footnote by deleting the note reference mark.

Whenever you move, copy, or delete a note reference mark, Word automatically updates the numbering of all the footnotes or endnotes in your document. Of course, you don't have to cut, copy, paste, or delete only the note reference mark; chances are you'll also be editing related surrounding text at the same time. The note reference mark moves with the surrounding text.

CAUTION

If you delete text that includes a reference mark, you delete the accompanying footnote or endnote as well.

NAVIGATING AMONG FOOTNOTES AND ENDNOTES

You've already learned that you can double-click any note reference mark to display the note pane. Whenever you click inside a footnote or an endnote in the pane, Word also displays the corresponding location in the main document.

You can move among notes in the main document without opening the note pane. To move to a specific footnote, click Edit, Go To (or press Ctrl+G or F5) to display the Go To tab of the Find and Replace dialog box. Choose Footnote in the Go to What scroll box; then, in the Enter Footnote Number text box, enter the footnote number you want to view, and click Go To.

A simpler method of just moving from one footnote or endnote to the next is to use the Browse Object buttons (see Figure 22.8).

Moves to previous footnote, endnote, or whatever
element you have selected in the Browser

Figure 22.8
Working with Select
Browse Object.

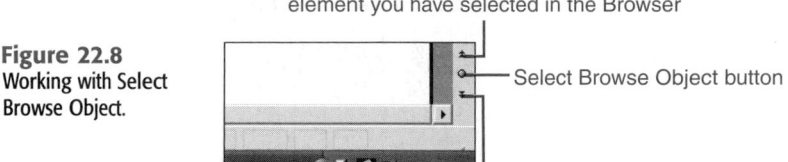

Select Browse Object button

Moves to next footnote, endnote, or whatever
element you have selected in the Browser

With these buttons you can use the double-down arrow to go to the next footnote or endnote in your document. Alternatively, the double-up arrow takes you to the previous one. First, however, you need to set either footnotes or endnotes as your browse object. Follow these steps to move from one footnote or endnote to the next:

1. Click the Select Browse Object button.
2. Click Browse by Footnote or Browse by Endnote (see Figure 22.9).

Browse by endnote

Browse by footnote

Figure 22.9
Using Select Browse
Object to move
between footnotes or
endnotes.

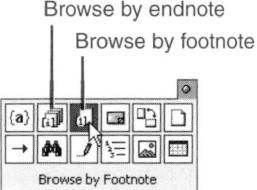

REFORMATTING FOOTNOTES AND ENDNOTES

Word builds footnotes using two built-in styles: Footnote Text for the contents of the footnote, and Footnote Reference for the reference mark (as it appears in both the document and the Footnote pane). For endnotes, Word uses Endnote Text and Endnote Reference. This means you can create a document in which all footnotes use one set of formatting instructions, and all endnotes use a different set of formatting entirely.

Follow these steps to change the appearance of either footnotes or endnotes in your current document, by changing their associated styles:

1. Select footnote or endnote text, or a note reference mark that you want to change.
2. Choose Format, Styles and Formatting. The Styles and Formatting task pane appears, displaying the name of the style that is being used by the text you selected.
3. In the Styles and Formatting task pane, click on the style name, and choose Modify. The Modify Style dialog box appears.

4. Select the style changes you want to make. For example, if you want, choose a different font in the Formatting area.

5. Check the Automatically Update check box if you want to change all appearances of the style in your existing document.

6. Check the Add to Template check box if you want the updated style to be added to the template associated with this document so that the updated style will be applied in future documents that use the same template.

7. Click OK.

→ To learn more about creating styles easily, **see** "Creating Paragraph Styles Easily with Style by Example," **p. 339**.

CONTROLLING FOOTNOTE AND ENDNOTE SEPARATORS AND NOTICES

By default, Word separates footnotes from the text of your document by inserting a line roughly one-third the width of a standard page margin. This is called the footnote or endnote *separator*.

If a footnote is so long that it must jump to the next page, Word separates it from the text on that page as well, using a footnote or endnote *continuation separator*. By default, this is a line that extends across the entire width of the page. You can see examples of both in Figure 22.10.

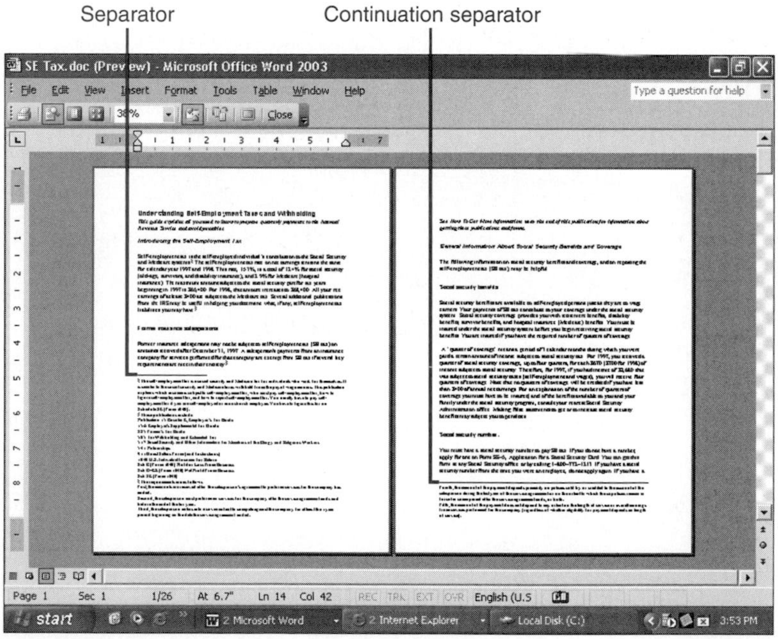

Figure 22.10
Word uses separators to divide footnotes and endnotes from other text in the document.

You can change the appearance of either the separator or the continuation separator. You can also edit them to include text. To do so, first display the Footnote or Endnote pane by double-clicking on any footnote or endnote reference mark in Normal view. From the Footnotes or Endnotes drop-down box in the notes pane, select the element you want to edit. The current setting appears, typically either a short or a long line. Figure 22.11 shows a footnote continuation separator as it appears after you select it from the Footnotes drop-down box. Edit the element to include the text, underlining, and/or formatting you want, and click Close.

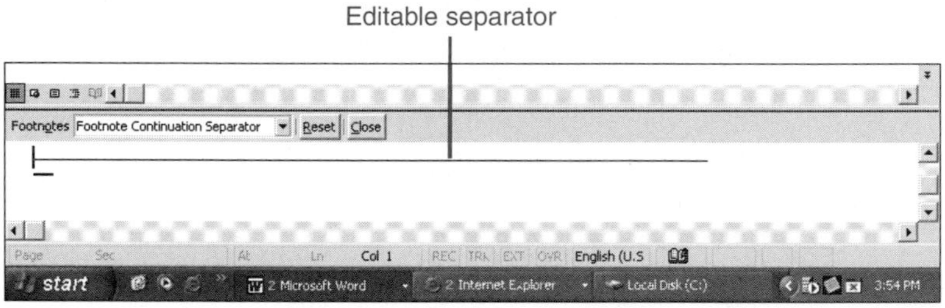

Figure 22.11
You can edit the separator by choosing it from the Footnotes drop-down box in the notes pane.

Editable separator

TIP

> If you want, you can also add text that tells users a note is jumping to the next page. With the Footnote pane open, choose Footnote Continuation Notice. (Or with the Endnote pane open, choose Endnote Continuation Notice.) Then enter and format the text you want. Click Close.
>
> By default, the Footnote or Endnote Continuation Notice is blank.

TIP

> If you work extensively with footnotes, consider a third-party bibliographic database product, such as ProCite 5.0 (www.procite.com) or Endnote 6.0 (www.endnote.com). Both products include sophisticated "cite while you write" Word macros that streamline complex footnoting.

If Word won't print endnotes on a separate page, see "What to Do If Word Won't Print Endnotes on a Separate Page," in the "Troubleshooting" section of this chapter.

If Word superimposes footers on top of footnote text, see "What to Do If Word Prints Page Footers on Top of Footnote Text," in the "Troubleshooting" section of this chapter.

If Word won't delete reference marks, see "What to Do If Word Won't Delete Footnote or Endnote Reference Marks," in the "Troubleshooting" section of this chapter.

USING BOOKMARKS

When you're working in a long or complex document, you often want a quick way to move back to a specific location—without having to remember page numbers, headings, or exact search text. That's where Word's *bookmarks* feature comes in handy.

22

Bookmarks don't just allow *you* to track blocks of text, but they allow Word itself to track blocks of text. By using the bookmarks you create, Word can

- Compile index entries that span multiple pages (see the section "Setting Page Numbers for Multiple-Page Index Entries" in Chapter 21).

- Build formulas that include references to numbers elsewhere in a document (see Chapter 12, "Structuring and Organizing Information with Tables").

- Create *custom properties* that reflect the changing contents of a document (see Chapter 34, "Managing Word More Effectively").

- Manage internal *cross-references* (discussed later in this chapter).

- Ask users for input and then display that input throughout the document (discussed later in this chapter).

- Build *hyperlinks* that connect to specific locations in external documents or the current document (see Chapter 24, "Using Word to Develop Web Content").

- Mark locations for later retrieval by a *field* or macro.

→ For more information about working with field codes, **see** Chapter 23, "Automating Your Documents with Field Codes," **p. 771**.

INSERTING BOOKMARKS

Word's bookmark feature allows you to flag any location or text in your document so that you can find the text later—or so that Word itself can find the text. This can be especially valuable if you're automating your document with cross-references, which are covered later in this chapter.

Follow these steps to insert a bookmark:

1. Select the text you want to associate with a bookmark, or click in your document at the location where you want to create a bookmark.

2. Choose Insert, Bookmark. The Bookmark dialog box opens (see Figure 22.12).

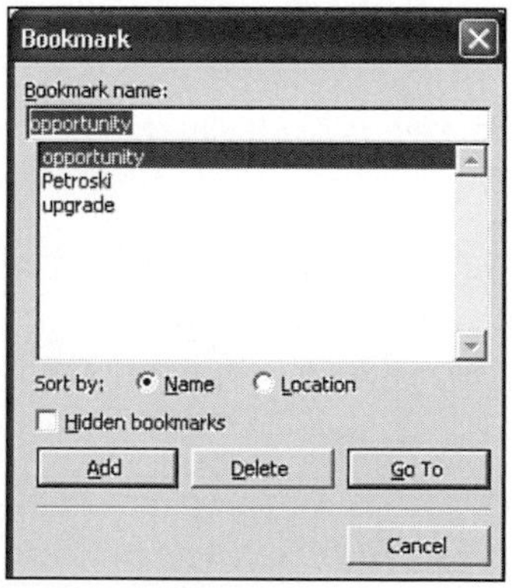

Figure 22.12
You can name and manage bookmarks from the Bookmark dialog box.

3. Enter a bookmark name. Bookmark names cannot exceed 40 characters, must begin with a letter, and can't include spaces or most punctuation—though they can include underscore characters (_).

4. Click Add.

VIEWING BOOKMARKS IN YOUR DOCUMENT

You may, at some point, want to view the borders of the bookmarks in your document. (For example, you may be editing text that you suspect is near the boundary of a bookmark. You also may want to know whether the text you add or delete is part of the bookmark.) To view the bookmarks in your document, choose Tools, Options, View; check the Bookmarks check box; and click OK. Text you bookmarked is now displayed within gray or black nonprinting brackets, depending on your computer and video card (see Figure 22.13).

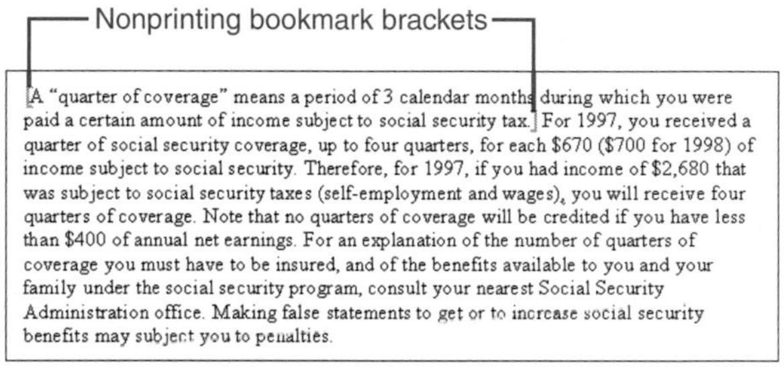

┌─ Nonprinting bookmark brackets ─┐

Figure 22.13
Gray brackets mark the boundaries of bookmarks within your document.

[A "quarter of coverage" means a period of 3 calendar months during which you were paid a certain amount of income subject to social security tax.] For 1997, you received a quarter of social security coverage, up to four quarters, for each $670 ($700 for 1998) of income subject to social security. Therefore, for 1997, if you had income of $2,680 that was subject to social security taxes (self-employment and wages), you will receive four quarters of coverage. Note that no quarters of coverage will be credited if you have less than $400 of annual net earnings. For an explanation of the number of quarters of coverage you must have to be insured, and of the benefits available to you and your family under the social security program, consult your nearest Social Security Administration office. Making false statements to get or to increase social security benefits may subject you to penalties.

NOTE

If you edit text that appears entirely within bookmark brackets, the bookmark will encompass all the text as you've edited it. However, if you cut text from within a bookmark and paste that text outside the bookmark, that text will no longer be encompassed by the bookmark.

FINDING BOOKMARKS

One of the key reasons to create a bookmark is to make it easy for you to find the bookmarked location or text later. There are two ways to find a bookmark after you've created it:

- You can choose Insert, Bookmark; select a bookmark; and click Go To.
- You can press F5 (or double-click on the page number in the status bar) to display the Go To dialog box. Then, choose Bookmark in the Go To What scroll box, select a bookmark name from the Enter Bookmark Name text box, and click Go To.

In both cases, when you go to a bookmark, Word selects all the text contained in the bookmark.

MOVING FROM ONE BOOKMARK TO THE NEXT

To browse your bookmarks, choose Insert, Bookmark to display the Bookmark dialog box; then sort your bookmarks by Location. One at a time, click each bookmark in the list and click Go To. The Bookmark dialog box remains open as you work (although you may want to drag it out of your way).

TIP

You can also browse for bookmarks using the Select Browse Object button under the vertical scrollbar. Click and hold the button; then choose Browse by Footnote or Browse by Endnote from the icons that appear. After you've done so, you can continue browsing to the next or preceding notes by clicking the double-arrows above or below the Select Browse Object button.

DELETING BOOKMARKS

Perhaps you created a bookmark temporarily, to track specific text while you were focusing on one element of your document. Now you want to delete the bookmark so that it no longer clutters up your bookmark list. To delete a bookmark, choose Insert, Bookmark; select the bookmark; click Delete; and click Close.

NOTE

If you delete all the text associated with a bookmark, the bookmark is deleted automatically.

NOTE

When you use certain Word features, Word adds its own hidden bookmarks; for example, if you cross-reference a heading, Word places a hidden bookmark where the heading appears in your document.

You'll rarely need to see hidden bookmarks, but if you need to, you can. Add them to your list of bookmarks by checking the Hidden Bookmarks check box in the Bookmark dialog box.

WORKING WITH CROSS-REFERENCES

Cross-referencing is a great way to help readers find relevant material scattered throughout a long document. However, many writers avoid manual cross-referencing because it is difficult to manage and update. Every time you edit your document and change its page numbering, who will go through the entire document and fix every cross-reference?

Word will. Word 2003 automates cross-references, making them exceptionally convenient and flexible. And if there's a cross-referencing task Word won't handle by itself, chances are you can still make it happen with field codes.

22

→ For more information on working with field codes, **see** Chapter 23, "Automating Your Documents with Field Codes," **p. 771**.

You insert nearly all your cross-references through the Cross-reference dialog box. To display it, choose Insert, Reference, Cross-reference. (If Cross-reference does not appear in the Insert menu, use the double-down arrow to make Word display its full menus.) Figure 22.14 shows the Cross-reference dialog box.

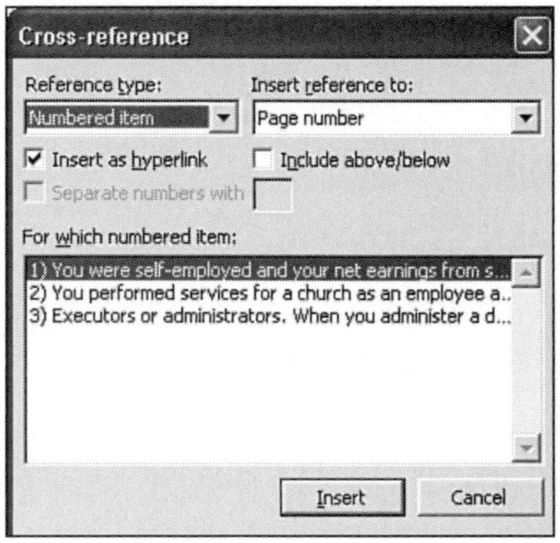

Figure 22.14
The Cross-reference dialog box can insert virtually all your cross-references.

This deceptively bare-looking dialog box packs quite a wallop: You can create cross-references to nine different elements of your document and customize the contents of any of them. More specifically, you can create cross-references to the following document elements.

> **NOTE**
>
> In these examples, the text in the monospaced font represents examples of text Word can insert as a cross-reference.

- Headings you formatted using one of Word's built-in heading styles. (Example: "For more information about Honus Wagner, see `Baseball in the 1920s`.") Headings are natural reference points within a document. They stand out due to size and formatting, so they're easy for your reader to find. Moreover, they define important topics in your document that are often worth referencing.

- Numbered items (paragraphs and/or headings) you numbered using Word's Outline Numbering feature. (Example: "See Section `I.2.a`.")

- Bookmarks. (Example: "See coverage on page `133`.") Occasionally, you'll want to cross-reference a block of text that doesn't correspond neatly to a document heading. For example, you might want to refer to an anecdote that was covered elsewhere in a different context; the anecdote may not have been important enough to warrant its own heading. Cross-referencing a block of text that is not a heading requires an extra step before proceeding. You must first select the text you want to cross-reference and use

22

Insert, Bookmark to create a bookmark. Creating bookmarks is covered in more detail earlier in this chapter.

- Footnotes or endnotes. (Example: "See Footnote 7.")

- Equations, figures, and tables for which you created captions using Word's Caption feature. (Example: "See Table 3.2: 1999 Quarterly Results.") If you captioned the equation, figure, or table using Word's Caption or AutoCaption feature, you can easily insert an automated cross-reference.

TIP

If you use heading styles and AutoCaptions, you make it much easier to create cross-references based on headings and captions.

To understand cross-referencing, it helps to first understand the steps involved in creating any cross-reference. After that, we'll take a closer look at the cross-references you're most likely to create: headings, bookmarks, footnotes, and figures.

CREATING A CROSS-REFERENCE

Whenever you create a cross-reference from the Cross-reference dialog box, you follow the same general steps:

1. Click the insertion point at the location in your document where you want your new cross-reference to appear.

CAUTION

In other words, *don't* click in the location containing the original text you are cross-referencing.

2. Add any text you want to appear next to your cross-reference. For example, if you plan to tell readers "see page 32," enter the words
   see page

3. Choose the specific element you want to reference from the Reference Type drop-down list box. For example, if you chose Footnote as your reference type, you now choose the specific footnote you want to use from a list of all footnotes you have already added to the document.

4. From the Insert Reference To drop-down box, choose which aspect of the document element you want to reference. For example, if you're referencing a footnote, do you want your reference to include the footnote number, the page number on which the footnote appears, or something else? The options available to you will vary, based on the reference type you choose. These are covered in greater detail in the following sections.

5. If you want your cross-reference to appear as a hyperlink that readers can jump to by pressing Ctrl and clicking on the cross-reference, check the Insert as Hyperlink check box.

6. Word can insert the word "above" or "below" in your cross-reference, depending on whether you're placing your cross-reference before or after the text you're referencing. Later, if you move either the cross-reference or the reference text, Word automatically adjusts—switching "above" to "below," or vice versa, if needed. If you want your cross-reference to have these capabilities, check the Include Above/Below check box.

TIP

> If you are referencing a numbered item or bookmark, you also have the option of inserting a cross-reference to the *complete* paragraph number associated with the numbered item or bookmark. This is known as the *full context* paragraph number. For instance, a reference to paragraph 3.(b)(iv) from anywhere in the document would be displayed as "3.(b)(iv)".
>
> To do so, choose Paragraph Number (Full Context) in the Insert Reference To drop-down box. When you select this option, the Separate Numbers With check box is activated. This allows you to enter a separator character (such as a period or dash) to appear between each component of the full context paragraph number.

7. Click Insert to place the cross-reference in your document.

The steps just listed may be slightly modified depending on the type of element you are cross-referencing.

The following sections review some of these differences more closely.

CROSS-REFERENCING A HEADING

To cross-reference a heading or bookmark, choose Heading or Bookmark from the Reference Type drop-down box in the Cross-reference dialog box. Then, in the Insert Reference To drop-down box, choose the aspect of the heading or bookmark you want to reference. The following options are available:

- If you choose Heading Text or Bookmark Text, Word inserts the entire text of the heading or bookmark.

- If you choose Page Number, Word inserts the page number on which the heading appears.

- If you choose Heading Number, Word inserts the heading number that appears in your document, but only if you already inserted heading numbers with Word's Outline Numbering feature (see Chapter 18, "Outlining: Practical Techniques for Organizing Any Document").

- If you choose Heading Number (No Context), Word inserts an abbreviated heading number (you must be in the same section as the text you're referencing). For example, if you're in section 6.F and you insert a cross-reference to heading 6.C, Word inserts the reference C rather than 6.C. You might use (No Context) if you think it would be redundant to include the section number. This setting has no effect if you cross-reference a document element elsewhere in your document. For example, if you're in section 6.F and you insert a cross-reference to heading 3.L, Word inserts 3.L no matter what—never just L.

- If you choose Heading Number (Full Context), Word inserts a full heading number, even if you're in the same section as the heading you're referencing.

- If you choose Include Above/Below, Word inserts the word "above" or "below" in your cross-reference, depending on whether you're placing your cross-reference before or after the text you're referencing. If you move either the cross-reference or the reference text, Word can automatically adjust—switching "above" to "below," or vice versa, if needed.

After you've selected the aspect of the heading you want to bookmark, you must establish any other dialog box settings you need. For example, if you want the reference to be inserted as a hyperlink, make sure that the Insert as Hyperlink check box is enabled. When you are finished, click Insert.

> **TIP**
>
> To really help readers find their way to your cross-reference, consider using two cross-references near each other: one that references the heading text, and another that references the page number. You can see how this works in the following example (both references are monospaced):
>
> For more information, see `The Retreat at Dunkirk`, page 146.

> **TIP**
>
> You may sometimes create a complex cross-reference that you expect to reuse throughout your document. In other words, you expect to repeatedly reference the same text in the same way. If so, insert the cross-reference, select it, and create an AutoText entry based on it. Then you can simply insert the AutoText entry wherever you need the cross-reference.

→ For more information on creating AutoText entries, **see** "AutoText: The Complete Boilerplate Resource," **p. 301**.

CROSS-REFERENCING A FOOTNOTE OR AN ENDNOTE

You may at times want to cross-reference a footnote or an endnote. To do so, display the Cross-reference dialog box, and choose Footnote or Endnote as the Reference Type. Establish your other settings; then, in the Insert Reference To drop-down box, choose the aspect of the footnote or endnote you want to reference:

- If you choose Footnote Number (or Endnote Number), Word inserts the number of the footnote or endnote.

- If you choose Page Number, Word inserts the page number where the footnote began.
- If you choose Above/Below, Word inserts the word "above" or "below" in your cross-reference, depending on where the referenced text appears.
- If you choose Footnote Number (Formatted) or Endnote Number (Formatted), Word inserts the number, formatted as if it were another footnote (or endnote) in your document. This enables you to create multiple footnotes or endnotes that refer to the same footnote text and use the same footnote or endnote number, as is often required by scientific journals. Because you're actually inserting a cross-reference that *resembles* a footnote, not a "true" footnote or endnote, the numbering of the other footnotes and endnotes in your document isn't affected.

When you're finished, click Insert to add the cross-reference in your document.

CROSS-REFERENCING A FIGURE (OR ANOTHER CAPTIONED ITEM)

To cross-reference a figure, a table, or an equation you've already captioned, display the Cross-reference dialog box, and choose Figure, Table, or Equation as the Reference Type. Establish your other settings; then, in the Insert Reference To drop-down box, choose the aspect of this document element you want to reference:

- If you choose Entire Caption, Word inserts the entire text of the caption, including its label and figure number.
- If you choose Only Label or Number, Word inserts the label and figure number, for example, Figure 1.1.
- If you choose Only Caption Text, Word inserts the text of the caption, excluding label and figure number.
- If you choose Page Number, Word inserts the number of the page where the figure, equation, or table appears.
- If you choose Above/Below, Word inserts only the word "above" or "below," depending on the figure's location relative to the cross-reference.

When you're finished, click Insert to add the cross-reference in your document.

LINKING CROSS-REFERENCES TO THE CONTENT THEY REFERENCE

By default, Word inserts cross-references into your document as links, which means that if you press Ctrl while clicking on a cross-reference, Word jumps to the spot in the document you cross-referenced.

NOTE

> If Ctrl+click doesn't work, choose Tools, Options, Edit; then check the Use CTRL + Click to Follow Hyperlink check box.

If you do not want to insert a cross-reference as a link, clear the Insert as Hyperlink check box in the Cross-reference dialog box. Note that Word doesn't format linked cross-references any differently than the surrounding text; they are not blue and underlined, like true hyperlinks. This is true even if you display your document in Web Layout view—and even if you resave the document as a Web page. In fact, the only difference between a linked cross-reference and one that isn't is the presence of an \h switch in the underlying field code.

TIP

> If you *do* want to insert a blue underlined hyperlink that will be visible to people reading your document in electronic formats, choose Insert, Hyperlink. Hyperlinks are covered in detail in Chapter 24.

You can add hyperlinking to a cross-reference by manually adding the \h switch, or checking the Hyperlink check box in the Cross-reference dialog box. You can remove a hyperlink from a cross-reference by deleting the \h switch, or clearing the Hyperlink check box.

Because hyperlinks look like ordinary text, there's rarely a reason not to format cross-references as hyperlinks. Even if you're creating a document for print, leaving Insert as Hyperlink checked makes it easier for you to move to the text you're referencing, making sure that your references are accurate and read as they should.

CAUTION

> If you are exporting your Word documents to other programs, such as desktop publishing programs, embedded hyperlinks could cause problems for those programs' import filters or converters.

Automating Cross-References with { ASK } Fields

You've learned that you can create a bookmark and use it to create a cross-reference. After you do this, Word can place the text you bookmarked in many locations throughout your document, wherever you insert a cross-reference to that bookmark.

Sometimes, however, you'll want to repeat text throughout your document, but you don't have an existing bookmark to work with. In fact, you don't know what text you want to repeat yet. What then?

Using the { ASK } Field to Create References That Reflect User Input

Imagine the following scenario: You have a standard boilerplate letter, as shown in Figure 22.15. As you can see, this letter offers a discount to a specific customer. What if you want to offer an extra-large discount to a specific customer? You can set up the letter to request input from whoever is preparing the letter. Word stores that information as if it were a bookmark and then inserts it anywhere your cross-reference looks for that bookmark.

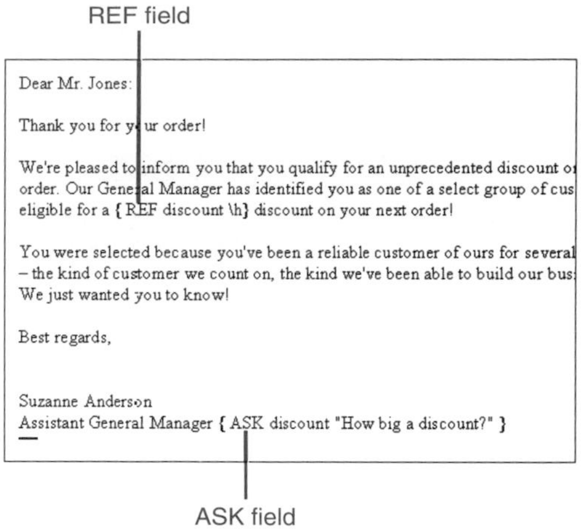

REF field

Figure 22.15
A sample letter that
can be customized to
specify the size of a
customer discount.

22

> Dear Mr. Jones:
>
> Thank you for your order!
>
> We're pleased to inform you that you qualify for an unprecedented discount on
> order. Our General Manager has identified you as one of a select group of cus
> eligible for a { REF discount \h} discount on your next order!
>
> You were selected because you've been a reliable customer of ours for several
> – the kind of customer we count on, the kind we've been able to build our bus
> We just wanted you to know!
>
> Best regards,
>
>
> Suzanne Anderson
> Assistant General Manager { ASK discount "How big a discount?" }

ASK field

To create a reference that reflects user input, follow these steps:

1. Choose Insert, Field.

2. Click on Ask in the Field Names scroll box, to create an { ASK } field that requests input and stores it in a bookmark.

3. In the Prompt: text box, enter the question you want the user to answer; for example, How big a discount?

4. In the Bookmark Name text box, enter the name of the bookmark you want Word to assign to the answer a user will enter later; in our example, we'll use discount.

5. If you want, you can enter a Default Response to Prompt. This is an answer that already appears in the dialog box that displays your question to a user. If the user clicks OK without editing the answer, Word uses the default response. In our example, we'll enter 20% as a default response. Figure 22.16 shows how the Field dialog box would look in our example.

6. Click OK. Figure 22.17 shows the Prompt dialog box that appears, based on the example in the preceding steps.

7. Click OK. (You must do this because the { ASK } field doesn't create the bookmark until you provide input.)

Now that you've created the { ASK } field and provided it with sample input, you can create your cross-reference.

Choose Insert, Reference, Cross-reference, and follow the steps described earlier to create a reference to a bookmark. Use the bookmark name you specified in the { ASK } field. Next, click Insert to place the cross-reference in your document. Repeat steps 1–3 to insert another identical cross-reference anywhere you want the same information to appear.

Entering the Prompt question that
will be displayed in a dialog box

Choosing the {ASK} field

Figure 22.16
The Field dialog box,
displaying the
{ ASK } field
options shown in this
example.

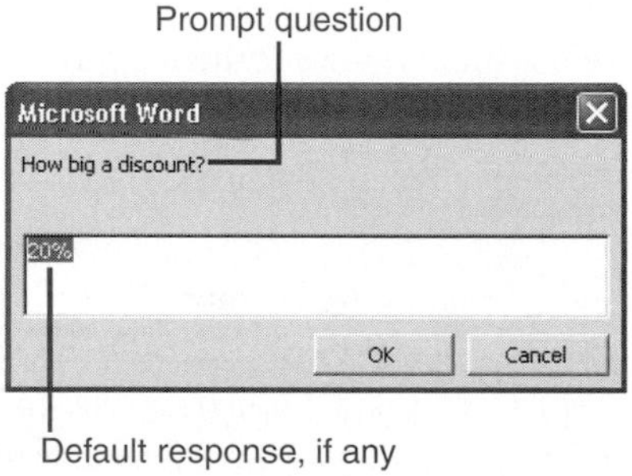

Entering the response
that will be used
by default

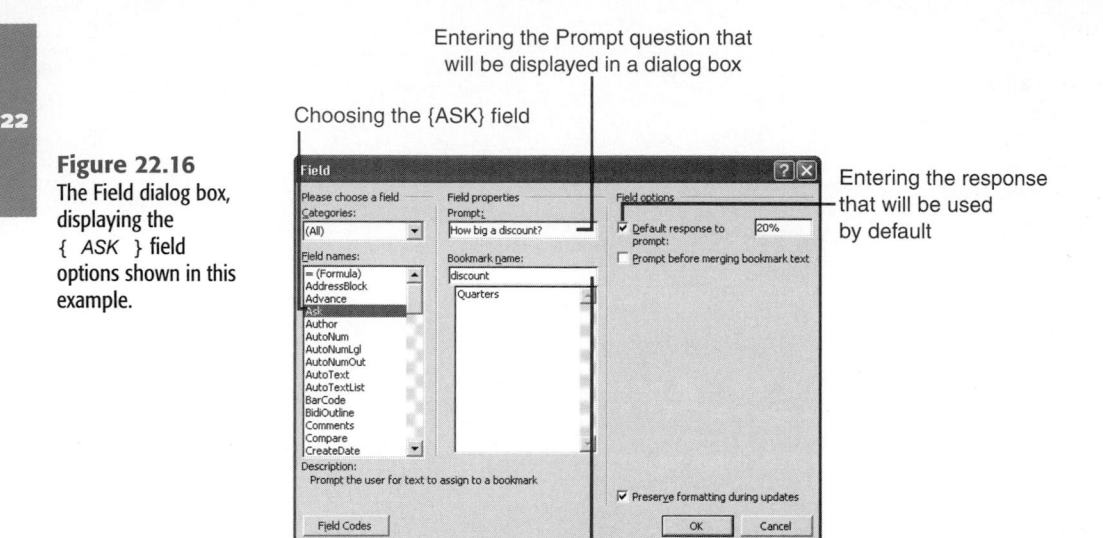

Entering the bookmark name you'll
use later, in your cross-reference

Prompt question

Figure 22.17
The { ASK } dialog
box displays the ques-
tion you included in
your { ASK } field.

Default response, if any

You're done—except for one thing. Like most fields, { ASK } must be updated in order to change its value. Unless a user presses F9, the Prompt dialog box will not display, and the user will not be given an opportunity to enter a new value.

Fortunately, there's a way to make sure that the dialog box displays when the file opens. You can record a simple macro that consists of the two commands needed to do this. Follow these steps:

1. Choose Tools, Macro, Record New Macro.
2. Enter the name AutoOpen in the Macro name box. This is a special macro name Word recognizes: it means Word should always run the macro when the document opens.

NOTE

If you plan to save the document as a template, and create new documents based on it, name the macro AutoNew and store it with your new template. The macro then runs every time you create a new document based on that template.

3. Click OK to begin recording the macro.

4. Press Ctrl+A (or choose Edit, Select All) to select the entire document.

5. Press F9 to update all fields in the document.

6. Click OK.

7. Click the Stop Recording button on the Stop Recording Toolbar.

→ For more information on recording macros, **see** Chapter 32, "Recording and Running Visual Basic Macros," **p. 1069**.

USING FIELDS TO CREATE MORE INTELLIGENT CROSS-REFERENCES

Until now, you've been using { ASK } and { REF } fields to enable users to customize letters one at a time. What if you could set up a cross-reference that would automatically know for what discount each customer was eligible, based on some other piece of information you provide, such as the size of the order the customer placed? You can, though it takes a little doing.

In this example, assume that customers who place orders larger than $10,000 are eligible for a discount of 10% on their next orders. Customers with smaller orders aren't eligible yet, but they will be if they reach the $10,000 threshold—and you'd like to encourage them to do so.

First, create an { ASK } field, as covered in the preceding section. This { ASK } field asks a user to specify the dollar value of a customer's orders to date. After the user responds, the information is stored in a bookmark named dollarvalue:

```
{ ASK dollarvalue "Value of customer's orders to date?" }
```

TIP

As discussed earlier, you can write a quick and easy macro that updates fields automatically when you open this document so that the dialog box requesting user input appears automatically.

Now that you've captured the value of a customer's order in a bookmark, you can use an { IF } field to show Word what decisions you want it to make—and what text you want it to place in your letter as a result. A generic { IF } field uses the following syntax:

```
{ IF test "DoIfTrue" "ElseDoThis" }
```

At the heart of an { IF } field is a test. You specify a condition, and Word sees whether that condition has been met. For example, the test might include a formula that asks, "Has the customer ordered at least $10,000 worth of merchandise?"

To create a formula such as this, first create a bookmark for the location in your document that contains the value you want to test. Often, you'll want to bookmark a table cell. In the following example, you create a bookmark named dollarvalue and use it in a formula that serves as the test:

```
IF dollarvalue >=10000
```

Next, the { IF } field specifies the text you want Word to insert if the condition has been met. In this example, you use the following text, surrounded by quotation marks:

```
"You've just qualified for a 10% discount on your next order!
Thanks for being such a great customer!"
```

Finally, the { IF } field specifies the text you want Word to insert if the condition has not been met. Again, this text should appear in quotation marks:

```
"Qualify for a 10% discount when you place $10,000 in orders!
You're well on your way!"
```

Now build the { IF } field by putting all three components together: the test, the text that should appear if the test comes back "true," and the text that should appear otherwise:

```
{ IF dollarvalue >=10000 "You've just qualified for a 10% discount on your
next order! Thanks for being such a great customer!" "Qualify for a 10%
discount when you place $10,000 in orders! You're well on your way!" }
```

After Word knows the size of the order, it also knows what text to add to the letter.

You might want to place the same text in several locations throughout your document, or perhaps on an accompanying envelope stored as page 0 of the same file. That's the easy part. Select the entire field (or field result) and mark it as a bookmark. In this example, the bookmark is named discount. Insert a cross-reference to the bookmark anywhere you want the text to appear.

TROUBLESHOOTING

What to Do If Word Won't Print Endnotes on a Separate Page

By default, Word places endnotes on the same page as the last text in the document. If you want them on a separate page, you have to add a manual page break (Ctrl+Enter) at the end of your document, before the endnotes.

What to Do If Word Prints Page Footers on Top of Footnote Text

This may happen if both the page footer and the footnote text exceed five lines and a section break appears on the same page. If you can't remove the section break, add some blank lines above the footnote text in the Footnote pane.

What to Do If Word Won't Delete Footnote or Endnote Reference Marks

You may have deleted the footnote text in the Footnote pane, but you also must select and delete the footnote reference mark in the document.

What to Do When You Can't Find the Heading You Want to Cross-Reference

Check: Did you format it with one of Word's built-in heading styles (for example, Heading 1 through Heading 9)? If not, do so. If you can't (or don't want to), select it as a bookmark and cross-reference it the same way you would cross-reference any other bookmark.

What to Do When Cross-References in a Master Document Return Error Messages

Make sure that the subdocuments your cross-references refer to haven't been removed from the document. Make sure that they are available and open.

→ For more information about working with master documents, **see** Chapter 19, "Master Documents: Control and Share Even the Largest Documents," **p. 653**.

CHAPTER 23

AUTOMATING YOUR DOCUMENTS WITH FIELD CODES

In this chapter

23

UNDERSTANDING FIELDS

A *field* is a set of instructions that you place in a document. Most often, these instructions tell Word to find or produce some specific text and place that text where you have inserted the field. In other cases, fields may be used to mark text, such as index entries, which you want Word to keep track of. In a few cases, Word fields can also tell Word to take an action that doesn't place new visible text in your document, such as running a *macro* that saves a file.

Using fields, you can delegate many details of assembling a document to your computer. For instance, suppose that your document contains figures and tables that need to be numbered consecutively. You can do this manually—and redo the numbering every time you insert or delete a figure or table. Or you can use a *field code* and let Word track it all for you.

Word disguises many of its field codes behind friendly dialog boxes. For example, when you insert a cross-reference, numbered caption, or table of contents—or tell Word to insert a date and time that can be updated automatically—you're inserting a field code. In fact, Word 2003 goes beyond any previous version of Word in helping users gain the benefits of fields without understanding the underlying codes themselves.

This chapter shows you exactly what can be accomplished using Word 2003's field tools. But you'll also get acquainted with the underlying field codes themselves, for two important reasons. First, you can still do many things by editing field codes that Word hasn't yet built into neat and clean dialog boxes. Second, if you need to enter many fields in your document, or troubleshoot fields you've entered or inherited, you'll be far more effective if you understand how they really work.

Fields come in several categories:

- *Result fields* give Word instructions about what text to insert in your document.
- *Marker fields* mark text so that Word can find it later—for example, to compile into an index or a table of contents.
- *Action fields* take a specific action—for example, to run a macro.

Each of these categories is covered next.

WHAT RESULT FIELDS DO

Fields that specify instructions that Word can use to determine which text to insert in your document are called *result fields*, and the information they generate is called *field results*. These field results can come from many sources, including the following:

- Information stored in the document's Properties dialog box, such as the author's name, or keywords you may have specified
- Information Word calculates from sources you specify, such as adding a column of numbers

- Information Word requests later
- Information Word produces based on what it finds in your document (such as page counts)
- Information found in other files
- Information found elsewhere in your document

Because your document stores the field instructions, not the actual information, Word can update the field results with new information whenever a change in your document calls for it. That's the magic of field codes—they handle details you might easily forget.

If Word is failing to update fields properly, see "What to Do When a Field Won't Update Properly," in the "Troubleshooting" section of this chapter.

WHAT MARKER FIELDS DO

Some fields simply mark text so that you (or another field you've inserted in your document) can find it later. For example, the TC field marks entries that later can be compiled into tables of contents; similarly, the XE field marks index entries that can be compiled into indexes.

WHAT ACTION FIELDS DO

Finally, some action fields tell Word to perform a specific action that doesn't place new visible text in your document. For example, when you click on a { HYPERLINK } field, Word jumps to the location indicated in that field. Similarly, the { MACROBUTTON } field places a button in the text. When you click it, Word runs a macro you've specified in your field code.

FIELDS THAT MIGHT ALREADY BE IN YOUR DOCUMENT

You've come across several field codes already, although you may not have realized it. When you place the date, time, or page number in a header or footer and instruct Word to update it automatically, Word places a { DATE }, { TIME }, or { PAGE } field code rather than text in the document. Whenever you update your fields, Word then checks your computer's built-in clock and updates the date and time to reflect what it finds there.

You can insert many fields easily if you use the specific Word menu commands, toolbar buttons, or dialog boxes, rather than inserting them directly as field codes. Table 23.1 lists these commands, buttons, and dialog boxes and the field codes that correspond to them.

Even if you enter a field code using a menu command, you might want to edit it later for precise formatting. But that's still easier than creating it from scratch.

TABLE 23.1   MENU COMMAND SHORTCUTS FOR SOME FIELDS

This Field Command...	Is Inserted by This Menu Command
{ BARCODE }	Tools, Letters and Mailings, Envelopes and Labels, Options
{ BOOKMARK }	Insert, Bookmark
{ DATE }	Insert, Date and Time
{ HYPERLINK }	Insert, Hyperlink
{ INCLUDEPICTURE }	Insert, Picture, From File
{ INCLUDETEXT }	Insert, Insert File
{ INDEX }	Insert, Reference, Index and Tables, Index tab
{ LINK }	Edit, Paste Special (Paste Link)
{ NOTEREF }	Insert, Reference, Footnote
{ PAGE }	Insert, Page Numbers
{ REF }	Insert, Reference, Cross-Reference
{ SEQ }	Insert, Reference, Caption
{ SYMBOL }	Insert, Symbol
{ TIME }	Insert, Date and Time
{ TOA }	Insert, Reference, Index and Tables, Table of Authorities tab
{ TOC }	Insert, Reference, Index and Tables, Table of Contents tab
{ XE }	Mark Index Entry (Alt+Shift+X or Insert, Reference, Index and Tables, Index, Mark Entry)
={ FORMULA }	Table, Formula

VIEWING FIELDS

Rarely do you see the fields themselves in your document. You typically see the information the fields find or create. Sometimes, however, you *do* want to see the underlying field codes. For example, you might want to edit a field so that it presents different information, or presents it in a different format. Or maybe a field isn't behaving the way you expect, and you want to troubleshoot it.

To view a field code, click inside it and press Shift+F9, or right-click inside it and choose Toggle Field Codes from the shortcut menu.

To view all the field codes in your document, press Ctrl+A to select your entire document and then press Shift+F9, the keyboard shortcut that toggles the display of field codes on and off. Or choose Edit, Select All; then right-click on a field and choose Toggle Field Codes from the shortcut menu.

Still another way to view all the field codes in your document is to choose Tools, Options; then choose the View tab. Check the Field Codes box in the Show area.

CONTROLLING HOW FIELD CODES APPEAR IN YOUR DOCUMENT

By default, field codes are shaded in gray when you select them. This shading doesn't appear in Print Preview, nor does it print. You can control how your field codes are shaded from the View tab of the Options dialog box. In the Field Shading drop-down list box, you can choose Never (in which case your field codes are never shaded, even when selected) or Always (field codes are always shaded, even when you haven't selected them).

When you need to see at a glance where all your field codes are (for instance, if you've extensively cross-referenced your document and you want to see where your cross-references are), choose Always. Conversely, if you're working in Print Layout view and you want to see exactly how your printed document will look—without being distracted by shading that won't print—choose Never.

VIEWING FIELD CODES AND FIELD RESULTS AT THE SAME TIME

You might occasionally want to view the field codes and the field results at the same time. You might, for example, want to check whether you've formatted a field the way you want. Open a second window on the same document (choose Window, New Window). Next, choose Window, Compare Side by Side With. If the Compare Side by Side dialog box appears, select the window you want to compare your open document with.

Your two windows will now appear as shown in Figure 23.1. In one window, choose Tools, Options, View. Check the Field Codes check box. Your screen displays field codes in one window and field results in the other.

INSERTING A FIELD USING THE FIELD DIALOG BOX

Although you can enter a field into your document directly, most people prefer to use the Field dialog box. Unless you're creating a simple field, or one with which you're especially familiar, working within the Field dialog box makes it easier to create field syntax Word understands, and it reduces your chances of making a mistake. Choose Insert, Field to display the Field dialog box (see Figure 23.2).

➔ For more information about entering a field directly, **see** "Placing Fields Directly into a Document," **p. 780**.

You can select the field code you want from a list of available fields in the Field Names box.

If you're not sure of the name of the field code you want, select a category of fields from the Categories drop-down box, and Word lists your choices for you. Word organizes its field codes into nine categories, listed in Table 23.2.

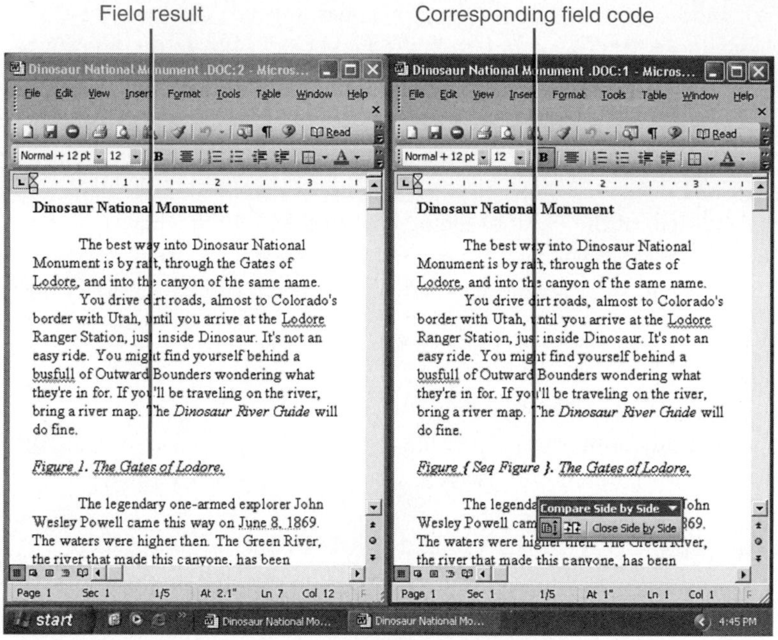

23

Field result   Corresponding field code

Figure 23.1
Displaying field codes
in one window and
field results in
another.

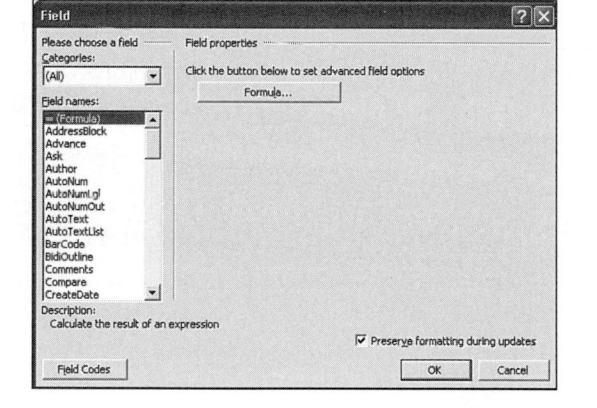

Figure 23.2
The default Field dia-
log box lists all avail-
able fields by
category.

TABLE 23.2   WORD'S FIELD CATEGORIES AND WHAT THEY COVER

Field Category	What It Covers	Which Fields Are Available
Date and Time	Fields that include the current date or time, or the date or time that an event relevant to your	{ CREATEDATE }, { DATE }, { PRINTDATE }, { SAVEDATE }, {TIME }, { EDITTIME }

Field Category	What It Covers	Which Fields Are Available
	document took place (for example, the last time you saved or printed)	
Document Automation	Compares values and takes an action (for example, runs macros, jumps to new locations, or sends printer codes)	`{ COMPARE }`, `{ DOCVARIABLE }`, `{ GOTOBUTTON }`, `{ IF }`, `{ MACROBUTTON }`, `{ PRINT }`
Document Information	Inserts or stores information about your document	`{ AUTHOR }`, `{ COMMENTS }`, `{ DOCPROPERTY }`, `{ FILENAME }`, `{ FILESIZE }`, `{ INFO }`, `{ KEYWORDS }`, `{ LASTSAVEDBY }`, `{ NUMCHARS }`, `{ NUMPAGES }`, `{ NUMWORDS }`, `{ SUBJECT }`, `{ TEMPLATE }`, `{ TITLE }`
Equations and Formulas	Creates and calculates the results of formulas; inserts symbols	`{ = (FORMULA) }`, `{ ADVANCE }`, `{ EQ }`, `{ SYMBOL }`
Index and Tables	Creates entries for, or builds, indexes and tables of contents, figures, and authorities	`{ INDEX }`, `{ RD }`, `{ TA }`, `{ TC }`, `{ TOA }`, `{ TOC }`, `{ XE }`
Links and References	Inserts information from elsewhere in your document, from AutoText entries, or from other documents and files	`{ AUTOTEXT }`, `{ AUTOTEXTLIST }`, `{ HYPERLINK }`, `{ INCLUDEPICTURE }`, `{ INCLUDETEXT }`, `{ LINK }`, `{ NOTEREF }`, `{ PAGEREF }`, `{ QUOTE }`, `{ REF }`, `{ STYLEREF }`

23

continues

23

TABLE 23.2   CONTINUED

Field Category	What It Covers	Which Fields Are Available
Mail Merge	Specifies information to be used in a Word mail merge, such as information from a data source	{ ASK }, { COMPARE }, { DATABASE }, { FILLIN }, { IF }, { MERGEFIELD }, { MERGEREC }, { MERGESEQ }, { NEXT }, { NEXTIF }, { SET }, { SKIPIF }, { ADDRESSBLOCK }, { GREETINGLINE }
Numbering	Numbers your document's pagesor sections, inserts information about your document's page numbers or sections, or inserts a bar code	{ AUTONUM }, { AUTONUMLGL }, { AUTONUMOUT }, { BARCODE }, { LISTNUM }, { PAGE }, { REVNUM }, { SECTION }, { SECTIONPAGES },{ SEQ }
User Information	Stores your name, address, or initials, or inserts them in a document or an envelope	{ USERADDRESS }, { USERINITIALS }, { USERNAME }

NOTE

> Notice the Preserve Formatting During Updates check box. If you mark this box and later make manual formatting changes to your field's contents, Word won't eliminate your manual formatting changes when it updates your field.
>
> For example, if you insert a field with this box checked and later format the field result as boldface, Word will retain the boldface. If you clear this box before you enter the field, Word eliminates the boldface.

USING WORD 2003'S FIELD DIALOG BOX

After you select a Field Name, the field name appears in the text box, and a brief description of the field's purpose appears at the bottom left of the Field dialog box. In most cases, Word 2003's Field dialog box also changes to display the options available for the field you've selected. Depending on the field, Word may present check boxes, scroll boxes, drop-down lists, text boxes, and other interface elements familiar to anyone who has worked with Windows software.

For instance, Figure 23.3 shows the Field dialog box as it appears when the { FILESIZE } field is selected. This field allows you to automatically update a document to display its size in kilobytes and megabytes.

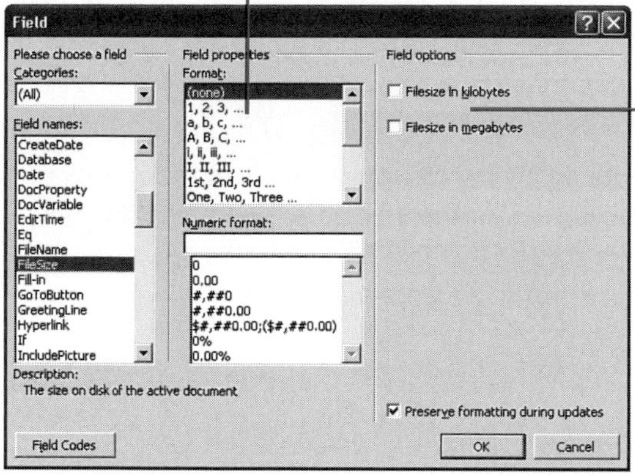

Field Properties usually relate to
how inserted text is formatted

Figure 23.3
The Field dialog box
as it appears when
the FileSize field is
displayed.

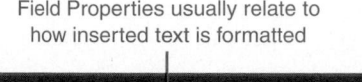

Field Options usually
relate to how the
field behaves

23

> **NOTE**
>
> In some cases, such as { INDEX }, the field that compiles an index and places it in
> your document, the Field dialog box displays a button in place of Field Properties and
> Field Options. When you click the button, Word closes the Field dialog box and opens
> the relevant dialog box associated with this Word feature. In this example, Word opens
> the Index tab of the Index and Tables dialog box.

The Field Properties settings that appear in the center of this dialog box allow you to control the formatting of the text that Word places in your document. In the { FILESIZE } field, you can control two aspects of formatting:

- The sequence used by the field—for example, 1, 2, 3...; A, B, C...; 1st, 2nd, 3rd; One, Two, Three; or other options. (Other fields may offer other options. For example, the { AUTHOR } field and other fields that display text in a document will offer case options, such as Uppercase, Lowercase, First capital, and Title case.)

- The numeric format used by the field—for example, whether decimal points, percentage marks, or dollar signs will be used. (Numeric formatting is covered in greater detail later in this chapter, in the "Using Word's Built-In Number Sequences" section.)

The Field Options settings that appear on the right side of the dialog box allow you to control unique aspects of the field's behavior—in this case, whether the field displays values as kilobytes or megabytes.

Sometimes, you won't need to make any adjustments to Word's default settings for a field. You can simply click OK, and Word will insert a field that does what you want. For example, if you want Word to insert the user's name, and you don't need to change the way the field results are capitalized, choose the { USERNAME } field and click OK.

More often, however, simply creating a field that consists of the field name won't accomplish what you intend. You'll find that you need to refine the field by choosing from the settings provided in the Field dialog box. When you change these settings, Word inserts text or "switches" that modify the field's behavior.

VIEWING AND EDITING THE FIELD CODE DIRECTLY

To see the entire field code as Word will insert it—or to make edits to a field code manually—click the Field Codes button at the bottom left of the Field dialog box. The Field dialog box now changes (see Figure 23.4), displaying the Advanced Field Properties area. Here, you can view the existing field code or enter switches of your own.

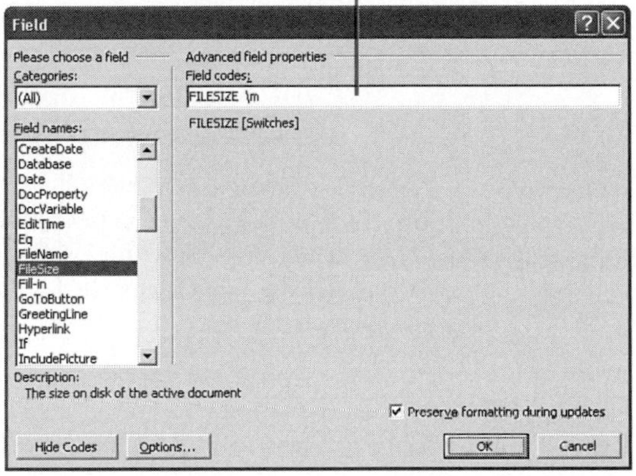

Enter field code syntax here

Figure 23.4
After you click the Field Codes button, the Field dialog box displays a text box where you can view field codes and manually edit them.

To discover the syntax Word expects you to use, look at the generic syntax Word displays in the Field dialog box, just below the text box where you type your field instructions. After you know what syntax to use, you can enter the correct text and switches in the text box in the Field dialog box.

Of course, there's a bit more to field syntax than this. Later in this chapter, you'll take a closer look at syntax you might need to add to your fields manually, and how you can do it.

PLACING FIELDS DIRECTLY INTO A DOCUMENT

It's possible to insert a field in your document manually, without using the Field dialog box at all. This can be faster, if you already know exactly what kind of field you need, and especially if the field is not complex.

For instance, if you want to insert a page count within your document text, the field you need is simple:

```
{ NUMPAGES }
```

By placing this field in your document directly, you save yourself the trouble of scrolling through a long list of field names in the Field dialog box.

To enter a field directly into your document, press Ctrl+F9. Word places two curly brackets around your insertion point and colors them gray to indicate that you're in a field (see Figure 23.5). These curly brackets are called *field characters*.

Field
brackets

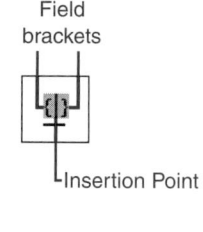

Figure 23.5
When you press Ctrl+F9 to insert a field, the field appears as two curly brackets; by default, these are highlighted in gray.

Insertion Point

23

NOTE

You can't insert field characters by pressing the curly bracket keys on your keyboard; you must press Ctrl+F9.

However, you can customize a menu, toolbar, or shortcut menu to include a command for inserting field brackets. From the Commands tab of the Customize dialog box, select the command InsertFieldChars and drag it to the toolbar or menu you want.

After you've inserted field characters, you can type any field names and any instructions inside the brackets. You can also cut and paste text into a field code from outside. Conversely, you can also cut or copy text from within field brackets to a location outside the field brackets. Keep the following syntax points in mind:

- You must leave one blank space after the left field bracket and before the right field bracket.
- After the first space, enter the field name; you can enter it in uppercase, mixed case, or lowercase.
- Leave one space between the field name and any switch.
- Leave one space between a switch and any parameters associated with that switch.
- If the field refers to a filename or specific text, enclose the filename or text in quotation marks.

TIP

Whenever you create a complex field instruction you might reuse, make it an AutoText entry. Then you have to enter it correctly only the first time; you can just copy it from then on.

→ For more information about working with AutoText, **see** "AutoText: The Complete Boilerplate Resource," **p. 301**.

WHAT GOES INTO A FIELD

Chances are that you will create most of your fields using the check boxes, scroll boxes, and other shortcuts that appear in Word 2003's Field dialog box. If you do, you may rarely see the field codes themselves; Word inserts them for you.

However, you may occasionally need to troubleshoot or slightly modify a field code. For those times, it's valuable to understand more clearly how they work.

You already know that every field has a name and that many fields require additional field instructions. Two of the most common field instructions are *arguments* and *switches*; these are covered next. More complex field instructions are covered later in this chapter, in the section "A Closer Look at Field Instructions."

USING ARGUMENTS TO GIVE WORD ESSENTIAL FIELD INFORMATION

In the example discussed earlier, you used { USERNAME } without any additional field instructions to insert the name of a user. When Word encounters this field, it inserts the username it finds stored in the User Information tab of the Options dialog box.

However, you can also use a { USERNAME } field to place a new name in the document and then permanently store that name in the User Information tab, where it can be used later for other purposes. If this is what you want to do, you have to tell Word what name to use. The syntax is as follows:

{ USERNAME "Robert Smith" }

The easiest way to create this field is to choose Insert, Field; select UserName from the Field Names scroll box; and enter Robert Smith in the New Name text box that appears. If you prefer, you can click the Field Codes button and enter the text manually.

In the example given previously, the field instructions in quotation marks after USER-NAME are a simple example of an *argument*. Arguments are text, numbers, or graphics that help a field decide how to act or what information to insert.

Arguments should always be enclosed in quotation marks. If you insert the fields using the check boxes, scroll boxes, and other shortcuts provided in the Field dialog box, Word enters the quotation marks for you.

If you enter the field codes manually—either by clicking Field Codes to display the Advanced Field Properties text box or by pressing Ctrl+F9 in the document to display field brackets—you then need to enter the quotation marks yourself.

> **NOTE**
>
> Word correctly recognizes one-word arguments without the quotation marks, but it's best to get in the habit of using quotation marks all the time. Quotation marks are required whenever you use an argument longer than one word, and if you don't use them consistently, you may forget to do so when necessary.

> **NOTE**
>
> Once in awhile, you may need to tell Word that you actually want real quotation marks to appear in the document. To indicate this, use backslashes, as in the following example:
>
> `{ TITLE "Start \"Loafing\" Around" }`
>
> This begs the question: What if you need to specify a document path, which already uses backslashes? (This might be necessary if you were using an `{ INCLUDEPICTURE }` field to insert a picture stored in a different folder on your drive or network.) The answer: Use *two* backslashes wherever you would otherwise have used one:
>
> `{ INCLUDEPICTURE "c:\\reports\\image12.jpg" }`
>
> By using quotation marks around the filename, you make sure that Word can read any filename, even if it consists of several separate words.

UPDATING YOUR FIELDS

One of the best things about fields is that you can update them automatically. F9 is the magic key:

- To update a single field, place your insertion point within it and press F9.

- To update more than one field, select the block of copy that contains all the fields you want to update, and press F9. Or, after you select all the fields, right-click on one of them and choose <u>U</u>pdate Field from the shortcut menu.

- To update all the fields in a document, press Ctrl+A and then press F9. In a long document, this can take a little while. If necessary, you can stop the process by pressing Esc.

- When you insert a field using Ctrl+F9, Word doesn't update the field until you press F9.

> **NOTE**
>
> Updating with F9 doesn't affect certain fields, whose functions don't require constant updates. This includes the following fields: `{ AUTONUM }`, `{ AUTONUMLGL }`, `{ AUTONUMOUT }`, `{ EQ }`, `{ GOTOBUTTON }`, `{ MACROBUTTON }`, and `{ PRINT }`.

 If Word fails to update fields properly, see "What to Do When a Field Won't Update Properly," in the "Troubleshooting" section of this chapter.

UPDATING FIELDS WHEN YOU PRINT

By default, Word does not update fields when you print a document. For many users, this makes sense: They want to stay in control of when their fields update, and not have Word do it for them without warning. However, if you want to make sure that your printed document always reflects the most current information available, you may want Word to always update fields before printing. To instruct Word to do so, choose <u>T</u>ools, <u>O</u>ptions and click the Print tab. Then, check <u>U</u>pdate Fields in the Printing Options area.

LOCKING FIELDS TO PREVENT THEM FROM UPDATING

Suppose that you want to temporarily prevent a field from being updated, even as you update fields surrounding it. For instance, suppose that you've prepared a report that uses an { INCLUDETEXT } field to display first-quarter results stored in a table in another document. One of these days, you might update the source table. But that doesn't mean you'll necessarily want the numbers in your executive report to change. If they did, your written analysis and the figures in the document wouldn't match.

To prevent a field from updating, you can *lock* it. First, place your insertion point in the field (or select text that includes several fields). Then, press Ctrl+F11 or Alt+Ctrl+F1. When you try to update this field, Word displays a message that the field is locked and cannot be updated.

To *unlock* a field so that it can once again be updated, place your insertion point in the field and press Ctrl+Shift+F11 or Alt+Ctrl+Shift+F1.

UNLINKING FIELDS TO REPLACE THEM WITH THEIR CURRENT VALUES

You might decide you *never* want to update a field. For example, imagine that you're completely finished with your document, and you're exporting it to a desktop publishing program that doesn't recognize Word field codes.

Word lets you permanently replace the field codes with the most recently updated field results. This is called *unlinking*. To unlink one or more fields, select them and press Ctrl+Shift+F9.

> **TIP**
>
> To be sure that the unlinked information is up-to-date before you unlink the field, first select it and then press F9 (or right-click and choose Update Fields) to update it.

Unlinking a field prevents an action field from working but has no effect on a marker field. For example, if you unlink all the fields in your document, you can still build an index based on { XE } index entry fields you inserted earlier.

> **CAUTION**
>
> Except for marker fields, after you unlink a field, the field is gone forever (unless you click Undo immediately or close the document without saving changes). If you have *any* reason to suspect that you might someday need the document automation provided by the field, save a duplicate copy of the file with all fields still in place.

SHORTCUTS FOR WORKING WITH FIELDS

Word provides various shortcuts for working with fields and navigating among them. These include shortcut menus, keyboard shortcuts, Select Browse Object, and Find/Replace/Go To. These techniques are covered in the following sections.

USING WORD'S FIELD SHORTCUT MENU

When you right-click on a field, the Field shortcut menu appears (see Figure 23.6). This includes the three most common tasks you might need: Update Field, Edit Field, and Toggle Field Codes. (*Toggling* a field switches between displaying the field code and displaying the field results.)

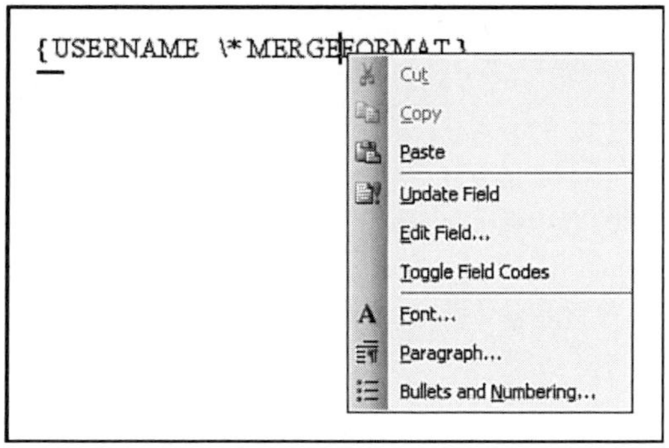

Figure 23.6
The shortcut menu appears when you right-click inside a field.

23

WORD KEYBOARD FIELD SHORTCUTS

You've already learned some of Word's keyboard shortcuts for inserting and managing fields, such as Ctrl+F9 for inserting field brackets in your document. All Word's relevant keyboard shortcuts are collected in Table 23.3.

TABLE 23.3   KEYBOARD SHORTCUTS FOR WORKING WITH FIELDS

Task	Key Combination	What It Does
Insert Field	Ctrl+F9	Inserts field characters { } so you can manually insert a field name and instructions
Update Field	F9	Produces a new field result
Go to Next Field	F11	Moves to next visible field
Go to Previous Field	Shift+F11	Moves to preceding visible field
View/Hide Field Code	Shift+F9	Toggles between displaying field codes and displaying their results
Lock Field	Ctrl+F11	Prevents a field from updating until you unlock it
Unlock Field	Ctrl+Shift+F11	Enables a locked field to be updated again
Unlink Field	Ctrl+Shift+F9	Replaces a field with its most recently updated results, eliminating the field code

continues

TABLE 23.3	CONTINUED	
Task	**Key Combination**	**What It Does**
Update Source (works with IncludeText field only)	Ctrl+Shift+F7	Updates selected text in another document that is linked to the current document by an IncludeText field
Perform Field Click (works with MacroButton field only)	Alt+Shift+F9	Performs whatever actions you've programmed into a MacroButton or GoToButton field or GoToButton
Insert Date Field	Alt+Shift+D	Inserts Date field with default format (in the U.S., 06/02/99)
Insert Page Field	Alt+Shift+P	Inserts Page field with default format (1, 2, 3...)
Insert Time Field	Alt+Shift+T	Inserts Time field with default format (in the U.S., 04:29 PM)

MOVING AMONG FIELDS

Word offers shortcuts for moving among fields. F11 moves to the next field and selects it; Shift+F11 selects the preceding field. Yet another way to move among fields is to click Word's Select Browse Object button at the bottom-right corner of the Word screen and choose Browse by Field.

FINDING AND REPLACING FIELD CONTENTS

Whenever the contents of field codes are displayed (as opposed to field results), you can use Edit, Replace to change those contents. This is invaluable if you ever need to change many field codes at once.

For instance, imagine that your document contains several { USERINITIALS } field codes, each designed to insert the user's initials in the document. Your department has grown; some people now share the same initials. You might decide to replace these fields with { USERNAME } fields that display the user's full name instead.

To display all field codes in your document, press Ctrl+A to select the whole document. Then, press Shift+F9 to display field codes. Now you can choose Edit, Replace to specify the changes you want to make.

Word's Replace feature is also ideal if you want to change the formatting of a specific kind of field that recurs throughout your document. For example, if your field is full of date fields and you want those date fields to also display the time, you could replace

M/d/yy

with one of Word's built-in date/time display options:

```
M/d/yy h:mm am/pm
```

Then, when you update your fields, all references to dates will also show times.

NOTE

> Some fields, such as index entries and table of contents entries, are automatically formatted as hidden text. As long as they are hidden, Word's field navigation and Find/Replace tools skip them. To show these hidden fields (and other hidden text in your document), choose Tools, Options; click the View tab; and check the Hidden Text button in the Formatting Marks area.

23

A CLOSER LOOK AT FIELD INSTRUCTIONS

Earlier in this chapter, you learned about *field instructions*: information that can be included with a field to adjust the way it behaves and the way it displays data in your document. You also learned about two of the most common types of field instructions: arguments and switches. Now you'll discover the power of two more kinds of field instructions:

- Bookmarks enable your fields to work with blocks of text stored anywhere in your current document or even in another document.
- Expressions enable you to build formulas into your field codes and have Word automatically update calculations just as a spreadsheet can.

CREATING FIELDS THAT CAN WORK WITH BLOCKS OF TEXT

In Chapter 22, "Using Footnotes, Bookmarks, and Cross-References," you learned that bookmarks are markers you can place anywhere in a document to identify a location or text you've selected. You can add a bookmark to some fields, thereby telling Word to go to that location or to use the bookmarked text for some purpose.

For example, the following { REF } field tells Word to insert text about Jones that you've bookmarked elsewhere in the document:

```
{ REF jones }
```

NOTE

> Bookmark names can be only one word, so you don't have to insert quotation marks when you insert a bookmark name in a field.

Or what if you don't want the bookmarked text to appear, but you want a cross-reference to the page number where the bookmarked text can be found? Use { PAGEREF }:

```
{ PAGEREF jones }
```

> **TIP**
>
> You can build this type of field using Insert, Cross-<u>R</u>eference, and then create an AutoText entry to quickly reuse it.

If you use the Field dialog box to select a field that uses a bookmark, a Bookmark <u>N</u>ame scroll box appears, displaying a list of the bookmarks in your current document. Choose a bookmark. If necessary, you can continue to edit your field. When you're finished, click OK to insert the field in your document.

You can also insert bookmark names manually; in fact, this is your only option if you are using { INCLUDETEXT } to insert text bookmarked in another document.

EXPRESSIONS: CREATING FIELDS THAT CAN CALCULATE

Expressions are field instructions designed to calculate—and to automatically update calculations when necessary—just as a spreadsheet program would.

The most basic Word expressions start with the = symbol. For example, if you enter the field

```
{ =24-8 }
```

Word displays the value 16.

Of course, this is a trivial example of what Word expressions can do. The real benefit of expressions is that you can base them on other information in your document—and when that information changes, the expression updates its results automatically. For instance, the field code

```
{ =joesales - bobsales }
```

tells Word to look for a bookmark named bobsales, which already contains a value, and subtract it from another bookmark named joesales, which also contains a value.

You can use the { IF } field to tell Word to display one kind of information if it finds one mathematical result, and different information otherwise. { IF } follows this syntax:

```
{ IF Expression1 Operator Expression2 TrueText FalseText }
```

In other words, you compare one value with another, and take one action if the resulting statement is true, another if it is false.

Consider the joesales/bobsales example. After you create the { =joesales - bobsales } field, you can bookmark it and name it joevbob. Now, you can build a field that pats Joe on the back if he outsells Bob. If not, it gently exhorts him to do better:

```
{ IF joevbob >0 "Congratulations, Joe, you're salesperson of the month!"
➡ "FYI, you're #2 this month." }
```

> **TIP**
>
> If you're working within a table, you can also use cell names (A1, A2, and so on) in place of bookmarks, so a table can perform many of the tasks of a spreadsheet.

NOTE

> If you want to reference one or more cells in another table, first select that table and bookmark it. Next, include the bookmark name in your formula alongside the cell reference. For instance, to include a reference to cell A4 in a table you've bookmarked as Table5, enter
>
> ```
> (Table5 A4)
> ```
>
> as in the following formula:
>
> ```
> =0.6*(Table5 A4)
> ```

23

A CLOSER LOOK AT FIELD FORMATTING

In this section, you'll learn some advanced techniques for controlling how field results appear. Suppose that you've made an important point somewhere in a large report. It's so important that you've boldfaced it for emphasis. Now you want to use a field to insert that phrase into your executive summary. But in that context, where everything's important, you don't want it to be boldfaced.

Well, you could insert the field result and reformat it manually—but it would then revert to the bold formatting anytime you updated your fields. Or you could lock that field—but if you ever want to update the substance of the field, then what? Obviously, neither of these solutions is ideal. Fortunately, Word provides field formatting switches that can do the job.

If you use a field that consists of only the field name, such as { NUMCHARS }, controlling the formatting of your field results is easy. Format the first character of the field name to look as you want your text to look. If you want bold italic text, your field should look like this:

```
{ NUMCHARS }
```

If the field also contains instructions, again format the first character of the field name the way you want it. Then add the following switch to the end of your field code:

```
\* charformat
```

For instance,

```
{ INCLUDETEXT "report.doc" \* charformat }
```

One more alternative is to manually format your field result and instruct Word not to change the formatting no matter what. This occurs when you check the Preserve Formatting During Updates check box in the Field dialog box—a check box that is checked by default. (If you enter a field manually, you must add the * MERGEFORMAT switch.)

There's only one catch to using Preserve Formatting During Updates or * MERGEFORMAT. When you do, Word counts words and takes their formatting literally. If you've formatted the fourth and fifth words in your field result as bold italic, then those words will always be bold italic—even if the field result changes and the fourth and fifth words happen to change. Let's say the field you insert consists of the following:

> According to Yankelovich, ***cohort marketing*** techniques can help you craft messages that address the emotional needs of the generation you need to reach.

Later, you edit the source copy a bit. You could wind up with something like this:

> Yankelovich cohort marketing ***techniques can*** help you craft messages that address the emotional needs of the generation you need to reach.

This literalism means you should use * MERGEFORMAT only when changing field results aren't likely to introduce a problem.

FORMATTING FIELD NUMBERS

You can use * CHARFORMAT and * MERGEFORMAT to format numbers as well. But numbers present some unique issues. What if a number should read one way in one location and a different way where a field inserts it? Or what if you need your field to return a number in an unusual format, with an unusual alignment, or in an unusual sequence?

In fields that typically return numbers, Word offers a wide variety of built-in number format options through the Field dialog box. And you can customize these options even further if you need to.

Figure 23.7 shows the Field dialog box for the { SECTION } field, which inserts a document's current Section number. Two types of number formatting options are available here:

- The options in the Format scroll box represent sequences of numbering you can use; Word inserts these with the * switch.

- The options in the Numeric Format scroll box represent formats you can use; Word inserts these with the \# switch.

The Format scrollbox lets you choose a sequence

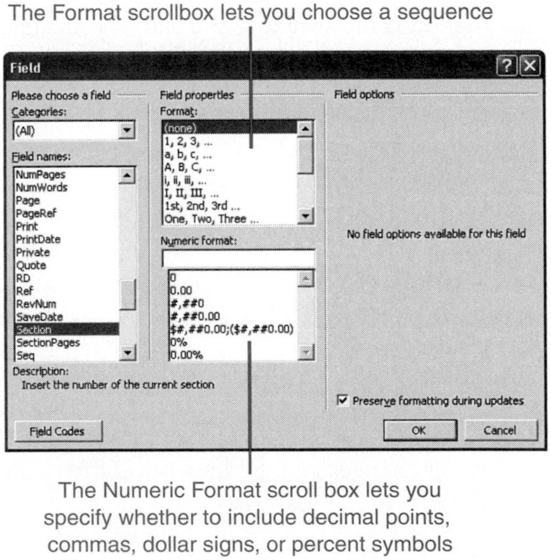

Figure 23.7
The { SECTION } field offers different kinds of number formatting in the Format and Numeric Format scrollboxes.

The Numeric Format scroll box lets you specify whether to include decimal points, commas, dollar signs, or percent symbols

The following sections take a closer look at each type of switch.

USING WORD'S BUILT-IN NUMBER SEQUENCES

Word provides several built-in sequencing options for the numbers that appear in field results. For example, you can format them as Roman numerals, convert them to words, or display them in a currency format such as you might see on a check or purchase order. Table 23.4 lists the primary choices Word offers.

TABLE 23.4   NUMBER SEQUENCES PROVIDED BY WORD

Sequence	Switch	What It Does	Example
1, 2, 3,...	* Arabic	Default format uses Arabic numbers	27
a, b, c,...	* alphabetic	Converts number into corresponding lowercase letters, "doubling up" letters after the 26th letter	aa
A, B, C,...	* ALPHABETIC	Converts number into corresponding uppercase letters, "doubling up" letters after the 26th letter	AA
i, ii, iii,...	* roman	Converts number into lowercase Roman numerals	xxvii
I, II, III,...	* ROMAN	Converts number into uppercase Roman numerals	XXVII
1st, 2nd, 3rd,...	* Ordinal	Converts number to follow ordinal sequence	27th
First, Second, Third,...	* Ordtext	Converts number to text that follows ordinal sequence	twenty-seventh
One, Two, Three,...	* Cardtext	Converts number to text that follows cardinal sequence	twenty-seven
hex,...	* Hex	Converts number to hexadecimal	1B
Dollar Text	* DollarText	Converts number to "check" format	Twenty-seven and 00/100

For example, if you want your field to report the section number as "three" rather than "3," you can select the A, B, C,... sequence from the Format scroll box. If you insert the field and then view it, you would see the following:

```
{ SECTION \* alphabetic }
```

Or you could use a { REVNUM } field to insert a sentence such as

```
NOTE: This is the fifth revision
```

where the word "fifth" was generated by the following field:

```
{ REVNUM \* OrdText }
```

USING WORD'S BUILT-IN NUMERIC FORMATS

What if you're perfectly happy with plain old Arabic numbers (1, 2, 3,...), but you need to control how many digits appear or where decimal points or commas are used, or you want to display a dollar sign before your field result? The options in the Numeric Format scroll box enable you to control these and other elements.

When you choose one of these numeric formats, Word inserts a \# switch and places the numeric format in quotation marks. For example, the following field inserts the file size, in megabytes (the \m switch specifies megabytes). The \# switch at the end of the field tells Word to use commas as separators between thousands (for example: 3,215 rather than 3215):

```
FILESIZE \m \# "#,##0"
```

CUSTOMIZING NUMERIC FORMATS TO YOUR SPECIFIC NEEDS

Word's built-in numeric formats are likely to be sufficient to handle most of your fields, but occasionally you may have to create your own:

- You may need to create a numeric format for an expression. Oddly, Word does not enable you to use the Field Options dialog box to do so; you must do so manually.
- You may need a format Word does not provide, such as a field result with three decimal places, or a field result that formats numbers with a foreign currency symbol such as # or ¥.

> **TIP**
>
> To insert a symbol into a dialog box such as the Field dialog box, insert it into your document using the Insert, Symbol dialog box; cut it into the Clipboard; open the dialog box where you want to paste it; and press Ctrl+V to paste it.

For situations in which you cannot use a built-in format, you must create the format manually. Word calls this *painting a numeric picture*.

Here's a simple example. Suppose that you're using fields to set up a list of numbers. If you use Word's default format, they look like this:

.8

15.96

29

18.2

That's sloppy—and if you choose to right-align your numbers you're no better off:

.8

15.96

29

18.2

You would prefer that each field result use the same number of decimal places so that they line up nicely when right-aligned:

.8

15.96

29

18.2

TIP

In some cases, you can achieve the same result using a decimal tab.

To create a numeric picture Word can use to create field results with three decimal places, you can use two of Word's built-in placeholders: # and 0. Within a numeric picture, the # symbol tells Word, "If there's no number in that location, insert a blank space." The 0 symbol tells Word, "If there's no number in this location, insert a 0."

Therefore, to get the cleaned-up list, use the following switch with each field:

`\# "###."`

NOTE

Quotation marks are optional unless you're combining the number with text.

NOTE

A numeric picture using # or 0 placeholders rounds off a fractional number that requires more digits than you allowed. For example, the field code { =1/3 \# "##".} by default displays the result 0.33.

Table 23.5 describes several placeholders and other characters you can use in numeric formats.

TABLE 23.5 CHARACTERS YOU CAN USE IN NUMERIC PICTURES

Character	What It Does	Sample Usage	Sample Field Result
[No switch]	Enters the value in the default format	{= 1/4}	0.25
#	Substitutes a blank space where no number is present; rounds off extra fractional digits	{=1/3 \# "$#.##"}	$ .33
0	Substitutes a zero where no number is present	{=1/4 \# "00."}	00.
$	Places a dollar sign in your field result	{=1/4 \# "$#.00"}	$0.25
+	Places a plus or minus sign in front of any field result not equal to zero	{=1/4 \# "+#.##"}	+.25
–	Places a minus sign in front of negative numbers (leaves positive numbers alone)	{= 1/4 \# "-#.##"}	–.25
.	Inserts a decimal point	{=1/4 \# "#.#"}	0.3
,	Inserts a comma separator (note: also use at least one 0 or #)	{=/2 \# "#,0"}	4,
;	Enables you to specify more than one option for displaying numbers, depending on whether the numbers are positive, negative, or zero (options should be specified in the order shown:positive, then negative, then zero)	{revenue-expenses \# "$###.00; ($###.00); 0"}	$.00 or ($.00) or 0 depending on actual field result
x	If placed on the left, truncates digits to its left; if placed on the right, truncates digits to its right	{ \# "#x##"}	75

Character	What It Does	Sample Usage	Sample Field Result
"text"	Includes text or symbols in numeric picture; places the entire numeric picture in regular quotation marks and the text in single quotation marks	`{= "#### 'lira'"}`	lira

FORMATTING DATES AND TIMES IN FIELD RESULTS

As with numbers, you can format dates and times in many ways. Usually, the quickest way to format date and time is to create your field with Insert, Field; the Field dialog box has most of the formats you need. However, as with numbers, you may occasionally need a specialty format.

The date-time switch is \@. Similar to what you've already seen with numbers, \@ creates a date-time picture—a model of how your dates and times should look. This date-time picture is usable with the following fields: { CREATEDATE }, { DATE }, { PRINTDATE }, { SAVEDATE }, and { TIME }.

You can use the characters in Table 23.6 and Table 23.7 in date-time pictures. You can also add separators, such as colon (:), dash (-), or slash (/).

CAUTION

> In date/time formatting, a character's meaning can change depending on its capitalization and the number of times you repeat the character. For instance, if you capitalize M in a date-time field, Word interprets that as *month*; lowercase m is recognized as *minute*.

TABLE 23.6   CHARACTERS YOU CAN USE IN DATE FORMATTING

Character	What It Does	Sample Usage	Sample Field Result
No switches (Default { DATE } field)	Inserts default date format	`{ DATE }`	7/6/99
M	Month in numeric format, 1–12	`{ DATE \@ "M" }`	7
MM	Month in numeric format, adding a zero to months that have only one digit; for instance, 01–12	`{ DATE \@ "MM" }`	07

continues

TABLE 23.6   CONTINUED

Character	What It Does	Sample Usage	Sample Field Result
MMM	Month as three-letter abbreviation	{ DATE \@ "MMM" }	Jul
MMMM	Month, spelled out	{ DATE \@ "MMMM" }	July
d	Day of month in numeric format, 1–31	{ DATE \@ "d" }	6
dd	Day of month in numeric format, 01–31	{ DATE \@ "dd" }	06
ddd	Day of week, as three-letter abbreviation	{ DATE \@ "ddd" }	Thu
dddd	Day of week, spelled out	{ DATE \@ "dddd" }	Thursday
y	Year (last two digits)	{ DATE \@ "y" }	99
yy	Year (all four digits)	{ DATE \@ "yy" }	

TABLE 23.7   CHARACTERS YOU CAN USE IN TIME FORMATTING

Character	What It Does	Sample Usage	Sample Field Result
No switches (Default{ TIME } field)	Inserts default time format	{ TIME }	12:15 PM
h	Hour, based on a 12-hour clock running from 1 to 12	{ TIME \@ "h" }	8
hh	Hour, based on a 12-hour clock running from 01 to 12	{ TIME \@ "hh" }	08
H	Hour, based on a 24-hour clock running from 0 to 23	{ TIME \@ "H" }	17
HH	Hour, based on a 24-hour clock running from 00 to 23	{ TIME \@ "HH" }	06
m	Minute, running from 0 to 59 (must use lowercase m)	{ TIME \@ "m" }	3

Character	What It Does	Sample Usage	Sample Field Result
mm	Minute, running from 00 to 59 (must use lowercase m)	{ TIME \@ "mm" }	03
AM/PM	Morning/afternoon data in the format AM or PM	{ TIME \@ "h:mm AM/PM" }	9:30AM
am/pm	Morning/afternoon data in the format am or pm	{ TIME \@ "h:mm am/pm" }	9:30am
A/M	Morning/afternoon data in the format A or P	{ TIME \@ "h:mm A/P" }	9:30A
a/p	Morning/afternoon data in the format a or p	{ TIME \@ "h:mm a/p" }	9:30a

Now for a couple of examples. Suppose that you want to automate the creation of a list of daily specials for your restaurant. You want a field that automatically inserts the correct day of the week in the following sentence:

```
Welcome! Here are our specials for today, Saturday:
```

You can build a { DATE } field that displays only the day of the week (not the month or date):

```
{ DATE \@ "dddd" }
```

Or perhaps you need to abbreviate the current month and day, but you don't need to include the year at all:

```
Mar 27
```

Use the following field:

```
{ DATE \@ "MMMM d" }
```

NESTING FIELDS

Sometimes, the best way to have one field's results affect another field is to *nest* the first field inside the second. This may sound abstract, but it is immensely useful.

To nest a field, first press Ctrl+F9 to create the field and edit the field as much as possible. Then, place the insertion point where you want the nested field to appear. Press Ctrl+F9 to insert a new field within your existing field. A sample (and simple) nested field follows:

```
{IF {DATE \@ "d-MMM"}="15-Apr" "Have you paid your taxes or asked for an
extension yet?" "Don't forget: tax preparation today can save you money
when April 15 rolls around!"}
```

In this example, the { IF } field checks the date returned by the { DATE } field. If the date and format match 15-Apr, Word inserts "Have you paid your taxes or asked for an extension yet?" If Word finds another date, it inserts "Don't forget: tax preparation today can save you money when April 15 rolls around!"

Here's a detailed example of how you can use nested fields to ask a user for an article name and then place that article name in the Summary Info tab of the Properties dialog box. After it's stored there, it can automatically be inserted anywhere else in the document you want, using another field.

Start by inserting a { SET } field, which sets a bookmark on the text that follows it. Call the bookmark Articlename:

```
{ SET ARTICLENAME }
```

Normally, the bookmark name would be followed by text. However, in this case, there is no text yet: You need to ask the user for it. You can use a nested { FILLIN } field that displays a dialog box asking the user to key in text:

```
{ SET ARTICLENAME { FILLIN "What is the article title?" } }
```

Next, create another nested field that stores Articlename in the Title box of the Properties dialog box. This field also places the data in your document. You might use it in a document header or footer to automatically place your document's title there:

```
{ TITLE { REF articlename } }
```

Using this nested-field technique, you can ask a user for any information and automatically place that information in the Properties dialog box, where other fields can retrieve it and place it anywhere in the document you want.

TROUBLESHOOTING

WHAT TO DO WHEN A FIELD WON'T UPDATE PROPERLY

First, try to update the field manually. Click inside it and press F9. If the information doesn't update, follow these steps:

1. Check to make sure that there really is new information available to replace the old information. For example, if a { FILESIZE } field doesn't change, make sure that the size of your file on disk has actually changed (this field's value won't change until you resave the file after adding or removing characters or other document elements).

2. Check to make sure that the field isn't locked. In some cases, Word beeps when you try to update a locked field. If you don't have sound enabled, try unlocking the field by selecting it and pressing Ctrl+Shift+F11. If the field still won't update, press Shift+F9 to view its contents. Delete the following characters if you find them present:
   \ !

If your field is contained in a text box, note that Word does not select text boxes when you select the text that surrounds them, or even if you select the entire document. To update a field code within a text box, select that text individually and press F9.

If you select text and press Shift+F9, but the field doesn't appear, it's possible that the field has been unlinked (replaced with ordinary text) or was never a field in the first place. For example, if you use Insert, Date and Time to enter the current date, but you leave the Update Automatically check box cleared, Word inserts the date in the form of text, not a field.

PART V

WORD, THE INTERNET, AND XML

CHAPTER 24

USING WORD TO DEVELOP WEB CONTENT

In this chapter

WEB PAGE DEVELOPMENT: WORD'S STRENGTHS AND WEAKNESSES

Word 2003 is a viable choice for the nonprofessional Web designer who may be already familiar with Word and reluctant to learn a new application. Using Word, even people with no HTML programming language experience can create basic Web pages with ease, including popular features such as scrolling text, frames, and cascading style sheets. However, Word lacks some of the high-end Web design features of an application like Microsoft FrontPage 2003 or Macromedia Dreamweaver MX, so someone who does Web design for a living would likely not choose Word for that work.

Word makes Web design easy by shielding the user from the raw coding, instead allowing the user to work in a familiar WYSIWYG (what you see is what you get) environment in which formatting can be applied with toolbar buttons and menu commands. Then when the document is saved, Word converts all that formatting to HTML coding that Web browser applications can understand.

WEB TECHNOLOGIES SUPPORTED IN WORD

Word 2003 is similar to Word 2002 in its Web design features. Word supports all the basic HTML codes that you would expect for formatting, plus several other technologies and scripting languages and supplementing traditional HTML code. The most notable improvement in Word 2003 is the enhanced support of XML (eXtensible Markup Language), covered in Chapter 25, "Using Word to Develop XML Content and Use XML Applications."

Word supports all these types of Web content:

- **HTML.** Hypertext Markup Language is the lingua franca (medium of exchange) of the World Wide Web. Almost every Web page is built with this language. HTML, a simple formatting and organizational language, is ideal for the display of text, simple graphics, and hyperlinks. It doesn't do anything fancy like search a database or pop up dialog boxes. The appeal of HTML lies in its ease of use and universal acceptance.

- **CSS.** Cascading style sheets are used to define the layout of a document precisely. Style sheets are more powerful than the styles found in Word because style sheets can also specify page layout. A style sheet can be a separate document, or it can be embedded in each HTML page. Because browsers have different capabilities in how they interpret these styles, they interpret what they can and ignore the rest; that is, they cascade down in their interpretation and display what they are able to.

- **XML.** EXtensible Markup Language is more robust and extensible (hence its name) than HTML. You can define new tags and their uses at any time and in any way by referencing them in an associated text document. The strength of XML is its capability to use these new tags to identify specific information. This technology vastly improves the users' abilities to find specific-subject Web pages and opens the Internet up to even more data mining. Chapter 25 deals with XML in detail.

- **VML.** Vector Markup Language uses text to define geometric shapes, colors, line widths, and so forth. These words are then interpreted and displayed as graphical images in browsers that understand VML (Microsoft Internet Explorer 5 and higher). No matter what size circle you want to display, you use the same amount of text to define it. VML reduces the bandwidth required to send a graphical image from a Web server to a browser. This improves the browser page load time, improves image quality, and helps reduce Internet or intranet network congestion.

- **JavaScript and VBScript.** Both of these script-style programming languages are in common everyday use on the Web right now. These languages handle simple programming tasks without having to load a separate application. JavaScript is supported by the vast majority of browsers; VBScript is supported by only Microsoft Internet Explorer browsers. These languages enable you to program interactivity into Web pages.

You don't need to know how to use each or any of these technologies to build or edit Web pages in Word 2003. However, if you are an experienced Web page designer, it's nice to have these tools supported in Word so that you need not turn to some other editing program simply because you want to use one of them.

WEB PAGE FILE FORMATS

When Word saves in Web Page format, it creates a file that contains all the HTML coding needed for display in a Web browser, *plus* all the Word coding needed for full-featured editing and display in Word. Therefore, you can switch freely between Word and a Web browser and the file will look the same in both places. Microsoft calls this interchangeability of file formats *round-tripping*, and it works with Word 2000 and higher.

NOTE

> Round-tripping applies only to Web pages created in Word. If any other Web page is edited in Word, it may or may not look like it originally did after it has been saved in Word.

This beefed-up Web page format that Word uses can display most Word features on a Web page. These supplementary technologies increase the capability of HTML so that Web pages can display Word-specific formatting and features that pure HTML does not support.

However, round-tripping comes at a cost: The file sizes of the HTML files generated by Word are larger than those for regular HTML because they contain all that extra code for Word support. Therefore, Word 2003 also offers an alternative mode called Web Page, Filtered that saves in pure HTML without round-trip support for Word. A filtered HTML file is identical to one you would create in a pure HTML editing application such as Dreamweaver.

Word also offers support for MHTML (MIME HTML), a file format that creates a single file out of a Web page that might ordinarily require support files. For example, suppose you have a Word document that contains a graphic. If you save it in either regular Web Page format or filtered format, Word will create an HTML file (.htm) and a support folder containing a separate picture file. This can be awkward to distribute to others via email. With the Single File Web Page (.mht) format, the Web page file contains both the text and the graphics with no need for support folders or files. The only drawback is that some older browsers are not able to display MHTML files.

NOTE

MIME is an encoding scheme for sending graphics and formatted text via email. It's been around for a long time, and most email programs support it.

WORD FEATURES LOST WHEN SAVING IN WEB FORMAT

Some weaknesses in Word's capability to translate all its features to Web pages still exist, even with the latest improvements. Here are a few Word features that do not transfer when you save in any of the Web Page formats:

- Versioning
- Passwords
- Word file headers/footers
- Newspaper-style column flow (though the text is unaffected)

When you use versioning, only the latest version number of the Word document is included in the HTML source. The reason for the lack of support for passwords is that typically on a Web site, the Web server controls passwords, rather than individual documents (or pages) doing so.

The lack of support for columns and headers/footers occurs because Web browsers simply have no functionality (that is, there is no HTML equivalent) to display these formatted items. When the Web page is reloaded into Word 2003, however, columns and headers and footers are restored. Because these "translation" problems are due to shortcomings in HTML or other Web technology, Microsoft simply cannot create a version of Word that is 100% compatible with Web pages.

TIP

If you plan to edit your Web pages in an HTML editor application, save them as filtered Web pages. Many HTML applications have trouble dealing with Word's extra formatting codes that it places in a standard Web page document.

WHY YOU MIGHT *Not* WANT TO USE WORD

When you have a choice between an application designed for a certain purpose and one designed for a more generic one, you will usually find that the specific program does its task better and with less effort. That's true with most of the higher-end full-featured Web design applications.

If you are designing a commercial Web site that will have a lot of pages and some complex linking requirements, you will find the job much easier in an application like FrontPage 2003 or Dreamweaver MX. These programs have all kinds of great shortcuts and wizards for creating, formatting, and debugging HTML code and active Web content. Although Word will serve as a vessel for many kinds of Web objects, such as JavaScript and VBScript, it doesn't help you generate those items in an automated manner.

CREATING AND SAVING A WEB PAGE IN WORD

In Word 2003, creating a Web page is much the same as creating a Word document. You do not need to open up a special environment or think differently about the contents of your page.

To begin building from a blank Web page, click on the Web Page link in the New Document task pane. A blank page opens, looking very much like (even identical to) a normal blank document. There are some differences, however, in some of the menu commands that are available when you are working with a Web page. For example, on the View menu there's an HTML Source command with a Web page. You will see other subtle differences as you go along. See the section "Adding Content to Web Pages in Word" later in this chapter for details.

NOTE

In Word 2002 there were a Web Page Wizard and a group of Web page templates you could choose from the New dialog box; however, these were cut from Word 2003.

Then what do you do? Just start creating your document. This is the beauty of Word: A Web page is mostly the same thing as a regular document in terms of basic typing, formatting, and layout. We'll get into some specifics that are exceptions later in the chapter.

PREVIEWING A WEB PAGE

As you are building your Web page, you can view or preview your Web pages using Web Layout view and Web Page Preview.

Web Layout view (choose View, Web Layout from the menu or click the Web Layout View icon in the status bar) presents your document like a Web page.

Web Page Preview enables you to preview your Web page in a browser without first having to save the file. Click File, Web Page Preview on the menu to initiate the process. The file in Word is opened in your default browser for viewing. This ensures that what you are building in Word is indeed being displayed the same way in the browser.

NOTE

Remember that just because your Web page looks good in one browser doesn't mean that it will look good in all browsers. Unless you know that everyone will be accessing

continues

your Web page with the same browser and version, it is a good idea to test your Web pages with the latest versions of Microsoft and Netscape browsers as well as earlier versions, if possible. Note that if some things do not show up in one browser (the scrolling marquee, for instance, is not supported by Netscape browsers), you may need to remove those elements or build browser-specific pages.

→ To see a list of browser-specific tags, **see** the book *HTML 4 Unleashed* (Rick Darnell, ISBN 1-5752-1299-4, Sams Publishing).

SAVING A WEB PAGE

When you start a new document as a Web page, and then save it, the default file format will be Single File Web Page. (Change to one of the other formats if you like.) You can also use File, Save As to save existing Word documents as Web pages.

As explained earlier, one of the nice things about Word is that it can save Web pages in any of three formats: Single File Web Page; Web Page; and Web Page, Filtered. Each of these is useful for different situations:

- Use Single File Web Page (.mht) when you are planning to send the Web page via email or distribute it as a document that you want people to be able to easily download and work with. Do not use this format if you think your users may be using very old Web browser software.

- Use the standard Web Page format (.htm) when you are planning to round-trip the page between Word and a Web browser, and if you don't mind that a separate folder for graphics and support files is required for page viewing. Don't use this format if you are planning to email the page to others, or if compatibility with other HTML editing software such as Dreamweaver is important.

- Use the Web Page, Filtered format (.htm) when you need the resulting file to be plain HTML with no special Word tags in it. For example, use it when you are going to integrate the page into a larger Web site created with Dreamweaver or FrontPage (although FrontPage does do a decent job of accepting Word Web content, because it's also by Microsoft). Don't use this format if you plan to edit the page in Word in the future.

The Single File Web Page (.mht) format is the default in Word 2003, but you can choose any of the formats from the Save as Type drop-down list in the Save As dialog box (File, Save as Web Page). See Figure 24.1. Notice that this is a special version of the Save As dialog box, not the standard one.

To save a Word document as a Web page, follow these steps:

1. Choose File, Save As Web Page. A special version of the Save As dialog box opens, as shown in Figure 24.1.

Figure 24.1
You have several file-type choices for Web pages in Word 2003.

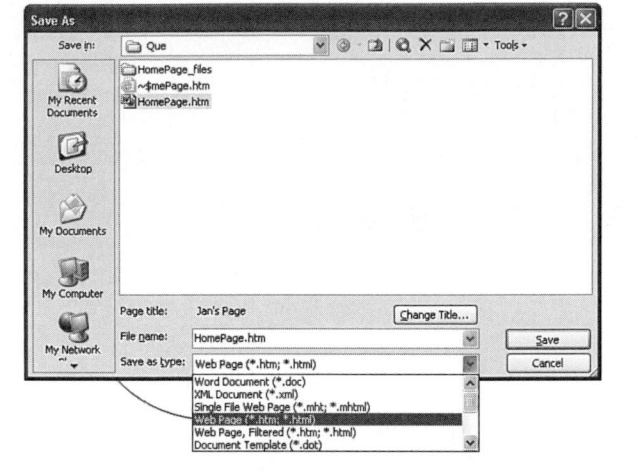

2. Open the Save as Type drop-down list and select the desired format.

3. Click the Change Title button. Type the desired title for the page and click OK.

4. If needed, change the location. You can save directly to a Web server, or save to a local hard disk and then upload to a Web server later.

5. Click OK.

This procedure doesn't provide much in the way of flexibility, but there are many ways of setting specific options when you save. The following sections address these options.

OPTIONS FOR WEB PAGE SAVING

Web options enable you to change the way Word saves Web pages. These are more subtle options, not the big ones like filtered/unfiltered or single page/multipage. Most people won't find it necessary to change them, but you should know about them in case a situation ever arises in which they are useful.

To open the Web Options dialog box, do this:

1. Choose Tools, Options.

2. Click the General tab.

3. Click the Web Options button.

You can also access this dialog box on-the-fly as you are saving a file; from the Save As dialog box, click the Tools button and then choose Web Options.

The following sections look at each of the tabs in this dialog box individually.

SAVING FOR COMPATIBILITY WITH SPECIFIC BROWSERS

Under the Browsers tab for Web Options, you can set your target browser. The target browser is based on version number and runs from Internet Explorer 3 and Netscape

Navigator 3 up through Internet Explorer 6 and higher. Select your default target browser based on the audience viewing your Web pages. To reach the widest audience on the Internet, use the lowest version numbers. You might choose Internet Explorer 6 as your target browser on a company intranet where everyone has standardized on the latest browser and you need these capabilities to support the content in your Web pages.

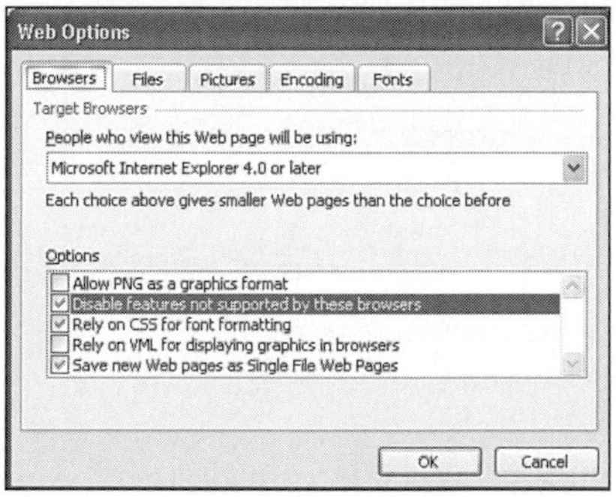

Figure 24.2
Set browser-specific Save options here, balancing compatibility with feature richness.

Each target browser setting enables or disables a set of supported features, including these:

- *Allow PNG as a Graphics Format.* This new format is not yet widely supported on the Internet but has advantages over GIF and JPEG files. See the following section for details.

- *Disable Features Not Supported by These Browsers.* For instance, no VML would be used in Web pages generated by Word 2002 because version 4 browsers do not understand VML. If you clear this box, every Web page feature built into Word 2003 is used without regard for whether any browser version can support it.

- *Rely on CSS for Font Formatting.* Only version 3 browsers cannot understand CSS. We recommend leaving this option on for the greatest flexibility in changing Web page formatting.

- *Rely on VML for Displaying Graphics in Browsers.* VML reduces overall Web page size, but browsers before version 5 do not understand it. See the following section for more on VML.

- *Save New Web Pages as Single File Web Pages.* This format has the advantage of storing all the files in a single file. You can, of course, override this option each time you save your Web page.

MORE ABOUT PNG AND VML

The most common graphics file formats used in Web pages are GIF (Graphics Interchange Format) and JPG (Joint Photographic Experts Group, also JPEG). Word automatically exports all images to these two formats when you save as a filtered Web page.

Word also supports the display of two additional graphics file formats in Web pages: VML (Vector Markup Language) and PNG (Portable Network Graphics).

VML GRAPHICS

Vector images are defined by equations. As such, they scale perfectly to any size. This is in contrast to bitmap images, in which each pixel has a defined position and color value. Bitmap images scale poorly because the graphics program must interpolate pixels as the image dimensions are changed. Items created in Word using the Drawing tools are drawn as vector objects. When you save as a Web page or a single file Web page (.mht) in Word, the graphical object is defined by the VML language. The primary advantage of using VML is economy of size, especially if you're using large images. But a significant disadvantage is that vector objects can be displayed only by Internet Explorer version 5.0 or later.

PNG GRAPHICS

PNG is basically an improved version of GIF. The idea behind this format is to solve the primary weaknesses of .gif and .jpg files: GIF can support only 256 colors, and JPG gains its small file size using a lossy compression scheme (that is, as you make your file smaller, you lose photo clarity and resolution as image data is discarded). Also, GIF supports transparency and animation, but JPG does not.

PNG supports 24-bit color, supports transparency, and uses a file compression scheme that does not reduce the file size at the expense of image clarity. The main reason that this format is not widely used now is that older browsers cannot read the PNG format.

SELECTING WEB PAGE FILE OPTIONS

From the Files tab of the Web Options dialog box, shown in Figure 24.3, you can change some filename options and make choices about Word 2003 being your default Web page editor.

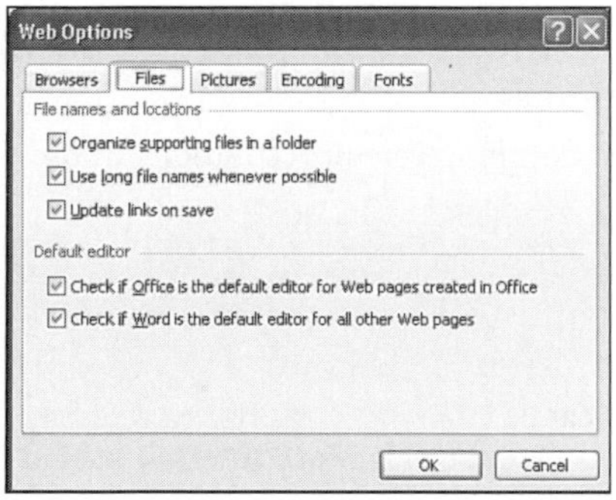

Figure 24.3
Setting filenames, locations, and default editor options using Web Options in Word 2003.

The first check box asks whether you want to organize supporting files in a folder. When Word 2003 saves a Web page, it sends many (though not all) supporting files—such as graphics—to a separate folder. If you deselect this check box, it places the supporting files in the same folder as the HTML file.

The Use Long File Names Whenever Possible check box is marked by default. The only operating system that does not support long filenames is DOS (with or without Windows 3.x). Unless you have many people using this operating system (which is unlikely), leave this check box checked.

The final check box in the section, Update Links on Save, updates links to supporting graphics and components in your Web page. It does not update or check hyperlinks.

The Default Editor portion of the Files tab under Web Options enables you to decide whether you want Office to be the default editor for Web pages created in Office (checked by default) or Word to be the default editor for all Web pages (not checked by default).

CHANGING PAGE SIZE

The Pictures tab, shown in Figure 24.4, defines the target monitor you want for your Web page.

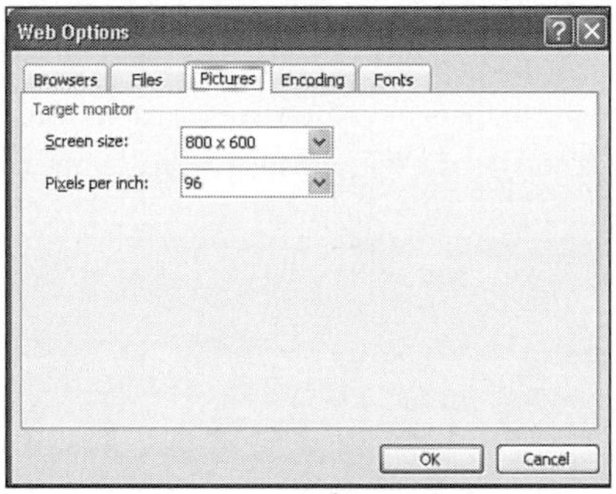

Figure 24.4
Choosing your target monitor size and resolution for display of your Web pages.

The target monitor refers to the screen resolution you want to optimize your Web pages for. This determines the "size" (width) of the page. Screen resolution is expressed in pixels, usually as width × height. The most common screen resolutions in use today on PCs are

- 800×600
- 1024×768
- 1280×1024

The larger the number, the more pixels (and thus more information) are displayed on the screen. If you choose a target monitor size of 800×600 for building your Web pages in Word and view the resultant page at 1280×1024, much of the screen will be empty space with most of the information crowded to the left side of the screen. On the other hand, if you design your pages at 1280×1024 and view it at 800×600, you will have to keep scrolling to the right to see all the information. The default of 800×600 is suitable for most uses, unless you're sure that most of your audience uses other screen resolutions.

You can also change the pixels per inch of your target monitor. Again, the default of 96 is suitable for most users. Using higher values greatly increases the size of your graphics and increases your Web page load time. Using a value of 120 slightly increases the detail in your Web page. A value of 72 gives you smaller Web graphics, but your Web page will have a slightly coarser appearance.

CHANGING LANGUAGE ENCODING

The Encoding tab in the Web Options dialog box (see Figure 24.5) enables you to choose the language code page from those installed on your machine. Choose the appropriate code page for the language you are using to build your Web page.

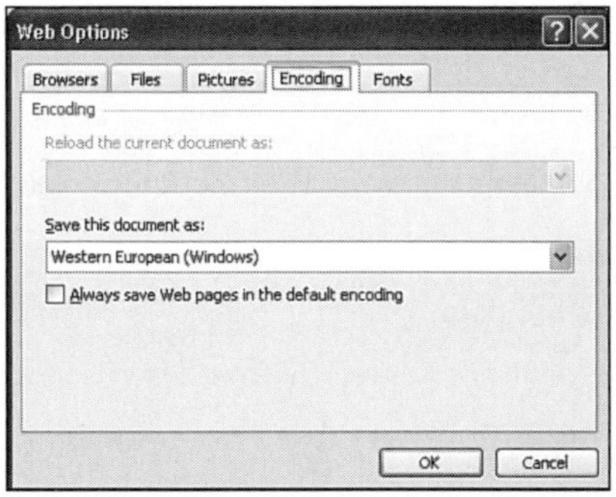

Figure 24.5
Choosing the language code page using Web Options.

CHANGING THE DEFAULT FONTS

You can set the default proportional and fixed-width fonts for your Web page from the Fonts tab, as shown in Figure 24.6.

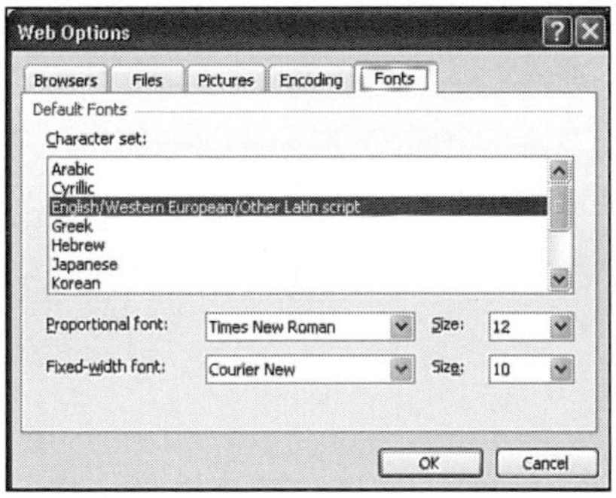

Figure 24.6
Changing the default font for your Web page.

Use common fonts for your defaults. If you use fonts in your Web pages that aren't installed on your viewers' PCs, their browsers can't render your fonts and will substitute their own default fonts. If you need to use a specific, unusual font, see the section "Using Nonstandard Fonts," later in the chapter.

WORKING WITH WEB PAGE PROPERTIES

When you build a Web page with HTML coding, you place all the text for the Web page itself in a section called <BODY>. There's also a <HEADER> section at the top of the file that contains some other information about the page, such as keywords that a search engine can use to index the page, and a page title.

The page title is important because it's what appears in the title bar of the Web browser when the page is displayed. When you save a Web page in Word, you have the option of changing the default page title by clicking the Change Title button, as you saw in Figure 24.1. But you can also change the page's title at any time, not just during the save operation, as well as specifying other header information.

To work with the page's header information, do the following:

1. Choose File, Properties. The Properties box for the document opens.
2. Click the General tab.
3. In the Title box, enter a title for the page.
4. In the Keywords box, enter one or more keywords that describe the content of the page. See Figure 24.7.
5. Click OK to close the Properties box.

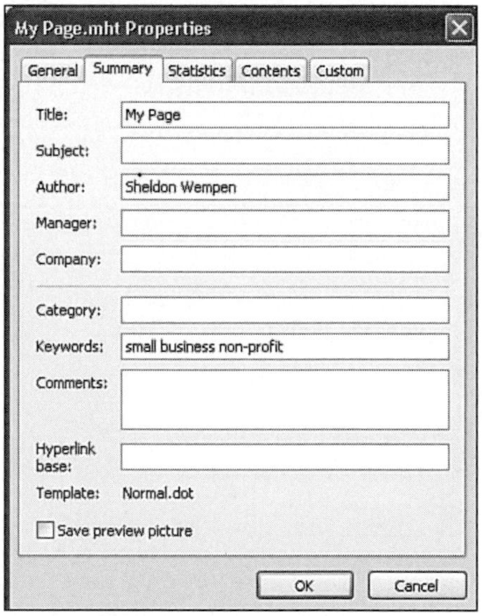

Figure 24.7
The Properties box controls the title and keywords reported to the Web browsers that will display the Web page.

VIEWING HTML SOURCE CODE

Whether you save a file as a Web page, a filtered Web page, or a single file Web page (.mht), the page information is saved as *HTML source code*. HTML source code is the actual code that a browser translates to display a Web page. In Word 2003, this is not only HTML but also includes XML, CSS, VML, and the scripting languages. If you want to access this code—for instance, to modify the JavaScript—you can access the code from the menu under View, HTML Source. The source code is displayed in Microsoft Script Editor window, as shown in Figure 24.8. Notice in Figure 24.8 that the keywords and title entered in Figure 24.7 appear in the <HEADER> section.

Figure 24.8
Viewing the HTML source code of a Web page in the Microsoft Script Editor.

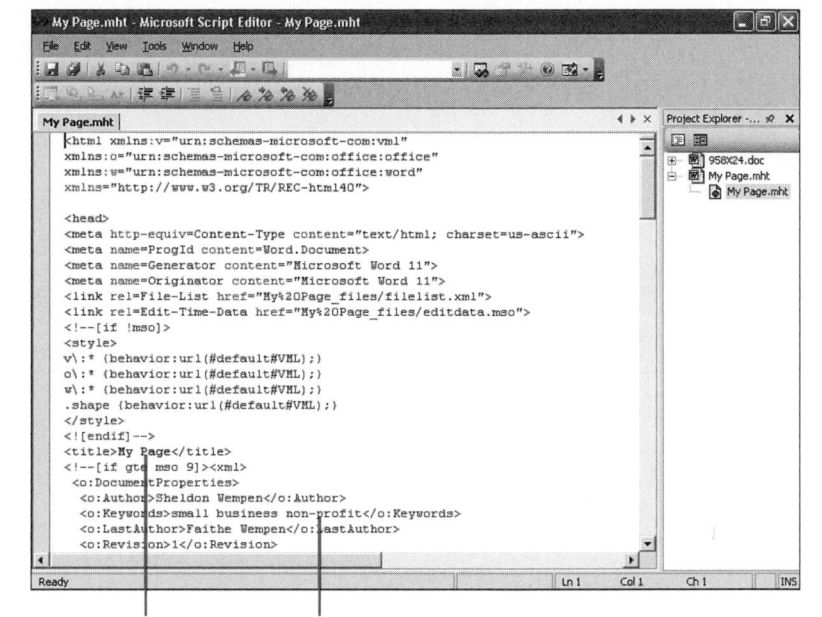

Title, author, and keywords were entered in the Properties box in Figure 24.7.

NOTE

> The Script Editor is not part of the default installation. The first time you activate this feature it initiates auto-installation, so keep your Word 2003 or Office 2003 CD-ROM handy.

As far as the HTML source code is concerned, you can search and edit the HTML source code from within the Script Editor as you want. To save your changes, choose File, Exit from the menu.

Directly modifying the HTML source from within the Script Editor is not recommended unless you are an experienced programmer or Web developer, or if you want to learn more about HTML by experimenting on prebuilt code.

ADDING CONTENT TO WEB PAGES IN WORD

A Web page and a Word document are similar in that their predominant content is usually words, sentences, and paragraphs. But Web pages include content not typically found in

Word documents. In this section, we'll look at how to create or apply many of the most common types of Web content and formatting in Word.

Creating Hyperlinks

A *hyperlink* is the combination of some descriptive text or an image and the location (also called the address) of a Web page or an object. Any text or image on a Web page can hold a hyperlink. Hyperlinks most commonly point to the following:

- Web pages
- Media objects such as sounds, video, or pictures
- Email addresses

The easiest way to create a hyperlink is simply to type it and let Word make it into a live hyperlink automatically. Whenever you type a string of characters that appears to be a Web or email address, Word automatically converts it for you. If it doesn't for some reason, or if you want to specify some options (such as ScreenTips), see the following sections.

Creating a Text Hyperlink

Any text phrase, word, or part of a word can be included in a hyperlink. To build a hyperlink, you need some text in a document and the exact location where you want the hyperlink to lead when it is clicked:

1. From a document in Word, highlight a text phrase. For instance, highlight "Microsoft" in the phrase "For more information, visit the Microsoft home page."

2. Click the Insert Hyperlink button on the Standard toolbar or choose Insert, Hyperlink to open the Insert Hyperlink dialog box, shown in Figure 24.9.

   You can also reach the Insert Hyperlink dialog box by using the keyboard shortcut, Ctrl+K, or by right-clicking on the selected text and choosing Hyperlink from the shortcut menu.

Figure 24.9
Filling in the Insert Hyperlink dialog box.

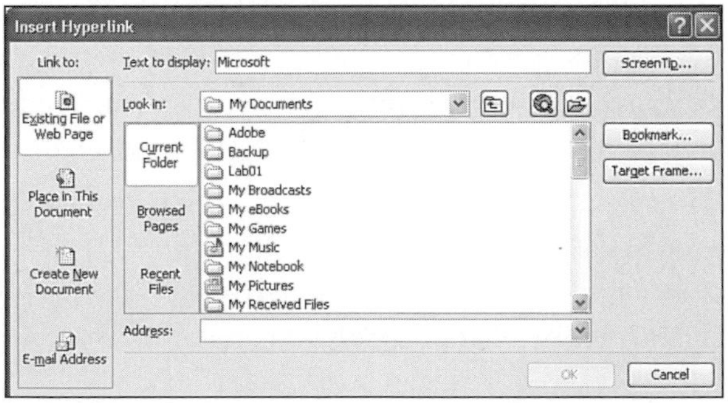

3. In the top box, labeled Text to Display, the text you highlighted is displayed. Change it if desired.

4. In the Address text box, enter the Web URL for the site to which you want the text to link.

5. (Optional) To add a ScreenTip to the hyperlink, click the ScreenTip button, type the text, and click OK. A ScreenTip is text that appears in a box when the user points at the hyperlink in a Web browser. If you do not specify a ScreenTip, the URL will be used as a ScreenTip.

6. Click OK. When you return to your document, the text you highlighted is now a blue color and underlined, indicating that it is now an active hyperlink.

NOTE

URL stands for uniform resource locator. It's the complete address to the Web page or other location being referenced. Web page URLs usually begin with `http://` and a great many of them (but not all) are then followed by www. Usually a company will place its Web pages on a server with the www designation, but some companies with large Web presences may have separate servers for support, sales, and so on. For example, to get support from Microsoft, the URL is `http://support.microsoft.com`.

ADDING A HYPERLINK TO AN IMAGE

A graphic can function as a hyperlink, such that when the user clicks on the image, a Web page loads. The process for building a clickable or hot image is similar to that for building a text hyperlink:

1. Select any clip art, picture, drawing object, or WordArt within a Web page.

2. Click Insert Hyperlink on the Standard toolbar to display the Insert Hyperlink dialog box. (Or use any of the other previously methods of opening the Hyperlink dialog box.) The Text to Display line will be dimmed because there is no text.

3. Type the address for the link in the Address box at the bottom.

4. (Optional) If you want a ScreenTip, click ScreenTip, type the text, and click OK.

5. Click OK to complete the hyperlink.

The picture will not look any different. If you view the Web page using File, Web Page Preview, the default cursor changes to a hand with a pointing finger when it hovers over the image to indicate that it is now clickable, and the ScreenTip appears.

CREATING AN EMAIL HYPERLINK

Besides referencing other pages, hyperlinks can start the user's email editor and begin a blank email message with the recipient name filled in automatically. This is useful for providing a hyperlink through which someone can email you to comment on your Web page.

Follow these steps to create an email hyperlink:

1. Select the text or choose an image for the hyperlink.

2. Click on the Insert Hyperlink button to display the Insert Hyperlink dialog box.

24

3. In the lower-left corner of the Insert Hyperlink dialog box, click on Email Address.

4. Enter the email address, as shown in Figure 24.10.

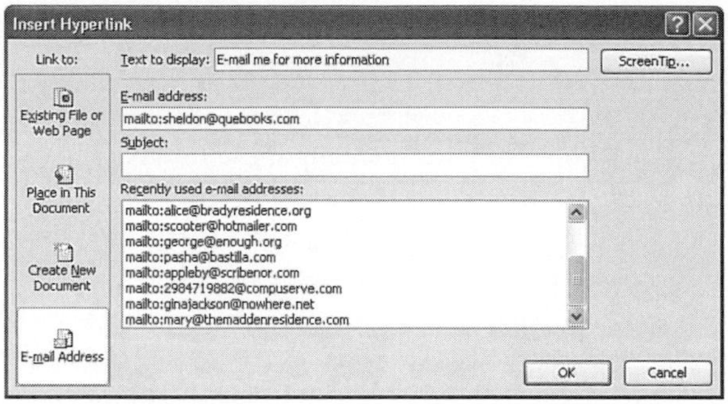

Figure 24.10
Hyperlinking to an email address.

Notice how the phrase `mailto:` is automatically added to the beginning of your email address.

5. Click OK to complete the link.

When the link is clicked, a blank, pre-addressed email is opened. The email hyperlink is a convenient means for letting visitors to your Web page send you feedback or questions.

INSERTING HORIZONTAL LINES IN A WEB PAGE

Word documents don't normally use horizontal lines (also called horizontal rules) to separate topical sections. This is, however, a commonly used convention in Web pages because there is no established page length for Web pages. A horizontal rule can help separate sections of a long page without having to break it up into separate pages.

To add horizontal lines to a Web page, follow these steps:

1. Click on the line in your page where you want to insert the horizontal line.

2. Choose Format, Borders and Shading from the menu.

3. Click the Horizontal Line button at the bottom of the resulting dialog box.

4. A list of lines from which to choose is displayed (see Figure 24.11).

5. Choose a line and click OK to insert it into your Web page.

NOTE

> Horizontal lines can be either the HTML element (<HR> tag) itself or, more commonly, a decorative graphic line. The ones you insert from Word are almost all graphical in nature, rather than using the simple HR tag. If you want to make sure you are getting a nongraphics line (for example, if you're trying to avoid using external graphics), manually edit the HTML code (using View, HTML Source) and add the <HR> tag.

Figure 24.11
Select a horizontal line to use.

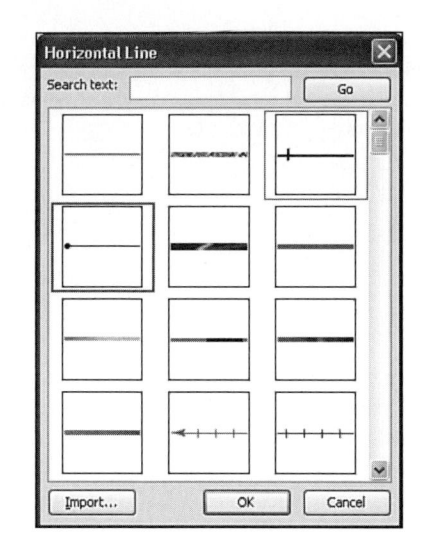

After you've inserted a horizontal line (an HTML tag or a graphic) that you like, you can edit the line by following these steps:

1. Select the horizontal line by clicking it; then right-click it and choose Format Horizontal Line from the menu. The Format Horizontal Line dialog box, shown in Figure 24.12, displays.

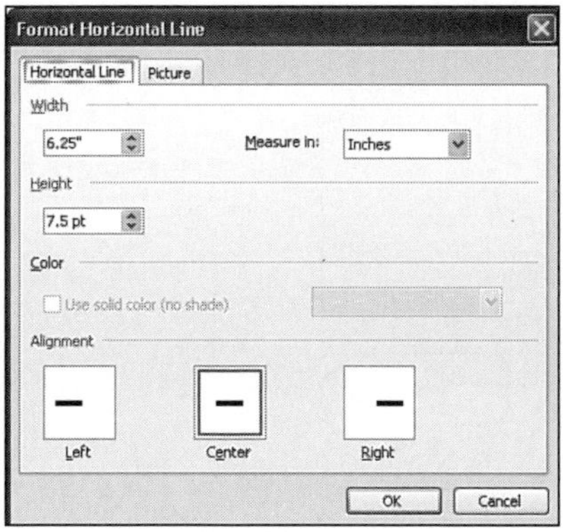

Figure 24.12
Changing the properties of a horizontal line.

2. The current width, height, and alignment of the line are displayed in the Horizontal Line tab. Color will also be displayed (and can be changed) if the horizontal line is the HTML tag and not a graphic image.

3. The other tab in this box, Picture (not present for the HTML tag-generated line), lets you change some of the picture qualities, including brightness and contrast. You can also crop the line from here. Make any changes desired.

4. Click OK to accept your changes to the horizontal line.

24

TIP

> After you have the line looking just as you want, use the Clipboard to copy and paste the line when you want to use it again. For consistency, use the same horizontal line throughout your Web site or section of a Web site.

Inserting Scrolling Text

Scrolling text is also called *marquee text*. Scrolling text marches stock-ticker style in a line across your Web page.

NOTE

> Before using scrolling text, remember that it is not supported in Netscape browsers and displays only partially or not at all. If you expect your Web page to be viewed with Netscape browsers, either don't use this feature or don't put any critical information in it.

Scrolling text is inserted via the Scrolling Text button (the rightmost button) on the Web Tools toolbar. (Right-click on a toolbar and select Web Tools if this toolbar isn't open.) Clicking the button opens the Scrolling Text dialog box, shown in Figure 24.13.

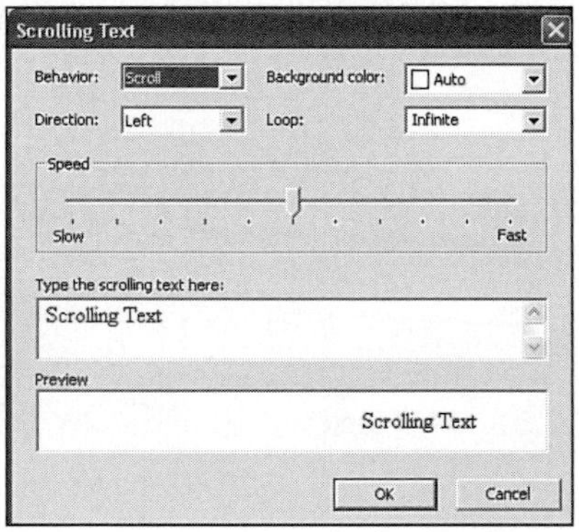

Figure 24.13
Adding scrolling text to a Web page.

To make the scrolling text move how you want and display your text, do the following:

1. Set your text behavior to Scroll (the default), Slide (which scrolls the text only once and stops on the opposite side of the screen), or Alternate (which bounces the text back and forth—like a Ping-Pong ball—between the left and right margins of your page).

2. For the Scroll and Alternate settings, you can choose how many loops to scroll or bounce with the Loop settings. Your only choices with this control are 1 through 5 times and Infinite.

3. Choose a background color for your control from the list. (Sorry, no custom colors are on this list.)

4. Choose the direction of your scroll: Left or Right.

5. The slider control in the middle of the box controls the speed of the scroll (or bounce). Drag it to change the setting.

6. Type the text you want to scroll in the Type the Scrolling Text Here box. The Preview area provides a preview of your scrolling text as you change the various options.

7. Click OK to place the marquee in your Web page.

After the marquee is inserted into your Web page, you can make more changes to it:

- Drag the marquee's border to change the length or height of the marquee (the text stays centered).

- Format the scrolling text using any of the standard font-formatting tools in Word.

- To temporarily stop the scrolling or bouncing (if it's driving you crazy as you work on the page, for example), right-click it and choose Stop. Right-click it and choose Play when you want to start it again.

- To reopen the Scrolling Text dialog box (Figure 24.13), right-click the marquee and choose Properties.

- To make the entire marquee a clickable hyperlink, select the marquee by clicking the Design Mode button (leftmost button) from the Web Tools toolbar. Then select the marquee and choose Insert, Hyperlink from the menu. Insert the correct Web address and click OK.

NOTE

> Marquees are great attention-grabbing devices for pointing people to new or important information. They can be irritating or distracting, however, if placed on a page where people also have to read a lot of text.

ADDING IMAGES, BACKGROUND IMAGES, AND BACKGROUND COLOR

Besides text, images are the second most common element found on typical Web pages. When used correctly, images can reinforce text messages, add a dash of color, or add content not possible with text. Images can also be used as page backgrounds to make text more readable and reduce the glare common with a white background on monitors. The background color of the page can also be changed to reduce glare or add more interest to the page.

ADDING GRAPHICS TO A WEB PAGE

Adding a picture to a Web page in Word is no different from adding an image to a Word document:

1. Place your cursor where you want to place the graphic.

2. Choose Insert, Picture and select the location of an existing graphic or tools to create a graphic (WordArt, for example) from the menu.

24

3. Choose or create your image and click OK to insert it into the page.

After the graphic is placed, you can resize it by clicking on it, grabbing the bounding boxes, and dragging the image larger or smaller.

TIP

> Bigger is not always better for images. Larger images can dramatically increase the load time for your Web page if your audience only has access to low bandwidth, such as a modem. Make the image only as large as needed to make your point.

→ For more information on working with images in Word, **see** Chapter 13, "Getting Images into Your Documents," **p. 437**.

USING A BACKGROUND TEXTURE

A small image repeated or *tiled* across the background of a Web page can give the illusion of texture, such as paper, cloth, stone, or wood.

You can select your own pictures for tiling, but Word comes with a nice assortment of pictures that are readily available and designed to look good when tiled. To add one of Word's background textures to your Web page in Word, do the following:

1. Choose Format, Background, Fill Effects from the menu. This brings up the Fill Effects dialog box.
2. Click the Texture tab to bring up the default list of textures, as shown in Figure 24.14.

Figure 24.14
Accessing the background texture graphics in Word.

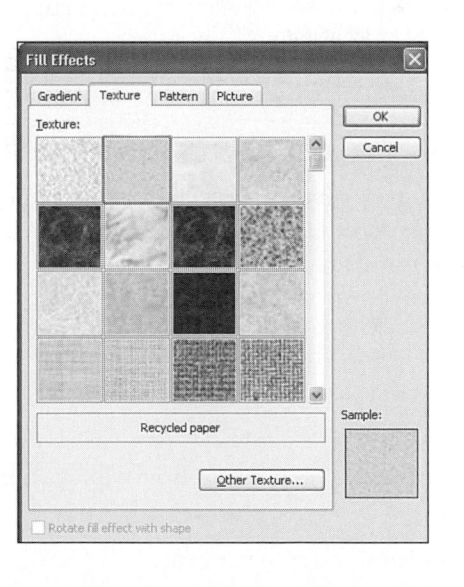

3. Scroll through the list until you find the texture you want, and click it to select it.
4. Click OK. The texture will now fill the background of your Web page.

If you want to use a picture of your own as the background texture, click the Other Texture button in step 3 instead of picking one of the existing ones.

Whenever you use a background texture, make sure that it contrasts with your font color. Dark text is best read against light backgrounds and vice versa. Also, background textures that contain too much definition or sharp patterns can make the page text difficult to read.

TIP

> The texture image files are specially designed to seamlessly tile—that is, tile without showing any boundaries between each image—across your Web page. It is often best to use images specially designed to be background textures; otherwise, the boundary between each tile becomes visible and spoils the illusion. You can find many free collections of background images suitable for textures all over the Internet. Search for terms like *Web backgrounds* or *textures*.

Adding Background Color to a Web Page

If you don't want to use a background texture, how about a solid color instead? Here's how to choose one:

1. With your Web page open, choose Format, Background from the menu.
2. You can choose one of the colors displayed or click More Colors to bring up more options.
3. After you've found a suitable color, click OK to apply it to your Web page background.

As with textures, you want your background color to have good contrast with your font color.

TIP

> Generally, it is a good idea to limit yourself to using about three colors. Your background color should be one that shows your text with good contrast. You should then reserve the second color for your main text color. You can use the third color to add accents and highlight those things that you want to grab the audience's attention. Using too many colors is distracting to the eye and detracts from the overall message. This would be a good time to use the company colors if they fit the profile. If the colors are difficult to work with, you can use just one or two of the colors and use a white background.

→ For more information on working with background colors and fills in Word, **see** Chapter 13, "Getting Images into Your Documents," **p. 437**.

Building Multi-Column Layouts with Tables

Web pages very commonly use tables to create multi-column layouts. The "traditional" organization of a Web page is to place a navigation bar at the left or top and the main content to the right or below. Figure 24.15 shows an example of the left/right layout, and Figure 24.16 shows an example of the top/bottom one.

Figure 24.15
A Web page that uses a table to create a left-right layout with links to other pages at the left.

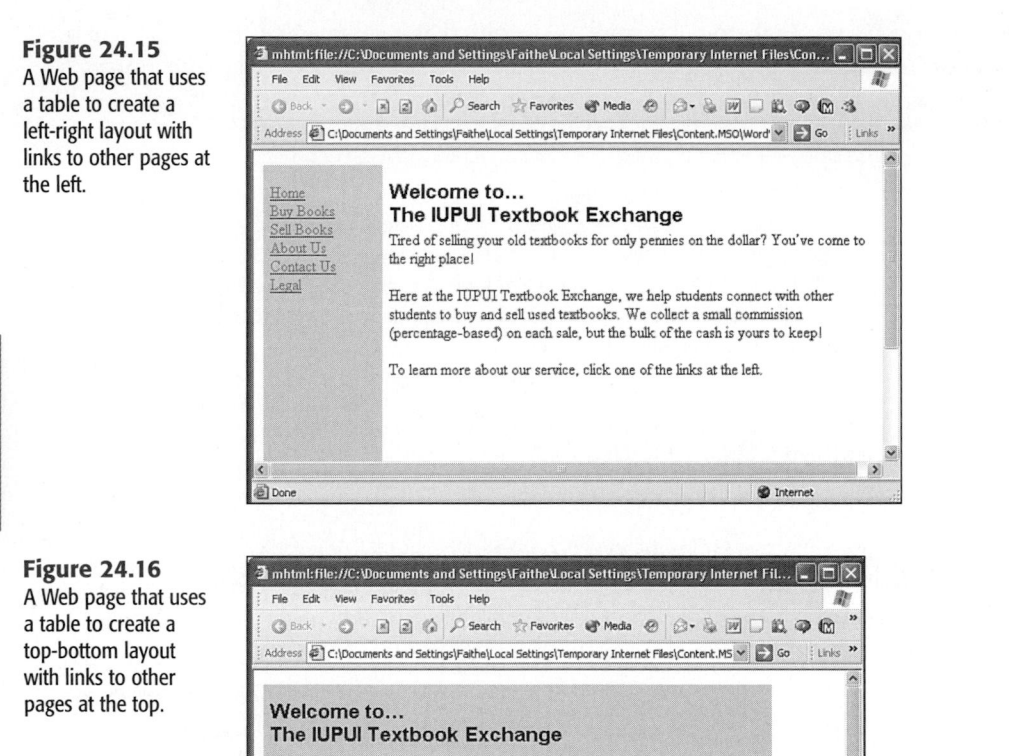

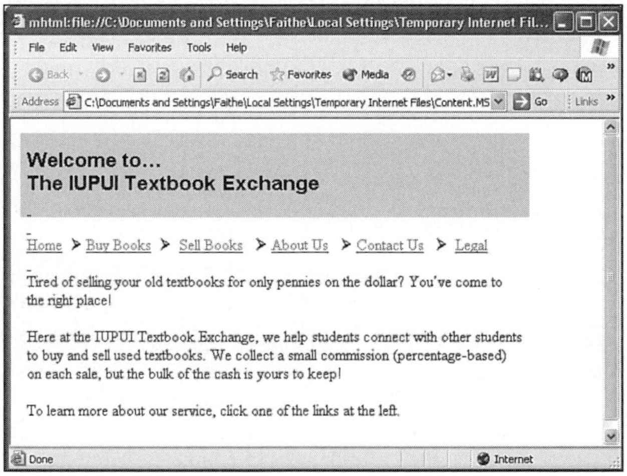

Figure 24.16
A Web page that uses a table to create a top-bottom layout with links to other pages at the top.

We won't go into table creation and usage here because Chapter 12, "Structuring and Organizing Information with Tables," covers the topic thoroughly. We will, however, explain in a big-picture way how to create a page like the ones in Figure 24.15 and Figure 24.16:

1. Start a new Web page and create a table. Size the table rows and columns as appropriate. To make a cell taller, click inside it and press Enter a few times.

   For example, you might want a large column at the right and a thinner one to the left that will hold navigation hyperlinks.

2. If you want any of the cells to have a colored background, click the cell and choose Format, Borders and Shading. On the Shading tab, select the desired color or shading, and then in the Apply To section, open the drop-down list and choose Cell. (See Figure 24.17.) Click OK when done.

Figure 24.17
Apply shading to an individual cell if desired.

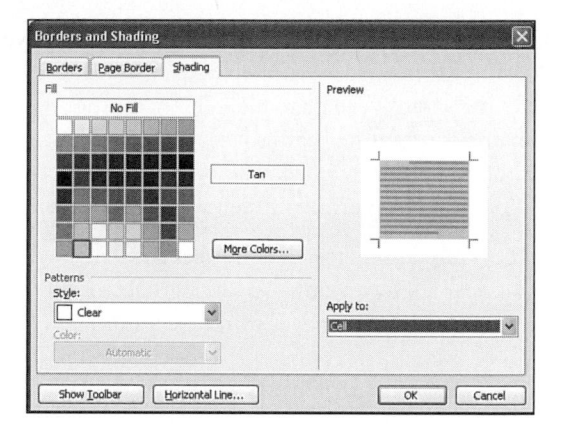

3. Remove the borders from around all sides of the table. (With the table selected, open the Borders drop-down list on the Formatting toolbar and choose No Border.)

4. Type or insert hyperlinks in the cell that you have decided will function as your navigation bar. If you want to hyperlink to other pages you have not created yet, decide what you will name them and then go ahead and create the hyperlinks for them.

> **NOTE**
>
> In the navigation bar cell, include a hyperlink to this page that you are on. Clicking it will do nothing, so it's okay to have it. The reason: You will probably copy this page and then edit the copy when you create the other pages in the Web site, and having the link to this page already in place will prevent your having to create it on each page later.

5. Type or insert the text for the main body of the page in the cell that will function in that capacity.

6. Save the page.

7. Save it again under a different name—one of the names you chose for the hyperlinks in the navigation bar.

8. Delete the main body content and enter the content for the new page. The navigation links should be able to remain the same.

9. Repeat until you have created all the pages for your site.

USING FRAMES

Frames are an alternative to tables in structuring a Web site's navigational system. They have both advantages and disadvantages over the tables-only method described in the preceding section.

With a frame system, you create a Web page with a *frameset* that will serve as the master template for the entire Web site. It is divided into separate sections called *frames*, and each frame pulls its content from a separate Web page file. The navigation bar for the site appears in a frame that remains constant no matter what other content is being displayed, so the navigation bar needs to be created only once. The other pages appear in other frames on the page that change based on which hyperlink in the navigation bar is clicked.

A frame system can make the Web designer's job easier because the navigation bar need not be manually repeated on each page. However, hyperlinking becomes more complicated because a hyperlink in the navigation frame needs to refer to a different frame as its target.

NOTE

> Not all Web browsers support frames, so it is considered good Web design practice to also develop a nonframes version of any Web site that uses frames. Therefore, you don't really save any Web design time by using frames; rather, you create twice as much work for yourself. If you ignore that guideline and create the frames version alone, however, you do save some time and effort.

ADDING FRAMES

You can create a set of frames on a Web page, either by choosing Format, Frames, New Frames Page from the menu or by opening the Frames toolbar. From the Frames toolbar, shown in Figure 24.18, you can choose to put a frame on any side of the existing page (above, below, left, or right). You can then drag the divider bar between the frames to adjust their relative sizing.

CREATING AND SAVING FRAME CONTENT

To create content to appear in a frame, click in that frame and start typing.

The frameset is a container page that tells the browser how to split the screen real estate among the pages in the set. For instance, a browser displaying two Web pages as frames is actually using three Web pages: one Web page for display in each frame and the third frameset page defining how the screen is split up between the other two pages.

Each frame's content will be saved in a separate file. Word will make up names for the files, but it's better if you name them yourself because that way you get to pick the name.

To save the content of a frame, follow these steps:

1. Right-click the frame and choose Save Current Frame As. The Save As dialog box appears.

2. Type a filename and click Save.

Figure 24.18
Adding frames to a
Web page.

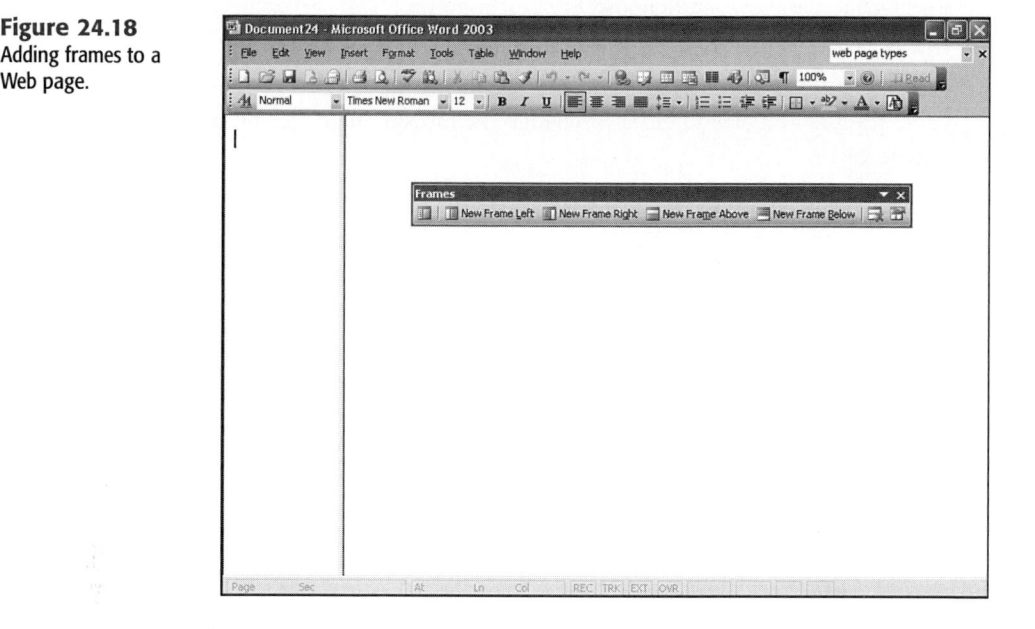

CAUTION

> If you resave a frame's content under a different name with Save As after saving it initially, the frameset's reference to it may not automatically update. To avoid that whole headache, try to stick with the original names for frame content.

SPECIFYING FRAME SIZES

After you have a frameset, you can drag the bar between frames to resize each frame manually.

Not precise enough? There's always the dialog box method. With it, you can resize the frame based on Percent, Inches, or Relative (that is, proportionately). For example, in Percent mode, you can define the current frame as 30%. Word resizes this window to take up 30% of the screen and automatically resizes the second frame to take up 70%. Using Inches simply resizes the frame to whatever width you enter. If you choose Relative, you are defining each frame in proportion to the others. A setting of 1 means a one-to-one (1:1) proportion between frames or each frame will fill half of the screen. A setting of 2 (2:1 proportion) means that the first frame will be twice as large as the second or fill two-thirds of the width of the frame.

You can also prevent people viewing the frameset in a Web browser from resizing the frames.

Follow these steps to access the frame properties that deal with sizing:

1. Right-click the frame and choose Frame Properties.

   If you are interested solely in preventing users from resizing frames, the frame you want in step 1 is the one to the left of or above the frame border you want to freeze.

2. Click the Frame tab, and enter or change the measurement for the frame's size. See Figure 24.19.

3. Click the Borders tab, and then, if desired, clear the Frame Is Resizable in Browser check box. See Figure 24.20.

4. Click OK.

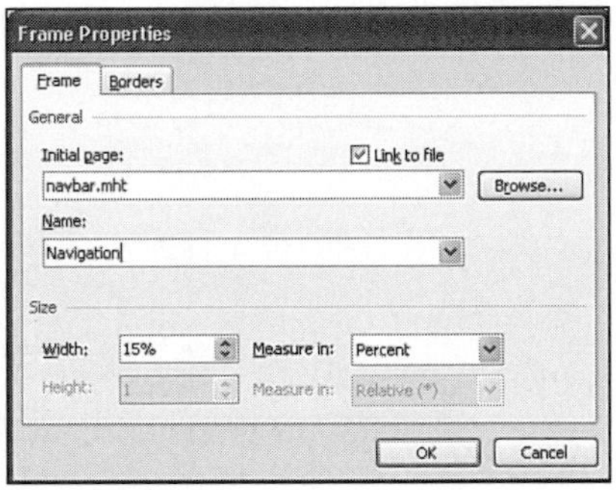

Figure 24.19
The Frames tab of Frame Properties.

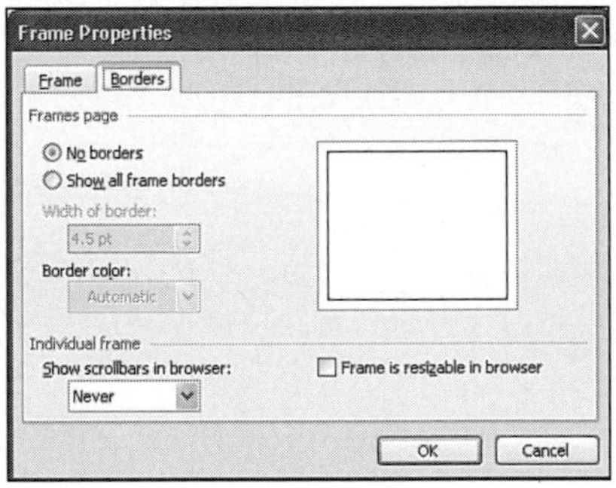

Figure 24.20
The Borders tab of Frame Properties.

CONTROLLING FRAME APPEARANCE

One of the reasons frames have gotten a bad rap in the past is that some people didn't know how to set them up attractively. That big thick default border between the frames has to go! And if a frame contains no more than one screenful of material (at any resolution), the scrollbar for it can go away too. With both of these formatting options applied, a page with a frameset is virtually indistinguishable from one created with tables.

> **TIP**
>
> For some particularly egregious examples of bad frame usage, check out
> www.sfwa.org/members/webspinner/BadFrames.html and
> www.arches.uga.edu/~macwoman/baddesign.html.

To change frame appearance settings, do this:

1. Right-click the frame and choose Frame Properties.
2. On the Borders tab (Figure 24.20), click No Borders.
3. (Optional) In the Show Scrollbars in Browser drop-down list, choose Never to hide the scrollbar.
4. Click OK.

> **CAUTION**
>
> Be cautious about turning off scrollbars completely. Even though the contents of one frame may not change (your navigation frame, for instance), it may not display the same in every browser, especially if you use text. Another browser may choose a larger default font. If you don't enable the scrollbars, your visitor won't be able to read the contents of your frame. Also, visitors using laptops or mobile computing devices with small screens may need the scrollbars just to view the entire content of a frame.

24

USING NONSTANDARD FONTS

You can apply any font available on your computer to the text on your Web page. You can also select any font size or weight you want just as you would for a Word document.

> **NOTE**
>
> HTML does not support using embossing or engraving in font styles—these won't be displayed in any browser.

Remember one important caveat when you choose fonts: The computer displaying any Web page you create must have the same fonts installed as are used on your Web page. If, for example, you choose Andale Mono as your font style under Windows, and your Web page is viewed on a Macintosh computer or under Unix, those viewers will not see the text displayed with the Andale Mono font. Their browsers will look for the font, and when it is not found, the browser will substitute a default font available on that machine. If the Andale Mono font is important to your Web page in terms of spacing or emphasis, note that both of these features will be lost on machines that don't have the Andale Mono font installed.

There are a few workarounds that allow you to use various fonts and have them display across multiple platforms and browser types:

- Manually mark up the font tag to support multiple fonts.

- Convert text to graphical images.
- Embed Web fonts into your Web page.

Each of these options is explained in the following sections.

MANUALLY MODIFYING THE FONT TAG

Most computers in use have three basic types of fonts installed: serif, sans serif, and mono-spaced. Examples of these fonts on the Windows platform include Times New Roman, Arial, and Courier, respectively. If, for example, you apply the Arial font to a line of text, the HTML code will appear as follows:

```
<font face="Arial">
```

However, on the Macintosh, the default sans serif font is Helvetica, and on many Unix installations, it is simply sans serif. You can manually add these font names to the font tag as follows:

```
<font face="Arial, Helvetica, Sans serif">
```

The preceding code will ask the browser to check first for Arial and use it if found; if it's not found, to check for Helvetica; and if neither of those is found, to use Sans serif.

You cannot tell Word to support multiple font names when it applies fonts to a Web page. You must make these changes within the HTML source using a global search and replace. Note that the font tag may be written differently within the source depending on whether you're working in a Web page, filtered Web page, or single file Web page (.mht). Again, Word may overwrite any manual changes you make to the HTML source if you later open and save the Web page from Word.

NOTE

Cascading style sheets (CSS files) or embedded style tags can be used to apply font information to text. Any fonts you specify with a style tag or CSS file must still be present on the viewer's computer to be rendered.

CONVERTING TEXT TO GRAPHICS

If you want to use a font that is not commonly found across multiple platforms, you have the option to add the text to your Web page as a graphical element. This completely eliminates the need for any user to have your font on his machine. There are a couple of serious side effects of this approach, though:

- If you display a large amount of text as graphics, the Web file size increases dramatically, slowing down page loading for users who have a slow connection.
- A search engine cannot index any text converted to graphics. The search engine simply sees an image; it cannot "read" the text.

Using text-as-graphics only for headers keeps your page size down. To make the text of the graphic searchable, you can add the text of your image to a Web page comment or a metatag, or manually edit the image tag to include the title attribute. Examples of these approaches are displayed here:

```
<!--Add the text of your graphic as part of a comment here -->
<meta name="Description" content="Text of your graphic here">
<img src="images/text.gif" title="Text of your graphic here">
```

Comments and metatags will not display in a Web browser, but a text indexer can read them. The metatag information must be placed between the `<head>` and `</head>` tags in your Web page. Again, all these changes must be made manually in the HTML source.

To create a graphic from text, you can use a bitmap editor such as Paint or Adobe Photoshop. Or you can create your text using WordArt and save your Web page as a filtered Web page. The WordArt is converted to a bitmap (.gif or .jpg) graphic during the save operation (unless you are saving as a single file Web page, in which case the graphic is integrated).

EMBEDDING WEB FONTS

Microsoft has developed a means for Web page authors to embed fonts directly into a Web page. When a browser reads a Web page, it accesses the embedded fonts on that page to display the text. So as an author, you no longer have to worry about which machines have which fonts. Using embedded fonts does increase the Web page file size somewhat, and not all browsers, especially older ones, can read the embedded Web fonts.

CREATING YOUR OWN WEB PAGE TEMPLATES

If you will be creating a lot of Web pages that share some similar elements, such as a navigation bar or a consistently sized table, creating a template can save you from having to re-create those elements each time, thus saving you a lot of time.

A template is a file you use to base new Word documents on. Can you just open a Word document and save it under a new name? Of course. But will you occasionally have a "duh" moment when you forget to save it under a new name and overwrite the original, causing yourself hours of rework? Undoubtedly. The beauty of a template is that it doesn't allow that kind of mistake to ruin your day.

To build a new Web page template, do the following:

1. From the New Document task pane, choose On My Computer to bring up the Templates dialog box.
2. Click Template in the lower-right corner.
3. Open an existing template or a blank Web page, whichever suits your needs best.
4. Save your template immediately.

NOTE

Notice that when you choose File, Save As from the menu, Word prompts you to save the template as a .dot file. You can use this format or save a template as a Web page (.htm) file.

Your template is saved to the path defined by the User Templates section in the Options dialog box (Tools, Options, File Locations tab). The default for this is the Documents and Settings/*username*/Application Data/Microsoft/Templates folder on the drive where Word 2003 is installed. You can change that location if desired from the dialog box.

5. Add whatever items you need to make a basic template. These might include

- A company logo
- One or more tables
- A background texture or color
- Font colors and styles
- A basic text outline
- Standard hyperlinks, such as one to your Web site home page
- AutoText entries

For instance, if your company has established colors and fonts, you could use those in your Web page template. You could use a company color as a background color on your Web pages. Your legal department might require you to include a hyperlink to a disclaimer in small text at the bottom of every page. These are the types of elements to include in a template to maintain consistency through all the Web pages on your site.

6. Save the template again with the items you just added.

USING WEB SCRIPTING

Web pages commonly use scripting languages to define actions and objects accessible from within a browser. The most common languages in use are JavaScript (Microsoft's version is called JScript) and VBScript (Visual Basic Script). To add JavaScript or VBScript code to a new Web page, do the following:

1. Choose Tools, Macro, Microsoft Script Editor from the menu. Or use the keyboard shortcut, Alt+Shift+F11. The Microsoft Script Editor opens up as shown in Figure 24.21, although with a different view from that in typical HTML source viewing.

If the Script Editor is not already installed, you will be prompted to install it; follow the prompts.

NOTE

The Script Editor view for typical HTML source (refer to Figure 24.8) does not open the Toolbox, Properties window, or Project Explorer window used to create or edit scripting code as shown in Figure 24.21.

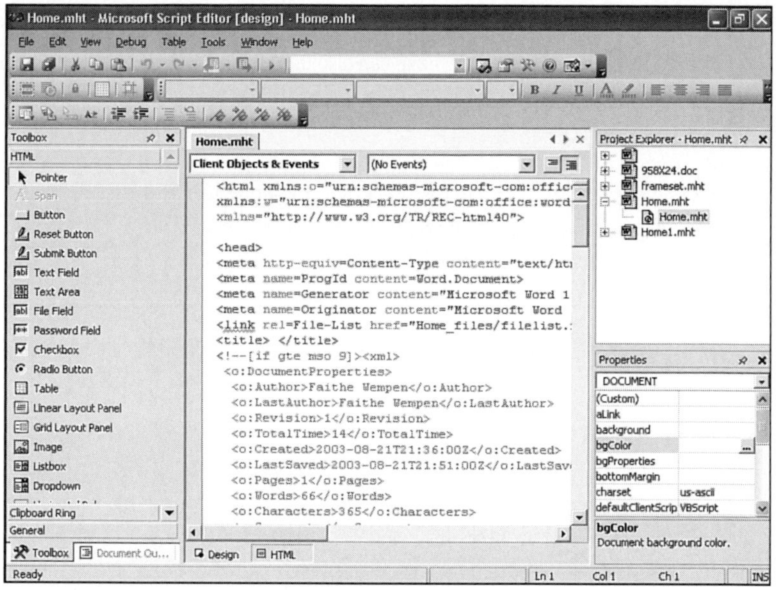

Figure 24.21
Adding script code to a Web page using the Microsoft Script Editor.

2. To choose the default language (either VBScript or JavaScript) in which to write a script, choose View, Property Pages from the menu (Shift+F4 from the keyboard). This affects scripts for which you do not explicitly specify a language. As shown in Figure 24.22, you can choose between VBScript and JavaScript (ECMAScript) for the Client.

CAUTION

JavaScript is the more universally supported language. VBScript works only in Internet Explorer, not in Netscape Navigator.

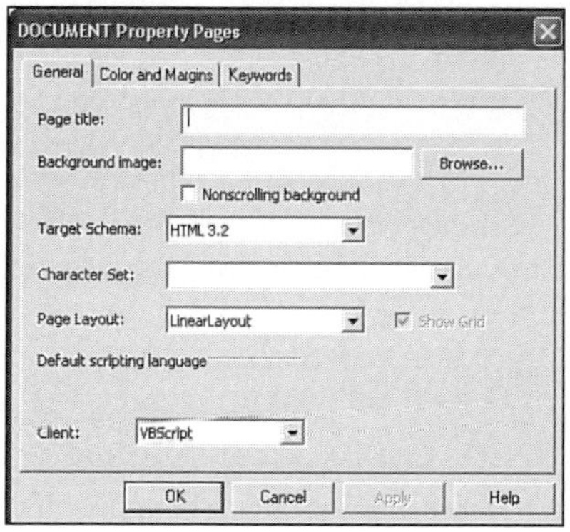

Figure 24.22
Choosing the scripting language to use in a Web page.

NOTE

Client-side scripts execute within the browser after the Web page has loaded; they are self-contained.

continues

continued

> The scripting language can also be changed in the Properties window of the Script Editor under defaultClientScript.

3. After you've selected a scripting language, scroll to the insertion location in the Web page. Right-click and choose Insert Script Block, Client. This command is also available from the menu under Edit, Insert Script Block, Client.

A typical blank scripting container for JavaScript would appear as follows:

```
<script language=javascript>
<!--

//-->
</script>
```

NOTE

> Those symbols `<!--` and `//-->` are used to enclose comments in HTML, so the HTML interpreter portion of a Web browser will not read them. This leaves other interpreters such as VBS or JavaScript free to claim them as their own and run them when the page loads.

4. After the container is created, you can start typing code.

If you prefer to select scripting functions from a list, click the Display an Object Member List button on the Text Editor toolbar (or press Ctrl+J). An object member list appears, as shown in Figure 24.23. Scroll and choose members as needed. After you've selected a member, you can click on the Display a Parameter List button in the Text Editor toolbar to view the proper syntax for a member.

The Microsoft Script Editor includes many of the amenities found in sophisticated programming environments, such as debugging and the capability to insert breakpoints. You can completely test and debug your script from within the Script Editor.

NOTE

> You may need to install the debugging features in the Script Editor before use. The Debug menu consists of only one item, Install Web Debugging, if debugging features aren't installed.

When the script works to your satisfaction, save the file and exit the Script Editor to return to Word.

CAUTION

> Word generates the HTML code. If you resave the Web page from within Word, any manual changes you made from the Script Editor may be overwritten and lost.

Display an Object Member List button

Display a Parameter List button

Figure 24.23
Choosing scripting members from a pop-up list.

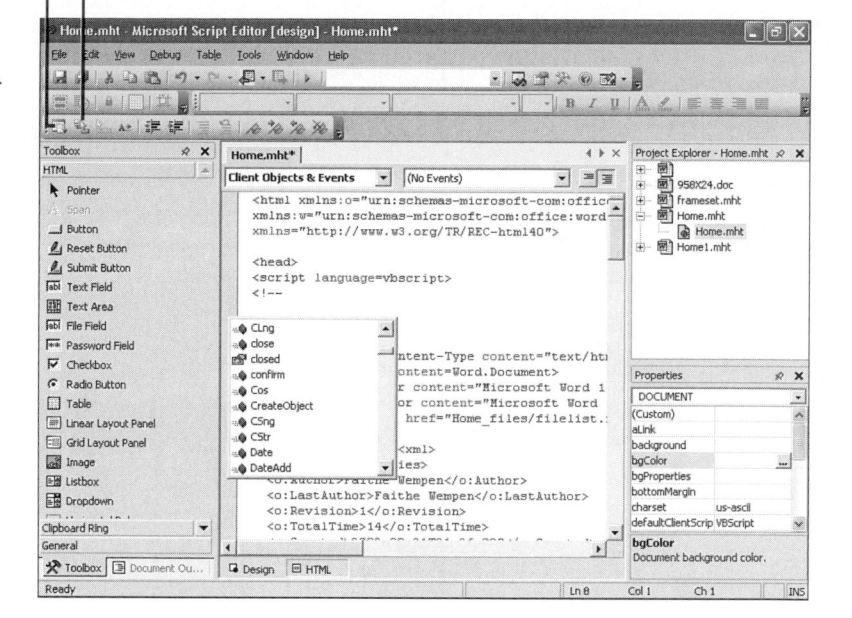

TROUBLESHOOTING

HOW TO SIMPLIFY YOUR WEB PAGES

A Web page saved from Word contains many complicated scripts, XML, and several extra files. You want to simplify this file and eliminate the extra files so that you don't have to keep track of them anymore.

To eliminate the complicated scripting and XML, you need to save your document as a filtered Web page:

1. With your document open in Word, choose <u>F</u>ile, Save <u>A</u>s from the menu.
2. From the Save as <u>T</u>ype list at the bottom, choose Web Page, Filtered.
3. Save your document.

To eliminate the extra files, save your document as a single file Web page:

1. With your document open in Word, choose <u>F</u>ile, Save <u>A</u>s from the menu.
2. From the Save as <u>T</u>ype list at the bottom, choose Single File Web Page.
3. Save your document.

There is no single file format available to simplify the HTML and eliminate the extra files associated with Web pages.

WHAT TO DO IF YOU NEED TO REARRANGE FRAMESETS

You have a frameset composed of a smaller page on the left and a larger, main window to the right. You want to move the left frame to the top so that you will have a smaller top frame and a larger main frame below it. How do you do this?

With your frameset open in Word, follow these steps:

1. Right-click in the left frame and choose Frame Properties. Make a note of the filename (it will usually have an .htm extension) listed in the Initial Page combo box. Cancel out of the Frame Properties dialog box.
2. Open the Frames toolbar.
3. Click in the main window (right frame). From the Frames toolbar, click New Frame Above to place a new frame above the main frame.
4. Click in the smaller left window. From the Frames toolbar, click Delete Frame. The selected frame disappears.

   You should now have a two-frame window with an upper, empty frame and the lower main frame.

5. Right-click in the upper, empty frame and choose Frame Properties.
6. Type the filename from step 1 (or browse to it) into the Initial Page combo box. Click OK.

   The upper, empty frame should now contain the content formerly seen in the left frame.

7. Adjust the borders between the frames by dragging or using Frame Properties.

WHAT TO DO TO SAVE MANUAL HTML CODE CHANGES FROM WORD

You made some changes to the HTML source in the Script Editor and saved it. You continued to work on the Web page in Word and saved the file. When you opened the Web page later, all your changes were gone. How can you keep your changes?

Word overwrites any changes you make because it regenerates the HTML source every time it opens the document. To avoid losing your changes, create them last. After saving your Web page in Word, do not open the page again in Word. If you must make further changes, use a text editor, such as Notepad, or an HTML editor application, such as FrontPage.

Using Word to Develop XML Content and Use XML Applications

In this chapter

AN OVERVIEW OF XML

A lot of attention has been given to the extensive support for XML that has been added throughout Microsoft Office and Microsoft Word. In this chapter we will discuss what XML is and what Word's support of XML can do for you.

NOTE

> XML features, other than saving documents as XML in the WordML schema format, are available only in Microsoft Office Professional and the standalone version of Microsoft Word.

WHAT XML IS AND DOES

XML is a text-based language created using the Standard Generalized Markup Language (SGML). XML is like HTML in that it uses a structure of "tags" to identify data elements in a hierarchical manner. Rules are implemented to control the relationships of these tags so that a predictable and consistent structure of information is produced. Because the information structure is consistent and well understood (thanks to widely accepted industry standards), the information can be shared across the world, and everyone can see and understand it.

So what makes XML different from HTML? These are some of the distinguishing features:

- The rules for creating XML documents are well structured and more rigidly enforced than those for creating HTML documents.

- XML is designed to describe the data and its structure, whereas HTML describes the presentation of the data. For example, you won't find an XML tag to make text bold. Instead, you'll find tags that specify what information *is*, what it *means*, and how it *relates* to other data.

- XML establishes extensible rule sets (a set of XML rules is called a schema) that can be used to create a virtually infinite number of markup languages for specialized purposes and environments. HTML is based on a specific and fixed set of rules that cannot be easily altered or extended.

XML'S ADVANTAGES OVER PREVIOUS APPROACHES

Because the rules for creating XML are more rigidly enforced, you can rely on XML to accurately communicate information between computer systems that cannot interpret HTML due to the inconsistencies and errors in the HTML documents. As a result, XML is rapidly becoming the data exchange format of choice for an enormous range of business applications. Word's XML support gives you the ability to build your own XML files and validate them against a schema, integrate that XML into normal documents for users, generate data for use by all of these XML-based applications, and access data those applications already contain.

Having a structure that describes the data instead of its presentation leaves you free to use the same source document for several different purposes without duplicating the information in various places. You simply attach a different style sheet or use a different transformation to provide new instructions for how to format and display each type of data contained in the document.

Duplication of data in different formats has long been a problem in businesses everywhere. Trip reports are entered in one place, read and retyped in another, and then read, summarized, and retyped in yet another. Expense reports are created on the road, and then the figures are retyped into an accounting system by the finance group when submitted. Numerous opportunities exist for errors to creep in, and many hours are spent performing the tasks. XML makes it possible to use the single source of information as originally entered for all these different uses without having to worry about the errors and inconsistencies that can be introduced as the data is reentered and reinterpreted at different locations.

As mentioned earlier, in Chapter 1, "What's New in Microsoft Office Word 2003," consider just a few examples of the many XML dialects that have already been created:

- XBRL, which standardizes the communication of financial reporting data among corporations
- MathML, which provides a standard format for mathematical equations
- WML, which provides a stripped-down markup language for displaying Web applications on wireless phones
- VoiceXML, which provides a standard language for controlling voice applications such as automated voicemail or call center systems
- SVG, which defines an efficient format for 2D vector graphics

Finally, the fact that XML is plain text cannot be overlooked as a huge advantage. In the not-too-distant past, developers trying to exchange structured data were forced to contend with mixing and matching options such as these:

- Complex network and authentication scenarios to allow binary connections
- Proprietary and/or binary file formats that required multiple conversion steps to use the data
- Text files containing character-delimited data (that is, tab-delimited flat files) that varied from site to site and had no good way to indicate structure or relationships

With the advent of the World Wide Web and HTML, networks are already configured to allow text-based traffic to easily move in and out with ease.

WHAT IS WORDML?

XML dialects (that is, schemas) provide a powerful tool to standardize the "data language" used by applications and organizations to communicate with each other. To support the enhanced XML integration in Word 2003, Microsoft has developed its own dialect for Microsoft Word documents that is appropriately named WordML.

To understand why this is important, think for a moment about what a document represents at a technical level. It's much more than just the contents of the document. Imagine trying to direct another person to create an exact duplicate of a document with your only method of communication being words and text. You would have to consider everything from document properties and settings (author, description, default printer, format, and so on) to content layout and presentation (headers and footers, paragraphs, text attributes, graphics, and so on).

That's exactly what WordML provides. What have in the past been proprietary formatted and binary documents can now be saved and exchanged in a format that is text-based in a structure that is fully and openly documented.

SCENARIOS AND APPLICATIONS FOR USING XML IN WORD

Before diving off into the mechanics of how Word supports XML integration, let's review some of the reasons why this might be useful:

- **Preparing content that can easily be repurposed in new ways**—If there were a way in today's business environment to calculate the cost of reentering and reprocessing information, it would be mind-boggling. If the data can be created originally in a structure that is consistent and can be queried for analysis, then the cost of using the data in new ways can be significantly reduced. Word provides this capability by allowing these original documents (trip reports, product orders, expense reports, and so forth) to be integrated with an XML schema.

- **Working with other productivity applications that recognize XML**—How many times have you tried to use a particular document type on a computer only to find out that the application needed was not installed, or that the right converter was not available to let you use it? The nature of XML structured documents is such that the content of the document can be modified without affecting the underlying structure needed by the specific application. Word provides this capability by allowing these XML files from other applications to be opened and edited while maintaining the original XML structure.

- **Generating data for business applications and processes**—As more critical business applications and processes become dependent on XML, the capability to generate data directly to support them becomes essential. Word provides this capability through XML Solutions by supporting one or many XSLT transformations to be integrated with the XML schema.

- **Using programmed "Smart Documents"**—Smart Documents are documents that include integrated programming to help you while you are using them. Existing templates in Word can have Smart Document programming added to them so that they become "process aware" and know at any given time what stage of the process they are in. This programming can include database access to store or retrieve information if needed. Smart Documents are implemented through XML Expansion Packs in Word.

WORKING WITH XML SCHEMAS

The full power of XML stems from combining the flexibility to create tags using whatever names you want and in whatever structure you want with enforcing strict compliance to that structure. The rules that are used to enforce this strict compliance are called XML schemas. Word provides you with the ability to manage the schemas you have available and to control which schemas are enforced for a given document.

UNDERSTANDING XML SCHEMAS

An XML schema is an abstract description of the structure you expect to use in an XML file. In the schema file (normally named with an extension of .xsd), you will find things such as these:

- Namespace definition
- Object/tag types (element, complex type, attribute, and so on)
- Object/tag names
- Data types (string, date, and so on)
- Object/tag relationships (hierarchy, min and max occurrences, and so on)

What you won't find in an XML schema is actual data, transformation or presentation logic, or information related to the implementation of the structure.

ADDING AN XML SCHEMA TO A DOCUMENT

Before Word can start applying a schema to a document, you need to add the schema to the document. You can add as many different schemas to a document as you need. To add a schema to your document, follow these steps:

1. Choose Tools, Templates and Add-Ins and then select the XML Schema tab (see Figure 25.1).

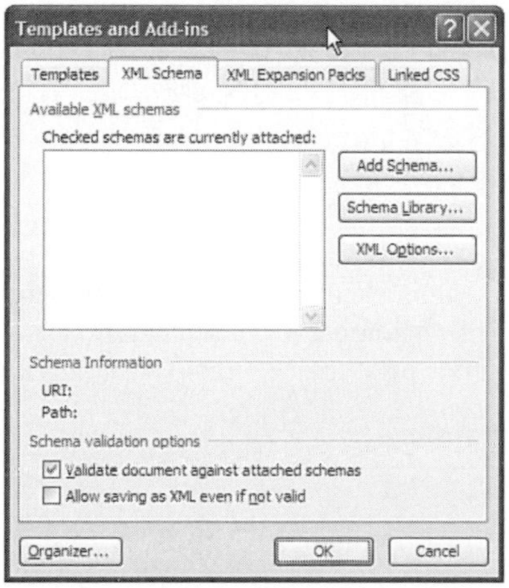

Figure 25.1
The XML Schema tab.

2. Click the Add Schema button to get to the Add Schema dialog (see Figure 25.2).

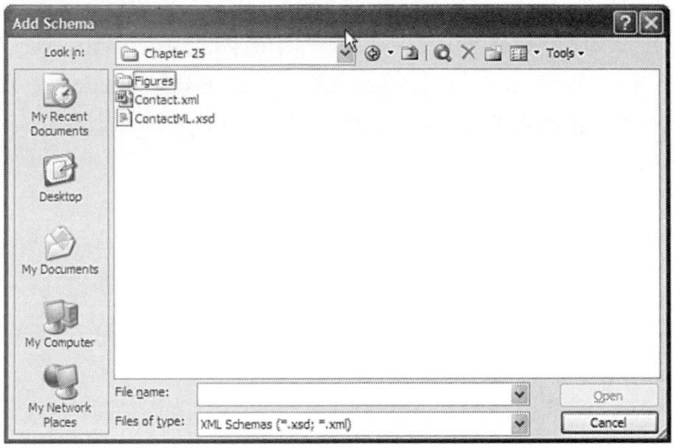

Figure 25.2
Selecting a schema file.

3. Browse to the schema file you want and click Open.

4. In the Schema Settings dialog (see Figure 25.3), enter an Alias name for the schema. This is not required but is highly recommended. If no alias is entered, the schema name will always be shown as the long namespace definition (starting with http://). This is not always easy to decipher later. If you enter a friendly alias name (like "Contacts List"), it will be more obvious what the schema controls when you have multiple schemas loaded.

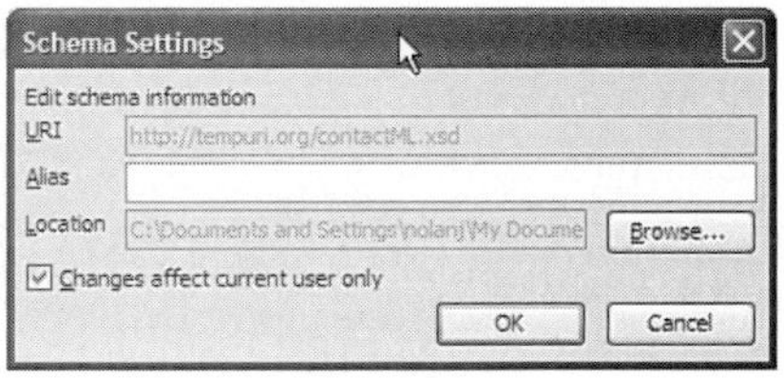

Figure 25.3
Setting the schema options.

5. If you want this schema definition to be available for all users, clear the Changes Affect Current User Only check box.

6. Click OK to add the schema.

> **NOTE**
>
> When you add a schema, Word references it using the local file path. If you move or rename the schema file after having added it to Word, you will need to update the schema settings to correct the path (see the section "Managing Schemas in the Schema Library," later in this chapter).

You'll now see the schema show up in the Available XML Schemas list (see Figure 25.4), and it will be checked, indicating that it has been applied to the document.

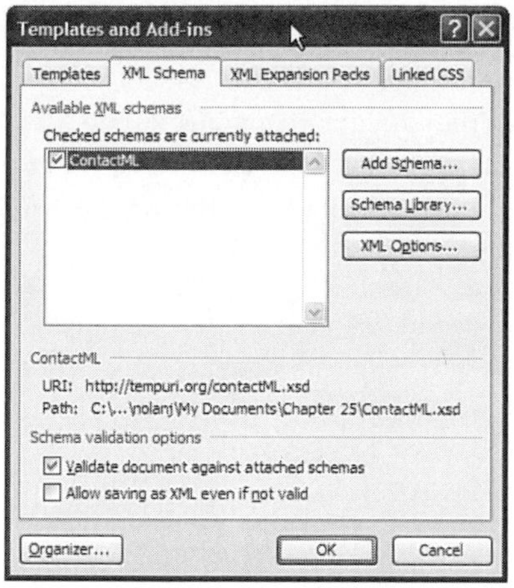

Figure 25.4
An XML schema applied to the document.

When applying a schema to a document, you also have some options that control how Word will validate your document (see Figure 25.4):

- **Validate Document Against Attached Schemas:** If you clear this check box, Word will not attempt to validate the XML content against the selected schemas. This can allow more flexibility when the specific rules of the schema don't match with how you want to construct the XML. You are not prevented from saving the changes; you just don't see the graphical display of the validation in the XML Structure task pane (see the section "Using the XML Structure Task Pane," later in this chapter). This option is checked by default.

- Allow Saving as XML Even If **N**ot Valid: If you clear this check box, Word will not allow you to save a document in XML format if the XML content cannot be validated against the schema. This setting can be very useful when you want to preserve your changes to the document before you have completed the entire XML structure. Technically, the XML you are saving is valid and well formed; it just does not adhere to the rules specified by the schema. After you have completed the data, you can turn this option back off to protect the integrity of the data. This option is not checked by default.

CHOOSING AN XML SCHEMA FOR A DOCUMENT

Anytime you add library (see the section "Managing Schemas in the Schema Library," later in this chapter). This makes it very convenient to use the schemas in the future. To choose an existing schema from the schema library to apply to your document, follow these steps:

1. Choose **T**ools, Templates and Add-**I**ns and then select the XML Schema tab (see Figure 25.4).
2. Locate the schema you want to apply in the Available **X**ML Schemas list.
3. If they are not already checked, check the boxes next to the schemas you want to apply.
4. Click OK.

MANAGING SCHEMAS IN THE SCHEMA LIBRARY

When you add an XML schema to a document, it is also added to Word's Schema Library. The Schema Library allows you to maintain your schema references as well as work with XML Solutions (see the section "Working with XML Solutions," later in this chapter). To access the Schema Library, click the Schema Library button on the XML Schema tab of the Templates and Add-Ins dialog (see Figure 25.4).

The Schema Library dialog is shown in Figure 25.5.

Figure 25.5
The Schema Library dialog.

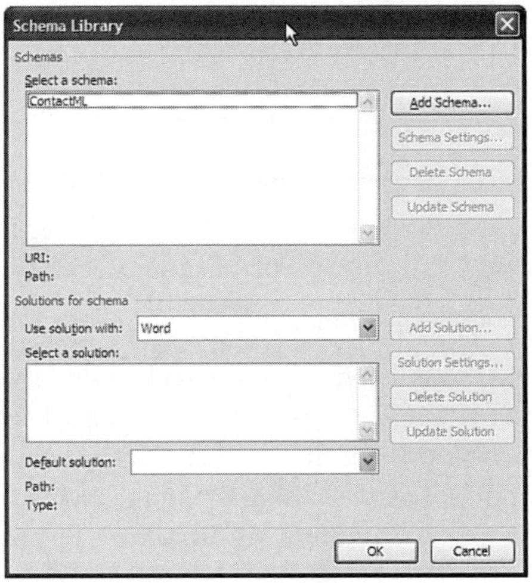

The Schema Library allows you to perform the following functions:

- Add a schema by clicking the Add Schema button (see the section "Adding an XML Schema to a Document," earlier in this chapter).

- Modify schema settings by clicking the Schema Settings button (see Figure 25.5). From the Schema Settings dialog you can modify the alias name used for the namespace, change the path to the schema file, or change whether your updates to the schema library affect other users.

- Delete a schema reference by clicking the Delete Schema button. This only removes the reference to the schema from Word. It does not remove the schema file from disk.

AN XML SCHEMA EXAMPLE

At this point you are probably wondering exactly what an XML schema looks like. We'll need a basic schema later in this chapter, so a sample schema for managing contact information is shown next. We'll call this XML contact dialect "ContactML."

```
<?xml version="1.0" ?>
<xs:schema id="ContactML"
    targetNamespace="http://tempuri.org/contactML.xsd"
    xmlns="http://tempuri.org/contactML.xsd"
```

```
    xmlns:xs="http://www.w3.org/2001/XMLSchema"
    attributeFormDefault="qualified" elementFormDefault="qualified">
    <xs:element name="ContactList">
        <xs:complexType>
        <xs:choice maxOccurs="unbounded">
        <xs:element name="Contact">
            <xs:complexType>
            <xs:sequence>
            <xs:element name="Fullname" minOccurs="1" maxOccurs="1">
                <xs:complexType>
                <xs:sequence>
                <xs:element name="prefix" type="xs:string"
                    minOccurs="0" maxOccurs="1" />
                <xs:element name="firstname" type="xs:string"
                    minOccurs="1"  maxOccurs="1"/>
                <xs:element name="middlename" type="xs:string"
                    minOccurs="0"  maxOccurs="1"/>
                <xs:element name="lastname" type="xs:string"
                    minOccurs="1" maxOccurs="1" />
                </xs:sequence>
                </xs:complexType>
            </xs:element>
            <xs:element name="Address" minOccurs="0" maxOccurs="unbounded">
                <xs:complexType>
                <xs:sequence>
                <xs:element name="company" type="xs:string"
                    minOccurs="0" maxOccurs="1" />
                <xs:element name="streetaddress" type="xs:string"
                    minOccurs="0" maxOccurs="2" />
                <xs:element name="city" type="xs:string"
                    minOccurs="0" maxOccurs="1" />
                <xs:element name="state" type="xs:string"
                    minOccurs="0" maxOccurs="1" />
                <xs:element name="zip" type="xs:string"
                    minOccurs="0" maxOccurs="1" />
                </xs:sequence>
                <xs:attribute name="type" form="unqualified" type="xs:string" />
                </xs:complexType>
            </xs:element>
            <xs:element name="editdate" type="xs:date"
                minOccurs="0" maxOccurs="1" />
            <xs:element name="email" type="xs:string"
                minOccurs="0" maxOccurs="1" />
            <xs:element name="Phonenumbers" minOccurs="0" maxOccurs="1">
                <xs:complexType>
                <xs:sequence>
                <xs:element name="Phonenumber"
                    minOccurs="0" maxOccurs="unbounded">
                    <xs:complexType>
                    <xs:sequence>
                    <xs:element name="number" type="xs:string"
                        minOccurs="1" maxOccurs="1" />
                    </xs:sequence>
                    <xs:attribute name="type" form="unqualified"
                        type="xs:string" />
                    </xs:complexType>
                </xs:element>
```

25

```
                    </xs:sequence>
                    </xs:complexType>
               </xs:element>
               <xs:element name="comments" type="xs:string"
                   minOccurs="0" maxOccurs="1" />
               </xs:sequence>
               </xs:complexType>
          </xs:element>
          </xs:choice>
          </xs:complexType>
     </xs:element>
</xs:schema>
```

If you are not familiar with XML schemas, take a few minutes to scan the example carefully. You will find that the structure is made to be a list of contacts, with each contact consisting of a full name, address, edit date, email, phone numbers, and comments. The full name is made up of a prefix, first name, middle name, and last name. An address has a type, company, street address, city, state, and ZIP. Phone numbers have a type and a number.

If you want to follow along to try out some of the examples shown later, create a text file now named contactml.xsd and enter the preceding schema information into it.

A full discussion of XML schemas is outside the scope of this chapter and indeed is a topic that can require an entire book itself.

SETTING XML OPTIONS

Word provides you with several options to control how it will save, validate, and display XML. These options can be set using the XML Options dialog. To access the XML Options dialog, click the XML Options button on the XML Schema tab in the Templates and Add-Ins dialog (see Figure 25.4).

The XML Options dialog is shown in Figure 25.6.

Figure 25.6
The XML Options dialog box.

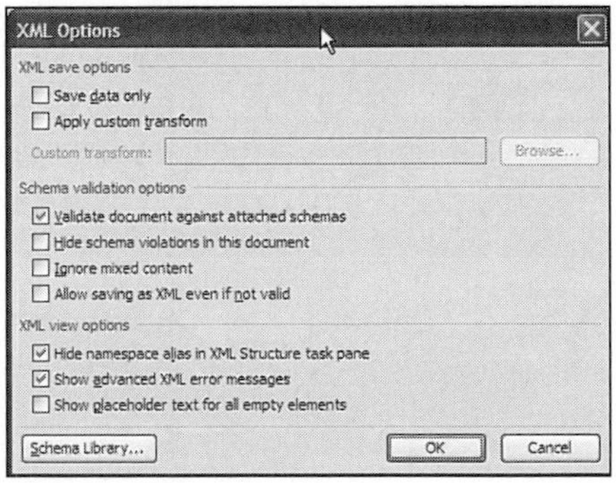

Using the XML Options dialog, you can control these settings:

- Save <u>D</u>ata Only: When this option is checked, Word will save only the data in the file that corresponds with the attached schema. No document properties, settings, and so on are included with the saved file. When this option is cleared, Word will save the file in XML format using the WordML schema so that all properties, settings, formatting, and so on are preserved.

- Apply Custom <u>T</u>ransform: When this option is checked, Word will apply the selected XSLT transformation to the file when it is saved. You can enter the full path for the XSLT file in the Custom transform text box or you can click on the <u>B</u>rowse button and navigate to it.

If you save a file using an XSLT transformation, Word saves only the result of the transformation. See "What to Do If You Lose Data after Saving Your XML File," in the Troubleshooting section at the end of this chapter.

- <u>V</u>alidate Document Against Attached Schemas: When this option is checked, Word will dynamically validate the XML using any attached schemas and display violations using various icons in the XML Structure task pane (see the section "Using the XML Structure Task Pane," later in this chapter).

NOTE

> This option does not affect Word's validation of the schema when saving an XML File. See the option Allow Saving as XML Even If <u>N</u>ot Valid in the following text.

25

- <u>H</u>ide Schema Violations in This Document: When this option is checked, Word will not display the wavy lines in the document that identify schema violations.

- <u>I</u>gnore Mixed Content: When this option is checked, Word will create valid XML documents without concern for any text formatting that may be inserted into the elements of the template. This is useful when saving document templates (.dot files) from which users will be entering data into an XML structure.

- Allow Saving as XML Even If <u>N</u>ot Valid: When this option is checked, Word will allow an XML file to be saved when the content cannot be validated against the attached schema(s). This is useful when you're filling in more complex XML structures and you want to save your interim changes without completing all the data. When this option is not checked, Word will present the dialog shown in Figure 25.7 if you attempt to save an XML file that has schema violations.

Figure 25.7
Trying to save an XML document with schema violations.

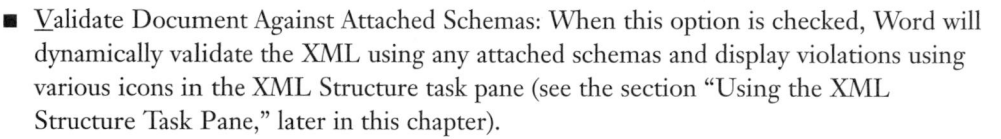

■ Hide Namespace Alias in XML Structure Task Pane: When this option is checked, Word will display only the element names from the attached schemas in the XML Structure task pane (see the section "Using the XML Structure Task Pane," later in this chapter). When this option is not checked, Word will append the namespace alias (or the full namespace if no alias is specified; see "What to Do If the List of Elements Is Hard to Read," in the Troubleshooting section at the end of the chapter) to the end of each element name. This is very useful if you have attached more than one schema to your XML file. Figure 25.8 shows an XML schema with the namespace alias displayed.

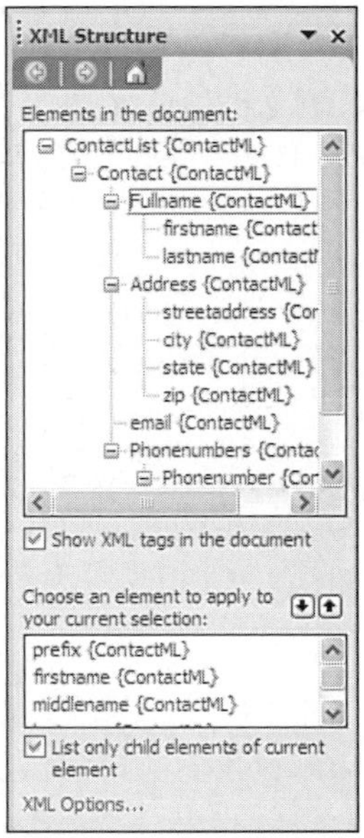

Figure 25.8
Showing the name-space alias in the XML Structure task pane.

■ Show Advanced XML Error Messages: When this option is checked, Word will display very detailed messages when schema violations are detected. When the option is not checked, Word will display a shorter summary of the problem. The advanced error messages are very valuable when debugging schema problems, but they can be confusing to general users if shown all the time. Figure 25.9 shows an example of an advanced message. Figure 25.10 shows the same error with this option turned off.

■ Show Placeholder Text for All Empty Elements: When this option is checked, Word will display a placeholder for all empty elements when display of the XML tags has been turned off (see the next section, "Using the XML Structure Task Pane"). This is a useful option when creating "fill in the blank" templates for users that you want to be entered based on a defined schema. The user can see what is expected to be filled in without having to deal with the distraction of seeing the XML tags in the document.

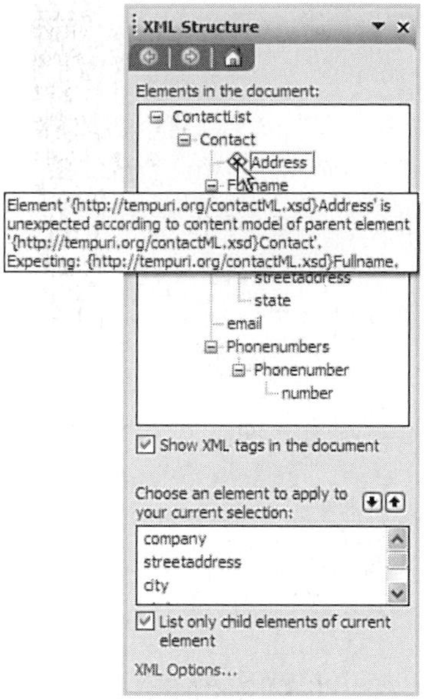

Figure 25.9
An advanced XML
error message.

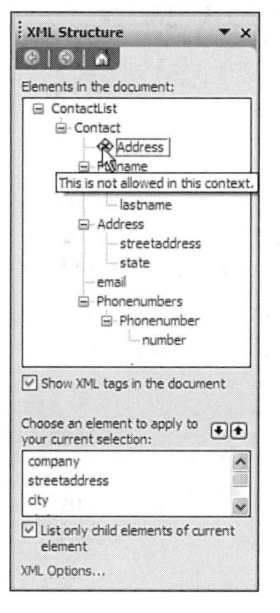

Figure 25.10
A non-advanced XML
error message.

25

USING THE XML STRUCTURE TASK PANE

So far we have discussed the flexibility of XML data, XML schemas and how they allow us to control the structure and content of the XML, and how to apply those schemas to XML content. By now you are probably wondering how to use Word to create the XML data to begin with. Word's XML Structure task pane is the answer to your question.

The XML Structure task pane gives you the ability to do these things:

- Construct your XML data (add and remove elements) based on the attached schemas
- View the subset of valid child elements for any existing element in the document
- Review the structure of new or existing documents in a hierarchical manner
- See any schema violations along with a description of the error
- Control display of the XML tags in the document

CREATING A NEW XML DOCUMENT

Let's get started by creating a new XML document based on the ContactML schema presented earlier in this chapter.

To create a new XML document, select File, New from the menus and click on the XML document link in the New Document task pane. You will see an empty document with the XML Structure task pane displayed, as shown in Figure 25.11.

Figure 25.11
Creating a new XML document.

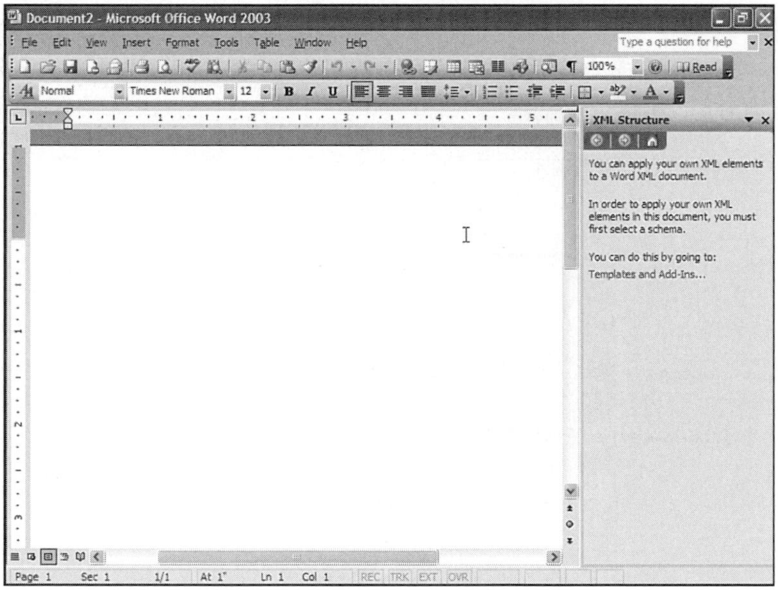

Looking at the XML Structure task pane, you can see that Word needs you to tell it what schema you want to use for the document. It's important to always remember that Word can allow you to modify the structure of any XML document only if you tell it what the schema of the document should be.

Click on the Templates and Add-Ins link to bring up the Templates and Add-Ins dialog and add the ContactML schema to the document. See the section "Adding an XML Schema to a Document," earlier in this chapter, for more information.

After you have added the ContactML schema to the document, the XML Structure task pane updates to show you the elements in the current document (which there are none of at this point) and the elements that are available to add to the document, as shown in Figure 25.12.

Figure 25.12
A new XML document with a schema attached.

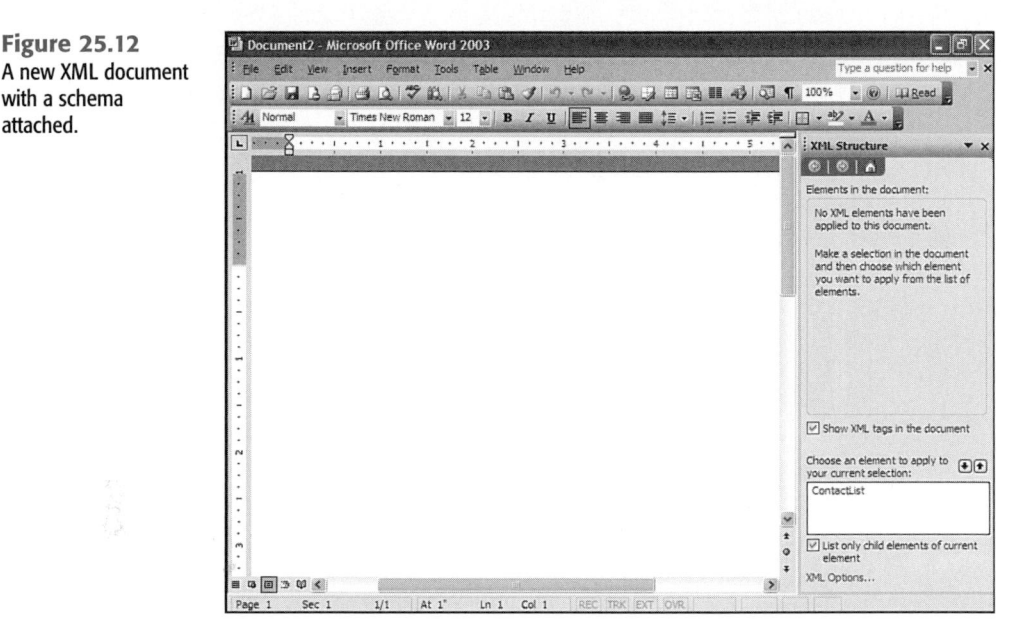

At the bottom of the XML Structure task pane is a check box named List Only Child Elements of Current Element that is normally checked by default. When this option is checked, Word will display only elements that are valid to apply to the element selected in the Elements in the Document list. Clear this check box now and see the effect it has (see Figure 25.13). Most of the time you will want to keep this option checked to help you in creating a valid XML structure. Note that you can apply any element displayed to your document, which means you are free to create a structure that is completely invalid based on your schema. Be sure to check this option before continuing.

At this point the available elements list should have only a single entry, ContactList. This makes sense because nothing has been added to the document yet, and well-formed XML can have only a single top-level root node. Click on this element name and it will be added to your XML document. Figure 25.14 shows the contact list element.

Looking first at the document itself, notice that the beginning and ending tags of the contact list are treated as objects. The insertion point will always be placed just inside the starting tag when you insert an element. You can use the arrow keys to move in and out of the element, double-click on the beginning or ending tag to select the element, or use the Enter and Tab keys to move the tag locations around.

Figure 25.13
Displaying all elements in the XML Structure task pane.

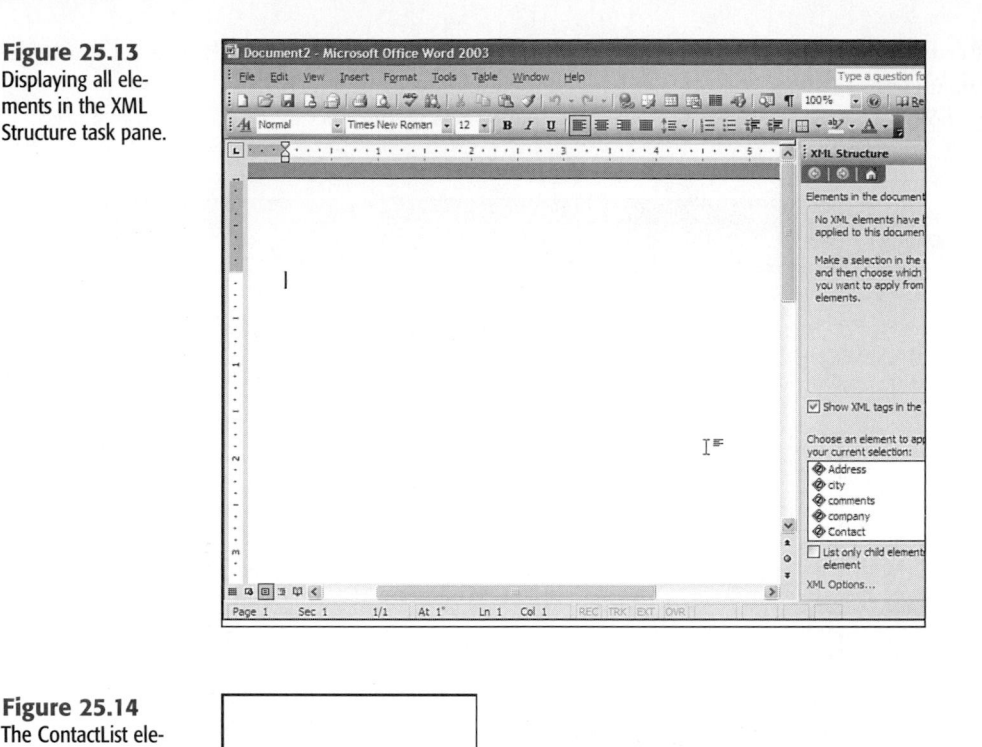

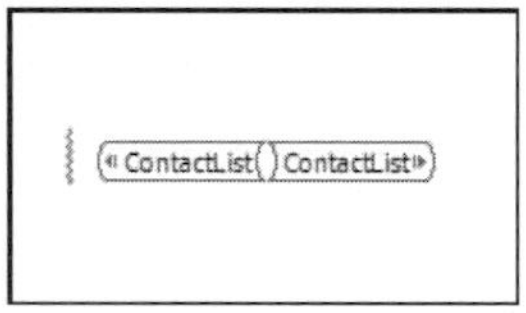

Figure 25.14
The ContactList element.

Now let's focus on something else Word is doing for you: schema validation. If you look closely at Figure 25.14, you will notice a purple wavy line on the far-left margin. Also, if you look at the XML Structure task pane, you'll see that the Elements in the Document list has started to build a structure for your document (see Figure 25.15). The yellow icon displayed to the left of the element name indicates that a schema validation problem has occurred.

To see exactly what the problem is, you can either right-click on the purple wavy line or hover the mouse pointer over the icon displayed in the XML Structure task pane. Figure 25.16 shows the error that has occurred, which in this case is not surprising because we have not added any child elements or data.

Finally, take a look at the list of available elements that is shown in Figure 25.15. It has been updated to have only one entry named Contact. If you look back at the schema we are using, you can see that the Contact element is the only valid child to the ContactList element. As you can see, the capability to limit this display to only valid child elements is a great help in building valid XML structures.

Now we are ready to add some more elements that will actually have some real data in them, but before we do there are a few issues about how Word handles the display of the XML to consider:

Figure 25.15
The ContactList element in the XML Structure task pane.

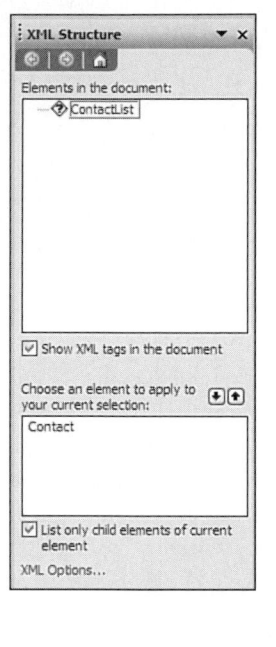

Figure 25.16
Displaying the schema validation error.

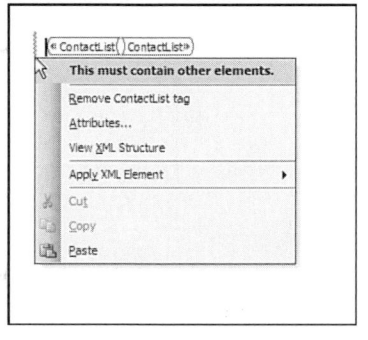

- When adding elements to the XML, Word inserts the element directly at the current insertion point and does not attempt to do any arranging of the XML to make it easy to read and follow (see Figure 25.17). If you like your XML displayed in a more structured manner, move the tags of the existing elements around before adding more elements (see Figure 25.18).

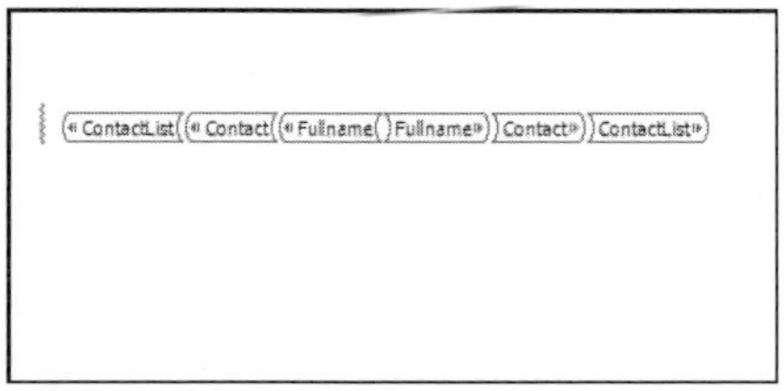

Figure 25.17
Inline XML construction can be hard to read.

25

Figure 25.18
Structured arrangement of XML tags.

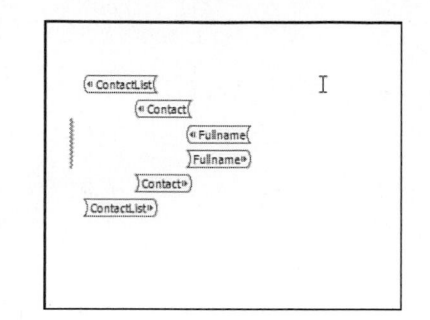

- When editing or arranging the XML content of the document, Word changes the presentation of the XML element to a single "self-closed" style of tags instead of separate opening and closing tags. See Figure 25.19 for an example of this display. This behavior happens if you insert two data elements adjacent to each other (like the prefix and firstname child elements of the Fullname element in our example) or if you place the cursor immediately to the left of an opening tag and press the Tab key. Also, when an element is changed to this self-closed format, all child elements are also changed. This has no affect on how the XML itself is saved, but it can be a little confusing if you are not prepared for it.

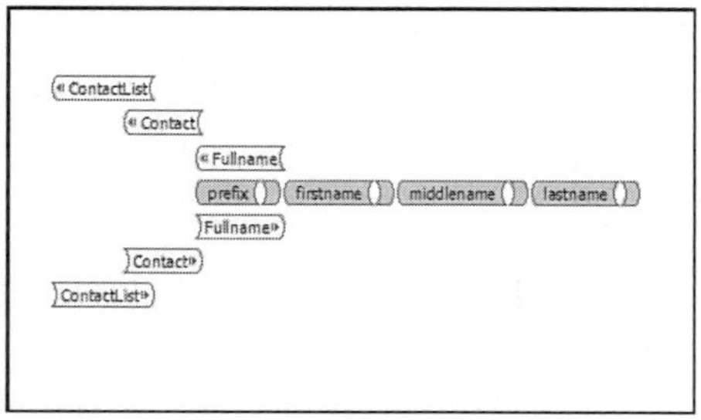

Figure 25.19
A self-closed XML tag display.

Now let's add a Contact and a Fullname structure for that contact. To add these to your document, follow these steps, keeping an eye on the schema validation icons along the way:

1. If it is not there already, place the insertion point inside the ContactList element.
2. Press Enter a few times to open up space for the Contact.
3. In the XML Structure task pane, click on the Contact element to apply it to the document. Notice that the list of available elements now shows several new things to add.
4. Press Enter a few times to open up space for the Fullname element.
5. In the XML Structure task pane, click on the Fullname element to apply it to the document.
6. Press Enter a few times to open up space for the prefix element.
7. In the XML Structure task pane, click on the prefix element to apply it to the document. Notice that the prefix element has no child elements.

8. Press the right-arrow key to move the insertion point outside the prefix element, and press Enter to get a new line.

9. In the XML Structure task pane, click on the firstname element to apply it to the document.

10. Repeat steps 8 and 9 to add the middlename and lastname elements.

When you have completed these steps, you should have a document that looks similar to that shown in Figure 25.20.

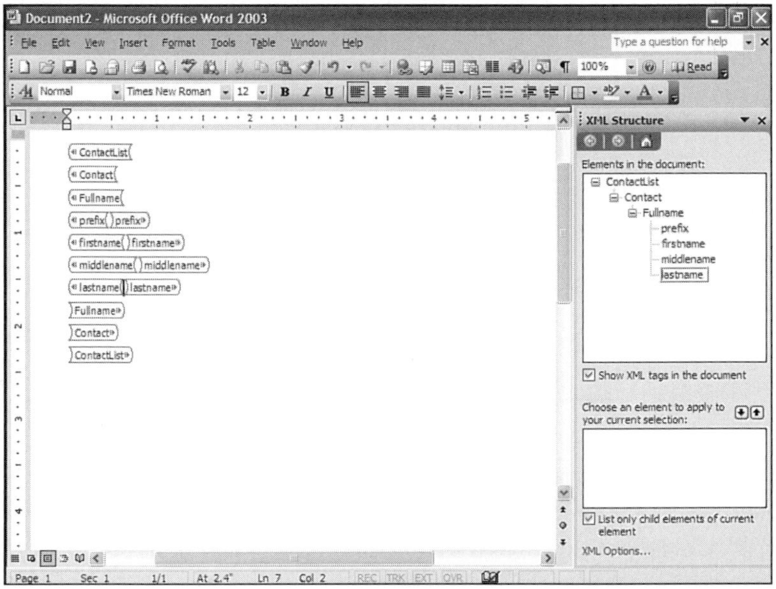

Figure 25.20
The Contact element with a Fullname.

Before moving on to complete the Contact structure, take a few minutes to see how Word handles navigating and selecting the XML elements. In particular, take note of these behaviors:

- In the XML Structure task pane, you can double-click on the plus or minus sign of the tree display to expand or collapse that element.

- In the XML Structure task pane, you can click on any element in the tree display and the contents of that element are selected in the document.

- In the XML Structure task pane, you can double-click on any element in the tree display and the entire element is selected in the document.

- In the document, you can click on the opening or closing tag of the element and the contents of that element are selected.

- In the document, you can double-click on the opening or closing tag of the element and the entire element is selected.

Using steps similar to those used to add the Fullname, you should now be able to complete the structure for the Contact. When you have added all the elements, you should have a structure that looks similar to what's shown in Figure 25.21.

Figure 25.21
The completed Contact XML structure.

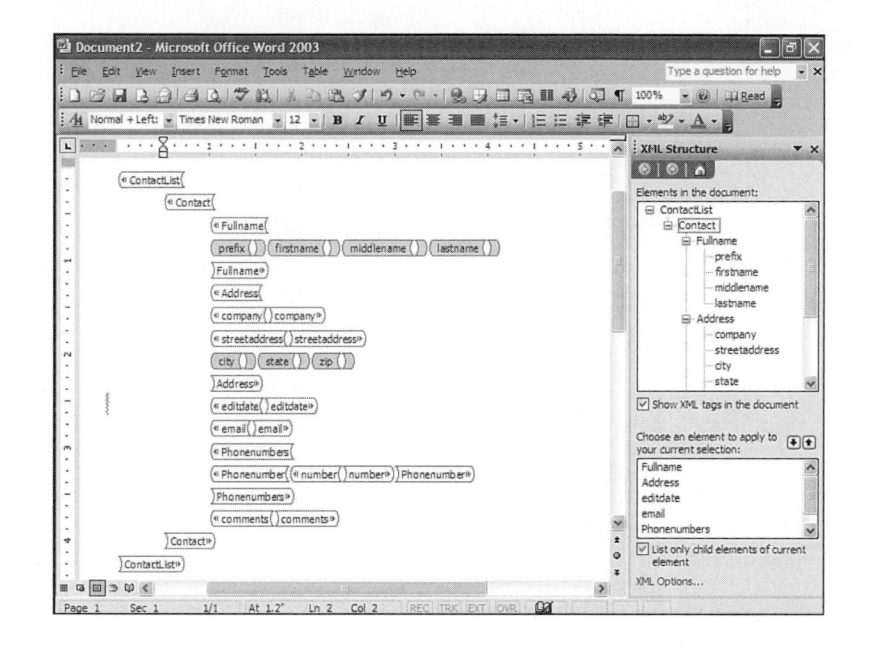

Now that you have a completed Contact structure, you can add some data into the various elements of the structure if you want. After you have done that, go ahead and save the document and name it ContactList. See the section "Saving to XML," later in this chapter, for more details on saving XML documents.

Congratulations! You've just constructed your first XML data structure and document.

EDITING AN EXISTING XML DOCUMENT

As with most data files that we deal with, the need to review or edit them will happen more frequently than creating them from scratch. When editing XML files in Word, we need to consider two scenarios: editing XML files saved as Word XML documents (using WordML) and editing standard (or data only) XML files.

EDITING A WORD XML DOCUMENT

Editing a Word XML document is pretty simple: Just double-click on the file in Explorer, or use the File, Open menu inside of Word and select the file. The file is opened and you can edit the document based on the same XML schema used to create it.

But what happens if you send this XML file to someone else or you want to edit it on a different computer? Remember that Word requires access to the XML schema file if you want to have full editing and validation of your XML structure. If the schema used to create the document is not available, Word will provide the same level of editing capabilities as provided for data-only XML files (see the next section, "Editing a Data-Only XML File"). Be sure that you include the schema file when sending the document to another person or when taking the document to a different computer.

EDITING A DATA-ONLY XML FILE

Obviously, there are many other sources of XML files out there than just those created in Word. You can open a data-only XML file using the File, Open menu and Word will present the XML structure along with the XML Document task pane, as shown in Figure 25.22.

Figure 25.22
The XML Document task pane.

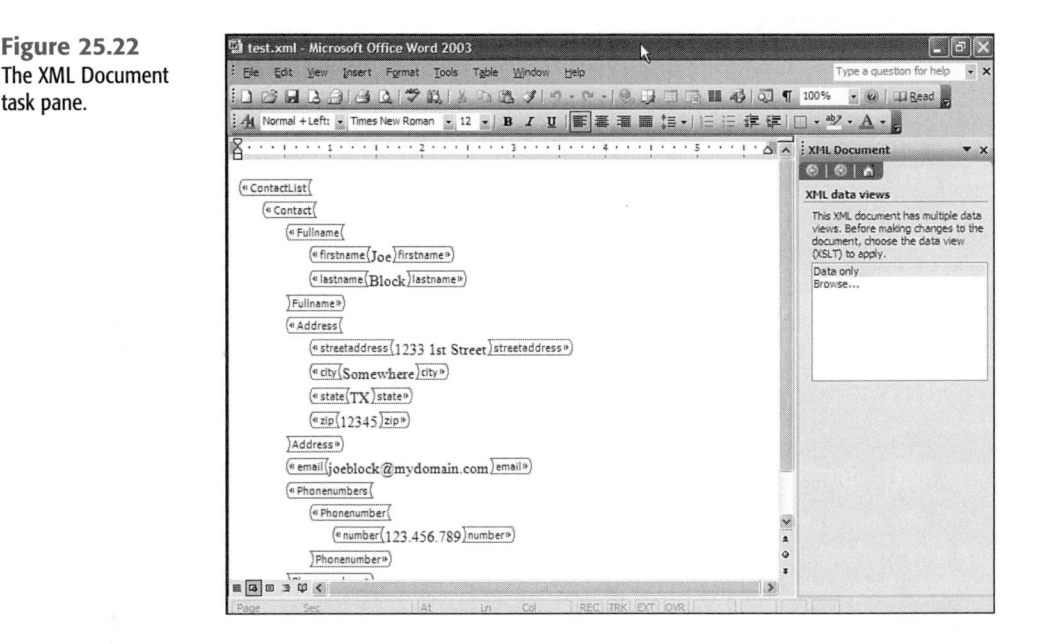

When opening a data-only XML file, Word gives you the option of using the full data structure (represented by the Data Only entry in the XML data views) or browsing to a separate XSLT transformation file. As soon as you make any changes to the data in the document, you are locked in to the view of the data that is currently presented. At that point the XML Document task pane will be removed completely for that editing session.

To apply a different transformation, or data view, follow these steps:

1. Click on the Browse entry in the XML Data Views list. The XSL Transformation dialog will be presented (see Figure 25.23).

2. Browse to the desired transformation (.xsl) file.

3. Click Open.

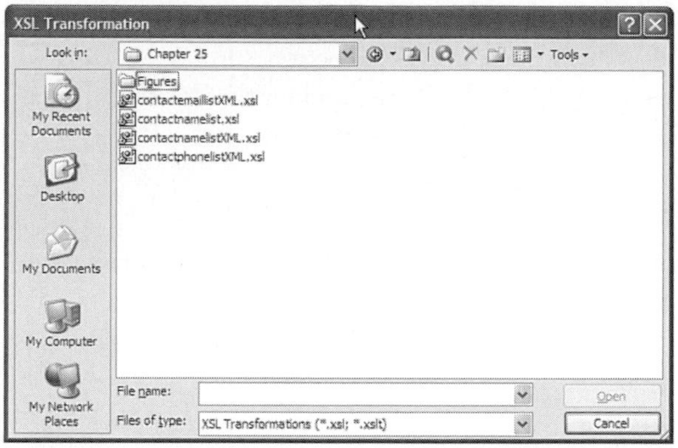

Figure 25.23
The XSL
Transformation dialog.

The new data view will be added to the XML Document task pane, and the transformation will be applied to the document. You can click between the data views that are loaded or add other data views if you choose. You can continue this process until any changes are made, at which time the XML Document task pane will be removed.

CAUTION

If you save a file using an XSLT transformation, Word saves only the result of the transformation. See "What to Do If You Lose Data after Saving Your XML File," in the Troubleshooting section at the end of this chapter.

APPLYING XML ELEMENTS TO AN EXISTING DOCUMENT

Up to this point we've established that Word has solid functionality dealing with XML data and XML schemas. Word's XML integration capabilities really shine, however, when you combine them with Word's existing document publishing capabilities. This powerful combination provides attractive and user-friendly documents driven by XML schemas for maximum benefit to everyone. Let's use our contact example to illustrate this capability.

If you've followed through the previous few sections, you have seen that although Word provides full editing capabilities of native XML data structures, the presentation and usability of the editing could use some improvement. What we would like to do is take a document like the one shown in Figure 25.24 and integrate it with our XML schema.

To apply our ContactML schema to this document, follow these steps:

1. Open the new contact record document.

2. Select Tools, Templates and Add-Ins, and click on the XML Schema tab.

3. Add the ContactML schema to the document (see the section "Adding an XML Schema to a Document," earlier in this chapter), and then click OK. The document should be similar to the one shown in Figure 25.25.

4. In the XML Structure task pane, click on the ContactList element name. The dialog in Figure 25.26 is then displayed. Click the Apply to Entire Document button.

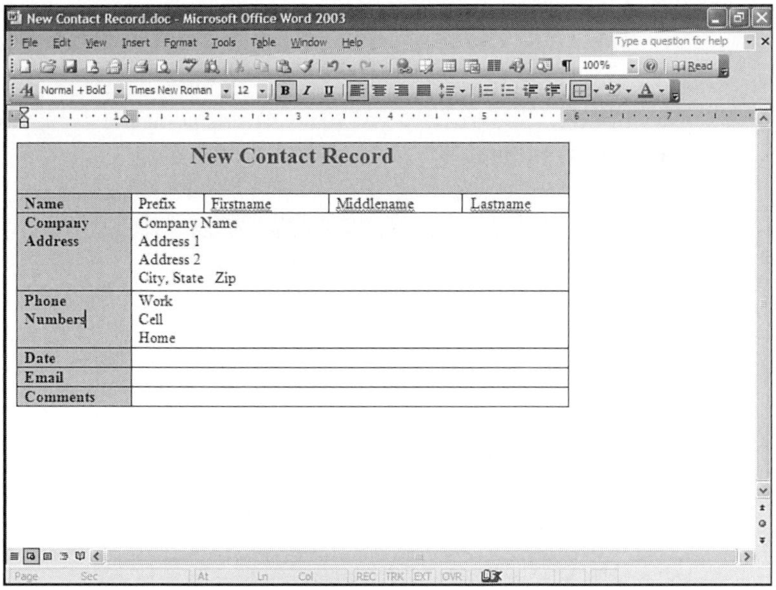

Figure 25.24
The new contact record document.

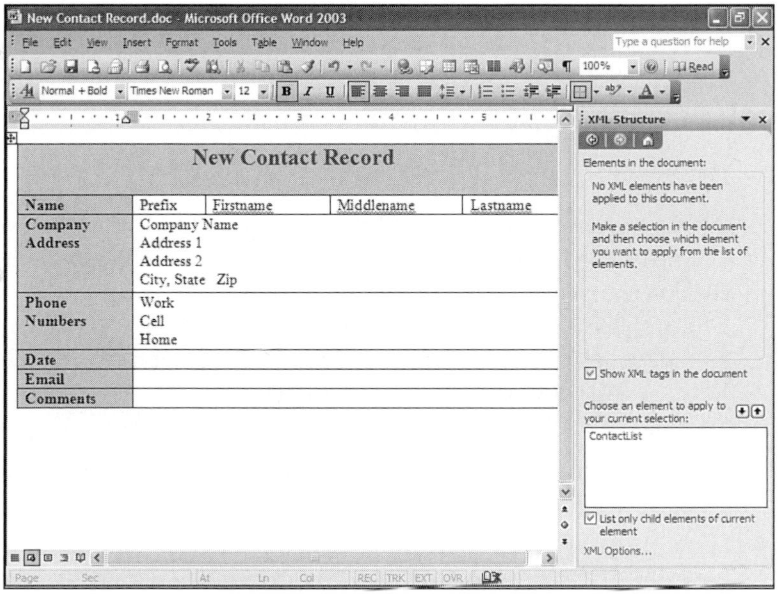

Figure 25.25
The new contact record document with schema applied.

Figure 25.26
Applying the ContactList element to the document.

25

5. With the contents of the ContactList element still selected, click on the Contact element in the XML Structure task pane.

6. Select the top row of the table that begins with Name and then click on the Fullname element in the XML Structure task pane. At this point the document should be similar to what's shown in Figure 25.27.

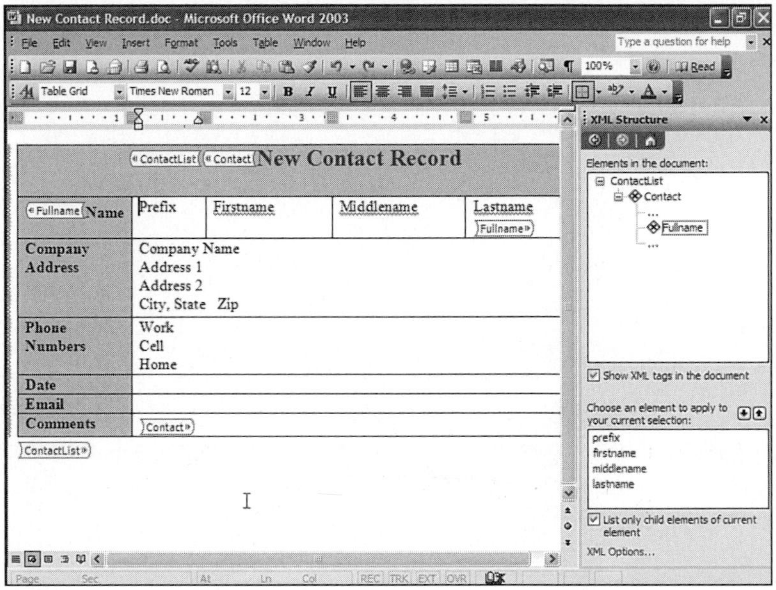

Figure 25.27
The new Contact document with some elements applied.

Take a moment to look at the Elements in the Document list of the XML Structure task pane. You'll see some unusual-looking errors and elements being displayed. If you click on the elements labeled as ". . ." the non-XML data parts of the form get selected. The problem being seen here is caused by what is called "mixed content." Mixed content means that there is a mixture of XML data and formatting text in the document. Word provides a way to deal with this in the XML Options dialog (see the section "Setting XML Options," earlier in this chapter). Let's keep going now.

7. In the XML Structure task pane, click the XML Options link to display the XML Options dialog, check the Ignore Mixed Content option, and click OK.

8. Select the rows of the table that contain the company name and address, and then click the Address element name in the XML Structure task pane. Continue to select the appropriate blocks of text and individual text items until you have completed the contact record. After you have completed the structure, your document should look similar to that shown in Figure 25.28.

Figure 25.28
The new Contact document with all elements applied.

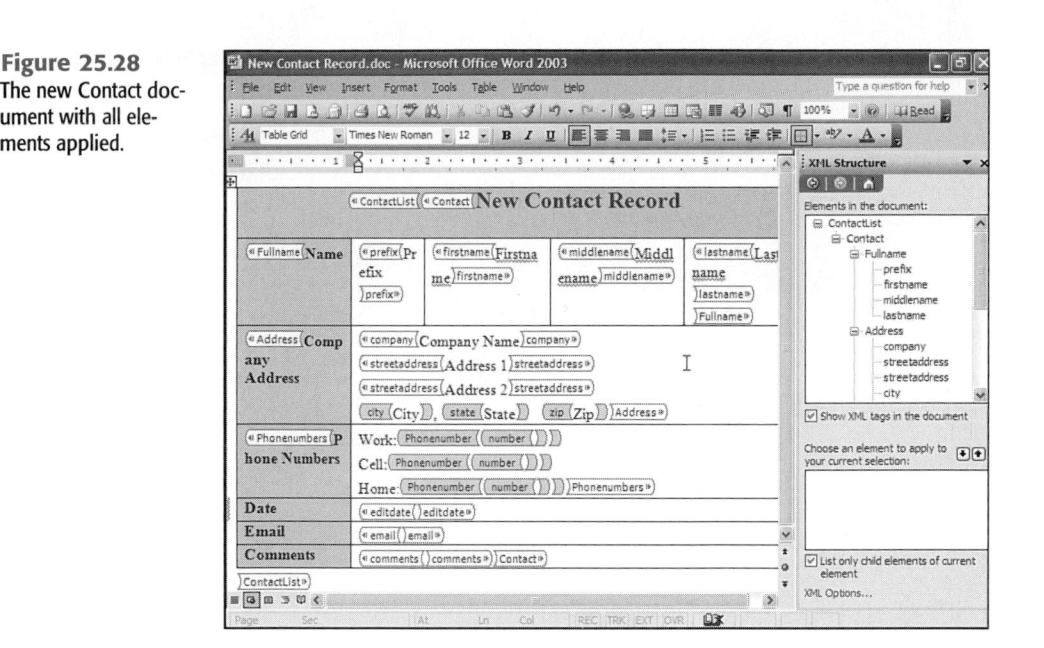

We've made progress, but it doesn't exactly look like the original document. Let's keep going and see whether we can get back to the format of the original document.

9. Return to the document and remove the placeholder text that was present in the original document (Company Name, Firstname, and so on).

10. In the XML Structure task pane, click on the XML Options link to display the XML Options dialog. If the Show placeholder text for all empty elements option is not checked, check it and click OK.

11. In the XML Structure task pane, clear the Show XML Tags in the Document check box.

After completing these steps, you should have a document that looks similar to the one shown in Figure 25.29. Select File, Save As and save this as a Word template (.dot file).

We now have an easy-to-use document template that can be used to record new contact records based on our predefined XML schema. The template can be saved as a Word XML document, and the data only can be saved in XML as well.

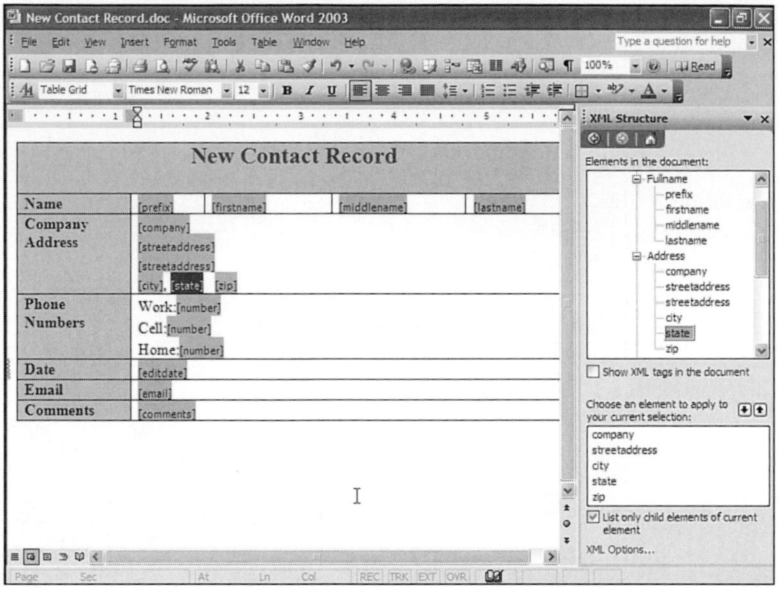

Figure 25.29
The new Contact form template.

SAVING TO XML

Word provides multiple options for saving XML files so that users have the flexibility to meet their business needs. XML files can be saved using the Microsoft Word document schema, WordML, XML data only based on the schema(s) attached to the document, or data only using a transformation.

SAVING AN XML DOCUMENT USING WORDML

To save an XML document that preserves all the Word document properties and settings, follow these steps (see Figure 25.30):

1. Choose File, Save As.
2. In the Save As dialog box, select XML Document in the Save as Type list.
3. Enter a filename in the File Name text box.
4. Clear the Save Data Only check box if it is checked.
5. Click Save.

SAVING AN XML DOCUMENT USING XML DATA ONLY

To save an XML document with only the data related to the attached schema, follow these steps (see Figure 25.31):

1. Choose File, Save As.
2. In the Save As dialog box, select XML Document in the Save as Type list.
3. Enter a filename in the File Name text box.

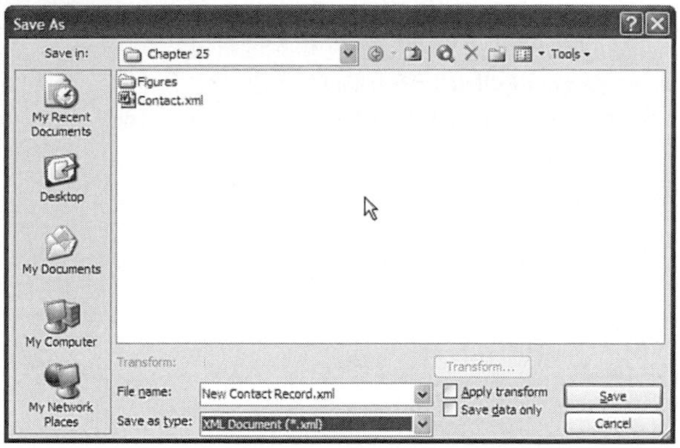

Figure 25.30
Saving an XML document using WordML.

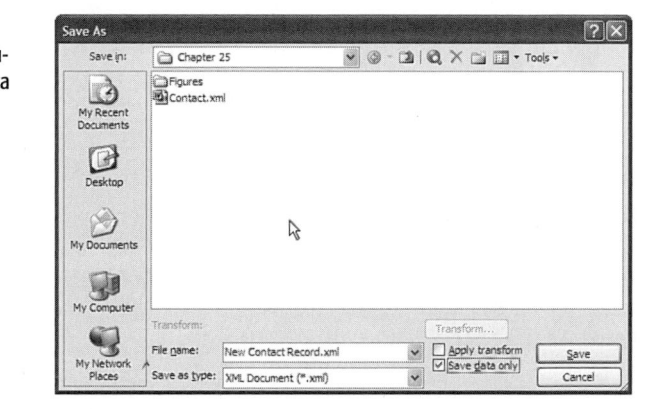

4. Check the Save Data Only check box if it is not checked.
5. Click Save.

Figure 25.31
Saving an XML document using XML data only.

SAVING AN XML DOCUMENT USING A TRANSFORMATION

To save an XML document using a transformation, follow these steps (see Figure 25.32):

1. Choose File, Save As.
2. In the Save As dialog box, select XML Document in the Save as Type list.
3. Enter a filename in the File Name text box.
4. Check the Save Data Only check box if it is not checked.
5. Check the Apply Transform check box is it is not checked, and then click the Transform button to select the transformation file (.xsl file) you want to use.

CAUTION

> When you save a document using a transformation, only the results of the transformation are saved. Word will discard all the data that is not used in the transformation. See "What to Do If You Lose Data After Saving Your XML File," in the Troubleshooting section at the end of this chapter.

6. Click Save.

Figure 25.32
Saving an XML document using a transformation.

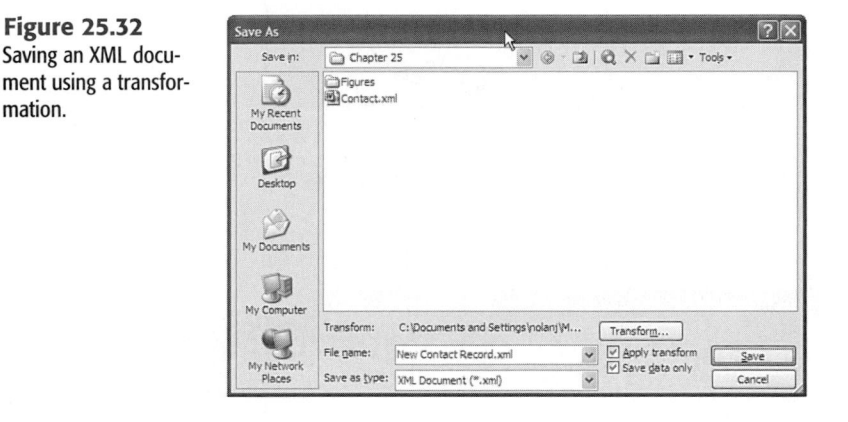

WORKING WITH XML SOLUTIONS

As you see from the simple ContactML XML schema presented earlier in this chapter, rigorous control of the data types, structure, and content arrangement is a key requirement of working in XML. We've discussed previously how Word's integration with XML also provides great flexibility. This flexibility is provided in part by XML Solutions.

UNDERSTANDING XML SOLUTIONS

In Word an XML Solution is an XSLT Transformation that is linked to a specific XML schema. This capability allows you to keep one set of data in an XML structure and link transformations representing different purposes of the data. When a new purpose (or solution) is identified, a new transformation can be added to the schema without having to move around any data.

MANAGING XML SOLUTIONS IN THE SCHEMA LIBRARY

XML Solutions in Word are managed from within the Schema Library. To access the Schema Library, select the Tools, Templates and Add-Ins menu, click the XML Schema tab, and then click the Schema Library button. XML Solutions are managed in the bottom half of this dialog (see Figure 25.33).

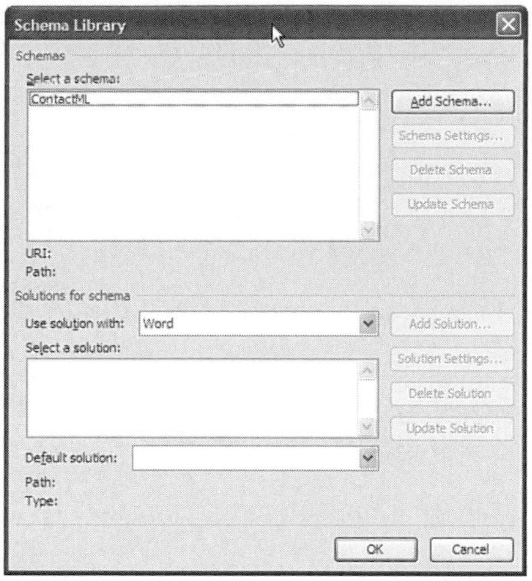

Figure 25.33
Managing XML
Solutions in the
Schema Library.

Follow these steps to add a solution:

1. In the <u>S</u>elect a Schema list, click on the schema to which the solution will be added.

2. Click the Add Solutio<u>n</u> button. The Add Solution dialog is displayed (see Figure 25.34).

Figure 25.34
The Add Solution
dialog.

3. Navigate to the XSLT transformation file (.xsl) and click <u>O</u>pen. The Solution Settings
dialog is displayed (see Figure 25.35).

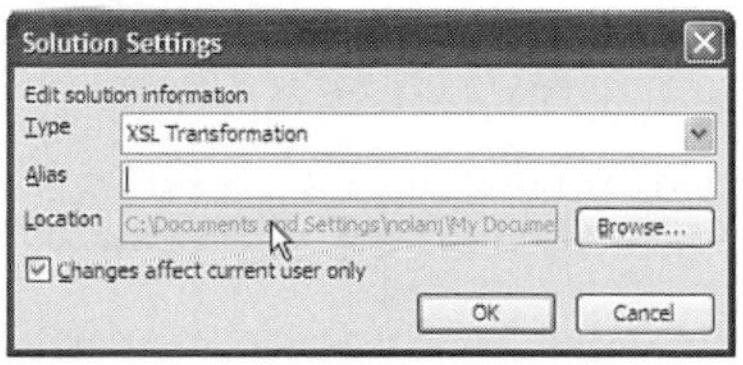

Figure 25.35
The Solution Settings
dialog.

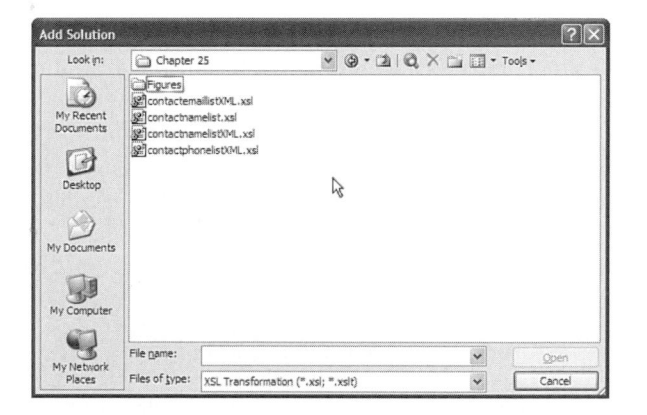

25

   4. Enter an alias name to identify the solution and click OK. The added solution will be displayed in the Select a Solution list. If this is the first solution to be added, it will also show up in the Default Solution selection.

To modify the solution settings, select the solution in the Select a Solution list and click the Solution Settings button. You can modify the alias name, change the path to the transformation file, or control whether this change affects all users (see Figure 25.35).

To delete a solution, select the solution in the Select a Solution list and click the Delete Solution button.

If you have multiple solutions attached to a schema, you can change the default solution using the Default Solution drop-down list.

After you have completed your changes to the Solutions, click OK to dismiss the dialog.

Managing Your Data with XML Solutions

We now have a good picture of how to create XML data based on a schema, what XSLT transformations represent, and how to associate them with a schema. Now how can we use that information to manage our data? Remember that our primary goals are to keep data in a well-defined structure, reduce duplication of input, and support repurposing of the information that has already been captured.

Let's think about our simple contact-list example and how this might apply. We have a friendly front end to enter the information with the data being saved in XML format based on an XML schema. We can include as many contacts in our list as we want and can extract the pure data (save as data only) anytime we want. After using this document for a time, we get tired of paging through all the contact records and realize that we need a simple list of names and email addresses. In the past we probably would have created a new document and then paged through the contact list copying and pasting entries into the other document. After this new document was created we would have duplicate sources of data that have to be separately maintained.

To produce our email list using XML, we can follow these steps:

   1. Use File, Save As to create a new XML file with data only.

   2. Create an XSLT transformation file (.xsl) with the following code:

```
<?xml version="1.0"?>
<xsl:stylesheet xmlns:xsl="http://www.w3.org/1999/XSL/Transform" version="1.0"
xmlns:cl="http://tempuri.org/contactML.xsd">
<xsl:template match="/">
<ContactList>
    <xsl:for-each select="cl:ContactList/cl:Contact">
    <Contact>
        <name><xsl:value-of select="cl:Fullname/cl:lastname"/>,
            <xsl:value-of select="cl:Fullname/cl:lastname"/>
        </name>
        <email><xsl:value-of select="cl:email"/></email>
    </Contact>
```

```
        </xsl:for-each>
    </ContactList>
    </xsl:template>
    </xsl:stylesheet>
```

3. Add the transformation file as a solution associated with the ContactML schema.

4. Open Word, select the File, Open menu, and pick the data-only XML file. When the file is loaded, you will be presented with the list of data views that are available (see Figure 25.36).

Figure 25.36
The email list solution for the contact list.

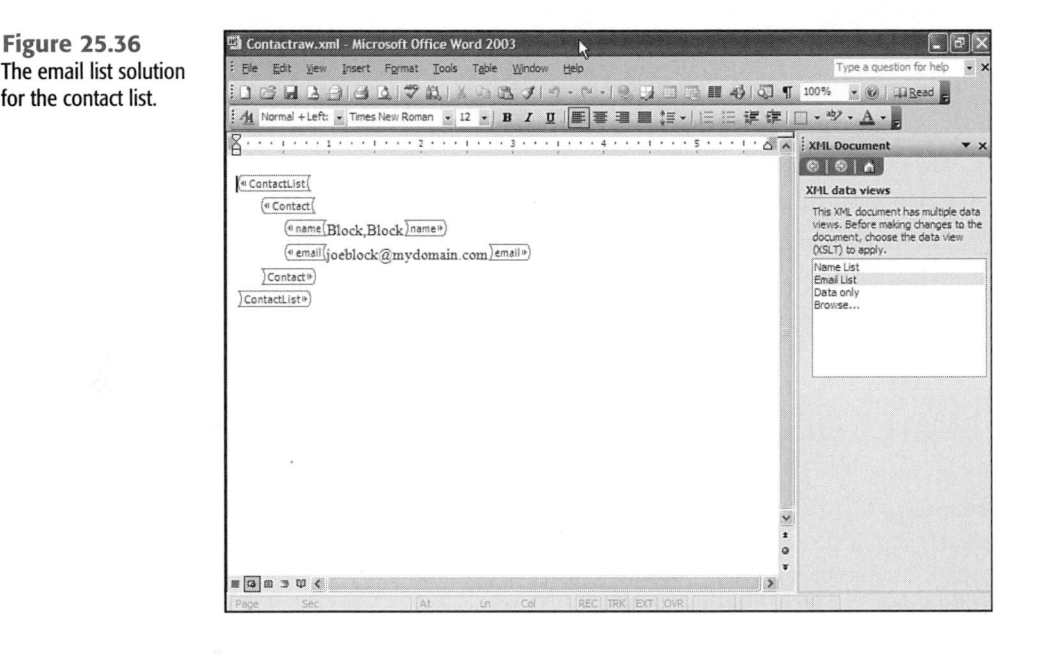

5. Select the Data Only and the Email List data views to see the two listings.

PUBLISHING CONTENT TO THE WEB VIA XSLT TRANSFORMATIONS

The XML integration provided in Word opens up many powerful and exciting capabilities for information sharing and distribution. These capabilities can be leveraged by using XSLT transformations to put the data in a form suitable for display on the Web.

Viewing through the Web would be a pretty boring experience if not for the ability to use colors, fonts, graphics, and layout to present the information in an attractive and interesting way. To support the expectations of viewing on the Web, the Word document attributes must be transformed into the corresponding HTML equivalents. Accomplishing this feat, however, is not a trivial task. You'll need to develop an understanding of XSLT style sheets, as well as how to translate the WordML schema into equivalent HTML formatting elements.

Extensive documentation on the WordML schema and its object model for representing a document is readily available, but much can be learned by some simple examination of the generated XML of the Word document. For most applications for transforming data to the Web, the number of different attributes that are needed is a small subset of the overall Word document object model.

You can follow these steps to learn a lot about the WordML schema:

1. Start with an empty Word document, and then enter a small amount of text and apply a single attribute of interest to it (like bold).

2. Save the document as an XML document.

3. Open the document in Notepad and remove the second line from the file that looks like `<?mso-application progid="Word.Document"?>`.

4. After saving these changes, double-click on the file and it will be displayed in Internet Explorer.

5. Locate the `<w:body>` root that represents the contents of the document.

6. Examine the contents of that element to learn which elements control the specific behavior desired.

THE LIMITS OF WORD'S XML SUPPORT

We've covered a lot of ground in this chapter regarding Word's support for and integration with XML. Clearly this integration expands the capability of Word to act as a source of business application data and an integration point for other XML-based resources. Even with all the integration capabilities we've discussed, there are still some limits to what Word can support.

WHEN TO USE MICROSOFT INFOPATH OR ANOTHER TOOL INSTEAD OF WORD

Microsoft InfoPath is a new product in the Microsoft Office System. Microsoft InfoPath was designed with teams and organizations in mind whose main purpose in their job is to collect and use information. Easy creation of powerful input forms that include business logic validation, auto correction, spell checking, and rich-text formatting as a front end to XML data sources are the strength of Microsoft InfoPath.

Consider using Microsoft InfoPath or another tool if

- You need fast and efficient data input
- You frequently need to build front-end forms for data input
- You need rich-text forms style formatting
- You need business logic validation
- You need automatic data-source updating without having to worry about file formats (that is, WordML versus data-only XML)

TROUBLESHOOTING

WHAT TO DO IF WORD CAN'T OPEN MY XML FILE

Several different problems can prevent Word from opening an XML file:

- An XML file must be well formed for Word to open it. If you see a message indicating that this situation exists, open the file in Notepad, fix the problem, and then try opening the file again.

> **TIP**
>
> If you have problems finding the specific location of an XML syntax error, try opening the file in Internet Explorer. It will attempt to validate the structure and provide more specific information about where the problem is.

- If you have created a document that does not have any XML structure elements in it and then choose to save data only, nothing will be saved. This is because the document text has no root node, and therefore a properly formed XML document cannot be created. When you try to open the file backup, it will be empty. If the content of your document does not contain valid XML, don't use the Save Data Only option.

- If you have specified an XSLT transformation and Word cannot use it, Word will try to apply any other transformation that is included in the document. If no others are available, Word will then try a default transformation to open the document. If all of these attempts fail, Word gives you a message indicating the problem. You must either use a different transformation file or open the XML file in Notepad and fix the source of the problem.

WHAT TO DO IF THE XML DOCUMENT TASK PANE DISAPPEARS

If you have selected a data view in the XML Document task pane and then open that file for editing, the data view is automatically activated. Because the data view is an XSLT transformation, you cannot reverse the process that results in removal of the XML Document task pane. To avoid this situation, make sure that you select the desired data view before you start editing.

WHAT TO DO IF INSERTING XML FROM ANOTHER FILE DOESN'T WORK

When using an XPATH expression to select data from another XML file, Word does not validate the syntax of the expression. If you enter an expression that is invalid or does not match anything in the XML file, nothing will be inserted and no error messages will be displayed. Keep these things in mind when using XPATH queries:

- Querying XML structures is a case-sensitive operation. Make sure you are specifying your element or attribute names with the correct case.

- If the XML file you are selecting data from was saved using Word's default WordML schema, your XPATH query must address that XML structure before it will work.

WHAT TO DO IF A DATA VIEW OR TRANSFORMATION DOES NOT FIND ANY DATA

Querying XML structures via XPATH or XSLT is not always a simple operation. If you enter an expression that is invalid or does not match anything in the XML file, nothing will be displayed and no error messages will be displayed. Keep these things in mind when working with data views and transformations:

■ Querying XML structures is a case-sensitive operation. Make sure you are specifying your element or attribute names with the correct case.

■ If the XML file you are selecting data from was saved using Word's default WordML schema, your XPATH query must address that XML structure before it will work.

WHAT TO DO IF YOU LOSE DATA AFTER SAVING YOUR XML FILE

If you save a file using an XSLT transformation, Word saves only the result of the transformation. The original data file is not saved. To prevent loss of data when using these transformations, keep a separate copy of the source XML file. Be sure to use the Save As menu when you apply your transformation.

WHAT TO DO IF THE LIST OF ELEMENTS IS HARD TO READ

Sometimes you may find that the element names in the XML Structure task pane have long strings on the end that start with {urn:,. This string is the namespace that the element belongs to. Although this is useful when multiple namespaces are used in the same document, it can also make the element names hard to read. You can turn off the display of the namespace by clicking on the XML Options, and then selecting the Hide Namespace Alias in XML Structure Task Pane check box.

WHAT TO DO IF NO ELEMENTS ARE AVAILABLE TO ADD WHEN EDITING AN XML DOCUMENT

Word requires access to a valid XML schema before it will allow any changes to be made to the structure itself. Make sure that the required schema has been added to the Schema Library.

THE CORPORATE WORD

CHAPTER **26**

Managing Document Collaboration and Revisions

In this chapter

AN OVERVIEW OF WORD'S TEAM WRITING TOOLS

Nowadays, few documents of any size are written entirely by one individual. In the corporate setting, most documents must be shepherded through a hierarchy; increasingly they must also be reviewed by cross-functional teams. Even freelance writers, of course, face the sharp red pencils of editors—often, more than one.

Word can't do much to make the substantive aspects of the review process easier. But it can work absolute wonders for the logistics of document review. If your review needs are especially simple, Word's Highlighting tool might be enough—just as a highlighter might have been enough for you in high school. We'll cover the Highlighting tool briefly at the beginning of this chapter.

However, most of this chapter focuses on Word's industrial-strength tools for complex document reviews—features that provide a comprehensive solution for ensuring that all input and feedback are reflected as efficiently as possible. These features include

- *Comments*, which enables reviewers to annotate your document with suggestions and recommendations without actually changing the text of the printed draft
- *Track Changes*, which helps you track changes made by multiple reviewers and then evaluate, incorporate, or reject them one at a time—or all at once
- *Protect Documents*, which enables you to prevent changes to your document other than comments or tracked changes
- *Versioning*, which enables you to maintain multiple versions of a document in a single file
- Close integration with Microsoft Outlook and Microsoft SharePoint to help you send file attachments to reviewers and track their progress

USING THE HIGHLIGHTER

Word's simplest reviewing tool is the Highlighter, which works just like the highlighting pen you might still use regularly with printed documents. For the most informal reviews, in which all you need to do is call attention to text, rather than make detailed comments about it, Word's Highlighter may be all you need.

NOTE

> For any more complex reviews, Track Changes makes it far easier to track, accept, and reject specific changes made by multiple reviewers. If you want to annotate a block of text with a suggestion or question, use Word's Comments tool.

To highlight one block of text, select it and click the Highlight icon on the Formatting toolbar. By default, your text is highlighted in see-through yellow. Figure 26.1 shows highlighted text in a document.

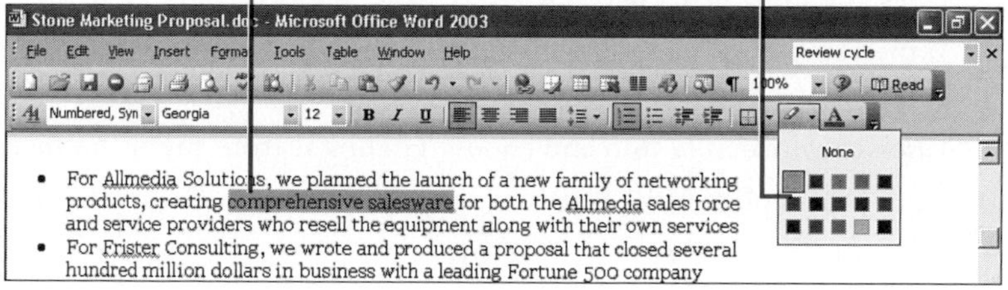

Highlighted text   Choosing a different highlighting color

Figure 26.1
By default, highlighted
text is marked in
yellow.

If you plan to highlight several blocks of text, click the Highlight button before you select any text. Then select the first block of text; Word highlights it. Select another block of text; Word highlights that one too. Word keeps highlighting text you select until you press Esc or click the Highlight button again.

If you prefer to use a color other than yellow, click the down arrow next to the Highlight button; a choice of 15 colors appears. Select the color you want to use. This becomes the default color for all highlighting you do until you change it again.

TIP

> Some highlight colors that are acceptable for online reading may be too dark when printed. Even if highlighted text is still readable, you may simply not want highlighting to appear in your printed drafts. To hide the highlighting both onscreen and in printed copies, choose Tools, Options and, on the View tab, clear the check box marked Highlight. Highlighting becomes invisible until you recheck the box.

NOTE

> When you save highlighted text as part of a Web page, Word stores the highlighting as part of Cascading Style Sheet information that can be understood by Microsoft Internet Explorer 3.0 and higher, as well as Netscape Navigator/Communicator 4.0 and higher. Earlier browsers may disregard the highlighting.

CHANGING THE COLOR OF HIGHLIGHTED TEXT

What if you add yellow highlighting throughout your document and then decide that your highlights should be a different color? Or what if someone else reviews the document using yellow highlights and you want to reserve yellow highlighting for yourself—displaying your colleague's highlights in another color, such as blue? You can use Word's Replace tool to change all the text highlighting in your document (no matter what color it is) to a different highlight color that you can specify. To do so, follow these steps:

1. Change the highlight color to the one you want.
2. Choose Edit, Replace.

3. Make sure that there's no text in either the Find What or the Replace With text box.

4. Click the Find What text box.

5. If the Search Options portion of the dialog box is not visible, click More to display it. If it is not already grayed out, click No Formatting.

6. Click the Format button and choose Highlight from the menu that appears.

7. Click the Replace With text box.

8. Repeat steps 5 and 6.

9. Click Replace All. Word replaces all the existing highlights in your document with new highlights in the color you've just specified.

REMOVING HIGHLIGHTING FROM YOUR DOCUMENT

There are three ways to remove highlighting from a document. The easiest is to remove all the highlighting throughout a document at one time. To do this, press Ctrl+A to select the entire document, click the down arrow next to the Highlight button, and choose None.

The other two methods are useful for removing highlighting from specific passages of text. In either case you must first select, exactly, the text with highlighting you want removed. From there you can click the down arrow next to the Highlight button and choose None (as described previously), or make sure that the selected color for the Highlight button matches the highlight you want to remove and click the button.

> **NOTE**
>
> If the color of the highlight button does not match the highlight color of the selected text, when you click the button this only changes the text highlight color to match that of the button.

INTRODUCING WORD'S REVIEWING INTERFACE

The next several sections cover two of Word's core reviewing features: comments and tracked changes. In Word 2002, Microsoft revamped Word's interface to both features, making them significantly easier to use. If you are upgrading from an older version of Word, you may first want to get comfortable with Word's current reviewing interface before getting into the details of working with comments and tracked changes.

> **NOTE**
>
> Microsoft sometimes refers to comments and tracked changes collectively as *markup*.

INTRODUCING WORD'S REVIEWING TOOLBAR

Word's Reviewing toolbar brings together all commands for marking up a document with comments, tracked changes, and highlighting, as shown in Figure 26.2.

Figure 26.2
The Reviewing toolbar.

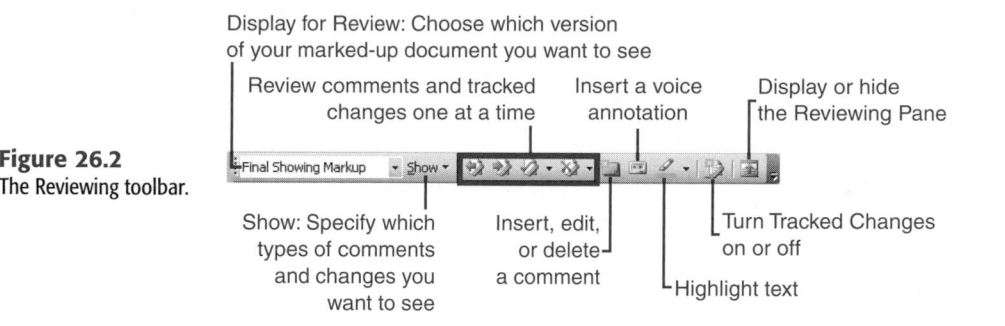

Two buttons on the Reviewing toolbar are especially worth mentioning: the Display for Review button and the Show button.

Display for Review allows you to control which version of your document you are looking at:

- Final Showing Markup shows the document in its current form, with all comments and tracked changes marked so that you can see what changes have already been made. Insertions that have been made are shown within the document, and deletions are shown in balloons or the Reviewing pane.

- Final shows the document in its current form, with no comments or tracked changes visible—in other words, the document as it would appear if you accepted every comment and tracked change.

- Original Showing Markup shows the document in its original form but also makes all comments and tracked changes visible so that you can see what changes have been *requested*. Deletions are shown as strikethroughs within the document, and proposed insertions are shown in balloons or the Reviewing pane.

- Original shows the document in its original form, with no comments or tracked changes visible—in other words, the document as it would appear if you rejected every comment and tracked change.

The Show button allows you to control several additional aspects of how your document displays material that must be reviewed.

By default, Word displays Comments, Insertions and Deletions, Formatting, and (if you are using a Tablet PC) any Ink Annotations you may have inserted. If the document is being reviewed by more than one person, by default, Word also shows each reviewer's changes at the same time. However, you can hide any or all of these items by clicking the Show button and clearing the corresponding check box (see Figure 26.3).

You might want to review formatting only after the document's content has been finalized; if so, clear the Formatting check box. Or you might want to review only comments from a single reviewer: Clear the All Reviewers check box and check only the name of the reviewer whose markup you want to see.

26

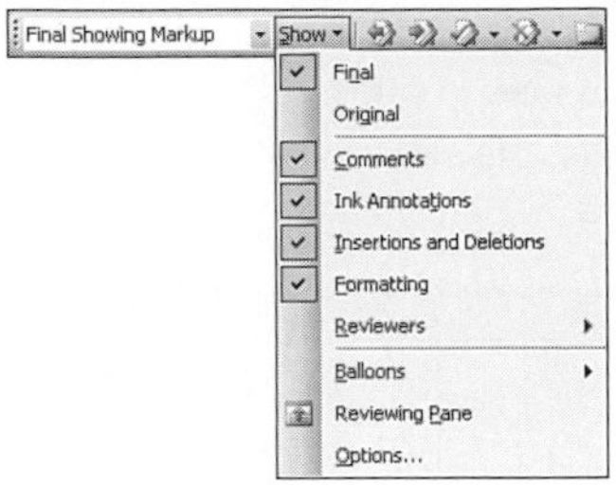

Figure 26.3
Choosing which sets
of changes to display.

WORKING WITH WORD'S REVIEWING PANE

Word's Reviewing pane (see Figure 26.4) makes it easy to scroll through all changes and comments made to the main document, headers and footers, text boxes, footnotes, and end-notes.

NOTE

> The Reviewing pane replaces the Comments pane that appeared in versions prior to Word 2002 and did not display tracked changes.

To display the Reviewing pane, click the Reviewing pane button on the Reviewing toolbar.

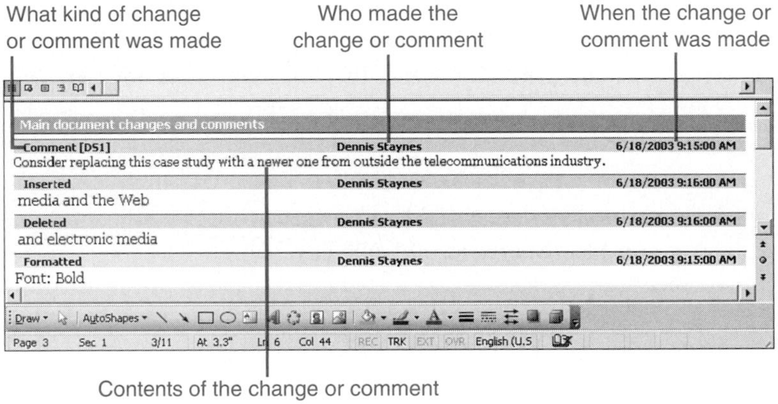

Figure 26.4
The Reviewing pane.

As you enter comments or make changes with Word's Track Changes feature turned on, your comments and changes appear in the Reviewing pane. You can use the Reviewing pane's vertical scrollbar to move through comments and changes. If you want to review the context in which a certain change was made, click on the gray line containing a description of the change, and Word's main editing window displays the surrounding text.

INTRODUCING WORD'S REVIEWING BALLOONS

When you work in Print Layout view or Web Layout view, Word also inserts balloons in your document displaying comments and tracked changes (see Figure 26.5).

Figure 26.5
Word inserts text balloons marking comments and tracked changes.

Balloon containing a comment

Dotted line connecting to comment

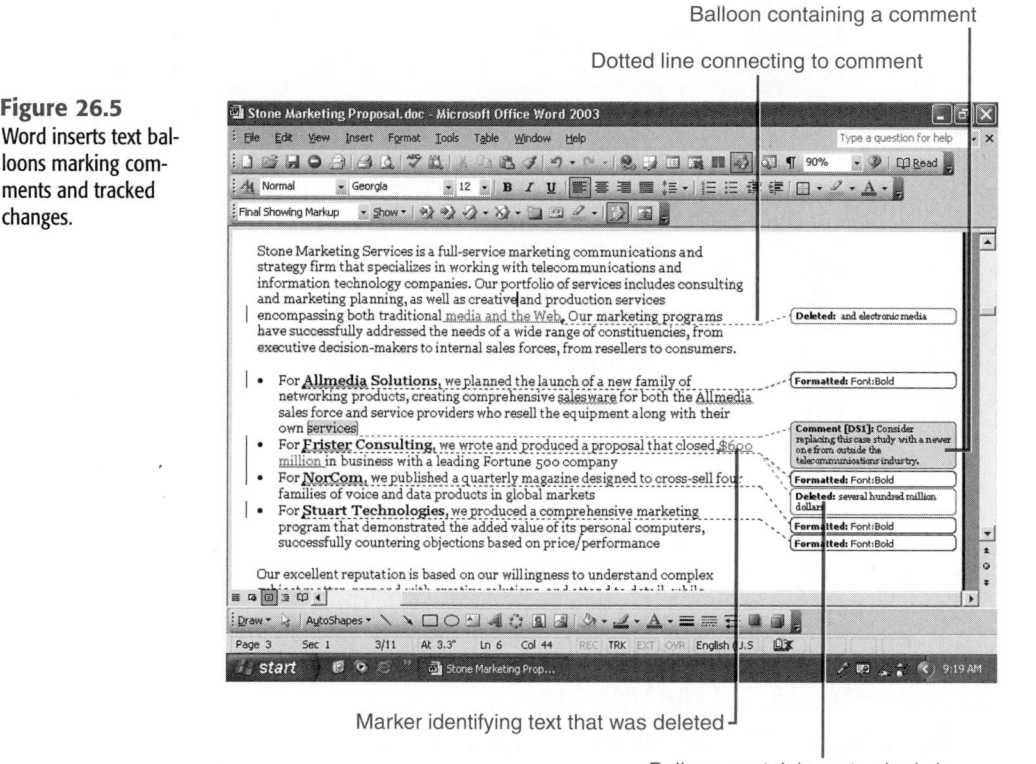

Marker identifying text that was deleted

Balloon containing a tracked change

26

Each reviewer's comments and changes appear in a different color. A dotted line points to the text being changed or commented on. When you click inside the balloon, the dotted line becomes solid. If you made the comment inside a balloon, you can edit it there.

→ To control where and how Comment and Track Changes balloons appear, **see** "Options for Controlling the Track Changes Feature," **p. 887**.

WORKING WITH READING LAYOUT

You may find it easier to review a marked-up document in Word's new Reading Layout, which enlarges the text of your document for easy readability, while providing a large space at the right for balloons containing tracked changes and comments (see Figure 26.6).

TIP

> If you work in Reading Layout view, you might find that the Reviewing toolbar is abbreviated to fit on the same row as the Reading Layout toolbar. To view all the options on the Reviewing toolbar, drag it below the Reading Layout toolbar.

Figure 26.6
Reviewing a document in Reading Layout.

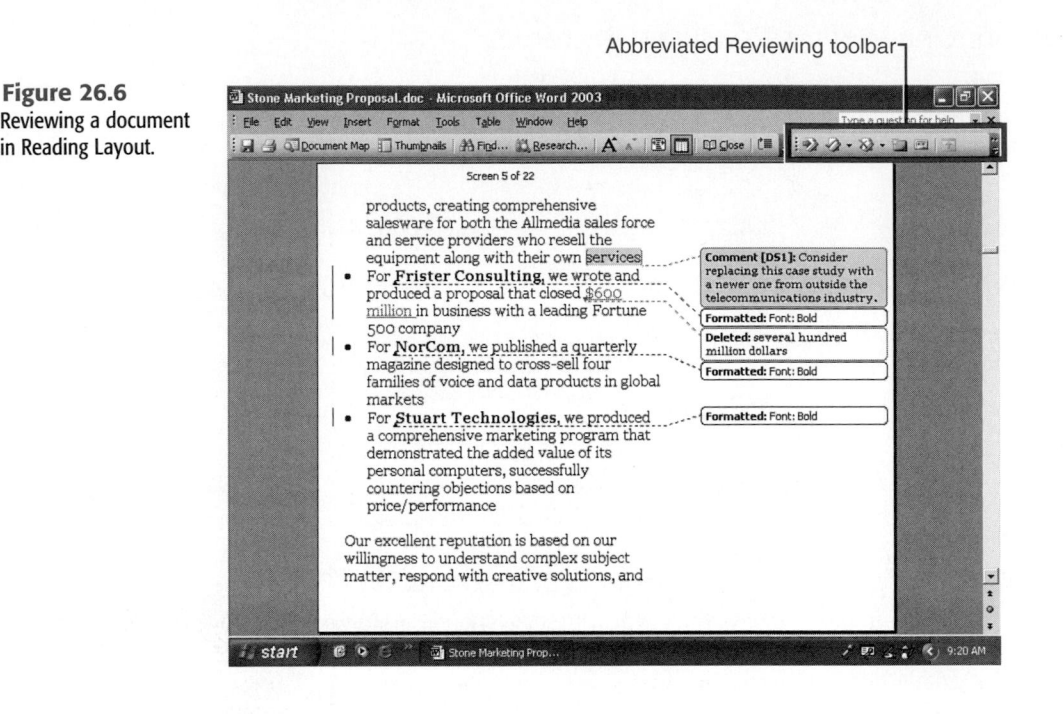

Now that you've become familiar with Word's Reviewing interface, let's take a closer look at the reviewing features that use it: comments and tracked changes.

WORKING WITH COMMENTS

It's a classic problem: How do you make (or invite) comments in a document without introducing text changes that have to be undone later? The solution is Word's Comments tool.

With Comments, your colleagues have a way of annotating your document that doesn't get in your way as you edit and format it. Whenever you're ready, their inserted comments are easy to view, print, and resolve.

TIP

> You can also use Comments to create notes to yourself about facts that need checking, additional text that needs to be added, and other unfinished business.

To insert a comment, either click where you want your comment to appear or select the text that relates to the comment you want to make, and then press Alt+Ctrl+M, or click the Insert Comment button on the Reviewing toolbar. (You can also choose Insert, Comment.)

If you are working in Normal view, a comment marker appears at the point in your document where you are entering the comment, and the Reviewing pane appears (refer to Figure 26.5 for an example). In Word, the word your insertion point was in appears highlighted;

this highlighting will not appear in the printed document unless you choose to print comments.

If you are working in Print Layout view or Web Layout view, a comment balloon also appears. You can now type your comment.

NOTE

> If you do not want to see comment balloons in your document, click Show on the Reviewing toolbar and clear the Comments check box.

INSERTING COMMENTS FROM MULTIPLE REVIEWERS

Several people can use Word's comments feature to annotate the same file. Word automatically places each reviewer's name above her comment marks, using the name that appears in the User Information tab of the Options dialog box.

TIP

> As mentioned earlier, Word displays your name above the comment in the Reviewing pane. If the name Word displays is incorrect, choose Tools, Options, User Information and enter your name in the Name text box.
>
> If you're using someone else's computer to make comments on a document, change the User Information to ensure that your name is associated with future comments. The change takes effect immediately; however, no name changes are made to comments that have already been inserted.

INSERTING VOICE COMMENTS

Occasionally, you might want to insert a brief audio comment in a file. For example, there may be a point you find it hard to explain in writing but easy to explain verbally. Or you may have a digitized quote you want to include. If you have a microphone and a sound card, Word makes it easy to add an audio comment. Even if your computer isn't audio equipped, you can insert WAV audio files you may have acquired elsewhere.

To record your own audio comment, follow these steps:

1. On the Reviewing toolbar, click Insert Voice. The Windows Sound Recorder applet opens (see Figure 26.7).
2. Click the Record button and speak.
3. When you finish speaking, click the Stop button.
4. Choose Exit & Return from the File menu.

 If the cassette icon is grayed out, preventing you from using it, see "What to Do If the Voice Comment Recorder Command Is Unavailable," in the "Troubleshooting" section of this chapter.

Figure 26.7
The Windows Sound Recorder opens whenever you want to insert an audio comment.

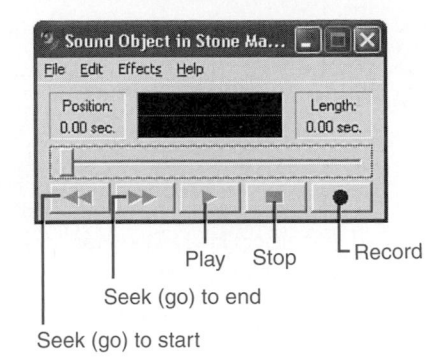

Seek (go) to end
Play Stop Record
Seek (go) to start

TIP

You can edit your sound file while Sound Recorder is open. For example, you can choose Edit, Insert File to insert another audio file into the comment. Or you can play your recorded file to the point where you made your most important point and choose Edit, Delete Before Current Position to edit out everything that came before it.

Your voice comment appears as a speaker icon both in the Reviewing pane and in a comment balloon (see Figure 26.8). You can include text along with an audio comment: Just enter the text to the right of the Speaker icon in either the Reviewing pane or the comment balloon.

To listen to an audio comment, double-click the icon. To edit the comment, right-click the icon; the shortcut menu appears. Choose Wave Sound Object, Edit, and the Sound Recorder applet opens.

CAUTION

Make your audio comments brief. Audio can dramatically enlarge the size of your files, reducing performance and straining your network.

Also keep in mind that your reviewer needs a sound card and speakers to hear your audio comments.

INSERTING INK COMMENTS

If you are running Word on a Tablet PC, you can insert handwritten comments with "ink," using the Tablet PC's stylus. (Note that this feature will not work on a regular PC even if the PC is equipped with a writing tablet.) To insert a handwritten comment, do this:

1. Click on the text or document element where you want to insert your comment. To comment on a paragraph, you can also tap at the end of the paragraph.

2. Choose Insert, Ink Comment. A comment balloon appears.

Speaker icon in Comment balloon

Figure 26.8
The Speaker icon sig-
nifies an audio com-
ment; double-click the
speaker to hear it.

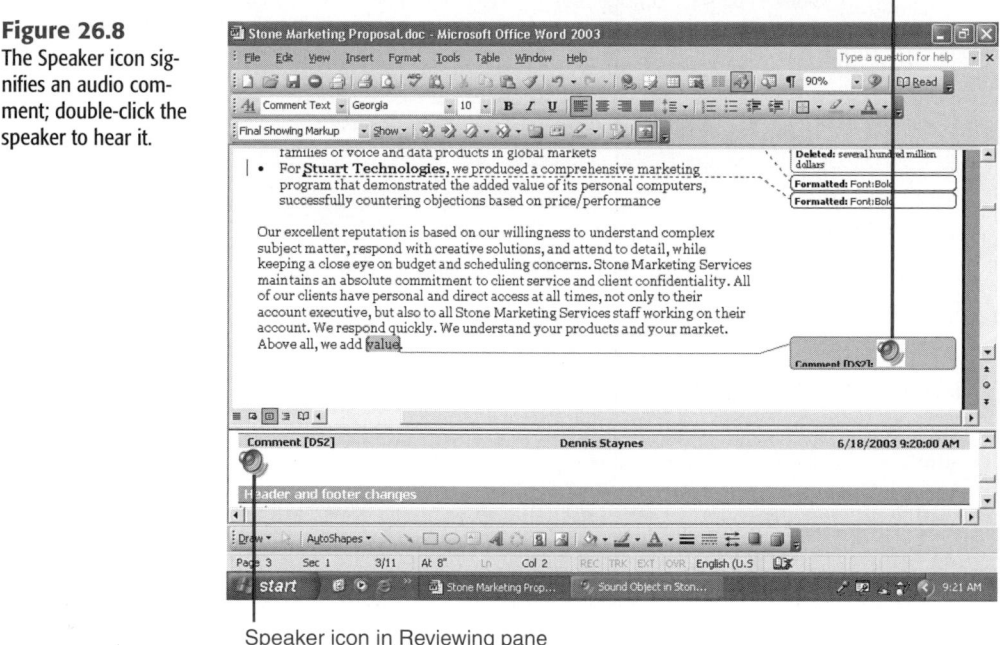

Speaker icon in Reviewing pane

3. Write your comment inside the comment balloon. If you need to erase part of your comment, tap Eraser on the Ink Comment toolbar; then drag the eraser across the ink you want to erase.

TIP

If you are working with a Tablet PC, you are not restricted to making ink comments inside comment balloons. If you switch to Print Layout or Reading Layout view, you can mark up the document just as if you were marking up a paper document.

For example, you might cross out, circle, or underline text; add marginal notes; or add handwritten text to be inserted within existing text.

Unlike Ink Comments, however, this markup cannot be reviewed one at a time through the Reviewing pane along with other typed comments.

VIEWING AND EDITING COMMENTS

So you've sent your document around for review, and you now have more comments than you know what to do with. Word makes it easier than ever to read, edit, and delete your comments. You can review all your comments systematically, in the Reviewing pane. Or you can review them more informally in the editing window.

TIP

> Before you start, consider saving a version of your file that contains all the comments as inserted by your reviewers. That way, you have a complete record of your document as it appeared before you decided what to do about each comment.
>
> To save a version, choose File, Versions and click Save Now. You'll learn more about versioning later in this chapter, in the "Using Word's Versioning Feature" section.

Reviewing Comments in the Reviewing Pane

To review comments in the Reviewing pane, make sure that the Reviewing toolbar is displayed (if necessary, choose View, Toolbars, Reviewing). Next, click the Reviewing Pane button.

By default, Word displays all the comments made by all your reviewers. In some instances, you might want to review all the comments made by a single reviewer, or walk through the document one reviewer at a time.

If your document has comments from multiple reviewers, you may find it helpful to focus on one set of reviewer's comments at a time. To view just one reviewer's comments, select Show, Reviewers on the Reviewing toolbar, and choose the name of the reviewer from the cascading menu.

→ For more information about these options, **see** "Introducing Word's Reviewing Toolbar," **p. 876**.

Whenever you click a comment within the Reviewing pane, Word displays the corresponding text in your document—making it easy to see to which text a reviewer is reacting. If a reviewer has suggested language you want to use in your document, you can select it from the Reviewing pane and copy it into your document. More likely, you will want to edit a comment before incorporating it; most of Word's editing tools are available in the Reviewing pane.

When you finish working in the Reviewing pane, click the Reviewing Pane button or press Alt+Shift+C to close it.

TIP

> If your document contains many comments, you might want to enlarge the Reviewing pane by dragging its top border higher in the editing window.

Reviewing Comments in the Document Window

You don't need to open the Reviewing pane to view and resolve comments: You can work with Word's comment balloons. To display comment balloons, first switch to Print Layout view or Web Layout view. If comments do not appear, click Show on the Reviewing toolbar and check Comments.

Comment balloons only identify comments by the reviewer's initials. However, if you hover your mouse pointer over a comment, a ScreenTip appears, showing the reviewer's full name and when he or she made the comment, as shown in Figure 26.9.

Figure 26.9
Viewing the ScreenTip associated with a comment balloon.

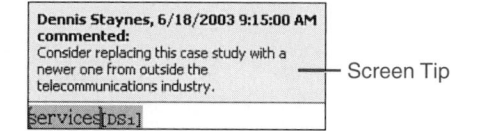

Screen Tip

T I P

> You can use Edit, Find to locate specific text in a comment, either in the Reviewing pane or in a comment balloon.

NAVIGATING AND RESPONDING TO COMMENTS

You've already seen that you can click a comment in the Reviewing pane to move to it in the document. The Reviewing toolbar offers a more systematic way to review comments. If it is not open, choose View, Toolbars, Reviewing to display the Reviewing toolbar. Then move from one comment to the next, using the Previous and Next buttons.

N O T E

> By default, clicking Previous or Next moves to either the next comment or the next tracked change (an insertion, a deletion, or a formatting change). If you do not want to review tracked changes, click the Show button; then clear the Insertions and Deletions and Formatting check boxes.

At some point as you navigate from one comment to the next, you'll find one that you think necessitates a response to the comment's author. Word allows you to respond to comments in various ways:

- You can copy text from within the comment into your document and, if necessary, edit it there.
- You can add new text to the document.
- You can reply to the comment with another comment.

Of course, you can also choose to disregard the comment.

After you've made your decision, you will generally want to delete the comment. To do so, select the comment balloon (or click on the comment's text in the Reviewing pane); then click the Reject Change/Delete Comment button on the Reviewing toolbar.

26

WORKING WITH TRACK CHANGES

Comments are invaluable when you or your reviewers want to make observations about the text in a document. But when it comes to line-by-line editing changes, Word offers a better tool: Track Changes.

With Track Changes turned on, you can edit a document normally, and Word keeps visual track of all the text you add and delete by color coding the changes based on the user making them. Then, you (or your colleague) can walk through the changes—deciding which to accept, which to reject, and which to modify.

The quickest way to start tracking changes is to double-click the TRK button in the status bar, or press Ctrl+Shift+E. If the Reviewing toolbar is open, you can also click the Track Changes button. (When Track Changes is on, you can use any of these methods to turn it off.)

No matter which procedure you use to turn on Track Changes, Word starts tracking changes in your document. By default, Track Changes behaves in the following manner:

- In all document views, new text you add appears in color, with underlining.

- If you are working in Normal view, existing text you delete remains visible but is formatted in the same color, with strikethrough applied. If you are working in Print Layout view or Web Layout view, existing text you delete is displayed in balloons at the right edge of the editing window. You can see an example in Figure 26.10.

- In all document views, new text added and then deleted by the same user doesn't appear in the document at all.

- In Print Layout view and Web Layout view, deletions are also marked with triangles pointing *down*. Formatting changes are marked with triangles pointed *up*.

- In all document views, wherever an editing change is made, a vertical line appears in the document's left margin. This makes it easier to find and focus on changes, especially in printed documents.

As discussed earlier, in the section "Introducing Word's Reviewing Toolbar," you can change several aspects of how Word displays tracked changes. For example, using the Display for Review drop-down box on the Reviewing toolbar, you can display the final document with all markup hidden. Or, using the Show button, you can display only the changes associated with a single reviewer.

As is covered later, in the section "Options for Controlling the Track Changes Feature," you can also adjust where balloons and changed lines appear, which colors are associated with changes, and other aspects of how Tracked Changes appear.

TRACKING REVISIONS IN THE BACKGROUND

If you're making extensive, line-by-line revisions, you may quickly find all these marks to be distracting; in fact, they can make a document very difficult to read. If so, you can hide them while you continue to mark the document. You therefore see how the document looks with the changes made—and Word continues to store the revisions in the background, so you can decide later whether you in fact want to keep each change.

Figure 26.10
With Track Changes turned on, new text is underlined, and deletions are marked with balloons.

Vertical line indicating change   Added text   Balloon indicating deleted text

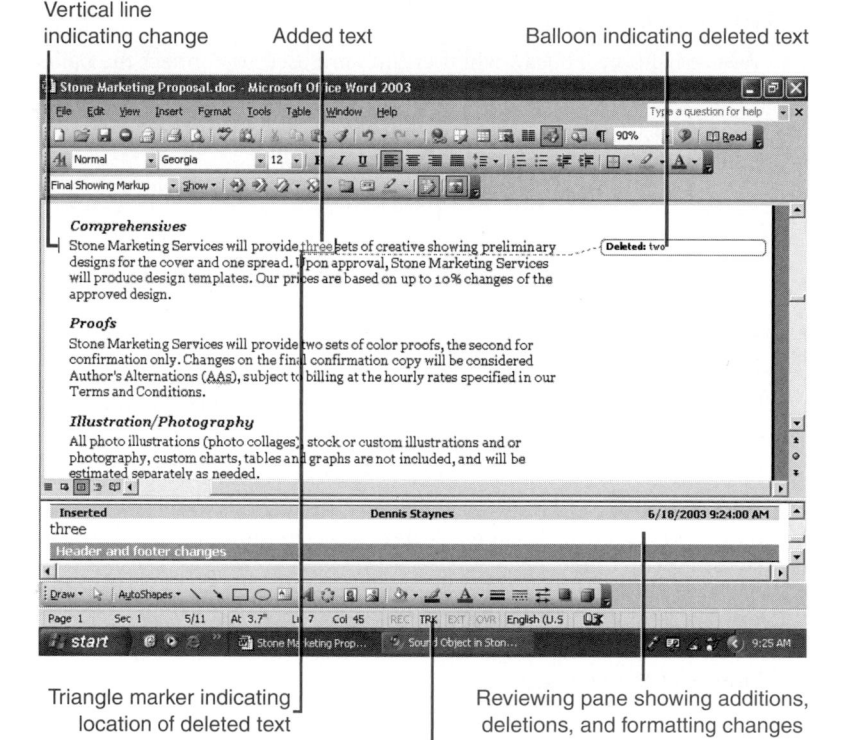

Triangle marker indicating location of deleted text

Reviewing pane showing additions, deletions, and formatting changes

TRK button on status bar indicating Word is tracking changes

Display the Reviewing toolbar if it is not already displayed. Click Show, and clear the Insertions and Deletions and Formatting check boxes. Word continues to mark all the changes in your document, but you don't see the change marks until you toggle these check boxes back on.

OPTIONS FOR CONTROLLING THE TRACK CHANGES FEATURE

You've already learned that you can control which sets of comments and tracked changes appear in your document through the Show button of the Reviewing toolbar, and that you can control whether markup appears in your document by making selections from the Display for Review drop-down box.

Using the Track Changes dialog box, you can also control several other aspects of how tracked changes and comments appear throughout your document. For example, you can control

- How insertions and formatting changes are formatted
- Which color is used to mark changes and comments
- Whether changes and comments are displayed with balloons in Print Layout view and Web Layout view
- Where balloons appear, whether lines are used to connect the balloons to text, and how large the balloons are
- Whether balloons are printed
- Whether changed lines appear in margins, and if so, where they appear and what color they are

There are many scenarios in which you might need to utilize these controls. For example:

- If your document already contains extensive underlining, you might want to distinguish change marks with double underlining.
- If you don't want to see reviewers' comments presented in different colors, you can specify the color Word will always use to display insertions, deletions, comments, and formatting changes on *your* computer. Even if you specify a single color for review on your computer, when others open your files, change and comment marks will be displayed based on the settings used by *their* computers.
- If you want to check a reviewer's formatting changes, you can specify that Word display all formatting changes in color, just as it displays Insertions, Deletions, and Comments. (By default, while Word *does* track Formatting changes, and *does* display them in balloons and in the Reviewing pane, it does *not* mark them with color in the document itself.)
- If you print interim drafts for distribution in three-hole binders, you can specify that changed lines always appear on the right margin, making them easier to see. Or, if you print documents on both sides of the paper, you can specify that changed lines always appear at the outside margin, away from the hole-punch.

To display the Track Changes dialog box, click <u>S</u>how, <u>O</u>ptions on the Reviewing Toolbar. The Track Changes dialog box appears (see Figure 26.11).

N O T E

> The new settings you establish in the Track Changes tab are global and apply not only to the current document but also to any others you open and use while these settings are in place.

The following sections cover the various features and controls found in this dialog box.

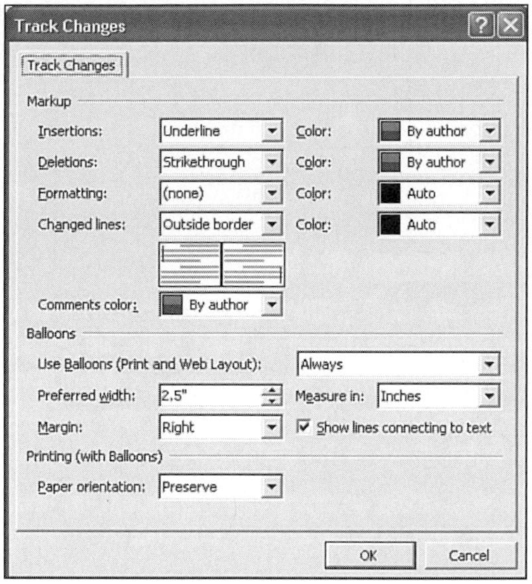

Figure 26.11
Setting options for how tracked changes appear.

CONTROLLING HOW INSERTED TRACKED CHANGES ARE FORMATTED

By default, when Word's Track Changes feature is turned on and markup is displayed, all tracked changes are shown as underlined text. To change the formatting Word applies to inserted text, choose different formatting from the Insertions drop-down box. You can instruct Word to format inserted text in bold, in italics, with double underline, or with color only. You can also specify (none)—in which case Word won't add any marks to indicate inserted text.

SPECIFYING HOW DELETED TRACKED CHANGES ARE FORMATTED

For the first time, Word 2003 also lets you control the appearance of text you delete while Tracked Changes is turned on.

By default, when Word's Track Changes feature is turned on and markup is displayed, all deleted tracked changes are shown as strikethrough text. To change the formatting Word applies to inserted text, choose different formatting from the Deletions drop-down box. You can instruct Word to format inserted text in bold, in italics, with underline or double underline, with color, as hidden text, or with either of the following symbols: ^ or #. You can also specify (none)—in which case Word won't add any marks to indicate deleted text.

CONTROLLING HOW WORD ASSIGNS COLORS TO REVIEWERS

By default, Word assigns colors to reviewers automatically. If Word runs out of colors, two reviewers have to share a color.

This system usually works well. However, you might want to permanently assign colors to individual members of your team so that you can tell at a glance who made each revision—

especially if you're looking at a document printed on a color printer. Although Word can't assign a specific color to a specific reviewer, it can assign a specific color for all changes tracked on your computer.

In the Track Changes dialog box, select the Color drop-down box and choose a color. Or, if you prefer that reviewed text appear in the same color that Word uses by default for other text in the document, choose Auto. This change is saved when you click OK.

SPECIFYING HOW FORMATTING CHANGES ARE MARKED

Word's Track Changes feature can track formatting changes as well as content changes. When you make a character formatting change to bold, italic, or underline, or a paragraph formatting change to bullets or numbering, Word inserts a vertical line in the outer margin, just as it would if you made a text change. In Print Layout view and Web Layout view, Word also displays a small down arrow at the point where the formatted change was made.

If you change the font, font size, color, or paragraph alignment, no vertical line appears. Even more strangely, a border applied to characters is shown as a change, whereas a border applied to a paragraph is not.

By default, Word does not add formatting (such as underlines) to indicate where a formatting change has been made. The rationale is simple: Users may find it hard to tell which formatting has been applied by the reviewer and which was added by Word to indicate the presence of a change. Word does, however, describe the formatting change in a Track Changes balloon.

Some users prefer to mark formatting changes with underlines or other formatting. To do so, return to the Track Changes dialog box and click the Formatting drop-down button. Using this list, you can specify that formatting changes be marked in boldface, italics, underline, double-underline, or strikethrough, or with color only.

You can also specify which color to mark formatting changes with. Click the Color drop-down box to the right of the Formatting drop-down box, and select the color you want to use.

SPECIFYING THE APPEARANCE OF CHANGED LINES

As you've learned, Word inserts a black vertical line at the outside border of any line of text that contains a tracked change. This is called a *changed line*. To control changed lines using the Track Changes dialog box, follow these steps:

1. From the Changed Lines drop-down box, choose the location where you want changed lines to appear: Outside Border, Left Border, or Right Border. If you choose None, no changed lines appear in your document.
2. To use a different color for changed lines instead of black, select it from the Comments Color: drop-down box. By default, Word uses a different color for each author.
3. Click OK.

SPECIFYING THE PRESENCE AND APPEARANCE OF BALLOONS

By default, Word marks comments and tracked changes with balloons that appear in Print Layout, Web Layout, and Reading Layout views. You can control several aspects of how these balloons appear. Use the Track Changes dialog box to make the changes you want:

- Choose when you want to see balloons through the Use Balloons drop-down box. If you always want to see them in Print, Web, and Reading Layout views, choose Always (the default setting). If you never want to see them, choose Never. If you want to see them only for comments and formatting, but not for other changes, choose Only for Comments/Formatting.

- By default, balloons are formatted as 2.5" wide; if necessary, Word automatically adjusts document margins to accommodate this width. To change the width of your balloons, set a new width using the Preferred Width scroll box. For example, if you have relatively few changes and you intend to print your document with wide margins, you may want your changes to appear narrower but deeper (see Figure 26.12).

Figure 26.12
Balloons adjusted to a narrower width (1.25") instead of 2.5").

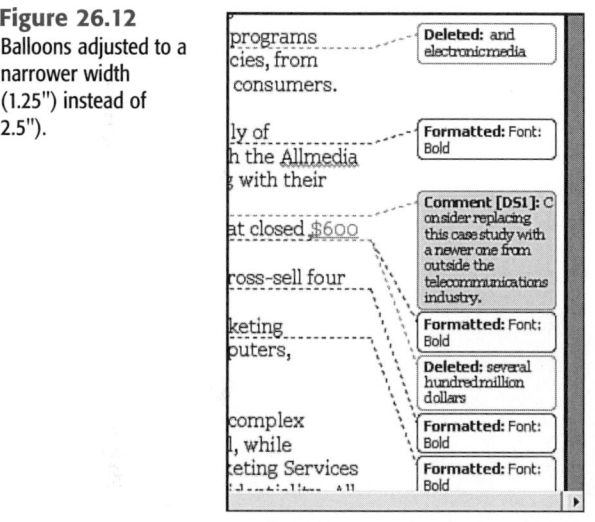

- By default, balloons always appear in the right margin. If you prefer to place them in the left margin, choose Left from the Margin drop-down box. (Word offers no option for placing balloons in inner or outer margins, as might be useful in booklets.)

- By default, balloons are always connected to the location in the document where the change or comment was made, via a dotted line. If you don't want the dotted line to appear, clear the Show Lines Connecting to Text check box.

- By default, Word preserves your current paper orientation (portrait or landscape) when you print a draft containing balloons. Word does so even if it has narrowed your margins to accommodate the balloons. If you are reviewing drafts, you might want to switch to landscape mode to make more room for the balloons (and for handwritten comments on hard copy). To switch to landscape, choose Force Landscape from the Paper Orientation drop-down box. If you want to give Word the *option* of switching to landscape if that will make the document more readable, choose Auto.

LIMITING THE CHANGES REVIEWERS CAN MAKE IN YOUR DOCUMENT

As you've learned, one of the main benefits of Word's Comments feature is that it prevents reviewers from cluttering up a document with text that must simply be deleted later. You can go beyond inviting reviewers to use Word's Comments feature. You can set up your document so that they can do nothing but make comments. Follow these steps:

1. Choose Tools, Protect Document. The Protect Document task pane opens (see Figure 26.13).

Figure 26.13
Using the Protect Document dialog box, you can prevent reviewers from doing anything except making comments.

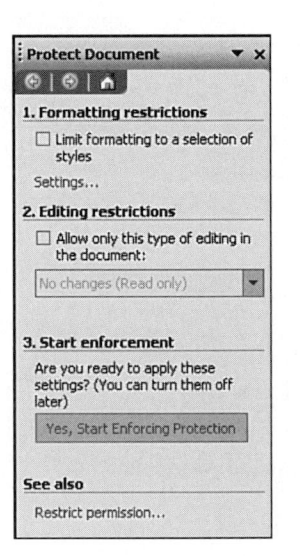

2. Check the Allow Only This Type of Editing in the Document check box. New options appear in the Protect Document check box (see Figure 26.14).

3. Choose Comments from the drop-down box.

> **TIP**
> To limit reviewers to making changes using Word's Tracked Changes feature, choose Tracked Changes instead.
>
> To limit reviewers to filling in Word forms, choose Filling in Forms instead.

Figure 26.14
When you begin setting editing restrictions, new options appear.

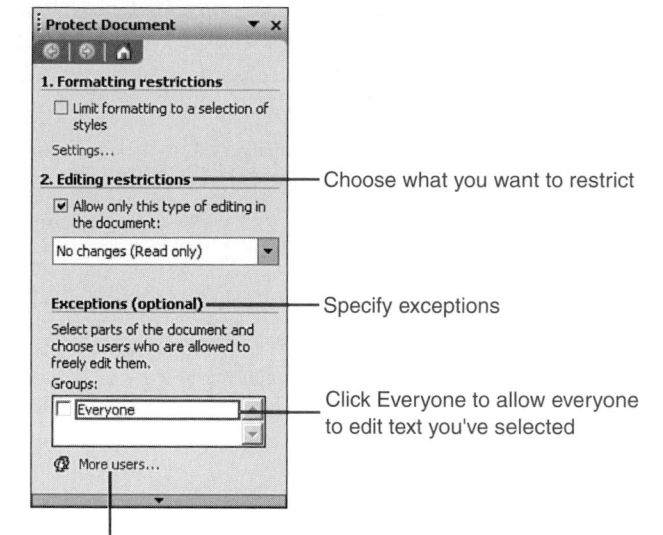

Choose what you want to restrict

Specify exceptions

Click Everyone to allow everyone to edit text you've selected

Click More Users to choose individual users who will be permitted to edit text you've selected

4. Click Yes, Start Enforcing Protection. (You may have to scroll down inside the task pane to see this option.) The Start Enforcing Protection dialog box appears (see Figure 26.15).

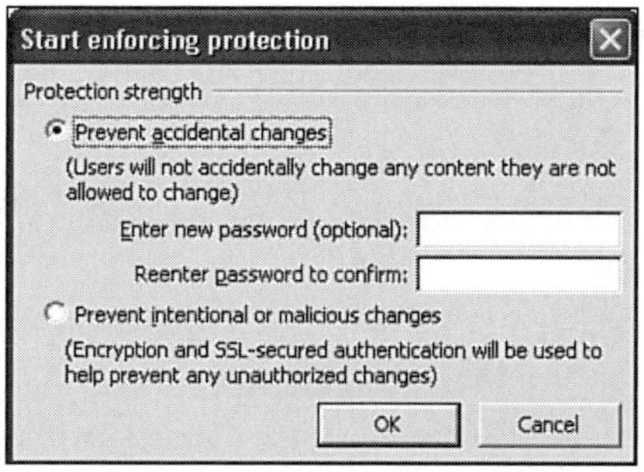

Figure 26.15
Using the Start Enforcing Protection dialog box, you can control the level of protection in your document.

26

5. Choose which level of document protection you want:

   • If you choose Prevent Accidental Changes, you can assign a password to your document. However, anyone who knows the password can remove it—and therefore remove the protection. Moreover, the document is not encrypted, so it may be at least partly readable in text editors such as Notepad. In fact, reviewers who can view your document in order to comment on it can *also* copy all of your document's text, images, and fields into another document that has no protection at all.

- If, on the other hand, you choose Prevent Intentional or Malicious Changes, the document will be encrypted. Moreover, Word will permit users to remove document protection only if they have been authenticated via an SSL-secured authentication system, such as Microsoft Active Directory.

6. If you chose Prevent Accidental Changes, enter a password in the Enter New Password (Optional) dialog box; then reenter the password in the Reenter Password to Confirm dialog box.

> **NOTE**
>
> If you do not use a password, when a reviewer opens the document he or she will still be restricted to making comments only. However, choosing Tools, Unprotect Document will unlock the document for any kind of editing.

7. Click OK. The protection is applied.

GAINING FINER CONTROL OVER EDITING RESTRICTIONS

Word allows you to select specific areas of your document and specify which users can freely edit those areas of the document. By doing so, you can restrict certain users to commenting on parts of the document you don't want them to edit. Meanwhile, you can specify individuals who will be permitted to edit as well as comment on the entire document.

To restrict different users in different ways, follow these steps:

1. Choose Tools, Protect Document. The Protect Document task pane appears.
2. Click the Allow Only This Type of Editing in the Document check box.
3. Choose Comments from the drop-down box.
4. In the document, select a block of text you want some or all document reviewers to be able to edit without restriction.
5. If you want everyone to be able to edit that text, check the Everyone check box in the Groups box (refer to Figure 26.15). If you want only some users to be able to edit the text you selected, click More Users. The Add Users dialog box opens (see Figure 26.16).

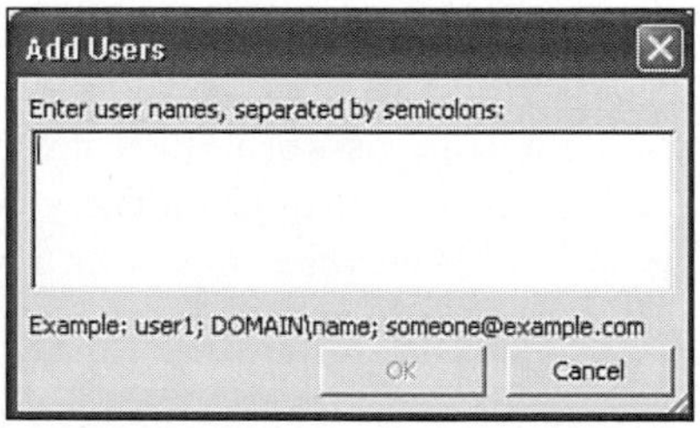

Figure 26.16
Adding specific users who will be permitted to edit the text you selected.

Add Users

Enter user names, separated by semicolons:

Example: user1; DOMAIN\name; someone@example.com

OK   Cancel

6. Enter user names corresponding to the users you want to give editing permission to. You can enter names by email address or Microsoft Windows user account:
   - If you intend to use Word 2003's strongest available protection (Prevent Intentional or Malicious Changes), use email addresses.
   - If you intend to use weaker password protection (Prevent Accidental Changes), use Microsoft Windows user accounts.

7. Click OK.

8. To give another individual (or individuals) editing rights to a different block of text, select the text, and repeat steps 5–7.

9. In the Protect Document task pane, click Start Enforcing Protection. (You may have to scroll down in the task pane to see this option.

10. The Start Enforcing Protection dialog box opens. Choose the form of document protection you want: Prevent Accidental Changes or the stronger Prevent Intentional or Malicious Changes.

→ For more information about these options, **see** "Limiting the Changes Reviewers Can Make in Your Document," **p. 892**.

11. If you chose Prevent Accidental Changes, enter a password in the Enter New Password (Optional) dialog box; then reenter the password in the Reenter Password to Confirm dialog box.

12. Click OK. The protection is applied.

WORKING WITH DOCUMENTS THAT HAVE BEEN RESTRICTED

If you open a document that has been restricted to comments (or to tracked changes or fill-in forms), the Protect Document dialog box will appear when you attempt to make an unauthorized edit (see Figure 26.17).

By default, the areas of text you are permitted to edit are highlighted in yellow and bracketed with brown brackets. You now have several options for working with the document:

- To select the next area of text you are currently permitted to edit, click Find Next Region I Can Edit.

- To select all the areas of text you are currently permitted to edit, click Show All Regions I Can Edit.

- To toggle highlighting on and off, check or clear the Highlight the Regions I Can Edit check box.

- To turn off protection altogether, click Stop Protection.

If the document was protected using Prevent Accidental Changes, and no password was used, the protection will be turned off. If a password was used, the Unprotect Document dialog box will appear (see Figure 26.18). Enter the password, and click OK.

26

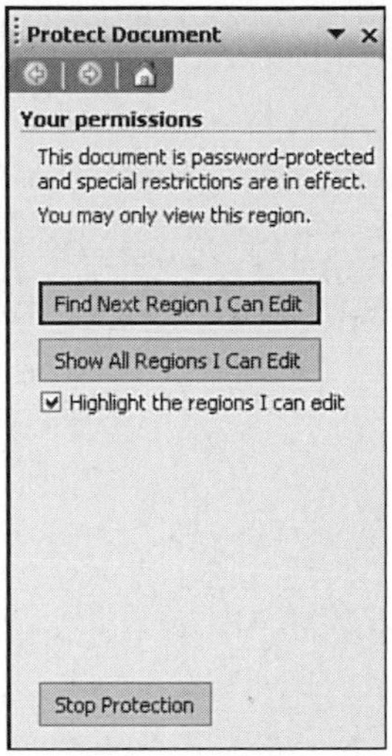

Figure 26.17
If you have been restricted from editing part or all of a document, the Protect Document task pane tells you so.

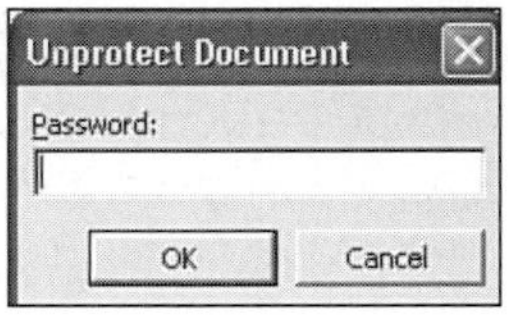

Figure 26.18
Enter your password in the Unprotect Document dialog box to stop enforcing protection.

PRINTING DOCUMENTS WITH MARKUP

By default, when you print a document containing markup, the markup is shown—balloons, underlining, and all. You can change this setting in two ways.

You can change the *version* of the document that is printed, by choosing a different version from the Display for Review drop-down box on the Reviewing toolbar. For example, if you want to print the original document with markup superimposed on it, you can choose Original with Markup. If you want to print the final document with markup indicating differences from the original, you can choose Final with Markup.

Alternatively, you can change what prints by choosing File, Print and choosing another option from the Print What drop-down box. The default setting, Document Showing Markup, prints the document with markup superimposed on it:

- If you prefer to print the final document as it would appear if all markup was accepted, choose Document.

- If you want to print a list of markup, as it appears in the Reviewing pane, choose List of Markup.

KEEPING TRACK OF CHANGES AMONG MULTIPLE DOCUMENTS

Imagine that you've asked someone to review a document, but you forgot to turn on Track Changes first. Have you forever lost the chance to see where changes were made and systematically resolve them? Not necessarily.

If you have a copy of the document in its original form (before the reviewer edited it), you can use Word's Compare and Merge Documents feature. When you're finished, you have a document that includes change marks wherever additions, deletions, and, optionally, formatting changes were made—just as if the edits were made with Track Changes enabled. Follow these steps:

1. Open the document where you want the change marks to appear.
2. Choose <u>T</u>ools, Compare and Merge <u>D</u>ocuments. The Compare and Merge Documents dialog box opens (see Figure 26.19).

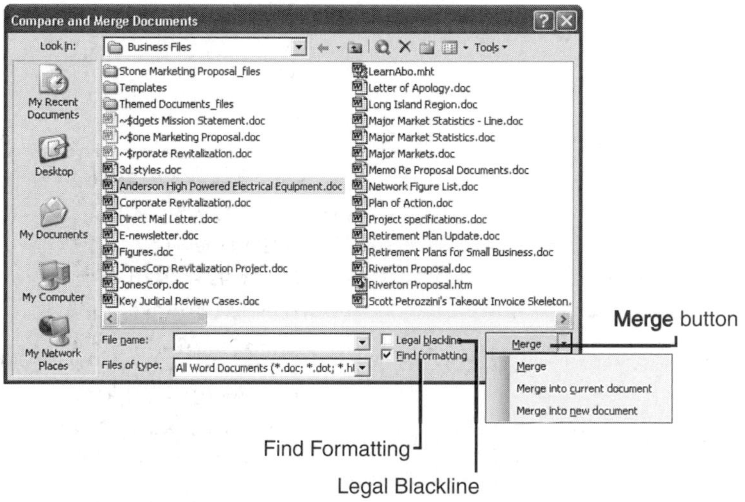

Figure 26.19
The Compare and Merge Documents dialog box.

Merge button

Find Formatting

Legal Blackline

26

3. Browse to and select the file you want to compare with the one you already have open.
4. By default, Word finds and tracks differences in formatting between two documents. If you don't want Word to do this, clear the <u>F</u>ind Formatting check box.
5. Choose where you want the differences between the documents to be displayed:
    - If you want the differences to be displayed in the "target" document—the one you selected through the Compare and Merge Documents dialog box—click Merge.
    - If you want the differences to be displayed in the "current" document—the one you opened before you selected a document to compare it with—click the down arrow next to the <u>M</u>erge button and choose Merge into <u>C</u>urrent Document.

- If you want the differences to be displayed in a brand-new document, click the down arrow next to the Merge button and choose Merge into New Document.

After you have merged the documents, all differences between them appear in purple as tracked changes. Balloons appear in Print Layout view and Web Layout view to describe the differences in more detail.

> **NOTE**
>
> To improve the accuracy of document comparison, Word inserts a hidden random number to help keep track of related documents. These random numbers could be used to identify related documents and potentially identify their authors.
>
> If you don't want these random numbers stored in your document, choose Tools, Options, Security; then clear the Store Random Number to Improve Merge Accuracy check box. Clearing this check box may reduce the accuracy of document comparisons.

MERGING REVISIONS FROM SEVERAL REVIEWERS INTO A SINGLE DOCUMENT

You've already seen one scenario for reviewing a document: You send a file to one reviewer who makes changes and then forwards it to another reviewer who makes changes that are recorded in a different color, and so on. When everyone is finished, the changes are returned to you in one rainbow-colored document.

In today's fast-paced business world, however, you may not have time to wait for each person to review a document consecutively. You may have to send a separate copy of the document to each reviewer and receive separate marked-up copies in return. You can use Word's Compare and Merge Documents feature to integrate all those changes into a single document, where you can resolve them all at once in an organized fashion.

Follow these steps to merge revisions from several documents into a document you already have open:

1. Choose Tools, Compare and Merge Documents. The Compare and Merge Documents dialog box opens (refer to Figure 26.19).
2. Browse to select the document you want to merge.
3. Click the down arrow next to Merge; then click Merge into Current Document.
4. Repeat steps 1–3 for each additional document with revisions you want to incorporate.

USING WORD'S LEGAL BLACKLINE FEATURE TO COMPARE DOCUMENTS

As you've just seen, Word's standard Compare and Merge Documents feature can be used to merge multiple sets of changes into a single document for review. Often, lawyers who need to review document changes have a slightly different problem: They must clearly see *only the differences between two documents*.

For this purpose, Word also provides a *Legal Blackline* feature. Unlike standard Compare and Merge, Legal Blackline treats requested changes as if they had been accepted. Unlike

Word's standard Compare and Merge Documents feature, Legal Blackline always creates a new document marking the differences between the two source documents.

To use Legal Blackline, carry out these instructions:

1. Choose Tools, Compare and Merge Documents. The Compare and Merge Documents dialog box opens.

2. Browse to select the document you want to merge.

3. Check the Legal Blackline check box. The Merge button changes to a Compare button.

4. Click Compare.

5. If tracked changes are present in either document you are comparing, Word displays a dialog box indicating that it will consider the tracked changes to be accepted for the purposes of the document comparison. Click Yes to continue comparing the documents.

6. Word displays a new document containing balloons marking every difference between the two documents you compared.

COMPARING DOCUMENTS SIDE BY SIDE

Before or after you merge two documents, you may want to compare them side by side. Word 2003 makes this easy:

1. Open both documents, and make sure one of them is displayed.

2. Choose Window, Compare Side by Side. The Compare Side by Side dialog box opens (see Figure 26.20).

Figure 26.20
The Compare Side by Side dialog box.

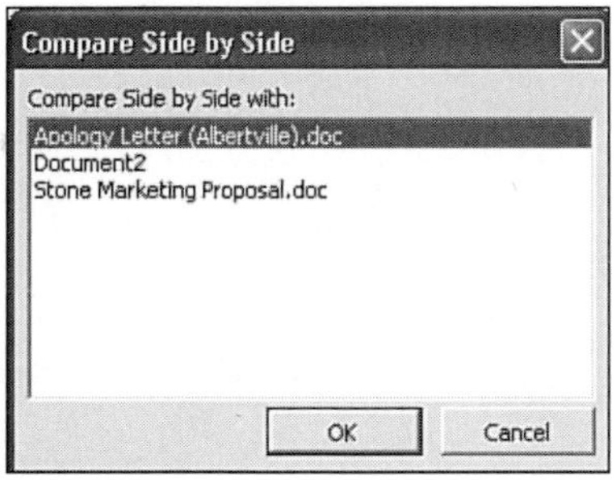

3. Choose the document you want to view alongside the document that is already displayed.

4. Click OK.

Both documents now appear side by side (see Figure 26.21). You can control them from the Compare Side by Side toolbar.

By default, when you scroll in one document, the other document automatically scrolls as well. Because the two documents may not be displayed at the same location in the document, this can be annoying. To prevent synchronous scrolling, click the Synchronous Scrolling button on the Compare Side by Side toolbar.

Figure 26.21
Documents displayed side by side.

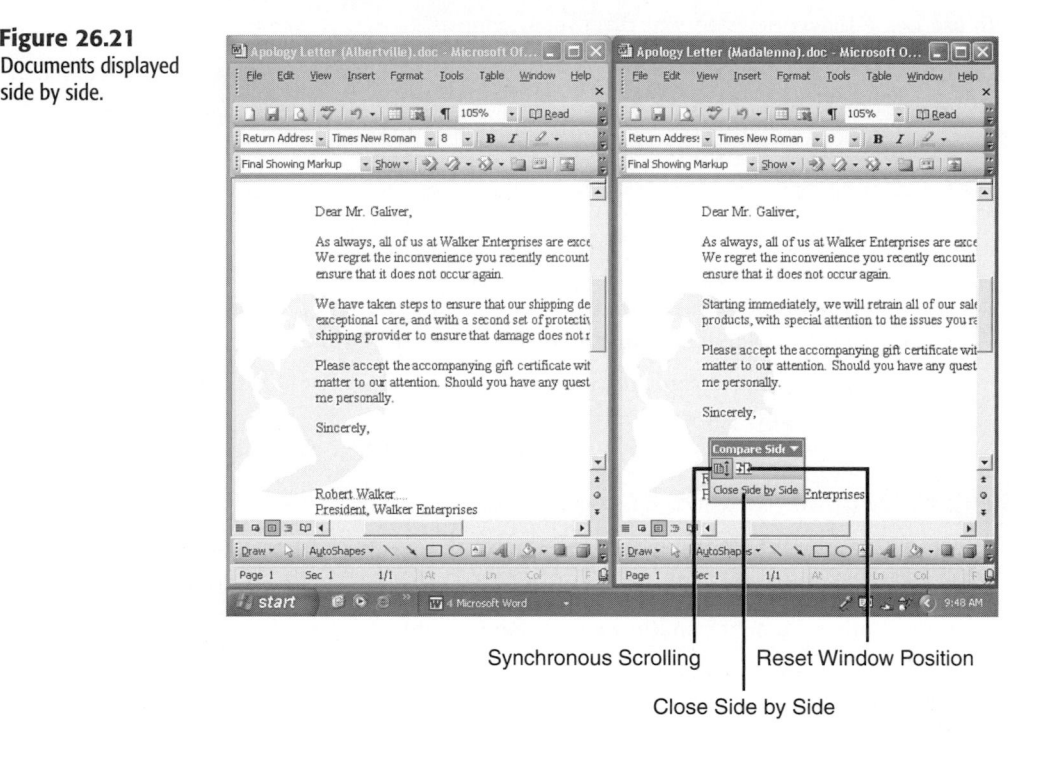

Synchronous Scrolling   Reset Window Position

Close Side by Side

You might occasionally resize one or both of the windows to see more or less of a single document. To return the documents to their original size—each taking up half of the available editing space—click Reset Window Position.

When you're finished viewing the two documents side by side, click Close Side by Side.

TIP

> You may find it easier to review the contents of both documents if you use Word's option to wrap text to the width of a window. Choose Tools, Options, View; then check the Wrap to Window check box, and click OK.

RESOLVING PROPOSED CHANGES

No matter how you get revision marks and comments into your document, the real beauty of Word's Track Changes feature comes later, when you see how easy it is to resolve the changes your reviewers have proposed.

Word provides a unified tool for resolving both tracked changes and comments: the Reviewing toolbar (choose View, Toolbars and check Reviewing (see Figure 26.22).

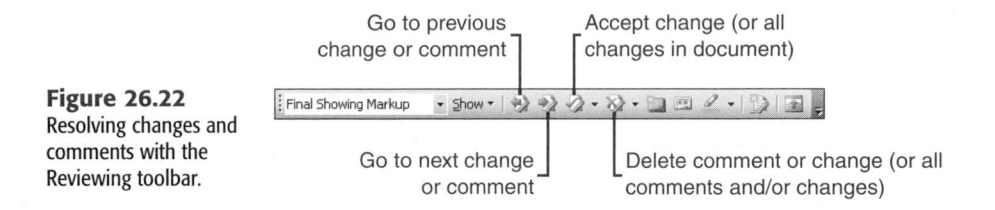

Figure 26.22
Resolving changes and comments with the Reviewing toolbar.

Go to previous change or comment

Accept change (or all changes in document)

Go to next change or comment

Delete comment or change (or all comments and/or changes)

RESOLVING CHANGES AND COMMENTS

Before you start resolving changes, you might want to press Ctrl+Home to move to the beginning of the document. After you've done so, click Next on the Reviewing toolbar, and Word selects the next tracked change or comment in the document. Word selects the tracked change or comment.

To accept a tracked change, click the Accept Change button.

To reject a tracked change or delete a comment, click the Reject Change/Delete Comment button.

> **NOTE**
>
> If you only want to resolve tracked changes and you don't want to review comments, click Show; then clear the Comments check box.

> **TIP**
>
> You don't have to resolve all your changes or comments at the same time; you can leave some unresolved until you get more information or speak to the right person. You might want to insert a comment reminding yourself why a change is still unresolved.
>
> You can also superimpose further edits on top of tracked changes, if you need to modify the changes a reviewer has made.

You can always undo a change you just accepted, rejected, or edited by clicking the Undo button on the Standard toolbar.

ACCEPTING OR REJECTING ALL CHANGES AT THE SAME TIME

It's unlikely, but you may occasionally be able to resolve all your revisions at the same time. Perhaps you (or your boss) will make an executive decision to disregard all the wrong-headed comments provided by someone in another department.

To reject all changes in a document, click the down arrow next to the Reject Changes/Delete Comments button on the Reviewing toolbar; then choose Reject All Changes in Document. To delete all comments in the document, click the down arrow to the right of the Reject Changes/Delete Comments button; then choose Delete All Comments in Document.

Conversely, on rare occasions, you may want to accept all the comments that have been made about your document, by all reviewers. Or, perhaps, only one individual has reviewed the document, but he or she is so important that you have no choice but to accept his or her comments. Click the down arrow next to Accept All; then choose Accept All Changes in Document. All the tracked changes slip seamlessly into your document as if they'd been there all along.

USING WORD'S VERSIONING FEATURE

Many Word users are in the habit of using File, Save As to save a new copy of every new draft they create. By doing so, they not only make sure of having a recent backup in the event of disaster, but also create an audit trail that helps identify when a critical change was made in case it is questioned later.

Nothing has changed the need for storing backups, but Word now has a more convenient, reliable way of providing that audit trail. You can now store each new version of your document in the same file so that older versions can't get easily lost, misplaced, or confused with the current version.

Follow these steps to save a new version of an existing file:

1. Choose File, Versions.
2. The Versions dialog box opens.
3. Click Save Now. The Save Version dialog box opens (see Figure 26.23).

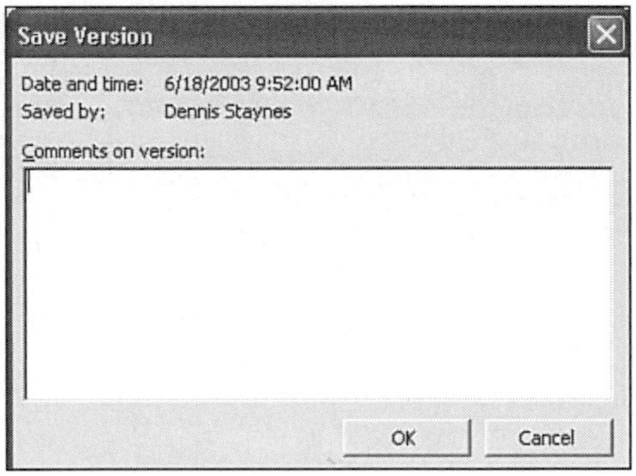

Figure 26.23
In the Save Version dialog box, enter detailed comments about why this draft was created and/or whose comments it reflects.

26

Save Version

Date and time: 6/18/2003 9:52:00 AM
Saved by: Dennis Staynes

Comments on version:

OK   Cancel

4. Enter comments on the version, such as whose changes it reflects, or why the new version was created. (Don't worry about entering the current date and time, or your own name—Word has already done that for you.)
5. Click OK. Word saves a new version of the document in the same file as the original.

CAUTION

> If you save a file containing multiple versions using a format other than the current Word format, the older versions will be lost. If you need to save the current version in an older format, first use File, Save As to make a copy of the file; then resave the copy in the older format you need. All the versions will, of course, remain in your original file.

NOTE

> In a file containing multiple versions, Word's document statistics apply to the current version only.

WORKING WITH MULTIPLE VERSIONS OF A FILE

After you've created one or more additional versions of a file, a Versions icon appears at the far right of the status bar (see Figure 26.24).

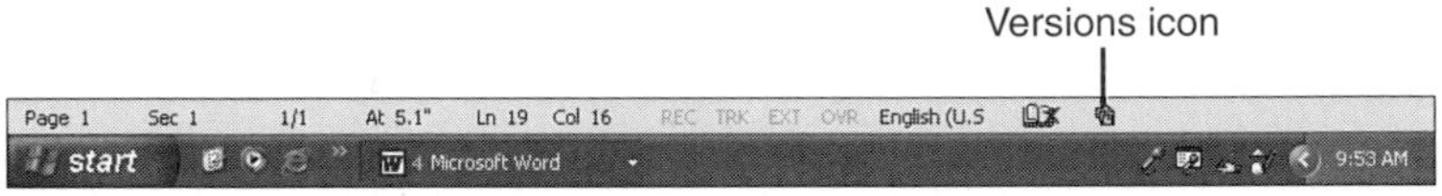

Figure 26.24
The Versions icon in the status bar indicates that a file contains multiple versions.

Versions icon

To work with your versions, you can double-click this icon, or choose File, Versions. This reopens the Versions dialog box. In Figure 26.25, you can see how this dialog box looks after multiple versions of a document have been created.

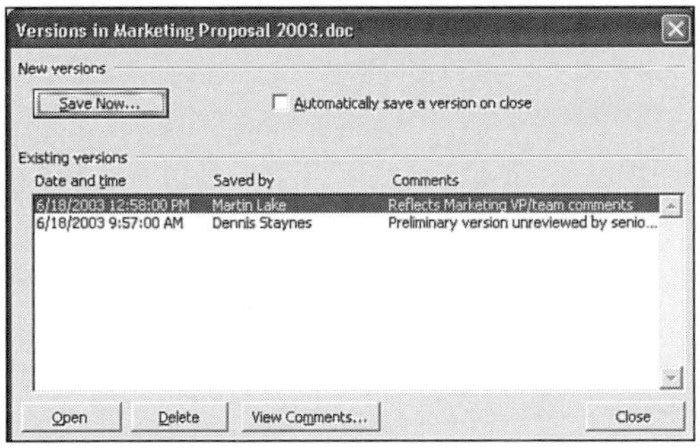

Figure 26.25
The Versions dialog box provides several new options after you have versions from which to choose.

26

To open any version, select it and click Open. To delete an old version, select it and click Delete; Word asks you to confirm the deletion and reminds you that you can't undo this action.

TIP

If you're planning to send a document out for review, you may want to delete all old versions to make sure that reviewers see only the current one. (Or, better yet, use File, Save As to create a new copy of the file and then delete the unwanted versions from the copy only.)

In the Versions dialog box, you can already see the first few words of comments about the file; if you want to see more, click View Comments. You can't edit comments made about a version that was saved previously; the comments are read-only.

SAVING A VERSION AS A SEPARATE FILE

When you open an older version of a file, Word displays the document in a separate editing window, which splits the screen as shown in Figure 26.26. Notice that the version you opened has a save date in its title bar—a gentle reminder that you're not working with the current version.

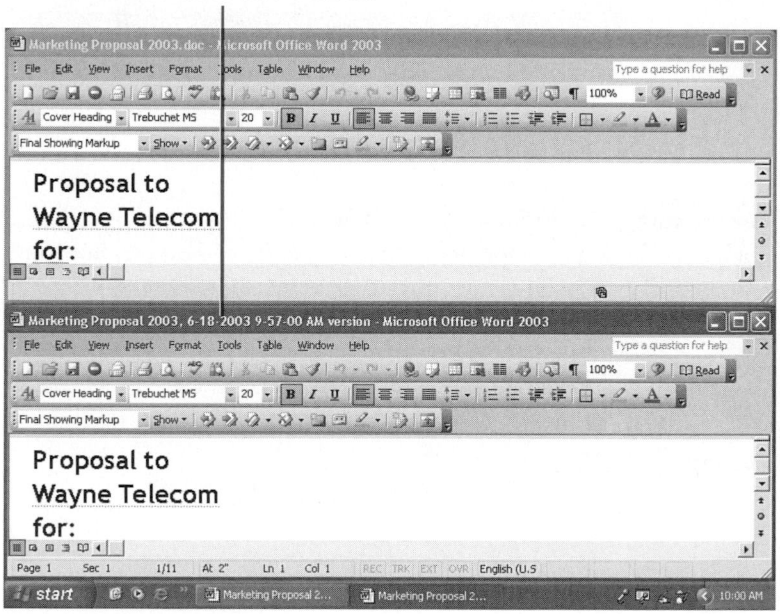

Version's creation date in title bar

Figure 26.26
If you open an older version, Word displays a new editing window and displays the version's creation date in the title bar.

If you make changes to the older version, Word won't save it in the same file any longer. When you choose Save, Word displays the Save As dialog box and shows the filename as it appears in the title bar with the version creation date. When you click Save, you get a new file containing only the version you edited.

TIP

> Unfortunately, you can't use Word's Compare Documents feature to compare two versions of a document within the same file. You can work around this limitation, however, by saving each version you want to compare as a separate file and then choosing Tools, Compare and Merge Documents.

→ For more information about comparing two documents, **see** "Keeping Track of Changes Among Multiple Documents," **p. 897**.

Automatically Saving New Versions

You may want to save a "snapshot" of your document each time you (or another editor or reviewer) finishes working with it. To do so choose File, Versions, and in the Versions dialog box, check the Automatically Save a Version on Close check box.

Versioning and Web Pages

Versioning is not available if you are editing a Web page. In addition, if you save an existing file in HTML (Web page) format, only the current version appears in the new HTML file. Word warns you that the older versions will be lost and offers to create a backup copy. Click Continue to save the backup copy and create a new Web file with only the current version.

Streamlining the Review Process with Microsoft Outlook

From within Word, you can forward a document for review—and if your colleague is using Word and Outlook, he or she can review it immediately on opening it.

To send a document for review, choose File, Send to, Mail Recipient (for Review). Word displays an Outlook message window, as shown in Figure 26.27; the attachment is listed in the Attach line. You can add the email addresses of your reviewer or reviewers in the To and Cc lines.

A follow-up message flag is automatically included with the message, indicating that the item needs to be reviewed, but specifying no due date or time. To set the due time or date, click the Message Flag button. The Flag for Follow Up dialog box appears (see Figure 26.28). Set a new date and time for follow-up in the Due By drop-down boxes, and click OK.

By default, Word sends a separate copy of your attachment to every email recipient. However, if you are using SharePoint Team Services or Microsoft SharePoint Portal Server with Word 2003, you also have the option of automatically creating a shared Document Workspace where you and your colleagues can work on a shared copy. To create a shared attachment, click Attachment Options. The Attachment Options task pane appears (see Figure 26.29).

26

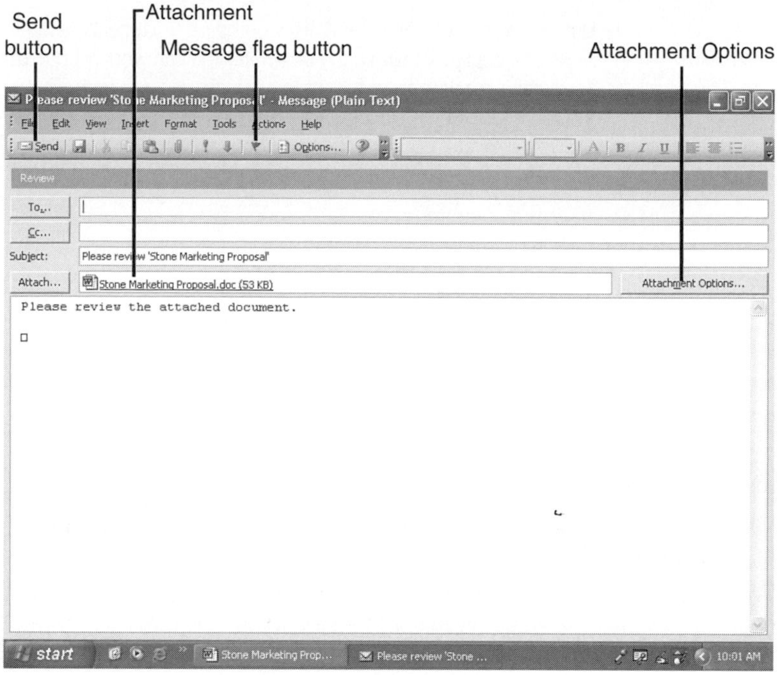

Figure 26.27
Word can include a copy of your document in an Outlook email message.

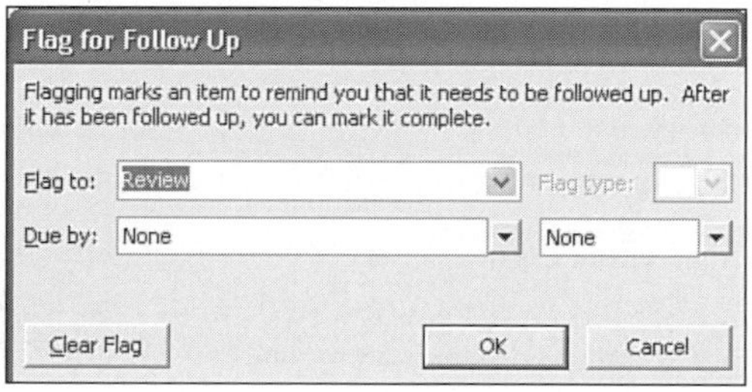

Figure 26.28
Controlling how Outlook flags a reviewed item for follow-up.

Click Shared Attachments. Next, type a URL corresponding to the location where you want the Document Workspace to be created.

When you're ready to send the message, click Send (refer to Figure 26.27).

When a recipient receives the message, he or she can double-click on the file attachment icon to open the file in Word, with the Reviewing toolbar already displayed. When reviewers return files to you, those files automatically prompt you to merge changes using the tools on the reviewing toolbar.

For files that have been sent for review, a new button appears on the Reviewing toolbar: End Review (see Figure 26.30). When you've finished merging changes from reviewers, click End Review to end the review cycle. After you've done this, Word will no longer prompt you to merge changes from reviewers.

Figure 26.29
The Attachment
Options task pane.

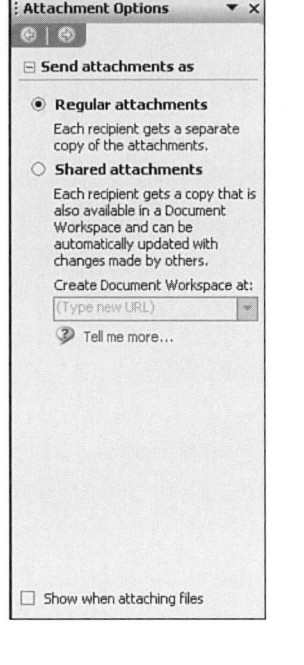

Figure 26.30
You can click End
Review to end a
reviewing cycle.

End Review button

TROUBLESHOOTING

WHAT TO DO IF THE VOICE COMMENT RECORDER COMMAND IS UNAVAILABLE

Check to make sure that your computer has a sound card and that the sound card is configured properly. You can check on this by clicking Start, Settings, Control Panel; double-
clicking on the System applet; and clicking the Device Manager tab. Look to see whether a
sound card is listed. If it has an exclamation point next to it, it is not configured properly;
try reinstalling the driver or checking for resource conflicts.

WHAT TO DO IF WORD WON'T LET YOU ACCEPT OR REJECT CHANGES

Most likely, your document is still protected for tracked changes. If so, choose Tools,
Unprotect Document. If you're asked for a password, enter it. If you don't have the password, you may not be authorized to accept or reject changes.

WHAT TO DO IF "AUTHOR" OR A GENERIC IDENTIFIER APPEARS INSTEAD OF A REVIEWER'S NAME

If Word displays Author in place of a reviewer's name in the ScreenTip or Reviewing pane item associated with a tracked change or comment, the reviewer has chosen to eliminate personal information from his or her files when they are saved. To store names, the reviewer must reenable the storing of personal information, like this:

1. Choose Tools, Options, and click the Security tab.
2. Clear the Remove Personal Information from This File on Save check box, and click OK.

If a generic identifier is present, the reviewer may not have set his or her name at all. To set a name, or update an erroneous one, follow these steps:

1. Choose Tools, Options, and click the User Information tab.
2. Enter a name in the Name text box, and initials in the Initials text box; then click OK.

WHAT TO DO IF YOU CAN'T SEE SOME CHANGES YOU'RE SURE EXIST

In Word it's easy to inadvertently hide some changes you intend to review. To make sure that all comments and tracked changes are visible, do the following:

1. Display the Reviewing Toolbar, and click Show.
2. Make sure that Comments, Insertions and Deletions, and Formatting are all checked.
3. Click Reviewers, and make sure that All Reviewers is checked.
4. If there are too many balloons displayed in Print Layout view or Web Layout view to read them all, review your comments in the Reviewing pane. On the Reviewing Toolbar, click Show, Reviewing Pane.
5. Make sure you aren't displaying the file in its Original form. On the Reviewing toolbar, click the Display for Review drop-down box, and choose another option—typically, Final Showing Markup or Original Showing Markup.
6. Certain changes may not be visible in Normal view; switch to Print Layout view or Web Layout view.

WHAT TO DO IF YOU'VE MERGED CHANGES INTO THE WRONG DOCUMENT

In Word you can merge changes into your original document, the "target" document you selected for comparison, or a new document. If you choose the wrong document, click Undo to undo the changes. If you've inadvertently merged to a new document, you can close that document without saving it.

NOTE

> If you don't realize the problem immediately, keep clicking Undo. Word can store 100 or more changes, and the document merge counts as only one change.

CHAPTER 27

ONLINE DOCUMENT COLLABORATION USING SHAREPOINT TEAM SERVICES

In this chapter

WHAT IS SHAREPOINT?

If you've been doing any reading about Microsoft's Windows Server 2003, you've probably heard the word *SharePoint*. You've probably heard it mentioned in several contexts: SharePoint Team Services, SharePoint Portal Server, SharePoint Web Parts, and SharePoint Dashboards. You might be confused about how these items interact and how they can help you. This chapter explains a bit about each of these technologies and goes into detail about how to use the various SharePoint technologies to collaborate with others both inside and outside your organization to share documents. Throughout this chapter, SharePoint Portal Server refers to SharePoint Portal Server 2003, and SharePoint Team Services refers to the SharePoint Team Services that works with Windows Server 2003.

Sharing documents is only one benefit to SharePoint. You can collaborate on meetings by creating shared meeting workspaces that can be accessed via the Internet, the corporate intranet, or even Outlook. For every meeting, you can store the agenda, documents, tasks, and objectives, and manage the attendees for your meeting. A detailed explanation of shared meeting workspaces is beyond the scope of this book, but we'll cover briefly how you can store and access documents to help you better prepare for and follow up on your meetings. Mostly, however, this chapter covers the features of Word 2003 that allow you to work directly with SharePoint technologies. Word users can benefit from SharePoint by utilizing the document collaboration features, implementing document versioning, and using the discussion features to update documents between multiple editors.

SHAREPOINT PORTAL SERVER VERSUS SHAREPOINT TEAM SERVICES

So what's the difference between SharePoint Portal Server and SharePoint Team Services? If you don't know off the top of your head, you're not alone. The gist of the difference is that SharePoint Team Services was designed for smaller teams collaborating over an intranet or the Internet. SharePoint Portal Server was designed to be used over an entire enterprise, allowing users to index and search for documents over a wide variety of portal sites. SharePoint Team Services can run on any existing Windows Server 2003 (including one being used for other roles such as a file server or database server). SharePoint Portal Server is a standalone server product. Table 27.1 illustrates some of the key differences between these two products.

27

TABLE 27.1 SHAREPOINT TEAM SERVICES VERSUS SHAREPOINT PORTAL SERVER

	Team Services	Portal Server
Primary Function	Team collaboration	Enterprise collaboration
Web Sites	Individual team Web sites	Enterprise portal Web site
Search Functionality	Documents within team Web site and subsites	Multiple types of data across multiple servers
Collaboration Features	Discussions, notifications, and surveys	Discussions and notifications

	Team Services	Portal Server
Customization	FrontPage 2003 and the SharePoint Team Services SDK	Web Parts and the SharePoint Portal Server SDK
Document Management Abilities	Publish documents, version control, check-in and check-out	Publish, version control, routing, check-in, and check-out
Security Roles	Administrator, Advanced Author, Author, Contributor, Browser	Administrator, Coordinator, Author, and Reader
Storage	SQL Server	Web Storage System
Licensing	FrontPage 2003 Server license, no separate client access license	SharePoint Portal Server license and client access licenses

The SharePoint Team Services technology allows users to quickly create and contribute to team or project-focused Web sites from within their browser or Office applications. With SharePoint Team Services, anyone on the team can create a quick Web site for sharing information that includes documents, calendars, announcements, and other types of information. Team members can easily customize and manage these Web sites through FrontPage 2003 and the SharePoint Team Services SDK.

SharePoint Portal Server 2003 allows administrators to create a portal Web site that allows users to share documents and search for information across the entire enterprise, including SharePoint Team Services sites. All of these sites can be searched and indexed through the SharePoint Portal Server main site. SharePoint Portal Server includes the document management features companies need to manage their business processes with their portal solution.

So what does this all mean? Well, if all you want to do is share documents with a limited group of people (either within your organization or outside your organization), you should probably implement SharePoint Team Services. You don't need client access licenses (CALs) and you can publish documents easily for everyone to access. If you need detailed version control and document routing, as well as the ability to access various data across multiple sites, you should look into SharePoint Portal Server 2003.

SHARING DOCUMENTS WITH SHAREPOINT TEAM SERVICES

This chapter's focus is SharePoint Team Services. However, most of the topics addressed here will work equally well with SharePoint Portal Server. A few of the topics covered in this chapter will work only with SharePoint Portal Server. Wherever that's the case, it will be noted in the text.

27

CREATING A SHAREPOINT TEAM SITE

Before you can use a SharePoint team site to collaborate on documents with colleagues, you might need to create the team site (in other cases, your SharePoint administrator might create the team site for you). For those responsible for creating their own team site, this section examines several methods you can use to create your team site.

CREATING A TEAM SITE FROM WORD 2003

You can create a SharePoint team site directly from Word 2003. When you create a team site from Word, you need to start with an existing document. Even though this might not be the only document you want to place on your team site, choose a document you want to place on your team site. To create a team site for the Network Infrastructure Upgrade Project, use the following steps:

1. Open the first document you want to place on your team site.

2. Select Shared Workspace from the Tools menu to display the task pane shown in Figure 27.1. The Shared Workspace task pane contains six tabs. We'll go through each of these tabs in detail later in this chapter.

Figure 27.1
Use the Shared Workspace task pane to create a new shared meeting workspace.

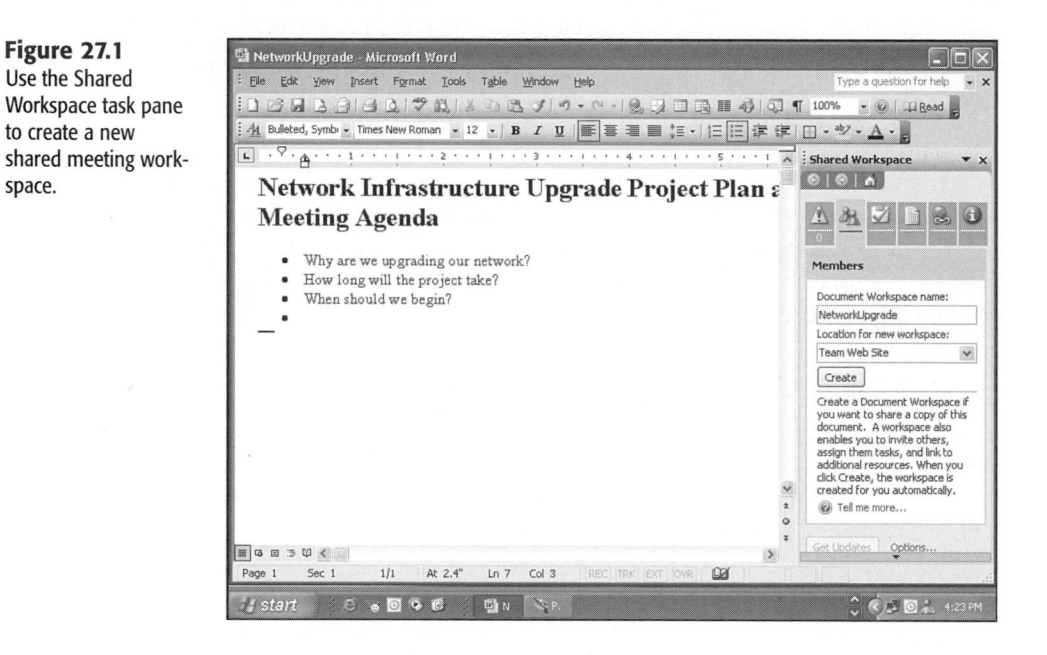

3. The Members tab is shown by default. You can choose a name for your shared workspace. When you first launch the Shared Workspace task pane, the name of the workspace defaults to the name of the current document. You can change the workspace name to reflect the entire project, such as Network Infrastructure Upgrade.

4. Choose a location for your shared workspace. If you have accessed a SharePoint Team Services Web site or a SharePoint Portal Server from this computer before, you'll be able to choose either site from the drop-down list. If you haven't, or if you want to specify a new site never accessed before, choose (Type a New URL) and enter the site's URL.

5. Click Create to create your shared workspace on the server.

Your task pane then changes to look similar to that shown in Figure 27.2.

Figure 27.2
After you create your shared workspace, you can manage tasks, members, documents, links, and information.

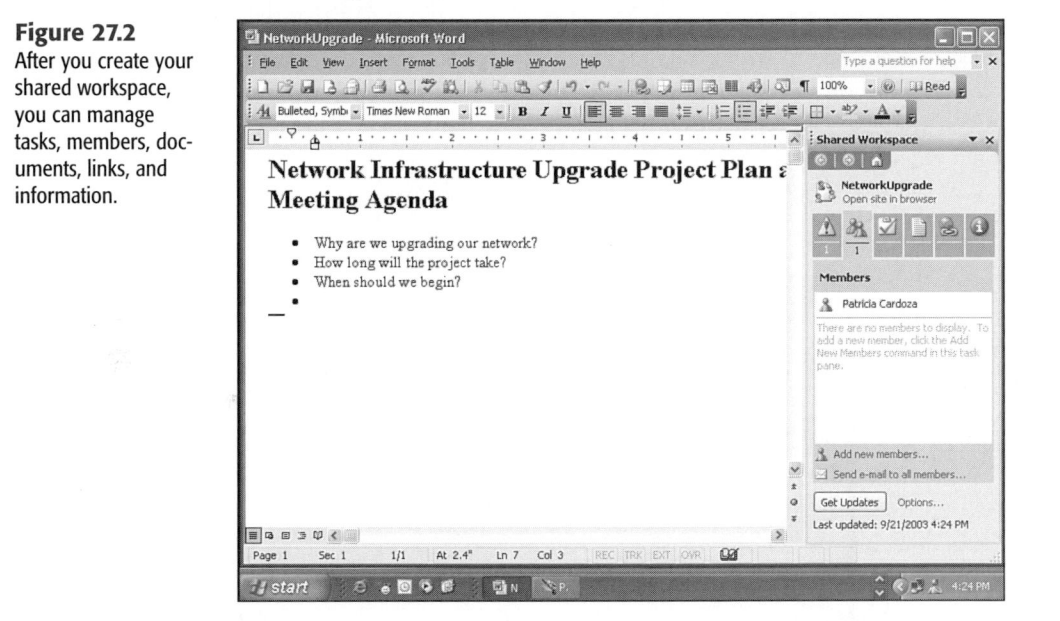

After you've created your workspace, you can add members to the workspace directly from the task pane. Just click on the Add New Members link on the bottom of the task pane to display the dialog shown in Figure 27.3.

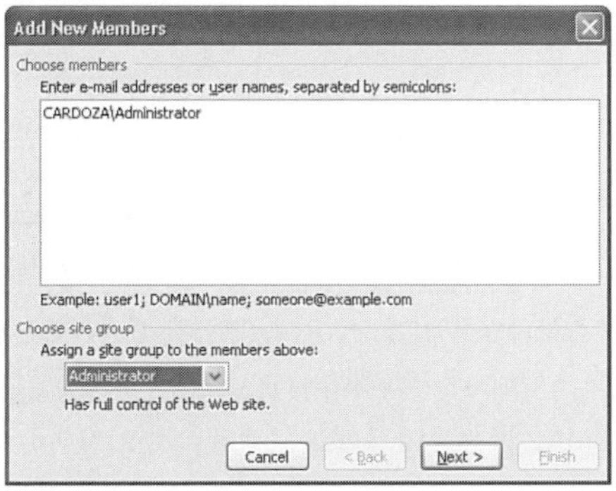

Figure 27.3
Use this dialog to add new users to your workspace.

27

Enter the email address or domain/username for the new user in the box provided. You'll need to specify a role for the new user. You can choose from the following roles for your new user:

- *Reader*—Has read-only access to the site.
- *Contributor*—Can add content to existing document libraries and lists.
- *Web Designer*—Can create lists and document libraries and customize pages in the Web site.
- *Administrator*—Has full control of the Web site.

Click Next to modify the email address or display name for your new user. You might not be able to edit all of this information. If you've entered a user in Active Directory, all of this information will be prefilled and read-only. Click Finish to add the user to your workspace. You'll receive a message asking whether you want to send an email to the user informing the user of the workspace. Choosing to do so displays an email message similar to that shown in Figure 27.4.

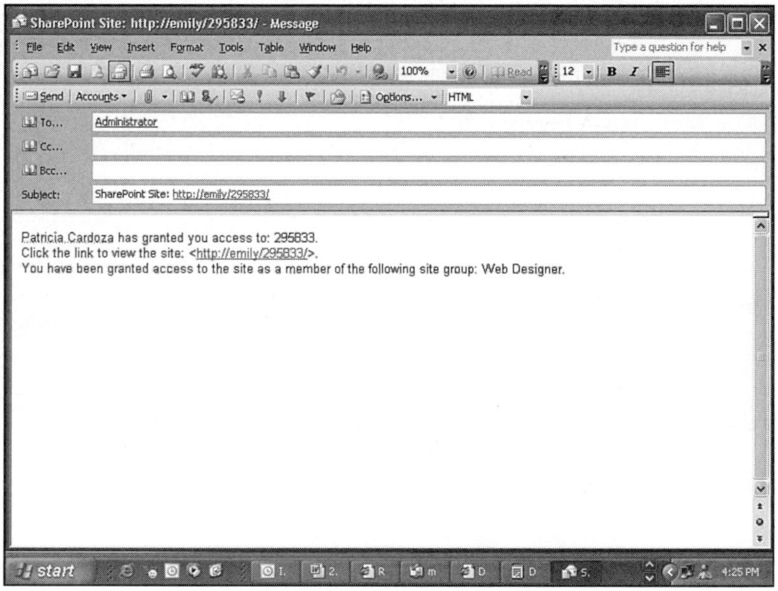

Figure 27.4
You can modify the email sent to members of your site.

When your new user receives the invitation email, he can click the link provided to log on to the workspace site.

CREATING A TEAM SITE FROM AN OUTLOOK 2003 MEETING REQUEST

You can create a team site from an Outlook 2003 meeting request to serve as the central collaboration tool for your upcoming meeting. One of the common uses for a SharePoint Team Services site is for a series of recurring meetings. Perhaps you have weekly meetings for the Network Infrastructure Upgrade project. You can send a link to the team site within the meeting request so that all of your attendees can access the agenda, project updates, and shared tasks in preparation for the meeting. Creating a team site for your meeting request allows you to store shared information for the meeting in a central location. You can upload agenda items to the SharePoint site, and add tasks, to-do lists, and documents for attendees to access at any time. This can often save precious time emailing documents back and forth between attendees, as well as preventing version conflicts when two attendees both update their own copies of a document.

To create a team site from an Outlook 2003 Meeting Request, use the following steps:

1. Click the Calendar banner in the Navigation pane to display Outlook 2003's calendar.

2. Click the New button on the toolbar to create a new appointment.

3. Click the Invite Attendees button to turn your appointment into a meeting request.

4. Click the To button to select other attendees from your Global Address List or Contacts folders. Add the required and optional attendees and any resources (such as a conference room or projector).

5. Click OK to return to your meeting request. At this point, all you have is a standard meeting request. The next steps add the link to the shared meeting workspace.

6. Click the Meeting Workspace button on the meeting request to display the Meeting Workspace task pane. If you've previously created a Meeting Workspace on this computer, the workspace you create for this meeting request will default to the previously used server. If you want to alter the server used, click Change Settings to specify a new SharePoint Team Services site.

7. Click the Create button to create the shared meeting workspace from your meeting request. When the process is completed, your meeting request will look similar to what's shown in Figure 27.5.

When the meeting attendees receive the meeting request, they can click on the link to the shared meeting workspace and upload or edit documents related to the meeting.

CREATING A TEAM SITE FROM YOUR SHAREPOINT WEB SITE

The last way to create a team site is directly from the SharePoint Web site. Navigate to the home page for your SharePoint Team Services site, as shown in Figure 27.6.

To create a new, shared workspace, use the following steps:

1. Click Create from the banner at the top of your SharePoint site.

2. Scroll down to the bottom of the page and click Sites and Workspaces to display the screen shown in Figure 27.7.

3. Enter a title and description for your shared workspace.

4. You'll need to enter a URL for your shared workspace. The first part of the URL is the base site address for your SharePoint site. You can choose the site name for your shared workspace.

27

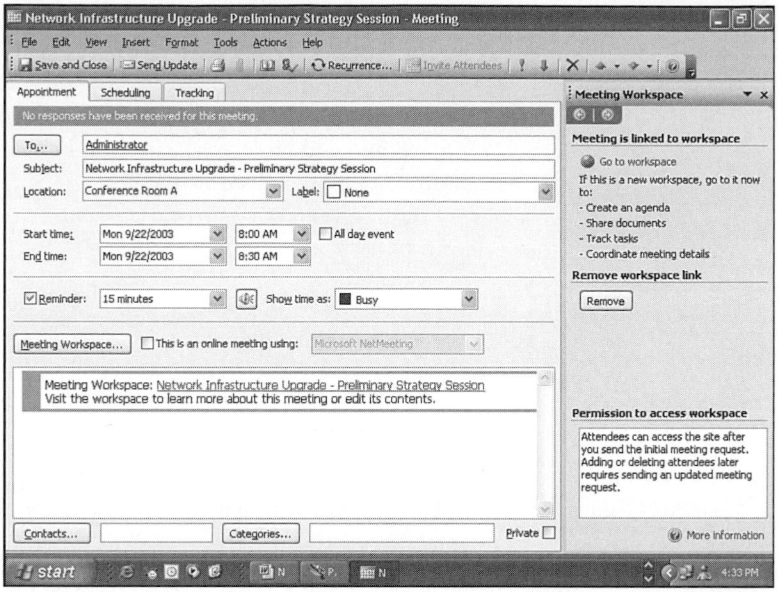

Figure 27.5
Click the link in the body of the meeting request to visit your shared meeting workspace.

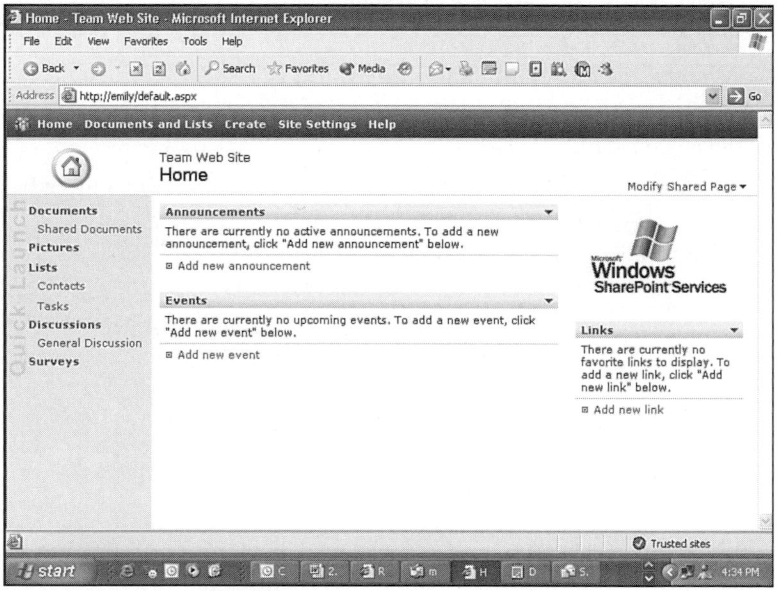

Figure 27.6
From your SharePoint home page, you can view meeting workspaces, add a new workspace, or manage your settings.

5. Click Create to display the screen shown in Figure 27.8.

6. Choose a template to use as the basis for your site. Click OK to apply the template and display the screen shown in Figure 27.9.

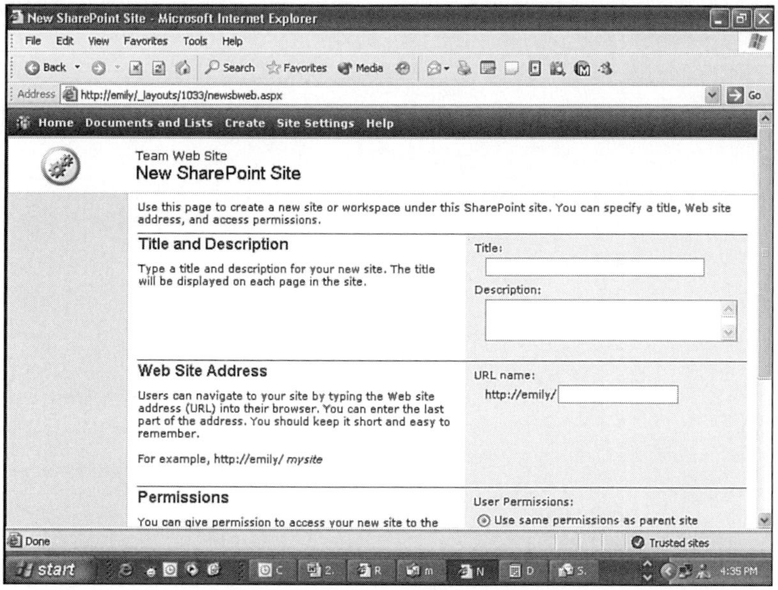

Figure 27.7
You can create a
shared workspace
from your SharePoint
Team Services site.

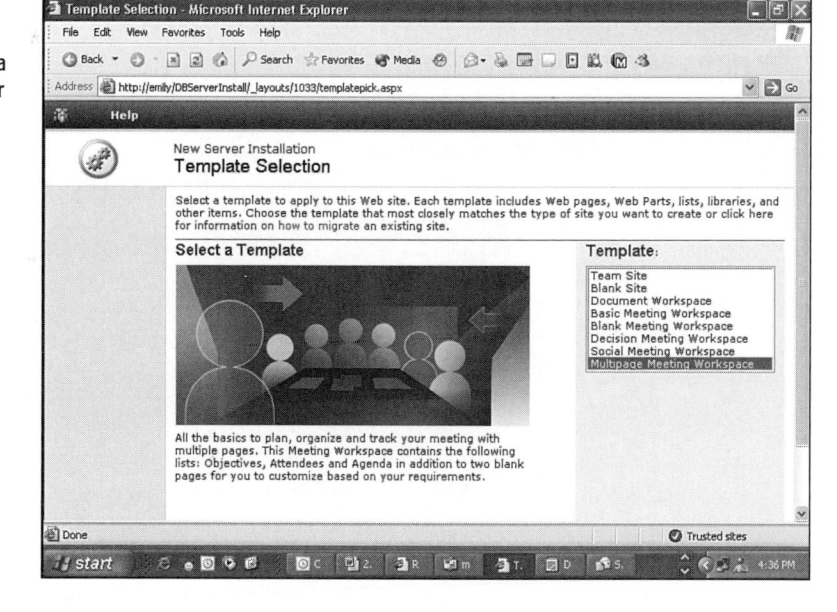

Figure 27.8
After creating your
site, you can choose a
template to base your
site's pages on.

27

Now that we've listed the various ways to create a SharePoint shared workspace, we'll examine how to work with your SharePoint site and how to share documents with your SharePoint site.

Figure 27.9
Your SharePoint shared workspace contains objectives, attendees, an agenda, and a document library.

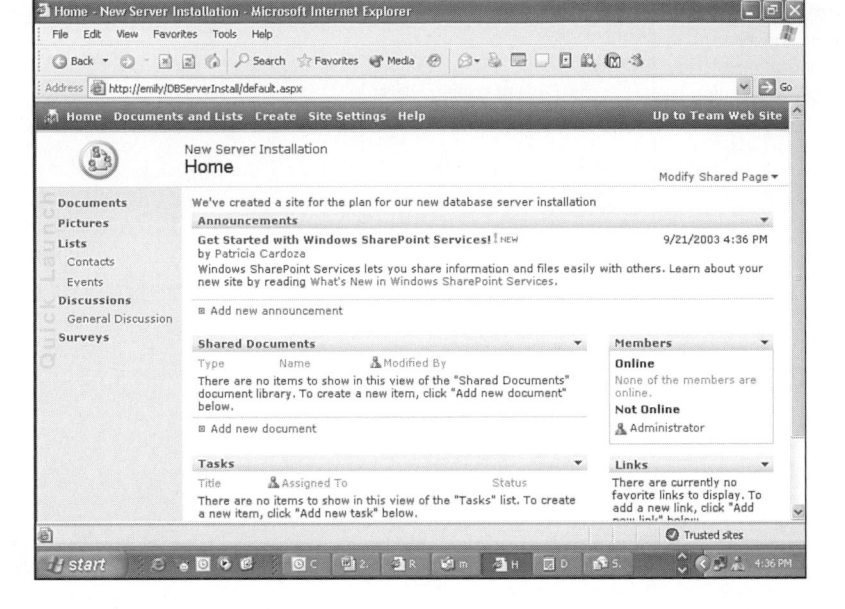

USING THE SHARED WORKSPACE TASK PANE TO WORK WITH YOUR SITE

From within Word, you can use the Shared Workspace task pane to work with your site. There are six action buttons (shown in Figure 27.2) you can use. The first shows the status of your workspace. For a currently open document, it will inform you that a copy of the document is stored in a document workspace. You can update the Workspace copy at any time by clicking the link provided.

The second button allows you to add or remove a member from the Workspace. We covered adding a member previously in this chapter. To remove a member, hover your mouse over the member's name and click the drop-down box that appears. Choose the option Remove Member from Workspace.

The third button allows you to manage the tasks associated with this shared workspace. You can add a new task or configure SharePoint to alert you about specific tasks. To add a new task, click the link at the bottom of the task pane to display the dialog shown in Figure 27.10.

You can enter a title, a status, a priority level, an assignee, and a description for your task. You can also assign a due date to your task. When you're done entering the information for your task, click OK.

The next action button, Documents, shows you all the documents associated with the shared workspace. Even though you created the Workspace from within your current document, you can add other documents to the Workspace by clicking the Add New Document link. You can also add a new folder to your shared workspace. Adding a folder allows you to categorize and separate your documents.

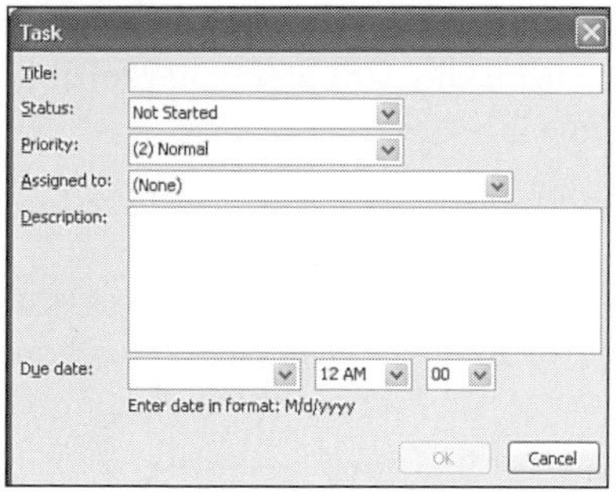

Figure 27.10
You can add new tasks to your SharePoint site from Word.

The Links button allows you to add external links to your shared workspace. You might want to add a link to the corporate intranet site or Internet sites used for research within your project.

The last action button, Document Information, displays information about who created the document, who last modified it, and when it was last modified. From this pane you can also restrict permission on the document, configure alerts, and view the version history for the document.

CREATING AND SAVING DOCUMENTS FOR A SHAREPOINT TEAM SITE

Now that you have a functioning team site, you can create new documents for the team site and upload existing documents for the team site. We've already examined how to create a team site from a document, but if you already have a team site created, you'll need to know how to upload a new or existing document to an existing SharePoint team site.

Creating a document in Word and saving it to the SharePoint team site isn't completely straightforward. To control the upload of documents directly from Word, you must first configure the team site as a network place in My Network Places in Windows XP. To add your team site to My Network Places, use the following steps:

1. Double-click the My Network Places icon on the Windows XP desktop, or choose it from the Windows XP Start menu.

2. Choose Add a Network Place from the task pane.

3. Click <u>N</u>ext from the Welcome screen. Windows will search for information on existing network providers.

4. Ensure that Choose Another Network Location is selected and click <u>N</u>ext.

5. Enter the URL for your team site. It should be in the format of http://*servername*/*teamsitename*. Don't worry about the team site's home page name, default.aspx. Click <u>N</u>ext.

27

6. Enter a name to associate with your team site. This name does not need to have anything to do with the name of your team site, although you probably want to keep a similar name for clarity. Click Next to continue.

7. Click Finish to complete the creation of your network place.

Now that you've added your team site to your My Network Places, you can save any Word document to the site. From within an existing document in Word, choose File, Save As to display the Save As dialog box. Choose the My Network Places icon from the shortcut bar. Double-click the network place you created to display the dialog shown in Figure 27.11.

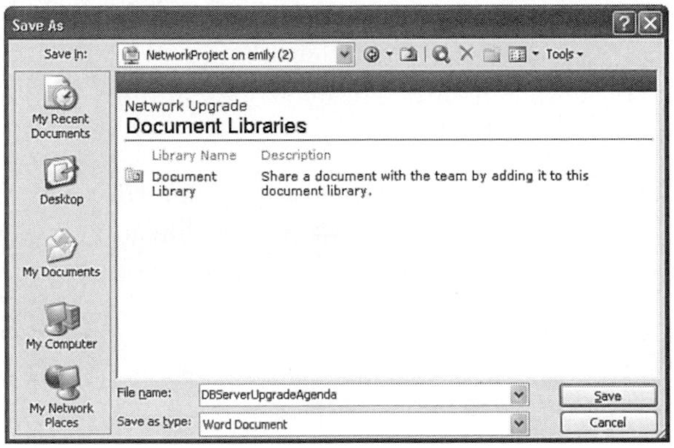

Figure 27.11
Every SharePoint team site has a document library.

Double-click on the Document Library shown in the Save As window. Enter a name for your file and click Save. Depending on the speed of your network, it might take several seconds to upload your document to the team site. When you're done saving your document, you can visit the team site, shown in Figure 27.12.

You'll see your document listed in the Document Library section of the team site. You can click the document to open it or click Document Library to display the screen shown in Figure 27.13.

To check out a document, hover your mouse over the name of the document and click the drop-down arrow that appears to the right of the filename. From this drop-down box, you can choose to edit the document in Microsoft Office Word, View Version History, or Check Out the document.

NOTE

> Checking out a document marks the document on the team site. Other members who want to access the document will be informed that you've checked out the document.

Although they can still open the document, it will be read-only for all users except the one who has checked out the document. After you check the document back in, others can edit the document. We'll cover more on checking out a document later in this chapter.

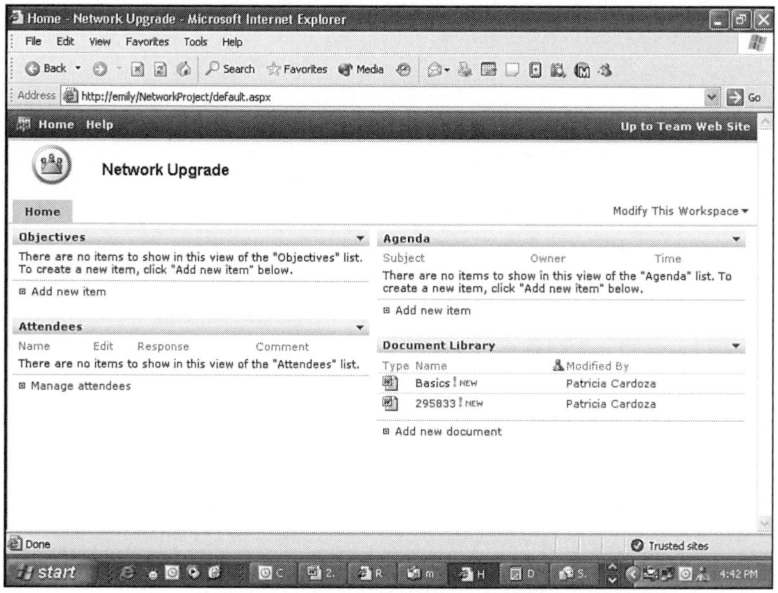

Figure 27.12
After saving documents to your team site, you'll see them listed on the home page.

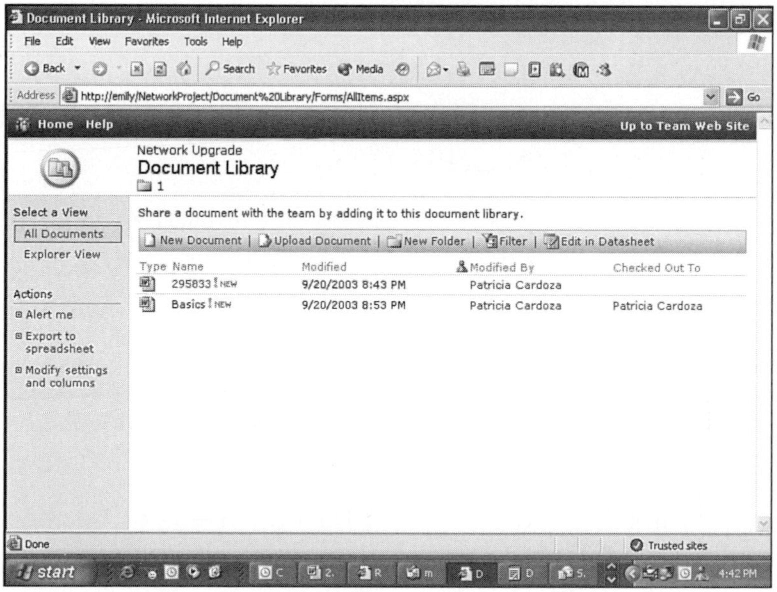

Figure 27.13
From the Document Library page you can check out documents for editing.

In addition to saving currently open documents to your team site through Word, you can use Internet Explorer to upload documents directly from your team site. To upload a document to your team site though Internet Explorer, use the following steps:

1. Navigate to your team site's home page in Internet Explorer.

2. Click the link Add New Document under the Document Library section of the team site.

3. You can type the name and path for a file directly in the Name box, or you can click Browse to locate the file on your computer.

4. If you want to upload multiple files, click the Upload Multiple Files link to display what's shown in Figure 27.14.

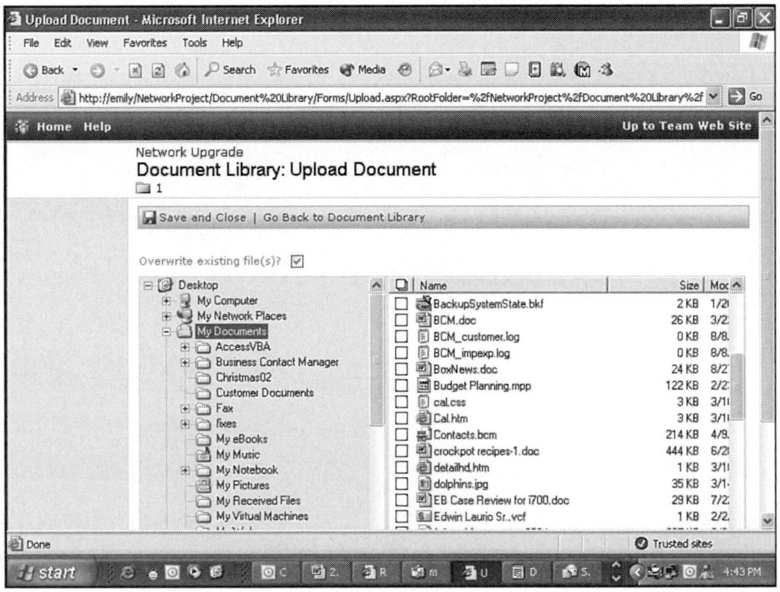

Figure 27.14
You can upload multiple files from various locations.

5. Use the treeview control on the left to navigate through your hard drive or network locations. Click the box next to the name of the file on the right pane to mark the file for upload.

6. When you're done selecting files, choose Save and Close from the top of the Web page. SharePoint will ask whether you're sure that you want to upload the files. Click Yes.

7. SharePoint will upload the files and return you to the team site's home page.

MANAGING YOUR DOCUMENTS USING DATASHEET VIEW

Your document library can be viewed in standard view (as shown in the previous images) or in datasheet view. To switch to datasheet view, click the Datasheet view button. The datasheet view, shown in Figure 27.15, allows you to change the display of your Document Library and filter your view to show only specific documents.

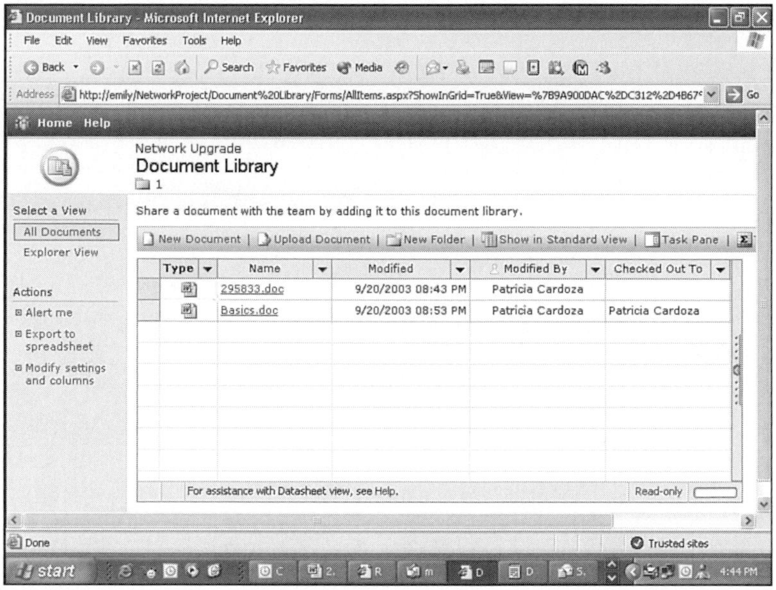

Figure 27.15
Datasheet view allows you to easily filter the display of your documents.

For example, if you want to show all the documents modified on a specific date, click the drop-down arrow next to Modified. You can choose any of the values in the datasheet, or you can click Custom Filter to display Figure 27.16. You can choose to display documents modified on a specific date and time, or before or after a specific date. When you're done creating your filter, click OK to update your display. Use the same process to filter your documents based on any criteria displayed on the datasheet. To clear your filter, use the drop-down, and click Show All.

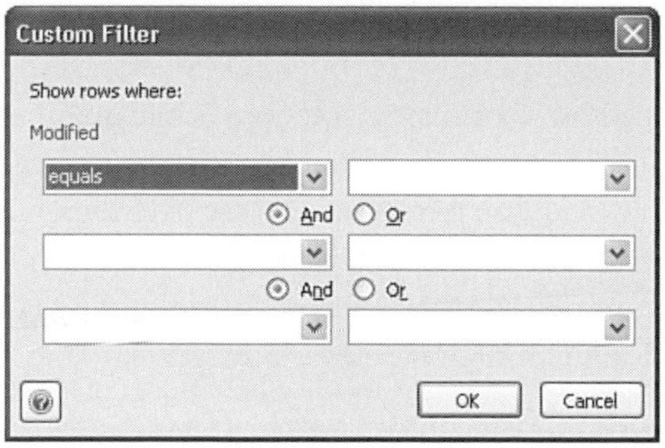

Figure 27.16
You can create a custom filter for your datasheet.

27

USING THE TASK PANE WITHIN YOUR TEAM SITE

While you're in datasheet view, you can display the task pane to help you work with your documents. Click Task Pane to display the task pane on the right of the datasheet view, as shown in Figure 27.17.

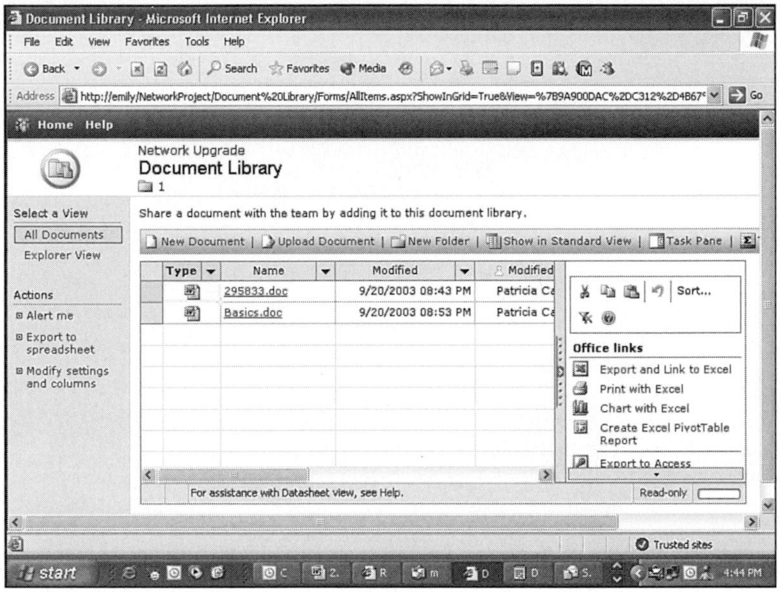

Figure 27.17
From the task pane, you can manipulate your existing documents.

You can perform various tasks from the task pane, including printing, creating a chart, exporting information to Excel, or creating a Microsoft Access report. You can also sort the information displayed in the datasheet.

SHARING DOCUMENTS USING SHAREPOINT TEAM SERVICES

After you have documents stored on a team site, you (and other members of the team site) can download and check out the documents for sharing purposes. Checking out a document is much like reserving a book at the library. You're marking the document as available only for you. Others can still view and edit the document; however, they will be working with the original copy of the document, rather than the checked-out copy. The following example illustrates the process of checking out and checking in a document.

Laura is the author of a Network Infrastructure Upgrade Agenda document. After creating the document, she uploads it to the local team site for viewing by all the members of her team. Two hours after she posts the document, she realizes that she forgot to add the Web site links she wants her team to review before the meeting. So Laura visits the team site and checks out the document. After the document is checked out, she opens the document for editing in Microsoft Office Word. In the middle of making her changes, Laura is called away to a meeting. She leaves the document open on her computer without checking the document back in to the team site.

Meanwhile, David decides to take a look at the agenda for tomorrow's meeting. He visits the team site and opens the document library. David can open the document for editing by simply choosing Edit with Microsoft Office Word from the document's drop-down menu. When David chooses to open the document, he's informed that the document has been locked for editing by Laura. He can open a read-only copy, or choose to open a local copy and save his changes locally. After David makes his changes, he saves the document to his local computer. Later, when Laura has checked in the document, David can choose to merge his changes with Laura's checked-in copy.

When Laura returns to her office after her meeting, she completes her changes to the document, saves it, and checks it back in to the team site. The next time David tries to open the local copy of the agenda, Word informs him that he is now able to access the server copy of the document. He chooses to merge his changes with the copy stored on the team site.

The next time Laura visits the team site, she takes a quick look at the Version History for the document. She hovers her mouse over the document name and chooses Version History to display the screen shown in Figure 27.18.

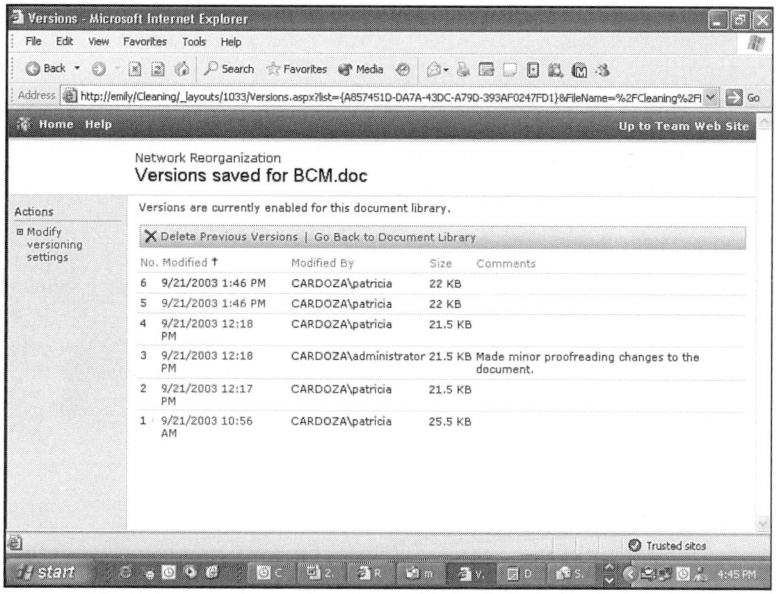

Figure 27.18
You can view multiple versions of the same file with version control enabled.

Hovering her mouse over each version allows Laura to choose three options from the version drop-down menu. Laura can view the version, delete the version, or restore it to the document library. The one function Laura can't perform is combining the versions.

THE IMPORTANCE OF VERSIONS

So if anyone can make changes to a document and combine their changes into the main document, why is versioning important? Well, whenever you have a document edited by multiple people, you have the possibility that someone will enter erroneous information or overwrite someone else's changes. Turning on version control can help an administrator recover previously saved changes to a document if necessary. Whenever a user checks a document back in, he can add comments to the checked-in version. This can provide an administrator with the information she needs to adequately understand which versions should be kept and which should be discarded.

RECEIVING ALERTS WHEN DOCUMENTS CHANGE

SharePoint Team Services has the capability to notify users when a document has changed. To receive an alert whenever a specific document changes, navigate to the Document Library. Hover your mouse over the document's name, and click the drop-down box that appears around the document's name. Choose Alert Me from the drop-down menu to display the screen shown in Figure 27.19.

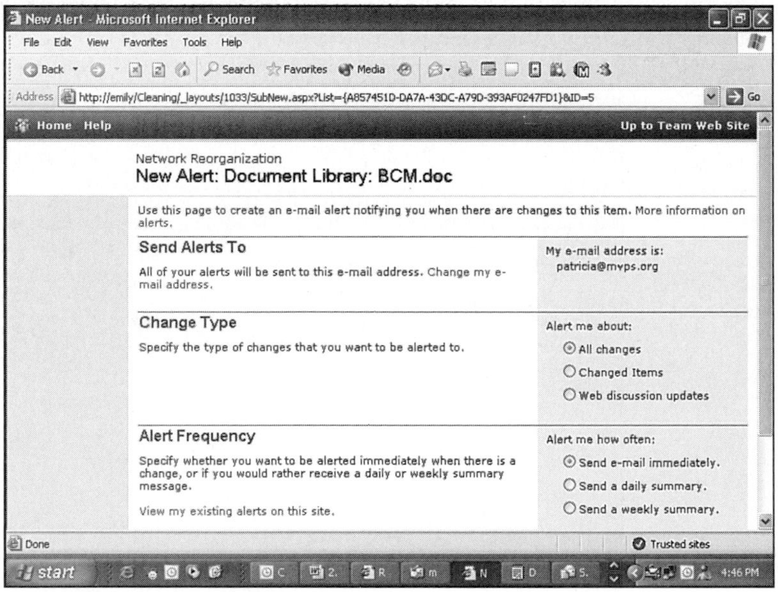

Figure 27.19
You can configure SharePoint to alert you whenever a document changes.

You can configure various settings to personalize your alert:

- *Send Alerts To*—You can have your team site alert you at any email address when a document changes. The email address you choose doesn't have to be the address you used to subscribe to the site, nor the one stored in Active Directory. Click Change My E-mail Address to specify a new email address.

- *Change Type*—Use this section to choose the types of changes you want to be notified about. You can select All Changes, Changed Items, or Web Discussion Updates.

- *Alert Frequency*—You can choose how often you want your SharePoint site to notify you of changes. You might not want to be informed of every change immediately when it happens. You can choose to get an immediate notification, a daily summary notification, or a weekly summary notification.

When you're done making changes to your alert settings, click OK to return to the Document Library.

CREATING A DOCUMENT DISCUSSION

One of the strengths of SharePoint Team Services is that it can be used to provide collaboration features such as document discussion. Multiple users of a team site can "meet" to discuss a document over the Internet. To open a discussion on a document from the Document Library, choose Discuss from the document's drop-down menu. In response to the prompt to open or save the file, choose Open to display the screen shown in Figure 27.20.

Figure 27.20
Multiple users can discuss a file over the Internet.

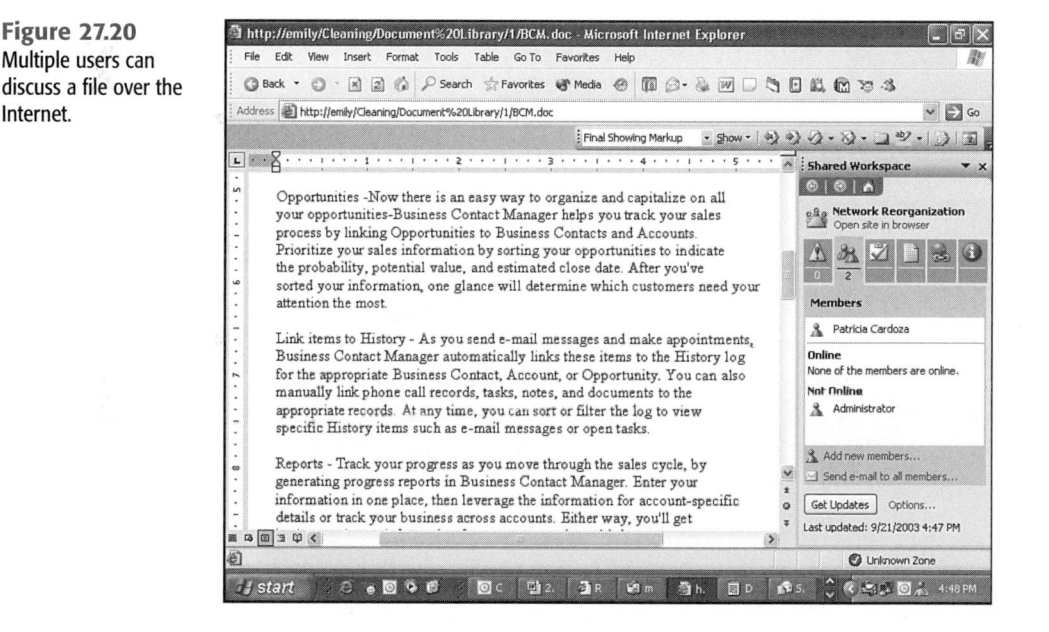

Multiple users can make changes to the documents or add new discussion topics. Use the discussion toolbar at the bottom of the document to add a new discussion to the document. When another user adds a discussion element, you won't see the element right away. You might need to refresh the discussions first. To do this, click the Discussions button at the bottom of the document and choose Refresh Discussions. You can also filter discussions and configure discussion options from this pop-up box.

After several discussions have been initiated about the document, your document might look similar to the one in Figure 27.21.

Figure 27.21
Multiple users can discuss many aspects of the document.

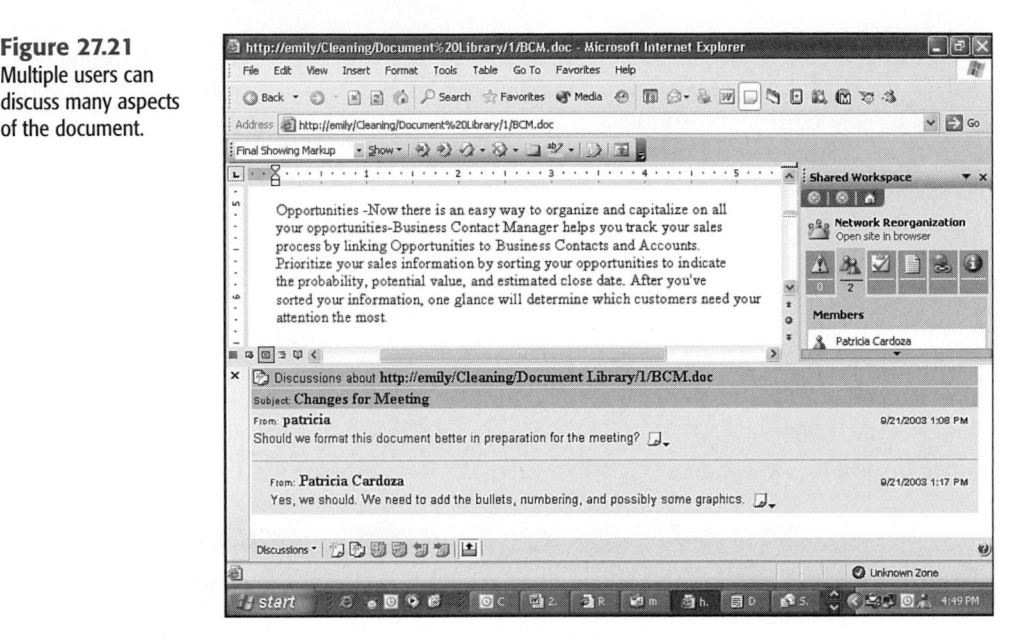

When you're done with a particular discussion, you can mark the discussion as closed. This removes the discussion from active view, yet leaves it as part of the document.

When you're done discussing the document, close the document. You won't be able to save your changes to the document on the team site; the document will be marked as read-only. This prevents multiple users from uploading changed versions simultaneously to the same location. You can, however, save changes to the document on your local computer and then upload the changed document back to the team site later.

CREATING A DOCUMENT WORKSPACE

In addition to uploading documents to a workspace, you can take an existing document and create a new document workspace. This workspace contains a copy of the original document and is designed to allow you to go into further discussion about the document without detracting from the purpose of the original team site. For example, you might create a team site for your Network Infrastructure Upgrade project that contains 10 documents. However, one of those documents is a proposal for the next phase of the project, the Network Software Upgrade project. Because this isn't even a project yet, but merely a proposal, you don't want to create a team site for the project. Because it will be a separate project with a different team and different objectives, you don't want to use your original team site for this new project either. So you can create a new document workspace for the Network Software Upgrade proposal. To create a new document workspace, click the drop-down arrow around the document's name and choose Create Document Workspace. Click

OK to create your document workspace. When SharePoint has created your workspace, it will display it in a new window, as shown in Figure 27.22.

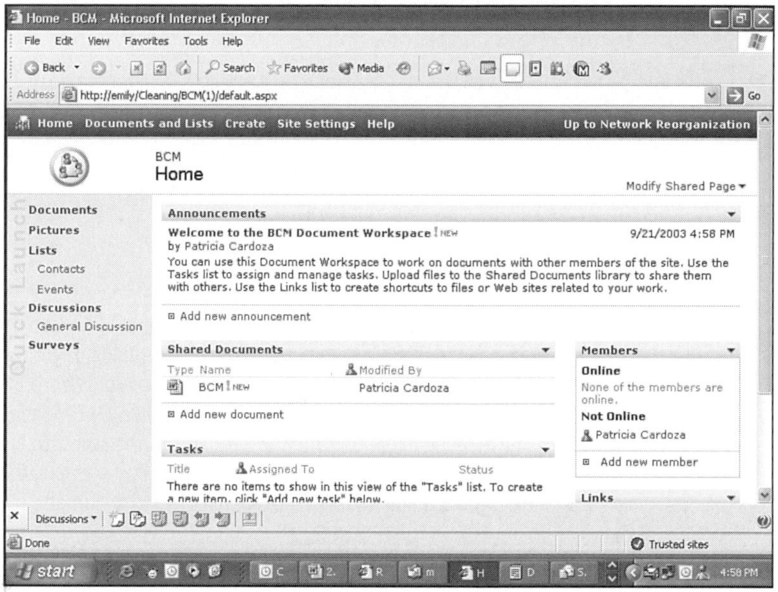

Figure 27.22
You can create a new document workspace from an existing document on a team site.

This document workspace contains shared documents, tasks, members, and links. Any changes you make to the document from this workspace remain separate from the original document in the original team site. You can work with this copy of the document in all the ways previously described in this chapter. You can manage alerts, check the document in or out, and discuss the document with users of your site. However, there's one more option you can use from your new document workspace. Clicking the drop-down box that appears around the document name allows you to choose to publish the document back to its source location. In this case, the source location is the original team site you used to create the new document workspace.

SEARCHING AND CATEGORIZING DOCUMENTS USING SHAREPOINT PORTAL SERVER

Even though this chapter is primarily about SharePoint Team Services, I'll briefly cover one major advantage to SharePoint Portal Server over Team Services. SharePoint Portal Server allows you to index and search for documents stored on the server.

You can perform two types of searches on SharePoint Portal Server: a simple search or an advanced search. A simple search allows you to search for keywords within the document. An advanced search allows you to search for keywords plus additional criteria such as specific property values in the document.

To perform a simple search, use the following steps:

1. Open Internet Explorer and navigate to the portal's home page (usually found at `http://server_name/workspace_name`).

2. Navigate to the Home, Categories, or Document Library tab of the portal page.

3. Click the Search drop-down list to select the scope of the search. The site administrator can create multiple scopes for searching. A scope can be defined as a subsite or a subset of documents.

4. Enter your search terms in the box provided and click Go.

5. Your search results are displayed below the search box.

> **NOTE**
>
> A site administrator can define multiple search scopes for a site. For example, in your site you might have multiple document catalogs. One catalog might contain all of your Excel files for the site. Another catalog might contain all of your Word files. Catalogs can also be defined by type of content. You can create a catalog for meeting minutes and another catalog for meeting agendas. When you're performing searches, it can save time and bandwidth if you search only the scope you need. For example, there's no need to search the Excel catalog if you're looking for a Word document.

To perform an advanced search, use the following steps:

1. Open Internet Explorer and navigate to the portal's home page (usually found at `http://server_name/workspace_name`).

2. Navigate to the Search tab of the portal.

3. Select the scope from the Search drop-down box.

4. Enter your search terms in the box provided.

5. Choose the document profile from the Search By Profile drop-down box to limit the search.

6. Further refine the search by choosing values of properties in the Search By Properties section of the search page. For example, you can search by document author.

7. If you want to refine your search to display only items either created or modified within a specific time frame, choose the Documents radio button in the Search by Date section. Use the drop-down provided to choose Created or Modified. Enter a time range you want SharePoint to search within.

8. Click Go to complete your search.

SUBSCRIBING TO DISCUSSIONS AND DOCUMENTS

Another feature available in SharePoint Portal Server is the capability for users to subscribe to documents. Subscribing to a document means that you'll be updated every time a change is made to the document. This feature is very much like the Alerts feature available in SharePoint Team Services. To subscribe to a document, use the following steps:

1. Navigate to the SharePoint portal site.
2. Click the Document Library dashboard tab.
3. Click Subscribe to display the New Subscription tab.
4. Give the subscription a name. By default, the name of the subscription will be the name of the document; however, you can change this name.
5. Confirm the email address you want to use to subscribe to the document. You can enter a different email address from the one associated with your site membership if you choose.
6. Choose how often you want to be notified of changes.
7. Click OK to confirm your subscription.

TROUBLESHOOTING

WHAT TO DO IF YOU MAKE CHANGES TO A CHECKED-OUT DOCUMENT AND THEY DON'T APPEAR ON THE TEAM SITE

If you made changes to a document someone else has checked out, you will be prompted to save a copy of the document locally. The next time you open the document, Word will ask whether you want to merge your changes back to the source document. If you don't re-open the document after it has been checked back in, you won't be prompted to merge your changes. So if you have to save the document locally, be sure to check back later to see whether the document is available for editing. If it is, merge your changes back into the main document.

WHAT TO DO IF CHANGES YOU'VE MADE TO A DOCUMENT ARE LOST BY ANOTHER USER

If the team site administrator has turned on versioning for your site, you can hover your mouse over the document name and click Version History. You can select an earlier version of the document to open or even replace the current version with the earlier version. Just be aware that if you replace the current version with an earlier one, you'll lose any changes made to the current version.

WHAT TO DO IF YOU CAN'T OPEN A DOCUMENT ON A TEAM SITE

Occasionally, you might run into problems opening a document from a team site. The most common problem in opening a document from a team site is that the document simply hangs on opening. This can be caused by several problems. Examine the potential problems to determine which one is the cause of your issues. First, make sure that you have a good-quality connection to the SharePoint server. If you're on a dial-up line with significant static, you might have problems opening a document, especially if the document is large. The static can interrupt the loading of the document, and the Web site will appear to hang without actually opening the document.

The second possibility is that your document is corrupted. Check out a previous version of the document to determine whether other versions will open. If so, see whether another user can open the current document. If not, you might need to abandon the current version and revert to a saved version.

The third possibility is that you're trying to open a subdocument of a master document stored on a SharePoint team site. Currently this functionality is not supported. You should be able to open a standard document, but subdocuments will not display properly; instead, only a blank browser window will open.

CHAPTER 28

CREATING FORMS

In this chapter

WORD'S FORMS CAPABILITIES: AN OVERVIEW

Word's sophisticated forms capabilities permit you to streamline various business tasks that once required paper forms. You can create forms that enable users to choose among lists of options, forms that provide online help, and even forms that guide users from start to finish. Best of all, users can fill in these forms without changing the underlying form itself. And if you're networked, you can use your network server or *intranet*—rather than some distant warehouse—as your central repository for forms.

WHEN TO USE WORD, WHEN TO USE ANOTHER TOOL

As you'll discover, building a printed or electronic form in Word 2003 is relatively easy. However, there may be times when it makes more sense to use another tool:

- Forms built in Word can perform calculations, but if your forms require extensive, complex calculations that go far beyond simple arithmetic, consider building them in Microsoft Excel rather than Word.

- Forms built in Word can transfer their data to a database such as Microsoft Access, but if integrating the information in your forms into a database is your central goal, consider building the forms in Access rather than Word.

- If you are using forms as a front end for applications that utilize XML, consider using the new Microsoft Office InfoPath.

- If the users who will fill out your online forms do not have access to Microsoft Word or Office, consider creating Web-based forms that can be accessed from a browser. Alternatively, consider using a traditional forms program such as FormTool or FormFlow.

> **NOTE**
>
> The tools Word provides for building Web forms—available through the *Control Toolbox toolbar*—can also be used in standard Word forms.

APPLICATIONS FOR WORD'S FORMS FEATURE

You can use Word's forms feature to build three types of forms:

- Standard electronic forms that are filled out in Word by users whose responses are limited to specific areas and types of information

- Guided electronic forms in which you display a series of questions and the forms can fill themselves in as the user provides answers

- Printed forms that can be completed with a typewriter or a pen

In addition to fairly obvious applications such as questionnaires and surveys, forms can be used in more traditional word processing functions such as automated document production. Lawyers use forms to fill out contracts, whereas bankers use them to complete loan applications.

In fact, Word's forms feature can help you build any document that is largely repetitive except for small areas of specific, individual information.

UNDERSTANDING THE WORKFLOW ASSOCIATED WITH BUILDING AND DISTRIBUTING WORD FORMS

Before you can begin building and using Word electronic forms, it helps to understand the workflow associated with them. In general, you should follow these steps in the order presented:

1. **Plan your form.** Understand its goals and the information it must elicit.

2. **Build a skeleton of your form.** Add all the text and images that won't change when a user fills out the form. Leave space for the form's interactive elements—the areas users will fill out. (At this stage, you might want to do preliminary testing of your form with colleagues who will ultimately be working with it.)

3. **Add interactivity with form fields.** In the spaces you've left for them, add *form fields* that provide your form's interactivity. These include text form fields that allow users to type text such as names and addresses, check box form fields, and drop-down form fields that allow users to choose from a list of options.

4. **Protect your form.** This prevents changes to its structure and functionality. After you've protected a form, users can enter information only in the areas you've provided for them.

5. **Distribute your form.** There are several options for doing this. For example, you can save your form as a template, and store it in the network location you use for global templates. Users can then create new copies of the form whenever needed, by choosing the form from the File, New dialog box. Alternatively, you can provide the form as a Word document, stored on an intranet or sent by email to users when they request it.

PLANNING YOUR FORM

Careful planning can make the difference between an incomprehensible form that users fill out improperly (or not at all) and a clear, usable form that delivers the information you need rapidly and effectively. Here are some ideas for building effective, usable forms.

- **Be clear about your goals.** As mentioned previously, make sure you understand exactly what your form is intended to accomplish, and what information it must request in order to accomplish its goals.

- **Organize the required information logically.** For example, place all contact details (name, address, phone, email) in one area; place all financial details in another. Separate fields with headings that are as clear and self-explanatory as possible. Avoid redundancy: The user should never have to fill in the same information twice.

- **Think about how users will work with your form.** For example, a form containing credit-card information will typically allow the user to specify which type of credit card

28

is to be used (MasterCard, Visa); then the credit-card number; and only then the expiration date.

- **Emphasize usability and readability.** Use readable typefaces, avoid print that's too small, avoid "ALL CAPS" text, and, if you use color, be sure to use high-contrast colors.

- **Leave sufficient space for user information.** This is doubly important if you're creating a printed form that will be filled in by hand.

- **Use conventions your users will expect.** For example, if you want users of an electronic form to select only one item from a list, use a drop-down box, not a series of check boxes that allow them to (incorrectly) select multiple items.

- **Help users avoid errors up front.** For example, if a form requires inputs to be in the form of dollars and cents, present a default setting in that format, use Word's tools for enforcing inputs—and give users help that explains specifically what you're looking for.

- **Test!** Try out the form with real live users—*and listen to what they tell you!*

BUILDING THE SKELETON OF YOUR FORM

Whether you ultimately want your forms to be used as hard copy or an online format, the first step is the same: creating a template containing the "shell" of the form. The shell is the text, layout, and formatting elements that remain constant whenever the form is used. To create a template from scratch, open a new blank document, click Save, choose Document Template from the Save as Type drop-down box, and click Save.

NOTE

> If you originally created a printed form in Word and you now want to turn it into an electronic form that can be filled out from within Word, open the original Word file and resave it as a template.

After you create your template, you must create a framework for your form. You can use all Word's editing, formatting, and drawing tools, just as if you were creating any other kind of document. Most forms make heavy use of the following features:

- Tables (see Chapter 12, "Structuring and Organizing Information with Tables")
- Text boxes (see Chapter 16, "Word Desktop Publishing")
- Borders and shading (see Chapter 5, "Controlling Page Features")

Leave empty spaces (or placeholder characters such as &&&&) for the areas of the form you want users to fill in. Later, you'll learn how to use form fields that transform those empty spaces with interactivity and automation, enabling users to enter information more quickly and accurately. Figure 28.1 shows the skeleton of a form with all structure, text, and graphics in place.

Figure 28.1
The skeleton of a form, awaiting the use of form fields.

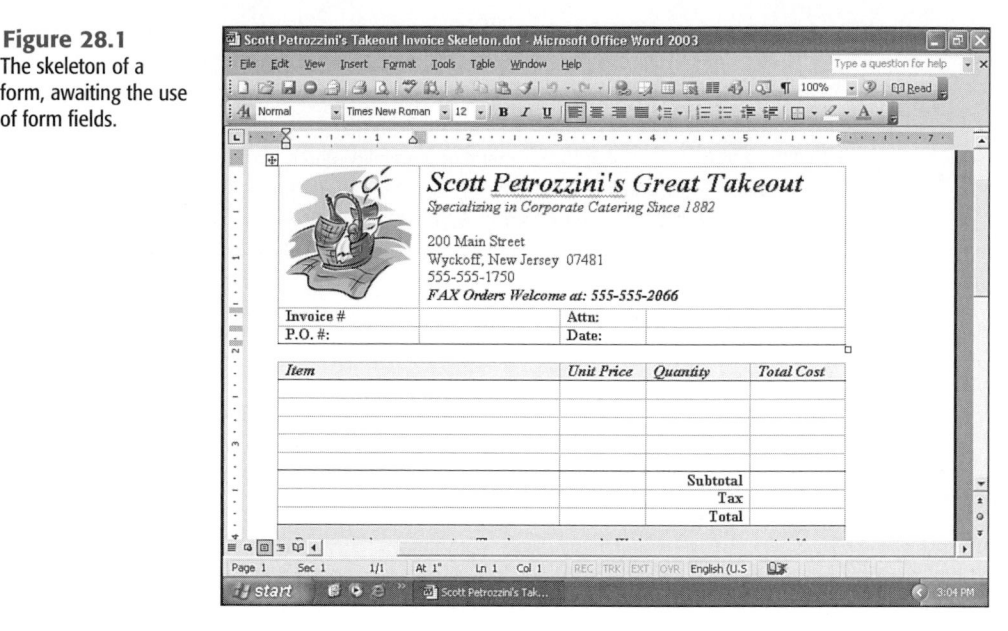

NOTE

Your form template should also contain any macros and AutoText entries you can create to streamline filling out the forms later.

 If you can't edit a form one of your colleagues has created, see "What to Do If Word Won't Allow You to Edit an Existing Form," in the "Troubleshooting" section of this chapter.

After you've built the skeleton for your form, be sure to save it as a template under a new name, preferably a descriptive one. If your organization numbers its forms, you might include the new form number in the name.

By default, Word saves all templates in the Templates folder; saving your file here makes it appear in the General tab of the New dialog box. You can also save it in any of the Templates subfolders, such as Letters & Faxes, Memos, Publications, and so on, which correspond to the other tabs of the New dialog box.

To enable users to access the form easily across a network, store it in a location to which they have access, such as the Workgroup Templates folder set up on your network. Of course, no matter how you choose to distribute your electronic forms, you should password-protect them so that they cannot be changed without authorization.

→ For more information on placing templates in a folder shared by an entire workgroup, **see** "Using Workgroup Templates," **p. 377**.

28

NOTE

> If you have a form that you want everyone to fill in, you can send the template as an email attachment, by choosing File, Send To, Mail Recipient (as Attachment). (Remember to add instructions on what to do with the form.)
>
> Outlook 2003 has its own form-generating capability, and if you need strong support for messaging and workflow—especially if your organization also uses Microsoft Exchange—consider building the form with Outlook instead of Word 2003.

If you want to edit the form's structure after completing it, you must open the template itself, not a document created from the template. To make sure that you're doing so, in the Open dialog box change the Files of Type to Document Templates to display Word templates instead of Word documents.

→ For more information about working with templates, **see** Chapter 11, "Templates, Wizards, and Add-Ins," **p. 355**.

ADDING INTERACTIVITY WITH FORM FIELDS

So far, you've seen only how to create a document that *resembles* a form—in other words, the skeleton of a form. In the rest of this chapter, you'll learn how to add interactivity and automation to your form with *form fields*. Form fields are special document elements that make it possible to fill out the form more easily and quickly, and to use the form's information after it's there.

WORKING WITH THE FORMS TOOLBAR

Working with forms requires access to a specific set of tools. Word 2003 has grouped the essential commands for creating and editing a form together in the Forms toolbar. You can display this toolbar as you would any other: Choose View, Toolbars, and then choose Forms from the submenu. Figure 28.2 shows the Forms toolbar.

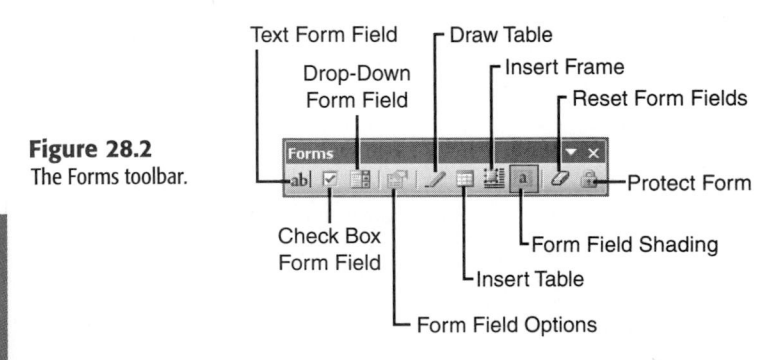

Figure 28.2
The Forms toolbar.

Ten buttons appear on the Forms toolbar:

- Text Form Field inserts a text form field where users can enter text, numbers, symbols, and spaces. You can also use text form fields to make calculations based on entries that users make in other form fields.

- Check Box Form Field inserts a check box in your document; users can either check the box or leave it unchecked.
- Drop-Down Form Field inserts a drop-down form field that gives a user a list of alternatives; the user is limited to choosing one of those alternatives.
- Form Field Options is used to specify the detailed settings for any form field after you've inserted it.
- Draw Table displays the Tables and Borders toolbar, which contains buttons the form designer can use to build tables more easily and activates the Draw Table tool.
- Insert Table inserts a table with a specific number of columns and rows, all of them the same height and width. This is the same Insert Table button that appears in the Standard toolbar.

→ To see how to draw or insert tables, **see** "Word's Multiple Approaches to Creating a Table," **p. 388**.

- Insert Frame includes a free-floating box in the form that you can format with a precise size and location. (Insert Frame does not insert text boxes.)
- Form Field Shading toggles your form's text, check box, and drop-down fields between medium gray shading and no shading.
- Reset Form Fields clears all entries that have been added to a form.
- Protect Form enables you to protect all areas of a form from change, except for those that users are intended to fill in.

> **TIP**
>
> As you build your form, you'll often want to use Protect Form to toggle between protecting the form (which shows how it will look and act when users work with it) and unprotecting the form so that you can make changes to it.

INSERTING A TEXT FORM FIELD

When it comes to basic forms, by far the most common type of entry is plain free-form text. Most forms, at a minimum, gather your name and address—and others may require widely varying types of information, much of which must be entered as text. Text form fields are the workhorses of forms.

To enter a standard text form field, display the Forms toolbar, position your insertion point where you want the field to appear, and click the Text Form Field button. You've just inserted a text form field; it appears shaded in your document (see Figure 28.3).

The generic 1/2"-wide Text Form Field button you've just placed in your document enables users to insert any text, of any length. But you may want to restrict what users can enter here—and give them some help in entering the information you need.

You control the options associated with a text form field through the Text Form Field Options dialog box, shown in Figure 28.4. This dialog box can be reached in two ways. You can select the field you want to edit and click the Form Field Options button on the Forms

28

toolbar, or you can right-click on the field and click Properties from the shortcut menu that appears.

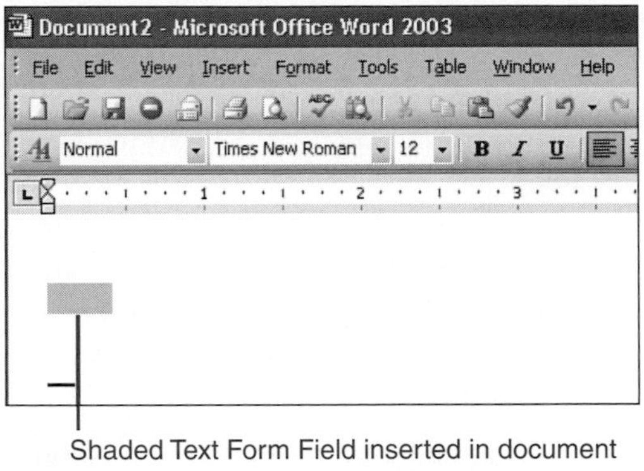

Figure 28.3
A text form field as it appears after being inserted in a document.

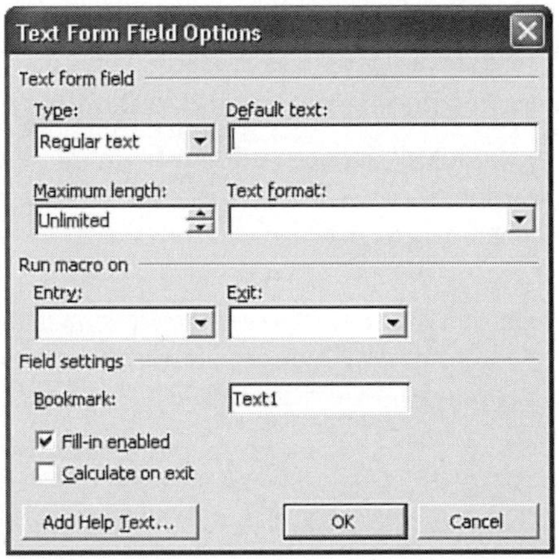

Shaded Text Form Field inserted in document

Figure 28.4
From the Text Form Field Options dialog box, you can control the behavior of a text form field.

PLACING A NUMBER, DATE, OR TIME IN A TEXT FORM FIELD

The first aspect of the text form field you can control is whether it should contain text. You can use the Type drop-down list box in the Text Form Field Options dialog box to specify several alternatives, including these:

- **Regular Text.** The default setting; users can enter anything they want.
- **Number.** This setting restricts entry to numbers and number-related characters and punctuation (for example, $ and : characters). If a user enters a character other than a number, the form stores the number zero instead.
- **Date.** This setting restricts entry to a valid date or time. An error message appears if the user enters something else.

- **Current Date.** This setting inserts a { DATE } field. The field is updated when the document is first opened or created, and afterward in accordance with the traditional Word field updating rules (for example, you can select the field and press F9 to update it).

- **Current Time.** This setting inserts a { TIME } field.

- **Calculation.** This setting tells Word you want the field to perform a calculation. As you'll see later in this chapter, in the "Using Calculations in Text Form Fields" section, if you use this setting, you have to create the equation as well.

SETTING DEFAULT INFORMATION FOR YOUR TEXT FORM FIELD

In many text form fields, users want to insert the same information most of the time. You can automatically provide this information, which then appears automatically in the form unless the user changes it.

To specify default information, display the Text Form Field Options dialog box and enter the information in the Default Text text box. You can enter text, numbers, symbols, or spaces, unless you've restricted the type of data that can be entered—for example, by choosing Current Date, Current Time, or Calculation.

The default information you specify will appear in the form as you typed it; the user can type over it to replace it with new information.

If your users are not familiar with Word forms, you may need to provide instructions that let the user know he or she can change this information.

CONTROLLING THE LENGTH OF USER INPUT

Many forms are designed to restrict the number of characters a user may enter in a specific area. For example, if your users are entering Social Security numbers, you should limit the number of digits to nine; any more digits than that, and the input is incorrect. You can set the length of a text form field in the Maximum Length scroll box in the Text Form Field Options dialog box.

CONTROLLING CAPITALIZATION IN TEXT FORM FIELDS

You apply most text formatting to form fields the same way you apply other text formatting: by manually applying it to characters or paragraphs, or by using styles. However, the Text Form Field Options dialog box does enable you to control the case to be used in regular text entries. Make sure that Regular Text is selected in the Type drop-down box; then choose Uppercase, Lowercase, First Capital, or Title Case from the Text Format drop-down box.

USING NUMERIC FORMATS IN TEXT FORM FIELDS

As you've already learned, you can limit a text form field to one of several types of information. One of the most useful types of information available to you is Number.

Specifying that data be entered as a number takes you one small step toward ensuring data integrity. Nobody can fill in alphabetical characters, for example, in a field that requires a dollar amount.

28

After you choose Number, you can also specify the format in which the number appears. Make a choice from the Number Format combo box. Among the options Word provides are options to

- Include decimal points; for example, `3.28`
- Add commas as thousands separators; for example, `12,516`
- Place negative numbers in parentheses; for example, `(132.14)`
- Use percentage symbols; for example, `38%`
- Use combinations of these symbols

Then, even if the user enters a number in a different format, Word automatically changes it to be consistent with all the other forms you're collecting.

NOTE

Some elements of the Text Form Field Options dialog box change their names depending on the type of information you choose to include in your text form field.

In the sample invoice shown in Figure 28.5, text form fields have been added to each table cell under Unit Price. These text form fields have been set to appear in dollars-and-cents format.

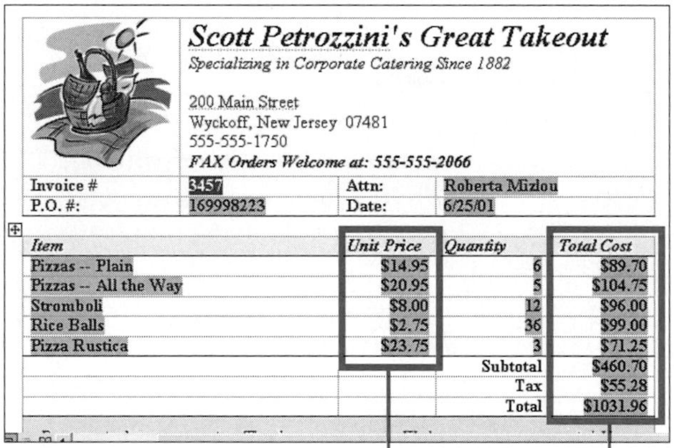

Figure 28.5
The text form fields have been formatted to appear as dollars and cents.

Text form fields formatted to appear as dollars and cents

TIP

You can go beyond standard numeric formats by adding a "numeric picture" in the Number Format combo box. The numeric picture ###.#, for example, tells Word to round off any entry to tenths. Numeric pictures are explained in the "Customizing Numeric Formats to Your Specific Needs" section of Chapter 23, "Automating Your Documents with Field Codes."

USING DATES AND TIMES IN TEXT FORM FIELDS

You can also specify that text form fields include dates and/or times. You can allow users to enter the dates or times, following date and time formats you specify. Or, if you prefer, you can time stamp your form with the current date or time when the form is first opened by a user.

To allow users to enter a date, display the Text Form Field Options dialog box, and choose Date from the Type drop-down box. Choose a Date Format from the drop-down box; if you want to include space for Time, choose a date format that contains h:mm.

→ For more information about choosing and customizing Word's date/time formats, **see** "Formatting Dates and Times in Field Results," **p. 795**.

In some cases, you want your form field to display the date when the form was opened for the first time, instead of permitting users to enter a date manually. To display the date when the form was opened, choose Current Date from the Type drop-down box. To display the *time* the field was opened, choose Current Time from the Type drop-down box.

CAUTION

Remember that a user can still circumvent your date and time settings by resetting the system clock, thereby making it appear that a form was filled out sooner than it really was.

CAUTION

When you're creating or editing your form, get in the habit of protecting your document before you test your changes. Otherwise, selecting the form field and then entering some text overwrites any default value you have established for the field. To quickly lock and unlock your form, use the Protect Form button on the Forms toolbar.

After you test a form field, be sure to clear all entries you don't want included in the final form. You can do this by clicking the Reset Form Fields button.

Other features of the Text Form Field Options dialog box are covered later in the chapter. In particular, adding Help Text is covered in the "Adding Help to Your Forms" section, and running macros is covered in the "Running Macros from Form Fields" section.

USING CALCULATIONS IN TEXT FORM FIELDS

In Chapter 12, you learned that Word can perform simple calculations within tables, much as a spreadsheet program such as Excel can. Forms can especially benefit from this capability. For example, you can create invoices that calculate totals based on how many of each item someone orders, and how much each item costs.

Use the Text Form Field Options dialog box to build calculations. First, choose Calculation as the Type of data you want to insert. To the right of the Type drop-down box, the Expression text box appears. An equal sign is placed in the text box. (All formulas in Word begin with an equal sign.) You can now use any of Word's basic calculation techniques.

28

To specify values in table cells, you can specify the table cells. The first row of a table is row 1. The first column of a table is column A. The cell at the upper left of a table, therefore, is cell A1. To add the contents of cells A1 and A2, enter

```
=A1+A2
```

Because every form field has a corresponding bookmark, you can also use bookmarks, such as

```
=Quantity1+Quantity2
```

You can also use any of the calculation functions Word provides. The simplest are SUM for addition and PRODUCT for multiplication. For example, to add the numbers in cells B1 and B2, enter

```
=SUM(B1,B2)
```

Or to add all the numbers above your current cell, enter

```
=SUM(ABOVE)
```

To multiply the numbers in cells B1 and B2, enter

```
=PRODUCT(B1,B2)
```

→ For more information about working with formulas, **see** "Calculating with Tables," **p. 427**.

USING CALCULATE ON EXIT TO AUTOMATE YOUR CALCULATIONS

If you've ever worked with a spreadsheet program such as Excel and then had to do calculations in a Word table, you've probably wished that Word could automatically recalculate formulas every time a value was changed. With the Calculate on Exit feature for form fields, Word can recalculate specific form fields whenever a user changes a value the field depends on. Calculate on Exit works when you click or tab away from the form field that contains this setting. (You don't have to wait until you exit Word or close the document.)

Because Calculate on Exit requires information from other fields in your form, setting this up is a bit more complicated than simply inserting a field. To use Calculate on Exit, follow these instructions:

1. Click the Text Form Field button on the Forms toolbar to place text form fields where you want to enter your numbers. Then insert a final form field to use for the value you are calculating.

2. In all but the final form field (where the calculated value is to appear), first change the Type from Regular Text to Number in the Text Form Field Options dialog box. Next, check the Calculate on Exit check box. If you want, you can also change the Number Format. Note the name of each form field in the Bookmark text box.

3. In the text form field that is to display the total, first change the Type to Calculation. Next, put your formula in the Expression text box. You can refer to the other form fields through their bookmark names. A typical formula that, for example, might add up the total of three form fields would read =SUM(TEXT1,TEXT2,TEXT3).

   Do *not* select the Calculate on Exit option for this final form field box.

4. After you close the text form field dialog boxes, lock the form by clicking the Protect Form button on the Forms toolbar.

Now, whenever a user enters or changes a number that is part of a calculated formula, the formula will automatically recalculate.

ADDING CHECK BOX FORM FIELDS

Check boxes are a handy way to enable users to select one or more options that are not mutually exclusive. For example, in Figure 28.6, check boxes indicate that a user can sign up for as many courses as he or she wants.

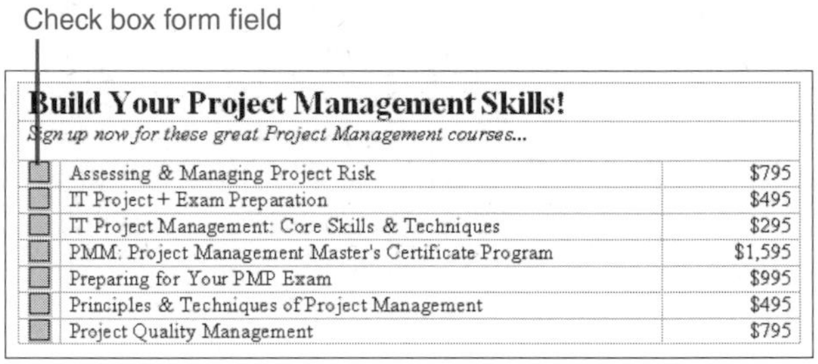

Check box form field

Figure 28.6
An example of how check boxes can be used in a form.

Build Your Project Management Skills!	
Sign up now for these great Project Management courses...	
Assessing & Managing Project Risk	$795
IT Project + Exam Preparation	$495
IT Project Management: Core Skills & Techniques	$295
PMM: Project Management Master's Certificate Program	$1,595
Preparing for Your PMP Exam	$995
Principles & Techniques of Project Management	$495
Project Quality Management	$795

Check boxes are generally used when it doesn't matter how many of the items in a group your user can select. For example, a check box is the method of choice when you see the phrase "Check all that apply" in a survey or questionnaire.

To insert a check box, place your insertion point where you want the check box to appear, and click the Check Box Form Field button on the Forms toolbar.

By default, Word displays boxes unchecked. If you want a box to appear checked by default, or to change other options associated with a check box, display the Check Box Form Field Options dialog box, shown in Figure 28.7. To do so, select the check box form field you just created and click Form Field Options, or right-click on the check box form field, and choose Properties from the shortcut menu.

To specify that a check box should appear checked by default, choose Checked in the Default Value area. While you're here, you may want to consider some other settings as well.

TIP

> Whether you prefer a default setting of Checked or Not Checked, there may be times when you want to prevent users from changing the default. For instance, you might want to include a check box in your form to indicate that you plan to make an option available in the near future, but prevent the user from checking the box until the option becomes available.
>
> To prevent the user from changing the setting you specify, clear the Check Box Enabled check box in the Field Settings area.

28

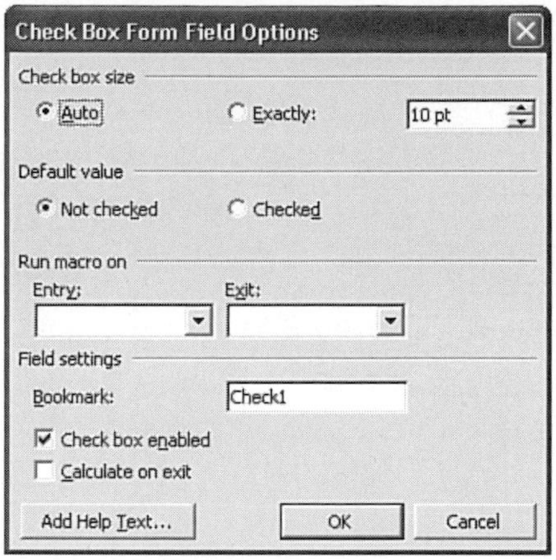

Figure 28.7
Controlling the behavior of a check box form field.

By default, Word keeps your check box the same size as the text that follows it; if that text changes size, so does your check box. The Check Box Form Field Options dialog box, however, enables you to change the size of the check box without changing the size of any surrounding text. For example, you could enlarge a box for emphasis.

To specify the precise size of a form field check box, choose the Exactly option button in the Check Box Size area. Then enter the new size in the spinner box.

Later, after you protect the form and make it available to users, they will see a square shaded box. To check it, they can click it once, or press either the spacebar or the X key. The same techniques uncheck a box that's already checked.

→ For information about adding Help and macro functionality to check box form fields, **see** "Adding Help to Your Forms," **p. 949**, and "Running Macros from Form Fields," **p. 951**.

ADDING DROP-DOWN FORM FIELDS

Often, you'll want to give users a specific set of options from which to choose—and prevent them from entering any other alternative. For example, you might create a form that asks your telephone customer-service representatives to specify which product family a caller is calling about. Word's drop-down form fields enable you to do this.

NOTE

The form must be unprotected for you to change the formatting of a form field.

In other forms software, round radio buttons are sometimes used to indicate that only one choice is possible (for example, a field that must be answered "Yes" or "No"). Word does not provide radio buttons for electronic forms; however, drop-down fields are a good substitute in forms that will be filled out electronically.

Drop-down fields are *not* an adequate substitute in forms designed to be printed and hand-filled, because some of the options provided by the drop-down field may not be visible on the printed form.

To add a drop-down form field to a form, display the Forms toolbar and click the Drop-Down Form Field button. This inserts a drop-down form field without any options for users to choose from.

You can supply the options by displaying the Drop-Down Form Field Options dialog box (see Figure 28.8). Select the drop-down form field you just created and click Form Field Options or right-click on the form field and choose Properties from the shortcut menu.

Figure 28.8
Creating options for a drop-down form field.

Now, populate the drop-down list with items that will be available to your form's users. One by one, type the items in the Drop-Down Item box and click Add. If you need to change the order of entries in the drop-down list, select an item you want to move, and click the Move Up or Move Down arrows.

Word treats the first item in your list as your default choice. That means it is the option that appears selected when the user opens the form, as shown in Figure 28.9.

Figure 28.9
Sample use of a drop-down form field.

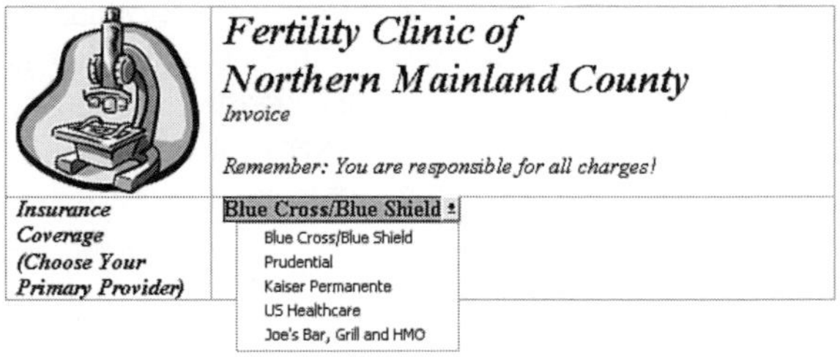

Suppose that you no longer need one of your options; perhaps you've discontinued a product or service. You can delete the option from your form by selecting it and clicking Remove.

As with check box form fields, there might be times when you want to specify choices but not allow users to access them. Perhaps you plan to make the choices available later, but for

28

the moment, only your default option is available. To disable the drop-down list box while still displaying the default option, clear the Drop-Down Enabled check box.

→ For information about adding Help and macro functionality to drop-down form fields, **see** "Adding Help to Your Forms," **p. 949**, and "Running Macros from Form Fields," **p. 951**.

FORMATTING YOUR FORM FIELDS

You can format form fields just as you would any other text characters: Select their contents and apply formatting using the Formatting toolbar, keyboard shortcuts, or menu commands. You can make text and drop-down form fields bold, italic, or underline; change the font name or size; and so on. The field itself retains the same gray shading. You can toggle this gray shading on and off with the Form Field Shading button on the Forms toolbar.

Most of the formatting you add—especially font formatting—isn't evident unless text appears in the field, either as a default setting or as entered by a user.

NOTE

The form must be unprotected for you to change the formatting of a form field.

CAUTION

When applying font formatting in a form, make sure that you use fonts that will be available on all the computers using your form. Otherwise, Windows may substitute fonts that look unattractive or are difficult to read.

This isn't a problem if you use basic Windows fonts such as Arial or Times New Roman. However, if you must use nonstandard fonts–perhaps to follow a corporate style guide– you may have another option. In some cases, you can embed the fonts you need directly in your form.

To do so, Choose Tools, Options, Save, and check the Embed TrueType Fonts check box. When enabled, this check box tells Word to actually store a copy of the font in the template.

Be aware that a template containing fonts increases the file's size, making it slower to open and close or send through email. Also, some fonts cannot be embedded due to manufacturer restrictions. To discover whether a font contains embedding restrictions (and to learn more about the detailed characteristics of a font), download and install the ttfext add-in available at Microsoft's Web site, at www.microsoft.com/ typography/property/property.htm.

REMOVING A FORM FIELD FROM YOUR FORM

As you create and modify form templates, you may find that some fields are no longer needed. To remove a form field from your document, first click on it to select it. The field turns a darker shade of gray than normal. After it's selected, pressing Delete removes the form field; you can also click Cut on the Standard Toolbar, press Ctrl+X, or choose Edit, Cut.

NOTE

> If your document is protected, you must first unprotect it. Choose Tools, Unprotect Document, or click the Protect Form button on the Forms toolbar.

CAUTION

> Although Cut works to remove an unwanted form field, you need to be more careful about using Copy and Paste to create multiple copies of a form field.
>
> If calculations are involved (as in a column of form fields that each calculate a line on an invoice), you need to manually update each form field to make sure it is calculating the correct bookmarked form fields.
>
> Also, if the form field you copy contains a bookmark, you need to manually create new bookmarks for all the copies.

ADVANCED FORM FIELD FEATURES

Word provides some powerful form field automation options that are available to you regardless of the types of form fields you're using. These include

- Adding help to your forms, including anything from a simple message in the status bar to a more detailed message that appears when the user presses F1. (Unfortunately, Word provides no way to add a ScreenTip to a form field—something your users might now be trained to expect.)
- Associating form fields with bookmarks.
- Running macros when users enter or exit a form field. This means that your form can help complete itself, based on the specific entries the user makes.

ADDING HELP TO YOUR FORMS

If you're in charge of helping people fill out their forms, you can cut down dramatically on the support you need to provide by adding built-in help to your online forms. Word's built-in help for forms can provide more detailed explanations than your form itself may have room for. You can use it to elaborate on the options you're offering, the information you want to collect, or how to use the form itself.

TIP

> You should give at least basic help in the form itself, where the help is visible for people who don't know how to look for it. Type language such as the following directly onto the form:
>
> To get help about any item, move to it with the mouse or the keyboard and press F1.

28

To add help text, create the type of form field you need, right-click on it, and choose Properties; its Form Field Options dialog box appears. Click the Add Help Text button. The dialog box shown in Figure 28.10 appears.

Figure 28.10
In the Form Field Help Text dialog box, you can specify where help comes from, where it appears, and what it says.

You now have two choices to make: where your help message appears and where its contents come from. If you want help to appear in Word's status bar, click the Status Bar tab. If you want it to appear when the user presses F1, click the Help Key (F1) tab.

NOTE
> You can create both kinds of help, by placing entries in each tab, as discussed in the next section, "Using Both Forms of Help Together."

No matter which tab you choose, you have the same two sources for your help text:

■ An existing AutoText entry containing boilerplate text you've already created. (Choose the AutoText entry you want from the AutoText Entry drop-down box, which lists all AutoText entries that are available to the template you're working in.)

■ New text (type it in the Type Your Own text box).

If you choose to use an AutoText entry, it's quite likely that this entry does not yet exist. To create an AutoText entry, type the text in your document; then choose Insert, AutoText, New. Enter a name for your AutoText entry, and click OK.

→ For more information about working with AutoText entries, **see** "AutoText: The Complete Boilerplate Resource," **p. 301**.

For simple "one-off" forms that aren't part of an extensive forms system, you'll probably want to use Type Your Own rather than a preexisting AutoText Entry. Type Your Own entries are conveniently stored with each form, and can easily be revised through this dialog box.

You might, however, use AutoText entries if you are creating a help entry you intend to use in multiple forms or multiple locations. This way, if you need to update the entry later, it will automatically be updated in all the locations where it appears.

CAUTION

> If you use an AutoText entry, be aware that neither the status bar nor these Help dialog boxes can contain graphics, even though graphics can be stored in AutoText entries.

When you finish creating help, click OK.

USING BOTH FORMS OF HELP TOGETHER

You don't have to choose between offering help in a dialog box and offering it in the status bar. For example, you might provide abbreviated help in the status bar, ending the status bar message with "Press F1 for more help." You could then associate more extensive information with the F1 key so that when the user presses it, Word displays the added help information in a special Help dialog box. (Status bar help is limited to 138 characters; help presented in a dialog box can be up to 255 characters in length.) Figure 28.11 shows how both kinds of help can complement each other in this fashion.

Help dialog box (appears when user presses F1)

Figure 28.11
Providing help to users of a form.

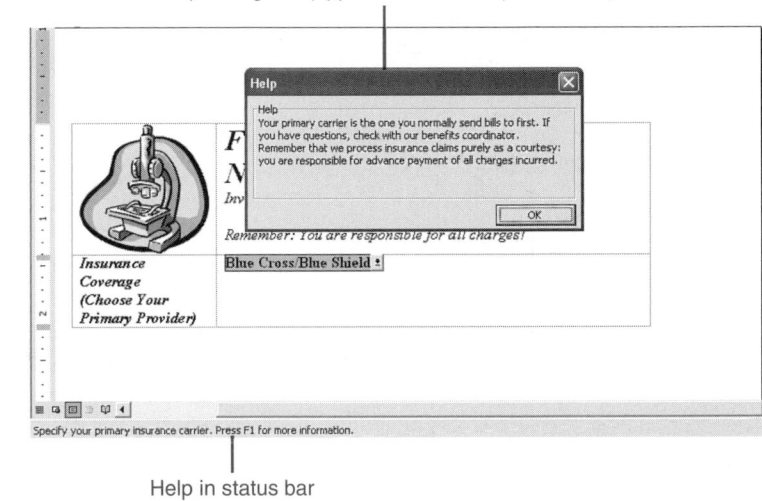

Help in status bar

Some users provide simple instructions on using the form in the status bar and provide background about how to interpret the form's questions in the dialog box.

For example, in a travel reimbursement form, the status bar might say "Enter total airline ticket cost," whereas the F1 key might summarize the company's travel reimbursement policies.

RUNNING MACROS FROM FORM FIELDS

You can instruct Word to run a macro whenever a user enters or leaves a field. In either case, you can select from macros available in your current document or template.

28

TIP

If you already have a macro you want to use, copy it to your form template using the Organizer.

→ For more information about working with the Organizer, **see** "Keeping Track of Styles with the Organizer," **p. 349**.

Figure 28.12 shows an example of how you might use this feature. In this example, a macro, ClickToPrint, has been recorded. ClickToPrint sends the form to a user's default printer. Whenever a user tabs to—or clicks in—the CLICK TO PRINT field, the file prints automatically.

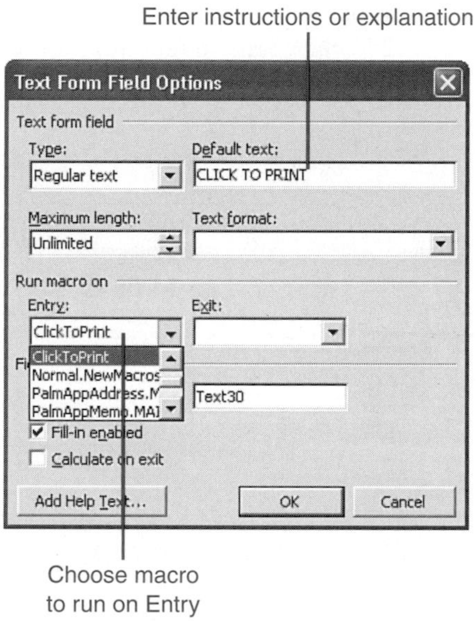

Figure 28.12
Creating a form that includes a Print button.

Enter instructions or explanation

Choose macro to run on Entry

Every form field is automatically assigned a bookmark name. This makes it easy to create Word macros that check the current contents of a bookmark and, based on what they find there, place corresponding contents in other fields. For example, when a user inserts a name, the macro can automatically look up that name in a database and insert the corresponding company and address. Or, when the user checks a check box, the macro can enable other form fields that were previously grayed out.

After your macro is written, you need to link it to a form field. First, double-click the form field to which you want to attach the macro, or right-click on the field and choose Properties. This displays the Properties dialog box associated with the form field.

NOTE

If double-clicking on the form field doesn't work, choose Tools, Unprotect Document to permit changes to form fields.

Second, in the Run Macro On section, choose either Entry or Exit (you can create different macros for each, if you want). Third, select the macro from those listed. Click OK, and you're finished. As always, be sure to lock the document using the Protect Form button on the Forms toolbar after you make your changes.

→ For more information about recording macros that can be used in forms (or elsewhere), **see** "Recording and Running Visual Basic Macros," **p. 1069**.

CONVERTING ELECTRONIC FORMS TO PRINTED FORMS

It's common to create forms that will be used both from within Word and in printed versions. Word delivers "What You See Is What You Get" formatting, so your forms appear in print exactly as they do onscreen. (There is one exception: The gray rectangles that mark form fields onscreen do not appear in print.)

However, the art of creating an easy-to-use printed form varies slightly from the techniques you need for electronic forms. Keep these pointers in mind:

- When users are working in Word, they can enter large amounts of data even in a tiny text form field (as long as you haven't limited the maximum length of their entries). Of course, this isn't true in print. Make sure that you leave sufficient space in your design for users to enter all the text they need to enter.

- You need to remove drop-down fields (so that defaults are not printed in your form, preventing users from making other choices). Then you need to reformat your forms so that users can see a list of the choices from which you want them to select.

- You may need to enlarge Word's default check boxes to make them easily visible and usable in print.

- If you're designing a form that will be filled out on a typewriter, make the font size 12 or 10 points. The type elements for most typewriters are usually one of these two sizes, and it makes aligning the responses much easier.

- The Drawing toolbar enables you to create various shapes perfect for forms: straight lines, arrows, boxes, circles, and numerous AutoShapes. Moreover, they can all be independently positioned and aligned.

- A table is an easy way to create a series of evenly spaced lines. You can turn off all but the bottom border and set the table height to be exactly a certain point size. The Forms toolbar has both Insert Table and Draw Table buttons.

- If you need to position an element of the form precisely, use a frame or a text box. To insert a frame, click the Insert Frame button on the Forms toolbar and drag the mouse pointer until you reach the approximate size you need. Then you can refine the size and position by right-clicking on the frame and choosing Format Frame from the shortcut menu.

- If your electronic form contains a time stamp, when you print it, the time stamp will represent the time of printing.

28

- Rather than using check box form fields, consider creating your check boxes through Format, Bullets and Numbering. Select the hollow square check box bullet. You can select any other symbol as a check box by clicking the Customize button on the Bullets and Numbering dialog box and then clicking the Bullet button. Click the Font button to change the bullet's size. Turn off your checklist by clicking the Bullet button on the Formatting toolbar.

PROTECTING AN ENTIRE FORM WITH EDITING RESTRICTIONS

When you have finished preparing your form, you need to protect it—preventing users from making unauthorized changes to the underlying form, while allowing them to fill out the form fields you have provided for them.

NOTE

> A form doesn't behave like a form until you protect it.

When you protect a form, some form fields that provide specific information can't be changed either. For example, in a protected form field, a user can't override the calculation you've built into a text form field.

To protect a form, first open it. Then choose Tools, Protect Document. The task pane shown in Figure 28.13 appears.

Figure 28.13
Protecting a form.

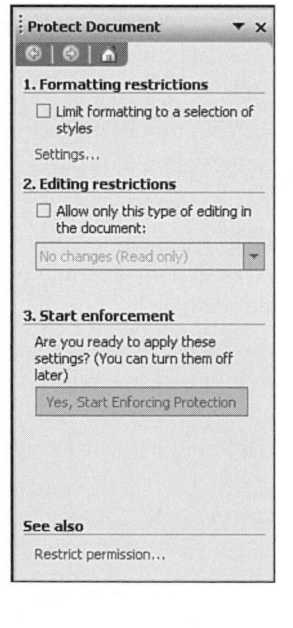

Check the Allow Only This Type of Editing in the Document check box. Then, choose Filling in Forms from the drop-down box. Click Yes, Start Enforcing Protection.

Word now displays the Start Enforcing Protection dialog box (see Figure 28.14). Here, you can protect your form with a password, if you choose. Include a password if there's any risk that your form might otherwise be edited inappropriately. (You don't want sabbaticals in Tahiti added to your benefits option form.)

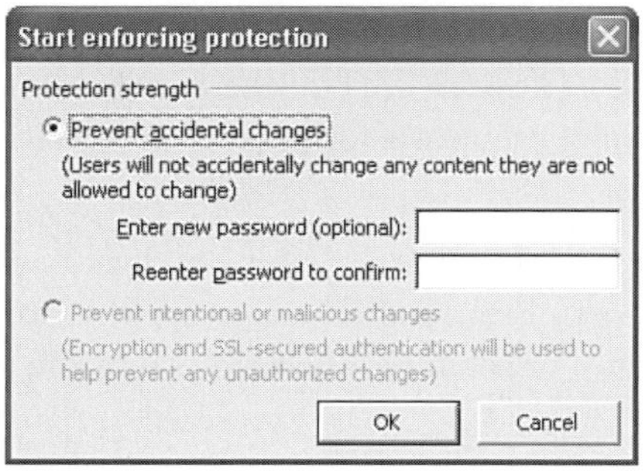

Figure 28.14
Setting a forms password.

Form passwords by themselves don't encrypt the document. Users can still open a password-protected form template; they just can't unprotect and edit it. To unprotect such a document, click Stop Protection on the Protect Document task pane. The Unprotect Document password dialog box opens, as shown in Figure 28.15.

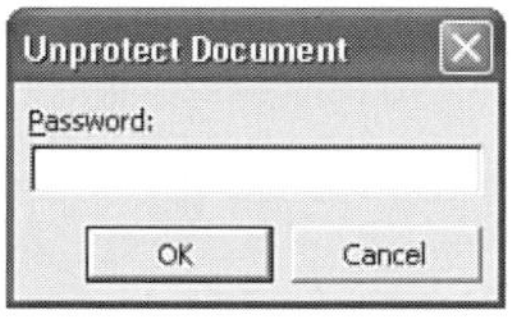

Figure 28.15
The Unprotect Document password dialog box.

As always when creating password names, choose a password you'll remember but nobody else can figure out. Don't write it down and leave it in an obvious location. And remember, after you create and confirm a password, you have no way to unprotect the document without the password.

To remove a password, first open the document (using its password). Then unprotect it using the Unprotect Document option on the Tools menu. Then protect it again by choosing Protect Document from the Tools menu. Choose Forms in the Protect Document dialog box. No password appears in the Password box. If you don't want the file to be protected by a password, click OK. When you save the file, it no longer requires a password. (If you want a new password, type it and confirm it. After you save the file, the new password goes into effect.)

28

TIP

> In some cases, you may not need "heavy-duty" protection against malicious changes: You may simply want to keep forms from being changed inadvertently while you're working with them. To quickly protect a form against inadvertent change, open the form. Display the Forms toolbar (View, Toolbars, Forms); then click the Protect Form button.

PROTECTING A SECTION OF A FORM

Word enables you to divide your document or template into multiple *sections* and protect only one section. This enables users to edit at will elsewhere in their form documents—but when they come to the section you've set up as a form, they're restricted to making changes in only the contents of form fields.

To protect only a section of your form document or template, start by separating your document into sections by choosing Insert, Break and choosing one of Word's section break types. (If you don't want extra page—or column—breaks in your form, choose Continuous.)

Then, to protect a specific section, follow these steps:

1. Choose Tools, Protect Document to display the Protect Document task pane.
2. Click the Select Sections hyperlink. The Section Protection dialog box opens (see Figure 28.16).

Figure 28.16
You can specify which sections of your form you want to protect.

3. Clear any sections you do not want to protect; check the sections you do want to protect.
4. Click OK when you're finished, and click OK again to close the Protect Document dialog box.

FILLING IN ONLINE FORMS

To fill in an online form, create a new document based on the template that contains the form. Each form field is shaded in gray. The first field is shaded in deeper gray; that's where your insertion point is.

Unless you specified a short maximum length for your field, the gray area extends as you type. If the field is located in a text cell, the text simply wraps when you reach the end of a cell.

After you fill in a form field, press Tab or the down-arrow key; both move you to the next form field in which you might make an entry. Word skips over form fields that it automatically calculates and fields in which you disable user input.

Table 28.1 shows Word's editing and navigation keys for editing forms. As you can see, some keys work a little differently in forms compared with other documents.

TABLE 28.1   WORD'S FORM EDITING COMMANDS

To Do This	Use This Key or Combination
Move to the next editable field	Tab or down arrow
Move to the preceding editable field	Shift+Tab or up arrow
Show the contents of a drop-down list	F4 or Alt+down arrow
Move up or down in a drop-down list	Up arrow or down arrow
Make a selection in a drop-down list	Enter
Mark or unmark a check box	Spacebar or X
Show help for a form	F1 (if you specified that Word display a dialog box to show help; otherwise, help appears in the status bar)
Insert a tab	Ctrl+Tab

After you've filled out the form, you can save it, print it, or forward it to whoever is responsible for processing it—for example, by using File, Send To, Mail Recipient (as Attachment).

SAVING ONLY THE DATA IN A FORM

One of the key reasons for using a form is to collect data. Data is best stored in a database where it can be sorted, filtered, and output in various forms. Word gives you an easy method to extract the information from filled-out forms in a format that makes it easier to import into a database. You can save only the data in a form (as opposed to the entire contents of the form, including the skeleton framework surrounding the form fields). To save only the data, do this:

1. After your form has been filled out, click the Save button on the Standard toolbar.

2. In the Save As dialog box, choose Tools, Save Options.

3. In the Save (Options) dialog box, check the Save Data Only for Forms check box and click OK. The file type changes to Text Only.

4. Choose a filename and folder location for your file. Click Save.

28

TIP

If you want your forms to be saved as data only, regardless of who uses them or how often, choose Tools, Options; click the Save tab; and then enable the Save Data Only for Forms check box. This way users don't have to worry about selecting Save Data Only for Forms in the Save As dialog box.

When Word saves just the form data, it uses comma-delimited fields. You might be familiar with the concept of a comma-delimited field if you've worked with mail merges. The information from each field is placed in quotes and separated by commas. For example, one data file might look like this: "John","Johnson","123 Somter Street","Avery","SC","29678". The data appears in Word's default tab order for the form's fields, or, if you set the tab order using macros, it saves in the order you specified.

TIP

Comma-delimited text is also easier to import into applications built on XML.

This file format is used for both text form fields and drop-down form fields; for drop-down fields, Word includes the item selected by the user. Information returned from a check box form field is handled slightly differently. A checked box shows up as a 1, whereas an unchecked box is a 0. Neither appears in quotes.

After you have saved your forms as data, the information can be imported into an existing database in a program such as Microsoft Access. Almost any database program can read comma-delimited fields saved in a text file. If you are comfortable writing Visual Basic for Applications code, you can write a macro to append the information in each form into one master file to make importing even easier.

→ For more information on working with macros, **see** Chapter 32, "Recording and Running Visual Basic Macros," **p. 1069**.

PRINTING ONLY THE DATA IN FORMS

Just as you might sometimes want to save only the data in forms, occasionally you might want to print only the data in a form. For instance, your form may be many pages long; you might want to have a quick printed record of your responses without printing the whole form. To print only the data, choose Tools, Options. On the Print tab, check the box marked Print Data Only for Forms.

NOTE

When you check Print Data Only for Forms, Word will print only the form's data until you uncheck this box.

This setting applies to the current form; if you save the form as a template, it also applies to new forms created based on this template.

TROUBLESHOOTING

WHAT TO DO IF WORD WON'T ALLOW YOU TO EDIT AN EXISTING FORM

The original designer of the form has probably protected it from changes. To unprotect the form, choose Unprotect Document from the Tools menu. If your colleague has created the form with a password, you need to know the password to gain access.

The sections "Protecting an Entire Form with Editing Restrictions" and "Protecting a Section of a Form," earlier in this chapter, cover protecting and unprotecting forms in more detail.

WHAT TO DO IF FORM FIELDS DISAPPEAR

Check to make sure that your forms are locked. If the form isn't locked, selecting a form field for entry is just like highlighting a word or a block of text; the next character you enter erases whatever is selected if you have Typing Replaces Selection enabled (Tools, Options, Edit). Always keep your Forms toolbar open and available when you are creating or editing a form. It's much easier to remember to click the Protect Form button than it is to choose Tools, Protect Document.

WHAT TO DO IF THE TAB ORDER IN YOUR FORM FIELDS IS INCORRECT

The easiest way of navigating a form when entering data is by using the Tab key. However, this is useful only if the order Word uses when tabbing from field to field is a logical one. By default, tab order follows the placement of form fields on the page, starting with the form field closest to the upper left of the page. From there, tabbing continues from left to right and down.

However, this may not be the best order for your form. For example, you may want users to answer all of a list of questions in a square area on the left of the form before they answer questions to the right. Forcing Word to go where you want requires you to manually build Visual Basic for Applications macros, and incorporate them in each form field to run on exit. You can find detailed instructions for doing this in Microsoft's Knowledge Base article Q212378, accessible at `http://support.microsoft.com/?kbid=212378`.

WHAT TO DO IF YOU SEE FIELD CODES SUCH AS { FORMDROPDOWN }

If you see field codes such as { FORMTEXT }, { FORMCHECKBOX }, or { FORMDROPDOWN } instead of the corresponding text boxes, check boxes, or drop-down boxes in your document, clear the Field Codes check box in the View tab of the Tools, Options dialog box.

HOW TO USE SYMBOLS IN { FILLIN } DIALOG BOXES

If you use the { FILLIN } field for prompting your users, you have to take extra steps to use certain characters in your prompt. For example, let's say that you wanted your prompt to say: "Type "M" or "F" in the box." If you entered that text directly in the Field dialog box, Word would see only the first pair of quotes, and your prompt would read *"Type"*. You must preface the quote with a backslash character to have it appear correctly. In the Field dialog box, you would enter the following text in the Prompt text box:

```
"Type \"M\" or \"F\" in the box."
```

Notice that the backslash goes before each quote, not just each quote pair. Similarly, if you ever want to have a backslash appear in your Fill-In prompt, you must use an extra backslash before it. For example,

```
"Name the file to be stored in c:\\Invoices\\1997."
```

LEVERAGING MICROSOFT OFFICE 2003'S POWER FROM WORD

In this chapter

29

WORD AND OFFICE: TIGHTLY INTEGRATED INTO A SINGLE SYSTEM

One of Word's most important strengths is its tight integration with Microsoft Excel, Access, PowerPoint, and the rest of Office 2003. These programs extend Word's power, and knowing how to use them with Word will make you much more productive. It's no wonder Microsoft has taken to referring to the "Microsoft Office System," rather than plain-old "Microsoft Office."

In Office 2003, Office's main applications are more tightly integrated than ever. In this chapter, you'll learn to leverage all of Microsoft Office to make Word an even more powerful tool.

NOTE

> To work with Excel, PowerPoint, Outlook, or Access, you must first install them, either as part of Microsoft Office or as standalone applications.

INTEGRATING EXCEL AND WORD

Word 2003 can perform a surprising number of calculations all by itself, as you learned in the "Calculating with Tables" section in Chapter 12, "Structuring and Organizing Information with Tables." However, it's not a dedicated spreadsheet program like Microsoft Excel.

Luckily, if you've installed Excel, you can call on it whenever you need extra number-crunching power, inserting Excel spreadsheets or charts instead of building them with Word. And, of course, you can take advantage of work you've already completed in Excel, so you don't have to redo it in Word.

This integration between Word and Excel is a two-way street. Excel offers tremendous mathematical prowess, but it's obviously more limited than Word when it comes to creating and formatting complex documents. You can use Word to present your Excel data in a format that communicates the information more effectively than Excel could alone.

Moreover, the connection between Word and Excel is as lively as you want it to be. If, for example, you link your quarterly report to sales data kept in three different files (gathered by three different sales representatives) on your company's network, every time you open or print the report, your numbers are updated. Just as important, you can also set the links to *not* update automatically. That way, you can always generate an accurate archival record of a project as it existed at a given point in time.

You can use several techniques to bring Excel data into Word. None is especially complicated, and some are downright simple. In the next section, you'll leverage Excel's mathematical capabilities in Word by integrating a new Excel worksheet into a Word document.

INSERTING A NEW EXCEL WORKSHEET IN A WORD DOCUMENT

In Chapter 12, you learned how you can use Word to add numbers in a table or insert a field that can calculate a formula anywhere in a document, using basic arithmetic operations and functions. You may well find, however, that you need to perform calculations beyond Word's capability. Fortunately, you can tap Excel's powerful capabilities without leaving Word.

INSERTING AN EXCEL WORKSHEET OF A SPECIFIC SIZE

If you need to create a new set of data that is reasonably compact, Word enables you to insert a blank Excel worksheet of specific proportions. The higher your screen resolution, the more rows and columns you can insert.

To insert a worksheet using the toolbar button, click in your document where you want the worksheet to appear and click the Insert Microsoft Excel Worksheet button on the toolbar. A grid appears (see Figure 29.1). Drag the mouse pointer down and across the grid to define the size of your worksheet. The worksheet appears in your Word document.

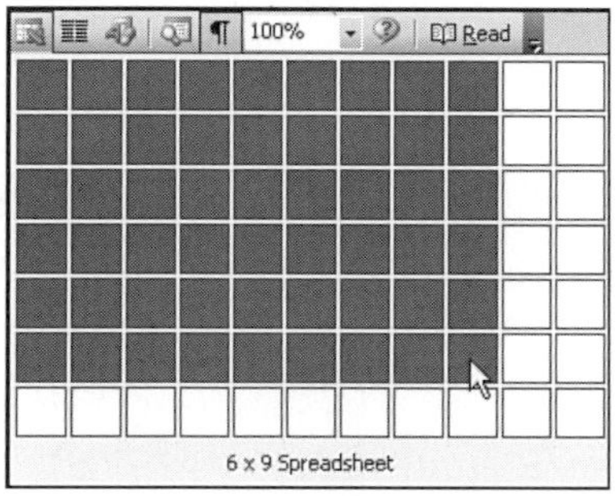

Figure 29.1
Dragging the Insert Excel Worksheet grid to insert a worksheet with specific proportions.

6 x 9 Spreadsheet

INSERTING AN EXCEL WORKSHEET THROUGH MENU COMMANDS

Another way to insert a new Excel worksheet is through menu commands. Choose Insert, Object to open the Object dialog box (see Figure 29.2). From the Create New tab, scroll down the Object Type list to select Microsoft Excel Worksheet. Click OK to insert the worksheet and close the dialog box.

The default worksheet is 7 columns wide by 10 rows high. Because this procedure can only insert a sheet of the default size, you may have to adjust the size manually afterward, by dragging on the sizing handles at the corner of the worksheet object.

NOTE

> You can use the Object dialog box to create an object corresponding to any Windows program that supports object linking and embedding (OLE), a Microsoft standard that allows you to create objects with one application and link or embed them in another. Simply choose the type of object you want to create in the Object Type scroll box.

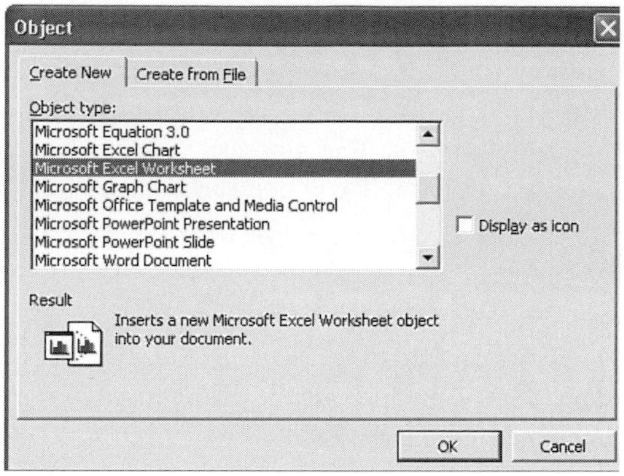

Figure 29.2
Inserting a new Excel
worksheet through
the Object dialog box.

Inserting a new worksheet through the Object dialog box gives you one option you don't
have if you use the Insert Microsoft Excel Worksheet toolbar button. You can choose to
insert the worksheet as an icon, rather than display the data itself in your document (see
Figure 29.3). To do so, check the Display as Icon check box.

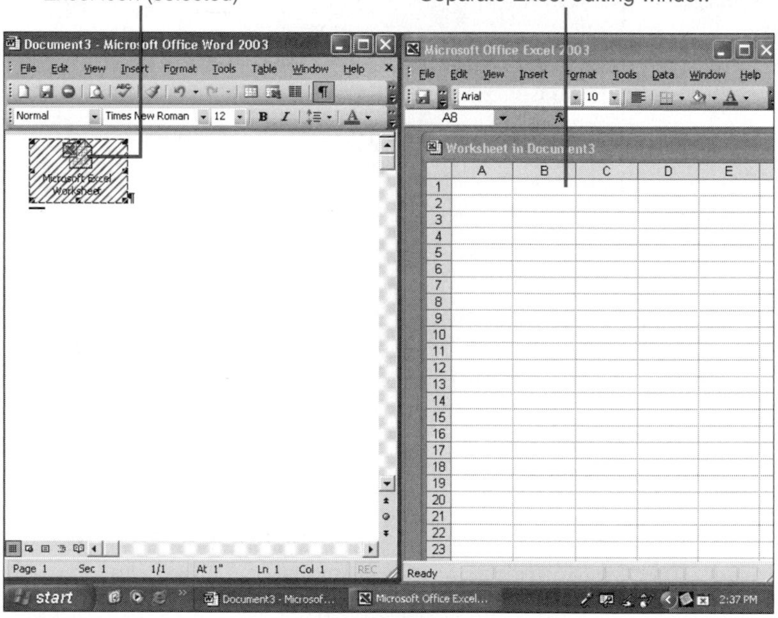

Figure 29.3
Displaying Excel data
as an icon in your
Word document.

After you insert the icon, you can double-click on it to edit the Excel worksheet in a separate Excel window.

When would you display a worksheet (or any other object) as an icon? When you won't
need to print it, and when you're running Word and Excel on a relatively slow computer.

You still have access to the live data, but Word runs a bit faster, because it needs to display only an icon representing the worksheet except when you are actually working with the data.

TIP

> If you choose to display worksheet cells in your document, and later decide you prefer to display an icon—or vice versa—you can easily swap between the two options. Right-click on the object to display the shortcut menu and choose Worksheet Object, Convert. The Convert dialog box appears. Check or clear the Display as Icon check box and click OK.

 If you open, edit, and save an Excel worksheet in Word and then cannot reopen it in Excel, see "What to Do If You Can't Open a Worksheet in Excel After You Edit and Save It in Word," in the "Troubleshooting" section of this chapter.

IMPORTING EXCEL OBJECTS

In the previous sections, you learned how to insert a blank Excel worksheet. But it's equally likely that you'll already have an Excel workbook containing the data you want to include. Many users prefer to create their data in Excel before inserting the data into a Word document.

If you already have an Excel worksheet, Microsoft gives you plenty of options for incorporating it into a Word document. For example, you can

- Import a copy of an entire existing Excel workbook
- Import a linked version of an existing Excel workbook
- Insert a range of cells from Excel as a table in Word
- Insert a range of cells from Excel into Word and retain all the Excel formatting
- Insert a range of cells as a link from Excel to Word

NOTE

> A word about terminology: An Excel file is called a *workbook*. Workbooks consist of one or more *worksheets*—individual "pages" of the spreadsheet that can be displayed separately.
>
> When you insert a blank worksheet into your Word document, Excel creates a workbook consisting of a single worksheet. If you insert an existing workbook, you need to pay attention to whether you're inserting one worksheet or several worksheets. Later in this section, you'll learn how to control which parts of a workbook you insert.
>
> When you insert a workbook with multiple sheets, only the active cells in the first sheet are visible, and only those cells print. However, if you double-click on the workbook to edit it, you can choose to display the active cells from a different sheet by clicking on that sheet's tab at the bottom of the Excel window.

IMPORTING AN ENTIRE WORKBOOK

To import an entire workbook that already exists, follow these steps:

1. Choose Insert, Object.
2. Click the Create from File tab (see Figure 29.4).

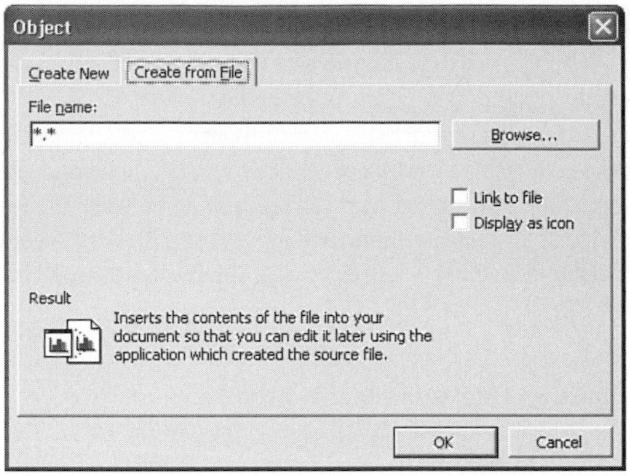

Figure 29.4
Creating an object
from an existing file.

3. Unless you know the exact filename and path, click <u>B</u>rowse. The Browse dialog box appears, which looks like a standard Open File dialog box. (If you know the filename and path, you can simply enter it in the File <u>N</u>ame text box, in place of the *.* characters that are present when you display this tab.)

4. Browse to and select your file.

5. Click In<u>s</u>ert.

6. Click OK.

> **TIP**
>
> You've already learned how to embed a Microsoft Excel object; you can do the same thing with any kind of object, including a PowerPoint presentation, a Visio graphic, or any other file created in an OLE-compatible application—from Microsoft or anyone else.

CHOOSING HOW TO IMPORT YOUR WORKBOOK

Word gives you three options for how to import a workbook as an object:

■ By default, Word embeds the workbook's contents in your document. You can edit them in Excel, but there is no connection to the original file; and if the original file changes, the change is not reflected in the Word document.

■ Check the Lin<u>k</u> to File check box in the Create from <u>F</u>ile tab. This not only inserts the contents of the Excel worksheet, but also establishes a link to the source file so that updates to the source file can be reflected in the Word document.

■ Check the Disp<u>l</u>ay as Icon check box in the Create from <u>F</u>ile tab. You've already learned that this option displays an icon in place of the worksheet cells; you can double-click the icon to open the worksheet in a separate editing window.

After you confirm your choice by clicking OK in the Object dialog box, a copy of the entire Excel workbook is inserted in your Word document as an object.

LINKING TO THE SOURCE FILE: ADVANTAGES AND DISADVANTAGES

When you choose Link to File, you're no longer working with a copy of the original file; you're working with the actual file. When you are working in Word and double-click the Excel object to edit it, Excel opens the workbook in another window, and any changes you make are incorporated into the source file. Likewise, with a linked object, any changes you make in the source file are reflected in the linked version.

Inserting a workbook as a linked file is both a blessing and a curse. The good news is that all your updates are centralized, and you don't have to worry about making changes in both Excel and Word. On the other hand, sometimes you want to lock in your report data after a certain point. Luckily, Word 2003 lets you have it both ways.

CAUTION

> Linking worksheets into a document creates a path to the spreadsheets on your local/networked drive. If you send a file containing links to a colleague via email or on a floppy disk, you need to send the linked files as well. If the linked files are in a different folder, you might need to place all the linked files in the same folder as the original file and edit the links to match for your colleague to adequately use the links.

If you cannot create a link to a worksheet you recently created, see "What to Do If You Cannot Link Cells from an Excel Worksheet," in the "Troubleshooting" section of this chapter.

MODIFYING AN OBJECT'S LINKS

After you have embedded a linked object into your Word document, the Edit, Links option becomes active. Choosing this menu option opens the Links dialog box, as shown in Figure 29.5. (You can also display the Links dialog box by right-clicking on the linked worksheet to display the shortcut menu and choosing Linked Worksheet Object, Edit Link.) From the Links dialog box, you can choose to update your link automatically, to update it manually, or to completely lock the link.

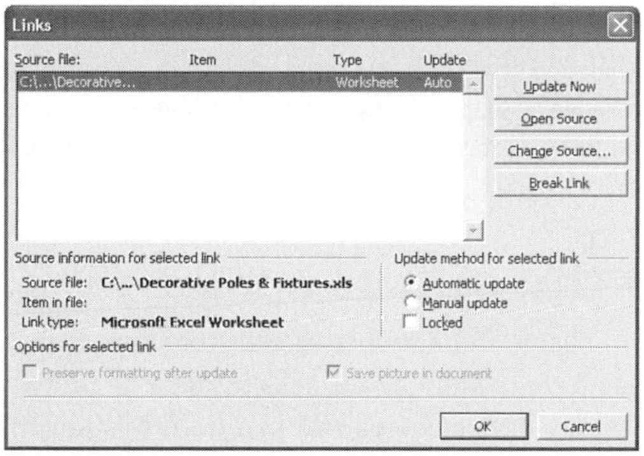

Figure 29.5
You can modify a linked object's status at any time through the Links dialog box.

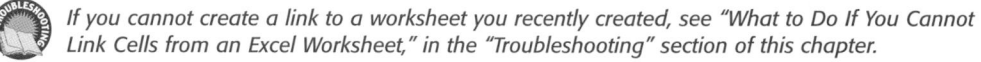

If the Manual Update option is chosen, you must select the object (or the entire document) and press F9 or click the Update Now button from the Links dialog box. Locking the link deactivates the Update Now button and prevents any updates from occurring until the link is unlocked. Your original Excel file can still be edited, but the Word file cannot be updated to reflect the changes.

Resizing a Worksheet to Fit Your Word Document

Often, after you insert an Excel worksheet, you'll discover that it is larger than your Word page. If this occurs, Word displays as much of your worksheet as it can, up to the edge of the page. Remaining cells beyond the edge are cut off and not displayed.

In some cases, making page setup adjustments can solve the problem. For example, to accommodate a worksheet that's too wide, you can change your page to Landscape mode. To change the page to Landscape, click on the worksheet object once to select, it and choose File, Page Setup. In the Margins tab, select the Landscape option button. Choose Selected Text in the Apply To drop-down box and then click OK.

If Page Setup changes are insufficient, Word gives you two ways to resize a worksheet object, which are covered in the next two sections.

→ For more information on sections and Landscape mode, **see** Chapter 5, "Controlling Page Features," **p. 157**.

Resizing a Worksheet Without Changing the Number of Cells Displayed

The first approach to resizing a worksheet retains the same number of cells but shrinks or stretches the contents of each cell, changing font sizes if necessary. This approach is especially helpful if you need to make minor sizing adjustments and cannot change the number of cells that appear in your document.

To resize the worksheet, click on the worksheet object once to select it—black sizing handles appear (see Figure 29.6). Click and drag a sizing handle to the proportions you want, and then release the mouse button.

CAUTION

Note that when you single-click an Excel worksheet in a Word document and drag its borders to change its shape, the existing cells are stretched or squeezed. If you need to shrink the worksheet extensively, the cells may become too small to be read comfortably.

Changing the Number of Cells Displayed in Your Document

Sometimes you may need to change the number of cells that appear in your Word document. For example, you may have to show fewer cells to make the information fit. Conversely, your worksheet may have changed and you need to show more cells. Perhaps you've added several new products and you need to display several additional rows of data about them in your Word document.

Figure 29.6
When you click on an Excel object, sizing handles appear within solid line borders.

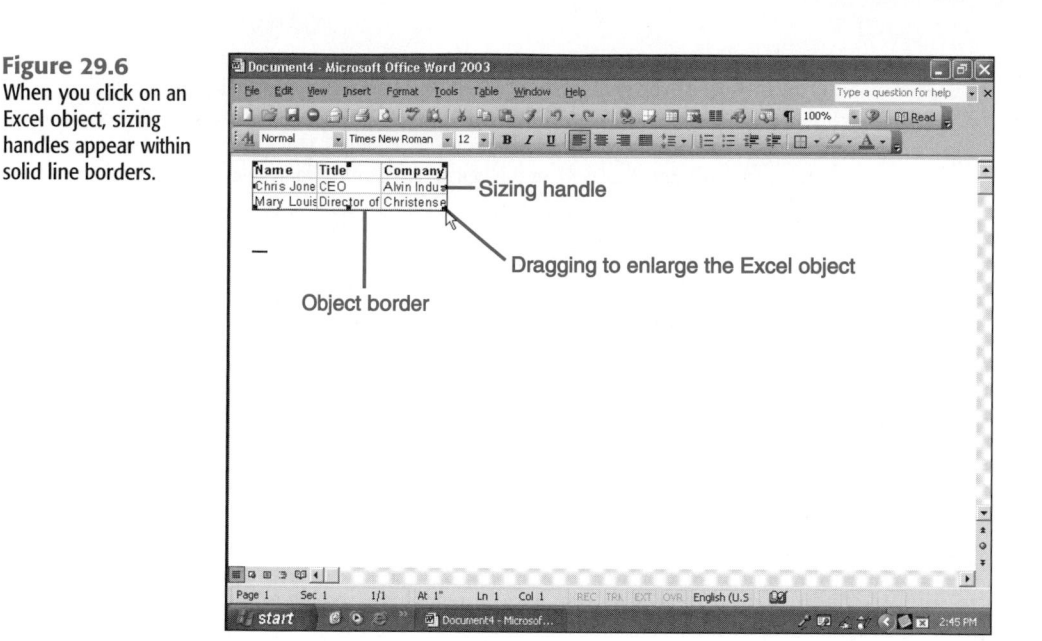

To adjust both the size of your worksheet object and the number of cells shown in it, follow these steps:

1. Double-click on the worksheet to edit it. Excel's menus and tools appear, and the worksheet is surrounded by diagonal cross-hatching (see Figure 29.7).

	A	B	C	D	E
1		Denver	Boston	Cleveland	Austin
2	1/1/2003	891.21	986.11	940.76	766.88
3	2/1/2003	351.70	480.03	532.94	846.52
4	3/1/2003	894.60	294.42	131.51	63.00
5	4/1/2003	47.55	739.04	196.82	150.96
6	5/1/2003	178.85	99.32	395.86	675.31
7	6/1/2003	348.48	767.41	227.83	364.28
8	7/1/2003	257.06	262.97	267.62	376.73
9	8/1/2003	666.84	342.24	572.73	216.88
10	9/1/2003	636.81	283.44	51.46	637.26
11	10/1/2003	121.51	477.70	564.76	495.81
12	11/1/2003	871.97	377.48	610.94	554.81
13	12/1/2003	841.91	483.44	251.55	675.94

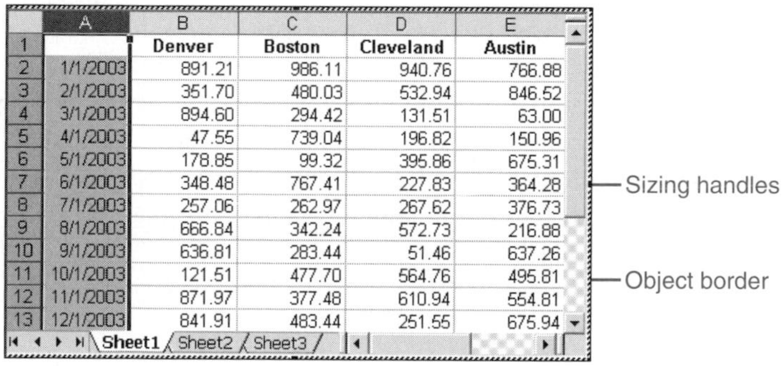

Figure 29.7
When you double-click on an Excel object, sizing handles appear within diagonal cross-hatch borders.

2. Drag one of the sizing handles inward or outward to adjust the proportions of the worksheet.
3. Click outside the worksheet; the new proportions appear in your Word document.

29

> **NOTE**
>
> Note that when you single-click an Excel worksheet in a Word document, and drag its borders to change its shape, the existing cells are stretched or squeezed. However, when you double-click an Excel worksheet to edit its contents, you can change the number of rows and columns displayed, or the height and width of individual rows and columns.

INSERTING A RANGE OF CELLS

Most of the time, you won't need to insert an entire Excel workbook into your Word document, just a specific range of cells. The process for doing this is one you're familiar with: cut and paste. As noted previously in the discussion of inserting a workbook, you can achieve three different results when you insert a range of Excel cells: They can appear as a Word table, as a worksheet object, or as a hyperlink. The following sections cover each of these alternatives.

PASTING CELLS AS A WORD TABLE

The simplest method of transferring data is to select and copy it from Excel and paste it into Word by clicking the Paste button on the Standard toolbar or pressing Ctrl+V. Cutting and pasting is a good alternative for simple, fixed data when there is little or no chance of the former formulas needing to be recalculated.

Your pasted entry is converted into a Word table. By default, numbers are right-justified and formulas become values. Most formatting is retained, with the exception of spanned columns, which can be simulated by selecting the cells in question and choosing Table, Merge Cells.

You can use Word's Paste Options button to control how information from an Excel spreadsheet is pasted into your document. Click the Paste Options button (see Figure 29.8) and choose the option you prefer. For example, if you are pasting Excel cells into an existing table that uses a Word table style, you can match the Excel cells to the formatting in the table style by choosing Match Destination Table Style and Link to Excel. If you want none of the formatting to import, you can choose Keep Text Only.

Figure 29.8
Using Paste Options to control how Excel cells are pasted into a Word document.

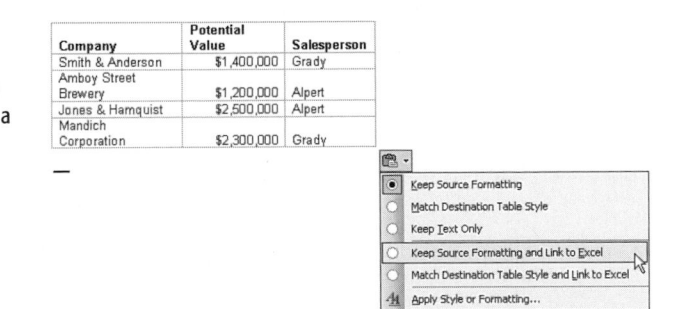

PASTING CELLS AS A WORKSHEET OBJECT

If you think it's even remotely possible that you'll need to update your numbers and recalculate your formulas, it's best to paste the Excel data as an object. The process is basically the same as regular cutting and pasting, with one little twist: You use Edit, Paste Special instead of the Paste command. Follow these steps to insert Excel information as an object:

1. From Excel, select the range of cells you want to insert.

2. Click the Copy button on the Standard toolbar.

3. Switch to your Word document.

4. Place the insertion point where you want the data to appear.

5. Choose Edit, Paste Special. The Paste Special dialog box opens, as shown in Figure 29.9.

Figure 29.9
Paste Special enables you to maintain all your Excel data's formulas and formatting.

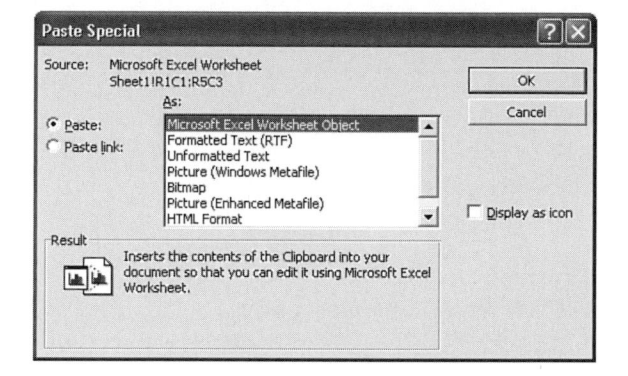

6. From the As list, select Microsoft Excel Worksheet Object.

7. If you want to establish a link to your source document, click the Paste Link option button; otherwise, leave the Paste option button selected.

8. If you want to display the worksheet as an icon, check the Display as Icon check box.

9. Click OK to insert the object.

> **TIP**
>
> You can also create a link using Paste Options. Paste the Excel cells into Word; then click the Paste Options button at the lower right of the pasted cells and choose either Keep Source Formatting and Link to Excel or Match Destination Table Style and Link to Excel.

INSERTING WORKSHEET CELLS AS A WORD HYPERLINK

If you click Paste Link in the Paste Special dialog box, Word displays a new set of options for the kind of links you can create. One of these is a Word hyperlink.

If you paste the worksheet cells as a Word hyperlink, the worksheet cells appear in your document at your insertion point, with blue underline formatting. When you press Ctrl and click on any of these cells, you're taken directly to the worksheet in Excel.

29

> **NOTE**
>
> To paste a spreadsheet into a document as a hyperlink, you can also select Paste as Hyperlink from the Edit menu.

WORKING IN A WORKSHEET YOU'VE INSERTED

Unless you insert your worksheet as an icon, the worksheet cells appear and are selected after you insert it. While the worksheet is selected, the standard Word menus and toolbars change to Excel menus and toolbars, as shown in Figure 29.10.

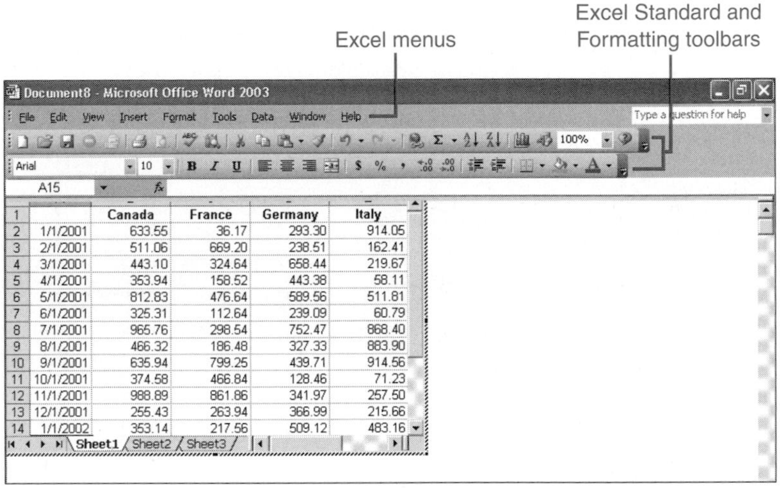

Figure 29.10
Word displays Excel's menus, toolbars, and other controls, and embeds a row-and-column worksheet within your document.

After you insert your worksheet, you'll notice the typical Excel layout with alphabetic column headings and numeric row headings. You can now enter and format your data and formulas in the worksheet's rows and columns as you would if you were working in Excel. You can also resize the columns just as you can in Excel—by moving your mouse pointer over the boundary of a column and then clicking and dragging the boundary to a new width.

> **NOTE**
>
> For all practical purposes, you are working in Excel—you just happen to be looking at it through a narrow portal that Word has provided.

> **TIP**
>
> You can move among multiple worksheets in an Excel workbook by clicking sheet tabs at the bottom of the Excel window.

When you finish editing inside the worksheet, click anywhere outside it, and your menus and toolbars return to their usual appearance, displaying Word commands. The borders of each cell are displayed in light, nonprinting gray. You can work inside the worksheet again at any time by double-clicking on it, or by right-clicking and choosing Worksheet Object, Edit from the shortcut menu.

If you've inserted the Excel worksheet cells with a link to an Excel workbook elsewhere, the changes you make to the worksheet cells are saved to the original workbook when you save your Word document. If you've inserted a new Excel workbook, the changes are saved only as part of the Word document, not as part of a separate workbook.

DELETING AN EXCEL WORKSHEET FROM A WORD DOCUMENT

To delete an Excel worksheet from your Word document, first make sure that you're in Word editing mode (if the Excel layout is active, click outside the worksheet into the regular document). Then select the object by clicking it once, and press Delete.

If you have inserted a workbook with several worksheets, you can delete a single worksheet from within Word. Double-click on the worksheet to select it for editing, and right-click on the worksheet tab you want to delete. Choose Delete from the Excel shortcut menu that appears.

CREATING CHARTS IN EXCEL

In Chapter 15, "Visualizing Your Message with Graphs, Diagrams, and Org Charts," you learned how to create charts in Microsoft Word, using the Microsoft Graph applet. However, you may have already built your charts in Excel. Word makes it easy to insert these charts into Word documents:

1. Starting in Excel, click on the chart to select it.
2. In Excel, click the Copy button on the Standard toolbar to copy the chart to the Clipboard.
3. Switch to Word and place your insertion point where you want the chart to appear.
4. If you don't need a link to the original chart, click the Paste button on the Standard toolbar. Otherwise, choose Edit, Paste Special.
5. If you want a link, click the Paste Link button.
6. Click OK.

In the Paste Special dialog box, Word gives you two options for the type of chart object you can create:

- **Microsoft Excel Chart Object**—This is the default setting, and it enables you to double-click on the chart to edit it in Excel.
- **Picture (Enhanced Metafile)**—With this option selected, your chart is inserted as a bitmap graphic that can be edited using tools such as Microsoft Paint or Microsoft Photo Editor.

Working with Access and Word

Much of an office's day-to-day business involves keeping track of data. Take an overdue invoice notice, for example. Although the letter you send to your debtor is typically a word processing document, the key data incorporated in it may well be stored in a database: the business name and address, invoice numbers, amount due, and so forth. Word's tight integration with Microsoft Access enables you to draw on the same data source to produce any report, mailing, or other document. For example, you may want to

- Incorporate specific, filtered elements of a database in a document you're creating, such as a discussion of new customers or sales opportunities

- Create a report based entirely (or largely) on Access data but utilize Word's more sophisticated formatting capabilities

Aside from mail merge, there are three ways to retrieve Access data for use in Word:

- You can use Word's Database toolbar to specify which Access data you want, and manage the data after you insert it. This technique often makes sense when you're incorporating Access data into a Word document that already exists.

- You can use Access's Publish It with Microsoft Word feature to build an RTF (Rich Text Format) file that can be edited and formatted in Word. If you're at least reasonably familiar with Access, this is the fastest way to create a Word document containing large amounts of Access data.

- You can use Access's standard data export tools, which enable you to specify the name, placement, and type of file Access creates when it exports data.

The following sections walk you through each of these techniques. But first, the next section provides some background about databases and how Access works with Word.

→ For more information on running mail merges, **see** "An Overview of Word's Mail Merge," **p. 584**.

Some Important Points About Access Databases

Remember that a database is made up of many records, each of which represents one business, person, or transaction. The records, in turn, are composed of various fields. Each field represents one unique aspect of a record, such as a first name, last name, street address, or ZIP Code. Databases are often represented as tables with each column representing a different field and each row a different record. The first row of the table is reserved for the field names and is called the *header row*.

In Access, you can enter field names of up to 64 characters with spaces and most special characters. However, if you're planning on using your database in Word, it's best to limit your field names to 20 or fewer characters and avoid spaces and any special characters other than the underscore. Otherwise, when you link your Word document with your Access database while setting up a mail merge, Word automatically truncates the field names to 20 characters and alters any spaces or special characters to the underscore character.

29

Word inserts your Access data just as it appears in Access. So if your AmountDue field isn't formatted to show dollars and cents in Access, it won't show up that way in Word. The same is true of date fields and text fields.

INTEGRATING MICROSOFT ACCESS DATA INTO AN EXISTING WORD DOCUMENT

Imagine that you're writing a report to management that describes all the new sales opportunities your division has generated in the past 30 days. You've already written plenty of glowing prose about your sales team's hard work. Now it's time to get down to cases: Which companies represent the largest sales potential? The data is stored in Access. You want to include it in your Word report, in the form of a Word table. In this section, you'll learn how to make that happen.

TIP

> If possible, familiarize yourself ahead of time with the specific Access database file you'll be using. For example, you need to know in which database tables the information you're seeking is stored, and which fields exist in those tables.

Follow these steps to import data into Word from Access:

1. Choose View, Toolbars, Database to display the Database toolbar (see Figure 29.11).

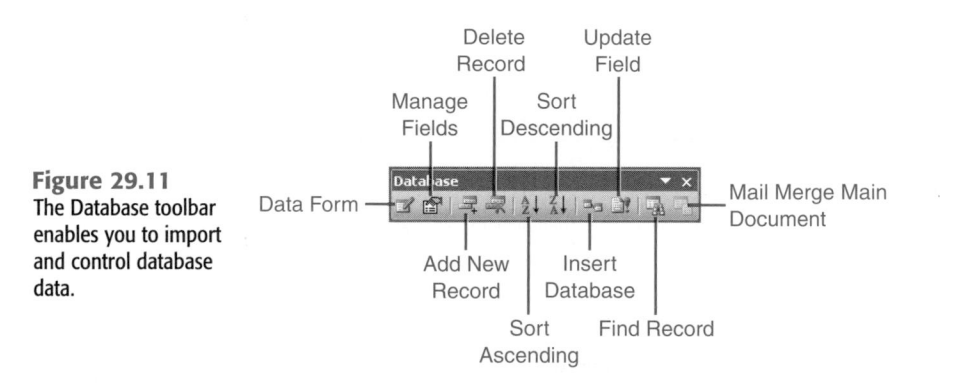

Figure 29.11
The Database toolbar enables you to import and control database data.

Delete Record
Update Field
Manage Fields
Sort Descending
Data Form
Mail Merge Main Document
Add New Record
Insert Database
Sort Ascending
Find Record

2. Click the Insert Database button. The Database dialog box opens (see Figure 29.12).
3. Click Get Data. The Open Data Source dialog box opens.

TIP

> If you want to insert another type of data source, such as an Excel worksheet, choose that option instead.
>
> If your data is actually stored in an SQL Server 2000 database accessed through a Microsoft Access front end, choose Access Projects from the Files of Type drop-down box.

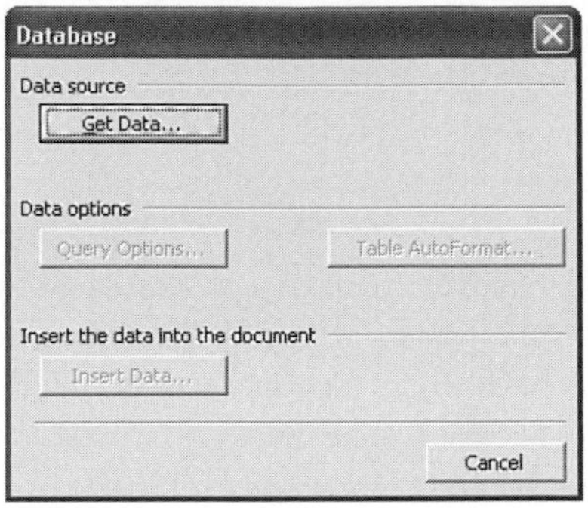

Figure 29.12
The first step in integrating Access data into a Word document is to click Get Data and retrieve the data you need.

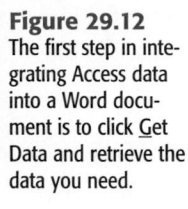

4. Browse to and select the database you want to use.

5. Click Open. If your database contains multiple tables, the Select Table dialog box opens (see Figure 29.13).

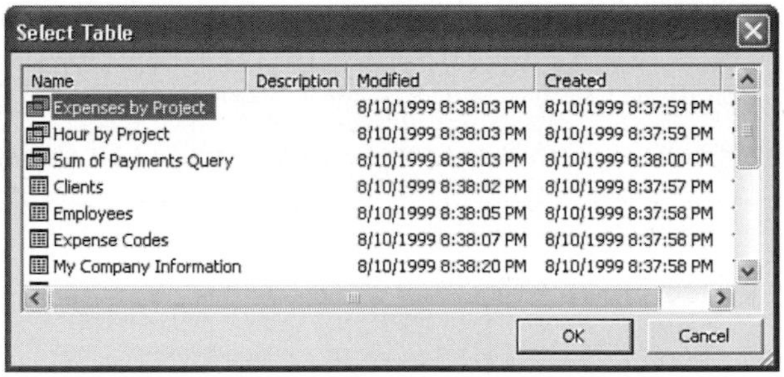

Figure 29.13
Choosing a database table or preexisting query.

6. Choose the table that contains the database fields you want to use. If a predefined query exists within Access that generates the data you want, choose that query instead.

7. Click OK.

You've now connected your Access database to your Word document, but you haven't actually inserted any data yet. At this point, you have a choice:

■ If you want to insert all the data stored in the database table you selected (or associated with the query you selected)—or specific consecutive numbered records from that table or query—you can click Insert Data in the Database dialog box and work from there. (See "Inserting Data Through the Insert Data Dialog Box," later in this chapter).

■ If you want to create a more complex query, sort the information placed in your document, or choose which fields to include, click Query Options in the Database dialog box. The Query Options dialog box opens, offering options for specifying which data to include in your Word document. Query Options are covered in the next section.

CREATING QUERY OPTIONS

As covered in the previous sections, you manage the process of importing data from Access through the Database dialog box. After you've selected the file that contains your data, you specify which data you want to use by clicking Query Options in the Database dialog box.

Most of Word's database Query Options are covered at length in Chapter 17, in the section "Advanced Filtering and Sorting." Briefly, however,

- In the Filter Records tab (see Figure 29.14), you can filter which data appears, based on any field in the database table you've chosen. You can also use comparisons such as "Equal to" and "Is Not Blank" to refine the data further. Finally, you can establish six criteria to widen or narrow the "data net" you're casting.

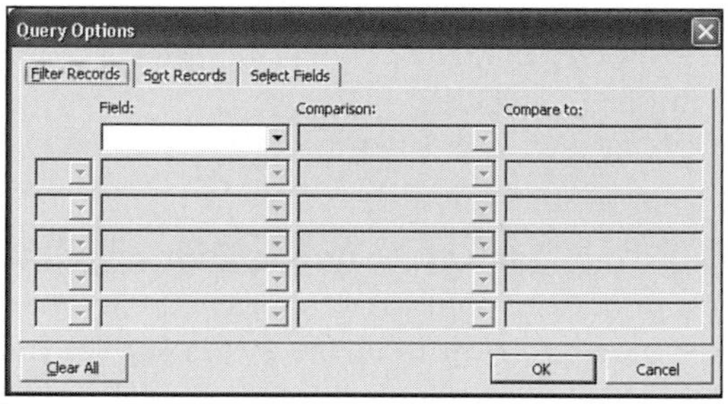

Figure 29.14
The Filter Records tab of the Query Options dialog box.

- In the Sort Records tab (see Figure 29.15), you can choose which field or fields to sort by. You can choose up to three sort fields and specify whether each of them sorts in ascending or descending order.

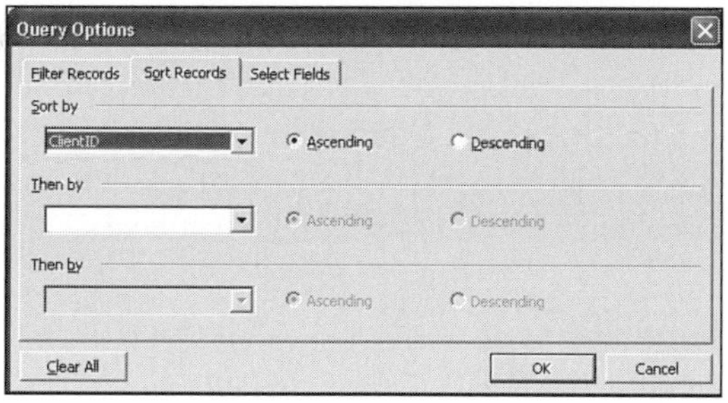

Figure 29.15
The Sort Records tab enables you to specify a sort order for your data, based on up to three fields.

- Finally, in the Select Fields tab—which is not available in mail merge—you can choose which fields from your data source are placed in your document. This tab is shown in Figure 29.16.

By default, every field in the data source is selected. To remove one field, highlight it in the Selected Fields scroll box and click Remove. To remove all fields, click Remove All. You can then add fields back one at a time. In the Fields in Data Source scroll box, highlight the

29

field you want to add. The Remove and Remove All buttons are replaced by Select and Select All buttons. Click Select.

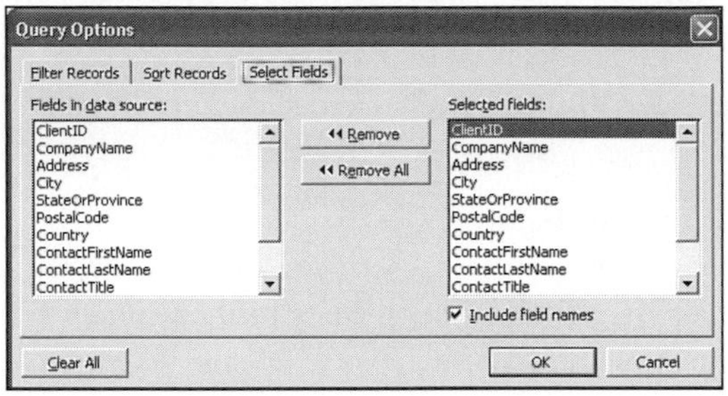

Figure 29.16
The Select Fields tab enables you to control which fields of data are placed in your Word document.

If you don't want a header row containing the field names, clear the Include Field Names check box. When you're finished, click OK.

AUTOFORMATTING YOUR DATA BEFORE YOU INSERT IT

In Chapter 12, you learned about Word's tools for AutoFormatting a table after you place it in your document. Because you might want to AutoFormat the information in the database you import, the Database dialog box (refer to Figure 29.12) enables you to choose Table AutoFormat before you place the information in your document.

After you complete the Get Data step and set Query Options (if any), click Table AutoFormat. The Table AutoFormat dialog box appears. Choose the Formats and other settings you want, and click OK to return to the Database dialog box.

INSERTING DATA THROUGH THE INSERT DATA DIALOG BOX

Now you're ready to insert the data. In the Database dialog box (refer to Figure 29.12), click Insert Data. The Insert Data dialog box opens (see Figure 29.17). Here, you have one last chance to refine your data. By default, Word searches the entire database for records that fit the query options you've already set. If you prefer to search only a specific range of numbered records, enter the range in the From and To text boxes.

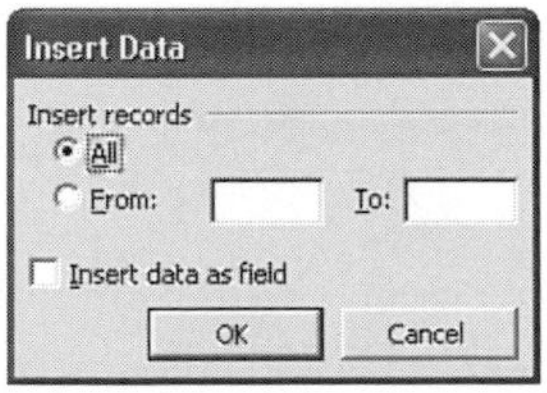

Figure 29.17
In the Insert Data dialog box, you can specify a range of records, or specify that data be inserted as an updateable field.

Finally, if you want the data to be inserted as a { DATABASE } field that can be updated based on the source database file, check the Insert Data as Field check box. When you're finished, click OK. The information appears in your document (see Figure 29.18).

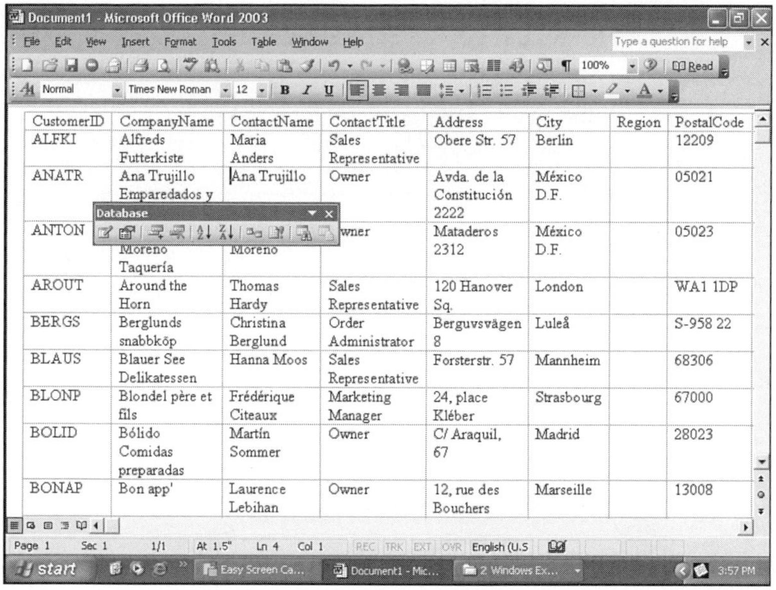

Figure 29.18
Formatted database
data inserted in a
Word document.

→ For more information about working with fields, **see** Chapter 23, "Automating Your Documents with
Field Codes," **p. 771**.

TIP

> If you've inserted a { DATABASE } field linked to a database file, you can update the
> database information at any time by clicking inside the data in your document and either
> pressing F9 or clicking the Update Field button on the Database toolbar.

USING THE DATABASE TOOLBAR TO MODIFY DATA PLACED IN YOUR DOCUMENT

After you've inserted database data in your document, the Database toolbar gives you tools
for managing it. The following sections cover each of the tools.

VIEWING THE DATA IN A FORM

To display the data through a data form, which makes it easier for you to move among records
and edit them, click Data Form. Figure 29.19 shows the navigation tools available in a data
form.

MANAGING FIELDS

To add, rename, or delete fields displayed in the table, click Manage Fields on the Database
toolbar. The Manage Fields dialog box opens (see Figure 29.20).

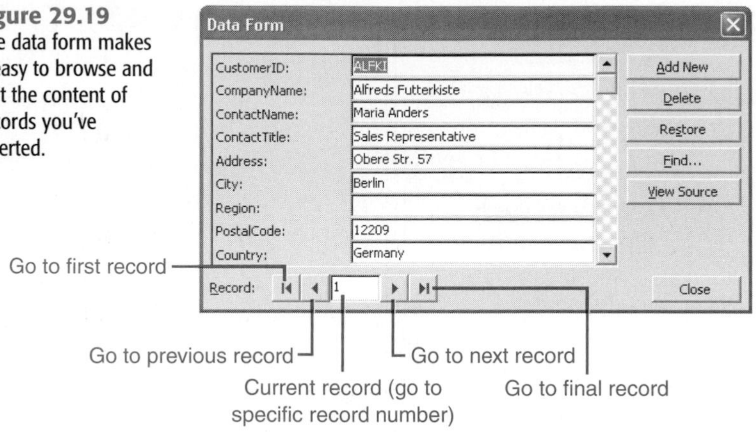

29

Figure 29.19
The data form makes it easy to browse and edit the content of records you've inserted.

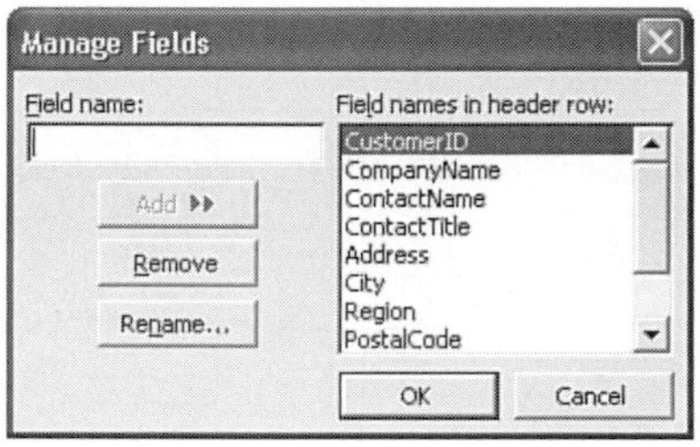

Go to first record

Go to previous record

Current record (go to specific record number)

Go to next record

Go to final record

Figure 29.20
In the Manage Fields dialog box, you can add, rename, or remove fields from the database data in your document.

From here, you can

- Add a new field by typing a new Field Name and clicking Add.
- Remove a field by selecting it in the Field Names in Header Row scroll box and clicking Remove.
- Rename a field by selecting it in the Field Names in Header Row scroll box and clicking Rename.

Adding, Deleting, and Sorting Records

To add a blank line where you can enter an additional database record, click Add New Record on the Database toolbar. This adds a new column to the Word table Access has entered in your document.

To remove an existing record, click inside it and click Delete Record.

To sort the records (excluding the header row), click in the column you want to sort by; then click Sort Ascending. To sort in reverse order, click Sort Descending.

PUBLISHING ACCESS DATA TO WORD VIA OFFICE LINKS

Microsoft Access contains a powerful shortcut for exporting data to Word: the Publish It with Microsoft Word feature, one of a family of "Office Links" features. To publish database information using this feature, open the Access database you want to use. You can publish to Word directly from an Access table, query, form, or report.

To publish to Word, select or display the item from which you want to publish. Then choose Tools, Office Links, Publish It with Microsoft Word. Access creates an RTF file containing a table of database information and immediately opens the RTF file as a table in a separate Word document window (see Figure 29.21). You can then save the RTF file as a Word document; copy the data into any other Word document; link or embed the Word file; or edit and format your file as needed.

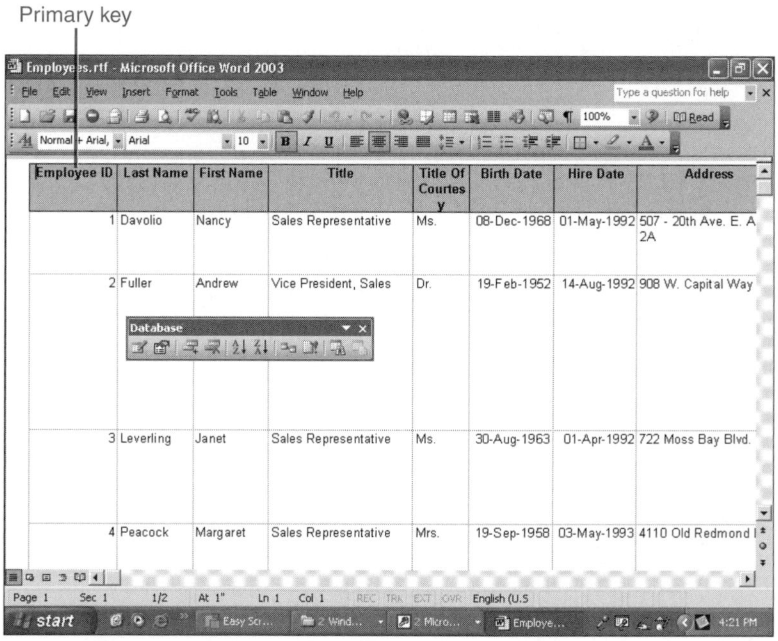

Primary key

Figure 29.21
An Access table, published to Word.

Keep the following points in mind:

- If you publish to Word from a report or form, the appearance of the Word table depends on the formatting you used in the Access report or form. You may find this unsatisfactory. If so, use Table AutoFormat or Word's manual formatting techniques to reformat the data after it appears in Word.

- As shown in Figure 29.21, a published Access table may include a column for the primary key, which you may not want. You can, however, manually delete this, by selecting the column and clicking Cut or pressing Ctrl+X.

- If you publish from an Access report, the information isn't stored in a Word table at all; rather, Access uses tabs to separate columns. You may want to immediately select the data and choose Table, Convert Text to Table to reformat the information in a Word table, which is almost always easier to manage.

- If you publish from a query or a report, you can refine the information you select using Access query and reporting tools, before inserting it in Word. Although there are many ways to build a query in Access 2003, you can often accomplish what you want by following these steps:

  1. Open Access 2003 and open your database.

  2. Choose Insert, Query.

  3. In the New Query dialog box, choose Crosstab Query Wizard, and click OK.

  4. Follow the instructions provided by the wizard.

- Regardless of which Access source you use, you may need to adjust column widths and alignments after your data is displayed in Word.

- Access automatically names the RTF file after the table, report, form, or query on which it was based, unless it finds an RTF file in the same directory that already uses this name. In that case, you're given a chance to rename the file.

- The published data does not retain any link to Access, so it is not automatically updated if the database is updated. Often, the best way to update information you've published to Word is to simply delete it and republish it using Access's Publish It with Microsoft Word feature again.

GETTING MORE CONTROL OVER ACCESS DATA EXPORT

Access's one-click Publish It with Microsoft Word feature is handy, but you may need more control over how you export Access data to Word. If so, open Access and select the form, report, table, or query you want to export. Then, from within Access, choose File, Export. The Export To dialog box, which looks similar to a normal Save As dialog box, appears.

From this dialog box you can

- Specify a File Name.

- Browse to the folder where you want the file to appear.

- Specify a file type (Save as Type); possibilities include Rich Text Format (RTF), Text Files organized for use in a Microsoft Word mail merge, HTML Documents, XML documents, or Active Server Pages designed for Web display using Internet Information Server.

When you're finished, click Save. You now have a file with the name you selected, in the format and location you selected, containing all the information from the table, form, report, or query. You can open or insert this file in Word and edit it there as you want.

USING POWERPOINT WITH WORD

Over the years, PowerPoint has developed into the multimedia center of Office. Not only can you use it to incorporate text and images in a slide format, but you can also add animation, sound, and movies to teach, explain, and persuade. Because both Word and PowerPoint are Office family members, you have a strong connection that enables you to share information in both directions.

Consider just a few of the ways you can use PowerPoint and Word together:

- You can draft your outlines in Word and then import them into PowerPoint.
- You can send presentation information from PowerPoint to Word, including outlines, notes, and handouts.
- You can take quick notes and mark action items in PowerPoint while you are making a presentation in front of an audience and then publish them to Word for editing and refinement.
- You can embed slides or an entire presentation into a Word document for inclusion in a report.

In the following section, you'll learn how you can use an outline from Word as the basis for a PowerPoint multimedia presentation.

USING WORD OUTLINES IN POWERPOINT

Often, the impetus for a PowerPoint presentation is a report drafted in Word. If you use heading styles or outline levels in Word, you can build your presentation with far less effort.

To export a finished Word outline to PowerPoint, open the document and choose File, Send To, Microsoft PowerPoint. You'll see a brief progress bar and then the presentation appears in PowerPoint, as shown in Figure 29.22.

Each paragraph or title, formatted with Heading 1 style (or Outline Level 1), can automatically become the title of a new slide. Each paragraph or subtitle, formatted with the Heading 2 style (or Outline Level 2), is transformed into the first level of slide text. Subordinate heading or outline levels are translated to correspondingly lower levels of slide text in your PowerPoint presentation.

TIP

If you haven't used heading styles or outline levels in Word, but you have used tabs to indicate headings and subheadings, save your document as a text file. Then, in PowerPoint, choose File, Open. Change the file type to All Outlines, select your text file, and choose Open. Each first non-indented paragraph becomes a slide title on a new slide; paragraphs with one indent become first-level text, and so forth.

29

Figure 29.22
Build your presentation's "talking points" by sending your Word outline to a PowerPoint presentation.

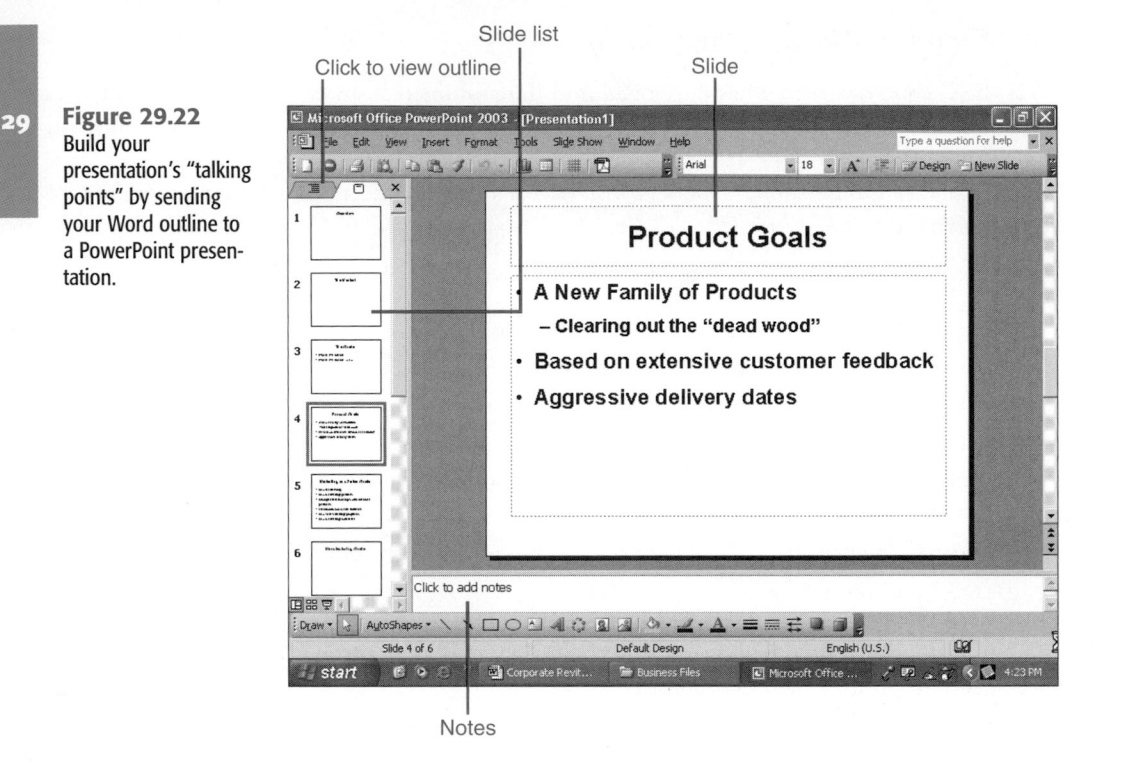

Click to view outline — Slide list — Slide

Notes

EXPORTING POWERPOINT FILES TO WORD

The slides are the flashy part of a PowerPoint presentation, but there's also a lot of supporting material: an outline, speaker notes, and handouts, for instance. PowerPoint makes it easy for you to export all this information and more to Word, where you can further modify it or incorporate it into an existing document.

When giving a presentation, it's useful to have a hard copy of your talk that tells you what slide comes next and what to say about it. After you've created your slide show, you can export it to Word so that you can further develop your speaker's notes. From PowerPoint's main menu, choose File, Send To, Microsoft Word. This opens the Send to Microsoft Word dialog box shown in Figure 29.23.

The Send to Microsoft Word dialog box comes with various layout options that govern not only how your notes will look but also what you are actually exporting. You can choose from the following options:

- **Notes Next to Slides**—With this option selected, Word creates a three-column table showing the slide number, a small image of the slide, and speaker notes. Three slides appear per page.

- **Blank Lines Next to Slides**—This option creates a three-column table showing the slide number, a small image of the slide, and a series of underscored lines for speaker notes. Three slides appear per page.

29

- **Notes Below Slides**—When this option is selected, Word puts each slide on its own page with a slide number and the speaker text.
- **Blank Lines Below Slides**—This option gives you each slide on its own page with a slide number and a series of underscored lines for speaker text.
- **Outline Only**—This option gives you just the outline for the presentation without a picture of the slide. The text of the presentation appears in the form of a Word outline, with each slide's main heading corresponding to a first-level heading in Word.

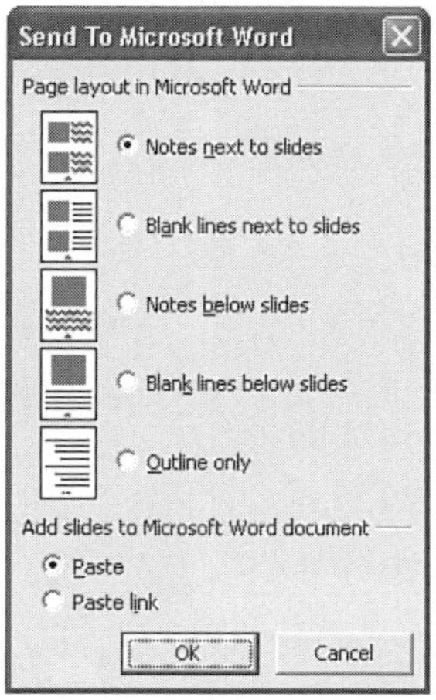

Figure 29.23
You can send your entire slide presentation along with any speaker notes to Word for further editing through the Send to Microsoft Word dialog box.

You'll notice that Paste and Paste Link options are available for all but the Outline Only selection. As with all embedded objects in Word, choosing Paste Link causes the document to be updated whenever changes are made to the source material, in this case a slide or presentation.

After you make your selections about how you want the PowerPoint presentation exported to Word, click OK. PowerPoint converts the file, and Word opens, displaying the file in the format you requested.

EMBEDDING A NEW POWERPOINT SLIDE IN A WORD DOCUMENT

PowerPoint comes with many templates and designs to give your message a professional edge. Word gives you full access to them: You can include slides in your documents at will, even if you have no intention of creating a full-fledged slide show. To insert a single PowerPoint slide as a graphic in a Word document, follow these steps:

1. In Word, position your insertion point where you want the slide inserted.
2. Choose Insert, Object to open the Object dialog box.
3. From the Create New tab, choose Microsoft PowerPoint Slide. The default slide appears as an object in your Word document.

29

In Word, whenever you double-click the slide, PowerPoint's menus and toolbars appear; you can now edit the slide using PowerPoint's menus and toolbars, as shown in Figure 29.24.

Figure 29.24
Word displays PowerPoint's menus and toolbars whenever you double-click on a slide embedded in your document.

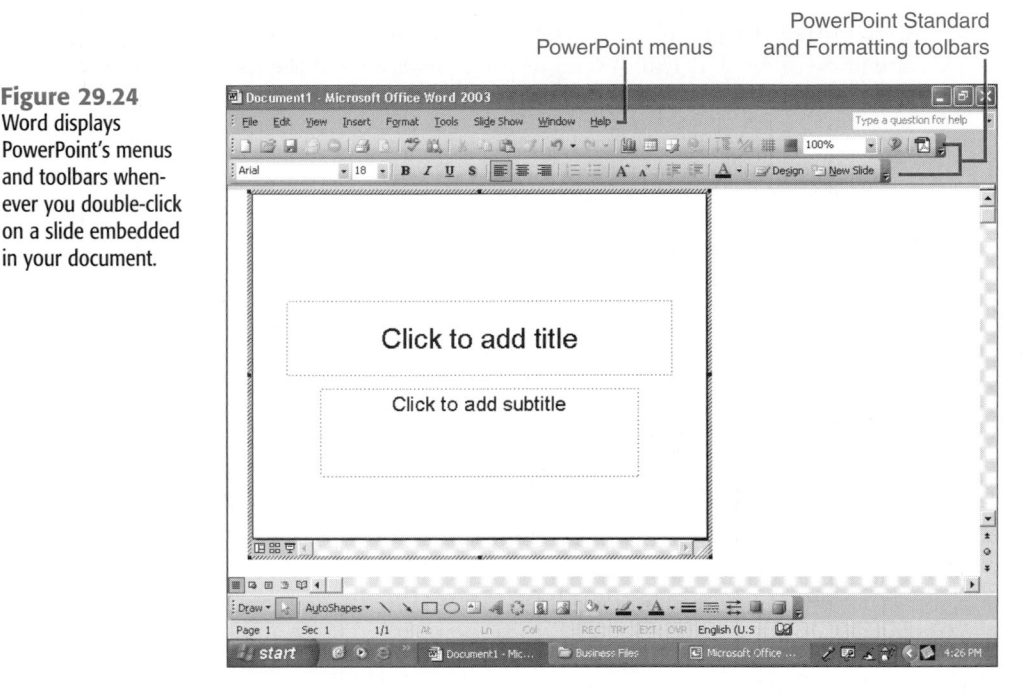

To quickly format the slide, right-click on it and choose Slide Design. In the Slide Design task pane (see Figure 29.25), choose the template you want to apply. (If you want larger previews, right-click on a design template and choose Show Large Previews.) When you're satisfied, click Apply.

You can now enter text in the slide. Editing text in PowerPoint slides is much like editing text in Word text boxes. You simply click next to a heading or bullet. A box that resembles a Word text box appears; start typing. When you're finished working in the slide, click outside it, and Word's menus reappear. You can work on the slide again by double-clicking it.

EMBEDDING AN EXISTING PRESENTATION IN A WORD DOCUMENT

You can also embed an entire PowerPoint slide presentation in a Word document. This works well for online training, manuals, and other documents that would benefit from a multimedia component.

Choose Insert, Object and click the Create from File tab. Next, browse to your existing presentation, select it, click Insert, and click OK. Word normally displays the first slide of the presentation in the document. To run the presentation, double-click the slide object.

29

Figure 29.25
Choosing a design template with which to format the slide.

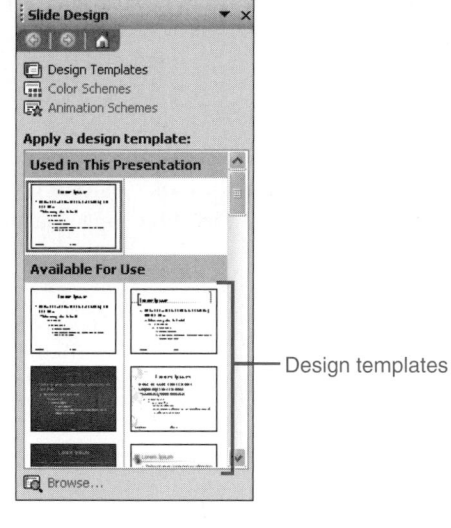

Design templates

NOTE

Of course, you can also incorporate any existing PowerPoint slide by using the Copy and Paste features. As with Excel and other objects, you can place a plain copy of your slide in your document by clicking the Paste button on the Standard toolbar.

You also can insert a linked copy of the slide by choosing Edit, Paste Special; selecting Microsoft PowerPoint Slide Object from the list; and then selecting the Paste Link option before you click OK. Now, whenever you update your PowerPoint slide, your Word document is also updated.

TIP

If you want to copy an entire PowerPoint slide into your Word document, make sure that you're in PowerPoint's Slide Sorter view (choose View, Slide Sorter).

If you're in Slide view (rather than Slide Sorter view), only the selected portion of your slide will be copied and pasted. You will lose formatting and text stored in the slide master (in other words, content that is applied to every slide in the presentation, not just a single slide).

USING OUTLOOK WITH WORD

Microsoft Outlook 2003, Microsoft Office's "personal information manager," is included in every version of Microsoft Office 2003. Outlook 2003 integrates with Word in three key ways that can make you more productive:

- If you use Outlook as your email client software, you can edit your email with Word. This gives you access to Word's extensive formatting and proofing capabilities. You can also send a Word file as an attachment, using the File, Send To, Mail Recipient (as

Attachment) command. Using Word as your email editor is covered in detail in Chapter 30, "Using Word as an Email Editor."

■ You can track your contacts in Outlook and use your contact information in a Word mail merge. (This is covered in detail in Chapter 17, in the section "Selecting an Outlook Contact List Containing the Names You Want to Use.")

■ You can track your Word documents through Outlook's Journal feature, making it easy to find out what files you worked on when, and for how long you worked on them. This is covered in the following section.

TRACKING WORD PROGRESS IN THE OUTLOOK JOURNAL

Did you ever wonder how much time you spent on a particular document over a series of days? Or maybe you're looking for a particular file you worked on sometime last Wednesday in the afternoon, but now you can't find it or remember its name. Outlook's Journal feature can keep track of all your work in Word (and Excel and PowerPoint), recording exactly what you worked on, when you worked on it, and for how long.

→ To learn how to turn on Outlook's Journal tracking feature, **see** "Controlling Whether Outlook Tracks Your Work" **p. 990**.

From within Outlook, it's easy to see which entries, if any, currently appear in your Journal: choose Go, Journal. If the Journal folder doesn't appear, choose Journal from the list of options in your current view. You'll see a timeline of days at the top of the Journal window and filenames at the bottom (see Figure 29.26).

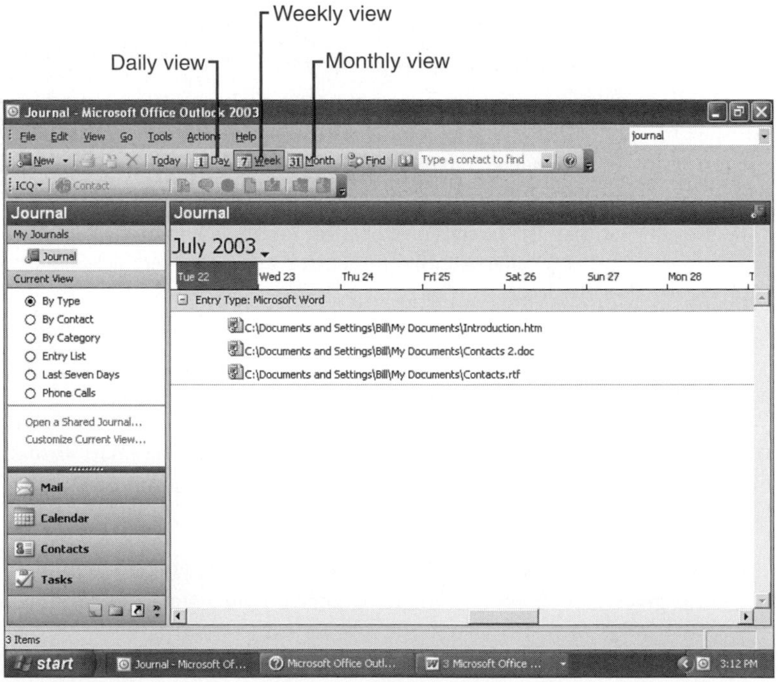

Figure 29.26
Word files tracked by the Outlook Journal.

You can choose a daily, weekly, or monthly timeline by clicking the appropriate toolbar button. Figure 29.27 shows a daily view. Each icon has a Duration bar above it to show when and for how long the document was open. By default, if you double-click the icon, the journal entry associated with the file opens. This journal entry contains information about the file, including exactly how long it was opened. It also contains a shortcut you can double-click to open the file itself.

Figure 29.27
The Journal shows how long you worked on a document and when.

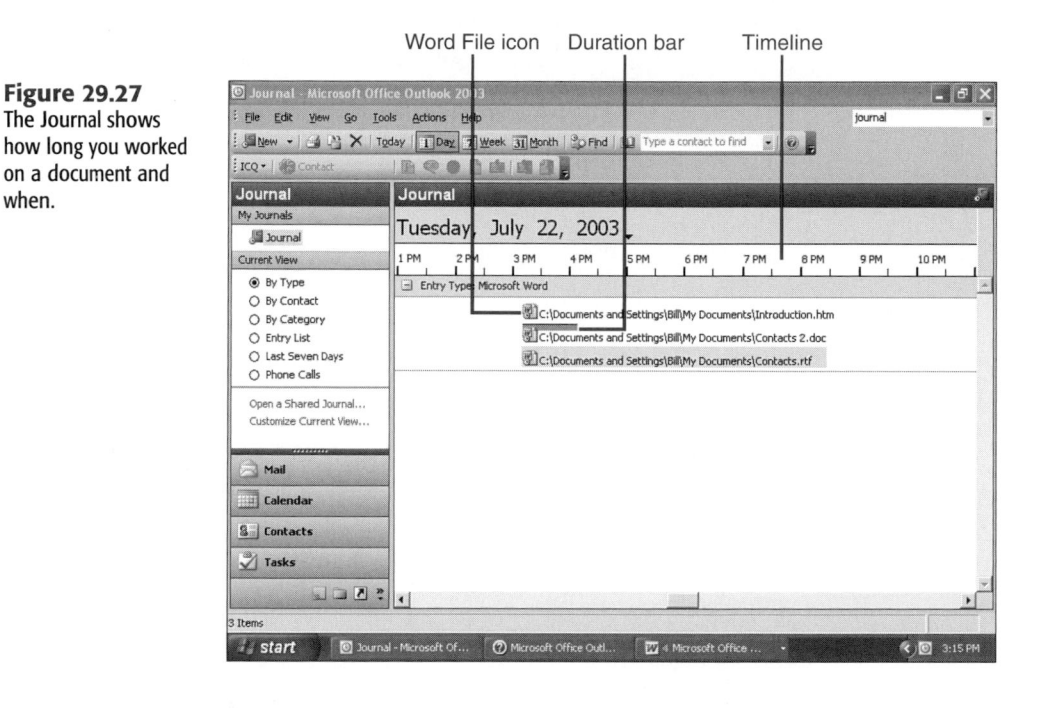

You can also right-click the journal entry for a list of options. For example, Open Item Referred To opens the file the journal entry refers to, without the extra step of displaying the journal entry.

WORKING WITH THE JOURNAL ENTRY

An Outlook journal entry contains much more than a filename and date. To work with the journal entry, right-click it. From the shortcut menu that appears, choose Open Journal Entry. The file's journal entry appears (see Figure 29.28).

Start Time shows when you started working with the file on that day. Duration shows how long the file was open. You can assign the file to a contact by clicking Contacts and selecting a name from your Outlook contact list. When you finish reviewing or editing the journal entry, click Save and Close.

29

Figure 29.28
A Word file's journal
entry in Outlook
2003.

Duration open

Document icon   Start time

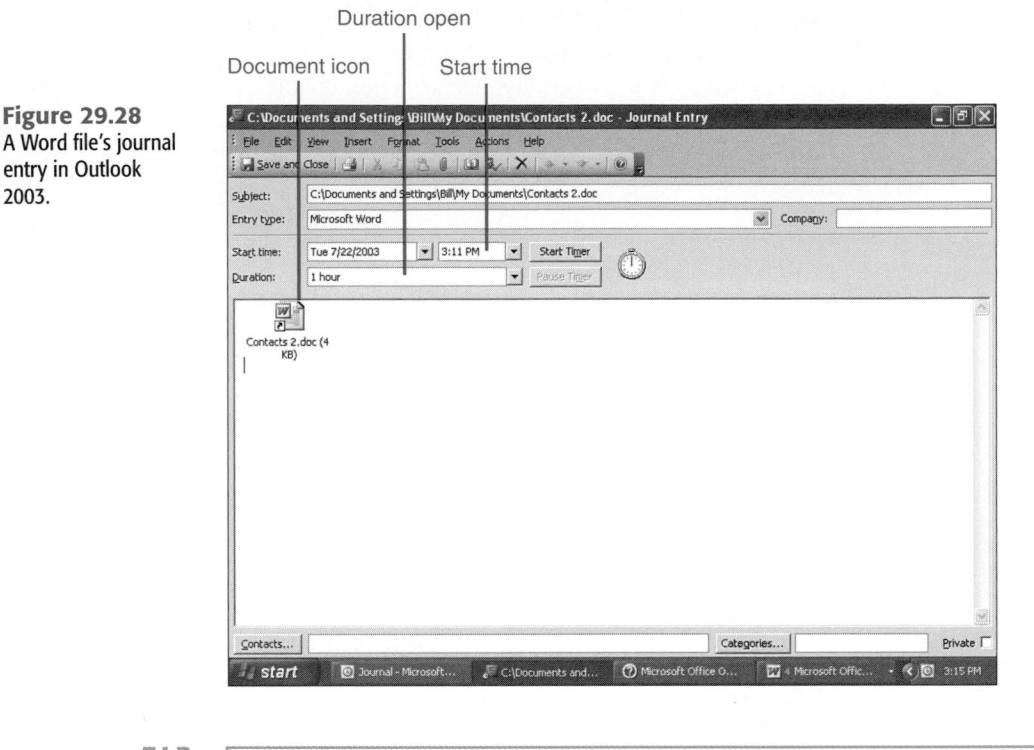

TIP

> You can open the Word file directly from within Outlook.
>
> From the Journal window, right-click on the journal entry and choose Open Item
> Referred To from the shortcut menu. The Opening Mail Attachment dialog box appears;
> click Open It and click OK.

From within the Journal Entry dialog box, double-click on the file icon. The Opening Mail
Attachment dialog box appears; click Open It and click OK.

TIP

> To link a document to a specific contact, enter the contact name in the document's prop-
> erty keywords.

CONTROLLING WHETHER OUTLOOK TRACKS YOUR WORK

By default, the Journal tracking feature in Outlook is turned off. To turn it on, or to make
sure that it is still turned off, follow these steps:

1. Open Outlook.
2. Choose Tools, Options.

3. If the Preferences tab isn't already open, click Preferences to display it.
4. Click Journal Options. The Journal Options dialog box appears (see Figure 29.29).

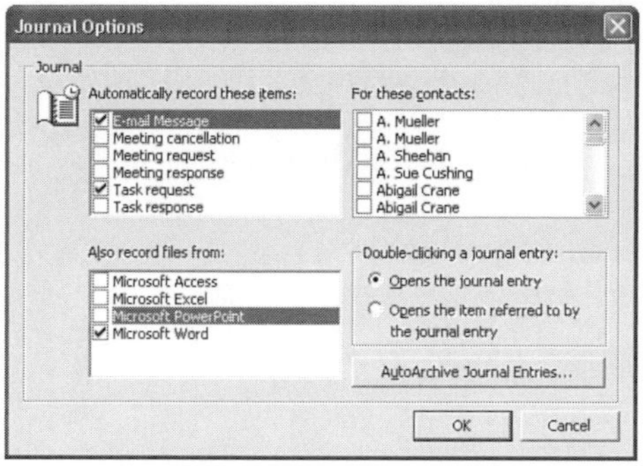

Figure 29.29
Changing the way
Outlook tracks your
work in Word.

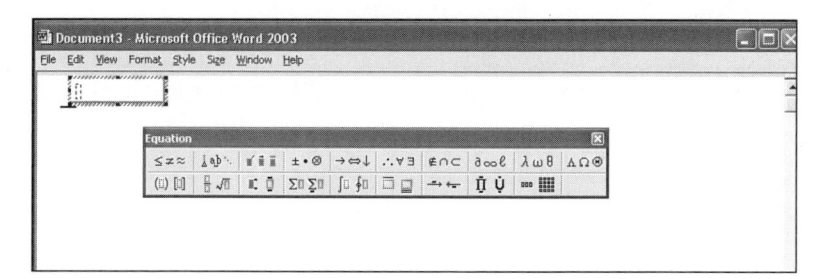

5. In the Also Record Files From box, check or clear the check boxes next to Microsoft
   Word and any other Office program you want Outlook to track or to stop tracking.
6. Click OK.

After you turn on tracking, Journal tracks your work whether or not you open the Outlook
application.

USING MICROSOFT EQUATION EDITOR 3.1

Microsoft Equation Editor 3.1 is useful for creating extended mathematical expressions.
Various mathematical symbols and templates simplify the process of constructing the most
complex formulas. Begin by choosing Insert, Object and selecting Microsoft Equation from
the option list. A working area, surrounded by a dotted box, opens on your screen, as does
the Equation toolbar shown in Figure 29.30.

Figure 29.30
Use the Equation
Editor for inserting
complex formulas in
your Word document.

Numbers, variables, and ordinary mathematical operators (such as =, +, −) can be typed
directly from the keyboard. To enter an operator or a symbol not available from the keyboard, click the appropriate button on the top row of the Equation toolbar and select from
one of the options that appear in the drop-down menu.

29

Complex expressions such as fractions, square roots, or integrals can be added by clicking the appropriate button on the bottom row of the Equation toolbar and choosing one of the drop-down options. Depending on the choice, an expression has one or more outlined boxes for inserting numbers or other symbols.

The relative spacing for the formula is handled through the Format, Spacing menu option. This opens the Spacing dialog box (see Figure 29.31), where you can control the line spacing, matrix row and column spacing, superscript height, subscript depth, and limit height between symbols.

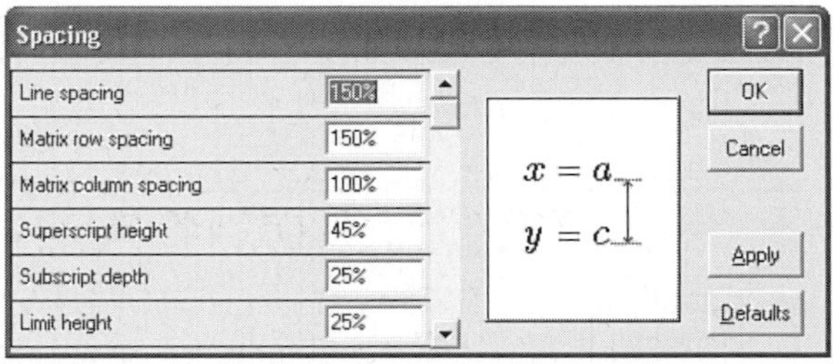

Figure 29.31
You can control a formula's overall spacing through the Spacing dialog box.

USING MICROSOFT OFFICE DOCUMENT IMAGING

Office 2003 comes with an applet, Microsoft Office Document Imaging, which provides basic scanning and optical character recognition (OCR) features. Microsoft Office Document Imaging makes it easy to use Word for editing documents you scanned from print sources or received as a fax and stored in TIFF format. Using Microsoft Office Document Imaging, you can perform these and other tasks:

- Read and search for text in a scanned document or received fax
- Export some or all of a scanned or faxed document's text to Word
- Archive text from a scanned or faxed document
- Rearrange pages in a scanned or faxed document

Microsoft Office Document Imaging contains two components that work together: a simple Scanning applet that allows you to scan any document, whether or not Word (or any other Office application) is open; and an Imaging applet that allows you to work with—and run OCR on—any document you scan or receive by fax. We'll cover both components in the following sections.

SCANNING A DOCUMENT USING MICROSOFT OFFICE DOCUMENT SCANNING

Assuming that you have a scanner connected to your computer and installed, you can scan a document using Microsoft Office Document Scanning. To do so, choose Start, Programs (or, in Windows XP, All Programs), Microsoft Office Tools, Microsoft Office Document Scanning (see Figure 29.32).

Figure 29.32
The Microsoft Office Document Scanning applet.

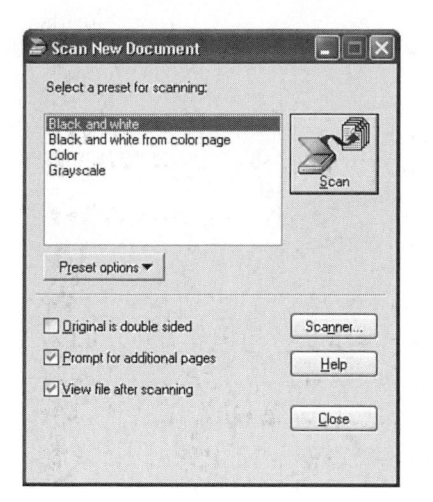

By default, Microsoft Office Document Scanning assumes that you are scanning a black-and-white document. If you are scanning a different type of document, choose it in the Select a Preset for Scanning box.

> **NOTE**
>
> Microsoft Office Document Scanning's four presets are designed to do a reasonable job with many kinds of documents. However, if you find that the results are not quite what you hoped for, you can adjust the program's settings.
>
> To do so, click Preset Options. To adjust an existing preset, choose Edit Existing Preset. To create a new preset, choose Create New Preset.

> **NOTE**
>
> If you are connected to more than one scanner, click Scanner to choose the one you want to use.

If you are scanning a document with multiple pages, check the Prompt for Additional Pages check box; Word then prompts you when it's ready for a new page. (If you don't check this box, Word ends the scan and displays the scanned page.)

If you are using a scanner with an Automatic Document Feeder (ADF) that can read both sides of a page, check the Original Is Double Sided box. Make sure that you insert pages in your document feeder so that the fronts of pages are scanned first. If you do, Microsoft Office Document Scanning collates the finished scanned pages in correct order.

When you've established the settings you need, click Scan. Microsoft Office Document Scanning will scan your document.

WORKING WITH A SCANNED DOCUMENT USING MICROSOFT OFFICE DOCUMENT IMAGING

29

When Microsoft Office Document Scanning has completed scanning your document, it displays the finished scan in Microsoft Office Document Imaging (see Figure 29.33). Here, you can work with the scan you've created.

Figure 29.33
The Microsoft Office Document Imaging applet.

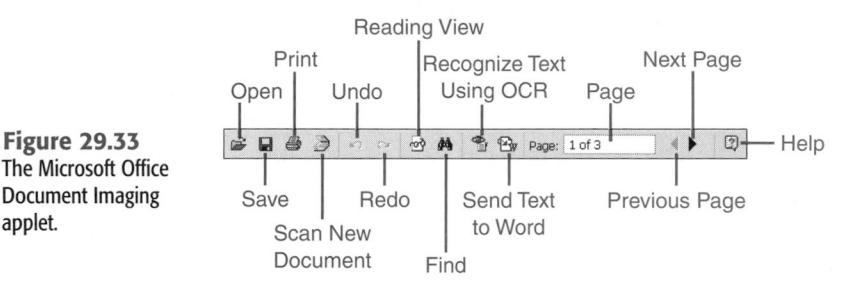

> **TIP**
>
> Sometimes you may want to open Microsoft Office Document Imaging without first creating a scan. For example, you may want to run optical character resolution on a fax you received through Microsoft Windows 2000 Fax Services.
>
> To run Microsoft Office Document Imaging on its own, choose Start, Programs (or, in Windows XP, All Programs), Microsoft Office Tools, Microsoft Office Document Imaging.

To view a scanned document more closely, click the Reading View button, or choose View, Reading View. The document is displayed in full size against a black background, making it easier to read (see Figure 29.34). When you're finished with Reading view, press Esc.

Figure 29.34
Viewing a scanned document in Reading view.

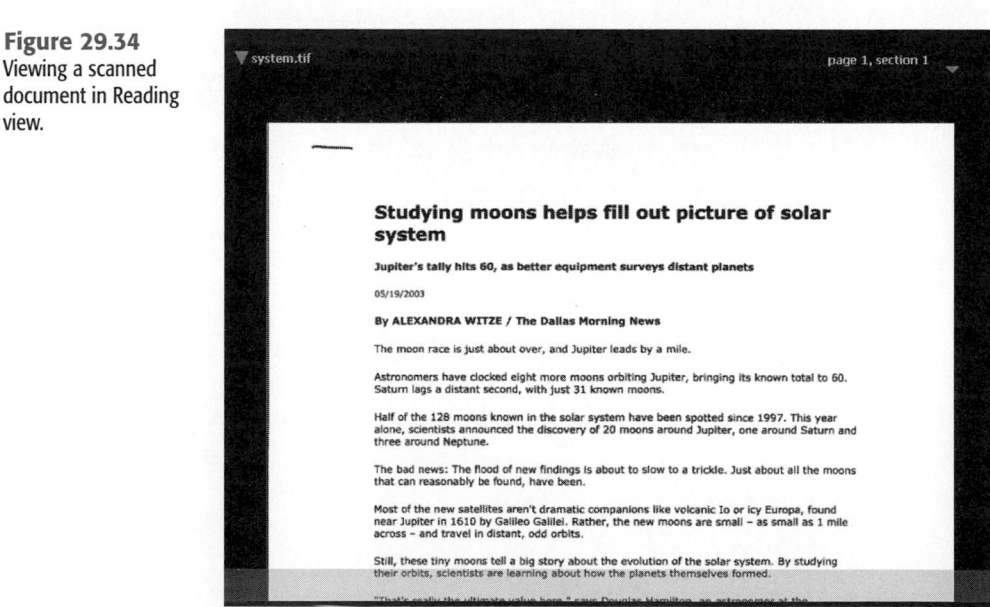

To save a scanned document, click the Save button. The document is saved as a TIFF graphics file that can be opened with a wide range of graphics software. A filename is assigned based on the first few words of text on the first page of the document.

To find text within a scanned document, click the Find button and enter the text in the Find box. Microsoft Office Document Imaging searches for the first instance of the text and displays it in reverse type, with a red rectangle around it.

CAUTION

> Because optical character recognition is not perfect, especially on printed documents of poor quality, such as second-generation photocopies or newspaper clippings, there is no guarantee that Find will locate every reference to specific text in a scanned document.

You can easily copy text from your scanned document into a Word document that can be edited. If you want to copy an entire file, click Send Text to Word, choose All Pages from the Send Text to Word dialog box (see Figure 29.35), and click OK. To copy only selected text, first select the text; then click Send Text to Word and click OK.

Word opens, displaying a new, unsaved and unnamed file containing the text from the scanned document.

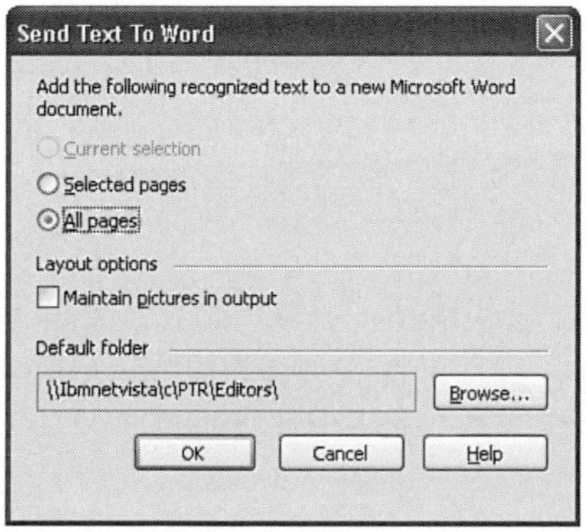

Figure 29.35
Choosing which text to send to Word.

TROUBLESHOOTING

WHAT TO DO IF YOU CANNOT LINK CELLS FROM AN EXCEL WORKSHEET

Make sure that you've actually saved the Excel worksheet; if the worksheet doesn't have a filename yet, the link won't work properly. After you've done so, create the link again, specifying the filename you just created.

WHAT TO DO IF YOU CAN'T OPEN A WORKSHEET IN EXCEL AFTER YOU EDIT AND SAVE IT IN WORD

Word enables you to open an Excel worksheet directly, by choosing it in the Open dialog box and clicking Open. If you do this, the cells are placed in your document in the form of a Word table. Because Word cannot save in Excel format, when you resave the file it is converted to a Word file, and Excel cannot read it. If you've made changes, you can copy them manually into Excel, though you'll have to reformat them. If you need to make changes that will be readable in Excel, use the techniques described elsewhere in this chapter to create a link to an Excel document, rather than opening it directly.

WHAT TO DO IF PARTS OF A POWERPOINT SLIDE DON'T APPEAR IN WORD

If you want to copy an entire PowerPoint slide into your Word document, make sure that you're in PowerPoint's Slide Sorter view (choose View, Slide Sorter). If you're in Slide view (rather than Slide Sorter view), only the selected portion of your slide will be copied and pasted.

This can cause problems, because you'll lose formatting stored in the slide master (in other words, most formatting that is applied to the entire presentation, not just a single slide).

WHAT TO DO IF YOU CAN'T SEND A WORD OUTLINE TO POWERPOINT

If you use File, Send To, PowerPoint, and Word displays an error message instead of opening PowerPoint, it's possible that you've recently installed the PowerPoint Viewer to view older PowerPoint files (perhaps files stored on the Internet or your intranet). You now need to reregister PowerPoint 2003 as the application you want to use with PowerPoint files. To do so, quit all Office programs and choose Start, Run. Then enter the following text in the Open box:

```
powerpnt /regserver
```

Click OK. If this does not work, run a maintenance install of Microsoft Office 2003 or Microsoft PowerPoint 2003.

WHAT TO DO TO IMPROVE THE ACCURACY OF OPTICAL CHARACTER RECOGNITION

The Microsoft Office Document Scanning applet is optimized to deliver the best possible optical character recognition for most scanned documents, and offers relatively few options for tweaking. However, there are a few things you can do if you're not satisfied with the accuracy of the OCR files generated from your documents:

- **Use the best preset**—The software's default setting is Black and White, for documents with black text on white paper. If your documents are colored—for example, magazine articles or text printed on a color inkjet—be sure to switch to Black and White from Color Page.

- **Increase resolution**—By default, Office scans at 300 dpi, which is usually the best trade-off between file size, speed, and OCR accuracy. However, most scanners support higher resolutions. To increase the resolution, display the Microsoft Office Document

Scanning dialog box. Click Preset Options, and choose Edit Selected Preset from the drop-down list. Display the General Tab, and click Advanced. In the Advanced Scan Settings dialog box (see Figure 29.36), choose a resolution higher than 300.

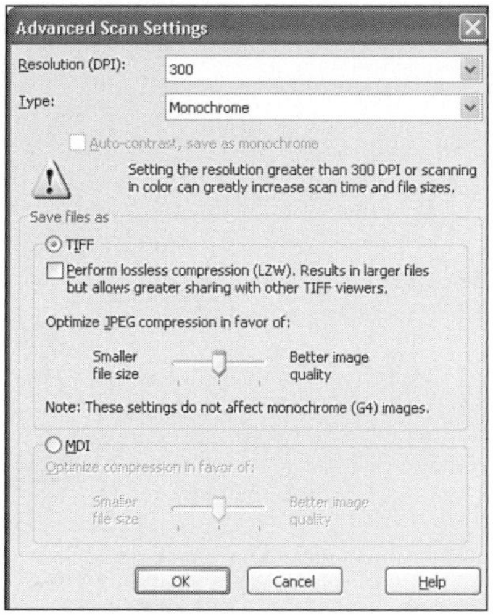

Figure 29.36
Changing scanning resolution in Microsoft Office Document Scanning.

CAUTION

Remember to switch back to 300 when you're finished scanning your current document; otherwise, future scans will be unnecessarily slow, and will create unnecessarily large files.

■ **Make sure that pages are being optimized for OCR**—In the Preset Options dialog box, choose the Processing tab (see Figure 29.37). Make sure that the Auto Rotate and Auto Straighten check boxes are checked.

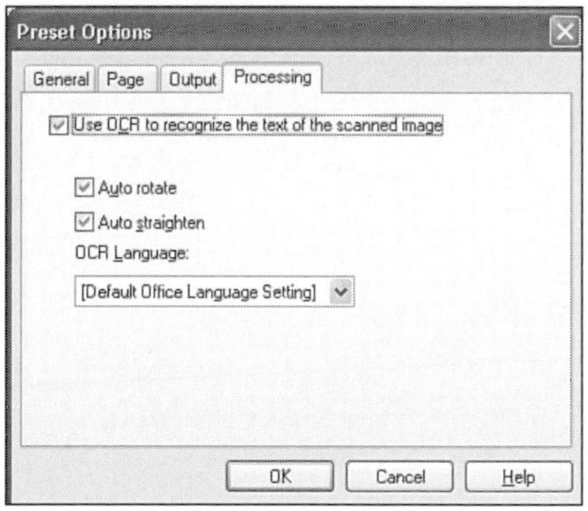

Figure 29.37
Checking Processing options in Microsoft Office Document Scanning.

NOTE

If you're scanning text written in a language other than your system's default language, also choose the OCR Language from the drop-down box on this tab.

CHAPTER 30

USING WORD AS AN EMAIL EDITOR

In this chapter

CREATING EMAIL USING MICROSOFT WORD 2003

When designing Outlook, Microsoft designed Word to serve as your primary email editor. There is tight integration between the two products as long as your versions of Word and Outlook are the same. Within Word, this means that you can edit new email messages or send documents you're already working on as email. It also means that, unless you specify otherwise, when you create a message within Microsoft Outlook 2003, Word opens to edit the message.

In the following sections, we'll review the different ways you can create an email from within Word.

CREATING A NEW EMAIL MESSAGE FROM WITHIN WORD

When you want to send an email, you'll most likely open Microsoft Outlook first and create the email from there. However, you can create a new email message directly from Microsoft Word. To create a new, blank email message while working within Word, select New from the File menu and then click Blank Email Message on the Task pane. A new, blank email message is displayed in a separate window (see Figure 30.1).

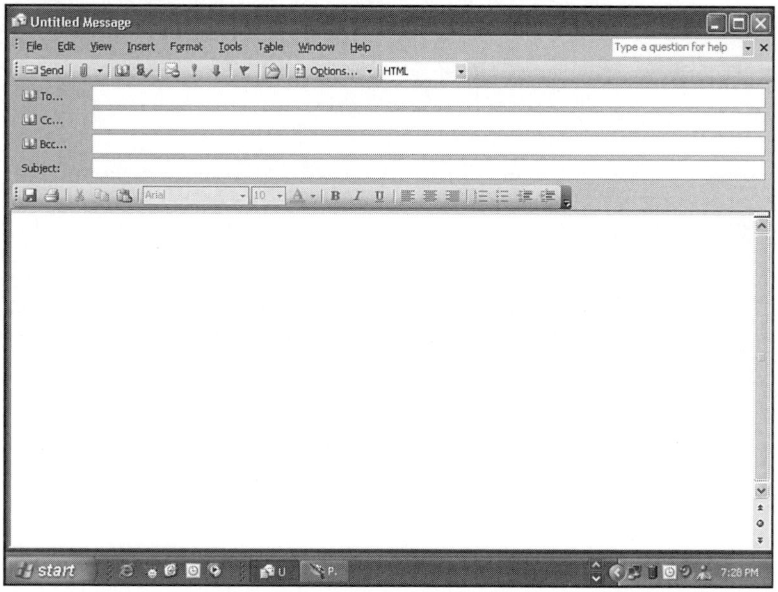

Figure 30.1
A blank email message.

NOTE

The buttons called out in this figure are referred to throughout this chapter.

CREATING AN EMAIL MESSAGE FROM A WORD DOCUMENT

In the preceding section, you learned how to create a blank email message from within Word. You can also create an email message directly from a document you're working on. To do so, display the document and either click the Email button on the Standard toolbar or choose File, Send To, Mail Recipient. This converts your document into an email message, displaying the same Word email editing window you saw in Figure 30.1, with one significant addition: an Introduction line that allows you to add information about your document without placing that information in the document itself (see Figure 30.2). The Introduction line appears in the message header only if the recipient's email client is Outlook 2003; otherwise, it appears at the top of the message body, separated from the document by a line.

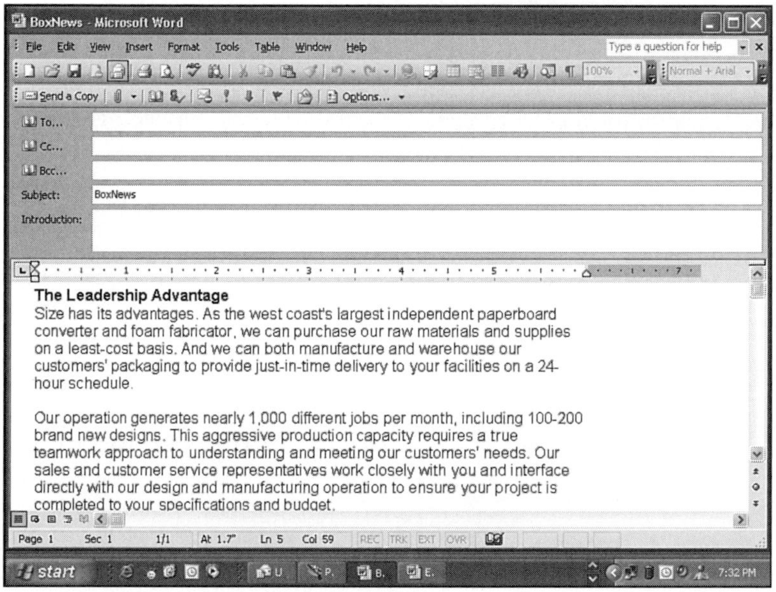

Figure 30.2
An email message based on an existing Word document.

The Email button appears on the Standard toolbar only if you have installed Outlook 2003 or another email program.

TRIGGERING A MESSAGE FROM WITHIN A DOCUMENT USING WORD SMART TAGS

NEW Word 2002 introduced Smart Tags, which allow you to trigger actions based on marked text in your document. Word 2003 improves on these Smart Tags by adding more functionality. Some of the additional functionality includes the capability for developers to create SmartTags with cascading menus, and the capability to associate Smart Tags with specific content. In particular, the online Office Marketplace has a large number of new Smart Tags available for users to download or purchase. With the enhanced flexibility of Smart Tag development in Word 2003, you'll see many more custom Smart Tags available. As you edit a Word document, Word marks certain text with a Smart Tag, which appears in your document formatted with purple dotted underlining. For example, it flags all names it recognizes as the recipients of email you've sent recently, and you can send messages directly from Smart Tags marked in this fashion.

NOTE

> If you want, you can specify that Word should flag *all* names it finds in your document, not those it recognizes as your recent email correspondents.
>
> Choose Tools, AutoCorrect Options, and choose the Smart Tags tab. Next, check the Person Names check box in the Recognizers scroll box, and click OK.

To send a message from a Smart Tag, follow these steps:

1. Hover the mouse pointer over a Smart Tag until the Smart Tag marker appears.

2. Click on the marker to display a shortcut menu of tasks you can perform (see Figure 30.3).

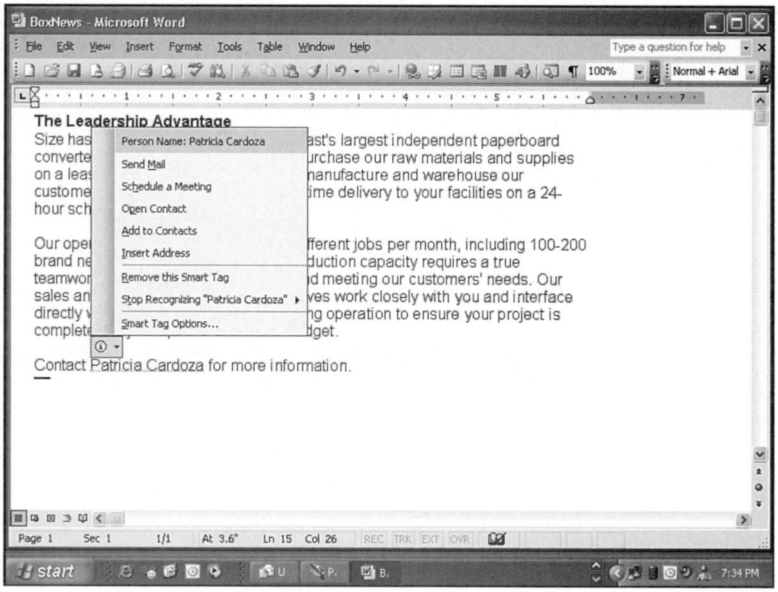

Figure 30.3
A list of options associated with a Smart Tag.

3. Click Send Mail to open a message with the recipient's name already displayed in the To box.

NOTE

> If the name of the recipient is not in your Outlook 2003 Contacts list, you'll still have to add a correct email address.

> However, as shown in Figure 30.3, you can also use Smart Tags to add a name to the Contacts list, displaying the Outlook 2003 Contact window and giving you an opportunity to add an email address to your Outlook 2003 Contacts list.
>
> After you've added the email address to your Outlook 2003 Contacts list, Word provides the address whenever you create a new message to the recipient—whether or not you use a Smart Tag to do it.

ESTABLISHING SETTINGS FOR YOUR MESSAGE

30

Whether you've created a blank email message or built one from a Word document, when you open Word's email tools, you can enter, edit, and format your message. You can also do the following:

- Specify recipients (primary, "carbon copies," and "blind carbon copies")
- Specify a subject for the message
- Add file attachments
- Set the importance of your message
- Check to make sure that you typed the recipients' names properly
- Create follow-up reminders for yourself
- Prepare a *blind carbon copy*, which prevents others from knowing that a given individual received it
- Add file attachments
- Set various other options

These tasks are covered in the following sections.

NOTE

> Much of the coverage in this chapter assumes that you are also running Microsoft Outlook 2003—either as part of Microsoft Office 2003 or as a program you have purchased and installed separately.

SPECIFYING HOW YOUR MESSAGE IS FORMATTED

Word supports three email message formats:

- **HTML.** Word's default setting, HTML allows you to format messages using the same types of graphics and text attributes found in Web pages. HTML-formatted messages can be read by most contemporary email client software, including Microsoft Outlook 2003 and Outlook Express, recent versions of Eudora and Netscape Messenger, and some versions of Lotus Notes.

- **Rich text.** This captures nearly all the formatting found in any Word document; in fact, it corresponds to the RTF format that has long been used to exchange Word documents.

- **Plain text.** This is the basic "lowest common denominator" ASCII character set virtually every messaging system understands.

HTML and rich text–formatted messages can communicate far more effectively than plain text messages. However, there are significant disadvantages to them, as well:

- Many people and companies still depend on email readers that can handle only ASCII text messages (though this is gradually changing). Although HTML support in email readers is widespread, using rich text is viable primarily in environments where you can be sure that all your recipients are using Microsoft Office. Borders, highlighted text, tables, bulleted lists, and numbered lists are especially troublesome for non-Office users attempting to read rich text emails.

- Some users prefer not to receive HTML or rich text messages, which take longer to download. This is especially the case for international users, who may be paying on a per-minute basis to download their messages.

- Other users prefer to avoid HTML messages due to privacy concerns. For instance, HTML messages can contain the same 1x1 transparent GIFs that many Web pages use to track their visitors. (This is not an issue with rich text messages.)

- When rich text messages are sent over the Internet, it's possible that formatting and attachments will be lost. Many email clients and servers can't interpret rich text messages. Instead a file, Winmail.dat, is included with the email message. If your recipients are receiving Winmail.dat files instead of the proper attachments, switch to HTML or plain text instead of rich text formatting.

NOTE

> Note, however, that Outlook 2003 deactivates scripts and ActiveX controls received in HTML messages. This means that HTML messages should be more secure than they were in earlier versions of Outlook. Outlook 2003 also includes built-in functionality to disable Web bugs embedded in HTML emails.

You can choose the format you want to use in your current message from the Message Format drop-down box (refer to Figure 30.1). To set a default format for all your messages, follow these steps in Outlook 2003:

1. Choose Tools, Options.
2. Click the Mail Format tab.
3. From the Compose In This Message Format drop-down box, choose the format you want to standardize on: HTML, Rich Text, or Plain Text.
4. Click OK and exit Outlook 2003.

CREATING FILE ATTACHMENTS

You'll often want to send file attachments with your message. These can take the form of any file: Office documents, graphics for review, saved Web pages, Acrobat PDF files, and many others. These are received as separate attachments that can be opened by the recipient using a wide range of email software, not just Outlook 2003 or Outlook Express.

SENDING AN OPEN WORD DOCUMENT AS AN ATTACHMENT

If you are editing a file in Word and want to send it as an attachment, choose File, Send To, Mail Recipient (As Attachment). A separate Microsoft Outlook 2003 email window appears, with the document listed as an Attachment (see Figure 30.4).

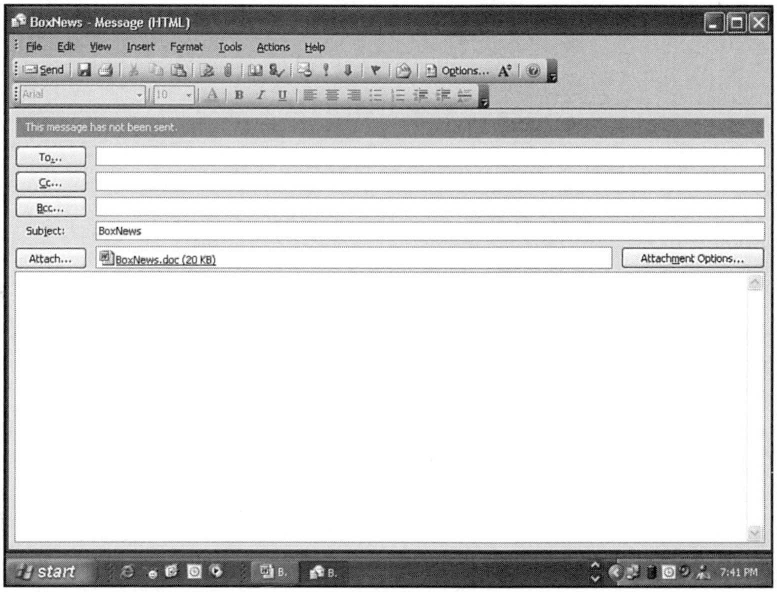

30

Figure 30.4
When you choose File, Send To, Mail Recipient (As Attachment), Word displays a new message with the file attachment contained in it.

> **TIP**
>
> You can also send a document For Review. It arrives as an attachment, and when an Office 2003 user opens it, it appears with Word's Reviewing toolbar displayed.

SENDING A DOCUMENT AS AN ATTACHMENT WITHOUT OPENING IT IN WORD

To create a message with a file attachment without first opening the file, right-click on the file in either Windows Explorer or Word's Open or Save As dialog boxes. Then, choose Send To, Mail Recipient from the shortcut menu. If you're asked to choose a Profile Name, choose your Outlook profile and click OK. An Outlook message window opens, with the file displayed as an attachment and the file's name appearing as the message's Subject, as well as in the message text.

ADDING A FILE ATTACHMENT TO AN OUTLOOK MESSAGE YOU'VE ALREADY CREATED

If you want to add a file attachment to an existing Outlook 2003 message you've already created, either click the Insert File button in the message window or choose Insert, File. If the Attach button is present in the message window, you can also click Attach.

The Insert File dialog box opens (see Figure 30.5). Browse to and select the file (or files) you want to insert; then click OK.

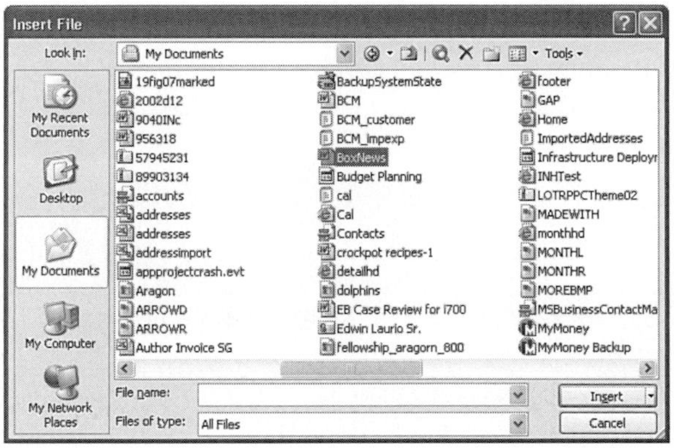

Figure 30.5
Choosing an attachment from the Insert File dialog box.

30

CONTROLLING MESSAGE PRIORITY AND OTHER OPTIONS

Word and Outlook give you extensive control over your messages. For example, you can mark a message with high or low importance; set message flags that help you follow up on your messages; and request delivery receipts. In the following sections, we review the options you're most likely to need as you create email messages with Word.

SETTING THE IMPORTANCE OF YOUR MESSAGE

Some messages are more important than others. To tell your recipient that a message is unusually important, click the Importance: High button. On those rare occasions when you know that a message can take low priority, click the Importance: Low toolbar button.

SETTING MESSAGE FLAGS

To create a message flag that reminds you (in Microsoft Outlook 2003) to check on the status of your message, click the Message Flag button. The Flag for Follow Up dialog box opens (see Figure 30.6). Then do this:

1. In the Flag To drop-down box, choose which kind of flag to set; for example, you can set a flag that calls for you to follow up the message, forward it to a third party, or just reread it.

2. To specify when you want to be reminded, click the Due By drop-down box and choose the date from the calendar that appears.

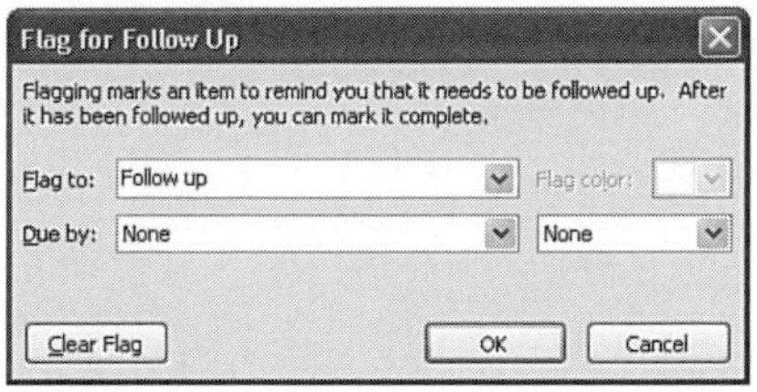

Figure 30.6
Requesting a
reminder about a
message you've sent.

3. When you're finished, click OK. Word returns you to the Microsoft Office Email editing window.

CREATING A BLIND CARBON COPY

Blind carbon copies give you a way to let someone in on a message you've sent to others—without letting those others know that that individual has seen the message.

Earlier, you learned that you can add a recipient of a blind carbon copy through the Select Names dialog box. You can also send a blind carbon copy from within the email message editing window. To do so, click Options on the Mail toolbar, and choose Bcc from the menu. A Bcc line appears below the Cc line in your message window. Add the recipients' names, either manually or from the Outlook 2003 Contacts list.

TIP

> Blind carbon copies can be used when you send a message to a long list of recipients and do not want every recipient's name to appear at the beginning of the message when it is opened. This can make messages more convenient, as well as more secure.

SETTING ADDITIONAL MESSAGE OPTIONS

Word and Outlook 2003 enable you to control several other aspects of how your message is sent and tracked. To control these aspects, click the Options button; the Message Options dialog box appears (see Figure 30.7).

You've already seen that you can flag the importance of your message; here, you can also flag its Sensitivity: Normal, Personal, Private, or Confidential.

CAUTION

> Flagging a message as personal, private, or confidential does nothing to ensure that your employer can't read it, or that it cannot be read by third parties in the event of a lawsuit.

You can also specify several tracking and delivery options:

■ Checking Request a Delivery Receipt for This Message triggers the recipient's email system to send you a message when your message is delivered.

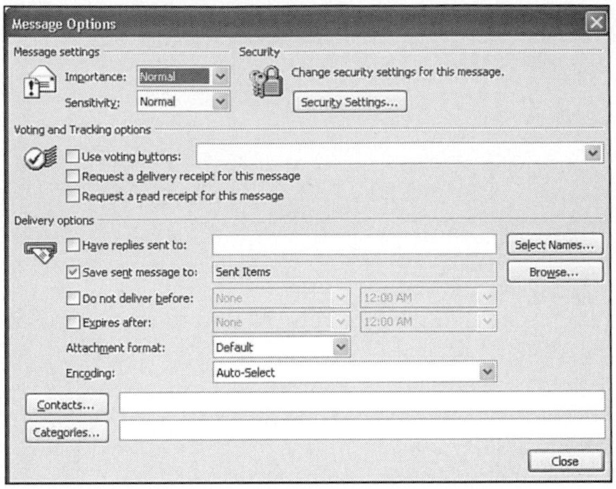

Figure 30.7
Controlling additional message options through the Message Options dialog box.

- Checking Request a <u>R</u>ead Receipt for This Message triggers the recipient's email system to send you a message when your recipient opens the message you sent (although nothing can guarantee that he or she actually *reads* it!).

> **NOTE**
>
> To request delivery receipts and/or read receipts for all your messages, follow these steps, in Outlook 2003:
>
> 1. Choose <u>T</u>ools, <u>O</u>ptions to display the Preferences tab.
> 2. Click E-mail Options.
> 3. Click <u>T</u>racking Options.
> 4. To request a Read receipt for all messages, check the <u>R</u>ead Receipt check box. To request a Delivery receipt for all messages, check <u>D</u>elivery Receipt. Delivery Receipts are available only if you are connected to a Microsoft Exchange email system.
> 5. Click OK.
>
> The same dialog box allows you to control how your computer responds to requests for read receipts. By default, Outlook 2003 asks how you want to respond. If you want to disregard all read receipt requests, choose <u>N</u>ever Send a Response.

> **NOTE**
>
> Even though you request a read or delivery receipt for your messages, there's no guarantee you'll receive one. If the recipient has Outlook 2002, Outlook 2003, or Outlook Express, the recipient can choose whether to send a read receipt. In addition, many email systems do not support the use of read or delivery receipts and won't return them.

> **NOTE**
>
> Another option, Use Voting B<u>u</u>ttons, allows the recipients of your message to vote up or down on the contents of your message. However, this feature works only if your Outlook 2003 email system is connected to Microsoft Exchange.

- Checking the Have Replies Sent To check box enables you to arrange for replies to be sent directly to a colleague or an assistant, rather than to you. To choose a name from your Outlook 2003 Contacts list, click Select Names and pick the name from the Select Names dialog box.

- Checking Save Sent Message To and clicking Browse enables you to specify a different Outlook 2003 folder in which to store a copy of this message after you send it.

- Clicking the down arrow next to Do Not Deliver Before enables you to hold off sending a message until a time you specify.

- Expires After enables you to specify a date after which the message becomes unavailable.

- Clicking the drop-down arrow next to Attachment Format allows you to specify how your message's attachment is coded for delivery across networks. The Default setting usually works well, but in certain instances, you may want to make a change. For example, if you are sending an attachment to a Macintosh user, especially one whose corporate email system is based on the Macintosh, you may want to use BinHex. If you are sending an attachment to an older Unix-based system, you may want to use UUEN-CODE.

- Clicking the drop-down arrow next to Encoding enables you to specify encoding associated with the region of the world that your message will be delivered to. Messages sent throughout North America, South America, and Western Europe utilize the default Western European (ISO) character set, but if your message is being delivered to the Baltics, Eastern Europe, the Middle East, or Asia, you might need to change this setting.

- Clicking Categories displays the Categories dialog box (see Figure 30.8), where you can set a category that helps you track your messages in Outlook 2003. For example, you might create a category for all messages associated with a specific project, or all messages associated with a specific personal goal you have. You can then later search your folders for all items of a specific category. Check the boxes that correspond to the categories to which you want the message assigned.

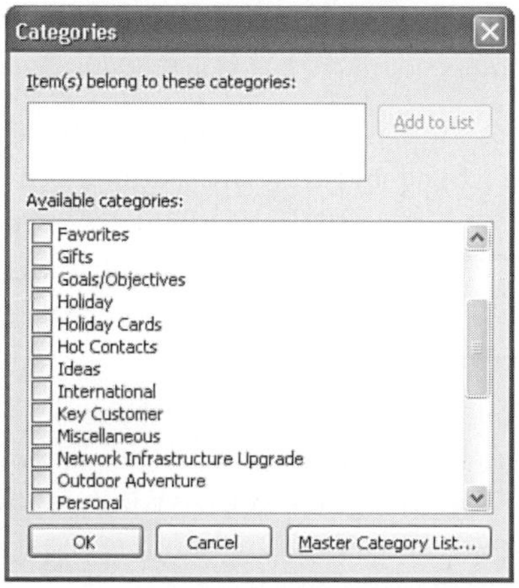

Figure 30.8
Assigning a message to one or more Outlook 2002 categories.

When you finish setting Message Options, click Close.

Still More Word and Outlook Options Affecting Email Handling

The preceding section discussed options that apply only to the specific message you are working on. Additional email options are scattered throughout Word 2003 and Outlook 2003.

Settings relevant to how Word formats all your email—especially settings for email signatures and digital stationery—are accessible by choosing Tools, Options, General in Word, and clicking the E-mail Options button. Settings for email signatures can also be accessed by clicking the drop-down arrow next to the Options button on the Mail toolbar and choosing E-mail Signature from the drop-down menu. Settings for Personal Stationery can also be accessed by clicking Options on the Mail toolbar and choosing Stationery from the drop-down menu. These settings are covered later in this chapter, in the section "Setting Formatting Defaults for All Your Mail Messages."

Settings that affect message formats can also be found in Outlook 2003. Choose Tools, Options and click the Mail Format tab. Several stationery, signature, and font settings in this dialog box overlap with options found in Word's email options dialog box. If you establish these settings in Word, Word's settings will apply here as well. (You can also specify that Outlook 2003 use its own built-in editor instead of Word for editing and formatting email. To do so, clear the Use Microsoft Word to Edit E-mail Messages check box.)

Settings that affect how Outlook 2003 connects to your email accounts, when it sends and receives, and how it stores email are accessible through Outlook 2003. To access these, Choose Tools, Options and click the Mail Setup tab.

Additional settings that affect how email is handled and tracked can be found in Outlook 2003. Choose Tools, Options; click the Preferences tab; and click E-mail Options.

Sending Your Message

After you edit and customize your message, sending the message is the easy part: Click Send a Copy. Word places the message in the Outlook Outbox, where it is sent automatically the next time Outlook sends messages (unless you have customized your Outlook settings).

If you don't want to wait, or if Outlook 2003 is not configured to connect to an server automatically, open Outlook 2003 and click Send and Receive. Outlook connects to your mail server to send and receive messages (see Figure 30.9), including the message you just created.

Routing a Document Through Your Email System

Suppose you have a document that you need to send to several people, and you want each person to review the document and send it on to the next person. If you're using Microsoft Exchange or another compatible email system, you can use Word's routing capabilities:

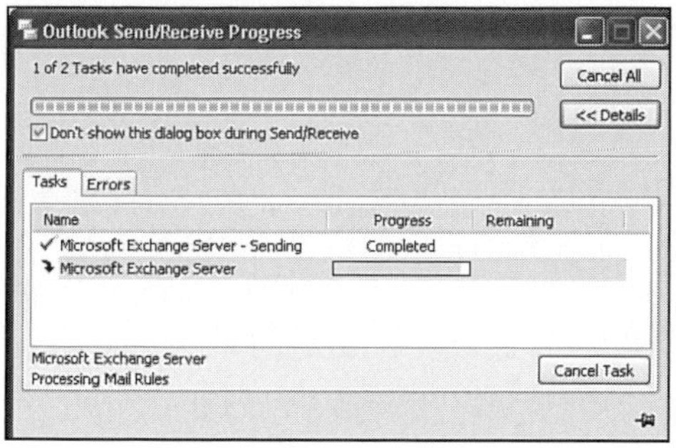

Figure 30.9
Sending and receiving messages in Outlook 2003.

30

1. Choose File, Send To, Routing Recipient. The Routing Slip dialog box appears (see Figure 30.10).

> **NOTE**
>
> If Word displays a dialog box questioning whether you want to give another program access to Outlook 2003's Contacts list, click Yes to continue.

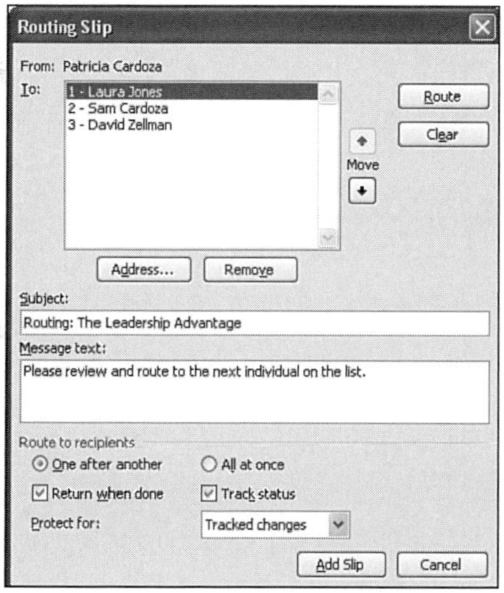

Figure 30.10
Word's Routing Slip dialog box.

2. Click Address to display the Address Book, from which you can choose names for routing.

3. When you finish selecting names, click OK to return to the Routing Slip dialog box.

4. Use the arrow you keys to change the order in which recipients are to receive the message.

5. Type text for an accompanying message in the Message Text box.

6. Choose whether you want to route the document to recipients One After Another or All at Once.

30

7. When you finish defining how you want to route the message, click Route, and Word delivers the message to the first recipient.

TIP

> You can prevent your recipients from making edits except with Word's Tracked Changes or Comments feature turned on. To do so, choose Tracked Changes or Comments from the Protect For drop-down box. (See Chapter 26, "Managing Document Collaboration and Revisions," to learn more about these features.)

NOTE

> For Word's internal and routing features to work, you must be connected to a compatible system. These include the following:
>
> - Full MAPI-compatible systems such as Microsoft Exchange or Microsoft Outlook 2003
> - Simple MAPI clients such as Outlook Express, Eudora, or Netscape Messenger
> - VIM-compatible systems such as Lotus cc:Mail
>
> Word and Office 2003's email and routing capabilities can vary depending on how your company has configured its email and messaging systems. For more information about using Office in Microsoft messaging environments, see *Special Edition Using Office Outlook 2003*, *Special Edition Using Microsoft Exchange 2000*, and *Special Edition Using Microsoft Exchange 2003*.

SETTING FORMATTING DEFAULTS FOR ALL YOUR MAIL MESSAGES

Earlier in this chapter, in the section "Setting Additional Message Options," you learned how to set options associated with a specific message. You can also set various options that control how *all* your messages are delivered. To do so, choose Tools, Options, General; then click the E-mail Options button. The E-mail Options dialog box appears, containing three tabs:

- **Signature.** Allows you to create, and if you want, format, a "signature" that appears at the bottom of all the messages you send.

- **Personal Stationery.** Allows you to establish visual formats and set fonts that will be used in all your messages.

- **General.** Controls three aspects of how Word prepares HTML messages.

Each tab is covered in the following sections.

CREATING AND SELECTING EMAIL SIGNATURES

Email signatures allow you to add a block of text—formatted or unformatted—to the bottom of all your email messages. This text can be used for various purposes; for example, it might be used to promote your company or its new product line.

To create and select an email signature, follow these steps:

1. In Word, choose Tools, Options, General, and click the E-mail Options tab. Make sure that the E-mail Signature tab is selected (see Figure 30.11).

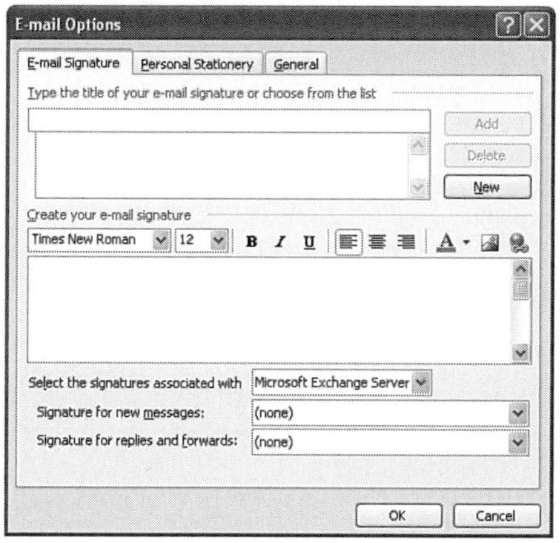

Figure 30.11
The E-mail Signature tab of the E-mail Options dialog box.

2. Enter a name for your email signature in the Type the Title of Your E-mail Signature or Choose from the List drop-down box. Keep it concise, but make sure that it's descriptive—so you'll be able to recognize it at a glance if you create several distinct signatures over time.

3. In the large scroll box at the middle of the dialog box, enter the text you want to appear in your email signature. Note that you're not limited to text: You can copy images from your document and paste them in the email signature scroll box. Be careful, however, not to bulk up your messages to the point that they inconvenience their recipients!

4. If you want, use the Create Your E-mail Signature formatting tools to format your email signature. Note that you can select and format individual words, not just the entire block of text. Of course, formatting will be disregarded in any message sent as plain text.

5. When you've finished editing and formatting your signature, click Add. The signature's title now appears in the list of signatures.

6. Click OK.

You can create as many signatures as you want. Word 2003 and Outlook 2003 include an additional often-requested feature: the capability to specify different signatures for each mail account in your profile. After you have created a signature, choose the account you'd like to use the signature and specify whether you want the signature to be used for new messages, replies and forwards, or both. If you create more than one signature, you can choose different signatures for your new messages, and for your replies and forwards. This way, those you correspond with won't see the same message as your email conversation continues.

30

TIP

If you're running *Outlook 2003*, you may also want to add a *virtual business card* (vCard) to your emails. To do so, create your signature in Outlook instead of Word. Sending a vCard with your signature ensures that everyone you correspond with can have all of your updated contact information when they receive your email. However, this process also increases the size of your email message, so think carefully about whether you want to do this.

First, create a contact entry with all your personal information. With the Contact displayed, choose File, Export to vCard File; enter a name in the VCARD File dialog box; and click Save.

Save and close your contact; then choose Tools, Options, Mail Format, and click Signatures. Click New to create a new signature. In the Create New Signature dialog box, enter a name for the signature and choose Next.

Enter your signature text and choose the vCard you created from the Attach This Business Card (vCard) To This Signature drop-down box. Finally, click Finish.

CREATING PERSONAL STATIONERY

Word gives you extensive control over the appearance of your HTML and rich text emails. To take advantage of these features, choose Tools, Options, General; click E-mail Options; and choose the Personal Stationery tab (see Figure 30.12).

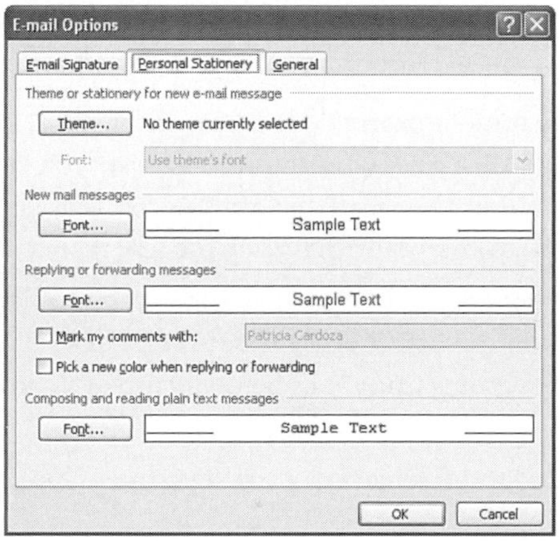

Figure 30.12
Establishing standard formatting for all your email messages.

CAUTION

As mentioned earlier, remember that heavily formatted emails can take longer to upload and download, drain system resources, and cause problems for email users who cannot display formatted email, or simply prefer plain text.

To attractively format your email in "one fell swoop," choose a theme, and Word takes responsibility for formatting fonts, bullets, background colors, horizontal lines, and images in all your messages.

Click Theme to display the built-in Web page and E-mail Themes Word provides (see Figure 30.13). Themes marked as (Stationery) are especially designed for email, but other themes can be used as well.

Figure 30.13
Choosing an email theme.

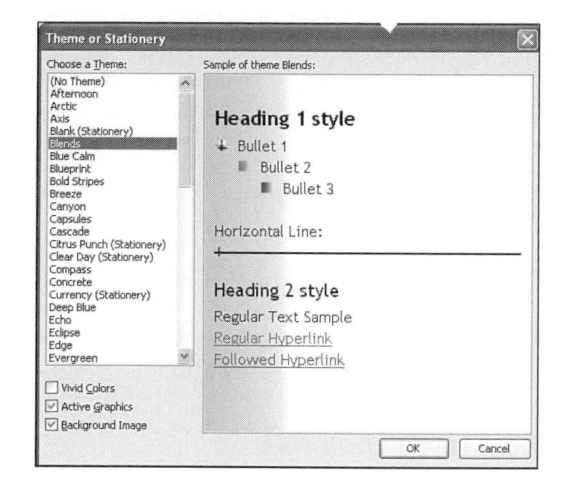

When you select a theme, it is previewed at the right. When you've chosen the theme you want to use, click OK to return to the Personal Stationery tab. The theme you chose will be listed, and fonts may have been adjusted accordingly.

If you prefer not to choose a theme, you can set fonts for New Mail Messages and for Replying or Forwarding Messages.

If you do choose a theme, you have a choice: You can use the fonts Word provides in the theme; disregard Word's fonts and choose your own; or compromise by specifying your own fonts only for replies and forwarded messages. After you choose a theme, these choices are available from a new Font drop-down box (see Figure 30.14).

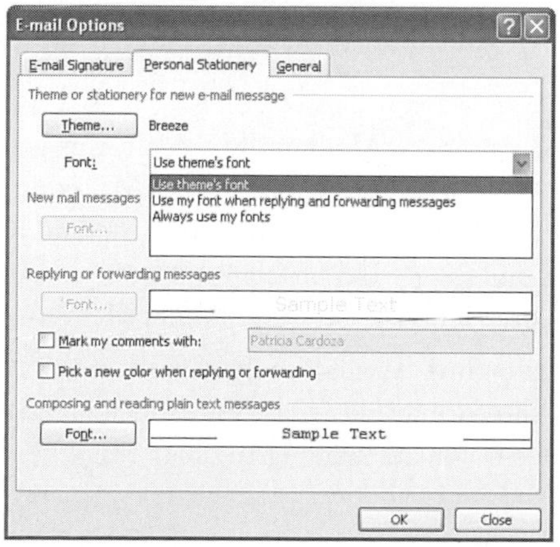

Figure 30.14
Choosing whether you want to supersede the font choices made in one of Word's themes.

The <u>P</u>ersonal Stationery tab allows you to control two other aspects of how your messages are formatted:

■ <u>M</u>ark My Comments With allows you to enter text that always appears at the beginning of comments you make within an email.

■ Pick a New <u>C</u>olor When Replying or Formatting makes it easier for recipients to tell replies from the original message.

Finally, even if you prefer to send and receive plain text mail, you can control the default font Word displays while you're editing and reading it. By default, that font is Courier New, but many Word users prefer to set this font to Times New Roman for improved readability.

SETTING ADDITIONAL OPTIONS FOR HTML MAIL

The <u>G</u>eneral tab of Word's E-mail Options dialog box contains three additional options for controlling the formatting of HTML email (see Figure 30.15).

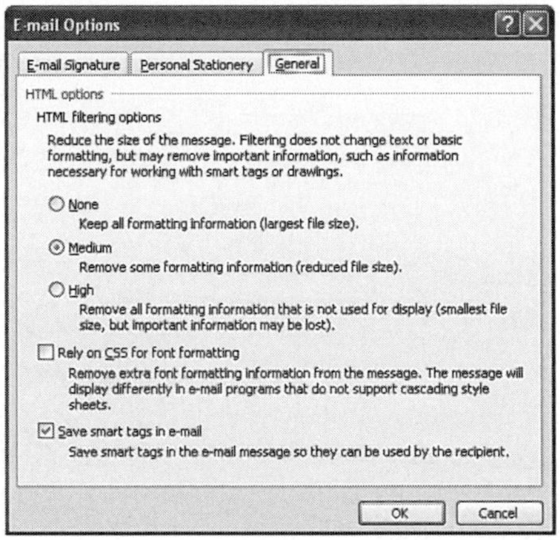

Figure 30.15
Controlling additional aspects of HTML-formatted email.

These settings are irrelevant if you send all your messages using plain text or rich text formats:

■ **<u>F</u>ilter HTML Before Sending.** Set to Medium by default, this group of options instructs Word to strip out some of the unique HTML/XML coding it otherwise sends with HTML messages to support advanced Word formatting and features. This reduces the size of messages and may avoid problems in how certain email editors display them. You can choose three levels of filtering: None, Medium, and High.

■ **Rely on <u>C</u>SS for Font Formatting.** Turned on by default, this instructs Word to use Cascading Style Sheets for font formatting. This results in smaller messages but causes compatibility problems if you are sending to older email clients that do not support CSS.

- **§ave Smart Tags in E-mail.** Turned on by default, this instructs Word to retain Smart Tags in email so that recipients who read the messages in Word 2002 or Outlook 2002 can use the Smart Tags. Of course, the Smart Tags will simply appear to be extraneous code to users of other email software.

TROUBLESHOOTING

WHAT TO DO IF YOUR EMAIL RECIPIENTS RECEIVE UNEXPLAINED ATTACHMENTS

You may have sent formatted RTF files to recipients whose email readers cannot handle them. Use plain text in your messages instead.

WHAT TO DO IF YOUR EMAIL RECIPIENTS CANNOT SEE FONTS, COLORS, TABLES, AND OTHER MESSAGE FORMATTING

Again, your recipients may be using email readers that can handle only text files. Send your messages as text, and if you need to send formatted information, send that information as a file attachment.

WHAT TO DO IF YOUR RECIPIENTS RECEIVE UNREADABLE EMAIL ATTACHMENTS CALLED WIN-MAIL.DAT

This occurs when you send messages using Rich Text Format (RTF) to people whose email programs cannot read RTF email messages. In Outlook, choose Tools, Options, Mail Format. Then, choose either HTML or Plain Text from the Compose in This Message Format drop-down box.

WHAT TO DO IF THE EMAIL MESSAGES YOU CREATE WITH WORD ARE TOO LARGE

Many email systems have limitations on the size of messages they will process. Certain aspects of Word's operation can easily lead to files that are too large to be sent, and will be "bounced back" by your system's email server. To reduce file size, consider these actions:

- Compress the pictures in your document (or, if the images are available on the Web, provide links instead of pictures). Right-click on a picture, choose Format Picture; click Compress; choose All Pictures in Document; and click OK.

→ For more information about compressing pictures, including potential drawbacks, **see** Chapter 13, "Getting Images into Your Documents," **p. 437**.

- Save the document to Word 6/95 format (which generally, though not always, leads to smaller documents).
- If you created the document using Word's speech or handwriting recognition features, choose Tools, Options, Save; clear the Embed Linguistic Data check box; and click OK. Then, resave the file without the accompanying voice and handwriting data that Word previously stored in it.

CHAPTER 31

CUSTOMIZING WORD

In this chapter

DECIDING WHICH WORD FEATURES TO CUSTOMIZE

Word is remarkably easy to personalize, and you can personalize it extensively—making your copy of Word look and function very different from the next person's. Of course, you wouldn't do that just for the sheer joy of it—few people have that much time to waste. On the other hand, judiciously applied customization can make Word more convenient, more comfortable, more productive, and even more fun.

If you use Word several hours a day, as you read this chapter think about the minor annoyances you've found in Word. Think about the tasks that seem to take longer than they ought, the toolbars that don't include the tasks you perform most, the automated actions you find yourself undoing. You just might be able to eliminate those annoyances.

If you're responsible for the way many people in your company use Word, you can use many of the same customizations to create a word processing program that more closely serves the needs of your colleagues and your organization as a whole.

CONTROLLING HOW WORD STARTS

You're probably accustomed to starting Word from the Windows Start menu, or perhaps from a desktop icon. But you have a good deal more control over how Word starts than you may realize. In the next two sections, for example, we'll show you how to automatically start Word whenever you start your computer—and how to start Word with a specific task or document.

STARTING WORD AUTOMATICALLY

For millions of people, it's a given: When they turn on their computers in the morning, they'll be working in Word. If you're one of those people, you can set up Windows to run Word automatically whenever you start your computer. You'll have a little more time to get coffee, and when you get back, Word will be all set for you to get started.

CAUTION

> The downside of adding startup programs is that Windows takes longer to finish loading at startup.

To run Word at startup, follow these steps:

1. Click Start, Microsoft Office to display shortcuts for all your Microsoft Office programs.
2. Right-click on the Microsoft Office Word 2003 shortcut, and choose Copy to copy it into the Clipboard.

3. Browse to and open the Startup folder associated with the All Users profile (typically, C:\Documents and Settings\All Users\Start menu\Programs\Startup.

4. Click Paste.

TIP

> If you're working on a long-term project that involves the same document day in and day out, you can place a shortcut to a Word document in the StartUp folder. Then, whenever you start your computer or log into Windows, Word opens with that document already displayed.
>
> These steps can also be applied to any other program that you want Windows to launch automatically when you start up or log in.

STARTING WORD WITH A PARTICULAR TASK

You've already learned that you can automatically start Word when you start your computer and that you can open a document at the same time. But what if you start with a few different documents? Imagine, for example, that on Tuesday and Wednesday you usually work on correspondence; on Thursday and Friday you work on a manual. You can create one desktop shortcut that runs the Letter Wizard when Word starts, and another that opens the master document where your manual files are stored.

To create a desktop shortcut that loads Word with a custom behavior, follow these steps:

1. In My Computer or Windows Explorer, browse to the Microsoft Word program file WINWORD.EXE. In a typical installation, its location is C:\Program Files\Microsoft Office\OFFICE 11\WINWORD.EXE.

2. Right-click on WINWORD.EXE to display the shortcut menu, and click Send To, Desktop (Create Shortcut).

3. On the Windows Desktop, right-click on the shortcut you just created, and choose Properties from the shortcut menu. Display the Shortcut tab if it is not already displayed.

4. In the Target box, edit the text to add an instruction or switch that corresponds to the behavior you want Word to perform at startup.

   For example, if you want Word to load a specific document, add the complete path to the document you want to load, within quotation marks. The following example shows how this would look if the document were stored in your My Documents folder. (You would substitute your account name for the word *Profile*.)

   ```
   "c:\Program Files\Microsoft Office\OFFICE 11\WINWORD.EXE " "c:\Documents and Settings\Profile\My Documents\startup.doc"
   ```

   If you want to instruct Word to start in a specific way, enter one of the switches shown in Table 31.1.

31

TABLE 31.1 WORD STARTUP OPTIONS

This Switch	Does This
/a	Loads Word without loading add-ins *or global templates*.
/l<addin name>	Loads Word with a specific add-in. (Follow /l with the add-in's file name and complete path, for example, /l"c:\Documents and Settings\Profile\ApplicationData\Microsoft\ Templates\sometemplate.dot".)
/m<macroname>	Loads Word without running any automatic macros (AutoExec and so on). (Follow /m with a macro name, and Word runs that macro instead.)
/n	Starts Word without opening a blank document.
/t<template name>	Starts Word and creates a new document based on the indicated template. (Follow /t with the name of the template—for example, /t"NewDay.dot".)

CAUTION

> Do not place the additional instructions within the quotation marks that already appear in the Target box.

5. When you're finished customizing Word's behavior, click OK.

6. Give the shortcut a descriptive name. On the desktop, right-click on the shortcut's current name (WINWORD.EXE), click Rena<u>m</u>e, and type a new name describing its purpose.

When might you use a startup option? You might run Word with the /a and /m options if you suspect that you have a macro virus infection (see Chapter 33, "Word Document Privacy and Security Options"). Or you might create a special desktop shortcut that runs Word and a specific custom macro that creates a unique editing environment for specific tasks. Figure 31.1 shows a Windows desktop with custom options for loading Word.

Figure 31.1
Sample custom options for loading Word from the Windows desktop.

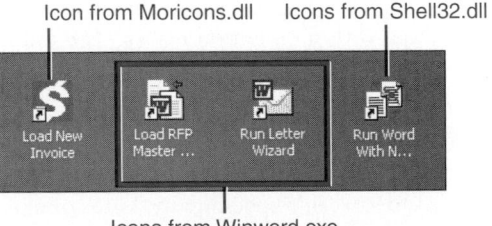

TIP

To run a specific wizard at startup, record a macro that loads the wizard (see Chapter 33 for more information on recording and running macros). Then create a desktop shortcut that runs this macro rather than any of Word's automatic macros. In the following example, the name of the macro is runwizard, and Word has been installed in the default location. You would enter the following in the Target text box of the Shortcut tab:

```
"c:\Program Files\Microsoft Office\Office11\WINWORD.EXE " /
➥mrunwizard
```

If you want, you can not only rename a shortcut but also assign it a new icon. After you create the shortcut, right-click on it and choose Properties; then click the Shortcut tab and click on Change Icon. A series of variations on the Word icon appears. You can select one of these or browse to another file containing icons. Windows typically includes two such files, Shell32.dll and Moricons.dll, both typically stored in the \Winnt\system32 folder.

After you've selected the icon you want, click OK in both of the open dialog boxes. The new icon now appears on your desktop.

31

CUSTOMIZING TOOLBARS AND MENUS

You can thoroughly customize any menu or toolbar to include exactly the commands you want, and you can create new menus or toolbars for any purpose you choose.

NOTE

Throughout the Customize dialog box, Microsoft calls menus "menu bars." We'll use the same terminology throughout this section.

The techniques for customizing both menu bars and toolbars are very similar, though not always identical. This isn't surprising, because under the hood, Word menu bars and toolbars are interchangeable. (The proof? If you so desire, you can place buttons on menu bars and menu commands on toolbars.)

In the following sections, we introduce the techniques you need to know to customize any menu bar or toolbar. You'll first discover how to add commonly used buttons to any existing toolbar. Next, we'll introduce the Customize dialog box, showing how to use it to make a wide variety of changes to menu bars and toolbars, including these:

- Adding commands
- Creating toolbar or menu items that insert pictures or load hyperlinks
- Removing commands
- Rearranging and organizing menu bars or toolbars
- Renaming commands or changing toolbar icons
- Adding or removing new toolbars or menu bars
- Adding or changing keyboard shortcuts associated with menu items

In particular, we'll introduce the new Rearrange Commands dialog box, which makes many interface customizations far more intuitive than they were in earlier versions of Word.

ADDING A COMMONLY USED COMMAND TO A TOOLBAR

You may occasionally want to add a command to a toolbar that is closely related to the commands that are already present—or, perhaps, a command that appeared on that toolbar in an earlier version of Word but has since been removed. For example, you know that the Standard toolbar contains an Open command; why not a Close command? Or, perhaps, you often create superscript and subscript text; why not place those commands on the Formatting toolbar?

Word makes it easy to make changes like this. To add or remove a commonly used button from a toolbar, follow these steps:

1. Click the Toolbar Options down arrow at the right edge of the toolbar containing the button you want to remove.

2. Position your mouse pointer over the Add or Remove Buttons command; then select the toolbar name from the cascading menu that appears. A list of available commands appears (see Figure 31.2). All the commands currently on your toolbar appear checked; all the related commands that do not currently appear on your toolbar appear without a check mark.

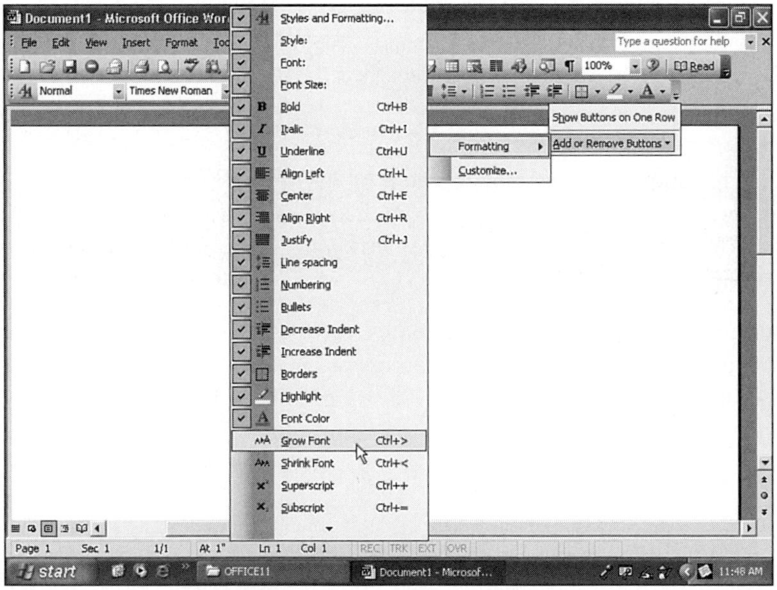

Figure 31.2
Adding a command to the Formatting toolbar.

3. To add or remove a command, toggle the check mark next to the appropriate button.

4. To finish, click anywhere outside the list of commands.

→ To learn how to reset a toolbar or menu item to its factory settings, **see** "Restoring Default Settings to a Menu Bar or Toolbar," **p. 1040**.

TIP

> If you're responsible for managing Word in an organization, you might want to delete toolbar buttons associated with features you don't want your colleagues to use. For example, if you want people to use Word's Track Changes and Comments features rather than simply highlight text in documents they review, you might remove the Highlight button from the Formatting toolbar.
>
> It's best to plan for these kinds of changes before you deploy Word 2003 throughout your company. If you plan in advance, you can create and install an official company template that reflects your changes to the Word interface, and you can train people based on your custom interface from the outset.

→ For more information about working with Word's workgroup revisions features, **see** Chapter 26, "Managing Document Collaboration and Revisions," **p. 873**.

→ For more information on administering Word installations throughout your organization, **see** Chapter 34, "Managing Word More Effectively," **p. 1113**.

NOTE

> Toolbar and button customizations may be stored in either the Normal template or whichever document or template is currently open.

→ For more information about working with templates, **see** Chapter 11, "Templates, Wizards, and Add-Ins," **p. 355**.

ADDING COMMANDS TO A TOOLBAR OR MENU BAR USING REARRANGE COMMANDS

Often, you may want to add commands to a toolbar that Word does not provide in its list of alternatives. For example, if you are working in a legal firm or department, you might want to add the Legal Blackline command to your Reviewing toolbar. Or you might want to add commands to a menu. For example, you might like the File menu to include a Save All command.

TIP

> This command actually *does* appear on the File menu if you press Shift when you select that menu.

You can add *any* Word command to *any* toolbar or menu bar. To do so, first make sure that the toolbar or menu bar you want to customize is displayed. Then continue this way:

1. Choose Tools, Customize to open the Customize dialog box shown in Figure 31.3 (you can also click the down arrow to the right of any toolbar, click Add or Remove Buttons, and click Customize).

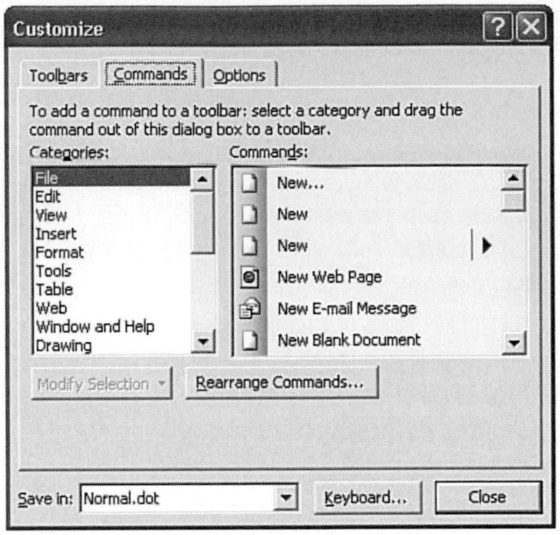

Figure 31.3
The Customize dialog box, with the Commands tab displayed.

2. Click Rearrange Commands to display the Rearrange Commands dialog box (see Figure 31.4).

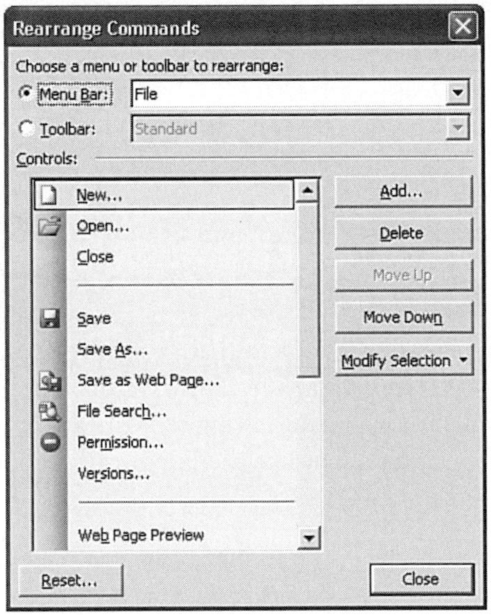

Figure 31.4
From the Rearrange Commands dialog box, you can change the commands appearing on any menu bar or toolbar.

3. Using the Menu Bar drop-down box, choose the menu you want to add a command to.

   If you want to add a command to a toolbar instead of a menu bar, click Toolbar. Then choose the toolbar from the Toolbar drop-down box.

4. Click Add. The Add Command dialog box appears (see Figure 31.5).

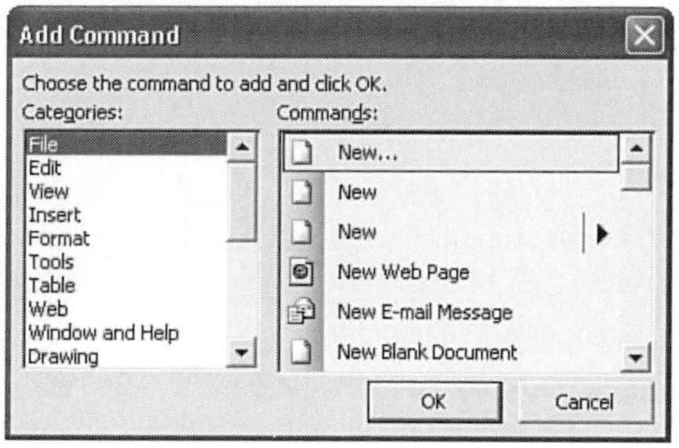

Figure 31.5
In the Add Command dialog box, you can choose which command to add to any menu bar or toolbar.

5. Click OK, and click Close to leave the Rearrange Commands dialog box.

6. When you're finished customizing toolbars and menus, click Close to leave the Customize dialog box.

Word places your new command at the end of the menu or toolbar.

→ If you want to move a command to a different location within the same toolbar or menu bar, **see** "Rearranging Commands on Any Toolbar or Menu," **p. 1030**.

It's worth taking a moment to look more closely at the Add Command dialog box, to see just how extensively you can customize Word. You can add commands from all the following Categories:

- The categories File, Edit, View, Insert, Format, Tools, Table, Window, and Help correspond to Word's menus of the same names. However, they include many options that don't appear on standard Word menu bars. For example, the File category includes items such as Close All and Save All—items that "didn't quite make the cut" to be displayed on the standard File menu.

- Several other categories, including Web, Drawing, AutoShapes, Borders, Mail Merge, Forms, and Control Toolbox, correspond to existing Word toolbars. Again, more options are typically available in the Customize dialog box than on the default Word toolbars. From the Commands tab, you can add these buttons to any toolbar you want.

- The All Commands category lists more than 400 individual commands Word can perform—everything from ApplyHeading1 (format selected text with the Heading 1 style) to WordUnderline (apply underlining to all selected words but not the spaces between them).

- The Macros category lists all currently available macros, allowing you to create a toolbar button or menu item for any existing macro.

- The Fonts category lists all currently available fonts, making it possible for you to create a toolbar button or menu item that automatically formats any selected text in any font on your system.

- The AutoText category lists all AutoText entries in all open templates, so you can create a toolbar button or menu item that inserts any AutoText entry you want.

■ The Styles category lists all available styles, including any custom styles you've created. You can create a toolbar button or menu item that applies any style you want.

NOTE

If you add commands to some of Word's longer toolbars—such as the Standard and Formatting toolbars—and your monitor displays at a low resolution, such as 640×480, you may not be able to see all the commands on these toolbars.

Consider using Add or Remove Buttons to remove commands you rarely use so that you can see all the commands you do use most. For example, if you use Word solely to write brief advertising copy, it's conceivable that you could live without the Insert Microsoft Excel Worksheet button on your Standard toolbar.

→ To create toolbar or menu items that insert pictures or load hyperlinks, **see** "Creating Toolbar Buttons or Menu Items That Insert Pictures" **p. 1035**, or "Creating Toolbar Buttons or Menu Items That Load Hyperlinks" **p. 1036**.

DRAGGING COMMANDS TO A TOOLBAR OR MENU BAR

With Word 2003, Microsoft has introduced the Rearrange Commands dialog box to simplify interface customizations. However, if you have customized earlier versions of Word, the procedures you already know still work. For example, you can still add a command to a toolbar or menu bar as detailed here:

1. Choose Tools, Customize.
2. If you are customizing a toolbar that isn't already visible, choose the Toolbars tab and check the box associated with that toolbar.
3. If the toolbar is partially hidden behind the Customize dialog box, drag the toolbar to a location that's more convenient.
4. In the Categories box of the Commands tab of the Customize dialog box (refer to Figure 31.3), choose the category of the command you want to add.
5. In the Commands box, select the command you want.
6. Drag the command out of the Customize dialog box and drop it on the toolbar or menu bar you want, in the location where you want it to appear. If you are adding a command to a menu bar, the menu will open when you drag the new command over it; you can then drag the command to the appropriate location.
7. Release the mouse button.
8. Close the Customize dialog box.

CAUTION

Be careful not to drag built-in menu items off a menu, or to drag an entire menu off the menu bar by mistake. If you're not careful, it's easy to lose commands you really need. Remember, Undo doesn't work on actions you take with the Customize dialog box open.

→ If you make an error and want to restore a toolbar or menu to its original conditions, **see** "Restoring Default Settings to a Menu Bar or Toolbar," **p. 1040**.

 *If you associate a button with a macro, and the button doesn't work after you copy it to a new template, see "What to Do If You Copy Custom Buttons Between Templates, but the Buttons Don't Work in the New Template," in the "Troubleshooting" section of this chapter.*

REMOVING COMMANDS FROM A TOOLBAR OR MENU BAR

Some people find Word's menus cluttered; they like to remove menu bar or toolbar commands they know they'll never use. Word's Rearrange Commands dialog box makes this easy. First, make sure that the toolbar or menu bar you want to change is displayed. Then, follow these steps:

1. Choose Tools, Customize to open the Customize dialog box (refer to Figure 31.3).

2. Click Rearrange Commands to display the Rearrange Commands dialog box (refer to Figure 31.4).

3. Using the Menu Bar drop-down box, choose the menu you want to remove a command from. If you want to remove a command from a toolbar instead of a menu bar, click Toolbar. Then, from the Toolbar drop-down box, choose the toolbar that contains the command you want to delete.

4. From the Controls scroll box, select the command you want to delete.

5. Click Delete. The command is deleted.

CAUTION

> There is no confirmation dialog box; the command is deleted immediately. If you found you've made a mistake, click Reset to restore the menu bar or toolbar to its original ("factory") settings.

6. Click OK, and click Close to leave the Rearrange Commands dialog box.

7. When you're finished changing toolbars and menus, click Close to leave the Customize dialog box.

TIP

> You can also remove a toolbar or menu item like this:
> 1. Open the Tools, Customize dialog box.
> 2. Move the mouse pointer to the toolbar or menu you want to change. If you move the mouse pointer to a menu, and then click on the menu, the menu will open.
> 3. Click the toolbar button or menu item you want to delete, and drag it off the toolbar or menu bar.

31

ORGANIZING ENTIRE TOOLBARS OR MENUS

So far, you've learned how to add or remove individual commands on menu bars and toolbars. Now step back a moment and look at the menu bars and toolbars themselves. Are they organized appropriately for easy use? In the following sections, you'll learn how to

- Rearrange commands on any toolbar or menu
- Copy or move commands from one toolbar or menu to another
- Widen or narrow boxes in a toolbar to improve readability
- Divide toolbar buttons or menu items logically for easy understanding

REARRANGING COMMANDS ON ANY TOOLBAR OR MENU

You may sometimes want to rearrange the commands on a toolbar or menu—perhaps to place the ones you use most often at the top. As with adding and removing commands, you can do this through the Rearrange Commands dialog box. Follow these steps:

1. Choose Tools, Customize to open the Customize dialog box (refer to Figure 31.3).
2. Click Rearrange Commands to display the Rearrange Commands dialog box (refer to Figure 31.4).
3. Choose the Menu Bar you want to rearrange from the Menu Bar drop-down box. Or, if you want to rearrange a Toolbar, click Toolbar, and choose the toolbar from the Toolbar drop-down box.
4. In the Controls list, choose the Control you want to move. Then, click Move Up or Move Down repeatedly, until the command appears where you want it to.

> **TIP**
>
> You can also choose any of the other options on the shortcut menu. Many of these are discussed in later sections of this chapter.

5. When you're finished rearranging your menu bar or toolbar, click Close to return to the Customize dialog box.
6. When you're finished making all your customizations, click Close to apply them.

COPYING OR MOVING TOOLBAR BUTTONS

You may occasionally want to move a toolbar button or menu item from one toolbar or menu bar to another, or copy the command so that it appears on more than one toolbar or menu bar. With the Customize dialog box open, you can do any of the following:

- To move a toolbar button, drag it from one toolbar to another.
- To copy a toolbar button, press Ctrl while you drag the button from one toolbar to another.
- To move a toolbar button within the same toolbar, click and drag it to its new location.

WIDENING BOXES IN A TOOLBAR

If you add the Font, Font Size, or Style commands (from the Format category), or (Web) Address command (from the Web category) to a toolbar, Word doesn't insert a button; rather, it inserts a drop-down box, just like the Style drop-down box that appears on Word's Formatting toolbar. You might find the box too wide or narrow for your purposes. For example, you might be in the habit of using exceptionally long style names. Or you might want to squeeze a font box onto a toolbar with little extra space for it.

To change the width of a box on a toolbar, make sure that the Customize dialog box is open. Then, place your mouse pointer on the left or right edge of the box so that the mouse icon shows a sizing handle, and then drag it to the width you want (see Figure 31.6).

Black borders show new width

Figure 31.6
Dragging a font, font size, or style box to the width you want.

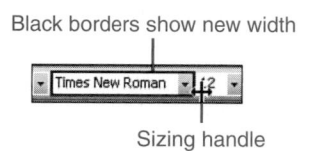

Sizing handle

31

DIVIDING TOOLBAR BUTTONS AND MENU ITEMS LOGICALLY

Perhaps you've noticed that Word's toolbar buttons and menu commands are grouped logically, with a group separator line between each group. (For example, you can find a group separator line between the Spelling and Grammar icon and the Cut icon on the Standard toolbar, and between the Print and Send To commands on the File menu.

You can add a group separator line of your own to make your custom toolbar buttons or menu commands easier to understand and use. To do so, choose Tools, Customize to display the Customize dialog box.

If you are adding a separator line to a toolbar, right-click the button immediately to the right of where you want the separator to appear, and choose Begin a Group from the shortcut menu. If you are adding a separator line to a menu bar, right-click the menu item immediately below where you want the separator to appear, and choose Begin a Group from the shortcut menu.

CHANGING THE APPEARANCE OF TOOLBAR BUTTONS AND MENU ITEMS

You may occasionally want to change the text or image used in your toolbar buttons or menu items. In the following sections, you'll learn how.

CHANGING THE TEXT OF A MENU COMMAND OR TOOLBAR BUTTON

Many of the commands you can add to a menu bar or toolbar have descriptions that are quite lengthy: for instance, names of styles, or typefaces. Left alone, they can take up too much space on a toolbar, or make a menu bar clumsier to use. In some instances—such as macro names—the labels Word assigns can be difficult to understand.

By default, if you place a command on a toolbar, Word will use a toolbar button for that command if one exists. But in many cases, no toolbar button exists. Of course, if you're adding a command to a menu bar, you'll most likely want to use text in any case.

You can edit the text of a menu item or toolbar button for brevity or clarity. To do so, carry out these steps:

1. Choose Tools, Customize.
2. Right-click on the toolbar button you want to edit. If you want to edit a menu item, click on the menu; the entire menu will appear. Then right-click on the menu item you want to edit. A shortcut menu appears (see Figure 31.7).

Insert an ampersand (&) before the letter
you want to use as a keyboard shortcut

Figure 31.7
You can change a toolbar button or menu item through the Customize shortcut menu.

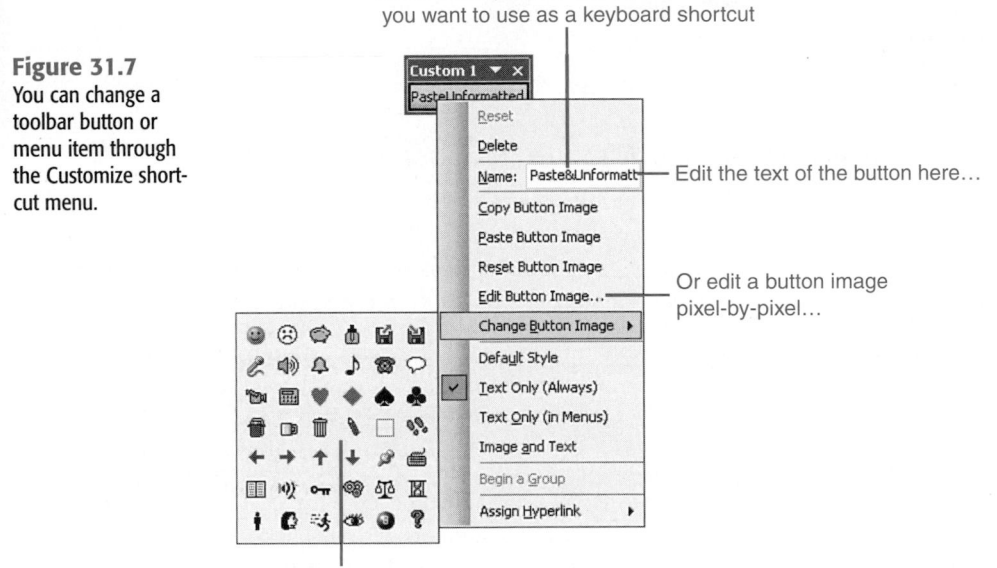

Edit the text of the button here...

Or edit a button image
pixel-by-pixel...

Or choose a different button image from Word's built-in library

NOTE

You can change the name or graphic for any button, not just the ones you've inserted.

3. Click inside the Name text box.
4. Type the new name you want. To assign a keyboard shortcut key, place the ampersand character (&) before the letter you want to serve as the keyboard shortcut.
5. Press Enter, and Word automatically changes the button accordingly.

CHANGING THE APPEARANCE OF A TOOLBAR BUTTON

If you want to change the appearance of a toolbar button (or add one to a command that doesn't have one), Word gives you all the tools you need to do so:

- You can assign a new button graphic in place of an existing image or text.
- You can copy and adapt an image from another button.
- You can create a button yourself, from scratch.

Each of these options is covered next.

COPYING AN IMAGE FROM AN EXISTING BUTTON

If you want to copy an image from an existing button onto any other toolbar button, follow these steps:

1. Make sure that the toolbar containing the image you want and the toolbar where you plan to place the image are both visible.
2. Right-click the toolbar button image you want to borrow or adapt, and choose Copy Button Image from the shortcut menu.
3. Right-click the button on which you want to paste the image.
4. Choose Paste Button Image.

USING A BUTTON FROM WORD'S BUTTON LIBRARY

If none of the button icons visible in your configuration of Word fits the bill, you can always browse through some of Word's other 42 generic buttons. To do so, follow these directions:

1. Right-click the button you want to change.
2. Choose Change Button Image. This brings up a submenu showing Word's other available button images (refer to Figure 31.7).
3. Select an image from the cascaded menu.

> **TIP**
>
> Using the Windows Clipboard, you can copy any bitmapped image onto a toolbar button, including images created in programs such as Microsoft Paint.
>
> 1. Open the graphics program and create or open the image you want.
> 2. Select all or part of the image and copy the selected image to the Clipboard (select the image and press Ctrl+C).
> 3. Switch to Word and choose Tools, Customize.
> 4. Right-click the toolbar button where you want to use the image.
> 5. Choose Paste Button Image.

continues

continued

> Be aware, however, that most images created elsewhere weren't designed for use on tiny, square toolbar buttons. The images that produce the best results are typically square (or roughly square) and have strong outlines with little internal detail.
>
> If Word's stock images aren't enough, try using the other Office programs. Excel, Outlook, PowerPoint, and Access have their own Tools, Customize dialog boxes, largely identical to the one in Word. You can copy an image from a toolbar button in Excel or PowerPoint and then paste it onto a toolbar button in Word.

In some cases, both an image and text are associated with a Word command, and when you assign the command to a toolbar button, both the image and the text appear. If Word displays both the image and the text, and you don't want to see the text, right-click the button and choose Default Style from the shortcut menu.

Thereafter, Word displays only the picture for that button.

EDITING EXISTING BUTTON IMAGES

It's possible you still don't have the right image for your custom toolbar button. In that case, you can create it yourself with Word's Button Editor—or better yet, adapt it from an existing image that's close but not quite right.

If you have an image you can use as a starting point, follow these steps:

1. Make sure that the Tools, Customize dialog box is open.
2. Open the image in any graphics program and copy the image to the Clipboard (Ctrl+C).
3. Switch to Word, right-click on the button, and choose Paste Button Image.
4. Then right-click on the button and choose Edit Button Image from the shortcut menu.
5. Word's Button Editor appears (see Figure 31.8). If you selected a button with an image, that image appears enlarged in the Picture box. If the button you selected had no image at all, the Picture box appears blank.

Figure 31.8
In the Button Editor, you can color or erase individual pixels within your button to get the exact image you want.

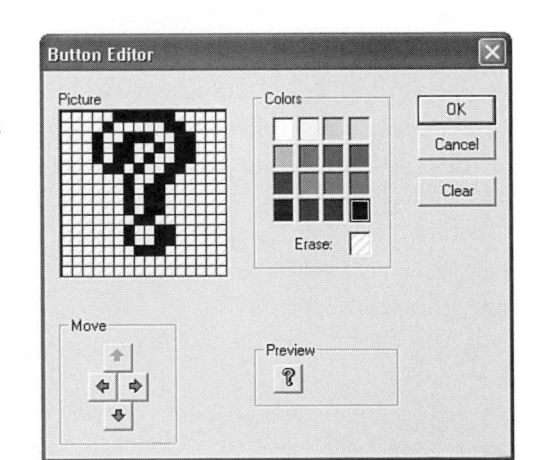

Now you can add or erase lines and colors from the picture, like this:

- To choose a color, click its square in the Colors area.
- To add color to the image, click and drag the mouse pointer across the individual pixels you want to color.
- To erase an existing part of the image, click on the Erase square in the Colors area and drag that across the individual pixels. Parts of an image that are left clear will appear transparent—in other words, they will be the same color as the button's background.

As you work, the button in the Preview area shows how your button now appears. If you're not happy with the results, you can click Clear to blank out the Picture box and try again.

This is painstaking work—which is why you're better off starting from a button image that can be adapted, wherever possible, rather than working from scratch.

Creating Toolbar Buttons or Menu Items That Insert Pictures or Hyperlinks

For the first time, Word 2003 allows you to add menu items or toolbar buttons that can be used to insert pictures into your documents, or to load documents from live hyperlinks.

If you have an image you use repeatedly—for example, a logo—consider adding a toolbar command that will enter it with a single click. Similarly, if you have a commonly used document, you might want to create a button or menu command that opens it via a live hyperlink. You can hyperlink to documents on your hard disk or network, your corporate intranet, or even a public Web site.

The following two sections cover adding toolbar buttons or menu items that insert pictures or hyperlinks.

Creating Toolbar Buttons or Menu Items That Insert Pictures

To create a toolbar button or menu item that inserts a picture, follow these steps:

1. Choose Tools, Customize.
2. Right-click on the toolbar button or menu item you want to insert a picture (instead of performing the task it currently performs).
3. On the Customize shortcut menu, choose Assign Hyperlink, Insert Picture. The Assign Hyperlink: Insert Picture dialog box opens (see Figure 31.9).
4. Browse to and select the image you want your toolbar button to insert.
5. Click OK.
6. Right-click on the button or menu item again to display the Customize shortcut menu again.

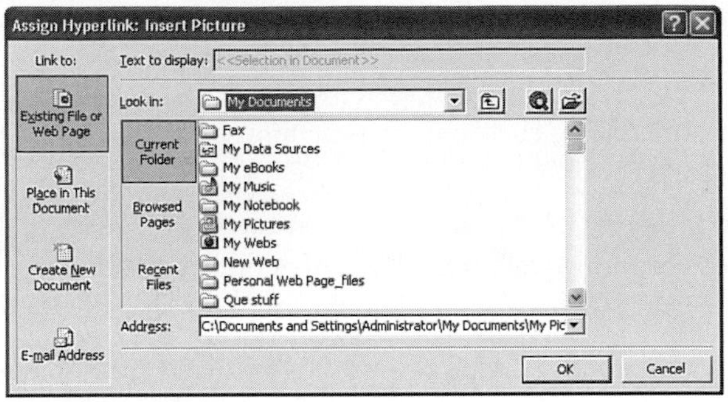

Figure 31.9
Choose a picture you want your toolbar button or menu item to insert.

7. In the Name box, rename the toolbar button or menu item to reflect the new image; or use one of the other Customize shortcut menu options to assign an appropriate image.

CREATING TOOLBAR BUTTONS OR MENU ITEMS THAT LOAD HYPERLINKS

To create a toolbar button or menu item that inserts a hyperlink, follow these steps:

1. Choose Tools, Customize.

2. Right-click on the toolbar button or menu item you want to insert a hyperlink (instead of performing the task it currently performs).

3. On the Customize shortcut menu, choose Assign Hyperlink, Open. The Assign Hyperlink: Open dialog box opens (see Figure 31.10).

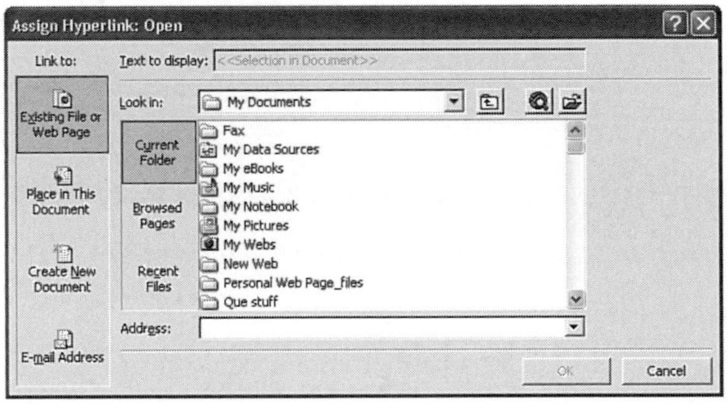

Figure 31.10
Browse to the location of the hyperlink you want your toolbar button or menu item to open.

4. Browse to and select the hyperlink you want your toolbar button to insert.

5. Click OK.

6. Right-click on the button or menu item again to display the Customize shortcut menu again.

7. In the Name box, rename the toolbar button or menu item to reflect the new hyperlink; or use one of the other Customize shortcut menu options to assign an appropriate image.

ADDING, RENAMING, AND DELETING CUSTOM TOOLBARS AND MENU BARS

Until now, you've worked on toolbars and menu bars that already exist. However, one of the most common ways to customize your user interface is to create your own custom toolbar or menu bar.

That way, you can leave the existing interface alone and avoid confusing people who don't understand why the buttons on the toolbars don't match the ones on their computer at home—or in the books they've purchased.

You can add sets of commands to custom toolbars or menu bars associated with specific tasks or clients. You can even store them in custom templates so that they appear automatically when you create documents based on those templates. For example, you can

- Create a toolbar associated with invoicing and attach it to your invoice template
- Create a "long document" toolbar with buttons for inserting bookmarks, index entries, tables of contents, and other elements
- In a law firm, create a special menu containing AutoText entries that insert contract boilerplate text and attach it to a contract template that all your lawyers, paralegals, and legal secretaries use
- Create a unique Company menu that contains forms, useful documents, and macros associated with your organization

ADDING A NEW (CUSTOM) TOOLBAR

To create a new custom toolbar, first make sure that the template where you want to store it is open. Then, follow these steps:

1. Choose Tools, Customize.
2. Choose the Toolbars tab.
3. Click New. The New Toolbar dialog box appears (see Figure 31.11).

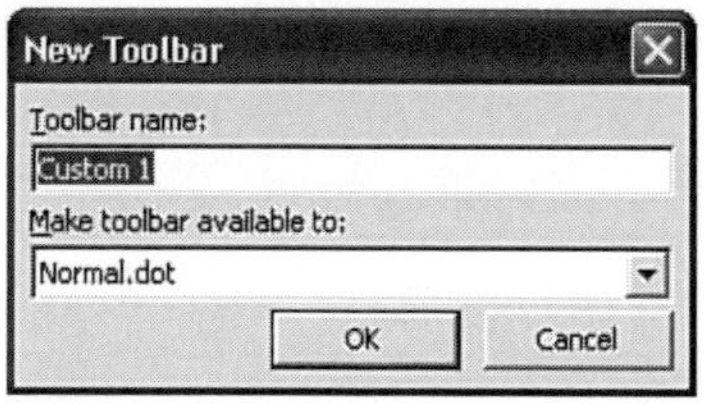

Figure 31.11
Enter the name of your new toolbar in the New Toolbar dialog box.

4. In the Toolbar Name text box, type the name of your new toolbar.
5. In the Make Toolbar Available To drop-down list box, decide whether to store the toolbar in Normal.dot, where it will be available at all times; in a different open template (a template must be open for you to assign a new toolbar to it); or in the current document.

31

6. Click OK. Word displays a new, empty toolbar (see Figure 31.12). Now you can add any buttons you want using the techniques described so far in this chapter.

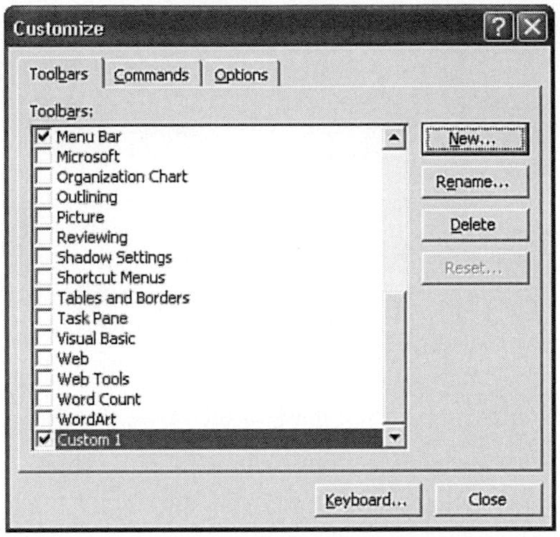

Figure 31.12
Word displays an empty toolbar; you can now move or copy buttons into it.

TIP

If you later decide you want to move a toolbar from one template to another, you can do so, using the Toolbars tab of the Organizer dialog box. You can get there by choosing Tools, Templates and Add-Ins; clicking Organizer; and choosing the Toolbars tab.

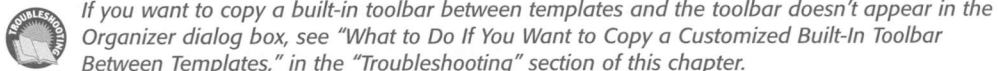

If you want to copy a built-in toolbar between templates and the toolbar doesn't appear in the Organizer dialog box, see "What to Do If You Want to Copy a Customized Built-In Toolbar Between Templates," in the "Troubleshooting" section of this chapter.

→ For more information on moving toolbars, styles, and other elements, **see** "Keeping Track of Styles with the Organizer," **p. 349**.

ADDING YOUR OWN MENUS

To create a new custom menu, first make sure that the template where you want to store it is open. Then, follow these steps:

1. Choose Tools, Customize and select the Commands tab.

2. In the Categories list, choose New Menu (the last item on the list).

3. If you want to store the menu in an open template other than Normal.dot, or in an open document, choose the template or document in the Save In drop-down box. (As mentioned earlier, the template must already be open for you to customize it.)

4. Drag the New Menu command from the Commands scroll box to where you want it to appear on the menu bar. It appears, bordered in black.

5. Right-click your new menu (or choose Modify Selection from the Customize dialog box).

6. Enter a new name in the <u>N</u>ame text box. If you want to have access to your new menu using a shortcut, don't forget to include an ampersand (&) before the letter with which you want to anchor the shortcut.

7. Press Enter.

After you've inserted a new menu, you can add menu items to it, as covered earlier in the "Adding Commands to a Toolbar or Menu Bar Using Rearrange Commands" section.

RENAMING CUSTOM TOOLBARS

You can't rename or delete any of Word's built-in toolbars. However, you can rename or delete a toolbar you've created. To rename a toolbar, follow these steps:

1. Choose <u>T</u>ools, <u>C</u>ustomize.

2. Choose the Tool<u>b</u>ars tab.

3. In the Tool<u>b</u>ars scroll box, click the toolbar you want to rename.

4. Click <u>R</u>ename. The Rename Toolbar dialog box opens.

5. Enter a new name and click OK.

DELETING CUSTOM TOOLBARS

To delete a custom toolbar, follow these steps:

1. Choose <u>T</u>ools, <u>C</u>ustomize.

2. Choose the Tool<u>b</u>ars tab.

3. In the Tool<u>b</u>ars scroll box, click the toolbar you want to delete.

4. Click <u>D</u>elete.

5. Click OK to confirm that you want to delete the toolbar.

RENAMING CUSTOM MENU BARS

You can't rename or delete any of Word's built-in menu bars. However, you can rename or delete a menu bar you've created. To rename a menu bar, follow these steps:

1. Choose <u>T</u>ools, <u>C</u>ustomize.

2. Right-click on the menu bar you want to rename.

3. Enter a new name in the <u>N</u>ame box on the shortcut menu.

DELETING CUSTOM MENU BARS

To delete a custom menu bar, follow these steps:

1. Choose <u>T</u>ools, <u>C</u>ustomize.

2. Right-click on the menu bar you want to delete.

3. Click <u>D</u>elete.

31

RESTORING DEFAULT SETTINGS TO A MENU BAR OR TOOLBAR

If you no longer want the toolbar or menu bar customizations that you or someone else has made, it's easy to return any menu bar or toolbar to its original settings.

If you want to reset a toolbar, first display it. Then, follow these steps to reset either a toolbar or a menu bar:

1. Choose Tools, Customize.

2. Click Rearrange Commands.

3. From the Menu Bar drop-down box, choose the menu bar you want to reset. If you want to reset a toolbar, click Toolbar, and choose the open toolbar you want to reset.

4. Click Reset. The Reset Toolbar dialog box opens (see Figure 31.13).

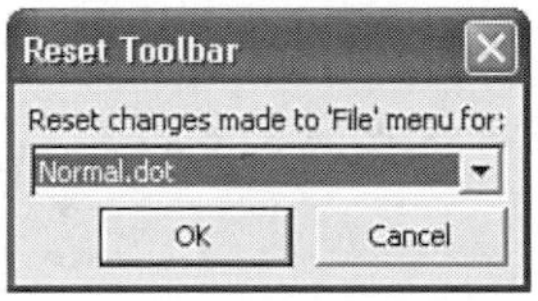

Figure 31.13
From the Reset
Toolbar dialog box,
you can eliminate
customizations in any
individual toolbar.

5. From the Reset Changes drop-down box, choose the template containing the toolbar you want to reset. When you reset a toolbar in Normal.dot, you reset it for all your documents which use that template.

6. Click OK.

TIP

> A quick way to eliminate *all* of Word's custom settings is to move your Normal.dot template to another folder where Word doesn't know to look for it—a folder outside the paths for User Templates and Workgroup Templates that are specified by default in the File Locations tab of the Options dialog box. This causes Word to generate a new Normal template based on its default settings, including default toolbars and menus.

ADDING A KEYBOARD SHORTCUT TO A MENU ITEM

In Word, every built-in menu command contains a letter designated as the shortcut key. For example, you can choose Save As from the File menu by pressing Alt+F, A. You can add a shortcut key to a custom command as well.

In many cases, Word includes a shortcut key automatically when you drag the command to a menu. If that shortcut key isn't already in use on the same menu, there's little reason to change it. If it is already used, however, you'll almost certainly want to change it.

NOTE

> If two or more commands on the same menu use the same shortcut key, when you enter the letter you get the command that appears closest to the top of the menu. If you enter the letter again, Word selects the next command that uses the same shortcut key, and so on.

To add or change a shortcut key, follow these steps:

1. Choose Tools, Customize to open the Customize dialog box.

2. Display the menu containing the command you want to change.

3. Right-click the command you want to change to display its shortcut menu (see Figure 31.14).

Figure 31.14
Add (or move) the ampersand symbol immediately before the letter you want to use as a shortcut key.

— Use an ampersand to designate a shortcut key

4. In the Name text box, Word places the existing name of the menu item (as it appears in the menu). To designate a shortcut, insert the ampersand (&) symbol before the letter you want to be your shortcut key. To change a shortcut, move the ampersand to precede the letter you want to use as a shortcut. (You might do this to avoid conflicts with another command on the same menu.)

5. Press Enter.

NOTE

> In the Name text box on the shortcut menu, you can edit the name of a menu item any way you want. You can also remove a keyboard shortcut by editing out the ampersand symbol.

CREATING NEW KEYBOARD SHORTCUTS

You probably know that Word contains hundreds of keyboard shortcuts: Ctrl+F for Find, Alt+Shift+X to insert an index entry, and so on. If you want, you can change those keyboard shortcuts or add new ones. When might you want to?

- When you're switching from another word processor whose keyboard shortcuts you're accustomed to

- When you find yourself often using a command or macro that doesn't come with a keyboard shortcut

ASSOCIATING KEYBOARD SHORTCUTS WITH COMMANDS, SYMBOLS, FONTS, MACROS, AND OTHER ELEMENTS

Many existing toolbar buttons and menu items already have keyboard shortcuts. Others that you use quite often may not. Or, perhaps, you're comfortable with toolbar buttons, menus, and keyboard shortcuts that Word provides, but you'd like more of them.

For example, how about adding a keyboard shortcut to apply a specific font or style you work with regularly? Or to insert a specific AutoText entry? Or to add a specific foreign-language accent mark or symbol you use every day? Or perhaps you recorded a macro that you didn't expect to use much, so you didn't bother to create a keyboard shortcut for it at the time. Now that you realize how useful your macro is, perhaps you want an easier way to access it.

→ For more information about recording macros, **see** "Recording Your Macro," **p. 1072**.

→ For more information about working with symbols and special characters, **see** "Inserting Symbols and Special Characters," **p. 565**.

To create a keyboard shortcut for elements such as these, follow these steps:

1. Choose <u>T</u>ools, <u>C</u>ustomize, and display the <u>C</u>ommands tab. Pick the template or document where you want the keyboard assignment to appear by selecting it from the <u>S</u>ave In drop-down list. (Note that keyboard assignments saved in Normal.dot are available all the time.)

2. Choose <u>K</u>eyboard. The Customize Keyboard dialog box appears (see Figure 31.15).

Figure 31.15
In the Customize Keyboard dialog box, press a keyboard shortcut to associate it with the command you've chosen.

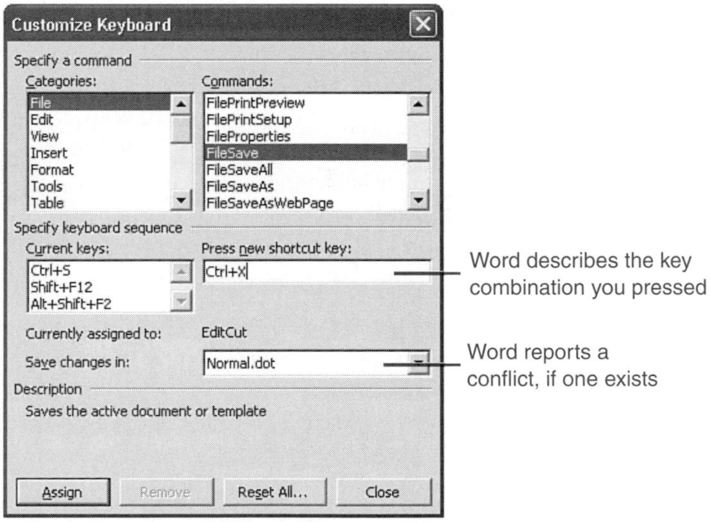

Word describes the key combination you pressed

Word reports a conflict, if one exists

3. In the <u>C</u>ategories scroll box, choose the category containing the command you want.

4. In the C<u>o</u>mmands scroll box, choose the command you want.

5. Press the keyboard shortcut you want to set as your shortcut. The combination appears in the Press <u>N</u>ew Shortcut Key text box.

6. The dialog box will change to display a Currently Assigned To area under the Current Keys scroll box. If the key combination is already in use, this area tells you which function it performs. If the key combination is not in use, the word [unassigned] appears.

7. If the key combination you pressed was already in use, and you don't want to overwrite it, press Backspace and try another key combination. If you do want to overwrite it—in other words, if you want to change what that keyboard shortcut does—move on to the next step.

CAUTION

Word does not display any confirmation dialog box if you ask it to overwrite an existing keyboard shortcut.

If you inadvertently overwrite a keyboard shortcut you intended to keep, you can reassign it manually, using the procedure described previously. Or you can restore an individual toolbar or menu bar to its original state, by choosing it in the Toolbars tab of the Customize dialog box, and clicking Reset.

8. After you have a shortcut key that fits your needs, click Assign. You'll see the new key combination in the Current Keys scroll box. Click Close.

RESETTING KEYBOARD SHORTCUTS

If you decide you no longer want one specific custom keyboard shortcut, display the Customize Keyboard dialog box using the Keyboard button on the Customize dialog box, select the command, and click Remove.

If you want to eliminate all custom keyboard shortcuts in the Normal template, display the Customize Keyboard dialog box and click Reset All. Because there is significant potential to wipe out a lot of work, Word asks you to confirm this action; click Yes.

CAUTION

Reset All eliminates all custom keyboard shortcuts stored in the Normal template, including keyboard shortcuts you may have created when recording custom macros.

Before you reset your keyboard settings, you may want to review them. If you want a simple list of custom keyboard assignments, click File, Print, and in the Print What drop-down box, choose Key Assignments.

For a more comprehensive understanding of your current keyboard settings, Word can generate a document containing either your current menu and keyboard settings or all Word commands using one of its built-in macros. To create such a document, follow these steps:

1. Choose Tools, Macro, Macros.

2. In the Macro Name text box, type listcommands and click Run.

3. The List Commands dialog box opens (see Figure 31.16). Choose to list either Current Menu and Keyboard Settings or All Word Commands.

4. Click OK.

Figure 31.16
The List Commands dialog box.

CONTROLLING WORD'S CUSTOMIZATION OPTIONS

Word offers several additional options for personalizing Word to your taste and convenience. One set of options enables you to control how Word's Personalized Menus and Toolbars behave. The remaining options cover various behaviors that might make Word simpler for you to use. To set these options, choose Tools, Customize and click the Options tab (see Figure 31.17).

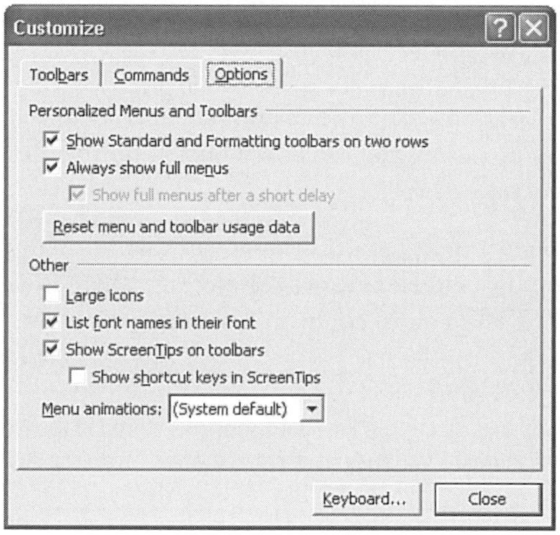

Figure 31.17
The Options tab of the Customize dialog box.

DISPLAYING FULL STANDARD AND FORMATTING TOOLBARS

Word's Standard and Formatting toolbars display on two rows by default. If you want, you can display an abbreviated version of the Standard and Formatting toolbars on a single row, showing only the most widely used buttons. This saves space, but it can be confusing—especially to experienced users, who want to know where the extra buttons went.

To display abbreviated Standard and Formatting toolbars on a single row, clear the Show Standard and Formatting Toolbars on Two Rows check box.

NOTE

> You can also toggle the Standard and Formatting toolbars between one and two rows:
>
> 1. Click the down arrow to the right of either the Standard or the Formatting toolbar.
> 2. Choose Show Buttons on One Row or Show Buttons on Two Rows.

CONTROLLING THE BEHAVIOR OF PERSONALIZED MENUS

Word's Personalized Menus feature keeps track of menu commands that you don't use and, after a set amount of time, hides them from view when you activate the menu. This is intended to make it easier to find the commands you *do* use frequently.

If and when you find yourself needing access to a hidden menu command, all you need to do is keep the menu selected for a few moments, and the remaining commands appear (you can also click the double-down arrow at the bottom of any menu containing hidden commands). When you use a hidden command, Word adds it to the default list of commands.

Although many users don't care for this feature, Word's Personalized Menus remain turned on by default: Word always shows an abbreviated list of menu options on a fresh install. If you don't like Personalized Menus, however, you can get rid of them.

NOTE

> If you're upgrading from Word 2000 or Word 2002 and you have already disabled Personalized Menus, these should remain disabled when you install Word 2003.

In the Options tab of the Customize dialog box, check the Always Show Full Menus check box. If you never want Word to display the long menus by hovering the mouse pointer over them for a short period, clear the Show Full Menus After a Short Delay check box. The double-down arrows that let you manually expand a menu do remain functional even if you clear this option.

If you are using Personalized Menus, but you want Word to forget what it has learned about the menu and toolbar commands you use, click Reset Menu and Toolbar Usage Data, and click Yes to confirm.

NOTE

> Reset Menu and Toolbar Usage Data eliminates only Word's stored record of the commands you use. It does not eliminate any manual changes you've made to toolbars, menus, or keyboard shortcuts.

DISPLAYING LARGE ICONS

When the Large Icons check box is checked in the Options tab of the Tools, Customize dialog box, all the buttons on your toolbars are enlarged (see Figure 31.18). Large icons are most helpful when you're working at higher screen resolutions. They may also helpful for those with less than perfect vision (though they can be blurry).

31

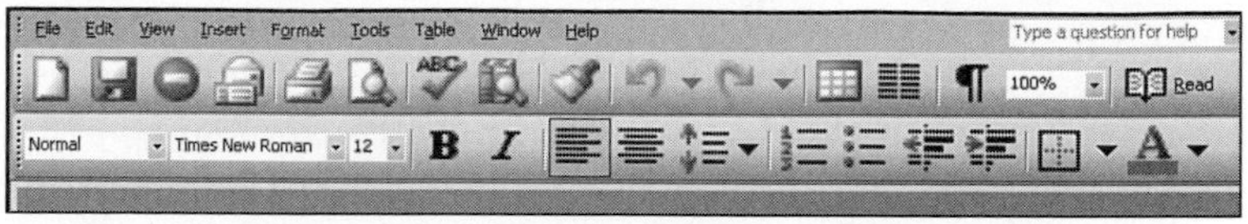

Figure 31.18
Large icons are easy to read but take much more space.

However, if you use large icons and a monitor with lower screen resolution, fewer buttons can fit on a toolbar, which means that some of the buttons you need might not be visible.

LISTING FONT NAMES IN THEIR FONT

By default, when you click on a Font list (such as the one in the Formatting toolbar, Word displays each font's name in that font, giving you a quick preview of how that font might appear in your document. This is convenient, but displaying a long list of fonts can take a long time on slower computers. If you find that font lists display too slowly, display the Options tab of the Customize dialog box and clear the List Font Names in Their Font check box.

CONTROLLING WORD'S SCREENTIPS

In the Options tab of the Customize dialog box there are two check boxes that control how Word uses ScreenTips. With the Show ScreenTips on Toolbars option turned on, when the mouse pointer hovers over a button in a Word toolbar, a brief description appears below the button. As you have likely guessed already, these descriptions are called *ScreenTips*. If you prefer not to see ScreenTips, clear the Show ScreenTips on Toolbars check box.

If you like ScreenTips, you can make them even more useful by telling Word to display the equivalent keyboard shortcuts along with the description (see Figure 31.19). Checking the Show Shortcut Keys in ScreenTips check box is a good way to learn the keyboard shortcuts you're most likely to use.

NOTE

Not all toolbar buttons have keyboard shortcuts, so even if you display Shortcut Keys in ScreenTips, shortcut keys often won't be present.

Figure 31.19
A ScreenTip that includes a keyboard shortcut.

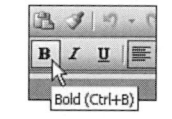

CHANGING WORD OPTIONS

Word offers a wide variety of other customization options: options that can help you eliminate Word behaviors you might find annoying or insecure; options that allow you to work more effectively in specific documents; options that allow you to save and find files more effectively, and much more. Word brings together the following 11 categories of customizable behaviors in the Options dialog box (click Tools, Options).

NOTE

> In the following list, items that include cross-references to other chapters are not covered in this chapter.

- **View.** These options control aspects of Word's appearance.
- **General.** This category includes options that Microsoft designers couldn't fit anywhere else.
- **Edit.** These options control Word's behavior as you edit.
- **Print.** These options control how and what Word prints. (See Chapter 6, "Printing and Faxing in Word.")
- **Save.** These options control Word's save behavior, including how and when Word saves files and what gets saved in each file.
- **Security.** These options control Word's features for password-protecting documents, using digital signatures, restricting macros, and eliminating document contents that you might not want others to see. (See Chapter 33, "Word Document Privacy and Security Options.")
- **Spelling & Grammar.** These options control how Word checks spelling and grammar. (See Chapter 8, "Making the Most of Word's Proofing and Research Tools.")
- **Track Changes.** These options control the formatting Word uses to represent revisions when it is tracking them. (See Chapter 26, "Managing Document Collaboration and Revisions.")
- **User Information.** These options store the information Word uses whenever it needs your name, initials, and mailing address.
- **Compatibility.** These options control aspects of how Word displays documents—allowing you to specify conventions that were used in previous versions of Word for Windows or Macintosh. Changes made in the Compatibility tab don't affect the document itself—only its appearance.
- **File Locations.** These options specify where Word looks for documents, images, templates, and other files it needs.

Throughout this book, you've come across many of the options available here. This section takes a systematic look at options that have been covered briefly (or not at all) elsewhere.

CHANGING VIEW OPTIONS TO CONTROL WHAT APPEARS ONSCREEN

Chapter 2, "Navigating Word 2003," discusses several ways to change Word's appearance. For example, it covers how you can choose View, Full Screen to hide all Word's menus and toolbars except for a Close Full Screen button—thereby enabling yourself to see much more of your document.

31

To control many other aspects of Word's appearance, choose <u>T</u>ools, <u>O</u>ptions, View. Figure 31.20 shows the default settings for View options.

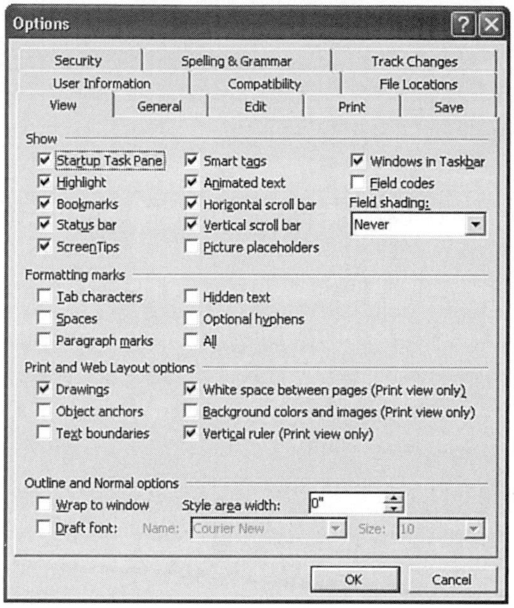

Figure 31.20
The View tab of the Options dialog box brings together various adjustments to Word's appearance.

CHOOSING WHICH USER INTERFACE ELEMENTS APPEAR

The selections in the Show category of View options control both document-specific features and user-interface features. For example, to make more space in your editing window, you can clear check boxes that control the display of the following:

- **Start<u>u</u>p Task Pane.** The Sta<u>r</u>tup Task Pane that appears at the right of Word's editing window when you first load Word and displays options for loading recent and new documents.

- **Stat<u>u</u>s Bar.** The Stat<u>u</u>s Bar at the bottom of Word's editing window.

- **Horizontal Scroll Bar.** The Horizontal Scroll Bar that is used to scroll left and right. (If you use the <u>W</u>rap to Window option, you'll rarely need the Horizontal Scroll Bar.)

- **<u>V</u>ertical Scroll Bar.** The <u>V</u>ertical Scroll Bar that scrolls up and down through documents.

You can also control several other aspects of Word's user interface:

- **<u>H</u>ighlight.** To make a heavily marked-up document more readable, you can temporarily hide highlighting by clearing the <u>H</u>ighlight check box.

- **Boo<u>k</u>marks.** Checking the Boo<u>k</u>marks check box adds gray brackets at the beginning and end of any text you've bookmarked. Displaying bookmarks can make it easier to build index entries, cross-references, and other automated features based on them.

- **Smart Tags.** To hide the Smart Tags dotted-line indicators (which alert users that they can perform tasks such as sending email to an individual named in your document), clear the Smart Tags check box.

- **Picture Placeholders.** To make Word run a bit faster, especially when you're focused on editing text and don't care about images, you can check Picture Placeholders. This instructs Word to display an empty box wherever you've inserted an image. When Picture Placeholders is turned off, Word spends time processing images for display, even if you're merely scrolling past them to another destination. The more images your document contains, the slower Word becomes.

TIP

> Because the placeholder boxes are the same size as the original images, you can use Picture Placeholders in Print Layout view to evaluate layouts more quickly when you don't need to view the pictures themselves.

31

Checking the Animated Text check box enables Word to display animation created in the Animation tab of the Format, Font dialog box, such as sparkle text. When this box is cleared, the animation disappears and the text appears as it will when printed (that is, without animation).

Clearing the ScreenTips check box turns off ScreenTips that appear when you hover the mouse pointer over a comment, a tracked change, a footnote, or an endnote.

NOTE

> To turn off the AutoComplete ScreenTips that appear when you start typing text that matches an AutoText entry, clear the Show AutoComplete Tip for AutoText and Dates Entry check box in the AutoText tab of the AutoCorrect dialog box. To turn off ScreenTips that appear on toolbar buttons, choose Tools, Customize, Options and clear the Show ScreenTips on Toolbars check box.

→ For more information about using AutoComplete with AutoText entries, **see** "Entering AutoText Entries Even Faster with AutoComplete," **p. 303**.

By default, Word displays each document in a separate box on the Windows taskbar. If you prefer to use only one taskbar box for Word, leaving the rest for other programs you may have open, clear the Windows in Taskbar check box.

Checking the Field Codes check box causes field codes to be displayed throughout your document, rather than the results they generate. You might use this when you're troubleshooting fields, such as cross-references or index entries that aren't delivering the results you expect.

TIP

Whether you've checked this box or not, you can still toggle selected field codes on and off by selecting them and pressing Shift+F9 (or Alt+F9 toggles all the field codes in the document). However, as long as the check box is turned on, new fields you enter will appear as field codes rather than results.

In the Field Shading: drop-down box, you can tell Word how to inform you of the presence of *field codes* in your document. The default option, When Selected, tells Word to display field codes in gray only when you've selected or clicked within them.

The Always option tells Word to show field codes and field results in gray all the time. Marking field codes in gray shows you where they begin and end and reminds you which information is being generated in your document automatically. However, you (or a colleague unfamiliar with Word field codes) might find the gray formatting distracting. If so, choose Never.

CAUTION

If you choose Never, you'll never know when you're typing text over a field code result. Thus, you could make changes to a document that will be overridden the next time field codes are updated; say, the next time the document is printed.

Controlling the Display of Nonprinting Characters

By default, when you click the Show/Hide Paragraph Marks button on the Standard toolbar, Word displays much more than paragraph marks; it also shows

- Tab characters
- Spaces (places a dot everywhere you typed a space)
- Hidden text (displays all hidden text, including hidden fields)
- Optional hyphens (shows where hyphens may appear in an automatically hyphenated document)

At times, this may give you more information than you want. For example, you might want to see all the paragraph marks in your document because you know they contain important paragraph formatting. However, you might not want to see an obtrusive dot between every single word on your page.

You can control whether each type of formatting mark appears by clearing the All check box and then checking each check box in the Formatting Marks area that correlates to marks you want to see.

TIP

Clicking the Show/Hide Paragraph Marks button does the same thing as checking the All box in the View tab of the Options dialog box.

All supersedes the settings in any of the other check boxes. This is a convenience; you can set up Word to display the nonprinting characters you want to see most of the time and then simply toggle All on or off when you need to see the rest of them, rather than adjusting each setting individually.

Controlling Print and Web Layout Options

The Print and Web Layout Options area controls six elements that can help you manage the way your document appears in print or when displayed in a Web browser:

- Clearing the Drawings check box hides any drawings you've placed in your document using Word's drawing tools—which are any drawings that "float above" the document in the drawing layer. (Drawings are already hidden when you work in Normal or Outline view.)
- Checking the Object Anchors check box displays object anchors so that you can see how drawings and other document elements are linked to specific paragraphs or other elements on your page.
- Checking the Text Boundaries check box displays your current margins with a thin dotted line. It also places dotted lines at column and object borders—giving you more visual feedback about where text can be placed.
- Clearing White Space Between Pages (Print View Only) hides the top and bottom margins of pages in Print Layout view (and also hides headers and footers). As a result, you can view more text.
- Checking Background Colors and Images (Print View Only) tells Word to print page backgrounds it would normally ignore in the interests of readability.
- Clearing the Vertical Ruler (Print View Only) hides the ruler that appears to the left of the editing window.

Controlling Text with the Outline and Normal Options

The Outline and Normal Options section of the View tab gives you control over certain aspects of how Word displays text.

In documents with narrow left and right margins, you may find that some text stretches past the far-right edge of the screen—requiring you to scroll back and forth on every line. Wrap to Window tells Word to make sure that all text appears within the width of your screen. Although this slightly reduces the "what you see is what you get" accuracy of Word's display, it eliminates the horizontal scrolling.

Because Wrap to Window tells Word to display widths inaccurately, it's unavailable in Page Layout and Web Layout views.

Draft Font enables you to display all the text in your document in a single font, with accurate spacing and paragraph indents.

If you have a slower computer, Draft Font may significantly improve Word's performance. You might consider using it for original writing and then turning it off when you need to work with formatting.

You can also control which font and font size to use as a draft font. The default setting is Courier New, 10-point, but you can choose a new font from the Name drop-down box and a new size from the Size drop-down box.

TIP

If you choose Print Layout or Web Layout view while Draft Font is turned on, Word displays all the correct fonts and formatting. But if you switch back to Normal view, the draft font is shown again. You can use this feature to quickly toggle back and forth between editing and formatting.

Style Area Width enables you to display the styles associated with each paragraph in a column to the left of your document text (see Figure 31.21). This makes it more convenient to identify and work with heavily styled documents. By default, this is set to 0"—in other words, no Style Area Width. If you set it to a higher number, such as 0.8", you see the style information.

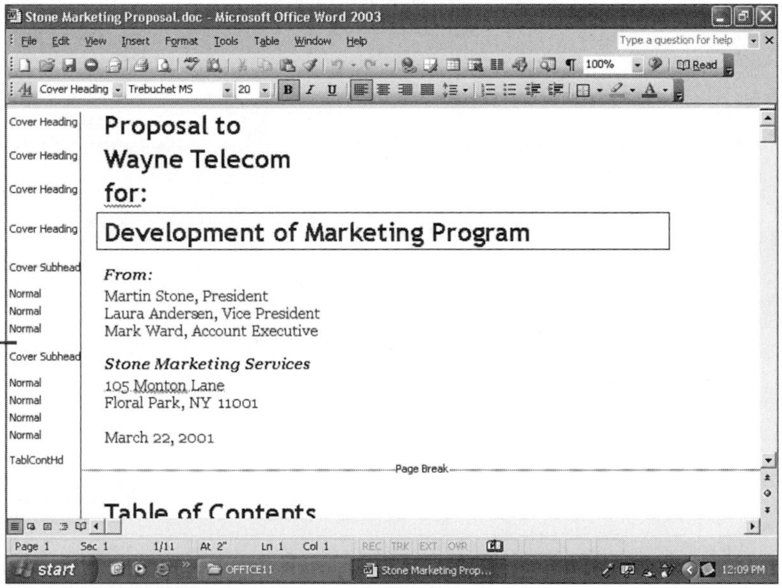

Figure 31.21
A document displaying styles in use at the left edge of the editing window.

CHANGING GENERAL OPTIONS

Quite simply, the General tab of the Options dialog box is where Word collects options that don't fit anywhere else. You can see its default settings in Figure 31.22.

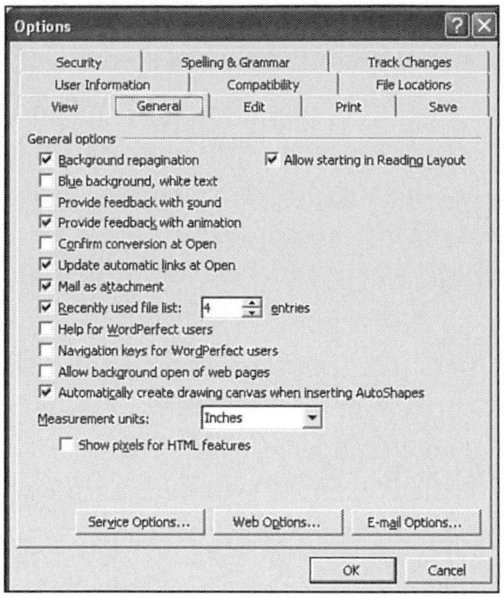

Figure 31.22
The default settings
for the General tab of
the Options
dialog box.

The options shown here include the following:

- **Background Repagination.** This option controls whether Word keeps track of page numbering continuously while you work. By default, it does. Like all of Word's automatic, on-the-fly features, this one takes a little bit of processing power. So if you're finding that Word runs too slowly on your computer, you might try turning off Background Repagination.

> **TIP**
>
> Background Pagination is always on in Print Layout view; otherwise, how could Word show true page layouts?
>
> If your computer is running Word too slowly, try working more in Normal view and less in Print Layout view.

- **Blue Background, White Text.** This option is designed to help WordPerfect users feel at home. It displays text in white against a blue, WordPerfect-like background. Some people who have never used WordPerfect still find this to be softer on their eyes; it's a matter of personal taste.

- **Provide Feedback with Sound.** This option tells Word to play sounds in response to specific actions or events, such as error messages. You need three things to play sounds: a sound card, speakers, and the sound files themselves. These files are not automatically installed as part of the Microsoft Office installation. You can use your own sound files if you have some, or you can follow Word's prompts to connect you to the Office Update Web site to download some basic sounds.

- **Provide Feedback with Animation.** This option is turned on by default and uses special animated pointers to tell you that certain automated procedures are in progress, such as AutoFormatting, background saves, and background printing. If you are running Word on an older computer (for example, a PC based on the original Pentium processor), turning off this option may slightly enhance system performance.

■ **Confirm Conversion at Open.** This an option may come in handy if you often work with files in other formats. In general, Word is capable of recognizing the source word processor of a document and using the appropriate converter to display it in Word. However, in rare instances, Word may choose the wrong filter, or you may want to choose a filter manually. If so, check this box. When you open a file in a different format, Word enables you to choose which converter to use.

■ **Update Automatic Links at Open.** This option is turned on by default and tells Word to automatically update any information in your document that is based on other files linked to your document. In general, you'll want to leave this enabled. However, if you prefer to see your document with the content it had the last time you worked with it, or if you suspect that the source document is no longer available, you can clear this check box to turn off automatic updating.

■ **Mail as Attachment.** This next option relates to the way Word integrates with MAPI-compatible email software (such as Microsoft Outlook) that may be installed on your computer. With this option turned on, if you choose File, Send to, Mail Recipient, Word opens an email message window and includes the formatted text of the document as the message. If you choose Mail Recipient (As Attachment), Word creates a new email message and attaches a copy of the current document to it. If you clear the Mail as Attachment check box, Word no longer offers a Mail Recipient (As Attachment) option; instead it offers Mail Recipient (as Text), which, as the name implies, copies the text of the document to the email message.

■ **Recently Used File List.** By default, Word displays the last four files you worked on at the bottom of the File menu. If you work on a great many files, you may want to increase the number of files displayed in this list. Conversely, if you have added custom items to the File menu, you might not even have room for four files. To make a change, click in the Entries scroll box and type a number from 1 to 9.

> **TIP**
>
> If you don't want any files listed in the Recently Used File List (possibly because you don't want others to know what you've been working on), clear the Recently Used File List check box.

■ **Help for WordPerfect Users.** When this option is turned on, Word's parallel help system for users transitioning from WordPerfect for DOS is also enabled (a common need in the mid-1990s). When you type a keyboard combination that corresponds to a WordPerfect feature, WordPerfect Help tells you how to perform the same task in Word and, in some cases, even demonstrates the feature.

■ **Navigation Keys for WordPerfect Users.** When this option is turned on, Word's Page Up, Page Down, Home, End, and Esc keys start behaving the way they would if you were running WordPerfect. For example, you would use Home, Home, Left arrow to move the insertion point to the beginning of the current line.

- **A̲llow Background Open of Web Pages.** When this option is checked, Word can open linked Web pages in the background while still displaying a document. This setting is cleared by default.

- **Automati̲cally Create Drawing Canvas When Inserting AutoShapes.** Checked by default, this setting automatically inserts a Drawing Canvas whenever you select an AutoShape from the Drawing toolbar. Drawing Canvases make it easier to create drawings that will not move in unexpected ways as you edit text and page breaks surrounding them. However, many users find Drawing Canvases distracting. If you clear this check box, they will not appear by default; however, you can still display one by choosing I̲nsert, P̲icture, N̲ew Drawing.

- **M̲easurement Units.** Settings in this box tell Word which measurement system to use in its rulers and in some of its dialog boxes: Inches, Centimeters, Points, or Picas. Note that not every measurement changes when you change this setting. For example, font size is still measured in points no matter which setting you choose.

> **TIP**
>
> In general, you can enter margins and similar information in any system you choose by adding the appropriate prefix or suffix. For example, if you enter 1" as your top margin while Word is set to display centimeters, Word inserts the appropriate margin setting and converts it to 2.54cm automatically. Conversely, if Word is set to inches, you can enter centimeters by adding cm after the number, and Word converts it to inches.

- **Show Pi̲xels for HTML Features.** This option tells Word to display measurements in screen pixels rather than inches.

→ For information about Web options, accessed via the Web Options button in the General tab, **see** Chapter 24, "Using Word to Develop Web Content," **p. 803**.

→ For information about email options, accessed from the Email Options button within the General tab, **see** Chapter 30, "Using Word as an Email Editor," **p. 999**.

CONTROLLING SERVICE OPTIONS

Word 2003's new Service Options allow you to control how you interact with Microsoft and how you collaborate with other users via SharePoint services. To control these settings, display T̲ools, O̲ptions, General; then click Ser̲vice Options. The Service Options dialog box opens (see Figure 31.23).

JOINING OR AVOIDING MICROSOFT'S CUSTOMER EXPERIENCE IMPROVEMENT PROGRAM

In the Customer Feedback Options tab, you specify whether you are willing to participate in Microsoft's anonymous "Customer Experience Improvement Program." If you choose to do so, Microsoft will collect information about your hardware configuration, how you use Microsoft's software and services, and the errors you encounter. Microsoft says it will do so anonymously; you will not be tied to the data it collects.

Figure 31.23
Setting Customer
Feedback Options in
the Service Options
dialog box.

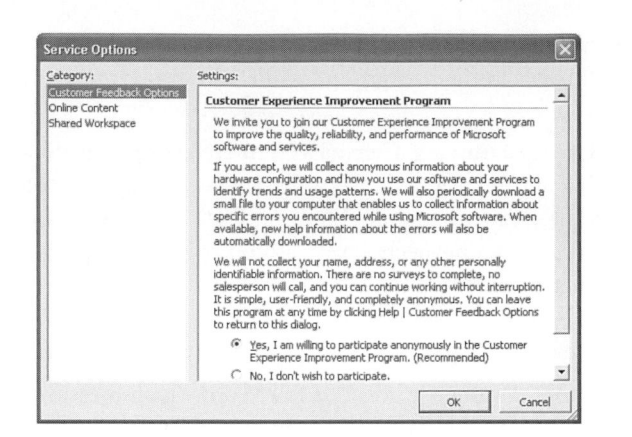

To participate, click Yes, I Am Willing to Participate Anonymously in the Customer Experience Improvement Program. To decline participation, click No, I Don't Wish to Participate. When you first install Word or Office 2003, neither box is selected.

CONTROLLING YOUR ACCESS TO MICROSOFT OFFICE ONLINE CONTENT

By default, Word shows content and links from Microsoft Office Online whenever they are available. It searches Office Online for new content whenever you are connected to the Internet; shows Office Online help whenever you open an Office Online template; and shows "Spotlight Links" calling your attention to new content or Office information.

To limit Word's use of Microsoft Office Online, display the Service Options dialog box, and choose Online Content from the list of categories. Here, you can take the following actions:

- To stop showing content and links from Office Online, clear the Show Content and Links from Microsoft Office Online check box.

- To show help for Word's online templates automatically whenever help is available, check the Show Template Help Automatically When Available check box.

- To stop displaying updated "Featured Links," clear the Show Microsoft Office Online Featured Links check box.

CHANGING EDITING FUNCTIONS IN THE EDIT TAB

If you're relatively new to Word, you may find some of its editing features, such as smart cut-and-paste, uncomfortable. In recent years, Word has also added new editing options associated with its newest features, such as the format checker. Editing behaviors such as these are controlled through the Edit tab of the Options dialog box (see Figure 31.24).

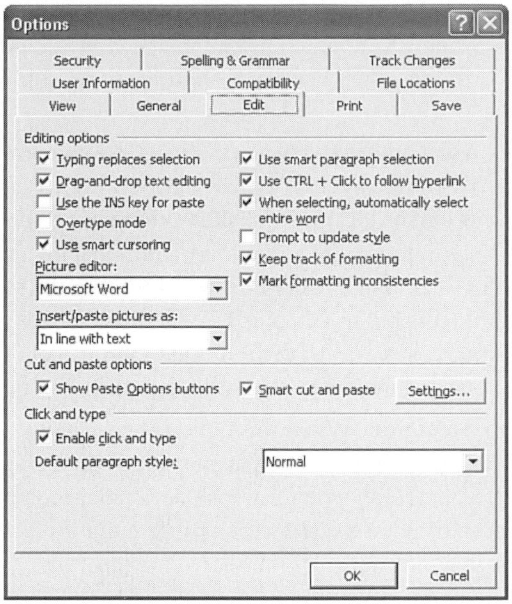

Figure 31.24
The Edit tab controls
how Word responds
as you enter and edit
text.

CONTROLLING EDITING OPTIONS

The first group of options found on the Edit tab lists a set of Editing Options:

- **Typing Replaces Selection.** This option is on by default, which means that you can replace text by selecting it and typing over it. That makes editing faster, and most people like it. Others find themselves deleting text they meant to keep. If you find that happening, clear the check box.

- **Drag-and-Drop Text Editing.** This option, which is also on by default, activates the Windows drag-and-drop feature. With this feature turned on, you can select text, click, and drag the text to a new location. Some people find drag-and-drop an especially intuitive way of moving text. Others find that they accidentally move text when drag-and-drop is enabled. If you want to turn it off, clear the check box.

- **Use the INS Key for Paste.** If this option is checked, the Insert key pastes text from your Clipboard into your document.

- **Overtype Mode.** By default, Word operates in Insert mode: It inserts text as you type and moves existing text to its right. In Overtype mode, Word instead replaces existing text, one character at a time, as you type "into it." You can turn on Overtype mode by double-clicking OVR in the status bar, or you can do it here by checking the Overtype Mode check box.

- **Use Smart Cursoring.** By default, your insertion point moves as you scroll up or down: when you press an arrow key, the insertion point responds at the page you're currently looking at, not where it was before you began scrolling. If you don't like this behavior, clear the Use Smart Cursoring check box.

■ **Picture Editor.** This drop-down box enables you to choose which drawing or image editing program opens when you double-click an image in your document. The default choice is Microsoft Word, but other Microsoft picture editing software appears if you have any installed.

■ **Insert/Paste Pictures As.** This drop-down box allows you to control how pictures are inserted or pasted into Word documents. The default setting, In Line with Text, inserts the picture at the current cursor location and allows the picture to move as text around it is edited. Word allows you to choose among five additional layouts: Square, Tight, Behind Text, In Front of Text, and Through. These are the same settings provided through Format, Picture (covered in Chapter 13, "Getting Images into Your Documents"). When you choose one of them in the Options dialog box, you establish a default setting for all your documents based on the template you're currently using.

■ **Use Smart Paragraph Selection.** When this option is checked, if you select an entire paragraph, Word selects the paragraph mark at the end of the paragraph. This helps make sure that cutting a paragraph won't leave an extra paragraph mark behind. It also makes sure that the formatting associated with a paragraph moves with the paragraph—something you may or may not want.

■ **Use CTRL + Click to Follow Hyperlink.** By default, to follow a hyperlink in a Word document, you must press the Ctrl key as you click on the hyperlink. This makes it easier to edit hyperlinked text. If you prefer for Word to jump to the hyperlinked document when you click on the hyperlink (without pressing Ctrl), clear this check box.

■ **When Selecting, Automatically Select Entire Word.** This option is a shortcut designed to make it easier to select large blocks of text. You don't have to precisely start at the beginning of a word to select the whole word. Rather, as soon as you select the space after a word, the program assumes that you intended to select the whole word. It works backward too; with this box checked, Word selects the word ahead of the selection if you have already selected one word and are starting to select another. Some people don't like Word to make assumptions about what they intend to select. If that's you, clear the check box.

■ **Prompt to Update Style.** If you want Word to display a confirming dialog box whenever you change a style, check this box.

■ **Keep Track of Formatting.** If you want Word to track formatting as you write, much as it keeps track of spelling, check this box.

■ **Mark Formatting Inconsistencies.** If you have specified that Word should keep track of formatting, check this box to have Word mark formatting inconsistencies in your document (with blue wavy underlines) as you enter them. (If you leave Mark Formatting Inconsistencies turned off, you can still check formatting all at once after you run a spelling and grammar check, through the Tools, Spelling and Grammar dialog box.)

CHANGING CUT AND PASTE OPTIONS

Word provides several options for controlling cut and paste behavior:

- **Show Paste Options Buttons.** By default, when you paste text into a document, Word offers options as to how you want it to be placed: whether the text should retain the formatting it had in its original document, match the formatting of the surrounding text, or be placed as text only. These options are accessible through a Paste Options button that appears in your document at the point where the item was placed. If you do *not* want the Paste Options button to appear, clear the Show Paste Options Buttons check box.

- **Smart Cut and Paste.** Checking this option tells Word to eliminate any extra spaces you might leave when you delete text or extra spaces you might insert when you paste text. In effect, Smart Cut and Paste makes sure that there is exactly one space between each word in a sentence. It's another way in which Word acts as if it knows better than you do. The fact is, Word is almost always right, but some people find features like these a little presumptuous.

- **Settings.** Clicking this button displays several additional cut and paste settings (see Figure 31.25). These include settings for how Word pastes tables, lists, and content from PowerPoint or Excel.

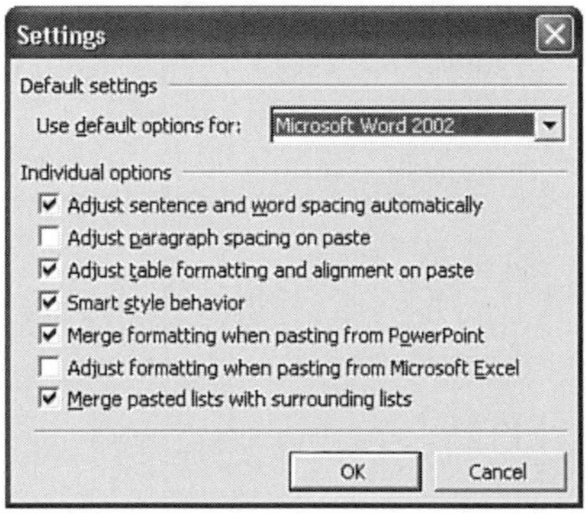

Figure 31.25
Additional cut and paste settings can be controlled from the Settings dialog box.

ADJUSTING CLICK AND TYPE OPTIONS

The Click and Type options group contains just two options for controlling Word's editing environment:

- **Enable Click and Type.** Without Click and Type, you can only click in a location where you've already placed text or graphics (the insertion point can't go beyond the end of the existing document). With Click and Type, you can double-click the insertion point anywhere. If you double-click beyond the end of the existing document, Word inserts paragraph marks in the intervening lines, and when it reaches the line where you double-clicked, it inserts a tab that extends horizontally across to where you double-clicked.

- **Default Paragraph Style.** This option enables you to choose which style Word should use for new paragraphs created when you use Word's Click and Type feature. (Existing paragraphs aren't changed.) For example, if you start with a new blank document and double-click in the middle of the document, the first paragraph remains in Normal style, but all the paragraphs inserted by the Click and Type feature—including the one that includes the insertion point—are formatted with the style shown in this box.

NOTE

The Default Paragraph Style drop-down box does not automatically display every built-in style available to a document. Instead, it shows Normal, Heading 1, and every style that's being used in the document, as well as any user-defined styles that are available. (To see a list of user-defined styles, choose Format, Style and in the List drop-down box pick User-Defined Styles.)

31 SETTING SAVE OPTIONS

In the Save tab of the Options dialog box (see Figure 31.26), you can control how Word saves files.

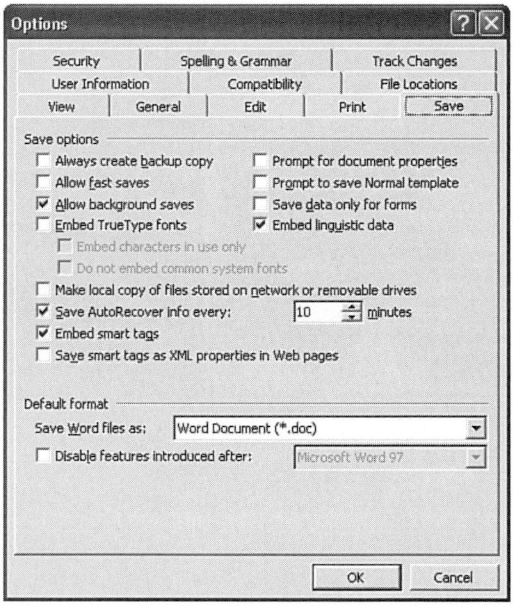

Figure 31.26
Use the Save tab of the Options dialog box to control Word's saving options.

Using this tab, you can control the following options:

- **Always Create Backup Copy.** Checking this box tells Word to rename the previous version of your document with a BAK extension and store it in the same folder as the new version it is saving.

→ For more information about automating backups of Word files, **see** "Creating Automatic Backups," **p. 92**.

- **Allow Fast Saves.** Checking this option enables Word to save time on most saves by recording all the changes to your document together, at the end of the document file. On occasion, even when Fast Saves is turned on, Word performs a full save, integrating all the changes throughout your document. You should clear Allow Fast Saves before saving a document file that will be used in another program, such as QuarkXPress or PageMaker.

CAUTION

Turn off Fast Saves if you're concerned about document security. With Fast Saves turned on, it's possible to use a text editor such as Notepad to read fragments of text that you thought you deleted from your documents.

- **Allow Background Saves.** Checking this option enables Word to save "in the background" as you work. While Word is saving, a pulsating disk icon is displayed in the status bar.

- **Embed TrueType Fonts.** Checking this box tells Word to embed the TrueType fonts you've used in your document. Check this box when you suspect that your file's recipients won't have access to the fonts you used to create your document. Keep a few things in mind, however. First of all, embedding fonts can dramatically increase file size. It's probably not a good option if your documents have many fonts and you're planning to send multiple copies across a network. Second, not all TrueType fonts can be embedded; font manufacturers have the power to prevent their fonts from being embedded as an anti-piracy measure, and some companies such as émigré have exercised that option. Third, PostScript fonts can't be embedded with this feature.

- **Embed Characters in Use Only.** Occasionally, you might want to embed a font you've used in only one or two document headlines. To save space, Word provides this option, which enables you to embed up to 32 individual characters from a font without embedding the entire font. If you've used more characters than this, Word embeds the entire font. Stay away from this option if you expect your recipients to edit the headline because they will not have access to other characters they may need.

NOTE

You can find out whether a font you own can be embedded—and more about your TrueType fonts—by using Microsoft's free Font Properties Extension, available for download at `http://microsoft.com/typography/property/property.htm`.

TIP

If you have a complex, heavily formatted document that you want others to read but not edit, consider using a program such as Adobe Acrobat to save relatively compact versions of your file, which can then be read and printed with fonts and formatting largely intact.

31

- **Do Not Embed Common System Fonts.** Even if you choose to embed fonts, you may not want to embed fonts virtually every Word user has, such as Courier New and Times New Roman. To instruct Word not to embed such fonts, leave this check box checked.

- **Make Local Copy of Files Stored on Network or Removable Drives.** If this box is checked, whenever you save a file across a network or to a removable drive, Word automatically stores a duplicate copy of that file on your computer's local hard disk.

- **Save AutoRecover Info Every.** The entry in this scroll box tells Word how often to create a document recovery file. You can set intervals from 0 to 120 minutes—if it's set to 0, Word saves AutoRecover information every time you pause typing.

- **Embed Smart Tags.** If you clear this check box, Word does not store Smart Tags in your documents.

- **Save Smart Tags as XML Properties in Web Pages.** If you check this box, when you save a document containing Smart Tags as a Web (HTML) page, Word creates an XML document header containing smart tag information.

- **Prompt for Document Properties.** Selecting this option causes the Properties dialog box to open whenever you save a document for the first time.

- **Prompt to Save Normal Template.** With this box checked, you are given a chance to abandon changes to default settings, AutoText entries, and macros before Word saves them to the Normal template at the end of your editing session.

- **Save Data Only for Forms.** With this option checked, Word saves only the text entered by the person filling out the electronic form, not the surrounding form itself. This information is stored in a tab-delimited, text-only format that is easy to import into databases.

→ For more information about saving only the data in forms, **see** "Saving Only the Data in a Form," **p. 957**.

- **Embed Linguistic Data.** If this option is checked, Word stores audio or handwriting input it received for purposes of voice or handwriting recognition. This can significantly enlarge your files, but it allows you to right-click on an error later, hear what was originally said or written, and help Word improve its recognition performance.

- **Save Word Files As.** In this box, you can specify a default format other than Word 2003 in which to save your files. You can choose any format for which you have installed an export filter.

- **Disable Features Introduced After.** If you check this box and choose either Word 97 or Word 6.0/95 from the drop-down box, you prevent Word from saving formatting, graphics, and text attributes that cannot be used in the older version of Word you specify. This is a helpful feature if you plan to share documents with users of older versions of Word. Before Word removes these features from a document, it warns you about what it will delete.

NOTE

The only way to eliminate formatting that older versions of Word (such as Word 6) can-not read is to save files in those versions of Word.

SETTING USER INFORMATION

Word uses your name, initials, and address in various ways. It stores your name as the Author in the Properties dialog box of any new document you create. It includes your name automatically in letters and envelopes you create using Word's wizards and templates; your initials are also included in letters. It attaches your name and initials to any changes or comments you insert using Word's Track Changes or Comments features.

To set or change your name, initials, or address, display the User Information tab of the Options dialog box (see Figure 31.27).

Figure 31.27

Use the User Information tab of the Options dialog box to change your personal information settings.

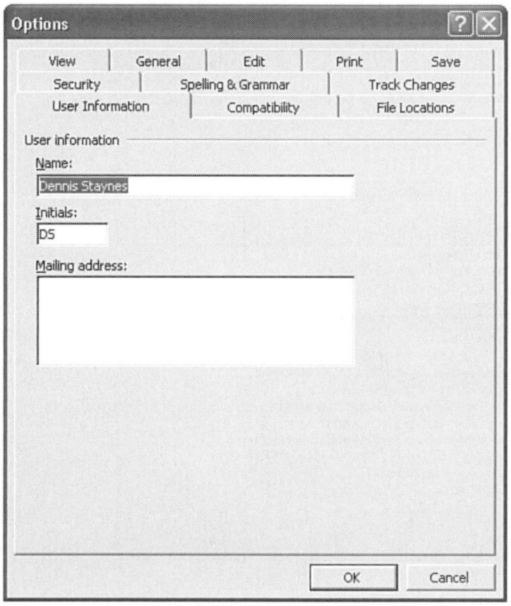

31

Enter your <u>N</u>ame, <u>I</u>nitials, and <u>M</u>ailing Address as you want them to appear when Word uses them. (For example, your initials don't have to correspond precisely to the name you enter in the name box—it's up to you.)

NOTE

Word also tracks your Company Name as you entered it during installation, but this information cannot be permanently changed from inside Word.

SETTING COMPATIBILITY OPTIONS

You might be accustomed to working with a different version of Word, or a different brand of word processor, such as WordPerfect. Or you may have documents that originated on a different system, such as a Macintosh running Microsoft Word 5.1. These programs differ subtly in the ways they display text.

These subtleties are almost all minor, but they can occasionally cause significant problems. For example, Microsoft 5.1 for the Macintosh uses larger Small Caps than Word 2003. This minor difference could conceivably affect where lines, or even pages, break—throwing off carefully created page layouts.

Using the Compatibility tab of the Options dialog box (see Figure 31.28), you can adjust Word to display your document as it would look if opened in a different program.

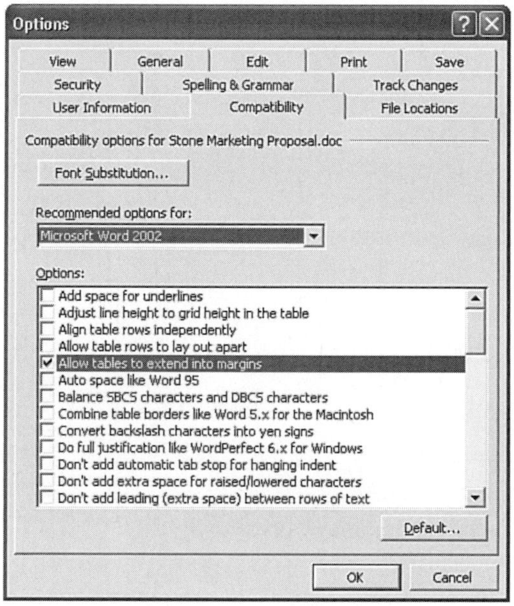

Figure 31.28
In the Compatibility tab, you can adjust Word's behavior to match that of older versions of Word for Windows, DOS, and Macintosh, as well as WordPerfect.

NOTE

These Compatibility settings don't actually change the contents of an existing file. They change only its appearance so that you can accurately format your document to reflect the software and computer from which it will eventually be used and printed.

If you know the program that created a file, the quickest way to ensure compatibility is to choose that program name in the Recommended Options For drop-down list box. Word has built-in options designed to reflect differences in appearance for the following:

- Word 2002
- Word 2000

- Word 97
- Word 6.0/95
- Word for Windows 1.0
- Word for Windows 2.0
- Word for the Macintosh 5.x
- Word for MS-DOS
- WordPerfect 5.x for DOS
- WordPerfect 6.x for Windows
- WordPerfect 6.0 for DOS

You can also choose Custom from the Recommended Options For drop-down box to create custom settings if you need them.

NOTE

For detailed information on most Word compatibility options, see Microsoft Knowledge Base article KB288792 (go to http://support.microsoft.com and search for this article number).

31

USING FONT SUBSTITUTION

If you've been asked to edit a file created with another word processing program, or on another type of computer, such as a Macintosh, you may find that you don't have all the fonts used in the original file. Word automatically substitutes fonts it does have for those it can't find.

In some cases, these font substitutions are no-brainers. For example, many Macintosh documents are created with PostScript fonts such as Times Roman and Courier. On standard Windows PCs that don't have Type 1 (PostScript) fonts installed, Word substitutes the TrueType equivalents, Times New Roman and Courier New.

Note that the substituted fonts are similar but not identical to the originals, so you might find unwelcome changes in line and page breaks. Also note that the original font names still appear in the Font drop-down box on the Formatting toolbar, so if you return the document to its source, the original fonts will automatically be in use.

Occasionally, you'll want to control the way Word substitutes fonts. For example, perhaps you've been handed a document formatted with the Eras Bold ITC font. You don't own Eras Bold ITC, and Word substitutes Lucida Sans Unicode, which looks quite different. However, you do have one of the many competitive "knockoff" fonts that resemble Eras Bold ITC. Your font has a name that Word doesn't recognize as being equivalent to Eras. You can tell Word to use that font rather than Lucida Sans Unicode whenever it comes across text formatted as Eras Bold ITC.

To use font substitution, click Font Substitution to open the Font Substitution dialog box (see Figure 31.29).

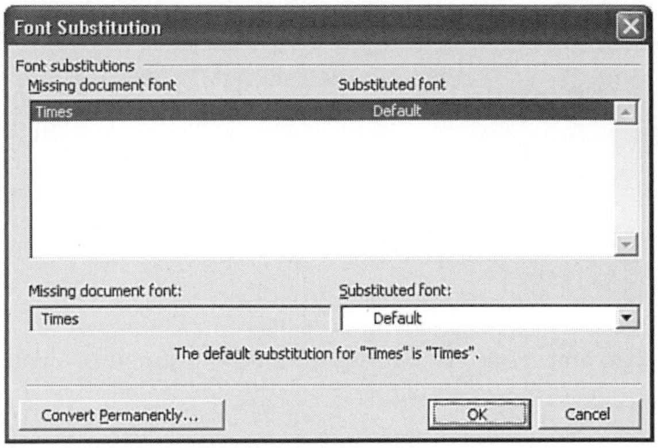

Figure 31.29
In the Font Substitution dialog box, you can control which fonts are used when you don't have the ones with which your document was formatted.

31

Font Substitution

Font substitutions
Missing document font   Substituted font
Times   Default

Missing document font: Substituted font:
Times   Default

The default substitution for "Times" is "Times".

Convert Permanently...   OK   Cancel

NOTE

If your document has no substituted fonts, Word won't display the Font Substitution dialog box. Rather, it displays a message telling you no font substitution is necessary.

The Font Substitution dialog box lists all the missing document fonts it has found and the fonts it has substituted. (Often, it simply substitutes a default font, typically Times New Roman.) To change a font substitution, select the row containing the missing document font and the font Word has substituted. Then in the Substituted Font drop-down box, select the font you want to use.

As you've already learned, when you substitute a font, Word displays and prints the document using the font you chose. However, the original font is still shown in the Font drop-down box. This is obviously welcome for documents that may be returned to their source. In other cases, however, it can be confusing. After all, the font you see onscreen no longer matches the font with which Word "says" the text has been formatted.

If you want to reformat the document using the fonts you've already chosen as substitutes, click the Convert Permanently button. Word pops up a quick confirmation dialog box, which only requires you to click OK to confirm the change. Wherever Word finds a substituted font in your document, it converts the document to use the substituted font name rather than the original one.

SETTING FILE LOCATIONS

There's one final Options tab: File Locations (see Figure 31.30), which specifies where Word looks for the files and documents it needs. You might find that you're piling up all sorts of documents in your My Documents folder, when most of the documents ultimately need to be moved to another folder. In this tab, you can tell Word to use a different default.

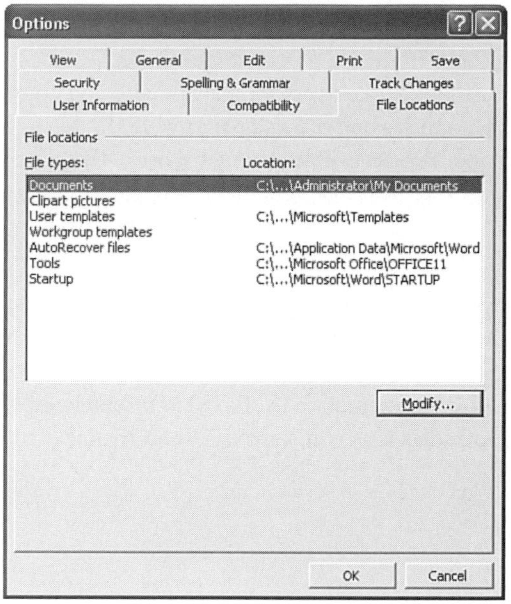

Figure 31.30
The File Locations tab enables you to change where Word looks for documents, templates, and tools.

TIP

If you know you'll be working primarily in a specific folder for a week or two, change the document's location to that folder. When you start Word and display the Open dialog box, Word automatically displays the contents of that folder.

In the File Locations tab, you can also control where Word looks for clip art, templates, workgroup templates shared across a network, AutoRecover files, tools, and templates or add-ins that should run at Startup.

→ For more information on deploying and using workgroup templates, **see** "Using Workgroup Templates," **p. 377**.

To change the location associated with a file type, select the row containing the file type and location, and click <u>M</u>odify. The Modify Location dialog box opens, allowing you to browse to the folder you want to use for the new location. After specifying it, click OK to enable the change.

TROUBLESHOOTING

WHAT TO DO IF WORD RESTORES COMMANDS YOU REMOVED IN AN OLDER VERSION OF WORD

If you open a template created in an older version of Word, you may find that menus and buttons you removed in that template reappear in Word 2003. To solve the problem, you must resave the template in Word's current format and then manually remove the commands and buttons again.

WHAT TO DO IF YOU COPY CUSTOM BUTTONS BETWEEN TEMPLATES, BUT THE BUTTONS DON'T WORK IN THE NEW TEMPLATE

If you've created toolbar buttons that run custom macros, and you copy the buttons to new templates, remember that you must copy the macros as well. To do so, use the Macro Project Items tab of the Organizer, accessible through Tools, Templates and Add-Ins, Organizer.

WHAT TO DO IF YOU WANT TO COPY A CUSTOMIZED BUILT-IN TOOLBAR BETWEEN TEMPLATES

Word's Organizer enables you to copy custom toolbars between templates, but it doesn't show built-in toolbars such as the Standard or Formatting toolbar—even if you've customized them. The workaround is to first create a new custom template and copy the buttons one at a time from the built-in template to the custom template. After you've copied the entire toolbar and organized as it as you want, use the Organizer to copy the custom toolbar.

CHAPTER 32

RECORDING AND RUNNING VISUAL BASIC MACROS

In this chapter

Macros: The Basics

A *macro* is a sequence of operations that Word can execute whenever you tell it to, with a keyboard shortcut, toolbar button, or menu command, or by executing the macro from the Tools, Macro, Macros dialog box. Word's powerful macro facilities enable you to automate just about anything you would do manually in Word. There are two general approaches to creating Word macros:

- Use Word's macro recorder to capture the steps in your macro as you perform them. After you save the macro, you can play it back at any time using one of the options listed previously.

- Write the code of the macro yourself in the Visual Basic for Applications (VBA) programming language. Word comes with a complete programming environment, the Visual Basic Editor, that you use to enter and edit your code, as well as powerful tools to help you debug and test your macros.

This chapter focuses on recording and playing back a Word macro. If you'd like to learn the fundamentals of VBA programming with Word, there are a number of books and websites you can use. I suggest a good VBA book such as VBA Developer's Handbook available from Sybex.

What Tasks Should You Automate with a Macro?

The most common purpose for macros is to speed your work, by taking a set of operations that you perform repeatedly and turning them into a one-step operation. Anytime you find yourself doing the same set of actions over and over again, you might have found a good candidate for a macro. Macros also make your work more reliable by ensuring that the steps of the macro are performed exactly the same way, each time the macro runs. Of course, that does mean it is essential to record the macro properly. Otherwise, it performs the same *wrong* set of steps each time it runs.

Before you take the step of creating a macro, however, you might want to consider some of the other timesaving features in Word that you can use instead of macros:

- If you often need to type the same text, such as your name or address, including formatting, you might want to use Word's AutoText feature, which lets you save named collections of text and formatting.

→ To learn about AutoText and other Word features to speed your work, **see** Chapter 9, "Automating Your Documents," **p. 287**.

- To quickly apply formatting in a consistent way through one or more documents, you can use styles.

→ To learn how to create and apply styles, **see** Chapter 10, "Streamlining Your Formatting with Styles," **p. 329**.

- To create neatly formatted standard documents, such as letters, rèsumès, or fax cover sheets, you can use one of the document templates or wizards that come with Word, or create your own template.

→ To learn about working with templates in Word, **see** Chapter 11, "Templates, Wizards, and Add-Ins," **p. 355**.

If none of Word's automated features alone will do the job for you, or if you want to use several of these features together, you can create a macro to carry out your commands. There is just about no end to the uses you might think of for macros. A few of the most common include the following:

- Applying complex formatting that you can't easily capture in a style, such as a mixture of font and paragraph formatting.

- Completing any task that takes several steps, such as creating a mail merge, applying complicated page setup, or requesting custom printing routines.

- Performing repetitive tasks in a long document. This is especially useful for documents that you have imported from other programs, or that other users have created. You can record a macro that finds and replaces special characters, removes extra paragraphs, or applies formatting.

- Performing commands normally found in Word's built-in dialog boxes. You might want to turn a display feature—such as the display of bookmarks—on or off as needed. Or you might want to quickly apply a format, such as strikethrough formatting.

DECIDING TO USE THE MACRO RECORDER

When you need to create a new macro, you have a choice between recording the macro and typing the VBA code yourself. Of course, if you don't know the VBA programming language, your only option is to record the macro. You can even use the recorder as a teaching tool by recording the macro and then studying the resulting VBA code. As mentioned, this book focuses on using the macro recorder.

It's worthwhile to know a little about how the macro recorder works before recording a macro. After you turn on the macro recorder, it captures just about everything you do in Word, including typing text, applying formatting, and performing menu commands. The recorder is very literal: It picks up just about every detail during the recording session. Don't be surprised, if you look at the VBA code that results from recording a macro, if it seems that Word recorded a lot more than you had in mind.

If you are, or become, proficient with VBA, you'll probably find that it is often useful to record a macro and then edit the resulting code to get it to work exactly as you want. As your VBA skills improve, you might even find that it's sometimes quicker and more accurate to type the code yourself in the first place.

PLANNING TO RECORD YOUR MACRO

It's always a good idea to take some time to think about exactly what you want your macro to do before you begin recording. You might even want to take a few notes on paper that you can refer to while you record the macro. Think about several things before recording your macro:

■ Consider how your document should be set up before the recording begins. For example, if your macro is to apply font formatting to selected text, you need to have the appropriate text selected before you start recording the macro. On the other hand, you might want to record the actual selection of the text. In many cases, the first action you record will be moving to the beginning of your document. This can ensure that the steps that follow are applied to the entire document.

■ Make sure that you know your keyboard shortcuts, especially the ones for moving through the document and for selecting text. Word doesn't record text selections or navigation you perform with the mouse, but you *can* use keyboard shortcuts to perform the same tasks. (You can still use the mouse to select toolbar and menu commands while recording.)

TIP

> If you want to record a macro that performs a series of actions to selected text, select some text before you begin recording the macro. Then record your macro as you normally would. For example, you could create a macro that makes selected text bold and italic. Select some text, begin recording the macro, click the Bold and Italic toolbar buttons, and stop recording. The resulting macro toggles the bold and italic setting for any selected text.

■ Think about the exact meaning of what you want to record. For example, to move to the beginning of the next paragraph while you are recording, press the shortcut key to move to the next paragraph (Ctrl+down arrow). If you simply use the arrow keys to move to the desired location, your macro records the arrow movements, not your intention to move to the following paragraph. When you run it in a different document, it replays the arrow movements, which may not have the same result in that document.

A good way to plan a macro is to take one or more "test runs" before turning on the recorder: Perform the commands and write down exactly what you did along the way. When you're satisfied that you've written down a workable list of steps, use it as a reference when recording the macro.

RECORDING YOUR MACRO

To begin recording a macro, choose Tools, Macro, Record New Macro, or double-click the REC marker on the Word status bar. The Record Macro dialog box appears, as shown in Figure 32.1.

Before you can begin recording the macro, you must give it a name and decide where you want to store it. You can also assign the macro to a keyboard shortcut or a custom toolbar button. Although you can change all these items later, it's far more convenient to make these decisions up front and enter them correctly now.

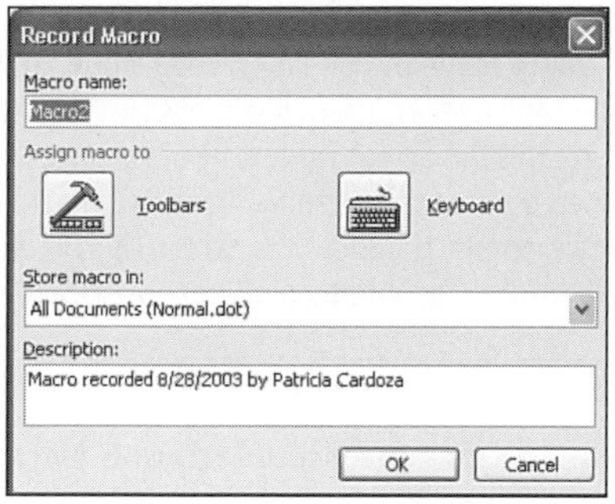

Figure 32.1
Enter the name and description of your new macro in the Record Macro dialog box.

NAMING YOUR MACRO

As you can see from Figure 32.1, Word suggests a name for your macro: Macro1, Macro2, and so on. It's usually much more useful to give your macro a more descriptive name so that it will be easy to identify when you want to use it later. Your macro name should describe the purpose of the macro and must follow these rules:

- Macro names must begin with a letter but can include numbers.
- Names can contain up to 80 letters and numbers. Spaces and other characters are not allowed.

NOTE

> According to Microsoft documentation, only letters and numbers are permitted in macro names. You can create a macro name that includes an underscore (_) such as New_Letter, to simulate spacing. However, this is not documented and might not work correctly in future versions of Word.

For example, the following macro names are legal:

    ApplyMyCustomFormatting
    Insert5BlankParagraphs
    TwoBOrNot2B

The following names are not legal:

    Create Letter
    2Spaces
    New?Document

Word 2003 does not give you any warning that your macro name is invalid until you click OK to start recording your macro. If your macro name contains invalid characters, Word will display a dialog box indicating Invalid procedure name. Simply click OK and launch the Record Macro dialog box again. Edit the name until it conforms to the naming rules. When it does, Word allows you to proceed.

TIP

> When you create a long macro name by running several words together, it's a good idea to begin each word with a capital letter. Then, if you assign the macro to a toolbar button, Word automatically creates the ScreenTip text by separating the macro name into its individual words, as defined by the capitalization. Naming a macro DeleteStrayCharacters, for example, produces the ScreenTip "Delete Stray Characters." Also note that embedded numbers generate an all-uppercase ScreenTip.

At the time you name your macro, you can also enter a description for the macro. Word's default description indicates the date the macro was recorded, and who recorded it. However, it makes sense to enter a more specific description for your macros. For example:

This macro goes to the top of the document and then performs a find and replace to eliminate the second space between sentences.

Deciding Where to Store Your Macro

Macros can be stored in templates and in individual documents. A macro is available for you to run only if the document or template that contains the macro is open. Macros can be stored in the following locations:

- *Normal.dot*—The simplest way to create a macro that you can run at any time, in any document, is to store the macro in your Normal template. As you can see in Figure 32.1, the Normal.dot template is selected by default as the storage place for recorded macros.

- *Active Document*—If you prefer to store the macro in the active document, click the Store Macro In drop-down list to select the document. The macro will be available for you to run only when this document is the active document.

- *Other Templates*—If you store a macro in a template other than the Normal template, the macro is available only when that template is open or when a document based on that template is open. For example, suppose that you have created a template for writing sales proposals. If you want to record a macro that you will use only when you are working on these proposals, be sure to select the template name in the Store Macro In drop-down list. The template, or a document based on the template, must be the active document at the time you record the macro.

Assigning a Macro to a Keyboard Shortcut or Toolbar Button

If you expect to use your macro often, and you want to save time when you run it, you can assign a shortcut key, menu command, or toolbar button for running the macro. Then you can run your macro quickly by pressing the shortcut key, selecting the command on the menu, or clicking the toolbar button.

NOTE

> Assigning a macro to a menu item is somewhat more involved than the process of assigning the macro a shortcut key or toolbar button. For that reason, it is covered later in this chapter.

Word does not require you to assign your macro to a shortcut key, menu command, or toolbar button: You can always run the macro using the Tools, Macro, Macros command. Although adding some form of shortcut can make a macro more accessible, you might prefer not to use up a key assignment or space on a toolbar for macros you use only rarely.

For commonly used macros, however, you probably should assign a keyboard shortcut or toolbar button. Several factors should enter into your decision, including these:

- Keyboard shortcuts are a great convenience for macros that you use often. If you use a macro only occasionally, however, you might find it difficult to remember the shortcut key. Also, if you're creating macros for other users, some users prefer shortcut keys, whereas others don't want to memorize anything.

TIP

> You can print a list of the custom key assignments associated with any document or template. To do so, choose File, Print; then choose Key Assignments from the Print What drop-down box and click OK. Word first prints all custom key assignments associated with the document itself, and then all custom key assignments associated with the template the document is based on.

32

- A button on a custom toolbar makes a macro readily available for use at any time. Many people prefer not to memorize many shortcut keys but don't mind clicking on a button in a custom toolbar.

- You can also add your macro commands to Word's menus. Internally, Word treats menus much like toolbars, and the customization process is also similar. You can add commands to the built-in menus, or add your own custom menus to Word's menu bar.

ASSIGNING A MACRO TO A KEYBOARD SHORTCUT   To assign a keyboard shortcut to the macro you're about to record, follow these steps while the Record Macro dialog box is open:

1. Click Keyboard in the Assign Macro To group. The Customize Keyboard dialog box appears, as shown in Figure 32.2.

2. Make sure that the correct template or document is selected in the Save Changes In drop-down list. In nearly every case, you'll want to save the keyboard shortcut in the same template or document the macro will be stored in. (Word's default setting is to store the change in the Normal.dot template, not the current document.)

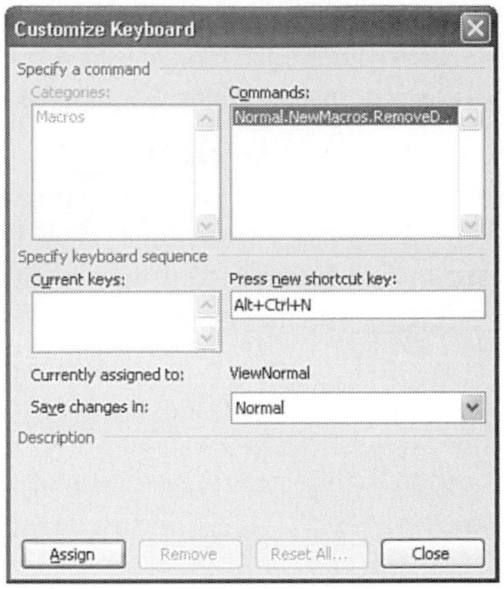

Figure 32.2
Use the Customize
Keyboard dialog box
to assign a key combi-
nation for your
macro.

3. Press the shortcut key combination you want to use for the macro. You can create keyboard combinations that include function keys F1 through F12, the Ctrl key, the Alt key, and the Shift key (but not the Windows key). The key combination you choose is displayed in the Press Underline New Shortcut Key text box. Under the text box, the current assignment for this key combination is displayed, or the combination is shown as *[unassigned]*.

CAUTION

Word allows you to override default keyboard shortcut assignments. In fact, it doesn't even require you to confirm this with a confirming dialog box. As soon as you click Close to start recording your macro, the macro replaces the default key assignment.

You should be very reluctant to change default key assignments. For example, if you decide to assign Ctrl+P as the shortcut key for your macro, you can no longer use that keyboard combination to print. If you store your macro in a specific document or a template you've created, the change in keystrokes will affect only the document, or documents, created with that template. In other words, the same keystrokes will perform different tasks at different times, which can be terribly confusing—for you and especially for others who may use your macro.

If you store the macro in Normal.dot, the change will affect all documents—but now, Word will behave differently from the way its online documentation (and this book) says it will.

4. To accept the new keyboard assignment, click Assign. The new assignment appears in the Current Keys list. You can assign more than one key combination for each macro if you want to, but remember that a relatively limited number of key combinations is available for everything Word has to do.

5. To complete the assignment and continue with the recording process, click Close.

TIP

If you find it difficult to identify unused keyboard sequences, try sequences that begin with the Alt key; most of these are unassigned.

Alternatively, you can obtain a list of shortcut keys assigned to existing Word commands. Select Tools, Macro, Macros. From the Macros In drop-down list, select Word Commands. This presents you with a list of Word commands. Scroll down to and select the ListCommands entry. Click the Run button. From the List Commands dialog box, select Current Menu and Keyboard Settings. Click OK, and a new document is generated containing all the commands and associated shortcut keys and menu items.

ASSIGNING A MACRO TO A TOOLBAR BUTTON To assign a toolbar button to run your macro, follow these steps when the Record Macro dialog box is displayed:

1. Choose Toolbars in the Assign Macro To group.

2. Make sure that the correct template or document is selected in the Save Changes In drop-down list. You will almost always want to save the toolbar assignment in the same template or document as that in which the macro will be stored.

3. The Customize dialog box appears, with the Commands tab selected, as shown in Figure 32.3.

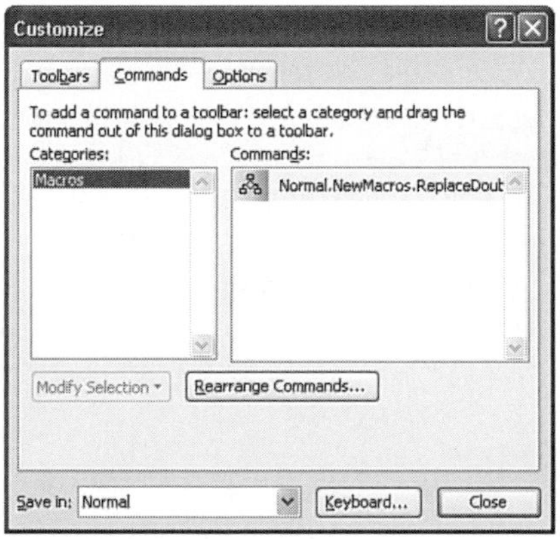

Figure 32.3
The Commands tab of the Customize dialog box.

4. If the toolbar you want to customize is not visible onscreen, click the Toolbars tab of the Customize dialog box. Check the box next to the name of the toolbar you want to use in the Toolbars list. Click the Commands tab to return to the list of macros.

5. In the Commands list, click the name of the macro you want to add to a toolbar, and drag the name to the desired position on the toolbar. The full name of the macro, including the template and module name, appears on the button that is added to the toolbar.

6. To edit the name of the button, right-click the new button on the toolbar. Edit the button's name using the Name text box on the shortcut menu that appears.

7. To continue with the macro recording process, click Close.

You can also customize your toolbars and keyboard shortcuts later, using the Tools, Customize command as described later in this chapter.

ADDING A MACRO AS A MENU COMMAND   You can also add a macro to a menu as a separate menu command. Because Word considers menus to be simply a variant on toolbars (albeit one that happens to contain text), adding a menu command is similar to adding a toolbar button—but not identical. Follow these steps:

1. Choose Toolbars in the Assign Macro To group. The Customize dialog box appears.

2. Click the Commands tab. The command name associated with the macro you're about to record appears in the Commands scroll box.

3. Drag the command name all the way to the menu bar at the top of the screen; then drag it over the menu you want to add it to. That menu appears.

4. Without letting go, drag the command name down to the location on the menu where you want the new command to appear.

5. Release the mouse pointer; the command name appears on the menu.

6. To edit the command so that it contains a name users will understand, right-click on the command, and enter a new name in the Name box on the shortcut menu. (To specify a shortcut key, place the & symbol before the letter you want to use as a shortcut; make sure you don't duplicate another shortcut key on the same menu.)

7. Press Enter; then click Close.

RECORDING THE STEPS FOR YOUR MACRO

If you chose to assign a keyboard shortcut, toolbar button, or menu command to your macro, after you click Close, Word turns on the macro recorder and displays the Stop Recording toolbar, as shown in Figure 32.4. If you decided not to make a keyboard or toolbar assignment, click OK in the Record Macro dialog box to begin recording.

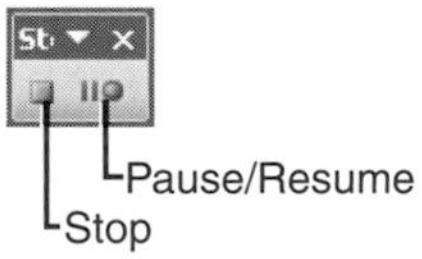

Figure 32.4
Use the Stop Recording toolbar to stop or pause your macro recording session.

Pause/Resume
Stop

When the macro recorder is active, you can perform most normal activities in Word, and those activities are recorded as part of your macro. Some examples of actions you can record in your macro include the following:

■ Typing and deleting text from a document.

■ Selecting text or navigating the document with keyboard shortcuts. You can't use the mouse to select text or navigate while you are recording. Instead, use the arrow keys to navigate, as well as the Home, End, Page Up, or Page Down keys, as needed. To select text, press and hold the Shift key while you use the arrow or navigation keys.

- Choosing menu commands or toolbar buttons and filling out the dialog boxes associated with the commands.

- Opening files, closing documents, or creating new documents.

- Choosing options, such as those found in the Tools, Options command.

NOTE

> You *can* still use the mouse to select menu commands and toolbar buttons while you're recording a macro.

Word displays the Stop Recording toolbar, shown in Figure 32.4, the entire time the macro recorder is on. When you have completed the steps of your macro, click the Stop Recording button.

If you want to pause your recording session and return to it later, click the Pause Recording button. Any actions you perform while recording is paused are not recorded. Click Pause Recording again when you're ready to resume your recording session.

Keep a few things in mind as you record your macros:

- The macro recorder captures the actions you perform, not the keystrokes you use to complete them.

- If you record a command that displays a dialog box, such as the Format, Font command, the dialog box doesn't appear when you run the macro. Rather, Word applies whatever settings you enter using the dialog box while you are recording the macro.

- Word records *everything* in the dialog box, so if you only want to turn on italic, it's better to press Ctrl+I or click the Italic button on the Formatting toolbar than it is to use the Format, Font command. Otherwise, Word also records other text attributes that apply to the current text—attributes you might not want to apply every time you run the macro.

- If you display a dialog box while you're recording, but you cancel the dialog box, Word doesn't record that command at all.

- Word records your actions literally. For example, if you record the File, Open command and select a file, Word records the exact filename you opened. When you run the macro, Word attempts to open the same file. If the file is not found, an error occurs, and the macro stops running.

When you finish recording your macro, you can turn off the recorder in the following ways:

- Click the Stop Recording button onthe Stop Recording toolbar.

- Double-click the REC text area on the status bar.

- Choose Tools, Macro, Stop Recording.

MAKING SURE YOUR MACRO IS SAVED

After you finish recording your macro, it is stored as part of the template or document in which you chose to save it. The macro is not actually saved, however, until you save that document or template. Because many macros are stored in the Normal.dot template, it's easy to forget to save your work. Of course, this template is saved when you exit Word, but you really should save your work more often that that, in case an application error or a power outage prevents you from safely exiting Word.

TIP

> An easy way to save the Normal.dot template is to use the hidden Save All command. To see this command, hold down the Shift key and then select the File menu. The Save All command now appears on the File menu. Select this command to save all open documents, including any templates that are open, especially Normal.dot.
>
> Of course, use the Save All command only if you want to save all the documents and templates that are open.

CREATING MACROS THAT RUN AUTOMATICALLY

In most cases, you should give your macro a name that describes its function so that you can easily remember its purpose later. There are, however, several special names you can give your macros. These names cause your macros to run automatically when certain events occur in Word:

- A macro named AutoExec runs when you start Word. For this macro to work, you need to store it in your Normal.dot template or another global template.

NOTE

> The capitalization used in this discussion isn't required; autoexec and Autoexec will work the same way as AutoExec. You cannot, however, give this function a completely new name.

- A macro named AutoExit runs when you exit Word. If you want a macro to run every time you exit Word, store this macro in Normal.dot or another global template.
- A macro named AutoNew runs when you create a new document. If you save this macro in a specific template, such as a memo template, then the macro runs each time you create a new document based on that template.
- A macro named AutoClose runs when you close a document. If you save this macro in a specific template, it runs when you attempt to close the template or any document based on the template.
- A macro named AutoOpen runs when you open the template that contains it or any document based on the template.

NOTE

> The names AutoNew, AutoClose, and AutoOpen are included for compatibility with earlier versions of Word, but similar functionality is provided by the VBA event procedures DocumentNew, DocumentClose, and DocumentOpen.
>
> Unlike AutoNew and the other "automatic" macro names, these VBA event procedures are not the *names* of macros, but rather the names of VBA *commands* that can be included in those macros. If you're not comfortable writing VBA code, use the automatic macro names instead.

RUNNING YOUR MACRO

Now that you have recorded and stored your macro, you can run the macro to perform the steps you have recorded. Use one of the following methods to run your macro:

- If you assigned the macro to a toolbar button, you can click the button to run the macro.

- If you assigned the macro to a menu command, you can select the command to run the macro.

- If you assigned a keyboard shortcut for the macro, press the key combination.

- To select the macro name from the list of available macros, choose Tools, Macro, Macros, or press Alt+F8. The Macros dialog box appears, as shown in Figure 32.5. Select the macro name that you want to run and click Run to execute the macro.

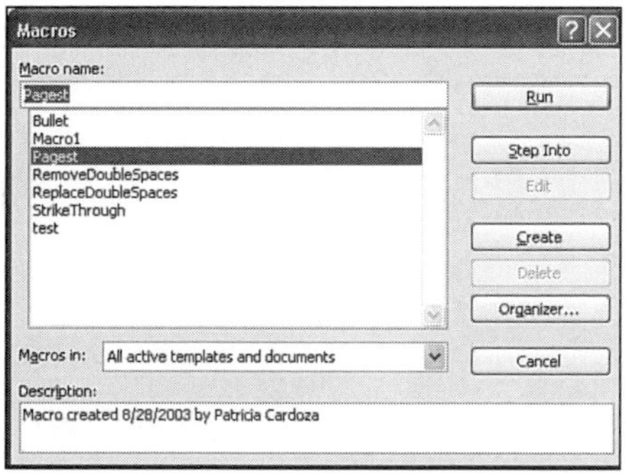

Figure 32.5
Use the Macros dialog box to select a macro to run.

TIP

> When you first display the Macros dialog box, Word lists all the macros currently available for you to run. The list can include macros in your Normal.dot template, macros in the active template or document, and macros in other global templates that are open.
>
> To shorten the list to include only those macros in one template or document, select the template or document in the Macros In drop-down list. To restore the full list of macros, select All Active Templates and Documents in the drop-down list.

DEALING WITH MACRO ERROR MESSAGES

When your macro runs, the statements you recorded are performed just as you recorded them. Sometimes, though, an error can occur. Suppose that you recorded a macro that tries to open a file name that no longer exists on your hard drive. If the macro can't find the file, it will cause an error, and display a message such as the one shown in Figure 32.6.

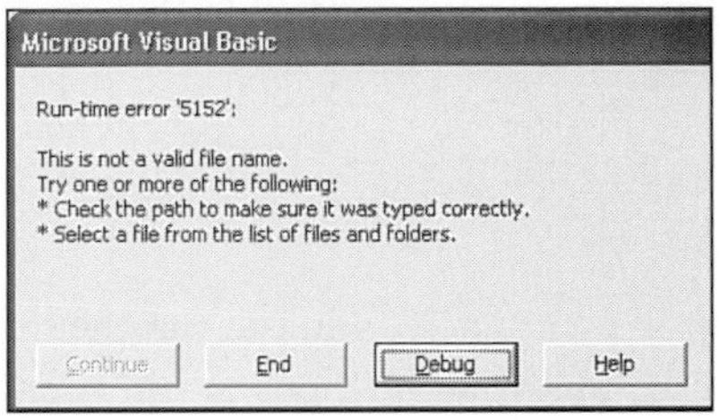

Figure 32.6
When a Microsoft Visual Basic error occurs, you can end the macro or debug it using the Visual Basic Editor.

If you're not interested in debugging the macro, click End. The macro stops running, and you are returned to the active document in Word. Examine your document carefully because some of the statements in your macro might have executed successfully, up until the point where the error occurred.

If you want to examine the VBA code in the Visual Basic Editor (VBE), click Debug in the error dialog box. The VBE is opened, and the line of VBA code in which the error occurred is highlighted, as shown in Figure 32.7.

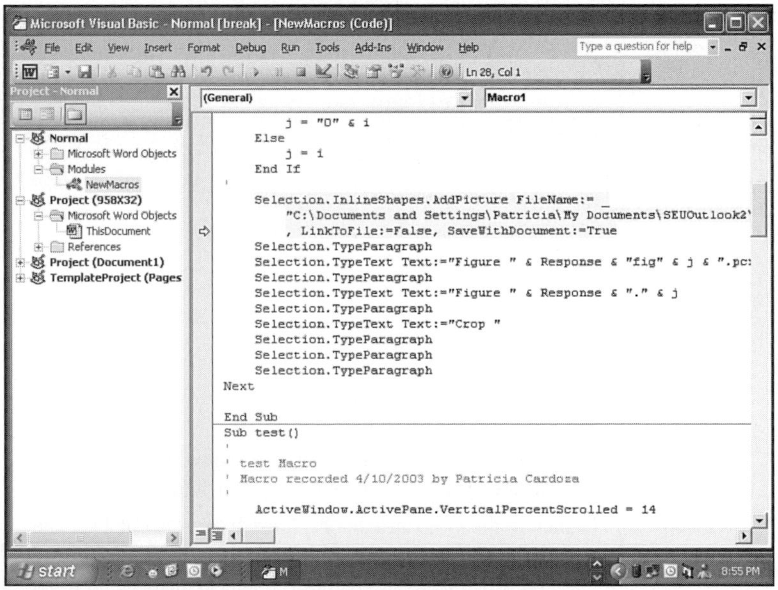

Figure 32.7
The line of code that caused the error is highlighted.

At this time, the macro is still running but is suspended in a state known as Break mode. Before you can resume normal operations, you must reset the macro project by clicking the

Reset button on the VBE's Standard toolbar, or by choosing Run, Reset from the VBE menus.

CAUTION

> Occasionally, a macro runs out of control, repeating its actions over and over. This is not likely to happen with a recorded macro, but it sometimes happens when there is a programming error in a macro you have edited. In this case, you can stop the macro by pressing Ctrl+Break. Again, this puts the macro in Break mode, and you must reset the macro project.

OPENING ADDITIONAL TEMPLATES TO RUN MACROS

If you want to run a macro that is stored in a different template, you can open that template as a global template. There are two ways to make sure that a template is loaded globally:

- Save the template in the Word Startup folder. This folder is listed in the Startup item in the Tools, Options, File Locations dialog box. Any template in this folder is opened invisibly, and as a read-only document, each time you start Word.

- Open a template globally at any time with the Tools, Templates and Add-Ins command. Click the Add or Remove buttons to load and unload templates from memory, as displayed in the Global Templates and Add-Ins list.

Clicking Add displays the Add Templates dialog box; browse to and select the template you want to load. After a template is loaded as a global template, its macros, toolbars, and keyboard shortcuts are available, along with those in any other templates and documents that are open.

32

MOVING PROJECT ITEMS AMONG TEMPLATES AND DOCUMENTS

VBA macros are stored in *projects*. A project is a collection of modules, and in Word, each document or template contains a single project. Within each project, macros are stored in *modules*. A module is a collection of VBA code, such as procedures, functions, and other declarations. A project can contain any number of modules. Each macro is stored as a procedure, or collection of VBA statements, in a module. Each module can contain as many individual macros as you want. When you record a macro, Word stores the VBA code in a module named NewMacros.

NOTE

> Modules can be added, renamed, and otherwise manipulated as required to obtain the desired functionality.

If you have a module containing some useful macros in a given template, you might want to reuse that module in another template. You can use Word's Organizer to copy macros from one project to another:

1. Choose Tools, Macro, Macros, or press Alt+F8, to display the Macros dialog box.

2. Click Organizer. The Organizer dialog box appears, as shown in Figure 32.8. This dialog box lets you display the modules in two templates or documents and copy modules from one list to another.

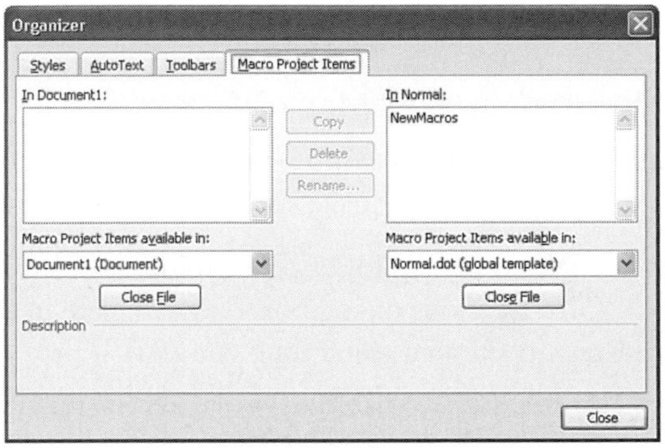

Figure 32.8
Use the Organizer to copy modules from one template or document to another.

3. Under either list, you can display a different template by clicking the Close File button, and then clicking Open File and selecting a different template or document.

4. To copy a module from one list to another, select the module that you want to copy and click Copy. The macro is copied to the destination list. If a module with the same name is already in the destination project, Word won't let you copy the module. If you still want to copy the module, you must rename it before copying it (see the next step).

5. To rename a module, select the module and click Rename. Type the new name for the module and click OK.

6. To delete a module from a project, select the module and click Delete. Word asks for confirmation that you really want to delete the module.

CAUTION

After you delete a module and save the template that contained it, there is no way to recover the deleted module.

7. When you are finished using the Organizer, click Close.

The Organizer copies, renames, and deletes only entire modules, each of which might contain many individual macros.

RUNNING WORD COMMANDS: WORD'S 400+ BUILT-IN, ONE-STEP MACROS

Word has more than 400 built-in commands that you can run as though they were macros. Many of these commands are the same as the commands already found on Word's menus and toolbar buttons. In some cases, though, there are commands that aren't found on any menu or toolbar button. In other cases, these commands provide a simpler or more effective approach to operations that you can perform with other commands.

Here are some of the built-in commands you might find useful:

- **Connect** displays a dialog box that enables you to connect to a network drive.
- **FilePageSetup** displays the Page Setup dialog box so that you can select a different printer or other printer options.
- **MicrosoftAccess**, **MicrosoftExcel**, **MicrosoftPowerPoint**, and similar commands start the desired program, or activate it if it is already running.
- **GrowFont** increases the font size of the current selection, and **ShrinkFont** decreases the font size accordingly.
- **Hidden** applies the Hidden attribute to the selected text, without applying other properties of the Font dialog box. Selecting the command a second time turns the Hidden attribute off.
- **SaveTemplate** saves the template that is attached to the current document.
- **InsertAddress** inserts an address from your Outlook contacts list or Personal Address Book.
- **ToolsCreateDirectory** creates a new folder under the current folder.

To run a built-in command as a macro, choose Tools, Macro, Macros (or press Alt+F8), and select Word Commands in the Macros In dialog box. Select the desired command in the Macro Name list and click Run.

NOTE

As you explore Word's built-in commands, you might choose to add them to your toolbars or menus, or to assign a keyboard shortcut to run them quickly. Using Tools, Customize, Command, select All Commands in the Categories list. The Commands list displays the full list of available Word commands for customization.

32

TROUBLESHOOTING

WHAT TO DO WHEN A BUILT-IN KEYBOARD SHORTCUT DOESN'T GIVE YOU THE RESULT YOU WANT

You probably assigned a macro to the keystroke combination. Review your macros and assign a different keystroke combination to the macro. Even if you don't have any macros saved in the current document, there might be macros available because they are stored in Normal.dot or because you have another document opened that has macros.

WHAT TO DO IF YOU CHOOSE THE WRONG COMMAND WHILE RECORDING

If you are in a dialog box and have made a mistake while the recorder is on, click the Cancel button of the dialog box or press Esc to close the dialog box. None of your selections in the dialog box will be recorded. If you have already completed the command or closed the dialog box, then choose Edit, Undo, and the last command will be removed from the macro. If too many commands have been chosen, use Edit, Undo, and edit the macro when you are finished recording it. Remember which command you want removed. The macro statement you want to remove will have a similar name.

CHAPTER 33

WORD DOCUMENT PRIVACY AND SECURITY OPTIONS

In this chapter

UNDERSTANDING AND USING WORD 2003'S PRIVACY AND SECURITY FEATURES

Companies and individuals are increasingly concerned about the security of their documents and computer systems. In this chapter, you'll learn about Word's many options for increasing document and computer security. If you store documents on network servers, you can combine Word's security features with the access restrictions built into your network operating system to tailor a security approach that meets the needs of your organization. Word's security features include

- Password-protected encryption of various strengths
- Privacy features that allow you to strip personal information and interim comments out of a document before you forward it to others
- New Information Rights Management features that allow you to control who can read and edit your document, and even give documents "expiration dates" after which they cannot be read at all
- Support for digital signatures that confirm the identity of individuals who have created a document
- Limited macro virus protection, largely intended to supplement third-party antivirus software, not replace it
- Improved document protection features that limit the changes that can be made to a document

Security begins, of course, with awareness—not just technology. If you are responsible for securing documents throughout a workgroup or an organization, you need to ensure not only that your colleagues understand Word's security features but that they understand the reasons to use them—and the limitations of these features, where they exist.

Word 2003 brings together its security features in a single location: the Security tab of the Options dialog box (see Figure 33.1). To display it, choose Tools, Options, Security.

REMOVING PERSONAL INFORMATION FROM WORD DOCUMENTS

Unknown to many Word users, Word stores a wide variety of personal information about you in the files you create—information that can be used to trace a document to you (and/or your colleagues).

For example, the first time you ran Word, you were asked for your name and initials; if you provided them, they have been stored in the Author field of the Summary tab of the Properties dialog box in all your documents. By default, Word also stores this additional personal information:

- The following Properties fields: Manager, Company, Last Saved By
- The names of individuals who have reviewed a document using Word's Tracked Changes and Comments features

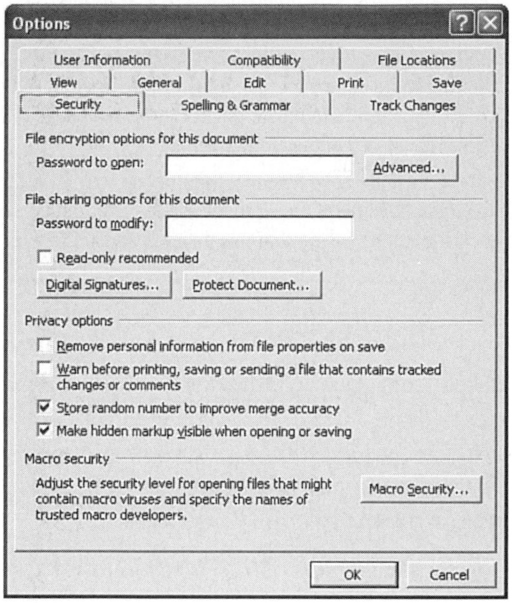

Figure 33.1
The Security tab of the Options dialog box brings together security features formerly scattered throughout Word, as well as security features new to Word 2003.

- The names that appear on a routing slip when you forward a document to others using File, Send To, Routing Recipient
- URLs stored in Smart Tags that can be used to download information from the Internet or corporate intranets
- Email headers created when you use Word as an email editor
- Information on who has saved each version of a document using Word's File, Versions feature

In Word 2003, you can strip all this personal information out of your documents whenever you save them. To strip the personal information out of an individual document, display the Security tab of the Options dialog box as described earlier, check the Remove Personal Information from This File on Save check box, click OK, and save the file.

Word removes all the individually identifiable Properties fields from the document. For document elements such as Tracked Changes, Word replaces individual names with the word "Author."

CAUTION

Checking the Remove Personal Information from This File on Save check box removes personal information only from your current document.

To remove personal information from all your new documents, you can record a macro named AutoNew, which checks the Remove Personal Information from This File on Save check box whenever you create a new document. Or, better yet, write a macro that

continues

33

continued

> creates this setting automatically, using VBA's New event. The VBA approach is more complex, requiring more coding, but it eliminates the risk that a different AutoNew macro stored with a different template might ever run in place of the macro you want. Either way, store the macro in the Normal template.
>
> Unfortunately, because Remove Personal Information from This File on Save is associated with individual documents, you cannot use the Office 2003 Resource Kit's System Policy Editor document to ensure that this policy is applied to every user or computer.

WARNING BEFORE SENDING A DOCUMENT WITH TRACKED CHANGES OR COMMENTS

If you ever use Word's Tracked Changes or Comments features, you may have noticed that it is all too easy to inadvertently leave interim notes and comments in your document that should be removed before they are saved, printed, or forwarded to a recipient by email. In Word 2003, you can set a warning to appear whenever you save, send, or print a file that still contains tracked changes or comments.

In the Security tab of the Options dialog box, check Warn Before Printing, Saving, or Sending a File That Contains Tracked Changes or Comments; then click OK.

After you check this box, you will be warned before you save, send, or print *any* files containing tracked changes or comments, not just the current file.

TIP

> If you are responsible for administering Word 2003 or Office 2003 throughout an organization, you can use the Office 2003 Resource Kit's System Policy Editor to enforce this setting for all users whenever they log on to their computers.
>
> The setting can be found in the Word11.ADM policy template, in the following location: Default User/Microsoft Word 2003/Tools | Options/Security/Warn Before Printing, Saving, or Sending a File That Contains Tracked Changes or Comments.
>
> For more information about creating system policies, see the Microsoft Office 2003 Resource Kit.

ELIMINATING TRACEABLE RANDOM NUMBERS WORD STORES IN DOCUMENTS

As covered in Chapter 26, "Managing Document Collaboration and Revisions," Word 2003 (and 2002) includes a powerful document comparison tool that is capable of identifying more changes than the comparable feature in earlier versions of Word. One way in which Word's new document comparison feature does this is by storing a random number in each document being compared. These numbers are hidden but can be uncovered and used to demonstrate that two documents were created by the same user or users.

You can instruct Word's document comparison feature not to store random numbers in your document—though this will sacrifice some accuracy in your document comparison. To avoid storing random numbers, follow these steps: In the Security tab of the Tools, Options dialog box, clear Store Random Number to Improve Merge Accuracy, and then click OK.

TIP

As discussed in the preceding section, you can use the Office 2003 Resource Kit's System Policy Editor to enforce this setting for all users whenever they log on to their computers.

The setting can be found in the Word11.ADM policy template, in the following location: Default User/Microsoft Word 2003/Tools | Options/Security/Store Random Number To Improve Merge Accuracy.

LEAVING OR JOINING MICROSOFT'S CUSTOMER EXPERIENCE IMPROVEMENT PROGRAM

With Word and Office 2003, Microsoft introduces the Customer Experience Improvement Program. Through this program, Microsoft collects information about your computer, your Office usage patterns, and errors you encounter running Word. Microsoft says it will use this information to improve Office's quality, reliability, and performance.

According to Microsoft, all information collected through this program is anonymous: "We will not collect your name, address, or any other personally identifiable information." Nevertheless, if you are concerned about security, you may want to avoid participating in this program simply because it represents another *potential* vulnerability.

By default, you do *not* participate in the Customer Experience Improvement Program. If you want to check or change your participation status, follow these steps:

1. Choose Tools, Options, General.
2. Click Service Options.
3. Choose Customer Feedback Options from the Category box.
4. To participate, choose Yes, I Am Willing to Participate Anonymously in the Customer Experience Improvement Program. To avoid participation, choose No, I Don't Wish to Participate.
5. Click OK.

CONTROLLING WHEN YOUR COMPUTER CONNECTS TO OFFICE ON MICROSOFT.COM FOR CONTENT

By default, when you run Word or any other Office application while you are connected to the Internet, Microsoft occasionally connects to your computer to display content and links from Microsoft Office Online. For example, Word's Getting Started task pane may display links to product news and new templates that have just been made available at Microsoft Office Online.

Again, however, if you are in a high-security environment, you may want to disable Internet connections that are not essential to your business. To disable this connection to your computer, follow these steps:

1. Choose Tools, Options, General.

33

2. Click Service Options.

3. Choose Online Content from the Category box.

4. Clear the Show Content and Links from Microsoft Office Online check box.

5. Click OK.

USING AND MANAGING WORD ENCRYPTION

Word makes it easy for users to encrypt their documents, using various encryption schemes, ranging from weak encryption to strong 128-bit RC4 encryption.

NOTE

> In France, 128-bit password protection is illegal. If Regional Settings are set to French in the Windows Control Panel, Word users cannot open 128-bit password-protected Word 2003 documents. If Regional Settings are reset to another locale, the files can be opened.

Follow these steps to encrypt a document:

1. Choose File, Save As.

2. In the Save As dialog box, click Tools, Security Options. The Security tab of the Options dialog box opens (refer to Figure 33.1).

3. In the Password to Open text box, enter a password. By default, passwords can be up to 15 characters long and can contain symbols and numerals as well as letters. For security reasons, Word displays asterisks onscreen as you type your password.

TIP

> In Word 2003, you can create a password up to 255 characters in length if you choose an RC4 security scheme, as discussed next.

4. To control what form of encryption to use, click the Advanced button. The Encryption Type dialog box appears (see Figure 33.2).

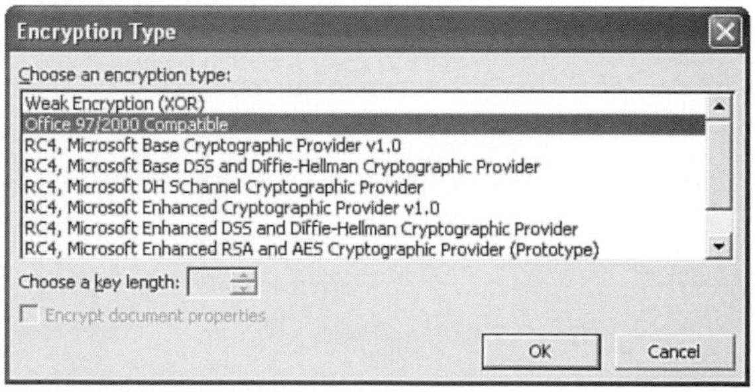

Figure 33.2
In the Encryption Type dialog box, you can choose what form of security to use.

5. Select a type of encryption from the Choose an Encryption Type scroll box.

6. If you choose an RC4 encryption scheme, you can also choose a key length and specify whether to encrypt document properties.

Take into account the following considerations in choosing an encryption type:

- If your document must be read on Office 97 or Office 2000 systems, you will typically need to select Office 97/2000 or Weak Encryption (XOR).

- XOR weak encryption, which was once the only type of encryption available for Word documents, is exactly what it says it is: notoriously weak.

- If you clear the Encrypt Document Properties check box, Word's Search feature will still be able to find files based on the contents of the Properties dialog box, though users without the correct password will not be able to open them.

- Although RC4 encryption is relatively strong, the strength depends on the key length you choose. As computers have become more powerful, 40-bit key length encryption has become far less secure. Fifty-six-bit key lengths take 65,536 times longer to crack, but even these are increasingly vulnerable. Expert recommendations now range from 90-bit to 128-bit key lengths and beyond.

7. Click OK to return to the Security tab.

8. Click OK. Word displays the Confirm Password dialog box (see Figure 33.3).

Figure 33.3
Confirm your password in the Confirm Password dialog box.

9. Reenter the password exactly as you typed it the first time. (Use the same capitalization; passwords are case sensitive.)

10. Click OK.

11. Click Save. Word saves the file.

Encrypted files cannot be indexed by the Windows file indexing services that may be running on your computer.

CAUTION

If you save a password-protected Word 2003 document to an older version of Word, such as Word 6/95, password protection is lost, and you have to reapply it in the older version of Word. This is true even though Word 6 and Word 95 also offered password protection.

CAUTION

After documents are encrypted, Word contains no feature for decrypting them without a password. In other words, if you forget your password, you will not be able to be open your document.

Even more serious, if one of your colleagues forgets a password, or leaves the company and does not share the password with someone, you will not be able to open his or her documents. If your workgroup uses passwords, make sure that copies of these passwords are stored securely—ideally, in a locked, fireproof, waterproof safe—where the company can access them in an emergency.

REMOVING PASSWORD PROTECTION FROM A FILE

If a file is encrypted using password protection, you can remove it. However, for obvious security reasons you have to open the file first (which requires entering the password). To remove a password from an encrypted file, take these steps:

1. Open the file and type the password when prompted.
2. Choose File, Save As.
3. In the Save As dialog box, choose Tools, Security Options.
4. In the Password to Open box, delete the asterisks corresponding to the existing password.
5. Click OK.
6. Click Save.

CAUTION

Clicking Cancel rather than Save in the Save As dialog box does not cancel the change to the password. It only cancels the Save operation. If Word should crash or if you close it without saving the file, the password protection remains in place.

SETTING A FILE AS READ-ONLY

Another way to secure a file from outside influence but still allow anyone to see it is to make it a read-only document. This way users can change a document only if they supply Word with the appropriate password. To do so, set the file to read-only as shown here:

1. Choose File, Save As.
2. In the Save As dialog box, choose Tools, Security Options.
3. In the Password to Modify text box, enter a password.
4. Click OK. Word displays the Confirm Password dialog box.
5. Reenter the password.
6. Click OK when asked to confirm your choice.
7. Click Save.

The Caution from the previous section also applies here: Cancel won't cancel the change of a password, and you can change the password in the Tools, Options, Security dialog box.

CAUTION

> Users who open a file as Read-Only can save it under a new name in Word 6/95 format; the new file will not be restricted to read-only status.

TIP

> You can also apply read-only status to a file from outside Word by setting the Read-Only attribute in the file's Properties dialog box. In Windows Explorer, right-click the file's icon and choose Properties from the shortcut menu. Then, click the Read-Only check box.
>
> You can't apply password protection this way, though the permissions you've set up on your network can prevent a user from altering the file's attributes.

CAUTION

> Unless you also use Word 2003's Permissions feature, nothing (other than perhaps limited network permissions) prevents a user from opening a read-only file, saving it under a new name, and changing it. The user can then close the new file, reopen it, and save it using the original file's name—thereby deleting the original file. The result is the same as it would be if the file had never been password-protected at all.

→ For more information about using Permissions, **see** "Using Permissions to Restrict Who May Use Your Documents," **p. 1096**.

"RECOMMENDING" READ-ONLY STATUS

You've just seen that you can password-protect a file as read-only, enabling users to read a file without a password, but making it more difficult for them to edit it. Word provides an even weaker form of protection that might be useful in circumstances in which you would prefer that a file not be edited but recognize that it may have to be. You can set a file as Read-Only Recommended.

When you set a file as Read-Only Recommended, if a user tries to open it, he or she sees a message like that shown in Figure 33.4.

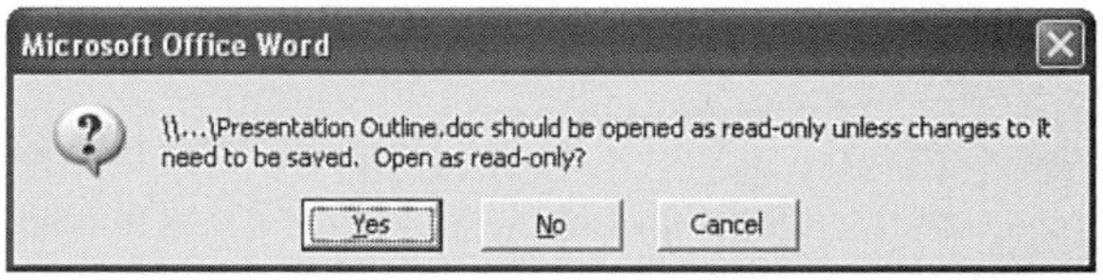

Figure 33.4
When a file is set as Read-Only Recommended, Word discourages—but doesn't prevent—users from editing a document.

Microsoft Office Word

\\...\Presentation Outline.doc should be opened as read-only unless changes to it need to be saved. Open as read-only?

Yes | No | Cancel

If the user clicks Yes, the file opens as read-only. If the user clicks No, the file opens normally, and the user can edit it.

To set a file as Read-Only Recommended, choose Tools, Options, Security; check the Read-Only Recommended check box, and click OK.

USING PERMISSIONS TO RESTRICT WHO MAY USE YOUR DOCUMENTS

Traditionally, you protected a document by restricting access to its location or contents via a password. However, after a document was opened with the correct password, you had no other way to restrict its usage or dissemination. The new Information Rights Management (IRM) feature built into Microsoft Office Professional Edition 2003 and standalone versions of Word 2003 changes that.

Using IRM, you can now associate specific permissions and restrictions with any document, giving users only the permissions they need to get their jobs done. For example, you can prevent people from

- Printing a document
- Copying content from a document
- Accessing the content of a document programmatically, with Visual Basic for Applications
- Accessing a document after a specific expiration date

You can establish different sets of permissions for each user. For example, you might allow one user to change a document but not print it; you might allow another user to use a specialized application to access selected document content, but not allow him to edit the document.

After you set permissions for a document, recipients will have only the permissions you give them, and individuals who have received no permissions will not be allowed to read, change, copy, or print your document.

You need significant Microsoft infrastructure to make full use of IRM. To authenticate users' identities, Microsoft requires you to be running either Windows Server 2003 (with appropriate Client Access Licenses) *or* Microsoft's Internet-based authentication service, which utilizes Microsoft Passport authentication.

Because older versions of Word and Office do not support IRM, they cannot be used to read and edit files with permissions. However, Microsoft is making available add-on software that will allow users with appropriate permissions to view IRM-protected files with Internet Explorer.

SETTING READ OR CHANGE PERMISSIONS

NEW To set permissions for a document, click the Permissions button on the Standard toolbar. The Permission dialog box opens. Check the Restrict Permission to This Document check box (see Figure 33.5).

Figure 33.5
The Permission dialog box displays access control options after you check the Restrict Permission to This Document check box.

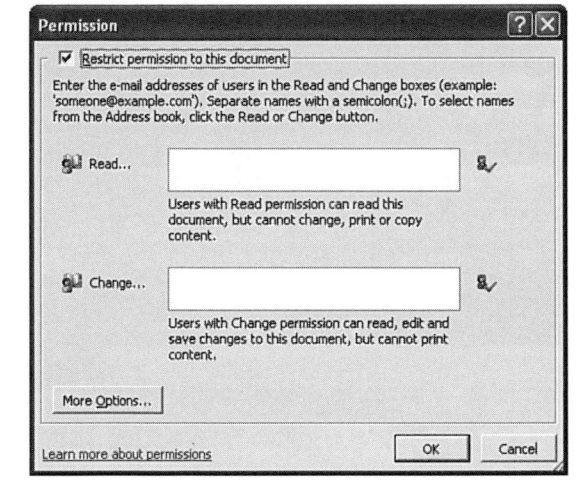

To restrict one or more users to reading a document but not changing, printing, or copying its content, enter their email addresses in the Read box. You may also click Read and select their names from the Select Names dialog box, which displays the names in your default Address Book, as shown in Figure 33.6. (If you are running Outlook, the default Address Book is probably your Outlook contact list.)

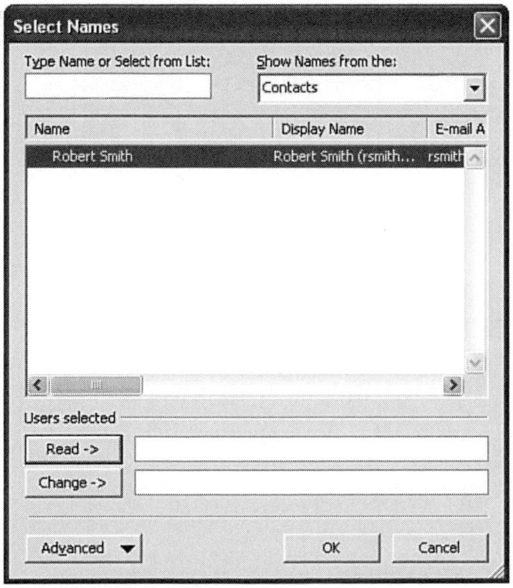

Figure 33.6
Selecting names from your address book.

33

CAUTION

Note that users who have permission to read a document but do not have permission to copy or print from it can *still* capture screens containing document text. Having done so, they can save those screens in a graphics program such as Microsoft Paint or Microsoft Document Imaging, and print from there.

Similarly, to permit users to read, edit, or save changes to the document—but prevent them from printing content—enter their names in the Change box. You may also click Change and select their names from the Select Names dialog box (refer to Figure 33.6).

PROVIDING ADDITIONAL PERMISSIONS AND RESTRICTIONS

In addition to the permissions you have already set, you can set additional permissions and Restrictions by clicking More Options. The Permission dialog box appears (see Figure 33.7).

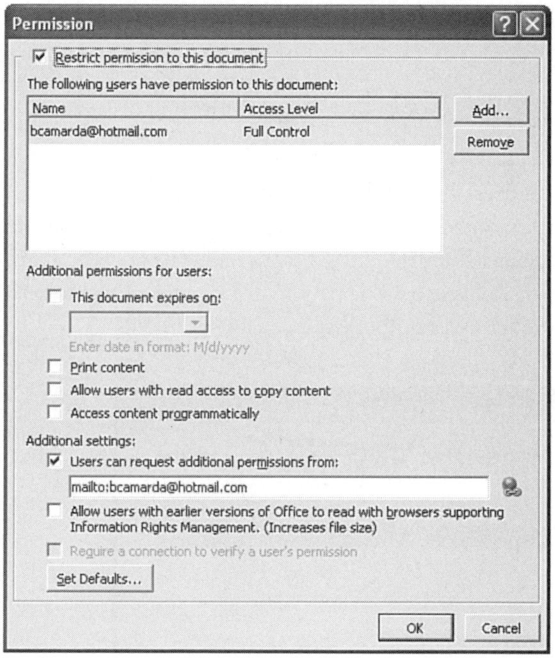

Figure 33.7
You can provide additional permissions through the Permission dialog box.

SETTING A DOCUMENT EXPIRATION DATE

You can set an expiration date for your document. After this date, your document will become inaccessible to everyone but you, even people you have given permissions to.

To set an expiration date, display the Permission dialog box shown in Figure 33.7. Check This Document Expires On. Then, enter a new date in the text box, or click the down arrow to choose a date from the built-in calendar. Then click OK.

GIVING USERS ADDITIONAL RIGHTS TO PRINT CONTENT

By default, if you give users Read rights, they cannot print your document. In certain cases, you may want to give them the right to print.

To do so, display the Permission dialog box shown in Figure 33.7. Check Print content; then click OK.

GIVING USERS ADDITIONAL RIGHTS TO COPY CONTENT

By default, if you give users Read rights, they cannot Copy your document's content into the Clipboard for use in other Windows programs. In certain cases, you may want to give them the right to do so. Display the Permission dialog box shown in Figure 33.7. Check Allow Users with Read Access to Copy Content; then click OK.

GIVING USERS ADDITIONAL RIGHTS TO ACCESS CONTENT VIA MACROS OR CUSTOM PROGRAMS

By default, if you give users Read rights, they cannot use custom VBA macros or programs that rely on information in your document. In certain cases, you may want to allow them to run such programs. Display the Permission dialog box shown in Figure 33.7. Check Access Content Programmatically; then click OK.

GIVING USERS A WAY TO REQUEST ADDITIONAL PERMISSIONS

Occasionally, one of your colleagues may legitimately need permissions you have not provided. You can give them a way to request those permissions. Check the Users Can Request Additional Permissions From check box, and enter mailto: followed by the email address where they can reach you.

By default, this check box is enabled, and the email address you are currently using for authentication purposes is entered in the text box under it. If you do not want to provide contact information for requesting permissions, clear the check box.

ALLOWING READ ACCESS TO USERS WITHOUT WORD 2003 OR OFFICE 2003

As mentioned earlier, Office 2003 Professional and the standalone Word 2003 are the first versions of Office and Word to support IRM. Therefore, users of older versions of Office or Word cannot use them to read IRM-protected documents. If a user attempts to open such a document, he or she will see the message shown in Figure 33.8.

Microsoft does provide an add-in that allows these users to read (but not edit) IRM-protected documents through the Internet Explorer Web browser. If you want to permit this, check the Allow Users with Earlier Versions of Office to Read with Browsers Supporting Information Rights Management check box.

SETTING DEFAULTS FOR DOCUMENTS WITH PERMISSIONS

After you've established a complicated set of permissions, you may want them to serve as the defaults for all Word documents, Excel workbooks, and PowerPoint presentations for which you assign permissions. To do so, establish all your permissions settings through both

33

Permission dialog boxes (Figure 33.5 and Figure 33.7). Then, click the Set Defaults button, and click OK.

Figure 33.8
The message that appears when a user attempts to open a document with permissions in an older version of Word.

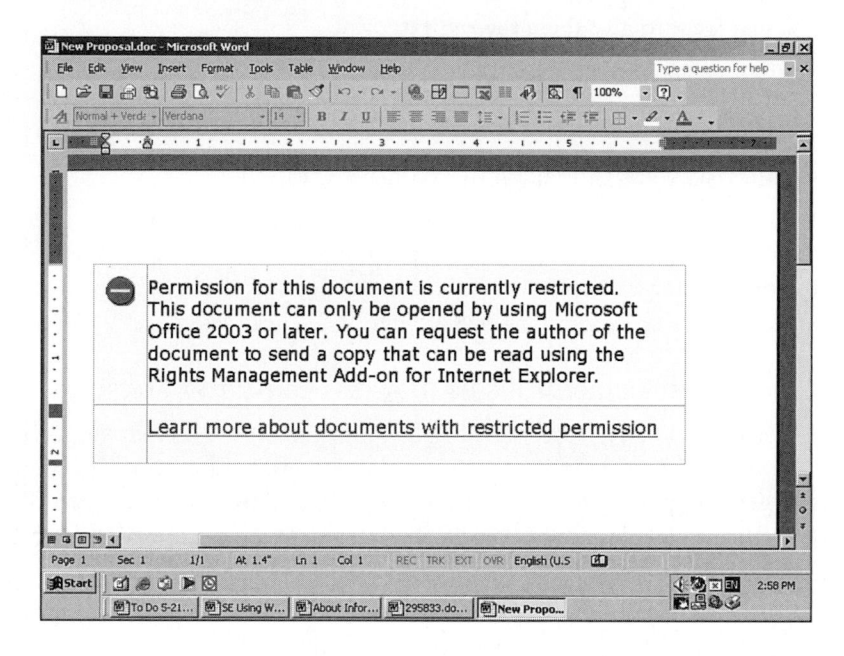

After you do so, when you click the Permission button on the Standard toolbar, your new settings will appear in the Permission dialog box. You can then adjust them as necessary.

WORKING WITH A DOCUMENT CONTAINING PERMISSIONS

When you open a document containing permissions, the permissions appear in the Shared Workspace task pane (see Figure 33.9). If you own the document, you can change permissions by clicking Change Permission and working in the Permission dialog box (refer to Figure 33.5).

If you have been sent material that requires you to authenticate using an account different from the one you are currently working with, click Change User. The Select User dialog box appears (see Figure 33.10). Select a different user account.

If only one account is available, click Add to select or establish another account. Then return to this dialog box, and select the appropriate account. When you're finished, click OK.

USING DIGITAL SIGNATURES

A *digital signature* is a unique piece of encrypted code associated with a specific individual. Individuals can attach this code to their documents, thereby verifying that they have in fact created the documents and that the documents have not been tampered with.

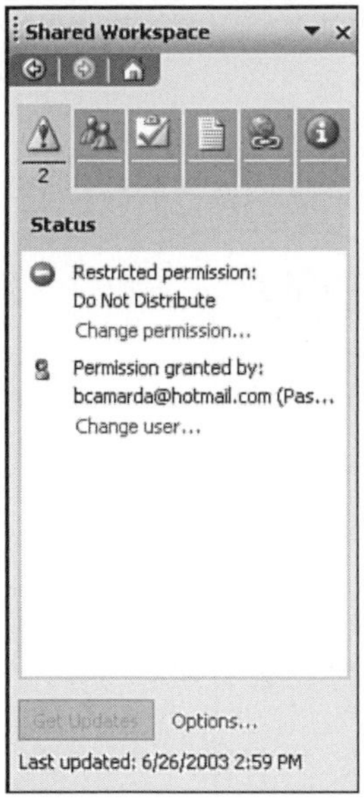

Figure 33.9
You can view your existing Permissions in the Shared Workspace task pane.

Figure 33.10
Changing the user account you use to access a document that has been protected by permissions.

Digital signatures are issued by commercial certification authorities, notably Verisign, Inc., and Thawte; some companies also maintain their own in-house digital certificate providers. Digital signatures are now legally binding in the United States in the same ways traditional handwritten signatures have been; in 1999, the European Union also agreed to phase in legal support for digital signatures. Word 2003 allows you to digitally sign any document.

NOTE

> If you want to experiment with digital certificates and signatures at no cost, you can create your own using Microsoft's free Selfcert.exe tool. Of course, nobody vouches for digital certificates you create yourself, and you cannot count on trusting digital certificates others create with Selfcert.exe.
>
> This tool is typically found in C:\Program Files\Microsoft Office\Office 11. If it is not present, you can install it by running a maintenance setup. (It appears under Office Shared Features, as Digital Signature for VBA Projects.)

After you have purchased or created your own digital certificate and installed it, you can add a digital signature to a document like this:

1. Choose Tools, Options, Security.

2. Click Digital Signature. The Digital Signature dialog box opens (see Figure 33.11).

Figure 33.11
The Digital Signature dialog box.

3. Click Add to display the digital certificates installed on your computer (see Figure 33.12).

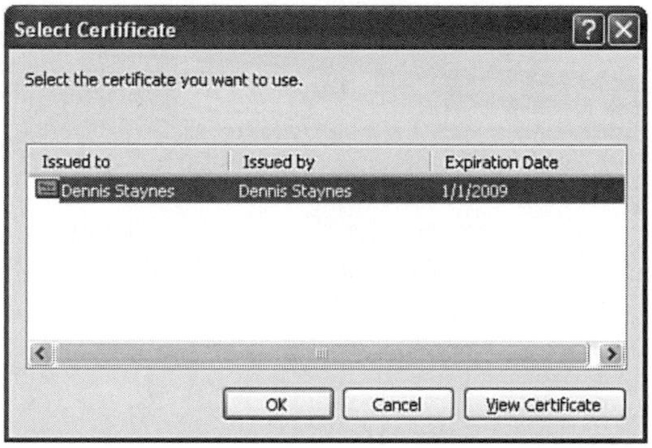

Figure 33.12
The Select Certificate dialog box.

4. Select the digital certificate you want to use.

5. If you want to view information about a certificate, click View Certificate (see Figure 33.13). Note that the certificate shown here is self-signed and therefore not truly secure.

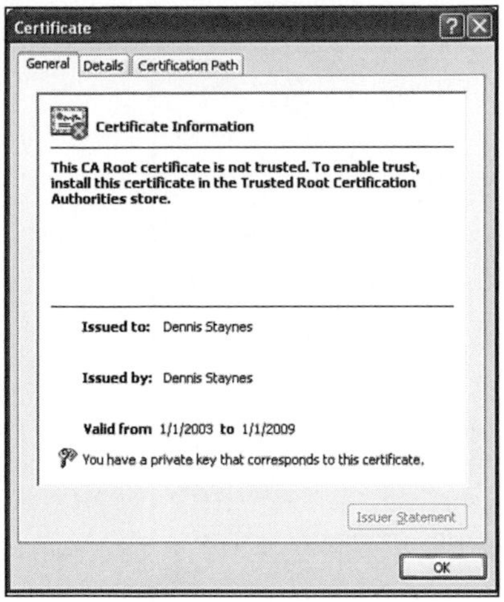

Figure 33.13
Viewing a digital certificate.

6. Click OK in the Certificate dialog box when you are finished viewing your certificate.

7. Click OK in the Digital Signature dialog box to select the certificate.

8. Click OK in the Security tab to apply your digital signature to the open document.

After you have signed a document, Word's title bar will include the word "(Signed)" whenever that document is open.

UNDERSTANDING SECURITY ISSUES ASSOCIATED WITH FAST SAVES AND OTHER SAVE FEATURES

Word 2003 provides several features designed to allow users to control how and where they save files. These features are controlled through the Save tab of the Options dialog box (see Figure 33.14).

Some of these features have security implications you should know about:

- Always Create Backup Copy stores a copy of the previous version of your document in the same folder as the original, using the file extension .wbk.

- Allow Fast Saves allows Word to save files more quickly, by storing all changes to a document at the end of a document. This means that text you have deleted from a document may still remain in the .doc file when that file is viewed from another program, such as a text editor.

- Make Local Copy of Files Stored on Network or Removable Drives allows users to automatically keep local copies of any files they create and store on the network.

- Save AutoRecover Info Every sets the elapsed time, in minutes, at which Word automatically saves unsaved information that might otherwise be lost in the event of a computer crash.

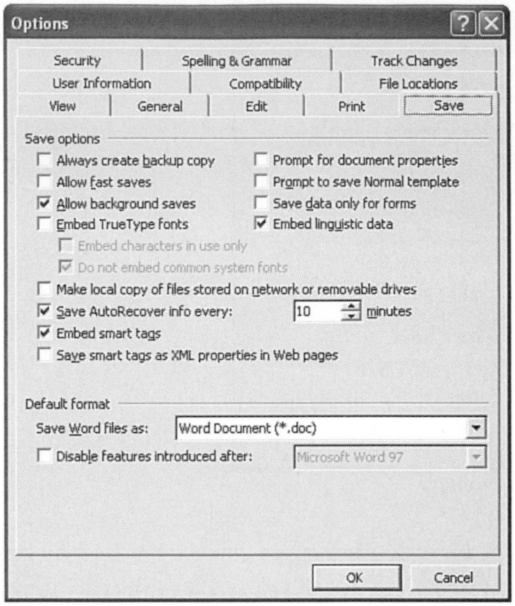

Figure 33.14
The Save tab of the
Options dialog box
includes Save features
that have security

If you are concerned about security, you may want to establish organization-wide policies concerning the use of these features.

CAUTION

> Be aware that regardless of how you use these Save options, older versions of your documents are likely to exist on your backup media. These should be carefully secured; many organizations also destroy old backup media after a certain period.

LIMITING THE CHANGES USERS CAN MAKE TO A DOCUMENT

You may want to allow a document to be edited but limit the types of changes that can be made—thereby making it easier to review or use the document later. With Word's Protect Document feature, you can limit users to any one of the following:

- **Tracked changes**—Users can only make revisions that are tracked by Word's Track Changes feature.

- **Comments**—Users can only add comments to a document, using Word's Comments tool.

- **Filling In Forms**—Users can only fill in the blanks in electronic forms but cannot change any other aspects of the form.

To protect a document for any of these elements, follow these steps:

1. Choose Tools, Protect Document (see Figure 33.15).

Figure 33.15
In the Protect Document task pane, you can protect a document for tracked changes, comments, or forms, and add a password, if you choose.

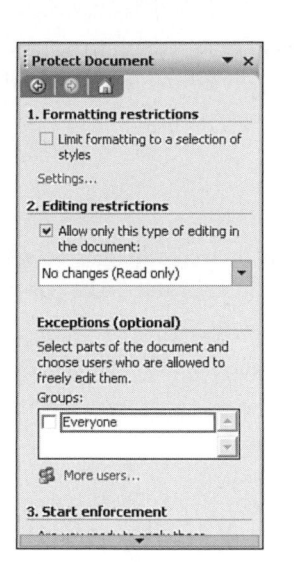

2. If you want to protect only part of the document, select the portion of the document you want to protect.

3. Check the Allow Only This Type of Editing in the Document check box. New options appear (refer to Figure 33.15).

4. Click the Allow Only This Type of Editing in the Document drop-down box, and choose Tracked Changes, Comments, or Filling In Forms.

5. If you want to identify specific users who will be exempt from your editing restrictions, click More Users; then enter the users' names by email address or Microsoft Windows user account:

   - If you intend to use Word 2003's strongest available protection (Prevent Intentional or Malicious Changes), use email addresses.

   - If you intend to use weaker password protection (Prevent Accidental Changes), use Microsoft Windows user accounts.

6. Click OK.

7. To give another individual (or individuals) editing rights to a different block of text, select the text, and repeat steps 2–4.

8. In the Protect Document task pane, click Yes, Start Enforcing Protection. (You may have to scroll down in the task pane to see this option.)

9. The Start Enforcing Protection dialog box opens. Choose the form of document protection you want: Password or User Authentication:

   - If you specify Password protection, the document is not encrypted, which means that it may be at least partly readable by a text editor. It also means that users with the correct password can remove the password protection entirely.

- If you specify User Authentication, Word encrypts the document and relies on your Windows Server's authentication services to ensure that the reader is who he or she claims to be. The document is encrypted, though authenticated users may remove the encryption.

10. Click OK. The protection is applied.

If you protect a document, any user can make the limited edits you've allowed without having the password. If you've specified a password, the user needs the password to make any other edits.

To remove protection from a document for additional editing, choose Tools, Unprotect Document, enter the password, and click OK. If no password was specified, choosing Tools, Unprotect Document automatically unprotects the document.

PREVENTING AND CONTROLLING WORD VIRUSES

Macro viruses have become an unfortunate fact of life for millions of Word users. Whether you are responsible for Word running on only your computer, or for an entire workgroup or organization, you need to be aware of them, and you need to take precautions to minimize the risk of becoming infected.

Macro viruses are viruses written in a Word macro language—originally WordBasic, but now Visual Basic for Applications. Like other computer viruses, they have the capability to reproduce themselves and spread to other computers that share files. And, like other computer viruses, some macro viruses are merely annoying, whereas others can cause serious data loss. Because Visual Basic for Applications can take advantage of virtually all of Word's capabilities, including the capability to delete files, macro viruses can use these features as well.

Macro viruses take advantage of the remarkable flexibility provided by Word's architecture and macro languages. The classic macro virus, Concept, established a pattern followed by most macro viruses since. When you open a file infected with Concept, the macro virus copies itself into the Normal.dot template, and from there copies itself into new files.

To prevent your computer from becoming infected, start with the same common-sense precautions that smart computer users have always known: Open only those documents that come from sources you trust. In the age of the Internet, this is more of a challenge than ever—and more important than ever. Beyond using caution, you should take two steps to prevent virus infections:

- First, use Word's built-in features, which deliver some protection against viruses but are not foolproof.
- Layer on additional protection by using third-party virus protection software—and keeping it updated to keep pace with new viruses.

Understanding How Word Uses Trusted Publishers

Microsoft's approach to providing macro virus security focuses not on identifying viruses placed in macros but rather on providing tools for ensuring that users run macros from only those publishers that can be trusted. As already discussed, Word and Office 2003 support digital certificates, which are the electronic equivalent of ID cards for documents and templates that contain macros.

When a user opens a document or template that contains a digital certificate, Word responds differently depending on the security level set for it. Setting security levels in Word 2003 is covered in the following section.

CAUTION

It's important to note that, in theory, a virus author may obtain a digital certificate, or a legitimate macro author might inadvertently embed a virus in a file before applying a digital certificate to the file. However, using digital certificates and trusted publishers does reduce the risks of virus infections substantially.

Setting Security Levels for Word 2003

To specify a security level in Word 2003, chose Tools, Macro, Security. The Security dialog box opens, displaying the Security Level tab (see Figure 33.16).

Figure 33.16
The Security Level tab enables you to specify how Word should react when it encounters a file containing macros.

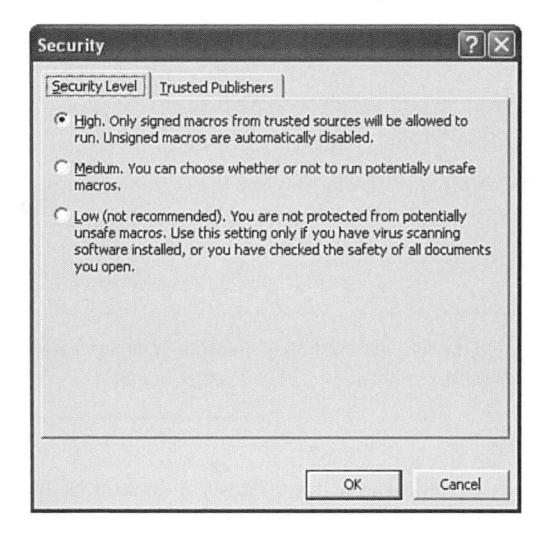

Here, you have three choices:

- **High**—This is Word 2003's default setting. Word automatically opens documents that contain macros only if these documents have digital certificates from publishers the user has already precertified as trusted.

If Word encounters a document with a digital certificate from another publisher, a dialog box appears, and the user is given the opportunity to add that publisher to the list of trusted publishers.

If a document contains a digital certificate but verification fails, the document is opened with all macros disabled, and the user is warned that it could have a virus.

In documents that contain macros without digital signatures, the document opens but the macros are disabled.

- **Medium**—Word behaves the same as it would if you set High Security, with one exception. If you attempt to open a document or template containing macros and that file contains no digital signature, you are given a choice whether to enable or disable macros, or not to open the document at all.

  Often, the macro is perfectly benign—Word can't tell the difference. However, you're likely to receive some documents from people who don't normally embed macros in their files intentionally. In this case, you can contact them to see whether the macro is legitimate. In the meantime, you can open the document without activating the macros—or simply not work with it. (Medium Security is the same as Word 97's Macro Virus Protection option.)

- **Low**—Word automatically opens all documents and templates with macros enabled.

> **NOTE**
>
> Regardless of the setting you choose, Word always opens files that do not contain macros.

REVIEWING WHICH PUBLISHERS WORD TRUSTS

To see which publishers Word already trusts, display the Trusted Publishers tab of the Security dialog box (see Figure 33.17). If you want to remove a publisher from the list of trusted publishers, click Remove.

> **NOTE**
>
> To add names to this list, you must open a document or template that is digitally signed and then respond Yes to the query about whether to trust it.

By default, Word 2003 trusts any add-ins or templates you have already installed manually. If you prefer to apply your security settings to these as well, clear the Trust All Installed Add-Ins and Templates check box.

> **TIP**
>
> If you're an administrator for multiple computers, you can specify trusted publishers that all of them will recognize, using the Internet Explorer 6 Administration Kit.

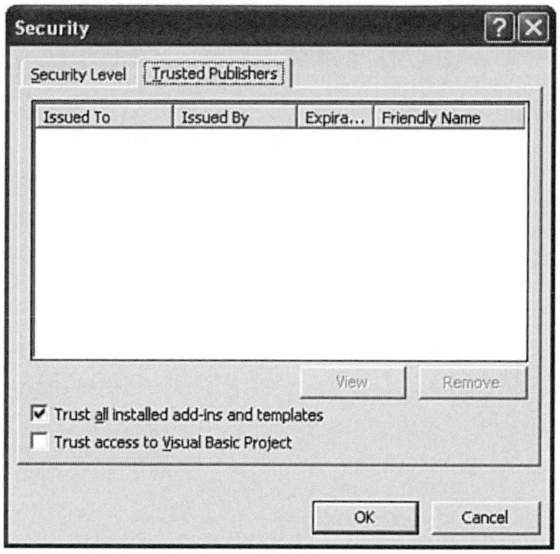

Figure 33.17
The Trusted Publishers tab shows which, if any, publishers of macros you have already stated that you trust.

HOW WORD 2003 AND WORD 97 HANDLE POSSIBLE VIRUSES IN WORDBASIC MACROS

If you are upgrading to Word 2003 from Word 6 or Word 95, you need to understand how Word handles the WordBasic macros that may be stored in your data files. When you open a Word 6 or Word 95 template that contains a macro, Word converts the macro to Visual Basic for Applications. If it recognizes the macro as a virus, it simply refuses to translate the virus to VBA. You aren't notified of this decision; it takes place automatically.

Most Word 6/95 viruses are caught this way. However, a few have slipped through. In several cases, a virus mutated by being translated from WordBasic to Visual Basic in a beta version of Word 97 that didn't yet include macro recognition features. Having mutated, it later became established in Word 97—making Word 2003 potentially susceptible as well.

THIRD-PARTY VIRUS PREVENTION

None of the Microsoft virus protection solutions is foolproof. You need a third-party antivirus program that is updated regularly to reflect the growing number of new viruses. The leading third-party antivirus software packages are

- Norton AntiVirus (www.symantec.com)
- Network Associates' McAfee VirusScan (www.mcafee.com)

Both companies now have packages designed specially for corporate use.

NOTE

In Word 2003 and Office 2003, Microsoft has provided an Anti-Virus Application Programming Interface (API) that enables antivirus software to check files for viruses whenever users open them.

CAUTION

> Although keeping your antivirus software up-to-date and avoiding opening files from untrusted publishers are the best precautions against virus infection, there are no certainties. New viruses are being written all the time, and each year fewer computers can be sufficiently isolated from the rest of the world.

BLOCKING PROGRAMMATIC ACCESS TO WORD AND OFFICE

In Office 2003, Microsoft provides an additional "brute force" solution for avoiding macro viruses: You can simply avoid using VBA at all. This is, in essence, equivalent to lobotomizing Word and Office: Features that require VBA—such as all of Word's wizards, many of its templates, and all of your custom commands—will simply no longer work. But if you have been suffering from ongoing virus infections and no other solution has been effective, you may want to consider this.

There are two ways to disable VBA:

- You can install Office without VBA (or run a maintenance install that removes VBA). Run Setup, choose Add or Remove Features, right-click on Visual Basic for Applications, choose Not Available, and click Update.

- You can centrally set system policies that disable access to VBA. Working with centralized system policies is beyond the scope of this book, but the system policies you are looking for can be found in Default Computer\Microsoft Office 2003\Security Settings. You can either disable VBA for all Office applications or set high security levels for Word and other individual Office applications. If you choose, you can instead disable VBA for a specific user, through Default User\Microsoft Office 2003\Security Settings\Disable VBA for ALL Office Applications.

OTHER METHODS FOR SECURING DOCUMENTS

There are other options for securing Word documents, which depend on the features of the underlying operating system you are running. For example:

- Files stored on Windows 2000 systems can be encrypted using Windows 2000's Encrypted File System (EFS).

- Files stored on any Windows system can be hidden by setting their file attributes. In Windows 2000 or Windows XP, follow these steps:

    1. Open Windows Explorer.

    2. Select and right-click the file you want to hide. The shortcut menu appears.

    3. Choose Properties from the shortcut menu.

    4. In the General tab, check the Hidden box.

    5. Click OK.

If the file is still visible, this means you have changed your Windows Explorer folder options so that they display hidden files. To change them back, follow these steps:

1. Choose Tools, Folder Options.
2. Click the View tab.
3. In the Advanced Settings scroll box, click the Do Not Show Hidden Files and Folders button.
4. Click OK.

When a file is hidden in Windows Explorer, it is also hidden in Word's Open dialog box. However, you can open it by typing its filename in the Open dialog box.

To make Windows (and Word) show all your files, go into Windows Explorer and choose Show All Files in the View tab of the Folder Options dialog box.

WINDOWS 2000/XP FILE-LEVEL SECURITY

If you maintain files on a network served by a Windows XP, Windows 2000 Server, or Windows 2000 Professional system that uses the NTFS file system, you have exceptional control over access to both folders and files.

Folder-level permissions include Full Control, Modify, Read and Execute, List Folder Contents, Read, and Write. Except for List Folder Contents, you can also set permissions for individual files stored on the NTFS partition.

In practice, this means that you can set general security for individual folders but tighten security beyond that for specific, sensitive files within those folders. (However, you cannot set tight security for a folder and loosen it for an individual file.)

File and Folder Level security are set from outside Word, using each file's and folder's Properties dialog box. (To control settings, right-click on the file or folder in Windows Explorer, choose Properties, and click the Security tab.)

NOTE

> Some security changes can be made only by individuals with administrator privileges.

TROUBLESHOOTING

WHAT TO DO IF YOU CAN'T ADD A NEW TRUSTED PUBLISHER

As you learned earlier in this chapter, Word allows you to add new trusted publishers: publishers whose digital certificates will certify that their macros can always be trusted. If you attempt to add a digital certificate and Word prohibits you from doing so, there are several possible causes:

- The certificate may have been created by the user himself or herself, using the Selfcert.exe tool provided with Office 2003. In this case, no third party is certifying that the user is authentic, and accordingly, Word does not acknowledge the certificate as authentic, except on the computer that created it.

- As a security measure, your system administrator may have prohibited you from adding trusted publishers, using system policies.

- You may have set security on your computer to Low. Security must be set to Medium or High for Word to add a trusted publisher.

What to Do If You Are Running Antivirus Software and Still Encounter an Infection

Antivirus software must be updated regularly to remain effective—ideally, once a week, but at minimum, once every two weeks. Use your software's automatic update feature to ensure that you have the most recent antivirus signatures. Also ensure that your antivirus software is configured to check against virus infection aggressively; in particular, ensure that it is configured to check attachments that arrive via email.

What to Do If Entering a Password Doesn't Work

Remember that Word passwords are case-sensitive: passtext is not the same as Passtext. Also, double-check to make sure that your Caps Lock key has not been inadvertently turned on, causing you to use the incorrect case.

What to Do If Text You Thought You Deleted Remains in a Word File

If Fast Saves are turned on, Word may not immediately remove text from a file after you delete it. Although the text is not visible while you are editing it in Word, it may be visible if viewed in a text editor such as Notepad. To make sure that Word immediately removes edits from your files, choose Tools, Options, Save; clear the Allow Fast Saves check box; and click OK.

Managing Word More Effectively

THE WORD 2003 FILE FORMAT

The Word 2003 file format has not changed substantially since Word 97, so you can freely exchange files between Word versions 97, 2000, 2002, and 2003, as well as Word 98 and higher for the Macintosh. This makes it easy and convenient to exchange files with people who use older Word versions. No special save procedure is required. Any 2003 features that the earlier version of Word might not support are simply ignored when the file is opened in the older software.

SAVING WORD FILES IN OTHER FILE FORMATS

Word's backward compatibility extends back only as far as Word 97 with its default file format. If you need to exchange files with colleagues who use Microsoft Word 95 (Word 6.0), you'll need to take special measures to ensure compatibility.

You can tackle such a problem from either side:

- You can give Word 6/95 users a filter that enables them to open Word 97 and higher files. The files can be read intact; however, if the user edits and resaves the files with the same name and location, any formatting supported only in Word 97 and higher is lost. This converter, MSWRD832.CNV, can be downloaded through Microsoft's Office Web site, at http://officeupdate.microsoft.com.

- You can specify Word 97-2003 & 6.0/95 - RTF as the file format when saving (from the Save as Type drop-down list in the Save As dialog box).

What a mouthful that file format is, huh! Let's break it down. Word 97-2003 is a generic name for the normal Word file format in use in Word versions 97 and higher. Word 6.0/95 was the version of Word that preceded Word 97. (It actually went by two names: Word 6.0 and Word 95.) RTF stands for Rich Text Format, a generic format for exchanging data between word processing applications. So this format with a huge name produces files that can be opened in virtually any version of Word as well as many non-Word applications such as WordPerfect and WordPad.

How does Word do it? Two words: *huge files*. Word saves the document with all the encoding needed for all the different versions, and fixes it so that whatever version opens the file will read the encoding appropriate to itself and ignore the rest.

Because this all-purpose Word 97-2003 & 6.0/95 – RTF format results in larger data files than regular Word format, you probably will not want to use it all the time unless you are constantly needing to exchange files with people who don't use Word 97 or higher.

CAUTION

> If you need to password-protect documents—or use protection for tracked changes, comments, or forms—these documents lose their protection when saved back to Word 97-2003 & 6.0/95 - RTF format (even though Word 6.0/95 does have its own password-protection feature).

34

SETTING A DEFAULT FILE FORMAT

If not everyone in your organization has upgraded to Word 97 or higher, you will not be able to share Word documents in the default Word 2003 format with some people.

If that's your situation, you can set up Word to save by default in the Word 97-2003 & 6.0/95 - RTF format. That's not the only format available, of course; you could specify HTML as your standard format, or a foreign-language Word format, or an older WordPerfect format such as WordPerfect 5.1 for DOS.

To specify a format other than Word Document (Word 97 and higher) as your default save format, choose Tools, Options and select the Save tab (see Figure 34.1). Choose the format you want to use from the Save Word Files As drop-down box and click OK.

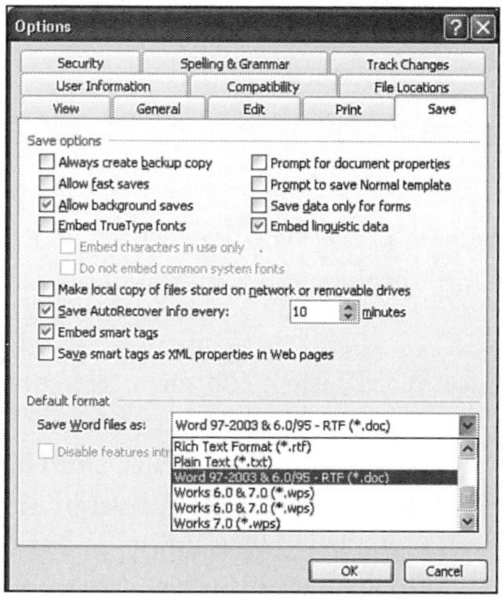

Figure 34.1
Choosing a different format as your default save format.

You can keep the file size a bit smaller by disposing of certain features in the saved file that were introduced before the bulk of your fellow file-exchangers' versions came out. For example, if almost everyone in your office still uses Word 2000, you could mark the Disable Features Introduced After check box and choose Word 2000 from its list.

NOTE

> The default format you specify affects only new files; when you resave an existing file, it is saved in its existing format.

CONVERTING FROM WORDPERFECT

If you are converting from WordPerfect—especially WordPerfect 5.1 for DOS, the word processing software that dominated the market a decade or so ago—Word 2003 comes with several features designed to make the transition easier. To access these features, choose

34

Help, WordPerfect Help. The Help for WordPerfect Users dialog box opens (see Figure 34.2). If Help for WordPerfect is not installed, you may be prompted to insert your Office 2003 CD.

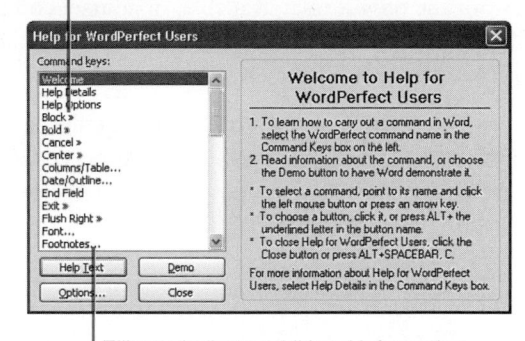

┌Double arrows indicate demonstrations

Figure 34.2
With the Help for WordPerfect Users dialog box open, people making the transition from WordPerfect can get detailed explanations of how Word features compare with WordPerfect for DOS.

└Ellipses indicate additional information

The Command Keys scroll box includes a list of WordPerfect for DOS command keys. When you select a command key, Word displays a description of how to accomplish the same task in Word 2003.

Where Word offers additional help for WordPerfect command key submenus, the command key is followed by an ellipsis. You can view the additional information (for all commands except the first three, which are Welcome, Help Details, and Help Options) by clicking Help Text. After you've drilled down to the bottom level of information, you can click Help Text again, and Word displays the help information on top of your editing window so that you can view step-by-step instructions at the same time you perform the task.

If Word has a demo available, and you want to watch the task performed, click Demo (or Demo Now). Word displays your current document and performs the action at your current insertion point. In some cases (see Figure 34.3), Word opens a dialog box and shows you what to do next.

34

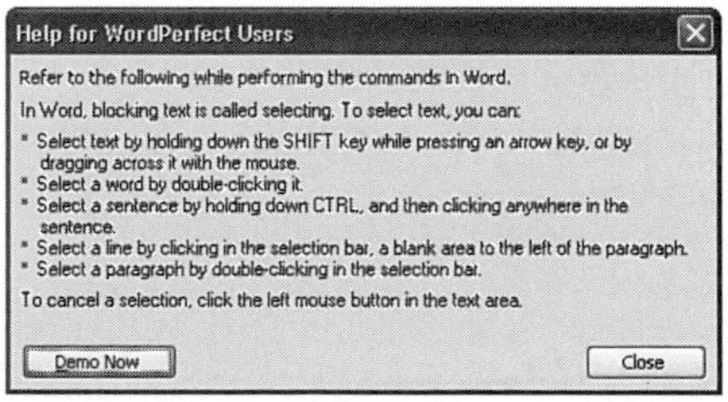

Figure 34.3
Word opens the appropriate dialog box and tells you exactly how to select text.

> **TIP**
>
> If WordPerfect Help performs an action you didn't intend, click the Undo button.

Setting WordPerfect Help Options

Word gives you options about how to use WordPerfect Help, based on how far along you and your users have come in transitioning from WordPerfect and DOS. To use these options, choose Help, WordPerfect Help and choose Options. The Help Options dialog box appears (see Figure 34.4).

Figure 34.4
You can control exactly how WordPerfect Help behaves.

Word displays or demonstrates instructions whenever you press a WordPerfect for DOS key combination. If you check the Navigation Keys for WordPerfect Users check box, Word changes the way its Page Up, Page Down, Home, End, and Esc keys behave to match the way they work in WordPerfect for DOS.

Depending on the speed of your computer, you may find that Word's feature demonstrations run too quickly—or too slowly. You can change their speed by choosing Fast, Medium, or Slow from the Demo Speed drop-down box.

NOTE

> If you or your users miss WordPerfect's Reveal Codes feature, remember that even though Word doesn't have equivalent formatting codes, you can get detailed information about the formatting associated with any text. Use Word 2003's Reveal Formatting feature.
>
> Click on or select the text you're interested in, and choose Format, Reveal Formatting. Word displays detailed formatting information in the task pane at the right.

→ For more information about Reveal Formatting, **see** Chapter 4, "Quick and Effective Formatting Techniques," **p. 107**.

Displaying Word 2003 Files on Computers Without Any Version of Word

Some of your computers may not have any version of Word installed. For example, individuals primarily responsible for data processing may not use Word. Investing in Word or

Office software licenses for their workstations would be expensive and unnecessary, and might require hardware upgrades.

NOTE

> Microsoft Works Suite comes with Microsoft Word as its word processor, so even if a user does not have the full Microsoft office, he or she might have Word.

As time passes, you may discover that these people can benefit from access to existing Word documents. For example, your corporate intranet may include manuals or sales guides written in Word. Giving customer-service representatives access to these resources may help them solve customer problems more effectively. For situations such as this, you have these options:

- Users can open Word 2003 documents in WordPad, the free word processing application that comes with Microsoft Windows. Some of the features of the Word document will not be visible, and you cannot save in Word format from WordPad. (However, you can save in Rich Text Format, which all versions of Word can open.)

- You can use Word 2003 to publish the data in HTML format, which can be read by anyone using a recent Web browser. (For more information on using HTML in Word 2003, see Chapter 24, "Using Word to Develop Web Content.")

- You can provide the Microsoft Word Viewer, a freeware application that can be copied and distributed. This small program, available at `http://office.microsoft.com/downloads/2000/wd97vwr32.aspx`, enables any Windows user to view and print any Word document. It supports many, though not all, Word 2003 features. For example, it supports Print Layout view, Outline view, Web Layout view, Document Map, zooming, headers, footers, footnotes, comments, and hyperlinks—but not toolbars.

You can't edit text in Word Viewer. However, you can copy the text into other applications through the Windows Clipboard.

You can think of Word Viewer as Microsoft's answer to Adobe Acrobat Reader. It has one major advantage compared with Acrobat Reader: Anyone who owns Word can author documents that can be read with Word Viewer.

It also has a major disadvantage, which limits its value as an Internet solution for distributing Word documents: It works only in Windows environments (not Macintosh or Unix).

TIP

> You can use Word Viewer as a helper application for viewing Word documents downloaded from the Internet. Word Viewer can also make it a little easier to work with customer and vendor organizations that have standardized on a different word processing platform.

34

CAUTION

> Although Word Viewer can coexist with Word on the same computer, it works best on computers on which Word isn't installed. Even though the Word Viewer Setup program is designed to ask whether Word or Word Viewer should be the default for opening Word files, you may sometimes find that the wrong application loads if they are both installed.

BATCH FILE CONVERSIONS

If you are upgrading your entire organization to Word 2003 at the same time, you may find it convenient to convert your collection of Word 6.0/95 files to Word 2003 format all at the same time. However, that's not the only time you may want to convert many files at once. For example:

- You might be migrating from WordPerfect and want to convert your WordPerfect files for use in Word 2003.

- You might be migrating from Macintosh to Windows and want to convert older Macintosh Word files for use in Word 2003.

- You might be upgrading a set of documents created in an earlier version of Word.

Word 2003 provides a batch conversion utility, the Conversion Wizard, for purposes such as these. With the Conversion Wizard, you can create Word 2003 documents from files in the following formats:

> Microsoft Works 6.0 & 7.0
>
> Outlook Address Book
>
> Personal Address Book (Outlook Express)
>
> Rich Text Format (RTF)
>
> Schedule+ Contacts
>
> Text
>
> Windows Write
>
> HTML
>
> Encoded Text
>
> Word 6.0/95 for Windows & Macintosh
>
> WordPerfect 5.x
>
> WordPerfect 6.x
>
> XML

In addition, Word can attempt to extract the valid text from any file, using the Recover Text from Any File option.

Similarly, you can convert documents from Word 2003 to the following formats:

34

MS-DOS Text or MS-DOS Text with Line Breaks

Rich Text Format (RTF)

Text or Text with Line Breaks

Word 97-2003 & 6.0/95 - RTF

Template

HTML

Encoded Text

Works 6.0 and 7.0

XML

The Conversion Wizard can convert all files in a specific folder. Before you use it, either place all the files you want to convert in the same folder or, if you want to convert files in their current folders, list the folders you want to convert and run the Conversion Wizard separately in each folder.

CAUTION

> Test your file conversions on a few sample documents before performing them en masse and putting the resulting documents into production.

To run the Conversion Wizard, choose File, New; click On My Computer on the New Document task pane; select Batch Conversion Wizard from the Other Documents tab; and click OK.

After you've displayed the Conversion Wizard, follow these steps:

1. Click Next. The From/To screen appears (see Figure 34.5).

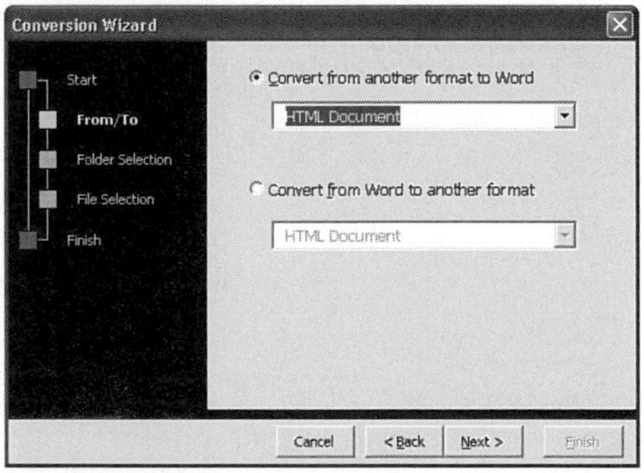

Figure 34.5
On the From/To screen of the Conversion Wizard, you specify to (or from) which format you want to convert your file.

2. If you want to convert files stored in another format into Word 2003 files, click Convert from Another Format to Word; then choose the format from the highlighted drop-down box. If you want to convert Word 2003 files into another format, click

Convert from Word to Another Format. A drop-down box becomes active under this button. From this drop-down box, select the format you want.

3. Click Next to move to the next window.

4. From the Folder Selection window (see Figure 34.6), click Browse (next to Source Folder) to specify the folder where your existing files are.

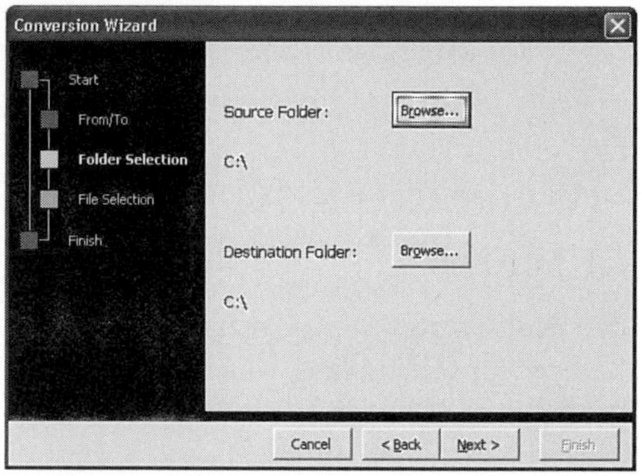

Figure 34.6
From the Folder Selection dialog box, you can choose both a source and a destination folder.

5. The Browse for Folder dialog box appears. Select a folder and click OK.

6. Click the Browse button located next to Destination Folder.

7. In the Browse to Folder dialog box, select a destination folder and click OK.

8. Click Next to display the File Selection window. From here, you can select the specific files you want to convert.

> **NOTE**
>
> If you choose the same folder for input and output, and you've chosen a conversion in which the file extension does not change—such as converting Word 6.0/95 to Word 2003 files—the old files are overwritten in the new format. Be careful to make sure that this is what you want to happen before you run the conversion.

9. To convert all the files in the folder you selected, click Select All. All the files now appear in the To Convert box.

> **TIP**
>
> If no files appear in the Available box, click the arrow next to the Type drop-down box to choose a different file extension.

10. To prevent a file from being converted, double-click it in the To Convert box.

11. When you finish selecting files, click Next.

34

12. Click Finish to perform the file conversions. A progress bar appears onscreen showing how far along in the conversion process the Conversion Wizard is. When the process finishes, the Conversion Wizard offers you an opportunity to run another conversion. If you click Yes, the wizard runs again.

NOTE

> Don't assume that the entire process will run unattended; check in every few minutes. The conversion process may occasionally stop to report an error message or, in some cases, to attempt to load a Web page included in a file being converted.

USING DOCUMENT PROPERTIES TO SIMPLIFY DOCUMENT MANAGEMENT

In Chapter 3, "Essential Document Creation and Management Techniques," you learned about Word's powerful capabilities for finding files, which are accessible by choosing Tools, Find from within the Open dialog box. You may recall that one of the ways Word can search for files is by document property. This section takes a closer look at document properties and shows you how to use them to your advantage—whether you're responsible for one desktop or many.

To work with document properties, choose File, Properties. The Properties dialog box opens (see Figure 34.7).

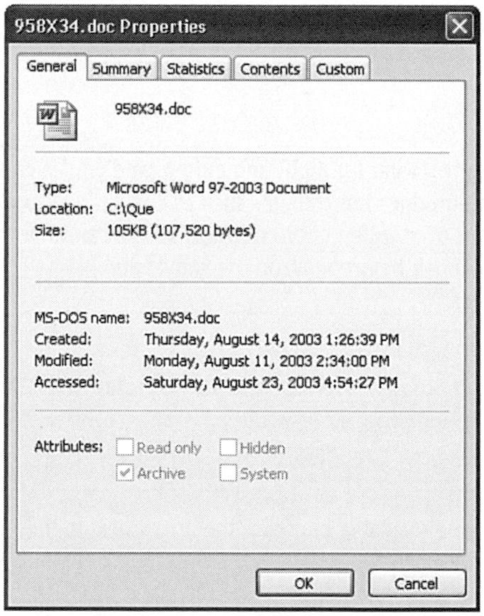

Figure 34.7
You can review a document's properties (and edit many of them) by displaying the Properties dialog box.

This dialog box contains five tabs:

- **General**—This tab includes information Word automatically stores about every document, including when it was created, how large it is, and where it is stored.

- **Summary**—This tab includes the document's title, comments, author, keywords, and other important document information.

- **Statistics**—This tab includes information Word compiles about the size and contents of a document, as well as how long it has been open and how many times it has been saved.

- **Contents**—This tab includes major parts of a document file.

- **Custom**—Options available on this tab enable you to create your own document properties or choose from 27 optional document properties Word can provide.

GENERAL INFORMATION STORED IN THE PROPERTIES DIALOG BOX

Display the General tab of the Properties dialog box when you want to know basic information about your Word document, including its current size and its MS-DOS "short" (8.3) filename, as well as when the file was created, last modified, and last accessed.

Most of the items in the General tab are self-evident, but a few are worth calling to your attention:

- **Type**—Ordinarily, this is a Microsoft Word 97-2003 document.

- **Location**—This displays the complete file path, whether on a local or networked computer.

- **Size**—This is the file's size in bytes, the amount of space it occupies on disk.

- **MS-DOS Name**—This is the old-fashioned 8.3 short filename stored with every file in Windows 98 and Windows NT—the name that stays with your file even if you send it to a Windows 3.x system or an older Macintosh or Linux/Unix system that doesn't support long filenames.

- **Modified**—This tells you when a file was last saved so that you can tell whether specific edits are likely to be reflected.

No general information is stored with a file until you save it for the first time.

WORKING WITH SUMMARY INFORMATION

Chances are that the Properties tab you'll use most is the Summary tab (see Figure 34.8). Here, you insert editable information about your file—including the categories by which you're most likely to search for it in Word's Tools, Find dialog box, such as Author, Comments, or Keywords.

If you've set up Word properly, much of this information can be entered for you automatically. Word enters a title based on the first line of text in your document—commonly a document's title. Word enters the Author based on the name stored in the User Information tab of the Tools, Options dialog box. If you ever run AutoSummarize, Word automatically copies the list of keywords it generates into the Keywords box. Finally, you can include Manager, Company, Category, and other information along with templates so that they are automatically included in every document built with those templates.

34

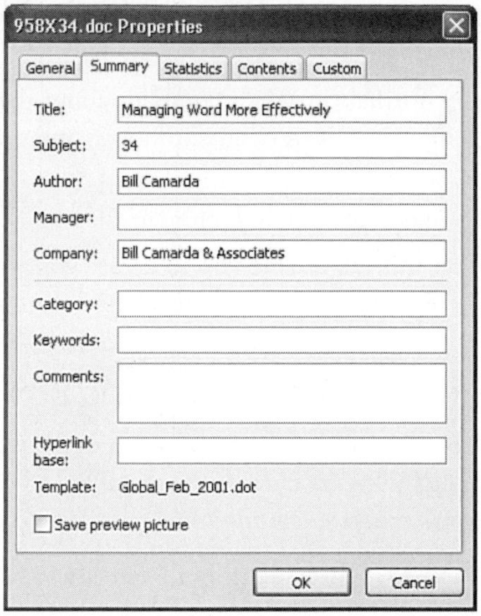

Figure 34.8
For most people, the Summary tab is the workhorse of the Properties dialog box.

958X34.doc Properties	✕

General | Summary | Statistics | Contents | Custom

Title: Managing Word More Effectively

Subject: 34

Author: Bill Camarda

Manager:

Company: Bill Camarda & Associates

Category:

Keywords:

Comments:

Hyperlink base:

Template: Global_Feb_2001.dot

☐ Save preview picture

[OK] [Cancel]

One more item on this tab is worth pointing out: Save Preview Picture. If you check this box, Word displays a thumbnail of the first page in the Preview pane of the File, Open dialog box, reflecting formatting. If you do not check the box, you can scroll through the text of the entire document in the Open dialog box's Preview pane.

TIP

> If nothing else, you might add your company name to the Summary tab of the Properties dialog box in Normal.dot. This provides an added measure of security by showing who owns the computer on which your documents were created. It's easy to remove this information—but many Word users don't even realize it's there.

NOTE

> The name specified in the Author box doesn't change if you forward the file to a colleague for editing on his or her computer. However, the Last Saved By name in the Statistics tab does change when your colleague saves the file.

34

If you are responsible for the documents created by an entire workgroup or organization, consider requiring (or at least actively encouraging) users to include Summary information along with their document. One way to do this is to have Word display the Summary tab of the Properties dialog box whenever a user saves a file for the first time. To do this, choose Tools, Options and select the Save tab. Check the Prompt for Document Properties check box and click OK.

Some Word users do not want to store this information with their documents, for privacy and security reasons. To remove it, along with other document information that can be traced to a specific user or computer, follow these steps:

Choose Tools, Options, Security; then check the Remove Personal Information from File Properties on Save check box and click OK.

→ For more information on this and other Word 2003 file security and privacy options, **see** Chapter 33, "Word Document Privacy and Security Options," **p. 1087**.

UNDERSTANDING AND USING DOCUMENT STATISTICS

The Statistics tab (see Figure 34.9) compiles several useful statistics about your document. You can see when your document was created, modified, and accessed—the same information you already saw in the General tab. Here, however, you can also see when your document was last printed—and who saved it last, even if it was saved by someone other than the author.

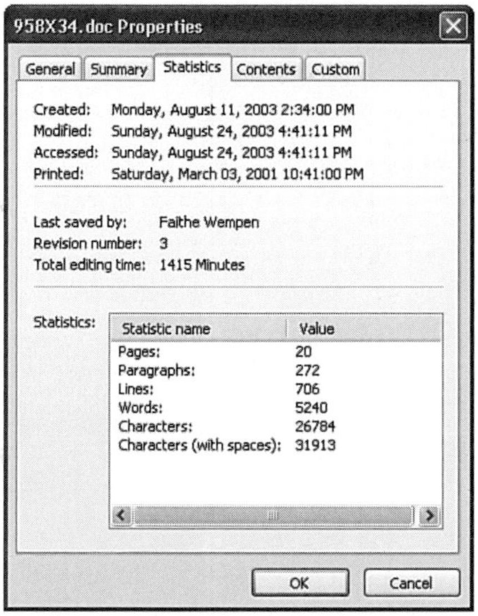

Figure 34.9
The Statistics tab gives you a quick look at the most important statistics associated with your document.

Revision Number tells you how many times you've saved the file. Because you may save a file every few minutes, it's easy to generate hundreds of revisions. If you want a true draft number, consider writing a Visual Basic macro that requests the current draft number and stores it in another Properties box, such as Comments. You can name the macro AutoClose so that it runs whenever you save a file associated with the template where the macro is stored.

The Statistics tab also reports Total Editing Time, which is actually the amount of time the document has been open. Of course, several other documents, or for that matter several different applications, may be open at the same time. Word doesn't care; it assumes that you're editing a document whenever it's open.

USING CONTENTS INFORMATION

As you saw earlier, if you check the Save Preview Picture check box in the Summary tab, the next time you look at the Properties dialog box, Word stores its headings in the Contents tab.

NOTE

> Unfortunately, several document elements you might reasonably expect to find here are not included. For example, Contents does not report on multiple document versions stored in the same file, macro modules stored with a file, or embedded graphics.

CREATING CUSTOM PROPERTIES

If the properties you've seen so far aren't enough, Word provides 27 more custom properties you can assign at will—or you can create your own. To work with custom properties, choose File, Properties and display the Custom tab (see Figure 34.10).

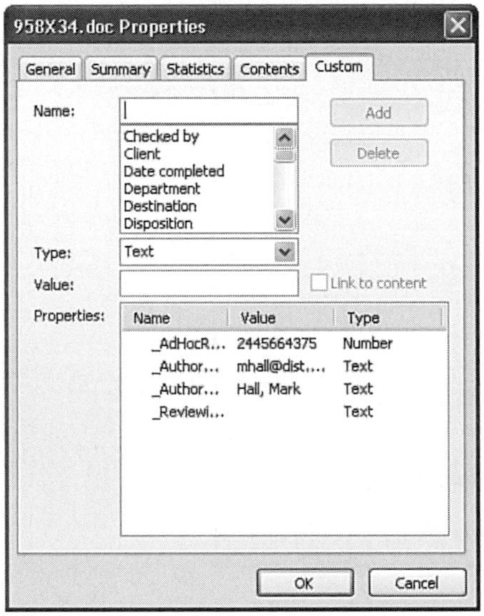

Figure 34.10
If you need a property that Word doesn't provide, you can add it in the Custom tab of the Properties dialog box.

Follow these steps to add a new category:

1. Choose a name for your custom property in the Name scroll box, or type a name of your own.

2. In the Type box, specify the kind of information you want your property to contain: text, a date, a number, or a Yes/No choice.

3. In the Value text box, enter the value with which you want your custom property to start. For example, if you've created a Date Completed property, you might enter the date 2/1/2003. The Value you insert must be in a format compatible with the Type you've just chosen.

4. When you're finished, click Add. The custom property, its type, and its value now appear in the Properties scroll box.

After the property has been created, you can modify it by selecting it in the Properties scroll box, entering a new Value or Type, and choosing Modify. Or you can delete it by selecting it and choosing Delete.

NOTE

> Because custom properties require a Value, you can't create an empty custom property. If you want to include a custom property in your document or template, insert a "dummy" value that users can later replace with a real one.

CREATING CUSTOM PROPERTIES THAT UPDATE THEMSELVES

You can create a custom property that knows how to update itself, based on changing information in your document.

Imagine, for example, that every division in your company sends you a monthly executive summary reporting new sales activity. Your reporting template includes a table; that table contains a cell listing the total value of all new customer sales made that month. You might want to search all those documents, quickly identifying the divisions where sales exceeded $10,000,000. However, you have dozens of divisions and you would rather not open each file individually to see the value stored in the table—you only want to know who has exceeded a certain threshold so that you can learn why.

To accomplish this task, you first create a bookmark associated with the text in your document that you want to attach to your property:

1. In your template, select the formula field that contains the calculation of total profits.
2. Choose Insert, Bookmark.
3. Type a bookmark name and click Add.

Next, create a custom property based on that bookmark:

1. Choose File, Properties.
2. Choose the Custom tab.
3. Check the Link to Content check box. (This box is grayed out unless your document contains at least one bookmark.) Notice that the Value box has turned into a drop-down box named Source.
4. In the Name text box, enter or select a name for your new custom property.
5. In the Source drop-down box, choose the bookmark to which you want to link your custom property.
6. Click Add. The new custom property appears in the Properties list. A Link icon appears next to it, indicating that this custom property is linked to a bookmark (see Figure 34.11).

34

Figure 34.11
You can create a custom property linked to bookmarked text in your document.

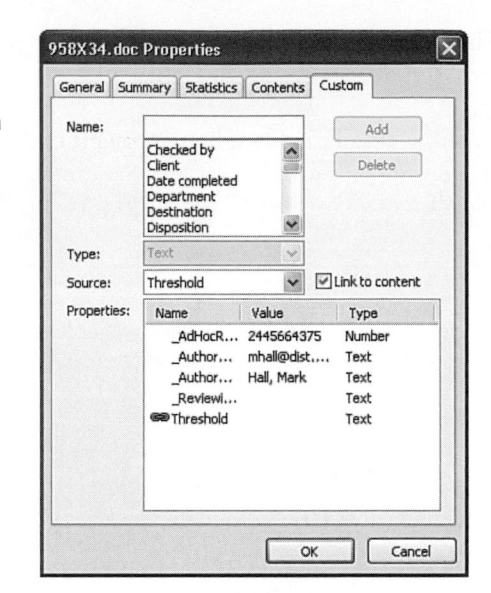

USING FIELDS TO DISPLAY PROPERTIES IN YOUR DOCUMENT

Many of the elements stored in the Properties dialog box can be placed in your document automatically, using fields. For example, you might want to create a cover sheet that prints with each of your documents. Table 34.1 lists fields that use information stored in the Properties dialog box. Of course, anytime you update your fields, changes in the corresponding Properties boxes are reflected in them.

TABLE 34.1 FIELDS THAT USE INFORMATION STORED IN THE PROPERTIES DIALOG BOX

Field	What It Displays	Notes
Author	Author data from Summary tab	
Comments	Comments data from Summary tab	
CreateDate	File creation date from General tab	
DocProperty	Information from any property you choose	Can also work with custom properties after you create them. Select the property in Insert, Field, Options.
EditTime	Editing time from Statistics tab	
FileName	Filename	\p switch adds full pathname.

Field	What It Displays	Notes
FileSize	File size	\k switch specifies kilobytes. \m switch specifies megabytes.
Info	Information from any summary	Select the property of your choice in Insert, Field, Options.
Keywords	Keywords data from Summary tab	
LastSavedBy	Last saved by data from Statistics tab	
NumChars	Number of characters in document	
NumPages	Number of pages in document	
NumWords	Number of words in document	
PrintDate	Print date from Statistics tab	
SaveDate	Last saved date from General tab	
Template	Template currently attached to document	\p switch adds full pathname of template.
Title	Title data from Summary tab	

→ For more information about working with fields, **see** Chapter 23, "Automating Your Documents with Field Codes," **p. 771**.

TROUBLESHOOTING

HOW TO SOLVE LINE- AND PAGE-BREAK PROBLEMS ASSOCIATED WITH FILE CONVERSIONS

Sometimes, line- and page-break problems are introduced after files are converted to Word 2003 format from other word processing programs and other platforms, such as the Macintosh. These may be associated with font substitutions Word makes when it cannot find the fonts originally used to create the document.

The best solution, if possible, is to install fonts that match those used on the system that created the original document. If this is not possible, you may sometimes be able to improve your results by changing the fonts Word substitutes. Doing so is covered in detail in "Using Font Substitution," in Chapter 31, "Customizing Word."

HOW TO FIX PROBLEMS ASSOCIATED WITH WORDPERFECT CONVERSIONS

Like most complex file converters, Word's WordPerfect import and export converters are not perfect.

Some inherent differences in the ways that Word and WordPerfect structure documents make it difficult for Microsoft (or anyone else) to implement a perfect converter. For example, WordPerfect places style definitions in a prefix for every document file, even if users don't specify styles. Word's conversion filter picks up these style definitions, sometimes using them in troublesome ways.

For example, WordPerfect style definitions that have the same name as Word's existing built-in style definitions override the Word definitions—so different documents with the same styles will look different, depending on where they were created.

The following resources may be helpful in understanding and troubleshooting WordPerfect conversions to Word:

- *Microsoft Office 2000 Deployment and Administration* (Que, ISBN: 0-7897-1931-2), Chapter 18, "Migrating from or Coexisting with Legacy Applications."

- Microsystems White Paper, "Making the Change from WordPerfect to Word in a Legal Environment," downloadable at www.microsystems.com/PDFS/whitepaper.pdf. (This page contains several excellent documents for troubleshooting unusual or buggy Word document behavior.)

- Microsoft's Office for Windows Support Center, currently located at http://support.microsoft.com/support/Office.

CHAPTER 35

USING WORD'S MULTILINGUAL AND ACCESSIBILITY FEATURES

In this chapter

An Overview of Language Support in Word, Office, and Windows

If your work requires you to edit in multiple languages, or to share your documents with others located outside the United States and English-speaking Canada, you will appreciate the multilanguage support that Word 2003 provides. Working together with international support features built into Windows, you can do all the following:

- Enter text in foreign languages, including special characters not normally found on an English keyboard.
- Use Word's Auto-Language Detect feature to automatically detect which language you are writing in and apply relevant formats and styles accordingly.
- Proofread in French and Spanish without purchasing any additional proofing tools, and proofread in more than 30 other languages by purchasing a single Microsoft add-on product.
- Display the Word and Office user interfaces and access Help in languages other than English.

In this chapter, you will learn how to customize your computer for international use by working with the features built into Windows and Word 2003, as well as optional products such as the Microsoft Office 2003 Multilingual User Interface Pack.

Setting Up Windows for International Environments

Some aspects of working with Office in an international environment are controlled in the Windows operating system; others are based on Office settings and components. The following sections walk you through some key elements that depend on Windows, including these:

- Regional settings, including how Windows handles dates, times, and punctuation
- Keyboard layouts

Controlling Windows Regional Options

When you use Word 2003, the application looks to the Windows Regional and Language Options to establish defaults for various settings that vary from country to country. For instance, Regional settings control number formats, currency formats, and how times and dates are displayed.

In Windows XP, for example, regional settings are controlled through the Regional and Language Options applet in the Windows Control Panel. To view it, open the Control Panel and double-click Regional and Language Options.

Figure 35.1 shows the Regional and Language Options dialog in Windows XP.

Figure 35.1
Choosing support for a specific language region in Windows XP.

In the United States, the default regional setting is English (United States). To change it, select a different regional setting from the drop-down box.

NOTE

> Windows may prompt you to provide the original installation media if you choose a regional setting that has not already been installed.

Later in this chapter, in the section "Using Foreign Dates and Times in Your Documents," you will learn how to override the default Windows settings for dates and times.

CHANGING YOUR KEYBOARD LAYOUT TO REFLECT A DIFFERENT LANGUAGE

If you are using a language that works with a different character set, you may need to change your keyboard layout to gain easy access to the characters that language uses. In Windows 2000, this can be accomplished from the Language tab of Keyboard applet in the Windows Control Panel. In Windows XP, the same is done from the Languages tab of the Regional and Language Options applet of the Windows Control Panel.

Figure 35.2 shows the Text Services and Input Languages dialog in Windows XP. You access this dialog by clicking the Details button on the Languages tab.

You can switch among the installed layouts by clicking on the Language indicator in the system tray at the right side of the Windows taskbar (see Figure 35.3). All available keyboards are shown, as are any Input Method Editors (IMEs) you may have installed to enter Asian languages. (IMEs are covered later in this chapter, in the section "Entering Asian Text with Input Method Editors.")

35

Figure 35.2
Adding a new keyboard layout in Windows XP.

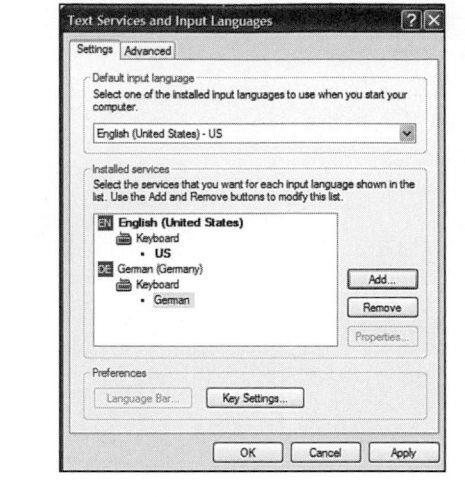

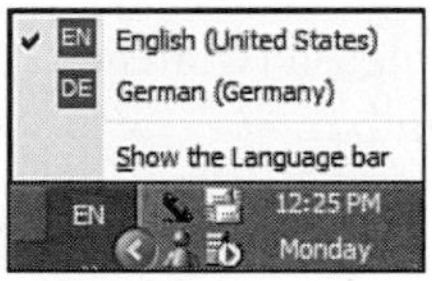

Figure 35.3
Switching between keyboard layouts in Windows XP.

NOTE

In Windows XP the Language indicator may not always show up in the system tray. If you have chosen to display the Language bar, it will be displayed as a floating toolbar on the desktop instead.

TIP

If you occasionally work with various Western European languages, but you do not work enough with any one language to switch to that language's keyboard, consider installing and using the US-International Keyboard. This keyboard replaces many rarely used English-language characters with the most common foreign-language characters.

WORD AND OFFICE MULTILINGUAL FEATURES

Now that you've reviewed key Windows features that you may have to customize to work with foreign languages, the next sections cover features and techniques specific to Word and Office.

TYPING TEXT IN A FOREIGN LANGUAGE

When it comes to entering and editing text in Word, foreign languages fall into one of three categories:

- Western European languages that include characters that do not appear on a standard English (US) keyboard

- Non-Western European languages, such as Greek, that require you to use a different keyboard layout to access the appropriate character sets

- Ideographic Asian languages that require the use of a special piece of add-on software called an Input Method Editor (IME)

Each of these categories is covered next.

TYPING TEXT IN A WESTERN EUROPEAN LANGUAGE OTHER THAN ENGLISH

If you work primarily in English, but occasionally you must enter a word, phrase, sentence, or paragraph in another Western European language, Word provides several ways to insert the accented (diacritical) characters you may encounter.

First, you can enter the characters through the Symbol dialog box. Choose Insert, Symbol; choose (normal text) from the Font drop-down box; click on the character you want; and click Insert.

Second, you can use a keyboard shortcut. For more information about these keyboard shortcuts, including a table listing all the shortcuts, see the Microsoft Office Word Help topic under "Keyboard shortcuts for international characters."

> **TIP**
>
> If you use a specific foreignlanguage word or phrase often, store it as an AutoText entry (see Chapter 23, "Automating Your Documents with Field Codes").
>
> If you use a specific foreign-language character often, consider assigning a macro as a button on your Standard or Formatting toolbar (see Chapter 31, "Customizing Word").

TYPING TEXT IN A NON-WESTERN EUROPEAN LANGUAGE

Many European languages use characters that either do not appear in the standard Windows character set or are difficult to access if you are typing more than a few characters.

To enter text in these languages, first install the appropriate keyboard layout for the language you need to use, through the Keyboard applet in the Windows Control Panel (see "Changing Your Keyboard Layout to Reflect a Different Language," earlier in this chapter). You can then switch to the appropriate keyboard in any of the following ways:

- If you've enabled automatic language detection and also enabled the language you want to use, Word will usually switch the keyboard for you automatically if it detects that you're using a language it has a keyboard available for. (To learn how to enable languages in Word and use automatic language detection, see "Having Word Assign Languages to Text Automatically," later in this chapter.)

35

- If you've set a keyboard shortcut for switching languages, Left Alt+Shift by default, use that shortcut.
- If you've displayed the list of keyboards in the system tray at the right edge of the Windows taskbar, click on it and choose the keyboard you want from the list that appears.

If Word switches you to the wrong keyboard without being told, see "What to Do If Word Switches Your Keyboard Setting Incorrectly," in the "Troubleshooting" section of this chapter.

If Word reformats your text in a language you don't want, see "What to Do If Word Formats Text in the Wrong Language," in the "Troubleshooting" section of this chapter.

Entering Asian Text with Input Method Editors

Documents prepared in ideographic languages such as Chinese, Korean, and Japanese can be read in Word 2003 if you have appropriate fonts installed, such as the Asian fonts. However, text cannot be entered in these languages using standard methods.

If you need to write extensively in Korean, Japanese, or Chinese, the best solution is to configure Word for these languages using the techniques discussed later in this chapter.

However, many users need to enter text in these languages only occasionally. For them, Microsoft's Language Pack provides *Input Method Editors (IMEs)*—add-on software that converts keystrokes into ideographic characters.

IMEs typically contain an engine that converts keystrokes into phonetic and ideographic characters, as well as a dictionary of the most widely used ideographic words. As you type characters based on the sounds of the spoken language, the IME attempts to guess which ideographic character or characters you want. The IME also provides tools for manually choosing characters one at a time.

For more information about IMEs, including how to install and use them, see the Microsoft Word Online Help under the topic "Input Method Editors."

Formatting and Proofing Text in Multiple Languages

Just as text in Word can be formatted with fonts and styles, so too can it be formatted with a specific language. Formatting text in a specific language tells Word which of your installed proofing tools to use and also helps Word choose the right formatting for dates, times, and numbering.

There are two ways to format text in a specific language other than English:

- You can use the automatic language detection feature to do it for you.
- You can do it manually, through the Tools, Language, Set Language dialog box.

HAVING WORD ASSIGN LANGUAGES TO TEXT AUTOMATICALLY

Word 2003's automatic language detection feature can identify the language in which you're writing by comparing the words you type against the proofing tools you've installed. If Word determines that you are writing in a different language, it can format the text automatically for that language.

Automatic language detection works one sentence at a time, so it doesn't get tripped up by foreign-language words or phrases you may use in an English-language document, or by Greek characters you might use in a formula. In detecting languages, Word considers only the languages that meet one of the following requirements:

- Enabled for editing (see the section "Enabling Languages in Office")
- Set as the default for documents created with the template you're using
- Associated with the keyboard you are using

ENABLING LANGUAGES IN OFFICE

To enable specific languages for use by Word and Office, you use a special utility program called Microsoft Office 2003 Language Settings. To access this utility, choose Start, All Programs, Microsoft Office, Microsoft Office Tools, Microsoft Office 2003 Language Settings. The Microsoft Office 2003 Language Settings dialog box opens, displaying the Enabled Languages tab (see Figure 35.4).

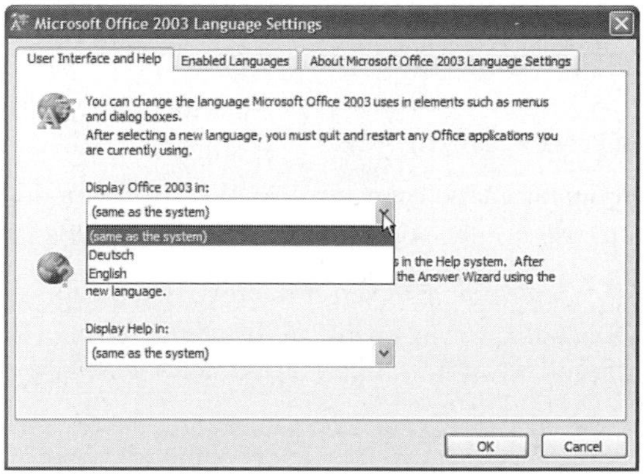

Figure 35.4
The Microsoft Office 2003 Language Settings dialog.

> **NOTE**
>
> In a default installation, the Language Settings tool is not installed, so you may need to wait for it to be installed the first time you access it.

35

In the Available Languages list, select the languages for which you want to install additional support. Use the Add button to add support for a language, or the Remove button to remove support for an already-enabled language. The languages appear in the Enabled Languages box at the right. When you're finished, click OK. The next time you open

Word, the language support is activated, and the language-specific styles and macros are automatically available.

TURNING ON AUTOMATIC LANGUAGE DETECTION IN WORD

Automatic Language Detection is enabled by default in Word 2003. If you find that the automatic detection is not working, turning on automatic language detection is simple. First, open Word. Choose Tools, Language, Set Language. The Language dialog box opens (see Figure 35.5). Check the Detect Language Automatically check box and click OK.

Figure 35.5
The Language
dialog box.

> **NOTE**
>
> If Word is open when you make changes to the language settings, you will need to close and reopen it for the settings to take effect.

MANUALLY ASSIGNING TEXT TO A LANGUAGE

If you do not want to set up automatic language detection, or if you do not have all the proofing tools you need to use it fully, you can still manually assign a language to your text.

To manually assign text to a language, first select the text. Then choose Tools, Language, Set Language. The Language dialog box opens. In the Mark Selected Text As scroll box, choose the language you want Word to use, and click OK.

> **NOTE**
>
> In the Mark Selected Text As list of languages, the languages you have installed proofing tools for are marked with a check-mark icon and the letters ABC, similar to the spell-check icon on the Standard toolbar.

35

SPECIFYING "NO PROOFING" ON SELECTED TEXT

Occasionally, you may edit in languages for which you do not ever expect to have proofing tools available or accessible. If so, you may want to specify that Word skip proofing all or part of your document to avoid having Word flag most of the words as incorrect. To do so, select the text that you do not want to be proofed. Next, choose Tools, Language, Set Language. The Language dialog box opens. Check the Do Not Check Spelling or Grammar check box and click OK.

CAUTION

> If automatic language detection is turned on, Word automatically skips proofing for text blocks it cannot identify as being written in a recognizable language.
>
> Use the Do Not Check Spelling or Grammar setting carefully. If it's used too often, misspelled words and bad grammar can creep into your documents unnoticed; this can present an embarrassing situation.

TIP

> Use the Do Not Check Spelling or Grammar option whenever you have long lists of product names, company names, or other text that Word would otherwise flag as potentially incorrect simply because it cannot find those words in its dictionary.

CHANGING WORD'S DEFAULT LANGUAGE

Word automatically creates documents using whatever language you set as the default; in the United States, this language is English (US). You can change the default language to any foreign or English variant, and Word adjusts its proofing tools as necessary.

To change the default language for all documents associated with the Normal template, follow these steps:

1. Choose Tools, Language, Set Language.
2. In the Language dialog box, choose the language you want to use.
3. Click Default. A confirmation dialog box appears.
4. Click Yes to confirm that you want to change the default language.

CHANGING PROOFING LANGUAGES DURING A SPELL CHECK

Earlier in this chapter, you learned that you can format text with a specific language, and Word will automatically use that language's proofing tools, assuming that they are installed. Occasionally, however, you may not notice a change in language until you run a spell check. This can cause a problem because many of the words will be flagged as incorrect. To resolve this problem while you're in the process of running a spelling or grammar check, Word allows you to change the proofing language it is using.

To do so, press F7 or click the Spelling and Grammar button on the Standard toolbar to display the Spelling and Grammar dialog box. Then choose a different language from the Dictionary Language drop-down box (see Figure 35.6). The change takes effect immediately.

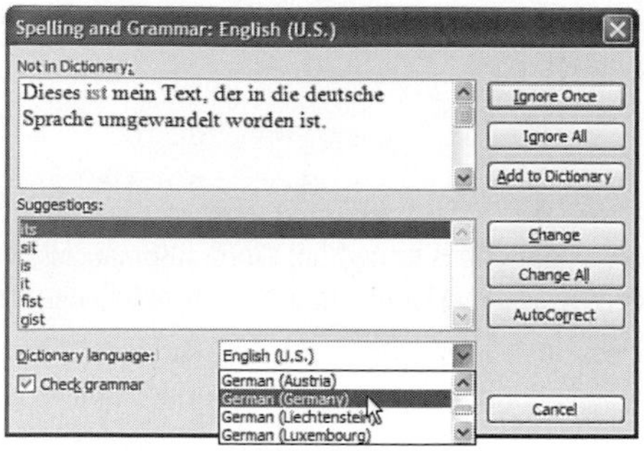

Figure 35.6
Manually changing
the language you use
for proofing.

If the <u>D</u>ictionary Language drop-down box does not appear, exit Word and use the
Microsoft Office 2003 Language Settings utility to enable the languages from which you
want Word to choose.

MICROSOFT OFFICE MULTILINGUAL USER INTERFACE PACK

The Microsoft Office Multilingual User Interface (MUI) Pack extends the capabilities
already discussed by providing text for menus, user interface, help, wizards, and templates in
the language of choice specified. When using the Office 2003 MUI Pack, you are working
in the English version of Office, but the commands, menus, templates, and so on are presented in a different familiar language.

NOTE

> The Office 2003 MUI Pack does not substitute for the localized versions of Word and
> Office that Microsoft will continue to produce. Rather, it is intended for use in organiza-
> tions that require either more extensive proofing coverage or multilingual user interfaces.

NOTE

> For more information on Office Multilingual Deployment, see the Office 2003 Resource
> kit article at www.microsoft.com/office/ork/xp/beta/four/default.htm.

WHAT'S IN THE OFFICE 2003 MUI PACK

The Office 2003 MUI Pack includes the following in several different languages:

- User interface components
- Help files

- Customized templates and wizards
- Proofing tools

> **NOTE**
>
> As mentioned earlier, Spanish and French proofing tools are already included in the standard version of Word 2003.

- Several TrueType fonts designed for international use

Installing the Office 2003 MUI Pack

The Office 2003 MUI Pack can be installed only over the English-language version of Word or Office. To install the tools in the Office 2003 MUI Pack, you must run the separate Setup program.

> **NOTE**
>
> For information about upgrading Office XP MUI Pack installations, see the Office 2003 Resource Kit article at `www.microsoft.com/office/ork/xp/beta/four/ch14/IntB04.htm`.

Changing Language Settings After You've Installed the Office 2003 MUI Pack

After you've installed the Office 2003 MUI Pack, you can add additional language support and switch user interfaces among the languages you've installed.

To work with the language settings, make sure that all Office applications are closed, and then open the Microsoft Office 2003 Language Settings dialog box and select the User Interface and Help tab. This tab will appear only after you have installed at least one MUI Pack.

From this tab you can select separate languages for Office 2003 and Help.

Using Foreign Dates and Times in Your Documents

In addition to controlling date and time settings, regional settings also control the way applications format numbers and currency values. However, after you install Word, you can change these defaults without changing them "Windows wide."

To change these settings only for Word, but not for the rest of Windows, follow these steps:

1. Enable the language you want to use, as discussed earlier in this chapter in the section "Enabling Languages in Office."

35

2. Choose Insert, Date and Time.

3. From the Language drop-down box, choose the language containing the options you expect to use most.

4. From the Available Formats box, choose the setting you expect to use most.

5. Click Default.

6. Click Yes to confirm that you want to change the default.

LANGUAGE FILE ORGANIZATION IN MICROSOFT OFFICE

Microsoft Office stores proofing tools and user interface components for each language separately. When you install only the English-language user interface, as is the case by default, all Office files related to displaying the user interface, including Help files, localized templates and wizards, and default AutoCorrect lists, are stored in the \Program Files\Microsoft Office\Office11\1033 folder. Grammar-checking files are stored in the \Program Files\Common Files\Microsoft Shared\Proof\1033 folder.

The number 1033 is the locale ID Microsoft has assigned to the U.S. version of the English language. In the default installation, Microsoft also creates corresponding empty folders named 3082 and 1036 where Spanish and French files will be installed if you use them.

Other languages are placed in folders that use their assigned locale names when you install proofing tools or user interface components with either the Microsoft Office Proofing Tools Kit or the Microsoft Office Multilingual User Interface Pack.

UNICODE AND INTERNATIONAL FONT SUPPORT IN WORD 2003

Word 2003 supports Unicode, a standard character set that includes all commonly used characters in virtually all the world's major languages, including Asian languages. This makes it much easier to create documents that are entirely, or partially, in languages other than English.

Word 2003 comes with one universal Unicode font, Arial Unicode MS (Arialuni.ttf), which covers all languages that Unicode supports.

NOTE

One disadvantage of standardizing on a true Unicode font such as Arial Unicode MS is its enormous size: several megabytes, compared with 100–200KB for most other TrueType fonts. Working with fonts this large can cause reduced performance, especially on slower systems with less memory.

Using Unicode fonts in your Word 2003 documents will also result in larger file sizes.

Word 2003's universal Unicode font enables you to use the same font to display documents in many languages, rather than reformat text in a specific language font. This means that you won't find yourself inadvertentlytransforming foreign-language text into gibberish when you change fonts.

TROUBLESHOOTING

WHAT TO DO IF WORD CANNOT FIND A PROOFING FILE YOU NEED

If you attempt to proofread text in a language for which you have installed proofing tools, and Word reports that it cannot find the appropriate files, check to make sure that you have not installed an older version of the proofing tools. You can install the new version over the older versions without any problems.

WHAT TO DO IF WORD SWITCHES YOUR KEYBOARD SETTING INCORRECTLY

If automatic language detection is turned on, Word might incorrectly determine which language you are writing in and switch your keyboard to the wrong language automatically. To switch your keyboard back, choose the correct keyboard from the keyboard indicator on the system tray, or use the appropriate keyboard shortcut (Left Alt+Shift by default).

WHAT TO DO IF WORD FORMATS TEXT IN THE WRONG LANGUAGE

Word's automatic language detection feature isn't perfect. It can encounter problems especially if you write sentences in multiple languages in the same paragraph or short document, or if you have enabled two similar languages.

If the problem occurs only occasionally, you can reformat the text manually by selecting it; choosing Tools, Language, Set Language; and choosing the appropriate language.

If the problem occurs repeatedly, try determining which language is causing the confusion—the one Word uses to reformat text in an undesired way. Then, if you rarely use that language, disable it using the Microsoft Office 2003 Language Settings utility.

WHAT'S ON QUE'S WOPR CD

In this appendix

A

This book includes a fully licensed copy of Woody's Office POWER Pack 2003, the legendary collection of Office add-ins that will help you work faster, smarter, and more productively. This latest version of WOPR includes updates of your favorite features from previous versions, plus a handful of indispensable new tools that you'll use every day.

The copy of WOPR 2003 on the CD is fully licensed at no additional cost to you. This isn't shareware, freeware, trialware, demoware, or limited in any other way. Previous versions of WOPR cost more than the price of this book, and now you are getting WOPR and this book for less than the cost of the software.

As with any other software, however, WOPR 2003 does have a license agreement. Be sure to read that and agree to it before using the software.

WHAT IS WOPR?

For more than a decade, WOPR (pronounced *whopper*) has led the way with incredibly useful extensions to Office—in fact, many of the features you see in Office today originated as WOPR utilities. If you rely on Office, you should be using WOPR, the one truly indispensable addition to your Office bag o' tricks.

WOPR 2003 brings dozens of new capabilities to Office 2003.

WOPR COMMANDER

In order to reduce the user interface clutter normally associated with having such a large and complex add-on package like WOPR installed into Microsoft Word, we've created the WOPR Commander. The WOPR Commander removes all of WOPR's user interface elements out of Microsoft Word's menus, toolbars, and so forth and places them on one convenient pop-up menu that is accessed via clicking on the WOPR Commander icon in the Microsoft Windows Taskbar's system tray area (that is, the tray notification area located by your system clock).

Each time Microsoft Word is started, the WOPR Commander's icon is automatically placed into your system tray. To access any of the WOPR utilities, simply right or left mouse-click on the WOPR Commander's icon (or use the CTRL+ALT+W hot key), and a pop-up menu will appear allowing you to control all aspects of the WOPR program (such as displaying the WOPR Tools or Lil'WOPR Tools toolbars, adding or removing the various WOPR components, running each of the WOPR utilities, and so forth).

ENVELOPER

Replace that wimpy Word envelope printer with an industrial-strength one-click wonder! Enveloper works in Excel, Access, and Outlook too.

Print logos/graphics, notes, and bar codes on your envelopes. Maintain multiple customized envelopes. Each envelope may be customized for a different situation: envelope size, return address, note, logo, fonts, and so on.

Enveloper lets you create custom envelopes and call them up when you need them. You can position the return address, addressee, bar code—even a logo or a note line—with a simple click and drag. One more click sets the font, and the whole process unfolds right before your eyes, so you can see how your envelopes will look before you print them. Most of all, Enveloper fits right into Office. There's no need to shell out to another program, or futz around with copying and pasting—Enveloper "grabs" addresses from your documents, worksheets, or Outlook Contacts, and churns out gorgeous envelopes in no time at all. You can pull addresses from Outlook or the address book of your choice, and even look up ZIP+4 Codes on the U.S. Postal Service Web site with a couple of clicks. Whether you print one envelope at a time, churn out thousands of envelopes for mass mailings, or just run the occasional holiday card mail merge, Enveloper helps every step of the way.

WORKBAR

WorkBar gives you a one-click listing of your key working documents right on Word's menu bar (or on a toolbar—it's your choice), automatically sorts the document list as you add documents, supports a variety of file formats (it will launch a file's parent application for you automatically so you're not limited to only Word documents on your WorkBar), and gives you control over how the document is opened in Word.

FILENEW POP-UP

This feature displays a list of useful commands that help you create new documents and interact with those documents' parent templates. It can

- Display the fully qualified filename of the current document's parent template, and allows you to open it with just a click
- Create new documents or templates based on the current document, the current document's template, Word's global template (Normal.dot), or any existing user or workgroup template
- Quickly find and open any user or workgroup template

FLOPPYCOPY

Working with documents on removable media (such as a floppy or Zip disk) can be a real pain—it's just plain slow. WOPR FloppyCopy makes working with documents on removable media easy. FloppyCopy steps in after you open a document from a removable media disk with Word's Open File dialog, and gives you the option of copying the document to your hard drive during editing. When you close the document, it is copied back to the removable media drive. You also have the option of keeping a copy on your hard drive for future editing.

LOOKUP ZIP+4

Lookup ZIP+4 is a utility for looking up ZIP+4 Codes from the U.S. Postal Service (USPS) Web site. Have you ever sent off a letter only to have it returned due to no ZIP Code or an incorrect ZIP Code? Have you ever wondered what the ZIP Code for a particular city was

A

or just wanted to find the ZIP+4 Code for your own or someone else's address? Well wonder no more; WOPR Lookup ZIP+4 comes to the rescue with a unique ZIP-finding utility that is designed to run exclusively from within Word. Simply enter an address (or partial address) into your document, fire up WOPR Lookup ZIP+4, and it will automatically grab the address, start your dial-up Internet connection, retrieve the correct ZIP+4 Code, and insert it into your document. WOPR Lookup ZIP+4 will even automatically disconnect from your Internet provider after a set amount of time or you can choose to remain connected. WOPR Lookup ZIP+4 has also been hooked into Enveloper's Find Zip button for easy access from within your envelopes.

INSERT PICTURE

Insert Picture gives you quick access to all of your graphic images, with more options and flexibility than Word's Insert Picture. With WOPR Insert Picture, you can

- Insert an image in its original size.
- Specify an exact size for the image before inserting it.
- Scale an image by any percentage before inserting.
- Insert an image into the drawing layer, where you can float behind or on top of your text.
- Insert multiple images by telling Insert Picture to remain open on your screen after each insertion.

TASK PANE CUSTOMIZER

Task Pane Customizer is a powerful tool that lets you customize the New Document, New Workbook, New Presentation, New File, and New Page or Web Task Panes in Microsoft Word, Excel, PowerPoint, Access, and FrontPage. With the Task Pane Customizer, you can add files or hyperlinks to, or remove files or hyperlinks from, any of the host Office application's New... Task Panes, rename existing files or hyperlinks, quickly move your files or hyperlinks to any of the four different Task Pane sections, and even clear the Task Pane's most recently used (MRU) document and template lists.

IMAGE EXTRACTOR/EDITOR

Ever want to grab the small 16×16 pixel icon out of an EXE file, DLL file, or from an Office application's command bar/toolbar? Well, WOPR Image Extractor lets you do just that. With Image Extractor, you can extract the small icons from any EXE, DLL, ICO, or BMP file, or from any Office command bar (toolbar or menu), edit them and use them in any Office application such as Word, Excel, PowerPoint, Access, FrontPage, and Outlook.

DOCUMENT NOTES

Document Notes is the electronic equivalent of paper sticky notes for all of your Word documents. The notes travel along with each of your documents and can even be password protected.

DATE AND TIME TOOLS

You can insert monthly calendars into your documents, calculate any date by selecting a start date and adding days, weeks, months or years with the date and time tools. They're a menu bar alarm/timer and much more!

POP-UP CONTACTS LIST

The Pop-up Contacts List lets you access all of your Microsoft Outlook contacts from within Microsoft Word, and insert various information about the contacts (such as their addresses, phone numbers, and so on) into your documents with just a couple of mouse clicks.

QUICKMARKS

QuickMarks is a one-key navigator for big documents that turns your number key pad into an instant document navigator.

SHOW/HIDE ALL

Show/Hide all transforms Word's built-in Show/Hide ¶ command found on the Standard toolbar into a fully customizable "Show Whatever You Want" power house. Without having to write a single line of code, WOPR Show/Hide All enables you to choose which View options to show or hide and which View State to display when Show/Hide All is toggled on or off.

FORMATTING TOOLBAR

The WOPR Formatting Toolbar is simply a better way to access your most-used formatting tools. The WOPR Formatting Toolbar features are

- **Enhanced Styles Menu**—Gives you quick access (via a plain-text preview) to all available styles, plus organizational fly-outs for Recently Used Styles, User Defined Styles, In-Use Styles, Built-In Styles, and All Styles. You can even manage your styles.

- **FastFonts**—Makes it fast and easy to find just the right font for your documents. FastFonts displays all available fonts on your system, with the font name in its actual typeface. You can even generate a printed sample of every available font! Very slick.

- **Format Font and Format Paragraph Menus**—Makes it easy to access commonly used font or paragraph formatting attributes.

- **Insert Symbol Menu**—Instant access to any available symbol. With just a couple of clicks, you can insert Math, Greek, Wingdings, and International symbols. There's also a Miscellaneous Symbols library that includes currency symbols (and the new Euro currency symbol, too), dots and daggers, publishers quotes, em and en dashes, trademarks and copyright symbols, and much, much more.

- **SuperSub**—Makes working with superscripts and subscripts fast and easy.

MODULE TOOLS

Module Tools is a custom toolbar containing a collection of tools for working with forms, modules, and macros in Microsoft Word. Features of WOPR Module Tools are

- **All Keys**—Generates a table of all available key assignments.

- **Rebuild File**—Rebuilds corrupted documents or templates. A real life-saver!

- **Import/Export**—Imports or exports multiple VBA project components (forms, classes, and modules) in a single shot!

- **All Command Bars**—Generates a table of all available command bar controls (menu bars, toolbars, and toolbar buttons).

- **FixXlate**—Fixes line-continuation character problems in WordBasic macros that have been translated to VBA by Microsoft Word.

- **Button Face IDs**—Displays all available button images for the built-in face ID numbers. You can copy the images to the clipboard, or print them out in a document.

CITY2AIRPORT SMART TAGS

City2Airport Smart Tags recognizes common city names as you type them into your documents and presents you with a pop-up menu that enables you to insert the city's airport name or code into your document, view an online map of the city or the city's airport region, get driving directions to or from the city's airport, and much more!

WOPR UPDATER!

This is the easiest way to make sure that you have the latest, most up-to-date version of WOPR.

LITTLE WOPRS LIBRARY

These are small, fast tools that you'll use everyday:

- **Active File Manager**—Gives you quick file management tools for working with the active document or template—move, copy, rename, or delete the active document/template with a few clicks. You can even create a shortcut to the active document/template on your desktop, Start menu, favorites folder, and more.

- **Digital Signatures**—Provides easy access for working with digital signatures in the active document or template. You can quickly add digital signatures to or remove digital signatures from the active document or template, and easily import digital certificate files (using Microsoft's PVK Import tool) for use in signing your documents/templates.

- **Print Selector**—Gives you quick access to all of your printer's settings, and makes printing only select portions of your documents a snap!

- **Calculator**—Takes whatever values are currently selected, calculates a result, and places the result immediately after the selection in your document. There's even a stand-alone toolbar based calculator that will paste the calculation result into your document in a variety of different formats.

- **Normal Quotes**—Converts Microsoft Word's "smart quotes" back into "normal quotes."

- **Fix Line Breaks**—Removes extra line breaks from imported ASCII text files.

- **Duplicate Style**—Lets you quickly make an exact copy of any existing style in the active document or template.

- **View Characters**—Tells you exactly what ASCII codes lie behind your inscrutable characters.

- **View Header/Footer**—Brings back the ol' Word 2.0 header/footer functionality.

- **Remove Personal Information**—Provides easy access to Microsoft Word's Remove Personal Information feature that removes all personal information from the active document or template's comments, revisions, and File Properties dialog box.

- **Change Date/Time Stamp**—Provides a quick and easy way to change any file's creation, last modified, and last accessed date and time stamps.

- **Toggle Showing Windows in Taskbar**—Provides easy access to toggling on or off Microsoft Word's Show Windows in Taskbar feature that displays a separate icon on the Microsoft Windows taskbar for each open window in Microsoft Word.

- **Edit Replace**—Allows you to kick off the find-and-replace process with the currently selected text.

- **Fast Find**—Finds the current selection *quickly*; just highlight your text and press the quick-keys.

INSTALLING WOPR 2003

To install WOPR 2003, make sure that you have Office 2003 installed, shut down all Office 2003 applications, insert the CD in this book into your CD drive, and run the WOPR2003.EXE program directly from the CD.

You must run the installer directly from the CD. If you copy all of the files on the CD to your hard drive and run WOPR2003.EXE from your hard drive, you'll need to insert the original CD into your CD drive before the installer will proceed.

The installer asks you to select which WOPR components you want to install. By default, all options are selected. (You might want to go ahead and install all WOPR tools because you can easily remove any unneeded components later.) Click Next to finish the first stage of the installation.

The Install Wizard starts Word to finish the installation. After it has completed the installation, Word will close. Most of the WOPR components install with no further prompts, but some, such as Enveloper, have their own additional installers, which run when you first attempt to use them.

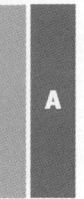

If you have an Internet connection active, WOPR 2003 can automatically check to see if there are any updates at the end of the installation.

If you performed a partial installation, and you want to install any component that you missed, select Add/Remove WOPR Components from the WOPR Commander's system tray menu (by the Windows system clock). Select any component that wasn't installed, and follow the prompts.

If you want to install WOPR on multiple PCs, please send email to mike@wopr.com for site-licensing terms.

SECURITY CONSIDERATIONS

Because of the security model in Microsoft Office 2003, it is possible that the security settings in Office might prevent some of the WOPR applications from running. Many of these applications are based on macros in templates. Although all the macros and templates on the CD are virus-free, Office security settings might prevent them from running anyway. If your Office security settings are set to High, unsigned macros will not run and you will not be given a prompt to change them. You can change this option by following the directions discussed in this book. If your company has "locked" your copy of Office to prevent you from changing this setting, you will need to contact your Office 2003 administrator to change this setting to allow these to run.

CAUTION

> Some of the macros have been signed with a digital certificate to authenticate who the creator was. With these, you might be prompted whether to run them and asked whether you "trust" the signer. You should accept the prompt to allow the template or macro to work correctly.

To uninstall WOPR 2003:

1. Close all of the host Office applications (Word, Excel, PowerPoint, Access, FrontPage, and Outlook).
2. Select the Add or Remove Programs applet from the Windows Control Panel.
3. Scroll down to WOPR 2003 and click the Add/Remove or Change/Remove button. Follow the onscreen prompts.

TECH SUPPORT

NOTE

> The technical support options listed here are for WOPR 2003 only! For support with the other items on this book's CD, contact support@quepublishing.com.

For technical support:

- Visit the FAQ (Frequently Asked Questions) page on our Web site at `http://www.wopr.com/wopr-xp/support/woprsupportfaq.htm`, and you'll likely find your answer.

- Visit our Online Technical Support page at `http://www.wopr.com/wopr-xp/support/woprsupport.shtml`.

- Post a message to your WOPR-using peers on the WOPR Peer-to-Peer forum in the WOPR Lounge located at `http://www.wopr.com/lounge`.

A

INDEX

paragraphs, 312
plain text Wordmail documents, 313
quotes, 312
Review AutoFormat
Changes dialog box, 314
running interactively, 314
Style Gallery, 315
styles, 313
superscripts, 313
symbols, 313
troubleshooting, 326-327

AutoFormat icon (Organization Chart toolbar), 547

AutoLayout feature (Diagram toolbar), 546

AutoMarking index files, 733-734

automatic backups, creating, 92-93

automatic grammar checking, turning off, 257

Automatic Language Detection feature, 1135
formatting, troubleshooting, 1143
keyboard setting, troubleshooting, 1143

automatic outline numbering feature, 636-637

automatic spell checking, 257

automatic style updating, reformatting index entries, 740

Automatic Text Detection feature (foreign languages), 1137-1138

automatically resizing tables, 410-411

automating
captions, 705-706
cross references, 764

AutoNew macro, 1080

AUTONUM, 572

AUTONUMLGL, 572

AUTONUMOUT, 572

AutoOpen macro, 1080

AutoRecover feature, 92

AutoShape command (Format menu), 574

AutoShapes, 573
callouts, 495
categories of, 491-492
Curve tool, 496
defaults, setting, 492
flowcharts, 493-494
formatting, troubleshooting, 554
Freeform tool, 497
freehand tools, 496
Lines submenu
Curve tool, 496
Freeform tool, 497
freehand drawing tools, 496
Stars and Banners, 493

AutoShapes button (Drawing toolbar), 485, 492, 530

AutoSum button (Tables and Borders toolbar), 427-428

AutoSum feature
overview of, 427-428
troubleshooting, 433

AutoSummarize dialog box, 318
Create a New Document
option, 319
Hide Everything But
Summary option, 320
Highlight Key Point
option, 319
Insert an Executive
Summary or Abstract
option, 319

AutoSummarize feature
accessing, 318
closing, 321
functionality of, 318
troubleshooting, 327
updating file properties
with, 321

AutoText feature
AutoText toolbar buttons,
302-303
built-in entries, 301
changing entries, 307-308
creating entries, 304
cross-references, using to
create, 762
entries
adding new categories
of, 306-307
creating, 302-304
displaying and storing
entries, 304
editing, 307-308
inserting, 301
moving between templates, 305-306
priting lists of, 307
saving in different templates, 305
updating, 308
inserting entries
AutoComplete, using,
303
automatically updating,
308
inserting options, 308
overview, 301
printing list of entries, 307
storing and displaying
entries, 304
adding categories of
entries, 306-307
saving entries to different templates, 305
selecting templates, 305
storing foreign words or
phrases as, 1135
storing tables as, 405

AutoTiling, 63

axes
Category, 523
Time-scale, 523

Axes tab (Chart Options dialog box), 523

axis titles, 520

How can we make this index more useful? Email us at indexes@quepublishing.com

editing
grouping and ungrouping, 506
moving, resizing or deleting, 505
selecting multiple, 505
inserting pictures in, 501
layering, 507
lining up, 507-508
nudging, 509
troubleshooting, text disappearing from, 510
working with, 484

Drawing toolbar, 39
3D button, 503
accessing, 485
Arrow button, 490
AutoShapes button, 492, 530
buttons, 485-486
Dash Style button, 489
Diagram button, 550
Diagram Gallery button, 542
Fill Color button, 497-499
Line button, 488
Line Color button, 497-498
Microsoft Graph, 530-531
Oval button, 490
Rectangle button, 490
Select Objects, 505
Shadow button, 502

drawings, handwritten
creating (Drawing Pad), 245
inserting (Drawing Pad), 245

Drop Cap command (Format menu), 564

Drop Cap dialog box, 564

drop caps, 120
adding, 564
defined, 564
example of, 564
fonts, selecting, 565
removing, 565
size of, changing, 564
using, 564

Drop-Down Form Field Options dialog box, 946

drop-down form fields, inserting, 946

drop-shadows, adding, 502

dummy text, inserting (AutoCorrect feature), 295

Duplicate Style feature (WOPR), 1151

E

E-Mail Options dialog box, 1016-1017

E-Postage, envelopes, printing, 212-213

Edit Button Image (Customize dialog box), 1034

Edit Category dialog box, 710

Edit menu commands
Copy, 76
Cut, 76
Find, 46
Go To, 46, 752
Import File, 541
Insert File, 882
Insert Script Block, 834
Keywords, 452
Links, 481
Office Clipboard, 76
Paste, 76
Paste as Hyperlink, 972
Paste Link, 540
Paste Special, 480
Replace, 46, 703, 875
Select All, 699
Undo, 79

Edit Picture command (shortcut menu), 505

Edit Replace feature (WOPR), 1151

Edit WordArt Text dialog box, 469

Edit Wrap Point option (Text Wrapping toolbar), 461

editing. *See also* changing; modifying
Access data in documents
Add New Record tool, 980
Data Form tool, 979
Database toolbar, 979
Delete Record tool, 980
Manage Fields tool, 979
AutoCorrect Backup Document, 300
AutoText entries, 307-308
button images on toolbars, 1034-1035
charts, 514
patterns, 529-530
titles, 522
comments, 883
custom dictionaries, 263
troubleshooting, 284
data forms, 594
data sources for mail merge, 594
datasheets, 532-533
dictionaries, 263-264
documents (Print Preview feature), 221-222
drawing objects
grouping and ungrouping, 506
moving, resizing, or deleting, 505
selecting multiple, 505
field codes, 718, 780
footnotes and endnotes, 746
formatting attributes, 109
forms
commands for, 957
troubleshooting, 959
frames in Web pages, 827
gridlines, 524
images, 456
keywords, 451
Print Quality option, 442
properties, 451
keywords, 452
lines, thickness of, 489
lines, horizontal, 819
list styles, 648
mail merge recipients, 600

How can we make this index more useful? Email us at indexes@quepublishing.com

revising automatically with OLE links to Excel, 541

revising automatically with OLE links to Word, 540

trendlines, using in, 537-538

datasheets
editing, 532-533
formatting data in, 534
moving data in, 533

default chart, 515, 518

Drawing toolbar callouts, adding, 530-531

editing environment, 514

Standard toolbar
Chart Type button, 515
Import File button, 515
Undo button, 515

Undo button, 515

Microsoft InfoPath (XML data tool), 868

Microsoft IntelliMouse
expanding or collapsing selected paragraphs, 635
scrolling with, 25

Microsoft Office Application Recovery dialog box, 93

Microsoft Office Document Imaging, 992-995

Microsoft Office Language Settings dialog box, 1137-1138

Microsoft Office MultiLanguage User Interface Pack
components of, 1140
installing, 1141
overview of, 1140

Microsoft Outlook, accessing addresses for envelopes, 205

Microsoft Publisher, 560

Microsoft Web site
Help task pane resources, 64-65

Font Properties Extension, 1061
Word Viewer, 1118

minor gridlines, 524

mirrored margins, setting, 165-166

missing fonts, locating, 156

misspellings, correcting (AutoCorrect feature), 290

mode section (status bar), activating/deactivating, 37

Modify Location dialog box, 378, 1067

Modify Style dialog box, 413, 648
accessing, 345
Automatically Update check box, 687

modifying
documents, number of cells (Excel), 968-970
font formatting in numbered lists, 147
number style for numbered lists, 147-148
position and alignment, numbered lists, 148
Web pages
default fonts, 813
size of, 812-813
WordArt objects, 469
content and style, 470
shape, 470

Module Tools Toolbar (WOPR), 1150

modules, 1083

monospaced fonts, adding to Web pages, 830

More AutoShapes (AutoShapes category), 492, 495

More button (Find and Replace dialog box), 48, 161

Most Recently Used file list, opening documents from, 96

mouse
Microsoft IntelliMouse, screen movement, 25
selecting text with, 74

move handles on toolbars, 43

Move Shape Backwards button (Diagram toolbar), 552

Move Up or Move Down buttons (Outlining toolbar), 630

moving
AutoText entries between templates, 305-306
between bookmarks, 758
between fields, 786
between screens
using Microsoft IntelliMouse, 25
using scroll bars, 24-25
cells in tables, 404
data in datasheets, 533
elements among templates, 374-375
footnotes and endnotes, 752
macros among templates and documents, 1083-1084
objects, 505
Organization Chart text boxes, 544
paragraphs within outlines, 629-630
shapes, 505
styles (Organizer), 351
subdocuments, 667-670
tables, 405, 433
text using drag and drop feature, 79
toolbar buttons, 1030
toolbars, 43, 66
toolbars between templates, 1038
within Organization Chart text boxes, 543

MSN Web Communities, storage space, 89

How can we make this index more useful? Email us at indexes@quepublishing.com

What's on the CD-ROM

The companion CD-ROM contains Woody's Office POWER Pack (WOPR) 2003, third-party software, book examples, Web resources, and a graphics library.

Windows Installation Instructions

1. Insert the disc into your CD-ROM drive.

2. From the Windows desktop, double-click the My Computer icon.

3. Double-click the icon representing your CD-ROM drive.

4. Double-click on start.exe. Follow the onscreen prompts to access the CD content.

NOTE

> If you have the AutoPlay feature enabled, start.exe will be launched automatically whenever you insert the disc into your CD-ROM drive.

License Agreement

By opening this package, you are also agreeing to be bound by the following agreement:

You may not copy or redistribute the entire CD-ROM as a whole. Copying and redistribution of individual software programs on the CD-ROM is governed by terms set by individual copyright holders.

The installer and code from the author(s) are copyrighted by the publisher and the author(s). Individual programs and other items on the CD-ROM are copyrighted or are under an Open Source license by their various authors or other copyright holders.

This software is sold as-is without warranty of any kind, either expressed or implied, including but not limited to the implied warranties of merchantability and fitness for a particular purpose. Neither the publisher nor its dealers or distributors assumes any liability for any alleged or actual damages arising from the use of this program. (Some states do not allow for the exclusion of implied warranties, so the exclusion may not apply to you.)